Studying Film

Nathan Abrams
(Wentworth College)

Ian Bell
(West Herts College)

Jan Udris
(Middlesex University and Birkbeck College)

Hodder Arnold

A MEMBER OF THE HODDER HEADLINE GROUP

Distributed in the United States of America by
Oxford University Press Inc., New York

First published in Great Britain in 2001 by
Hodder Arnold, a member of the Hodder Headline Group,
338 Euston Road, London NW1 3BH

http://www.hoddereducation.com

Co-published in the United States of America by
Oxford University Press Inc.,
198 Madison Avenue, New York, NY10016

The advice and information in this book are believed to be true and accurate
at the date of going to press, but neither the authors nor the publisher can
accept any legal responsibility or liability for any errors or omissions.

British Library Cataloguing in Publication Data
A catalogue record for this book is available from the British Library

Library of Congress Cataloging-in-Publication Data
A catalog record for this book is available from the Library of Congress

ISBN 978 0 340 76134 2

5 6 7 8 9 10

Production Editor: James Rabson
Production Controller: Bryan Eccleshall
Cover Design: Terry Griffiths

Typeset in 9.25/14pt News Gothic by J&L Composition,
Filey, North Yorkshire
Printed and bound in India

What do you think about this book? Or any other HodderArnold title?
Please send your comments to feedback.arnold@hodder.co.uk

£8.99

ilm

This book is to be returned on or before the last date stamped below or you will be charged a fine

e r i e s
l i v a n

Contents

Preface

The field of Film Studies is already large but is still growing in popularity. An increasing number of schools, colleges and universities are also adopting film as an area of study. Numerous courses are devoted to the study of aspects of film and film history and many disciplines are also actively integrating the use of film, among them Media Studies, English, Historical Studies, American Studies and Cultural Studies, to name just a few.

But do we need yet another book on Film Studies? While there are any number of academic texts covering many different areas of Film Studies, there are relatively few textbooks which explain basic concepts in a lucid manner suitable for students at the very beginning of their studies. For example, at the time of writing only a single textbook is available for British A level students. *Studying Film* provides an alternative core text for the new AS/A-Level specification in Film Studies. The text is also designed to provide a useful tool for undergraduate students both in Film Studies and cognate degree courses. It will also assist teachers of Film Studies and those with a general interest in film alike, providing additional information outside the syllabus's scope for those wishing to learn more.

Acknowledgements

We would like to thank the many people who in various ways have helped in the development and completion of this book. They include family and friends, colleagues and students, readers, Tim O'Sullivan, Lesley Riddle, Emma Heyworth-Dunn and the team at Arnold. Their contributions range from patience and understanding to help and advice. We would also like to thank Kobal and the BFI for permission to reproduce photographs.

Illustrations and Tables

Tables

Introduction

Why study film? Shouldn't films be enjoyed rather than studied? Doesn't studying films destroy their entertainment value? Arguably film was the major art form and entertainment of the twentieth century and shows no sign of giving up this status as we enter the twenty-first. Most of us have been watching films since childhood and have consequently developed an informal literacy in the language, grammar and syntax of film. Studying film can help to formalize and deepen this informal cineliteracy, as well as broadening the medium's entertainment value. The increasing popularity of academic and specialist film journals, as well as of TV programmes and documentaries about the making of films, indicates this. Studying film can also develop an understanding of production techniques, how films communicate meaning, how we as audiences both respond to films and influence the types of films made, and how the industry functions in terms of ownership, control, finance, marketing and exhibition.

How to study film? Film can be studied within three key but interrelated areas: industry, text and audiences. Films can be studied as cultural products, texts that carry particular values and beliefs which are open to a number of different interpretations. They can powerfully affect or influence us, their audience, while satisfying our desires. Films can also be regarded as an integral part of the global media industry and thus are central to the economic activities of an increasingly concentrated range of multinational conglomerates.

The field of Film Studies is already large but is still growing in popularity. The GCE Advanced Level in the subject has already been running for several years and an increasing number of universities are also adopting film as an area of study. In many universities, a range of second and third year modules are devoted to the study of aspects of film and film history and many disciplines are also actively integrating the use of film, such as Media Studies, English, Historical Studies, American Studies and Cultural Studies, to name just a few. *Studying Film* is aimed at students taking such courses. It will also assist teachers and those with a general interest in film alike, providing additional information for those wishing to learn more.

Studying Film aims to aid systematic study of cinema and film based on the key concepts, terms and issues that have informed Film Studies and film criticism. It focuses on how cinema functions as an institution for the production and distribution of social knowledge and entertainment, the very specific ways in which film images and sounds generate meaning, and the relationship between audiences and cinema as institution, as films, as texts. Although most attention will be paid to dominant forms of popular cinema – Hollywood – alternative or less 'popular' cinemas will also be addressed. Consequently, *Studying Film* aims to cover a broad spectrum of topics within Film Studies from a range of perspectives;

hence the inclusion of other areas of cinema outside Hollywood, in particular British cinema. Although this coverage is neither comprehensive nor exhaustive of the huge range of film movements that exist, it will indicate some of the alternatives to mainstream Hollywood cinema. In doing all this, each chapter provides case studies, summaries, suggestions for further reading and exercises, some of which are questions for discussion but others of which may be suitable for essay work. A list of suggested websites, a glossary and an index are supplied. As a result, this textbook will provide an invaluable resource for the student and teacher alike.

Studying Film aims to stimulate appreciation, enjoyment and understanding of a wide range of different types of film together with an awareness of the nature of cinema as a medium, art form, and social and economic institution. It aims to encourage an under-standing of the nature of personal responses to film and to deploy the critical languages that have been developed to analyse the ways in which films and spectators construct meaning. It will provide a critical and informed sense of the contexts in which films are and have been produced, disseminated and consumed, within both mainstream and alternative cinema. It aims to instil a thorough knowledge of the critical and technical terms used in film produc-tion and practice. Finally, it will develop a critically informed sense of the history and devel-opment of film conventions, both mainstream and alternative.

STRUCTURE OF THE BOOK

The book is divided into four main sections covering Cinema as Institution, Film as Text, Critical Approaches to Film, and Film Movements and National Cinemas.

Part 1 (Cinema as Institution) examines cinema in relation to the social context within which it operates, in particular the interaction between the cinema as an industry and the audience. It considers the determining factors behind film form, paying particular attention to the industrial and economic basis of commercial cinema, particularly its business and profit motives. Its principal focus is Hollywood, but not to the exclusion of other cinemas.

Part 2 (Film as Text) provides an introduction to the basic terms of visual communication and perception as well as to the technical terms specific to cinema. In doing so, it begins to analyse how images and sounds produce and communicate meaning.

Part 3 (Critical Approaches to Film) examines the major critical approaches towards understanding film and aims to discover the complex relationship between film as text, cinema as institution, and the audience. The chequered history of theories about how indi-vidual spectators 'read' films is also considered.

Finally, Part 4 (Film Movements and National Cinemas) explores other forms of cinema outside Hollywood that have been vital to the development of film. It looks at the range of different cultural and institutional contexts for cinema and seeks to understand the different, sometimes explicitly oppositional forms of film associated with them.

A note on one or two conventions and other choices about usage which we have adopted for this text. English language titles are given first (except where the meaning of the foreign title should be evident), as well as the original titles in most cases; directors and dates are given for most films. We have decided to use the word 'film' to refer both to individual films and to the celluloid, the material of the original medium. The term 'movie' is used sparingly, principally in reference to particularly American contexts. The Glossary explains some key terms.

The future for Film Studies? Although there is an emerging discipline, 'Screen Studies' – the objects of which include TV, video, video games and whatever happens on a monitor screen as well as film itself – Film Studies will surely remain relevant and must surely inform the new Screen Studies. To be sure, rapid changes in production and projection technologies and viewing contexts are now evident, and these are addressed at a number of points in this volume.

Cinema as Institution

Hollywood Cinema

In this opening chapter we shall focus on the American film industry which goes by the name of Hollywood. The precursors to and origins of Hollywood are examined elsewhere, in Chapter 7 on Early Cinema and Film Form; here we shall be examining Hollywood from its heyday, the 'mature' Studio System between the years 1930 and 1949, through to what has variously been called post-1948 Hollywood, New Hollywood or contemporary Hollywood. While tracing the development of Hollywood, we shall also look at the growth of the 'independents' and their relationship to the major studios in terms of finance, distribution and exhibition.

Histories of Hollywood have changed over time. Early histories were little more than first-hand accounts of the industry, written by individuals who were often part of the very system they claimed to analyse. This raises questions of the objectivity and usefulness of such accounts. From the 1970s onwards, however, a new academic form of Film History emerged from the university campuses which sought to revise the earlier, often uncritical, histories. In turn, these histories were themselves challenged in the late 1970s and 1980s and scrutinized by others who had adopted Marxist–materialist perspectives. Then by the mid-1980s, another mode of Film History, which focused upon institutions, began to emerge. Academic understanding of Hollywood, therefore, has developed as the writing of film history itself has changed. Our intention is simply to focus upon certain key periods; we acknowledge that the boundaries that mark different periods in Hollywood's history (and, indeed, what to call them) are still in dispute, but we shall not enter into that debate here.

THE STUDIO SYSTEM

The origins and early history of the motion picture industry in Hollywood will be discussed in other chapters; our emphasis here will be on the years between 1930 and 1949, which have been described as the 'Golden Age' or the 'Classical Era' of Hollywood film. To understand why this is so, we need to examine the nature of Hollywood film production during this period, which Thomas Schatz (1998) has referred to as 'the genius of the system'. It is during this period that we see Hollywood trying to remove any element of surprise or unpredictability from the film-making process at every level from a film's conception to its exhibition. It must be pointed out here, however, that many of the techniques that were so effective during the heyday of the Studio System were being developed from 1909 onwards and were already firmly in place by 1930.

Oligopoly

By 1930 eight studios dominated the Hollywood film industry in the form of an oligopoly: a situation where the market is completely dominated by a small number of companies, resulting in limited competition. These companies were divided into the 'Majors' or 'Big Five', which were Warner Brothers, Loew's-MGM, Fox, Paramount and Radio-Keith-Orpheum (RKO) (see Figure 1.1), and the 'Minors' or 'Little Three': Columbia, Universal and United Artists (UA). The major studios were vertically integrated, which means they exercised control over production, distribution and exhibition, whereas the minors generally concentrated on production.

Hollywood's position as the film capital of the world was made possible partly by the advent of the First World War in 1914. The war temporarily destroyed European competition, particularly in France and Italy. For the next four years Hollywood dominated the film world, establishing an impressive global distribution network. It has been estimated that in 1914 Hollywood produced 50 per cent of the world's films; by 1918 it produced nearly all of them. By 1925 foreign film rentals amounted to 50 per cent of total Hollywood revenues.

Figure 1.1   *RKO: disbanded in 1957 (BFI Stills, Posters and Designs)*

Vertical Integration

Vertical integration meant that the major studios dominated film production, distribution and exhibition. They made, released and marketed their films, even owning the cinemas in which they were shown: exhibition was the most profitable sector of the film industry. In the days before television and VCRs, box-office sales were the source of income for recouping budgets spent on making films. The heads of the major studios wanted to ensure that there was a constant outlet for their product, and this led to a series of initiatives designed to dominate the industry.

In 1916 Adolph Zukor developed a system of 'block booking' for film distribution. He forced theatre owners to rent Paramount's star vehicles along with groups or 'blocks' of other less desirable and less commercially viable films. Zukor thus ensured a steady outlet for his films regardless of their quality, meaning that money was made on everything Paramount produced.

Within a year every major production company had adopted this practice. The studios already controlled production and block booking represented an attempt to control distribution and exhibition as well. This desire to dominate exhibition was extended by the studios' attempts to acquire as many cinemas as possible during the 1920s. By the 1930s the majors were pouring most of their investments into exhibition, and as a result between 1930 and 1949 they owned almost three-quarters of first-run US cinemas. The majors had divided the country into 30 markets and these were again subdivided into zones, in which the cinemas were classified as first-run, second run, and so on. First-run cinemas showed films as soon as they were released. They tended to have large numbers of seats, were situated in key locations in urban areas, and charged higher admission prices. Each film had to be shown for 14 to 42 days before it could move to the next zone, and this meant a maximum profit for the majors from each release. The majors' ownership of theatre chains, in particular first-run cinemas, together with block booking practices, ensured maximum exhibition of their films.

As mentioned above, the studios had already established an impressive global distribution system by the 1920s, and a major factor in their success was an international market for their films. The major studios dominated this distribution network as a direct result of their control of exhibition. The minors had some involvement in distribution, most notably United Artists, which was set up in response to Zukor's block booking initiatives by Mary Pickford, Douglas Fairbanks, Charlie Chaplin and D.W. Griffith in 1919 for the exclusive distribution of their films. However, they had to co-operate with the majors' system of distribution, and in practice this meant that the majors ensured that their own films received priority over those of the minors. It was these initiatives that increased cost-effectiveness and guaranteed profits and helped to account for the commercial success of the Hollywood Studio System after 1930.

Assembly Line Production

During the 'Golden Age' of Hollywood, the studios produced one film each per week per year. At its height, the studio system released 350 films in a single year. The studios were able to achieve such remarkable production figures through rationalization of working practices.

Adopting a 'scientific management' approach to film production, the studios began to model themselves on factories, employing assembly-line techniques, hierarchical structures, and a strict division of labour; the 1920s also witnessed hundreds of Model T Ford cars as well as an array of other consumer items rolling off assembly lines. In fact Thomas Ince had initiated such practices in the film industry as early as 1908 in the first Hollywood studio, Inceville. Each studio had its own back lot, wardrobe department, props and contract actors. At first, studio heads exercised almost total control over film production, holding responsibility for approving the original film concept and its budget, allocating the director and team of writers, approving the completed screenplay, supervising casting and hiring of other personnel, checking the film's progress, and overseeing the editing.

In 1931, however, Columbia announced the introduction of a producer-unit system whereby a head of production was responsible for running the studio; directly beneath him/her were several associate producers responsible for supervising a number of films and delivering them to the head of production. These methods were designed to save money since each associate producer could now monitor his/her own projects more closely than one central figure could. Often, the producer was the only person to see the film through from conception to completion. In addition to this, particular specialisms could be developed under particular associate producers, which led to more innovation, creativity, and ultimately better quality films. Altogether, these new working practices improved the efficiency and consistency of film production in the Hollywood Studio System.

At Warner Brothers, for example, as many as 20 writers would work on a single script. The script was prepared to an extremely detailed standard and the writers were usually present on set. Once the producer had approved the completed screenplay, the stars/actors were cast and the director, art director, composer, camera operator and editors were appointed. During the studio era the director rarely had any say over any of these personnel; directors were salaried employees 'there to make sure the actors hit their marks while the camera was running' and who left production once shooting had been completed (Biskind, 1998, p.19). The film was then passed on to the editing department, which cut it according to a set of general specifications. Indeed, the style of each film owed more to the values of the studio as a whole than to those of any particular individual working on it.

As the largest, most profitable and productive of the studios during the 1930s, MGM mainly produced melodramas, musicals and literary/theatrical adaptations notable for their high key lighting, rich production design and middle-class American values (*The Wizard of Oz*, 1939; *Gone with the Wind*, 1939). In contrast, Paramount had a definite 'European' feel since many of its directors, craftspersons and technicians had come from Germany. It made sophisticated and visually lavish films such as 'sex-and-violence' spectacles, musical comedies, and light operas (*The Sign of the Cross*, 1932; *The Love Parade*, 1930). Warner Brothers had a reputation as the studio of the working class and focused on low-life melodramas and musicals with a Depression setting (*The Public Enemy*, 1931; *Wild Boys of the Road*, 1933; *Gold Diggers of 1933*, 1933). Under Busby Berkeley, the musical flourished at Warner Brothers (the *Gold Diggers* series) while RKO became the home of the Fred Astaire–Ginger Rogers musical as well as of literary adaptations (*Flying Down to Rio*, 1933; *The Hunchback of Notre Dame*, 1938). 20th Century Fox films such as *The Grapes of Wrath* (1942) were characterized by their 'hard, glossy surfaces' (Cook, 1996, p.292). As for the minors, Universal produced low-budget features designed for the double bill, but did make a niche for itself in the horror-fantasy genre (*Dracula*, 1931). Columbia specialized in westerns, while UA became more a distributor for independent directors than a production company (*City Lights*, 1931; *The Front Page*, 1931).

Style

It was during this period that the studios developed a set of film techniques known as the 'continuity system'. Films of the studio system were constructed in a particular way to ensure that everything was made clear to the viewer. Techniques included psychologically rounded characters with clear goals, character-driven action, the removal of 'dead time', a cause-and-effect, chronological linear narrative, a sense of closure, continuity editing and verisimilitude. This enabled the viewer to suspend disbelief while watching a smooth flowing narrative with a clear ending. These techniques became known as 'classical' film form and will be described in Chapters 6–8.

Genre

Another form of standardization that facilitated the use of factory production-line techniques during the studio era was the development of genre. Genre simply means a type or cate-gory of film (or book or other artwork; the term is not restricted to Film Studies). Genres provided the formulae for making films during the studio era, and, as noted above, each studio specialized in a particular genre or set of genres in an attempt to attract customer brand loyalty through product differentiation. Genres suited the nature of the studio system for two main and connected reasons. First, they offered a financial guarantee. They were formulaic, they contained conventions and they were repetitive (see Chapter 10). Consequently, they could easily be recycled over and over again, promising standardized consistency. Once a formula had been tried and tested, it was hoped that future success could be guaranteed. Why innovate when past experience based on a specific formula had been profitable? This allowed the studios to successfully target, select and predict audiences. Generic films could be pre-sold to an audience along with a particular star. Generic differences allowed the easy identification of audiences for which specific films could be made, which in turn facilitated standardized production. The audience would recognize the characteristics of that genre and the promise that its storyline would develop with a measure of predictability, thus pro-viding the desired outcome and hence providing satisfaction and fulfilling desires.

Second, genres provided a means for the studio to save money. With the establishment of a particular formula, the sets, props, equipment, techniques, storylines and stars could be re-used time after time and frequently were. For example, RKO producer Val Lewton (known as the 'Sultan of Shudders') outlined his recipe for horror: 'Our formula is very sim-ple. A love story, three scenes of suggested terror, one scene of actual violence and it's all over in less than 70 minutes' (quoted in Burman, 1999, p. 9).

Genre, therefore, was one of the ways in which the studios sought to eliminate the unpredictability that is the nature of a creative medium like film. Principal examples of genre in the studio system were: western (*Stagecoach*, 1939); horror (*Frankenstein*, 1931); musical (*42nd Street*, 1933); gangster (*Little Caesar*, 1930) and film noir (*The Maltese Falcon*, 1941).

The Contract System

As mentioned above, the American film industry was rationalized and subject to scientific management techniques. This included a highly specialized division of labour designed to facilitate mass production of films. Accordingly, during the years 1930 to 1949 the studios employed all personnel, even their stars, on long-term or permanent contracts. The stars, directors and crew were contracted to a particular studio and even those who had established a reputation in the industry were employed on a contract basis. This meant that individuals could be assigned to their roles with ease, speed and minimal expense. Contracts tied stars to a particular studio, which helped to target and attract a big audience for the studio's films. If, however, a star refused to work on a particular film then s/he was not given an alternative and had to sit out for one and a half times the duration of that production while suffering loss of income. As a result many seven-year contracts were extended to twice that length. Often, however, stars were loaned out to other studios; Columbia regularly borrowed stars from its rivals. The contract system may have been a source of bitterness for many Hollywood stars during these years, but it contributed to the success of the studio system.

New Technologies

During this period new technologies were developed which had a significant effect on promoting the success of the studio system. Of paramount importance were the introduction of sound technology from 1926 onwards, of cameras with greater mobility, depth of field photography and colour film. These are dealt with in more detail in Chapter 5 on Film Technology.

Context

What must not be ignored in explaining the success of the studio system is the context within which the films were made and consumed. It must be remembered that between the years 1929 and 1949 the United States underwent a series of traumas: the Wall Street Crash of 1929, the Great Depression, and the Second World War. In 1929 the Stock Market crashed, plunging millions of Americans into poverty. Banks were closed, farms were ruined, and many lost their jobs in the subsequent depression, the likes of which had never been witnessed in American history. The Depression felt even worse because it came immediately after the prosperity and consumer boom of the 1920s, which many have labelled 'the Jazz Age'. During this time of despair and stress, the movies provided a means of escape from the harsh realities of American life and Hollywood films, with a few exceptions, tended to downplay the worst aspects of the Depression. In part, this was due to the strictures of the Hays Office (see p. 57 below). What is more, under the New Deal, Franklin D. Roosevelt's series of initiatives designed to get America back on the road towards recovery, the restrictive practices of the film studios were tolerated. Similarly, during the Second World War, while other industries either nationalized or closed down (vacuum cleaners and motor cars, for example), Hollywood was not only left untouched, instead it flourished because the government deemed it an 'essential industry'. Not only did it provide a diversion from the war, but its help was also enlisted in fighting the war. Studios helped to sell war bonds, they made training and information films, and assisted in producing and disseminating propaganda co-ordinated by the Office of War Information's Bureau of Motion Pictures, such as Frank Capra's 'Why We Fight' series.

Casablanca (Michael Curtiz 1942) (Warner Brothers)

Casablanca has been described as one of the most typical products of the Hollywood studio system. Warners produced it for $953,000, Michael Curtiz directed it and it starred Humphrey Bogart, Ingrid Bergman, Paul Henreid and Claude Rains. The film was an instant success and became one of the biggest hits in studio history, winning Oscars for Best Picture (1942 and 1943), Director (1943) and Screenplay (1943); its producer, Hal B. Wallis, won the Thalberg Memorial Award.

Plot: *Casablanca* is set in neutral French Morocco, North West Africa in late 1941, where refugees from Europe anxiously await exit visas to escape to Lisbon and from there to America. The action focuses around the *Café Américain* owned by Rick (Bogart). Victor Laszlo (Henreid) arrives in Casablanca with his wife Ilsa (Bergman), both trying to escape the Nazis. We learn that Rick had previously had an affair with Ilsa in Paris. The Nazis, as represented by Major Strasser (Conrad Veidt), are desperate to prevent Laszlo from leaving Casablanca and the chief of police, Captain Renault (Claude Rains), is asked to assist (see Figure 1.2).

Casablanca: the star system at work (BFI Stills, Posters and Designs)   Figure 1.2

Production: Warners' mode of production was highly centralized. As Executive in Charge of Production, Hal B. Wallis had first pick of story properties, directors, performers, and any other contract talent. The Head of the Studio, Jack Warner, also agreed to hire any additional talent that Wallis felt was fundamental to the production. Finally, Wallis had total control to edit the film. As producer, therefore, Wallis had a huge amount of control over the film. Furthermore, Warners' directors were adjusted to the assembly-line mode of production; they were expected to work on four to five films per year with little active participation in pre- and postproduction. They were excluded from story and script development as well as from editing. Their role was confined almost exclusively to intensive filming, and when most of a film had been completed they were assigned to another project. They had little creative freedom since they were subject to an inflexible studio organization and strict production schedules. This was the case even for Warners' 'star' directors like Curtiz, who had become the studio's top staff director by 1941 having made films such as *Angels with Dirty Faces* (1938), *The Front Page* (1935), *Captain Blood* (1935) and *The Adventures of Robin Hood* (1938).

Genre: *Casablanca* is a love/romantic story and a thrilling adventure/war story in the classical Hollywood style. It is simultaneously two films, allowing for dual readings and different levels of enjoyment for different audiences.

Style: *Casablanca* exemplified the Warners' style which, more than that of any other studio in the 1940s, tended towards *film noir*. Warners had already made *The Maltese Falcon* (1941), starring Bogart as a hard-boiled detective in an espionage thriller. Curtiz, who was appointed to direct *Casablanca*, developed a *noir*ish style for the film which continued in his later films *Passage to Marseilles* (1944) and *Mildred Pierce* (1945). The *noir*ish style was based on expert camera movement, low key lighting, rapid pacing and shadows, including many night scenes. Such cinematography fitted in with Warners' strict budget policy and helped to disguise cheap sets, particularly during wartime when materials for set design were lacking and films had to be made in more austere conditions. *Casablanca* illustrates this well: location work was avoided and most of the shooting occurred in a studio. The action rarely leaves Rick's café and most scenes are either interior shots or set at night. The final sequence demonstrates the creativity of the set designers in creating the illusion of a fully operational airport. Filmed on a stage, the view from the hangar depicts a cardboard model plane in the distance. In order to achieve 'realism' and to maintain the perspective, midgets acted the roles of the mechanics.

Script: The film was based on an unpublished play, *Everybody Comes to Rick's* by Murray Burnett and Joan Alison. It was then adapted for the screen by a series of writers before shooting began. Aeneas Mackenzie and Wally Kline began the initial treatment; they were later removed by Wallis and replaced by Casey Robinson, Warners' in-house expert on romantic melodrama. Finally, Warners' 'top script doctors' Julius and Philip Epstein were officially appointed and credited with the screenplay while Robinson received no official recognition for his work. During filming, Wallis appointed Howard Koch to rework the character of Rick, for which he received a credit. And when preview audiences expressed disappointment with the ending, Wallis himself is alleged to have added the last line of dialogue: 'Louis, this could be the beginning of a beautiful friendship.'

Stars: Bogart was selected for the role of Rick and on 1 January 1942 he signed a seven-year deal with Warners for $2,750 per week. Bogart was chosen because he was the Warners tough guy – cynical and self-reliant. Although he became a top star at Warners and won an Oscar nomination for his role, he was still tied to his seven-year contract and went on to make a series of war films. David O. Selznick loaned Bergman to Warners for $15,000 per week and Paul Henreid was loaned out by RKO against his will.

Exercise 1.1

Take any film from the 'mature' studio era (1930–49) and examine how it was produced under studio conditions. You may wish to consider the following elements: producer, script, genre, style, director, stars, set design and sound. How did these elements combine to form a successful film?

DECLINE OF THE STUDIO SYSTEM

In 1949, the studio system began to decline as a result of a number of interrelated factors:

- Divorcement in 1948 effectively ended vertical integration as the US courts required the 'Big Five' studios to divorce production and distribution from exhibition because the practice broke anti-trust laws; this brought to an end the oligopoly of the studio era. In the 1940s the studios had already agreed to end other restrictive practices such as block booking and blind selling.
- The huge demand for films during the 1940s led to a rise in independent production, and in an attempt to reduce overheads the majors subcontracted production to such companies.
- Stars began to seek greater independence from the studios. In 1943 Olivia de Havilland took Warner Brothers to court over her contract; this resulted in the development of fixed-term rather than unlimited contracts. Stars and crew now had greater freedom than ever before.
- Costs of production rose as a result of wage increases brought about by the growth of trade unions in the industry.
- Import tariffs were imposed on Hollywood films, as foreign countries wanted to prevent the export of dollars while audiences were growing more interested in European art cinema.
- During the 1950s many Americans moved to the newly established suburbs; this had an adverse effect on audience figures, as cinemas were mainly located in urban rather than suburban areas. Although drive-ins were introduced, this did not help to arrest the declining trends since such enterprises tended to favour independent films.
- Television competed with cinema after 1948 and attendances fell as TV became the focus for leisure activity.

Together, these seven factors combined to increase the costs of production while decreasing the revenues which films brought in. Audiences fell by half between 1946 and 1956, approximately 4,000 cinemas closed, and there were massive staff cuts. This led to the end of the 'factory' production-line system as the studios had no guaranteed outlet for their films. Facing competition from the independents, the studios discovered that their structure was too expensive to maintain. In 1957 RKO, for example, was disbanded. In place of the studio system a new structure for the film industry gradually emerged.

HOLLYWOOD FROM 1948 TO THE PRESENT

Divorcement and the newly established television networks led to increased competition and decreased integration in the film industry. As a result, film production became more and more fragmented as independent film production was boosted and new smaller companies began to supply low-budget films (see the section below on 'Independent American Film' for more detail). The majors increasingly subcontracted production and were eager to lease studio space to these companies, which further exacerbated the fragmentation of Hollywood. During the 1950s the major studios also increasingly moved into producing TV programmes.

Although structural changes in the mode of film-making from the 1950s onwards may have resulted, it can still be debated whether this actually constituted a decisive break with the traditions of the studio system. The term 'New Hollywood' may be widely used to refer to post-1950s Hollywood, but there is a great deal of debate over what is actually 'new' compared with the earlier studio system. Labels and periodizations that seek to divide Hollywood into distinct periods are continuously in dispute and an academic consensus has not yet been reached.

Oligopoly

Film production at the start of the twenty-first century is still dominated by seven major studios: Warners, Paramount, Disney, MCA/Universal, MGM/UA, 20th Century Fox and Columbia Tristar. Together they produce 33 per cent of films in the USA, but receive 90 per cent of revenue. Furthermore, the majors have continued to control domestic and international distribution, and although the theatre chains had been split off in 1948 they still continued to dominate exhibition. Douglas Gomery has called this new arrangement a 'bi-lateral oligopoly', replacing the oligopoly of the period 1930–49.

Vertical Integration

The anti-trust legislation of 1948 forced the majors to divorce their lucrative exhibition arms, resulting in a major loss of revenue. In 1985, however, this legislation was overturned, reflecting President Ronald Reagan's more tolerant attitude towards big business, once again allowing the major studios to buy profitable theatre chains. Thereafter Coca-Cola (the owners of Columbia) bought the Walter Reade chain; MCA/Universal bought a 49 per cent share in Cineplex Odeon; Columbia/Sony bought Loew's Theaters; and Paramount and Time-Warner Brothers both bought their own cinemas.

The Package Unit System

In place of the studio system and its mass production of films, a new 'package unit system' developed in the 1950s whereby individual productions were wholly or partially financed by a studio. Under the studio system ideas were developed almost entirely *within* the studio, but now 'packages' were developed *outside* the major studios, which then became sources of labour and materials for film production. In the absence of mass production, major companies had to compete for projects initiated outside their studios. Independent producers assembled a package consisting of a script, director and stars on a one-time-only basis in order to acquire finance. The producer, rather than a mogul or studio executive, was now responsible for a film, overseeing its progress from conception to exhibition (see Chapter 2). Alfred Hitchcock, for example, had a contractual agreement with Universal to use their studio staff and equipment.

Film-makers, however, were still reliant upon the majors for finance, production and distribution. Studio executives, with little experience of industry, gambled on *bankable* producers, directors, and stars with strong track records. This caused a shift in power away from the major studios towards new 'star' producers, directors and actors. Film-making is now increasingly dominated by 'the deal' negotiated between the producer and the studio. Nowadays the star may also receive a percentage of the profits. As control has shifted from the studios to the producers and directors, responsibility for the budgets has moved away as well, with the result that the influence of producers and directors has increased. Furthermore, many directors now enjoy more creative freedom to pursue their personal and artistic vision.

The major studios have been willing to tolerate this trend towards expanding budgets. Since the early 1950s Hollywood has been increasingly hit-driven following the success of big-budget, star-studded blockbusters such as *The Ten Commandments* (1956) (Figure 1.3)

The Ten Commandments: an early blockbuster (BFI Stills, Posters and Designs)   Figure 1.3

and *The Sound of Music* (1965). The budget for the former ($12m) broke the all-time record for a film at that time.

From the 1960s onwards the major studios have followed a 'boom or bust' philosophy and this trend has become particularly marked since the 1970s as it was matched by increasing box-office figures. Thomas Schatz argues that not only has the blockbuster mentality significantly intensified among the major studios, but since the release of Steven Spielberg's *Jaws* (1975) (Figure 1.4), it has also been consolidated. According to Schatz, *Jaws* underlined the value of saturation booking and advertising and the increased importance of a film's box-office performance in the opening weeks of its release. It set new standards for popular cinema and convinced Hollywood that an expensively produced and highly publicized film will automatically turn into a blockbuster (Schatz 1993, pp. 17–25). Compare this to the tight budgets and schedules of the studio system era.

Today the industry's success is based upon very few films. Approximately one film in 10 makes a profit on the first run, and so the majors release only 150 films per year between them in an attempt to minimize their financial risks. Compare this to the 350 films that were produced in one year at the height of the studio system. In planning new productions studios increasingly look for sequels, prequels, series and copies of other successful formulae to try to build upon an already proven formula.

Style

In contrast to the 'classical' film form of the studio era, films that came out of post-1948 Hollywood did not always follow mainstream film techniques. While classical conventions

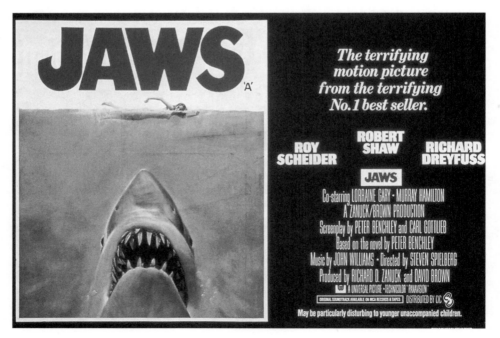

Figure 1.4   *Jaws: consolidated the blockbuster mentality (BFI Stills, Posters and Designs)*

were and are still in evidence, greater individuality and creativity on the part of the director, together with an increased willingness to incorporate European art cinema, led to the appearance of more 'alternative' films (see Chapter 8 on Mainstream and Alternative Film Form). A new generation of directors was emerging whose styles had been shaped by influences very different from those of the studio system. Many of these new directors had been through film schools and had encountered alternatives to Hollywood. Directors such as Coppola, Scorsese, Lucas and Spielberg were labelled the 'movie brats' because of the way they challenged established Hollywood directors and film styles. However, this initial challenge soon came to be seen as Hollywood's saviour. A number of the 'movie brats' films of the 1960s (*The Graduate, Bonnie and Clyde, Midnight Cowboy, Easy Rider*) embodied alternative and 'art' techniques. These films were relatively low budget but were very popular with teenage audiences because of the issues covered, the styles used and the frequent use of contemporary music. The studio was no longer responsible for the style of a film. Whereas before the studio could be distinguished by a film's 'look', under the new conditions it was very difficult to discern a film made by a particular studio as there was no consistency.

Genre

Under the new Hollywood structure, the standardized conventions of genre were largely discarded. Instead of the formulaic genre mode of film production of the studio system, Hollywood has increasingly espoused innovation and hybridity. Despite the blockbuster mentality, the success of two relatively inexpensive and unconventional films, *Butch Cassidy and the Sundance Kid* (1969) and *M*A*S*H* (1969), caused Hollywood to begin changing direction. More innovation was introduced as a new generation of American-based directors including Robert Altman, Arthur Penn, Mike Nichols, Bob Rafelson, Stanley Kubrick and Roman Polanski emerged, influenced by the European art cinema of Bergman, Fellini, Truffaut and Antonioni, to join forces with the movie brats.

Without the restrictive walls of genre, such directors were able to experiment with as well as challenge generic conventions. This has also taken on an economic dimension for the major studios since mixing genres could broaden the potential appeal of a film. As we have seen, *Casablanca* was an early example of this, blending a love story, a romantic thriller and an adventure-war story. More recent examples include *Star Wars* (1977), a mix of science fiction, western, action and war; *Blade Runner* (1982), science fiction, action/adventure, detective, *film noir* and horror; and *Pulp Fiction* (1994), gangster and comedy. Under New Hollywood, genres have become blurred and often hybrid, particularly since the emergence of postmodernism (for more detail see Chapters 10 and 12).

Free Agents

The ending of studio contracts for creative personnel in the early 1950s meant that important stars, directors, writers and other talent could now negotiate their own deals with the production companies. Increasingly, agents negotiated deals with studios on behalf of individuals, thus ending the restrictive contracts of the studio system. The most powerful talent agencies today are the Creative Artists Agency, the William Morris Agency, International Creative Management and MCA.

The end of the contract system and the decline of the rigidly hierarchical studio mode of production combined to give more creative autonomy to the director. Freed from the restrictive directives, budgets and schedules of the studio moguls and executives, a director could impose a more personal imprint upon a film. S/he now had more input into pre- and post-production, overseeing story and script development, casting and editing. This new power was validated by the emergence of *auteurism* (see Chapter 9 on Authorship).

Similarly, it can also be argued that actors can now have more input into their roles, interpreting them with more individuality than was possible under the studio system. The power of star actors has also increased massively since the ending of the restrictive contract system. It has even been suggested, notably by John Boorman (*Deliverance*), that five or six key stars have usurped the studios in the Hollywood hierarchy. This power has translated into bigger fees, and many stars now have creative control over a film, including approving its final cut (see Chapter 11 on Stars). The overall effect has been a shift in power away from the studios and an increase in film budgets.

New Technologies

Since the Studio System era, Hollywood has continued to see new technologies developed which played a significant part in the success of the industry. This happened in two ways. First, improvements in camera, sound, colour, viewing and computer/digital technologies have led to the creation of more technologically sophisticated films which have helped attract audiences back into the cinemas (see Chapter 5 on Film Technology).

Second, the major studios sought to maximize the potential of the rapid growth of new media technologies, in particular cable, satellite and video technology. Cable and satellite stations were eager to pay large sums to screen Hollywood films and increasingly most films now recoup initial budgets on video sales and rentals. Altogether, the revenue from cable TV, satellite and video has begun to overtake that from theatrical release.

Context

As was the case during the days of the studio system, Hollywood films continued to be significantly determined by the context in which they were produced. The onset of the Cold War in 1947, the investigations of the House UnAmerican Activities Committee (HUAC) into Hollywood in 1947 and 1951, and the hysteria of the McCarthy years combined to produce a climate of fear and a blacklist in Hollywood. The result was a decline in socially conscious films and the rise of the anticommunist and science fiction feature. The ending of the blacklist by the end of the 1950s re-energized Hollywood film production. By the late 1960s anti-establishment and counter-cultural tendencies are clearly evident in American film, no doubt influenced by the assassination of JFK, by the Beatles, the pill, drugs, American involvement in Vietnam, and the high profile assassinations of Martin Luther King and Robert F. Kennedy. Furthermore, the Production Code had been liberalised since the early 1960s, and was formally dropped in 1968 (see p. 58). By this point the Civil Rights movement of the 1950s had become more militant and violent, transforming itself into Black Power, and this was matched by the students' and women's struggles. These issues spilt over into the 1970s, exacerbated by continued involvement in Vietnam. Watergate compounded America's troubles by revealing the presidency to be flawed and corrupt. In the 1980s, however, Reagan sought to restore confidence in the United States and its foreign policy, and this decade saw a renewed Hollywood interest in Vietnam and other conflicts. This was the period of 'high concept' film-making (see Wyatt, 1994). By the 1990s the end of the Cold War led Hollywood to seek new enemies both outside and within America.

CASE STUDY

Apocalypse Now (Francis Ford Coppola 1979)

The production of *Apocalypse Now* demonstrates the dramatic changes in film production following the decline of the studio system. United Artists produced it for more than $30m, Francis Ford Coppola directed it and it starred Marlon Brando, Robert Duvall and Martin Sheen (Figure 1.5). The film was a box office success, taking in over $37m, receiving favourable critical reviews and winning Oscars for Best Cinematography and Sound (1979).

Plot: *Apocalypse Now* can be read both as a physical journey, up a primitive river in the quest for a man whose discovery promises revelation, and as a metaphorical journey into the darkest recesses of the human mind. During the Vietnam War, Captain Willard (Sheen) is sent along a tributary of the Mekong into a tip of Cambodia to assassinate Colonel Kurtz (Brando), once a promising young officer but now insane and surrounded by a gang of worshippers. Coppola's stated reason for making the film was to assist Americans in 'putting the Vietnam experience behind them'. It has since emerged as a provocative and influential film that closely approximates the horror as well as the emotional and physical upheaval of the American experience in Vietnam. *Apocalypse Now* demonstrates the combination of astute political comment with spectacular aesthetics.

Apocalypse Now: Coppola directs Brando (BFI Stills, Posters and Designs)   Figure 1.5

Production: Coppola was one of the 'movie brats': a film school educated director (in this case UCLA) influenced by European art cinema who had directed *The Rain People* (1969) and the first two parts of *The Godfather* (1972, 1974). In contrast to the tight production schedules of the studio system, preproduction began in mid-1975 and postproduction ended in 1979. The film was originally scheduled to be shot over six weeks and to open in 1977, but various setbacks, such as a typhoon that destroyed the sets, and financial overruns, plagued filming and shooting lasted 16 months instead. Overall, production lasted for four years. Similarly, the initial budget was $12m, far in excess of earlier studio budgets, and this rocketed to $31.5m.

Genre: Although it can be classified as a war story, the film's philosophical implications, which examine the horror and madness of war, take it beyond the traditional war genre. Its controversial political comment, for example, widened the boundaries of the war genre, as *Casablanca* had done. It has also been described as a 'quest' film that moves through several other genres such as thriller, horror, adventure and even comedy.

Style: In contrast to the studio influence on products of the 1930s and 1940s, UA was not responsible for the style of *Apocalypse Now*. The film owes its particular style to the vision of Coppola and cinematographer Vittorio Storaro, combining art cinema with popular entertainment. It contains some spectacular set pieces, such as the opening dissolves and superimpositions of Sheen's face with a ceiling fan and a helicopter attack; the 'Ride of the Valkyries' battle sequence; and the napalm destruction of Kurtz's compound during the final credits of the film. In contrast to earlier productions that were almost entirely filmed on studio sets, *Apocalypse Now* was filmed on location in the Philippines.

Script: *Apocalypse Now* was a loose adaptation of Joseph Conrad's novel *Heart of Darkness* (1899) co-written by Coppola and John Milius (the latter went on to make militaristic films such as *Red Dawn* (1984)). Michael Herr, who had written *Dispatches* (1977) using his experiences as an army correspondent in Vietnam, provided additional material. As a result, the film displays a clear ambivalence in regard to its view of the Vietnam War, displaying both pro- and anti-war sentiments. Many scenes and cinematic techniques work to further a pro-military, pro-war interpretation of the conflict, but these are always balanced by anti-war, dove-like sentiments. These opinions are never wholly reconciled and lead to what can be described as a somewhat surreal and confusing ending that did not leave critics completely satisfied.

Stars: Harvey Keitel was originally cast as Willard, but two weeks into production Sheen replaced him. In contrast to the studio contracts, Brando was paid $1m in advance to be in the film. He turned up on set late, overweight and allegedly drunk, having read neither the script nor the book on which the film was based, illustrating the new power held by key stars. The film also featured many young actors who would later become Hollywood stars, such as Dennis Hopper, Larry Fishburne and Harrison Ford.

Exercise 1.2

Look at the production of a particular Hollywood film after the 1960s. What are the differences and similarities between films made under the new system and the studio system? How do differences in the structure of the film industry affect the film itself?

INDEPENDENT AMERICAN FILM

Independent American film is not a new phenomenon. It has existed since the early days of Hollywood; indeed, many of the major studios began life as independent production companies. During the height of the studio system independent film companies known as 'poverty row', such as Disney, Republic, Monogram and Tiffany, supplied B-features for double bills.

Divorcement in 1948 boosted independent film production and companies like Allied Artists and American International Pictures began to supply low-budget films for the growing teenage market. In this period, the majors were eager to lease studio space to independent production companies and increasingly subcontracted production to them; this resulted in such films as *Marty* (1955) and *The Bachelor Party* (1957), which were produced by the Hecht-Lancaster company established in 1947. UA, which was the distribution company for such films, released several notable films including *Kiss Me Deadly* (1955), *The Night of the Hunter* (1955), *The Sweet Smell of Success* (1957) and *Paths of Glory* (1957).

In the 1960s, the relaxing of the Production Code (see Chapter 3 on Cinema, Audiences and Society), together with the further decline of the majors, favoured the independents. In 1960, John Cassavetes made *Shadows* entirely outside the studio system and hence has been described as the 'father' of independent American film, drawing upon a long history of maverick film-making that was pioneered in Hollywood by Orson Welles and *Citizen Kane* (1941). During the 1970s, companies began to specialize in certain genres: martial arts, action, erotica, blaxploitation and horror. Many of today's independent film-makers cut their teeth on the low-budget films of the 1970s.

Fuelled by the expansion in home video and cable, independent films have been ever more prominent since the 1980s, emerging from companies such as Circle Films, Hemdale, Island Pictures, New Line Cinema, Cinecom, Cannon, De Laurentis, New World and Miramax. Low-budget productions could be financed entirely from presales to video, thus missing out the need for cinema release and going straight to video. Some of these companies attempted to work outside the sphere of the majors and accordingly fared badly. During the mid- to late 1980s, however, a new pedigree of 'neo-indies' emerged. Carolco, Morgan Creek, Castle Rock, Imagine Entertainment and Largo all possessed sufficient finance to produce their own films outside the major studios, but they worked very closely with them for distribution and exhibition. Independent film is very much alive in Hollywood today, enjoying both critical and box-office success.

How do we define Independents?

Can independents be defined economically? A truly independent company, it is argued, can finance, produce and distribute its own films. It operates outside the control of the majors and competes directly with them for a share of the film market. However, even the large independents are not truly independent, as they are reliant on exhibitors, often the majors, for their films to be screened. In reality, independent film-makers choosing to work outside the constraints of the major studios, whose films are mostly low-budget in order to retain creative freedom, are closer to being fully independent as their films are often screened outside the exhibition chains owned by the majors.

However, independent production companies are often owned by a larger company; for example, much of Castle Rock's initial funding came from Coca-Cola, which used to own Columbia. Castle Rock is now a subsidiary of Warners. Furthermore, independents are reliant on the majors for distribution and exhibition (Castle Rock uses Columbia) and some may even receive studio backing, which surely militates against their total freedom. What is more, independent films are often planned in close co-operation with the majors for exhibition and distribution rights as well as finance. Although Spike Lee's *Do the Right Thing* (Figure 1.6) contains some alternative aesthetic and ideological elements and was produced by his own independent production company, 40 Acres and a Mule, it was made for MCA/Universal. Nor are all independent production companies small or low budget. Companies like Carolco, Morgan Creek, Castle Rock, Imagine and Largo were respectively responsible for these big-budget, star-studded blockbusters in 1991: *Terminator 2, Robin Hood, City Slickers, Backdraft* and *Point Break*. Most independent companies agree that the label 'independent' is somewhat misleading (see also Chapter 8). While it is agreed that an independent is defined by its capability to finance its own films, most do not operate outside the established studio system; instead they usually enjoy close ties. Today most independent film companies can be described as simply 'outgrowths' of the majors.

Exercise 1.3
Pick an independent film of your choice and assess how this may have shaped the values and content of the film. Does it have any unusual features or striking storylines that set it apart from mainstream Hollywood films? Consider how far any film can be truly independent.

Figure 1.6   *Do the Right Thing: independent or major studio project? (BFI Stills, Posters and Designs)*

Conclusion

We have seen in this chapter how Hollywood has changed over time. The American film industry has developed from a highly structured, centralized, factory-style studio system to a more fragmented package unit system in which individual films are pitched by independent producers to competing studios. The result has been a shift from assembly-line production, with its formulaic use of genres, studio styles and stars, to a system in which directors, stars and others have more creative freedom to work outside the limitations of genre, studio style, budgets and other restrictions. Beneath the surface, however, there are some essential continuities and similarities between these two periods of American film history. Despite a short interlude, Hollywood today, like the old studio system, is still essentially a vertically integrated oligopoly. In addition, the studios both of the past and of today have utilized new technologies to maximize profits and to bring audiences into cinemas. Independent film has always existed in the United States but flourished particularly during and after the 1950s following the decline of the studio system. While it may now be hard to distinguish an independent from a major studio, independent films are still a key part of America's film output.

SUMMARY

- Both the Studio System and post-1948 Hollywood can be described as 'oligopolies', dominating through vertical integration.
- The studio system was structured according to assembly-line production, leading to a high number of films each year. Post-1948 Hollywood is arranged around a 'package unit system', producing fewer films and more blockbusters.
- Each studio developed its own style and favoured particular genres, but today this is not so evident.
- The contract system which tied directors, crew and stars to the studio has now ended, leading to greater creative autonomy.
- Studios have maximized the potential of new technologies to benefit film production.
- Hollywood films have always benefited from the context in which they were made.
- Independent American film has existed since Hollywood's origins, but was boosted by 'divorcement' in 1948, the relaxing of the Production Code in the 1960s and the expansion of home video and cable.
- Economic independents finance, produce and distribute their own films, which are often but not always small and low-budget, operating outside the control of the majors. However, larger companies often own independents and the majors work very closely with them.

References

Peter Biskind, *Easy Rider, Raging Bulls: How the Sex 'n' Drugs 'n' Rock 'n' Roll Generation Saved Hollywood* (London: Bloomsbury, 1998).

Mark Burman, 'The Val of death', *The Guardian Review* (15 October 1999), pp. 8–9.

David A. Cook, *A History of Narrative Film* (3rd edn, New York and London: W.W. Norton & Co., 1996).

Douglas Gomery, *The Hollywood Studio System* (London: Macmillan, 1986).

Thomas Schatz, 'The New Hollywood', in Jim Collins, Hilary Radner and Ava Preacher Collins (eds), *Film Theory Goes to the Movies* (London and New York: Routledge, 1993), pp. 8–36.

Thomas Schatz, *The Genius of the System: Hollywood Film-making in the Studio Era* (London: Faber & Faber, 1998).

Justin Wyatt, *High Concept: Movies and Marketing in Hollywood* (Austin: University of Texas Press, 1994).

Further Reading

Tino Balio, *The American Film Industry* (Madison, WI: University of Wisconsin Press, 1985).

Peter Biskind, *Easy Rider, Raging Bulls: How the Sex 'n' Drugs 'n' Rock 'n' Roll Generation Saved Hollywood* (London: Bloomsbury, 1998).

Pam Cook and Mieke Bernink (eds), *The Cinema Book* (2nd edn, London: BFI, 1999).

Douglas Gomery, *The Hollywood Studio System* (London: Macmillan, 1986).

Jim Hillier, *The New Hollywood* (London: Studio Vista, 1992).

Annette Kuhn and Susannah Radstone (eds), *The Women's Companion to International Film* (London: Virago, 1990).

Richard Maltby, *Hollywood Cinema: An Introduction* (Oxford: Blackwell, 1995).

Steve Neale and Murray Smith (eds), *Contemporary Hollywood Cinema* (London and New York: Routledge, 1998).

Thomas Schatz, 'The New Hollywood', in Jim Collins, Hilary Radner and Ava Preacher Collins (eds), *Film Theory Goes to the Movies* (London and New York: Routledge, 1993).

Thomas Schatz, *The Genius of the System: Hollywood Film-making in the Studio Era* (London: Faber & Faber, 1998).

Janet Wasko, *Hollywood in the Information Age* (Cambridge: Polity, 1994).

Further Viewing

A Personal Journey with Martin Scorsese through American Movies (BFI, 1995).

Hearts of Darkness: A Film-maker's Apocalypse (Bahr & Hickenlooper 1991).

The Universal Story (Universal, 1995).

Darryl F. Zanuck – 20th Century Filmmaker (20th Century Fox, 1995).

Hitchcock, Selznick and the End of Hollywood (Thirteen/WNET, 1998).

Production, Distribution and Exhibition

How does a film eventually reach the screen? In this chapter we shall examine the process of making and showing a film, from original idea to screening. We trace the life of a film from its earliest stages of finance, preproduction, production and post-production while explaining key roles in the film industry. The process by which films are distributed, classified, promoted and marketed to the audience will then be explored. Finally, we shall look at where and how films are exhibited as well as at reviewing and criticism. Although film production, distribution and exhibition are global phenomena, our focus here will be on the contemporary US and British situations. In particular, we shall be looking at the period from the end of the First World War to the present day and at those elements that are not covered in other chapters on Hollywood and Early Cinema and Film Form.

PRODUCTION

This section will trace the process by which an idea is transformed into a celluloid reality. The process of production itself is subdivided into four further stages: finance, preproduction, production and postproduction.

Finance

Film is a blend of creativity and commercialism. It must always be remembered that most film production is an 'industry', a business designed to make money through entertainment. The profit motive of the industry cannot be stressed enough. America's film industry, for example, is the country's second largest source of export. At the same time film production is very expensive and involves high overhead costs. Finance, therefore, is essential to every stage in the life of a commercial film and those who provide the money – investors, financiers, distributors and exhibitors – have great influence over the film itself.

Investors

The types of investors for any one film can vary considerably. If a major studio such as Warner Brothers, Columbia TriStar or Dreamworks produces the film, it will already have enough capital to finance production through other previously successful and profitable films. On the whole, American studios finance their own development and production out of their cash flow and loans. Independent producers also usually have a contract with a studio. *Extreme Measures* (1996) and *Mickey Blue Eyes* (1999) were both made under a *house-keeping deal* between Liz Hurley and Hugh Grant's Simian Films and Castle Rock (a subsidiary of Warners). They developed the projects using Warners' finances, giving them first refusal on the film. On acceptance Warners fully financed the production.

When seeking finance a film company will usually approach the *executive producer* of a studio or a production company. For independent film production, however, this capital is not guaranteed and thus it must be secured from a variety of sources such as banks, private investment companies, the government, self-financing wealthy individuals, foreign sales, distribution pre-sales, television rights and equity finance. Sid Sheinberg, ex-head of MCA/Universal, described the difference between securing finance for a Hollywood studio and for an independent production as 'the difference between flying a 747 and one of those devices that people in the Middle Ages used to put wings on, flap and jump off cliffs' (quoted in Mcnab, 1999, p. 12). It is hard to pinpoint why exactly investors invest in a particular film, but the script, the producer, the director, the stars or any combination of these elements may appeal to them. They may have what is known as *bankability*, that is, it is felt that they can guarantee an audience, which will provide a good financial return on the original investment.

CASE STUDY

INVESTMENT IN THE UNITED KINGDOM

The Government

In many European countries, and particularly in France, film-making is a state-funded activity with plenty of government subsidies for production, distribution and exhibition. Through a combination of taxes, tax incentives and government contributions the French film industry is the most vigorous in Europe. Although government funding for film-making in the UK is small, there has been increasing recognition of the need to finance the industry: direct funding rose from £14.9m in 1988 to £27.7m in 1994. Government money is provided through several sources:

- *The Arts Council's* National Lottery subsidies and film franchises have provided £67m since 1995 to those films that qualify as 'British' under the terms of the 1985 Films Act and which are intended for UK release, such as *Wilde* (1997) and *Ratcatcher* (1999).
- *British Screen Finance Ltd* is a film investment company backed by both the state and private sectors. Its contribution rarely exceeds £500,000 and is never more than 30 per cent of a film's budget. It has financed *Fever Pitch* (1996).

- *The British Film Institute* co-financed films between 1951 and 1998, awarding grants to 'culturally significant projects', aiming to recover its investment through the films it financed, such as *Beautiful People* (1998).
- *The European Co-Production Fund* was set up in 1991 to promote collaboration between British and European Union producers. One of its projects was Louis Malle's *Damage* (1992).
- *The National Film and Television School* is directly funded by the government.
- *The British Film Commission* was between 1991 and 1999 an independent organization funded by the government to market the British film industry to overseas film-makers and to provide support for the overall UK film infrastructure.
- *The Film Council*, which was set up in April 2000, is a new strategic body for film funded by the Department of Culture, Media and Sport. Headed by director Alan Parker (*The Commitments*, 1991; *Evita*, 1996), it absorbed the British Film Commission, BFI production, the Arts Council of England's Lottery Film Department and British Screen Finance.

Television Companies

Television companies are an important source of funding for films; as well as a financial return on their investment they receive the broadcast rights after the film has been released in cinemas. The arrival of pay TV (satellite, cable and digital) has led to an increased demand for films. Abroad, major players such as HBO (USA) and Canal + (France) have been financing film production for some time. In comparison to their foreign counterparts, however, TV investment in the UK is low. The major investors in the UK are the following:

- *Channel 4,* through its feature subsidiary *Film Four*, is the biggest TV investor in Britain and has contributed to over half of all British films made since the 1980s. Approximately 10 per cent of its annual programming budget is spent on new British films and it aims to co-produce 15–20 feature films per year. Since its launch in 1982 it has made more than 300 films, including *Four Weddings and a Funeral* (1994) and *Brassed Off* (1996).
- *BSkyB* has the pay TV rights to all British films that are theatrically released. It also agreed an arrangement with British Screen Finance (see above) to finance a few British productions in return for the broadcast rights, for example, for *Tube Tales* (1999).
- *BBC Films* has a relatively small budget, but funds film-makers through its *10x10* initiative. Examples would include *The Van* (1996) and *Billy Elliot* (2000).
- *ITV Companies* generally do not fund film production, but some noticed Film Four's critical success and began to invest. For example, Granada Television co-financed *My Left Foot* (1989).

Foreign Investment

Often UK film-makers look abroad for foreign investment, most of which is provided by the major American studios. Foreign studios financed all the following 'British' films: *Chariots of Fire* (1981), *A Fish Called Wanda* (1988), *Sense and Sensibility* (1995), *Emma* (1996), *Hamlet* (1996) and *The English Patient* (1996). Many countries offer finance or tax incentives if a significant proportion of the main photography is done there.

Private Investment

Private investment is another way of financing a film. This is uncommon since the high costs of producing a film are beyond the capacities of most private investors. Until 1993 the Business Expansion Scheme attracted many small-scale private investors by allowing significant tax relief on investments of up to £40,000, leading to the production of low- to medium-budget films such as *Henry V* (1989). This scheme was replaced in 1994 by the Enterprise Investment Scheme – a tax-based investment programme. Using this scheme, Paradise Grove plc offered investors roles in the film as extras if they invested at least £1,000. Films that benefited from the Enterprise Investment Scheme were *The Scarlet Tunic* (1998) and *An Ideal Husband* (1999). Production companies can also meet production costs by negotiating special fees with crew members and equipment suppliers and by securing *product placement* deals. This provides a symbiotic relationship between film-maker and advertiser. While the latter gets valuable coverage of a product, the former does not have to pay for use of that product, although some do charge for placement. Recent examples include Tom Cruise swigging Red Stripe lager in *The Firm* (1993) and Tommy Lee Jones and Will Smith wearing Ray-Ban Wayfarer sunglasses in *Men in Black* (1997). Bond movies have long benefited from use of product placement (see Figure 2.1): Dom Perignon and Bollinger Champagnes, Stolichnaya and Smirnoff vodkas, Samsonite luggage and the BMW Z8.

The producer

It is the job of the producer to secure finance for the film and then to supervise its expenditure. The producer is involved in every stage of a film's development from conception to exhibition and is engaged in the film longer than any other person; this continuity is essential for effective production. The producer deals with the idea, which may originate from a writer, director, producer, book or play, and must clear the screen rights for the material and then secure finance by assembling a package that includes an outline script (detailed storylines, possible stars, locations), proposed budget, a *storyboard* of several scenes, the director and any potential stars. The producer presents the package in such a way that it stands out from the competition in order to attract investment. This process of selling the package is known as the pitch. A successful package will not only appeal to financiers and investors; it will also reassure them that a return on their investment is possible. If the pitch is successful, a deal is struck between the producer and the investors.

Figure 2.1   *Bond films have typically relied on product placement to recoup production costs (Eon Productions, courtesy Kobal)*

Exercise 2.1

Do you think the British government should fund film-making? What are the main sources of production finance for British film-makers or for film-makers outside the Hollywood system working on low or relatively low budget productions?

PREPRODUCTION

Preparation

Once the funding has been secured, the film can enter the next stage of its life: preproduction. Research and planning for production can begin and development money is used to develop the outline script. The producer then assembles a complete package, overseeing and assisting in the hiring of the director and technical crew, in casting and in choosing locations. It is now the task of the producer to steer the film into production, and his/her role can be summarized as the conduit between the idea, the script and the marketplace. The producer has overall responsibility for production and mediates between the film and its financiers, yet beyond this the role is not precisely defined and can vary considerably. Some producers take a 'hands on' approach during production while others delegate to an associate producer who directly supervises the daily shooting. Sometimes there is a credit for an executive producer, usually the head of a studio or a production company, who will not be too closely involved as s/he will be supervising several films in various stages of production.

The producer works closely with the director. A good working relationship between them is essential to the film's smooth progress, for where the producer is responsible for financial decisions the director is only concerned with artistic and technical ones. Since film-making is so expensive, a great deal of time and effort is spent meticulously planning and scheduling the shooting of the film in order to ensure that it runs as smoothly as possible. Planning covers all of the activities involved in preparing, editing and filming the script, including casting, finding locations, hiring technicians and other crew, organizing insurance, designers, accommodation and travel equipment. During preproduction the script will have been developed into a detailed *screenplay*, which is broken down into scenes and then storyboarded. This involves visualizing the script's narrative in a series of drawings that indicate the content of each shot and may also include audio information and camera instructions. A shooting schedule is then prepared, and before filming begins a production script is likely to be required. This not only gives script information but also provides written details on how the script is to be filmed, such as camera instructions, further audio information and guidance to actors. Once production has begun, a more precise budget than that proposed during the pitch will be finalized. Budgeting is divided further into above-the-line and below-the-line costs. Above-the-line costs include the salaries of the director, actors and crew whereas below-the-line costs refer to any other expenditure such as film stock, equipment hire, hotel costs, food, scenery and costumes.

PRODUCTION

Production is the actual process of shooting the film. It is usually the most expensive stage in a film's life as it involves a large number of staff; hence the long credits at the end of a film! If the planning during preproduction has been carefully done, then the production should run smoothly and according to schedule. This is not always the case, however, and length of production varies from film to film. Kevin Costner's *Waterworld* (1995), for example, ran well over schedule and budget as it involved filming on the open sea subject to favourable weather conditions (see also *Apocalypse Now*, p. 22).

Key Production Roles

The following list is by no means comprehensive and does not cover all of the roles on a film. Some of the most important roles in production, however, are:

- The *producer*: see above.
- The *line producer* is responsible for the daily running of the production, in particular the day-to-day budget.
- The *scriptwriter* develops the original script/screenplay. Some films may employ more than one writer as the script is written and rewritten even as the film is being shot (see the section on *Casablanca*, p. 14).
- The *director* is the individual responsible for translating the script into a film. Arguably s/he is the most important individual on the set. S/he usually takes the artistic decisions regarding camera angles, type of shot, shot length, lighting, how the actors should interpret their roles, and editing. As with the producer, the role of the director varies according to each individual. Some may be described as *metteurs en scène*, basically skilled technicians, while others are referred to as *auteurs* – more like artists who attempt to stamp their own personal imprint upon the film (see Chapter 9 on Authorship).
- The *art director* or *production designer* is responsible for set design (*mise en scène*) and graphics.
- The *cinematographer* is also known as the *director of photography* or *lighting cameraman* and is responsible for the 'look' of a film, as s/he is in charge of camera technique. S/he translates the director's vision onto the screen, advising the director on camera lenses, angles, lighting and special effects.
- The *costume designer* conceptualizes and supervises the characters' outfits and works closely with the art director.
- The *casting director* selects and hires the support cast and negotiates fees with agents.
- The *camera operator* physically operates the camera under the guidance of the cinematographer.
- The *assistant camera operator* will help with camera movement, setting up the camera and operating controls, such as 'pulling focus'.
- The *assistant sound technician* will often be involved in operating a boom microphone, which is directional, meaning that it only picks up sound from the area the operator is pointing it towards.

Director and camera operator at work on Apocalypse Now (Zoetrope/UA, courtesy Kobal)   Figure 2.2

- The *locations manager* finds suitable locations for filming and negotiates their use.
- The *unit publicist* promotes the film during production and collects useful publicity materials.
- The *sound technician* is responsible for the complex process of recording sound. When recording 'live' sound during filming, recording levels have to be set low enough so as not to introduce distortion and high enough so that dialogue can be heard. Sound checks are carried out before recording.
- The *gaffer* is responsible for the lighting under the direction of the cinematographer.
- The *best boy* is the gaffer's assistant.
- The *key grip* is in charge of all other stagehands, who are known as *grips*.

POSTPRODUCTION

The final part of the overall production process is postproduction. Once approved, the *rushes* (film shot that day) will be sent to the editor, who will begin to put together a *rough cut* of the film. Once filming is complete, the shots are selected and put together to form the completed film. All recorded material is logged; *shot* and *take* numbers are indicated with times, descriptions of each shot and appropriate comments on the quality of each take. The completion of the log sheet is followed by an edit decision list. This identifies the takes that have been selected for the final edited film, gives their order and includes any other information that is needed at the editing stage. Editing is the process of joining together the chosen takes in the appropriate order with the inclusion of any extra audio-visual material.

Film Editing

The role of the editor is possibly the most important in imposing a narrative structure on the film. S/he supervises the splicing or cutting together of the many rolls of film shot during production into their final structure and will work closely with the director to ensure that his/her vision is fulfilled. The editing process includes the selection, shaping, and arrangement of shots, scenes, sequences and special effects. The editor will assemble a rough cut from the daily *rushes* during production, and this will then be refined in postproduction to achieve the finished edit or fine cut.

Sound Editing

The dubbing mixer, much like the editor, assembles a single soundtrack from the multiple soundtracks recorded during production such as dialogue, music and sound effects (all sounds that are neither music nor dialogue). During film production sound is recorded separately from the film, and the two must then fit together so that the sounds match the images on screen. The soundtracks must also be mixed together at appropriate volumes. This may involve additional alterations to the tone of dialogue and frequently actors are recalled (sometimes months after production has finished) to re-record their lines. Sound effects are the responsibility of the foley team, who create appropriate noises for the images. The sound is then optically or digitally added to the film stock.

The composer will work closely with the director to achieve the 'feel', atmosphere, mood, tension and emotion of the film. Frequently s/he will compose and often conduct an original score for the film in accordance with the director's wishes. Increasingly soundtracks are assembled from existing popular and classical music. The sound designer creates sounds for the film, many of which are specially created as they are not reality/earth-based (e.g. spaceships, extraterrestrial beings, etc.).

The Special Effects Department creates a range of illusions to enhance the film that are unobtainable during production. These involve using optical effects such as *front* and *rear projection,* models, mechanical or physical effects such as fires, explosions, flying or falling objects, and increasingly computer-generated imagery. Graphic artists work on the titles and credits of the film.

DISTRIBUTION

Once the director has approved the final cut, a preview screening is arranged for the distribution company. The distributor aims to exploit the film in order to profit from it or at the very least to recover the initial development and production costs. Effective distribution is fundamental to the film's success and many potentially prosperous films have failed at this point. In order to make a profit, a film must make roughly two and a half times its production costs at the box office. A distributor can acquire the distribution rights to a film by investing in it, by buying the rights after it has been made, or by being part of a larger company responsible for both production and distribution, such as a major Hollywood studio. Often the rights to distribute the video are acquired at the same time, which is a large source of revenue. A distribution company is subdivided into Publicity and Marketing (promotion), Film Sales (booking films into cinemas) and the Print Department (making copies of the film). The major distributors in the USA and the UK are UIP, Buena Vista, 20th Century Fox,

Warners and Columbia Tristar. Independent distributors include Entertainment, Polygram, Guild, Film Four, Rank, First Independent, Artificial Eye and Electric.

Based on an estimation of what a film will make at the box office and through rentals, the print and advertising budget (referred to as the P & A budget) is created for marketing. This determines the amount the distributor is able to spend on promoting the film and getting it into cinemas. Again this is divided into above-the-line costs, such as advertising, and below-the-line costs such as publicity, merchandise and flying in the stars. The distributor typically receives about 40 per cent of box office revenues, 30 per cent of which is spent on marketing, promotion, prints, certification and administration. Any money left over will then be paid to the producer, who will in turn pay the film's investors, artists, creditors and crew.

The tasks of the distributor include:

- acquiring a film;
- negotiating both the number and timing of the prints to be released to the exhibitors (distributors send hundreds and sometimes thousands of copies of each film to individual cinemas around the world, at approximately £1,000 per print. This can cost more than £3m for a film on wide release);
- arranging the distribution of these prints to the exhibitors;
- supplying the publicity material, advertising and trailers to the exhibitors in order to promote the film;
- arranging promotional partnerships to tie in with the film (known as tie-ins);
- dubbing and subtitling foreign language films;
- arranging and paying for a certificate;
- acquiring the rights to distribute the film on video.

Certification/Classification

Before a film can be screened to a paying audience in Britain it is a legal requirement that the British Board of Film Classification (BBFC) classifies it. In the United States there is a similar rating system which, although not a legal requirement, makes it unlikely that a film will be screened without a certificate (for more on this process see the section on Regulation and Censorship below). Certification is important when targeting an audience since it will determine the age of the audience at which the marketing will need to be pitched. A distributor may want to maximize the potential audience and aim to achieve a particular classification, as lower categories are on the whole believed to be more commercially advantageous. *Monty Python and the Holy Grail*, for example, generated some amusing (and probably not untypical) correspondence about how much swearing to 'lose' (see Figure 2.3).

The producers of the Bond films targeted the young teenage audience throughout the 1990s. In another instance, the distributors of *The Mummy* (1999) (Universal) wanted a '12' certificate for the film in the UK, but a hanging scene was deemed too graphic for such an audience. Universal were given a choice either to cut the offending scene or accept a higher classification. Since Universal wanted to maximize the potential audience, it cut 14 seconds from the scene and got its '12' classification. Similarly, *Lethal Weapon 4* (1998) was

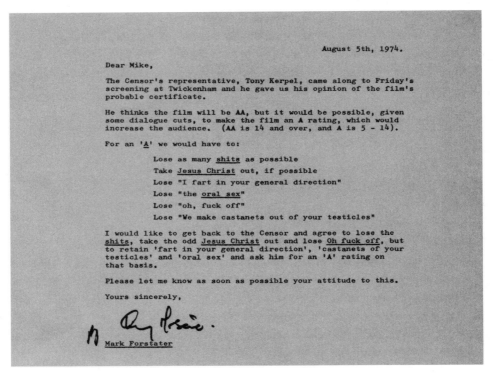

August 5th, 1974.

Dear Mike,

The Censor's representative, Tony Kerpel, came along to Friday's screening at Twickenham and he gave us his opinion of the film's probable certificate.

He thinks the film will be AA, but it would be possible, given some dialogue cuts, to make the film an A rating, which would increase the audience. (AA is 14 and over, and A is 5 - 14).

For an 'A' we would have to:

        Lose as many <u>shits</u> as possible
        Take <u>Jesus Christ</u> out, if possible
        Lose "I fart in your general direction"
        Lose "the <u>oral sex</u>"
        Lose "oh, fuck off"
        Lose "We make castanets out of your testicles"

I would like to get back to the Censor and agree to lose the <u>shits</u>, take the odd <u>Jesus Christ</u> out and lose <u>Oh fuck off</u>, but to retain 'fart in your general direction', 'castanets of your testicles' and 'oral sex' and ask him for an 'A' rating on that basis.

Please let me know as soon as possible your attitude to this.

Yours sincerely,

Mark Forstater

Figure 2.3   *Monty Python, swearing and certification*

voluntarily re-edited at the request of the UK distributor in order to obtain a '15' certificate instead of the less profitable '18'. This was also because, in the words of the BBFC, 'the British audience preferred its entertainment with the blood-letting toned down' (BBFC, 1999 Report, p. 9). Voluntary cuts in trailers are often made to achieve a wider category in order to appeal to a broader audience. The BBFC has tried to encourage these commercial motives where they can be made to operate in the public interest. The standard cost to the distributor for the certification process is £837 (plus VAT) for a 90 minute English language feature film, which means that the per minute cost is about £9.

Marketing

Once a film is finished it becomes a product – something that needs to be sold. The aim of marketing is to raise awareness of the product. Audiences must be informed that a film exists, their interest in it must be aroused and they must be persuaded to go and see something they neither necessarily need nor want. This is the job of the distributor. Marketing a film often begins months before a film is released, creating anticipation in audiences that it is coming to a nearby cinema soon.

    The distributor devises a marketing strategy so that the film finds its audience, and needs to determine the prime target audience at which the film will be aimed. In order to do this the distributor conducts audience research. Preview screenings are set up whereby the distributor can receive a range of opinions and reactions to the film, which can be a good indication of the prime target audience. The distributor will also turn to regular weekly research known as tracking undertaken by the National Research Group.

The process of marketing can be divided into three areas.

- **Advertising**: the distributor devises an advertising campaign using trailers, posters and radio, newspaper and TV spots, all of which are carefully tested. Interviews are conducted to ascertain a response and TV and radio slots are scheduled in order to reach the target audience. The campaign must be consistent so that the audience receives a single message about the film. Usually this message is based around a film's unique selling point (USP) – that single thing that differentiates it from other films – which could be the director, the stars, the plot or the special effects. Trailers are particularly important as they allow audiences to sample the film first hand. An effective trailer will generate interest in a film while a poor one may dissuade viewers completely.

- **Publicity** is free advertising that either cannot be bought or is too expensive to buy, such as the front pages of newspapers, magazine covers (see Figure 2.4), newspaper editorials, television and radio coverage. This involves press kits for journalists, photographs, star interviews, press screenings, gala premieres and free public screenings. New films can gain valuable publicity at film festivals held around the world, such as Cannes and the Sundance Festival.

- **Promotional merchandising** has become an important feature of marketing films following the phenomenal success of *Star Wars* (1977). Video sales and rentals are important, but initial budgets are now also recouped by sales of promotional merchandising, tie-ins and Original Sound Tracks. This has been accelerated by the trend towards conglomeration in the film industry, as a film is now often perceived as only one part of a product line of toys, clothes, food and drink, video and computer games, novels, comics and other spin-offs. Sales of these items also help to promote the film, while the film encourages sales of merchandise.

The most effective marketing method is word of mouth as it not only costs nothing, but also reaches its prime target audience successfully. Personal recommendations from friends, relatives or acquaintances, particularly those with shared tastes, are the most powerful devices for getting people into cinemas. Increasingly this is being replaced by word of mouse whereby films are marketed via the Internet. Today most major releases have a website. Together word of mouth and of mouse combined to create the unprecedented hype surrounding the release of *The Phantom Menace* (1999). Officially tolerated and unofficial fan-based websites created an expansive source of information about the film prior to its release, even including a scene-by-scene breakdown of the film. *The Blair Witch Project* (1999) was almost exclusively marketed on the web in the United States prior to its release there. Similarly, *The Omega Code* (1999) benefited from strategic promotion on the Internet without a single frame being shown to the mainstream press.

The timing of release is vitally important in determining a film's box office success. Many factors are taken into consideration: genre, subject matter, and also other films due for release either by the distribution company or its competitors. The peak release dates are

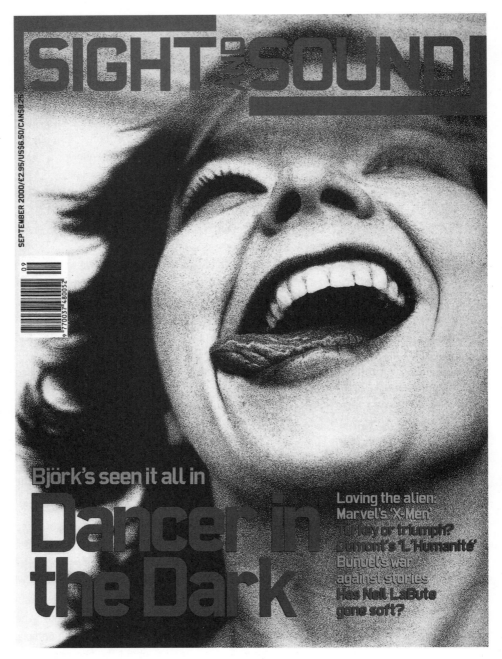

Figure 2.4   *Free publicity is essential to film promotion (BFI Stills, Posters and Designs)*

summer and winter holidays as these provide maximum leisure time for families. *The Blair Witch Project* was released in the UK to coincide with Halloween. The release may also be timed to coincide with the Oscars or other film festivals as these can have an important impact on box-office performance. *The English Patient* was released in the USA in March 1996 to coincide with the Oscar nomination period of February onwards. It was then later released in the UK deliberately to feed upon its Oscar successes in the USA. In contrast, 20th Century Fox deliberately delayed the release of the controversial *Fight Club* (1999) in order to avoid the Senate hearings on how to curb violence in films and thus to evade any adverse publicity that the film may have received. Ultimately, however, despite the best efforts of those promoting and marketing the film, it is the public who decides if a film will be a success or not.

Exercise 2.2

Compare and contrast the routes through distribution and exhibition of a typical mainstream Hollywood film and a smaller British film. Does the latter have the same options and opportunities as the former?

EXHIBITION

The next stage in a film's life is where the real money is made. Exhibition is the key stage since it is the first outlet for the film product and is where the distributor earns revenue from the public. Exhibition is essential to a film's success, as it is the shop window in which films are sold to their audiences. A film must also, therefore, be 'sold' to the exhibitor, who works very closely with the distributor to promote the film to an audience.

Once the exhibitor has viewed the film, a release pattern and financial deal will be arranged to rent the film from the distributor. It is the task of the film booker to find films that will attract an audience and in turn create large box-office returns, and usually the exhibitor and the distributor will work together closely to ensure this. Mainstream films are usually booked between three and six months prior to release, but sometimes they can be booked up to a year in advance. The exhibitor will then advertise the film locally in order to attract as large an audience as possible. This will be done through listings in local magazines and newspapers, posters, competitions, trailers and other promotional material. Once the audience member has paid for his/her ticket, the cinema typically subtracts about 60 per cent to cover its running costs (the 'house nut') and its profit margin. The rest (about 40 per cent) is paid back to the distributor. In order to ensure a profit, the exhibitor also sells concessions (ice creams, hot dogs, sweets, drinks, etc.); this is a particularly important source of revenue if the film is a failure.

A Brief History of British and American Exhibition

We shall look at the history of exhibition until the end of the First World War in Chapter 7 on Early Cinema and Film Form. Here we shall look briefly at the history of exhibition in Britain and the United States after 1918. Following the war, the Hollywood studios dominated US exhibition through a system of vertical integration and continued to do so until divorcement in 1948 (see the section on the Hollywood Studio System in Chapter 1). In Britain, the Cinematograph Act of 1927 attempted to prop up the flagging film-making industry in the

UK by requiring that a quota of British releases be shown. Deals were then made between the large US distributors (who received about 25 per cent of the total gross from the UK), British film-makers, and the emerging cinema circuits such as Provincial Cinematograph Theatres – England's first national circuit (established 1919). Three other large circuits soon appeared: Gaumont (1926), Associated British Cinemas (1928) and Odeon (1930s), resulting in the construction of many elaborate cinemas.

However, the Second World War stopped cinema building in the UK and, by the time restrictions had been removed in 1954, cinema attendance was in decline as a result of changes in leisure activity, the move to the suburbs and greater disposable incomes (see Chapter 3 on Cinema, Audiences and Society). In the United States, audiences declined as a result of a combination of TV and increasing suburbanization. In reaction, the major studios introduced new technologies in an attempt to lure audiences back into the cinemas. There was increased use of colour processes in the 1950s followed by the introduction of widescreen and 3D technologies. From the 1970s onwards, sound quality improved as stereo and Dolby playback were developed (see Chapter 5). However, the decline in audience figures was accelerated by the introduction of home video in the late 1970s. Many cinemas closed down and were converted (in Britain) into bingo halls, pubs, night-clubs or supermarkets or were pulled down and replaced by housing.

By 1985 vertical integration had returned in the United States and the ownership of the theatre chains, such as Walter Reade, Cineplex/Odeon and Loew's Theaters, was still concentrated among a small number of companies like Universal, Columbia, Paramount and Warners (see Chapter 1). In the UK the major cinema operators became Cinven (ABC and Odeon Cinemas), UGC (Virgin), National Amusements (Showcase Cinemas), UCI (owned by CBS/Viacom and Seagram), Warner Village and Cine UK (see Table 2.1).

The Multiplex, Multi-screen and Megaplex

By the mid-1980s British cinema appeared to be in terminal decline as video rentals, combined with dingy cinemas, poor audio-visual quality and high ticket prices, kept potential

Table 2.1   *Major UK exhibitors*

Exhibitor	Screens 1997	Screens 1998	Screens 1999
Odeon Cinemas (UK)	410	452	460
UCI (US)	253	294	317
UGC (France)	208	266	303
Warner Village (US/Australia)	152	192	266
National Amusements (US)	197	197	211
ABC Cinemas (UK)	206	208	180
Cine-UK	66	116	146
Independents	857	856	875
Total	2349	2581	2758

Source: Dodona Research (2000)

cinemagoers at home. The average Briton visited the cinema approximately once a year. As audiences dwindled, profits were affected, and the major US distributors recognized the need to revitalize the European exhibition sector. In the 1960s the major studios, such as Universal, Warners and Paramount, had begun to invest in refurbishing cinemas, improving audio-visual facilities and increasing the numbers of screens per cinema. This led to the launch of the *multiplex* – two or more screens housed in a single building – by AMC Entertainment in America in 1963, soon to be followed by Cineplex's development of the *multi-screen* in 1979. The watershed for the film industry in Britain was 1985, when the first multiplex cinema opened in Milton Keynes. Since then cinema-going has changed irrevocably. New 'fast-food-style' multiplexes housing up to 20 screens sprang up across the country. Older large single-auditorium cinemas were divided into smaller screens, giving rise to the multi-screen cinema housing between three and eight screens. And soon there emerged the *megaplex*, which housed more than 16 screens, with retail outlets, restaurants and other leisure activities.

Since 1985 multiplex expansion has been unrelenting as the major cinema operators have channelled their energies into this sector. Multiplexes with more than seven screens account for more than half of Britain's cinema screens. Almost 1,400 new cinema screens have opened at 140 multiplex sites in the UK and approximately 50 per cent of these opened in the years 1997–2000 alone. In 1998 almost 300 screens were opened (more than in any 12-month period for 15 years) and nearly 700 new screens were opened in 1999 and 2000. This trend is increasing as the major operators have yet more multiplexes planned. At present, multiplexes dominate the UK exhibition sector – about half of the UK's population is no more than 20 minutes' drive away from a multiplex and about 60 per cent of all cinemagoers now attend multiplexes on suburban town fringes. In turn, this increased competition has gradually forced smaller inner-city and high street local cinema operators out of the market. In 1999, for example, the ABC in Golders Green (originally the Ionic), which was built in 1912, closed down because of the competition from two nearby Warner Village multiplexes. The future suggests that smaller operators will be swallowed by the bigger chains, leaving just several large exhibitors and a decreasing number of independent competitors.

Following Virgin's lead, the major cinema chains have been rebranding themselves in order to attract customers away from other operators and to encourage customer brand loyalty. As a result, many now offer premium screens, 'arthouse' screens, cafés, bars, cappuccino shops, merchandising, children's facilities and other spending attractions in order to set them apart from the competition. Concessions now provide revenues of £125m per year, representing a 25 per cent increase over 5 years. Advertising revenues are also increasing and account for 20 per cent of box office takings. Meanwhile, average ticket prices have increased from £3 in 1994 to £3.75 in 1999.

Despite the huge growth in cinema admissions and screens (see Table 2.2) the actual number of films widely available in the UK has not increased significantly. Rather than expanding the range of films, cinemas have tended to focus on exploiting a limited number of blockbusters. Films will play on multiple screens with multiple staggered start times, and despite early promises of maintaining an arthouse screen, many operators have passed this over in favour of offering another screen for the blockbuster.

Table 2.2   *Cinema screens in the UK, 1950–99*

Year	Multiplex	Traditional	Total
1950	0	4583	4583
1955	0	4483	4483
1960	0	3034	3034
1965	0	1971	1971
1970	0	1529	1529
1975	0	1530	1530
1980	0	1562	1562
1984	0	1275	1275
1985	10	1345	1355
1986	18	1315	1333
1987	45	1290	1335
1988	142	1320	1462
1989	288	1310	1598
1990	390	1325	1715
1991	518	1285	1803
1992	562	1280	1842
1993	624	1280	1904
1994	689	1275	1964
1995	725	1280	2005
1996	864	1358	2222
1997	1089	1260	2349
1998	1357	1224	2581
1999	1617	1141	2758

Source: Central Statistical Office, Dodona Research (2000)

One of the reasons why Britain's film industry is so weak is of course due to American ownership of the cinema chains. American exhibitors tend to block British products and, as a result, approximately 85 per cent of films screened in the UK are American. The US distributors, rightly or wrongly, believe British films to be unpopular with mainstream audiences and, consequently, low-budget and British films find it difficult to find exhibition opportunities outside independent and 'arthouse' cinemas.

Exercise 2.3

Carry out a survey among your class asking why people went to the last film they saw. What factors did they take into account? Did they feel that they had a real choice of films or were there many films that they did not want to see?

Arthouse cinemas began to appear in the early 1950s and by the early 1960s there were approximately 500 in the USA. They are distinguished by their specialist programming policies and the range of films that are shown. They can be defined as cinemas that feature foreign-language, independent, avant-garde, retrospective or classic films. In the UK they are also often referred to as 'repertory' cinemas. Such cinemas are generally small and rely on a select and discriminating clientele, but have nonetheless helped to increase cinema-going. They are generally owned by individuals, smaller companies (e.g. Oasis, Apollo and Robins), or are subsidised by the government, operating apart from the major chains. Since the 1960s they have greatly decreased in number as the distinction between American and foreign films has become less significant and foreign films have had a very difficult time at the box office. However, in the face of competition from the multiplexes, many owners have refurbished their cinemas to offer a different experience including cafés, restaurants and bookshops. Some of the most notable of these cinemas are the National Film Theatre on London's South Bank, the Phoenix in East Finchley, the Tricycle in Kilburn and the Electric Cinema in Birmingham.

Reviewing and criticism are important elements in the life of a film as they may help to determine its success. When a film is marketed, press screenings are arranged in the hope of positive write-ups from the critics. The typical film review will contain a concise summary of the plot, background information, a set of condensed arguments about the film and an appraisal. When reviewing a film, the critic will usually be looking for compositional, 'realistic', intertextual and artistic motivation, as well as social and entertainment value as both narrative and spectacle. Film reviewing also has other functions. It informs readers about the latest news and releases. It advertises and publicizes the film, encouraging readers to see it or to avoid it. And it analyses, describes and evaluates the film. The actual impact of the critic/reviewer, however, is hard to pinpoint. Extracts from positive reviews are often included in the poster campaign of a film, but what effect does reviewing have on the potential audience? Are we persuaded to see a film or dissuaded from seeing it because of what someone else has written about it? Who writes about films and why are their reviews read? These are questions that cannot be easily answered, but they will be considered in the next chapter.

Exercise 2.4

For a new release of your choice, read/collect as many different reviews as you can (including a wide range of newspapers and magazines). Try to account for the differences of approach.

THE FUTURE OF CINEMA

What does the future of cinema-going hold? Experts have already predicted that the number of screens in the UK will reach saturation point somewhere between 2005 and 2010. Increasing capacity has overtaken the rise in cinema attendance, and pockets such as Bolton, Swindon and Sheffield are reportedly already unable to sustain any more new cinemas as a result of what has been called 'consumer fatigue'. Multiplexes are also expensive and many have been struggling to make profits. In addition, new planning laws in the

UK (which encourage investment in town centres and reduction of car travel) have forced many operators to reconsider plans for stand-alone multiplexes on town fringes or in suburbs. The major cinema operators, such as Cinven (ABC and Odeon), Viacom and Seagram (UCI), Hoyts and UGC (Virgin), are delaying and withdrawing from planned projects in the UK and some are getting out of the market altogether. The suggested forecast is that smaller operators will be swallowed by the bigger chains or will simply drop out of the UK market.

Cinema-going has been revolutionized over the years not only by new cinemas but also by changes in technology, particularly with the advent of VCRs, the Internet and DVDs. The merger of AOL and Time-Warner suggests that the Internet may become the primary site for film exhibition in the near future, shifting viewing to the home. Exhibitors will undoubtedly react, as they have always done, with the introduction of improved audio-visual technology, which we shall look at in Chapter 5 on Film Technology. *Toy Story 2* (2000), for example, was screened in the UK using digital projection, which may make the need for what have been perceived to be unwieldy and costly reels of film redundant. Soon this may become the norm. The introduction of IMAX and OMNIMAX technologies may also affect the way we watch films in the future. But will these technologies have a significant impact or will the allure of viewing films over the Internet within the comfort of the home prove too strong?

S U M M A R Y

- **There are three main stages in film-making: production, distribution and exhibition.**
- **Production involves the following:**
  - **finance: a producer seeks to find investors and financial backing for a film package;**
  - **preproduction: includes research, planning, budgeting, hiring director and crew, casting, finding locations, scripting and storyboarding;**
  - **production: shooting the film;**
  - **postproduction: editing, sound design, sound editing and dubbing, special effects and graphics.**
- **Distribution: the distribution, marketing, advertising, promoting and classification of the film.**
- **Exhibition: exposing the film to the audience, whether it is in a one-screen, multiplex, multi-screen, megaplex or arthouse cinema; also includes reviewing and criticism.**

REFERENCES

BBFC *Annual Report 1998* (London: BBFC, 1999).

Geoffrey Mcnab, 'Hey, you wanna buy a movie?', *The Guardian* (21 October 1999), p. 12.

FURTHER READING

Angela Bell, Mark Joyce and Danny Rivers, 'The British film industry', in *Advanced Level Media* (London: Hodder & Stoughton, 1999), pp. 130–47.

Gill Branston and Roy Stafford, 'Case study: making films outside the mainstream', in *The Media Student's Book* (2nd edn, New York and London: Routledge, 1999), pp. 369–76.

Eddie Dyja (ed.), *BFI Film and Television Handbook 2000* (London: BFI, 1999).

The Film Industry Pack (London: Film Education, 1999).

Douglas Gomery, *Shared Pleasures: A History of Movie Presentation in the United States* (London: BFI, 1992).

Nicholas Garnham, *Emancipation, The Media and Modernity: Arguments about the Media and Social Theory* (Oxford: Oxford University Press, 2000).

John Hill and Pamela Church Gibson (eds), *The Oxford Guide to Film Studies* (Oxford: Oxford University Press, 1998).

Jill Nelmes (ed.), *An Introduction to Film Studies* (2nd edn, New York and London: Routledge, 1999).

Picture Palaces: New Life for Old Cinemas (London: English Heritage, 1999).

Janet Wasko, *Hollywood in the Information Age* (Cambridge: Polity, 1994).

FURTHER VIEWING

The British Film Industry (Film Education, BBC2, 1999).

The Distributor's Tale (Film Education, BBC2, 1999).

The Film Industry in Britain (Film Education, BBC2, 1999).

The Making of a Blockbuster: The Bond Phenomenon and Preproduction (Film Education, Channel 4, 1999).

The Making of a Blockbuster: The Bond Phenomenon and Production (Film Education, Channel 4, 1999).

The Making of a Blockbuster: The Bond Phenomenon and Postproduction (Film Education, Channel 4, 1999).

Marketing Movies (Film Education, BBC2, 1999).

Cinema, Audiences and Society

The relationship between films and their viewers is central to Film Studies. '[I]t is through the existence of an audience that film acquires social and cultural importance' (Jostein Gripsrud, quoted in Hill and Church Gibson (1999), p. 203). It is precisely because of this powerful relationship that the film industry has been subject to censorship and regulation from its earliest days. Similarly, there has been an interest in the impact that a film has upon its audience from the turn of the twentieth century onwards, as well as in who constitutes that audience. The study of these matters falls into two main areas: audience research and spectatorship. In this chapter, we shall be considering the 'audience' rather than 'spectatorship' (the academic study of how individual viewers/subjects relate to and decode film texts), which is examined elsewhere in this book.

This chapter is divided into two parts. In the first section, 'Film Consumption', we will examine contemporary film demand and consumption in the UK, encouraging the reader to reflect on her/his own viewing habits. In the process, both the commercial and cultural significance of film consumption will be considered. Film consumption includes not only cinema-going, but also video, television and other situations of film viewing. In the second section we will consider how regulation and censorship have affected both producers and audiences and impacted upon the relationship between them, particularly in imposing limitations. As we shall see, the history of both topics – audiences and censorship/regulation – follows a similar pattern, as both have fluctuated and changed according to political, social, economic and cultural circumstances.

FILM CONSUMPTION

We know that people watch films and that films have audiences. An audience is essential to the continuing production of films, as that is where profits are made and initial investments are recouped. But what is an audience and what do we actually know about audiences? First, a warning: the concept of the audience is slippery, shapeless, evasive, and rather hard to define, but we can distinguish the audience from the spectator. Where the spectator is an individual, the audience is a collection of individuals transformed by a shared experience;

where the spectator is constituted by psychological and textual relations, the audience is organized around categories of ethnicity, class, gender, age, education, and so on. Furthermore, the audience is a construct and can never be understood in a 'pure', unadulterated form. The ideological perspective of those who are looking for the audience – film producers, marketers and distributors, pressure groups or governmental agencies – shapes their particular conception of the audience.

When seeking to understand the audience we have to consider who watches films and how, when and where they are watched. How many people watched the film and what did they do afterwards? What role do films play in our lives? How do we actually watch them and with whom? How do we use and talk about our film experiences? We cannot treat the audience as a single, monolithic, undifferentiated mass. Rather, we must understand that the audience is heterogeneous and can contain many people from various groups, that different films are enjoyed and hated by different people at different times, and further that films are watched in widely differing circumstances: in cinemas, at home on the TV, video or DVD, over the Internet, on aeroplanes, with friends, or alone, and so on. Our enjoyment of a film will also vary according to mood, different social occasions, whether we are alone or with others, and whoever is watching with us. Perhaps the best way to understand what we mean by the audience is to be aware of your own responses and behaviour when engaged in the social practice and cultural phenomenon of cinema.

Constructing Audiences

Although the concept of the audience is difficult to pin down accurately, a great deal of what is called quantitative research has been devoted to doing just that. The first audience research was prompted by fears about the social effects of cinema's huge popularity, particularly with youngsters. And there has long been an interest in audience composition, particularly for early audiences. Studio executives pay large sums to audience research groups to measure the success of their films and to provide 'what people want'. The commercial and competitive nature of Hollywood and other film industries has ensured a constant flow of research about numbers of viewers, information about who they are and what they make of what they see (and hear). Furthermore, the film industry has always sought to relate cinema audiences to wider society and its tastes and composition. Audiences have thus been categorized in two ways:

- demographics, which segments social groups according to class, gender, age, family, nation, and ethnicity, education, religion, political allegiance, region, urban/rural background etc.;
- psychographics, whereby the consumer is categorized in terms of needs and desires (e.g. those who aspire to a richer lifestyle or those who want to make the world a better place).

Film producers, distributors and exhibitors (who are often ultimately part of the same company) have attempted to construct audiences from the very beginnings of the film industry. As we have seen in the section on distribution in Chapter 2, once a film is finished it becomes a product that needs to be sold. An audience is targeted, selected and constructed; today this has become an industry in its own right. Profiling, market research, advertising, tracking and psychological testing are all used to build and construct an audience, and vast sums of money are spent doing this.

Understanding Audiences

Academics, governmental agencies and pressure groups, while interested in the audience, are particularly concerned with the *effects* of film consumption and the *uses* to which it is put, and a range of theories have been developed which seek to explain these processes. Some of these models are looked at in Chapter 12 on spectatorship; however, below we list those that have sought to understand how audiences read and use films.

- Opinion leaders and two-step flow: early research suggested that audiences were neither passive nor uniform. While audiences did accept media messages, they were also as likely to be influenced by their own situations or others' opinions as by the content of a film text. It was shown that opinion leaders played a key role in affecting individual views (see Lazarsfeld *et al.*, 1944).
- Selective influence: this research indicated that the effects of films were neither direct nor uniform. Further, audiences' selection of films was typically based on their social category (e.g. class, age, gender), their individual psychology and social relationships, which were more influential on their opinions than the media. The research indicated that to maximize profit, films should be targeted towards specific groups.
- Modelling: this research suggested that audiences may gradually emulate behaviour that was clearly rewarded and appealing, which in turn could be reinforced by frequent observation of such behaviour or by discovering that it actually produced results. This approach is evident in the concern over cinematic and 'designer' violence.
- Media consumption within social environment explores who controls the viewing and how people actually watch and talk about their experiences. This presumes an active viewer watching in specific social circumstances and sharing audio-visual experiences in an equally social context (see Morley, 1986).
- Historical reception studies: Reception Theory looks at audiences as individuals who actively make sense of media texts. Stuart Hall, head of the Centre for Contemporary Cultural Studies in Birmingham, suggested that how we *decode* information contained in the text will depend on our background and factors like class, ethnicity, gender, age, status, job, region, religion, experience and beliefs. These factors will influence our response regardless of what a producer may have *encoded* within a film. In analysing encoding and decoding in media texts, Stuart Hall, using a Cultural Studies approach, noted that while a text may have a preferred reading encoded within it, this is not always accepted. Rather, there are three types of audience response: *dominant readings* in which the audience accepts the preferred reading; *negotiated readings* in which the audience generally agrees with dominant values, but may disagree with certain aspects; and *oppositional readings* in which the audience rejects dominant values (see Hall *et al.*,

1980; Morley, 1980). Umberto Eco has gone further in claiming that all media texts, including films, can also be *aberrantly decoded*. Historical reception studies analyse the varying responses of audiences to certain films at specific historical moments, taking into account social history, audience composition, reviews, commentary, fandom, star images, tie-ins, scandal and any other events/publicity that impact on the reception of a film (see Staiger, 1992). A good example of such an approach is Staiger's own 'Taboos and totems: cultural meanings of *The Silence of the Lambs*', in Collins *et al.*, (1993).

A Brief History of UK Cinema-going

In 40 years UK cinema attendance has changed dramatically (see Table 3.1). The peak point of cinema attendance was 1946 when there were 1,635 million admissions, representing 31.5m people going once a week. By 1984, however, cinema attendance had sunk to a post-war low of 54m (over 70 per cent of the population had not been to see a film once that year!).

What happened over these years to change a nation's leisure habits? Those who went to the cinema in 1946 were mostly working-class, urban and young and lived near to local cinemas. Young children grew up going to the cinema, particularly on Saturday mornings, encouraged by their relatives. By the mid-1950s, however, the growth of the suburbs took people away from local cinemas and their extended families. Furthermore, a growth in leisure time and greater disposable income meant that people had a far greater range of consumer products to distract them. Inner-city cinemas closed down and failed to relocate to the new housing estates. Meanwhile, though the young working classes were still the main consumers of films, they were also absorbed in other activities like music, dressing up and drinking, which grew out of a distinctive youth culture. Although television appeared in the 1950s, it was at first restricted to the middle classes (who had never constituted a significant part of cinema audiences) and did not have a major impact until the early 1960s with the advent of ITV and (later) colour. Thereafter, the home became the focus of leisure activity. By 1984, then, most people in the UK preferred to watch films at home. As we have seen in our section on exhibition, dingy cinemas, poor audio-visual quality and high ticket prices kept potential cinemagoers at home and the average Briton visited the cinema only once a year. By this time, cinema had also ceased to be a primarily working-class activity.

Video, Pay TV, DVD

The advent of video in the mid-1970s revolutionized access to films and may also have kept cinemagoers at home. Rather than depending on the local cinema or BBC and ITV, people could choose a wide range of films to be viewed in the comfort of their own homes. Video viewing is suited to family life as it is cheaper than multiple cinema tickets, parking/public transport and the obligatory refreshments, and can cater for the whole family's tastes and preferences. Video can also compensate for the lack of choice at the cinema and provide for niche or culturally specific tastes. Furthermore, video gives greater power to the consumer to choose when, where and how to watch – a trend that can only increase with the

Table 3.1   *UK cinema admissions 1933–98*

Year	Admissions (millions)	Year	Admissions (millions)
1933	903.00	1966	288.80
1934	950.00	1967	264.80
1935	912.33	1968	237.30
1936	917.00	1969	214.90
1937	946.00	1970	193.00
1938	987.00	1971	176.00
1939	990.00	1972	156.60
1940	1,027.00	1973	134.20
1941	1,309.00	1974	138.50
1942	1,494.00	1975	116.30
1943	1,541.00	1976	103.90
1944	1,575.00	1977	103.50
1945	1,585.00	1978	126.10
1946	1,635.00	1979	111.90
1947	1,462.00	1980	101.00
1948	1,514.00	1981	86.00
1949	1,430.00	1982	64.00
1950	1,395.80	1983	65.70
1951	1,365.00	1984	54.00
1952	1,312.10	1985	72.00
1953	1,284.50	1986	75.50
1954	1,275.80	1987	78.50
1955	1,181.80	1988	84.00
1956	1,100.80	1989	94.50
1957	915.20	1990	97.37
1958	754.70	1991	100.29
1959	581.00	1992	103.64
1960	500.80	1993	114.36
1961	449.10	1994	123.53
1962	395.00	1995	114.56
1963	357.20	1996	123.80
1964	342.80	1997	139.30
1965	326.60	1998	135.50

Source: Screen Digest/Screen Finance/BFI

expansion of pay TV services, particularly BSkyB and digital TV, which now allow the viewer to select from a range of films on offer, and DVD, which is set to replace video.

It will be interesting to see how these developments will affect cinema attendance over the coming years, especially as the relationship between video and a decline in cinema attendance is not as straightforward as it appears. Cinema attendance began to rise in 1985 – reaching 75m compared to 54m the previous year – just when video ownership was reaching its peak. Video ownership, therefore, may actually indicate a resurgence of interest in the cinema, not least because those who own VCRs are also most likely to attend the cinema and may only use their machines for timer recording.

Multiplexes and Multi-screens

When the first UK multiplex opened in Milton Keynes in 1985, it was during what was labelled 'British Film Year'. Since then cinema-going has changed irrevocably and cinema attendance has risen, seemingly as a direct result of the increase in the number of cinema screens. In 1998 the attendance figure reached 135.5m, totalling £507m in box-office takings. *The Full Monty* lifted British cinema attendance to a record 139.5 m in 1997, but this fell in the following 12 months with the top British film, *Sliding Doors*, only managing to take £12.3m in comparison to *The Full Monty*'s £40.8m. The American-produced *Notting Hill* boosted audiences in June and July 1999 to levels not seen since the 1970s. Audiences were forecast at 140m for 1999, which only just signals a return to the attendance figures of the 1970s. Although Britain has nearly as many screens as in 1960, attendance has dropped by 75 per cent. The average Briton now goes to the cinema about 2.3 times per year in comparison to 9.6 visits per year in 1960. In contrast, the average American attends the cinema more than five times a year and the United States is described as having the world's most developed cinema market.

Cinema-going has witnessed a shift in class allegiances, becoming more of a middle-class than working-class activity (see Table 3.2). In the UK those aged between 15 and 24 were the most regular cinemagoers in 1998, followed closely by 25–34 year olds and then 7–14 year olds, a total of 24.33m people (see Table 3.3). Research has shown that the 15–24 age group has the most time and money to go the cinema and they will be deliberately targeted by film-makers, distributors and exhibitors. Interestingly, the largest demographic group – 35+ (representing 30.15m people, well over half the population) – visits the cinema the least, as their time and disposable income may be decreased as a result of other responsibilities. Since the rise of the multiplex the audience has become more family-centred since such cinemas are conveniently located (a short drive from most homes) and are near to shopping and other leisure facilities. In terms of gender, the figures are almost identical: 82 per cent male and 84 per cent female.

Why do we watch?

The type of film available to us is determined by a number of factors: where we live, how much we can afford to spend, what is on TV, whether we have pay TV, a VCR or DVD player, and what

Who goes to the Cinema? UK cinema screens and admissions, 1960–98   Table 3.2

Year	Admissions (million)	Admissions (per person)
1960	500.8	9.6
1970	193.0	3.5
1980	101.0	1.8
1990	91.0	1.6
1995	108.0	1.8
1996	124.0	2.1
1997	139.5	2.4
1998	135.5	2.3

Source: Dodona Research

Table 3.3   *Frequency of UK cinema-going 1998*

Age group	7–14	15–24	25–34	35+	ABC1	C2DE	Male	Female
No. of people (m)	8.30	6.96	9.07	30.15	26.39	28.09	26.79	27.69
Once a month or more (%)	31	53	33	11	27	20	24	22
Less than once a month (%)	48	37	44	33	41	34	37	39
Once a year or less (%)	13	7	18	30	20	25	21	23
Total who ever go to the cinema (%)	92	97	95	74	99	79	82	84

Source: Screen Finance/X25 Partnership/CAVIAR

Notes:

A = upper middle class, successful business, higher management or professional

B = middle class, middle management or administration or professional

C1 = white collar, lower middle class, junior management or supervisory or professional, small tradespeople or non-manual workers

C2 = blue collar, skilled working class, manual

D = semi- or unskilled manual workers

E = unemployed or casual workers or pensioners or those dependent on social security

is available at the local video rental shop. In rural areas, there are less cinemas than in urban areas. Similarly, in larger cities there is a greater choice of cinemas, including more repertory/arthouse cinemas. Cinema-going tends to be greater in areas where there is a large number of screens offering a wide choice of films than in locations with a limited selection. The quality of the cinema experience, its proximity to other attractions, easy access and parking are all other reasons why people go to the cinema. However, increased ticket prices and the cost of food, popcorn, etc. have begun to undermine the perception that cinema is cheap.

Some of the main reasons for going to the cinema are that it provides the best setting for viewing films, access to new films while they are still 'fresh', and a pleasurable, undemanding and cheap chance for going out. On the other hand, improved home viewing technology, greater access to films through film channels and video hire, and shorter post-cinema release times have lessened the appeal of going to the cinema, making watching at home seem cheaper, easier and more comfortable and relaxing than going to the cinema. Cinema-going competes against other forms of leisure; for some people it does not have the convenience of watching at home, while for others it is not as social or exciting as going out for a drink, to a party or a club or eating out. It has a low priority as it is seen to be continuously available, low key and neither routine nor special enough to make it first option. Cinema-going, therefore, is increasingly combined with other leisure activities as one part of a larger night out. However, there are occasionally 'must-see' films which transform cinema-going into a leisure activity in its own right.

The most intensive periods for watching films in the UK are the Christmas and summer holidays, the peak leisure times when both TV and cinema audiences are at their highest. Weekends usually generate the most video rentals.

Choosing Films

According to the Film Policy Review Group (FPRG, 1998), 'Film is regarded [by the audience] as the most complete story-telling medium; watching an enjoyable film is still one of the most satisfying, absorbing and appealing forms of entertainment'; but how do audiences decide what films to see?

A survey of UK cinema-going habits conducted by the FRPG in the 1990s showed that cinemagoers were rather cautious when choosing films, tending to avoid those they might not like. As there is a large choice of films which spectators know they should enjoy, there was only limited interest in taking risks by exploring films beyond the mainstream, and a tendency to stick with 'their kind of film'.

The study found that in general terms, younger (18–30) C1C2 audiences prefer more mainstream, big budget, star-studded action films with impressive special effects rather than gritty realism, small-scale and low-budget 'message' films, which are perceived as 'depressing'. Older audiences, on the other hand, like subtlety; men prefer action films while women prefer human interest stories. C2s favour easy-watching escapist films while BC1s want to be challenged more. Older and more educated Bs like realistic films about characters and settings they can identify with and period films, classics and films about social issues.

Beyond these broad tastes, mood, occasion and company can also have an impact, and we are likely to be influenced by the presence of a favourite star or director, the plot, special effects or music. Our choices are also influenced by how and by whom the film has been recommended. Despite the vast sums of money spent on marketing films, word of mouth is a particularly important factor in choosing a film, though reviewing and criticism clearly also play a part. Specific choices and judgements are made on the basis of a wide variety of evidence, such as genre, title, poster, stars, director and publicity.

Exercise 3.1
Think about your own film-watching behaviour: when do you go to the cinema and why? When do you watch films on TV and when do you rent videos? Also, consider occasions when you have watched films other than on TV or at the cinema.

REGULATION AND CENSORSHIP

Censorship – erasing or blocking parts of or whole publications, correspondence or theatrical performances – has a long history stretching back to ancient times. Every society has had customs, taboos or laws by which speech, play, dress, religious observance and sexual expression were regulated, and laws have evolved concerned with restricting the expression, publication and dissemination of information, particularly in wartime.

Public complaints often accompanied the emergent medium in the 1890s, but it was not until the expansion of permanent cinemas from 1905 onwards that public and governmental interest took hold and censorship was enforced. Initially it was the responsibility of the police and the local authorities, using the existing laws and powers covering places of entertainment, to censor films. But as film developed into a global phenomenon, film-makers had difficulty dealing with the variable standards applied from one country to another and sometimes within their own country too. In response, each country's film industry usually set up its own voluntary censorship organization with which film producers were expected to co-operate. In most European countries censorship remained a local police responsibility for far longer than in the UK or the USA. In countries with totalitarian or autocratic governments, however, there has been central government control of all films, as was the case in Nazi Germany and the Soviet Union.

Censorship bodies usually develop guidelines about what is prohibited in films, and these have changed over time according to changing circumstances. In particular, public attitudes have changed, and more explicitly violent and sexual representations are tolerated now than in the past. As the power of religious bodies has declined, religion and morality do not appear to be subjects for censorship.

Exercise 3.2

As a member of an audience, how far do you feel that an external body has the right to censor and regulate what you see? In what situations are censorship and regulation not only necessary, but also desirable?

CASE STUDY

Censorship in the United Kingdom

At present, film and video are regulated (and in some cases censored) by the British Board of Film Classification (BBFC) – an independent, non-governmental body, funded by charging for the service it provides to the film industry. Although the BBFC gives the certificate for a film, any local authority has statutory power to overrule its decisions. Local authorities generally accept the Board's decisions, except on rare occasions such as when Westminster Council, for example, refused to allow the screening of *Crash* (Cronenberg, 1996) in its cinemas, or when Camden showed *The Texas Chainsaw Massacre* (Hooper, 1974) without approaching the Board. Several local authorities also banned the screening of *Monty Python's Life of Brian* (1979) on grounds of blasphemy, with the result that in 1979/80 one could see the film in Leeds but not in Harrogate. All films normally require a certificate, which must be clearly displayed in advertising, at the cinema entrance and on the screen immediately before the film is shown. Local authorities can, however, allow an uncertificated film to be screened, but face the possibility of legal action, for example under the Obscene Publications Act. Cinemas have to be licensed before they can screen films and are thus unlikely to risk losing an exhibition licence (see Figure 3.1) by screening a film which a local authority is likely to object to.

The BBFC age certificates   Figure 3.1

Initially, it was the responsibility of local authorities to censor films, but this led to confusion as widely differing standards were applied. Among the first councils to ban a film outright was London County Council, which took objection to a film of the recently contested world heavyweight boxing championship, in which a white man had been beaten by a black opponent (see Richards, 1997, p. 167). In 1912 the British Board of Film Censors was established by the film industry to provide uniform national standards of censorship. The Board has never had a written code of practice although it has published its classification guidelines. The history of regulation and censorship shows, however, that the Board's standards have changed as society has changed. In 1913 there were two certificates: 'U' (universal) and 'A' (more suitable for adults). In 1916, BBFC President T.P. O'Connor compiled a list of 43 rules that covered censorship. At that time, Britain was involved in the First World War and Russia was close to a revolution. These concerns were reflected in his guidelines that films should not depict 'realistic horrors of warfare' or 'relations of capital and labour'. The rules also exhibited a fear of immorality, particularly sex, and outlawed items such as 'nudity' and 'indelicate sexual situations'. The rules governing cinema were strict at this time, not least because the audience was perceived by the very paternalistic and morally old-fashioned Board as an immature, working-class mass, susceptible to corrupting influences. A notable example of censorship after the war was the banning of the Soviet film, *Battleship Potemkin* (Eisenstein, 1925), in 1926 because of its violent and revolutionary aspects. These were seen as particularly relevant in Britain at that time as the General Strike held the possibility of striking workers overthrowing the government.

Between the two world wars, the BBFC was mainly concerned with horror and gangster films and those that dealt with sexuality. In 1932 the category 'H' was introduced to indicate potential unsuitability for children. By 1951, the emergence of the 'teenager' as an economic force and a major part of cinema audiences, coupled with fears of teenage gangs and crimes, prompted the introduction of a new category: 'X' excluded children under 16. *Rebel without a Cause* (1955) was heavily cut so that it could be screened, and *The Wild One* (1954) was banned altogether, as it was seen as a threat to traditional family values. Over the next two decades, partly in response to growing numbers of serious 'adult' films with sexual themes from mainland Europe, the Board were obliged to accept directorial intention and artistic merit as valid criteria; the standards changed once again partly also to incorporate teenagers' specific concerns: 'X' was raised from 16 to 18, 'A' allowed the admission of 5 year olds whether accompanied or not, 'AA' allowed in those aged 14-17 if accompanied by an adult, and 'U' was wholly suitable for children of all ages.

In 1982 these categories were again changed when the BBFC modified its classifications to correspond with the American system: 'A' became 'PG', 'AA' became '15', 'X' became '18', and a new category of 'R18' for material of a sexually explicit nature was introduced. The category of '12' was added in 1989 to bridge the gap between 'PG' and '15' and the category of 'Uc' (particularly suitable for children) exists solely for video. Reflecting concerns over the rise of so-called 'video nasties', in 1984 the Video Recordings Act was passed and a year later the BBFC was empowered to classify all videos for sale and rental. The Board changed its named to the British Board of Film Classification to reflect its new role. In 1994 the Criminal Justice and Public Order Amendment to the Video Recordings Act of 1994 required the BBFC to consider if a video can cause 'harm to potential viewers' or 'harm to society through the viewers' behaviour' in its treatment of 'criminal behaviour', 'illegal drugs', 'violent behaviour and incidents', 'horrific behaviour and incidents' and 'human sexual activity'. The standards applied to videos have always been much stricter, as access to them is much easier than to a cinema, which is required to operate an age bar and can lose its licence for not doing so. The Board's video classification also has more direct legal force.

The BBFC only censors/cuts about 7 per cent of the films submitted for classification. The current BBFC President, Andreas Whittam Smith, recognizes that cutting is not easy to do without the audience realizing that the film has been censored: 'I originally thought "Oh well, if there's a problem, we can cut our way out of it." That's not really an option. Anything good is too intricately made to cut' (quoted in Pendreigh, 1999, p. 7).

In terms of classification the BBFC has three main areas of concern: language, sex and violence. It must also apply legislation to films and videos before they can be classified, and its guidelines have changed as new laws have been passed. These include the Cinematograph Films (Animals) Act 1937, the Protection of Children Act 1978, the Obscene Publications Act 1959 and 1964, the Race Relations Act 1976, Blasphemy, the Hypnotism Act 1954 and the Human Rights Act 1988. Now, the BBFC also has to take into account the right to free expression under the European Convention of Human Rights.

Changing Times: the 1990s

As a sign of changing times, the BBFC has passed uncut several films which have featured explicit sex scenes that seem to have crossed over the line of what was previously thought in good taste, particularly *Romance* (1999) and *Idiots* (1999); but *Happiness* (1998), *American Pie* (1999) and *There's Something About Mary* (1998) have also tested the boundaries. Furthermore, the Board has classified films that had caused controversy on their original release in the 1970s. *Straw Dogs* (1971) and *The Exorcist* (1973) received video classifications for the first time; *The Texas Chainsaw Massacre* (1974) and *A Clockwork Orange* (1971) – the latter withdrawn by Stanley Kubrick himself – were both passed for cinema screening, while *The Driller Killer* (1979), demon of the 'video nasties' hysteria of the 1980s, was passed and screened after the distributing company itself made cuts. In 1998 the proportion of '18' films dropped to 16 per cent and cuts were required in only 14 films, 3.6 per cent of the total. Both statistics represent the lowest recorded proportions on record. In 2000, following a six-month consultation period involving the public, the BBFC relaxed its guidelines, saying that it would 'only rarely' cut explicit sex scenes, thus reflecting a mood that the public would rather make up its own mind about what was acceptable. Does this indicate that the BBFC is becoming more liberal in its decisions, reflecting contemporary circumstances, or that film-makers are treating adult subject matter in what some may consider to be a more responsible and socially acceptable fashion?

Exercise 3.3
In *Ali G: Da Video*, Ali G expressed the opinion that if his video did not receive the '18' certificate then he would be in grave danger of losing his street credibility. How far are we guided by a film's classification? Would you watch or ignore a film because of its classification?

CASE STUDY

Censorship in Hollywood

In the United States, the Constitution and the First Amendment, which guarantees free speech, protect film. However, individual states can censor films if they are 'obscene' and classify them if it is felt they may harm children. Initially, the National Board of Censorship was set up in 1909 to pass films as suitable for exhibition, whether censored or uncut. Unlike the BBFC it did not classify films as suitable for particular audiences. In 1922, however, following growing public concern about film content and some Hollywood scandals, the American film industry set up the Motion Picture Producers and Distributors of America (MPPDA),[1] headed by Will Hays. The MPPDA administered a 'voluntary' code of self-regulation in both pre- and postproduction, which became known as the 'Production Code' or the 'Hays Code'.

The Production Code

In 1930 a more formal set of rules called the Motion Picture Production Code was introduced in Hollywood but this was not enforced until 1934. During those four years, censorship was lenient and film-makers took full advantage, with the result that sex and violence routinely found their way onto the screen. In 1934, however, the studios were under intense pressure to 'clean up' or face government legislation and they agreed to self-regulation through the Code. The studios were feeling the effects of the Great Depression and radio's growing popularity. In an attempt to appease religious groups engaged in box-office boycotts and to ward off the possibility of costly governmental censorship, the MPPDA instead amended the 1930 Code 'to give it coercive power over member producers'. The amendments were formally adopted on 12th July 1934. Self-regulation was quickly and generally accepted for three reasons: its standards were uniform and national, it saved the studios huge editing and distribution costs and the resulting 'wholesome family pictures' were extremely profitable, and the advent of the enforcement of the Code coincided with Hollywood's rapid return to financial prosperity. Any infraction, however small, was punished by a $25,000 fine. The Code attempted to tie film production to a Judaeo-Christian standard of morality by instituting the following guidelines: the sympathy of the audience should never be drawn to the side of crime, wrongdoing, evil or sin; excessive and lustful kissing and embracing and suggestive gestures and postures and explicit nudity were unacceptable; and swearing, such as the use of 'Damn', 'God' and 'Hell', was unacceptable.

HUAC and the 1950s

The 1950s were a fascinating decade in American film history. In addition to the Production Code, a number of political, economic, cultural and social factors coincided to produce an almost unprecedented situation of self-regulation and self-censorship. In 1947 and later in 1951, the House UnAmerican Activities Committee (HUAC) began to investigate possible communist influence in the motion picture industry. The Committee was motivated by the number of communists employed by Hollywood, and to ensure publicity for itself it called the most popular film stars of the day to testify in Washington. The refusal of a group of directors and writers, known as 'the Hollywood Ten', to co-operate with HUAC produced panic within the film industry. In the new Cold War climate communism was unpatriotic and tantamount to treason and any director, writer or actor found to have such sympathies would suffer a boycott of their films by religious and other right-wing groups. Faced with potential commercial failure, Hollywood's investors on Wall Street pressured the industry to fire such individuals, producing an unofficial blacklist from November 1947 onwards. The Motion Picture Association of America (formerly the MPPDA until 1945), rather than the government, imposed the blacklist. Anyone caught refusing to testify before HUAC was blacklisted, which meant a loss of work and usually led to social ostracism. Effectively, Hollywood purged itself of some of its most talented individuals, as those who were blacklisted fled or were forced to work under pseudonyms. The blacklist did not ease up until 1960, but many careers had been destroyed by then.

The studios were afraid to produce any film that could be interpreted as communist or even left-wing; this led to a decline in serious-issue and social comment films. There was a fear of anything too new or too different, as uncertainty and apprehension fuelled by the Cold War, the atom bomb and the political tirades of Senator McCarthy characterized the 1950s. It was a time of safe, uncontroversial, bland and timid movies. In particular, two genres thrived: the anticommunist film, which lauded the American authorities, in particular the FBI (*My Son John*, 1952; *I Was a Communist for the FBI*, 1951), and the science fiction B-movie. Where the former genre was quite clearly pro-American in its sensibilities, the sci fi genre allowed for more ambiguity. Submerged in metaphors and analogies, these films dealt with themes such as atomic radiation (*The Day the Earth Stood Still*, 1951), usually signified by shrinking/growing humans (*The Incredible Shrinking Man*, 1957) or by creatures exaggerated to gargantuan proportions (*Them!*, 1954), and communist invasion depicted by alien attack (*Invasion of the Body Snatchers*, 1956; *Invaders from Mars*, *War of the Worlds*, both 1953). It was not until 1960 that public hysteria regarding communism had declined sufficiently to allow the film industry to return to its pre-1950 days.

The Production Code was formally dropped in 1968 (although in practice it had been liberalizing since the early 1960s and Kubrick had tested it with *Lolita* in 1961), as it was recognized that cultural values had changed from those of the 1930s. The MPAA abandoned censorship altogether and instituted an advisory rating system instead. The Code and Ratings Administration (renamed the Classification and Ratings Administration in 1977) replaced the Production Code, introducing four categories: 'G' (General), 'M' (Mature), 'R' (Restricted) and 'X' (no under-18s permitted). *Midnight Cowboy* (1969) was the first major American film to carry an X certificate and to win Oscars nonetheless. These categories were eventually replaced by the following, which are still in current use: 'G' (General), 'PG' (Parental Guidance), 'PG-13' (Parental Guidance although some material may not be suitable for under-13s), 'R' (Restricted) and 'NC-17' (No-one under 17). Recently, power has been devolved to the local level and the central body only classifies films with respect to their content as suitable for various age groups. Since the MPAA dropped its censoring function, it is sometimes argued that there is no censorship in America, only classification. But how far is this the case given that film-makers work within the framework of an advisory system? Particular classifications still have potential commercial advantages over others; for example, the under-17 audience is crucial to box-office success while the 'NC-17' rating is dreaded, as some cinemas refuse to screen such films, TV networks won't carry their trailers and print ads are hard to place. This means that film-makers will act as self-censors in order to conform to a specific audience rating. Furthermore, some contracts oblige the production of films for distributors that are not above the 'R' rating. As a mark of this, only a handful of controversial films have been awarded 'NC-17', including *The Cook, the Thief, His Wife and Her Lover* (1989) and *Henry: Portrait of a Serial Killer* (1986). Recently *American Psycho* (2000) initially received the 'NC-17' rating, but eight minutes of a sex scene were cut to appease market forces and its final rating was 'R'.

We could say that the American system represents a form of preproduction self-censorship, rather than the external censorship of the UK where many cuts occur in postproduction. A surface comparison between the two countries suggests that it is easier to see how censorship and regulation affect film producers in the USA than in the UK.

Exercise 3.4

Using any national cinema of your choice, investigate how far film censorship and regulation have influenced film content at one specific point in history. You may wish to compare this with another national cinema at the same moment, or compare it with another moment from the same national cinema.

Conclusion

The topics of audiences and censorship and regulation are similar in several respects. They both help to shape film content in one form or another. Film producers, particularly in mainstream cinema, are concerned to understand their audiences in order to provide them with what they want or like. Similarly, censors, classifiers and regulators wish to protect film audiences from what they see as the harmful effects of particular film messages, but at the same time they are willing to account for the audience's attitudes, beliefs and values. Approaches to both the audience and censorship have changed over the course of the first hundred years of film history as the understanding of them has shifted according to changing circumstances. What was felt to be dangerous and how it affected those who watched it at the beginning of the twentieth century is very different in the twenty-first century. Although we do not know exactly where audience research and attitudes towards censorship are moving, we can be certain that they will develop and shift over the next hundred years.

SUMMARY

- The concept of the audience is difficult to define and has changed over time, but it is essential to both the film industry and Film Studies, and can be distinguished from spectatorship.
- Audiences are not passive or uniform; rather, they are constituted by a number of factors and exist in very different circumstances.
- Film consumption is also influenced by a number of factors. In the UK it declined after the Second World War and then recovered dramatically in the mid-1980s.
- Regulation of film content and censorship have changed according to different social circumstances and have affected film content.
- The BBFC operates an external, postproduction classifying service for the UK film industry, while in the United States censorship and regulation have been voluntarily adopted by film producers themselves.

NOTE

[1] This is the name given for the MPPDA by the majority of sources. Thompson and Bordwell's *Film History* (1994), however, refers to the Motion Picture Producers and Distributors Association.

REFERENCES

BBFC *Annual Report 1998* (London: BBFC, 1999).

Jim Collins, Hilary Radner and Ava Preacher Collins (eds), *Film Theory Goes to the Movies* (London & New York: Routledge 1993).

Eddie Dyja (ed.), *BFI Film and Television Handbook 2000* (London: BFI, 1999).

Umberto Eco, *The Role of the Reader* (London: Hutchinson, 1981).

A Bigger Picture: The Report of the Film Policy Review Group (London: Department for Culture, Media and Sport, 1998).

Jostein Gripsrud, 'Film audiences', in John Hill and Pamela Church Gibson (eds), *The Oxford Guide to Film Studies* (Oxford: Oxford University Press, 1999), pp. 202–11.

Stuart Hall *et al.* (eds), *Culture, Media, Language* (London: Hutchinson, 1980).

Paul Lazarsfeld, Bernard Berelson and Hazel Gaudet, *The People's Choice: How the Voter Makes up his Mind in a Presidential Campaign* (2nd edn, New York: Columbia University Press, 1944).

David Morley, *The Nationwide Audience* (London: BFI, 1980).

David Morley, *Family Television* (London: Comedia, 1986).

Brian Pendreigh, 'Everything was in place for a clampdown on sex and violence. So where is it?', *The Guardian* (30 April 1999), pp. 6–7.

Jeffrey Richards, 'British film censorship', in Robert Murphy (ed.), *The British Cinema Book* (London: BFI, 1997), pp. 167–77.

Janet Staiger, *Interpreting Films: Studies in the Historical Reception of American Cinema* (Princeton: Princeton University Press, 1992)

Kristin Thompson and David Bordwell, *Film History* (New York: McGraw-Hill, 1994).

FURTHER READING

Martin Barker (ed.), *The Video Nasties* (London: Pluto Press, 1994).

Gregory Black, *The Catholic Crusade Against the Movies, 1940-1975* (New York: Cambridge University Press, 1998a).

Gregory Black, *Hollywood Censored: Morality Codes, Catholics and the Movies* (New York: Cambridge University Press, 1998b).

Francis G. Couvares (ed.), *Movie Censorship and American Culture* (Washington and London: Smithsonian Institute Press, 1996).

Tom Dewe Matthews, *Censored. What They Didn't Allow You to See and Why: The Story of Film Censorship in Britain* (London: Chatto & Windus, 1994).

Thomas Doherty, *Pre-Code Hollywood: Sex, Immorality, and Insurrection in American Cinema, 1930–1934* (New York: Columbia University Press, 1999).

Richard Falcon, *Classified! A Teacher's Guide to Film and Video Censorship and Classification* (London: BFI, 1994).

Stephen Farber, *The Movie Rating Game* (Washington, DC: Public Affairs Press, 1972).

Ros Hodgkiss, *Media Effects and Censorship* (London: Film Education, 1999).

Lea Jacobs, *The Wages of Sin: Censorship and the Fallen Woman Film 1928–1942* (Madison, WI: University of Wisconsin Press, 1991).

Charles Lyons, *The New Censors: Movies and the Culture Wars* (Philadelphia: Temple University Press, 1997).

Janet Staiger, 'Taboos and totems: cultural meanings of *The Silence of the Lambs*', in Jim Collins, Hilary Radner and Ava Preacher Collins (eds), *Film Theory Goes to the Movies* (London and New York: Routledge, 1993).

Tana Wollen, *Film and Audiences* (London: Film Education, 1988).

FURTHER VIEWING

Sex, Censorship and the Silver Screen (11th Day Entertainment, 1995).

Cinema, the Media and Globalization

As a study of film, this book focuses on films as texts that communicate meanings, audiences as consumers of films, and cinema as an industry that produces films. This chapter is concerned with issues of ownership and power within cinema, while also placing the latter in the wider context of the media as a global phenomenon. What has become known as 'the media' consists of a number of industries including television, radio, print, music and of course cinema. It is increasingly the case that these industries cannot be seen as separate areas of activity; rather, they are often interlinked in terms of ownership and how they operate. Nor can we think of media industries and companies as functioning simply within individual countries. Media companies are increasingly multinational, and exist and operate across several countries. Furthermore, the marketing, distribution and consumption of media products have become globalized, with productions from one area of the world often being experienced elsewhere in very different cultures.

OWNERSHIP OF THE MAJOR STUDIOS

The major studios are well known to us already and have been referred to in Chapter 1. The names have been with us for more than 80 years: Columbia, Disney, MGM, Paramount, 20th Century Fox, United Artists, Universal, Warner Brothers. However, while the economic function of these companies essentially remains the same, their structure and conditions of ownership have changed dramatically. The above studios are, quite rightly, identified as large production companies in their own right; however, the size of these studios is put into perspective when we realize that they are just small parts of much larger multinational conglomerates that own a vast range of other companies, often with interlinking interests. As Richard Maltby notes, this restructuring of the film industry is nothing new and is now well established:

> In the late 1960s many of the majors merged with, or were taken over by, large corporations with diverse interests. This was only the first stage of a gradual reorientation in which

film production and distribution companies have become components in multimedia conglomerates geared to the marketing of a product across a number of interlocking media.

(Maltby, 1995, p. 75)

Columbia Pictures (Figure 4.1) has existed since the early days of cinema, but the company's structure and ownership have changed considerably. In 1982 the Coca-Cola company
bought Columbia, and in the same year Columbia itself formed TriStar Pictures as a means
of diversifying its production facilities. Five years later the two companies were merged,
resulting in what is now known as Columbia TriStar. Coca-Cola's venture into film production
ended in 1989 when the Sony Corporation bought Columbia TriStar. Sony intended to ensure
that its media hardware production would be complemented by media software, an area
where it had failed when it developed its video system in the 1970s.

Disney was not one of the original major studios and did not begin film production until
1923. However, the Walt Disney Company is now one of the biggest media groups in the
world, its most profitable activities being the theme parks in the United States and Europe.
The company had originally expanded into TV production in the 1950s, in association with
ABC, in order to fund the development of its Disneyland theme park. Disney also formed the
Buena Vista distribution company in 1953. In the 1980s it expanded its film production
further with the creation of Touchstone Pictures in 1984. The 1990s saw further growth with
the acquisition of Miramax Pictures in 1993 and ABC TV in 1996.

Two other studio names that have survived from Hollywood's heyday are MGM and United
Artists, though both companies have had their problems. By the 1970s MGM had virtually
ceased film production and in 1980 United Artists was severely weakened after the costly
mistake of *Heaven's Gate*, which resulted in a $40 million loss. The following year the two
companies amalgamated to form MGM/UA. This company went on to form the distribution
giant United International Pictures (UIP) in partnership with Paramount and Universal.
MGM/UA has made a slow but steady recovery, though rumours of take-overs have never
been far away. The 1990s saw the company re-establish itself through funding and distribution of the James Bond films.

Columbia: an old company in a modern world   Figure 4.1

Paramount was one of the original major studios and was used as the test case for the 1948 anti-trust legislation. Like the other major studios, it is now part of a large multimedia conglomerate. In 1966 Paramount was bought by Gulf & Western and was eventually renamed Paramount Communications Inc. Viacom took over the company in 1994, bringing together television, publishing, radio and film interests. Viacom also owns the MTV channel and the international video rental company, Blockbuster.

20th Century Fox has existed in one form or another since 1915. In 1985 Rupert Murdoch applied for American citizenship in order to acquire American media interests. In the same year he bought 20th Century Fox. His multinational company News Corporation already had significant media interests around the world, including television and satellite companies and the UK based News International newspaper company.

Universal Studios dates back to 1912 and has also been through several changes over the years. Universal was taken over by the Music Corporation of America (MCA) in 1962, although this was often perceived as a merger because of the use of the title MCA-Universal. However, MCA itself was bought up in 1990 by Sony's Japanese competitor, Matsushita, who hoped to match media production with media technology, which was their area of specialization with equipment such as TV sets, VCRs and CD/tape players. Matsushita had been successful with the launch of its video home system (VHS) in 1977. Although their video system was regarded by many as technically inferior to those of its competitors (Sony's Betamax system and Philips' V2000 system), it ensured success with the rights to more films for video release. Matsushita was less than successful with its venture into film though, and in 1995 it sold MCA and its assets, including Universal, to Seagram, a Canadian drinks company. In 1998 Seagram expanded its media empire with the purchase of Polygram, which produces films and owns 13 music companies, from Philips, who decided to concentrate on producing media hardware. In 2000 Vivendi, a French company with telecommunications interests, merged with Seagram to create Vivendi Universal, bringing together film, TV, satellite and Internet business interests.

Warners' beginnings were in film production but the company eventually expanded to become co-partner of the world's largest multimedia conglomerate, Time-Warner Inc. Warners was already a conglomerate with a range of media interests by 1973, the year in which it renamed itself Warner Communication Inc. (WCI). In 1989 WCI merged with Time Inc. to create Time-Warner, a company with interests in film, video, television, music, distribution, exhibition and publishing. Time-Warner's position as world leader was further reinforced through the merger in 2000 with America On-Line (AOL), the Internet service provider, to form AOL-Time Warner.

Exercise 4.1

Look at your video collection or recall the last five films you have seen. What percentage of the films belong to / were produced by the six major studios?

MEDIA CONGLOMERATE STRATEGIES

There are particular reasons for the trend towards amalgamating companies into multinational conglomerates. The ultimate purpose of such companies, as business enterprises, is of course to make a profit, to be commercially successful. Large companies have the advantage of being able to provide the financial resources necessary for further expansion, developing new products or marketing existing products. Smaller companies can find it hard to compete with the economic power of large conglomerates; amalgamating companies through mergers and buy-outs concentrates ownership and can reduce competition, thus increasing the likelihood of financial success.

Bringing together a range of media companies has its own particular benefits. The media are all about communication, and having interests in a variety of media industries places a conglomerate in a position where the various companies can in many instances promote the other areas of the conglomerate via, for instance, television, radio, newspapers, magazines or general marketing facilities. It is also the case that particular media products are often to be found duplicated in various media forms so that a film may have a television spin-off, a music soundtrack and magazines based on the original concept. The low-budget success *Lock, Stock and Two Smoking Barrels* (1998) was turned into a British television series in 2000. It is to be noted that there has also been an increasing trend for television programmes to make the transition to film: *The Addams Family, The Flintstones, Batman, Mission Impossible*.

With regard to media conglomerates, the links between hardware and software are becoming increasingly important. Media products such as films on VHS and DVD, television programmes and music CDs need technology such as VCRs, DVD players, TV sets and CD/tape players for them to be consumed. The entertainment industry, now largely constituted by media conglomerates, has already made major moves into acquiring hardware and software interests. With the growing importance of computer systems and digital technology, as seen in the advances made in digital television and Internet access, further inroads are likely to be made into media hardware industries. The multinational and global nature of the contemporary media industries is illustrated by the locating of media companies in a variety of countries and by the consumption of media products around the world, but is also well served by the growth of telecommunications technology ('tele' literally meaning 'over a distance'). The previously mentioned multinational conglomerates have been quick to take advantage of the possibilities offered by becoming 'multimedia'. For example the merger of AOL and Time-Warner means they are poised to take full advantage of the Internet. Increasing conglomeration has accelerated the trend towards perceiving films as only one part of a product line of toys, clothes, food, drink, video, computer games, comics, magazines and soundtracks (see Chapter 2).

By 2000, News Corporation had developed extensive cross-media ownership, and owns 20th Century Fox and News International, as well as Fox Television, BSkyB satellite broadcasting and Star TV in Asia, and interests in Internet services, Australian newspapers and Latin American television. Murdoch's cross-media interests are frequently used to promote other areas of his media empire. His British newspapers, for example, often refer to his BSkyB satellite services.

SONY.®

Figure 4.2   *Sony: a vertically integrated multinational conglomerate with media cross-over for synergy*

The Sony Corporation (Figure 4.2) had originally concentrated on the production of media hardware such as TV sets, VCRs, CD and tape players, but with the acquisition of Columbia it expanded into software production. Sony's software interests have since developed beyond film production, with interests in exhibition through Loew's Theaters, TV production, video sales, and the purchase of CBS Records. The Sony Playstation systems have given the company a further foothold in hardware and software in the computer games industry. Behind Sony's expansion has been a strategy of *synergy*, whereby the various industries under its control are brought together to mutually benefit each other. Thus Sony televisions may be bought and used for screening its TV productions, Columbia's films, possibly on Sony videos, or for viewing a Playstation game. Similarly, music released by Sony's CBS division may be played on Sony CD or tape systems.

AOL-Time Warner are ideally placed to practise synergy. It will readily be seen that a Warners' film may use a soundtrack produced by Warners' music division, use its distribution company, be screened at Warners' cinemas, be publicized in Time-Warner magazines, release the film via its video company and no doubt screen it on a Warners' television channel. AOL-Time Warner also plans its own shops for film merchandise and computer games based on its films. Time-Warner has on occasions also cleverly resurrected and re-used old products in new films. The company owns *DC Comics*, in which the original Batman character appeared, and of course produced four Batman films. Similarly, the original Warner Brothers cartoon characters were relaunched in *Space Jam* (1997), which combined cartoon characters such as Bugs Bunny with actors through the use of computer technology.

Vivendi Universal is a typical example of a vertically integrated company as a result of the previous activities of one of its subsidiaries, MCA. In 1977 MCA and Paramount jointly formed the Cinema International Corporation (CIC) as a film distributor. Co-operation between film companies has become increasingly common as a means of pooling resources and specialisms to maximize profits (in 1975 20th Century Fox and Warners had co-produced *The Towering Inferno*). In 1987 MCA-Universal obtained part control of the Cineplex Odeon chain and went on to form United Cinema International (UCI) as an exhibition chain with Paramount. Thus Vivendi Universal is a well-established, vertically integrated company, capable of producing films, distributing them and screening them in its own cinemas. Like the other major media conglomerates, Vivendi Universal also has music, television, Internet and publishing interests.

Viacom is another company with elements of vertical integration, mainly due to the activities of its subsidiary, Paramount. Through its interests in the UIP distribution company and UCI exhibition chain, Paramount, like most of the major film companies, is again vertically integrated. The 1948 anti-trust legislation ending vertical integration in the USA was repealed in 1985 by the Republican administration, headed by B-movie actor Ronald Reagan. His administration pursued a *laissez-faire* economic policy which sought to reduce government intervention in the economy, leaving the financial markets to govern themselves. Viacom's merger with CBS in 1999 ensured guaranteed access to television for Paramount films.

The Disney Company provides an example of horizontal integration in the film industry: the purchasing of companies that are operating in the same area of production; in effect buying out a competitor. Thus when the Disney Company, as a production company, bought Miramax Pictures, it was expanding horizontally, in contrast to the previously mentioned examples of companies expanding vertically into other areas of the industry.

Exercise 4.2

Which of the films you have seen over the past year have been linked to other media forms through CD soundtracks, video copies, magazine articles, television screenings or documentaries?

CONCENTRATION OF OWNERSHIP

Continued horizontal integration would ultimately result in one company monopolizing a particular industry. However, it is unlikely that this will happen in the film industry, if only because anti-monopoly legislation should prevent such a development – though it is worth bearing in mind that, as we have seen, legislation preventing vertical integration was eventually repealed.

Although the film industry is not monopolised by one company, it can certainly be described as an oligopoly, an industry that is dominated by a small number of companies. Essentially six companies control the international film industry: Disney, News Corporation, Vivendi Universal, Sony, AOL-Time Warner and Viacom (North America is the most profitable cinema market and in 1997 these companies accounted for 80 per cent of that market). Thomas Schatz sees no signs of change in the current media conglomerates' strategy of buying into the film industry and notes that 'Because movies drive the global marketplace, a key holding for any media conglomerate is a motion picture studio; but there is no typical media conglomerate these days due to the widening range of entertainment markets and rapid changes in new technology' (Schatz, 1993, p. 30). Ownership could become even more concentrated with the continuing expansion of telecommunications companies such as AT&T and Cable & Wireless and further amalgamations or take-overs involving software, hardware and distribution networks.

Current trends and possible future developments with regard to ownership raise the question of whether concentration of ownership within the film industry and media as a whole is desirable. From a purely economic perspective, it could be argued that large multinational conglomerates are necessary nowadays as they are able to supply the huge budgets that contemporary films often seem to require. Smaller companies could not match the resources of the larger conglomerates. From a political perspective it could be argued that ownership has become concentrated in relatively few companies because they are the best at what they do and are the most competitive. From a capitalist perspective, a free market is desirable as competition results in the most effective companies surviving and consumers (so the theory goes) getting the best deal possible.

However, it could also be argued that conglomerates are basically a cartel which tends to protect the position of each company and that in effect the companies do not really compete with each other. The power of the conglomerates makes it difficult for smaller independent companies to compete on equal terms, thus ensuring the survival of the conglomerates. Production companies that are referred to as independent are usually dependent on the major companies for finance or distribution, and they often end up being bought by majors or going bankrupt in the face of unfair competition; Orion went bankrupt in 1992 and Disney bought out Miramax in 1993. The increasing power of multinationals is thus undemocratic and undesirable. From a Marxist perspective, multinationals are the logical result of an economic system based upon profit rather than need. The concentration of capital is predictable and self-perpetuating and while the types of films and media products made are intended to meet consumer demand, that demand is itself created by expensive marketing campaigns. A Marxist analysis may also suggest that the media products supplied tend to embody values and beliefs that reinforce the position of a political and economic dominant class.

GLOBALIZATION

The concept of globalization is not new, and was foreseen by Marshall McLuhan in the 1960s when he referred to the 'global village' in which communication from one part of the world to another effectively eliminated physical distances, as if we were all living in the same community. The 1960s saw international communications networks expanding, a high point being satellite communication with its possibility of instantaneous mass communication between different countries via satellite and television. Such communication was, however, limited to developed areas of the world which possessed the requisite technology. Global, albeit not instantaneous, communication had of course been taking place for most of cinema's history through films; films are imported and exported to and from all parts of the world, in effect, providing an exchange between cultures.

However, the obvious point to be noted is that the exchange is somewhat unbalanced. It tends to be American films and Western culture that are propagated around the world, with little in the way of non-American films and non-Western culture being allowed to return. An indication of the marginalization of films made outside Hollywood is the film category of 'World Cinema' used in many video rental shops in Britain, a handy label used to cover virtually anything made outside the USA, usually including British films. It is also interesting to note that when (in Britain) we refer to 'foreign films', we usually mean a film that uses a language other than English, ignoring the fact that (in the UK) American films are also 'foreign'. This illustrates the extent to which we have accepted American films and culture as being similar to our own.

There isn't of course anything necessarily wrong with American films being consumed in all corners of the world; indeed, it could be claimed that US hegemony with regard to films is simply the result of Hollywood's production of the types of films that people around the world want to see. The suspicion remains, however, that as long as studio ownership and control of distribution and marketing generally remain with the USA, American films are likely to remain dominant. The implication behind such a scenario is that choice is limited. Although they question the degree to which cultural domination has taken place, Held *et al.* concede that:

> within the West there has been some degree of homogenisation of mass cultural consumption, particularly among the young, and that it is spreading to the more affluent strata of the developing world, especially in East Asia and Latin America. In popular music, film and television a single product will be consumed in a multiplicity of places. There is also some evidence to suggest that this has, as a consequence, squeezed some domestic alternatives out of the market. The most obvious impact of US domination of, say, the UK film market is that it has become harder for UK film-makers to produce and distribute movies in Britain.
>
> (Held *et al.*, 1999, p. 373)

The Indian film industry has shown remarkable resistance to American cinema, no doubt because of the long and well-established history of film production in India, but the point to note is that Indian cinema remains relatively isolated and Bollywood cannot compete globally with Hollywood.

The subject of globalization has led to fierce debate because of the claim that the imbalance in global communications amounts to cultural imperialism. In effect, the values and beliefs and ways of life represented in American films are, it is argued, gradually eroding the traditional values and beliefs of other cultures. This does not just apply to non-Western cultures but also to Britain where, since the 1950s, it has been claimed by cultural theorists such as Richard Hoggart that there has been a gradual 'Americanisation' of society. Thus the replacement of indigenous cultures by what is argued to be predominantly American culture is seen as a form of imperialism in which one culture is controlled by another. The means by which this cultural imperialism is achieved extend beyond cinema and the media to the general exporting of consumer goods from one area of the world to another. A Marxist analysis identifies the relentless drive towards expansion, control of markets and the increased profits central to capitalist social organization as inevitably resulting in inequalities between developed and underdeveloped areas of the world in terms of economic and cultural independence.

However, the argument is perhaps not quite as straightforward as it first seems. We could for instance question the status of traditional culture, as it could be claimed that a people's way of life is always changing in one way or another, is always in a state of transition. Is there then an identifiable culture to be undermined? Annabelle Sreberny-Mohammadi has suggested,

> [a] conceptual challenge to the 'cultural imperialism' model, stemming from new modes of analysing media effects which question the 'international hypodermic needle' assumption

preferred by the 'hegemonic' model ... diverse audiences bring their own interpretative frameworks and sets of meaning to media texts.

(Sreberny-Mohammadi, quoted in Curran and Gurevitch, 1991, p. 122)

Certainly, different cultures may well interpret films in ways that suit their own values and beliefs (see Chapter 12 on Meaning and Spectatorship). In other words, American ideology will not necessarily be interpreted as such by another culture; rather, that culture may extract meanings from a film different from those intended by, for instance, an American studio. The marketing departments of the major studios are aware of cultural differences between audiences that may watch Hollywood films. The James Bond films of the 1980s and 1990s used different advertising campaigns depending on which countries they were promoting the films in; this was especially noticeable in the publicity posters used.

None of this of course changes the fact that there is a far greater flow of films out of the United States than into it. Financial support from governments for their indigenous film industries would help redress the balance, but many countries do not have the surplus wealth necessary for such an initiative. But, then, a capitalist analysis emphasizes how competition, market forces and supply and demand ultimately determine what films are consumed, and where.

Exercise 4.3

1. What is the percentage of American films that you have seen over the last six months compared with non-American films?
2. Discuss your responses to US films. Do you think you 'read' such films in the same way as an American spectator would?

SUMMARY

- **Cinema as a central part of the international entertainment industry is continuing to expand.**
- **Multinational conglomerates concentrate ownership in fewer and fewer hands, the emphasis being on creating huge multimedia companies that match the various areas of media production to each other in order to strengthen their position.**
- **Synergy and vertical integration are common strategies within these multinational conglomerates.**
- **Film production and media ownership are concentrated in the Western world, especially the United States, and this has been accompanied by a globalization process which has resulted in films and media goods tending to make their way from Western cultures to other cultures around the world.**
- **The tendency towards a one-way cultural transfer has arguably led to cultural imperialism by which Western values and beliefs perhaps undermine and replace indigenous cultures.**

REFERENCES

Jim Collins, Hilary Radner and Ava Preacher Collins (eds), *Film Theory Goes to the Movies* (London: Routledge, 1993).

James Curran and Michael Gurevitch, *Mass Media and Society* (London: Edward Arnold, 1991).

David Held, Anthody McGrew, David Goldblatt and Jonathan Perraton, *Global Transformations* (Cambridge: Polity Press, 1999).

Richard Maltby, *Hollywood Cinema* (Oxford: Blackwell 1995).

Thomas Schatz, 'The New Hollywood', in Jim Collins, Hilary Radner and Ava Preacher Collins (eds), *Film Theory Goes to the Movies* (London: Routledge, 1993).

FURTHER READING

Tino Balio (ed.), *The American Film Industry* (Madison, WI: University of Wisconsin Press, 1985).

James Curran, David Morley and Valerie Walkerdine (eds), *Cultural Studies and Communications* (London: Arnold, 1996).

Jim Hillier, *The New Hollywood* (London: Studio Vista, 1993).

Garth Jowett and James Linton, *Movies as Mass Communication* (Thousand Oaks, CA: Sage Publications, 1989).

James Lull, *Media, Communication, Culture: A Global Approach* (Cambridge: Polity, 1995).

Richard Maltby, *Hollywood Cinema* (Oxford: Blackwell Publishers, 1995).

Annabelle Sreberny-Mohammadi, Dwayne Winseck, Jill McKenna and Oliver Boyd-Barrett (eds), *Media in Global Context* (London: Arnold, 1997).

Janet Wasko, *Hollywood in the Information Age* (Cambridge: Polity, 1994).

FURTHER VIEWING

Global Culture (BBC, 1992).

Film as Text

Film Technology

In this chapter we shall focus on the ways in which film as a specific form of communication requires technology. In Chapter 7 on Early Cinema and Film Form, we shall examine the emergence of photography, the development of the zoetrope and its provision of the first moving images. Here we shall trace the main developments in film technology over the last century, focusing on the camera, sound, colour, deep field photography, projection technologies and computer and digital technologies.

TECHNOLOGY, INDUSTRY AND AUDIENCE

In some senses, the history of film is a hundred-year tale of innovation as film-makers attempted to translate stories into moving images. Film has always relied upon technology; as a form of art, it is one of the most technological. Arguably, cinema *is* technology and thus examining technology is crucial to understanding film itself. Technological developments have affected film-making in two ways: film-makers have utilized new technologies to make films, and films have consequently increasingly reflected on the consequences of the use of such technology. As media guru Marshall McLuhan put it, 'the medium is the message'.

It is not our intention, however, to present technological developments as a simple or uninterrupted linear progression. As will be seen, improved film technology was not always welcomed initially or used immediately upon its emergence. Indeed, in many cases, the technology already existed some years (even decades) prior to its widespread adoption. The explanation behind this delay can partly be explained by the studios' assessment that the initial expense was too great and too risky and would disrupt the financial status quo.

The adoption of new processes closely mirrored their context. The initial financial risks of investing in new technology were later justified by potentially greater losses in revenue by not doing so. Thus, rather than being led by the new technology itself, the film industry reacted to social, economic and cultural factors (usually declining audiences) by utilizing new processes. In this way, it sought to regenerate itself and to present cinema as a 'novel' experience. As in any industry, complacency could lead to stagnation. Furthermore, just as the studios had specialized in particular genres or sets of genres in an attempt to attract customer brand loyalty through product differentiation (see Chapter 1), the adoption of new technologies led to each studio attempting to outdo its rivals in the bid for a greater market share.

THE CAMERA

The camera is the device with which the cinematographer captures a series of progressive images on a strip of film. Early pioneers in cinematography struggled with the problem of capturing clear, sharp moving images and were indebted to a combination of three constituent technologies, two of which were not particularly new. Lens manufacture, for example, had already become a healthy industry in the years since 1827, when photography was invented.

The technology for rapidly repeated exposure of a light-sensitive emulsion to light admitted through an aperture had also existed for some time: all that was needed was a motor designed to turn at the appropriate speed which triggered repeated opening and closing of the aperture, initially 16 or 18 times per second (24 after the coming of sound in 1927–29), to take this number of photographs each second. It was a relatively simple matter to adapt the kind of mechanism used in a sewing machine, which had been invented in the 1840s.

The last piece of the technological jigsaw to be developed was the flexible celluloid emulsion-coated strip which could weave its way through the motor without breaking. Early experiments such as those of Eadweard Muybridge and Jules Marey (who were interested in studying movement rather than inventing film) in the 1880s had generally been carried out with non-flexible plates, but in 1888/89 George Eastman developed the first flexible film, made first of paper, then celluloid. He christened this 'Kodak'.

Over a century later it is too easy to forget how established much of the early technology was to become. Although the Lumière camera-projector was hand-cranked (and so could be used in the most remote locations with no need for electricity), basic camera technology had changed little a century later; the four-sprocket 35mm film developed by Edison has remained standard and the earliest films can easily be shown on the most modern film projectors.

Initially, cameras were static, and most movement was restricted to panning and tilting from a fixed tripod. There were early experiments such as placing the camera on a boat or a train; the Lumière brothers and D.W. Griffith moved their cameras, but to a limited extent. The cinematographer of F.W. Murnau's *The Last Laugh* (*Der letzte Mann*, 1924), Karl Freund, however, was the first to move the camera backwards and forwards, up and down and side to side, to great dramatic effect. The style of German Expressionism (of which Murnau was an exponent) gradually found its way into Hollywood film.

The introduction of sound, however, introduced particular problems for camera movement. Omni-directional microphones often picked up the sound of the noisy camera. As a

result, cameras were encased within soundproofed, static 'iceboxes', which limited movement, allowing only 30-degree tilts and pans.

During the 1930s, dubbing or post-synchronization released the camera from its icebox.
Camera mobility was further facilitated by the invention of the *blimp* – a lightweight, soundproof casing that muffled the whirr of the camera's motor. Tracking was made easier by the
introduction of a wide range of camera supports, manoeuvrable dollies and boom cranes.
It is alleged that the first actual crane shot was developed for Paul Fejos' *Broadway* in 1929,
but perhaps its finest moment came in *Gone with the Wind* (1939) when the camera tracks
Scarlett O'Hara walking among the Civil War casualties at the railroad station.

Crane shots give a remarkable scope of choices to the film-maker; s/he can follow an
actor up a flight of stairs; pass over crowds of people and focus on a single person; track
an individual from a distance; move over obstacles; move off from heights and into space
or provide an aerial view of a scene.

In 1922 and 1923 respectively, 9.5mm cameras and 16mm film stock (in contrast to the
professional 35mm) were introduced, which meant smaller and lighter cameras and less
expensive filming. Cameras became (just about) light enough to be hand-held, significantly
assisting the development of documentary film. During the 1940s, a new generation of
documentary film-makers became increasingly dissatisfied with the sedate tripod-restricted
techniques of established documentary, and encased the camera in lighter metal to make it
more portable. In 1960, André Coutant used a prototype of a silent-running, hand-held
16mm camera to make Jean Rouch's *Chronicle of a Summer* (*Chronique d'un été*); the new
camera was marketed as the Éclair in 1962. This allowed film-makers to move into areas
once too restrictive for filming and allowed close tracking of movement. Hand-held camera
movement produces an unsteadiness which can be used for a variety of effects, such as
'realism', immediacy or grittiness, as it can represent a character's point of view or emphasize the camera operator's situation amidst the action.

The introduction of the steadicam by Garrett Brown in 1973 allowed for hand-held-style
shots combined with smooth movement. Rather than using dolly track to produce smooth
camera movement, the camera was strapped to its operator by means of a hydraulic brace
incorporating a series of shock absorbers. This removed the shakes and bumps that accompanied footage recorded by a hand-held camera, allowing free movement over rough terrain
or where track could not be laid, for example on steps. Steadicam was used notably to follow Sylvester Stallone running up the steps of the Philadelphia Museum of Art in *Rocky*
(1976). Its most notable user was Stanley Kubrick, who used it for several sequences in *The
Shining* (1980).

Exercise 5.1

Look at sequences from *Rocky*, *The Shining* and/or *Breaking the Waves* (von Trier,
1996) and any other films of your choice. Try to identify the types of camera movement used.

Advances in camera mobility seem to have been derived principally from aesthetic rather than commercial choices, the impetus being from the individual film-maker who desired to create a certain effect. Indeed, where camera mobility conflicted with commercial considerations like the introduction of sound, it was readily discarded as sound film was seen to be a greater crowd puller than camera movement.

SOUND

The transition from silent to sound film was not a harmonious one. Experiments with sound began with the birth of motion pictures itself and between 1900 and 1925 sound systems proliferated. The studios, however, were unwilling to invest the sums needed to convert to sound production and they did not want to tamper with a profitable business. Initially, it was feared that conversion to sound might herald the collapse of the film industry itself. New sound studios would have to be constructed, cinemas would have to be wired for sound, a huge back catalogue of silent films would become redundant, the foreign market would collapse as easily translated titles would have to be dubbed and stars would need to be retrained. Sound was also vigorously opposed by film theorists and directors such as Münsterberg, Arnheim, Chaplin and Kurosawa, who felt that cinema might be permanently hindered by the public's fascination with a passing fad.

Two studios, however, perceived the situation somewhat differently, acknowledging that sound enhanced the film-viewing experience, but that full-scale pit orchestras and Wurlitzer organs were too expensive. After the First World War, the search for a cheap but effective way of recording film sound intensified. Fox Film Corporation began developing their own sound system – Movietone – at the same time as Warners, believing that the introduction of sound in their studios and cinemas would allow them to compete with the pit orchestras of their rivals, had acquired a sophisticated sound-on-disc system called Vitaphone. In 1926 they presented *Don Juan* in Vitaphone followed by *The Jazz Singer* in 1927, heralding the introduction of sound in terms of music and effects. Just prior to *The Jazz Singer*, Fox had presented *Sunrise* (1927) using their competing system, Movietone.

This sound technology, however, was only single-track, meaning that it was not possible to have both soundtrack music and dialogue at the same time. Audiences, therefore, still had to wait for speech, as the dialogue-only sections of the film were still communicated by titles. Warners, though, shrewdly allowed some of Jolson's ad-libbed dialogue to remain in the finished film and audiences were amazed not only by the singing and dancing Jolson, but also by his informal and spontaneous speech. At one point, he tells the audience, 'You ain't heard nothing yet.' *The Jazz Singer* was an international success grossing over $3.5m. This was followed by the release of *The Lights of New York* – the first completely sound commercial film – in 1928.

The popular success of these films showed that sound attracted large audiences and, therefore, could not be ignored. In a bid to catch up with Fox and Warners, the other studios rapidly converted to sound production. In part, the impetus was economic. Audiences had been declining since 1926, 1927 had been a bad year for Hollywood (with the exception of

Warners) and the forecast for the following year was worse. The public seemed to be bored by formulaic production methods and heavily promoted stars. In addition, cinema was facing competition from the wider availability of cars and radios. Following the Wall Street Crash of 1929, the United States was thrown into an economic depression which further affected the film industry, and sound was the new attraction to lure audiences back into the cinemas. By 1932, silent films had been largely forgotten and 'talkies' helped to distract American audiences from the harsh realities of everyday life. The major Hollywood studios were also keen to extend their grip over the film industry abroad and so began converting European cinemas to sound in order to capitalize on sound's popularity. The UK, in particular, became the major foreign market for Hollywood sound films.

The effect of sound on the film industry was radical. The camera's mobility became restricted as it now had to be enclosed in a soundproof booth, actors were grouped around concealed microphones, and close ups and complex editing were all but abandoned. Many silent film stars lost their jobs as their voices were not adequate and they were replaced by a new wave of Broadway actors, accompanied by scriptwriters who could write dialogue – the 1952 musical comedy *Singin' in the Rain* addressed exactly this subject. Sound led to the creation of new genres and the decline of old ones. The comedies of the Marx brothers and W.C. Fields replaced those of Charlie Chaplin and Buster Keaton. Musicals, in particular, benefited immensely from the developments in sound technology. Initially, musicals were little more than unsophisticated, photographed versions of Broadway productions, but they developed so quickly that by 1933 they had become a major Hollywood genre. The acoustic interiors of cinemas were transformed from concert halls to spaces with fewer echoes, thus increasing the comprehensibility of the dialogue. By the mid-1930s, soundtrack dubbing (whereby other soundtrack elements like music and sound effects would automatically be lower in volume under the recorded dialogue) and post-synchronization (post-recording sound, particularly dialogue, after the film has been shot and edited so that the new sound is synchronized with the on-screen images) had been perfected. This allowed film-makers to include overlapping lines, off-screen dialogue and voice-over narratives. Films could now be dubbed into foreign languages easily, which meant that Hollywood films could be enjoyed around the globe.

Initially, the soundtrack was recorded on discs that were synchronized with the film, but this proved to be unreliable and gave way to the optical recording of sound onto the film stock itself. By the 1950s this was in turn replaced by sound recorded on magnetic tape and played back in optical stereophony to accompany the new widescreen formats (see below). Indeed, it was the arrival of these formats that led to the almost total conversion from optical to magnetic sound recording. In the following decade more improvements such as the Dolby System were developed; this reduced background noise, producing better fidelity for the soundtrack. Sound designer Walter Murch pioneered the use of sound technology to revolutionize film soundtracks in such a way that music and other sound effects combined with visual images to produce a harmonious whole. Using multi-track sound, Murch filled the cinema with noise, for example, the synthesized whirr of the helicopter blades in *Apocalypse Now.* Such techniques, though taken for granted today, were innovative at that time.

Originally stereophonic, Dolby has now become Surround Sound, filling cinemas with sound effects and music from speakers located both to the side and to the rear of the audience. During the 1980s two rival systems were introduced: George Lucas' THX Sound System, premiered with his *Return of the Jedi* in 1983, and Digital Theatre Systems, which is by far the more popular format. Currently, in 2000, sound is being digitized, which has made postproduction simpler and more flexible while giving greater clarity, resonance, range and fidelity inside the cinema. Although some films are still released with only an analogue soundtrack, more and more are released for digital audio systems.

In the early days of film sound, dialogue and singing were privileged, but newer sound technology allows the recording of multi-track sound, of complex layers on the same soundtrack. Now, sound, music and dialogue can co-exist, lending a heightened 'realism' and greater emotional power.

Exercise 5.2
Discuss how far technological advances have contributed to the success of the film industry.

COLOUR

Again, as was the case with sound, colour technology was experimented with from the earliest days of the cinema (Méliès hand-tinted his films), but was rarely used because of technical difficulties, the time-consuming nature of hand-colouring and the expense involved. Even the commercial success of Technicolor's first two-strip feature, *The Toll of the Sea* (1922), did not lead to a major conversion to colour production; nor did use of improved Technicolor in films like *On with the Show* and *Gold Diggers of Broadway* (both 1929). By 1932 production of Technicolor films had all but stopped as audiences were unsatisfied with the two-colour process, but in 1934 Technicolor bounced back with Rouben Mamoulian's *Becky Sharp*, using a three-strip of cyan, magenta and yellow. Its commercial success led to the release of further three-colour films culminating in *Gone with the Wind* (1939) (Figure 5.1) and *The Wizard of Oz* (1939), the latter of which dramatically highlights the transition from black and white to colour as Dorothy enters the fantastic land of Oz.

Earlier, in 1937, Walt Disney had released *Snow White and the Seven Dwarfs* – the first animated colour feature film. The commercial viability of colour had been established, but its rise was interrupted by the onset of the Second World War.

Film-makers began to use colour widely during the 1950s for two main reasons. First, the newly developed Eastmancolor was both cheaper and more convenient and had successfully challenged Technicolor's monopoly. By 1953, it had replaced Technicolor as the most widely used colour film stock. Second, the increased competition from television is the primary explanation for Hollywood's speedy shift from black-and-white to colour

Early Technicolor was a major attraction (Selznick/MGM, courtesy Kobal)   Figure 5.1

production between 1952 and 1954. The major studios attempted to respond to the advent of television, which had enticed 30 per cent of the cinema-going audience away from the big screen, by singling out and highlighting film's advantages over black-and-white television: size (see below) and colour. In 1947 approximately 12 per cent of Hollywood's films were in colour, but by 1954 this had increased to over 50 per cent. Nonetheless, by the end of the 1950s 50 per cent of Hollywood films were still in black and white, which was only abandoned when television converted to colour in the 1960s.

Although colour had become the norm for high-budget productions, low-budget films, particularly the independent science fiction and horror B-movies of the 1950s, tended to remain in black and white primarily as a result of commercial considerations. Since the 1950s, colour cinematography has vastly improved in subtlety and sophistication and today the overwhelming majority of mainstream commercial films are in colour. Those that remain in black and white are so either for financial reasons (e.g. independent films like *Clerks*, 1993) or for aesthetic ones (e.g. *Schindler's List*, 1993). Such aesthetic choices are also often linked to '*diegetic motivation*': the choice between black and white and colour can be explained in terms of the narrative. The black-and-white *vérité*-style footage in *The Blair Witch Project* can be 'explained' as student research material.

DEEP FIELD PHOTOGRAPHY

Just as there was for sound and colour technologies, there was a gap between the technological possibility of deep field photography and its acceptance and use. Deep field photography had always been possible in sunlight and even the Lumière brothers had used it, but Hollywood cinematographers resisted departures from the established style of soft tonal qualities and shallow depth of field. The emergence of deep focus cinematography as an acknowledged visual style is usually dated to Gregg Toland's cinematography for *Citizen Kane* (1941), but Jean Renoir had employed deep focus in the late 1930s (*La Grande illusion*, 1937; *Rules of the Game/La Règle du jeu*, 1938), as had John Ford in *Stagecoach* (1939). But it was *Citizen Kane* that introduced the technique to the wider public (see also

Chapter 6 on the Language of Film). Deep field cinematography simultaneously keeps all planes of an image – foreground, middleground and background – in equally sharp focus, giving the viewer the whole scene without guiding his/her attention. In contrast, shallow focus guides the audience's viewing by emphasizing a single plane of the image, usually the action, behind or in front of which everything else is blurred.

The emergence of deep field photography (see also next chapter) can be traced to two main considerations. The first factor in the use of deep focus was the rise in photojournalism and the social realist and documentary film movements of the 1930s. Influenced by these movements, film-makers increasingly made an aesthetic decision to replicate the perspective and realism of this photographic style. The second factor was the availability of new film-making equipment. From the mid-1930s to 1939, improved carbon arc lights replaced the silent Mazda incandescent tungsten lamps (another side-effect of the coming of sound), and faster film stock (which was more sensitive to light), enhanced emulsion types and new lens coatings allowed light to be used more efficiently, leading to more effective screen illumination, image contrast and sharpness of focus. These technological developments enable a fast shutter speed to be combined with a small aperture, which results in deep focus. Although the use of deep focus seems to derive from an aesthetic choice based on the accessibility of new technology, an economic dimension on the part of the studios can also be observed as they strove to improve their market position by developing a new look for their films.

PROJECTION TECHNOLOGIES

Since the earliest days of film, film entrepreneurs have struggled with different ways of exhibiting films. Projection refers to the process whereby photographed images are projected on a screen (and thus enlarged) so that their rapid consecutive appearance creates the illusion of movement through persistence of vision (and/or via the phi-phenomenon). It was the Lumière brothers – whose ownership of a factory manufacturing photographic materials was no doubt a great help – who developed the projection system which immediately spread all over the world. The remarkable feature of the system was its simplicity and compactness: the same basic hand-cranked motor served to operate both the camera and the projector, which formed a portable unit. The same system could also be adapted for developing and printing the film.

In the first year of their operations, the Lumière brothers trained several dozen camera operators/projectionists, who promptly travelled to all parts of the world, where they filmed the early 'actualities', developed and printed the film themselves, and often projected the results for the amazed locals. During the silent era films were filmed and projected at the rate of 16–20 frames per second (fps), the speed being variable as the motor was at first cranked by hand. With the advent of sound and the need for standardization to enable sound–image synchronization, a common speed of 24 fps was agreed on (and for films converted to video this has become 25 fps). This is why characters in silent films screened at 24 or 25 fps seem to move so quickly!

For the remainder of this chapter, we will concentrate on the film industry's response to declining audience trends from the 1950s onwards, which led it to release new films in new formats and to introduce new projection and viewing technologies, the most significant being widescreen, 3D, IMAX/OMNIMAX and digital projection.

Widescreen

Widescreen refers to any film screening for which the ratio of the width of the projected image to its height (called the aspect ratio) is greater than 4:3 or 1.33:1 – the standard ratio used in the industry from silent film until the early 1950s, also called the Academy format. During the 1920s there were experiments with several different widescreen systems in Hollywood, such as Magnascope, Fox Grandeur, Vitascope and 70mm Wide Film, but these processes were expensive and did not provide high quality pictures. Meanwhile, in France, *Napoléon* (1927) was screened using 'Polyvision', whereby three projectors showed a trip-tych of images across three screens to create a panoramic shot. This process was improved in 1952 when Cinerama (based on Gance's Polyvision) introduced a curved screen, stereophonic sound and three projectors. The screen went beyond the field of vision, which is 160 degrees, giving the illusion that the audience was actually 'in' the film. In the following year, 20th Century Fox brought out *The Robe* using its cheaper widescreen alternative, CinemaScope, which required only a single camera with a special anamorphic lens (again such lenses had already been made in the nineteenth century) that squeezed an image onto standard 35mm stock, which was then stretched back to its original format dur-ing projection. Screens were double the width of the normal screen and slightly curved to give the illusion of depth. CinemaScope was so successful (by 1955 more than 20,000 cinemas around the world had installed it) that foreign companies copied the system, using similar names – Franscope (France), Ultrascope (Italy), Agascope (Sweden), Sovscope (USSR) and Tohoscope (Japan).

Paramount responded by introducing its own process, VistaVision, and this was soon joined by Todd-AO. From 1960 onwards, however, Robert Gottschalk's Panavision gradually superseded all of these widescreen processes, so that it is now almost the only process used in 35mm widescreen filming.

Despite its expense and difficulty of use, the studios were keen to invest in widescreen during the 1950s because audiences, unable to resist the allure of television, were declin-ing: cinema attendance dropped from 90m per week in 1948 to 51m in 1952. It has also been argued that during the post-war period, American audiences had a greater choice of leisure activities and many were now moving to the newly established suburbs, away from city-centre cinemas. As a result, films had to engage their audiences in a more spectacular fashion. The 1950s widescreen, employing a ratio of at least 1.66:1, provided a visual experience that television could not emulate, and this was exploited by film-makers. The new, altered screen formats led to a dramatic change in *mise en scène* as directors began to use horizontal space much as depth of field was explored during the 1940s. Editing became secondary to shooting long, uninterrupted scenes, as each frame was now wide enough to display a close up, a medium shot and a wide angle simultaneously. The viewer was involved in the space of the film and brought closer to the action with a greater immediacy than ever before. Particular genres, such as historical or epic dramas (*The Ten Commandments*, 1956) and westerns (*The Searchers*, 1956) became natural choices for the widescreen format. Indeed, post-studio system Hollywood's taste for the blockbuster was facilitated by the new technology (see Chapter 1 on Hollywood).

3D

3D, whereby the three-dimensional illusion of depth is created by making the foreground stand out in relation to the other planes of the image, was experimented with as early as the 1920s. It did not take off, however, until the 1950s, when Hollywood used the technology as a further ploy to draw audiences away from their TV sets and back into the cinemas. In 1952, 3D projection called Natural Vision was introduced with Arch Obeler's *Bwana Devil*, and 69 Natural Vision films were made by the end of the following year. Other studios released 3D productions and soon more technical innovations were pioneered: Vistarama, Superscope, Naturama, AromaRama and Smell-O-Vision. These processes, however, were flawed, expensive and failed to attract a lasting audience. They were novelties that were deemed not to be worth the expense and they died out after a few years. During the 1960s, the main advance was the new optical system, Panavision, which allowed 35mm film to be enlarged to 70mm width without the need or expense of wide film production.

IMAX and OMNIMAX

The above widescreen processes have, however, been improved upon and surpassed by the advent of IMAX 3D technology, which premiered in 1970 in Japan, and the first IMAX cinema opened at Ontario Place's Cinesphere in Toronto the following year. 'IMAX' stands for 'image maximization' or 'maximum image', as it fills the field of human vision by producing an image as large as 20 metres high and 26 metres wide. IMAX uses a 15-perforation/70mm film format, which is not only supposedly the largest in the world, but is ten times bigger than that of conventional 35mm film. The size and scale produce extraordinary clarity and sharpness. A six-channel Surround Sound soundtrack is synchronized with the film, and the audience sits on a series of elevated rows at a 30–45 degree gradient and so feels immersed in the picture. Since 1996 approximately 200 IMAX cinemas have opened world-wide, including the BFI cinema at Waterloo, London.

Reflecting the 1950s, IMAX technology can project films in both 2D and 3D. The spectator wears a special headset with left and right liquid-crystal lenses and a 'personal sound environment' that encases the six-channel soundtrack. OMNIMAX (or IMAX DOME) uses the same system, but with a fisheye lens for projecting a 165-degree image on a giant dome screen surrounding the viewer with high-fidelity sound, thus increasing the spectator's feeling of immersion. IMAX technology has not, however, spread throughout the industry. Films must be specially shot and are shown in purpose-built cinemas. The system's use of 3D is still some distance from 'realism' and the screen at times proves to be too large for comfortable viewing.

Digital Projection

In the summer of 1999, *The Phantom Menace* was the first film to be screened in the United States using digital projection equipment. Computers, microchips and liquid-crystal displays replaced the traditional projector and reels of film. Where traditional analogue projection uses a signal corresponding to the original light and sound waves of the subject, digital projection converts the image and sound into an electronic coding through a binary series of zeroes and ones. In 2000, *Toy Story 2* was the first film screened in the UK using digital projection. As Michael Atkinson stated, it was 'the first time in the history of the 104-year-old medium that a movie made its way from conception to execution to projection without ever involving a single foot of film' (2000, p. 9). Atkinson does not make the point, however, that arguably the medium itself is no longer 'film' *per se* as it no longer always uses film. Digital projection hints at the end of the traditional pattern of film production and distribution that has been the norm for over a century. No longer will image and sound need to be captured on moving reels of negative film that are then developed, cut and spliced together, and transported to cinemas to be projected by bright light onto giant white screens. Instead, digital films can be beamed directly via satellite from studio to exhibitor with no loss in quality. At present, film distribution is vastly expensive and hence a whole industry has grown around it. Hundreds, if not thousands, of copies of films are distributed around the world at a cost of £3m for a global release. Since the advent of digital technology, however, such inconvenience and expense may become redundant. Digital projection may soon become the norm, not least because digital 'film' is much cheaper to shoot, and the new technology allows the film-maker to capture much more footage than do conventional film and cameras.

COMPUTER AND DIGITAL TECHNOLOGY

Unlike most of the technologies considered in this chapter, computer and digital processes are relatively new developments. But as for the other technologies, their adoption by the film industry has involved a combination of commercial and aesthetic considerations. Digital technologies have provided the means for creating new and different special effects images through computer generated imagery (CGI) (it should be noted that the initials are also used to refer to 'computer graphic interface' or to 'computer gateway interface'). They have made production and postproduction techniques more efficient. They have allowed the creation of new types of entertainment product, such as video and computer games, theme rides and virtual reality (VR) experiences. And finally, they have provided new avenues for distribution: CD-ROM, the Internet, satellite and cable, laser discs and DVDs.

Special Effects

The desire to create artificial yet plausible worlds for their films has occupied film-makers since the beginning. This led to *photorealism*, the attempt to produce images of photographic appearance and quality. Méliès developed 'trick film' or special effects for his films during the first years of cinema, but though special effects were attempted, often they were not very photorealistic. Even 60 years on during the 1950s, for example, the science fiction genre, which relied heavily on special effects to create its extra-terrestrial props and settings, was relegated to B-movie status because of the poor quality of these effects. It was not until 1968 that Stanley Kubrick was able to create a 'virtual reality', and in doing so he revolutionized the genre and the use of special effects. His *2001: A Space Odyssey* was the product of innovative use of sophisticated technology such as blue screen photography, travelling mattes, scale models and front and rear projection. Kubrick set new standards and it was almost a decade before anyone attempted to emulate him.

George Lucas' *Star Wars* used computer-co-ordinated camera movement ('Dykstraflex') to produce a seamless fusion of special effects and live-action footage. By the end of the 1970s film had integrated special effects, which had originally begun as mere spectacle, as central to both narrative and *mise en scène*.

Exercise 5.3

Do technologies that result in films achieving greater 'realism' reduce the need for the audience to use its imagination, thereby resulting in less involvement in the production of meaning?

CGI

It was not until the 1980s, however, that computer technology had advanced sufficiently to allow film-makers to incorporate wholly computer-generated imagery into their films. Disney's *Tron* (1982) was the first film to combine live-action footage with 3D CGI, which took up a total of five minutes of screen time. The film both used and reflected upon this use of CGI, as its protagonist was a computer whizz-kid trapped inside his computer. Although the film's *mise en scène* was relatively primitive and based on limited technology, it had a profound effect on film-making, in particular in the science fiction genre.

In 1984, *The Last Starfighter* incorporated 27 minutes of CGI. From the late 1980s onwards, computer and digital processes then developed with amazing rapidity, reflecting the growth of and advances in the high-tech industries. Almost annually a new technique was, and still is, introduced into film-making. These developments can only be described as a 'digital revolution'.

In 1989, a vastly improved CG effect known as *morphing* appeared in James Cameron's *The Abyss* in the form of a fluid 3D seawater creature, known as a 'pseudopod', capable of mimicking any organic or artificial form in its surroundings. At that time, morphing was an experimental process and the creature only appeared in the film's climax.

In 1991, however, Cameron advanced this technique to an entirely new level of impressiveness in his sequel to *Terminator* (1984), *T2: Judgement Day* (1991). In *T2*, Cameron introduced the T1000 cyborg – a humanoid android capable of morphing into almost any animate or inanimate thing – as a central plot device. Not only did the T1000 appear throughout the film, but the quality of its morphing was also extremely sophisticated. The integration of the special effects with the actors was almost seamless and the film has been seen as 'groundbreaking in its digital special effects, in particular the sophistication and photorealistic quality' of its imagery (Michael Allen, 1999, p. 63).

Throughout the 1990s, many films incorporated CGI into their narratives; often the special effects themselves became the main feature. In 1993 Steven Spielberg's *Jurassic Park* created the first CG dinosaurs and the following year *The Mask* employed some of the same tools to produce effects that had previously only been seen in animation. CGI is also used in postproduction to add colour, to remove support wires used for stunts, to insert images or to integrate separate photographic images into a film. This is known as *electronic compositing* – the manipulation of film images. *Forrest Gump* (1994), for example, uses computer and digital technology to place its eponymous hero in a variety of historical settings with a range of historical characters. Since then, CGI has made unlikely, and probably unobserved, appearances in many films, such as *Elizabeth* and *Waking Ned Devine* (both 1998). Perhaps the high point of digital and computer technologies during the twentieth century came with *Titanic* (1997) and *The Matrix* (1999). In the former, the entire ship is resurrected from the seabed and brought back to life, whereas in the latter, the protagonist, Neo (Keanu Reeves), is seen to walk up walls, hover through the air and dodge missiles in 'a breathtaking mode of temporal mangling known as "bullet time"' (Bennun, 1999, p. 29).

'Bullet time' is the appearance of people or objects being suspended or moving slowly in mid-air while the camera seems to track around them to give different visual perspectives. The effect is achieved by placing a large number of still or movie cameras in an arc around the subject, then operating them at exactly or almost the same time. The almost simultaneous shots from each camera are then edited together and synchronized using computer technology to create the impression of a camera tracking round the subject while it is suspended, or moving slowly, in mid-air.

Pixar

Animation in particular has benefited from the advances in computer and digital technology as the new processes are less expensive, speedier and more versatile than traditional methods. In 1986 Pixar released its first fully realized digitally animated short film, *Luxo Jr.* The landmark in digital animation, however, arrived in 1995 when Disney's *Toy Story* was the first ever feature-length film to rely exclusively on 3D CGI. Using Pixar technology, *Toy Story* was made entirely on computer with not one single frame being shot using conventional methods. Nonetheless, the film still preserved the tempo and illusion of camera movement and sophisticated live action. Since then several other fully digitally animated films have been produced (*Antz* and *A Bug's Life*, both 1998), and *Toy Story 2* (2000) amazed critics and audiences alike with its advances in animation.

While it is the product of an aesthetic choice, the use of CGI also reflects one of Hollywood's long-held concerns – economy. The use of digital and computer processes is sometimes cheaper than building an entirely new set or filming on location. In *Fight Club* (1999), for example, budget restrictions determined that CGI would be more cost-effective than building a giant kitchen for one particular sequence. In other films like *In the Line of Fire* (1993), *Forrest Gump* and *Titanic*, CGI was also used to generate large crowd scenes using only a small number of real extras who were duplicated and multiplied, saving money in wages and crowd control. Such technology is thus increasingly used as one of the ways in which production costs can be minimized. At the same time, films using these special effects have been immensely popular with audiences, and therefore some commentators see a link between the use of such technology and maximizing a film's revenues and argue that elaborate special effects are so bankable that rather than being used to tell a narrative, new films are written around them. Many of the films mentioned above have been high earners, suggesting a link between sophisticated special effects and box-office figures.

Exercise 5.4

Look at any film which relies on CGI (e.g. *Titanic*, *Independence Day*). Are the effects achieved 'photorealistic'? Can you see a difference between the real actors and props and the special effects; do they blend together seamlessly or is there a noticeable difference?

Tech *Noir*

Just as advanced technologies have emerged for creating improved special effects, the very films that have used them to greatest effect have also reflected on the potential of technology. Science fiction films in particular have tended to reflect on the latest technological developments and on possible future technologies. Space travel was the subject of Georges Méliès' *Journey to the Moon* (1898), while Fritz Lang's *Metropolis* (1926) (Figure 5.2)

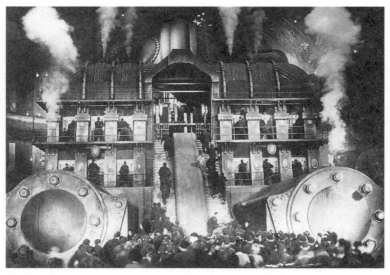

Figure 5.2   *Metropolis: futuristic technology (BFI Stills, Posters and Designs)*

envisaged a future set in the year 2000. The future and space and time travel have continued to fascinate film-makers ever since. In the 1950s, the classic sci fi 'B-movies' meditated on atomic and nuclear technology, particularly on the effects of radioactivity. In 1968, Kubrick's *2001* (its title a homage to *Metropolis*) examined the implications of computer malfunction (in this case the computer is called HAL, which some have read as standing for IBM – think about it) at a time when computers were still confined to the military-industrial complex (Figure 5.3).

The revolution in computerization since the 1970s, however, has led to the emergence of an entirely new sub-genre: 'tech *noir*'. Building on Kubrick's *2001*, tech *noir* began to emerge in the 1970s and 1980s. While reflecting on the implications of technology and manifesting a fascination with high-tech industry, computer technology, artificial intelligence, genetic engineering and virtual reality, it projected a dystopian, pessimistic view of the future. Films of this genre include *THX 1138* (1970), *Westworld* (1973), *Logan's Run* (1976), *Blade Runner*, *Terminator* and *T2*. Kathryn Bigelow's *Strange Days* (1995), using the device of VR, was a sophisticated self-reflexive study of voyeurism, spectatorship, the psychic dangers of vicarious entertainment and the nature of the cinematic medium itself. Other films which have examined the implications of VR are *The Lawnmower Man* (1992), *eXistenZ* (1999) and *The Matrix* (1999).

THE FUTURE

In a famous essay in 1949, André Bazin characterized the advance of film technology as an inevitable and graceful progression towards greater screen realism. In doing so, however, he ignored the socio-economic context in which each development was grounded. Up to that point, the prime impetus behind each major technological innovation had been commercial rather than aesthetic, as enterprising studio heads recognized new technology as a means to maximize profits while simultaneously distinguishing their product from the competition.

2001: a celebration of space technology (BFI Stills, Posters and Designs)   Figure 5.3

Computer and digital technologies have advanced further than any other innovation considered in this chapter over the past 20 years. If they continue to progress at this rate, the age of complete 'realism', with CG images more realistic and more 'real' than the world we inhabit, may soon be achieved. Will this signal the end of traditional actors and settings? *Casper* (1993) featured the first CG talking lead figure while *The Phantom Menace* (1999) depicted another CG character in Jar Jar Binks. While in *Casper* the character was merely a friendly ghost, the huge leaps in computer and digital technology suggest that it may be the beginning of a new trend. Eventually, special effects technology will be able to replace live actors with resurrected dead stars, while any setting will be creatable within a computer. Although current technologies may point to such developments in the future, will they manage to achieve the level of 'realism' that many demand?

Exercise 5.5

Take each of the six new technologies outlined in this chapter. Find out who introduced them; what was their reason for doing so? Who was responsible for their adoption? Was it the studios, individual film-makers or outside companies? Consider how far they were introduced for commercial or for aesthetic reasons.

SUMMARY

- Technological developments have affected film-making in two ways: film-makers have utilized new technologies to make films, and, as a result, films increasingly reflect on the consequences of the use of such technology.
- The adoption of new technology was and is not a simple or uninterrupted linear progression.
- Developments in film technology were not always welcomed initially or used immediately upon their emergence. In many cases, the technology already existed some years (even decades) prior to its widespread adoption.
- The adoption of new processes closely mirrors their context.
- The main technological developments have been: camera mobility, sound, deep field photography, colour, projection technologies (widescreen, 3D, IMAX/OMNIMAX and digital) and computer and digital technologies.

REFERENCES

Michael Allen, 'Technology', in Pam Cook and Mieke Bernink (eds), *The Cinema Book* (2nd edn, London: BFI, 1999), pp. 45–64.

Michael Atkinson, 'Cinema's secret history', *The Guardian Guide* (1 January 2000), pp. 4–9.

Erik Barnouw, *Documentary: A History of the Non-fiction Film* (Oxford: Oxford University Press, 1974, reprinted 1993) (Chapter 1).

André Bazin, 'The myth of total cinema', in *What is Cinema?* Vol. 1 (transl. Hugh Gray, Berkeley: University of California Press, 1967).

David Bennun, 'One day soon, all actors may be made this way', *The Observer Magazine* (12 December 1999), pp. 24–30.

Marshall McLuhan, *Understanding Media: The Extensions of Man* (London: Abacus, 1974).

Christopher Goodwin, 'The digital explosion', *The Sunday Times Culture* (14 November 1999), pp. 55–7.

John Hill and Pamela Church Gibson (eds), *The Oxford Guide to Film Studies* (Oxford: Oxford University Press, 1998).

Ira Konigsberg, *The Complete Film Dictionary* (2nd edn, London: Bloomsbury, 1997).

Richard Maltby, *Hollywood Cinema: An Introduction* (Oxford: Blackwell, 1995).

James Monaco, *How to Read a Film* (3rd edn, Oxford: Oxford University Press, 2000).

David Parkinson, *History of Film* (London: Thames & Hudson, 1995).

Kristin Thompson and David Bordwell, *Film History* (New York: McGraw-Hill, 1994) (Chapter 1).

Chris Webster, 'Film and technology', in Jill Nelmes (ed.), *An Introduction to Film Studies* (2nd edn, London: Routledge, 1999), pp. 59–87.

FURTHER READING

David A. Cook, *A History of Narrative Film* (3rd edn, New York and London: W.W. Norton & Co., 1996).

FURTHER VIEWING

The Making of The Mummy (Universal, 1999).

The Language of Film

There have been at least nine different TV and feature films made about the sinking of the Titanic. These range from a silent version made within months of the disaster (*Saved from the Titanic*, 1912), to the dryly titled *A Night to Remember* (1958), to *S.O.S. Titanic* (1979), to two films imaginatively called *Titanic* (1953 and 1997). The reason for mentioning these films is not to indicate the long history of the disaster movie genre but to highlight the fact that there is more than one way to tell a story in a film. The scripts for each of these films would of course have been very different, but essentially the story was the same: unsinkable ship makes maiden voyage, ship hits iceberg, ship sinks with a few passengers escaping.

An understanding of how there can have been several versions of the *Titanic* story can be gained by studying the 'language of film'. All forms of communication have their own language. This book is communicating using the English language; music uses the written language of musical notation; photography communicates meanings by using a language that consists of concepts such as composition, framing, camera angle, shot size, lighting, contrasts between black and white, varying tones of colour; a radio programme may use the English language combined with an audio language consisting of practices such as fading volume up and down at appropriate times and mixing dialogue, music and sound effects together at various volume levels depending on what meaning is intended. Whatever the language being used, it consists of *codes* and *conventions*. Codes are particular methods for communicating meanings and conventions are the ways in which those codes are usually used. The English language uses particular words and grammatical structures.

Film has its own 'language'. A range of techniques are available to a film-maker and those techniques are used to present a narrative through the medium of film, a narrative being a chain of events that are (usually) causally linked. The language of film is used (usually) to tell stories. A film's form is determined by the ways in which the story is told by the film, and is a combination of style and content. The content is structured by the narrative and style is shaped by the film techniques employed. The previous chapter covered film technology, which can be regarded as the 'tools of the trade'. Film techniques are the ways in which film technology is used; this chapter aims to identify what the language of film consists of and how film techniques produce meanings.

The film production process can be divided into preproduction, production and post-production. Preproduction includes scriptwriting – putting into words the types of narratives we have already looked at. This is followed by storyboards which visualize the script's narrative in a series of drawings that indicate the content of each shot. The production stage is when filming takes place, and the editing of filmed material is referred to as postproduction (see Chapter 2 on Production, Distribution and Exhibition). With regard to film techniques, we are interested in the specific practices that take place during production and postproduction. These techniques are covered by four terms: *mise en scène*, cinematography, editing and sound, each of which subsumes a range of subsidiary techniques.

MISE EN SCÈNE

This term originally developed in relation to theatre and literally translates as 'putting on the stage'. For our purposes it refers to 'placing within the shot'. A significant part of the meaning produced by a film comes from the visual content – this is to a large extent how the story is told. What a shot consists of is therefore crucially important. As James Monaco writes, '[b]ecause we read the shot, we are actively involved with it. The codes of *mise en scène* are the tools with which the filmmaker alters and modifies our reading of the shot' (1981, p. 148). The elements covered by *mise en scène* are: setting, props, costume, performance, lighting and colour. But in addition to choosing what is to be included in a shot, someone also has to decide how the elements are to be arranged. In other words, composition is also central to *mise en scène*.

A director needs to make a number of decisions when deciding on shot content and arrangement. It needs to be recognized, however, that though the director is the person ultimately responsible for such matters, film conventions established over time can also play a large part in shaping *mise en scène*. Genre films tend to require particular elements, thus restricting the director's freedom (see Chapters 9 and 10 on Authorship and Genre). We also need to be aware that while we may try to determine the meanings produced by a shot, it is very likely that other spectators will interpret differently, especially when viewing from a different cultural perspective. In other words shots can be *polysemic*; they can have many meanings (see Chapters 3 and 12 on Cinema, Audiences and Society and on Meaning and Spectatorship).

Setting

The setting provides the space in which all the other elements of *mise en scène* are situated. The setting, like props and costume, sets up expectations for the viewer and can instantly produce meanings; it signifies certain things. This is especially the case with genre films (see Chapter 10 for more detail). A shot of a relatively barren landscape with a small town consisting of wooden buildings including a saloon bar and sheriff's office will immediately indicate a western. Setting can be provided by filming on location, in a setting that actually exists, or by set design where the location is built for the specific purpose of the film. Typically, films use both studio sets and location filming, but many of the films from the Hollywood studio system era were filmed entirely within the studio. By comparison *Tilaï* (1989) was filmed entirely on location around a small village in Burkina Faso in Africa.

Props

Props are the inanimate objects placed within the setting. They may remain static or may be used by the characters in the film. Props may simply serve to strengthen the effect of the setting by making the environment in which the action takes place visually more convincing. Los Angeles in 2019 as the setting for *Blade Runner* (1982) is made more convincing by the addition of hi-tech equipment, flying craft and futuristic gadgets. Props may also have a more active function. The phone that we see at the beginning of *Scream* (1996) is a prop that immediately plays a very active part in that it directly links the viewer and Casey to danger.

Costume

Costumes help create an actor's character. They can place an actor within a particular historical period, indicate social class or lifestyle, and even determine what is possible and what is not. A space suit makes survival in space possible. A cowboy wearing a gun can survive a shoot-out. This example indicates that there can be an overlap between props and costume – at what point does the gun cease to be prop and become part of a costume? As with the previous two categories, costume can also help define the genre of a film.

Performance

What an actor does within a shot obviously contributes significantly to the meanings produced. The way an actor moves could indicate confidence, uncertainty, panic, friendliness. The actor's facial expressions may show fear, anger, happiness, sadness. In addition to these examples of body language or non-verbal communication, and to the clear differences in the speech patterns of different actors, a performance may have a particular effect because of what the actor has previously done in other films. Actors may be identified with certain types of characters, and actors with celebrity status can bring connotations to a film that emanate not only from previous films but also from their lives outside the films (see Chapter 11 on Stars). When we see Madonna in a film, is it possible to ignore her previous roles and what we know of her personal life?

Lighting and colour

Lighting illuminates the above-mentioned elements in a shot while itself also becoming an element within the shot. It has long been suggested that the human eye is drawn towards movement and towards the brightest area in a shot. A memorable shot from *Citizen Kane* (1941) illustrates the importance of movement and light. In the first flashback to Kane's early life, we see his mother and Thatcher in the foreground discussing his future. In the distant background we see Kane playing with his sledge. Despite the close proximity and important dialogue of Mrs Kane and Thatcher, we can't help but notice Kane in the distance because of the character's movement and because he is framed by a window against a bright backdrop.

Lighting is usually thought of in terms of high key (balanced) lighting and low key (*chiaroscuro*) lighting. High key lighting is usually used when a relatively normal, everyday scenario is being filmed – we generally attempt to illuminate the situations we typically find ourselves in. Illumination exposes detail and provides visual information. However, in many films a mellow and subdued atmosphere is called for if suspense and fear of the unknown are required. The latter is often achieved by providing a lack of visual information and by hiding detail; this can be obtained through low key lighting, lighting from one source so as to create shadows and strong contrasts. *The Blair Witch Project* (1999) provides an extreme example of the use of low key lighting as a method for creating fear. During the night-time scenes the only source of light is a torch or video camera light in the darkness surrounding the characters. Only being able to see a small part of the forest emphasizes how little the characters can see.

When high key lighting is desired in a film, lighting from at least two sources is used. In reality at least three lights are usually employed (see Figure 6.1): a *key light* as the main

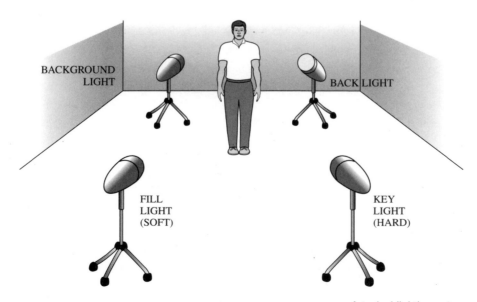

A typical lighting set up   Figure 6.1

source, a *fill light* to remove shadows, and a *background light* to create a sense of depth between the main subject and the background. A fourth light, a *back light*, may also be used, placed behind and facing towards them. It has the effect of highlighting the edges of a figure, usually the head. The key light is usually placed at approximately eye level; however, it can be placed above the actor as top lighting or below the actor as under lighting. Top lighting tends to enhance the actor's features whereas under lighting distorts the features.

Colour has long been thought to affect mood; for instance, light green is believed to be a relaxing colour; red is a 'restless' colour. But as well as having a psychological effect, colours can also symbolize emotions and values, thus producing meanings in a text. White and black have respectively been used to represent good and evil, red can symbolize passion, romance and anger. Blue can symbolize detachment, alienation and a lack of emotion: futuristic, dystopian films such as *Blade Runner* and *RoboCop* (1987) use blue light to a significant degree.

Composition

Having selected all the above elements for inclusion in a shot, the director then has to place them as required. The arrangement of elements within a shot is known as composition. Symmetrical composition places elements of a similar shape and size in similar positions on either side of the shot. Asymmetrical composition achieves an overall balance by having each side of the shot generally equate with the other in terms of areas of visual significance. A balanced composition is usually regarded as visually pleasing as opposed to unbalanced composition, which may make us feel uneasy or uncomfortable. Unbalanced composition can, however, be a useful creative device.

A fascinating shot for analysing *mise en scène* comes from *Psycho* (1960) during the scene when Marion and Norman converse in his room. The setting is a small room cluttered with props such as a table, chairs, pictures, ornaments, candlesticks, a chest of drawers, curtains and a table lamp, all of which are typical everyday items; yet combined with the setting they create a somewhat claustrophobic atmosphere. The props that stand out as unusual are several stuffed birds. The lighting is slightly low key but the only strong shadows are cast by the stuffed birds illuminated by under lighting. Interestingly, Hitchcock chose to film *Psycho* in black and white even though colour film had been available for 25 years.

Norman's costume does not appear to be of particular significance, but his performance is full of meaning. The mid-shot of just Norman concentrates our attention upon his performance. It is a low angle shot which gives us an unusual view of Norman, distorting his appearance. He is talking animatedly, using his hands, and has an intense, obsessed look on his face. Norman does not appear normal. Our doubts about his sanity are enhanced by the predatory birds on the wall, which indicate his obsession with taxidermy and symbolize his potential for preying on Marion. The composition of the shot is also unsettling in that while Norman is looking left towards Marion, his face is placed on the left-hand side of the screen. This is unbalanced composition because there is nothing on the right-hand side of the shot to balance out the left. It also introduces tension because Norman has no 'looking space' within the shot. Normally a character looking left would be positioned to the right to create space for him/her

Mise en scène and shot composition in Some Like it Hot (BFI Stills, Posters and Designs)   Figure 6.2

to look through. When Norman is placed up against the left side of the shot we have no idea if something is placed directly in front of him or not. It creates uncertainty because we are visually uninformed. All in all this shot shows highly effective *mise en scène*.

The still from *Some Like it Hot* (Figure 6.2) contains a wealth of information that we identify through a reading of the shot's *mise en scène*. Marilyn Monroe, as Sugar, is talking to Tony Curtis (Joe) on the beach. Joe is wearing a ship's captain's uniform and sits formally in a sheltered chair, separating himself somewhat from the informally dressed occupants of the beach. He has an appearance of authority and status, albeit not a very convincing one. Sugar is sitting in close proximity to Joe and gazes up at him with a look of admiration and interest; Joe avoids her gaze and seems to be trying hard not to show any interest in her. The brightly lit beach carries connotations of leisure, pleasure and playfulness, as epitomized by Sugar, while Joe's appearance and his position above Sugar emphasize his comical attempt at cool detachment and composure.

Exercise 6.1

Describe the ways in which the *mise en scène* contributes to the meaning of one sequence in a horror film of your choice.

CINEMATOGRAPHY

If *mise en scène* refers to what is placed in front of the camera, then cinematography is concerned with recording the elements within the shot. While photography is the recording of a static image, cinematography is the recording of a moving image. In order to obtain the desired images, the cinematographer must attend to two areas: control of lighting and oper-ation of the camera. The images consist of reflected light and the camera records light. Indeed, in Britain a cinematographer (the person responsible for lighting and camerawork) is sometimes known as the lighting cameraperson or as the director of photography.

Framing

A key ingredient of cinematography is *framing*. This refers to the edges of a shot, in that fram-ing determines both what is included and what is excluded. There is indeed a close link between framing, composition and *mise en scène*. *Mise en scène* refers to what is to be filmed and how it is arranged and therefore in effect defines what the framing will be; however, strictly speaking, the framing is only realized when the shot is filmed through the camera lens.

To refer back to the Norman and Marion conversation scene from *Psycho*, Hitchcock could have chosen to widen the framing so that we could see both Marion and Norman. How-ever, this would have entailed including more height in the shot, which would perhaps have meant meaningless space and detail. The tighter framing chosen by Hitchcock means we get a mid-shot of Norman's reactions as he speaks to Marion. Hitchcock nevertheless briefly gives us a long shot of both Marion and Norman at the beginning and end of the scene to provide us with a sense of the spatial relationship between them.

Shot Size

Shot size in turn is determined by the framing. There are many possible choices of shot but we can think in terms of five basic shot sizes with intermediate shots in between (see Figure 6.3). Shot sizes can be closely tied to narrative development, notably to the progression of scenes. Typically a film, and often a scene, will begin with an *extreme long shot* (ELS). Just as narratives tend to begin slowly in order to acquaint us with characters and locations, so films visually use an ELS (sometimes called an *establishing shot*) to place things in context. An ELS allows us to see a subject in relation to her/his surroundings. *Blade Runner* begins with several ELSs which gradually introduce us to Los Angeles in the twenty-first century, fol-lowed by the introduction of themes and characters.

A film can begin with an *extreme close up* (ECU); this could be used to make us inquisi-tive, or it may simply be an impressive shot because of its content, but more often than not it won't make much sense. *The Good, the Bad and the Ugly* (1967) famously begins with an ELS which is immediately transformed into an ECU as a character walks into shot and looks straight to camera. The shot is interesting and intriguing while also being disconcerting; however, it makes no obvious sense in the context of the film. It does not enable us to get to know the character in greater depth, which would arguably be a pointless exercise any-way as he dies a couple of minutes later. The choice of shot seems to be more to do with style and experimentation than with illustrating the narrative. Furthermore, having a charac-ter look straight to camera is usually identified as a technique of alternative cinema (see p. 146 below).

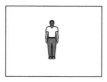

EXTREME LONG SHOT
(ELS)

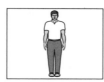

LONG SHOT
(LS)

MID SHOT
(MS)

CLOSE UP
(CU)

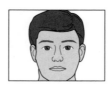

EXTREME CLOSE UP
(ECU)

The five main shot sizes   Figure 6.3

A first *close up* is usually found some minutes into a film when we are already accustomed to characters and locations. Typically a CU will concentrate our attention on an important detail to ensure that the desired meaning is communicated, or else a CU will be used as a reaction shot to show someone's response to an incident. It is common to find a CU of someone's face when their expression tells us something or a CU on an object that is to have a crucial function in the film. *Scream* in fact begins with a potentially confusing shot, a CU of a telephone; however, we do hear a phone ringing and we don't have to wait long for it to take on relevance. The camera tracks back to show Casey picking up the phone. These introductory shots are also soon followed by an exterior ELS (albeit a threatening one) of Casey's home to provide us with context.

Length of Take

If shot sizes tend to be large at the beginnings of films and scenes, an equivalent characteristic can be noted for shot duration or the length of a take. The average duration of a shot is approximately 6 seconds, but introductory shots are often at least twice this length. Again, the pace tends to be slower in order to allow the viewer more time to become acquainted with characters and locations. If we look at 2 minutes from near the beginning of *Cinema Paradiso* (1989) we find only five shots. Within this time we are introduced to the main character Salvatore and his wife, who informs him that an old friend, Alfredo, has died. This leads into a flashback to his youth which goes on to provide his childhood memories, which constitute the bulk of the film. If we then look at a 2-minute period from the climactic section of the film, when Salvatore saves Alfredo from a fire in the village cinema, we find 52 shots. The narrative *allows* short takes because we know the location and characters well, and the narrative also *requires* short takes because the scene involves action and panic. Imagine the effect if we reversed the shot durations: 52 shots in 2 minutes to introduce characters and only five shots to cover 2 minutes of fast-moving action.

There can be other reasons for long takes in a film. Orson Welles famously, and Jean-Luc Godard infamously, have used long takes. In Godard's *Weekend* (1968) one shot lasts 8 minutes and gradually reveals to us a long line of cars in a traffic jam. As well as also helping to ensure that the film is 'alternative', which was no doubt part of the director's intention, the shot also helps make one of Godard's points about cultural life and consumerism in 1960s France – the point being that while the trend of going away for the weekend grew, it increasingly resulted in people spending the weekend in traffic jams.

Welles began *Touch of Evil* (1953) with a shot that lasts over 3 minutes. It begins with a close up of a bomb being planted in a car. The camera then rises to give us a bird's eye view of the situation, including the car driving off. The camera tracks to catch up with the car, then drops down to enable us to hear a banal conversation between a border guard, a woman and a man. This technique builds suspense as we are expecting an explosion, which soon follows and brings the shot to a close. Being the exception to the rule begs the question: why use a long take instead of editing together several shots covering the same action? It could be argued that in this instance we are given an overview of what is happening in adjacent locations simultaneously as a way of providing us with the bigger picture. However, if this is the intention, then why is the technique not used more frequently?

Alternatively it could be argued that such a shot was motivated more by style than by the requirements of the narrative, which is not necessarily undesirable. For now it is sufficient to note that it is a technically impressive shot with incredibly complex timing which has certainly gained a place within the study of film. As Richard Maltby notes:

> [V]isual style is not usually so conspicuous an element in a movie's performance. In *Touch of Evil* we notice the emphasis on the camera as an active agent in the manipulation of the audience precisely because we are used to the more anonymous and self-effacing strategies associated with Hollywood camerawork. Long takes or extravagant camera gestures stress the existence of an instrumental, manipulative presence.
>
> (Maltby, 1995, p. 246)

Having suggested that the long take at the beginning of *Touch of Evil* may be more to do with style than with content, it would be wrong to assume that this is always the case. *Tilaï* regularly uses takes throughout the film of almost a minute's duration. However, the length of the takes is not particularly noticeable because they seem to suit the narrative. The film is set in a small, rural community in Africa. The pace of life is slow and the story is not action-driven. The cause–effect processes within the film develop gradually. The narrative *requires* long takes. What is also noticeable is the lack of camera movement in many of these long takes. The camera allows the narrative to unfold in front of it without trying to add meaning through movement. A further reason for these long takes, which often tend to be long shots too, is the location of the film. The village is surrounded by wide open spaces; there is little to interrupt the vast horizons. Director Idrissa Ouedraogo allows events to unravel against this backdrop of uninterrupted space with a minimum of interference, whereas within the more enclosed confines of most film locations, there is a need to switch to different camera angles and shot sizes, if only to cover all the action.

Hitchcock took the long take one stage further in *Rope* (1948). A reel of film normally lasts no longer than 10 minutes and Hitchcock filmed so that each reel was one complete take. What is more, he began and ended each reel with someone or something passing close to the camera lens so that the screen went dark. At these points the reels were edited together so that the whole film appears to be one long continuous take lasting 80 minutes. The camera continually tracks around the apartment in which the film takes place, following characters and actions to give a variety of perspectives.

Camera Movement

As has already been mentioned in the above example, long takes usually involve camera movement of some sort, as it would be difficult to justify a long take in which the camera was static unless the action within the frame was sufficiently interesting to be able to hold our attention (one of the characteristics of early films was long takes with static cameras; see Chapter 7 on Early Cinema and Film Form). There are four main types of camera movement: in a *pan* shot the camera rotates horizontally around a fixed position (often used to follow movement); a *tilt shot* moves the camera vertically around a fixed position (typically used to indicate height); a *tracking* shot involves a horizontal movement of the camera in which it changes location, usually fitted to a device called a *dolly* that runs on rails; a *crane shot* enables the camera to be raised and lowered and moved horizontally. In addition to the above, it is also possible to use a hand-held camera or to utilize the *zoom* facility, which strictly speaking is not a camera movement but movement within the camera – repositioning the lens in relation to the aperture.

The problem with hand-held camerawork is that the shots can be unsteady, but the use of *steadicam* equipment can overcome this problem and provide smooth moving shots (see Chapter 5 on Film Technology). However, films like *The Blair Witch Project* and those of Dogme 95 achieve their impact partly through unsteady hand-held camerawork. The viewer is linked more directly to the person filming, first because we usually see exactly what s/he sees via the camera but also because we are reminded of their presence through the shaky camerawork.

Crane shot

In Martin Scorsese's opinion, one of the greatest shots of all time is a crane shot lasting more than a minute, used by Hitchcock in *Young and Innocent* (1937). In this film a murder has been committed and those investigating believe the culprit is in a ballroom; the only clue they have is that the murderer has a facial twitch. Hitchcock gives the viewer information the investigators don't have with a crane shot that begins with an ELS of the ballroom, then moves over the heads of the dancers towards the band on the stage, ending with an ECU of the drummer's face, which begins to twitch.

Tracking shot

The penultimate shot from *Psycho* (see Figure 6.4) contains a good example of a tracking shot, combined with unusual framing. Norman Bates has been caught and is being held in a cell. We see a long shot of Norman, but the framing produces an awkward composition in which he is placed to the left of the shot and his lower legs are out of the frame. It is an uncomfortable shot visually. The long shot emphasizes Norman's isolation in a bare, white room. The camera gradually tracks in to a close up of Norman's face in the centre of the screen, at which point he slowly looks up from under his eyebrows with an evil grin. At the beginning of the shot we feel safely distanced from Norman, but by the end of the tracking shot we are close to him and feel threatened.

Zoom and tracking shots

It will immediately be realized that a tracking shot is one way of bringing a subject closer by physically moving the camera nearer. However, another technique which produces a similar effect is that of a zoom, the main difference being that the camera does not physically move closer but the lens alters its focal length. But while both techniques bring the subject closer, they differ in how they deal with perspective concerning the relationship between what is in the middle of the shot and what is at the edges of the frame.

Hitchcock experimented creatively with this difference in *Vertigo* (1958). When Scottie, who suffers from vertigo, is running up the tower in the final scene, he twice looks down the centre of the stairwell. The film cuts to his point of view and brilliantly imitates the experience of light-headedness and nausea through fear of heights by distorting the perspective between the edge of the frame and the centre of the shot. Hitchcock achieved this through a *reverse-track zoom*. As the camera zooms back from the bottom of the stairwell, it also tracks in to ensure that the edges of the frame stay exactly the same. The effect is to have the centre of the shot stretching away from the edges of the shot. Similar techniques have since been used by Scorsese himself and by Mathieu Kassovitz (*La Haine*, 1995) among others.

Figure 6.4   *Psycho: the unbalanced Norman Bates (Paramount, courtesy Kobal)*

Camera Angle

Camera angle provides another means of producing different meanings. Normally the camera angle is horizontal and at eye level: we usually communicate with each other at something approximating eye level and subconsciously expect to relate to the characters in films in the same way. However, high and low camera angles can be used too. A high camera angle can be useful for providing a general overview of a situation. A low camera angle may be required because of the position of a character in relation to something else. High and low camera angles can also be used to represent a power relationship between characters in a film or to emphasize the subordinate or dominant nature of a character to the audience. An example of this technique is found in *Citizen Kane* when Kane is arguing with Susan. As Kane is talking, a low angle is used; he towers over Susan and over us. When Susan is talking, a high angle is used; we look down on her. Kane's power is symbolized further in this scene when his shadow gradually eclipses Susan. However, the meanings behind high and low camera angles remain linked to the narrative context.

An angled shot can also provide a distorted view. In *Psycho*, during Norman's conversation with Marion Crane, at one point a low angle shot is used of Norman which has the effect of exaggerating his 'strangeness'. We already suspect he is odd from the things he says and from his obsessive, unpredictable character. At another point in the conversation Marion stands up and a high angle shot of Norman is used. This has the effect of reducing him to looking like a small child where before he was threatening, thus emphasizing his split personality.

Depth of Field

One last aspect of cinematography remains, this being *depth of field*. Depending on shutter speed, aperture and the amount of light available, a camera can focus on just a small part of what is in the frame or on the whole scene. Focusing on only part of a frame is known as shallow focus and is often used as a device for encouraging the audience to concentrate on a particular part of the scene. Conversely, seeing everything in focus, from foreground to background, is known as *deep field photography* or *deep focus*.

This technique has probably never been shown more clearly than in the scene referred to earlier (p. 95) from *Citizen Kane* when Kane as a small boy is seen playing in the snow in the background while his mother and Thatcher talk in the foreground. The shot begins as an exterior shot of Kane. The camera then moves back through a window and past Kane's mother and Thatcher. The camera continues to track back through a doorway, at which point Mrs Kane and Thatcher move to sit in front of the camera (Figure 6.5). The shot was arranged and filmed by cinematographer Gregg Toland so as to be in focus from foreground to background. It is difficult not to suspect that the shot was contrived to illustrate deep focus; as with other techniques in *Citizen Kane*, such as use of low key lighting and extreme camera angles, the deep focus here is hardly subtle and can leave the viewer remembering the style of the film rather than its narrative. This is a criticism Robert McKee makes of Welles, claiming that *Citizen Kane* is all style and no content; in effect, style is the film's content, our eye stops at the screen and does not get through to the narrative. For McKee style should provide access to the narrative and strengthen it.

Figure 6.5   *Citizen Kane and deep focus: Kane's parents decide his future as he plays in the background (BFI Stills, Posters and Designs)*

Exercise 6.2
Compare and contrast the camerawork in the opening and closing scenes of a non-Hollywood film of your choice.

EDITING

After the completion of filming, the final stage is editing, the selection and piecing together of shots to form the completed film. Just as a range of choices exists for the cinematographer when manipulating light and using a camera, so editing offers many possibilities.

Continuity Editing

One of the key principles is *continuity editing*. Most films, in one way or another, attempt to have us fully engrossed in what we see. The intention is that we escape into the film for the duration of the screening. The concept of 'willing suspension of disbelief' sums up the experience of much film-going. We know that what we see on the screen isn't real, in other words, we disbelieve it, but in order to fully engage with the film we willingly suspend that disbelief – we happily ignore our doubts about the authenticity of what we see. We allow ourselves to enter the world (the *diegesis*) of the film.

In order that we can experience films in this way, it is important that we are not reminded that we are watching a film and that we are not confused by an incomprehensible presentation of events in the narrative. Annette Kuhn writes: 'Continuity editing establishes spatial and temporal relationships between shots in such a way as to permit the spectator to "read" a film without any conscious effort, precisely because the editing is "invisible".' (in Cook and Bernink, 1999, p. 40) For this to be possible, it is essential that the shots flow smoothly from one to another and that our attention is not drawn to the edit points. In effect, the shots support each other. One shot logically leads to the next and to a degree we expect the next shot: there is a continuity between one shot and the next. A number of techniques help make this possible.

Movement and Speed of Editing

To ensure such 'transparent' editing, it is necessary that the locations, props, actors and movement in one shot are consistent with what has gone before. The speed at which something happens and the space within which it occurs should be consistent across the relevant shots. In effect, continuity editing supports the meanings produced by the audio/visual interpretations of the narrative.

This principle can be illustrated by reference to a scene mentioned previously, the climactic moment in *Cinema Paradiso* when Salvatore rescues Alfredo from the fire that has started in the cinema projection room. The pace of editing is fast, people are panicking, events move with speed. Within this scene there is a consistency with regard to time and movement and similarly there is a consistency in the locations and space within which the events unravel. Failure to maintain this consistency would interrupt our involvement in the film and draw attention to the artificial and constructed nature of film.

Shot Size and Editing

This particular scene also serves to illustrate another common principle behind editing, the use of a variety of shot sizes. On one level a variety of shot sizes helps maintain our interest visually through avoiding repetition, but it also serves another function. We have already noted the various meanings that shot sizes can produce, and through editing a logical progression is created out of shot size. In the scene from the above example we are provided with an extreme long shot of the village and cinema to provide context. The shots are then edited together to eventually take us onto a more personal level as we see Salvatore in extreme close up battling his way through the crowds to Alfredo.

Shot/Reverse Shot Editing

Editing also helps to clarify situations by joining together shots from different angles to provide us with different perspectives, thereby creating a fuller understanding. This is common during conversations where a *shot/reverse shot* edit is frequently used. The shots themselves are often 'over the shoulder shots' in which we see part of the back of one person's head and shoulders and the front of the other person talking to them. The editing provides an understanding of the spatial relationship between the characters while also giving information on movement and facial expression.

Eye-line Match

Conversations, and for that matter any interaction between characters, will usually also require an *eye-line match* in order to maintain continuity between edits. If character A is in a chair looking up at character B who is standing, when we cut to a close up of character A s/he should still be looking up, even if character B is out of shot – and vice versa for a close up of character B. In other words, the direction of a character's gaze needs to be matched to the position of the object they are looking at.

Match on Action

Another form of edit that provides additional information about an event is a *match on action*. Here the edit brings together two shots from different angles or shot sizes of the same action being completed. Again, this gives us a slightly different perspective on an action and can often provide us with more detail through the use of a close up. We see a hand raise a gun – next we see an extreme close up of a finger pulling the trigger.

Cutaway Shots

A *cutaway* shot may be edited into a scene. This type of shot is not directly related to the action taking place but it has an indirect link. We may see two people having a conversation in an apartment and, while we still hear their dialogue, for several seconds we may see a shot of the exterior of the apartment before returning to the conversation. The shot cuts away from the action but still retains some connection to the scene.

Cross-cutting

Cross-cutting is an invaluable editing technique and is commonly used for building suspense. It consists of editing together shots of events in different locations which are expected eventually to coincide with each other. We shall look in Chapter 10 at the way omniscient narration can build suspense by providing an overview of different areas of action, and cross-cutting is the realization of such a narrative approach. At the end of *Lock, Stock and Two Smoking Barrels* (1998) we are aware that Tom is desperately trying to get rid of two shotguns which he believes are incriminating evidence. However, we then cut to a pub where his associates have just learned that the guns are worth a fortune. Suspense is built through editing between Tom trying to dump the guns into the Thames and his associates desperately trying to phone him to stop him getting rid of the guns. In one respect, cross-cutting breaks the film's continuity by suddenly jumping to another scene; however, the close linking together of the two scenes ensures coherence.

The 180 Degree Rule

There are a couple of important 'rules' associated with editing. The *180 degree rule* specifies that the camera should not have 'crossed the line' of action when two shots are edited

together. This is particularly important during a scene where two characters are interacting with each other in some way. We will have subconsciously noted that one character is
on one side of the screen while the other is on the opposite side. The *line of action* is an
imaginary line passing through the two characters. If the camera were to be placed on the
other side of the action in the next shot, then the position of the characters would be
reversed (see Figure 6.6). It could take the viewer a second or two to realize what had
happened and this might interrupt involvement in the film. In reality audiences are fairly
adept at quickly ascertaining what has happened in such an edit; indeed, it is increasingly
common to see the line crossed. In the café scene when Jimmy and Henry meet towards
the end of *GoodFellas* (1990), the camera crosses the line but our involvement is not dramatically disrupted. The two ways of safely crossing the line are to either track across the
line in one continuous shot or have an intermediate shot on the line in between the two
shots.

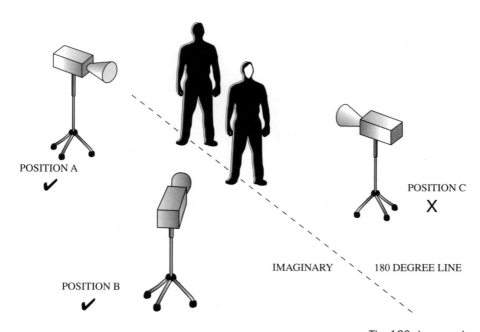

The 180 degree rule   Figure 6.6

The 30 Degree Rule

The *30 degree rule* (Figure 6.7) indicates that if two shots of the same location or action
are edited together, then either the camera should move position by at least 30 degrees or
the shot size should radically change. If this does not happen then the effect is a *jump cut*.
The elements within the shot appear to jump slightly, producing a disconcerting effect on
the viewer.

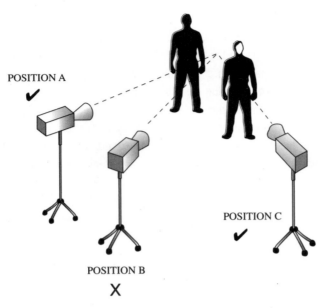

Figure 6.7   *The 30 degree rule*

Alternatives to Cutting

Other techniques can be used at the editing stage to create a seamless unity for the film, whose narrative will usually contain many scenes within the overall story. If scenes were edited straight up against each other, then the transition from one to another could be confusing. The usual convention is to use a *fade* to black and a fade from black to end and begin a scene. Fades are introduced during the editing stage. *Dissolves* and *wipes* are often used too: one shot gradually gives way to another to indicate a transition, sometimes from one scene to another, but more often than not this is used to indicate the passing of time.

Discontinuity Editing

If most editing can be described as continuity editing, then it is equally true that a minority of films use *discontinuity editing*. As the name implies, there is no smooth flow to the shots that are edited together; there is a disruption between one shot and the next. However, discontinuity editing can be used to good effect. If continuity editing principally supports the meanings residing within the shots that represent the narrative, then discontinuity editing can be regarded as producing meanings from the ways in which the shots are linked together. The shots are not necessarily unified; rather, meaning comes from the way in which the shots interact.

Montage

The best known example of discontinuity editing is *montage*, which was much used by Eisenstein, most famously in *Battleship Potemkin* (1925) in the Odessa Steps sequence (see also Chapter 14). Here the shots that are edited together do not flow smoothly; instead they clash: they conflict with each other. The sequence switches, in a spatially disorientating way, between views of the Tsar's advancing troops and views of the fleeing citizens. The troops are armed, menacing and inhuman; the citizens are unarmed, vulnerable and all too human. The juxtaposition of meanings between the shots results in new meanings, produced by the viewer on seeing the montage of shots that are pieced together.

It is also possible for the pace of editing to create a rhythm which itself produces meaning. In the shower scene in *Psycho* there is no logical progression to the way in which the stabbing of Marion is visually presented; it is a montage of shots. The shots are short and are filmed from a variety of angles – a rhythm is set up by the editing which emphasizes the frenetic rhythm of the stabbings. The knife comes from different directions and these shots are intercut with short shots of Marion struggling. The effect of the sequence is to create a feeling of confusion, madness, panic. No doubt precisely what Hitchcock wanted.

Graphic Match

Another editing technique that can break continuity is that of linking shots containing similar visual content. The shower scene in *Psycho* ends with a *graphic match* when the camera zooms in to a close up on water swirling down the circular drain in the shower and then dissolves to a revolving close up of Marion Crane's eye. Shot size, movement, shapes and composition are matched.

Symbolic Insert Edit

As the name implies, this term describes a shot which is edited in between other shots and which indirectly represents something else. Godard used this device in *Weekend*. Rather than show the murder of Corrine's mother, Godard inserts a shot of a dead rabbit covered in blood. The edit breaks the film's continuity as it makes no obvious sense in the context of the accompanying shots – it comes from outside the world of the film. However, throughout the film the editing frequently lacks continuity, and time and space often lack coherence from scene to scene.

Freeze Frame

One final technique remains to be mentioned that is achieved at the editing stage. The freeze frame for obvious reasons creates a discontinuity – the moving image suddenly comes to a standstill. It is not a common technique but can be a useful device. In *Jules et Jim* (Truffaut, 1962), at one point Catherine is pretending to pose like a model. Truffaut momentarily freeze frames the shots of her poses to create the impression of a photograph. At the beginning of *Trainspotting* (1996) several freeze frames of the characters are used, with a voice-over providing information about the characters. A freeze frame can usefully give us time to analyse an image. Finally, and less problematically, since Truffaut's own *The 400 Blows* (*Les 400 coups*, 1959), a freeze frame can often be used to signal the end of a film.

Exercise 6.3
Analyse the editing in the climactic scenes of a science fiction film and a romance, and identify the similarities and differences in technique.

SOUND

Sound is of vital importance at both the filming and editing stages. Film is both a visual and an aural medium. The most important sound within a film is likely to be the dialogue, plus any accompanying sounds such as those caused by movement of characters or objects. These sounds will give us a lot of information, helping us to follow the story and complementing the images we see on the screen. However, it is likely that other sounds will be added to the film to further emphasize the meanings it is hoped the film will communicate.

Diegetic and Non-diegetic Sound

Sound originating from the world within the film is known as '*diegetic*'. Typically this consists of dialogue and sounds emanating from action within the shot, including background or ambient noise. *Non-diegetic* sound has a source outside the film's narrative. Most obviously this includes incidental music but it also refers to voice-overs. Non-diegetic sound is added at the editing stage and can hold great importance for the edited images. However, diegetic sound may also be modified or added during editing, for instance, the sound of a car crash. Two films whose narratives revolve around suspect manipulation of sound are *The Conversation* (Coppola, 1974) and *Blow Out* (De Palma, 1981).

Sound can also be used to help hold together edited shots, which are rarely continuous; they often hide an *ellipsis*, a period of time which is omitted from the film. It is, for instance, unlikely that a film would cover in real time someone leaving a house to get into a car. Parts of this action would be excluded, and continuous sound can help provide a smooth join between the discontinuous shots.

Sound Effects

The use of sound effects is common in films; such effects usually function as diegetic sound in that they appear to originate from elements within the film, even though such sound is often added during post-production. Sounds can be regarded as signs that produce meanings, just as visual elements are signs. The sound of a creaking door or the gradual approach of footsteps can create suspense and fear of the unknown just as can low key lighting. We wonder what is opening the door and fear its entry into the space of the film. We wonder whose footsteps we hear and what their arrival will bring.

Ambient Sound

Ambient sound is also recorded at the end of filming in a location: it is what is heard when there is no dialogue or movement. This background sound can be added at the editing stage if it is judged that there is too much silence. A lack of sound can be just as noticeable as the presence of sound, and it is rare that we experience complete silence in a film.

Music

A soundtrack is usually essential for a film; it creates mood and strengthens meaning. A classic example of incidental music supplementing visual content while also creating meaning is the series of short, sharp, high pitched screeching sounds produced from a violin in *Psycho*. It is not an easy sound to listen to. It is of high volume and high frequency, and is discordant: it puts us on edge and makes us feel uncomfortable. When the film begins with this sound, accompanying the title sequence of light and dark lines slicing the screen horizontally, expectations are immediately set up. Famously the music returns during the shower scene when Marion Crane is repeatedly stabbed. The music itself is sharp and stabbing and provides at least as much meaning as the shots it accompanies. To grasp the importance of music, one may try imagining the *Psycho* music being replaced with the theme tune from *Star Wars*. What effect would it have upon the visual content? It would seem inappropriate and would undermine the importance of what we see on the screen.

The soundtrack for *Trainspotting* is atypical. A film's music is usually not noticed; it is incidental, and supports the narrative by reinforcing the intended meaning. We are often not conscious of its presence. *Trainspotting* places the music up front alongside the visual content. The soundtrack consists of popular contemporary tracks from the mid-1990s and is no doubt as much to do with targeting an audience as with supporting the narrative. Not all music in *Trainspotting* is non-diegetic, however. There are a couple of scenes set in clubs and the accompanying music is diegetic because it originates from the club locations.

However, not all films have an accompanying music soundtrack. *The Blair Witch Project* contains no music to supplement its narrative and for good reason. The film is supposed to be documentary footage, roughly edited together having been found several years later, which records 'real' events. The addition of music, even if appropriate to the building of suspense, would have ruined the basis of the narrative, that the events witnessed really happened. We become so accustomed to the lack of non-diegetic music that the addition of abstract sounds during the end credits may seem odd.

Voice-overs

Voice-overs are added at the postproduction stage and are typically used to anchor the meanings in a film and give guidance to the audience. *Trainspotting* and *Lock, Stock and*

Two Smoking Barrels both use voice-overs at the beginning, the former to set the scene and raise issues for the film to deal with, the latter to introduce characters and indicate their possible roles in the film. Films such as *Blade Runner* and *Double Indemnity* (1944) use voice-overs throughout as a way of supplementing what we learn from the images and dialogue while also providing insights into the main characters.

Parallel and Contrapuntal Sound

Usually the sound we hear in a film directly accompanies what we see on the screen; it is appropriate sound, it is the sound we expect. The music in *Trainspotting* matches what we see in the film and seems relevant to the characters, their lifestyles, and the pace of the film. In other words, the music works in parallel with the visual content of the film. However, this is not always the case. In both *A Clockwork Orange* (1971) and *GoodFellas*, horrific acts of violence are accompanied by bright, happy, energetic music rather than the sinister, threatening incidental music we may expect. This is an example of contrapuntal sound. The sound works against what we see on the screen. In these particular cases the effect is to emphasize the characters' casual, sometimes gleeful attitude to violence while also shocking the viewer.

Sound Bridges

The editing of a film normally ensures that sounds coincide with the shots they relate to. However, postproduction audio mixing can place a sound earlier or later than the image to which it relates. This device is used fairly often for linking two scenes together. We may be watching the end of one scene when we hear dialogue from the scene which we cut to a moment later. Similarly, we may cut to a shot from the next scene while still hearing dialogue from the preceding scene. In both cases we are prepared for the scene to follow. This technique, often used as a variation on the convention of a fade to indicate the ending or beginning of a scene, is known as a sound bridge. It can help smooth over the edit point between two shots.

FORMALISM AND REALISM

Two perspectives that are closely linked to the topic of film form are *formalism* and *realism*. Each has a particular view of what film should be for and how it can achieve its purpose. Formalism began to take on coherence in the 1920s in the Soviet Union, and its two key theorists were Sergei Eisenstein and Rudolf Arnheim. The theorization behind realism gained strength during the 1930s and its later proponents included André Bazin and Siegfried Kracauer. Although the debate between these perspectives may not have really taken off until the 1930s, there has always been a division in the ways in which the medium has been used. Between 1895 and 1901 the films of the Lumière brothers aimed to record scenes from everyday life, while Méliès used film as an expressive medium that centred on the importance of *mise en scène* in the construction of fantasy.

Formalism emphasizes film's potential as an expressive medium. The available film techniques are of central importance – use of camera, lighting, editing. For the formalists, film should not merely record and imitate what is before the camera, but should produce its own meanings. Primary importance is attached to the filmic process, and it is suggested that film can never fully record reality anyway, if only because it is two-dimensional compared to reality's three dimensions.

We have already looked at examples which can be described as formalist in the work of Eisenstein and Hitchcock. The Odessa Steps sequence from *Battleship Potemkin* consists of montage editing. Eisenstein was not content to merely show us what happened on the Odessa Steps; instead he expressed the meaning of the events through the choice of shot content and the way he edited the shots together. He produced meaning from a dialectical process between shots, by producing associations from shots, by using symbolic shots, all of which requires the viewer to make sense of what is seen, to think through a sequence. Eisenstein wrote of the editing of shots: '[t]he juxtaposition of these partial details in a given montage construction calls to life and forces into the light that general quality in which each detail has participated and which binds together all the details into a whole' (Eisenstein, 1942, p. 11).

The shower scene from *Psycho* uses a formalist strategy of montage editing. The scene is not shot and edited in a continuous, linear style. The meaning and effect come both from the content of shots, namely a knife flashing across the screen at different angles towards Marion Crane, and from the editing of the shots, which produces a series of short shots that juxtapose the knife and Marion with their different directions of movement. Further examples of formalism are to be found in German Expressionism. Films such as *The Cabinet of Dr Caligari* (1920) are non-realist: the expressive nature and meaning of these films tend to rely upon the *mise en scène*, on the selection and arrangement of elements within shots. It will be noticed that the formalist approach to film-making necessarily emphasizes the importance of the director as someone who intervenes in the film-making process. In other words, a film is a vehicle for personal expression.

Realism, by contrast, emphasizes film as a medium for directly recording what the camera 'sees'. Film techniques are important, but not for producing meaning within the film. The function of the camera is to record what is in front of it and to allow the content to speak for itself for the audience to draw their own conclusions. Bazin believed realist cinema was a more democratic form of film in that it did not manipulate the audience. The use of deep focus allows the audience to clearly perceive a number of elements within a shot instead of being guided towards a particular element. The use of long takes reduces the need for intervention by the director in the construction of the film. Less editing means less fragmentation of time and space. Film is seen as having the potential to reveal the world to audiences. 'For the first time, between the originating object and its reproduction there intervenes only the instrumentality of a nonliving agent. For the first time, the image of the world is formed automatically, without the creative intervention of man' (Bazin, 1967, p. 13).

This Bazin quote comes from an essay entitled 'Ontology of the Photographic Image'. *Ontology* is central to any kind of realism, concerned as it is with the 'reality status' of objects and representations. Is a documentary more 'real' than a Hollywood film? Can any film be 'real'? What does 'real' mean'? These are not idle questions: from personal experience we can affirm that many people (in response to a direct question) think of soap operas as 'real'. The ontological question is in turn linked to the matter of *epistemology*, which is about the meaning of 'knowledge'. How do we know what we know? Again, this question is much deeper and more far-reaching than it may appear: do I 'know' something because I have experienced it (*empirically*), because I have sensory (*phenomenological*) information about it, or because I believe what I have read or heard... or seen in a film or on TV?

Exercise 6.4

Consider the Gulf War. How do you know what you know about it? What are the sources of your knowledge? How confident are you that your knowledge is 'true'?

The use of film as a means of addressing ('real') social issues gained impetus in the 1930s with the growth of documentary film-making and the 'realist' films of Jean Renoir. Renoir's films tended to deal with social issues and used deep focus and long takes as a way of reducing directorial intervention. A film such as *La Grande Illusion* (1937) typifies Renoir's concern with themes of class inequalities and the futility of war. John Grierson, who spearheaded British documentary film-making, was similarly concerned with revealing social issues in 1930s Britain. However, it must be noted that the use of realist film techniques does not necessarily imply social issue films. Orson Welles, for example, is well known for his use of long takes and deep focus but produced films as entertainment, and while *Citizen Kane* contains realist techniques, it also extensively uses formalist devices such as expressive lighting and unusual camera angles.

The concept of realism remains problematic. If long takes result in greater realism, then presumably one continuous take with no editing would be the ideal, yet this has rarely been tried. Even with such an approach, there is still directorial intervention in terms of decisions about when the take begins and ends. Similarly, although deep focus means the audience is not guided towards a particular element, choices are still made about what is in the shot and how it is composed. Add to this the fact that realist films often make very effective use of music, as in the case of *Bicycle Thieves* (1948), and the case for a realist aesthetic looks untenable. This is not to say that there is no place for realist techniques in film, but it does indicate the limits that exist for realism. What audiences regard as 'realistic' also changes over time and varies from culture to culture.

FILM TECHNIQUES, FILM FORM AND NARRATIVE

The question was posed at the beginning of this chapter of how several film versions of the *Titanic* story could have been made, each different from the others. Having looked at the language of film and how film techniques are combined with narratives, we are now in a position to look again at this question. We have noted that form is the result of the inter-action between content and style, and is determined by the narrative and the way in which it is presented to us. This is what gives a film its shape.

Let us consider two of the Titanic films, *A Night to Remember* (1958) and *Titanic* (1997), both of which deal with the *Titanic* story from before passengers board the ship until after the sinking when some passengers are rescued. *Titanic* also includes contemporary footage dealing with underwater exploration of the sunken ship and with the recollections of one of the surviving passengers.

The contemporary footage immediately results in a difference between the two films' methods of narration. *Titanic* is told using flashbacks. The exploration of the sunken ship results in Rose, a survivor of the disaster, contacting the research team, and this in turn creates the possibility of the story being told through her recollections. *A Night to Remember* does not give us a personalized account of the *Titanic*; it uses objective rather than sub-jective narration (see pp. 142–3 below), although both films use omniscient narration too. We are aware of events happening to different people in different locations.

A Night to Remember uses documentary footage of the *Titanic* being launched and its voyage at sea at several points as a way of establishing context and atmosphere and to provide a degree of authenticity. *Titanic* makes little use of documentary footage. *A Night to Remember* gives what appears to be a more straightforward account of the ship's voyage, while *Titanic* is very consciously telling the story in a fictionalized way. *A Night to Remember* does not have the embellishments of *Titanic*. The latter film spends a long time introducing and developing characters; the iceberg is not hit until more than 90 minutes into the film, compared with *A Night to Remember*, in which the iceberg intervenes after half an hour.

Both films have characters for us to follow, both films have elements of romance, and both contain class as an issue; however, each film deals with this content in a very different way. The characters in *A Night to Remember* are not developed far – it is the events that we really follow – whereas in *Titanic* the events are subservient to the characters (and to spectacle). *Titanic* conforms to Propp's observations on character types: Jack as the hero, Cal as the villain and Rose as the princess (see pp. 139–40). Hence we can see that the same essential story is constructed and told in very different ways.

The same can also be noted for the film techniques used. While the *mise en scène* of some shots, essentially those establishing locations, is strikingly similar, the types of shots, use of camera and editing techniques are very different. *A Night to Remember* tends towards allow-ing meaning to emerge from the content of the shots (and is thus rooted firmly in the British 'realist' tradition), whereas *Titanic* goes further in producing meaning from the conscious use of camera and editing techniques such as close ups, crane shots, tracking and cross-cutting.

Finally, the eras in which the two films were made also account for some of their differences. *A Night to Remember*, made in 1958, is a black-and-white film and uses what now seem like primitive special effects and models. The *Titanic* of 1997 employs complex and convincing models and special effects, heavily based on digital technology and computer-generated images. We have the same story, but visually it is told very differently in each film. Thus we can see how a film's form emerges from the way its narrative is structured and presented through the language specific to film.

From the small number of examples referred to in this chapter it should already be clear that many different types of film are possible. New films are always being made, and audiences never seem to tire of watching them because the permutations within and between narratives and film techniques are endless, which should ensure continuing innovation and originality. The language of film can be used in many different ways, some of which will be explored in the rest of this book.

SUMMARY

- **There is more than one way to tell a story – a range of possibilities exist and choices have to be made.**
- **A film's form is the result of a multitude of variables, which are themselves the result of decisions taken by those involved in the film's production.**
- **Decisions are taken as to how the narrative is to be structured and how it will be narrated.**
- **The content of each shot requires careful consideration, the result of which is the shot's *mise en scène*.**
- **The techniques used to film each shot need much thought in terms of camera movement, angle and shot size.**
- **The editing together of shots and the use of sound also play a vital part in the construction of a film's form as they produce, enhance and communicate meanings vital to the film's story.**

REFERENCES

André Bazin, *What is Cinema?* Vol. 1 (Berkeley and Los Angeles, CA: University of California Press, 1967).

Pam Cook and Mieke Bernink (eds), *The Cinema Book* (2nd edn, London: BFI, 1999).

Sergei Eisenstein, *The Film Sense* (New York: Harcourt Brace and Co., 1942).

Richard Maltby, *Hollywood Cinema* (Oxford: Blackwell, 1995).

James Monaco, *How to Read a Film* (Oxford: Oxford University Press, 1981).

FURTHER READING

David Bordwell and Kristin Thompson, *Film Art: An Introduction* (New York: McGraw-Hill, 1997).

Noël Burch, *Theory of Film Practice* (London: Secker & Warburg, 1973).

Peter Cowie, *The Cinema of Orson Welles* (New York: Da Capo Press, 1973).

James Monaco, *How to Read a Film* (Oxford: Oxford University Press, 1981).

Jill Nelmes (ed.), *An Introduction to Film Studies* (2nd edn, London: Routledge, 1999).

David Sterritt, *The Films of Alfred Hitchcock* (Cambridge: Cambridge University Press, 1993).

FURTHER VIEWING

A Personal Journey with Martin Scorsese through American Cinema (BFI, 1995).

Close-up on Battleship Potemkin *by Roger Corman* (BBC2, 1995).

Reputations: Alfred Hitchcock (BBC2, 1999).

Visions of Light (The American Film Institute, 1992).

Without Walls: J'accuse Citizen Kane (Channel 4, 1992).

Early Cinema and Film Form

When film emerged in 1895 as a new form of communication, there was little idea of what its future might hold. It was unclear how it might be used, what its purpose should be and how people would react to it. In effect, film production was an experiment. Audiences were certainly amazed by the new phenomenon but film-makers wondered how long its novelty value would last. We now know, of course, that film has become a global industry. Cinema is a central part of our lives and over time a range of conventions have developed for making films. This chapter looks at how cinema began, what its characteristics were and how conventions gradually developed. The main focus is on film form in early cinema, with film production placed in context through reference to the developing industry and audience trends of the time.

THE INDUSTRY

Inventions are rarely realized in isolation. Developments in the recording and projection of moving images were being pursued in several countries at the same time, but just as important were the inventions that pre-dated cinema. The means to view moving images had been developed by 1834 by William Horner with the *zoetrope*, but the images were a series of drawings which mimicked the various stages of motion of a moving object, typically someone running. The ability to produce images that recorded the natural world had been realised in 1827 by Joseph Niépce with the invention of photography. Cinema was the result of bringing together techniques for showing moving images and the technology of recording aspects of the real world (see Chapter 5 on Film Technology).

Camera and Projection Systems

In 1893 Thomas Edison had unveiled his Kinetoscope moving image system, as developed by W.K.L. Dickson. Edison is also believed to have built the first film studio (called the 'Black Maria'), with sections in the roof to let in light and with the whole building revolving in order to be able to follow the sun. Edison's method of screening films only catered for individual viewers, though, and as such was not a projection system. Other equipment designs were developed in 1896 in Britain and the United States, but it is Auguste and Louis Lumière who are regarded as having produced the first widely used successful camera and projection system in 1895, the *cinématographe* (see Figure 7.1).

It is also the Lumière brothers who are usually credited with having made the first films in 1895 and with having held the first public screening on 28 December of that year, at the Grand Café in Paris. In fact Max Skladanovsky had screened a film on 1 November of the same year in Germany, but his contribution to developing film technology is often forgotten; his camera/projection system was cumbersome and impractical and developed no further, leaving the Lumières to perfect their system. Other camera and projection designs had also been experimented with in other countries around the same time.

Europe

Cinema may have been dominated by the United States for most of the twentieth century, but the early years belonged to Europe. American cinema was outstripped by the film output

Figure 7.1   *The first camera and projection system: the cinématographe (BFI Stills, Posters and Designs)*

of France, England, Denmark and Italy, and it was only during the First World War that the United States began to dominate the international film industry (see Chapter 1). Production companies such as Nordisk from Denmark, Cines from Italy and Cecil Hepworth's company in England produced and exported many films but France's Pathé Frères and Gaumont led the field. By 1905 Pathé Frères was already vertically integrated, but their control of production, distribution and exhibition was soon to be mirrored by companies in the United States.

The United States

By 1900 the three key companies in the United States were American Mutoscope and Biograph, Vitagraph and Edison's company (Figure 7.2). They had a large domestic market to satisfy, though that market was at the time also being fed by European film companies. In the United States the battle was soon on for supremacy within the industry. The Edison company took legal action to prevent other American companies from using cameras and projectors for which Edison claimed the patents. American Mutoscope and Biograph used a different type of camera, however, and they battled with Edison for control of the industry. Both forced other companies to pay for the right to use their equipment designs.

The MPPC

The rivalry continued until 1908, when the two companies formed the Motion Picture Patents Company. The new company also included Vitagraph, Essanay, Kalem, Lubin and Selig, all of whom had to pay the two main companies for continued use of patented designs. Although the MPPC aimed to reduce the number of foreign films coming into the country to enable American producers to expand their own share of the market, a deal was struck which allowed Pathé and the Méliès company to join. Screenings of foreign films declined in the United States as a result of the increasing power of the MPPC but European cinema continued to dominate the rest of the world.

Company logos: American Mutoscope and Biograph, Vitagraph, and the Edison Company (BFI Stills, Posters and Designs)   Figure 7.2

The MPPC ensured that fees had to be paid by production companies using their camera designs, by distribution companies dealing with their films, and by theatres showing their films and using their projection systems. Thus the MPPC soon became an oligopoly; its small number of companies controlled the emerging American film industry. The stranglehold on the industry was tightened further when Eastman Kodak signed an exclusive deal with the MPPC for supply and use of film stock.

The Independents

Nonetheless a thriving independent sector managed to grow within the United States, prompting the MPPC to respond by forming the General Film Company to release exclusively all MPPC films. However, 1912 saw the beginning of the end for the MPPC when a court ruling rejected its claim to exclusive rights to the camera and projection equipment designs. The final blow for the MPPC came three years later in 1915, when it was declared to be undermining competition within the industry and was required to cease its restrictive practices.

The independent companies were now in a strong position: their main competitor was weak and the fact that they had not previously been tied into a rigid production structure meant they were more flexible. They made early moves towards producing feature films instead of short one-reelers and many companies, realizing that the most profitable part of the industry was exhibition, reorganized accordingly. Many of these 'independents' in turn became vertically integrated themselves and developed the same monopolistic practices as had the MPPC before them. By 1915, the origins of companies such as Paramount, Fox, Universal, MGM and Warner existed, all of which were to become the core of the Hollywood Studio System during the 1930s and 1940s (see Chapter 1). Initially the American film industry had been mainly based on the East coast and in Chicago, but by 1915 the majority of companies had relocated to the Los Angeles area, which included a district called Hollywood. The weather was more suitable for location shooting – filming was much easier with reliable sunshine – and a greater variety of landscapes was available.

The European film industry had also developed monopolistic practices. In France, Pathé Frères and Gaumont dominated, while in Britain most films were exhibited by the Gaumont-British company and the Associated British Pictures Corporation. With the start of the First World War in 1914, however, the film industry in Europe was severely disrupted. The next few years saw the United States establish itself as the dominant international power in the cinema.

THE AUDIENCE

The beginnings of cinema were characterized by uncertainty, as several camera and projection systems existed and film techniques were little more than experimental. It did not take long, however, for those concerned to realize that there was a potentially huge audience for the new form of communication. Cinema audiences were perhaps initially more interested in what the technology could do than in how it was used, since moving images were such a novelty – they could surprise and shock, they could provide a spectacle rather than tell stories. Nonetheless, the possibilities for film as entertainment were soon realized.

Exhibition

The first cinema was opened in France in 1897 by the Lumière Brothers, while the first US cinema did not open until 1902. Early cinemas were basic, often consisting of nothing more than a screen, a projector, a piano and several rows of chairs. Initial doubts about the viability of public screenings of films soon disappeared and by 1905 the United States had approximately 1,000 cinemas, a figure which had risen to 5,000 by 1908. The industry continued to expand and by 1910 weekly cinema attendances numbered 26 million, a figure which almost doubled over the next five years to reach 49 million by 1915. Cinema building continued apace, led by entrepreneurs such as S.L. Rothafel.

Cinemas in the UK were similarly basic and initially had little more than rows of benches surrounding a primitive projector. The Cinematograph Act of 1909 changed this with its requirements of fireproofing and separation of the projection box from the auditorium and the installation of fire exits and toilets. The worst halls closed down and many theatres were converted into cinemas, with 3,500 in existence in the UK by 1915. However, many cinemas closed down during the First World War.

In the USA prior to 1905, films tended to be shown wherever facilities existed for entertaining the general public: thus theatres, music halls, vaudeville houses and even funfairs were regularly used. It was common for vaudeville shows to begin and end with short films, but this practice was soon reversed in cinemas where it became common for a vaudeville act to perform while reels were being changed. By 1905 purpose-built venues had become the norm, and these early exhibition theatres were referred to as nickelodeons rather than cinemas, the cost of admission typically being a nickel. Nickelodeons were relatively small and had minimal facilities; they provided cheap entertainment and were well suited to their audience, which tended to be working class. Films provided popular entertainment just as music halls and circuses had done previously, while classical concerts and plays at the theatre tended to be more expensive and remained a middle-class leisure activity.

Entertainment

Initially most films were non-fiction. Film's ability to record movement in the real world was sufficiently impressive for it to be entertaining and when films were unable to record actual events, the events were often re-staged to provide a representation of what had happened – typically of a news item of interest to the public. Re-enactments of historic moments were also frequently made and *actuality* films, especially travelogues, were popular. Fiction films soon became common, though, and proved to be very popular with audiences, who came to look for entertainment and escapism in addition to the information and novelty they were used to. The fiction narratives were usually simple and frequently took the form of comedies. The lack of sound in a film was often compensated for by a piano performance or the use of a gramophone, and actors sometimes spoke dialogue behind the screen to match the actions in the film. Sound effects were similarly added.

Until about 1905, production companies tended to sell copies of their films to exhibitors, which meant that films had to be screened repeatedly for the initial investment to be recouped. When the practice of renting films replaced that of purchasing them, exhibitors were able to show a greater variety of productions. Audience interest grew again with the arrival of feature films around 1910, which were usually between four and six reels long (60 to 90 minutes) and were often released as serials, with titles like *The Perils of Pauline*, one reel per week. Serials were in effect a transition between one-reelers and full feature films.

Stars

Audiences were thus initially attracted to the cinema by the novelty of experiencing moving images, and soon after by the provision of entertaining stories on film. A further attraction was added by the rise of film stars when audiences began to identify particular actors and admire their performances. By 1909 two stars were already established: Florence Lawrence the 'Biograph Girl' (Figure 7.3) and Florence Turner the 'Vitagraph Girl'. Whereas previously audiences tended to identify films by the production company name, increasingly stars helped to sell films, and film posters came to highlight the featured star. By 1915, stars were regularly pulling in the crowds. Theda Bara was signed to the Fox company as their studio star and Charlie Chaplin became known as the loveable tramp with bowler hat and cane.

Censorship

Some sections of society were nevertheless expressing concern at the rise of cinema as a new form of entertainment. Many felt that cinema was a powerful form of communication and believed it was likely to have an effect upon the audience. At a basic level this was illustrated by audiences who momentarily believed that a train hurtling towards them on a cinema screen was actually about to hit them, but the real concern was with the portrayal

Figure 7.3   *The Biograph Girl, Florence Lawrence (Courtesy Kobal)*

of crime, violence and romance on screen. Concerned US citizens claimed that nickelodeons were likely to become breeding grounds for criminality, violent behaviour and loose morals. There was also a fear from sections of the establishment that film could be used as political propaganda to create social unrest (see Chapter 3 on Cinema, Audiences and Society). However, governments themselves soon turned to using film as propaganda with the onset of the First World War.

The developing film industry was aware of growing concern and acted to halt legislation being passed by government. In the United States the major production companies co-operated with an organization calling itself The National Board of Censorship, which was set up in 1909. Wanting to seem responsible, film companies submitted films for preview before releasing them. The production of more serious films – based on literary classics, Shakespeare and religious stories – helped to hold the censors at bay and indeed allowed the industry to censor itself. A similar situation existed in Britain where the British Board of Film Censors, funded by the industry, was founded in 1912.

Exercise 7.1

In what ways would film-viewing during the era of early cinema have been different from your own experience of film-viewing?

THE FILMS

Film form changed dramatically between 1895 and 1915. The beginnings of cinema were marked by simple narratives and primitive film techniques. Initially little importance was attached to camerawork and editing; the emphasis was on *mise en scène*. Particular films have been recognized as indicating major steps in the development of film techniques, but, as with film technology, it is important to remember that new techniques were being explored by many different film-makers in many different countries. There was much cross-fertilization of ideas as film-makers influenced one another.

Movement and the Moving Image

The first five years of cinema produced few films with identifiable narratives. Films tended not to contain stories in which events were clearly explained and linked together. Shots often seemed to exist in isolation and there was a lack of logical progression in the actions on the screen. None of this should surprise us since the initial fascination with film resulted from its ability to record movement; that it could do this at all was often enough to impress an audience. The first task for film-makers was to understand the different ways in which a camera could be used; only coming to terms with using cameras could film-makers begin to think about telling coherent stories on film. As Kristin Thompson notes: '[D]uring most of the primitive period, films appealed to audiences primarily through simple comedy or melodrama, topical subjects, exotic scenery, trick effects and the sheer novelty of photographed movement' (Bordwell *et al.*, 1985, p. 157).

The earliest films were very much the creations of the camera operators, who were usually also the director and scriptwriter. However, the emphasis gradually changed over the years as control shifted from the camera operator to the director and/or the producer. Film-making was from the outset very much a male-dominated profession, with the notable exception of Alice Guy from France, who was making films by 1896. Also from France, and best known for their early work, were the Lumière brothers and Georges Méliès. Their productions were radically different, though, with the Lumières tending towards non-fiction films whereas Méliès concentrated on fiction.

It is perhaps not surprising that travel was a common theme in early films. Not only were modes of transport such as cars and trains rapidly developing at that time, which in turn led to speculation about future modes of travel, but transport is of course about movement, which was exactly what the new cine-cameras could capture on film. What did *not* provide movement in early films was the camera itself, which usually remained static. This is partly explained by the cumbersome early cameras which were not easy to move during filming, but it is perhaps also explained when we think of the types of popular entertainment that preceded film. Music-hall and theatre performances took place on the stage with action statically framed by the stage curtain, and early films often have the appearance of a recording of a stage performance. This is especially true of many of Méliès' films.

Georges Méliès

In *Journey to the Moon* (1902) Méliès used a static camera and extreme long shots. It would be easy to believe that the events we see take place on a stage, as characters walk on from and off to the sides of the frame and the action takes place against what is obviously a backdrop. The film is typical of much of Méliès' work; it is a mix of comedy and fantasy and could be claimed as the first science fiction film: a group of scientists travel in a rocket to the moon (Figure 7.4).

The Impossible Journey was made by Méliès the following year and deals with similar themes. Passengers board a train, the train takes to the skies and eventually flies into the sun, where the passengers emerge from the crashed train and end up on a submarine which submerges into the sea. Méliès built his own studio, in which he constructed elaborate, fantastic sets. His complex stage designs were complemented by the frequent use of models, especially for simulating travel scenes in fantasy worlds. He often created magical effects on film through the use of stop motion techniques to join together different takes. In *The Impossible Journey*, stop motion is used to link together actions where the join is disguised through the use of smoke and fire. The film's fantasy world is emphasized through the use of strong colours which were used by Méliès to hand-tint the film, making it stand out from the usual repertoire of black-and-white films. As before, takes are static – though a pan shot is used at one point to follow movement – and shot sizes are very long throughout. The film lasts for six and a half minutes and contains fourteen takes, meaning an average of approximately 30 seconds per take; moreover, so skilful is Méliès' use of stop motion that it is

Journey to the Moon (1902): an early fantasy film with extensive use of tableau shots (BFI Stills,   Figure 7.4
Posters and Designs)

sometimes difficult to ascertain exactly when he has used it. He also makes extensive use of dissolves to link shots together. Such early examples of special effects engendered those of today (see Chapter 5).

The use of long takes was a common characteristic of early cinema, as it was for Méliès' films. An individual take was often referred to as a *tableau*. The take commonly covered a whole scene and its length, combined with its being a static extreme long shot, tended to isolate it from the rest of the film. The individual takes, or tableaux, were virtually autonomous as editing did not link takes closely together. Editing was not used to produce or clarify meaning, the content of the takes alone providing meaning. The lack of coherence in some early films is not surprising, partly because of historical and cultural differences for a modern viewer, but especially because the use of long shots and the lack of close ups means that detail in these films is often unrecognizable.

The Lumière Brothers

Travel was also a theme for other film-makers. One of the Lumières' first films was *L'Arrivée d'un train en gare* (1895). A static camera framed a station platform and an arriving train with an extreme long shot to record the passengers disembarking. The film was most memorable for its depiction of diagonal movement towards the camera by the train. Most early films lacked a sense of perspective and emphasized two dimensions only.

The Lumières' very first film from 1895 was *Workers Leaving the Factory*. The Lumières owned a large photographic company and filmed their employees emerging through the factory gates: a typical example of an actuality film, which is what the Lumières concentrated on. They did, however, also produce fictional comedy films, their best known being *The Waterer Watered* (*L'Aroseur arosé*, 1895). A gardener is watering plants until a boy stands on the hose pipe to stop the water, at which point the gardener looks quizzically at the end of the hose pipe; the boy steps off, leaving the water to suddenly shoot out over the gardener. As far as is known, this was the first comedy film.

Experimentation

Early cinema had no conventions; it was all about experimentation. Once the obvious visual possibilities of film had been recognized, some film-makers began to realize the further potential of the medium. The emphasis on recording the real world gradually gave way to attempts at creating the impossible on film. We have already seen examples of this in Méliès' work; he was a professional magician and was already skilled in creating illusions. As noted above, Méliès used stop motion, using editing to create a kind of jump cut in which elements within a shot suddenly change position, appear, or disappear. In addition, film-makers experimented with running film backwards, with speeding up and slowing down time and with multiple exposures, which involved running the film through the camera more than once to superimpose different images on top of each other. Méliès himself used multiple exposures to brilliant effect in his 1900 film *The One Man Orchestra*. A man walks on stage to play an instrument and then the same man walks on seven times to play seven different instruments, at which point the orchestra is complete.

Early British Films

Britain also had its share of film pioneers and experimenters. One of the earliest British films was *Rough Sea at Dover,* made by Birt Acres in 1895. It contained a static long shot of Dover harbour during a storm and was impressive for its primitive recording of movement. G.A. Smith's *Grandma's Reading Glass* (1900) broke new ground in the techniques used. The film shows a boy borrowing his grandma's magnifying glass and looking at various objects. The film was interesting in that the action was broken up into several takes, including extreme close ups from the boy's point of view through the magnifying glass (Figure 7.5). This was radically different when compared to the usual long shots that covered all the action in other films.

Another notable British film from 1900 was James Williamson's *The Big Swallow*. This begins with a man becoming aware that he is being filmed. He gradually becomes more irate until he moves towards the camera, mouth wide open, and appears to swallow the camera as his mouth blanks out the screen. At this point an edit takes us to a shot of the cameraman falling into a black hole, followed by another shot of a black screen from which the camera tracks back as it seems to emerge from the man's mouth. The transitions from shot to shot are well timed and hardly noticeable.

To return to the theme of travel, Cecil Hepworth made two films in 1900 with cars as the main theme. *How it Feels to be Run Over* shows a car driving towards the camera; just as the car fills the screen an edit cuts to a black screen on which appears the message 'oh, mother will be pleased'. *Explosion of a Motor Car* uses stop motion. A car travels down a road and a large cloud of smoke billows from the car. At this point an edit cuts to another take in which a

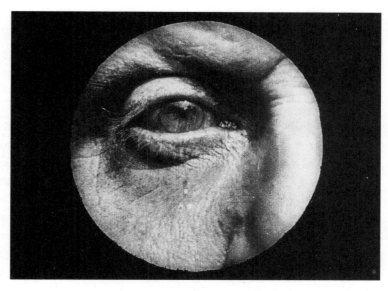

Grandma's Reading Glass (1900): an early example of an extreme close up shot (BFI Stills, Posters and Designs)   Figure 7.5

very similar cloud of smoke clears to reveal bits and pieces of a car lying on the ground. The two shots appear as one continuous take. This is followed by a policeman looking into the sky and from off screen parts of the car's passengers fall down. Such reference to events outside the camera frame was unusual. R.W. Paul's *The Motorist* (1906) contains several examples of stop motion and includes the use of models to make the impossible appear on screen. A policeman is caught on a car's bonnet; a convincing dummy falls off in front of the car, which runs over it; the policeman stands up again and runs after the car. Where the running-over seems to be a continuous take, it is in fact two, the second one beginning with the policeman getting up having apparently been run over. Other stop motions in the film create the illusion of a car driving up the front of a house and a car being transformed into a horse and cart. The use of models has the car driving over clouds and around the moon.

Cecil Hepworth's 1905 *Rescued by Rover* was notable for editing that was more complex than that usually found at that time. The film tells the story of a baby that is stolen. The parents are alerted by their dog, Rover, who leads them to the place where the baby has been hidden. There is a coherence to the way the story is told which is lacking in other early films. The editing provides consistency of direction and pace of movement between each shot. Time and space are presented in a way that makes the film's narrative intelligible. The film was so popular that it was remade twice after the negatives wore out from producing so many copies.

Edwin S. Porter

To return to the United States, another film that broke new ground in the methods used to tell a narrative was Edwin S. Porter's *The Great Train Robbery* (1903). A gang of outlaws rob a train; a telegraph operator alerts the sheriff, who rounds up a posse to track down the outlaws. The innovation was in the use of cross-cutting when the film shows the outlaws robbing the train but then cuts to the telegraph operator sending a message. We assume he is trying to alert someone to the robbery. At another point we see the outlaws fleeing on horseback, then after a cut we see the sheriff and his posse; the cross-cut edit indicates to the viewer that there is likely to be conflict. However, the effect is partly lost because of the difficulty of knowing which set of characters we are looking at, since the predominance of extreme long shots makes character identification difficult. Another scene in the film, a tableau, is also made fairly incomprehensible by reliance on an extreme long shot: when the outlaws order all the passengers off the train, the passengers are presumably being robbed by the outlaws but the lack of detail makes it difficult to ascertain if this is the case. The uncertainty of the shot is increased by the fact that it lasts almost 2 minutes.

Another unusual element in the film is the inclusion at the end of a close up of one of the outlaws looking straight to camera and firing a gun, effectively at the audience (Figure 7.6). The shot exists outside the narrative, but has the effect of reminding us of the complex relationship between the film and the audience by transforming the viewer into the one being viewed by a character in the film – a technique which has remained unusual throughout cinema history, though we should note the clear *homage* at the end of Scorsese's *GoodFellas*!

Film Techniques and Narratives

The lack of clarity in some early films, partly due to the lack of sound, was the reason why inter-titles were often used, either to explain the situation within which events were happening or to elaborate upon an interaction between characters. Similarly, the acting in early

Figure 7.6   *The Great Train Robbery (1903): an unusual shot which has no relation to the narrative but serves to remind the audience of the presence of the camera (BFI Stills, Posters and Designs)*

films frequently seems exaggerated and theatrical rather than naturalistic because in the absence of sound it too could help clarify the narrative. The increasing use of genres also helped explain narratives and raise particular expectations in the audience. Common genres of the time were fantasy, comedy, crime, melodrama, chase and actuality (see Chapter 10 on Genre).

By 1905, films were regularly built around narratives which had an identifiable beginning, middle and end, contained motivated characters and concluded with some kind of resolution. However, this highlighted the problem of how to clearly tell a visual story. Thompson and Bordwell have identified this issue and the film-makers' response as follows:

> Filmmakers came to assume that a film should guide the spectator's attention, making every aspect of the story on the screen as clear as possible. In particular, films increasingly set up a chain of narrative causes and effects. One event would plainly lead to an effect which would in turn cause another effect, and so on.
>
> (Thompson and Bordwell, 1994, p. 39)

Over the next ten years conventions were to become established which aided the coherent presentation of film narratives.

Exercise 7.2

What are the key differences between the characteristics of early cinema and the conventions of Hollywood Studio System films?

Film Form and Conventions

Movement takes place over time and within space. It was necessary that time and space be dealt with appropriately if films were to be able to tell stories clearly. Camera and editing techniques were to provide the solution. The content and function of shots were clarified through the breaking up of scenes into several takes using different shot sizes and camera angles. The increasing use of close ups provided information and detail to the viewer and made it easier to identify characters and develop greater characterization. Variety of camera angles gave a stronger sense of space through the provision of different perspectives on action and location. However, using a greater variety of shot types meant that how the takes were edited together became more important. Consistency in shot content was necessary in terms of speed and direction as well as of location and props. An eye-line match also became necessary when editing between one person and another as they interacted with each other. Cross-cutting also became more common (see Chapter 6).

The emphasis on consistency between the takes that were edited together resulted in the concept of continuity editing (see p. 104 above). The types of shots filmed and the way they were edited together needed to present a smooth flowing narrative that progressed logically and clearly so that the story could be easily understood by the audience. By 1915 these techniques were in common use and were in effect film-making conventions, identified by Noël Burch as the 'Institutional Mode of Representation', as distinct from the 'primitive' mode of representation that had gone before. Film form had changed radically since the birth of the medium.

Two films that neatly sum up the results of the evolution of film form between 1895 and 1915 are Chaplin's *The Tramp* and D.W. Griffith's *Birth of a Nation*, both made in 1915. *The Tramp* is the story of how a vagabond saves a girl who has been attacked and is then taken in by her family. He comes to believe that she is in love with him, as he is with her, but his heart is broken when her lover arrives. The film makes extensive use of close ups and achieves a depth of characterization unusual in early cinema. The effectiveness of the character development resulted in Chaplin being recognized and remembered for his ability to get an audience to empathize with his character on screen (Figure 7.7). *Birth of a Nation* is set during the American Civil War and while its racism is objectionable, its use of film techniques is admirable. Griffith brought together and refined the techniques that had been developing since 1895. The use of camera and editing not only provided a clear narrative but also managed to involve the viewer emotionally. Variety of shot size and of camera angle were employed throughout with effective use of cross-cutting, the principles of continuity editing were applied to ensure narrative coherence, and characters were well developed and given a depth not often present in films of the time. The film was an epic: it lasted over three hours and cost $110,000 to make.

It is important, however, not to see early films as nothing more than a stage in the development of what we now see as mainstream conventions. Early films existed in their own right as expressions of individual film-makers' creativity and expertise; they also had a particular relationship with audiences of their time and reflected aspects of their respective cultures and societies. It must also be remembered that, in contrast to our own contemporary entertainment cinema, the main aim of early cinema was not to tell coherent narratives. The principal urge was to explore and experiment with the possibilities of the moving picture medium.

Figure 7.7   *The Tramp (1915): effective use of characterization and empathy (BFI Stills, Posters and Designs)*

Exercise 7.3

What similarities can you identify between early cinema and contemporary film-making?

SUMMARY

- In 1895 film form was fluid as there were no conventions, and early film-makers had no guidelines – these manipulators of light were working in the dark.
- The new medium had a primitive form; narratives were simple and film techniques crude; telling a story via film was difficult and tended to result in a lack of clarity.
- Film-makers often opted to simply record the world in front of the camera rather than construct a story on film, and it took several years for film to become the basis of a new industry.
- With the gradual development of sophisticated camera and editing techniques, it became possible to present complex narratives on film.
- The types of stories and the style of film-making in place by 1915 were to make a major contribution to the established conventions that still underpin much of today's film-making.

REFERENCES

David Bordwell, Janet Staiger and Kristin Thompson, *The Classical Hollywood Cinema* (London: Routledge, 1985).

Kristin Thompson and David Bordwell, *Film History: An Introduction* (New York: McGraw-Hill, 1994).

FURTHER READING

Tino Balio (ed.), *The American Film Industry* (Madison, WI: University of Wisconsin Press, 1976).

Noël Burch, *Theory of Film Practice* (London: Secker & Warburg, 1973).

Noël Burch, *Life to Those Shadows* (Berkeley, CA: University of California Press, 1990).

Pam Cook and Mieke Bernink (eds), *The Cinema Book* (2nd edn, London: BFI, 1999).

Thomas Elsaesser, *Early Cinema: Space, Frame, Narrative* (London: BFI, 1990).

James Monaco, *How to Read a Film* (Oxford: Oxford University Press, 1981).

Jill Nelmes (ed.), *An Introduction to Film Studies* (2nd edn, London: Routledge, 1999), pp. 15ff.

Barry Salt, *Film Style and Technology: History and Analysis* (London: Starword, 1992).

Kristin Thompson and David Bordwell, *Film History: An Introduction* (New York: McGraw-Hill, 1994).

FURTHER VIEWING

Cinema Europe (BBC2, 1995).
Early Cinema: Primitives and Pioneers (BFI, 1992).
The Last Machine (BBC1, 1995).

Mainstream and Alternative Film Form

By the 1920s particular conventions had become well established for making films. Mainstream techniques such as the organization of time and space through 'invisible' continuity editing and the verisimilitude resulting from particular uses of *mise en scène* and from cause and effect structures and character motivation began to dominate film-making, as exemplified by the output of Hollywood. In this chapter we shall examine the principal ways in which these and other practices contributed to what Noël Burch has called the 'Institutional Mode of Representation', though the more commonly used term is 'Classical Hollywood Narrative' (see Bordwell *et al.*, 1985). This chapter will also discuss the development of alternative narrative forms. Using the ideas of Peter Wollen in particular, we shall describe alternative techniques such as non-linear narratives, lack of character identification, and the attack on conventional forms of pleasure represented by counter-cinema.

MAINSTREAM NARRATIVE AND FILM FORM

Narratives are central to our existence. Not only can our individual lives be seen as stories, but much of our time is spent telling people stories or informing them of things that have happened. Stories consist of people and events, actions, occurrences. Narratives can be defined as 'chains of events'. They contain actions and events that are linked together and which usually revolve around people, the characters within the story.

We shall be dealing here with narrative fiction. Although documentary films also usually contain narratives and are often structured in similar ways, these are briefly considered elsewhere (see Chapter 15). Our concern in this first part of the chapter will be the Classical Hollywood Narrative (which has already been signposted particularly in the last two chapters).

Structure

Narratives are about things happening, usually about people doing things. We may follow a narrative because the events interest us or because we can relate to the characters.

However, if we are to clearly understand the content of a film narrative or fully comprehend the meanings intended by the film-maker, the narrative needs to be structured appropriately.

Cause and effect

Most narratives are what we can call linear narratives. They move forward in a straight line from beginning to end. The events in such a narrative are linked together via a cause and effect relationship. An event takes place which causes an effect upon something else, thus resulting in a new situation; in turn this new situation has an effect upon other elements within the narrative, again resulting in further change. So taken for granted is this basic narrative requirement that we usually do not think about its function. But consider what would happen to a narrative without this cause-effect process: it would stop, the story would remain static. We would have what is called 'dead time'.

Another way of viewing progression within narratives is as a dialectical process. Dialectics, from Plato to Hegel and Marx, is a method for explaining and creating change. It can be summed up by the idea of a thesis which is challenged by an antithesis (an opposite or opposing position); the result of this conflict of ideas or situations is the synthesis, a new concept or situation. The cause and effect structure of narrative works in a similar way, leading us from beginning to end via events, and these events take place within time and space. They occur in particular locations for a certain duration.

The centrality of cause and effect, of change, can easily be identified by looking at the opening scene of *Scream* (1996). Casey is spending a quiet evening alone at home. It is unlikely that we would sit through the whole film if that situation remained unchanged, and of course it does change. Casey's quiet evening is interrupted by the phone ringing. She answers the phone. A threat is made. This results in a new situation: Casey is scared. The cause and effect process is under way. Her fears are then realized by the attack that takes place in her garden: yet another situation. This in turn leads to further actions: attempts to find the attacker, further attacks.

The logical way in which this cause and effect process develops is not usually questioned by the viewer, but a different arrangement of elements, a different ordering of events, would soon result in an incomprehensible storyline. If *Scream* began with the attack in Casey's garden and then cut to her having a quiet evening alone we would soon be confused, or would at the very least be expecting a very different type of film.

Chronology

Narratives thus tend to develop in a linear way, and this, crucially, tends to give us a chronological ordering of events. Events unravel in a logical manner over an ordered period of time. Time is a crucial ingredient in film narratives, not only because the medium itself consists of moving images which give films their duration, but also because the relationships between events and characters only become meaningful as they develop over a period of time.

The events in *Scream* are presented chronologically. The story's progression takes place from beginning to end through time in a linear manner. We can easily make sense of the film.

This is how most film narratives are structured. However, Quentin Tarantino's *Pulp Fiction* (1994) interrupts this chronological structure and gives us a non-linear narrative (Figure 8.1). The usual chronological development of narrative is disrupted. *Pulp Fiction* begins and ends with a scene that is split in two and which chronologically occurs half way through the story. The film opens with Honey Bunny and Pumpkin conversing in a café. We learn that they have previously carried out armed robberies. The film ends with a continuation of this scene in which the couple carry out an armed robbery of the café which is interrupted by Vincent and Jules. In the body of the film the chronological beginning and end of the story are brought together. A young Butch is given a watch that belonged to his father and an older Butch then wins his fight and settles a score with Marsellus. As this latter scene is presented in the film it appears as a flash-forward to the future.

We can speculate about why Tarantino chose to reorder the narrative sequences. Certainly it forces us to think more deeply about what we are watching and possibly engages

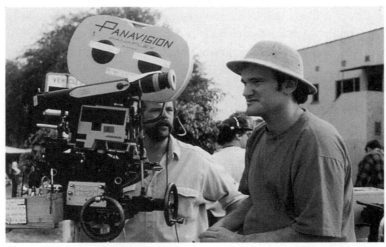

Figure 8.1   *Quentin Tarantino makes play with narrative in Pulp Fiction (BFI Stills, Posters and Designs)*

us more fully with the narrative. We are encouraged to be active viewers; we have to question what we see. Or perhaps it was a *homage* to Stanley Kubrick's *The Killing* (1956), which had already experimented with narrative chronology.

Flashbacks

A common method of interrupting chronology is through *flashbacks*. The flow of the story might be interrupted with references to things that have happened in the past. We are taken out of the present of the narrative. Interruptions of narratives, such as those caused by flashbacks, are usually explained and justified so that they do not necessarily disrupt the narrative; indeed they can clarify it. *Citizen Kane* (1941) tells the story of a powerful newspaper proprietor, Charles Foster Kane. The film begins with Kane's death, followed by journalists looking at newsreel footage of Kane's life. This is followed by the journalists planning to investigate the life of the recently deceased Kane. This is the 'present' of the narrative and we follow one journalist's investigations and interviews with people who knew Kane. However, the interviews consist of reminiscences, which means that much of the film's narrative consists of flashbacks. In this instance the film's initial situation is Kane's death and the short documentary about his life. The disruption comes with the journalists' mission to find out who the real Kane was and, most importantly, why the last word he spoke was 'Rosebud'. The implication of course is that if the journalists want to know, then so do we. Resolution is achieved when we, the viewers, find out the secret of 'Rosebud', which is revealed to us in the present but not to the journalists. The flashbacks have served to tell us about Kane's life and what lay behind the secret of 'Rosebud'.

Story, plot and screen duration

The *temporal* nature of narratives – how they are placed in *time* – is further elaborated by Bordwell and Thompson. They clarify the difference, with regard to time, between a film narrative's *story* and its *plot*. They define the story as all the events that we see and hear, plus all those that we infer or assume to have occurred, whereas the plot is the film's actual presentation (which includes the *style*) of certain events in the narrative.

We can clearly illustrate the difference between story and plot by looking at *High Noon* (1952). Plot time begins at 10.30 a.m. when news breaks that Frank Miller, who was imprisoned 5 years before by Marshall Will Kane, is due in town with the rest of his gang on the noonday train to seek vengeance. Plot time ends at noon with the shoot-out. In other words plot time is 90 minutes. However, story time is over five years, as the film refers to Miller's imprisonment by Kane, though we do not see this. The film is interesting for a further reason. Films usually compress time. A film usually has between 90 and 120 minutes to deal with events often lasting at least several days. *High Noon* is an exception, as it comes close to presenting the plot in real time: screen duration is 80 minutes compared to the plot time of 90 minutes. Time is clearly integral to the film as we get several glimpses of clocks to remind us of the approach of noon as a method for building suspense. *Rope* (1948) goes one step further by presenting the plot in real time in just one location. The film appears to be one continuous shot (see p. 101 above).

Exercise 8.1
For any three films of your choice, compare the story time and the plot time. How are they related in each of the films?

It is also the case that time can be expanded in a film. *The Untouchables* (1987) contains a shoot-out scene on the steps of a town hall, part of which is shot in slow motion. The sequence lasts 2 minutes, whereas the fast-moving events would probably have lasted less than half that time. The expansion of time emphasizes the speed of the action by only making it comprehensible when it is slowed down. The sequence is also a *homage* to Eisenstein's *Battleship Potemkin* (1925) and the famous Odessa Steps sequence in which time is also expanded. The attack by the Tsar's troops on the citizens of Odessa is illustrated from various perspectives and points of view; events happening simultaneously are shown to us one after another. The effect is to create a stronger impression of slaughter and savagery. The importance behind these observations is the realization of how time is managed within narratives, how it is manipulated and rearranged in films.

Plot is more than story information, however. The style of a film (the *mise en scène*, editing, cinematography and sound) works ceaselessly to provide the viewer with other information, for example about character, about relationships, about mood. Thus the plot of *Pulp Fiction* informs us at one point that Jules accidentally shoots a captive while talking in the car, then argues with Vincent. This is part of the storyline. But it is the style's contribution to the plot that makes us party to the absurdly matter-of-fact tone of Jules and Vincent's conversation and the (comically) brain-splattered interior of the car. In *Citizen Kane*, when Kane and Susan talk/argue in Xanadu, plot information includes style: the expressionist lighting, the framing and camera angles accentuate Kane's power and Susan's powerlessness. This difference between story and plot information can be shown in Table 8.1.

Beginnings, middles and ends

The beginning of *Scream* and the film's subsequent events also serve to illustrate another key aspect of narrative theory. Tzvetan Todorov regarded narratives as typically consisting of three different stages. A narrative usually begins with an *equilibrium*, a state of harmony

Table 8.1   *Story and plot information*

Type	Order	Result
story	explicitly presented events rearranged into chronological sequence	inferred events built into the sequence of explicitly presented events
plot	explicitly presented events, not necessarily in chronological sequence	added stylistic/non-diegetic material

or balance in which the audience is introduced to key characters and locations. We get to know characters and perhaps identify with them. The next phase of the narrative sees a *disruption* of the initial equilibrium as a problem is introduced. This is one way in which the audience can be 'hooked' into the storyline. It is intended that we will want to follow the key characters through the story until they have solved the problem. This brings us to the third stage of a narrative: a *new equilibrium* is achieved, the problem is resolved, harmony and balance are restored. Traditionally this equates with a happy ending, with closure as the story is brought to an end. We can note that this also fits neatly with the cause and effect nature of a typical narrative which we identified earlier in this chapter.

Analysis of *Scream* confirms Todorov's model as appropriate to this particular narrative. The equilibrium is Casey intending to have a pleasant evening at home, a situation with which we can probably identify. The disruption is clearly the phone call followed by the attack. Casey has a problem and soon her friends have one too. The narrative is driven by the attempts to identify the killer, with a few more attacks along the way to add greater urgency. The new equilibrium, or restoration of harmony, is achieved with the unmasking of the source of the attacks. The problem is solved, a resolution is obtained. The narrative essentially conforms to Todorov's model, as do most film narratives. Closure is provided.

Open and closed narratives

However, while we may experience *Scream* as a complete narrative with closure, there has of course been a *Scream 2* (1998). This obviously places a question mark over the degree of closure in the first film. The financial attraction of sequels is obvious, but the potential for a sequel is unknown until the degree of popularity of the initial film is established. It is a risky strategy to make a film with an obviously open ending which may prove unsatisfactory. For example when John Sayles' *Limbo* (1999) ends with a fade to white and no evident narrative closure, there have often been loud groans from the audience!

In reality, film-makers are now adept at making films that appear closed but hold the possibility of continuation. Nor is this a recent strategy. *Star Wars* (1977) is one instalment in a six-part story. No doubt George Lucas perceived this particular section of the story as having the best chance of success. As a film it stands on its own as a complete story. However, as we now know, it is the fourth of six episodes; in other words, it is also an open-ended narrative. In this respect it is not such a typical narrative.

Being just a part of a larger narrative also explains why the beginning of *Star Wars* is at variance with the conventions of film narratives. As we have seen, an equilibrium is normally found at the beginning of a narrative, yet *Star Wars* begins *in medias res* (a Latin expression which means 'in the middle of things'), with action, with a battle in space, which visually strikes the viewer as a disruption. The only thing that would stop us defining it as a disruption is the fact that we have no knowledge of what came before and therefore do not know what could have been disrupted. We now know that *Star Wars* begins this way because it is a continuation of episode three. No doubt another good reason for beginning *Star Wars* this way is that it immediately launches us into the action, which is one of the key elements of its narrative. We have virtually no time to consider the narrative itself. Events move quickly and conflict is everywhere. Thomas Schatz summed up *Star Wars* and the film trend that followed as 'plot-driven, increasingly visceral, kinetic and fast paced, increasingly reliant on special effects, increasingly "fantastic".' (Schatz, 1993, p. 23).

Single- and multi-strand narratives

If the essential storyline of *Star Wars* moves rapidly from point A to point B, the same cannot be said of all film narratives. While most films contain one main storyline, *Do the Right Thing* (1989) can be described as a multi-strand narrative. There are several storylines running throughout the film which occasionally cross paths with one another. In many respects *Do the Right Thing* is like a soap opera narrative; it is even left open-ended. Although Mookie, played by Spike Lee, may be the central character, at least twelve other characters who regularly crop up have key roles within their own storylines, as well as within the narrative as a whole. They raise various issues and present a range of messages on race, parenthood, family, unemployment, enterprise and gender. It is a different type of film in both its narrative structure and the imaginative film techniques used. However, it is far from being an 'alternative' film; it still provides a coherent and entertaining narrative, albeit with political messages that often challenge mainstream beliefs.

Characters and Actions

While the events within a narrative may well catch our attention, action on its own is unlikely to be enough to carry us all the way through a film. The number of films based primarily on action may have increased in recent years, but characters are usually required to involve us fully in a film. This is partly because most actions are initiated by characters anyway, but also because as human beings we tend to link into a film much more easily through the representation of other human beings within a narrative.

Characters as protagonists

Almost invariably it is the main characters who are the protagonists in a film. They are the people within the story who cause things to happen. Exceptions are films where the driving force is a natural disaster that causes events. Yet even in such films individual human agency is usually woven into the narrative. In *Twister* (1996) it is tornadoes that provide the disruption. However, while on one level the equilibrium is a community before it is hit by a tornado, on another level the equilibrium is the lead character intending to settle down with his girlfriend. For the communities the arrival of the tornadoes is the disruption, while for the lead character the disruption is him being drawn back into 'tornado chasing' with his old friends, which poses a problem for his relationship. For the communities the new equilibrium is provided by the departure of the tornadoes, while for the lead character the new equilibrium is him agreeing to leave his fiancée and return to his previous lover, who is a kindred spirit, a fellow tornado chaser. This provides resolution, closure and a happy ending.

Motivated characters

For a film to involve the audience fully it will normally need to deal with the lives of individuals. As individuals in a relatively individualistic society, this is what we are likely to relate to. What we really follow in *Twister* is the lead character and his associates. They are motivated; they want encounters with tornadoes. This in turn makes them protagonists in that their motivations lead them to make things happen through the decisions they take. It is intended that we will identify with their desire for adventure and follow them through their dangerous adventures.

Exercise 8.2

For any three films you have seen recently, examine the motivations of the central characters. How do their drives and desires make the narrative go forward?

Character functions

Vladimir Propp has provided an interesting analysis of the kinds of characters contained by certain kinds of narratives. He analysed hundreds of Russian folk stories and identified eight main types of characters in terms of what their functions were within the narrative: the hero, the villain, the donor, the helper, the princess, the princess's father, the dispatcher and the false hero. While we need to be careful in judging the relevance of such analysis because of cultural and historical differences, the research having been undertaken in the Soviet Union in the 1920s, Propp's conclusions can be seen to be useful, even though he was only looking at a particular type of narrative. 'Proppian' analyses have been carried out, for example, on Hitchcock's *North By Northwest* (1959) and on the James Bond films, and a film-friendly model has been developed by ex-scriptwriter Christopher Vogler (1992).

A cursory glance at *Star Wars* soon reveals how the first five of Propp's character functions or types are appropriate. The hero is Luke Skywalker, the villain is Darth Vader, the donor is Obi Wan Kenobi, who gives Luke the 'force'; the helper is Han Solo, and the princess is Leia. Princess Leia is not of course the typical helpless princess of fairytales; she could not afford to be in a 1977 film, given the changes in gender values that had occurred as a result of the feminist movement. However, if we take account of changes in gender representation by broadening out the categories of hero and princess to encompass heroines and 'princes', Propp's model is still surprisingly appropriate.

Lucas' *Star Wars* provides clear examples of the roles of characters and actions within a film. This is especially the case with Luke Skywalker. When we first meet him he is living with relatives, helping run a mundane business buying, selling and repairing robots. Luke is restless; he is in his teens, he wants to break away, to be independent, to prove himself a man and to have adventures (and is therefore also an ideal identification figure, especially for adolescent males). In other words, he is already motivated but needs a definite purpose, a clear goal. This is provided by the discovery that Princess Leia has been caught and is seeking help. Luke requests the help of the wise old Obi Wan Kenobi, who aids his rites of passage in this story, seeing Luke safely on his way from boyhood to manhood. Luke is the protagonist, the main character who has a purpose. However, on its own this is not enough for an interesting story. An antagonist is needed, someone who opposes Luke's intentions. Once we have met the evil Darth Vader and the Empire, we are well placed to take the side of Luke against the villain. We identify with Luke and his mission to see good triumph over evil.

Good versus evil implies conflict, and this is a regular feature of *Star Wars*. The conflict drives the narrative forward, as it does in many classical narratives. Princess Leia is rescued but her planet is still threatened with destruction. Finally our hero saves the planet by destroying Darth Vader's (and the Empire's) base. The hero is rewarded by the princess. Happy ending.

Some Aspects of Style

Narratives can be considered in terms of content and structure. They consist of events which are organized in a particular way. The process of presenting a narrative is called narration, and the way in which a narrative is presented can be identified as its style. The principal components of film style (*mise en scène*, cinematography, editing and sound) have been described in Chapter 6 above and much of their relevance to narrative has been considered; here we shall briefly consider how a few particular aspects of style contribute to mainstream narrative.

Voice-over

We experience a film's narrative largely through what we see characters doing and what dialogue we hear from them. Other audio-visual elements such as written text and music are used to add meaning to the film. Usually these forms of communication are sufficient to produce a coherent narrative and create the desired effect. However, another method for helping to deliver the narrative is voice-over narration, which tends to be used for two reasons. First, it may be used to reinforce the account of an 'omniscient' narrator. Second, it may serve to provide a personal interpretation of narrative events.

Voice-over narration was particularly common in crime/detective films and *films noirs* of the 1940s. The voice-over narration supplements what we see and hear. We get a personal point of view of the events, though not usually a visual point of view. An example of this technique can be found in *Double Indemnity* (1944). In this particular film the narration is built into the actual narrative. Walter Neff records his confession and explanation of a murder he has become involved in. The narration supposedly comes from the recording we see him begin to make at the start of the film. The voice-over then accompanies the story of how Neff became embroiled in helping to murder Phyllis Dietrichson's husband in order to make a life insurance claim. The story could have been told without voice-over narration but then we would not have had such a personal interpretation of events.

Blade Runner (1982) also uses a voice-over. The voice-over narration is supplied by Deckard, the main character. Deckard has supposedly retired as a cop whose job was to kill rogue replicants, cyborgs built to perform human tasks. He is forced back into his old job to eradicate some new and dangerous replicants. The narration takes us through his thoughts and retells the story. *Blade Runner* is an interesting example because Ridley Scott later released *Blade Runner: The Director's Cut* (1991), in which the voice-over had been removed. The effect of this is to distance us from Deckard, making it easier for us to see things from the perspectives of other characters in the film. Without voice-over narration we are required to think more about what we see and hear. Things are not explained so clearly, and the viewer has to be more active.

However, we are most likely to come across voice-over narration in documentary narratives. A documentary usually aims to investigate a particular subject and to reveal information. Although interviews may be used, it is often the case that not all the required information is revealed through the shots and dialogue. A voice-over may be added to supplement the 'raw' information. Examples of this practice are to be found in the classic documentaries produced by John Grierson in the 1930s and 1940s. He saw documentaries as having a potentially democratizing effect through their educational value and ability to expose social inequalities. In one way or another the documentaries he produced tended to deal with the living and working conditions of the British working class, among the most famous films being Cavalcanti's *Coalface* (1935) and *Night Mail* (1936). Voice-over narration was used to provide greater detail and to guide the audience towards a particular interpretation, and such techniques have since been and remain very common in TV documentaries.

Restricted and unrestricted narration

Other choices also need to be made about how narratives are to be presented. The narrative information given to us can be *restricted* or *unrestricted* (the latter is also sometimes called 'omniscient' narration; see p. 208 for discussion of the 'classic realist text'). Each method can be used to powerful effect. As Warren Buckland notes: 'in restricted narration, the spectator only knows as much as one character, resulting in mystery. In omniscient narration, the spectator knows more than the characters, resulting in suspense' (1998, p. 34). Although restricted narration links the narrative to one character, it is not necessarily from their perspective. This form of narration can create mystery because we are unaware of what is happening elsewhere. We are left guessing; we do not know everything. At the end of *Scream*, it appears that the two murderers, Stewart and Billy, have been killed and we begin to relax as the threat seems to be over, but we and Sydney are shocked by the sudden appearance of Randy in a close up shot of Sydney. Again we relax, only to be startled twice more by Billy suddenly coming to life – an effect we may see as comic, but only after we have recovered from the shock. We are as surprised as Sydney because the presentation of the narrative has not prepared us for these interventions; information has been withheld and restricted.

Unrestricted narration, on the other hand, links the viewer to several characters and locations. We move from one to another. We can see how characters and events may coincide and have an effect upon each other; the viewer is in a privileged position. This form of narration is very capable of creating suspense because we may see what is about to happen while the characters may not. Towards the end of *Psycho* (1960) we are aware that Norman has put his mother in the fruit cellar. Lila, sister of the murdered Marion, has made her way to the house to question Norman's mother. She believes Norman's mother is harmless; the spectator has been led to believe she is a murderer. We are aware of something Lila does not know. We follow Lila around the house and it seems that she has managed to avoid the fruit cellar. However, she finds it by accident when she has to hide from Norman. Hitchcock continues to tease us by having Lila begin to walk down the steps to the cellar, only to stop and turn around, then finally continue down to the cellar. This creates suspense. We foresee two situations coinciding and feel like telling her to turn around and escape. While restricted narration is more likely to be used for shock, unrestricted narration is ideal for suspense – as Hitchcock himself knew very well. In a famous interview with French director François Truffaut, Hitchcock explained it thus:

> We are now having a very innocent little chat. Let us suppose that there is a bomb beneath this table between us. Nothing happens, and then all of a sudden, 'Boom!' There is an explosion. The public is *surprised*, but prior to this surprise, it has seen an absolutely ordinary scene, of no special consequence. Now, let us take a *suspense* situation. The bomb is underneath the table and the public *knows* it, probably because they have seen the anarchist place it there. The public *is aware* that the bomb is going to explode at one o'clock and there is a clock in the décor. The public can see that it is a quarter to one. In these conditions this same innocuous conversation becomes fascinating because the public is participating in the scene. The audience is longing to warn the characters on the screen: 'You shouldn't be talking about such trivial matters. There's a bomb beneath you and it's about to explode!'
>
> In the first case we have given the public fifteen seconds of *surprise* at the moment of the explosion. In the second case we have provided them with fifteen minutes of *suspense*. The conclusion is that whenever possible the public must be informed.
>
> (Truffaut, 1978, pp. 79–80, original emphasis)

A good example in which this principle is illustrated graphically is when three bombs are planted and we anxiously wait for them to explode in Gillo Pontecorvo's *Battle of Algiers* (1966).

In reality, films often mix restricted with unrestricted narration, depending on the scene and on the requirements of the narrative. *Star Wars* generally uses unrestricted narration but occasionally we receive restricted narration, as in the final battle scene when we share Luke Skywalker's point of view during his attempt to blow up the Death Star, and do not realize that he is being backed up by Han Solo in the *Millennium Falcon*.

Objective and subjective narration

Narrative information can also be presented subjectively or objectively. Subjective narration tells the story from a character's point of view; this is not necessarily their optical point of view but may be their mental perception of events. An example occurs in *The Cabinet of Dr Caligari* (1920). The narrative is presented as known by Francis. The film tells his story, of how Dr Caligari hypnotizes his accomplice Cesare to commit murders. Francis intends to expose what Caligari is doing. He tracks Caligari, who goes into hiding in a lunatic asylum. However, by the end of the film we return to objective narration and learn that Francis is an inmate of the asylum and Caligari is his doctor.

Battleship Potemkin provides a very objective narrative. We do not get close to any of the characters. We do not see things from their perspectives, although we do see a range of characters as part of the events that are shown to us. The film is a fictionalized account of a sailors' mutiny against the Russian Tsar's regime and the support given to the sailors by the townsfolk of Odessa. The film's narrative has no individual protagonists as such, preferring to present the events as the result of political developments within society. The film provides an overview of this particular incident from 1905 rather than a character's personalized account.

Many films mix objective with subjective narration. For instance, in *Citizen Kane*, the narration from the beginning of the film to the start of the journalists' investigations is objective. We observe events. However, when the characters interviewed provide us with their flashbacks, we initially experience subjective narration, although the flashbacks too eventually resort to objective narration. Thus within a particular flashback, events may be shown or described which the flashback's 'narrator' could not have seen or experienced. For example, at one point during the account of Susan's disastrous singing career, an apparent crane shot (which is in fact a cleverly edited fabrication) takes us from Susan on stage up to beneath the roof to show two stage hands silently expressing their disgust: these two characters would have been invisible to anyone else.

Subjective and objective narration are often combined with restricted and unrestricted narration. Close analysis is sometimes required to identify which is being used. A voice-over might give us a subjective viewpoint of events from a character's perspective, or it could be an objective description of events that is not personalized. It also needs to be remembered that using restricted narration which shows us events linked to one particular character is not necessarily subjective. We may not see events from the character's perspective. Similarly, unrestricted narration which presents events in relation to several characters is not necessarily objective, as the presentation of various events and characters may be retold from a very personal point of view.

ALTERNATIVE NARRATIVES AND FILM FORM

The vast majority of films, whether American, British, Brazilian or Japanese, have been structured around the kind of mainstream narrative described above. Such narratives tell stories about characters who are 'believable' (either because they are 'realistic' or because they correspond to accepted genre stereotypes) as they experience a series of events within a relatively coherent time and space. It may be worth repeating that such films, as part of the commercial film industry, are made with profit in mind: the aim is to make money. As is stressed elsewhere, this also tends to mean that such films are likely to belong to a genre and to contain stars, as both these factors tend to help in targeting a large audience.

Throughout most of cinema's history, though, some film-makers have refused this mode of film-making and have experimented with other kinds of narratives; indeed some have refused narrative altogether. Among famous examples of narratives being constructed quite differently from the dominant model outlined above were the Soviet Montage films and Surrealist films of the 1920s; these will be considered in Chapters 14 and 15.

A Further Note on 'Independent Films'

'Independent' is a term which has often been applied particularly to American films since the 1960s, as in 'US Independents'. But what does 'independent' mean in the cinema? We may recall that the early years of American film-making were dominated by the Motion Picture Patents Company, and it was only when the MPPC's activities were judged illegal in 1915 that other struggling companies became successful. These fledgling companies included Warner Brothers and Paramount, who were at the time the 'independents' of American cinema.

Some 50 years later, as the studio system had to find ways to adapt to the 1948 anti-trust legislation, changing lifestyles and television competition, increasing numbers of films were produced by 'independent' companies: companies set up, sometimes by maverick film-makers, for the production of a single film; such companies hired facilities from the studios but were otherwise financially independent. However, as successful production companies were established, and as the restriction on vertical integration was eroded during the Reagan years, powerful commercial concerns came to dominate all sectors of the industry, most noticeably distribution (see pp. 66–7 above). It is thus very debatable whether the films of Tarantino and Jarmusch, for example, can really be called 'independent'; *Pulp Fiction*, for all its innovation, was co-financed by Miramax, as was Jarmusch's *Dead Man* (1995).

Perhaps the only productions which can be considered 'independent' are those dependent neither on Hollywood or multinational conglomerate finance nor on state sponsorship. Truly independent films would thus not be purely commercially driven, and would be produced for aesthetic or political reasons. The style and content of such films would challenge mainstream conventions and ideologies. Truly independent cinema stands apart from popular or commercial mainstream film and is generally considered to be marginalized, alternative, or oppositional.

Though films which refuse the dominant rules of story-telling form a tiny percentage of all films ever made, they have been (and continue to be) an important part of film history and culture. Why is this?

Form and Ideology

Films have a deep sensory appeal and have often been compared with dreams. It is this unconscious aspect of the film experience which has provoked much suspicion and criticism of classical narrative film form – and which has also inspired the use of film as propaganda. In this section we shall look at some of the criticisms levelled at mainstream narrative entertainment films and at some examples of alternative film forms: films which demonstrate a refusal of the kind of narrative described thus far in this chapter.

The appeal to the unconscious was an important part, for example, of the Surrealist project, in film and in other art forms. Here we shall be concerned mostly with the attacks on mainstream narrative coming from a more political critique which was first mounted in the 1970s; we shall also briefly consider the contributions made by 'art cinema'.

Since Brecht and Eisenstein, it has been argued that film, theatre and indeed written narratives in western cultures have been constructed in such a way as to seduce the reader/spectator into accepting the dominant ideologies of the age. Among these have been assumptions about heterosexual, monogamous relationships within 'nuclear' family units which, so the argument goes, are designed to reproduce the class, gender and race relations suitable for capitalist exploitation. If poor, downtrodden spectators 'buy into' a social system which actually oppresses them and keeps them poor and enslaved, it is in large part because they unconsciously absorb messages about 'how society has to be' which are disguised as innocent entertainment. Millions of words have been printed arguing about how exactly this happens (and a few more are printed in Chapter 12, in which we shall consider ideology in slightly more detail), but there is a persistent belief, shared here, that this is indeed the job that ideology does through the media representations which surround us.

The very form of narrative as exemplified by Hollywood came under attack in a 1970s argument between Guy Hennebelle and James Monaco over whether it was possible to make responsible films about political subjects within a conventional narrative format. While Hennebelle argued that films such as those of Constantin Costa-Gavras (Z, 1969; State of Siege, 1973; Missing, 1982) would be consumed principally as thrillers and that their political 'message' would therefore be lost, Monaco argued that the narrative 'hook' was essential to get audiences to see the films in the first place: as George Bernard Shaw pointed out, if there is a pill to be swallowed, it is best that it be sugar-coated. The debate was not so much about the 'obviously' progressive/anti-establishment values and beliefs promoted in films such as The China Syndrome (Bridges, 1978) and Hidden Agenda (Loach, 1990), but rather about whether the use of mainstream narrative techniques somehow neutralized the political effectiveness of such films.

Godard and Counter-cinema

While there was no shortage of critics and theorists engaging in these arguments, a number of film-makers – predictably outside Hollywood – put theory into practice and made films which deliberately rejected conventional narrative forms. Among these was Jean-Luc Godard (see also pp. 264–5), particularly in the films he made between 1967 and 1972.

In an influential article written in 1972, Peter Wollen advanced the term counter-cinema to describe Godard's (and others') anti-narrative films. He organized the differences between conventional narrative film and counter-cinema into seven oppositions.

1   *Narrative transitivity* versus *narrative intransitivity*: conventional narrative has a coherent plot with events following one another in a cause and effect structure – this will serve as a definition of 'transitivity'. In counter-cinema, events do not follow each other in a logical cause and effect structure; there is likely to be digression and (deliberate) incoherence. *Pulp Fiction* is not an example of counter-cinema because despite Tarantino's games with chronology, the film is still composed of large narratively coherent chunks, which have only to be placed in the correct order for the puzzle to be solved. In Jean-Marie Straub and Danièle Huillet's *Not Reconciled* (*Nicht versöhnt*, 1965), on the other hand, the action takes place in at least three historical periods (corresponding to a character's youth, middle age and old age); yet it is extremely difficult to work out 'what is going on' as jumps in time are not signalled as they usually are by fades, by character motivation or cinematography (a zoom in to a face may usually signal a memory flashback, for example). In addition, no attempt is made to provide an illusion of passage of time by showing younger or older characters or by evoking a historical period: characters tend to look the same and to speak in the same way whether they are 20 or 70 years old! Needless to say, part of the aim here is to force the spectator to actively work out what is happening. The same 'active spectatorship' is necessary for such Godard films as *Weekend* (1967), *Wind from the East/Vent d'est* (1971) and *One Plus One/Sympathy for the Devil* (1969); in the last of these, shots of a Rolling Stones recording studio session are intercut with scenes exploring themes such as black power and feminism.

2   *Identification* versus *estrangement*: characters in mainstream narratives are generally constructed, made up, costumed and filmed in such a way as to encourage audience identification. Such characters may 'represent' social groups or positions, and they will often act naturalistically, or at least in a way we would expect according, say, to the genre. The spectator is also likely to be drawn into a conventional narrative to identify with events and situations: part of the 'reality effect' of film. By contrast, counter-cinema rejects such identification; the work of 'drawing in' and identification of conventional narrative are seen as central to the passing of ideologies referred to above. Instead, characters are often fragmented; no attempt is made to make them 'believable'; the same actor may play more than one role (this was a common practice in Brecht's theatre). Actors may look/stare at the camera – this has been called the 'fourth look' – perhaps while they and the spectator listen to a speech by another character, highlighting their 'role' in the film and breaking any identificatory spell. *Weekend* contains many such moments. Finally, voices may not match characters; sometimes it is difficult to work out 'who' is speaking. Marguerite Duras' *India Song* (1975) contains plenty of dialogue, but *none* of it is synchronized; again, the spectator needs to work hard to make meaning.

   An important way in which most mainstream films bind in the viewer and encourage identification is through continuity editing and especially through shot/reverse shot sequences (see Chapter 6 above). These are also commonly refused in films such as *Weekend* and *Sympathy for the Devil*. Completely different editing patterns are used, and the long take or shot-sequence (a shot lasting 10–20 minutes) is common.

3   *Transparency* versus *foregrounding*: just as in most films characters are constructed so as to seem 'believable', the overall *mise en scène* is likely to conceal the artifice of

film-making and to promote the illusion. An ever greater degree of 'realism' is demanded (not least by audiences) in the representation of fights, bodily mutilations and transformations, accidents, blood, etc., not to mention the assumed verisimilitude of the film's settings. In just the same way as with acting and character, counter-cinema refuses such illusionism and is not afraid to declare 'this is a film'. Props and settings may not seem 'realistic', and cameras, sound booms and other film-making equipment (and personnel) may be part of the film itself. In Godard's *Vent d'est* and *Sympathy for the Devil*, characters who are meant to be tortured or beaten up have red paint thrown at them. When a character in *Weekend* is murdered, a dead fish is shown in a puddle of red paint. *Vent d'est* contains a sequence in which the production personnel hold a chaotic meeting about how to proceed with the film. In this and a wider variety of films, the use of freeze frames, direct address to camera, hand-held camera and jump cuts and other discontinuities draws attention to the film's status as film and helps to break the habitual mainstream narrative illusion. Again, though, it is a matter of degree: if such techniques are used superficially (as a way of 'showing off' or as a kind of director 'signature'), they cannot be said to be counter-cinematic.

This strategy (again also frequently used in Brechtian theatre) also has literary roots: the Russian Formalists of the early twentieth century urged such foregrounding with the notion of 'making strange' (*ostranenie*). Since Brecht, such an anti-illusionist strategy has also been termed the 'alienation-effect' (*Verfremdungs-Effekt*). It *distances* the spectator, promoting contemplation and analysis rather than involvement and identification.

4 *Single diegesis* versus *multiple diegesis*: most film narratives take place in a single 'world': *Scream* and *Citizen Kane* both take place in and around the USA of the central characters. Sometimes, as in *The Wizard of Oz* or even *The Deerhunter*, two (or more) 'worlds' may be very different, but there is *narrative motivation* for movement between them: in *The Deerhunter* we spend the first hour of the film getting to know the main characters in a small industrial town, before being plunged into the Vietnam nightmare: this is clearly motivated as we know three of the characters are about to leave for Vietnam. Some counter-cinema films, by contrast, move between narrative 'worlds' without apparent motivation: again the spectator must make sense of it. In *Weekend*, two central characters are on a journey through central France, but meet characters in nineteenth-century costume and become involved with a band of anarchist cannibals living in a forest. The existence of these different diegetic worlds is not motivated by events in the narrative.

5 *Closure* versus *aperture*: mainstream narrative films usually concern a relatively closed and self-contained world, and references to other worlds and texts are generally integrated into the narrative. The narrative closure of most films reinforces this sense of the film as a unity – a unity which some writers have called 'organic'. By contrast, counter-cinema's frequent references to other films/texts does not seek to integrate such references into an 'organic' whole, but indulges in the references for their own sake or just to make a point. Thus many Godard films are full of cinematic, cultural and literary references or 'quotes'. We shall return to this aspect of counter-cinema when we discuss postmodernism in Chapter 12.

6   *Pleasure* versus *unpleasure*: though it may seem strange (even incomprehensible?), this is a crucial aspect of counter-cinema and of critical discussion of entertainment films. According to the counter-cinema argument, the pleasures of mainstream entertainment films seduce the spectator into a state of passive receptivity so that ideologically reactionary/conservative 'messages' are allowed free passage. By contrast, some critics and film-makers have insisted on the need to dismantle this kind of pleasure, and have called openly for its destruction:

> It is said that analysing pleasure, or beauty, destroys it. That is the intention of this article. The satisfaction and the reinforcement of the ego that represent the high point of film history hitherto must be attacked. Not in favour of a reconstructed new pleasure, which cannot exist in the abstract, nor of intellectualised unpleasure, but to make way for a total negation of the ease and plenitude of the narrative fiction film.
>
> (Laura Mulvey, in Nichols, 1985, p. 306)

While the political and ideological analysis of such theorists and filmmakers has been sound enough, they have ultimately perhaps overestimated the number of people prepared to see films which require hard work. A sequence in *Weekend* consists of a single 8-minute tracking shot showing a (non-'realistic') traffic jam with horns blowing throughout (Figure 8.2); a single shot in Godard's *Tout va bien* (1972) tracks repeatedly to and fro past the many checkouts of a hypermarket to portray a slowly escalating disturbance in the aisles. Such writers and film-makers have no doubt also tended to underestimate the human need for 'pleasure'; following George Bernard Shaw, even Brecht recognized the strategic importance of providing pleasure for the audience: 'Erst kommt das Fressen, dann kommt die Moral' [loosely translated, 'First the eats, then the moral']. How effective can counter-cinema and oppositional films be if most people do not want to see them?

Figure 8.2   *An everyday traffic jam in Godard's Weekend (BFI Stills, Posters and Designs)*

The whole issue of how pleasure is produced and why we sometimes experience pleasure (and sometimes not) is a complex one which will be considered further in chapter 12 below.

7 *Fiction* versus '*reality*': it can be argued that *all* films, including documentaries, are 'fiction'. Since it is impossible to 'show reality' on film, the aim of counter-cinema has been to force the audience to confront reality: the reality of the film-making, the reality of the viewing experience, each spectator's own social and individual reality. Such is the aim of all the strategies outlined above. Films such as Godard's *Vent d'est* and *Struggle in Italy* (*Lotte in Italia*, 1969) and the early films of the American Jon Jost (for example, *Speaking Directly*, 1974) feature a direct address and implication of the spectator which systematically refuse the usual fictionalizing pleasures of the cinema.

ALTERNATIVE FORM AND ART CINEMA

After his French New Wave films of the 1960s, Godard gained fame and notoriety with his Maoist/Marxist-Leninist-inspired 'difficult' period of 1968-72, corresponding to the 'counter-cinema' described above. He was not alone in his politicized rejection of the status quo, but not all film-makers were so dogmatic in their politics. A contrast is provided, for example, by the work of Marguerite Duras, a French writer who turned to film-making in 1971 and proceeded to make some 20 films (see p. 163). While her films conform to a number of aspects of counter-cinema (especially the refusal of identification and of simple narrative structure), her motivation was less a political or ideological programme than simple disgust with the illusionism of conventional film form. More recently, Derek Jarman took the counter-cinema oppositions to the limit with *Blue* (1993), a meditation on life, death and AIDS and art conducted through an otherwise imageless blue screen: meaning is here almost entirely carried by the voice-over and music soundtrack.

In some ways almost all 'art' cinema can be seen as more or less rejecting Hollywood's narrative conventions, sometimes in the pursuit of more indigenous story-telling forms. 'Art' films, where they use narratives at all, typically do not contain fully developed 'characters' in the classical sense, and the cause and effect chain is often weak or non-existent. The distinction needs to be made, though, between those film-makers who are clearly critical of conventional narrative forms and those whose motivation is some version of personal creativity. While directors such as Godard, Duras and Jarman and also avant-garde structuralist-materialist film-makers such as Michael Snow and Peter Gidal have clearly rejected conventional forms as inadequate (if not downright oppressive), others such as Raul Ruiz and Peter Greenaway have been less obviously political in their playful experiments with narrative forms. The case of film-makers working outside the so-called 'developed countries' and the major film-producing centres (such as Ousmane Sembene, Med Hondo and others) will be considered in Chapter 14.

While (well-known) directors like Godard, Straub and Fassbinder pursued their political agendas in the glare of critical scrutiny, the 1970s also saw an explosion of film-making in Western

Europe by relatively unknown individuals and collectives who were equally committed to political change and to re-educating the spectator. Many of these films became 'unfashionable' over the Thatcher years (1979–94) and some people now treat them as a kind of political freak show. Nevertheless film-makers like Werner Schroeter, Marc Karlin, the Berwick Street Collective, the Newsreel Collective and Laura Mulvey herself (*Penthesilea*, 1974; *Riddles of the Sphinx*, 1977) (to name but a few) contributed an important chapter to the evolution of film form.

Conclusion

It can certainly be argued that the distinctions drawn here between Classical Hollywood Narrative and alternative forms are less clear than they once were. According to Richard Maltby, following the collapse of the classical Hollywood Studio System and the need for innovation during the spread of television in the 1950s, the following two decades (from 1960 to 1980) saw a considerable loosening of the Classical Narrative conventions as they have been outlined in the above pages, a loosening which was hastened by the lifting of many censorship restrictions and by growing social liberalization. It is interesting to note, however, that Maltby (1995, pp. 221–8) also notes evidence of a return to classical Hollywood storytelling in 1980 (his example is *Ordinary People*), and links this to a return to more conservative family and other ideologies, also evidenced by the political regimes in Britain and the USA during that decade. If the narrative landscape of commercial films has evolved since the 1980s, perhaps incorporating and neutralizing some aspects of the previously revolutionary counter-cinema, it is perhaps time to introduce the notion of the *postmodern* . . . but we shall have to wait until Chapter 12 to do so.

Exercise 8.3
Try applying the counter-cinema definitions to a recent commercial film. If the film seems to fit in with some counter-cinema criteria, how would you explain this?

Finally it is worth stressing that counter-cinema films were (on the whole) not made as part of some cruel, perverse joke. Many counter-cinema films are rich, dense texts which can reward the work necessary in watching and studying them. But such films are rarely 'entertaining'.

SUMMARY

- **Whatever the exact structure, style or content of a mainstream narrative, particular film techniques tend to be used in order that the narrative may be presented coherently, so that the audience does not have to work too hard to understand.**

- These techniques were consolidated with the rise of the Hollywood Studio System: continuity editing ensures that the narrative is easily understandable by arranging shots in a certain order; appropriate use of shot sizes guides the viewer through the narrative.
- These film techniques, together with the narrative techniques we have been looking at, gave rise to Classical Hollywood Narrative.
- Alternative narratives and styles have rejected the classical narrative model.
- These alternative modes of film-making have often been politically motivated and have rejected ideologies associated with 'entertainment'.
- Peter Wollen's idea of 'counter-cinema' provides a useful way of analysing oppositional film-making strategies.

REFERENCES

Warren Buckland, *Teach Yourself Film Studies* (London: Hodder Headline, 1998).

Richard Maltby, *Hollywood Cinema: An Introduction* (Oxford: Blackwell, 1995).

Bill Nichols (ed.), *Movies and Methods* (Berkeley, CA: University of California Press, 1976).

Bill Nichols (ed.), *Movies and Methods II* (Berkeley,CA: University of California Press, 1985).

Thomas Schatz, 'The New Hollywood', in Jim Collins, Hilary Radner and Ava Preacher Collins (eds), *Film Theory Goes to the Movies* (London and New York: Routledge, 1993).

François Truffaut, *Hitchcock* (London: Paladin, 1978).

Christopher Vogler, *The Writer's Journey* (London: Boxtree Books, 1992).

Noël Burch, *Theory of Film Practice* (London: Secker & Warburg/BFI, 1973).

Jean-Louis Comolli and Jean Narboni, 'Cinema/Ideology/Criticism', in Bill Nichols (ed.), *Movies and Methods* (Berkeley, CA: University of California Press, 1976).

Pam Cook and Mieke Bernink (eds), *The Cinema Book* (2nd edn, London: BFI, 1999).

Guy Hennebelle, 'Z-Movies, or what hath Costa-Gavras wrought?', in *Cineaste*, vol. 6, no. 2 (1974), pp. 28–31.

Richard Maltby, *Hollywood Cinema: An Introduction* (Oxford: Blackwell, 1995).

James Monaco, 'The Costa-Gavras syndrome', in *Cineaste* vol. 7, no. 2 (1976), pp. 18–22.

Laura Mulvey, 'Visual pleasure and narrative cinema', originally in *Screen*, vol. 16, no. 3. (Autumn 1975), reprinted in Bill Nichols (1985).

Steve Neale and Murray Smith (eds), *Contemporary Hollywood Cinema* (London: Routledge, 1997).

Bill Nichols (ed.), *Movies and Methods* (Berkeley, CA: University of California Press, 1976).

Bill Nichols (ed.), *Movies and Methods II* (Berkeley, CA: University of California Press, 1985).

Thomas Schatz, *Hollywood Genres: Formulas, Filmmaking and the Studio System* (New York: Random House, 1981).

Christopher Vogler, *The Writer's Journey* (London: Boxtree Books, 1992).

Martin Walsh, *The Brechtian Aspect of Radical Cinema* (London: BFI, 1981).

FURTHER READING

Martin Barker, *Comics: Ideology, Power and the Critics* (Manchester: Manchester University Press, 1989).

David Bordwell, Janet Staiger and Kristin Thompson, *The Classical Hollywood Cinema: Film Style and Mode of Production to 1960* (London: Routledge & Kegan Paul, 1985).

David Bordwell and Kristin Thompson, *Film Art: An Introduction* (5th edn, New York: McGraw-Hill, 1998).

Peter Wollen, *Signs and Meaning in the Cinema* (London: Secker & Warburg 1969, 1972, 1987) (also London: BFI, 1997).

Peter Wollen, 'Godard and counter-cinema: *Vent d'Est*', originally in *Afterimage*, no. 4 (Autumn 1972); reprinted in Peter Wollen (1982).

Peter Wollen, *Readings and Writings* (London: Verso, 1982).

FURTHER VIEWING

A Personal Journey with Martin Scorsese through American Cinema (BFI, 1995).

Visions of Light (The American Film Institute, 1992).

Critical Approaches to Film

Authorship

[T]he cinema is the work of a single man, the director . . . A film is what you write on the screen. (Orson Welles, quoted in Wollen, 1969, p. 26)

This chapter will examine the role of the director in relation to the complex structure of finance, production, genre and stars. In particular, it will look at the influence of the *Cahiers du cinéma* articles in which Jean-Luc Godard, François Truffaut and others developed their '*politique des auteurs*' and the subsequent application of these ideas to Hollywood cinema.

As we have seen, film-making is almost always a complex team activity, and the idea of authorship may seem a strange one to use in such a collaborative medium. Nevertheless, as we shall see below, the idea of the author has been crucial to much thinking about film for at least the past four decades. But what is an author?

SOME GENERAL REFLECTIONS ON AUTHORSHIP

In common usage the idea of an author seems unproblematic: it is the person who writes; usually the word is used to refer to the writer of a published work, be it a book, an article or a letter. Yet even this is perhaps not as straightforward as it may seem. Many books are listed under the person who has 'edited' a series of chapters or articles by different writers; clearly the writers of the separate chapters/articles are the collective authors, but the person credited for the book is the 'editor', who may have written just a short introduction.

Then there is the problem of copying and plagiarism – an important area for any student or writer to negotiate. If for the purposes of this chapter in this book I copy or rely heavily on someone else's book/text, then can I be said to be the 'author' of the chapter? If a student copies large chunks from, say, Bordwell and Thompson's *Film Art* in an essay, who is really the 'author' of the essay? Such plagiarism and stealing of other peoples' ideas and words have of course long been a subject of dispute: two quite different sorts of examples would be the controversy about 'was Shakespeare really the author of the plays that are attributed to him?' and the increasing numbers of long (and expensive) court cases (for example, that involving Bruce Springsteen) fought over alleged theft/plagiarism of relatively obscure fragments of music. Indeed, with the popularization of rap and sampling techniques since the 1980s, and with the increasing availability of written text, recorded sound and moving images through the Internet since the 1990s, another kind of major threat to common-sense ideas of authorship (and of course to the idea of copyright) has emerged. Of what, for example, is rapper Will Smith the 'author'? It is also to be noted, of course, that plagiarism in examination work is often punished with a 'Fail' grade.

The idea of the writer/painter/artist as gifted creator/'author' of his/her work of art is in fact a comparatively recent one in the history of humanity. Though the names of a number of artists and writers have of course been recorded over the centuries, the idea of the 'gifted artist' as 'author' of her/his (historically usually 'his') work really dates from the Renaissance of the fifteenth and sixteenth centuries: before then the ultimate 'creator', or the source of inspiration, was most often seen as God (or some equivalent). Painters, sculptors and writers were principally seen as craftsmen.

Though it comes at the end of a (very) long history of ideas about writing/literature, the idea that Mary Shelley was the author of *Frankenstein*, Dickens of *David Copperfield* and Brett Easton Lewis of *American Psycho* can now be taken for granted. By extension, it is fair to see Leonard Cohen as the 'author' of *The Future*, John Lennon of *Imagine*.

These examples, however, begin to illustrate another kind of difficulty with the idea of an author. While obviously some authors/artists have created their work in private and with the aim of expressing their creativity (Rubens and Gauguin in painting perhaps, Virginia Woolf and Salman Rushdie in literature, to take a few random examples), this has certainly not been the norm. Most painting and sculpture before and after the Renaissance was commissioned either by the Church or by wealthy patrons – the 'artist' was thus basically doing a job for someone. Much music was also written/composed in the same way, and indeed many post-Renaissance composers, Mozart and Wagner among them, continued to rely on commissions and patronage to earn a living.

With the development of capitalism in the eighteenth and nineteenth centuries (and of course throughout the twentieth), a new kind of market was created, works of art became commodities, and the artist/author's name became a label which could be used to sell the product: a painting, a book, a theatre production. The idea of the author as gifted creative individual is thus (in the grand scheme of things) a relatively recent development which fits perfectly into the dominant capitalist culture which has developed most particularly in Europe and North America over the last two centuries.

Possible 'Authors' in Film

All of this is relevant to film because cinema was born at the end of the nineteenth century into a set of developed capitalist economies in France, Britain and the United States. The new medium (see Chapter 7 for more detail) was almost immediately developed along capitalist lines as a commodified entertainment.

The initial attraction of film was as a novelty, and film-makers (the distinction between director, producer, company, etc. only becomes useful after about 1907 with the development of the first film studios in North America) and exhibitors were not slow to exploit the entertainment and exploitative possibilities of the new medium. American nickelodeons between 1905 and 1915 ran continuous programmes, typically from 8 o'clock in the morning until midnight; programmes were often sensationalist and were advertised stridently. The emphasis was thus on the experience and the novelty – in much the same way that Virtual Reality arcades, computer games and indeed perhaps still the circus are advertised/consumed today – and the idea that individuals/artists could produce films was at first nowhere in sight.

Film companies

If anything gained fame/notoriety during this period, it was the film company (for example, Edison, Vitagraph, Biograph), which would typically be the only 'credit' attached to the film. Indeed, until around 1910 the upstart film shows were not 'respectable' entertainment at all, and many of those appearing in the films were actors who could not secure work on the more legitimate stage. There was thus a certain stigma attached to acting in films, and indeed film producers were at first reluctant to publicize nascent 'stars' since this would lead to claims for higher wages.

Actors

The first credits for individual actors began to appear in 1910, and this has been seen as arguably the first step towards recognizing authorial agency in film. Perhaps it is not surprizing that actors were thus recognized before directors, since they are the most publicly *visible* personnel in film-making.

But can an actor be seen as the 'author' of a film? If actors could then be seen by audiences as a film's most significant individuals – as of course they often still are – which other persons may be candidates for the 'authorship' of a film?

Exercise 9.1

List the major roles which have to be fulfilled by individuals in the making of a film. For each one, note in what ways that individual could be considered as the 'author' of the film. It may help to think about specific examples which could support your choices.

The earliest films (for example, those credited to Georges Méliès, Edwin S. Porter, R.W. Paul) were made by very small groups of people: in the Lumière tradition at least, the principal task was simply to operate the camera. While individuals continued to experiment (increasingly in other countries further and further away from France and the USA), a significant event was the setting up of Thomas Ince's New York Picture Company studios in California and the development of production control and scientific management practices aimed at the efficient production of films (see Chapter 1). The important innovation at Ince's studios was the division of film-making labour into specific tasks – tasks which had been roughly developed previously but which had never been so clearly defined within an industrial and management structure. While the size of Hollywood studios increased a hundredfold over the coming half-century, Ince inaugurated working methods which, though they evolved with time, were to become the bedrock of the American film industry.

The principal personnel in film-making in the studio system – apart from the actors of course – became the studio head, the producer, the scriptwriter(s), the director, the cinematographer, the camera operator and the editor. Even in the studio set-up some of these functions were sometimes combined, and perhaps the most interesting contested task in the present context is that of the editor.

Although it will become clear (if it is not already) which of these roles can best be and most usually is called 'authorial', a limited case (usually based on the evidence of relatively few films) can be made for some of the others.

Moguls

It could, for example, be argued that studio production heads ('moguls') such as Irving Thalberg (at Loew's-MGM between 1924 and 1936) and David O. Selznick (who worked at RKO and MGM between 1931 and 1936) stamped a recognizable 'identity' or 'look' on nearly all films produced in their studios during that particular period and so should be given (at least joint) 'author' status. It is reported that Thalberg in particular read all scripts, saw the rushes of all films, and oversaw the production of Universal and MGM films to an unprecedented degree. In common with other producers, Thalberg and Selznick also controlled the editing of most films (except those entrusted to the most experienced directors or those who dug their heels in and refused studio 'interference'). Thalberg's reputation is thus typified by his sacking Erich von Stroheim before the editing stage when, already a respected director, the latter had run massively over budget on the production of *Foolish Wives* in 1922. Selznick was also famed for the hundreds of memos he would send during the production of a single film.

Scriptwriters/screenwriters

An obvious case could also be made for the authorial status of many scriptwriters. This is not only because scriptwriters actually write and are thus more easily thought of as 'authors', but also because scripts sometimes 'make' films. Among scriptwriters whose work has most often been seen as crucial to a film are Dalton Trumbo (*Spartacus* and *Exodus*, both 1960) and T.E.B. Clarke, who wrote the scripts for many of the Ealing comedies. Another interesting case is Ruth Prawer Jhabvala, part of the Merchant–Ivory–Jhabvala 'authorial' team: an unusual case of joint 'authorship' being proclaimed through the triple-barrelled label attached to such films as *A Room with a View* (1985) and *Howards End* (1991). Richard Curtis' writing of *Four Weddings and a Funeral* (1994) and *Notting Hill* (1999) shows considerable 'authorial' continuity. The list could go on.

Authors of 'source' books

The 'quality' adaptations of the Merchant–Ivory team also remind us that the author of the original written text can be given some author-status in a film in an effort to boost its cultural prestige: thus *Bram Stoker's Dracula* (Coppola, 1992), *Mary Shelley's Frankenstein* (Branagh, 1994) and *William Shakespeare's Romeo and Juliet* (Luhrmann, 1996).

Cinematographers

Perhaps less obviously, the cinematographer and photographer (in early films these functions were often combined by one person) have also sometimes been hailed as 'authors', as having the greatest influence on how a film turns out. Thus most famously, Gregg Toland's work on *Citizen Kane* has often been seen as more significant than Orson Welles' well-publicized direction (though it is true that Welles also co-scripted and starred in the film). The deep field photography, allied to the lighting systems and the camera angles and framing, were highly innovative at that time and, perhaps rather belatedly, Toland's is now being seen as the determining contribution.

Another interesting example from film history is the camerawork of Karl Freund, whose experiments with 'das entfesselte Kamera' (the 'unchained' camera) in films such as *The Last Laugh (Der letzte Mann)* in 1924 were a revolutionary liberation of the camera from its previously ponderous movements. Thus, another arguably 'authorial' contribution. Many more recent films have also boasted the services of celebrated photographers: for example, (see Figure 9.1) Raoul Coutard worked consistently with Jean-Luc Godard between 1959 and 1967; Sven Nykvist was closely associated with Ingmar Bergman before going on to work with a number of other well-known directors. And although 'author' status never came his way, Billy Bitzer was the expert camera operator with whom D.W. Griffith (see below) made almost all 'his' films.

Editors

Before we move to the role in film-making which has most consistently been associated with authorship, we should note the crucial role of the editor. While Alfred Hitchcock and John Ford, for example, insisted on tight control of the editing in 'their' films, countless other films have been edited, in effect, by studio personnel, by professional editing staff who would have been virtually unknown to those actually shooting the footage on set or out on location, or to the audience. Sometimes – indeed, more often than not in the major studios of the 1930s, for example – editing was personally supervised according to a strict set of guidelines by the producer and/or the studio head. Though the editor is not normally thought of as an author, then, it is nevertheless clear that the overall look/shape of a film depends enormously on the editing.

Figure 9.1   *Godard's innovation, Sven Nykvists's photography: A Bout de souffle (BFI Stills, Posters and Designs)*

Interesting case studies are provided by *Performance* (Cammell and Roeg, 1970) and *Blade Runner*. Warner Brothers executives hated *Performance* so much (Richard Schickel's review in *Time*: 'the most disgusting, the most completely worthless film I have seen. . .') that they tried to have it drastically re-edited, to the dismay of Cammell and Roeg. Only under pressure from Cammell did they agree for re-editing to be done by Frank Mazzola, to whom Cammell gives much of the credit for the eventual version. *Performance* was then deliberately released in the USA in the 'dead' month of August 1970 and sank without trace; in Britain it was released in January 1971, received good reviews and became a cult classic (see Figure 9.2). The editing of *Blade Runner* was delayed by endless controversy and argument especially among Ridley Scott (the director), Hampton Fancher and David Peoples (the scriptwriters), Michael Deeley (the producer) and the representatives of the financing companies (see Sammon, 1996). The film was first released in 1982 having been edited by Terry Rawlings, not without pressure and interference from Tandem, the 'completion bond guarantor' company. It was not until 1992 that Ridley Scott was able to re-edit the film and change the soundtrack, and *Blade Runner: The Director's Cut* was released.

More extreme cases of editor-authorship are of course provided in cases where films depend largely or entirely on archive/found footage. A famous example of this was the case of the Soviet film-maker Esfir Shub, several of whose films, including *Fall of the Romanov Dynasty* (1927), were composed entirely of such pre-shot archive film. Apart from the (often unknown) camera operators who had shot the original material, therefore, she was the sole 'author' of her films. Interestingly, however, the Soviet film administrators Sovkino refused to recognize Shub's right as author.

Editing problems: Jagger and Fox in Performance (BFI Stills, Posters and Designs)   Figure 9.2

THE DIRECTOR AS 'AUTHOR'

This brings us, finally, to the person most commonly accorded film 'author' status: the director. In the remainder of this chapter we shall trace the way in which the idea of directorial authorship developed, and particularly the debate which followed a series of articles about the *auteur* in the French journal *Cahiers du cinéma* and which had a widespread effect on theories of authorship.

It is not generally wise to overvalue the importance of single individuals. Whatever influence the individual has and whatever the 'effect' on history, the individual must always be seen in a historical, social and economic context. As we have noted, the idea of the gifted creative artist is historically a relatively recent one, and the concept indeed needs to be seen in the context of the Renaissance, of a gradual retreat from religious explanations of human agency, and of a slowly developing capitalist society.

D.W. Griffith as *Auteur*

Nevertheless, the contribution of David Wark Griffith to film history was an important one. If he was in some way a 'genius', this was because his talents were ideally suited to the early industrial context of film-making: the early studio system which provided a tight production structure but in which innovation (especially technical) was vital and would benefit all concerned: the audience with the excitement of a developing entertainment/art form, the studio bosses/owners with increasing profits, and film-making employees with new technical and aesthetic challenges. For some, of course, this meant fame, and D.W. Griffith became famous.

Griffith's innovative career is also considered elsewhere in this volume; the relevant point here is his development of the role of the director as person in overall charge of shooting a film. At the time of Griffith's debut in film-making in 1908 – he had drifted into the film industry when his career as a theatre actor failed to blossom – the directorial function was in its infancy; since the advent of cinema in 1895 the person who 'made' the film had been the camera operator. At the turn of the century, of course, editing was also quite rudimentary and consisted of the sequencing of 'tableaux', sometimes into a narrative progression, sometimes not. Although by 1906, following Edwin S. Porter's *The Great Train Robbery*, intercutting between scenes was being developed (in America and elsewhere), when Griffith began his career in 1908 editing was in its infancy. The camera remained static. The camera operator was concerned with light levels, with the distance of the camera from the actants/subject (framing) and indeed often with organizing what was happening in front of the camera (the *mise en scène*).

Griffith was instrumental in changing this. Though constrained in the 450 films which he made between 1908 and 1913 by Biograph's insistence on one-reelers and the studio's reluctance to venture into 'serious'/'artistic' subjects, Griffith was nevertheless responsible for much innovative work on film language (see p. 130) and was the first to establish a reputation as director which rivalled those of stars of the day such as Theda Bara, Douglas Fairbanks and Mary Pickford. Indeed, he was the first director to accord *himself* authorial status by placing his directorial credit before the names of well-known stars. Related to this, it is not insignificant that he took his own writing talents seriously: he soon began composing his own (sometimes rather pompous) inter-titles and placed his own logo on each inter-title for all to see.

Griffith's status as star director enabled him to put pressure on Biograph to let him make longer and more ambitious films (*Enoch Arden* and *Judith of Bethulia*) but Griffith was unhappy with the company's marketing of these films, which did not help them to be successful. In 1913 he left Biograph and was able to complete two ambitious projects, *Birth of a Nation* (1915) and *Intolerance* (1916), both considered to be major landmarks of film art. After some financial hiccups, together with Charlie Chaplin, Douglas Fairbanks and Mary Pickford he set up United Artists in 1919 and immediately directed *Broken Blossoms*, perhaps his last major film.

Griffith was thus the first high-profile director who could be accorded 'author' status. If there have been many other directors since then who may be considered 'authors', the story has become complicated by an important distinction which can be seen to have some roots in the Griffith case: this is the distinction between 'art cinema' and the commercial or mainstream cinema of (initially) Hollywood.

Art Cinema

Outside and in parallel with the industry of commercial cinema, art cinema has always been concerned less with entertainment and more with artistic experimentation and expression. Art cinema (like its cousins avant-garde and independent cinema) has been closely linked with the idea of film as an expression of the vision of an individual director-artist. Working outside industrial structures, some directors have made films entirely alone: Steve Dwoskin, for example, made films in the 1970s partly as social commentary but also as intensely personal (and political) documents. At the same time and into the 1980s, structural-materialist avant-garde artists such as Peter Gidal, Peter Kubelka and Michael Snow produced experimental films which explored the possibilities of the film medium: 'images' were created on film not only by unconventional combinations of lighting, camera movements and angles, but by physical manipulation of the celluloid: film was scratched, deliberately scorched, treated with acid, mould was allowed to grow on the celluloid surface. . . It is easy to see the self-expression and products of such film-makers in the same way as those of, say, the painter-artist.

Other directors have worked more or less professionally with other film personnel: with recognized camera operators, actors etc. Nevertheless such directors maintain(ed) a good deal of control over the production process and over the final product, and so their films have been recognized as expressions of their artistic sensibility. Carl Dreyer, for example, famously insisted on total control over all aspects of production in the relatively few feature-length films he completed (six between 1928 and 1964, an average of six years for each feature film). Though (most) other 'art' directors had a more complicated relation to the broader film industry, we are used to talk of 'an Ingmar Bergman film' or 'the latest Jarmusch'.

There is an interesting commentary on 'authorial' control at the end of *Speaking Directly* (Jon Jost, 1974) in which Jost, a steadfastly outspoken and independent film-maker, painstakingly thanks all those involved in making his (very cheap) film. He lays out and describes all the equipment he has used, explains where he borrowed each item from, thanks the spectator for watching, but also explains that to credit everyone involved in the film would involve thanking the people who physically developed his film stock, the mine workers who obtained the minerals necessary for the film emulsion, and so on. . .

There have been and are many such film 'authors'. One further interesting case was Marguerite Duras, a French writer and film-maker who died in 1996 as author of much literature and of over 20 films. One of her avowed reasons for making films was a strong hatred for the limitations and conservatism of conventional film story-telling, and almost all her films (for example, *India Song*, 1974; *Le Camion*, 1977; *Les Enfants*, 1985) were thus refusals of the conventional treatment of time, character and space. While following a very personal agenda both in terms of the films' subject matter and in her filming methods, the thing to stress in the case of Duras is the collaborative nature of the work; perhaps a kind of seduction in which the directness and the honesty of a charismatic artist, though often 'difficult' to deal with, generally produced a closeness and a sense of shared purpose in all those involved.

The media 'fame' of a film-maker (and here we effectively return to Griffith) may, as in the case of Duras, be related to her/his other work, for example, as a writer, or to a flair for self-publicity (no doubt true of Griffith but also, for instance, of Orson Welles). The artistic aura of others such as Ingmar Bergman, Carl Dreyer or Stanley Kubrick has been at least partly due to their perceived mysteriousness and *lack* of self-publicity in the rarity of interviews, for example.

The 'Author' and the Hollywood Studio System

We thus return to the world of commercial/entertainment cinema with its publicity and its marketing: an 'image industry' in that it produces filmic images, but also in the sense that it produces 'star images', usually of star actors but also sometimes of directors (think of Quentin Tarantino).

As we have seen, then, film production in the Hollywood Studio System which dominated world cinema from the 1920s until around 1950 was a highly organized and collaborative enterprise, and we have also remarked that it might even be possible to see a studio head of production such as Irving Thalberg as having the greatest personal influence on any particular MGM film of the time. Since the studio system became a more or less universal organizational model throughout the world, considerable influence thus also fell, for example, to Michael Balcon at Ealing Studios and to the 1930s producers at the massive 'Tollywood' studios at Bombay in India.

If, since Griffith, the director could therefore sometimes be seen as imposing his/her ideas on a project, as definitively shaping a film to an 'authorial' purpose, it has also been clear that the studio system with its rigid divisions of labour made this very difficult. Thus though the quality of the films would also have been a factor, while some directors became known either partly because of a previous acting career (Charlie Chaplin), through doggedly insisting on greater control (John Ford, Alfred Hitchcock) or largely through self-publicity (Orson Welles), the fame of the great majority of directors ended with seeing their name in the credits; the film was a Warner Brothers gangster film or a Universal horror film. It is largely with retrospect that names such as Todd Browning, James Whale, Mervyn Le Roy, Lloyd Bacon and hundreds of others are now well known to film historians, and that many directors of Hollywood and elsewhere have become 'authors'. How and why did this happen?

Cahiers du Cinéma, the 'Politique des Auteurs' and Auteur Theory

The seeds for a reappraisal of the director's role were sown in an article written in 1948 by Alexandre Astruc for *Cahiers du cinéma* entitled 'The Birth of a New Avant-garde: la caméra-stylo [camera-pen]'. This established the idea that film-making was analogous to writing, so it was not long before filmic equivalents for the literary author were sought. The moment which sparked a major shift in assessment of a director's contribution to the film-text was an article by François Truffaut entitled 'A certain tendency of the French cinema', which appeared in *Cahiers du cinéma* no. 31 in January 1954.

The position advanced in the Truffaut article and in subsequent pieces in the same journal by Jean-Luc Godard, Jacques Rivette, Claude Chabrol and Eric Rohmer became known as the '*politique des auteurs*'. It is often wrongly called the '*auteur* theory', which as we shall see below was principally the responsibility of the American writer Andrew Sarris. The French writers' texts were put forward as a *polemic*, as an argument intended to provoke debate and change, not as a 'theory'.

The starting-point of this polemic was the cinematic unimaginativeness of the French cinema of the time as perceived by Truffaut and his young colleagues. Theirs was a thirst for a cinema which would innovate and explore the cinematographic possibilities of the medium, and for them the model of such experimentation was to be found in Hollywood films. The love of Hollywood films as a form of cinematic art, itself a view perhaps peculiar to French *cinéphiles* (lovers of film), was, however, also linked to growing suspicion about the relative values of 'high art' and popular or mass culture: the traditional dismissal of the latter (as trivial and unworthy of serious critical attention) at the expense of the former (as uplifting, concerned with 'serious' matters). While the exporting of American culture (particularly after the Second World War) can certainly be seen and denounced as cultural imperialism, here the French writers' focus was on the *democratizing* and aesthetic possibilities of popular cinema; a reappraisal of the artistic merits of a popular form was begun in reaction against the widespread class-snobbery of 'high art'.

This led the *Cahiers* group to examine the films made by a particular director to try to find common themes or signs of a characteristic film-making style. Feeling confident that they could indeed find, for example, common themes and preoccupations in many of John Ford's films, and a coherent characteristic use of *mise en scène* in the work of Vincente Minnelli, they boldly argued what had not been argued before: that many directors (in Hollywood but also by extension elsewhere), despite working in a 'scientific management' industrial system, nevertheless managed to shape 'their' films so that the films which they had directed had something in common; the director's 'style' or world-view was a kind of 'authorial' signature linking her/his films. While not denying that any film was subject to many other influences, the *Cahiers* group asserted that the director was an *auteur* – or, failing this, a *metteur en scène*. The distinction was between those directors (*auteurs*) whose films showed a more or less consistent set of themes or preoccupations which was developed through many or all of their films in a coherent, individual way, and those directors whose 'authorship' was detectable principally at a stylistic level but whose films lacked a coherent 'world-view': these were the *metteurs en scène*.

Many of the films of Douglas Sirk, for example (and especially *All I Desire*, 1953; *Magnificent Obsession*, 1954 ; *All that Heaven Allows*, 1956 and *Written on the Wind*, 1957), consistently explore family and gender relations in middle-class America; Sirk's use of the melodrama/'women's weepie' genre is now widely agreed to have enabled a biting critique of American society which would probably not have been possible in other genres of the time. Many of John Ford's films (most of which were westerns or war films) explore the place of a certain kind of masculinity in American culture. This means that Sirk and Ford have been seen as *auteurs*.

CASE STUDY

Alfred Hitchcock

The British director Alfred Hitchcock made some 57 films in a career spanning over 50 years; his first film as director was *The Pleasure Garden* (1925) and his last was *Family Plot* (1976), completed at the age of 76.

Having established himself as a 'master of suspense' in Britain by 1938, and at a peak in terms of reputation, Hitchcock then gave in to the lure of Hollywood. After some hits and some misses in the 1940s, he then entered his most successful phase working at Warner Brothers, Paramount and Universal. His films during this period included *Strangers on a Train* (1951), *I Confess* (1953), *Dial M for Murder* (1954), *Rear Window* (1954), *The Trouble with Harry* (1955), *The Man Who Knew Too Much* (1956), *Vertigo* (1958), *North by Northwest* (1959), *Psycho* (1960), *The Birds* (1963), *Marnie* (1964) and *Torn Curtain* (1966).

Among the themes which have excited the attention of film critics and theorists are guilt and religion, knowledge, looking and voyeurism, and obsessive/troubled relationships between men and women, and particularly their mothers . . . a potent brew!

If it is possible to play the amateur psychologist (see p. 211) and point to Hitchcock's strict Catholic upbringing and to his troubled relationship with his own mother, these are not the main aims of the *auteur* theorist. The important point in establishing Hitchcock's status as *auteur* is to analyse and chart how the above themes run through many of his films.

Thus, for example, the theme of guilt is evident as early as *The Tenant* (1926) and *Blackmail* (1929). The latter is usually described as the first British sound film; it also involves some rudimentary special effects (quite innovative at the time) which helped Hitchcock to develop the pursuit scenes which were to mark a number of his later films.

'Guilt' here is much more than the common plot device of 'is he guilty?' or 'will her guilt be discovered?'. Many of Hitchcock's films are complex examinations of the very idea of 'guilt', whether 'real' or imagined. The religious (Catholic) dimension of feelings of guilt is explicitly explored, for example, in such films as *I Confess*, but is never far below the surface, for instance in *Strangers on a Train* and *Vertigo*.

Many of Hitchcock's films are concerned with investigation, thus with watching and spying and the relation between knowledge, looking and voyeurism. In *Rear Window* the central character is played by James Stewart; the fact that he is hardly referred to by name may indicate his status as an 'everyman' voyeur. Confined to his room with a broken leg, he indulges his investigative drive (he is a photographer/reporter) by watching his neighbours, eventually through binoculars and then using a telephoto lens. The viewer thus shares his observation of several minor narratives; these include a lonely woman who almost attempts suicide after failing to meet a man through a lonely-hearts agency, and a couple of newlyweds on honeymoon. . .

He begins to suspect foul play in an apartment facing his own across the courtyard, but is unable to convince his police friend to take it seriously. Instead, his (female) nurse and his girlfriend (played by Grace Kelly) become his accomplices and do his legwork. When his girlfriend risks her own safety by entering the suspected murderer's flat to find evidence, she is discovered by the killer. He hastens to Stewart's apartment to kill him, but the latter outwits the killer (by *blinding* him with flashbulbs). Though he breaks his other leg in the ensuing fight, Stewart solves the case and the killer is caught. The last shot of the film seems to tell us that our voyeur has decided to give up spying on the neighbours: he is resting, asleep at the open window. But this is how the film began. . .

Attached to the convenient hook of a murder mystery, *Rear Window* is in fact itself a complex investigation of the act of looking and its pleasures. Through manipulation of point of view and through editing, the spectator is obliged to (at least partly) identify with the central character's peeping tom activities (see Figure 9.3). The critique of cinematic voyeurism may be less radical and more playful than in *Peeping Tom* (Michael Powell, 1960), but *Rear Window* is more about looking than it is about a simple detective story.

Other Hitchcock films which involve explicit themes of looking/voyeurism would have to include Norman Bates watching Marion Crane through a hidden spyhole in *Psycho*, Scottie's

Are we all voyeurs? Rear Window (Paramount, courtesy Kobal)   Figure 9.3

obsession with recreating an image of Madeleine in *Vertigo*, and themes of spying and perform-ance in *North by Northwest*.

The third important theme in Hitchcock's films is the often troubled relationship of a central (usually male) character with women, and particularly with an (often strange) mother. Among early examples would be the threatening mother-figure in *The Man Who Knew Too Much* (1934) (and in Hitchcock's own 1956 remake). The theme is taken up in earnest in the American films between 1951 and the late 1960s. In *Strangers on a Train* Bruno (Tony Curtis) has a very odd relationship with his mother. The spy-thriller plot involving smuggled microfilm in *North By Northwest* is a good example of a 'McGuffin', a plot red herring; the central theme and subject of the film is the work-ing through of Roger Thornhill's (Cary Grant's) Oedipal relationship with his mother. Norman Bates (Anthony Perkins) in *Psycho* of course has the unhealthiest relationship of all with his mother. The mother figures in *The Birds* and *Marnie* (the latter the mother of a *female* character) are also con-structed as disturbing figures.

Effects of the *Politique*

The discovery of common strands – both thematic and stylistic – in a director's work is rather more complex than it may seem here. In the 1970s and beyond, psychoanalytic theory and semiology were used to carry out many detailed analyses of the work of Hitchcock and many other directors (see Further Reading for this chapter and for Chapter 12) and to explore their contributions as *auteurs*.

By contrast, other directors were praised for their mastery of the filmic art of storytelling, but were seen to lack the thematic coherence of the *auteur*. A good example would be William Wyler, whose exploration of the social problems exposed by soldiers returning from the Second World War in *The Best Years of Our Lives* (1946) was seen as a masterpiece of *mise en scène*, but whose other better-known work included films from a number of quite different genres: the dangerous-female melodrama *Jezebel* (1938), the in-praise-of-British-war-spirit *Mrs Miniver* (1942), the western *The Big Country* (1958), the Roman Epic *Ben Hur* (1959), and a musical: *Funny Girl* (1968). Directors such as Wyler, Minnelli, Michael Curtiz and John Huston could then be seen as expert technicians, in contrast to the *auteurs* who succeeded, against the industrial odds, in expressing something of their own sensibility, and were therefore closer relations to the more obvious 'authors' of the art cinema.

While the *Cahiers* polemic of course shocked the French cinematic Establishment, the *politique* had important effects on film-making itself as well as on ideas of authorship in film theory. We shall look a little more at the French New Wave in a later chapter; here we can note that the *Cahiers* articles were instrumental in launching the film-making careers of several of the journal's writers, most importantly those of Truffaut, Godard, Chabrol, Rohmer and Rivette.

The effect on thinking about film was less immediate but no less profound. While *Cahiers du cinéma* continued to examine the films of Ford, Minnelli, Hitchcock, Huston and many others, and engaged in a debate with the rival left-wing journal *Positif* about the value of the *politique des auteurs*, theorists elsewhere and particularly in Britain and North America digested the work.

An important factor in the 'migration' and assimilation of 'theory' in other countries/ intellectual cultures has always been availability of texts in translated form. While the Internet is clearly able to drastically reduce the time needed for a text to become available in translation, the 'history of theory' has been much shaped by this factor in the past. Thus the *Cahiers* articles which appeared in the early 1950s were only published in English in the mid-1960s. While theoretical arguments continued (and have not ended) over the exact *extent* to which a Hollywood director could be considered an *auteur*, the study of directors became intellectually acceptable, indeed fashionable.

The *Auteur* Concept in Britain

The *auteur* concept was taken up in different ways in Britain and in the USA. British films have often been described in terms of their more 'realist' traditions and indeed a preference for 'uncinematic' cinema; there is a long history of disparagement of British cinema (rather like its cricket team really. . .). One quote may stand in for many others: 'I do not think the British are temperamentally equipped to make the best use of the movie camera.' (Ray, 1976, p. 144.)

Put another way, British cinema had, since the documentary influence of Flaherty and Grierson in the 1920s and 1930s, been generally less concerned with 'film as art' than with film as some kind of reflection of/commentary on the reality of social life. This persistent tradition was evident in initial reactions – in both film-making and film criticism – to the *Cahiers* polemic. While much British film production continued to seek to inflect Hollywood's commercial working practices with a particularly British (or rather English) sensibility, the direction taken by 'independent' film-making was much more concerned with 'social realism' and less concerned with authorial investigation of film as 'art'. The key moments of British cinema of the late 1950s and early 1960s were thus the 'Free Cinema' of Lindsay Anderson, Karel Reisz and Tony Richardson, and the British New Wave which explored naturalist 'kitchen sink' realism (see Chapter 13).

British film criticism and theory, though also heavily influenced by the documentary/realist tradition, did begin to address the issue of authorship, and three journals were central to this critical debate. *Sight and Sound*, originally founded in 1932, had during the 1950s come to concentrate on art cinema and the aesthetic, and thus on the art film director as an art *auteur*; the journal was on the whole hostile at the time to the idea of treating Hollywood directors as *auteurs*. A rival journal, *Movie*, though quintessentially British, was, as its name implies, more favourable to American films and between its beginning in 1962 and well into the 1970s developed its own brand of auteurist criticism, exemplified in the work of Victor Perkins.

The third and 'youngest' journal, *Screen*, though it only began in 1971, became the lead-ing British film theory journal of the 1970s and 1980s (in a history of the politics of the editorial policies of film journals, *Screen* would merit several chapters). As part of this devel-opment it increasingly promoted and engaged with French film theory and was instrumental in the evolution of a British strain of 'structuralist *auteur* criticism' (also heavily influenced by Marxist and psychoanalytic theory) which sought to extend French *auteur* analysis through *structuralist* analysis of film-texts, exemplified by the work of Peter Wollen on Hitchcock, Godard and others (see Chapter 8). It is interesting that while this kind of 'cine-structuralism' sought to unearth previously undiscovered themes common to particular directors through structuralist methods derived from Claude Lévi-Strauss, Vladimir Propp and others, it also (sometimes explicitly, sometimes implicitly) stressed 'the death of the author': the 'author' was an 'effect of the text'; the 'author' 'Hitchcock' (in inverted commas) was to be found *in the text*; the simpler words Alfred Hitchcock were reserved for the real flesh-and-blood person. These assaults on the concept of authorship are discussed further below.

The 'Auteur Theory'

By comparison with the sometimes obscurely theoretical turn of events in film culture in Britain, the influence of the *Cahiers politique* in the United States was no less important. It was writer/critic Andrew Sarris who, between 1962 and 1968, elaborated the '*auteur* theory' which has so often been confused with the original *politique*. His championing of the *auteur* idea involved a rejection of the then-dominant 'social realism' writing of most American critics, and was related to the growing availability of (old) films on television (and subsequently on video). This increased availability of previously dismissed films for a wider audience (including film critics and theorists) facilitated a reappraisal of those films and their directors.

Having dispensed with the finer points of the *Cahiers* argument, Sarris proceeded to elab-orate his criteria for a 'pantheon' – amounting to a kind of league table of directors, placing most known directors in one of several categories:

> I am now prepared to stake my critical reputation, such as it is, on the proposition that Alfred Hitchcock is artistically superior to Robert Bresson by every criterion of excellence, and, further, that, film for film, director by director, the American cinema has been con-sistently superior to that of the rest of the world from 1915 through 1962. Consequently, I now regard the *auteur* theory primarily as a critical device for recording the history of the American cinema, the only cinema in the world worth exploring in depth beneath the frost-ing of a few great directors at the top.
>
> (Sarris, 1962/3, pp. 5–6)

It is to be noted that there is in Sarris's categories a strong evaluative sense (some directors are great, some others are better than the rest. . .) which is almost completely absent from the more structuralist British approach and which runs counter to the polemical thrust of the original *Cahiers* writers, whose principal aim was the critical rehabilitation of Hollywood directors as a species.

POSTSTRUCTURALISM AND RECENT DEVELOPMENTS

Subsequent poststructuralist and postmodern theoretical developments (see Chapter 12) have posed further difficult questions about the concept of authorship. Is the 'author' the real person called Quentin Tarantino, is it an effect of the film-text (the 'Quentin Tarantino' of *Pulp Fiction*, say), or is it something that lives in the reader/viewer's head (Figure 9.3)? Indeed, after Roland Barthes, are we not *all* 'authors' who 'write' our own films in our heads as we watch them? And apart from the theoretical argument, the advent of video and more recently DVD means that it is now possible (for some spectators) to control the experience of film viewing in strange new ways: 'interactive' DVD systems will enable viewers to literally construct their own narratives from, say, an image/sound bank labelled '*Pulp Fiction*'. One of the websites listed at the end of this book enables the student of film to re-edit the shower sequence from *Psycho* almost at will.

At the same time, the distinction between 'art' and commercial/entertainment films has, since the late 1950s and the start of the *auteur* debate, become increasingly blurred as mainstream films continue to adopt formal strategies which were once seen as avant-gardist and 'arty' (see p. 150). Whether it is Ford or Hitchcock, Tarantino or

Figure 9.4   *Quentin Tarantino or 'Quentin Tarantino'? (BFI Stills, Posters and Designs)*

Lynch, Jarman or Duras, the idea of the director as the most significant creative influence on a film has passed into everyday mythology; while some would have gone to see *Eyes Wide Shut* for the sex, some for the stars and some more problematically for the genre, few would have been unaware of Kubrick's reputation as a director – or at least of his recent death.

Indeed, the increased celebrity status of many 'Hollywood' directors can, as we have already suggested, be dated to the breakdown of the classic Hollywood Studio System in the 1950s and the threat to cinema-going posed by television and other social/demographic changes which affected choice of leisure activities. The fame and quasi-'art cinema' author-status of the 'movie brats' such as Scorsese, Spielberg and Coppola who emerged between 1971 and 1974 (and of more recent 'name' directors) are largely due to the lack of permanence/stability in contemporary studio and industrial structures. Most particularly, it is now the director who has taken over many of the functions previously carried out by the producer and which arguably made the latter something of an 'author'. While producers of the 1930s and 1940s would typically find story material, see it developed into a screenplay, do the casting and oversee production and postproduction/editing, the producer since the 1960s has increasingly become 'an agent, a packager, a promoter, or a financial man' (Pandro Berman, producer at RKO and MGM, quoted in Kent, 1991, p. 182).

Conclusion

Finally and in summary: should the student of film accept the idea of director as 'author'? The answer seems to be no and yes. In stressing the terms film *industry*, show *business* and dream *factory*, Richard Maltby has asserted that 'authorship remains an inadequate explanation of how movies work' (1995, p. 33). Yet by analysing ways in which individual directors were/are able to produce a stylistic or thematic 'signature' in 'their' films, the *auteur* concept has reasserted the possibility of individual agency in the context of the corporate capitalism of the studio system of the mid- and late twentieth century.

As a postscript to this chapter, and echoing earlier remarks about other sources of 'authorship' in film, we should perhaps note that the very concept of director has been called into question by recent films. For example, Daniel Myrick and Eduardo Sanchez are credited as directors, screenwriters and editors for *The Blair Witch Project*. Yet almost all the footage for the film was shot without the directors present. . . Given the proliferation of public access programmes and channels on TV (particularly in the USA), are the days of the director as currently defined numbered? Just as rappers deliberately sample other texts and DJs such as Carl Cox attain star status by sampling and mixing music 'authored' by music artists, will films also become just another source for postmodern recycling?

Exercise 9.2

1. Discuss the *auteur* status of any director of your choice; how does the director's contribution compare to the contributions of others (e.g. scriptwriter(s), camera-person, editor) who work on a film?
2. Is the 'world-view' expressed in a film that of the director? Is it an important mark of 'authorship'?
3. Compare a recent/contemporary director (e.g. Tarantino, Cameron, Bigelow) with one from classic Hollywood cinema (e.g. Hitchcock, Ford, Curtiz). How has the 'authorial' role of the director changed?

SUMMARY

- The idea of individual authorship is a problem in a collaborative medium such as film-making.
- The idea of the talented author is itself historically specific.
- It is possible (particularly for pre-Second World War films) to argue authorship status for a number of film-making personnel such as camera operator, producer, studio head, etc.
- There are important differences between the director's role in Hollywood and other mainstream entertainment films on the one hand and 'art' films on the other.
- The idea of Hollywood director as author/*auteur* dates from arguments first presented in the French journal *Cahiers du cinéma* in the 1950s.
- A distinction can be made between Hollywood directors who are/were expert technicians ('*metteurs en scène*') and true '*auteurs*' whose films can be seen to express some kind of 'artistic vision'.
- The idea of directorial authorship was taken up in different ways in Great Britain and the USA.
- The 'cult of the director' is flourishing as we enter the twenty-first century, but the reasons may be less to do with authorship than with brand-name marketing.

REFERENCES

Nicholas Kent, *Naked Hollywood: Money, Power and the Movies* (London: BBC, 1991).

Colin MacCabe, *Performance* (London: BFI Film Classics, 1998).

Richard Maltby, *Hollywood Cinema* (Oxford: Blackwell, 1995).

Satyajit Ray, *Our Films, Their Films* (Bombay: Orient Longman, 1976).

Paul M. Sammon, *Future Noir: The Making of Blade Runner* (New York: Harper, 1996).

Andrew Sarris, 'Notes on the Auteur theory in 1962', in *Film Culture*, no. 27, Winter 1962/63.

Peter Wollen, *Study Guide No. 9: Orson Welles* (London: BFI Education Department, 1969, reprinted 1977).

FURTHER READING

David Bordwell and Kristin Thompson, *Film Art: An Introduction* (5th edn, New York: McGraw-Hill, 1998).

Gill Branston and Roy Stafford, *The Media Student's Book* (London: Routledge, 1996).

Pam Cook and Mieke Bernink (eds), *The Cinema Book* (2nd edn, London: BFI, 1999).

John Hill and Pamela Church Gibson (eds), *The Oxford Guide to Film Studies* (Oxford: Oxford University Press, 1998), Part 2 Chapter 7, pp. 310–26.

Jill Nelmes (ed.), *An Introduction to Film Studies* (2nd edn, London: Routledge, 1999).

Michael O'Pray, 'The big wig', in *Sight and Sound*, vol. 9, no. 10 (October 1999), pp. 20–2 (on Andy Warhol).

Victor Perkins, *Film as Film* (Harmondsworth: Pelican, 1974).

George Turner, 'Sharp practice', in *Sight and Sound*, vol. 9, no. 7 (July 1999), pp. 24–6 (on Gregg Toland).

Sight and Sound has long been a good, 'respectable' film journal; since the 1970s, however, a number of more 'theoretical' (and difficult) journals began to appear. It is recommended that, where your own educational institution's resources allow it, you try to have a look at back numbers of some of the following British journals: *Screen, Framework, Film Form, Undercut* and *Block*. Among equally prestigious North American journals of the time were *Jump Cut, Wide Angle, Cineaste, Velvet Light Trap* and *Camera Obscura*. It should be noted that these theoretical film journals, almost without exception, assumed a Marxist, feminist, anti-establishment position.

FURTHER VIEWING

Hitchcock on Hitchcock (BBC2, 1999).
Reputations: Alfred Hitchcock (BBC2, 1999).
Scene By Scene: Roman Polanski (BBC2, 2000).
Scene By Scene: Woody Allen (BBC2, 2000).

Genre

The use of genres within the film industry is so common that we usually do not question their function. We tend to use genre categorizations without being aware of them. Video stores physically divide up space through classifying videos by genre, and film promotional campaigns, whether trailers in cinemas, adverts on television or posters on billboards, often explicitly refer to a film's genre and at least implicitly indicate what type of film it is. What we don't often think about is *why* films tend to be divided up into genres and how they can be identified as belonging to a particular genre. Nor do we tend to concern ourselves with how genre conventions structure films and how the industry and audiences use genres. This chapter looks at these issues and some of the debates surrounding the theory and practice of film genre. The ways in which genres change over time are identified along with an evaluation of the usefulness of genre studies.

GENRE AS REPETITION AND DIFFERENCE

Genre is a French word meaning 'type', and film genres have existed since the early days of cinema. Films were frequently categorized as being crime, romance, comedy, fantasy or actuality. It is to be noted though that the descriptions given to particular types of films have frequently changed, along with the identification of new genres. Edwin Porter's *The Great Train Robbery* (1903) was initially described as a crime/chase movie but is now regarded as a western. Similarly, Méliès' *Journey to the Moon* (1901) was referred to as fantasy whereas nowadays it would be identified as science fiction. Classification of films into genres helped the industry to organize production and marketing in terms of making use of available and suitable props, locations, actors and production staff, as well as promoting films as being of a particular type. Audiences in turn used the marketing descriptions of films as a guide to what to expect.

However, while the use of genre has a long history in film, it has a far longer general history which dates back to Ancient Greece, at which time Aristotle categorized theatre plays by type. Nowadays most cultural production, be it television, magazines, music, painting or literature, ends up being assigned to one genre or another. In all cases what makes a genre possible is the existence of common elements across a range of productions. In other words, it is the identification of repetition across a series of productions that results in them being described as being of a particular type. An important term in genre analysis is 'convention', meaning the way in which something is usually done. Because certain films tend to do things in particular ways, we recognize similarities between them and consequently describe them as belonging to a particular genre.

If repetition is a key requirement for the identification of a particular genre, then so too is difference. When watching a film we become aware not only of how it is similar to other films but also of how it differs. Genres exist not only because there is repetition across a number of films, but also because there are differences across a range of films. The demarcation of films by genre emphasizes the differences between these types.

The concept of difference has further significance for genre categorization. It was noted earlier that genres had importance for both industry and audience during the formative years of cinema, and this became even more the case as the industry established itself further, especially with the consolidation of the American film industry during the 1930s through the Hollywood Studio System (see Chapter 1). The industry had become adept at demarcating the market, with accompanying benefits both for production and for targeting audiences through the use of genre conventions. However, the problem for the industry was that genre production could easily result in films that were repetitive, predictable and formulaic. Indeed, the emergence of art cinema, which tends to consist of non-genre films, was seen by many as a reaction to the over-use of successful formulas by the industry which stifled creativity and experimentation in film. It was therefore imperative that difference be an ingredient within genres as well as between genres. Genre films had to be not just 'more of the same' but also 'something different'; they needed variation, innovation, flexibility and change, albeit within the general parameters of the genre.

Style often results in difference being created within a genre, but it can also result in difference between films of the same genre that are basically telling the same story. Many of the classic horror films from the 1930s, such as *Dracula* and *Frankenstein*, both from 1931, have been remade several times over but in different styles. The originals were no doubt frightening at the time of their release and visually their influence can been seen in later versions, but the originals now appear rather slow, theatrical, tame and uncontroversial. The remakes by Hammer Films essentially told the same story but were stylistically very different. *Dracula* (1958) updates the vampire tale for a new generation of cinemagoers in a new cultural context. The 'X' certificate rating enabled Hammer to go further in trying to shock, which they attempted to do through more violence and gore and greater emphasis on the sexual nature of Count Dracula's relationship with his female victims. The many horror films made by Hammer in effect established a sub-genre of Hammer horror through considerable continuity in style, actors, themes and directors. More recent remakes of 1930s horror films have included *Bram Stoker's Dracula* (1992) and *Mary Shelley's Frankenstein* (1994), both of which tell more complex tales than had the earlier versions.

While remakes are fairly common, usually a significant period of time elapses before a film is reinterpreted, as with the above example. However, a recent notable exception is *Nikita* (1990). It is the story of a drug addict who shoots a policeman and is sentenced to death, but is pardoned so long as she agrees to become a government assassin. The film is by the French director Luc Besson. However, a Hollywood remake was released just three years later; *The Assassin* (1993) told almost exactly the same story, to the point where repetition becomes noticeable; stylistically, however, the two films are radically different despite having a common story and genre. *Nikita* is widely regarded as the 'better' of the two, perhaps because it not only tells an interesting story but also contains impressive direction of camera, lighting, music and acting. By contrast, *The Assassin* concentrates on telling the story as clearly as possible and thus perhaps loses some of the subtlety of the original while not being as visually memorable.

Another remake which differs stylistically from the original is *Shaft* (2000). The original *Shaft* of 1971, though belonging to the crime genre, carried the label 'blaxploitation'. It was made during the US era of Black Power politics and the main black detective character was a break with stereotypes of blacks as subservient and second-class. The 2000 remake no longer needs to challenge such stereotypes in the same way and concentrates on being an action/crime film. With its big budget and well-known stars, the new version is a mainstream movie; the original was a cult film with a political message.

Unsurprisingly Hollywood succeeded in combining repetition and difference in its films, at least to the point where audiences regularly returned to view genre films. A further way in which Hollywood has categorized films is through the use of stars as a means of identifying and targeting films and audiences (see Chapter 11). A film would be referred to as a John Wayne film rather than as a western, a Marilyn Monroe film rather than a comedy/romance. In contemporary Hollywood, categorization has often come to include reference to the director (see Chapter 9 on Authorship). We get a Scorsese film rather than a gangster movie, a George Lucas film rather than a science fiction film. However, the main problem with categorizing films by reference to individuals is that we are restricted to a particular era of films. With such a classification, we cannot trace changes over an extended period of time in the way we can with genre classification.

The ultimate effect of the repetition, common elements and conventions found within genres is to create particular repertoires of elements, a range of possibilities all of which in effect limit what is possible. The conventions of individual genres define the parameters within which a genre film will normally operate. The choices available within the western genre would not normally include song and dance routines and slapstick comedy, and if we came across such a film it would probably be *Blazing Saddles* (1974) by Mel Brooks or the earlier *Cat Ballou* (Silverstein, 1965) and would be referred to as a western spoof or pastiche.

The use of a repertoire of elements ends up creating a self-contained world structured by genre conventions. For the duration of a film we experience a world defined and limited by these conventions. Consistency is essential if this 'genre world' is to be believable, so in effect genre films need to create realism within the confines of their conventions. The term *verisimilitude* describes the quality of being believable, the appearance of being real, plausibility. However, this believability is placed very much within a fictional world and is dependent upon maintaining consistency in the elements used in the genre film. Verisimilitude can be contrasted with *realism*, which is the representation of a reality, a world that recognizably exists outside the film itself. However, the concept of realism is problematic and there is often disagreement about its definition (see Chapter 6).

Exercise 10.1

With reference to your own favourite genre film, list its generic features and note how it differs from other films of the same genre. What do you find appealing about the film?

FILM GENRE, IMAGE AND SOUND

Genre categorization can also be problematic, however. On one level, understanding genres is simple; we can identify recurring elements with regard to narrative themes, characters, plots and visual content such as location, props and costume; sound can also be a recurring element, particularly in terms of music appropriate to a particular genre. However, we soon come up against the problem of films that don't quite fit a genre, films which seem to cover several genres and films that appear to be a particular style of a particular genre. Thus while we can refer to the western genre or crime/detective genre, some films may be identified as spaghetti westerns or *film noir*. Such films are often referred to as belonging to a sub-genre, a genre within a genre, although in the case of *film noir* this is disputed by some who see it as a style of the crime/detective genre but think it sufficiently different to have its own genre, a point we will return to later in this chapter.

The most immediate way in which we identify a genre is usually by the visual elements in a film. The film's narrative may take a while to reveal the genre but the visual signification tends to be immediate. However, it is possible that sound could first indicate genre through theme music at the beginning of a film, and with comedy, romance and melodrama, the narrative, rather than the iconography, could well indicate the genre. The theme music of *Blade Runner* (1982) hints at the science fiction genre before we see any images; the music would seem out of place if used to introduce another genre. If used at the beginning of *Notting Hill* (1999), the music would raise inappropriate expectations. Similarly, the placing of a spacecraft in *Notting Hill* would undermine the expectations raised by the comedy/romance genre.

Sound and image indicate genre through the use of signs. Signs represent and communicate particular meanings, and audio-visual content functions as signs. However, for a sign to be readily understood by an audience, it needs to be a part of a well-established system of communication, in effect, a part of a language system belonging to a genre. If the film-maker uses audio-visual signs appropriately, then an audience that is aware of the genre conventions will generally understand the intended meanings. Intended meanings are encoded into signs by the film-maker and the audience decodes the signs to reveal the meanings. It is the regular use over a period of time of particular signs that establishes them as conventions and builds up the language system for a particular genre.

Although we have identified the role that 'sound signs' have within genres, film tends to be primarily regarded as a visual medium, and so attention often concentrates on the visual signs found within genre films, a point elaborated on by Colin McArthur in his analysis of the gangster genre.

> The recurrent patterns of imagery can be usefully divided into three categories: those surrounding the physical presence, attributes and dress of the actors and the characters they play; those emanating from the milieus within which the characters operate; and those connected with the technology at the characters' disposal.
>
> (1972, p. 24)

The study of visual signs and their meanings is known as *iconography*, icons being visual representations. Icons, as visual signs, give away the genre of a film. Iconography is about the meanings carried by genre elements such as location, props and costumes.

This may sound very similar to *mise en scène*, as both are obviously concerned with what elements are placed within a shot. However, iconography refers to how location, props and costume produce meanings through the broad cultural agreement that exists about what these visual signs refer to – meaning is collectively determined. *Mise en scène* emphasizes the way in which the director produces meanings through the selection and arrangement of location, props and costume – meaning is more individually influenced. The contrast between iconography and *mise en scène* can be broadened out into the opposing perspectives of genre analysis and authorship, the former having been elaborated on by Jim Kitses and Will Wright among others, the latter theorized in the French journal *Cahiers du cinéma* in the 1950s. Genres are seen as relying upon a general understanding of the conventions used and the meanings they produce, whereas authorship focuses on the ways in which meanings originate with the director or possibly with a star or cinematographer. Similarly genres may be associated with restricting what is possible through their structuring tendencies – manifesting themselves, for instance, in the conventions of a western – while authorship is seen as allowing personal creativity and vision; hence the existence of genre cinema and art cinema. However, as we saw in the last chapter, attempts have also been made to reconcile both perspectives, with directors being seen to manipulate genre parameters and use them creatively.

One of the richest genres for iconography is the western, from obvious icons such as barren landscapes, horses and guns to the occasional appearance of windblown tumbleweed (Figure 10.1). It would be misleading, however, to imagine that specific genres require specific visual elements, because iconography can be relatively flexible. As mentioned earlier, one distinctive type of western is the spaghetti western, so called because these productions were based in Italy as costs were lower than in the USA. Filming often took place in Spain, again for financial reasons, and this gave such westerns a different look – the impressive mountainous scenery of many traditional American westerns was often replaced

Unforgiven: western location, props and costume (Warner Bros, courtesy Kobal)   Figure 10.1

by flat desert locations. Spaghetti westerns, especially those directed by Sergio Leone (*The Good, the Bad and the Ugly*, 1966), were noticeably stylized in contrast to mainstream American westerns. The use of extreme camera angles and of cutting from extreme long shots to extreme close ups, not necessarily for any obvious reason, gave such westerns a different look compared with the American western. However, the identification of visual stylistic differences highlights the limits of iconography in its ability to identify and explain visual content. Iconography cannot account for the use of camera or for editing, which also crucially shape a film visually. These film techniques are to be found across a range of genres and are not necessarily specific to one genre.

Exercise 10.2
What possible meanings do the lighting, props, location and actors carry in the shot from *Double Indemnity* illustrated in Fig 10.2?

Double Indemnity: low key lighting and a femme fatale with murder in mind   Figure 10.2
(Paramount, courtesy Kobal)

Film noir is strongly identifiable by its iconography; regardless of whether it is a genre, sub-genre or style of the crime/detective genre, it is unusual in that its categorization was created by film theorists as a descriptive tool rather than by the industry as a marketing tool. Visually, *noir* films, as you would expect from the name, are dark. Low key lighting is frequently used, with resulting silhouettes and shadows, and light is often fragmented through Venetian blinds with alternating black and white shafts of light splayed across walls and ceilings. An urban setting is the usual location, with the addition of rain to complete the forbidding picture. Cigarettes and glasses of whisky are common props. *Double Indemnity* (1944) uses such iconography extensively. It is a classic example of *film noir*, complete with deep shadows, strong contrasts between light and dark and gloomy, forbidding locations (Fig 10.2). However, it needs to be noted that the use of low key lighting has also been explained as necessary in order to hide the fact that set designs were often of low quality as a result of material constraints. Certainly *film noir* characteristics have persisted through stylistic variations, resulting in the label *neo-noir* being applied to films such as *The Long Goodbye* (1973) and *Chinatown* (1974), and the *tech noir* of *Blade Runner* (1982) and *The Matrix* (1999).

FILM GENRE AND NARRATIVE

However, *film noir* is more than just the iconography mentioned above. Its narratives contain particular themes, characters and plots, and these can indicate genre too. The seductress is a central character in *film noir* narratives; the *femme fatale* is a deadly woman whose function is to tempt the lead male into committing a heinous crime, usually a murder, from which she will benefit. However, the *femme fatale* is usually outwitted, caught and punished in some way. The male lead tends to be a world-weary, cynical loner, often the archetypal 'hard-boiled' detective alienated from the society he lives in, as in the Sam Spade and Philip Marlowe characters created by Dashiell Hammett and Raymond Chandler. A common sound convention of *film noir* is the use of voice-over narration as a reflection on what has taken place. In *Double Indemnity*, the male lead provides a commentary to explain events, delivered in a hard, emotionless voice.

Morbid themes are central to *noir* narratives: the cold-blooded planning of murders, detail being dwelt upon and a lack of remorse are common. Underlying the plot and themes lies a paranoid wariness, a distrust of other human beings. Deceit and double-crossing accompany the other narrative elements and visual signifiers. Why such narratives, themes and visual style should have appeared between 1941 (*The Maltese Falcon*) and 1958 (*Touch of Evil*) is an interesting question which has been analysed by Colin McArthur, among others. Genre analysis looks for explanations within the society in which the film was produced. Is it possible that *noir* films were an expression of unease about changes within American society, especially against the backdrop of the Second World War? Women had gained greater independence, they increasingly held a strong position in the job market and their lives were not necessarily dedicated just to home and family. From a male perspective, this could have been seen as a challenge, as unsettling. American involvement in the war provided more space for women to take up employment as many males were called up, and the war itself raised dark issues, uncertainty and anxiety, all identified within *film noir*. The end of the Second World War was marked by the first use of an atom bomb, and the ensuing post-war angst about the possibility of global nuclear war also contributed to growing uncertainty and increased anxiety. It can therefore be seen that *film noir* provides a good illustration of how genre categorization is dependent upon more than visual conventions.

Thomas Schatz has written extensively on the importance of narrative in relation to genre categorization. He shifts attention away from iconography as the determining factor towards narrative themes, plots and characters. However, he goes further than many would by proposing that essentially there are only two categories of genres, 'genres of social integration and indeterminate space' and 'genres of social order and determinate space'. Schatz writes:

> Ultimately, genres of indeterminate, civilised space (musical, screwball comedy, social melodrama) and genres of determinate, contested space (western, gangster, detective) might be distinguished according to their differing ritual functions. The former tend to celebrate the values of *social integration*, whereas the latter uphold the values of *social order*.
>
> (1981, p. 29)

According to Schatz, the genres of social order/determinate space include westerns and gangster and detective films. Typically such films have a narrative that contains a male hero whose individual actions involve the use of violence to resolve conflicts within a society. A key theme in such films is lawlessness, and the problems developed within the narrative are ultimately resolved by the protagonist who creates or restores order by the end of the film. Such narratives also tend to take place within a clearly defined space or setting, necessitated by the narrative theme of gaining control over a particular community or locale. Iconography tends to be central to such narratives in that visual signifiers help define the contained world within which action takes place. A western such as *Unforgiven* (1992) is set in a relatively lawless society, as exemplified by the cowboy who attacks and injures a prostitute but goes unpunished by the sheriff. Justice and order are restored by Clint Eastwood, who shoots him. *Star Wars* (1977) centres on the conflict created by Darth Vader and the Death Star, who are destroying whole civilizations. It takes Luke Skywalker and friends to restore order to the universe through the destruction of the Death Star. *GoodFellas* (1990), as a gangster film, is concerned with gangsters as a lawless element within American society and with conflict in the gangster community, in which order is achieved through violence. A degree of order is achieved at a societal level when Henry gives evidence against his former gangster partners, thus ensuring that justice is done.

Schatz's genres of social integration/indeterminate space encompass musicals, comedies and melodramas. In such films there is a strong likelihood of the lead character being female, or the lead role may even be a collective position taken up by two or more characters rather than an individual male lead. The setting for the narrative tends to be stable and consensual as opposed to being based on conflict and opposition; thus the space within which the action takes place may not be clearly defined, because location is not necessarily a key issue. Similarly, iconography may be less important as the centrality of visual signifiers is displaced by an emphasis on emotions and ideological issues. The problems raised within the narrative are emotional and will generally be resolved through agreement or by co-operation rather than by physical and violent action. The key theme running through films belonging to this category is the peaceful resolution of conflict which results in the film's characters being integrated into a consensual community. Thus, in the musical *The Wizard of Oz* (1939), the temporarily wayward Dorothy is welcomed home by her family and community at the end of the film. The conflict in *Notting Hill* (1999) arises from the central characters' problematic relationship: Anna Scott is a wealthy American film star with a boyfriend; William Thacker is a book-shop owner struggling to make ends meet. Their emotional crises are resolved by the end of the film when Anna agrees to settle in England with William.

However, while such an approach is useful for concentrating attention on recurring themes, values and beliefs across several types of film, the two categories cannot always be clearly distinguished. *Alien* was a ground-breaking film in 1980 in terms of gender representation and complicated the idea of a genre of order by having a female lead in a science fiction film. Sigourney Weaver as Ripley is also attempting to preserve a 'community' in space, albeit through physical violence (Figure 10.3). The film is more than science fiction though, clearly encompassing horror with the inclusion of the alien as a monster. Horror films could generally be problematic for Schatz's categories; where, for instance, would you place a film such as *Scream* (1996)? While there is a violent resolution to the film and order is restored, key characters are female, relationships are an important theme and the community within which the narrative is set is generally integrated. It is of course also a comedy. *Thelma and Louise* (1991) also seems to suit both categories. Although the film is about the establishment of order through the shooting of a rapist, the film has two heroes who are female, and emotions, along with relationships, are key themes.

Schatz's categories nevertheless provide a useful approach to studying genre and can perhaps be thought of in terms of *genres of conflict*, in which a resolution is provided through violent confrontation, and *genres of consensus*, in which a resolution is provided through emotional agreement, with the possibility existing of a cross-over between both categories.

Figure 10.3   *Alien: gender role reversal (20th Century Fox, courtesy Kobal)*

> **Exercise 10.3**
> Choose one gangster film and one romance film. Note how far each film's narrative
> has developed before you can identify its genre and what narrative elements confirm
> that genre.

FILM GENRE, INDUSTRY AND AUDIENCE

Cinema, like all industries, is about the production of goods and services. The vast majority
of films are produced as commodities to be consumed, for profit. Films are big business,
subject to the 'laws' of commercial supply and demand. The industry will make films as long
as people want them. As with other industries, profits are maximized through efficient production methods, accurately matching supply to demand, and effective marketing. From an
industry perspective, genres have several uses which help fulfil these economic imperatives.

If genre films are particular types of film, it follows that such films require particular types
of scripts, acting, locations, props and costumes, and often need specialist equipment and
production staff for the actual shooting and editing. In effect, genre films lend themselves
to specialization at all levels of the production process and this increases the likelihood of
being able to maximize profits through the efficient use of existing resources. Genres are
about standardization, an industrial practice. The film industry aims to identify successful
formulas and recycle them, albeit in different guises.

Directors and stars will often work on particular types of film, and the industry will use
the reputations and expectations attached to directors and stars to help market films and
create demand (see Chapters 11 and 9 on Stars and Authorship). Genres enable the industry
to divide up the range of films that can be made; the market is demarcated. Market research
and the monitoring of audience trends inform the industry of what types of film are likely to
do well at the box office; genres can therefore be targeted at the audience that exists for
particular types of films.

The flip side of the industry using genres to target audiences is of course that the audience in turn uses genres to target particular films. Being able to identify the genre of a film
enables a cinemagoer to determine whether s/he is likely to enjoy a film or not. This raises
the question, however, of why audiences gain pleasure from genre films. Considering the
predictable elements in genre films, we can assume there are certain narrative themes and
visual elements that audiences are attracted to. This attraction can be analysed at a
psychological level, at the level of subjectivity, while also being linked to the social world,
the objective world of social relations, cultural values and ideology (see Chapter 12).

If we accept that there are certain attractions that draw audiences to see genre films,
how is the attraction maintained over a sustained period of time? Pleasure is often gained
through obtaining what we want and in the case of genre films, having one's expectations
met results in pleasure. We get what we want and our knowledge of the genre's characteristics is confirmed. In other words, we seek repetition of a past pleasure; we will, to a

degree, be able to predict what will happen, what characters will do. The use of recognizable character types and plots can also make a film easier to understand. However, as noted earlier, difference is also an integral part of genre production. The audience gains pleasure from
the introduction of variations on a theme and through identifying the ways in which conventions are reinterpreted and reinvented within the general parameters of the genre.

Though we should not ignore those films which, because of their non-adherence to
generic conventions, cannot easily be categorized, it must be noted that non-genre films
constitute a minority of films made and distributed and that, by and large, such films are not
hugely popular.

Tom Ryall's (1978) approach to genre has de-emphasized the importance of identifying
particular genre characteristics and has concentrated on the relationship between film, film-
maker and audience and the role that all three areas have in the production of meaning,
albeit within the general conventions of a genre. Although a film may be placed within a particular genre, the film-maker makes decisions about how to use the conventions, and ultimately the audience interprets the film for itself. Ryall also highlighted the importance of the
production context of a genre film in terms of finance and ownership, which then needs to
be placed in the overall social context of production and consumption. Thus for Ryall there
are a number of variables such as film, film-maker, audience, studio, industry, economy and
ideology, all of which need to be borne in mind when evaluating the function and effect of
genres. In other words the genre conventions to be found in a film and how they are used
are the result of a multiplicity of influences.

Steve Neale (1980) similarly focuses on industry, film and audience and their relation to
genre, while also emphasizing the function of expectations, conventions, repetition and
difference. However, Neale is not interested in the categorization of films as such and sees
overlap and flexibility between genres as the predominant feature. He also sees the need for
a psychoanalytic approach to genre study in order to identify the ways in which pleasure,
identity and the relationship of the subject to society are reflected, reinforced or shaped in
genre productions. Thus the determining potentials of the subconscious and of ideology are
important in Neale's perspective, which takes account of audience desire and its origins in
relation to the functions of genre films.

FILM GENRE, SOCIETY AND HISTORY

The previous section raised the question of why audiences tend to be drawn to genre
films, and also referred to the position of genres within the wider social context. In identifying the relationships between audiences, genre films and society, it is worth emphasizing that genre films, as cultural products, may very well carry the dominant ideologies
of the societies in which they are produced. Given the economic imperatives of the
industry, it is likely that cultural production will reflect societal values and beliefs. Moral
issues are raised, questions are asked and answers given. We are invited to evaluate a
character's actions and decisions, and imaginary solutions are offered to real problems
within society.

Genre films, and the stories or myths they tell, can be regarded as a society or culture communicating with itself, reflecting on what it consists of, explaining the world to itself, perhaps learning about itself by retelling aspects of the culture's experiences. It could be claimed that such films are not 'reflections' of society but are particular perceptions of a society. How we see such films might ultimately be determined by whether or not recurring patterns and themes can be identified.

In the case studies from the science fiction genre that follow, we shall see how it is possible to claim that the themes addressed by genre films do deal with issues and values predominant within a culture. Perhaps the most important point to note is that although a genre remains recognizable over an extended period of time, the style and themes within that genre change, reflecting changing beliefs. The values that are prevalent within a society can be reproduced within the structures of meaning in a film.

CASE STUDY

Science Fiction Case Studies

The science fiction genre rests upon what has become known as the 'what if?' question. We are encouraged to speculate about what life would be like if certain things happened, in other words, what our future would hold for us if our present world were radically transformed by the advance of science and technology or, of course, visitors from another planet. The science fiction genre enables contemporary issues relating to technological developments to be considered with regard to how they might change our future world. However, as we shall see, it can also be used to symbolize other concerns that are not related to scientific advances but which are very much to do with ideology.

Metropolis (Fritz Lang, Germany, 1926)

This German Expressionist film is set in the year 2000. The ruling class of Metropolis live above ground in luxury while the masses work below ground keeping the city functioning and their rulers living in luxury. The workers rebel and start destroying the machinery on which they work. Meanwhile a scientist is developing a robot that can do the jobs of the workers, and so the rulers are content to let the workers destroy the underground city. The film ends somewhat simplistically with both sides making peace, although what that peace involves is not really explained.

The early part of the twentieth century had seen social upheavals in Germany with continuing industrialization, high unemployment, an authoritarian government and defeat in the First World War. These issues were reflected in this film with its portrayal of an unjust, divided class society and a ruthless dictatorship. Distrust of authority and its misuse are key themes throughout Metropolis. The huge technological advances being made at the time created uncertainty for many and did not augur well for the future, and a fear of the future was the result of these rapid changes. This film reflects those fears about the potential of technology, especially when it is in the hands of an authoritarian government.

X the Unknown (Leslie Norman, UK, 1956)

Soldiers are searching for radioactive waste in a remote part of Scotland. An explosion occurs just before they return to base, leaving a gaping hole in the ground and soldiers suffering from radiation burns. Scientists discover that the fissure contains a mysterious creature that feeds on radiation; several deaths take place after this discovery. The creature grows in size and emerges from the hole to attack the army base and the local village. The creature is finally destroyed.

This is a film which dealt with contemporary issues and fears. Science and technology had made awesome advances in the study and use of the atom, with the resultant threats of nuclear war and exposure to radiation. These fears were given added urgency as the 'Cold War' was well under way by 1956, with the threat of war breaking out between the United States and the Soviet Union. Although the 'threat' of communism was not as big an issue in Britain as it was in the United States, there was still an element of 'red scare' paranoia that suggested communists could be among the British people, trying to take over. In this film the fear of atomic radiation is linked to the threat of the expanding creature taking over the army base and village but then possibly moving on to other areas of Britain.

2001: A Space Odyssey (Stanley Kubrick, UK, 1968)

2001 is a film that celebrates space, science and technology while also warning of what could happen if we lose control of such technology. In the film, HAL, the spaceship's central computer, takes over control of the spaceship from the crew. The space technology ends up inadvertently enabling the surviving astronaut to gain an insight into the nature of existence after an encounter with a form of extra-terrestrial. The film, like its source book, speculates on the origins of life, on the universe, on time and space.

The 1960s had seen successful missions into space and space travel was a strong contemporary issue. Space exploration was generally seen as a positive use of resources, but since humans had not yet landed on another planet, there were uncertainties about what was out there. The film deals with this fear of the unknown and warns of the danger of technology taking over. The film also coincided with the psychedelic era of the late 1960s and consciously used psychedelic imagery in some sequences.

Blade Runner (Ridley Scott, USA, 1982)

Blade Runner is set in Los Angeles in 2019. Replicants (robots/androids that look human but have superhuman abilities) have escaped and are to be hunted down by Deckard (Harrison Ford). There are points in the film when we are encouraged to wonder whether in fact the replicants are more humane than the humans. The replicants are denied the right to live as long as humans through a built-in life expectancy of four years; however, at the end of the film the last replicant, Roy, catches Deckard but saves his life just as his own is coming to an end.

Throughout the film this dystopian world always seems overcast and it is almost always raining. The film contains typical sci fi iconography but also has a dark, sombre urban setting with a strong use of low key lighting which is strongly reminiscent of film noir. The replicants are dangerous and are a product of scientific progress, much like the monster of Frankenstein; there are thus elements of the horror genre in Blade Runner, through the representation of the replicants as monstrous. The process of hunting down the replicants creates similarities with the crime/detective and action/adventure genres, and romance is provided by Deckard's relationship with the replicant Rachel.

In the early 1980s there was widespread concern over nuclear weapons and their continuing proliferation. The possibility of nuclear war raised the prospect of a 'nuclear winter' in which the skies would be darkened from the explosive fall-out, resulting in continual darkness and rain.

These concerns are mirrored through the location and lighting in *Blade Runner*. Debates had also developed about the nature of human subjectivity: what is it and where does it come from? The film investigates the issue of identity – what does it mean to be human? Can a replicant be just as human as we are? This debate is given urgency in the film with the proposal that in 2019 it will be possible to construct cyborgs that appear to be human; scientific and technological advances since 1982 may well have reinforced such a view.

From the above examples it can be seen that genres are flexible. While the iconography remains relatively similar, the narrative themes and styles can change over time as cultural values change and different ideological issues arise within society. However, it is perhaps important to recognize that genre films do not automatically reflect a society's dominant ideologies. It could be argued that genre films can challenge dominant ideas and question cultural values. Certainly, such a view could be regarded as more positive and optimistic as it would imply that we are not helplessly tied into a society's belief system. Our conclusions as to whether cultural products such as genre films reflect, reinforce or challenge a society's values will no doubt depend on the examples used, the analytic methods employed and the perspective from which we approach genre study.

Exercise 10.4

Choose two films of the same genre that were made at least twenty years apart. Identify the similarities and the differences between the two films, and try to link these to their historical contexts.

CONTEMPORARY FILM GENRES AND POSTMODERNISM

It will be noticed from the last example in the previous section, *Blade Runner*, that several genres have been identified in the film. Just as we have seen how genres are flexible as they change over time, it can perhaps also be claimed that flexibility and change can be introduced into genres by combining them. Although multi-genre films are nothing new (*Casablanca* contains at least three), it has been claimed that more recent films aim increasingly consciously for genre cross-over. Rick Altman notes that:

> Hollywood's early mixing of genres for publicity purposes was rudimentary at best, typically involving a small number of genres combined in an unspectacular and fairly traditional manner. Only rarely was attention drawn to disparities among the genres thus combined. Recent films, on the contrary, often use intertextual references and conscious highlighting of genre conventions to stress genre conflict.

(1999, p. 141)

This phenomenon has been identified as one aspect of what has been called the *postmodern* (see also pp. 223–5).

The term *postmodernism* begs an obvious question: what is modernism? Modernism is a term that has been used to describe developments in the arts and is one aspect of modernity. Modernity was built on the values of the eighteenth-century Enlightenment which foresaw a new age of science, reason, liberation, freedom and progress. The new outlook that emerged in the modern era was wide-ranging and encompassed the arts, science, philosophy, economics and politics. A strong element in this new outlook was the desire to explain the world, to provide answers.

From the perspective of film as cultural production, it is art that we are concerned with and modernist art became identified as such in the early twentieth century. Its initial theory and practice were based on progress and experimentation, which manifested themselves in film as well as other art forms. However by the 1980s some cultural theorists were claiming that the spirit of experimentation and progress had come to a halt around the 1950s. The implication was that there was nowhere else to go with art, everything had been tried, that modernism had come to an end.

The era that has followed is often referred to as postmodern. Its general approach has been to reject the notion that explanations and answers can be universally applied to humanity or to this world. Everything is regarded as relative, there are no valid 'grand theories', nothing is certain, there are no absolute truths and, from the point of view of the production of meaning through iconography and signs, there are no fixed meanings. All we have are *floating signifiers*. From the perspective of art and film, the inevitable conclusion is that if there is no more space for progress, no new ground to break, then the only possibility is to reuse and recycle, perhaps in different combinations, what has gone before. This is what we quite often get in contemporary cinema.

Several key concepts and practices have emerged in contemporary cinema which could be described as postmodern. As mentioned earlier, genre cross-over, resulting in multi-genre films, is common. This practice of genre amalgamation results in a mixing together of already existing types and styles of films and opens up new possibilities. Meaning can be produced in different ways; different types of stories can be told, new combinations are possible. The mixing together of genres is often referred to as *bricolage*: elements from various film types can be selected and pieced together. Such films are *hybrids*; they are eclectic in that there is no specific set of conventions to shape the film; the film-maker picks and chooses from a range of available influences. *Pastiche* is the result of bringing together unusual influences and types of material that often draw on genres and styles from cinema's past; this technique is marked by its deliberate and self-conscious nature. The result is an *intertextuality* in which films interact with each other rather than with issues taken, in one form or another, from the world outside the film. This can lead to a somewhat self-contained world which may be entertaining and interesting but runs the risk of heavy reliance on irony and of having little that is of relevance to the viewer.

Whether films that use postmodern techniques are successful or not may still depend on how well the genres and styles are integrated into a coherent, unified piece of cinema. A film such as *From Dusk Till Dawn* (1996), which deliberately and noticeably joins two completely different genres together in the middle of the film, obviously runs the risk of losing the audience's involvement in the storyline. *Blade Runner,* on the other hand, integrates the different genres into the narrative, and visually the different genres are not too difficult to separate from each other. The latter film also deals with postmodernity in relation to issues such as subjectivity, authenticity (the real versus the copy, human versus replicant) and the lack of answers or solutions; it is a fatalistic, dystopian film.

The Coen brothers are film-makers who regularly use postmodern techniques. Visually and thematically their films frequently employ some of the devices described above. *Barton Fink* (1991) contains the usual rich array of entertaining characters and dark humour associated with the Coens in a story set in 1930s Hollywood which follows several weeks in the life of a young scriptwriter. Thematically it is the film industry looking at itself, albeit via a comedy and across a time period of 60 years. *The Big Lebowski* (1998), another Coen brothers film, is again a successful comedy/thriller with an entertaining variety of characters. The most notable postmodern device is the use of occasional voice-over narration provided by an observer of the events who talks like an old western ranch hand, and when we eventually see him on the screen he matches our expectations with his cowboy attire. The laid-back cowboy drawl suits the film in many ways while visually being out of place; the borrowing of western iconography ultimately probably works because of the comic nature of the film. The beginning of the film completely misleads the viewer as the camera tracks over a typically barren western landscape, accompanied by some rolling tumbleweed that the camera follows, all of which is followed by the cowboy's introductory voice-over.

The references to postmodernism here have emphasized the aesthetics of film with regard to genre; it is, however, also possible to place postmodern cinema in an economic context. A good example is *Star Wars*, which could justifiably be described as postmodern in that it is a pastiche of different genres, from science fiction and action/adventure through to elements of the western, war movie and romance, with the consequent intertextuality. Thomas Schatz refers to *Star Wars'* 'radical amalgamation of genre conventions and its elaborate play of cinematic references' (Schatz (1993), p. 23). The film has been a huge success for over 25 years in terms of entertainment and box-office takings. It could be argued that its success is partly due to the wide range of genres that it evokes, the effect being to broaden its audience appeal. In this respect, the application of postmodernism to film-making could have an economic imperative as well as an aesthetic purpose.

SUMMARY

- The majority of films have been genre films and genre categorization has existed throughout cinema's history.
- Genres can be identified through visual content and narrative themes and it is the repetition of common elements across a number of films that makes categorization possible.
- Difference is also necessary in genre films to ensure innovation and novelty as well as predictability.

- Genre categorizations are not static, and themes and styles evolve to match social change.
- Genres are useful for the industry in targeting audiences, and for the audience in terms of being able to identify the types of films that will be liked.
- Genre study is useful in that it enables us to determine whether, and how, genre films reflect values, beliefs, issues and ideas that are prevalent within a society at any given moment.
- The study of genres enables us to identify the common elements in films belonging to a particular genre in terms of iconography, music and narrative themes, and to examine structures and variations that occur within and between genres.
- Genre study can highlight the ways in which common characteristics can appear in films of different genres, indicating that genres can overlap and can be combined.

REFERENCES

Rick Altman, *Film/Genre* (London: BFI, 1999).

Colin McArthur, *Underworld USA* (London: Secker & Warburg/BFI, 1972).

Steve Neale, *Genre* (London: BFI, 1980).

Tom Ryall, *Teachers Study Guide No. 2: The Gangster Film* (London: BFI Education, 1978).

Thomas Schatz, *Hollywood Genres* (New York: McGraw-Hill, 1981).

Thomas Schatz, 'The New Hollywood', in Jim Collins, Hilary Radner and Ava Preacher Collins (eds), *Film Theory Goes to the Movies* (London: Routledge, 1993).

FURTHER READING

Rick Altman (ed.), *Genre: The Musical* (London: Routledge & Kegan Paul, 1981).

Edward Buscombe (ed.), *The BFI Companion to the Western* (London: André Deutsch Ltd., 1988).

Joan Copjec, *Shades of Noir* (London: Verso, 1993).

James Donald (ed.), *Fantasy and the Cinema* (London: BFI, 1989).

Jim Kitses, *Horizons West* (London: Secker & Warburg/BFI, 1969).

Steve Neale, *Genre* (London: BFI, 1980).

Tom Ryall, *Teachers Study Guide No. 2: The Gangster Film* (London: BFI Education, 1978).

Will Wright, *Sixguns and Society* (Berkeley, CA: University of California Press, 1975).

Stars

In this chapter we shall examine the functions and meanings of stars within the film industry and Film Studies. Stars have not always been deemed essential to the production of films. The avant-garde aside, it was not until the 1920s in Hollywood that the value of the star was widely acknowledged. Throughout the 1930s and 1940s Hollywood stars were placed at the centre of the film industry, but by the 1950s their role had changed somewhat. In recent times, certain star actors have held far greater power in Hollywood, particularly in terms of production. Similarly, stars have not always been seen as a particularly important part of Film Studies and star studies are still in an early stage of development.

Early writing on stardom was little more than biography (of which there is still plenty being produced). Often such writing mythologized the stars, simply serving as a means to promote the star's image. In the 1950s and 1960s, stars were looked at as symbols of the larger society. It was not until the late 1970s that stars began to become a topic for film theorists when Richard Dyer suggested that stars were economic elements within and manufactured by the Hollywood Studio System and other film industries like Bollywood. Dyer has helped to direct attention towards the figure of the star not only within film, but also as part of a wider social context.

Thanks to Dyer, Christine Gledhill and others, it is now recognized that the star is more than just talent, beauty, glamour and charisma. There are at least five key elements to be considered when studying stars. These five elements – the star as a real person; the star as a form of economic capital or commodity; the star in performance, as someone who takes on roles and characters; the star as an image, a persona, a celebrity, and the star as a form of representation – will be examined in turn here. While we may tend to focus on Hollywood, if only because it was responsible for the primary model of film stardom, it is hoped that the reader will go beyond its boundaries to look at stars from other national cinemas.

THE REAL PERSON

How much does the 'real' person behind the star really matter? When we watch a film we know that a real person called Keanu Reeves (if that is actually his real name) undoubtedly exists, but does it impact upon our understanding of the film? In some cases, where we know that the star uses a stage name (Winona Ryder/Horowitz), the gap between the real person and the star is evident. Sometimes films can confuse these identities. In two recent British films, *Final Cut* (1999) and *Love, Honour and Obey* (2000), the names of the actors were used, so Jude Law's character was called 'Jude', Sadie Frost's 'Sadie', and so on. The relationship between the real identity and the star can get more complicated, as in *Notting Hill* (1999) where Julia Roberts plays a film star called 'Anna Scott', or when a star plays another star's 'real' identity, for example, Jim Carrey as Andy Kaufman in *Man on the Moon* (2000). Do we get here a rare glimpse of the 'real' Roberts or Kaufman or are we merely observing an image of the image that is Julia Roberts or Andy Kaufman? In a recent class discussion a student said that he could never look at Hugh Grant the same way again after the episode in the back of his Mercedes. In this case, the 'real' person has interfered with the viewer's reception of his character. However, Dyer would argue that the real identity of the star is inconsequential, for we only really know her/him through other media products (newspapers, TV, magazines, etc.), and that the rare insights into a star's character offer us nothing in the understanding of a film. Guest appearances by film stars on TV shows such as *Friends, Seinfeld* and *The Larry Sanders Show* are now regular occurrences. In some episodes they appear as themselves, as the 'real' person. Think about what this says about modern stars. Is there a gap between their star image and the real person? Do we learn something about the real person or do such stars appear as we expect them to? The study of stars does not seek to discover the real/true person/identity behind the media facade, but rather attempts to analyse the function of the star within the film industry in particular, and the star's meaning and function in society in general. Like films, stars are perceived as texts that exist within particular socio-economic contexts and hence must be studied accordingly.

ECONOMIC CAPITAL/COMMODITY

Film stars have not always been with us. Prior to 1910 actors' names did not appear in film credits or publicity as it was felt that they might demand higher fees. Instead, the spectacle, technology and story of the film were promoted. It soon became clear, however, that films which named the 'featured players' were more successful with audiences, and during the period from 1915 to 1920 the importance of the actor was more widely appreciated. The Famous Players Company and the introduction of major theatrical actors into *'films d'art'* began to focus attention on the body and life of the actor, changing the way that film actors were perceived. The print media also began to publicize the off-screen lives of these actors, transforming hitherto nameless screen bodies into actual film stars with names and identities that went beyond their on-screen roles. The presence of a particular star in a film helped to differentiate it from the competition, and soon the Hollywood Studio System had adopted the star. By the 1920s a fully formed star system had emerged.

As we have seen in the chapter on Hollywood, stars were considered central to the success of a film. We still often go to the cinema to see particular actors and actresses regardless of the films they are actually in. Some have become more popular than others, and a star name on the credits may become a guarantee of a degree of financial success (bankability). A star, therefore, is someone who contributes to a film's box-office success. Significantly, though, a star is someone who can do this over a number of films, rather than just one, as there have been many examples of what can be called 'one-hit wonders'.

Stars are part of the labour force that produces a film: the raw material from which films are made. The real person needs to be transformed into a star; hence the talent schools and dialogue coaches, beauticians, hairdressers and fitness instructors who serve to fashion the raw individual into a star image/product. The film industry perceived stars as a means of drawing audiences into the cinemas. Accordingly, stars were seen as a form of *capital* or commodity and the studios employed them on long-term and permanent contracts. Stars were tied to a particular studio, which then prepared them to fit the styles and genres of that studio. They had almost no say in which roles they were cast for or the films they would be in, and if they refused they could be suspended without pay.

Stars were contracted because they helped to target and attract a large audience for their films. Their performances contained a set of conventional elements such as standard gestural and behavioural patterns, which would be repeated over a number of films. Audiences then expected a certain type of performance and were able to predict what the star was most likely to do. Stars were also closely linked to genre, in particular through iconography, visual style and placement within the structure of the narrative. Humphrey Bogart, for example, symbolized the hard-boiled detective and lone alienated figure of *film noir*. Alternatively, the star was the basis for recognition by audiences through a readily identifiable image ('Humphrey Bogart in . . .'). Often the stars were loaned out to other studios; for example, Vivien Leigh and Clark Gable were loaned to David O. Selznick for *Gone with the Wind* (1939), one of the most successful films in history. Since the audience expected a certain type of experience, film posters would create expectations by placing the star against a background of scenes from the film.

The studios deliberately used stars to increase demand for tickets. They often generated publicity around stars' off-screen lives which was designed to complement their onscreen images. The studios often packaged stars such as John Wayne, Marilyn Monroe, Clark Gable and Cary Grant as untouchable, mythic figures, identified by their typical screen roles, which were often in truth fairly superficial. This is what is known as the star's 'image', which we will look at in more detail below. Stars were also seen as an *investment*, a protection against possible loss of revenue. A poor story or a remake could be improved by the presence of one or more stars. In order to maximize the potential of a star, the studios constructed an image or persona for him/her: we can think of Bogart, who was often seen wearing a fedora hat and smoking a cigarette, or of Marilyn Monroe with her skirts blowing over an air vent (Figure 11.1).

Figure 11.1   *Marilyn Monroe. During the studio era stars were seen as little more than commodities; economic capital to be exploited (Courtesy Kobal)*

Following the decline of the studio system, the power of star actors has increased massively with the ending of the restrictive contract system. Stars have effectively become free agents and talent agencies increasingly negotiate deals with studios on their behalf. Stars now have more power to select which films they appear in; indeed, they make fewer films than under the Hollywood Studio System. The increasing trend towards big-budget and star-studded features, as well as the increasing competition from the television and music industries, has facilitated 'star power'. Some stars have set up their own production companies and have used their economic power to control the films they appear in, often producing and directing themselves. However, this is not a new development. In 1910, Fox wooed Florence Lawrence away from the Biograph Studio by fulfilling her demands for a larger salary, a larger dressing room and a job for her boyfriend. In 1919 Charlie Chaplin, Mary Pickford (Figure 11.2) and Douglas Fairbanks, together with D.W. Griffith, established United Artists so that they could exercise more control over their own careers. During the 1950s, Marilyn Monroe set up her own company in order to produce her own films.

It has been suggested that five or six key stars have now usurped the power of the studios, directors, producers and agents in the Hollywood hierarchy; indeed, we now talk of 'star power'. Actor Nick Nolte has condemned this state of affairs: 'The star system sucks. The big studios have boiled Hollywood down to four male leads . . . it's not creative. They get the stars before they get a script' (quoted in Gibbons, 2000, p. 9). Director John Boorman further explains:

> Because films go out to hundreds of cinemas across America at the same time, they need very expensive advertising. This means the audience needs a recognition factor of a simple story and stars they can identify with. Films now have to succeed on that first all-important weekend and, because they can open a picture in that way, this has given a handful of stars enormous power. They choose the projects; they are the people in charge.
>
> (quoted in Dewe Matthews, 1999, p. 2)

Mary Pickford: early star power (BFI Stills, Posters and Designs)   Figure 11.2

This power has translated into bigger fees per film, and many stars now have control not only over how a film is made, but also over how it is marketed. Stars can determine which films are made, they can demand script alterations, select their co-stars and even approve the final cut (known as the 'actor's cut'). Recent examples are Edward Norton and *American History X* (1998) and Mel Gibson and *Payback* (1999). Stars have become so powerful because studio executives believe that the right actors make the difference between success and failure. As films have become more expensive, studios, producers and financiers have increasingly relied upon star attraction to protect their investments. Since stars are now free to pick and choose projects and the major talent is spread fairly thinly, the power is in their hands. In an attempt to retain them, production companies strike deals as a means of rewarding their most valuable performers. The value of a star is now measured in terms of how much money her/his films make, particularly over the opening weekend. This is known as *insurance value* to the investor. Echoing the contracts of the studio system, the major studios attempt to 'buy' their own personal film stars, but despite their attempts, it seems to be a stars' industry. As producer Tim Bevan put it, '[y]ou can't expect somebody in the studio's position or in our position, who's being asked to put up $40–$50m, not to reduce their risks and look for an insurance policy, and in our business, the insurance policy is a star . . . at the end of the day, the stars have got a monopoly because there are so few of them' (quoted in Dewe Matthews, 1999, p. 2).

The history of stardom in India (in particular the Hindi cinema of Bombay) parallels that of Hollywood. Star power grew bit by bit; initially stars were tied to studios with strict discipline and rigorous contracts, but this began to break down in the 1940s, with the result that today stars command even more power than their Hollywood counterparts. It is an entrenched axiom in Indian cinema that stars are an essential element in the success of any mainstream film. And since the 1960s an entire magazine industry has emerged which spreads lewd gossip about these stars in many languages.

Since the rise of the multiplex, video and DVD, it could be argued that the role of the star has changed yet again, that their role is simply to make money. Lately, however, there has been concern that stars are failing to fulfil their function and are no longer bankable. After the success of the $200m blockbuster *Titanic* (1997), its stars, Leonardo DiCaprio and Kate Winslet (see case study below), have both appeared in box-office failures (*Celebrity*, 1998; *Hideous Kinky*, 1998).

In the second half of 1999, five major stars – Harrison Ford (*Random Hearts*), Kevin Costner (*For Love of the Game*), Bruce Willis (*The Story of Us*), Nicolas Cage (*Bringing out the Dead*) and Robin Williams (*Jakob the Liar*) – all suffered poor box-office returns. In contrast, the low-budget, independent *The Blair Witch Project* (1999), featuring three unknowns, was a massive hit, as was *American Pie* (1999), suggesting that audiences like to be surprised occasionally. There are ultimately no guarantees that the mere presence of a star will generate income. Nonetheless, the question is: do stars still constitute a form of capital, and if so, who owns them: the production companies, their agents or themselves?

Exercise 11.1
Compare and contrast a star from the studio system with one from Hollywood today. What are the differences and what are the similarities?

ROLE, CHARACTER AND PERFORMANCE

In this section we will consider the following question: what specific meanings do stars bring with them to the roles they play? A key part of the star is her/his performance. Figure movement and expression within the *mise en scène* is another way in which actors 'signify' – convey or express meaning. The star, like the director, may be considered an '*auteur*' in his/her performances in that s/he may bring qualities to a film independent of the script and generic conventions. For the audience, interpreting a performance involves assessing how far the actor has 'become' the character, which may then be discussed in terms of how far it was 'believable', 'truthful' or 'realistic'. A film is often a vehicle for the star, giving him/her the chance to demonstrate his/her unique qualities in a particular role, situation or context. An actor may on the one hand submerge his/her personality to create a character, or may let his/her own personality create the character. Acting ability, however, is not always a prerequisite for stardom. A common criticism levelled at Arnold Schwarzenegger (which is not shared by all critics) is that he can't act. Consider how many times you have seen a film and said the same thing about the main actors/actresses.

The star's ability to act or to play certain roles and characters gives a *production value* to the film-maker, who then knows what to expect from a certain star. The character may be adapted to fit the star, or the former's characteristics may happen to correspond to those of the star. Few of us really believe, however, that the star and the character they are playing are actually the same thing (although, as we have seen above, a character's name may accord with that of the star, causing some confusion). Richard Dyer has categorized three relational possibilities between the star and role/character. First, cases where the character makes 'selective use' of the star's persona; second, when the character and the star seemed to be a 'perfect fit'; and third, when the star and character are mutually opposed or a 'problematic fit'.

As we can see, there is a relationship between the star and the role/character s/he is playing. A role is created for a star or a star is put into a particular role. Eventually, the star becomes associated with a particular type of role (e.g. James Bond and Sean Connery/Roger Moore/Pierce Brosnan). These recurring elements lend a measure of predictability to the film and go some way to fulfilling the audience's expectations. Think of Schwarzenegger, Clint Eastwood or Sharon Stone and certain roles/characters will spring to mind. There is a circular relationship between the star and her/his role within a particular genre. A star often emerges within a particular genre. Stars, therefore, can be productively studied with reference to genre.

Performance is an important part of stardom and can be broken down into two categories:

- Impersonation: This type of acting/performance is usually associated with the theatre. The actor constructs a role using her/his imagination and specific skills and is judged on how successfully s/he submerges her/his 'real' personality by the number and scope of roles s/he adopts, and how far s/he is acknowledged as being psychologically realistic.
- Personification: Hollywood more often utilizes this type of acting/performance. The actor plays a role that matches his/her physical appearance, what Dyer refers to as a 'perfect fit', and success is judged not by what s/he does (acting), but rather by what s/he 'is' (identity).

Since the early days of film, the role of the star has gradually changed as a result of considerable changes in acting styles. During the silent era, actors were not required to speak while acting. The introduction of sound after 1926–27, however, meant that many silent actors lost their jobs and were replaced by East Coast theatre actors. Since the subsequent decline of the studio system from the late 1940s onwards it can be argued that actors have had more input into their roles as well, interpreting them with more individuality than was previously possible. Indeed, this is reflected in the arguable *auteur* status which international stars such as Marlene Dietrich, Gérard Depardieu, Jackie Chan, Raj Kapoor and Clint Eastwood (among others) have enjoyed.

In Hollywood, the mannered, heavily stylized enunciation of previous decades was gradually replaced by a more spontaneous, more naturalistic approach, as demonstrated by Marlon Brando, Rod Steiger, James Dean, Paul Newman, Geraldine Page and Joanne Woodward. They had trained at the Actors Studio, New York, which embraced the Stanislavsky technique, stressing emotional truth and realism in the performing arts. Stanislavsky's teachings were preached by Lee Strasberg and Elia Kazan and became known as 'Method Acting', or simply 'the Method'. The Method seeks to break down the distinction between the actor and the role (for more detail see Maltby, 1996) and is a more extreme and advanced form of personification whereby the actor physically embodies the role in appearance, gesture and movement. When Kazan's *On the Waterfront* (1955) won seven Oscars, including a Best Actor award for Brando, the Method had arrived in Hollywood and by the 1960s it had been almost completely absorbed into mainstream Hollywood.

As a result of these changes, some stars are now considered to be more believable, more 'real', and are more likely to be appreciated for their acting skills as their on-screen roles tend to have more depth. A contemporary actor committed to the Method is Robert De Niro, who researches the background of his character, seeks real-life models for the character he portrays and attempts to transform himself physically into the role he is playing. In *Raging Bull* (1980), for example, he gained a great deal of weight in order to physically personify an ageing and out-of-shape boxer, as well as turning in a savage performance as the same boxer in his fighting prime.

Appearing in the same role/character can lead to *typecasting*, and audiences may become bored with the constant repetition. For a star to survive s/he must be willing to adapt or change, and as a consequence stars, like genres, can change over time as the star moves over several genres. Bruce Willis, for example, has successfully broadened his appeal by making comedies as well as action/adventure films.

But does the star generate meaning through acting ability (i.e. voice and body) alone? One way of testing this is through what has been called the *commutation test* (see also p. 218): this works by imagining swapping one actor for another in a particular role to see if this makes any difference for the spectator. Any changes point to what is unique about one actor compared with another. What is more, elsewhere we discuss how genre and authorship play an important role in signalling meaning for the spectator. In the 1920s, Soviet film theorist Lev Kuleshov intercut a shot of an expressionless actor with various objects. He argued that because the spectator then saw emotions in the actor's face (depending on whether the actor had been intercut with a bowl of soup or a young child, for example) this had to be a result of editing rather than of the actor's performance alone. To this it can be added that action as perceived is a product of camera angles and movement, lighting and music, as well as of voice and body. Is the actor/actress constrained by the director, genre and film technique, or will her/his performance transcend those boundaries? What factors determine how we read a performance?

Exercise 11.2
Discuss how far an actor's performance alone generates meaning. You may wish to consider the roles of the director and the casting director as well as the actor's acting ability.

IMAGE

Although stars belong to the raw material from which films are made and are part of the labour force that produces a film, they are distinguished from the rest of the crew by their image. The image of a star is vitally important to the film industry, as the star is used to market and publicize a film as an enticement to come to the cinema. As the Film Policy Review Group notes, '[t]he presence of certain stars can endorse a film and provide clues about its likely nature and appeal and a favourite star is a defining factor in choice for some cinema goers.' The star image is constructed through promotion, marketing, advertising, publicity, film roles and characters and critical commentary on those roles. Today, the star is extensively promoted through the mass media in interviews, features, reviews, news and so on. Media promotion of the star plays upon a set of contradictions – stars are both ordinary and glamorous, they are like us and yet not like us, they are a real person and a mythical economic commodity. It is often claimed, therefore, that stars carry meaning in the persona independently of the particular roles they may play.

Like genre, director and even special effects, stars are used to sell films and so the star's image dominates film posters and trailers and appears in hundreds of magazines and newspapers. Image gives the star extra value as it can attract investment, and signals to the audience and the exhibitor that this is a particular type of film. This is known as *trademark value*. Stars provide a sense of expectation for the audience and consequently they are used both by the industry to target audiences and by audiences to target the type of film they wish to see. Thus stars are designed to conform to certain generic expectations just as films are, and we expect a certain type of performance from a particular star. Consequently, stars can play a part in the standardization of films just as genre categorization does, as they can carry particular roles with them from one film to another. It may be argued that popular audiences identify and value films according to their stars and star performances rather than their directors. The presence of certain stars gives us important clues to the nature of the film, and may suggest genre, narrative and mood before we have even seen the film.

But who exactly determines the star's image? Do we as the audience simply accept the image that is constructed for us by the star, the role and the publicity, or do we have a more active role in deciding upon the image? It can be argued that the meanings and responses generated by stars are much less fixed than film producers and casting directors may imagine and that the audience plays a more creative part in the process of star understanding. The sheer number of unofficial and fan-based websites for major film stars suggests that fan behaviour in responding to stars is outside the control of the film industry. On the other hand, while the expansion of the Internet may have empowered many to create their own websites about their favourite actors and actresses, it has simultaneously fuelled the fetishization of stars created by the media in the first place.

Exercise 11.3

Consider your own behaviour as a 'fan'. How far are you responsible for constructing the image of your favourite star and how far is the distributor/marketer responsible?

REPRESENTATION AND MEANING

Why are certain stars popular at certain times? It is hard to pinpoint exactly why an actor/actress becomes a star, but there can be a measure of luck in simply appearing in the right film at the right time. Stars are people the audience can identify with, relate to and admire. They allow us the vicarious pleasure of identification: they are there to do the things that we can never do and to live the lives we can never lead. As James Monaco has put it, '[s]tars were – and still are – the creation of the public: political and psychological models who demonstrate some quality that we collectively admire' (1981, p. 222). Furthermore, stars often settle ideological conflicts that cannot be resolved in real life, and these fantasy solutions serve to comfort the viewer. Indeed, audience identification with the hero/ine and audience and conflict resolution are both central aims of mainstream cinema.

Particular stars may also be the direct or indirect reflection of the needs, drives and dreams of their particular society. We can point to the success of Chuck Norris, Sylvester Stallone (Figure 11.3) or Arnold Schwarzenegger, for example, during the Reagan years; their success has since declined as times have changed. According to the BBFC's report of 1998, there seems to have been a shift in what we watch. The action/adventure heroes of the 1980s and 1990s such as Seagal, Van Damme and Schwarzenegger had aged or fallen out of favour except on video. Film stars can participate in the spread of dominant ideological values by embodying or personifying the dominant ideology, and may be seen as role models – they represent beliefs and values which largely reflect those of their society. In looking at stars, we must consider representation in order to understand how stars generate significant meanings and responses and thus may embody various values and ideologies.

But *can* we simply say that stars are reflections of dominant social values? Although this is a common belief, current star studies reject this idea as simplistic: film stars can also participate in the alteration of ideological values. In Indian cinema, for example, stars often behave in a 'shocking' fashion (both on and off the screen) that would seem to undermine the rigid social patterns of Indian society. Thus Madhuri Dixit was one of seven actresses whose 'obscene' performances recently prompted an unsuccessful prosecution in India for 'eroding the cultural fabric of the country'. Rather than simply suggesting that the star is a

Figure 11.3   *Sylvester Stallone: embodiment of 1980s Reaganism (courtesy Kobal)*

mere reflection of dominant social values, we can say that the star generates many m
ings within a particular context.

Current star studies seek to analyse these meanings in relation to ideologies of class,
race and gender. Typically, the female actor/body has been the focus of many star studies,
including those of Marilyn Monroe, Greta Garbo, Shirley Temple, Jean Harlow, Rita Hayworth,
Kim Novak, Judy Garland, Mae West, Bo Derek and Demi Moore in the west, and 'Fearless
Nadia', Nargis Dutt and Smita Patil in the east. In many cases, it is argued that female stars
are constructed to appeal to male desire (*voyeurism* and *scopophilia*), but such studies have
been criticized for their assumption of a male spectator and masculine viewing position.
What if the spectator is female and the observed a male? Recently, there has been an
increased interest in masculinity as viewed from both female and male perspectives. For
example, what are we to make of the frequent close ups of the body of Brad Pitt within
genres that primarily appeal to young males?

Using a semiological approach, Richard Dyer's influential work of the 1980s and
1990s has studied stars as texts, as bundles of analysable signs. According to Dyer, in
any single instance, a star can signify a *polysemy* – a range of different possible meanings – which has been manufactured through four main types of media texts: promotion,
publicity, film roles/characters and criticism/commentary on these roles. For Dyer, the
presence of a star in more than one media text – intertextuality – is vital to studying
stars. Indeed, a star must appear in a range of media texts; otherwise s/he is not truly
a star. It is this intertextuality that distinguishes the star from the non-star known only
for one role (this is the case with many soap characters when we either forget or do
not even know their real names). Today, Hollywood stars cut across far more media
texts than they did in the days of the Studio System. Will Smith, for example, started
out as a rapper before starring in the TV sitcom *The Fresh Prince of Bel Air*. Since then he
has continued with his musical career while starring in big-budget Hollywood blockbusters
(see case study below). As we mentioned above, film stars regularly also make guest
appearances on TV shows.

What is central to understanding the star's representation and meaning is the audience.
Frequently the audience is either omitted entirely from star studies (which tend to treat the
star as a text) or presumed to be passive. Both approaches are inadequate and it is important to try to understand how audiences might read stars within specific historical and cultural settings. This move beyond simply considering the function of stars within particular
film texts has been exemplified by Richard Dyer's *Heavenly Bodies*, an effective sequel to
his own ground-breaking *Stars* (see Further Reading).

CASE STUDY

Kate Winslet

Co-star of *Titanic* (Cameron, 1997), Kate Winslet was thrust into stardom; but what kind of a star
is she? Many Hollywood stars of the studio period did not go by their original names: John Wayne
was born Marion Morrison, Marilyn Monroe started life as Norma Jean Mortenson. Cary Grant's
original name, Archibald Leach, was deliberately used for the Archie Leach character in the British

comedy *A Fish Called Wanda* (Crichton, 1988) played by John Cleese, whose name would have been John Cheese if his father had not changed his own name before going into the army in 1915. By contrast, recent stars have perhaps more often retained their own names, so the person who is 'Kate Winslet' is also called Kate Winslet.

Winslet acted in a number of TV and film roles before she was 20, including an episode of the BBC hospital soap *Casualty*. The breakthrough into major roles came with *Sense and Sensibility* (Lee, 1995), *Jude* (Winterbottom, 1996) and *Hamlet* (Branagh, 1996); *Titanic* and record-breaking success beckoned. It is interesting that subsequent films such as *Hideous Kinky* (MacKinnon, 1998) and *Holy Smoke* (Campion, 1999) have not been successful and have not enhanced Winslet's star status. Why should this be?

At least four different kinds of factors may have contributed to Winslet's relative lack of prominence since the success of *Titanic*. First is her relative 'ordinariness': like Johnny Depp, say, she appears approachable. This in turn may be linked to her Englishness and to her apparent wariness of Hollywood: several of her films, from *Heavenly Creatures* (Jackson, 1994) to *Enigma* (2001), have been at least partly British, often with French, Australian, or New Zealand/Aotearoa connections: *Holy Smoke* was directed by Jane Campion, the New Zealand/Aotearoa director who made *The Piano* (1993).

This lack of Hollywood exposure could also, of course, have been forced by a third factor: the relative weakness of her perceived celebrity image, which has a number of possible explanations which are likely to overlap. Is there something non-photogenic about Kate Winslet's appearance? Despite the success of *Titanic*, were there reservations about her acting in the film or about the meanings generated by her character and performance? Could it be that *Titanic* hit the jackpot *despite* its female lead and not because of her?

Or, finally, does Kate Winslet herself refuse to conform to the conventional star image, with its photo-opportunities, emphasis on image, glamour and gossip-fodder? Inconceivable though it may be to marketing executives, it may be that she is simply not interested in being the kind of star they have in mind. The characters she plays are often strong-willed, independent-minded free spirits; could it be that these qualities in a woman are still threatening to some?

Figure 11.4   *Kate Winslet: in some ways a star, in others not? (Photograph by Stephane Fefer, courtesy Kobal)*

C A S E   S T U D Y

Will Smith

Willard Christopher Smith Jr was born in 1968 and grew up in middle-class West Philadelphia. He allegedly earned the nickname 'Prince' because of the way he could charm his way out of trouble, and began his career as the rapper 'Fresh Prince' performing with DJ Jazzy Jeff. He then went on to star in his own sitcom, *The Fresh Prince of Bel Air*, from 1991 to 1996. In this sitcom he played himself in the title role of a streetwise and tough kid from West Philadelphia who is sent to live with his middle-class cousins in Bel Air.

Meanwhile, Will Smith appeared in the films *Where the Day Takes You* (1992), *Six Degrees of Separation* (1993), *Bad Boys* (1995) and *A Thin Line between Love and Hate* (1996), but it was not until the blockbuster *Independence Day* (Emmerich, 1996) that he emerged as a leading Hollywood actor. Since then he has appeared in *Men in Black* (1997), *Enemy of the State* (1998), *Wild Wild West* (1999), *The Legend of Bagger Vance* and *Men in Black: Alien Attack* (both 2000). Although he has played a variety of roles and characters (confidence trickster, police officer, military captain, lawyer, Civil War hero and even a golf caddy), Smith seems to stick to certain genres. Using his comedic TV persona, Smith has appeared in films that integrate comedy with other genres such as action, thriller and science fiction. Across all of these roles, however, one can detect his trademark brashness.

As an important bankable commodity he now commands a fee of approximately $15m per film. What is more, Will Smith is seen as a good investment because he can also provide the soundtrack: on at least two of his films, *Men in Black* and *Wild Wild West*, he wrote and sang the title track.

Why has Smith emerged as such a success? Certainly there has been a history of African American actors in Hollywood, such as Paul Robeson, Sidney Poitier (incidentally in *Six Degrees* Smith plays a man who pretends to be his son) and more recently Eddie Murphy and Denzel Washington. But Smith's success as a leading actor in the mid- to late 1990s may signal a transformation not only in Hollywood, but also in American society in general. As an African American, it is possible that Smith could only have reached this level of stardom within a more liberal and open-minded society, perhaps mirrored by the liberal Clinton Administration, than those of his predecessors Reagan and Bush. His gentler, more comedic persona has replaced the white, macho, patriotic action-adventure heroes of the late 1980s and early 1990s such as Schwarzenegger, Stallone and Van Damme. Perhaps Smith's stardom reflects a new era and an American society that is more pluralist and tolerant of ethnic minorities.

Unlike Winslet, Smith seems to conform to the conventional image of the star. As a musical and TV performer he fulfils Dyer's condition of intertextuality necessary for stardom, and he has continued to perform as a rapper, releasing a string of successful hits such as 'Will2K' and 'Summertime'. His various images as a successful rapper, TV performer and film star have overlapped to create a very marketable persona. Since some of these characteristics seem to have been drawn from his real life, we may feel we are actually offered a glimpse of the 'real' Will Smith, particularly as we may have seen him before he emerged on the big screen. His cool rebellious character, as indicated through his dialogue, music and dress style, has an obvious appeal for a teenage audience that frequently has similar concerns, while his comedy and occasional moral messages perhaps attract an older audience too.

Conclusion

Star study is a relatively new and complex part of Film Studies. In looking at the five components which make up the star – the real person, economic capital/commodity, performance, image/persona/celebrity and representation – we can say that the meanings and responses generated by stars are not stable or fixed. Nonetheless, the study of stars, alongside genre and authorship, is not only productive when looking at the film industry, but also sheds light on our understanding of film. Yet there is a possibility that stars will not always be with us. Things have shifted drastically since the days of Florence Lawrence the Biograph Girl; while a few stars may dominate Hollywood or Bollywood today, since the arrival of CGI we may no longer need stars in the conventional sense. Rather than investing in physical human labour, film executives may deem it cheaper and less complicated to res-urrect dead stars or to create them entirely from scratch. During the production of *Gladiator* (Ridley Scott, 2000), for example, Oliver Reed died. CG depictions of his head were matted onto another actor's body.

SUMMARY

- Star studies attempts to understand the function of the star in both film and society.
- It is important to understand the role of the audience when studying stars.
- The star is a real person, but how far does this matter?
- The star was and maybe still is deployed as a form of economic capital or commodity to increase the success of a film.
- The star is someone who takes on roles and characters and may often be judged by the quality of his/her acting.
- The star has an image, a persona and a celebrity, which may be different from the real person and the roles/character, which is used to publicize a film.
- The 'value' of a star can be broken down into three categories: insurance value (for the investor), production value (for the producer) and trademark value (for the audience).
- The star also operates as a form of representation and produces meaning within a particular society.

REFERENCES

Gill Branston and Roy Stafford, 'Case study: making stars', in *The Media Student's Book* (2nd edn, New York and London: Routledge, 1999), pp. 308–15.

Jeremy G. Butler, 'The star system and Hollywood', in John Hill and Pamela Church Gibson (eds), *The Oxford Guide to Film Studies* (Oxford: Oxford University Press, 1998), pp. 342–53.

Tom Dewe Matthews, 'They're not just rich and famous. They're in charge', *The Guardian* (19 November 1999), p. 2.

Richard Dyer, *Heavenly Bodies: Film Stars and Society* (London: Macmillan, 1986).

Richard Dyer, *Now You See It* (London: Routledge, 1990).

Richard Dyer, *Stars* (new edn, London: BFI, 1998).

FPRG, *A Bigger Picture: The Report of the Film Policy Review Group* (London: Department of Culture, Media and Sport, 1998).

Fiachra Gibbons, 'Stars demanding up to $30m a film', *The Guardian* (17 May 2000), p. 9.

Christine Gledhill (ed.), *Stardom: Industry of Desire* (London: Routledge, 1991).

Stephen Kruger, *Film and the Star System* (London: Film Education, 1985).

Richard Maltby, *Hollywood Cinema: An Introduction* (Oxford: Blackwell, 1995).

James Monaco, *How to Read a Film: The Art, Technology, Language, History, and Theory of Film and Media* (rev. edn, New York and Oxford: Oxford University Press, 1981).

Damon Wise, 'Money for nothing?', *Screen: The Observer* (14 November 1999), pp. 6–7.

FURTHER READING

Jeanine Basinger, *A Woman's View: How Hollywood Spoke to Women, 1930-1960* (London: Chatto & Windus, 1994).

Richard Dyer, *Heavenly Bodies: Film Stars and Society* (London: Macmillan, 1986).

Richard Dyer, *Now You See It* (London: Routledge, 1990).

Richard Dyer, *Stars* (new edn, London: BFI, 1998).

Christine Gledhill (ed.), *Stardom: Industry of Desire* (London: Routledge, 1991).

Stephen Kruger, *Film and the Star System* (London: Film Education, 1985).

Geoffrey Macnab, *Searching for Stars: Rethinking British Cinema* (London: Cassell, 2000).

Jackie Stacey, *Star Gazing: Hollywood Cinema and Female Spectatorship* (London: Routledge, 1994).

John O. Thompson, 'Screen acting and the commutation test', *Screen*, vol. 19, no. 2 (1978).

Ginette Vincendeau, 'Brigitte Bardot', in John Hill and Pamela Church Gibson (eds), *The Oxford Guide to Film Studies* (Oxford: Oxford University Press, 1998).

FURTHER VIEWING

Gary Cooper – the Face of a Hero (BBC2, 2000).

Marilyn Monroe – The Mortal Goddess (20th Century Fox, 1996).

Omnibus: Sidney Poitier – One Bright Light (BBC1, 2000).

Hollywood Legends: The Collection (series) (20th Century Fox).

Humphrey Bogart: Behind the Legend (Millennial Entertainment Inc., 1994).

Meaning and Spectatorship

In this chapter we shall examine the major critical approaches towards understanding film. We shall try to understand the complex relationships between film as text, cinema as institution, and the spectator. This will involve considering the chequered history of theories about how individual spectators 'read' films.

It is important to note straight away that we shall *not* be considering the 'audience' here (see Chapter 3). You will often hear the term 'audience response' used apparently to refer to the way individuals react to or 'read' a film. This is, though, perhaps a little misleading since the principal aim of such studies/research (which is often commissioned by production companies or other media organizations for economic reasons) is usually to establish *statistical* information about *audiences* which can be used to change the ending of a film prior to general release or to try to predict what kind of film is likely to be a hit next Christmas. By contrast, spectatorship studies refers to the more academic study of how individual viewers (or *subjects* as they/we are sometimes called) relate to and decode film texts.

This involves theorizing the spectator and the nature of the viewing experience. Who or what is a spectator? What does watching a film involve? Are there different ways of watching a film? How do we create meanings when we watch a film? These are actually difficult and complex questions which also depend on first defining what we mean by a 'film text'; fortunately much of this task has been achieved, and Chapters 5–7 have been devoted to establishing this. We have seen how a film text can be defined in terms of the use of *mise en scène*, cinematography, sound and editing to produce a more or less narrative audio-visual representation.

WATCHING A FILM

Before the Copernican revolution in the sixteenth century, it was obvious to everyone that the Earth was flat. When the Lumière brothers first projected a film of a train arriving at a station in 1895, it was obvious to spectators that a train was about to mow them down: there was panic in the room.

Anything which seems obvious needs to be approached with care. The act of watching a film can never be 'just entertainment'; there is always important social, ideological and psychological work being done. We need to keep asking the questions: who is this spectator who is watching? What goes on during the viewing experience? How exactly do we watch a film?

Theories of spectatorship have made use of concepts drawn from a number of areas, some of which may at first sight seem a little far-fetched; nevertheless this has enabled a great deal of important and interesting work to be done, and in the latter part of the twentieth century these ideas of how we watch films were very influential – though they were certainly contested. In the following pages we shall be looking very briefly at how psycho-analytic theory, semiology, structuralism, the concept of ideology and more recently 'cognitive' approaches have contributed to spectatorship theory. But first let us take a look at the early days.

EARLY MODELS

There were some early pioneers of writing on film spectatorship, among them Hugo Münsterberg and Rudolf Arnheim. Although the theories advanced by such theorists have been largely ignored (partly because they wrote only about pre-sound film and partly because in most cases film was not their principal concern), they are currently being redis-covered and reread: see pp. 112–14 on formalism and realism. Their impact on approaches to spectatorship studies, however, was for much of the last century far less significant than that of more sociological approaches addressed to the larger concern with audiences for mass culture.

'Effects' Approaches

Since the early days of film and of mass media, there has been a strong assumption that media have an 'effect' on the spectator; this assumption has been most noticeable in the various moral panics which punctuated the twentieth century, most obviously the early anxiety about film itself, the debate around the so-called 'video nasties' in the 1980s and the more general concern about representations of violence (see Martin Barker's *A Haunt of Fears* and *The Video Nasties*); among the more high-profile films which have run into trouble have been *Peeping Tom* (Michael Powell, 1960) (Figure 12.1), *Straw Dogs* (Sam Peckinpah, 1971), *A Clockwork Orange* (Stanley Kubrick, 1971) and *Natural Born Killers* (Oliver Stone, 1994).

The mechanisms by which films/media may have an effect, however, have been far from clear, and a number of explanations have been used. An early model was the *hypodermic syringe model,* so called because of the strength of the underlying idea: the media get under the skin and 'inject' values and beliefs into the spectator. Yet this model did not begin to explain *how* this could happen.

Figure 12.1   *Peeping Tom: too challenging for its time (BFI Stills, Posters and Designs)*

A more elaborate (sociological) approach was provided by Katz and Lazarsfeld in the 1940s; they argued that according to the *two-step flow* model it was only certain individuals (called 'opinion leaders') whose learning or world-view was affected by the media, and these opinion leaders then passed on this 'effect' to their less active peer groups.

Central to subsequent developments in 'effects' theory are theories of psychoanalysis and ideology (see below), but one other model should be mentioned here. The idea of the *classic realist text* was applied to films (first by Colin MacCabe in *Screen*); according to this idea, all narrative films (which means virtually all films that 99 per cent of the public go to see) are structured in such a way (through a hierarchy of discourses) as to provide a secure position of knowledge for the spectator: stylistic codes involving editing, camerawork, *mise en scène* and sound are used to place the spectator in an unthreatening position of virtual power. According to this model, the spectator position itself can be seen simply as a *textual effect*: the range of meanings which it is possible for any spectator to produce is severely limited by the narrative and stylistic form.

Uses and Gratifications

It was largely as a reaction against the pessimism of such models (called deterministic because they seemed to allow no freedom of interpretation and saw meaning as largely pre-determined within an ideological system) that the uses and gratifications approach developed in the 1970s. Here there was a greater stress on the more or less conscious uses which individuals make of the media and on the kinds of pleasures which can gratify a variety of needs. Thus watching a soap opera such as *Eastenders*, for example, can be an exciting addition to a boring everyday routine, it can be an escape from the problems of one's own everyday life, it can enable a lonely person to feel part of something, it can enliven conversation with friends or colleagues the following day (did you see. . . ?). Media users can then be described as belonging to *interpretive communities*: groups who use a particular programme in a similar way. Uses and gratifications work in the 1970s and 1980s focused predominantly on TV audiences and how/why viewers watch: see especially the work of David Morley and Ann Gray.

Cultural Studies

If uses and gratifications approaches were not so evident in Film Studies, this was due partly to the continuing sway of so-called '*Screen* Theory', but also to the emergence in the 1980s of Cultural Studies, an approach which sought to transform '*Screen* Theory' in combining it with more sociological methods, for example those emerging from the work of the Centre for Contemporary Cultural Studies in Birmingham. The first issue of the journal *Cultural Studies* in 1987 thus carried the following statement:

> *Cultural Studies* will publish articles on those practices, texts and cultural domains within which the various social groups that constitute a late capitalist society negotiate patterns of power and meaning. It will engage with the interplay between the personal and the polit-ical, between strategies of domination and resistance, between meaning systems and social systems.

In the 1990s, the study of meaning-making in films was much influenced by this approach, as indeed it continues to be. Film is seen as one (changing) medium among many, con-sumed/used in a variety of social contexts, so that how meanings are produced will depend on the individual and on her/his social history as well as on the specific film text.

This discussion has perhaps taken us a little away from this chapter's focus on individual spectatorship. Let us return to some areas which have been influential in theorizing the individual spectator's relation to film.

PSYCHOANALYTIC MODELS OF THE VIEWER AND OF THE VIEWING ACTIVITY

Since the time of Sigmund Freud (1856–1939), the relevance of psychoanalytic theory to many other disciplines (and indeed its very validity) has been hotly contested. While Film Studies has been no exception, we propose here to accept (one hopes not too controver-sially) that the unconscious exists, that we as human beings ('subjects') are by definition largely unaware of much that happens in our unconscious minds, and that it can be fruitful to analyse what 'hidden' mechanisms are at work in films.

The typical film-watching experience (and this is still so as we begin the twenty-first century) takes place in the dark. While some viewers do occasionally indulge in conversation, mobile phone-calls, popcorn-eating and other sensuous activities during a film, the typical relationship with what unfolds on the screen remains of a rather special kind (see John Ellis, 1982). It is not for nothing that Hollywood has been called the Dream Factory. The 'effect' of relatively large moving images, usually involving human figures, since 1929 usually with sound, since the 1950s usually in colour, and more recently often with Dolby/stereophonic sound and a widescreen format, can be seen as dreamlike. Indeed, it is interesting that the drive of this ever-growing 'reality-effect' is precisely to encourage the spectator to 'believe in' the illusion being presented on the screen – though we should also note the 'distracted mode of viewing' or 'back-seat viewing' theorized by Christine Geraghty (1997, p. 155).

It is not possible to consider the details of Freudian theory here, but we can outline some of the main ways in which psychoanalytic ideas have been used in the area of film. The first two of these are of less theoretical importance than the last three.

Film-makers and Psychoanalysis

A perhaps surprisingly large number of films have been 'touched' by psychoanalytic ideas; these can be identified principally in three historical periods. First, some European 'art' and avant-garde films of the 1920s and 1930s were made within or influenced by the 'Surrealist movement', for which techniques for exposing the unconscious directly in art were central. The most important films – which are still remarkable to behold – were *The Andalusian Dog* (*Un chien andalou*, Luis Buñuel and Salvador Dali, 1929) and *L'Age d'or* (Buñuel, 1930) (Figure 12.2). It is interesting that Quentin Tarantino, a self-taught 'film freak', named his one-time production company (notably for *Pulp Fiction*) 'Large Door': a clear *homage* to the 1930 Buñuel film.

Figure 12.2   *L'Age d'or: sexual dynamite in code (BFI Stills, Posters and Designs)*

A further group of films influenced by psychoanalytic theory emerged in the 1970s and 1980s, this time mostly in Britain and North America. This time the influence was more explicitly theoretical, and these avant-garde films tried to work against dominant models of narrative, identification and spectatorship (see p. 146). Among these many films were *Riddles of the Sphinx* (Laura Mulvey, 1977), *Thriller* (Sally Potter, 1979), and the films of Jackie Raynal. These films reached only small audiences of intellectuals and political activists and required very specific watching skills!

A third group of films, however, was very much part of the Hollywood production of the 1940s and 1950s. This was a period when Freudian psychoanalysis became popular and indeed fashionable in the USA, and a number of studio personnel and film-makers saw the potential of drawing on such ideas. Several films worked directly with (popularized and simplified) psychoanalytic notions such as repression, neurosis, mother-fixations, split personalities or the Oedipus complex. These films included *The Secret Behind the Door* (Lang, 1948), *The Cobweb* (Minnelli, 1955), *Shock Corridor* (Fuller, 1963) and *Marnie* (Hitchcock, 1964). Many other films of the period (particularly those of Alfred Hitchcock, for example), though they did not deal explicitly with such issues, lent themselves to analysis in psychoanalytic terms.

The 'Nosographic' Approach

There has been some writing which attempts more or less to psychoanalyse a film director; the director's films can be treated as 'symptoms' which can be used to analyse, for example, the director's repressed sexuality or mother-fixation. Such an approach has been used, for instance, in writing about Alfred Hitchcock and about Howard Hawks. You will often find this attitude underlying film reviews and biographies, but it has not generally been considered a very useful approach in academic work.

'Apparatus Theory'

As we have already hinted, it is possible to see the mechanism of watching a film (at least at a cinema) as somehow dreamlike, engaging unconscious processes. Indeed, the illusory nature of film viewing was foreshadowed over two thousand years ago by the Greek philosopher Plato in a 'thought experiment' which is now referred to as 'Plato's cave'.

Plato imagined a situation in which spectators (who can be taken to represent humanity in general) sit in an enclosure facing a wall and in front of another wall which it is impossible for them to climb; what is behind this wall is unknown to them, indeed, they are basically unaware that there is anything behind the wall (see Figure 12.3). On the wall/screen in front of them the spectators see shadowy images, which are in fact the shadows projected by figures moving and dancing in front of a fire behind/above the spectators: a scene to which they have no access and of which they have no knowledge.

Plato's imagination seems to have provided a remarkable premonition of cinema: spectators in an auditorium watch images projected from behind them by a mechanism which is startlingly similar to the figures moving in front of a fire in Plato's cave. Most importantly, the watchers of film seem to ignore (we refer to it as a 'suspension of disbelief')

Figure 12.3   Plato's cave (François Millepierres, Platon – La République VII et VIII, collection Traductions Hatier, © HATIER, Paris 1966)

the projection mechanism which creates the illusion. This supports the idea that film-viewing is largely unconscious, and is also linked to ideas about how *ideology* operates; we shall return to this later in this chapter.

The 'cinematic apparatus' thus puts individual watchers in a position of specularity, where the drive to look or watch (the clinical word for this is scopophilia) is satisfied. But of course this is not the end of the story.

What does 'Looking' Mean?

It is significant that in the cinema this drive to look remains largely private: although there may be hundreds of spectators looking at the same screen, each individual ('subject') sits in the dark and enjoys an intimate scopophilic relationship with the screen.

A significant step in the use of psychoanalytic theory in Film Studies was taken in 1975 when Laura Mulvey used the ideas of Jacques Lacan (an influential analyst who effectively rewrote Freud for the late twentieth century) to argue that in the classical Hollywood narrative the spectator is constructed as male. Over most of the history of Hollywood films the 'hero' or central character has usually been male, and female characters have been there principally to be looked at or to be saved. This was of course a reflection of gender power relations common in western (and other) societies for most of this century; but it was also, Mulvey argued, a product of complex (male) fears revolving around castration anxiety (again we must stress that these fears and anxieties are profoundly unconscious). As a result, male characters – from John Wayne's cowboys and heroic soldiers to Dirty Harry (Figure 12.4) and Rambo – were typically active, investigative narrative agents inviting *identification*, while female figures in film – from Marlene Dietrich in von Sternberg's 1930s films to Marilyn Monroe (Figure 12.5) and

Dirty Harry Callaghan: whose identification figure? (BFI Stills, Posters and Designs)   Figure 12.4

Figure 12.5   *Monroe in Gentlemen Prefer Blondes: who is she performing for? (20th Century Fox, courtesy Kobal)*

Brigitte Bardot – were often *fetishized* as objects of a male gaze. We need only think of macho heroes saving swooning virginal damsels or of half-dressed women displaying themselves for the spectator to see which films Mulvey was concerned with.

Mulvey's original ground-breaking work generated much intense debate and writing. She herself and many others have modified and extended her ideas; others have argued against such a psychoanalytic approach (see p. 226).

Two related areas of enquiry in relation to the 'male spectator' are of interest. First, since the 1970s films have increasingly featured central female characters, from *Alien* (Ridley Scott, 1979) to *Blue Steel* (Kathryn Bigelow, 1990) to *Thelma and Louise* (Ridley Scott, 1991). Second, many women writers have questioned the validity of the 'male spectator' position outlined by Mulvey, arguing that there are pleasures and other ways of looking available to women; and indeed there have (again since around 1980) been more and more films which also seem to offer the *male* body (for example, Sylvester Stallone/Rambo, Arnold Schwarzenegger, Brad Pitt) as an object of desire. Nevertheless, it may be argued that for every *Thelma and Louise* or *Desperately Seeking Susan* there are still more *Die Hards* and *Lethal Weapons*, and that even where the male body is offered for spectacle it generally retains narrative control.

Exercise 12.1

Arrange yourselves into groups in which each member has seen the same (recent) film. Discuss to what extent the film addresses the spectator as 'male' (or female?). Discuss the presence (or absence) of active/central female characters. Is it possible for female spectators to identify with male characters (and vice versa)? Are male characters there 'to be looked at'?

Psychoanalytic theory has also been used (again controversially) to explain the way in which spectators are drawn into shot/reverse shot editing, to analyse ideas of acting 'performance' in relation to the 'performance' of gender roles, to analyse virtually every aspect of cinematic pleasure. If psychoanalytic approaches to film are still often rejected and ridiculed, a good reference point may be the world-famous film made by one of Britain's finest directors which explicitly dealt with the more disturbing links between voyeurism and film: *Peeping Tom* (1960) was immediately banned for over 20 years and Michael Powell never made another film.

Exercise 12.2

Discuss the 'difficulty' of psychoanalytic approaches. Is it more likely that such approaches are 'wrong' or that (because they deal with unconscious processes) they are threatening (to individuals and to the social status quo)?

Analysis of Individual Films

The most important and productive use of psychoanalytic theory has been in the analysis of individual films and the ways in which they prompt the production of meaning. This has often meant the application of fairly standard psychoanalytic concepts, but these have been adapted to gain insight into specific films.

The so-called Oedipus complex is one example. According to classical Freudian theory, in order to become fully socialized (heterosexual) adults, male and female infants have to (eventually) renounce their primary love-object (their opposite-sex parent) and accept that another man or another woman will do instead. To oversimplify, the boy typically 'feels' a sexual attachment to his mother, would like to eliminate/kill his father who is his rival, but has to 'learn' the difficult lesson that the father-figure represents 'the Law' and that he cannot himself take the father-figure position unless he accepts symbolic 'castration' and submits to the 'Law of the Father'. He must (symbolically) lose his masculinity (by submitting to a father-figure) so that he can in turn wield the phallus (and the patriarchal power that goes with it) himself. A similar (but different) journey awaits the infant girl. This 'Oedipal journey' results in adulthood.

The Oedipal journey can be found in many narratives, filmic and non-filmic. For example, in *North By Northwest*, Roger Thornhill's perilous journey can be shown to follow an Oedipal model very closely. He begins the film attached to his mother, struggles with (symbolic) father figures throughout the film, and reaches sexual maturity at the end of the film when he is saved from death by the forces of law and order and a new Mrs Thornhill takes the place of the mother in his life. Many (some have argued all) films contain traces of such an Oedipal journey, and of course, the more such ideas have passed into critical circulation, the more film-makers have begun to *deliberately* play with and subvert generic expectations to do with the 'hero's journey' (*Back to the Future*, 1985; *Last Action Hero*, 1993).

Exercise 12.3

1. List some films you have seen which contain traces of such an Oedipal journey.
2. In a recent film of your choice containing a central male character, discuss his 'journey'. What Oedipal elements can you find?
3. Choose a recent film with a central female character. How does her narrative 'journey' compare with that of a typical male central character?

MORE WAYS OF DESCRIBING A FILM: SEMIOLOGY

Both spoken and written languages are made up of signs. The social science of *linguistics* developed in the late nineteenth century as a means of studying language systems. Methods were developed for studying the sounds (*phonetics*) of a language, its grammar, its vocabulary, its historical development, and its relation to other languages. What was new was the *systematic* nature of the subject, which many writers treated as a kind of science.

But if language is a system of signs, then what about painting? What about photography? And what about film? It became clear in the second half of the nineteenth century that all cultural products are made up of signs, and indeed that we are surrounded by various kinds of signs in everyday life. Charles Sanders Peirce (pronounced 'purse'), for example, was among the first to analyse such everyday signs; from him we have the division of all signs into three types:

- iconic: signs which (in some respects at least) look like the things they refer to: for example, some road signs, some 'male' and 'female' toilet signs, figurative painting, and of course photographs.
- indexical: signs which have some causal link with what they signify: for example, a weathervane indicating wind direction, a footprint, smoke signifying fire.
- symbolic: signs which are *arbitrary*: this means that there is no apparent causal link between the sign and what it refers to. Examples include Morse code and, of course, words and the letters/sounds of which they are made. 'D-o-g' and 'c-h-i-e-n' both refer to (more or less) the same thing, but the choice of letters/sounds for the word seems arbitrary.

Peirce is seen as the founder of *semiotics*, which is really the American word for what is called *semiology* in Europe. The beginnings of the latter were developed by Ferdinand de Saussure, a Swiss professor of linguistics, in the late nineteenth century. There is sometimes some confusion because Peirce and Saussure worked independently and sometimes used the same words to mean slightly different things.

It is to Saussure that we largely owe a different model of *signification*:

- signifier: that which signifies: the word, the letters on a page, an image, a sound.
- signified: that to which the signifier refers: the idea of 'a dog' perhaps, or something more precise like the idea of 'a rotweiler'.

- sign: the combination of the *signifier* and the *signified*. Saussure nicely compared these two 'sides' of the sign to the two sides of a sheet of paper: both necessary for the sheet to exist, but impossible to separate.

In the second half of the twentieth century semiology came to be closely associated with *structuralism*, a method of study with the following principles:

- Structuralists were concerned with the *text* (film, novel, advertisement, painting. . .) and not with the author or the audience.
- The approach was non-normative: this means that it made no attempt to evaluate or judge whether texts or artworks were 'good' or not. Studying beer-mats could be seen as just as useful as studying Picasso's paintings.
- Meanings were seen as produced by particular sign systems interacting with their context.
- Structuralists saw their work as systematic and as more 'scientific' or 'objective' than more traditional approaches to the study of culture.

The 1960s and 1970s saw the most intensive attempts to apply the methods of semiology to film (and to television). It is only possible to mention two aspects of the mountain of study, but among the chief figures were Roland Barthes, Raymond Bellour, Christian Metz and Peter Wollen.

One kind of work concerned analysis of how signification is coded in individual frames or shots in particular film texts. In this respect film analysis was quite similar to structuralist-semiological analysis of other products; for example, Roland Barthes gained public prominence with a series of semiological meditations on things like the Citroen Déesse car and the face of Greta Garbo. In films, the focus came to be on how elements of the image such as iconography, *mise en scène*, camera and lighting 'make meaning'. The low key shadowy lighting and strange camera angles of *film noir* help to signify a threatening and uneasy atmosphere; the use of red colour in *Marnie* (blood, a bouquet of flowers) is clearly used to signal the central character's mental fragility. An iconography including crucifixes, garlic, knives and tombstones can be used to analyse the horror genre. It is worth remembering that much everyday reviewing and critical writing on films has now absorbed semiological assumptions; indeed, students generally already 'think semiologically'. Here it is simply a matter of making the origins of such thinking explicit.

The second application of semiology was more ambitious. One of the main questions which concerned such theorists was whether and how film could be described as a 'language' – indeed, one of the unresolved questions remained whether linguistics is a branch of semiology or whether semiology is a kind of linguistics. By the 1960s it had already become common to speak of close ups, camera angles and different kinds of editing as part of the 'language' of film (as we have done at some points in this book), but what interested Christian Metz in particular was whether it was possible to see these and other elements as part of a more systematic 'grammar', to see film as a language *system*. In keeping with the structuralist principles listed above, Metz used *Adieu Philippine* (a relatively obscure film directed by Jacques Rozier in 1960) to develop a typology or grammar (which he called a '*syntagmatique*') which attempted to show all the different types of shot combinations which could be used in a narrative film. The terms *syntagm* and *syntagmatic* entered the critical vocabulary, and referred to any fragment of a text (in the case of film, frame, shot, scene or sequence) and how such elements were linked together to form a narrative. At the same time, any element in a text could also be seen as a *paradigm* or as *paradigmatic*, in which case the emphasis was on how the element (the high angle for the shot of the village about to be attacked in Hitchcock's *The Birds*, for example) was chosen in preference to other alternatives. The effectiveness of such paradigmatic choice could then be checked against other possible options (in this case a low angle shot) using a commutation test (see also p. 198).

Metz's work gave rise to much further research and debate which eventually cast doubt on the validity of seeing film in such rigid 'grammatical' terms, but his work remains an excellent example of the strengths (and weaknesses) of the structuralist-semiological approach.

STRUCTURALIST APPROACHES TO NARRATIVE

We have already referred in the chapter on Mainstream and Alternative Film Form to models of narrative developed by Vladimir Propp and by Tzvetan Todorov. As they deal principally with the structure of the narrative, and tend to ignore the 'content' and themes (what the story is 'about'), such approaches are often described as structuralist. At this point we shall deal briefly with two other structuralist approaches to narrative which have been influential.

Lévi-Strauss and Binary Oppositions

Though anthropologist Claude Lévi-Strauss did not work on or write about film, his studies of myth and meaning-making in a variety of cultures have been widely used in narrative studies. Lévi-Strauss proposed that myths (and by extension narratives) are structured around *binary oppositions* which are significant for the particular society or culture. While Lévi-Strauss studied oppositions such as light and dark, sun and moon and raw and cooked in South American and other cultures, his ideas and analysis can readily be applied to films and other media/cultural artefacts.

In a western such as Clint Eastwood's *Pale Rider* (1985), for instance, significant binary oppositions include the following:

law	disorder
knowledge	lack of knowledge
male	female
individual	town/community
civilization	wilderness

These binary oppositions interact and change in the course of the narrative; more interestingly, comparison of how similar oppositions work in other westerns tells us how narrative themes change from film to film, from one historical period to another. This is a way of looking, for example, at the role of the individual hero central to most westerns: why did audiences want John Wayne in the 1930s and 1940s but go for Clint Eastwood in the 1970s and 1980s?

Exercise 12.4

1. Choose two films of the same genre and map out their binary oppositions. How do the oppositions develop and interact in the films? What are the differences?
2. Are such binary oppositions so easy to detect in more recent films (since 1990, say)? What does this tell you about the narratives of more recent films? How is this linked to genre?

Roland Barthes and Narrative Codes

A second approach which has been called structuralist is that developed by Roland Barthes, a French writer and cultural theorist who wrote widely from the 1950s until his death in 1980. Once again (though Barthes did also write about film) some of his influential ideas originally concerned narrative in literature, but have been extensively applied to film.

In a book entitled *S/Z*, Barthes outlined the workings of five *narrative codes*; while some of the names he chose are Greek and may be difficult, he also sensibly provided abbreviations (see Table 12.1). It is possible to see how Barthes' codes are relevant to a number of

Roland Barthes' narrative codes   Table 12.1

Code	Abbreviated	What the code organizes
1 hermeneutic	HER	code of puzzles, enigmas and mysteries; 'what happens next?'; 'how will this end?'; clues (which may be misleading) are provided, resolutions are delayed; this code draws the reader/spectator through the narrative.
2 semic	SEM	code of character construction: characters are built up through iconography, gesture and speech and usually establish apparent individuality.
3 proairetic	ACT	code of actions (hence ACT) related to recognizable behaviour; this code operates retrospectively as actions can be seen to have been organized into sequences.
4 cultural	REF	code of references (hence REF) to bodies of knowledge outside the text, e.g. accents, knowledge about particular places, parody of other texts/films.
5 symbolic	SYM	code of broad themes and motifs often structured in oppositions (cf. Lévi-Strauss), for example light/dark, good/evil, male/female; patterns of symbolic meanings run through the text.

preceding chapters: we have already considered the nature of narrative cause and effect (which involves the hermeneutic code), the nature of plot and story events (which refer to the proairetic code) and character (semic code); the binary oppositions of Lévi-Strauss are clearly ideal for Barthes' symbolic code. The cultural code focuses on knowledge which a viewer brings to a film: the colour red may signify danger, passion or 'stop'; the Big Mac conversation in *Pulp Fiction* depends on audience knowledge of hamburgers (and of McDonald's!); it can even be argued that we use the cultural code to recognize that a close up signifies intensity or attention to detail.

Detailed analysis of a single film using Barthes' codes is a long and exhausting procedure – see *Jump Cut* no. 12/13 (Dec 1976) for a very difficult but fascinating analysis of Jean Renoir's *The Rules of the Game* (*La Règle du jeu*, 1939). If we limit ourselves to a single sequence or to the start of a film, though, we can learn a great deal about the narrative organization of the film and about how a viewer decodes that narrative.

CASE STUDY

Barthes' Codes and the Opening 6 Minutes of *Scream*

The credit sequence of any film already activates the codes and influences the viewer's under-standing of the narrative, and *Scream* is no exception. The lurid lettering of the title, the scream, metallic (knife) sounds and heartbeat on the soundtrack instantly appeal to cultural knowledge of the horror genre [REF code]. We may also (unconsciously?) register the colours used in the title lettering: red, white and blue: the colours of the US flag. . . [REF and SYM codes]. As with most titles, there are also immediate questions: Who will scream? Why? [HER code]; here an additional question may be 'Is that really the end of the credits?!'

After the sound of the phone ringing bridges from the title to the start of the narrative proper, and the camera pans as Casey picks up the receiver and answers the call (Fig 12.6), many view-ers would recognize Drew Barrymore [REF]. The SEM code also immediately comes into action as we begin to build an idea of the character: her appearance, clothing (chunky-but-tight-fitting white sweater) and manner tell us she is young, blonde, attractive, confident in her surroundings, perhaps friendly. The SEM code, however, also enables us to begin to imagine the man who is

Figure 12.6   *Scream: Casey answers the phone (Miramax, courtesy Kobal)*

calling: initially polite, pleasant... but perhaps already just a little unsettling. Why is he calling? What does he want? Is it important? These are all HER code questions.

After another phone call (which involves the SEM code to continue to establish the caller as threatening), the camera zooms in to and lingers for a moment on the window. . . we (more or less unconsciously) recognize this as significant [REF] and continue to wonder what will happen next [HER]. The extreme long shot of the house which follows acts partly as a delayed establishing shot but also confirms [REF] a sense of unease familiar to horror fans.

Casey lights the gas and starts to prepare some popcorn. The REF code is activated as this evokes film-viewing, and it is clear from what she says during her third conversation with the mystery caller that she is a 'normal' horror-film fan: this could be you! Here there are also shifts involving both SEM and HER: she is (implausibly?) friendly and even flirtatious with the caller, and the viewer surely wonders what her changed manner will lead to. Casey walks through from the kitchen to the living room while she discusses horror films with the caller; she turns off a light as she does so; the camerawork here subtly reinforces the dialogue, which is about *Halloween* and the Freddy films [REF].

An important HER moment occurs as the caller says 'I want to know who I'm looking at': the threat is clear and is immediately underlined by a subtle zoom towards Casey [REF perhaps] and the sound of dogs barking, accompanied by threatening music. Another important HER element throughout this opening sequence is the state of the popcorn: the repeated cutaways to the popcorn getting hotter and hotter and about to burst clearly parallel [SYM] the overall tension of the sequence. It is significant that she is just about to turn off the gas when the killer calls one more time and things become really nasty.

The rest of the sequence clearly continues to develop the characters [SEM] but also clarifies the ACT code: a young woman is harassed on the phone, then she and her boyfriend are murdered by an unknown killer. While the ACT code could in principle be reduced to smaller actions (she picks up the phone, she smiles. . .), it is usually used to split up a narrative into larger chunks (phone harassment; murder).

The REF code is also rampant throughout the whole sequence: Casey plays with a large carving knife as she happily talks to her killer about *Halloween*, preparing the viewer for the knowing self-reflexive 'quiz' which the killer imposes on her. The REF code here is clearly complicated by the many overt ('postmodern') references to the film's own genre, for example 'You should never say "who's there", don't you watch scary movies?'. A further indicator of the REF code is the TV set (switched on but imageless . . .) which is often (and very deliberately) placed in the background in many shots.

The SYM code tends to operate over an entire film. In *Scream*, one significant symbolic opposition seems to be light and dark: Casey gradually turns off most of the lights as she is increasingly terrorized and ends up hiding behind the TV set, and this can perhaps be linked to her own blondeness and white jumper (the killer taunts her with 'blondie'). A broader symbolic opposition may be peace/stability and mayhem, a staple of the slasher sub-genre. Visibility and invisibility are also an important symbolic opposition; the killer wants to know who he is looking at; his taunting of Casey ('can you see me?') is subtle because he can only ask the question because he knows/can see where she is. . . and of course for the spectator everything on the screen is visible.

IDEOLOGY AND POSTMODERNISM

What is Ideology?

We have already come across the idea that films have an ideological function. But what is this stuff called ideology? When the word was first introduced by Antoine Destutt Tracey in 1812 in the aftermath of the French Revolution, it referred to 'the study of ideas'. Before long, however (in Destutt Tracey's own lifetime – he was imprisoned for his writing), it became clear that those in power generally did not like the 'ideas' underlying their power being analysed. Given the different interests of the power 'élite' and of those being oppressed by that power (the working class), it is not surprising that the definition of ideology has been a theoretical battleground ever since. In the process, 'ideology' has come to refer not so much to the study of ideas as to the 'ideas' themselves. (It is interesting to compare this transformation with what has happened to other 'ologies': 'the ecology of a forest' no longer refers to the study of the forest; 'the biology of the cockroach' is now more likely to refer to the life-processes of the creature than to their study.)

There are many definitions of ideology which are all more or less 'correct'. The following exercise is adapted from a longer list of definitions provided by Terry Eagleton.

Exercise 12.5

Working individually, read through the following list of possible 'definitions' (courtesy of Terry Eagleton) of ideology. Select three which seem most 'correct' to you.

Then, in pairs, select three definitions on which you agree. Finally, in groups of 4–6, compare choices; each group must (through reasoned discussion, seduction, haranguing or bribery) come up with a shortlist of three preferred 'definitions'. In class discussion you will see if there is any consensus. Your teacher may also contribute her/his preferred definitions.

(a) the process of production of meanings, signs and values in social life
(b) the body of ideas characteristic of a particular social group or class
(c) ideas which help to legitimate a dominant political power
(d) false ideas which help to legitimate a dominant political power
(e) systematically distorted communication
(f) forms of thought motivated by social interests
(g) socially necessary illusion
(h) the medium in which conscious social actors make sense of their world
(i) action-oriented sets of beliefs
(j) the indispensable medium in which individuals live out their relations to a social structure

---

Much of the development in theories of ideology in the nineteenth century was influenced by Karl Marx, whose aim was the overthrow of capitalism and the establishment of a socialist society governed by the people. Considering the anti-democratic interests of capitalism, it is not surprising that throughout most of the twentieth century, 'ideology' was seen (in Europe and North America at least) as a fanatical or fundamentalist set of ideas (a grotesque caricature of Destutt Tracey's original definition of the term). So the official view was that the Soviet bloc, as well as China, Cuba and others, were in the grip of 'ideology', whereas the liberal democracies of most of Western Europe and North America were (and are) ruled by rational 'common sense', free of ideology.

This last view was ridiculed and exposed as itself ideological by political theorists, particularly in the 1960s and 1970s. It has become clear that many 'common-sense' beliefs and assumptions are profoundly ideological, from the once-commonplace racist beliefs about white supremacy over 'savages' to the old chestnut of 'women drivers' (and the ideological function of racist and chauvinist jokes is of course far from negligible). As we have already noted, it is wise to suspect the 'obvious'.

The tradition of Marxist writing on ideology was continued by Antonio Gramsci, Georg Lukacs, and Herbert Marcuse, Theodor Adorno and Max Horkheimer of the Frankfurt School, among many others. Throughout the middle of the twentieth century, theories of ideology were developed which, it must be said, had little effect on film theory at the time.

This changed with the advent of Jacques Lacan and Louis Althusser. While Lacan developed a complex – some would say incomprehensible – psychoanalytic reworking of Freud, Althusser sought to marry Marxism and psychoanalysis. The result was a particularly complex theory according to which ideology is seen as unconscious, as an *imaginary* relation to real conditions of social existence.

All representations (whether part of the mass media, 'art' or personal communication) are thus ideological: they carry ideological 'messages' which overwhelmingly reinforce the status quo. The individual subject has some limited 'choice' (insofar that s/he may have come to oppose dominant ideologies) to decode representations 'oppositionally', but the emphasis of the Althusser model of ideology is on the fundamentally conservative nature of most media representations as carriers of dominant ideology.

The immediate effect of the work of Lacan and Althusser in the 1960s and 1970s – and we need to remember that several years passed before their writing was translated into English – was a massive reassessment and revaluing of Marxist theory, together with a wealth of related writing on film, particularly in the journal *Screen*.

Much of the theoretical writing of the 1970s has (some would say unjustly) now joined flared trousers, platform heels and Slade as a 'fashion casualty' of that time. It is possible, though, to see the subsequent marginalization and dismissal of Marxist theory (and of film theory built on Marxism and/or psychoanalysis) as part of a backlash which itself can only be described as ideological – a backlash which gained much strength from the 'end of socialism' rhetoric associated with the fall of the Berlin Wall in 1989 and the dissolution of the Soviet Union in 1991.

Postmodernism and Postmodernity

There is no space here to consider the postmodern in any detail. Even the (obvious?) idea that it follows the modern (see p. 188) has been disputed, and the writing of postmodern theorists is notoriously hard to understand.

The distinction between postmodernism and postmodernity needs to be made, however. Postmodernism refers to art (painting, architecture, films, writing) which is part of an explicit rejection of or alternative to modernism; there have been few (if any – *Blade Runner* may be a candidate. . .) 'postmodernist' films – as a label the term has more readily been attached to architecture, paintings and literature, increasingly since the 1970s. On the other hand, postmodernity is a term used to describe the culture which Western societies increasingly live in, and the word 'postmodern' can thus be applied to films, TV and other aspects of turn-of-millennium life independently of the label attached to the particular product.

The following are some of the characteristics associated with postmodern culture. Film titles are included where they show signs of the particular characteristic.

1. Loss of faith in the so-called *grand narratives* of human progress (including Marxism, Darwinian evolution, Freudianism, feminism, perhaps even rationality and science).
2. A loss/lack of a sense of history (*Absolute Beginners*, 1986; *Plunkett and MacLeane*, 1999).
3. Borrowing of fragments from other texts (including paintings, film, etc.) and using them with no reference to their original context (*bricolage*); this is closely linked to the idea of *intertextuality*, which is about references to other texts/paintings/films (*Orlando*, *Pulp Fiction*; use of famous paintings in posters, for example the Mona Lisa smoking a joint).
4. Pastiche and playfulness: 'Modernist' texts often had/have a serious purpose and often use(d) *parody* to satirize or attack a person or an institution. Postmodern pastiche does not have any serious target but tends to imitate and play with past texts/forms just for the fun of it (*Austin Powers: International Man of Mystery*, 1997; *Austin Powers: The Spy Who Shagged Me*, 1999).
5. *Irony* and *knowingness* are closely linked to most of the above (*Orlando*).
6. Divorcement of the image from reality: it has been increasingly argued since Baudrillard that (in western cultures) we are losing touch with reality (whatever that is) and that electronic images (TV, video and now the Internet) have become the new reality: a *simulacrum* of reality (a simulacrum is an image which cannot ultimately be linked to a specific referent or object being represented). In David Cronenberg's *Videodrome* (1982), a character called Brian O'Blivion says as much:

> The battle for the mind of North America will be fought in the video arena – the Videodrome. The television screen is the retina of the mind's eye. Therefore the television screen is part of the physical structure of the brain. Therefore whatever appears on the television screen emerges as raw experience for those who watch it. Therefore television is reality and reality is less than television.

While the narrative of *Videodrome* is explicitly about television, other more recent films such as *eXistenZ* (Cronenberg, 1999) and *The Matrix* have begun to play explicitly with notions of 'reality', building on such earlier alternative-reality films as *Total Recall* (Verhoeven, 1990).

7. Fragmentation of the individual subject: while until (roughly) the 1970s/1980s most individuals (again, it has to be stressed that this applies to western cultures) saw themselves as unitary, coherent subjects, the trend is now to a more fragmented subjectivity

(matching an increasingly fragmented society) in which individuals have a different personality for each day of the week.
8. 'The end of ideology': Francis Fukuyama infamously suggested in the aftermath of the events of 1989 that the 'victory' of western liberal democracy and the fall of the Soviet regime effectively signalled the end of history.

Exercise 12.6
In small groups and then as a whole group, discuss the ways in which some recent films may be described as 'postmodern'.

Of course it is possible to argue that some of the above strategies are not new, but the last three points in particular (whether we want to accept them or not) seem to signal quite a radical shift in the way many people see films, and, indeed, the world.

Indeed, such aspects of the postmodern can also be seen as part of the *poststructuralism* which, naturally enough, followed the structuralist impulse of the 1960s and 1970s. If structuralism did have a tendency to study a cultural product in isolation, and was often open to the charge of ignoring the social context in which such products were produced and consumed, it is also fair to say that much structuralist analysis has always been acutely aware of the limits of its methodology: Barthes' *S/Z*, which furnished the narrative codes (see Table 12.1) which have been much used in film analysis, was itself marked by a poststructuralism which insisted that there was no single meaning, no way of simply stating how any spectator or reader would decode a text.

If the text was central to the structuralist approach, it is the very idea of a 'text' which has been *deconstructed* in poststructuralism. If *The Matrix*, say, is an audio-visual text, it is also part of a larger 'text' which would have to include the previous biographies and work of the film-makers, their financial and artistic relationship with the backers of the film (including the distributors, Warners), the production process itself, and indeed the biographies and social positioning of all of its spectators. In poststructuralism and for Cultural Studies, the 'text' becomes global: the whole of the world and of reality becomes a 'text'.

Yet if poststructuralism has been intent on deconstructing cultural artefacts and analysing their relation to the societies which produce and consume them, it could not have done so without the tools and the vocabulary provided by structuralism. It can be argued that the vocabularies of semiology, structuralism and psychoanalysis remain vital to understanding how films 'work'.

COGNITIVE APPROACHES

Since around 1990 a number of writers (principally North American and most notably David Bordwell and Noël Carroll) have contested the apparent dominance of so-called 'Screen Theory' (named after the British film journal), of which semiology, psychoanalysis and ideology were important components. Indeed, the hostility of many of the critiques of 1970s theory has led some to refer to the new approaches as 'Anti-theory'. The title of the book edited by Bordwell and Carroll, *Post Theory* (1996), is itself provocative.

Nevertheless it would be quite wrong to say that the new 'Post-theory' approach has no theoretical foundations. While rejecting much 'established' *Screen* theory and its post-structuralist developments, such writers favour an approach based on Cultural Studies, reader response and cognitive theories. Cognitive theory (or 'cognitive science') aims at detailed (scientific) explanation of the links between perception (of film images and sounds, among other things) and the emotions produced. This approach is partly based on sciences of (visual) perception and Darwinian adaptation and evolution.

The old (and admittedly poorly understood) 'persistence of vision' explanation for how films produce an illusion of movement has thus been discarded in favour of the 'phi-phenomenon'. While the former attributed the illusion to an automatic mechanism beyond the viewer's control, the latter stresses the *active* nature of the work done by the brain in 'filling in the gaps' between the film's frames (Maltby, 1995, p. 490).

If both the *Screen*-derived and cognitivist approaches claim to provide more accurate explanations of how individual spectators create meaning from films, the single central thing which separates the two camps seems to be an insistence on or an indifference to the role of our old friend the unconscious.

In the words of Noël Carroll, '[t]he mere plausibility of a cognitivist theory gives it a special advantage over psychoanalytic theories of the same phenomenon. . . . [W]here we have a convincing cognitivist account, there is no point whatsoever in looking any further for a psychoanalytic account' (Bordwell and Carroll, 1996, p. 65). On the other hand, as we have already seen, this kind of assertion seems to deny the possibility that the plausible (or obvious) may be 'wrong' and that a psychoanalytic approach may be necessary to expose *why* perception works as it does.

NEW FORMS OF SPECTATORSHIP

At the beginning of the new millennium, new film-making and screening technologies are bound to entail new relationships between spectator and film text. Some of these have been suggested in Chapters 2 and 5 above, but it may be worth considering some other changes in spectatorship which are likely to be with us in the next decade or two.

Film projectionists (of whom there are surprisingly many) will no doubt mourn the eventual disappearance of celluloid and of 'film' in the physical sense. Film projection is a technical skill requiring considerable training and expertise. With the advent of digital technologies, of videotape, CD-ROM and more recently of DVD, however, it is possible that screenings in cinemas will depend only on someone capable of pressing the right buttons.

How will this affect spectatorship? Superficially, perhaps very little at first. The spectator's relation to the screen will remain much as it is now. The ritual of watching a film in a cinema may remain relatively unchanged. But there are at least four further aspects of the new digital technologies which are likely to have far-reaching effects on spectatorship.

For the first of these, we do not need to leave the cinema. With increasing use of CGI in films, the screen image loses its 'depth' and becomes 'flatter', a less effective simulation of 3-dimensional space. What will be the implications for feeling 'part of the action'? How will this affect identification with character or action? Will films come to resemble TV or computer games?

Second, and remaining in the cinema, the very nature of characters and the actors/stars who play them is likely to change radically. Already, characters have been entirely computer-generated: in *Titanic*, the crowd seeing off the voyage is a computer figment; in *Eyes Wide Shut*, the version distributed in the USA features a group of computer-generated characters walking in front of an orgy scene which would have been unacceptable for the rating which the distributors wanted. This means that the images of people which are shown on the screen have no *referent*; this is not a picture of a real person (which of course has serious effects on the kind of semiological analysis that is possible!). Again, this is likely to have implications for how we think about identification with characters, or with actors or stars. It is likely that in the future there will be cyberstars (or 'synthespians') who have no material existence. Existing stars may also sell the rights to their images to computer-imaging companies so that their (computerized) images can be recycled in future films. . . As Barbara Creed points out (2000), as Arnold Schwarzenegger was fond of saying, 'I'll be back!'

The other likely effects on film spectatorship move us out of the cinema and into the domain of private viewing. While since around 1980 (in the UK) widespread access to VCRs and videotape has revolutionized private film viewing (not least for academics and teachers!), the effect of DVD, following that of CDs in audio, may well be even more radical. Not only do DVDs usually come complete with additional 'documentary' material about the making of the film, profiles of actors and creative technicians, etc., but the facility of being able to drop into the film at almost any point (and indeed of watching scenes in any order) further weakens the incentive to watch the whole film. The development of interactive technology also means that spectators will soon be able to choose which narrative (for a named film) they wish to follow. . .

Finally, the above developments will, of course, also be transferable to film viewing on the Internet. Here, in addition to the DVD options, there are likely soon to be sophisticated databases linked to individual films. At the time of writing, prototype Internet programmes exist which allow DVD viewing on part of the screen, and simultaneous analysis on other parts of the screen. For example, it is possible, at a click of the proverbial button, to identify all cuts or shots for a sequence or for the entire film and to generate sample frames from the shots. It is possible to summon texts from a database of reviews and articles in which sections dealing with particular aspects of the film (for example, the central character, lighting, *mise en scène*) have been highlighted; a click on the highlighted section can then call up the sequence referred to. Some films in production are already having all technical information about shooting automatically stored on computer. Internet sites (and perhaps DVDs) will thus contain shot-by-shot catalogues of shot sizes, camera angles, lighting and various aspects of *mise en scène*, in addition to dialogue and other script details.

With such wide-ranging changes in strategies of spectatorship, it is likely that theories of spectatorship will also need to change. It will be for a new generation of film spectator-theorists to develop appropriate models. These will no doubt need to draw on much of the theoretical legacy outlined above. . . but the recipe will be different.

SUMMARY

- Spectatorship refers to the individual spectator, while 'Audience Studies' refers to social groups of spectators.
- Over the course of the twentieth century, 'effects' studies gave way to uses and gratifications and Cultural Studies approaches.
- Alternatively, the spectator's position can be seen as an effect of the text itself.
- Psychoanalytic models of the spectator have been influential since the 1970s, but have recently come under attack, particularly from a cognitivist perspective.
- Semiology/semiotics (the study of sign systems) and structuralism have provided important tools for textual analysis of films.
- The concept of ideology has been at the centre of arguments over how films produce meaning in relation to individual spectators/subjects.
- The idea of the postmodern has led to suggestions that we have reached the end of history and of ideology.

REFERENCES

David Bordwell and Noël Carroll (eds), *Post Theory* (Madison, WI: University of Wisconsin Press, 1996).

Cultural Studies, vol. 1, no. 1 (1987).

Christine Geraghty, 'Women and sixties British cinema', in Robert Murphy (ed.), *The British Cinema Book* (London: BFI, 1997).

Richard Maltby, *Hollywood Cinema* (Oxford: Blackwell, 1995).

FURTHER READING

It is not possible here to give a full sense of the amount of detailed analysis which has been carried out on individual films from a psychoanalytic perspective (or indeed from many other theoretical perspectives). There is a vast iceberg of theoretical literature just waiting for the unsuspecting student. . . Some of the texts suggested here are perhaps more 'difficult' than many of those listed in other chapters.

Dudley Andrew, *The Major Film Theories* (Oxford: Oxford University Press, 1976) (Part 3).

Martin Barker, *A Haunt of Fears* (London: Pluto Press, 1984a).

Martin Barker (ed.), *The Video Nasties* (London: Pluto Press, 1984b).

Martin Barker (with Thomas Austin), *From* Antz *to Titanic* (London: Pluto Press, 2000).

Roland Barthes, *Mythologies* (transl. Annette Lavers, London: Paladin, 1973).

Roland Barthes, *S/Z* (transl. Richard Miller, New York: Hill & Wang, 1974).

David Bordwell and Noël Carroll (eds), *Post Theory* (Madison, WI: University of Wisconsin Press, 1996).

Leo Braudy and Marshall Cohen (eds), *Film Theory and Criticism: Introductory Readings* (5th edn, Oxford: Oxford University Press, 1999).

Pam Cook and Mieke Bernink (eds), *The Cinema Book* (2nd edn, London: BFI, 1999).

Barbara Creed, 'The cyberstar: digital pleasures and the end of the unconscious', *Screen,* vol. 41, no. 1 (Spring 2000).

John Ellis, *Visible Fictions* (London: Routledge & Kegan Paul, 1982).

Anne Gray, 'Reading the audience', *Screen,* vol. 28, no. 3 (Summer 1987).

John Hill and Pamela Church Gibson (eds), *The Oxford Guide to Film Studies* (Oxford: Oxford University Press, 1998), Chapters 6–11.

Judith Mayne, *Cinema and Spectatorship* (London: Routledge, 1993).

David Morley, *The Nationwide Audience* (London: BFI TV Monograph, 1980).

David Morley, *Family Television* (London: Comedia, 1986).

Robert Stam, *Film Theory: An Introduction* (Oxford: Blackwell, 2000).

Peter Wollen, *Signs and Meaning in the Cinema* (London: Secker & Warburg, 1969, 1972, 1987) (new edition, London: BFI, 1997).

PART 4

Film Movements and National Cinema

British Cinema

British cinema has existed since 1895, and many of its innovative and memorable films have attracted international acclaim. It has covered many different themes, styles and genres and produced numerous stars, from Charlie Chaplin to Kate Winslet, and *auteurs* from Alfred Hitchcock to Ridley Scott who have gone on to work in Hollywood and elsewhere. This chapter aims to identify what exactly is meant by the term 'British cinema' and to trace its history in terms of the films, the industry and the audiences. British cinema has taken different forms at particular moments in the nation's history, and these trends and developments are to be identified and explained. There is not, of course, just one British cinema; the countries that make up Britain – England, Scotland, Wales and the disputed territory of Northern Ireland – all have very different cultures and film industries. The reality is that film production has been, and still is, concentrated in England, as illustrated by the preponderance of references to English films in this chapter. Case studies will be used to identify how aspects of British culture and society have been represented in British films, in terms of class, race, gender, sexuality, age and national and regional identity.

WHAT IS BRITISH CINEMA?

There are two principal approaches to defining British cinema: the first approach emphasizes the role of the film industry, while the second is concerned with the films' representations of British cultural life. The British film industry has existed in one form or another since the beginning of the twentieth century and as such can be regarded as an institution – it is well established, even though it goes through periodic changes. When we talk of British cinema as an institution, we are concerned with the industry in terms of ownership and control, of how films are financed and who produces, distributes and exhibits films. The institutional definition of British cinema, as determined by government, has changed much over the years but has essentially referred to finance and production. Thus, for a film to be classified as British, it has been necessary that a certain percentage of the finance, production staff and actors be British.

Film Finance

Using this approach to determine the national characteristics of a film results in *The Full Monty* being classified as only partly British as its finance was supplied by 20th Century Fox. Similarly, *Chariots of Fire*, despite looking every inch a British film, was in fact mainly financed from the USA and Egypt. We might also imagine that the Bond films are British because of the nationality of their hero, the nationality of much of the production staff and the location of many of the storylines, but in fact the latest Bond movies were financed and thus are owned by MGM/UA, an amalgamated American company. Nor is the director useful as an indication of the nationality of a film. Ridley Scott and Alan Parker are British, as of course was Alfred Hitchcock, but most of their films have been American, in that they were financed by American companies. Again, using the economic and production-based definition, *Land and Freedom,* a film set in Spain about the Spanish Civil War, is classified as British because of the source of its funding (Film Four, the film finance wing of the TV company Channel 4, Figure 13.1), plus the nationality of its director, Ken Loach, and of much of the production staff.

While the majority of films screened in Britain are funded by American companies, a significant number of low-budget films have drawn their funding from British companies, and some have gone on to be successful. Film Four has become the main source of funding in Britain and financed successes such as *Secrets and Lies* (Mike Leigh, 1995) and *Trainspotting* (Danny Boyle, 1995), as well as co-financing Mike Newell's *Four Weddings and a Funeral*; however, the follow-up, *Notting Hill,* was financed without Film Four by Universal and Polygram. Co-financing is now common in Britain and has seen the British Film Institute partly funding Ken Loach's *Riff-Raff*, the Arts Council contributing to David Caffrey's *Divorcing*

Figure 13.1   *The Channel Four logo*

Jack and the BBC funding Lynne Ramsay's *Ratcatcher*. A further source of funding is the National Lottery, which has made significant contributions via the Arts Council to Pathé Productions, The Film Consortium and DNA Film Ltd. However, a significant number of films made by small production companies who have received lottery funding have been critical and financial failures. Merchant–Ivory have also been a consistent source of funding for what has been called 'heritage cinema'. However, some sources of funding have unfortunately disappeared, such as Goldcrest and Palace Pictures, both companies folding in the 1980s. Production costs for British films are extremely low when compared with Hollywood films, for which costs have run as high as $600 million. Average production costs for British films made during 1998 were £5.72 million (Dyja, 1999, p. 19).

British Culture

The institutional approach to British cinema clearly leads us towards some important observations about Britain's film industry in terms of finance and ownership, but the cultural approach is also useful in providing an understanding of British cinema, although the emphasis is on the films themselves rather than the industry. The British Film Institute's annual review of the film industry provides five categories of British films, all of which refer to elements of finance and production personnel as originating from Britain, while two of the definitions also refer to aspects of British culture being featured in the films. The categories are as follows:

Category A: Films where the cultural and financial impetus is from the UK and the majority of personnel are British.

Category B: Majority UK co-productions. Films in which, although there are foreign partners, there is a UK cultural content and a significant amount of British finance and personnel.

Category C: Minority UK co-productions. Foreign (non-US) films in which there is a small UK involvement in finance or personnel.

Category D: American-financed or part-financed films made in the UK. Most titles have a British cultural content.

Category E: US films with some British financial involvement.

(Dyja, 1999, pp. 20–2)

The UK Department of Culture, Media and Sport has also concerned itself with defining what constitutes a British film. It commissioned a report from the Film Policy Review Group, and proposed two categories. The first category relates to film finance and identifies a film as British if '75% of total production expenditure is incurred on goods supplied or services performed in the UK' (FPRG, 1998, Annex 2). The second category classifies a film as culturally British with reference to a points system, with points allotted if key production staff are British and if the subject matter of the script is about Britain.

A cultural definition is concerned with how films represent aspects of British life, especially with regard to social groups and ideologies that exist within British society. Thus the cultural approach looks at how issues relating to class, race, gender, sexuality, age and national and regional identity, as well as values and beliefs about social institutions and practices such as family, work, leisure, religion, education and politics in Britain, are depicted in films. A cultural approach enables films such as *Chariots of Fire* and *The Full Monty* to be interpreted as British films, even though their finance came from outside the UK, because they deal with aspects of British culture.

Representation is a central issue in every sector of the media, be it film, television or some other media form, because the media mediate; they show things. Representation is an important and often controversial topic in studies of the media because there is always more than one way to represent something; choices are always made. Representations can be positive or negative, dominant or alternative. Thus there is always the possibility of an individual, or a social group, believing that they have been represented inaccurately or unjustly, in other words, misrepresented. Behind representations lie ideologies; values and beliefs shape how things are shown to us. Film, like other media, is a form of indirect communication: we experience an interpretation of the world second-hand. The messages we receive are mediated; the process of production comes between us and the things being represented within a film. It is always possible that our perception of the world, of British society and the social groups it contains, could be shaped and influenced by the representations we experience in films. What appear to be natural ways of seeing aspects of British society may in fact be no more than selective interpretations. For this reason, the latter part of this chapter focuses on identifying representations and stereotypes in British films that have perhaps resulted from the repeated use of particular representations over a period of time.

AN OVERVIEW OF BRITISH CINEMA

One of Britain's first film-makers was Birt Acres, who began by making actuality films, one of which was *Rough Sea at Dover* (1895). G.A. Smith tended more towards short stories such as *Grandma's Reading Glass* (1900). Experimentation was an important element in early British films and both Cecil Hepworth (*Explosion of a Motor Car,* 1900) and James Williamson (*The Big Swallow,* 1901) developed a range of special effects for their early films, which tended to be comedies (see Chapter 7 on Early Cinema and Film Form).

It was at least ten years before an identifiable film industry emerged in Britain. The above film-makers had established their own production companies, the main ones being the Hepworth Manufacturing Company, the Sheffield Photographic Company, Williamson's Kinematograph Company and George Albert Smith Films. Exhibition of films was led by the Associated British Pictures Corporation and Gaumont-British (a subsidiary of the French company). By 1912 the British film industry was deemed large enough for it to require a national organization to monitor and regulate the content of films, and the industry set up the British Board of Film Censors in 1912. However, the First World War interrupted the development of the British film industry. Before the war 15 per cent of films screened in Britain were British, with 50 per cent being supplied by Europe and the remaining 35 per cent coming from the United States, but by the end of the war the US figure was 80 per cent (Murphy, in Barr, 1986, pp. 50–1).

The British Studio System

The dominance of American cinema in Britain has steadily grown since the First World War, despite intermittent attempts to hold back the power of American production, distribution and exhibition. The British government passed the Quota Act in 1927, decreeing that exhibitors had to ensure that at least 5 per cent of films screened were British and that this figure should rise to 20 per cent by 1936 (Murphy, in Barr, 1986, p. 52). In fact, the quota percentages were often exceeded, but many of the British films shown were of poor quality and were cheap, rushed productions (known as 'quota quickies') whose sole purpose was to meet the quota target. These films were often made by British companies financed by Hollywood studios. However, many of the new companies that emerged as a result of the quota legislation went bankrupt with the ending of the silent era as they could not afford the sound technology required to keep pace with larger production companies.

While the Hollywood Studio System had clearly taken shape by the late 1920s, a British version was also emerging which consisted of two 'majors', British International Pictures and the Gaumont-British Picture Corporation, and three 'minors', British and Dominion, London Film Productions and Associated Talking Pictures. Michael Balcon and Alexander Korda were key figures during this era of British cinema, establishing international reputations as studio heads. Balcon established Gainsborough Studios as a source of popular films, which continued with film production through to the post-war years and became an associate production company as part of the Gaumont-British Picture Corporation. In 1938 Balcon took over as head of production at the newly established Ealing Studios, remaining there until 1959. Major studio facilities were built at Shepperton and Pinewood.

British International Pictures amalgamated with the exhibition company Associated British Cinemas, and in 1929 produced the first major British sound film, which was also Alfred Hitchcock's first 'talkie', *Blackmail*. Other studios moved into producing sound films, some of which became popular abroad as well as in Britain. *Sally in Our Alley* (Basil Dean, 1931) was popular with audiences and was unusual in that it focused on working-class life at a time when films tended to avoid themes relevant to contemporary Britain. Alexander Korda, a Hungarian film-maker, built his own studios at Denham and attracted significant financial backing, especially from United Artists. When, in 1933, his London Film Productions made *The Private Life of Henry VIII*, its commercial success in the USA was indicative of the growth of the British film industry. This expansion in film production capacity resulted in a number of studios being built in the Elstree area, which subsequently became known as 'the British Hollywood'. Another company to join the burgeoning British film industry in the 1930s was British National Films, formed by J. Arthur Rank in 1934. It became a vertically integrated company in 1935 with the formation of General Film Distributors. By the mid-1940s, Rank's company was the most powerful in the British film industry.

Although feature fiction films constituted the vast majority of productions in Britain, an influential documentary film movement was initiated in the late 1920s. As a director and producer, John Grierson was central to the growth of documentary film-making; he believed that films could have an educational, informative and social function. As an employee of the Empire Marketing Board, he was paid to promote trade within the Empire, but his first film,

Drifters (1929), stands in its own right as a documentary film rather than a marketing exercise. The film revealed the tough life of fishermen at sea and combined documentary footage with imaginative film techniques to produce a successful documentary film. The Empire Marketing Board was dissolved in 1933 and the film unit transferred to the General Post Office, with Grierson at the head of the GPO Film Unit. One of the most popular films from the unit was *Night Mail* (Watt and Wright, 1936), which covered the overnight mail train's journey from London to Glasgow and provided exterior shots of the British country-side and interior shots of the train and of its crew at work. Another key documentary from this period was *Housing Problems* (Anstey and Elton, 1935), which was sponsored by the Gas, Light and Coke Company in an effort to expand its business through the modernization of housing. The film exposed the poor housing conditions in much of Britain through location shooting, combined with interviews and voice-overs.

Films for Victory

The Second World War was soon to have a huge impact on the British film industry, on both feature and documentary cinema. The GPO Film Unit came under the control of the Ministry of Information and the Unit made documentaries that aimed to strengthen the war effort and maintain morale. *London Can Take It* (Watt, 1940) documented London during the Blitz and illustrated how Londoners coped with the nightly bombing raids by German planes. The Ministry of Information also co-financed some feature films with the aim of uniting the nation and building patriotism. Michael Powell and Emeric Pressburger worked together on several wartime films and caused controversy with *The Life and Death of Colonel Blimp* (1943), to the point where Churchill tried to ban the film. In addition to exposing the old-fashioned ('blimpish') inefficiency of parts of the war effort, the film features a German refugee who has chosen to escape from Nazi Germany and highlights the hostility that can greet a foreigner arriving in Britain.

Wartime films were generally intended to help hold the nation together, to create a unity of purpose against the enemy and prepare the nation for victory. *Went the Day Well?* (Cavalcanti, 1942) tells the story of a complacent English village which is unexpectedly invaded by German paratroopers, supported by a traitorous country squire. The film's message was clearly a plea for all to be vigilant and prepared. *Millions Like Us* (Launder and Gilliat, 1943) emphasizes the common experiences of wartime Britain, using a fictional story to illustrate home life, life at work and leisure activities. There is a strong emphasis on women making the transition from working at home to taking up employment previously carried out by men. *This Happy Breed* (David Lean, 1944) similarly provides a sense of common purpose and shared experiences. David Lean and Noël Coward directed *In Which We Serve* (1942), in which the crew of a sunken British ship are adrift on a liferaft. The survivors on the liferaft include an upper-middle-class captain, a lower-middle-class officer and a working-class rating. These characters, who represented the British class system, shared their experiences and lives and their immediate situation as an example to the rest of Britain about the need for unity across divisions within society for the sake of the war effort (Figure 13.2).

In Which We Serve: class unity during wartime (BFI Stills, Posters and Designs)   Figure 13.2

Gainsborough Studios continued film production throughout the war years, but tended towards melodramas and historical films, which provided an escape from the common realist aesthetic of other wartime films. *Madonna of the Seven Moons* (Arthur Crabtree, 1944) focuses on changing values with regard to femininity and convention, sexuality and repression, as symbolized by mother and daughter. *The Wicked Lady* (Leslie Arliss, 1945) challenges conventional expectations of female behaviour. The female protagonist marries a friend's lover, has an affair, seeks adventure as a highwaywoman, kills someone, and has another affair before being killed herself. These films, and other Gainsborough productions, were popular (particularly with women) perhaps because they raised questions about female identity at a time when such issues were becoming increasingly topical, partly because of the changes in lifestyle that women had experienced during the war years.

The year after the end of the Second World War saw Britain's highest ever cinema attendance figures, with an average of over 31 million admissions per week throughout 1946. The main cinema chains were ABC (owned by the Associated British Picture Corporation, whose production wing was BIP) and Odeon and Gaumont-British (owned by Rank). Rank's production facilities had been gradually expanding over the years, with Pinewood Studios being supplemented with the purchase of Gainsborough's Shepherds Bush studios in 1941 and a finance and exhibition deal being signed with Ealing Studios in 1944.

However, Britain's film production capacity had been weakened by the war as a result of resources being redirected and of many employees being called up for national service. In the post-war years American films dominated the British market and this prompted the government, in 1948, to introduce a quota whereby 30 per cent of screenings had to be British films. The Eady Levy was introduced, taking a percentage of box-office receipts for reinvestment in the film industry. This state intervention by the post-war Labour government was mirrored in other areas of society such as health, education and housing, where the government invested and reorganized rather than leaving the free market to decide.

One of the major directors to emerge in the post-war years was David Lean, who was responsible for many popular films through to the 1960s, including *Brief Encounter* (1945), *Great Expectations* (1946), *Oliver Twist* (1948), *Hobson's Choice* (1953), *Lawrence of Arabia* (1962) and *Doctor Zhivago* (1965). Carol Reed also made his name in the late 1940s with films such as *The Odd Man Out* (1947) and *The Third Man* (1949), both of which contained elements of an expressionist style. Powell and Pressburger continued working together after the war, making films such as *Black Narcissus* (1947) and *The Red Shoes* (1949), which through its effective use of expressionist techniques became an unusual example of popular art cinema.

From Comedy to Horror

Ealing Studios continued to be a source of popular films, with 1949 seeing the release of *Passport to Pimlico* (Henry Cornelius), *Kind Hearts and Coronets* (Robert Hamer) and *Whisky Galore!* (Alexander MacKendrick). Further successes followed, including *The Lavender Hill Mob* (Charles Crichton, 1951) and *The Ladykillers* (MacKendrick, 1955). These films and others like them became known as 'Ealing comedies'. Actors who came to prominence through these films included Stanley Holloway and Alec Guinness. The studio's success was aided by the agreement previously signed with Rank, but by the mid-1950s cinema attendances were falling, partly reflecting the increasing availability of entertainment via television: there were 2 million television sets in Britain by 1953. In 1955 Ealing Studios was sold to the BBC. The studio left a legacy of memorable comedy films, identifiably British (or mostly very English) in their style and content, typically dealing with ordinary people in everyday situations, frequently consisting of individuals challenging authority, and often using class and status as key ingredients.

Just as the 1940s saw new directors, actors and film styles coming to prominence, so too did the 1950s. Hammer Films was a small independent film company that produced successful low-budget horror and science fiction films. Hammer took advantage of the X-certificate rating which had been introduced by the British Board of Film Censors in 1951, which allowed for more explicit sex and violence in films. Among the successful science fiction films were *The Quatermass Experiment* (Val Guest, 1955), *X the Unknown* (Leslie Norman, 1956) and *Quatermass II* (Guest, 1957). Hammer's popular early horror productions included *The Curse of Frankenstein* (1957), *Dracula* (1958) and *The Mummy* (1959), all directed by Terence Fisher. Christopher Lee and Peter Cushing achieved fame through their roles in Hammer horrors, which were often remakes of Universal Studios' 1930s horror films.

These films tended to appeal to teenage audiences who saw the realist style of 1940s films and the innocent humour of Ealing comedies as unadventurous and irrelevant to their generation. The phenomenon of the 'teenager' appeared in the 1950s as an awareness of a 'generation gap' grew, manifesting itself in terms of different values and beliefs, especially with regard to sexuality and the role of the individual in society. Teenagers were a cultural market to be targeted because of their relative wealth in terms of disposable income and interests in music, film and fashion. Hammer's last film was *To the Devil a Daughter* (Peter Sykes, 1976) and the company, suffering a decline shared by much of the film industry in the 1970s, went bankrupt in 1980.

Another distinct form of British cinema also began in the 1950s and ended in the 1970s: the Carry On films. There were twenty-eight in all, the first being *Carry on Sergeant* (Gerald Thomas, 1958) and the last *Carry on Emmanuelle* (Thomas, 1978); an attempt to resuscitate the genre with *Carry on Columbus* (like all the Carry Ons, directed by Thomas in 1992) was unsuccessful. The same actors usually appeared in each film and included Sid James, Kenneth Williams, Charles Hawtrey, Joan Sims, Barbara Windsor, Kenneth Connor, Jim Dale and Hattie Jacques. The films' humour arises from the use of sexual innuendo, double meanings, embarrassing situations, stereotyping of gender, sexuality, class and race, and a strong disregard for authority and accepted standards of decency and morality. The films were made possible by, and no doubt found their appeal in, the general questioning of morals that had gradually gained pace in the years after the war and the growth of a more 'permissive' society. The Carry On films declined in the late 1970s, perhaps because this process of moral change had been generally concluded and the particular brand of smuttiness which they embodied had been overtaken by more explicit representations of sexuality (for example, in the *Confessions of* series).

Sex, Pop and Realism

While the Carry On films were light-hearted, cheeky entertainment, a new type of film emerged the following year which took a very different form. Social realist cinema, or 'kitchen sink cinema' as it came to be known to reflect the common use of domestic locations such as kitchens in the films, presented a gritty, raw interpretation of everyday life. Typical themes were alienation, frustration, fighting the system, and ambition for a better life away from the drudgery of everyday life. As John Hill has noted, 'one of the most striking characteristics of the British cinema towards the end of the 1950s was its increasing concern to deal with contemporary social issues' (1986, p. 67).

The 1950s had supposedly ushered in a new era of affluence within a meritocratic society, but the world presented in these films is a class society with far more limited possibilities. The protagonists are usually male, working-class and angry. The 'angry young man' had become a common character in plays written and performed during the mid-1950s, the best known being *Look Back in Anger* by John Osborne. This play was turned into a film in 1959 by Tony Richardson and was the first film to be made by Woodfall Films.

The company's three principal directors were Lindsay Anderson, Karel Reisz and Tony Richardson. They had previously worked together in the early 1950s in the Free Cinema movement, which had sought to politicize cinema by using it to analyse contemporary society through documentary forms, with the aim of exposing injustices and proposing alternatives. These directors were responsible for a number of social realist films. They were Britain's answer to France's 'new wave', in terms of the unusual style and content of the films they made. Amongst their best-known films are: *Look Back in Anger* (Richardson, 1959),

Saturday Night and Sunday Morning (Reisz, 1960) (Figure 13.3), *A Taste of Honey* (Richardson, 1961), *The Loneliness of the Long Distance Runner* (Richardson, 1962) and *This Sporting Life* (Anderson, 1963). These films helped establish actors such as Rita Tushingham, Albert Finney and Tom Courtenay. As a film movement it was short-lived, lasting only from 1959 to 1963, but it influenced other directors, most notably Ken Loach.

By 1963 pop culture was well established, and audiences tended to be more interested in entertainment than social issue films. This was the year the Beatles came to fame and the following year they were to make their own film, *A Hard Day's Night* (Richard Lester, 1964), which showed the 'fab four' as representatives of British youth, resisting and mocking the outdated and unnecessary restrictions of British society. This was the 'swinging sixties' and life was meant to be 'fun'. Also well suited to this new era was the suave, sophisticated yet rugged womanizer, James Bond. The first Bond film, *Dr No,* had been made in 1962, with Sean Connery in the starring role. Bond smoothly combined being a British spy with an international playboy image which mirrored the supposed sexual permissiveness of the 1960s together with the espionage of the Cold War.

However, although mid-1960s British cinema was often characterized by the themes of fun, pleasure, promiscuity, adventure and escape, some films took a slightly more critical approach and others chose to deal with completely different issues. *Alfie* (Lewis Gilbert, 1966) focused on a Cockney character and his sexual exploits. The film begins by revealing the promiscuous lifestyle he leads and the fun he has as he moves from woman to woman. However, by the end of the film he is revealed as a friendless, isolated man who has no meaningful relationships. In the same year, Ken Loach made *Cathy Come Home.* The film was a far cry from the celebrations of pop culture and the swinging 1960s; instead, it

Figure 13.3   *Saturday Night and Sunday Morning and the angry young man: 'What I'm out for is a good time. All the rest is propaganda.' (BFI Stills, Posters and Designs)*

revealed the harsh reality of homelessness in Britain and the injustices many people suffered.

Ken Loach had been influenced by the work of the social realists and the documentaries of the Free Cinema movement. He began making films at the BBC, including *Up the Junction* (1965) and *Cathy Come Home* (1966), before moving on to cinema releases with *Poor Cow* (1967) and *Kes* (1969). Loach has often made use of hand-held camerawork to add to the 'realism' and believability of his films. He continues to make social issue films from a left-wing perspective.

One of the key social realist directors from the early 1960s had adopted a very different style of film-making by the late 1960s, though arguably with a similar motive of exposing social injustice. Lindsay Anderson made *If. . .* in 1968 as a statement about class privilege in Britain, as revealed through a story set in a private school. The film was very much of its time, the revolutionary inclinations of the three main protagonists mirroring the revolutionary upheavals of the same year across Europe and the USA. However, the film was far from the realism of Anderson's early films and the story frequently slips into bafflingly surreal scenes.

Decline and Fall

Many British films of the 1960s were made with American money, but by the end of the decade such finance had declined, thus weakening British cinema. There was also an exodus of British directors and stars who sought work in the American film industry or on British television, and most box-office hits in Britain were American films. Two of the most prominent directors to leave for Hollywood were Alan Parker, who made *Midnight Express* in 1978, and Ridley Scott, who made *Alien* in 1979.

Ironically Stanley Kubrick had made the reverse journey, basing himself in Britain, and began the decade with *A Clockwork Orange* (1971), a controversial film set in a violent future Britain. The James Bond films continued to be produced, but *Diamonds are Forever* (1971), *Live and Let Die* (1973) and *The Spy Who Loved Me* (1977) were American productions and were released by United Artists, as they always had been.

Pop culture music films, which came into their own in the 1960s, continued to be popular in the 1970s. Ken Russell directed a film version of the Who's rock opera, *Tommy*, in 1975. In the latter half of the decade the influence of punk sub-culture made itself known, effectively moving into mainstream pop culture with *The Great Rock 'n' Roll Swindle* (1979), a film about the Sex Pistols directed by Julian Temple. Derek Jarman made *Jubilee* (1978), which also employs aspects of punk style to critique modern urban life.

A more overtly political form of cinema also developed in Britain in the 1970s as a continuation of the revolutionary perspectives that had emerged in the late 1960s, alongside student and worker strikes and occupations in Britain, Europe and the USA. Small, radical, independent production companies such as Cinema Action and Amber Films made films throughout the 1970s which focused on political issues and campaigns in working-class communities, often covering industrial disputes with the intention of providing an alternative perspective to that offered by the mainstream media. A focal point for independent film production was the London Film-makers Co-operative, which was founded in 1966 and became established during the 1970s. Feminism was perhaps the main radical movement of the decade, with film-maker and theorist Laura Mulvey among those who raised gender issues and moved the debate forward. It is no coincidence that the London Women's Film Group emerged during the 1970s. Mulvey's *Penthesilea* (1974) and *Riddles of the Sphinx* (1977) and Sally Potter's *Thriller* (1979) analyse the role of women in a patriarchal society, in the home and the workplace in terms of power relationships, identity and resistance.

The latter three themes were also the driving force for the Black British Cinema which began to find its feet in the 1980s. Individual black directors began to deal with themes of black culture and identity and of racism (Horace Ové with *Pressure* (1975), Menelik Shabazz with *Burning an Illusion* (1981)), but the most important films arguably emerged eventually from the Black Audio Collective (BAC) and from Sankofa. These were film/video production groups in which tasks were rotated and shared, but the principal directors were Sankofa's Isaac Julien (*Territories*, 1985; *Young Soul Rebels*, 1991) and BAC's John Akomfrah (*Handsworth Songs*, 1986).

With regard to mainstream film production the 1970s were a lean period for the British cinema. Audience figures declined dramatically from 501 million per year in 1960 to 193 million per year in 1970 (Dyja, 1999, p.30 – see also Table 3.2 above). Throughout the 1970s cinemas were frequently converted for multi-screen exhibition to attract audiences back by offering greater variety, although it is questionable just how much choice was available. The last Carry On film was made in 1978 and the last Hammer Film in 1976. However, studios such as Pinewood and Shepperton were still used by American companies for production and *Star Wars* was partly filmed at Elstree Studios. Among the more popular British films from this decade were the innovative gangster film *Get Carter* (Hodges, 1971) and the alternative humour of *Monty Python and the Holy Grail* (Gilliam and Jones, 1975) and *Monty Python's Life of Brian* (Jones, 1979), two films which earned the comedy team an international reputation. A popular contemporary director who began making films at the time is Mike Leigh, whose first feature film was *Bleak Moments* (1971).

Something from Nothing

After a range of successful work for television, Mike Leigh firmly established himself in the 1980s with *High Hopes* (1988), which contained his usual mix of simple storyline, everyday situations, social comment and amusing, if somewhat stereotyped, characters. The 1980s also saw success for British cinema as a whole, which is ironic given that the Conservative government elected in 1979 had made things even tougher for the industry by abolishing the Eady Levy and the National Film Finance Corporation, both of which had provided finance for film production.

One particular group of films that proved successful in the 1980s became known as 'heritage cinema', the stories being set in Britain's resplendent past. Among the best known were *Chariots of Fire* (Hugh Hudson, 1981) and *A Room with a View* (James Ivory, 1985), both produced by newly formed companies, Goldcrest and Merchant–Ivory respectively; however, the bulk of funding for *Chariots of Fire* (Figure 13.4) came from the USA and Egypt. *Chariots of Fire* was in many respects ideally suited to the early 1980s. Thatcher's

Chariots of Fire: celebrating the 1980s British film renaissance? (BFI Stills,   Figure 13.4
Posters and Designs)

Conservative government emphasized, in both its rhetoric and its legislation, the importance of nationality, Britain's 'greatness' and individualism. The film itself harks back to an age when Britain was still a world power and still had its Empire. Furthermore, the film focuses on the individual endeavours of two athletes, with the emphasis on initiative and hard work, both supposedly key elements in that government's ideology. However, the film also deals with issues that were not at the heart of the Thatcher regime's concerns, namely class injustice and racism. The issues of class and race emerge in the bigotry shown by the university and sports establishments towards the working-class Scot, Liddell, and the middle-class Jew, Abrahams. The film is very 'English' not only because of its location but because of its use of supposedly English attributes such as reserve, fair play, gentlemanly conduct, stoicism, and perseverance in the face of adversity.

The other area of success in British cinema could not have been more different, dealing as it did with the reality of contemporary Britain. After five years of planning, Channel 4 was finally launched in 1982 with a remit to provide programmes that catered for minority tastes. This ethos spilled over into the channel's funding of film productions, via its Film Four subsidiary. Two of the company's biggest successes were *Letter to Brezhnev* (Chris Bernard, 1985) and *My Beautiful Laundrette* (Stephen Frears, 1986), both dealing with working-class life, in Liverpool and in South London respectively, and with issues relating to class divisions, race, nationality and sexuality.

Many other memorable and successful films emerged from 1980s British cinema. *Gregory's Girl* (1980) is a Scottish comedy about football and teenage love directed by Bill Forsyth, who had another success two years later with *Local Hero,* which tells the tale of a wise old Scotsman who outwits a large multinational oil company. *Defence of the Realm* (David Drury, 1985) follows a journalist's encounters with the secret establishment when he tries to expose an MP as a spy and reveal a nuclear cover-up by the government. *Distant*

Voices, Still Lives (1988) is set in post-Second World War Liverpool and follows the lives of an extended working-class family; however, Terence Davies' style is a far cry from the raw, documentary techniques of social realism and Ken Loach, showing instead a more self-conscious and artistic approach. The renaissance of British cinema during the 1980s is all the more surprising because most of these films were low-budget, usually costing less than £3 million compared to the average Hollywood budget of ten times as much. The Conservative government's philosophy of non-intervention in industry left the British film industry weak compared with Hollywood and other national film industries. The success of British cinema in the 1980s is also surprising when set against trends in cinema attendances at that time, which reached an all-time low in 1984 of just over 1 million per week, contrasting starkly with the all-time high figure of 31 million admissions per week in 1946.

Small Films, Big Movies

Channel 4's successes continued into the nineties with its involvement in a range of films. *The Crying Game* (Neil Jordan, 1992) tells an unusual story which deals with the politics of Northern Ireland and with transvestism. *In the Name of the Father* (Jim Sheridan, 1993) also addresses the politics of Northern Ireland, in relation to the British state, the security services and the legal system. It tells the story of the Guildford Four, falsely imprisoned for fourteen years having been found guilty, on faked evidence, of planting a bomb. In reality, a prolonged campaign for their release was eventually successful. *Bhaji on the Beach* (Gurinder Chadha, 1993), the first British feature film to be directed by an Asian woman, deals with issues such as mixed race relationships, gender relations, conflict between generations and multiculturalism within an Asian community and Britain as a whole. The film takes an imaginative, comic and perceptive look at race and culture in contemporary Britain. Sarita Malik writes:

> In *Bhaji on the Beach*, we see an ensemble of Asian women temporarily inhabiting a public sphere (Blackpool beach) which is predominantly associated with 'Englishness' and 'whiteness'. The quintessential 'Englishness' of Blackpool is juxtaposed with the 'Indianness' of the female protagonists, both culturally and visually. At the same time, we do not get the sense that any one culture has 'crossed over' or been assimilated, but that a new form of cultural identity is emerging. This hybrid identity is 'British-Asianness', a fluid evolving entity, which cannot be reduced to any one thing.
>
> (1996, p. 213)

Derek Jarman's *Blue* (1993) consists of a blue screen accompanied by a meditative soundtrack and voice-over narration, and tells the story of his experiences of dying from AIDS. *Trainspotting* (Danny Boyle, 1995) was a phenomenal success which cost £1.7 million but took over £60 million. The film takes the issue of heroin addiction and, through the effective use of a mix of characters and contemporary music, manages to tell an entertaining story that doubles as a warning about drugs (Figure 13.5). *Brassed Off* (Mark Herman, 1996) turns to another social issue, unemployment, and the destruction of traditional working-class communities. *Twin Town* (Kevin Allen, 1997) is set in Swansea and focuses on two twin brothers and their everyday lives. It is an uncompromisingly black comedy that moves

Trainspotting: the advance of British cinema... (Figment/Noel Gay/Channel 4, courtesy Kobal)   Figure 13.5

across a range of issues from unemployment, police corruption and violence to joyriding, drug-taking and murder. *East is East* (Damien O'Donnell, 1999) is a comedy based on a Pakistani family living in 1970s Britain which experiences upheaval as the children drift away from a traditional Muslim upbringing in response to other cultural influences.

Channel 4 went on to set up its own satellite film channel Film Four, screening films from outside the mainstream. The BBC also continued to fund films and found critical success with Lynne Ramsay's *Ratcatcher* (1999), which follows the lives of children in Glasgow during the 1970s; the film also obtained some lottery funding. The BBC followed this success with co-production *Billy Elliot* (2000). The film's story takes place during the 1984 miners' strike and explores issues of class and sexuality through Billy's attempts to transcend the conventions of his working-class roots by developing a career in ballet which requires him to move to London to lead a different life among a different class. *Lock, Stock and Two Smoking Barrels* (Guy Ritchie, 1998) used several financial backers and proved to be yet another low-budget, high earning British film.

The two largest grossing films to emerge from Britain during the 1990s were *Four Weddings and a Funeral* (Mike Newell, 1994) and *The Full Monty* (Peter Cattaneo, 1997), both of which were heavily marketed and proved popular in the USA. *Four Weddings* was part funded by Film Four, cost £3 million to make and made £210 million. *The Full Monty* was made for £2.2 million and took £50 million in its first year alone, before video sales and rentals and television screenings are taken into account. However, both these films were mainly funded from abroad. *Notting Hill* (Roger Mitchell, 1999) attempted to cash in on the success of *Four Weddings* with a similar form of humour, the same male lead star (Hugh Grant) and a rather quaint view of England that presents a polite, white, middle-class world no doubt manufactured as much for foreign viewing as for the British.

The 1990s were also to be a phenomenal decade for Ken Loach, who made no less than seven films, five of which were set in Britain and dealt with the political and social issues that Loach habitually weaves into his storylines. His first film of the decade, *Hidden Agenda* (1990), was unusual in that it was a political thriller. Set in Northern Ireland, it focuses on deceit and corruption in the armed forces, security services and government. *Riff-Raff* (1991) deals with the effects of the political legacy of the 1980s which had undermined trade unions and in this particular film had resulted in the growth of temporary contract labour in the building industry, where workers often had no employment rights and frequently worked in dangerous conditions. *Ladybird, Ladybird* followed in 1993, *Raining Stones* in 1994 and *My Name is Joe* in 1998. Mike Leigh was also to have a productive decade with *Life is Sweet* (1990) and *Naked* (1993), the latter darker and less humorous than most of Leigh's films, although the usual array of strong character types are present. *Secrets and Lies* (1996) won several awards in film festivals around the world including the Academy Awards and Cannes, and this was followed by *Career Girls* (1997).

Cinema attendances generally improved through the 1990s, with the annual figure reaching 136 million in 1998 (Dyja, 1999, p. 30; see also Table 3.2 above). The growth of multiplexes continued apace and exhibition was dominated by six companies: Warner, Odeon, Virgin, UCI, ABC and Cine UK. With the election of a Labour government in 1997, some progress was made towards further funding of the film industry. The Arts Council was given the role of deciding how National Lottery money was to be used as a source of finance for production companies, and the first three recipients were DNA Films Ltd., the Film Consortium and Pathé Productions. In 2000 the Film Council was set up to lobby for and administer lottery funding.

CASE STUDY

British Films, Culture and Ideology

The following films, covering a period of over 50 years, provide useful examples of the various ways in which values, beliefs and social groups have been represented in British films. It will be seen not only that there have been changes in how society's morals, ideas and cultures are shown to audiences over time, but that at any particular moment there are a range of possible ways of representing such ideologies.

Brief Encounter (David Lean, 1945)

Laura Jesson is a mother and a housewife and is happily married until she meets Alec Harvey at a railway station. By coincidence they meet again and from then on their encounters are intentional. Although Laura and Alec's relationship is never obviously consummated, she is filled with guilt about betraying her husband. Compared to her husband, she finds Alec interesting, humorous and exciting. Their relationship does not last long, however, and they soon return to their respective partners.

Although the story appears rather tame now, in 1945 the film was dealing with something that would not normally be discussed; in fact, it is possible to see this 1945 film as being very relevant to its time. The Second World War had resulted in many women living without their partners and many men being conscripted, leaving women to do their jobs. In effect, women had more independence and were perhaps more open to temptation. The film acknowledges this reality while ultimately upholding traditional morals. Laura's return to being a faithful wife can be interpreted as reflecting the situation at the end of the war when men returned to their jobs and (most) women returned to the home.

The ways in which gender, class and sexuality are represented result in particular values being reproduced by the film. Laura and Alec's relationship, as a male/female relationship, consists of

Brief Encounter: social class and sexual restraint (BFI Stills, Posters and Designs)   Figure 13.6

active and passive roles. Alec is the active partner, taking the initiative, suggesting they meet, go for walks, go to the cinema. Laura is the passive partner, submitting to his advances, desiring a better marriage.

Class becomes an issue through the ways in which Laura and Alec are represented as middle-class and the station porter and café woman as working-class. The most immediate way in which we identify their class is through accent, though the café woman does noticeably attempt a 'refined' voice, indicating the desirability but impossibility of the working class attaining middle-class status. Employment also indicates class, the porter and café woman undertaking manual labour whereas Alec's profession of doctor involves study, skill, knowledge and responsibility, and Laura lives comfortably from her husband's income. Of more interest though is what is *said* about class. The working class is represented as unintelligent through the conversations of the porter and café woman. Their contributions to the film consist of inane comments and mindless trivia typical of people who don't think before they speak. In other words, the working class is represented negatively. By contrast, Laura and Alec's conversations appear to be thoughtful, intelligent and well informed, thus representing the middle class positively.

In *Brief Encounter* representation of sexuality appears to be linked to class and gender. Laura's sexual desire results in feelings of guilt and is integrated into her desire for a satisfying marriage. For Alec, sexual desire seems to exist in its own right with no connotations of guilt or marriage. However, the couple ultimately act 'responsibly'; they restrain their desires. When they are compared to the working-class porter and café woman, clear differences in representation become apparent; the latter two do not exhibit the same degree of restraint with regard to their sexuality. Their suggestive conversations are not hidden and their implied sexual relationship outside marriage could be seen as representing the working class as immoral and irresponsible.

Alfie (Lewis Gilbert, 1966)

In many respects *Alfie* epitomizes 1960s British cinema more than any other film. It embodies aspects of the 'swinging sixties' through its portrayal of sexual promiscuity and use of pop music contemporary to that time, both of which are interwoven with what is, at times, a gritty drama that reveals the influence of social realism in its depiction of the reality of everyday life. Out of this combination come issues relating to sexuality, gender and class, occasionally underpinned by strong moral messages.

Alfie, as a character, is summed up in the first five minutes of the film. We see Alfie and Siddie emerging from a car, presumably after sexual intercourse: Siddie forgets to put her knickers back on and Alfie refers a couple of minutes later to 'having it off'. Alfie shows a lack of concern for the feelings of the women he has brief relationships with, dropping them as soon as he is satisfied. At the beginning of the film, although Alfie is with Siddie he has an intermittent conversation with the audience, talking to camera, referring to Siddie as 'it' and revealing that 'she won't be around for much longer'. On leaving Siddie to return to her unexciting husband, Alfie makes his way to see Gilda, who is described as a 'standby'.

The first few minutes of the film use such representations to establish characters and themes. What we find is that men are represented as either dominant, macho and sexually active, as in Alfie's case, or submissive, timid and passive, as with Siddie's husband, and these representations are repeated elsewhere in the film. In contrast to Alfie, the female characters are represented as subservient to him; they are less active, yet more interested in developing a relationship. However, Alfie eventually meets his match in Ruby. She chooses to have a brief relationship with Alfie, dropping him in favour of a younger man. It is to be noted though that Ruby is not typical of the female characters in the film, in that she is wealthy and American.

Sex is dealt with in a noticeably different way compared with the previous decade. There is no restraint; sexual desire is satisfied, in keeping with the popular perception of the 1960s as the decade of sexual freedom. However, sexuality can perhaps also be linked to social class in the film. The characters in *Alfie* can be identified as working-class by their accents, their employment and their homes, and the film can be read as implying that those from the working class tend to be sexually active, placing sex at the centre of their lives.

Later in the film, Alfie's life of pleasure gradually declines. When Lily becomes pregnant, he helps to arrange an abortion, which leaves him feeling guilty and briefly sorrowful. Gilda later also becomes pregnant, again leaving Alfie with the prospect of responsibilities, marriage and decisions to make, none of which come easily to him, as his whole life has been focused solely on himself. Alfie declines marriage and so Gilda eventually marries someone else who will help bring up Alfie's son. By the end of the film, Alfie is a lonely character with a rather empty life. He admits that he does not have 'peace of mind'.

East is East (Damien O'Donnell, 1999)

Immigration and racism were big issues in Britain throughout the 1970s. Asian families had been settling in Britain and racists, encouraged by Enoch Powell's 'rivers of blood' speech, were calling for repatriation, claiming that different cultures could not live alongside one another.

The film's story is set in Manchester in 1971. Although *East is East* is a comedy it manages to raise and expose social issues and problems, albeit in a humorous way. The film focuses on the Pakistani Khan family whose father, George Khan, wants his children to have a traditional Muslim upbringing. Thus his sons must be circumcised, mustn't eat bacon, are to co-operate with arranged marriages and abide by the Koran. However, the rest of his family, apart from one of his sons, have different ideas. The eldest son breaks off an arranged marriage at the last moment, leaves home, and ends up helping his gay partner run a fashion boutique (echoes of *My Beautiful Laundrette*. . .).

The father then arranges to introduce his next two sons to the daughters of a family living in Bradford, where Pakistani culture is much more common. The lack of identification with such a culture by George Khan's children is emphasized through them referring to the 'Pakis' in Bradford, in effect indicating they are a different people. The two sons are more interested in going to discos and going out with the local white girls. The daughter is far from being his model daughter either, showing more interest in playing football than in following Islam; at one point she kicks a football through a racist neighbour's window.

George Khan becomes increasingly agitated by the failure of his family to adopt the religious and cultural values that he espouses. He beats his wife Ella when she defends the children, and the son who is attempting to follow Islam is caught between supporting his father and defending the rest of the family. Towards the end of the film the sons defend their mother when their father again attacks her. After George Khan has despaired of how his family ignores his wishes and rejects his beliefs, he finally realizes how hated he is. The film ends with him appearing to reconsider his life, his beliefs and his family; he finally has doubts about whether he has been right.

The film promotes multiculturalism through its positive representation of white and Asian youth mixing, and indeed Ella Khan is herself white (though it is perhaps hard to believe that a fundamentalist like George would have married a white woman outside his faith). The film can also be regarded as multiculturalist in its rejection of fundamentalist interpretations of Islam and of the racism of some sections of British society, both of which are represented negatively. Multiculturalism also raises the issue of national identity; in a country of increasingly diverse lifestyles and ethnic groups, what does it mean to be British? George Khan's identity is shaped by Pakistan and Islam while the local racists see their national identity being eroded; most of the youth in the film are, to varying degrees, open to various cultural influences.

However, the film does perhaps rely on stereotypes to deliver its messages and tell its story, to the point where it is frequently amusing, but perhaps at the cost of the messages being almost lost. George Khan and Islam are portrayed simplistically and are defined principally by intolerance, dietary law, circumcision and arranged marriages, where believable representations would have to be more complex. There are liberal as well as fundamentalist interpretations of Islam, and George Khan is far from being a coherent example of Islamic culture.

SUMMARY

- Although British films have never been central to world cinema, they have consistently, in one area or another, been influential.
- From early special effects films, through documentary cinema, Hammer horror films, Ealing comedies and social realism to the low-budget independent films of the 1980s and 1990s, British cinema has left its mark.
- Despite a consistent lack of significant financial support for the industry, films continue to be made that entertain, challenge, and deal with contemporary social issues.

> Social groups and issues, institutions and cultural practices, ideologies and ideas and values and beliefs have been shown in a variety of ways, both positively and negatively, resulting in both dominant and alternative representations of aspects of British life.

Exercise 13.1

1. Compare two British films that are separated by at least 20 years and determine whether/how the values and beliefs represented within them differ from each other.
2. Identify a British film which in your opinion contains 'alternative' ideas, and indicate which elements within the film are represented positively and which negatively.
3. With reference to any British film, identify the ways in which it reinforces dominant ideology. Indicate any stereotypes that are used.

REFERENCES

Eddie Dyja (ed.), *BFI Film and Television Handbook 2000* (London: BFI, 1999).

FPRG, *A Bigger Picture: The Report of the Film Policy Review Group* (London: Department for Culture, Media and Sport, 1998), Annex 2.

John Hill, *Sex, Class and Realism* (London: BFI, 1986).

Sarita Malik, 'Beyond "The Cinema of Duty"?', in Andrew Higson (ed.), *Dissolving Views* (London: Cassell, 1996).

Robert Murphy, 'Under the shadow of Hollywood', in Charles Barr (ed.), *All Our Yesterdays* (London: BFI, 1986).

Geoff Hurd (ed.), *National Fictions* (London: BFI, 1984).

Colin McArthur (ed.), *Scotch Reels: Scotland in Cinema and Television* (London: BFI, 1982).

Robert Murphy, *Sixties British Cinema* (London: BFI, 1992).

Robert Murphy (ed.), *The British Cinema Book* (London: BFI, 1997).

Lance Pettitt, *Screening Ireland* (Manchester: Manchester University Press, 2000).

Jeffrey Richards, *Films and British National Identity* (Manchester: Manchester University Press, 1997).

Screen, vol. 26, no. 1 (Jan/Feb 1985) ('British Cinema' issue).

Sarah Street, *British National Cinema* (London: Routledge, 1997).

John Walker, *The Once and Future Film: British Cinema in the Seventies and Eighties* (London: Methuen, 1985).

FURTHER READING

Charles Barr (ed.), *All Our Yesterdays* (London: BFI, 1986).

Lester Friedman (ed.), *British Cinema and Thatcherism* (London: UCL Press, 1993).

John Hill, Martin McLoone and Paul Hainsworth (eds), *Border Crossing: Films in Ireland, Britain and Europe* (London: BFI, 1994).

John Hill, *British Cinema in the 1980s* (Oxford: Oxford University Press, 1999).

FURTHER VIEWING

Brit Pix (Film Education, 1999).

Omnibus: Made in Ealing (BBC, 1986).

Typically British (BFI TV and Channel 4, 1994).

World Cinema and National Film Movements

Most of this book has been concerned with Hollywood cinema and its influence, which is a reflection of Hollywood and US dominance since the 1920s. Nevertheless, there have been moments when other national cinemas have attracted the interest of film theorists, critics and historians (and indeed of audiences), and in this chapter we shall explore some such moments, both historical and more recent. First, however, we should reconsider the meaning of 'national cinema' (see also Chapter 13).

NATIONAL CINEMA

If it is rare to find the term 'American Cinema' used, this is largely because the dominant modes of cinema *are* American; as we have seen, this is reflected in the influence of Hollywood on film-making practices and on 'film language', in the way films are marketed and consumed and in film financing and media ownership. When we speak of 'British cinema', 'Indian cinema', 'Finnish cinema' or any other national cinema, part of its meaning is thus in some kind of *opposition* to the dominance of the United States. Indeed, the term 'World Cinema', which we have reluctantly used as a chapter heading, is highly problematic: it is commonly used to refer to non-American cinema; but is it not ideologically significant that American films somehow stand apart and are not to be considered as part of the 'world'? As has been the case with values and ideologies associated with maleness and white imperialism in the past, American cinema is all the more powerful for being unnamed and for being taken as a norm.

But *why* can we say that 'French Cinema' is French? What makes a film 'French'? Is it because all or most of the money to make the film came from France? Is it because the director was French? Because the principal actors were French? Because the film was made in France? What about the technicians? Or is it because the film is *about* French characters, society or history?

Another way to approach the notion of national cinema is to ask what relation a group of films has with the film institutions (the government, the production, distribution and exhibition structures) of the country. Colin Crofts, for example, adapts Andrew Higson's work to produce a list of possible defining characteristics of any national cinema, on which the following modified list is based (Table 14.1). This may be compared with the 'official' list noted above (p. 235).

Table 14.1   *Criteria for defining national cinema*

Criterion	Key questions
Production	How nationally specific are the production practices? To what extent do they depend on American practices and finance?
Distribution and exhibition	What percentage of 'home-made' films are shown? How does this compare with films from America or elsewhere?
Audiences	Which films are 'popular'? Why?
Discourses	How do critics and theorists write about the films of a country? Are they seen as entertainment in competition with American or multinational productions or as expressions of a 'national' voice?
Textuality-cultural specificity	Are themes of nationality or national identity treated in the films? How are cultural identities within a nation dealt with?
The role of the state	How much is the state involved in regulating the nation's film industry? To what extent do subsidies, quota legislation, censorship etc. 'protect' the indigenous film industry?

The complexity of writing about national cinemas dates, of course, from the 1980s and the rapid growth of globalization; before then it was a little easier to identify films and film movements as coming from, say, Germany or Brazil.

Exercise 14.1

Select any three non-American films made at different times (perhaps one from the 1960s, one from the 1980s and one recent release), and discuss how easy or difficult it is to describe each as (for example) a British, Indian or Italian film. If there is time, you may want to do some research on the films' production contexts and exhibition (box-office figures etc.).

THE MAJOR NATIONAL CINEMA MOVEMENTS

Before going further we should note a difficulty with the word 'movement'. Though we use it here in a loose sense to indicate a coherent group of films (and film-makers), strictly speaking, the term should only be used where the film-makers *defined* themselves as a 'movement'. While some of the groups of films which we shall discuss certainly can be said to be part of a 'movement', others cannot, and are linked by style rather than by any agreed programme or aims. Nevertheless for the sake of simplicity we have followed a common practice and retained the word as a general term. Be warned!

Historically, then, a number of 'national cinema movements' have emerged as significant to the development of new film styles or as particular manifestations of a particular country's social/historical context at a particular time. There are as always some problems of definition (are the 1930s German 'mountain films' best described as a 'movement', a genre or a sub-genre?) and it would be impractical to look at every conceivable 'movement'.

The national film 'movements' most frequently mentioned in textbooks tend to have originated in Europe, representing as they do a version of film history which has been produced almost entirely by European and North American writers about film. The omissions would thus be those Asian, African and South American national cinemas which have imposed themselves (usually only during the 1980s and 1990s) as significant objects of study.

Space will not permit a complete examination of all the major 'national cinema movements'. We shall here have to limit ourselves to a brief look at a selection of the significant 'movements' from Europe, Asia and Africa.

German Expressionism

Although the first German Expressionist film, *The Cabinet of Dr Caligari* (Wiene, 1920) (Figure 14.1), was a startling success, it did not come as such a surprise. The reason for this was that Expressionism had been an important current in theatre and painting (and, indeed, in literature) since around 1906. Nevertheless Wiene's film was clearly different from anything that had been seen before, and was the first of a cycle of commercially successful and critically praised German Expressionist films culminating in Fritz Lang's *Metropolis* in 1927 (released as a restored and re-edited print in 1984 with a rock music soundtrack which has met with mixed reviews).

The 'Expressionism' which developed in Europe (and especially in Germany) at the beginning of the twentieth century was principally a reaction against and a rejection of the realism which had come to dominate art at the turn of the century, and the methods of expressionist

The Cabinet of Dr Caligari: expressing insanity (BFI Stills, Posters and Designs)   Figure 14.1

theatre were successfully transferred to the cinema. The *mise en scène* featured distorted buildings and interiors, with non-vertical walls and hardly a right angle in sight. Theatrical backdrops featured disorientatingly garish colour compositions. The acting was anti-realist and (in the theatre) involved screaming and shouting as the expression of extreme mental states and of 'inner feeling'. Actors' movements were choreographed so as to complement the jarring *mise en scène*. Although lighting was predominantly 'flat', there was often an effective use of shadows for frightening effect.

There is disagreement about whether only those films which show the above character- istics should be described as expressionist, or whether others, where the narratives and the characterizations can be read as consistent with expressionist themes of mental disinte- gration, can be included. In any case, after *The Cabinet of Dr Caligari*, the principal German Expressionist films included *The Golem* (Wegener and Boese, 1920), *Destiny* (*Der müde Tod*, Fritz Lang, 1921), *Nosferatu the Vampire* (Friedrich Murnau, 1922), *Dr Mabuse the Gambler* (Lang, 1922), *Die Niebelungen* (Lang, 1924), *Faust* (Murnau, 1926) and *Metropolis*.

While these silent films are fascinating in themselves, there are two further ways in which they are significant. In his massively detailed (and not undisputed) book *From Caligari to Hitler*, Siegfried Kracauer saw German Expressionism as a symptom of the German people's readiness for Hitler: the evocation of evil and the forces of darkness, the threat to sanity, the reimposition of a healthy order through efficiency and through symmetry. The over- whelming use of geometrical symmetry in the interiors of *Algol* (Werckmeister, 1920), the trees in *Die Niebelungen* and the architecture of *Metropolis* seem to look forward to the fas- cist *mise en scène* of Leni Riefenstahl's *Triumph of the Will* (1935), with its construction of Hitler as a god-like figure and feverish rendering of his mass appeal. To be fair to *Caligari*, however, it can be read as a critique of power and authority, even if power remains in place at the end of the film. Similarly, *Metropolis* is an attack on dictatorship (though again with a cop-out ending) rather than a plea for order and efficiency.

If there is some truth in Kracauer's general sense of the Germany of the 1920s, the fate of many of the film-makers of that time tends to tell another story. Few of the artists (in film or indeed in any other medium) stayed in Germany to find out what Hitler would bring; they had already guessed. Those who stayed were on the whole either dedicated idealists or Nazi sympathizers. Those who left Germany bring us to the other important consequence of German Expressionism.

Among those who emigrated to the United States from Germany (under various degrees of pressure) were Fritz Lang, his cameraman Karl Freund and scriptwriter Carl Mayer, Friedrich Murnau, Billy Wilder and Otto Preminger. Some of these were established and respected directors and technicians, others (like Wilder and Preminger) were just beginning their careers in film-making. It would perhaps be wrong to see the link as too straight- forward, but it has often been suggested that the visual style of *film noir* (see p. 180 above) was indebted to the arrival of European (largely German) film-making talent in Hollywood in the 1930s. Certainly the sense of threat and of mental instability of many *films noirs*, from *The Maltese Falcon* (Huston, 1941) to *Kiss Me Deadly* (Aldrich, 1955), was well comple- mented by the low key lighting and the unusual and disconcerting camera angles; while these were not necessarily typical aspects of German Expressionism, it has been argued that, in the contemporary United States context of anxiety about the Second World War, and subsequently about the role of men and about atomic weapons, the *mise en scène* and camerawork of *film noir* were a reworking of the aesthetics of German Expressionism.

If we also consider the later development of *tech noir* in the 1980s (*Blade Runner*, 1982/1991), and the self-conscious use of 'expressionist' sets and lighting in, for example, the *Batman* films, we can see that the indirect influence of German Expressionism has been great indeed.

CASE STUDY

Nosferatu the Vampire (Friedrich Murnau, 1922)

Though firmly identified with German Expressionism, Murnau's *Nosferatu*, the first and most celebrated of vampire films based on Bram Stoker's *Dracula* written in 1897, is in fact not an entirely typical Expressionist film.

The emphasis on horror and menace is certainly in keeping with the Expressionist style (and in this sense the film is quite different from the post-1960s Dracula cycles which increasingly emphasized the camp and sexually deviant aspects of the character, as well as concentrating on special make-up effects). The grotesqueness of Dracula's body, his costume and movements, is expressionistic.

The lighting in *Nosferatu*, however, is not so typical; though the use of shadow is certainly effective, it is not common to other Expressionist films. *Nosferatu* was also shot largely on location, with the sense of threat being created through cinematography and editing rather than with the distorted *mise en scène* of *The Cabinet of Dr Caligari*, for example. This led Lotte Eisner to praise Murnau for creating 'expressionist stylisation without artifice' (1965, p. 102).

Soviet Montage cinema

If German Expressionism was to influence the *mise en scène* of later Hollywood films, the other major European film movement of the 1920s set itself up in opposition to Hollywood. The aftermath of the 1917 Russian Revolution saw years of struggle before the noble aims of communism were extinguished under the tyranny of Stalin in the 1930s. What is of interest here is the political and intellectual struggle of the 1920s over the forms and uses of 'art' (including cinema). By 1934 Stalin's support had ensured that the 'realist' tendency became official policy (though Soviet Socialist Realism was a very strange kind of 'realism'), but in the more open and stimulating 1920s, the 'realist' camp had to compete with two other strong tendencies: those who argued that art had to be directly at the service of the workers (the *proletariat*), and should be a tool of education and propaganda, and those who argued that the very nature of art had to be transformed before new revolutionary ways of seeing the world could be produced. This latter argument has usually gone under the umbrella term of Formalism (see also pp. 112–13 above), and in its effect on film it is perhaps best remembered for Soviet Montage theory.

The five names most attached to Soviet Montage (though there were several others) were Lev Kuleshov, Alexander Dovzhenko, Vsevolod Pudovkin, Dziga Vertov and Sergei Eisenstein, but it is the last of these who produced by far the most comprehensive writing on theories of montage and whose films are best known.

Indeed, it was a time of excitement and experiment (see Further Reading) and there was little clear agreement among the Formalists. While Kuleshov was an important and dynamic teacher about film (at the time, between 1919 and 1924, material shortages in the Soviet Union were so severe that students at the new Film School had to make films in their heads, without any film), he made few films and disagreed strongly with Eisenstein. His approach was closer to that of Pudovkin (*Mother*, 1926), for whom montage and editing in films had to remain at the service of the narrative: an approach rather closer to the 'classical narra-tive' of Hollywood. Dziga Vertov was a documentary film-maker who dismissed entertain-ment narratives as 'cine-nicotine' and for whom the camera and the lens (the 'film-eye') should be instruments of 'kino pravda': 'film truth'. When lighter cameras and better sound recording equipment later revolutionized documentary film-making in the early 1960s, the new methods were called *cinéma vérité* in honour of Vertov, who himself glorified the camera and made it a 'star' in his films (most famously in *Man With a Movie Camera*, 1929).

The most influential figure, however, was Sergei Eisenstein (*Strike*, 1925; *Battleship Potemkin*, 1925; *October*, 1928). While Pudovkin (and Kuleshov) spoke of shots in terms of 'elements' or 'building bricks' which could be linked or built into a text, Eisenstein spoke of shots as 'cells', and saw the potential relationships between shots in terms of *conflict* and *collision*. For Eisenstein the arrangement of shots into narrative sequence was only one special case (and a not very interesting one at that). In his theoretical writing, eventually published as *Film Sense* (1942) and *Film Form* (1949), he explores the various ways in which pairs of shots can 'collide' to create new meaning: the dialectical process we mentioned in Chapter 8.

The 'conflict' between shots could, for example, be graphic or geometric: Eisenstein recognized that shots with similar diagonal lines in the frame or with similar lighting would fit together harmoniously (the common Hollywood approach), while what interested him more was the sense of conflict or unease which could result from deliberately jarring juxta-positions of diagonals, of patterns of light or of the balance of objects in the frame (see Figure 14.2).

Montage could also create the illusion or sense of movement or change of some sort (Eisenstein would have been aware that this was an extension of the illusion of movement on which cinema itself is based). In *Battleship Potemkin*, for example, a shot of a woman with pince-nez glasses is soon followed by a shot of her screaming with blood running down her face: she has been shot. Less 'logically', more metaphorically, soon after this there are three consecutive shots of different statues of lions who appear to 'rise' from sleep to a roar-ing posture: here Eisenstein symbolizes the awakening of the sailors of the *Potemkin* to revolutionary action.

Through most of his discussion of montage, Eisenstein stresses the importance of graphic matches between shots in achieving montage 'effects' (for example, direction of movement, shapes in the frame, patterns of light and shade). He was not afraid of frag-menting time and space, of sacrificing the continuity editing being developed in Hollywood to create new kinds of meanings. The famed Odessa Steps sequence of *Battleship Potemkin* thus takes rather longer (some $5\frac{1}{2}$ minutes) than it would take the soldiers to march down the steps: events overlap, different shots of the same event are juxtaposed, and a variety

Battleship Potemkin: 2 shots indicating Eisenstein's graphic conflict (BFI Stills,   Figure 14.2
Posters and Designs)

of camera angles are used to create a highly effective (though not conventionally 'realist') representation of the massacre. A 'smaller' (but interesting) instance of fragmentation of time and space occurs earlier in the film when a sailor angrily smashes a plate: 11 rapid shots from a variety of angles show overlapping fragments of the action, and an action which would have taken about a second takes up about 3 seconds of screen time. Though made in entirely different entertainment-oriented contexts, the shower murder in *Psycho* and the final shoot-out in *The Untouchables* (De Palma, 1987) are clearly indebted to Soviet Montage, the latter a clear pastiche of the Odessa Steps.

Montage could also be put to emotional effect, for what Eisenstein called *emotional dynamization*. Thus the significance of a conference (in *October*) is 'dynamized' by intercutting shots of delegates arriving with rapidly spinning motorcycle wheels. A clearer emotional impact is achieved at the end of *Strike* by the intercutting of shots of strikers being killed by police with shots of a bull being slaughtered in an abattoir.

Eisenstein and the other Formalists were producing work which, though it naturally looks dated some 75 years later, foresaw some of the film experiments and debates which occurred many decades later. The films are a reminder of one of the most important moments in film history; it is also worth remembering that many free-thinking radical Soviet artists of the 1920s were eventually thrown into prison or sent to Siberia; several died there. Eisenstein himself survived at the cost of formally denying his previous films and writing, and was obliged to co-operate with the Stalinist regime in directing the masterful but 'realist' *Alexander Nevsky* (1938) and *Ivan the Terrible* (*Parts 1 and 2*) (1944, 1946).

Exercise 14.2

Discuss recent films in which time and space are fragmented: can you think of examples where screen time is greater than event duration? How do recent films carry the influence of early experiments with montage?

Italian Neorealism

The warning about 'movements' at the beginning of this chapter is particularly relevant to Italian neorealism: a group of films and film-makers was identified and celebrated by critics in the middle and late 1940s, but there was (at the time at least) no 'programme', no explicit statement of shared purpose.

The Italian neorealist films of 1945–51 were a stark contrast to the bland entertainment films of the fascist period, sometimes referred to as 'white telephone films' because of their storylines concerned with the lifestyles of the sophisticated rich, often symbolized (as in some Hollywood films) by the use of white telephones as props in the films. Although Mussolini's Italian fascist regime (which was in power from 1922 until the Spring of 1945, shortly before the end of the Second World War) was less brutal and more tolerant of artistic experiment than Hitler's Nazism in Germany, the end of the war in 1945 brought a sense of release to most Italians, and the 'Italian Spring' began. With the main Rome film studios (Cinecitta) all but destroyed and with severe shortages of equipment and film, a number of directors made a virtue of necessity and began filming on location, producing stories about ordinary working people struggling to survive in the poverty of post-war Italy.

In fact two of the first neorealist films, while dealing with everyday stories and shot entirely on location, were made before the end of the war and were concerned with the impact of the war on ordinary people: *Rome Open City* (1945) and *Paisa* (released 1946), both directed by Roberto Rossellini. The other major Italian neorealist films included *Germany Year Zero* (Rossellini, 1947), *Bicycle Thieves* (Vittorio De Sica, 1948), *The Earth Trembles* (*La terra trema*, Luchino Visconti, 1948), *Bitter Rice* (Giuseppe De Santis, 1948), *Stromboli* (Rossellini, 1949) and *Umberto D* (De Sica, 1951). This last film, dealing with a retired civil servant and his struggle against eviction and depression, was at the time described by the eminent French critic André Bazin as 'one of the most revolutionary and courageous films of the last two years . . . a masterpiece' (1967, p. 79)

If these films were praised by critics like Bazin for their 'realism' and won prizes in international festivals, they were not especially popular with Italian audiences, who generally preferred Hollywood films (of which they had of course been deprived during the war years). The Catholic Church and conservative elements of the coalition government were also very hostile to such films, claiming that they created a 'slanderous' image of Italy.

Indeed, the 'Italian Spring' ended in 1948 as the Christian Democrats won a general election and engineered legislation (the 1949 'Andreotti Law') which increased economic protection for the Italian film industry but signed the death-knell of the neorealist style by insisting on vetting scripts as a condition for state finance: a form of preproduction regulation and censorship.

The 'neorealist' directors (chief among them Rossellini, De Sica and Visconti) in fact came from different backgrounds and did not necessarily share the same political views: Visconti, though from an aristocratic family, was a Marxist, Rossellini later had difficulty denying his links with Christian Democrat ideology, De Sica was a Social Democrat. Nevertheless their films of the neorealist period were similar in significant ways. We can discover these by looking in a little detail at a humble, unspectacular film from 1948 which still regularly makes its way into the top 10 or so films of all time.

CASE STUDY

Bicycle Thieves (Ladri di biciclette) (Vittorio De Sica, 1948)

An important characteristic of neorealism has already been mentioned in passing above: the use of locations. *Bicycle Thieves* was filmed largely in the streets and buildings of Rome, though not a Rome which visitors would have recognized: the focus here was on poverty and unemployment. The bulk of neorealist filming was done on location, most famously Rossellini's *Rome Open City* and *Paisa*, both of which were shot during the war in some secrecy. Some films did make limited use of studios (we should remember that studio space was in very short supply), and the most notorious examples of 'false' use of locations occur in *Germany Year Zero*, in which a boy wanders the derelict streets of post-war Berlin: a number of the sequences in this film represent action which supposedly happened in Berlin, but which was shot in Italy against back-projected footage of Berlin streets.

We have also already referred to the downbeat subject matter of the neorealist films: the struggles of everyday Italians at the end of the war, poverty, the underprivileged. The narrative of *Bicycle Thieves* is deceptively simple: the father of a poor family manages to get a job putting up posters, uses all the family savings to buy back his bicycle, then has the bicycle stolen on his first day at work. The rest of the film follows him and his young son as they search hopelessly for the missing bicycle (without which he cannot do the job), until in an act of despair he himself tries to steal a bike. Shaken and ashamed, he walks off with his son into the anonymous crowd, again reduced to an unemployment statistic (Figure 14.3).

The neorealist directors shared a post-war social concern to exorcise the fascist years and to create a better society. However, the individual and political approaches of these directors were,

Figure 14.3   *Bicycle Thieves: a hard life without a bike (BFI Stills, Posters and Designs)*

as we have noted, quite different. *Bicycle Thieves* itself, though effectively portraying the postwar poverty and social problems of Rome, has been criticized from a more left-wing perspective for not providing any effective political *analysis* of the *sources* of the problems.

A third characteristic shared by most neorealist films is the use of non-professional actors. The elderly civil servant of *Umberto D* was played by a university professor; Antonio Ricci and his son Bruno in *Bicycle Thieves* were played by a factory worker and a boy whom De Sica cast because of the way he looked walking next to his 'father'. Although De Sica (having himself been a successful actor) was careful in his casting, in this sense he was much closer to the neorealist ideal than Rossellini, who combined non-professionals with star names (Anna Magnani in *Rome Open City*, Ingrid Bergman in *Stromboli*).

Lighting and camerawork in neorealist films were unspectacular and designed to further the 'realist' illusion of simple observation. The ideal was to use natural light and to avoid artificial lighting set-ups, though this was sometimes not practical. Dramatic camera angles and sudden camera movements were avoided; close ups were sparingly used. The scene in *Bicycle Thieves* where Antonio and Bruno walk the streets of Rome and Antonio fears that Bruno may have drowned in the river is a good example of 'undramatic' camerawork: one need only imagine how the suspense of such a scene could have been manipulated by, say, Hitchcock. This apparent artlessness, however, was not unprepared: most neorealist films were very carefully planned and scripted, and up to six cameras were used for a number of the outdoor sequences of *Bicycle Thieves*.

Editing in neorealist films was typically slower and again less concerned with manipulating dramatic tension than in most films. Though takes were not especially long (as they would become in later experiments with realism), editing was designed simply to further the impression of observation of a unified diegetic space. There was relatively little use, for example, of point of view shots, or of shot/reverse shot methods for conversations compared with Hollywood films. While this trend is clearly visible in *Bicycle Thieves*, it has to be pointed out that there are also moments when the spectator's attention *is* being directed and manipulated: thus, for example, when Antonio and Maria go to redeem his bicycle, the editing is different and puts the spectator in the couple's position as they watch an employee climb the enormous stack of bedsheets which have already been pawned: a clear symbol of the desperate poverty of the working class.

A final point to be made about Italian neorealist films (and one which clearly undermines their 'realist' status) is that virtually all Italian films of the period were post-synchronized: voices were dubbed onto the image tracked in a sound studio. In addition, most neorealist films (*Bicycle Thieves* is no exception) were accompanied by a sentimental, melodramatic music score, which further undermines the claims to 'transparent representation of reality' which have been made on behalf of Italian neorealism.

Italian neorealism is an important and interesting moment in film history, but its influence on future film-makers has also been considerable. Many Asian, South American and African directors made deceptively simple films about their own societies and cultures; excellent examples include the Indian director Satyajit Ray's *Apu* trilogy, made between 1955 and 1960 (see p. 271 below), *Salaam Bombay!* (Mira Nair, 1988), also from India, *Central Station* (Walter Salles, 1998) from Brazil, and a number of other African, Latin American and recent Iranian films. Gillo Pontecorvo's Italian-Algerian co-production *The Battle of Algiers* (1966) was inspired by Italian neorealism. The neorealist impulse has also continued in Europe, not least through the British New Wave of 1959–63 and the work of British directors who continue to be active in the new millennium such as Ken Loach.

The French New Wave

This term (*nouvelle vague* in French) is used to describe the French films made between 1959 and the mid-1960s by two slightly different groups of film-makers. One was a group of enthusiastic young men with little experience of making films; the other was a slightly older group of men and women, sometimes referred to as the 'Left Bank' (*Rive gauche*), committed to 'art' but not exclusively to the cinema, who had made films before and whose reputations were enhanced by the *nouvelle vague*.

The French New Wave was largely a product of critical impatience with 'le cinéma de papa' as expressed in *Cahiers du cinéma* (see Chapter 9). Youthful exuberance certainly helped, but the film-making careers of Jean-Luc Godard, Claude Chabrol, François Truffaut, Eric Rohmer and Jacques Rivette were indebted to at least two other factors.

The first was the unexpected success of *And God Created Woman* (*Et Dieu créa la femme*, Roger Vadim, 1956), which alerted financiers and distributors to a potential new youth market which may have tired of the 'classics' of the 1940s and 1950s. Without Vadim's success it is unlikely that Godard and the others would have secured funding for their early films. The second factor was the development at the time of far more portable cameras and sound recording equipment, which increasingly freed filming from the studio and gave far more creative freedom to the director.

It is not possible to give any coherent overview of the New Wave here: between 1959 and 1968 Godard made or collaborated on some 20 films, Truffaut 9, Chabrol 18. The older group of Agnès Varda, Alain Resnais, Georges Franju and others remained active. It is possible in these pages only to evoke some of the innovative and exciting techniques used in a few of the early films; the word 'exciting' is appropriate because, in contrast with Italian neorealism, the French New Wave films of the 1960s were popular with both critics and audiences.

The films of the new directors were quickly and cheaply made; they experimented with film style so that the camerawork and editing were highly innovative at the time – see, for example, the hand-held camerawork and freeze-frames of *Jules et Jim* (Truffaut, 1962). The narratives were often built around apparently chance events and were often digressive and open-ended. Characters were typically young, somehow dissatisfied with life. Dialogue was idiosyncratic and fragmented and often included lengthy meaningful silences. Little family life was ever shown. Settings were contemporary, often urban (and most often Paris). In keeping with the ex-critics' intellectual passions, many of their films (and particularly those of Godard) became intensely *intertextual*, constantly 'quoting' books, art and other films.

If there were common characteristics in the early French New Wave films, the careers of the three most significant directors soon took different paths to different kinds of world fame. Claude Chabrol established a reputation for archetypally French psychodrama crime thrillers (*Le Boucher*, 1970; *Blood Wedding* (*Les Noces rouges*, 1973)), and has often been compared with Hitchcock; having made over 40 films and several TV episodes by the mid-1990s, he emerged as the most commercially flexible of the New Wave directors. The films of François Truffaut (who had experienced a traumatic childhood and had been largely brought up by Bazin), though stylistically very much part of the New Wave, were much more personal, from his semi-autobiographical *The 400 Blows* (*Les 400 coups*, 1959), *Stolen Kisses* (*Baisers volés*, 1968), *Bed and Board* (*Domicile conjugal*, 1970) and *Love on the Run* (*L'Amour en fuite*, 1979) to films such as *The Wild Child* (*L'Enfant sauvage*, 1970), which were also intensely personal. His aim was perhaps not so much to transform French cinema as to revive it. Truffaut died in 1984.

Jean-Luc Godard is perhaps seen as the most 'typical' French New Wave director: unpredictable, innovative, provocative and prolific (he is still an active director and producer as we enter the new millennium). As Thompson and Bordwell observe, 'the inconsistencies, digressions and disunities of Godard's work make most New Wave films seem quite traditional by comparison' (1994, p. 525).

C A S E   S T U D Y

A bout de souffle (Godard, 1959)

Godard's *Breathless* (*A bout de souffle*, 1959) was the first of many films in which he used an increasingly experimental and fragmented style to challenge the spectator's assumptions: a favoured saying of Godard's at the time was: 'ce n'est pas une juste image, c'est juste une image' (it's not a 'just' image, it's just an image).

Jean-Paul Belmondo in A bout de souffle (BFI Stills, Posters and Designs) Figure 14.4

The 'hero' of *A bout de souffle* is a petty crook Michel (played by Jean-Paul Belmondo, (Figure 14.4), who went on to a profitable career based on such characters), who is wanted for shooting a policeman; he becomes attached to a young American woman, Patricia (played by Jean Seberg, the first of many 'foreigners' in Godard's films), in Paris and they agree to run away together, but our hero must first pick up some money from a very elusive debtor. He eventually manages to get the money, but as the police close in, Michel restates his commitment to Patricia and is killed as he runs from the police.

What is (still) disconcerting and surprising about the film is the way this apparently straight-forward plot is narrativized. Michel's killing of the traffic policeman is casual and barely explained; his meeting with Patricia is accidental and their relationship seems casual; there are no conventional indicators of 'love'. Jump cuts and discontinuity editing abound. Most of the film is concerned with unfocused conversations between Patricia and Michel and with the latter's unconvincing attempts to find his money. The spectator never really learns anything about the underworld or the reason why the money is not forthcoming. Stripped of conventional narrative and psychological 'motivation', *A bout de souffle* became the archetypal New Wave film: art for a new generation.

The initial *Cahiers* infatuation with Hollywood (which as we saw in Chapter 9 was important in the development of the *auteurist* approach) soon became for Godard a love-hate affair as love for the stars and icons of Hollywood gradually gave way to a politicized hatred for American imperialism. Thus in *A bout de souffle* the main characters go to see American films and the otherwise typically French hero clearly has a Humphrey Bogart fixation; by the time of *Contempt* (*Le Mépris*) of 1963, a story set in Hollywood and with veteran German Expressionist Fritz Lang playing a tyrannical director, commercial film-making is seen as a heartless, exploitative business which leads to suffering and death.

Exercises 14.3

1. One of Quentin Tarantino's production companies for *Pulp Fiction* was named 'A Band Apart' (the title of a 1964 Godard film). What signs are there in Tarantino's films of his interest in Godard's early work?
2. Watch Godard's *A bout de souffle* and Jim McBride's 'remake' starring Richard Gere, *Breathless* (1983). Compare the style and the narratives of the two films.

Japanese Cinema

The history of Japanese cinema is in fact longer than that of Hollywood. The first studios were built in 1905 and soon led to a studio system very similar to that in the United States. While from the 1920s Hollywood had its 'Big 5', in Japan the two biggest studios (Nikkatsu and Shochiku) were joined in the 1930s by Toho to create the 'Big 3'. As in the USA, from a very early stage the industry was vertically integrated. While in the USA early films portrayed vaudeville acts and began to develop rudimentary western and crime genres, early Japanese films showed traditional *kabuki* plays and 'swordfight' narratives. These were extremely popular, and enabled Japan to cement its commercial dominance in Eastern Asia. It is worth noting that Japan is virtually the only country in the world whose domestic product was not overshadowed by American films; despite rapid westernization during the 1920s and 1930s, Japanese cinema-goers preferred to see Japanese films. It was not until much later, in 1976, that American films came to dominate Japanese cinemas.

An interesting difference in the silent period was the presence for many screenings in Japan of commentaries spoken by professional speakers called *benshi*: films were thus accompanied by spoken explanations of dialogue and action which were often performances in themselves. Indeed, the union strength and influence (and popularity) of the *benshi*, and the Japanese reluctance to be dominated by US technology, meant that the replacement of silent film by synchronized sound was considerably delayed. While Hollywood moved rapidly into sound film production between 1927 and 1929, it was not until 1931 that the Japanese Tsuchihashi sound system had been developed, and a series of strikes by the *benshi* also delayed effective distribution of new sound films. By 1935 half of Japanese films were still silent. This should not, however, simply be seen as blinkered conservatism; the few Japanese silent films which survive indicate that the 1920s, though marked by reliable genres such as swordfight films, comedies and family dramas, were also a period of dynamic experiment in narrative, camerawork and lighting, comparable to the better known European 'movements' such as German Expressionism.

The two most significant Japanese directors of the 1930s were Yasujiro Ozu and Kenji Mizoguchi. Both established themselves with 1930s genre films before gaining international recognition with their contrasting styles in the 1950s (Ozu with *Tokyo Story* (1953), Mizoguchi with *The Life of Oharu* (1952) and *Ugetsu Monogatari* (1953)). Mizoguchi's style was expansive and dramatic. His subject matter was epic, the drama heightened by a refusal of close shots and a preference for relatively long takes in long shot.

By contrast, though he began by making a wide variety of different genre films, Ozu soon developed a very personal style which was to become his trademark. Dealing principally with life's little stories, his films contain little camera movement; every shot is very carefully framed, and many shots are held for a few seconds after significant action or dialogue has finished: it has been suggested that emptiness and absence reflect a specifically oriental or Zen philosophy to be contrasted with western emphasis on presence. There are very few high or low angle shots; virtually all shots are filmed horizontally from a height of about one metre, significantly lower than is usual. It is likely that this is at least partly influenced by the traditional Japanese practice of sitting or kneeling on the floor. Another Ozu trademark is the cutaway shot, often to an object or an exterior detail, which serves no narrative function but which evokes a relevant emotion.

The careful frame composition works together with the editing in a unique way. Ozu was one of the first directors to systematically break the 180 degree rule (Nagisa Oshima was to do so much later, in *Death By Hanging* (1968)). Ozu worked according to his own system whereby camera angle changes could be any multiple of 45 degrees, which meant that space was constructed quite differently from that built up by continuity editing. At the same time, it is graphic matches and contrasts that determine the editing. Thus in films such as *Passing Fancy* (1933) the figures may occupy identical positions in the frame. According to David Bordwell: 'Ozu instructed his cameraman to film medium shots of different-sized characters from different distances, so that the figures would be the same size in each shot. . . . Even the eyes had to be in the same position from shot to shot' (1988, p. 98). The 180 degree rule is broken, yet the spectator is not entirely disorientated. It is interesting to compare Ozu's use of such graphic matching with Eisenstein's concern with such matches and contrasts in Soviet Montage.

After the devastation suffered during the Second World War, Japan's restructuring was dominated by the United States until 1952. Many wartime Japanese films were destroyed, but the structure of the film industry remained more or less intact and by the mid-1950s production had returned to pre-war levels. The films of Ozu, Mizoguchi and Akira Kurosawa (*Rashomon*, 1950; *The Seven Samurai*, 1954 (Figure 14.5); *Throne of Blood*, 1957; *Yojimbo*, 1961; *Ran*, 1985) gained recognition at international festivals and began penetrating overseas markets, while domestic consumption was well served by comedies and melodramas, which were not so exportable, and then from the mid-1950s by the monster genre inaugurated by *Godzilla* (1954), which was.

The early 1960s saw the Japanese New Wave, which stimulated the careers of Oshima, Shohei Imamura and Yoshishige Yoshida. Though this was superficially similar to the French New Wave of the same period, the significant difference is that while the French movement was a reaction against tradition, the Japanese New Wave was manufactured by the industry itself. The modernist experimentation of the directors was real enough, and the assaults on traditional values were severe, but in the Japanese case the revolt was managed by the industry itself. As in France, however, the popularity of the films dropped off after 1964 in face of the competition from television. The studios began to struggle and, as in the United States, survived by letting out studio space and by investing in ·TV and other productions. The studios thus survived, but there was an explosion in 'independent' film-making.

Figure 14.5   *Japan enters the world stage with The Seven Samurai (BFI Stills, Posters and Designs)*

The studios also survived by cashing in on highly successful formulaic genres such as the monster movie and by investing in foreign (including American) productions. Indeed, the international careers of Kurosawa, Imamura and Oshima were largely dependent on international projects.

By the 1980s Japanese film production had become much more fragmented but nevertheless remained internationally successful and exportable. Post-apocalyptic *anime* animations, *manga* and visceral heavy-metal sex-and-violence were the stuff of the 'New Japanese Cinema', itself a post-punk reaction against the experimental and intellectual modernism of the 'New Wave'.

Since 1976, however, most cinema admissions in Japan had been for American films. If Japanese films now retained their popularity, it was surely in large part by (often very effectively and inventively) mimicking the entertainment values of the foreign imports. Films for the 1980s home market were produced very cheaply to appeal to an affluent youth market, and according to Thompson and Bordwell (1994, p. 758) at least half of the films produced around 1980 were soft pornography.

Since the 1990s, American companies have moved into exhibition in Japan by opening their own multiplexes, while powerful Japanese companies have taken over American entertainment companies such as Columbia and Universal. If Japanese directors and films no longer carry the prestige of Ozu or Kurosawa, there is a lot of Japanese money and influence in the increasingly globalized media industries.

Hong Kong

Though the Hong Kong film industry only began in the 1950s, its success and international standing have been considerable, particularly considering the size of the previous British Crown Colony which was returned to China in 1997.

Until 1970, the virtual monopoly of Run Run Shaw's 'Shaw Brothers' studios turned out a successful series of swordfight films, melodramas and films inspired by Chinese opera traditions; the vertically integrated company dominated the market in south-east Asia. When a new martial arts genre was developed in the 1960s (borrowing from Japanese samurai films, spaghetti westerns and Chinese opera), competition appeared in the form of Raymond Chow's 'Golden Harvest' company, which unleashed Bruce Lee on the world.

As well as achieving massive domestic popularity with his genuine but balletically chore-ographed kung fu skills (he was also an explicit pro-Chinese and anti-Japanese symbol in a number of his films), Bruce Lee brought Hong Kong cinema to international attention with *Fists of Fury* (1971), *Enter the Dragon* and *Return of the Dragon* (both 1973). His untimely (and unexplained) death in 1973 increased his cult hero status.

The 1970s thus saw Hong Kong cinema producing over 100 films a year and with far-reaching market influence: its profitability was aided by cheap production methods and by the 'forbidden' appeal of films made in an area with relatively liberal censorship regulations. The films did very well both at home and abroad. Gradually the martial arts genre declined, though despite desperately contrived parodic excesses it also retained popularity, much as did the Italian spaghetti westerns. Thrillers, comedies and 'underworld' action films became the favoured genres, and, more significantly, these were resolutely set in a modern urban environment.

It is in this context that Hong Kong's 'First New Wave' appeared in the late 1970s. While the French New Wave and other European cinema had clearly influenced directors such as Ann Hui, Shu Kei, Tsui Hark, Patrick Lam and John Woo, the innovation of the Hong Kong directors was concerned less with the development of a new kind of cinema than with see-ing how far they could go with existing popular genres.

At the risk of 'New Wave overload', it may be worth stressing at this point the difference of Hong Kong cinema compared with neighbouring Chinese cinemas. There was, for example, a resurgence in Taiwanese cinema in the 1970s, sparked by King Hu's very challenging *A Touch of Zen* (1971). Very different, on the other hand, was the story of Chinese cinema itself (which it is not possible to go into here); following the so-called 'Cultural Revolution' of 1966–76 (dur-ing which very few films were made in China), a 'Fifth Generation' of film-makers were trained in Beijing, whose 1980s films, though sometimes subject to various forms of censorship in China, found a ready audience in the West. Among these were *Yellow Earth* (Chen Kaige, 1984) and *Red Sorghum* (Zhang Yimou, 1987). With the drastic and continuing suppression of civil rights symbolized by the events of Tiananmen Square in 1989, some Chinese directors made their way to the West, including Chen Kaige (*Raise the Red Lantern*, 1991).

While the distinction between 'mainstream' and 'alternative' films had in fact always been rather blurred in Hong Kong, there was a second 'New Wave' in the 1990s, typified by the more experimental and idiosyncratic films of Wong Kar-Wai, aided and abetted by his equally creative Australian camera operator Chris Doyle (*Ashes of Time*, *Chungking Express* (both 1994)) (Figure 14.6). In an age of media saturation and omnipresent video images, Wong's films questioned the very nature of cinema as cinema, and were perhaps suitable signs of the 'culture of disappearance' in pre-1997 Hong Kong. Yet despite the imminent take-over by China, Hong Kong films were already widely available on the mainland.

Figure 14.6   *Chungking Express: Hong Kong streetlife (BFI Stills, Posters and Designs)*

India

The Indian film industry has often been described as 'the biggest in the world' in terms of production output. It also has a long history dating from its roots in 1896 and from the work of Dadasaheb Phalke, who directed the first Indian feature film (*Raja Harishchandra*) in 1913. By the 1920s Indian studios were already producing over 100 films a year, considerably more than either the British or French industries. Output was prolific but, perhaps partly hampered by the variety of cultures and languages of the subcontinent, the major production companies were unable to secure any measure of vertical integration to consolidate their position. Though the studios (most typically those at Tollygunge in Calcutta which were nick-named 'Tollywood') were modelled on Hollywood, they retained a 'family' ethos, and the most favoured (and highly popular) genres were the 'mythological' or religious tales, 'stunt' adventure films and a smattering of socially responsible romantic melodramas. Most significantly, virtually all films, of whatever genre, were punctuated by (apparently non-diegetic) song and dance numbers.

By the eve of the Second World War in 1939, the Indian film industry had attained a deceptive position of apparent strength. Some 200 films were being made each year, yet though many of the films were popular within India, they were not dominant in the way that Japanese and (later) Hong Kong films dominated their home markets. This was no doubt partly due to the wide variety of Indian cultures and languages (which made it impossible for a single film to appeal to a truly massive audience), but must also have been exacerbated by the financial instability of the film companies themselves, which were prey to corruption and nepotism as studio heads were increasingly held to ransom by star actors and actresses demanding exorbitant fees.

Though the old Indian studio system collapsed in the 1940s and hundreds of small independent companies sprang up, little changed in the post-war years; by the early 1960s some 300 films were being produced each year by an intensely competitive industry (with its principal bases in Bombay and Madras), conforming largely to the same genres, with the addition of the 'historical' genre inaugurated by *Chandralekha* (Vasan, 1948). This genre complemented the 1950s moves to censor representations of sexual activity, particularly wanton kissing and 'indecorous' dancing – though dancing and singing, of course, remained essential ingredients of almost all Indian films, aimed as they were at a rural audience which was at the time still largely illiterate.

Nevertheless, the 1950s also saw some changes, with some directors beginning to experiment deliberately with European influences. Thus while Raj Kapoor's comedy dramas were popular and populist, the *mise en scène* was new to Indian audiences. More innovative still were the films of Satyajit Ray, a writer and commercial artist who turned to film after seeing *Bicycle Thieves* – it is clear that Ray was in no way 'typical' of Indian film-making of the time. His semi-autobiographical trilogy *Pather Panchali* (1955), *Aparajito* (1956) and *The World of Apu* (1960) introduced the methods and ideals of Italian neorealism to Indian cinema: no songs, no dancing, but a careful, undramatic but sensitive and beautiful observation of the hardships of a poor family (Figure 14.7). When De Sica's scriptwriter Cesare Zavattini saw *Pather Panchali*, he responded: 'at last, the neorealist cinema that the Italians did not know how to do' (quoted in Das Gupta, 1981, p. 61). While Ray's films have probably been appreciated more in western 'art cinema' circles than in rural Indian cinemas, his influence on later Indian films (for example, Mira Nair's *Salaam Bombay!* (1988)) has been considerable. Indeed, even *Mother India* (Mehboob Khan, 1957), at the time the greatest Indian box-office hit of them all (and still playing occasionally on British terrestrial TV), despite its use of song and dance, was perhaps more 'realist' than previous films of the genre.

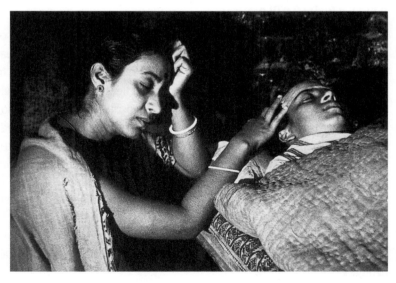

A child dies in Pather Panchali: the neorealist influence on Indian cinema (BFI Stills, Posters and Designs)　　Figure 14.7

Though the song-and-dance formula continued to be popular (and, indeed, still is), and the 1960s saw a consolidation of home markets and the beginning of profitable exports, there were government attempts to move Indian cinema beyond its entertainment base. From 1969, Film Finance Corporation funds were provided for a Bombay-based 'Parallel Cinema', which became the 'New Indian Cinema' of the 1970s. This was a more self-consciously experimental, artistic and politicized cinema, made by directors such as Satyajit Ray but also by Mrinal Sen (*Bhuvan Shome*, 1969), Ritwik Ghatak (*Reason, Argument and Tale*, 1974) and Basu Chatterji (*The Whole Sky*, 1969). The influence in these films of European attitudes to material otherwise censorable in India, and of leftist critiques severely critical of ruling ideologies, led (perhaps not surprisingly) to increased censorship of such 'alternative' films and to revised guidelines for allocation of finance for funding such projects. A further problem was the lack of any alternative distribution system for such relatively challenging films.

In a country of (then) over 500 million people, however, it is no surprise that such marginal films continued to be made (largely in the more left-wing/communist states such as Kerala), side by side with the staple entertainment: by 1980 Madras had become 'the most prolific filmmaking capital in the world' (Thompson and Bordwell, 1994, p. 771). Export markets continued to grow (particularly with the boom in video sales) and soon included Indian populations in Europe, Canada and Australia as well as in East Africa; in Britain's Birmingham and London and elsewhere, specialist cinemas showed (and continue to show) Indian and Pakistani films to full houses night after night; Bollywood is clearly more popular than Hollywood in some parts of the world. In 1990 some 950 Indian films were made; although a number of these were international co-productions, this is still some kind of record.

African Cinema

It is clearly not technically correct to treat African cinema as a 'national' cinema, as Africa comprises over 50 nation-states. Yet with the exception of the Mediterranean countries such as Egypt, Tunisia, Algeria and Morocco, and to some extent South Africa (the relative prosperity and contact with Europe of these countries having enabled the development of some film-making – indeed, Egypt has a rich and varied film history), almost no indigenous film-making took place in the continent for most of the twentieth century, and indeed until the 1980s or so there were very few cinemas and virtually no attention was paid by individual governments to developing film industries. When one considers the more pressing problems of drought, starvation, war, and the repayment of crippling debts to western governments and banks whose imperialist policies were a large part of the problem in the first place, however, it is perhaps not so surprising that developing national cinemas was not such a high priority. Despite obvious variations in the histories and cultures of many of the countries, it has been common to treat 'Black African Cinema' (as it should perhaps be called) as a critical category.

Prior to the start of Black African film-making, and indeed since that time, the overwhelming bulk of films shown in Africa have been distributed by American and European companies; the entertainment agenda has been dominated (increasingly so since the spread of satellite TV and video in Africa) by cheap American films and by Egyptian, Indian and more recently Hong Kong products. Insofar that such films addressed African issues at all, they did so only in crude and caricatural terms: even 'respectable' films like *Out of Africa* (Pollack, 1985), *Gorillas in the Mist* (Apted, 1988) and *Cry Freedom* (Attenborough, 1987) did not escape this judgement.

The first steps towards the development of Black African film-making were taken with the establishment of Film Festivals at Carthage in Tunisia in 1966 and, more crucially, in Ouagadougou in Burkina Faso in 1969. These festivals secured the essential outside finance needed to launch indigenous film-making, and it was in the French-speaking Senegal and the Ivory Coast that the first films were made and shown – it would be interesting to explore the possible legacy of the pioneering French documentary film-maker Jean Rouch, who made a number of films throughout much of central and West Africa between 1946 and 1977.

The first group of Black African film-makers included Med Hondo (Mauritania), Paulin Vieyra (Senegal), Désiré Écaré (Ivory Coast), Oumarou Ganda (Niger) and the 'father' of Black African film, Ousmane Sembene of Senegal, who is credited as having directed the first Black African film, the 20-minute *Borom Sarret* (1963). Several of the early African films made surreal use of documentary and neorealist techniques to mount biting attacks on the ills of postcolonial African societies; many of this first generation of Black African film-makers had been trained in Europe and so were influenced by European 'movements' such as Soviet Montage theory and Italian neorealism, and had also developed a revolutionary left-wing political analysis (Ousmane Sembene, for example, had studied in Moscow). When these film-makers began to explore the African past in the 1970s and 1980s, the films were powerful critiques of colonialism and imperialism.

The problem, however, was not just getting films made; there was at the time almost no distribution network for such films, which found their audiences almost entirely in the 'art cinema' circuits of Europe and North America. The result was that films such as Ousmane's *Emitai* (1972), *Xala* (1974) and *Ceddo* (pronounced 'Yeddo', 1976) and Hondo's *Sarraounia* (1968) and *Soleil O* (1970) were too often written about and analysed as if they were European art films, and their specifically African nature was sometimes forgotten.

Yet despite the European influence, and despite the growth of some 'western' style film-making/genres such as comedy and thrillers in some countries with stronger western links such as Nigeria and Cameroun, a specifically 'African' cinema was slowly born. Constructions of space and time are different; the work of 'magic' (such as characters suddenly appearing or disappearing, for example in *Emitai* and *Sarraounia*) is integrated into some films in a matter-of-fact way; and perhaps most significantly, oral story-telling techniques (often involving a story-teller or *griot*) are woven into the narration (*Ceddo* is an excellent example).

These themes, and perhaps especially the narration of time and space, were taken up by the next generation of Black African directors, who included Safi Faye of Senegal, Souleymane Cissé of Mali (*The Wind* (*Finyé*), 1982; *Brightness* or *The Light* (*Yeelen*), 1989) and Idrissa Ouedraogo of Burkina Faso (*Grandmother* (*Yaaba*), 1989; *Tilaï*, 1990). There has also been some debate about the status of some other black film-makers such as Haile Gerima and

Sarah Maldoror: not resident in Africa, should they and other *diaspora* figures (a term used to describe those who have spread – for whatever reason, in this case originally through slavery – throughout the world) be included in 'African' cinema?

The films mentioned above reflect the increasing photographic quality made possible by the modern technical facilities in Burkina Faso, and they accordingly did well on the European art circuit. Nevertheless, as well as exploring universal themes, a film such as *Tilaï*, for example, is also intensely specific to the culture in which it was made (Figure 14.8). When a traveller returns to find that his father has married the woman of his own desire, an affair develops between the traveller and his stepmother. Is this incest? Should the couple try to run away to avoid the man's death which is demanded by custom? What are their rights and their obligations in their society? While lyrical and contemplative in its camerawork, *Tilaï* is an exploration of cultural questions very relevant to Burkina Faso.

Questions of culture, relevance and adaptation to a rapidly changing world are central to debates about the future of African cinema. At the 1995 Ouagadougou Festival, a 'queer' South African film dealing openly and provocatively with homosexuality sparked a mass walk-out by the Black African audience. Among the urgent tasks facing Black African film-makers and cinema is engaging with such relatively 'new' moral and cultural issues. In this they may, finally, be helped by the increasing links being formed with other black film-makers abroad, with the diaspora.

Figure 14.8   *Tilaï: exploring customs through storytelling (Films de l'Avenir/Waka/Rhea, courtesy Kobal)*

SUMMARY

- 'National cinemas' are usually defined in opposition to the dominance of US/Hollywood cinema.
- The best-known European film 'movements' include 1920s German Expressionism and Soviet Montage, the Italian neorealism of the 1940s and the French New Wave of the early 1960s.

- Indian films (particularly those of the studios known as 'Bollywood') have, in terms of audience figures and popularity, arguably been more successful than those of Hollywood.
- Despite their considerable success, other Asian cinemas, particularly those of Japan and Hong Kong, have generally been critically neglected in the West.

REFERENCES

André Bazin, *What is Cinema?* Vol. 1 (transl. Hugh Gray, Berkeley, CA: University of California Press, 1967).

David Bordwell, *Ozu and the Poetics of Cinema* (London: BFI, 1988), pp. 88–105.

Colin Crofts, 'Concepts of National Cinema', in John Hill and Pamela Church Gibson (eds), *The Oxford Guide to Film Studies* (Oxford: Oxford University Press, 1998).

Lotte Eisner, *The Haunted Screen: Expressionism in the German Cinema* (London: Secker & Warburg, 1965).

Chidinanda Das Gupta (ed.), *Satyajit Ray* (New Delhi: Directorate of Film Festivals, 1981).

Kristin Thompson and David Bordwell, *Film History: An Introduction* (New York: McGraw-Hill, 1994).

FURTHER READING

André Bazin, *What is Cinema?* Vol. 2 (transl. Hugh Gray, Berkeley, CA: University of California Press, 1971).

Peter Bondanella, *Italian Cinema: From Neorealism to the Present* (New York: Continuum, 1996).

Leo Braudy and Marshall Cohen (eds), *Film Theory and Criticism* (5th edn, Oxford: Oxford University Press, 1999).

Sergei Eisenstein, *Film Form* (transl. Jay Leyda, New York: Harcourt Brace Jovanovich, 1949).

Lotte Eisner, *The Haunted Screen: Expressionism in the German Cinema* (London: Secker & Warburg, 1965).

Teshome Gabriel, *Third Cinema in the Third World: The Aesthetics of Liberation* (Ann Arbor, MI: University of Michigan Press, 1982).

John Hill and Pamela Church Gibson (eds), *The Oxford Guide to Film Studies* (Oxford: Oxford University Press, 1998).

Jay Leyda, *Kino: A History of the Russian and Soviet Film* (London: George Allen & Unwin Ltd., 1973).

Mira Liehm, *Passion and Defiance: Film in Italy from 1942 to the Present* (Berkeley, CA: University of California Press, 1984).

Gerald Mast and Marshall Cohen (eds), *Film Theory and Criticism* (Oxford: Oxford University Press, 1974) (see also Braudy and Cohen).

Robert Murphy (ed.), *The British Cinema Book* (London: BFI, 1997).

David Overbey (ed.), *Springtime in Italy: A Reader on Neo-Realism* (London: Talisman, 1978).

Kristin Thompson and David Bordwell, *Film History: An Introduction* (New York: McGraw-Hill, 1994).

Frank Ukadike, *Black African Cinema* (Berkeley, CA: University of California Press, 1994).

FURTHER VIEWING

Cinema Europe (BBC2, 1995).

Cinema Cinema: The French New Wave (Channel 4, 1992).

Close-up on Battleship Potemkin *by Roger Corman* (BBC2, 1995).

Alternative Cinema and Other Film Styles

We looked in Chapter 8 at how some films, such as those of counter-cinema, stand apart from mainstream entertainment cinema in their partial or total refusal of narrative conventions and commercial film techniques. In this final chapter we shall briefly consider some other groups of films – some bigger than others – which in their different ways have challenged dominant film conventions.

SURREALISM

Like German Expressionism, Surrealism was an artistic tendency which developed in the early years of the twentieth century. It inspired a small number of film-makers to make 'surrealist' films, and the surrealist influence still echoes strongly in the films of Terry Gilliam and David Lynch, for example.

Surrealism developed from dada into an art form which valued the spontaneous and the unconscious. Very influenced by Freudian ideas (though in a way which disgusted Freud himself), the Surrealists had by the mid-1920s developed into a group of painters, poets, writers and musicians with very fragmentary but passionately held beliefs; the group published a manifesto in 1924 and was constantly splitting as artists accused one another of betraying the cause, of not being 'true' Surrealists. Among important figures in the group, which was based in Paris, were Paul Éluard, Louis Aragon and André Breton. A few film-makers began to experiment with dream-states on the screen, for example Man Ray (*Emak Bakia*, 1928) and Germaine Dulac (*The Seashell and the Clergyman*, 1928).

In 1928, however, two young, then relatively unknown members of the group made a film which tore up the cinematic map: *The Andalusian Dog* (*Un chien andalou*). Salvador Dali was to become arguably the most famous (and most notorious) twentieth century artist, and Luis Buñuel would go on to make over 30 films: more of him later.

A man stands on a balcony, watching thin slivers of cloud cut across the moon. A razor is sharpened. A woman sits passively, her eye is held open, and, echoing the clouds passing across the moon, the razor slices open the eye (Figure 15.1). So begins *Un chien andalou*, which was intended to scandalize French audiences and succeeded. The sliced eye can be seen as symbolizing the sexual act; ants crawling into a hand symbolize decay; the female character has a choice between remaining with her tame, rational suitor or following lust and passion with his alter ego or other side. She opts for the former and the film ends with the couple buried to their necks in a sandy beach: the living dead. Though there were other possible readings of the film, it was clearly a savage assault on religion and on bourgeois values. The film was also not given a UK censors' certificate until 1968. Filled with images symbolizing sexual desire and frustration, *Un chien andalou* is said to have been written by Buñuel and Dali in such a way that any scene which made rational or logical sense was discarded; much of the film is based literally on its creators' dreams. Indeed, it remains a disturbing, dreamlike film: dreamlike not in the soft-focus Hollywood sense but because of the dreamlike 'logic' which guides the narrative.

Buñuel and Dali then collaborated again in 1930 on *The Age of Gold* (*L'Age d'or*), another exploration of sexual passion and its suppression which was attacked violently: a screening of the film in December 1930 was disrupted by fascists and anti-Jewish groups: paint was thrown at the screen and many books and art-works in an exhibition were vandalized. Members of the audience were beaten up. Interestingly, the police did not intervene and the film was banned for a time.

These films are still seen as the founding moments of surrealism in the cinema. They were followed by Jean Cocteau's *The Blood of a Poet* (*Le Sang d'un poète*, 1932). Though such films remained on the margins of film exhibition, we must remember that over the next decade or two Freudian theories about dreams, the unconscious and their social significance were to become part of conventional wisdom in the US and Europe (see also Chapter 12).

Though the number of genuinely 'surrealist' films was small, their influence was great, and was aided in no small measure by the subsequent career of Luis Buñuel. Though he made many other films in a remarkable career, his *Viridiana* (1961), *The Discreet Charm of the*

Un chien andalou: the shock of Surrealism (BFI Stills, Posters and Designs)   Figure 15.1

Bourgeoisie (1972) and particularly *That Obscure Object of Desire* (*Cet obscur objet du désir*, 1977) marked a successful fusion of French/Spanish 'art' cinema with Buñuel's abiding surrealist impulse. The latter film (his last) is interesting not only because it continues and develops Buñuel's scathing attacks on the hypocrisy and moral bankruptcy of the bourgeoisie and of the Church, but also because two actresses are used to play a single character, symbolizing different aspects of the central male character's desire.

The object of desire usually remains obscure: if we think we desire a man, a woman, a bar of chocolate or a Porsche, it usually hides a desire for something else. Insofar that some recent film-makers have been aware of this, they have sought to integrate such Freudian–surrealist insights into their own films. David Lynch, for example, in his *Eraserhead* (1976) (Figure 15.2), *Blue Velvet* (1986) and *Lost Highway* (1996), has explored the dark unconscious underside of the American psyche; his TV series *Twin Peaks* (1990–91), though more comedic and playful, occupies the same territory. And though postmodernism may also have something to do with the questioning of 'reality' and of consciousness in films like *eXistenZ* and *The Matrix*, the surrealist legacy also retains a strong influence.

The surrealist influence is more diluted in films which may be described as 'fantasy cinema'. Finding inspiration in dream but less rigorous in their exploration of the psychological or social significance of the unconscious, such films would include the early *Orphée* (Cocteau, 1950), *Alice* (Jan Švankmajer, 1988), *Institute Benjamenta* (Brothers Quay, 1995), *Delicatessen* and *The City of Lost Children* (Jean-Pierre Jeunet and Marc Caro, 1990 and 1995), several of Raul Ruiz's films (especially *Shattered Image*, 1998), and perhaps even those of Pedro Almodovar. Such films blur the boundaries between dream, fantasy and 'reality', but generally leave the door open for a rational interpretation of the film's events.

Figure 15.2   *Henry has a problem in Eraserhead (BFI Stills, Posters and Designs)*

DOCUMENTARY FILM

When we think of film we usually have in mind works of fiction, which indeed account for the vast majority of films; yet the birth of cinema was heralded by documentary, a form which has been with us ever since. The simplest definition of documentary, as film of unmanipulated reality, can easily be picked apart, but here we propose to simply provide brief snapshots of some important documentary moments.

There are many types of documentary film and they serve different functions. The Lumière Brothers' early work consisted of 'actuality' films such as *Workers Leaving the Factory* (1895), which were recordings of events from everyday life. As film-makers they simply recorded what was in front of the camera. Actuality footage is the principal raw material of documentaries but can be edited and presented in a variety of ways to serve particular functions.

Soviet film-maker Dziga Vertov documented aspects of life in the Soviet Union during the 1920s, but his films already presented their material in ways not usually associated with documentaries. He used experimental postproduction techniques that included superimposed images, animation, split screens (see Figure 15.3) and editing together shots that have visual associations. *Man with a Movie Camera* (1929), for example, is an unusual mix of information, propaganda and entertainment. By the end of the film we are as aware of Vertov's style of film-making as we are of aspects of Soviet society. The film celebrates much about the Soviet Union but celebrates film-making too.

Another innovative documentary film-maker and producer was Scotland's John Grierson (see also Chapter 13), who did not merely document events in his films, but ensured that material was creatively shot and that imaginative editing presented the film's subject matter

Man with a Movie Camera: early documentary experiments (BFI Stills, Posters and Designs)   Figure 15.3

so that it was coherent, interesting and entertaining. *Drifters* (1929) does more than show us fishermen at sea; the shots are visually stunning, the editing produces drama; the film is informative and educative but also moving and gripping.

Leni Riefenstahl's 1930s documentaries had a somewhat different purpose: she was employed by the Nazis to produce propaganda films. *Triumph of the Will* (1935) is a record of a Nazi rally but does far more than simply record events. The *mise en scène*, camerawork and editing serve one function: to praise Hitler, the Nazi party and the Aryan race. The camera captures the choreographed speeches and the massed, geometrically arranged ranks of obedient citizens and soldiers; all in all, a stunning performance. The editing ensures that the message does not escape the viewer: Hitler as saviour and leader, backed by a strong party (and an army), with the purpose of making the heroic and mythologized German people victorious and great again. This is clever propaganda and effective documentary.

Ten years later in Italy, Roberto Rossellini found another use for documentary. He had supported the Italian partisans during the Second World War and made fictional films about life in Italy during the Nazi occupation and their defeat in 1945. *Paisa* (1946), one of the first neorealist films, consists of six fictional stories, but the closeness to reality of each episode is emphasized through the use of actuality footage from Italy's war years. Common documentary devices in the film include the use of archive footage and a voice-over to provide explanation.

Another typical documentary technique is the combining of actuality footage with interviews. In the mid-1950s Lindsay Anderson, Karel Reisz and Tony Richardson, of the British-based Free Cinema movement, established themselves with films that documented and analysed contemporary working-class issues. They produced innovative films such as *Momma Don't Allow* (1955), *Every Day Except Christmas* (1957) and *We are the Lambeth Boys* (1959). The group had been strongly influenced and inspired by Grierson's work and they wanted their documentaries to be informative and provocative, analytical and revealing.

Not all documentaries have a social or political purpose, however; many have entertainment as their priority. Music documentaries ('rockumentaries') came to prominence in the 1960s and one of the most memorable is *Don't Look Back* (1966), which documented Bob Dylan's British tour. The film used 'direct cinema' techniques in that the use of mobile cameras enabled the unfolding events to be filmed directly rather than situations being set up for the camera. The camera operator wasn't a part of the events but merely an observer. *Woodstock* (1970) is also regarded as a landmark film in its recording of events at a music festival by several cameras and with innovative editing. However, music documentaries tend to be well planned and are far from being transparent recordings of events. This is not of course to say that such documentaries are worthless; indeed, *Stop Making Sense* (1984) is a carefully crafted recording of a Talking Heads performance that is widely regarded as a classic of its kind. *The Buena Vista Social Club* (1999) has similarly been claimed as a quality documentary in its use of direct cinema techniques, interviews and live recordings to investigate the lives of some old Cuban musicians, the narrative culminating in a reunion concert.

Another documentary style, *cinéma vérité*, also makes use of mobile cameras and sound equipment but holds open the possibility of the camera operator being part of events through his/her involvement with people filmed. Jean Rouch's *Chronicle of a Summer* (*Chronique d'un été*, 1960) is often regarded as the first *vérité* film. Andy Warhol's *Chelsea Girls* (1966) provides an unusual example of the technique in that visitors to his open art studio in New York were given cameras to record events, resulting in a poorly filmed record of rather tedious conversations. A more purposeful use of *cinéma vérité* is found in *Harlan County, U.S.A.* (1977), which documents a strike by Kentucky coal-miners for trade union rights. The film-makers lived with the mining community and became part of the events, with the result that the film has a closeness to the action and issues unusual in documentaries.

A further documentary device is fly-on-the-wall filming. Here the camera is often fixed in position, thus doing away with the need for a camera operator; the camera can record events without people being reminded of its presence. This technique tends to be reserved for television documentaries rather than film, though the fictional *Truman Show* (1998) took the concept to an extreme with Truman being unaware of his 24-hour surveillance by a multitude of cameras. The intention of fly-on-the-wall documentaries is that we see an unmediated reality in that the presence of the camera does not interfere with the people being filmed and does not influence their behaviour. However, as with all films, documentary and fiction alike, decisions are made that in effect mean we only get a representation of reality. The positioning of the camera immediately shapes what we see but more importantly, fly-on-the-wall footage is normally edited, again involving choices which influence what we see in the completed documentary. The popular Channel 4 series *Big Brother*, broadcast in 2000, employed several fly-on-the-wall cameras, but these were located in carefully selected positions, and the programmes were obviously heavily edited to condense 24-hour footage from many cameras into a series of half-hour programmes.

The term 'non-fiction' is of course itself a problem, and some commentators have all but abandoned the distinction between 'factual' subject matter and 'fiction'; all that really remains is the documentary *style*. What then do we make of what is termed *faction*, the reconstruction (common on TV) of (usually recent) 'real' events? Recent examples (among many) would include films such as *In the Name of the Father* (Sheridan, 1993) (about the 'Guildford Four') and *Apollo 13* (Howard, 1995) (about the spacecraft launch disaster), and TV films such as the Channel 4 reconstruction of the David Irving libel trial and that of TNT about the Nüremberg Trials. Can any reconstruction, however faithful, be called a documentary? Again (see pp. 113–14 above) we are faced with *ontological* questions.

Exercise 15.1

In small groups, discuss any recent film or TV drama-documentaries you may have seen. Are the events portrayed 'real'? Can such programmes or films be described as documentaries?

Even if documentaries contain non-fiction material, it is impossible for them to be completely objective. Participants are usually aware of the camera, footage is usually edited, camera position provides a particular perspective, interviews structure what verbal information is to be revealed, and postproduction voice-overs guide us towards particular interpretations and understandings. However, this is not necessarily undesirable. A well-planned and intelligently produced documentary can analyse a topic, reveal information about a subject, develop understanding and still be entertaining.

FEMINIST FILM

Throughout the history of film, as of the other arts, the vast majority of those associated with the medium have been men. In part this is simply a reflection of a patriarchal culture which guards male privilege and allows women into film only as objects of the gaze (see pp. 213–14 above); perhaps, though, the technical complexity of film (and indeed of more recent developments via video, CGI and DVD) has also reinforced the idea of 'toys for boys'. The vast majority of computer enthusiasts are also male.

There have always, however, been a few pioneering women film-makers. Leni Riefenstahl, despite the fascistic content of her best-known films (*Triumph of the Will*, 1935; *Olympia*, 1938), was a gifted director. Maya Deren (*Meshes of the Afternoon*, 1943) (Figure 15.4), influenced by Surrealism and interested in voodoo, was among the first famous female film

Figure 15.4   *Maya Deren's Meshes of the Afternoon: American avant garde cinema (BFI Stills, Posters and Designs)*

artists. Dorothy Arzner was the first female Hollywood director (*Dance Girl Dance*, 1940) whose career was re-excavated in the 1970s. Ida Lupino (*Outrage*, 1950) and Stephanie Rothman (*Knucklemen/Terminal Island*, 1973) were other rare female directors of commercial films.

Though women directors in mainstream production remained rare, the 1960s, 1970s and 1980s saw a marked increase in numbers of women making 'art' or alternative films. Among the best known of these were Agnès Varda, Marguerite Duras in France, Margarethe von Trotta, Helma Sanders-Brahms and Ulrike Ottinger in (then West) Germany, Laura Mulvey and later Sally Potter in Britain, Jackie Raynal and Yvonne Rainer in North America, Chantal Akerman in Belgium, and Marleen Gorris (pronounced 'Horris') in the Netherlands.

The emergence of female film-making was clearly linked to a general loosening of previous social prejudices and assumptions, and to the almost-revolutionary events of May 1968, when through strikes and direct action students and workers (particularly in France but to some extent in other western countries) came very close to bringing down governments; it is difficult for later generations to grasp the excitement of that time when anything seemed possible; the subsequent disillusionment of social revolutionaries was deep indeed; in France there were many suicides.

In such a climate – which, influenced in the USA by the Civil Rights and New Left movements and inspired by Betty Friedan's *The Feminine Mystique*, also gave birth to the Women's Liberation Movement – an important concern for alternative film-makers (both male and female) was to explore the nature of capitalism and patriarchy and to create a new kind of oppositional or counter-cinema. We have already looked at some aspects of such films in Chapters 8 and 12 above, but an additional dimension was the feminist concern with changing the way a gendered spectator was addressed by a film, indeed, with changing how gender was itself constructed.

This involved dealing with new subjects, but for many of these female directors it also involved dealing with them in radically new ways: it meant searching for a new 'language', a women's language. Akerman's *Jeanne Dielman, 23 Quai du Commerce, 1080 Bruxelles* (1975), for example, concerns the everyday household activities of a housewife-prostitute. Activities such as cooking and cleaning are shot in long takes which correspond to the monotony of the tasks; the camera remains at head-height to share the character's perspective. Duras and Varda both developed highly individual styles which rejected most mainstream narrative conventions; Varda coined the term *cinécriture* ('film-writing') to describe her own style. A good example of the latter is *Vagabonde* (*Sans toit ni loi*, 1985), which uses flashback to recount the events leading to the death of the central female character Mona, portrayed as an uncaring, selfish vagrant who eventually freezes to death in a ditch. The flashback contains episodes which overlap in a complex way, with a variety of interview-style remarks from people who have come across Mona. Most of the tracking shots of Mona walking through a cold, desolate landscape are (very unusually) from right to left; many such tracking shots begin without Mona in the frame and end after she has left the frame.

Vagabonde is a challenging work, like many of its feminist sister-films. Among the other best-known examples are Varda's own *Happiness* (*Le Bonheur*, 1965), Akerman's *News From Home* (1976) and *Les Rendez-vous d'Anna* (1978), Duras' *Nathalie Granger* (1972) and

India Song (1975), Mulvey's *Penthesilea* (1974) and *Riddles of the Sphinx* (1977), von Trotta's *The German Sisters* (*Die bleiende Zeit*, 1981), Ottinger's *Ticket of No Return* (*Bildnis einer Trinkerin*, 1979), Susan Clayton and Jonathan Curling's *Song of the Shirt* (1979), Connie Field's *Rosie the Riveter* (1980), Potter's first film, *Thriller* (1979) and Gorris's *A Question of Silence* (1982) (Figure 15.5).

While Hollywood and the mainstream film industry are still overwhelmingly male, the 1980s and 1990s saw a few more women taking creative (and, indeed, executive) roles in the film industry. Kathryn Bigelow (*Blue Steel*, 1990; *Point Break*, 1991; *Strange Days*, 1995) was making action/adventure films: an example of 'genre-bending' with a female director making action-packed and sometimes violent genre films. Jane Campion made *An Angel at My Table* (1990) and *The Piano* (1993).

Jane Campion is one of the few female directors who are referred to as *auteurs*. Her work is closer to art cinema than it is to mainstream cinema yet her work has achieved commercial success. Campion's films defy easy genre categorization and their recurring themes and visual techniques have resulted in her work having an identifiable style. She has made five feature films to date: *Sweetie* (1989), *An Angel at My Table* and *The Piano*, *The Portrait of a Lady* (1996) and *Holy Smoke* (1999). *The Piano* was awarded several Oscars and earned Campion an international reputation.

There are elements of melodrama in her work, with a strong emphasis on relationships, family, and exploring characters' emotions, sometimes through an effective use of dark humour. The frequent criticisms of patriarchal society and the strong female protagonists of her films have led to her being regarded as a 'feminist' director. The central female characters tend to be obstinate and independent free spirits, often troubled and frequently searching for meaning and spirituality in their lives. Other themes in her films include analyses of the effects that society has on individuals, observations on the relationships between men, women and power, and a reversal of perspective that provides a female view of the world. Jane Campion's films are visually and aesthetically impressive, with imaginative use of cinematography, occasionally using expressionistic devices and symbolism which further mark her work off from mainstream cinema.

Figure 15.5   *A question of murder: three women against a man in A Question of Silence*
(Sigman Films, courtesy Kobal)

Mainstream films, however, did start to deal with issues of gender and sexuality; indeed, male directors also seemed to begin making films which could be described as 'women-friendly'. *Thelma and Louise* (Ridley Scott, 1991) concerns two women who end up on the run from the police after their weekend outing goes wrong when Louise (Susan Sarandon) shoots and kills a rapist in defence of her friend Thelma (Geena Davis). Most men in the film are stupid, violent or weak (or all three); even the otherwise sympathetic cop played by Harvey Keitel is ultimately powerless. The viewer's sympathy is surely with the women as they opt to drive over a cliff rather than return to such a stupid male-dominated society. Though there is no overt physical contact between Sarandon and Davis and their characters are clearly signalled as heterosexual, the bonding between the women indicates a clear lesbian subtext.

Other films also began to deal with gay and lesbian representations more explicitly. Thus *Desert Hearts* (Donna Deitch, 1985) is told as a fairly straightforward love story, lesbian sex scenes and all. The postmodern disintegration of stable gender identity was explored in the much more British film *Orlando* (Sally Potter, 1992), an adaptation of the Virginia Woolf novel. The film follows the experiences of the male Orlando (played by the female Tilda Swinton) who lives through various experiences in the seventeenth and eighteenth centuries (without ageing), changes in sleep from male to female ('same person, no difference at all . . . just a different sex'), and who then passes through some more episodes to arrive in late twentieth century Britain, an androgynous woman with a daughter who films her happiness with a video camera. The film is full of ironic commentary on male and female gender roles, suggesting that such roles are obsolete and a thing of the past.

The feminist experiments with film form continue but reach only small audiences. Hollywood/mainstream cinema has taken on previously controversial issues of sexuality, gender and violence against women. But does this mean that feminist films which continue to struggle for a new mode of expression are no longer of any interest? It could be argued that such alternative film-making remains more vital than ever; mainstream entertainment films may have more active female heroes and may deal with tougher issues, but the under-lying forms and ideologies remain the same; female sexuality is still used to sell films as the female body is exhibited and objectified. We should remember what happened to Patricia Charbonneau after her lesbian role in *Desert Hearts*: she was unable to find work for several years.

THIRD CINEMA

We have given some attention in Chapter 14 above to the cinema of what used to be called the 'Third World' (is the term 'Developing Countries' any less patronising?). The label 'Third Cinema' has been applied to films produced principally in South America, Asia and Africa, but also to some extent in Europe, which promote indigenous and/or ethnic minority cultures but which stand in opposition to western imperialism.

The best known of these cinemas is perhaps the South American 'Cinema Nôvo' ('New Cinema') of the 1960s: *Os Fuzis* (Ruy Guerra, 1964), *Antonio-das-mortes* (Glauber Rocha,

1969). At a time when the Brazilian and other South American film and TV industries were buying in cheap American films and soap operas, the 'Cinema Nôvo' film-makers ran considerable risks in making and promoting their films. They had to compete not only with hostile US media interests, but with CIA-backed state terrorism which put their lives at risk. Solanas and Getino's epic *Hour of the Furnaces* (1969) was filmed secretly and made the directors marked men for Argentina's CIA-funded military regime.

While in South America (and in parts of Africa and Asia) such 'Third Cinema' was (and in some cases still is) produced at considerable physical risk, other films of this type have been made in more benevolent or at least tolerant environments. The Cuban films of Tomas Guttierez Alea (*Memories of Underdevelopment*, 1968) and Santiago Alvarez (*79 Springtimes*, 1969), for example, attacked American imperialism from a democratic socialist Cuba. Curiously, British films such as *Territories* (Isaac Julien/Sankofa, 1985) and *Handsworth Songs* (John Akomfrah/Black Audio Collective, 1986) could also be seen as 'Third Cinema' in their oppositional stance in relation to the institutional racism of white British culture.

AVANT-GARDE AND STRUCTURAL-MATERIALIST FILM

The avant-garde of any art form, be it literature, painting or film, is concerned with stretching the limits of the medium. In theoretical terms, this perhaps places such artists close to the formalists (among them Eisenstein and Arnheim) who felt that film could only be 'art' if it made maximum use of its possibilities: to use sequences of photographic images to manipulate space and time rather than to try to reflect 'reality'.

Many early avant-garde film-makers were thus concerned with film as a plastic art rather than with any recording of 'reality'. For Man Ray, Fernand Léger, René Clair, Oskar Fischinger and the surrealists, the emphasis was clearly on what could be done with the (then still relatively new) medium.

Exercise 15.2

If it is possible, look at one or more avant-garde films of the 1920s or 1930s, for example *Entr'acte*, *Le Ballet mécanique* or *Un chien andalou*. Compare it/them with recent experimental TV work and with pop videos and credit sequences. The technical differences are obvious enough, but how are technological innovation and video 'art' treated and sold now? Compare the present production and consumption situation with the time at which such films were made.

The best-known avant-garde films of the mid-century were produced in the United States, by Maya Deren, Stan Brakhage, Jonas Mekas, Bruce Conner and others. Then came Kenneth Anger's *Fireworks* (1947) and *Scorpio Rising* (1964), both troubled explorations of the director's sadomasochistic homosexuality (Anger went on to write *Hollywood Babylon*, a vitriolic exposé of the dark side of Hollywood). Anger's films gave impetus to what became known as 'Underground' cinema, at first a US phenomenon but then spreading to other industrialized countries. Underground films were marked by shock value and by a quasi-documentary focus on sex: George Kuchar and Jack Smith became notorious, the latter's *Flaming Creatures* (1963) being banned (though this did not stop the film being shown clandestinely).

And then of course there was Andy Warhol. The ground-breaking *Sleep* (1963) and *Empire* (1965) were minimalist 'concept' films: these and many other Warhol films contain little or no camera movement or editing; the camera simply (?) 'observes' a man sleeping or several hours in the stony life of the Empire State Building in New York. Warhol was also responsible for 'The Factory', which produced such indulgences as *Chelsea Girls* (1967) (Figure 15.6) and *Lonesome Cowboys* (1968) and launched the troubled careers of Joe Dallesandro, Paul Morrissey and the Velvet Underground. Warhol also saw the commercial potential of what would later become postmodernism earlier than most, commissioning and exhibiting the famous Roy Lichtenstein pop-art cans of beans and his own endlessly reproduced 'portraits' of Marilyn Monroe.

If artistic personal expression led some avant-garde artists inexorably back to Hollywood and Babylon, other film-makers took a different path. The 'structural-materialist' films of the 1960s and 1970s more clearly developed the formalist concerns of the 1920s pioneers: little or no narrative, no characters, just an exploration of the possibilities of film. Thus

Andy Warhol's Chelsea Girls: no narrative, no direction (BFI Stills, Posters and Designs)   Figure 15.6

Michael Snow's films (*Wavelength*, 1967; ↔ (also called *Back and Forth*), 1969; *Central Region*, 1971) were explorations of the images created by rigorously and mathematically controlled camera movements; *Wavelength* appears to be a 45-minute zoom from one end of a room in to a close up of a picture on a wall, which nevertheless teases the audience as the soundtrack indicates that events seem to occur off camera which encourage speculation about a possible narrative. Hollis Frampton's *Zorns Lemma* (1970) is constructed according to strict mathematical principles. Ken Jacobs' *Tom, Tom the Piper's Son* (1969) is a 'documentary' exploration of a short 1905 silent film which brings film-making centre-stage much as did Dziga Vertov. Peter Gidal's more personal explorations of everyday space were often difficult and disorientating, with their strange camera angles and abrupt camera movements. Where any kind of narrative is used, it is invariably deconstructed, as in Malcolm Le Grice's *Blackbird Descending* (1977), in which very similar (but not identical) events are repeated over and over again as the spectator learns that in its own way each event is a recording of a recording of a recording. . .

Other film-makers explored the nature of the film medium itself: images were painted or drawn directly onto the film (recalling the experiments of Georges Méliès in the earliest years of film), the film was etched with acid, fungus was grown on it, 'hairs in the gate' and other foreign bodies were integrated into the viewing experience; in this connection it is difficult to know if the Monty Python line about one of their films being 'made entirely on wood' was the usual Python absurdity or a knowing reference to avant-garde film-making!

While such films were interesting experiments, not surprisingly they were seen by few people. The advent of video, however, means that since the 1980s video installations have found a niche in galleries and exhibitions, often as part of a multimedia environment, and artists such as Bill Viola and Steve McQueen have reached a new kind of audience. Instead of being screened at specific times, experimental video works of whatever length (Douglas Gordon's *24-Hour Psycho* is a projection of Hitchcock's *Psycho* at an eighth of its proper speed) are now shown on a continuous loop, with gallery visitors arriving and leaving at any point. Through programmes such as *10x10* and *Fourmations*, such films/videos have also received exposure on terrestrial television.

DOGME 95

A small but important recent example of 'alternative' film-making emerged in 1995 when a small group of Danish directors launched a manifesto entitled 'Dogme 95'. The group's self-imposed 'vows of chastity' are given in Figure 15.7.

Though the 'manifesto' was clearly at least partly a publicity stunt, it did result in a number of films which generated a great deal of debate and which have led some other film-makers to reconsider their methods. In addition to making the cult-destined *Kingdom* (1994) and *Kingdom II* (1998), Lars von Trier achieved international recognition with *Breaking the Waves* (1996) and *Idiots* (1999) (the lack of director credit demanded by the manifesto has clearly not impeded his career!). While the hand-held 'scope camera-work' of *Breaking the Waves* has reportedly induced something like seasickness in some

Dogme 95

Film-makers must put their signature to this:

I swear to the following set of rules drawn up and confirmed by Dogme 95:

1. Shooting must be done on location. Props and sets must not be brought in. (If a particular prop is necessary for the story, a location must be found where the prop is to be found.)

2. The sound must never be produced apart from the images or vice versa. (Music must not be used unless it occurs where the scene is shot.)

3. The camera must be hand-held. Any movement or immobility attainable in the hand is permitted. (The film must not take place where the camera is standing; shooting must take place where the film takes place.)

4. The film must be in colour. Special lighting is not acceptable. (If there is too little light for exposure, the scene must be cut or a single lamp attached to the camera.)

5. Optical work and filters are forbidden.

6. The film must not contain superficial action. (Murders, weapons, etc. must not occur.)

7. Temporal and geographical alienations are forbidden. (That is to say the film takes place here and now.)

8. Genre movies are not acceptable.

9. The film format must be academy 35mm.

10. The director must not be credited.

Furthermore, I swear as a director to refrain from personal taste! I am no longer an artist. I swear to refrain from creating a 'work', as I regard the instant as more important than the whole. My supreme goal is to force the truth out of my characters and settings. I swear to do so by all the means available and at the cost of any good taste and any aesthetic considerations. Thus I make my vow of chastity.

Copenhagen, Monday 13th March 1995

The Dogme 95 Manifesto   Figure 15.7

spectators, it is with *Idiots* (officially entitled *Dogme 2*) that von Trier most effectively challenges barriers of 'taste' and aesthetics.

As part of their provocation of bourgeois prejudices, the members of an experiment in communal living 'pretend' to be mentally disabled in public places. As well as scandalizing the local public, this is also supposedly part of a liberating and emancipatory 'discovery of the inner idiot'. As frictions and disagreements develop in the group, however, and as a party develops into an orgy (with penetrative sex displayed on the screen), it becomes troublingly unclear whether the film's characters are 'acting' or whether they really are taking part in some kind of psycho-social 'experiment'. Although such ambiguity is not entirely new (and indeed strangely echoes the ambiguities of Larry Clark's *Kids* (1995) and Harmony Korine's *Gummo* (1997)), the Dogme 95 approach perhaps makes it particularly disturbing.

The first film 'officially' produced according to Dogme principles, *Dogme 1* (*Celebration* (*Festen*, Thomas Vinterberg, 1998)), uses Dogme 95 methods to full effect: a patriarch's birthday party goes badly wrong when one of his sons accuses him of sexual child abuse in front of all the guests. Again the hand-held pseudo-documentary camerawork, lack of any 'superficial action' and 'here-and-now' nature make this a particularly powerful film (though it is at times clear that the camera is *deliberately* being shaken to increase the tension. . . one may wonder if there were lessons here for the makers of the *Blair Witch Project*).

While the Dogme 95 method does indeed impose constraints on how a film is made, it says nothing about two crucial areas: how actors are to be deployed in a narrative, and how the film is to be edited. The status of the 'acting' in *Idiots* remains unclear, while for *Festen*, Vinterberg reportedly rehearsed actors for the birthday scenes but did not tell them about the shattering allegations that the son would make, so the shock of the party guests is in a sense 'unacted'. There is in fact an additional degree of manipulation on top of the already strong narrative, about the writing of which the manifesto is silent. And editing is crucial to both *Idiots* and *Festen*; while shooting is limited to one or more hand-held cameras with ambient light and direct sound, there are (as with any other film) otherwise few limits to how shots can be recombined.

CULT FILMS

Finally, and at the very last to stray a little from the beaten path, there is a body of films (ill-defined to be sure) which has recently become a focus for study, perhaps partly because the significance of these films rests less in their own qualities than in the ways they have been used by their audiences. Cult films may be defined by the passionate devotion they inspire, by fans' obsessive and encyclopaedic knowledge of such films and of their plots, by ritualistic viewings sometimes involving dressing up in appropriate costume (the best-known example must be *The Rocky Horror Picture Show* (Sharman, 1975) which for many years was screened at the Baker St 'Screen' cinema and in a Paris cinema as part of a *Rocky Horror* New Year's Eve Party. . .), sometimes by the existence of societies and fan clubs devoted to particular films.

The origins of cult films may lie in the star-worship of early Hollywood, but at least three further factors have been important. First, marginal subcultures (which are also 'interpretive communities') found that celebrating shared tastes gave them strength and solidarity. A good example of this (explored to excellent effect by Richard Dyer) was the popularity of icons like Judy Garland and James Dean among the gay community, particularly before the legalization of homosexuality in the UK in 1967.

A further impetus to cultishness was provided by the advent of widespread access to video from the mid-1970s onwards: favourite films could be recorded or bought, viewed repeatedly, and more or less memorized, and the resulting familiarity shared with other fans. Finally, the Internet has provided an easy means for sharing cult knowledge through societies, fan clubs, etc., a facility which has of course not been lost on advertising and marketing companies, so that 'cult' is already becoming another empty marketing category.

Exercise 15.3

In groups of 3 or 4, discuss some of your favourite films (especially films which are not massive commercial successes). How well do you know them? Do you have friends who share your affection for the film(s)? How do you share your pleasure with others who like the film?

Nevertheless it is not entirely clear what makes a genuine 'cult' film. 'Good' (or critically acclaimed) films can attain cult status (*Casablanca*, *Blade Runner*), but so can 'bad' or critically undervalued films (those of Russ Meyer or Ed Wood for example: Wood's *Plan 9 From Outer Space* (1956) has often been described as the worst film ever made). It has been suggested that three ingredients are necessary for a film to attain cult status (irrespective of its initial commercial success or failure).

First, a (relatively specific) interpretive community must be addressed: (sci fi cinephiles for *Blade Runner*; ageing ex-1960s students (or their successors) in the case of *Withnail and I*; a gay or camp audience in relation to *The Wizard of Oz*). Second, the film should contain episodes and characters which can be 'memorable' when taken out of narrative context: thus for example Monty Python's 'Parrot Sketch', most of *Monty Python's Life of Brian* (1979), sections of *Dune* (Lynch, 1984) and the public toilet in *Trainspotting*. Finally, and surely most obscurely, the film needs to contain 'quotable' dialogue and catchphrases, familiarity with which can become a sign of membership of the cult. The Jules–Vincent dialogue about the Big Mac and the Royale in *Pulp Fiction* is an obvious recent example, as is 'You're the money' in *Swingers* (Liman, 1996); but 'I feel unusual', 'It's resting' and 'That's a *damn* fine cup of coffee' are cult folklore.

SUMMARY

- 'Alternative' films are marked by their rejection of mainstream narrative conventions.
- Feminist films represent a rejection of a film style which is seen as perpetuating patriarchal and male-dominated ideologies.
- Previously experimental and marginal film-making techniques have now been largely absorbed into mainstream film-making.

FURTHER READING

Erik Barnouw, *Documentary: A History of the Non-fiction Film* (Oxford: Oxford University Press, 1974, 1993).

Pam Cook and Mieke Bernink (eds), *The Cinema Book* (2nd edn, London: BFI, 1999).

Richard Dyer, *Heavenly Bodies* (London: BFI, 1987).

Umberto Eco, *Travels in Hyperreality* (New York: Harcourt Brace Jovanovich, 1983).

Teshome Gabriel, *Third Cinema in the Third World: The Aesthetics of Liberation* (Ann Arbor MI: University of Michigan Press, 1982).

Peter Gidal (ed.), *Structural Film Anthology* (London: BFI, 1976).

John Hill and Pamela Church Gibson (eds), *The Oxford Guide to Film Studies* (Oxford: Oxford University Press, 1998).

Rosemary Jackson, *Fantasy* (London: Methuen, 1981).

Kevin Macdonald and Mark Cousins, *Imagining Reality* (London: Faber & Faber, 1998).

Chris Rodley (ed.), *Lynch on Lynch* (London: Faber & Faber, 1997).

Kristin Thompson and David Bordwell, *Film History: An Introduction* (New York: McGraw-Hill, 1994).

Linda Williams, *Figures of Desire* (Berkeley, CA: University of California Press, 1981).

FURTHER VIEWING

Arena: Scene By Scene (BBC2, 1999) [Lynch on Surrealism].

This Film is Dogma 95 (Channel 4, 2000).

Further Resources

This is a basic list of websites and a few addresses which will be of use to both student and teacher alike. It is by no means comprehensive or exhaustive and website addresses and the information contained in them are subject to change.

Ain't It Cool News
http://www.aint-it-cool-news.com/
For reviews and gossip relating to films only recently, or not yet, released.

Alfred Hitchcock Scholars/'MacGuffin' Site
http://www.labyrinth.net.au/~muffin/
Dedicated to the work of Hitchcock.

American Film Institute
http://www.afionline.org/
Includes a list of the 100 'best' films and other film information.

The Art and Craft of Movie Making
http://www.bbc.co.uk/education/lzone/movie/index.htm
Interviews with film directors and a guide to low budget digital film-making.

Artists Rights Foundation
http://www.artistsrights.org
Lists films that have been edited for TV.

Bafta Awards
http://www.bafta.org
Official site for the Bafta awards, with lists of nominees and winners.

BBC Education
http://www.bbc.co.uk/plsql/education/webguide/
Links to Film and Media information for students.

BKSTS - The Moving Image Society
http://www.bksts.com

British Board of Film Classification (BBFC)
http://www.bbfc.co.uk
3 Soho Square
London W1V 6HD
Tel: 020 7439 7961
Fax: 020 7287 0141

British Council – British films
http://www.britfilms.com/britfilms99

British Film Commission
http://www.britfilmcom.co.uk

British Film Institute (BFI)
http://ww.bfi.org.uk
21 Stephen Street
London W1P 2LN
Tel: 020 7255 1444
Fax: 020 7436 0349

BFI National Library
http://www.bfi.org.uk/nationallibrary

British Universities Film and Video Council (BUFVC)
http://www.bufvc.ac.uk/
Lists of individual libraries, researchers and facilities aimed at higher education and research.

Broadcasting Standards Commission (BSC)
http://www.bsc.org.uk

Cinemachine
http://www.cinemachine.com/
Reviews for current films from US newspapers and magazines.

The Cinema Connection
http://online.socialchange.net.au/tcc
A large list of film subject links.

Cinepad
http://cinepad.com/
A creative film site, including film extracts, an
index for the *film noir* genre and a library of recommended film criticism.

Classic Movies
http://www.geocities.com/Hollywood/9766/
A reference guide to selected Hollywood films,
1939–69.

Close Up: The Electronic Journal of British Cinema
http://www.shu.ac.uk/services/lc/closeup/
title.htm

Department for Culture, Media and Sport (DCMS)
http://www.culture.gov.uk/

Empire
http://www.empireonline.co.uk/

Entertaindom.com
http://www.entertaindom.com
Time Warner site.

Entertainment Weekly Online
http://www.ew.com/ew/

European Cinema On-Line Database
http://www.mediasalles.it
A database of companies involved in European
cinema.

Feature Film Forum
http://gewi.kfunigraz.ac.at/~blimp/FFF/
Abstracts of articles appearing recently in
European film journals.

Film.com
http://www.film.com/backlot/filmfests/archive/
default.htm

The Film Council
http://www.filmcouncil.org.uk
Useful information on the UK film industry,
statistics, funds and a resource section.

Film Education
http://www.filmeducation.org
Alhambra House
27–31 Charing Cross Road
London WC2 0AU
Tel: 020 7976 2291
Fax: 020 7839 5052

Film Four
http://www.filmfour.com/

Film Societies
http://www.filmsoc.org
A resource for people involved in film societies.

FilmUnlimited
http://www.filmunlimited.co.uk
The Guardian film site offering coverage of all
films, listings and reviews for the UK.

Golden Globes
http://www.goldenglobes.org
Lists winners since 1944 and this year's nominees.

Golden Raspberry Awards
http://www.razzies.com/
The worst films of the year.

Greatest Film Site
http://www.filmsite.org
Includes a list of the classic Hollywood films of
the twentieth century.

Hammer Film Productions Limited
http://www.hammerfilms.com
Official studio site for Hammer, including star
interviews and archive material.

Images: a journal of film and popular culture
http://www.imagesjournal.com/

Internet Movie Database
http://uk.imdb.com
http://www.imdb.com
Essential, comprehensive and exhaustive site of
film information.

Kinema, A Journal of History, Theory and
Aesthetics of Film and Audiovisual Media
http://arts.uwaterloo.ca/FINE/juhde/
kinemahp.htm

The Knowledge
http://www.theknowledgeonline.com
Information on all aspects of the British film
industry.

Masterclass
http://www.bbc.co.uk/education/lzone/master/
index.shtml
Frank insights into the feature film industry

The Movie Clichés List
http://www.moviecliches.com/
Examples of mainstream film clichés.

Museum of the Moving Image (MOMI)
http://easyweb.easynet.co.uk/~s-herbert/
momiwelcome.htm
Information about pre- and early cinema.

National Museum of Photography, Film and
Television
http://www.nmpft.org.uk

Noir Films
http://www.noiralley.com/main.htm
Alphabetical listing of *films noirs* from 1939 to
1959.

Oscars
http://www.oscars.org/
http://www.oscar.com
Information on the Academy Awards.

Pop.com
http://www.pop.com
Imagine Entertainment and DreamWorks SKG site.

Premiere
http://www.premieremag.com/index.html

Psycho Studio
http://www.saulbass.co.uk/psychostudio/
Re-edit the shower scene from *Psycho* and learn
more about Hitchcock and film technique.

The Rosebud Project: An Evolving Digital
Resource Site for Film Studies
http://www.inform.umd.edu/rosebud/
Information on film studies, history, criticism,
theory and concepts and definitions.

Scope: an online journal of film studies
http://www.nottingham.ac.uk/film
Articles on film history and reviews.

Screening the Past
http://www.latrobe.edu.au/www/screeningthe
past/index.html
Contains articles on visual media and history.

Sheffield Hallam University (School of Cultural
Studies) Internet Resources: Film and Media.
http://www.shu.ac.uk/services/lc/subjects/
lcfilm1.html
Links to significant film organizations, online film
journals, and screenwriting and script sites.

Short Films
http://www.proteinTV.com
Offers a monthly selection of shorts, animations
and promotionals.

Silent Films
http://www.mdle.com/ClassicFilms/
Comprehensive and authoritative site dedicated
to silent film.

Skillset
http://www.skillset.org
The National Training Organization for Broadcast,
Film, Video and Multimedia
91–101 Oxford Street
London W1R 1RA
Tel: 020 7534 5300
Fax: 020 7534 5333

Glossary

180 degree rule The camera should normally stay on the same side of the line of action for successive shots. The imaginary line of action passes between characters or objects; if shots are taken from opposite sides of the line (this is called crossing the line) then the spatial relationship between the characters or objects is reversed.

30 degree rule If shot size and content remain similar for successive shots, then the camera should move position by at least 30 degrees; failure to do so results in a **jump cut** when the edited shots are viewed together.

abstract Non-figurative. Abstract films do not contain representations of identifiable objects; they are likely to consist of colours, shapes and rhythms and to have no narrative.

alienation Estrangement. Feeling distanced from something. Inability to feel as though one is a part of something. Some films are intended to alienate the spectator by preventing involvement in the film; the spectator is discouraged from identifying with the action in the film and is kept at a distance.

analogue film production The recorded material is analogous or similar to the actual subject matter filmed; film as a recording medium has the quality of being continuously variable in its ability to respond to variations in light intensity and colour (see **digital film production**).

aperture The hole through which light passes from the lens to the film. The size of the hole is varied by adjusting a diaphragm. A greater **depth of field** is obtained by using a small aperture, which in turn requires either greater illumination to ensure sufficient light reaches the film or a more efficient lens and faster film stock.

art director Responsible for set design and costumes.

auteur A person, usually a director, who is credited with being responsible for the thematic and stylistic characteristics of a range of films.

avant-garde An advance beyond what has gone before. At the cutting edge of artistic experimentation. Avant-garde films use new techniques and ideas to produce alternatives to the mainstream.

back light A soft light placed behind and above or below an actor to produce a slight aura of light around the edge of the actor.

background light A light that is placed behind an actor and directed towards the background to create a sense of depth and distance between actor and background.

balanced lighting (see **high key lighting**).

best boy Assists the **gaffer**.

bricolage The piecing together of a variety of different elements and influences. As a technique, this manifests itself in films as a mixing together of genres and styles (see **postmodernism**).

camera obscura　Literally means darkened room. An early form of the still image camera. It consists of an enclosed box with a pinhole on one side through which the light from an exterior object is projected onto the opposite interior face of the box.

capitalism　The economic organization of society whereby the means of production are privately owned. The primary motive for producing goods and services is to make a profit. In theory, competition between producers should result in more choice and lower prices, but in practice competition is weakened through the trend towards concentration of ownership, leading to oligopolies and monopolistic trends (compare with **communism**).

chiaroscuro lighting (see **low key lighting**).

chromakey　(colour separation overlay) An electronic technique that can be used in video production, where a chosen colour (usually a 'blue screen' background) can be ignored by the camera so that another image can be 'keyed' in to replace it. The video equivalent of a film **matte**.

cinematographer　Is responsible for deciding how the camera and lighting are to be used.

cinéma vérité　Literally means 'cinema truth'. A documentary style developed in France in the 1960s that made use of mobile, lightweight camera and sound equipment. The camera operator was seen as potentially part of the events being filmed through his/her interaction with, and influence upon, the participants.

close up　When framing a human face, such a shot would range from just above the top of the head to just below the chin.

codes　Systems of audio and visual signs that enable communication to take place. Particular types of objects, shot sizes, camera angles, lighting, editing and music in films tend to produce particular meanings for those who understand the codes. The codes are widely understood because they have become **conventions**.

cognitivism/cognitive theories　As the name implies, this recent approach (which spread from North America in the 1990s) values conscious recognition and knowledge and rejects many of the more complex psychoanalytic and structuralist assumptions of *Screen* Theory; most cognitive theory writers are intensely hostile to the notion of the unconscious. The links between perception (of films for example) and emotion are analysed using rational, scientific models.

communism　The economic organization of society whereby the means of production are publicly owned. Goods are produced for need rather than profit. In theory, ownership and control are spread throughout society, but in practice power has tended to become concentrated in the hands of a small élite. Marx's analysis of capitalism led him to propose a communist form of society (compare with **capitalism** and see **Marxism**).

composition　The arrangement of elements within a shot.

connotation　The associated or implied meaning of an image, sound or word.

continuity editing　The editing together of shots such that the action flows smoothly. Content, position and direction of movement are consistent between shots and the editing ensures that attention is not drawn to the construction of the film itself.

conventions　The customary ways of doing things. Films normally use conventional methods for structuring and communicating their narratives, such as story resolution, the inclusion of certain objects and locations, and particular use of camera, sound, lighting and editing. Genres consist of conventions that have become established over time. Conventions result in **codes**, accepted ways of understanding and communicating meaning.

crane shot   The camera is mounted on a crane, enabling it to move up and down, backwards, forwards and sideways.

cross-cutting   Editing together shots which alternate between action happening simultaneously in different locations.

cross-media ownership   Owning companies in different media industries. Makes **synergy** possible.

crossing the line   (see **180 degree rule**).

cut   This has two related meanings: it describes the end of a filmed take (as when a director calls out 'cut!'). It also describes a simple transition between two shots which have been edited together.

cutaway shot   A shot inserted between other shots in a scene which is not directly related to the scene.

deep focus   Everything within a shot is in focus, from foreground to background (compare with **shallow focus**).

denotation   The direct and literal meaning of an image, sound or word.

depth of field   The range within which objects in an image are in focus.

dialectics   The process whereby ideas and situations are challenged and result in new ideas and situations. The initial concept is a thesis, which is challenged by an anti-thesis, which leads to a synthesis, the outcome of the conflict. Progress, in the real world or in a narrative, can be regarded as a dialectical process.

diegetic   That which originates from within a film's narrative such as dialogue, sound effects and music played by a character (see **non-diegetic**).

digital film production   The recorded material is an approximate but incomplete copy of the actual subject matter filmed because digital electronics does not have the quality of being continuously variable in its ability to respond to variations in light intensity and colour. The colour range of television and video technology is less than that of film, but digital equipment tends to be cheaper and more flexible than film equipment (see **analogue film production**).

direct cinema   A documentary style developed in the USA in the 1960s reflecting the belief that the availability of mobile, lightweight camera and sound equipment made it possible to make documentaries that revealed social realities in a more truthful way as the filming of events did not need to be planned and was therefore more direct and unmediated. The camera operator does not play an active part in the events.

director   Responsible for the creative aspects of a film's production; determines how the narrative is to be translated onto film.

director of photography   (see **cinematographer**).

dissolve   A transition from one shot to another by fading out the first shot as the second shot fades in.

DVD   Digital versatile disc. A method of storing audio, video and computer data which is now replacing the use of magnetic tape.

dystopia   A future world that would be an unpleasant place to live in; the opposite of a utopia.

editing   Selecting the required takes from the filmed shots, arranging them in the required order and joining them together.

ellipsis   A narrative jump in time. The time not shown/described can be many years (the trick cut from childhood to adult life in *Citizen Kane*) or a second or less (the matched shots showing someone from either side of a door).

empiricism   A view of knowledge which privileges direct experience. Empirical knowledge is based on personal experience (see **epistemology**).

epistemology   The study of the meaning of knowledge. What does it mean to 'know' something? (see **empiricism**).

establishing shot   A shot, usually at the beginning of a scene and often an extreme long shot, which provides a visual context within which action is to take place.

extreme close up   A shot that provides detailed visual information. When framing a human face, such a shot would range from just below the top of the head to just above the chin.

extreme long shot   A shot that provides context but little detail. When such a shot is centred on a person we may also see other people, objects and an indication of the location.

eye-line match   When a character looks offscreen in one shot, we may expect the next shot to indicate what they were looking at. We would also expect the direction and level of the character's gaze to be consistent with what we see in the next shot.

fade   A common device for indicating the end and beginning of a scene. The last shot of a scene may well fade to black and the beginning of the next scene fade from black into the first shot.

feature film   The custom is that a film must run for 75 minutes for it to be classified as a feature film.

fetishism   The displacement of sexual desire onto an object or body part which stands in for the disavowed object of desire. One argument in film theory has been about the extent to which representations of the female body, in so far that they focus on bits of the body rather than on the overall (female) character, reflect a fetishization of the female body which goes hand in hand with the active male hero who drives the narrative forward. The male character, so the classical psychoanalytic argument goes, is a figure for identification; the female body is an object of fetishistic **scopophilia**.

fill light   A soft light that is placed on the opposite side of an actor to the **key light** with the function of reducing shadows by balancing out the overall level of lighting.

fly-on-the-wall   A form of documentary in which the intention is that the camera records events without the participants being aware of its presence.

focal length   The distance between the lens and the recording material, e.g. film in a film camera and a charge coupled device (CCD) in a video camera.

focus   The degree of sharpness of an image.

form   Generally refers to the means by which communication takes place, as in media forms such as television, radio, newspapers, magazines and film which use particular methods for producing meanings. For film, form refers to the use of moving images and sound to communicate meanings that are shaped by a film's **narrative** and **style**. The narrative may be structured by a genre or may be relatively free of **conventions**. The style may consist of mainstream film techniques or may employ alternative techniques.

formalism   Emphasizes how film as a specific form of communication can be used to produce particular meanings. The formal properties of film mean that shot size, camera angle, lighting and editing all influence meaning. Formalism can be contrasted with **realism**.

framing   Relates to the edges of a shot and what is included and excluded.

front projection   An improved version of **rear projection**. A filmed location is projected onto a half-silvered mirror set at an angle of 45 degrees in front of the camera and projected onto a screen behind the actors. The camera records the action and the location through the mirror. Lighting is adjusted so that the projected images are not visible on the actors.

gaffer   The chief electrician who is in charge of operating the lights.

graphic match   Two shots edited together which are visually similar.

hegemony   It is argued that those with power (the ruling class or a political and economic élite) obtain support for their ideas, and can thus gain ideological dominance, through cultural influences rather than force. Although society consists of different social groups, it is run in the interests of a minority. The media, such as cinema, can promote values and beliefs that come to be seen as common sense, whereas in reality other alternative **ideologies** may well be at least as appropriate. It could be argued that Hollywood has hegemony over the international film industry with regard to the conventions used in film-making and in terms of the values and beliefs contained in such films.

high angle shot   The camera is placed above the subject.

high concept movie   A film that is based on a simple idea that is easily summarized, understood and marketed.

high key lighting   Lighting that avoids creating shadows by using two or more light sources on opposing sides of the subject.

horizontal integration   A company specializing in one area of production buys up another company with similar interests. A film production company that takes over another production company expands horizontally.

hypodermic model   An approach that believes the media are powerful and that they 'inject' meanings into the audience. Media texts such as films are seen as having an effect on a passive audience; the text is the stimulus and the audience responds (contrast with **uses and gratifications model**).

iconography   The way in which visual signs and referents create meanings. Especially important in genre studies where the selection of particular locations, props and costumes is linked to **conventions** that are intended to communicate particular messages.

ideology   A set of ideas, values and beliefs that are often taken for granted and go unchallenged through their being regarded as natural and true despite the fact that other alternative ideologies may exist. Dominant ideology is the general set of values and beliefs widely held throughout society and may be seen as helping to sustain particular power relations in that society.

institutional mode of representation   The established way of showing things. By 1915 a broad range of conventions had become established for the production of films with reference to shot size and duration, camera angle and movement, lighting and editing, especially with regard to mainstream cinema.

intertextuality   Texts cease to exist as isolated texts and are linked to other texts through references and influences. Films increasingly make implicit and explicit references to other films (see **postmodernism**).

jump cut   An edit between two shots which results in an abrupt and conspicuous change in the shot content (see **30 degree rule**).

key grip   In charge of the stage hands on a film set. Organizes the film set in terms of lay-out of equipment and set design.

key light   The main source of illumination, usually a hard light, placed on the opposite side of an actor to the **fill light**.

lighting cameraman   (see **cinematographer**).

long shot   When framing a person, such a shot would range from just above the head to just below the feet.

low angle shot   The camera is placed below the subject.

low key lighting   Lighting that creates shadows by using one main light source, thus making the lighting unbalanced; there is a strong contrast between light and dark.

Marxism   A wide-ranging body of thought based on the writings and activities of Karl Marx, a German philosopher (1818–1893). Marx claimed that the bourgeoisie, who own the means of production, live off the profits of goods produced and sold, and promote an **ideology** that is intended to perpetuate its power and control. The proletariat (work-ing class) sells its labour in order to survive. Marx's analysis of **capitalism** as an eco-nomic system revealed contradictions that inevitably resulted in periodic crises. He also highlighted the social injustice and exploitation inherent in a class system. Marx proposed a classless society in which the means of production are owned by all (see **communism**).

master shot   A long take, usually a long shot, that generally covers all the action in a scene. It is usually intercut with mid shots and close ups.

match on action   Two shots of different sizes or angles that are edited together to provide continuous coverage of an action.

matte   The combining of two different filmed images within one frame by masking out a part of one image and replacing it with another.

medium or mid shot   When centred on a person, such a shot would range from just above the head to the waist.

mise en scène   What is included in a shot. The selection and arrangement of elements in front of the camera, all of which are contained by the framing of a shot. Includes location, props, costumes, make up, acting and lighting.

modernism   Refers to developments in the arts at the beginning of the twentieth century that were epitomized by experimentation and innovation in cultural production. Film was a relatively late artistic form but modernist influences clearly emerged in the 1920s as a challenge to mainstream techniques.

montage   Literally (in French) means editing or piecing together various elements to make a complete artefact. A key technique of discontinuity editing. Consecutive shots are not continuous but are often juxtaposed so that meaning is created through the contrast between the different shots.

narrative   The linking together of events that usually have cause and effect relationships in space and time.

naturalism   An approach to film-making and art in general that aims to accurately reproduce surface appearances (compare with **realism**).

non-diegetic   That which is added to a film and does not originate in the narrative, such as soundtrack music and credits (see **diegetic**).

Oedipus complex   A concept central to Freudian psychoanalytic theory: child (unconsciously) desires/loves opposite-sex parent, has to learn that such love is 'impossible', and relinquishes the parental love-object to find a socially acceptable partner. For a boy, this means accepting the father-figure's prior claim to the maternal love-object and accepting the 'Law of the Father'. The traces of Oedipal attachments and anxieties are rarely fully resolved. Many (some say all) narratives are about the quest for or journey towards a new love object.

oligopoly   A small number of companies control an industry, resulting in reduced competition, as is the case with the American film industry.

ontology   The study of the reality status of an object or representation. How 'real' can an image (or a film) be?

pan shot   A horizontal movement of the camera around its axis.

paradigm   One of the range of possible elements that could be used in place of each other in a particular text. An appropriate sign is selected from the available set of choices in order to communicate a message. A concept used in **semiology** (see **syntagm**).

parody   The imitation of someone else's work in a humorous or mocking way. The films of Mel Brooks are usually parodies.

pastiche   The reuse of existing styles, often mixed together. Films may be identified as postmodern because of their recycling of previous film styles and influences (see **postmodernism**).

persistence of vision   A phenomenon whereby the retina of the eye retains an image for a split second after it has disappeared until a new image appears. This explains the illusion of a continuous moving image produced by a film, even though the film consists of separate images each lasting one twenty-fourth of a second. This process is seen as automatic or 'passive' (see **phi-phenomenon**).

phallus/phallic   These terms are central to Freudian (and Lacanian) psychoanalytic theory and have been much used in film theory. The 'phallus' is a symbolic representation of the penis, both in films (guns, knives, big cigars, thrusting engines, skyscrapers, big budgets) and in psychoanalytic accounts of patriarchy and the 'Law of the Father'.

phenomenology   A strand of art reception theory which emphasizes 'knowledge' of the environment through direct sensual perception (see **empiricism** and **epistemology**).

phi-phenomenon   The process by which the brain uses intermittent images (as in a film) to construct a represented simulation of movement. For the cognitivists, this is an 'active' process (see **persistence of vision**).

plot   Everything that is directly presented to us in a film. **Style** shapes the plot and the **story** may not be portrayed chronologically. Referred to as *syuzhet* by the formalists.

pluralism   It is argued that power is distributed among a variety of social groups. Society is believed to be heterogeneous rather than homogeneous, and a pluralist conception of society emphasises how the media, such as cinema, produce a diverse range of products to meet the interests of all social groups. Pluralism also identifies the need for a variety of political parties reflecting the interests of all social groups.

point of view shot   A shot that represents the viewpoint of a character in a film. Most shots are taken from the point of view of an uninvolved observer. Optical point of view shots which show exactly what a character sees are relatively rare.

polysemy   The quality of having many meanings. Although a film may have been made with a particular message in mind, different viewers will extract different meanings from it.

postmodernism   Whereas **modernism** was epitomized by experimentation and innovation in cultural production, such as film-making, postmodernism emphasizes the reworking of existing ideas and styles as typified by the techniques of **pastiche** and **intertextuality**. The boundaries between different styles are also broken down through an eclectic approach that uses various influences embodied in the technique of **bricolage**.

poststructuralism   An approach which stresses that although society contains structures within which meanings are produced and ideas are communicated, there is a multiplicity of structures resulting in a variety of values and beliefs being propagated. The power and constituting effects of these wide-ranging structures negate the concept of ideology as there are no sets of ideas as such. The meanings that can be extracted from a film are seen as more free-floating than they are using a **structuralist** approach.

post-synchronization   Adding sound (dialogue, music, sound effects) to a film after the shots have been edited together.

preferred readings model   The producers of media texts, such as films, encode particular meanings into texts with the intention that the audience will decode the texts accurately and accept the meanings; in other words, media texts have preferred readings. However, while a viewer may make a dominant reading of the text that accepts the intended meaning, s/he could make an oppositional reading rejecting the intended meaning or a negotiated reading that only partially accepts the intended meaning.

producer   Responsible for the administrative aspects of a film's production such as getting financial backing for the film, booking locations and equipment, hiring actors and film crew.

psychoanalytic film theory   The use of ideas derived from Freudian psychoanalytic theory to study how films (in general and in particular) interact with the unconscious mind. Films can be seen as potentially powerful in that they are generally viewed in the dark on a large screen that is usually placed above the spectator, all of which concentrates vision on overwhelming images. Such spectatorship has been compared to a dreamlike state.

realism   Emphasizes how film as a form of communication has unique properties that enable it to make an accurate recording of reality. The view that meaning is produced from the content that is filmed rather than from the film techniques that are used can be contrasted with **formalism**. Realism as a film style is usually associated with the recording of everyday situations, often dealing with social issues, and is often thought of in terms of whether a film accurately records or imitates what we identify as the real world. With regard to fiction, realism also refers to the degree to which a film conforms to our expectations in terms of surface appearance, character actions and narrative events (see **verisimilitude** and **naturalism**).

rear projection   A filmed location is projected onto a screen behind the actors so that they appear to be in that location.

representation   The process of showing something. The media represent aspects of the world, both fiction and non-fiction; however, when we use the media we experience things indirectly, second hand. Choices are made (consciously or unconsciously) as to how to represent things, which can result in controversy if social groups are represented positively or negatively compared to other social groups; hence frequent claims of bias or misrepresentation. There tend to be ways in which things are represented that have become established as dominant representations and could be regarded as reflecting dominant ideology. **Stereotypes** are often used in media representations. Representations tend to change over time; an example is the different ways in which the 'wild west' has been portrayed in westerns over the past hundred years.

reverse-track zoom   A complex use of the camera in which the camera tracks out as the lens zooms in, so that the framing remains the same but the centre of the image is magnified, resulting in a distortion of perspective. A reverse-zoom track zooms out while tracking in so that perspective appears to stretch away.

scopophilia   Pleasure, often sexual, gained by looking. While voyeurism refers to a hidden activity usually related to a particular object or sexual obsession, scopophilia is related to the general act of looking. With regard to cinema, feminist theorists have claimed that films tend to be made for the male viewer so that pleasure is gained either by looking at a female character who is there for the male's sexual gaze, or by identifying with an active male character who may well be the hero.

semiology/semiotics   (The first word is used in Europe, the second in the USA). The study of signs. Analysing the audio-visual content of a film, in the context of cultural practices and social conventions, can reveal how meanings are produced and communicated.

sexuality   The sexual desires people have and how they express themselves sexually. Linked to heterosexuality and homosexual/gay/lesbian issues.

shallow focus   Only a small area on one plane of the image is in focus (compare with **deep focus**).

shot   A continuous period of action filmed in a single **take**.

shot/reverse shot edit   The editing together of two shots that provide different perspectives on action, most commonly a conversation between two people in which each shot shows a character talking or reveals the expression on their face. Such an edit provides visual information that clarifies the spatial and emotional relationship between the characters. Such edits must normally obey the **180 degree rule**.

social realism   A style of film-making that attempts to represent the typical everyday lives of most people in society. The subject matter is usually the working class and related social issues.

socialist realism   A style of art and film-making that developed in the Soviet Union during the Stalinist era as a form of propaganda, with the purpose of promoting the interests of the supposedly socialist state.

stereotypes   Simplistic categorizations of social groups and ideas that are easily under-stood but usually inaccurate. A stereotype is the result of a regularly repeated **representation**. Early westerns stereotyped Native Americans as barbaric, uncivilized and unjust.

story   A chronological account of all events in a narrative, including the **plot** plus events that are inferred, hinted at or assumed. Referred to as *fabula* by the **formalists**.

structuralism   An analytic approach which sees society as containing underlying structures. Language systems organize how meaning is produced and determine how it can be communicated. The various forms of communication carry the values and beliefs of a society. Language carries (usually dominant) ideology. Cultural products, such as films, can only be understood by reference to their relationships to the structures within which they are produced and consumed; meaning is shaped by the structures within which communication takes place (compare with **poststructuralism**).

style   The particular way in which something is done. Different directors or film movements may use particular film techniques in certain ways. Film style can be analysed in terms of *mise en scène*, camerawork, editing and sound.

subject   In film/media theory, this refers to the individual (viewer) and her/his analytic and social position.

synergy   The use of various media interests to the mutual benefit of each area. **Cross-media ownership** makes synergy possible; a company could use its different media interests to make a film, promote it in its newspapers, screen it on its television channel and produce computer games based on the film.

syntagm   The arrangement of chosen elements into an appropriate sequence to construct a particular text. The signs are organized into a suitable order to communicate a message. Depending on the object of analysis, a syntagm in a film may be the series of frames in a shot, the shots making up a sequence, or the sequences in the entire film text. A concept used in **semiology** (see **paradigm**).

take   A filmed shot. It is common for several takes to be filmed of a **shot**.

tilt shot   A vertical movement of the camera around its axis.

tracking shot   The camera is mounted on wheels attached to a device called a dolly which runs on tracks, enabling it to move backwards, forwards and sideways.

unconscious   The central idea in Freudian psychoanalytic theory: part of our mind is not directly accessible to us, and we are unaware of the deep-seated reasons for much of what we want, do or say, or indeed of many of the complex meanings that films hold for us. While much film theory has accepted this view, some recent writing has begun to reject the importance of the unconscious (see **cognitivism**).

uses and gratifications model   An approach that sees the audience as powerful and as using the media to satisfy needs and wants. The audience is seen as active and may consume media texts such as films for various reasons and in a variety of different ways (contrast with **hypodermic model**).

verisimilitude   Believability or plausibility, often structured by particular conventions. Although we will not have experienced a future reality, we will happily accept the world presented in a science fiction film if it uses the expected conventions (see **realism**).

vertical integration   A company specializing in one area of production, distribution or exhibition buys up another company with interests elsewhere in the chain of commercial activities. A film production company that buys into exhibition expands vertically.

voyeurism   A perversion of scopophilia. The ('natural') drive to look becomes a desire to look secretly. It is possible to see film-watching (particularly in a dark cinema) as voyeuristic.

wipe   A shot transition (see also **cut**, **fade** and **dissolve**) in which one shot replaces another by spreading horizontally or vertically over the screen.

zoetrope   A pre-cinematic device that creates the illusion of a moving image. It consists of a series of images, each slightly different from the preceding one, on the inside surface of a cylinder that has a thin vertical viewing slit between each image. When the cylinder is revolved and the viewer looks through the viewing slits, the images appear to create a continuously moving image.

zoom/reverse zoom   Achieved by altering the **focal length**. Increasing the length produces a telephoto zoom that makes objects appear closer but decreases the angle of view. Decreasing the length produces a wide angle reverse zoom that makes objects appear further away but increases the angle of view.

Index

The following selective index contains entries only for those words, names and films which are more or less substantively discussed in the text, and does not have entries for those which are mentioned only in passing

'This book is outstanding. It comprehensively addresses the broad range of key aspects of both policy and practice in the primary curriculum. With contributions from acknowledged experts in individual fields, it really is an essential companion for trainee teachers and NQTs. More experienced practitioners and teacher trainers who are keen to remain up to date with developments in primary teaching and learning, and to improve their own practice, will likewise find it invaluable.'

Angela McLachlan, *University of Manchester, UK*

'*Learning to Teach in the Primary School* is an invaluable book for those in primary initial teacher education. It covers all the most important topics and issues, and supports students in reflecting on and deepening their learning. This is an essential text.'

Helena Gillespie, *University of East Anglia, UK*

'A comprehensive text that will support the student teacher during training and beyond. Written by academics who are respected in their field, this is an authoritative text that synthesises pedagogy with practice and provides a solid foundation on which to build a reflective practitioner approach to teaching.'

Elizabeth Broad, *University of Roehampton, UK*

'This book is a valuable collection of essential reading for any beginning or training teacher embarking upon their new career. The extensive literature covers topical issues prevalent in all primary classrooms and the wide variety of contributors indicate a breadth of knowledge and research that guide the teacher in many pedagogical areas. I would highly recommend the book and both Teresa Cremin and James Arthur should be commended for offering so much updated and current material within this third edition.'

Shauna McGill, *University of Ulster, UK*

'*Learning to Teach in the Primary School* provides valuable support to all trainee teachers in developing understanding of all aspects of the role and achieving the Teachers' Standards. This understanding is essential in becoming an outstanding, flexible, effective and creative primary school teacher whichever route is chosen in joining the profession. Recent developments are discussed and practical advice is offered throughout.'

Karen Russell, *University of St Mark and St John, Plymouth, UK*

LEARNING TO TEACH
IN THE PRIMARY SCHOOL

Flexible, effective and creative primary school teachers require subject knowledge, an understanding of their pupils and how they learn, a range of strategies for managing behaviour and organising environments for learning, and the ability to respond to dynamic classroom situations.

This third edition of *Learning to Teach in the Primary School* is fully updated with reference to the new National Curriculum, and has been revised to provide even more practical advice and guidance to trainee primary teachers. Twenty-two new authors have been involved and connections are now made to Northern Irish, Welsh and Scottish policies. In addition, five new units have been included on:

- making the most of your placement
- play and exploration in learning
- behaviour management
- special educational needs
- phonics.

With Masters-level reflective tasks and suggestions for research-based further reading, the book provides valuable support to trainee teachers engaged in learning through school-based experience and through reading, discussion and reflections as part of a teacher education course. It provides an accessible and engaging introduction to knowledge about teaching and learning that every student teacher needs to acquire in order to gain qualified teacher status (QTS).

This comprehensive textbook is essential reading for all students training to be primary school teachers, including those on undergraduate teacher training courses (BEd, BA with QTS, BSc with QTS), postgraduate teacher training courses (PGCE, SCITT) and employment-based teacher training courses (Schools Direct, Teach First), plus those studying Education Studies.

This textbook is supported by a free companion website with additional resources for instructors and students and can be accessed at www.routledge.com/cw/Cremin.

Teresa Cremin (previously known professionally as Grainger) is Professor of Education (Literacy) and Education Futures Research Cluster Director at The Open University, UK.

James Arthur is Head of School and Professor of Education and Civic Engagement in the School of Education at the University of Birmingham, UK.

THE LEARNING TO TEACH IN THE PRIMARY SCHOOL SERIES
Series Editor: Teresa Cremin, The Open University, UK

Teaching is an art form. It demands not only knowledge and understanding of the core areas of learning, but also the ability to teach these creatively and foster learner creativity in the process. *The Learning to Teach in the Primary School Series* draws upon recent research which indicates the rich potential of creative teaching and learning, and explores what it means to teach creatively in the primary phase. It also responds to the evolving nature of subject teaching in a wider, more imaginatively framed twenty-first-century primary curriculum.

Designed to complement the textbook, *Learning to Teach in the Primary School*, the well-informed, lively texts offer support for student and practising teachers who want to develop more creative approaches to teaching and learning. The books highlight the importance of the teachers' own creative engagement and share a wealth of innovative ideas to enrich pedagogy and practice.

Titles in the series:

Teaching English Creatively
Teresa Cremin

Teaching Science Creatively
Dan Davies

Teaching Mathematics Creatively
Linda Pound and Trisha Lee

Teaching Geography Creatively
Edited by Stephen Scoffham

Teaching History Creatively
Edited by Hilary Cooper

Teaching Music Creatively
Pamela Burnard and Regina Murphy

Teaching Physical Education Creatively
Angela Pickard and Patricia Maude

LEARNING TO TEACH IN THE PRIMARY SCHOOL

Third edition

Edited by
Teresa Cremin and
James Arthur

Routledge
Taylor & Francis Group

LONDON AND NEW YORK

Third edition published 2014
by Routledge
2 Park Square, Milton Park, Abingdon, Oxon, OX14 4RN

and by Routledge
711 Third Avenue, New York, NY 10017

Routledge is an imprint of the Taylor & Francis Group, an informa business

First edition published by Routledge 2006
Second edition published by Routledge 2010

British Library Cataloguing in Publication Data
A catalogue record for this book is available from the British Library

Library of Congress Cataloging in Publication Data
Learning to teach in the primary school/edited by Teresa Cremin and
    James Arthur. – Third edition.
    pages cm
    1. Elementary school teaching – Great Britain. 2. Elementary school teachers –
    Training of – Great Britain. I. Cremin, Teresa II. Arthur, James, 1957-.
    LB1556.7.G7L43 2014
    372.11020941 – dc23
    2013045628

ISBN: 978-0-415-81818-6 (hbk)
ISBN: 978-0-415-81819-3 (pbk)
ISBN: 978-1-315-81296-0 (ebk)

Typeset in Interstate and Helvetica
by Florence Production Ltd, Stoodleigh, Devon, UK

CONTENTS

Introduction   **1**
TERESA CREMIN AND JAMES ARTHUR

> What is primary teaching? • How can this book help me? •
> What's in the book?

SECTION 1
BECOMING A TEACHER   **7**

1.1 Primary teaching: a personal perspective   **9**
COLIN RICHARDS

> 'Acrostic' teaching • A sense of style • Teaching: science, craft or art?
> • Enactive, pre-active and post-active primary teaching • The personal qualities
> and knowledge required of primary teachers • The purposes of primary
> teaching

1.2 Professionalism and trainee teachers   **21**
DENIS HAYES

> Background • Principles underpinning the standards • Wider ('extended')
> professional responsibilities

1.3 Making the most of your placements   **35**
JANE WARWICK AND MARY ANNE WOLPERT

> Establishing effective dispositions • Reflective teaching • Evaluations
> • Working within the school community • Working with school mentors
> • Making the most of learning conversations • Trainee progression through
> placements

SECTION 3

PLANNING AND MANAGING LEARNING   145

ILLUSTRATIONS

FIGURES

TABLES

TASKS

CONTRIBUTORS

Carrie Ansell has taught widely in multicultural early years and primary settings in England, Sweden and Crete. She acted as a Literacy Advisory Teacher for Bristol Local Authority, before becoming a Senior Lecturer at Bath Spa University for the primary and early years PGCE English programme. She is currently a Lecturer in Primary Language and Literacy at Plymouth University. Her research interests are in the field of literacy, social diversity and bilingualism. She shares the role of South West Regional Representative for the United Kingdom Literacy Association with her colleague Deborah Nicholson.

Professor James Arthur is Head of the School of Education and Professor of Education at the University of Birmingham. He has written on the relationship between theory and practice in education, particularly the links between communitarianism, social virtues, citizenship, character and education. He is Editor of the *British Journal of Educational Studies* and Director of the Jubilee Centre for Character and Values at the University of Birmingham. His publications include *Education with Character: The Moral Economy of Schooling*, *Social Literacy, Citizenship, and The National Curriculum*, *Teaching Citizenship Through History*, *Subject Mentoring in the Secondary School*, *Schools and Community: The Communitarian Agenda in Education*, *Teaching Citizenship in the Secondary School* and many other texts published by Routledge and RoutledgeFalmer. He has written *Of Good Character* for Imprint Academic and a number of other texts for other publishers, as well as a range of chapters and articles.

Dr Jonathan Barnes has wide experience in all sectors of education. His current role in teacher education involves teaching music and geography and researching the relationships between the arts and well-being. He is author of *Cross Curricular Learning 3–14* and writes regularly on creative approaches to staff and student development.

Eve Bearne's research interests while at the University of Cambridge Faculty of Education have been concerned with diversity and inclusion, specifically gender, language and literacy. She edited *Differentiation and Diversity* (Routledge) and has written and edited a range of books about language, literacy and inclusion, the most recent being *Literacy and Community: Developing a Primary Curriculum Through Partnerships* (co-edited with Rebecca Kennedy) and *Inclusive Approaches to Teaching Literacy in the Secondary School*, both for the United Kingdom Literacy Association.

Dr Des Bowden is former Head of Geography at Newman University, Birmingham, and a Director of B and C Educational (www.primary-school-resources.com). He and his business partner produce and publish their own global teaching resources, offer curriculum consultancy to primary schools, and lead groups of primary teachers and heads to The Gambia as part of their CPD course on the global dimension in the curriculum.

Jo Bowers is Senior Lecturer in Primary Education and Literacy Coordinator for the School of Education at Cardiff Metropolitan University. She teaches English and history courses to PGCE primary students and a number of other literacy-related courses on undergraduate education programmes. Her subject specialism is Primary English. Prior to this appointment, she was a primary school teacher for 20 years and a Literacy Coordinator for 15 of them. She is the Welsh regional representative for the United Kingdom Literacy Association (UKLA) and is on the editorial board for the English Association's literacy journal for primary teachers, *English 4-11*. She has a lifelong interest in children's literature and developing children's reading for pleasure and currently co-leads a children's literature Special Interest Group with two UKLA literacy colleagues. She has recently completed a research project supporting student teachers' subject knowledge of children's literature. Her other main areas of interest are using philosophical enquiry to develop thinking skills and talk in the primary classroom.

Julie Bowtell has taught in a range of educational settings: nursery units, primary schools and FE colleges. She has experience as an early years practitioner, as a KS1 class teacher, reading recovery teacher, family literacy coordinator and an advisory teacher for early literacy. She is currently involved in initial teacher education at the University of Hertfordshire.

Dr Cathy Burnett is a Reader in the Department of Teacher Education, where she leads the Language and Literacy Research Group. She has worked as a primary teacher, for a local education authority and, for many years, as a teacher educator. She has a particular interest in the role of research in professional development.

Carrie Cable was Senior Lecturer in Education at The Open University. She was director of a government-funded research project examining the teaching of languages in primary schools from 2007 to 2010. Carrie has been involved in teaching and research related to primary and early years education for many years and has written chapters and co-edited books in these areas.

Jenny Carey is Course Leader for the Early Years Teacher Specialism at the University of Strathclyde, which provides Masters-level study for early years practitioners. She also works on both undergraduate and postgraduate initial teacher education courses, contributing to teaching and learning and to language and literacy programmes. Her work with undergraduate and Masters-level students has guided her interest in teacher reflection and curriculum implementation. Jenny's current research explores factors that affect 9-year-old children's engagement with learning in school settings, focusing on the perspectives held by children and teachers about the learning opportunities, pedagogical approaches and interactions.

Professor Simon Catling is Emeritus Professor of Primary Education at Oxford Brookes University. His teaching, research and advisory activities have been largely in geography in primary education. His early career was as a primary teacher and he worked for thirty years in primary teacher education with undergraduates, postgraduates, masters and doctoral students. A Past President of the Geographical Association and Past Secretary to the International Geographical Union Commission on Geographical Education, he has written widely for children, teachers, teacher educators and researchers on geography curriculum, teaching and learning.

Roland Chaplain is a Chartered Psychologist and Associate Fellow of the British Psychological Society. He has experience as a teacher, head teacher and senior lecturer at Cambridge University, where he designed and teaches the Behaviour Management Training and Support Programme to all PGCE trainees. The quality of this programme has been highlighted in all recent Ofsted inpections at Cambridge. As an educational consultant, Roland also provides behaviour management training to schools and ITT providers. He has produced many books, chapters and journal articles on classroom management, behaviour disorders and teacher stress.

Pam Copeland is former Citizenship Lead at Newman University, Birmingham, and a Director of B and C Educational (www.primary-school-resources.com). She and her business partner produce and publish their own global teaching resources, offer curriculum consultancy to primary schools, and lead groups of primary teachers and heads to The Gambia as part of their CPD course on the global dimension in the curriculum.

Professor Teresa Cremin is Professor of Education (Literacy) at The Open University. She is an Academician of the Academy of Social Sciences, a Fellow of the English Association, Past President of the United Kingdom Literacy Association and a Board Member/Trustee of Booktrust, the Poetry Archive, the Cambridge Primary Review Trust and UKLA. She is also currently a coordinator of the British Educational Research Association's Special Interest Group on Creativity and a member of the Economic and Social Research Council (ESRC) Peer Review College. Teresa's sociocultural research, teaching and consultancy focus mainly on teachers' literate identities and practices, pedagogies of reading and writing for pleasure, and creativity in teaching and learning from the early years through to higher education. Additionally, she has recently explored contemporary enactments of Vivian Gussin Paley's work with young children scribing and enacting their own narratives, the literary discussions of extracurricular reading groups, and, through working with practitioners as researchers, she has investigated the everyday literacy practices of young people in the twenty-first century. Teresa has written and edited more than twenty-five books and numerous papers and professional texts, most recently publishing, with Debra Myhill, *Writing Voices: Creating Communities of Writers* (2012, Routledge) and editing, with colleagues Kathy Hall, Barbara Comber and Luis Moll, *The International Handbook of Research into Children's Literacy, Learning and Culture* (2013, Wiley Blackwell).

Dr Lyn Dawes taught in secondary and primary schools as Class Teacher and Science Coordinator. After completing a PhD in educational computing, Lyn taught at the Universities of Bedford, Northampton and Cambridge on PGCE and BA(QTS) courses. Lyn is part of the Thinking Together team and is now an Education Consultant. She has a special interest in 'Talk for Learning' and provides workshops in talk-focused classroom learning around the UK. Lyn has authored several books for teachers, including *Talking Points: Discussion Activities in the Primary Classroom* (2012, Routledge) and *Talking Points for Shakespeare Plays* (2013, Routledge).

Bernadette Duffy OBE is Head of the Thomas Coram Centre and author of *Supporting Creativity and Imagination in the Early Years*. Bernadette has been a member of a number of advisory groups for the Department for Education, including the revised EYFS, and was on the advisory committee of the Cambridge University Primary Review.

Justine Earl is a Senior Lecturer in Primary Education at Canterbury Christ Church University, where she is Programme Director for the PGCE part-time programme and responsible for English across the PGCE programmes. She has worked in primary education for 20 years, including time as a teacher and a local authority adviser. Her areas of specialism include English, primary languages, professional studies and music.

Dr Tony Eaude was the Head Teacher of a multicultural first school for 9 years, before completing a doctorate. For the last 10 years, he has worked independently, focusing on research, writing and professional development and continuing to teach in Key Stage 2. He has written books about children's spiritual, moral, social and cultural development, pedagogy and teacher expertise. More details are available at www.edperspectives.org.uk.

Dr Sue Ellis is a Reader in Education at the University of Strathclyde. Her first degree was in theoretical linguistics and language pathology, and her current work involves research, teaching and consultancy in language and literacy assessment, curriculum, pedagogy and policy. She is interested in how children learn to become literate, but also in how the literacy curriculum is framed, developed, taught and assessed.

Dr Sally Elton-Chalcraft is Reader in Education at the University of Cumbria. She has responsibility for MA dissertations, is course leader for the Religious Studies QTS specialism and teaches on a range of QTS programmes. She has published in the areas of race and equality (*It's Not Just About Black and White Miss: Children's Cultural Awareness*, 2009, Trentham), research methods (*Doing Classroom Research: A Step by Step Guide for Student Teachers*, with Hansen and Twiselton, 2008, Open University Press), and creative teaching and learning ('Measuring challenge, fun and sterility on a "phunometre" scale: evaluating creative teaching and learning with children and their student teachers in the primary school', with Mills, 2013, *Education 3-13: International Journal of Primary, Elementary and Early Years Education*). Currently, she is involved in a collaborative project investigating teacher values (including fundamental British values) as espoused in the 2012 Teaching Standards. She lives in the Lake District with her husband, three children and cat.

Professor Deborah Eyre is Education Director at Nord Anglia Education, a premium international schools organisation. Working with governments and schools across the world on issues around educational quality and advanced cognitive performance, she is a leading figure in gifted education. She was formerly the Director of the National Academy for Gifted and Talented Youth and an academic at the Universities of Warwick and Oxford Brookes University.

Professor Kit Field is currently the Head of Academic Practice at the University of Wolverhampton, after serving as the Dean of the School for Education Futures for 6 years. Kit has a publications record relating to the teaching and learning of modern foreign languages, middle leadership in schools and continuing professional development.

Dr Robert Fisher taught in schools in the UK, Africa and Hong Kong, before becoming Professor of Education at Brunel University. His many books include *Teaching Thinking*, *Teaching Children to Think*, *Teaching Children to Learn*, the *Stories for Thinking* series, *Creative Dialogue* and *Brain Games for Your Child*.

Professor Caroline Gipps was, until July 2011, Vice Chancellor at the University of Wolverhampton. Previously she was Deputy Vice Chancellor at Kingston University and Dean of Research at the Institute of Education, London. Trained as a psychologist, test developer and a qualified teacher, she carried out research on assessment in the school system for more than 20 years. Research projects have included a 6-year study of the introduction of the National Curriculum assessment programme into primary schools; a seminal study of teacher feedback to learners; and the teaching, assessment and feedback strategies used by 'expert' classroom teachers.

Stephen Griffin is Senior Lecturer in the Department of Education and Professional Studies at Newman University, contributing to both undergraduate and postgraduate courses. Previously, Stephen worked in a range of educational settings from KS1 to KS3 and was a Deputy Head Teacher. His research interests focus on the implementation of neuroscientifically informed learning theory in the classroom and its efficacy. Stephen is currently completing his doctoral thesis.

Professor Kathy Hall is Head of the School of Education at University College Cork. A former primary teacher, she researches in the areas of learning, inclusion and assessment. Her most recent, co-authored publication, *Networks of Mind: Learning, Culture, Neuroscience* (2013, Routledge), critically explores sociocultural and neuroscientific standpoints on learning.

Dr Eleanore Hargreaves is Senior Lecturer in Education at the Institute of Education, London University, where she has worked since 1995. She leads the MA in Effective Learning and Teaching, focusing her research and teaching on learning in classrooms. Her main focus is the improvement of learning for both students and teachers. She has written widely about assessment for learning and has run development courses for teachers in the UK, as well as in Pakistan, Somalia and Hong Kong, to support the use of assessment for learning in schools. She is currently involved in a TEMPUS-funded project exploring teacher professional development in Egypt, Palestine and Lebanon.

Dr Denis Hayes was formerly a Professor of Education and is now a freelance writer and speaker. Denis worked for many years in a variety of schools before spending 20 years in higher education. He has spent much of his career helping trainee and inexperienced teachers develop effective classroom teaching skills.

Donna Hazzard has worked in the Education Department of St Mary's University College in Belfast for the past 15 years, where, as a Principal Lecturer, she holds the posts of Literacy Course Team Leader and Masters-Level Co-ordinator. Donna is the United Kingdom Literary Association's Northern Ireland representative.

Suzy Holding is a Senior Lecturer in English in Primary Education at the University of Hertfordshire. She is the professional lead for primary English and oversees the undergraduate and postgraduate English teaching and learning in the School of Education. Her MA in Children's Literature investigated the impact of multimodal texts and popular culture on reading for pleasure in KS2. Her current interests are working with schools to maintain and develop speaking and listening as a priority in literacy development.

Dr Jenny Houssart has a background in primary teaching and is now Reader in Education at the Institute of Education, London, where she works on a range of undergraduate and postgraduate courses. She is author of *Low Attainers in Primary Mathematics* and has written a range of research and professional publications.

Dr Peter Kelly is an Associate Professor of Education at Plymouth University. He teaches mostly on Masters and Doctoral programmes. He is particularly interested in comparing language, literacy and mathematics teaching and assessment in European schools, and has worked in Denmark and Germany and England. Before moving into higher education, he spent 15 years teaching in primary and middle schools in London and south-west England.

Rebecca Kennedy is an independent consultant specialising in literacy. She has a range of experience in teaching and supporting primary schools, working alongside local authorities as well as on national research projects. Previously, Rebecca was a Regional Adviser for the National Strategies. Her professional interests are children's reading and writing, multimodality and children's literature. She has contributed to several United Kingdom Literacy Association publications, co-editing *Literacy and Community: Developing a Primary Curriculum Through Partnerships*, and is on the editorial board of the magazine *English 4-11*.

Dr Andreas O. Kyriakides works as a primary school teacher in Cyprus. He is also a Scientific Collaborator at the Department of Educational Studies of the European University Cyprus. In the field of teacher education, he is interested not only in training prospective teachers to acquire the necessary knowledge base but also in sharpening their sensitivity to the complexities of learning and directing their attention to practices and constructs that can inform preferences when teaching.

Cynthia Martin has over 25 years experience in the field of primary languages, since first participating in a research project in 1989. She was formerly a Senior Lecturer in Modern Languages Education in the Institute of Education at the University of Reading. Cynthia has taught French in a local primary school, worked in curriculum development for a variety of government agencies, and co-ordinated support groups for primary practitioners. She has been President of the Association for Language Learning and is an active member of the Association's Special Interest Group In Primary Education.

Dr Jane Medwell is Associate Professor of Education at the University of Nottingham. She has published widely, and her current research interests include the development of handwriting and its relationship to composing, the teaching of modern foreign languages in primary schools and the teaching of Chinese as a second language.

Dr Elaine Millard began her career as an English teacher working in a variety of 11–18 comprehensive schools in Sheffield and Nottingham. From 1998 to 1990 she worked as an advisory teacher for Nottingham LEA, preparing both primary and secondary schools for the introduction of the English National Curriculum. In 1991 she joined Sheffield University's School of Education and was one of the main originators of its influential Masters degree in Literacy. Elaine is past chair of the National Association for the Teaching of English. Her most influential publication is *Differently Literate* (Falmer Press), which presents research into the differences between boys' and girls' responses to the reading curriculum.

Deborah Nicholson taught in primary schools in London and Cardiff, and has worked as an advisory teacher for the Centre for Literacy in Primary Education. She is currently a Senior Lecturer at Bath Spa University, in the primary and early years PGCE English programme. Her research interests include children's literature, writing and social diversity. She shares the role of South West Regional Representative for the United Kingdom Literacy Association with Carrie Ansell.

Anny Northcote spent many years teaching in London primary schools and as an adviser for supporting bilingual pupils, before moving to higher education as a tutor for PGCE and undergraduate education studies. Her main interests are in language, literacy and literature, and she has been engaged in a Big Lottery-funded research project on *Dyslexia and Multilingualism*, published in 2012.

Alison Pickering taught in primary schools in inner London and Sydney, Australia, prior to her appointment as Deputy Head Teacher of a primary school in Richmond-upon-Thames. She was Course Director for undergraduate routes into teaching at the School of Education, Kingston University. Her main areas of interest are primary science, cross-curricular approaches to learning and creative approaches to assessment.

Dr Noel Purdy is Head of Education Studies (including Special Educational Needs) and Chair of the Primary BEd programme at Stranmillis University College, Belfast. He is currently Chair of the Northern Ireland Anti-Bullying Forum and Vice-President of the National Association for Special Educational Needs (Nasen) in Northern Ireland. His research interests include disability and bullying, and his edited volume, *Pastoral Care 11–16: A Critical Introduction*, was published by Bloomsbury Academic in 2013.

Chris Randall is Primary Partnership Director at the University of Wolverhampton and has been in this role for 6 years. He previously worked in school improvement and is a trained HEI Ofsted Inspector. Chris has a record of delivering and supporting CPD locally, nationally and internationally, recently working in India with an alliance of schools. He is a member of two teaching schools and a trust.

Professor Colin Richards is former primary school teacher, senior HMI and Professor of Education at the Universities of Cumbria, Warwick, Newcastle and Leicester. As an inveterate letter writer and critic of government education policies, he is a frequent contributor to the national media. He is chair of governors of a Cumbrian school and a national leader of governance. He is a non-political member of the Socialist Education Association and a firm opponent of academisation in both the primary and secondary phases of education.

Christopher Robertson is a Lecturer in Inclusive and Special Education at the University of Birmingham, where he leads the postgraduate National Award for Special Educational Needs Coordination programme. His teaching and research interests include education policy, international perspectives on special and inclusive education and all aspects of teacher education. Christopher has written extensively on the role of the special educational needs coordinator. He has also co-authored books on special educational needs and written articles on a wide range of issues pertaining to special and inclusive education, including: initial teacher education, autonomy, quality of life, teacher stress and the social theory of disability.

Dr Carol Robinson is a Principal Research Fellow at the School of Education, University of Brighton. Her research interests combine theoretical and empirical work focusing on the voices, experiences, rights and empowerment of children and young people. Carol has taught in a range of secondary schools and schools for children with special educational needs. She has led a number of Pupil Voice projects in primary and secondary schools, and also led the 'Pupils' Voices' strand of the University of Cambridge Primary Review of Education.

Dr Sue Rogers is Head of the Department of Early Years and Primary Education at the Institute of Education, London. Her research interests include play, curriculum and pedagogy, young children's perspectives and child–adult interaction. She has published widely in the field of early childhood education, including three books: *Inside Role Play in Early Childhood Education: Researching Children's Perspectives* (with Julie Evans, 2008), *Rethinking Play and Pedagogy: Concepts, Contexts and Cultures* (2010) and *Adult Roles in the Early Years* (with Janet Rose, 2012).

Dr Janet Rose is a Principal Lecturer and Award Leader for the Early Childhood Education undergraduate and postgraduate degrees at Bath Spa University. She has over 20 years' experience of working in the early years, both in England and internationally. She has recently co-written a book on *The Role of the Adult in Early Years Settings* and will soon publish a book on *Health and Well-being in the Early Years*. Her particular interests include child development, supporting children's behaviour and the adult role. She is currently leading a research project that is implementing a community-wide, cross-disciplinary approach to promoting children's resilience and well-being and is developing a project called Attachment Aware Schools, which is a comprehensive programme of support for children affected by early attachment difficulties, trauma and neglect.

John Ryan is a Lecturer in Professional Studies at the University of Birmingham. He has previously worked as a Senior Lecturer in Education and Professional Studies at Newman University. His research interests are currently focused on professional identity, gender and pedagogical approaches in the primary curriculum. He is due to complete his doctorate very soon and has over 20 years' teaching experience.

Dr Kieron Sheehy has a background in teaching and educational psychology. He has a particular interest in inclusive education pedagogy and new technologies. He is currently Programme Leader of the Doctorate in Education Programme at The Open University.

Sandra Smidt is a writer and consultant in early years education. Her most recent books include: *Introducing Paulo Freire* (forthcoming, 2014); *The Developing Child in the 21st Century*, second edition (2013); *Introducing Malaguzzi* (2012); *Introducing Bruner* (2011); *Playing to Learn* (2010); *Planning for the Early Years Foundation Stage* (2009); *Key Issues in Early Years Education*, second edition (2009); *Introducing Vygotsky* (2008); *Supporting Multilingual Learners in the Early Years* (2007) and *A Guide to Early Years Practice*, third edition (2007), all published by Routledge.

Marcelo Staricoff is the Head Teacher of Hertford Infant and Nursery School in Brighton and part-time Lecturer in Education at the University of Brighton. Marcelo has published a book, *Start Thinking*, and a number of articles that describe how a learning-to-learn and enquiry-based approach can be integrated into the daily life of a primary classroom. He was formerly a member of the Academy for Gifted and Talented Youth's Think Tank.

Jo Trowsdale is Associate Professor in Education at the University of Warwick, where she has been engaged in the development of teachers, including those specialising in drama for the primary and secondary ages, over several decades. For 7 years, she led a Creative Partnerships organisation supporting teachers, schools and artists to work together to develop creative learning to address identified needs. For example, the Reggio Emilia-inspired Second Skin project in early years enabled staff and artists to develop pedagogies and practice that supported independent and creative learning through stimulating physical environments. Jo has been involved in the professional development of artists and teachers, research and evaluation projects with local authority education departments and with cultural organisations. Her research interests concern the relationship between arts, creativity, culture and education, and she is currently researching into the value of creative learning and developing a creative engineering partnership with primary schools.

Professor Peter Twining is a Professor of Education (Futures) at The Open University. He was the Director of Vital, a £9.4 million DfE-funded programme to support practitioners in enhancing their teaching about and/or with digital technology. Peter has been the Head of the Department of Education at The Open University and the Co-Director of the Centre for Research in Education and Educational Technology.

Professor Samantha Twiselton is Director of the Sheffield Institute of Education at Sheffield Hallam University. Her interests and research centre on student teacher development and curriculum development and she uses this to inform the development of the portfolio in the Institute. She was a primary classroom teacher for a number of years. She is a primary English specialist, a passionate believer in the importance of evidence-based teaching and strongly encourages all her students to see research as central to good practice.

Jane Warwick taught in primary schools for 15 years and was a support teacher for PE and a local authority science adviser. For the last 7 years, Jane has been the Early Years and Primary PGCE Course Manager at the University of Cambridge. She teaches Professional Studies and has responsibility for preparing trainees for school placements. Research interests include professional development of trainees and mentors.

Professor Janice Wearmouth has many years' experience of teaching in mainstream schools, as well as teaching and research in universities in the UK and internationally, focusing on issues related to behavioural concerns, literacy difficulties and inclusion. She combines a concern for learners whose educational experience is problematic with a concern for professionals who deal with the problems and facilitate opportunities for learning. Currently, she is Professor of Education at the University of Bedfordshire.

Louise Wheatcroft is a Senior Lecturer in Primary English at Birmingham City University. She has worked in education for over 20 years, primarily in primary schools as a literacy coordinator. She worked for Voluntary Services Oversees in the Maldives in teacher training, developing training materials and carrying out research. Her main research interests are in the field of primary literacy, including home and school literacies, popular culture and digital literacies.

Ben Whitney is an Independent Education Welfare Consultant, providing training and support for schools on attendance and child protection. Prior to that, he worked for over 20 years in senior positions in two local authorities and was the author of several books of practical advice for schools. He is a member of the Oaktree Co-operative, a group of current and former local authority officers committed to promoting pupil welfare. In addition to his professional work, he also writes on 'humanist spirituality' and can be contacted via his website at www.ben-whitney.org.uk, where he also offers a regular blog on educational and social issues.

Mary Anne Wolpert taught for 12 years in primary schools, latterly as an English specialist, and was a local authority English consultant. She has worked in teacher education at the University of Cambridge since 2005 and, as Deputy Course Manager for the Early Years and Primary PGCE, focuses on developing partnerships with schools, preparing trainees for placements and coordinating the Professional Studies course. Research interests include children's literature and reading comprehension.

David Wray is Professor of Literacy Education at the University of Warwick. He has published over fifty books on aspects of literacy teaching and is best known for his work on developing teaching strategies to help pupils access the curriculum through literacy.

Professor Dominic Wyse is Professor of Early Childhood and Primary Education at the Institute of Education, University of London. The main focus of his research is curriculum and pedagogy. Key areas of work are the teaching of English, language, literacy and creativity. Dominic has led or been participant in more than twenty funded research projects. Dominic is author of more than 40 research articles and chapters, and 20 books. These include major international research volumes on the teaching of English, language and literacy, for which he is the lead editor, and bestselling books for teachers and educators that are now in their third edition. One of his most recent books, *Creating the Curriculum*, is the first to compare the national curriculum in the four nations of the UK.

ACKNOWLEDGEMENTS

The editors would like to thank Helen Pritt, Helen Marsden and Holly Davis from Routledge, who have been an invaluable support in undertaking this substantial new edition with twenty-two new authors involved; some joining established writers, others replacing previous authors, and ten authoring and co-authoring new chapters in response to current primary phase concerns. Each of the original and new authors involved in offering research-informed advice and practical guidance is also gratefully thanked for their time and talent. We trust the professional resource that this third edition represents will enable student teachers across the four nations of the UK to develop the knowledge and understanding, skill, energy and creativity needed to teach effectively in the primary phase.

INTRODUCTION

Teresa Cremin and James Arthur

WHAT IS PRIMARY TEACHING?

Teaching in primary schools has sometimes been thought of as having lower status than 'real' teaching – that is, teaching a proper subject in a proper school, which means a secondary school. Primary teaching, so folklore tells us, is just looking after young children until they attend 'proper' school – showing them how to hold a pencil, wiping their noses, telling them a story or two, but not actually teaching them much of real importance. Those (rather rare) teachers who have made the change from teaching in secondary schools to primary schools often find that parents, even children, ask them why they have 'moved down', the idea that someone might voluntarily choose primary teaching over secondary being a hard one to grasp.

Thankfully, at least in official quarters, the image of primary teaching has changed, and it is now recognised that the primary years and primary schooling represent a crucial period, perhaps the most crucial, in children's learning. During this time, they need to be taught the complex skills that are the foundation of all the learning they will do in the rest of their lives. It is primary teachers who teach children to read, to write, to manipulate numbers and to observe, record and question their experiences of the world, and who provide them with opportunities that stimulate their imaginations and expand their worlds. It is also primary teachers who help to foster positive attitudes and creative learning dispositions, as well as develop children's interpersonal skills and collaborative capacities. Far from being seen as childminders with little expertise, primary teachers are now more commonly viewed as professional learning enablers, highly skilled educators possessing a wide subject knowledge base, a rich understanding of child development and a commitment to fostering effective and creative teaching and learning, both within and beyond the classroom.

However, even when the complexity of the job is recognised, there are still a number of different ways of conceptualising what makes a good primary teacher. A description that is often used is that primary teaching is a vocation – rather like the priesthood, you have to have a calling in order to be a good primary teacher. This view produces such ideas as the belief that good teachers are born, not made, and that, to become a teacher, all you really need to do is to work for a while alongside another experienced teacher and copy what he or she does. This used to be referred to as the 'sitting with Nellie' approach to becoming a teacher. It does have the merit that, if Nellie *is* a good teacher, watching and copying what she does will almost certainly pass on some pretty good habits of classroom practice.

But what if Nellie's classroom changes, as classrooms have changed, radically, over the past 20 years? If Nellie is to remain effective as a teacher and make learning meaningful, relevant and engaging to the young, those good habits will need to change as well. And the trouble with habits, as all the nail-biters and chocoholics among you will know, is that they can be extraordinarily resistant to change. Nellie will need to have an understanding about why she does what she does, why it works now but might not work in the future, and how she will go about changing and developing her practice. Having a sense of vocation will only get her so far. Successful teaching needs more than a feeling of being 'born to teach', and it is also true that many teachers develop into highly effective practitioners without ever feeling such an inner calling.

Another popular way of conceptualising teaching is to describe it as a craft, with the implication that it consists of an integrated collection of skilful activities. Other crafts include such activities as plumbing and wood-turning, both very skilful in their own right (and in some cases more lucrative as careers than primary teaching!). A craft view of teaching allows for changes in practice to a much greater extent than might a vocation view. In the same way that plumbers have to change their practices to accommodate innovations (such as plastic rather than copper piping), so teachers have to adapt their skills to cope with the changing nature of literacy, for example, in this new media age. Naturally, there is a large element of craft involved in the role of the primary teacher. For most beginning teachers, learning these craft elements looms pretty large in their early experiences of teaching. Learning to talk to large groups of pupils in an authoritative yet approachable way, learning to ask questions, learning to model curiosity and artistry, learning to plan appropriate activities for all the children, learning how to write informative reports to parents about the progress of their offspring – all these have a significant craft element to them, and many beginning teachers see their principal aim in their first years of teaching as mastering these and other skills, and becoming craftsmen/women of the classroom. Yet this is not all there is to successful primary teaching, nor to the process of becoming a successful teacher. The two simple facts that set teaching apart from other crafts are the two Cs – consequence and complexity.

Let us take consequence first. What is the consequence of a plumber failing to do a job properly? Well, the worst-case scenario is a flooded house, which may be costly to put right but, in the end, is usually repairable. But the consequence of a teacher failing a pupil or group of pupils can be much, much more serious. Struggling children can easily develop a negative self-image, one that incorporates failure even – a view of themselves that can persist throughout their lives and radically limit the development of their potential. Teachers who fail to teach their pupils to read or write, or who fail to foster positive attitudes to learning, do far more damage than any plumber who fails to connect two pipes together properly. The consequences of teaching are greater and longer lasting than those of most other crafts.

In terms of complexity, the craft of teaching also outdoes most others. Indeed, teaching is so complex an activity that it is sometimes almost impossible to predict what will happen as you engage in it. A plumber might weld together two pipes and, 99 times out of 100, if the job is done carefully, the result will be the same. A teacher, on the other hand, can teach the same lesson twice to different groups of pupils, and with one achieve success, but with the other have a disaster. Why? Well, it might be because the groups were different, with different personalities, abilities, interests, aptitudes and moods. The performance of the teacher may also have been subtly different, depending on his or her mood and/or capacity to respond flexibly to the needs and interest of the children. In addition, other variables such as the physical environment, the time of day and the previous knowledge of the children may alter the curriculum experience. The point here is that any act of teaching is an incredibly complicated affair – there are so many things that can influence it. One of the key characteristics of really effective teachers is the ability to hold a lot of this complexity in their minds as they plan, develop and evaluate their teaching. Another significant difference between the craft of teaching and craft activities such as pottery or plumbing is that, whereas pipes are inert, children have personalities of their own. They are unique young thinkers, with their own thoughts, interests and needs. By concentrating on practical teaching skills and methods – the mechanics of teaching – it is more than possible to produce a mechanistic 'teacher' who is able to manage a class and instruct pupils with a fair show of competence. The emphasis here is on what the teacher can do (a trade), rather than what the teacher is and can become (an educator). You need to be aware of the wider social setting, to develop the flexibility to anticipate change and adapt your teaching methods to new demands and different learners.

Teaching in a primary school is, above all, a professional and artistic enterprise. Pupils spend a large part of the day with their teachers, and so you will have significant opportunities to influence them. The time spent by pupils in the company of teachers is inevitably personal and formative. Good teachers are connected to their pupils, for, at the heart of the practice of education, is the relationship between teacher and pupil. It is this relationship that sets the tone for everything that happens in the classroom, and it is this relationship that influences the development of positive attitudes and dispositions, as well as growth in knowledge, skills and understanding.

For all these reasons, when we talk about teaching, we use the notion of professional decision-making to represent it.

So our third way of conceptualising primary teaching, and the approach we use in this book, is to conceive of teaching as a professional activity. This term implies a number of attributes within the teacher, including:

- high levels of relevant knowledge about what is being taught and the children to whom it is being taught;
- knowledge of, and skill in using, a range of strategies to enable learning;
- the capacity to engage flexibly and thoughtfully in the classroom, taking into account the needs and responses of the learners as they develop and manifest themselves;
- an understanding of the importance of learners' attitudes towards what they are learning;
- an ability to influence and develop these attitudes; and
- the ability and willingness to learn from a variety of sources about effective teaching and to adapt practices to fit this ongoing learning.

It is one of the aims of this book to help you begin to develop such professional attributes, dispositions and competences.

HOW CAN THIS BOOK HELP ME?

From what we have just said, you may already have realised that the book you are holding is not a collection of 'tips for the beginning teacher'. It is true you will find within its pages a great deal of very practical advice about primary teaching, strategies to support you and activities you can use within the classroom, but the book goes far beyond this. In compiling it, we aimed to offer you practical advice and support, but also a rationale for why such advice might be useful, where it comes from, on what basis it has been formulated and how you might evaluate its usefulness. In short, this book is intended to be both practical and theoretical, a professional resource that is a prompt for reflection, a source of new knowledge and support for tomorrow. This reflects a view of teaching as a highly skilled, knowledgeable, professional activity.

The book, therefore, will help move you on in your development as a professional by providing you with background insights into a range of issues that affect the decisions you make in the classroom, and illustrating how such insights affect your classroom practice. Our intention is that this book will work alongside the other experiences within your initial teacher training/education course, both in university- or college-based sessions and in the classroom.

WHAT'S IN THE BOOK?

The aim of this book is to provide vital support to student teachers, their tutors and their mentors, particularly with reference to the professional studies part of the course and during the school placement element of their initial teacher education. It provides a practical introduction to the necessary knowledge, skills, understanding and attitudes that a student teacher will need to acquire, and to the theories underpinning them.

The book is divided into key sections, each explaining critical issues, such as teaching and learning, curriculum and assessment. Each unit within these sections contains an introduction to the key concepts and several learning activities for student teachers, presented in the form of tasks. Tasks that are appropriate for Masters-level (M-level) study are referred to as M-level challenges.

There are also annotated lists of suggested reading for students, tutors and mentors who want to explore topics in more detail.

Section 1: becoming a teacher

This section includes units focusing on:

- the nature of teaching, both formal and informal;
- the standards required for QTS, with particular emphasis on professional values;
- placement opportunities in school and how to make the most of them.

Section 2: exploring the nature of learning and teaching

This section includes units focusing on:

- theories of child development in order that you can provide appropriate learning opportunities for children;
- conceptualisations of learning and the implications of these for teaching;
- insights into learning and teaching strategies that respond to these;
- effective early years practice and the principles and theories underpinning this;
- the significance of play and exploration in learning.

Section 3: planning and managing learning

This section includes units focusing on:

- planning classroom work, for medium- and long-term periods;
- planning for the short term, including lesson planning and evaluation;
- managing and organising the classroom for learning;
- managing children's behaviour;
- handling difficulties in children's social, emotional and behaviour development;
- organising effective classroom talk;
- organising and managing learning outside the classroom.

Section 4: approaches to the curriculum

This section includes units focusing on:

- the aims of primary education;
- conceptions of the school curriculum and its formal, informal and hidden aims;
- the rationale for and framing of the National Curriculum in England;
- the current Scottish Curriculum at the primary phase.

Section 5: assessment

This section includes units examining:

- the nature of ongoing, formative assessment of pupils' progress – assessment for learning;
- approaches to summative assessment – assessment of learning.

Section 6: diversity and inclusion

This section includes units focusing on:

- provision for inclusion and barriers to learning and participation;
- providing for special educational needs;
- responding to difference, diversity and differentiation;
- responding to cultural diversity;
- exploring gender differences and their impact upon school experience and achievement;
- recognising and building upon children's linguistic diversity.

Section 7: recent developments

This section includes units exploring:

- the voices and views of young people;
- languages learning and teaching;
- creative teaching and teaching for creativity;
- thinking skills and the concept of multiple intelligences;
- provision for children who are gifted and talented;
- e-learning within and beyond the classroom;
- early reading and phonics.

Section 8: partnership in practice

This section includes units examining:

- the changing role of the primary teacher;
- working in partnership with a range of adults in the classroom;
- partnerships with parents to support learning and others;
- the teacher's pastoral role and child protection issues.

Section 9: your professional development

The final section of the book includes units on:

- applying for a job and what to expect in induction;
- professional development and career opportunities;
- connecting teaching and research, and considering further qualifications.

HOW CAN I USE THE BOOK?

There are a number of ways in which you might use this book. You might, of course, want to find yourself a comfortable space and a mug of steaming coffee and just read it from cover to cover. We anticipate, however, that, as gripping a read as this book is, you will probably not want to approach it in quite that way!

It is more likely that you will want to read units from the book separately. It has been designed so that each of them, while written to be part of a coherent whole, is also free standing. So the text can be used in a very flexible way. You might use a number of approaches, for example:

- You might prepare for a particular college or university session by reading the relevant unit in advance. You are likely to find the session much more rewarding and useful if you have prepared in this way by developing your background knowledge of the area to be covered.
- You might read a particular unit after you have touched upon similar material in a taught session. The unit will then serve as a revision of material you may have covered in the session, and/or extend your understanding of this material.
- You might find that, because of the pressure of time on a course of teacher training (as in the case of most PGCE courses, for example), there simply is not enough college or university time available to cover some issues in any more than an introductory manner. In this case, this book will help you ensure that you do not miss anything really important, and you can read units to widen your understanding and expertise.
- You might choose to read a unit in preparation for your work on a placement in school or as a result of conversations you take part in with your school-based mentor or the class teacher with whom you are working.
- You might choose to share a unit with your school-based mentor, to debate the issues and discuss ways forward for children in the class for whom you are responsible.

However you use this book, we hope it will help inspire in you the same deep interest in education, and primary education in particular, that is felt by every one of our contributors. *Learning to Teach in the Primary School* is now in its third edition, and, in inviting our original contributors to extensively update their units (twice!), and indeed in adding five new units, we have sought to retain the enthusiasm and commitment that was so evident in the first edition back in 2006. Our contributors have sought to share their individual and collective passion for primary education and offer you their informed understanding and not inconsiderable expertise, based on many years of experience as primary educators.

Education is an endlessly fascinating subject, and, of course, teaching children is a highly challenging activity. Enjoy the experience – we hope it will be engaging and satisfying for all involved and that this book will support you on your professional learning journey as you commence your career as a primary teacher.

BECOMING A TEACHER

PRIMARY TEACHING

A personal perspective

Colin Richards

INTRODUCTION

Primary teaching is an immensely complicated business – much more complicated than government ministers and most other politicians realise. It involves the interplay of so many elements, including interpersonal, intellectual, physical, spiritual, even aesthetic dimensions. It changes in form and substance from hour to hour, lesson to lesson, class to class and year to year. Some people see it as scientific in orientation, involving the selection of the best ways to 'deliver' material to young minds; others stress its artistic side and place emphasis on the 'feel' or style of teaching. So what is this enterprise called primary teaching? It is the purpose of this introductory unit to open this up for discussion.

OBJECTIVES

By the end of this unit you should be beginning to:

- form a view of the nature of primary teaching;
- develop an awareness of the personal qualities and skills you require as a primary teacher;
- form views as to the purposes of primary teaching;
- be overawed at the responsibility of being a primary school teacher.

'ACROSTIC' TEACHING

When you begin teaching you will be surprised at the range of different types of writing that the children are expected to engage in. Children have to learn to write narrative accounts, imaginative stories, descriptions of their 'experiments', diaries, letters, poems, etc. Many are introduced to acrostics and enjoy the challenge these present. What are acrostics? They are poems or other compositions in which certain letters in each line form a word or words.

I use an acrostic when giving an introductory talk to students at the beginning of their course of teacher education. You will notice that I don't call them 'trainees' and I don't talk of 'teacher training'. Like you, they are not being introduced to a simple straightforward activity in which they can be trained to perform like machine operators on a production line or like circus animals.

They are being inducted into a very complex professional activity – illustrated, for example, by the fact that the text you are reading contains over thirty units and is just an introduction! It is not the easy, straightforward activity beloved of politicians in search of sound bites and easy votes. It's a very demanding set of activities that require intellect, emotional intelligence, imagination and sensitivity – all of which are not easy acquire or to assess. I used to present the following:

```
T   . . . . . . . .
E   . . . . . . . .
A   . . . . . . . .
C   . . . . . . . .
H   . . . . . . . .
I   . . . . . . . .
N   . . . . . . . .
G   . . . . . . . .
```

and ask the students to characterise primary teaching (as they see it) using eight adjectives corresponding to the eight letters.

Task 1.1.1 The nature of primary teaching

Try the task for yourself. What do you think primary teaching is like? What does it feel like? What kind of activity is it? Make your list and share it with fellow students.

Of course, there are no right or wrong answers, and an activity as complex as primary teaching cannot be captured in eight words. As 'a starter for eight', I offer you the following:

T iring: Primary teaching is very demanding work – demanding physically, as you have to cope with a class of very active, growing human beings; demanding emotionally, as you have to deal with the myriad social interactions occurring in a crowded classroom; demanding intellectually, as you have to translate complex ideas in your head into terms that children of a particular age can understand.

E xhilarating: Primary teaching is equally (but paradoxically) invigorating work – when both you and the children get 'fired' up with enthusiasm for a particular activity, project or piece of work. The 'buzz' needs to be experienced to be appreciated. That 'buzz' cannot be measured, but it can be experienced and treasured.

A musing: Primary teaching is enlivened by countless amusing incidents during the course of a day or a week. Some children are natural and conscious comedians; others are unintentionally so; primary classrooms provide endless scope for amusement. 'Never a dull moment' captures this characteristic.

C haotic: Primary teaching can appear (and sometimes is) chaotic, as unforeseen circumstances arise and have to be coped with, as the government, parents, the head teacher and children make conflicting demands that have somehow to be met, and as the daily business of managing the learning of twenty or thirty lively and, to a degree, unpredictable youngsters has to be conducted.

H ectic: Primary teaching occurs in an extremely busy place called a classroom, where a multitude of activities (some intended by the teachers, others unintended!) take place, and where nothing or nobody stands still for long. Stamina, patience, resilience and an ability to cope with the unexpected are at a premium. These qualities are impossible to 'train' or 'measure', but they can be fostered and appreciated.

I nspiring: Primary teaching can be inspiring. You can be inspired by the amazing abilities children can reveal, for example in the creative arts; you can be inspired by the personal qualities of kindness and consideration children can show to one another and to you; you can be inspired by the fact that children with unbelievably difficult home circumstances come to school and manage to learn at all; you can be inspired by the work of your colleagues in your own school and in others from whom you can learn so much.

N ever-ending: Primary teaching is not a 'nine till four' occupation. In fact, it's not so much an occupation as a way of life. It is never complete, never mastered, never perfected. There is always more to learn and more to do for the children in your class. Teaching can take over your whole life with its never-ending demands, but you have to learn to temper these demands with your own personal needs. Doing this can be conscience-wracking, but is absolutely essential – to your own and, indirectly, your children's well-being.

G ratifying: Primary teaching can be intensely gratifying (despite some inevitable frustrations). Teaching a child to read, seeing another child's delight on mastering a skill, telling a story that captivates the whole class, having a lesson that goes really well – such activities can and will give you tremendous satisfaction. But don't expect it from every single lesson. You cannot be outstanding all the time or expect outstanding results from every child all the time – despite the fact that some inspectors seem to expect this.

A SENSE OF STYLE

You can see from my acrostic that I believe that primary teaching is an extremely complex activity. It's an amalgam of so many elements – emotional, intellectual, physical, spiritual, even aesthetic. It changes subtly in form, substance and 'feel', hour to hour, lesson to lesson, class to class, year to year. It involves notions such as 'respect', 'concern', 'care', 'commitment' and 'intellectual integrity', which are impossible to define but which are deeply influential in determining the nature of life in classrooms. The ends and means, aims and methods of teaching are inextricably interwoven. As well as being a practical activity, it needs to be conducted with moral purpose. The word 'style' captures something of what I am trying to convey – a sense of considered professional judgement, of personal response, of quality, of distinctive style – which each practitioner (including you!) needs to foster. You need to develop your own style; don't be misled into believing that there is an 'approved' style that will 'deliver' (horrible word!) the results. Primary teaching involves far more than the routine repetition of established procedures; it goes well beyond establishing and maintaining patterns of classroom organisation. It cannot be pinned down in a few straightforward sentences or in a political sound bite or in a brief inspection report (or in my simple acrostic!).

TEACHING: SCIENCE, CRAFT OR ART?

Some educational researchers, such as Muijs and Reynolds (2001), argue that it is possible to create a science of teaching. They believe that it is possible to study teaching by comparing the results of different methods in terms of the outcomes they produce in children, and thereby arrive at objective findings as to which teaching methods are effective in which contexts. You will come across books with titles such as *Effective Teaching*, which claim to provide scientifically defensible evidence on which to base decisions about how to teach. But don't be afraid to question their conclusions.

Some educationists, such as Marland (1975), regard teaching as essentially a craft – a set of difficult and complex techniques that can be picked up from, or taught by, skilled practitioners and that can be honed and perfected over the years. Currently, many politicians also have this view of teaching, though they tend to see it as much more straightforward than the educationists do. You will come across government documents such as 'The importance of teaching' and books with titles such as *The Craft of the Classroom* that embody this approach. Be questioning of these too.

Still others, such as Eisner (1979), regard teaching as essentially an art – a complex creative activity concerned with the promotion of human learning and involving imagination, sensitivity and personal response and an indefinable element of professional judgement, none of which can be taught directly by another person (though they can be learned indirectly). He talks of the need to 'recognise the contingent nature of educational practice, to savour its complexity, and to be unafraid to use whatever artistry we can master to deal with its problems' and he warns against 'pseudoscience' (p. 33). Treat Eisner's views with respect, but question them too.

Task 1.1.2 Teaching: science, craft or art?

Based on your experience of teaching at school, at university or on this course, how would you characterise teaching – as science, art or craft? Try to justify your answer to fellow students.

Again, as in the response to Task 1.1.1, there are no absolutely right or wrong answers.

From what I have written already, you can see that I characterise teaching as an art, although an art also involving some craft skills that can be taught and even trained for. I do not see that there can ever be an 'objective' science of teaching, involving the rigorous definition of methods and the clear measurement of outcomes in national tests or through other means. I believe that such a science is logically impossible, as 'the power to teach' is a highly complex amalgam of judgement, technique and personal qualities whose assessment is inevitably subjective and can never be susceptible to quantification or measurement. However, that perspective is my own personal one. Treat it critically. Other educationists have different ideas of the nature of teaching, including some who subscribe to the notion of 'the science of the art of teaching'!

ENACTIVE, PRE-ACTIVE AND POST-ACTIVE PRIMARY TEACHING

What activities are involved in being a primary teacher? What should the balance be between the different kinds of activity?

To outsiders (government ministers in particular!) and perhaps to most primary age children (though we don't know because we haven't asked them!) 'teaching' conjures up an image of a teacher in front of class describing, explaining, instructing or demonstrating something to his or her pupils. This is enactive teaching – teaching in action, the full frontal interaction of teacher and children. Of course, enactive teaching doesn't only take place in classrooms – it occurs in the hall, in the school grounds and on school trips. Nor does it always involve direct interaction with a class of children – the teacher may be teaching individuals or groups, or may be setting up activities where children learn for themselves, for example. There has been a considerable amount of research into enactive teaching in English primary schools – referred to in other parts of this book. However, there is far more to teaching than enactive teaching, even though the latter is the core activity.

There is pre-active teaching, involving the preparation and planning for children's learning, the organisation of the classroom, the collection and organisation of teaching resources, the management of visits or activities outside the classroom and the briefing of other adults who work with children. Interestingly, there has been little research into how primary teachers actually plan, prepare and organise their work. Pre-active teaching is essential to the success of enactive teaching – hence the emphasis on planning and managing learning in a later section of this book.

There is also post-active teaching, which involves considered reflection on practice, writing up evaluations, marking children's work, making assessments of children's progress and keeping records. At its best, this feeds into pre-active teaching as reflection and assessment inform planning and preparation. There is plenty of advice available on assessment and record-keeping (see Section 5) but, again, a dearth of research into how teachers actually engage in post-active teaching – you might consider undertaking some research of your own later in your career!

But there is still more to primary teaching as a professional activity. Teachers have to engage in a variety of extra-class activities – administrative tasks, staff meetings, clubs, consultations with parents and attendance at professional development courses, which relate indirectly to teaching but can't be fitted into my neat (too neat?) threefold classification.

There was some interesting work carried out 20 years ago by Campbell and Neill (1994) into the nature of primary teachers' work, especially the amount of time devoted to a variety of activities. The research makes interesting reading, although the categories the researchers used are rather different from my classification, and the findings are now dated. Campbell and Neill found that, on average, the 374 infant and junior teachers in their study spent 52.6 hours a week on professional activity – subdivided into 18.3 hours for teaching (i.e. enactive teaching), 15.7 hours for preparation/ marking (i.e. an amalgam of pre-active and post-active teaching), 14.1 hours on administration, 7.2 hours on professional development (including staff meetings and reading) and 4.5 hours on a ragbag of other activities that didn't fit into any of their other categories. Clearly this research gave the lie to the idea of primary teaching as a '9 to 3.30 occupation'!

To many, including the researchers, one of the most surprising findings was the relatively small proportion of the teachers' total work time devoted to what I have called enactive teaching, that is, about a third. It is interesting to speculate whether the figures would be any different were the research to be conducted today. It's a pity that such research is not being undertaken, but, even if it were, I doubt if there would be any substantial changes except for a large (I would say 'disproportionate') increase in the amount of time devoted to assessment and record-keeping. Enactive teaching requires a large input of pre-active teaching if it is to be successful, and it needs to be followed up by considerable, though somewhat less, post-active activity to ensure a professional cycle of planning – teaching – assessment – reflection – planning – teaching – assessment . . . ad infinitum. Remember, primary teaching is 'never-ending'!

THE PERSONAL QUALITIES AND KNOWLEDGE REQUIRED OF PRIMARY TEACHERS

There has been little research into how children view good teachers. Over 40 years ago, Philip Taylor asked both primary- and secondary-aged children and received very similar answers from both. In his words:

Pupils expect teachers to teach. They value lucid exposition, the clear statement of problems and guidance in their solution. Personal qualities of kindness, sympathy and patience are secondary, appreciated by pupils if they make the teacher more effective in carrying out his primary, intellectual task . . . there appears to be little demand by pupils that teachers shall be friends or temporary mothers and fathers.

(Musgrove and Taylor, 1969: 17)

Much more recently, the Cambridge Review asked children what they looked for in a good teacher:

Children described the best teachers as being those who listened, were kind and 'understood how you feel'. A good teacher, they suggested, should:

- 'really know their stuff'
- be able to make learning fun
- know everyone's names
- tell you things in advance so that you know what a lesson is about
- give you a permanent record of what you learn
- be able to explain things clearly so that you understand
- have lots of energy and enthusiasm.

(Alexander, 2010: 148)

How do these two sets of findings compare with the results of your small group discussions?

Task 1.1.3 The characteristics of a good teacher

In a small group, consider what makes a good teacher, and what knowledge and personal qualities are needed.

Would children come up with the same answers? Discuss the issue with a small group of primary-aged children.

The knowledge required to be a primary teacher has changed very considerably since the introduction of what was then teacher training in the nineteenth century, but the personal qualities needed have remained the same. The following paragraph captures something of what is required:

Teaching involves a lot more than care, mutual respect and well-placed optimism. It demands knowledge and practical skills; the ability to make informed judgements, and to balance pressures and challenges; practice and creativity; interest and effort; as well as an understanding of how children learn and develop.

(Department for Education and Skills and Teacher Training Agency, 2002: 4)

In a letter published some years ago in the *Times Educational Supplement* (circa 2004), I characterised the expectations of teachers held by the government and the wider society as representing:

a set of demands which properly exemplified would need the omni-competence of Leonardo da Vinci, the diplomatic expertise of Kofi Annan, the histrionic skills of Julie Walters, the grim determination of Alex Ferguson and the saintliness of Mother Teresa, coupled with the omniscience of God.

Admittedly this is over the top, but it does represent the inflated expectations of us as teachers. None of us is a perfect human being (nor, for that matter, are the children in our classes, their parents or our politicians), but those inflated expectations are a powerful influence on how many teachers view themselves and on causing so many to feel guilty about falling short. We can aspire to educational sainthood but hardly hope to achieve it. However, in its pursuit, we can at least aspire to show such qualities as 'care', 'respect', 'optimism', 'interest' and 'effort', required of us, quite properly in my view, by officialdom.

The knowledge required of you as primary teachers is of seven kinds – each important, though one (the second) is, in my view, more important than the others. As the government emphasises (rather too much?), you certainly need subject content knowledge – an understanding of the main concepts, principles, skills and content of the areas that you will have to teach. That's a tall order, given that the curriculum you are required to teach in Key Stages 1 and 2 comprises a large range of subjects, as well as cross-curricular areas such as personal and social education and citizenship, and given that the curriculum required in the Early Years Foundation Stage comprises seven areas. You can't assume that you have the required subject knowledge as a result of your own education, whether at school, college or university. You will need to audit and, where necessary, top up your subject knowledge by reading or attending courses. Begin now in a small way, if you haven't done this already.

The second kind of knowledge involves the application of subject knowledge in teaching your children – sometimes termed, rather grandly, 'pedagogical subject knowledge'. This crucially important area involves knowing how to make the knowledge, skills and understanding of subjects accessible and meaningful to children – how best to represent particular ideas; what illustrations to use; what demonstrations or experiments to employ; what stories to tell; what examples to draw on; what kinds of explanation to offer; how to relate what needs to be taught to children's experiences or interests, and so on. You will begin to develop this applied expertise in your course of initial teacher education; you will need to add to it through continuing professional development and through your own reading; and, over time, you will add to it from 'the wisdom of practice' – your colleagues' and hopefully your own. Membership of associations such as the National Association for Primary Education (NAPE) or the Association for the Study of Primary Education (ASPE) can also enhance your expertise and wider understanding of primary education. Application of subject knowledge also draws on knowledge of children's development, including aspects of how children learn and what motivates them; of developmental sequences (in so far as we can identify them); and of learning difficulties and other special needs (see Sections 2 and 6 of this book).

You also need to develop curriculum knowledge, that is, knowledge of National Curriculum requirements; of policies, guidelines and schemes of work; and of the range of published materials and sources available as 'tools of the trade' to help you teach your class. You cannot be expected to keep abreast of developments in every area, but you can be expected to know to whom to turn for advice and to give advice in turn in any area of the curriculum where you act as a coordinator.

There are still other areas of professional knowledge you need to acquire. According to Shulman (1987), these include general pedagogical knowledge (including teaching strategies, techniques, classroom management and organisation), knowledge of educational contexts (ranging from the workings of small groups and the ways in which schools are organised, run, financed and governed, to the characteristics of communities and cultures) and knowledge of educational ends, purposes and values.

You can see that primary teaching involves much more than a knowledge of how to teach 'reading, writing and number' – a view too many politicians, local and national, seem to hold. Being a primary teacher involves lifelong learning!

THE PURPOSES OF PRIMARY TEACHING

The state first provided elementary education for children of primary-school age in the latter half of the nineteenth century. The state system complemented a rather chaotic and ad hoc collection of schools established earlier by religious organisations. Now over 95 per cent of children aged 4 to 11 attend state primary schools and are taught by teachers in local authority (LA) schools or in primary academies. LA schools have to work to, and primary academies have to 'have regard to', national requirements and guidelines, such as the National Curriculum and testing arrangements.

Over that period of time, primary teaching has served a variety of purposes, although the relative importance of these has changed from time to time. As a primary teacher, you will play a part in fulfilling these purposes. You will need to form your own view of their relative importance and decide how best to fulfil them, or possibly subvert aspects of them, in the best interests of your pupils.

One major purpose of primary teaching has been, and is, *instruction* – here broadly conceived to include the fostering of:

- procedural knowledge:
  - helping children to acquire and use information, e.g. learning and applying the four rules of number, learning how to spell, learning facts in science or history;
- conceptual knowledge:
  - helping children to understand ideas;
  - helping children to understand principles, e.g. learning how to conduct fair tests in science; learning the importance of chronology in history;
- skills acquisition:
  - helping children to acquire manipulative and other physical skills, such as cutting, handwriting or gymnastics;
  - helping children to acquire complex skills such as reading;
- metacognitive knowledge:
  - helping children to be more knowledgeable about how they learn and how they can improve their learning.

Over time, the relative importance of these components has changed. In the nineteenth century, most emphasis was placed on *procedural knowledge* and *skills acquisition*, often of an elementary kind. The latter half of the twentieth century saw an increasing emphasis on *conceptual knowledge* and more advanced *skills acquisition*. Currently, there is a growing interest in fostering *metacognitive knowledge* (see Section 2), but also a re-emphasis by the government on procedural knowledge. As a primary teacher in the early part of the twenty-first century, you will need to foster all four components – not an easy task!

A second major purpose of primary teaching has been, and is, *socialisation*. Children need to be introduced into a wider society than the home; they need to be able to relate to their peers and to work with them. They need to be inducted into the norms and values of British society, but also be aware of wider international values such as sustainability and human rights. They need to be socialised into the 'strange' world of school, which operates very differently from most homes and involves a great deal of fundamental but often unacknowledged learning – graphically captured (for all time?) in Philip Jackson's brilliant first chapter in his *Life in Classrooms* (1968). As a teacher, especially if you are an early years teacher, you will be a most significant agent in children's socialisation. This process has always been a major purpose of primary teaching, especially in the nineteenth century, when large numbers of children entered formal education for the first time and had to be compelled to 'accept their place in society', as the Victorians might have put it. But it is still very significant today – partly as a result of our increasingly complex, rich, multicultural society, in which the values of tolerance and respect for others are so much needed and where they can be fostered and reinforced from the minute children enter school. Contemporary children need to find a place – a comfortable, affirming, respected place – in our society. Primary teachers need to help them find it and make it their own.

Linked to socialisation is another function of primary teaching. Teachers are concerned with children's *welfare* – physical, mental, emotional and social. Primary schools are the most accessible 'outposts' of the welfare state as far as most parents and children are concerned. They are crucially important points of contact, especially for economically disadvantaged families. In the late nineteenth and early twentieth centuries, primary teachers were particularly concerned for children's physical welfare – as illustrated by the introduction of school meals and medical inspections and the emphasis placed on physical training. In very recent years, there has been a resurgence of concern about children's welfare. Especially in the area of welfare, it is not easy to decide on the limits of teachers' care for their children (Nias, 1997). This is yet another dimension to primary teaching – no wonder your course of teacher education is so crowded, and this book so long!

There is a fourth function of primary teaching – and one with which I feel uncomfortable. Traditionally, primary teaching has also involved the *classification* of children in order to 'sort' them out for their secondary education. Classification wasn't a major purpose in Victorian times – the working-class children who were taught in the state elementary schools were not expected to go on to any form of secondary education. However, in the first three-quarters of the twentieth century, primary teachers played a major part in identifying children of different abilities and preparing them for different forms of secondary education – grammar, secondary modern and, to a far lesser extent, technical education. That classification function still applies in those parts of the country that retain selective schools. Yet I would argue that, currently, a more insidious form of classification influences the practice of many primary teachers as a result of the introduction of national testing and the sorting of children into so-called 'levels'. Too often, children are described as 'level twos', 'level fours', etc., are classified as such and are given a subtly different curriculum, so that these levels begin to define them in ways that narrow their views of themselves and their ability to learn. The government is intending to replace these levels at some point, but still proposes to grade children's attainment in mathematics and English in some way or other. As a primary teacher, you will need to work within the system as it is, but you also have a professional duty to work to change it, if, like me, you feel it works against the interests of children in your care.

Task 1.1.4 The purposes of primary teaching

In pairs, consider the relative importance of the four purposes of primary teaching. Make a list of the kinds of activity teachers engage in related to each of the four purposes. Primary teachers in other countries do not necessarily see their role in these terms (see Alexander, 2000). Should any of these purposes *not* apply, or be given far less emphasis in primary teaching in the United Kingdom? Why?

SUMMARY

The importance of primary teaching

I hope that, by now, you have realised how demanding primary teaching is and how important it is, especially to the children themselves. Philip Jackson reminds us that children spend around 7,000 hours in primary school, spread over 6 or 7 years of their young lives. There is no other activity that occupies as much of the child's time as that involved in attending school.

> Apart from the bedroom there is no single enclosure in which he spends a longer time than he does in the classroom. During his primary school years he is a more familiar sight to his teacher than to his father, and possibly even his mother.
>
> (Jackson, 1968: 5)

As a child's teacher, you are an incredibly (and frighteningly!) significant person: your teaching will help shape attitudes to learning at a most sensitive period in children's development. After all:

> These seven years are among the most vivid of our existence. Every day is full of new experiences; the relatively static seems permanent; time seems to last much longer; *events and individuals leave deeper impressions and more lasting memories than later in life.* Without discussing what are the happiest years, we may at least agree that every stage of life should be lived for its own sake as happily and fully as possible. *We must above all respect this right on behalf of children, whose happiness is a good deal at the mercy of circumstances and people beyond their control.*
>
> (Scottish Education Department, 1946: 5; my italics)

To return to my acrostic, becoming a primary school teacher is demanding, difficult and exhausting and at times can be a fazing experience. But it is also immensely rewarding, incredibly fascinating, never for a moment boring (unless you make it so!), often very humorous and, because never-ending, always unfini . . .

Hopefully, you are up for it?

 ## ANNOTATED FURTHER READING

Alexander, R. (2000) *Culture and Pedagogy: International Comparisons in Primary Education*, Oxford: Blackwell. A fascinating analysis of primary teaching as practised in France, Russia, India, the United States and England.

Alexander, R. (2010) *Children, Their World, Their Education*, London: Routledge.
> The most recent and authoritative review of English (not UK) primary education – full of valuable and fascinating information and ideas, though less good at getting 'inside' what it is to be a primary teacher.

Campbell, R.J. and Neill, S. (1994) *Primary Teachers at Work*, London: Routledge.
> Though almost two decades old, its findings provide plenty of food for thought as to the nature of the demands, responsibilities and work of English infant and junior teachers.

Cremin, T. (2009) 'Creative teachers, creative teaching', in A. Wilson (ed.) *Creativity in Primary Education*, 2nd edn, Exeter: Learning Matters, pp. 36–46.
> This explores the characteristics and personal qualities of creative teachers and creative primary teaching.

Jackson, P. (1968) *Life in Classrooms*, New York: Holt, Rinehart and Winston.
> This offers a complementary but rather different characterisation of teaching primary-aged children from that offered in this unit. Forty years on, it is still the most evocative description of life as lived in classrooms.

Nias, J. (1989) *Primary Teachers Talking: A Study of Teaching at Work*, London: Routledge.
> This gets 'under the skin' of being a primary teacher and is based on in-depth interviews carried out over a number of years.

FURTHER READING TO SUPPORT M-LEVEL STUDY

Nias, J. (1997) 'Would schools improve if teachers cared less?', *Education 3-13*, 25(3): 11–22.
> This is a challenging, critical perspective on the role of education and care in the education of primary-aged children.

Richards, C. (2011) 'What Could Be – for contemporary policy and practice: challenges posed by the work of Edmond Holmes', *Forum* 53(3): 451–61.
> This discusses critically the role of the primary school teacher – from both a contemporary perspective and from a historical one. It illustrates some of the perennial issues facing primary education.

REFERENCES

Alexander, R. (2000) *Culture and Pedagogy: International Comparisons in Primary Education*, Oxford: Blackwell.

Alexander, R. (2010) *Children, Their World, Their Education*, London: Routledge.

Campbell, R.J. and Neill, S. (1994) *Primary Teachers at Work*, London: Routledge.

Department for Education and Skills (DfES) and Teacher Training Agency (TTA) (2002) *Qualifying to Teach: Professional Standards for Qualified Teacher Status and Requirements for Initial Teacher Training*, London: DfES/TTA.

Eisner, E. (1979) *The Educational Imagination*, New York: Collier-Macmillan.

Jackson, P. (1968) *Life in Classrooms*, New York: Holt, Rinehart and Winston.

Marland, M. (1975) *The Craft of the Classroom*, London: Heinemann Educational.

Muijs, D. and Reynolds, D. (2001) *Effective Teaching: Evidence and Practice*, London: Paul Chapman.

Musgrove, F. and Taylor, P. (1969) *Society and the Teacher's Role*, London: Routledge and Kegan Paul.

Nias, J. (1997) 'Would schools improve if teachers cared less?', *Education 3-13*, 25(3): 11-22.

Scottish Education Department (1946) *Primary Education*, Edinburgh: His Majesty's Stationery Office.

Shulman, L. (1987) 'Knowledge and teaching: foundations of the new reforms', *Harvard Educational Review*, 57: 1-22.

PROFESSIONALISM AND TRAINEE TEACHERS

Denis Hayes

INTRODUCTION

You are probably reading *Learning to Teach in the Primary School* – and this unit in particular – because you are numbered among those who have a burning desire to become a teacher and use your knowledge, skills and personality to motivate children and young people. In your quest to teach, you are aspiring to become an *excellent* teacher, not an average one.

To achieve this worthwhile aim, you will need to understand how, as a trainee teacher, you can develop the qualities and expertise needed to attain the prescribed teaching standards (Department for Education, 2012) and become a fully fledged professional. In the light of these requirements, this unit will principally help you to: (a) explore ways to improve your classroom practice; (b) develop appropriate relationships with adults and children in school; and (c) foster your professional development.

To assist you in understanding and negotiating these fundamental roles, you are first given a set of eight 'expectations' upon which your progress as a teacher can be built. Second, you are encouraged to look beyond the walls of the classroom and accommodate a range of wider professional responsibilities that relate to the well-being of pupils, colleagues and parents. Your ability to incorporate the expectations and extended professional responsibilities into your work will determine whether you meet the standards required of trainee teachers, and so you are advised to read this unit diligently.

OBJECTIVES

By the end of this unit, you should be able to:

- understand the requirements for becoming a member of the teaching profession;
- acknowledge the principles underpinning professional life and their implications for teaching;
- recognise the nature and demands of teachers' extended responsibilities as staff members.

BACKGROUND

Terminology

Over recent years, the use of the term 'professional' has expanded to embrace almost any job requiring specialist skill, such that everyone, from footballers to plumbers to electricians to chefs, is included. This plethora of references to professional and professionalism raises the issue of what is distinctive about teaching such that teachers should not only be referred to as professionals but also as members of *a profession*. In so doing, it is helpful to distinguish between someone acting professionally – that is, someone who competently uses his or her technical skills – and a person who is *in a profession* – that is, someone who has not only gained accredited qualifications that demonstrate practical competence, but also possesses behavioural attributes, insights and what might be termed 'educated intuition' in applying theory to the task of teaching, and responding to the particular needs of the pupils concerned.

During the middle years of the twentieth century, educators fought hard for teaching to be accepted as a profession in much the same way as then applied to law and medicine. Over time, there were improvements in training, conditions of employment and salary, which were eventually deemed sufficiently rigorous for teaching to merit the status of a profession. It is now assumed that you, as a trainee teacher, will not only show a keen awareness of the need to adopt a professional attitude towards your work, but will also strive to qualify as a member of the teaching profession through proficiency in: (a) classroom practice, (b) relating to colleagues and parents, and (c) extending your knowledge and expertise by means of continuous study.

Professional practice

Research was commissioned by the General Teaching Council for England to discover how teachers identify their strengths and weaknesses, and to whom they turn for support and advice (Poet *et al.*, 2010a, 2010b). Findings from the report, *How Teachers Approach Practice Improvement*, included the predictable fact that nearly all teachers were keen to improve their professional practice, specifically with respect to:

- doing the best job they can and meeting the needs of all the pupils;
- learning about effective ways of presenting information to children;
- improving their subject knowledge;
- utilising reflection and peer support in developing their practice;
- being observed and receiving constructive feedback;
- collaborating with colleagues and also doing independent research;
- accessing formal development through courses that address school-identified development needs;
- engaging with development activities that have a positive impact on self, school and pupils;
- using colleagues as a source of first-hand support and inspiration.

It was also noted in the report that: (a) the ethos and management style of senior staff have an impact on the type and level of support available to teachers; (b) the professional standards are not regularly used to monitor progress; (c) lack of time is the biggest barrier to teachers. Other factors included levels of funding, the culture of the school (e.g. whether positive and aspirational, or generally depressed) and the attitudes of colleagues (e.g. whether supportive and collegial, or self-centred).

One of the least contentious report findings was that teachers' energy levels impacted on their motivation to improve classroom practice. An exhausting schedule led to a 'treading water' approach, in which teachers were kept at full stretch in dealing with their regular commitments, let alone enhancing their expertise through course attendance, further study and the like. On the basis of the above findings, the implications for your own work as a trainee teacher are as follows.

1   Make up your mind to adopt a positive approach during your school placement and avoid complaining.
2   Be an excellent time manager; always do the essential things first – lesson planning, assessing pupil progress and keeping records.
3   Learn to pace yourself in your work and increase your effectiveness through greater efficiency.
4   Seek to be friendly, co-operative, reliable and willing to learn from colleagues.

In 2011, the Department for Education (DfE) launched a national scheme to support professional development, known as the Professional Development (PD) Scholarship Scheme, to create expectations within the sector about the importance of scholarship throughout a teacher's career, and share learning, knowledge and expertise across the school system.

Teachers' Standards

The *Teachers' Standards* (Department for Education, 2012), henceforth referred to as *the standards*, requires that all trainee teachers must satisfy certain criteria before gaining qualified teacher status (QTS), though certain exemptions are permitted for teachers who work in independent schools and in academy schools. The remainder of this unit focuses on the principles underpinning effective practice and ways in which your professionalism can be expressed through extending your role beyond the classroom. Note that the process and practicalities of ongoing study and ways of furthering your knowledge will be referred to only briefly, but see Expectation 5 under 'Principles underpinning the standards', overleaf.

Task 1.2.1 Professional characteristics

Order the following list of your professional characteristics with the strongest first.

(a)   Your study and work ethic.
(b)   Your relationships with others: pupils, colleagues and parents.
(c)   Your diligence in lesson preparation, teaching and assessment.
(d)   Your attention to detail in recording pupil progress.
(e)   Your willingness to learn from others and extend your knowledge.
(f)   Your self-evaluations of progress.
(g)   Your expectations and determination to succeed.
(h)   Your support for pupils and colleagues.

What factors governed your decisions about the list order? Suggest ways in which you can actively demonstrate a more professional approach in each of the areas.

In September 2013, the government created more rigorous entry tests for people wanting to become teachers in a bid to raise the quality and standing of the profession. The tests include mathematical problems, to be solved without the help of calculators, and longer written exercises, rather than straightforward word identification. Candidates are also tested on spelling, grammar and punctuation.

There are questions in verbal, numerical and abstract reasoning, which take the form of on-screen and verbal tests to assess a candidate's ability to solve problems, recognise patterns, think laterally, evaluate and analyse issues. A candidate must pass the tests before commencing a training course.

PRINCIPLES UNDERPINNING THE STANDARDS

The list of standards is prefaced with a preamble from which eight broad principles can be elicited regarding a teacher's attitude, knowledge and skill level. To gain QTS, you must demonstrate the following attributes:

1   Make the pupils' education your top concern.
2   Be accountable for achieving the highest possible standards in work and conduct.
3   Act with honesty and integrity.
4   Possess strong subject knowledge.
5   Keep your knowledge and skills up to date.
6   Be self-critical.
7   Forge positive professional relationships.
8   Work with parents in the best interest of pupils.

The above list presents a challenging set of requirements and highlights the wide-ranging demands made of anyone aiming to be a member of the teaching profession. They do not show you how to *achieve* these worthy aims; instead, they offer a view of what is needed to act professionally through possessing the knowledge and technical skills to teach effectively, and the necessary character attributes, social skills and relational competence to facilitate your work as a teacher. The eight expectations are designed to provide the foundation stones of education principles and agreed teaching aims upon which your progress as a teacher can be built. The standards are not intended to be an abstract, blanket set of regulations. They are written as a guide for individuals like you, who have a yearning to teach and want to become the very best practitioners. Each of the eight points is explored below.

Expectation 1: to make the pupils' education your top concern

No doubt you are pleased to see that pupils' education is at the top of the list, though determining what constitutes a good education is far from easy. In Hayes (2012: 95-6), I offer the following description:

> Fully educated children are not just the ones who pass examinations and gain top marks but also those who develop the skills, knowledge and abilities to foster their physical, social, mental and emotional wellbeing in all aspects of life, and help others to do the same. Such pupils have a desire to achieve their full academic potential but also a growing awareness of their responsibilities as significant members of a community.

Although your principal role is to impart knowledge and assist children to gain understanding, you must always be conscious of the fact that you have influence that extends beyond academic goals and measurable scores. True professionals concern themselves as much with the individual as with the person's achievement.

Expectation 2: to achieve the highest possible standards in work and conduct

Notice the phrase 'highest *possible* standards'. There are numerous factors affecting pupil achievement, some of which (e.g. temperament, background, personality) will be beyond your immediate control to change. The impact of these external factors is significant in affecting pupils' success, though politicians and policymakers sometimes dismiss them as excuses for low expectations, rather than reasons for explaining under-achievement. In reality, children from unsettled backgrounds or with a poor attitude to school, who are not easily managed or motivated to learn, provide teachers with the severest challenge. Nevertheless, as an aspiring professional, you have to find strategies to cope with a wide spectrum of pupil abilities, attitudes and behaviour, which together constitute both the thrill and the demand of being a teacher. Inclusion of the word 'accountable' in the above statement is significant, for, although teaching offers a great deal of pleasure and fulfilment, it is, after all, a service to the community for which teachers are paid. If we fall short of expectations, it is not unreasonable for those with a vested interest in children's education to ask searching questions of us. Once you are in the classroom, you share the accountability load with the other staff, however inexperienced or inadequate you might feel.

Expectation 3: to act with honesty and integrity

Honesty and integrity as a teacher involve more than telling the truth. They consist of twelve elements: (1) dealing with situations in a fair and informed manner; (2) showing impartiality, while exploring the rights and wrongs of a circumstance; (3) demonstrating concern for the welfare of children and adults with whom you have contact; (4) being a decent and reliable person; (5) sparing no effort in seeking resolution of a problem; (6) being someone of your word; (7) offering encouragement to others; (8) evaluating fairly your progress as a teacher; (9) being transparent yet wise about disclosing your feelings and thoughts; (10) giving yourself credit for doing well, while acknowledging areas requiring development; (11) being generous in word and deed; and (12) avoiding being judgemental or sceptical. In summary, to be the kind of person and colleague that *you* would like to work alongside! In a world riddled with selfishness, your integrity involves more than behaving admirably. By setting a good example, you can help to transform attitudes, inspire others and – to use a popular but apt sentiment – make the world a better place.

Expectation 4: to have strong subject knowledge

The issue of subject knowledge for a primary teacher is more complicated than for a secondary colleague, who normally has a limited range of subjects to teach, howbeit with higher intellectual demands. At one time, primary teachers asserted that they taught children, not subjects! However, the situation has changed markedly over recent years, and every primary teacher, including those working with early years pupils, is now expected to have a good grasp of each curriculum subject, together with an in-depth understanding of language (especially reading techniques), mathematics and ICT.

Your subject knowledge must develop in four ways. First, through improving the quality of your factual knowledge, such as mastering historical data and multiplication facts ('times tables'). Second, having knowledge of where and how to access facts through a variety of media (books, Internet, journals, and so forth). Third, possessing teaching and learning strategies by which children can gain knowledge and grasp the related concepts (e.g. through collaborative discussion). Finally, having knowledge of specific techniques to facilitate learning (e.g. the use of phonics for reading, or problem-solving in science and mathematics). It is important to acknowledge that, however well informed you may be, there will always be weaker areas of your knowledge that require dedicated study and improvement. In addition, some children have a surprising depth of knowledge about a subject and should be encouraged to contribute what they know (e.g. by use of 'be the expert' sessions in which a child shares with classmates information and experiences relating to an area of interest).

Expectation 5: to keep knowledge and skills up to date

An important aspect of being a member of a profession is a willingness to study and enhance your existing knowledge and learn about ways to enhance your skills that relate to: (a) classroom practice, (b) relationships with pupils and colleagues, (c) communicating information effectively, (d) making informed decisions about priorities in learning, and (e) good time management. As a trainee teacher, you will probably have more than enough to think about in completing the present course, let alone considering further study, and yet, as someone who aspires to be a member of the teaching profession, you must develop an instinct to seek out fresh knowledge, ideas and ways to enhance your effectiveness. You are well advised to adopt a 'sponge mentality', in which you are ready and willing to soak up and evaluate every scrap of information and advice that is available. For instance:

1 Glance through regularly, and make notes from, a mainstream education publication.
2 Listen to, observe and learn from colleagues.
3 Ask questions about specific aspects of classroom practice that you observe.
4 Take every opportunity to work alongside a staff member with specialist teaching skills.
5 Consider how the new knowledge you have gained through steps 1–4 above might affect your classroom practice.

The final point is particularly significant, as pursuits of the kind listed above are of limited worth if they do not translate into improved teaching, so spend time exploring the links between theory ('explaining why') and practice ('showing how').

Expectation 6: to be self-critical

Being self-critical is not the same as finding fault or being gloomily introspective, and must not be confused with damaging and negative *criticism*. Unless you have already been voted teacher of the year, there will always be areas of your practice and relationships that need to be adjusted, enhanced and improved. Think back to the best teachers you had when you were at school. Although you were unaware of the fact, it is almost certain that their success was due to the habit they cultivated of regularly examining and evaluating every aspect of their work as a teacher, to gauge what was going well and where subtle improvements needed to be made. Years of experience in the job count for a lot, but the time must be spent productively in gaining knowledge and skills that contribute to effective practice. The length of time that you spend in front of a class is important, but does not guarantee advancement, so make it your aim to introduce small improvements to your classroom practice at every opportunity by: (a) reflecting upon what you do, as you do it; (b) reflecting upon what you have done, after you do it; and (c) drawing from the knowledge and experience of others to guide your decisions about your future actions.

Qualifying as a teacher is not an end point in itself; rather, it is the first major step on the path to becoming a top professional. Some qualified teachers seem happy to amble along well-trodden paths and never have the joy of experiencing new ways of working. Their classroom practice is adequate but bland, because they lack the spark and creativity to inspire children to achieve their best. You will not wish to join their ranks!

Finally, remember that being self-critical is also an opportunity to celebrate your progress and competence. Give yourself credit for what you are doing. It takes courage and tenacity to be a teacher, so avoid focusing on your shortcomings at the expense of celebrating your victories.

Expectation 7: to forge positive professional relationships

A generation ago, it was possible to separate yourself from the rest of the staff, emerging briefly from your room during break times and hurrying off home at the earliest opportunity when school ended. In reality, such teachers were few and far between, but isolation was an option for those who chose it. Today, such behaviour would rightly be considered unprofessional and even subject to disciplinary procedures. As a trainee teacher, the majority of your time is spent learning how to manage and teach a class of lively children, complete paperwork and hand in work to your tutor before the deadline. However, as in every profession, the way in which you relate to pupils, parents, support staff and colleagues is vitally important and used as an 'unofficial' indicator of your suitability for teaching.

As a student teacher, it is accepted by staff and tutors that you are still learning 'on the job', and that mistakes are an inevitable part of your professional development. Nevertheless, it is also assumed that every trainee teacher will be courteous, pleasant, receptive and co-operative when relating to others. Despite the caricatures of grumpy lawyers, pompous doctors, hard-nosed detectives and arrogant teachers that appear in the media, the truth is that few such people exist, and those that are so inclined are likely to be unhappy and inept. As a successful professional, you need to be efficient and effective, but not at the expense of personal relationships, for the simple reason that you must work as part of a unit if the corporate endeavour is to be achieved. The very best schools are characterised by closely knit team membership, a mutually supportive climate and active collaboration across the whole staff. It takes time to stand and listen to an anxious colleague's woes or make an effort to be especially helpful to an anxious parent or laugh at the caretaker's latest funny story when there are more pressing needs. In doing so, however, you are not only responding to situations positively but also demonstrating that you value the person concerned. You might not have a deep interest in seeing yet another picture of the teaching assistant's grandchild, hearing the 6-year-old's description of her birthday party, chatting to mums in the playground after school about reading books or sitting in the staffroom to celebrate a birthday – but such involvement is all part of building professional relationships for mutual benefit. Bear in mind, too, that the most effective teachers are nearly always the most likeable and approachable, so that time spent on being person-centred, receptive and fostering a good rapport with everyone invariably reaps its rewards.

Expectation 8: to work with parents in the best interest of pupils

The concept of working with parents is hardly a new idea but has been given fresh impetus in that they now have an entitlement to receive detailed and relevant information about their children's progress. Additionally, head teachers are obliged to consult parents on a variety of school-based decisions, and parents are strongly represented on governing bodies. During inspections, the visiting inspectors take the views of parents seriously, and a summary of their comments is included in the final report.

In your endeavour to become a top teacher, you must leave no stone unturned to ensure that every child enjoys learning. In doing so, you need to provide relevant teaching and associated pupil activities during the lesson, but also to look for ways in which learning can be developed and enhanced beyond the timetabled lessons. One of the best ways to accomplish this last aim is to involve parents in the learning process. For example:

1 setting homework for pupils towards which parents can contribute, should they wish to do so;
2 talking informally to parents about their children's work and areas for development;
3 inviting parents to help in the classroom or to assist with outdoor pursuits, as advised by the regular teacher;
4 discussing pupil progress in the formal setting of a parents' evening in conjunction with the regular teacher.

The younger the children, the more likely that the informal contacts noted in point (2) will predominate during the time that parents collect their children, though you should always be cautious about sharing confidential information about a child in public places. Although the regular teacher will normally take responsibility for (3) and (4), you should be aware of the processes and procedures involved, and be willing to contribute when invited to do so. Naturally, you should never disclose information about a child to anyone other than the parent.

Task 1.2.2 Present achievements

Using the eight major headings listed earlier, rate your present achievement in each area using one of four descriptions: (a) doing well, (b) broadly on track, (c) tending to struggle, or (d) short of experience.

- What evidence do you possess to justify your selections? Are they based on your instinct or on feedback from a tutor or colleague?
- Write down one practical action that would specifically strengthen or improve your position in each area.
- Repeat the rating exercise in a week's time and evaluate the effectiveness of your actions.

Meijer *et al.* (2011) suggest that all inexperienced teachers experienced highs, lows and transformative moments. However, it was during times of crisis that they were forced to re-affirm their commitment to teaching and, in most cases, regain their motivation for the job. During such times, support from mentors and colleagues can make the difference between despair and a determination to continue. A willingness to persevere when challenges arise requires courage and determination, but seeking advice and acting on it are prerequisites for progress.

WIDER ('EXTENDED') PROFESSIONAL RESPONSIBILITIES

A glance at the eight points explored above that form the bedrock of true professionalism indicates that there is more to being a teacher than the act of teaching. It is certainly true that no one devoid of classroom expertise will be given entry to the profession, but it is also the case that, even as a trainee, you are a temporary member of the staff team and expected to play your part in fostering harmony and co-operation. You may not *feel* as if you are a member. You may not *think* that you are a member. One or two of the existing staff might not be enthusiastic about welcoming you as a member. Nevertheless, you *are* a staff member, howbeit a junior one, and must behave accordingly.

Standards for extended professional responsibilities

The standards refer to five specific aspects of your wider professional responsibilities (WPRs) of significance, as follows:

1 Make a positive contribution to the wider life and ethos of the school.
2 Develop effective professional relationships with colleagues, knowing how and when to draw on advice and specialist support. See also Expectation 7, page 27.
3 Deploy support staff effectively.
4 Take responsibility for improving teaching through appropriate professional development, and responding positively to advice and feedback from colleagues.
5 Communicate effectively with parents with regard to pupils' achievements and their well-being. See also Expectation 8, page 27.

It is fair to say that even the most experienced teachers sometimes find these sorts of wider responsibility to be time consuming and requiring a great deal of effort and perseverance, so don't feel discouraged if the list looks daunting. There are a number of key points to note for each of the five standards that will assist you in meeting them.

WPR 1: make a positive contribution to the wider life and ethos of the school

Trainee teachers normally spend time in a variety of school settings, each with its unique characteristics and ways of doing things. It takes time to adjust to the new environment, but, as you do so, it is essential to play your full part in contributing to every aspect of school life. In particular, take note of the following:

1 Be a bright and positive presence around school. In particular, use good eye contact, smile and sound as naturally cheerful as possible.
2 Look for positive features rather than focusing on negative ones. Be ready to encourage others and enthuse about situations rather than look for faults.
3 Make an effort to acknowledge anyone you meet in school. A breezy, courteous greeting is invariably beneficial and will impress visitors.
4 Be willing to work hard and contribute your knowledge, insights and skill to enhance the children's education and support your colleagues. Always be ready to lend a hand with basic tasks, but keep in mind that you are training to be a teacher, not to be an assistant.
5 As soon as you have got your regular teaching commitments under control, volunteer to help with extra-curricular activities. The host teachers will be impressed by your willingness to 'get stuck in', but beware lest your classwork suffers because you spend too much time on extra-curricular tasks.

Even if you are only in the school for a few days or weeks, you are still one of its representatives, so make every effort to be punctual, neatly dressed, conscientious and creative. Keep your file in order, tidy up any mess you make and do everything you can to aid the smooth running of the classroom. Be aware that you are always in the public eye – inside the school, in the playground and out in the street – so maintain a high standard of speech and behaviour at all times.

WPR 2: develop effective professional relationships with colleagues, knowing how and when to draw on advice and specialist support

The use of the word 'professional' in the title highlights the fact that, even if you do not like a colleague or do not approve of her or his attitude or teaching approach, the task of providing a good education for children must not be adversely affected. In other words, personality or philosophical differences between staff members cannot be allowed to hinder the educative process, which must always be subject to the maxim, 'best for pupils' rather than 'best for teachers'.

The reality of school life is that, in such an intimate environment, there is little room for harmful tensions, disagreements or conflicts between adults that undermine morale. When head teachers and governors make staff appointments, they are highly sensitive as to whether the newly appointed person will 'fit in' with the existing staff; there are similar hopes for trainees on placement. Although you are not expected to be a helpless onlooker during your time in school, it is wise to make every effort to accommodate the existing norms and ways of doing things, rather than becoming unnecessarily assertive and sceptical. First and foremost, it is the regular teacher and tutor whom you have to satisfy; however, other members of staff will also be watching and noting your actions, and so it pays to be alert.

Most teachers enjoy offering advice and expertise to trainees, but, in seeking their assistance, bear in mind two factors. First, teachers are willing to help, but are also extremely busy, so don't be upset if they seem a little abrupt on occasions; it is probably that their minds are grappling with a dozen other things at that moment. Second, be cautious about asking questions of the 'what should I do?' kind, unless a procedural matter is involved. If, for whatever reason, you decide to ignore or modify the advice, the colleague concerned will probably wonder why you bothered to ask in the first place and be less inclined to offer help on future occasions. By contrast, there is an expectation that you will use every opportunity to learn from experienced colleagues about aspects of the job, including class management, ways to teach different subject areas, and completing paperwork. Keep a record of what you learn from others in a file called 'professional development' and, as ever, note likely implications for classroom practice.

WPR 3: deploy support staff effectively

The number and variety of assistants have grown significantly, and, in early years settings, it is now quite common to see several adults (including parents) involved in the children's education. Teaching assistants (TAs) are normally female, self-motivated and well-educated people. About 10 per cent of TAs in school are qualified teachers who, for one reason or another, decided not to teach. In primary settings, it is likely that a percentage of assistants will be parents of children in the school. There are usually more TAs working with younger pupils per class than with older ones, unless individuals have specific educational needs that require regular adult support. Assistants are often 'shared' between classes, so that you cannot assume that they will be available. Higher-level teaching assistants (HLTAs) have greater responsibility for aspects of learning; for example, they may have specialist knowledge in a subject area or be allowed to plan and teach a group of pupils.

It is not easy for a newcomer to assume responsibility for managing the work of assistants, as patterns of working will already be in place when you join the school, and so it pays to become familiar with them before rushing in with your own ideas. In practice, it is advisable to adopt a 'please support me in what I'm doing' attitude to assistants, rather than a strongly directive approach. For example, imagine that you are establishing three groups in mathematics and want the TA to supervise the most able group, while you supervise the other two groups. In such a situation, it is better to say something like, 'Are you happy to work with group one?', rather than, 'I want you to work with group one'. To assist your relationship with the TA, ensure the following:

1   The TA is clear about your expectations.
     The assistant will not only want to know what pupils are supposed to do, but also have a reasonable idea about what is commonly referred to as 'learning outcomes': that is, what you intend the children should learn as a result of your teaching. (Note: learning *intentions* will almost

always differ from the actual learning *outcomes*.) If you want the assistant to record anything about, for example, general lack of understanding or an individual's speed of working or application to task, warn her beforehand, so that, when you consult her after the lesson, she is in a position to give an informed answer.

2   The TA knows whether she is teaching or supervising.
This point is significant, as it is unreasonable to expect an assistant to teach something without warning and the chance to prepare thoroughly. Although most assistants are extremely adaptable, others will resent being asked to do what they consider to be the teacher's job, especially if they then struggle to cope. The mantra is: 'Never assume, always inform'.

3   The task accommodates early finishers.
It is not always possible to precisely 'match' the task with the time available, and pupils soon get restless if they are underoccupied, and so it is worth thinking through what happens if there is time to spare at the conclusion of an activity. Having a simple extension task will save the TA having to find something bland to occupy the children or interrupting you to ask what should be done.

A happy and satisfied TA is an asset for hard-pressed teachers, so make every effort to express your appreciation, invite her opinion, give her ample opportunity to use her skills and enhance her expertise. Give her the respect she deserves and offer your quiet thanks for her efforts on the children's behalf.

Task 1.2.3 Relating to adults in school

Keep a mental note of the adults with whom you communicate during the school day and categorise your response to each one from the following list.

1 a nodding encounter;
2 exchanging a few words;
3 an extended conversation.

Over the next few weeks, make an effort to improve the depth and quality of your communication by moving more of response (1) into (2), and more of response (2) into (3). Monitor how attitudes and relationships develop as a result.

WPR 4: take responsibility for improving teaching through appropriate professional development, responding to advice and feedback from colleagues

Simply spending time in the classroom does not ensure that you will make strong progress and become a good teacher. The best teachers never stop learning and are always hungry for information and ideas that will enhance their work. Part of your role as a trainee teacher is to observe more experienced teachers but also to *understand* what is happening. After several years in the classroom, most teachers do things so instinctively that they rarely have the time or inclination to stop and analyse why they act and behave as they do. Rather, they judge the strength of their teaching in terms of the quality of pupil behaviour and measurable progress. Teachers gradually adjust their teaching approach with respect to 'what works' and 'what does not work', rather than what is promoted by policymakers or educationists.

However, as the novice, you have the challenging and exciting task of not only observing what more experienced teachers do, but also extracting the principles that guide their actions. For example, you observe a teacher speaking sternly to a boy who is daydreaming, with the result that he concentrates on his work again. On the basis of the observation, you might conclude that the best strategy for ensuring on-task behaviour is to speak sternly to the individual concerned. However, an analysis of the situation needs to take account of questions such as:

- Did the teacher use a stern voice because 'softer' methods had failed?
- How long did the pupil concentrate on his work after the rebuke?
- Did the boy's quality of work improve after being told off?
- Was the stern voice a desperate measure or a strategic one?

Merely replicating the teacher's methods in the hope that they will 'work for you' is unlikely to prove satisfactory, unless you are clear about the purpose underpinning the strategies you employ, which you can shape to suit your style of teaching over time. In short, be a professional learner and implementer, and not a mimic.

Eady (2011) refers to your *personal professional development* and recommends that you actively engage in further study to structure your own learning, and view it as part of the everyday role of teaching and reflecting. Consequently, you need to step back from the situation, evaluate your strengths and areas for development, and modify your teaching approach, after viewing the circumstances and taking account of what others have advised. This professional approach, though challenging, is preferable to one in which you simply plan more of the same, work harder and only succeed in compounding the same errors.

WPR 5: communicate effectively with parents with regard to pupils' achievements and well-being

We noted earlier that parents are in a unique position to assist their children in learning, though you will need to accept that a small percentage of them grumble that it is the teacher's job to teach, not theirs. When communicating with parents, always adhere to the following practices:

1   Be sensitive to the fact that the pupil's welfare and educational progress is the parent's number one concern.
2   Be as natural and friendly as possible, smile a lot and maintain gentle eye contact.
3   Stay bright and cheerful in your speech and conduct, but avoid exuberance or behaviour that might be perceived as immature.
4   Stress the pupil's positive attributes and achievements more than the weaker areas.
5   Avoid giving the impression that you are 'telling tales' about the child to the parent.
6   In the rare event of reporting a pupil's poor behaviour to the parent, have a suggested remedy available and an explanation as to why you failed to notify the parent earlier.
7   Avoid being drawn into an extended discussion about trivial issues, while being alert to the fact that what is inconsequential to you may be important to the parent.
8   Never promise something that you cannot possibly deliver.
9   Refer complex or controversial issues to the regular teacher.
10 End a conversation positively and encouragingly.

Once parents perceive that you are someone of significance, you become a legitimate target for their questions, suggestions and, occasionally, their complaints. Although you need to maintain openness with parents, be aware that your words will be seized upon and discussed at length outside the classroom. You may be shocked to know how much you will be quoted by parents and pupils, and so it pays to exercise discretion and wisdom in expressing your opinion. On the whole, it is better to stick to facts ('pupil performance') and potential, than to explore personality, other than making commending comments (e.g. 'We enjoy Sam's great sense of humour'). Remember, too, that parents talk at length to one another, so do not imagine that a supposedly confidential discussion will remain so.

Finally, bear in mind that the regular teacher is striving to foster a positive relationship with parents, so maintaining a close liaison with them is essential. Always inform the host teacher about any significant conversations you have had and bear in mind that the incumbent teacher has to work with parents long after you have left the school.

SUMMARY

In this unit, you have been encouraged to think carefully about the many demands made of trainees before they can become a qualified teacher and a member of the teaching profession. Although successive governments have emphasised achieving academic results with pupils as the single most important factor in determining the level of professionalism, membership of a profession places responsibilities on your shoulders that go beyond the core ability of teaching competence. It is possible to be proficient as a classroom teacher, yet fail to recognise your role with respect to both children's and adults' welfare, self-worth and motivation. Make sure that you not only help children to achieve the best they can do academically, but also make their time with you memorable and inspirational. In short, try to become the sort of trainee teacher that colleagues and pupils will be sorry to see leave when you move on.

 ## ANNOTATED FURTHER READING

Ellis, G., Morgan, N.S. and Reid, K. (2013) *Using Values-Based Education to Promote Positive Learning*, London: Routledge.

By using case studies in real school settings, the authors show how their Family Values Scheme has been successfully put into practice. The book links with social and emotional aspects of learning (SEAL) and demonstrates how schools and organisations can create effective partnerships with families and the community in an exciting and sustainable way.

Hayes, D. (2012) *Foundations of Primary Teaching*, 5th edn, London: David Fulton.

The book provides a comprehensive introduction to all aspects of primary teaching, blending theory and practice to foster effective pedagogy and stimulate thinking. *Foundations of Primary Teaching* is principally aimed at trainee and newly qualified teachers who aspire to become effective practitioners and highly skilled professionals.

Reardon, D. (2013) *Achieving Early Years Professional Status*, 2nd edn, London: Sage.

The second edition of Reardon's book encompasses the Teaching Agency 2012 new-era Early Years Professional Status (EYPS) standards and provides up-to-date advice and guidance grounded in current reading, research and government policy for people training to achieve EYPS.

FURTHER READING TO SUPPORT M-LEVEL STUDY

Cushman, P. and Cowan, J. (2010) 'Enhancing student self-worth in the primary school learning environment', *Pastoral Care in Education*, 28(2): 81–95.

> The authors stress the importance of teachers gaining an understanding of the inherent uniqueness of their own classrooms and how the dynamics of relationships between themselves and their pupils, and between pupil and pupil, influence self-worth and motivation to learn.

Marcos, J.M., Sanchez, E. and Tilema, H.H. (2011) 'Promoting teacher reflection', *Journal of Education for Teaching*, 37(1): 21–36.

> Marcos *et al.* evaluated a range of studies concerned with teacher reflection and discovered that too many of them were prescriptive and not rooted in classroom practice. The authors conclude that reflective accounts offered as part of teachers' development programmes are ineffective, because there is insufficient guidance about the way in which they might lead to modifications in existing teaching methods.

RELEVANT WEBSITES

Department for Children, Schools and Families: www.gov.uk/government/uploads/system/uploads/attachment_data/file/222236/DCSF-RW076.pdf

> A review of literature concerning beginner teachers' experiences of initial teacher preparation, induction and early professional development.

Early Years Teachers' Standards: www.gov.uk/government/publications/early-years-teachers-standards

> This Department for Education document outlines what standards early years teachers must reach. It also provides statutory assessment guidance.

European Journal of Teacher Education: www.tandfonline.com/doi/abs/10.1080/02619768.2012.662638

> An article concerning trainee teachers and the Code of Conduct and Practice in England.

Trainee Teachers Emerging Concepts of Professionalism: www.escholar.manchester.ac.uk/uk-ac-man-scw:116040

> Paper presented at the International Conference on Learning, 6 July 2010, Hong Kong.

REFERENCES

Department for Education (2012) *Teachers' Standards*, London: Crown Copyright.

Eady, S. (2011) 'Personal professional development' in A. Hansen (ed.) *Primary Professional Studies*, Exeter: Learning Matters.

Hayes, D. (2012) *Advanced Primary Teaching Skills*, London: Routledge.

Meijer, P.C., de Graaf, G. and Meirin, J. (2011) 'Key experiences in student teachers' development', *Teachers and Teaching*, 17(1): 115–29.

Poet, H., Rudd, P. and Kelly, J. (2010a) *Survey of Teachers 2010: Support to Improve Teaching Practice*, London: General Teaching Council for England.

Poet, H., Rudd, P. and Smith, R. (2010b) *How Teachers Approach Practice Improvement*, London: General Teaching Council for England.

MAKING THE MOST OF YOUR PLACEMENTS

Jane Warwick and Mary Anne Wolpert

INTRODUCTION

> The steepest learning curve for a student teacher naturally takes place in the classroom itself.
>
> (Chris, a primary PGCE trainee)

In this unit, we examine how you can capitalise upon the opportunities afforded by your placements in schools as you train to be a teacher. Through day-to-day experience of working with children on school placements, you will gain understanding of how theory and scholarly research are integral to effective teaching. We discuss the importance of being a reflective practitioner who takes responsibility for their learning, and we examine how the dispositions you present, and the relationships you develop on placement, are key factors to the successful outcome of your course. As the quotation from Chris above suggests, school placements provide crucial, yet sometimes challenging, learning experiences in your professional development. We offer vignettes of recent PGCE trainees reflecting on various significant aspects of their school placements and, in the last section of the unit, we return to Chris's reflections on how, with the help of scaffolded school experience throughout the training year, he was able to develop the competencies required of a qualified teacher.

OBJECTIVES

This unit will help you to:

- understand dispositions that will maximise your learning during school placements;
- develop as a reflective practitioner during school placements;
- have a greater understanding of the role of the mentor in your professional development;
- understand the importance of lesson evaluations;
- understand how learning conversations with professional colleagues can inform your practice;
- understand the nature and progression of school placements.

As seen in Unit 1.1, teaching is a highly complex amalgam of judgement, technique and personal qualities. Pollard (2010) argues that what teachers do – the quality of their pedagogy – is of fundamental importance. For Alexander (2009: 28), pedagogy is, 'the why, what and how of teaching. It is the knowledge and skills teachers need in order to make and justify the many decisions that each lesson requires. Pedagogy is the heart of the enterprise'.

Pollard *et al.* (2010) break down the elements of pedagogy into three interconnected key components:

1   *Craft* is seen as the repertoire of teachers' skills, strategies, methods, approaches and practices from which they select and to which they continue to add through a lifetime of professional work.
2   *Science* is seen as teachers' knowledge, understanding of, and engagement in, evaluation, reflection and research, in search of evidence to inform the professional choices and decisions they make.
3   *Art* is seen as teachers' moment-by-moment responses to what is happening in the classroom in ways that are secure, grounded, creative or innovative, as the occasion demands.

Pedagogy, therefore, is the very essence of teachers' professional practice. It is during school placements that an understanding of the practical application of pedagogy – the craft, science and art of teaching – is developed. Let us first consider the importance of developing effective professional learning dispositions while on school placement.

ESTABLISHING EFFECTIVE DISPOSITIONS

In order for you to make sense of and integrate your experience across placements during your course, it will be helpful to understand your own dispositions towards your learning. Hagger *et al.* (2008), in their study of 1-year PGCE trainees, noted that the nature and extent of trainee learning varied considerably. As a result of their research they define five different dimensions that, they

TABLE 1.3.1 Five dimensions according to which the variation among the student teachers' accounts of their learning from experience were analysed

Dimension		Orientation		
Intentionality: the extent to which learning is planned	Deliberative	←	→	Reactive
Frame of reference: the value ascribed to looking beyond their experience in order to make sense of it	Drawing on a range of sources to shape and make sense of experience	←	→	Exclusive reliance on the experience of classroom teaching
Response to feedback: disposition towards receiving feedback and the value attributed to it	Effective use of feedback to further learning	←	→	Tendency to be disabled by critical feedback
Attitude to context: attitude to the positions in which student teachers find themselves and the approaches they take to the school context	Acceptance of the context and ability to capitalise on it	←	→	Tendency to regard the context as constraining
Aspiration: the extent of their aspirations for their own and their pupils' learning	Aspirational as both learners and teachers	←	→	Satisfaction with current level of achievement

Source: Hagger *et al.* (2008: 167)

argue, lead to a better understanding of the range of approaches that trainee teachers take to professional learning (see Table 1.3.1). We argue that having an understanding of these dimensions and their associated orientations will leave you better equipped to become a competent professional learner and teacher.

Hagger *et al.* (2008) argue, first, that the degree of intentionality, the extent to which the learning is planned, is a key issue. One end of the continuum is represented by a 'deliberative' approach to learning, and the other by an approach that relies on a reaction to each experience. Trainees who take the first, proactive approach, actively seek feedback on their teaching or advice from more experienced colleagues and show an 'enthusiasm to experiment with their teaching' (2008: 169). In contrast, trainees with a 'reactive approach' show 'an abdication of responsibility' for their own learning (2008: 168) and have difficulty identifying their future learning needs.

Within the second dimension, 'frame of reference', they found clear differences in the extent to which trainees recognised the value of looking beyond their own experience in order to make sense of it. Trainees with a 'proactive' disposition drew on other sources, such as wider reading of appropriate research findings and discussions with mentors and tutors, whereas those exhibiting a 'reactive' disposition restricted the range of sources from which they drew.

In terms of the third dimension, 'response to feedback', dispositions towards receiving feedback ranged from those trainees who made effective use of feedback and those who had a tendency to be defensive and see the feedback as criticism. We explore this dimension more fully below.

Attitude to the school context is similarly characterised as a continuum ranging from trainees who accepted and capitalised on the position in which they found themselves, and those who regarded the context as a constraint on their progress. We discuss this further in section 4, below.

Finally, Hagger *et al.* (2008) identified an aspirational orientation. At one end were trainees who constantly sought to develop professional practice and the ways in which they, and pupils, learn. At the other end were those who were complacent about both their own level of performance and those of the learners. As Rawling (2003) usefully summarises, teacher professionalism can be described as a continuum ranging from the 'restricted professional' to a 'fully developed professional'. Rather than assuming that experience on placement alone will automatically lead to learning, we would argue that adopting a proactive or deliberative approach will enable you to make the most of your school placements.

Task 1.3.1 Dimensions and their associated orientations

In relation to Table 1.3.1, consider the five dimensions and their associated orientations. Where would you place yourself on each continuum? What evidence do you have to support this judgement? Thinking about your personal context, what actions do you think might be necessary for you to move towards more positive orientations in each of the dimensions?

REFLECTIVE TEACHING

> Teaching is a complex and highly skilled activity which, above all, requires classroom teachers to exercise judgement in deciding how to act.
>
> (Pollard *et al.*, 2008: 5)

Having discussed the range of dispositions trainees present, in this section we argue that while on placement, you need to develop the skills that will enable you to analyse and reflect upon your practice in a systematic way in order to make increasingly appropriate judgements about teaching and learning. Teachers' Standard 4 (Department for Education, 2012) requires teachers to 'reflect systematically on the effectiveness of lessons and approaches to teaching'.

So what does it mean to reflect?

Reflection about an episode in the classroom starts as a series of 'questioning thoughts' (McGregor and Cartwright, 2011: 1), which will help you to understand what, when and how the event happened. These initial thoughts will become more purposeful when you start to analyse why the event happened in the way it did, especially as you become more familiar with the context and the children with whom you are working. Such questions need to be followed by consideration of how you might have behaved or done things differently, and how to improve the situation in future. This is not to suggest that reflection should only happen when things go wrong; the 'habit of reflection' is something that needs to be developed in relation to all aspects of your professional work. Through conscious engagement in the process, your reflections will move from being descriptive to analytical.

Cartwright states that reflection should be a conscious activity: 'Reflection at its most effective comes with growing professional knowledge based on the acquisition of theory and its critical application to practice' (Cartwright, 2011: 56). Drawing on your reading of educational research is essential to help you reflect on, and make sense of, your classroom experiences. According to Pollard *et al.* (2008), there are seven characteristics of reflective teaching (see Figure 1.3.1). Through engaging in reflective action that stems from professional thinking, rather than merely having intuitive reactions to classroom situations, teachers can raise their standards of professional competence. This process, Pollard *et al.* argue, is cyclical in nature, is mediated through collaboration and dialogue with colleagues and arises through evidence-based enquiry. While you are on placements, discussions with your mentor and other more experienced staff will help you to gain confidence in analysing and reflecting on your teaching.

This concept of reflection in and on activity has been extended to include the notion of reflexivity as a specific example of being reflective (Sewell, 2008). Through being reflexive, one shows 'not just the ability to reflect about what has happened and what one has done, but the ability to reflect on the way in which one has reflected' (Moore, 2004: 148). Reflexivity is about acting on your reflections, rather than just suggesting what you could have done or what you might do next. In addition, when you are being reflexive, you take into account the impact and implications that you as a teacher will bring to, and have on, a particular learning situation (Sewell, 2008). This means that you consider how your values, dispositions and possible biases might influence your teaching. While on placement you will need to show evidence of your reflective and reflexive practice through discussion and recordings in more formal documentation; lesson evaluations are one tool for helping you to do this. In the next section, we show examples of trainees' evaluations of their teaching, their identification of the next steps for the children's learning and the ways in which they express implications for their future practice.

Reflective teaching:

1 implies an active concern with aims and consequences, as well as means and technical efficiency

2 is applied in a cyclical or spiraling process

3 requires competence in methods of evidence-based classroom enquiry

4 requires attitudes of open-mindedness, responsibility and whole-heartedness

5 is based on teacher judgement, informed by evidence-based enquiry and insights from other research

6 along with professional learning and personal fulfilment, is enhanced through collaboration and dialogue with colleagues

7 enables teachers creatively to mediate externally developed frameworks for teaching and learning

FIGURE 1.3.1 The seven characteristics of reflective teaching
Source: Pollard *et al.* (2008: 14)

Task 1.3.2 Surprising events

Think about an unexpected or surprising event that happened while you have been in school and replay it in your head. Identify:

- what happened
- when
- how.

Then consider:

- Why did it happen that way?
- How could you have behaved or done things differently?
- What was the impact of your actions on the learning situation?

EVALUATIONS

> The lesson does not end when the bell goes!
> (Hattie, 2012: 145)

Lesson evaluations are a fundamental part of the planning, teaching and assessment cycle; no lesson is complete without one. Evaluations are also key to promoting and demonstrating reflection and, therefore, should help you to understand and develop your practice. They could take the forms of reflective journals or diaries, annotations of individual lesson plans and sequences of lessons, or detailed, 'formal' evaluations of individual lessons. Beginner teachers often have a tendency to focus their reflections on aspects of their own performance in the classroom and, most notably, how they manage behaviour (Furlong and Maynard, 1995). Burn *et al.* (2000) found trainees focused on four categories related to their own practice: 'their actions, their planning, the resources used (materials they had made themselves or existing resources) and their own affective state (usually judgements about their nervousness, but sometimes reflections on their sense of exhaustion)' (2000: 272). We argue that the focus on pupil learning is a crucial element of lesson evaluations.

So, what should be included in a lesson evaluation if it is to focus on both pupil learning and your teaching?

Cohen *et al.* (2010) list a number of elements for teachers to consider in their evaluations:

- what the trainee teacher has learned about the children, which might include their interests, motivations, behaviour, abilities, progress, achievements, self-esteem and independence;
- what the trainee teacher has learned about organisation, resources, behaviour and relationships with colleagues;
- the organisation of the classroom – e.g. layout, seating arrangements;
- the curriculum – content, coverage, differentiation, structure, sequencing and progression;
- the pedagogy – the structuring of activities, the use of experiences, teaching styles, resources, use of display and ICT;
- assessment and monitoring.

However, if you are to have time to teach, it is impossible to reflect upon all these elements after every lesson! If evaluations are going to be effective and formative, i.e. highlight implications for future plans, it is important that they focus on specific elements and avoid repetition and description. They should also link to previous targets set by your mentor, other school colleagues, tutors or yourself. In order to ensure that your lesson evaluations are not too lengthy, or consist primarily of descriptive narrative, it might be helpful to consider the following in structuring your evaluations:

1   the successes of the lesson;
2   the children's learning;
3   your teaching;
4   implications for your future practice.

Let's consider each of these in more detail.

The successes of the lesson

Beginning teachers tend to make sweeping judgements about the successes of the lesson. For example, comments such as 'all the children enjoyed the lesson and understood the learning objective' or 'the lesson went well' are typical. Compare these brief comments with the example below to see how the analysis can be developed to a more appropriate level, and how specific evidence supports the judgements made.

The children's learning

When reflecting upon and analysing children's learning, consider the following questions:

- What did the children actually learn and do?
- To what extent did the children meet the learning objective?
- To what extent did children maintain interest and effort?
- Were there any misconceptions/errors for all children? If so, how will they be addressed?
- Were there any barriers to learning?

TABLE 1.3.2 An example of appropriate comments that highlight successes of a lesson

Question	Comment	Specific evidence
What were the successes of the lesson?	Most of the children really enjoyed the day and took a lot of pride in their work and made a lot of effort. Children were engaged in the lesson and able to work in pairs, threes or independently effectively. For the majority of the day the timings were well planned and children were occupied throughout the day. The lesson was accessible to all pupils with self-differentiation taking place in the creative writing of poetry. Higher ability learners were able to work on their own if they wanted to while less confident pupils could support each other. Children learnt about some important aspects of poetry such as the importance of reading it aloud and listening to it being read. The children carefully presented their work and all wanted to read their poems to the rest of the class, which demonstrated how much they had enjoyed the lesson.	Our mentor was very pleased with the letters and said that she thought it had gone well. She said the children were really enjoying themselves and that we had carefully planned it, although she had a few points which we could adapt and improve upon for another time. The final pieces of work were finished on time and were of a satisfactory or good standard.

> *It is important to get feedback from other professionals*

> *The quality of the children's work forms a key source of evidence*

TABLE 1.3.3 An example of appropriate comments that relate to children's learning

Question	Comment	Specific evidence
What did the children actually learn and do? Were there any unexpected outcomes?	The children learnt to identify characters and their emotions and descriptions. Some learnt to predict what would happen next in the story	The work produced showed a clear understanding of the characters' emotions, and the following lesson for literacy showed that the concept of character descriptions had been learnt through the application in a different context (which was commented on by the teacher). Children also showed they had learnt to predict what would happen next by the discussion I had with a few of them while they were completing the work, and some managed to draw what they thought would happen next.

> *Evidence from a range of sources supports judgements*

In the above examples, the trainees have identified explicitly what the children learnt; this would be linked to the lesson learning objectives and success criteria. The judgement made is based on the children's outcomes, rather than an assumption that may or may not be correct. Names of individual children and groups have been removed.

Your teaching

When you first start, analysing your own teaching tends to be easier than reflecting on the children's learning. However, in order to avoid writing a descriptive narrative that focuses on you, it might be helpful to consider the following questions through the eyes of the children:

- How effective was the lesson/activity plan?
- How effectively did I manage behaviour?
- To what extent was my modelling and explanation clear throughout the lesson?
- Was the timing appropriate?
- Was the use of other adults efficient and did it support the learning?

TABLE 1.3.4 An example of critical comments that relate to an evaluation of the teaching

Question	Comment	Specific evidence
How effective was the lesson/activity plan? Consider: (1) timings; (2) pace	The pace of the lesson went well. The activities were relatively short (10–15 minutes each) to encourage the children to maintain interest whilst still allowing them time to apply their skills. The resources were already prepared before the lesson, and included the use of whiteboards and worksheets. However, I am aware that the children spent a large proportion of time on the carpet. This is partly due to the layout and size of the class. At times I would have preferred the children to return to their class seats, but if this happened I would not have been able to speak to all of them effectively – they would struggle to hear me and it would be more difficult to engage them. Therefore, I will try to keep the activities on the carpet short and snappy to maintain interest and levels of concentration.	Teacher feedback, observations

> *Reflections explicitly state an issue that will have impacted on children's motivation and concentrations levels. Importantly a change of practice has been identified.*

Question	Comment	Specific evidence
To what extent was my modelling and explanation clear throughout the lesson?	I modelled the process of creating words related to the toy helicopter and then after the process of joining words together to create a line of poetry. I used the words 'sneaky', 'sly' and simile 'as slow as a turtle' to show that it didn't have to be a literal description; I wanted the children to tell me what words/images the toy helicopter evoked for them. This worked well; most children came up with interesting words and used comparisons and alliteration. However, the blue group, Jim, Jess and Joseph simply copied the words I wrote down. In the future I need to be clearer about what I expect the children to do, and to ask the children who struggled to understand what this is to repeat to me what they think it is they have to do with an example.	Teacher feedback, pupil response

> *Individual children who either exceeded or did not meet the learning objective are identified which will inform future planning.*

Implications for your future practice

This is at the heart of why you are asked to spend time writing lesson evaluations, i.e. 'so what?'. How are you going to change your practice or develop the work for the children next time? If the lesson evaluation is going to be formative, and therefore have an impact on your future teaching, then it is helpful to structure an action plan that focuses both on children's learning and on your own practice.

Task 1.3.3 Lesson evaluation

Using the suggested four sections of a lesson evaluation outlined above, reflect upon and evaluate a recent lesson you have taught. What evidence have you found to support your analysis? Discuss this with your mentor and identify an aspect of your lesson evaluation that informs your targets for development.

TABLE 1.3.5 An example of the implications for future practice identified after teaching a lesson

Children's learning	The importance of modelling both pushes and pulls before asking the children to do each task. I learnt how time consuming practical investigations are – in future I will allocate longer. I learnt how important it is to keep the focus on science and make recording as simple as possible, therefore, in future I will keep the written aspect to a minimum. I also learnt how valuable the interactive science clips are on the IWB. I will definitely use these in the future.
In my role as a teacher	If children aren't giving me the answers I am hoping for, I will use t hinking time, talk partners and group discussions. I will add this into future plans.
	To have confidence to keep discussing concepts and extend the discussion if the children are still engaged.

It is important to be aware that:

*   Evaluation skills can be learnt; mentors and tutors can support you with this process through discussion.
*   In deconstructing and evaluating your practice, you need to ensure that you are analytical and critical, rather than descriptive.
*   Every lesson evaluation should have a specific focus. This will avoid superficial, subjective judgements that are not supported by evidence or rigorous analysis.
*   Lesson evaluations are more effective if you reflect on the impact of the lesson through the learners' eyes, not just your own.
*   Every lesson should identify a 'so what?' – the implications for your future practice.

WORKING WITHIN THE SCHOOL COMMUNITY

> The way we do it here.
>
> (Nias, 1989)

A key factor in the success of your placement will be the extent to which you feel absorbed into a 'community of practice' (Lave and Wenger, 1991). Some of the difficulties experienced by trainee teachers are in relation to how to conform to the expectations placed on school staff and in understanding the individual characteristics of the different school settings during their course, especially as these may vary considerably. For some trainees this process may be likened to 'walking on eggshells' (Hayes, 1998). This is because, in addition to your responsibilities around planning, preparation and teaching, contextual elements will also affect your emotional well-being and impinge upon your teaching performance. Three elements that are highlighted in Hayes' research (1998: 69) are:

*   fitting in with the school situation;
*   the quality of relationships with teachers;
*   the ability to interpret the micro-political dimensions of school life.

It is important to realise that school placements are not just about developing teaching skills, but also, importantly, about learning to recognise, interpret and respond appropriately to a variety of contextual, personal and social factors (Hayes, 2001).

This process of enculturation (Hayes, 2001) is complex. Calderhead and Shorrock (1997) identify four factors that may help you deconstruct this process:

1   sociocultural – taken for granted practices within the school;
2   personal – trainees image of themselves as teachers and their beliefs about effective teaching;
3   technical – the methods and strategies used;
4   quality of mentoring – by example, coaching, practice-focused discussion, structuring the context, emotional support, devising learning experiences.

As Hayes (1998) argues, it is imperative that you recognise and adjust to different school situations and see this as part of your professional development. As a trainee teacher, you will be supported by your mentor in interpreting and responding appropriately to the individual school culture. Therefore, the relationship you develop with your mentor will influence the success of your placement. We now turn to consideration of the trainee–mentor relationship.

Task 1.3.4 Enculturation in schools

Look at the four factors identified by Calderhead and Shorrock (1997) that may influence you while on placement. Make brief notes about the taken-for-granted practices, methods and strategies used in the school and the processes of mentoring that seem evident in your relationship with your mentor. Reflect on these in relation to your personal beliefs about effective teaching. If possible, discuss these with your tutor to help you identify the specific elements that are unique to your current school. Compare these with previous school settings you have worked in and consider the adjustments you need to make in order to become part of the 'community of practice'.

WORKING WITH SCHOOL MENTORS

> My mentor was one of the most important, if not the most important, element of learning how to teach.
>
> (Charlotte, a primary PGCE trainee)

We use the term mentor to describe the school-based colleague who supports and guides your progress on a daily basis while you are on placement. The 'National Framework for Mentoring and Coaching' (Department of Education and Skills, 2005) defines mentors as experienced colleagues with knowledge of the requirements of the role. The mentoring process should be structured and sustained and will enable you to respond to the changing demands of your placements. Mentors will provide you with access to a range of increasingly self-directed learning opportunities to scaffold your development. Because of the extent of their role in your professional development, it can be helpful to conceive of them as 'significant narrators' (Sfard and Prusak, 2005: 833) who have a major role to play in the building of your emerging professional identify as a teacher.

According to Laker et al. (2008), in their research involving 4-year BEd trainees in southern England, trainees value immediate professional support and advice from their school mentor. Then, as they progress through a series of school placements, Laker et al. identify a definite pattern of progression that moves from formal to more informal sources of support, namely fellow trainees and teacher colleagues in the wider school community. Forming these social relationships is vital in helping you move from somewhat 'peripheral participation' (Lave and Wenger, 1991) in the school workforce to becoming a member of a community of practice.

During your placements, mentors will provide explicit modelling and then articulate and discuss their practice to raise your awareness of the complexities of teaching generally and also alert you to specific elements of practice in relation to the context or individual children involved. They will support you in identifying learning goals, providing guidance, feedback and, when necessary, direction. Your mentor will work to provide you with a range of support within the school context, which may include setting up observations of specialist colleagues, organising for other staff to observe your teaching and provide feedback or directing you to appropriate external agencies. As you progress through the placements, mentors will enable you to develop increasing control over your learning.

In this vignette, Charlotte reflects on her experiences of working with mentors during her training:

> In my first two placements, my mentor was one of the most important, if not the most important, element of learning how to teach. Mentors can facilitate your pathway into the teaching profession as they allow you to see the role of a teacher from the inside out. I learnt from observing, discussing and questioning about what goes on in the classroom with my mentors. By making their practice explicit through modelling and explanation, they helped me to develop my practice and understand what was happening in the classroom.
>
> My mentors guided me but I also realised that it was essential that I took responsibility for finding out as much as possible from their wealth of knowledge and experience in the precious time I spent with them. This involved me asking questions and for advice, but also going to them with ideas.
>
> My mentors were there to encourage, to give insight and, when necessary, to redirect. I shared my plans with my mentor which gave me the opportunity to explain my vision and ideas. This allowed them to see how I was thinking and moreover, how I had taken on board advice and used it to adapt my planning and teaching. At times I did not fully understand what my mentors were saying and quickly learned that I shouldn't feel embarrassed about asking what I sometimes thought were obvious questions. For anybody who has ever walked into any new profession, the feeling of being 'new' means that some pieces of advice can remain dormant for some time, until that 'eureka moment' when the suggestion gains its meaning.
>
> It is natural to want to take advantage of the opportunity to learn from your mentor. Nevertheless, a trainee is another element to an already intense and busy environment for any mentor. It was important that I understood I could only demand so much time from my mentor and respect that they needed space to manage all the other facets of being a teacher. Nonetheless, a positive relationship is essential for the trainee to benefit most from their mentor and it helped me to realise that this relationship wasn't one way and that I could also be an extremely useful resource in the classroom for my mentor.

MAKING THE MOST OF LEARNING CONVERSATIONS

So, how do you think the lesson went?

Learning to teach is a challenging and complex process; in order to make sense of this, it is vital that this process is scaffolded through dialogue with more experienced practitioners. Having feedback, both verbal and written, on your teaching from mentors, other school colleagues and tutors is essential to supporting your progress during school placements.

Receiving and responding to feedback is intrinsically linked with beliefs about learning. The term feedback may seem to imply a one-way process or receptive-transmission model, in which feedback discourse is characterised by the 'expert' giving information to others to help them improve. In other words, feedback could be seen as a 'gift' (Askew and Lodge, 2000: 4). Askew and Lodge offer a second model of discourse in which feedback is a two-way process, with expanded discourse enabling others to develop their understanding and make connections through the use of open questioning and shared insight. We prefer to consider Askew and Lodge's third model of feedback – a co-constructive discourse that involves a reciprocal process of learning. In this instance, feedback is a dialogue, formed by 'loops' connecting the trainee and the mentor that illuminate learning. We, therefore, use the term learning conversation, as this indicates the necessary active involvement of the trainee in the dialogue.

The nature of the learning conversation you have with school colleagues, their frequency and the manner in which they are conducted will vary. These conversations may not always be positive and straightforward. It is important here to understand that 'feedback thrives on error' (Hattie, 2012: 115). Hattie argues that this is not deficit thinking, nor concentrating on the negative:

> Error is the difference between what we know and can do, and what we aim to know and do – this applies to all (struggling and talented; students and teachers). Knowing this error is fundamental to moving towards success. This is the purpose of feedback.
>
> (Hattie, 2012: 115)

However, research shows that trainees present different dispositions, which will influence the effectiveness of the learning conversations on their professional development.

Dweck (1986) outlines the motivational processes that affect learning and how learners vary in their beliefs about success, their 'goal orientation' about learning and their responses to difficult tasks. She defines a 'positive learning orientation' as one that focuses on 'improving one's competence', with a belief that effort leads to success and a belief in one's ability to improve and learn. On the other hand, a more negative pattern focuses on 'performance orientation', in which one is more concerned with 'proving one's competence'. This is associated with negative effects for learners, such as greater helplessness, reduced help-seeking and reduced use of learning strategies.

Dimension	Orientation		
Response to feedback: disposition towards receiving feedback and the value attributed to it	Effective use of feedback to further learning	← →	Tendency to be disabled by critical feedback

As we have seen earlier in this unit, Hagger *et al.* (2008) characterise trainee teachers' dispositions in relation to feedback and the value attributed to it as a continuum. At one end, trainees make full use of the learning conversation; the expertise of mentors and tutors is valued, so that changes in planning and teaching in the light of the suggestions received are made. Trainees are receptive to professional critique, whatever form it takes, and look for further challenges, actively seeking more critical advice and opportunities for their thinking and understanding to be challenged. At the other end, Hagger *et al.* present examples of trainees who 'adopt a defensive stance' and 'those who cannot distinguish between criticism of their teaching and criticism of themselves', regardless of the nature of the learning conversation. In these conversations, trainees with this disposition have a tendency to blame others, including the pupils, to explain their difficulties or lack of progress.

Teacher Standard 8 (Department for Education, 2012) states that teachers need to 'take responsibility for improving teaching through appropriate professional development, responding to advice and feedback from colleagues'. The preceding discussion illuminates how this responsibility should be conceived and how advice and feedback should be responded to in order to optimise your learning during placements.

Pollard *et al*. (2008) identify two characteristics of reflective teaching that need consideration in relation to learning conversations (see Figure 1.3.1 earlier): attitudes of open-mindedness, responsibility and whole-heartedness, and the importance of collaboration and dialogue with colleagues in enhancing professional learning and personal fulfilment. In this vignette, Nicola reflects on learning conversations with her mentor and how this enabled her to make her placement a success. As you read this, consider how Nicola's positive dispositions were essential to this process.

> I was apprehensive as I drew up my chair for the initial feedback meeting with my mentor. I was acutely aware that this very experienced, very capable teacher had not just closely observed everything I had done in my first lesson but also scrutinised my careful planning that underpinned it. 'So', he asked 'how do you think the lesson went?' Admittedly, the whole lesson had gone by in a blur. Now, however, finding myself more self-conscious than when I had actually been standing up in front of the Year 6 class, I responded with a hopeful 'Ok?' Together we reviewed and analysed several aspects of the lesson: the lesson plan and timings, resources and class layout, how I moved around the class, what I said, differentiation and behaviour management. I quickly realised that my work wasn't being pulled apart and criticised, instead it was being looked at objectively and comments were considered and drawn on years of experience. Positives were highlighted whilst areas of improvement tactfully suggested.
>
> One observation my mentor made was that I hadn't made full use of the classroom teaching assistant. This really surprised me, I had considered that my planning for the teaching assistant was good and had spoken to her just before the lesson. To help clarify his point, my mentor showed me the comprehensive directions he'd written on his own lesson plans for his teaching assistant and explained how resources and worksheets had been modified for her to use. Later, in lessons, I paid closer attention to his interaction with adult classroom support. Arrangements were even made for me to spend a few hours shadowing a teaching assistant, observing how she worked and discussing what we could do to help each other in the classroom. I discovered how much I had taken the role for-granted, lesson planning around an aspect of the classroom that I hadn't actually clearly understood. Realising this shortcoming had really helped; I now found myself far better placed to support classroom staff, which would, in turn, support me and ultimately benefit all of my pupils. In the next feedback session I acknowledged that my mentor's original observations had been quite right. He was pleased with my progress and we moved on to identify new areas of development for the coming week.
>
> The mentoring feedback process prevented me from being insular, at times even a little defensive about my teaching. Instead I became reflective about my practice and open to suggestions. The professional relationship we struck would prove absolutely fundamental in not just making my placement a successful one but in helping me become a more able, confident and rounded trainee, ready to make the move to qualified teacher.

In summary, it is important to be:

* receptive, open-minded and active in these learning conversations;
* aware of how you learn and the strategies you find effective in order that you can talk explicitly to your mentors about the approach that suits you;
* sensitive to when it will be most appropriate for you *and* your mentor to have learning conversations;
* aware of your attitude towards engaging with learning conversations. This includes how you present yourself through your body language, tone of voice and level of engagement.

TRAINEE PROGRESSION THROUGH PLACEMENTS

Throughout this unit, we have emphasised the need for you to be an active participant while on placement, shaping your own progress and reflecting on your learning to enhance your practice. Learning to teach does not merely involve acquiring a body of knowledge, but requires changes in cognition and perception and the development of skills to interpret school experience. It is helpful at this point to consider the general stages of progress that most trainees seem to go through, to illustrate how reflection can help you to make sense of your placements.

Furlong and Maynard (1995) have identified five different stages in trainees' development.

1   Idealistic view – trainees are highly idealistic as they start the course and will have an image of the sort of teacher they want to be. This involves wanting to identify closely with pupils and with their needs and interests. Reflection at this stage should lead trainees to begin to recognise that there is no one way of 'good' teaching. This leads to the realisation that teaching is not as easy as it looks but is 'an evolving interaction that can be successfully managed in different ways' (Fletcher, 2000).

2   Personal survival – at this stage, trainees find it difficult to make sense of what is happening in the classroom and may feel there is too much to remember and cope with. Managing the class becomes an overriding concern, as many find it hard to think of themselves as an 'authority figure'. They feel uncomfortable about taking on the role of teacher because, as a result, they think the pupils won't like them. Frequently, trainees do not know what they are supposed to be looking at when asked to do observations.

3   Recognising difficulties – at this stage, most trainees begin to act like a teacher; they learn how to control and engage the pupils in some purposeful activity and achieve a basic level of competence. They begin to grasp the complexities of teaching, although they may start to do things that other teachers do, on the basis of their observations, without really knowing the reasons why.

4   Hitting the plateau – at this stage, trainees have found a way of teaching and are reluctant to make any changes. Lessons can become formulaic and mechanistic. In order to move on from this stage, trainees' reflections need to focus on the pupils' learning.

5   Moving on – as trainees gain in confidence, they take increasing responsibility for their own development and experiment with their methods of teaching, taking risks with their teaching strategies. At this stage, they are more autonomous and initiate reflection.

It is important to understand that the stages can be of differing duration and are not linear. For most trainees, the features of the first three are generally evident during the initial part of training, and the remaining stages are encountered as the trainee gains further experience in schools. However, as you move within a school or to a different school, you may find that you feel your practice has seemingly regressed – this is perfectly natural and to be expected, because, as we discussed previously, there are challenges to be met in the process of enculturation within the new setting.

Although there may be some benefit in reviewing these five stages to help you to understand your own professional development, there has been some debate that casts doubt on the notion that trainees pass through these five discrete stages. Burn *et al.* (2000) suggest that trainees are not so preoccupied with issues of classroom management and control that they do not consider the pupils' experience of the lesson and their learning. In addition, Burn *et al.* noted that, even early on in their course, trainees were developing an appreciation of the 'complex understandings' that need to inform practice (2000: 276).

In this vignette, Chris describes his route through a 1-year PGCE course. As you read this passage, consider how the features of placements analysed in this unit are evident in his narrative, enabling him to develop professional competencies and to achieve QTS.

> The first few days of my initial placement were spent familiarising myself with the school, the staff and the pupils, ascertaining established routines and behaviour management policies, and learning as many names as possible. At first, I was asked to work with small groups of six to ten children on short, specific tasks initially prescribed in some detail by the classroom teacher. This allowed the opportunity to put key strategies into practice especially with regard to time-keeping and discipline, whilst being closely observed by my mentor. I was soon aware of becoming a self-reflexive practitioner, capable of evaluating lessons critically, learning from mistakes and growing in confidence in my handling of situations that arose within the classroom.
>
> Having firmly established my competence early on during the placement, my mentor's role became less prominent, allowing greater freedom and flexibility to develop my own strategies and explore a range of techniques to improve aspects of my pedagogy. As part of the development of my teaching style and persona, I built up my bank of resources and techniques to provide a myriad of ways to present topics creatively and memorably and to cater for pupils of all abilities. Regular classroom teaching gave me the opportunity to vary my approach and to become more consistent in my delivery.
>
> Next, I was entrusted with the teaching of the whole class and encouraged to take on additional responsibilities where appropriate. These included responsibility for transitions to and from the classroom throughout the school day, preparation of wall displays, break time supervision, and attendance at staff meetings and training sessions, as well as participation in extra-curricular activity.
>
> During my final placement, I was able to assume the mantle of the teacher in its entirety, embracing all facets of the role of the teacher in that class. I was ultimately responsible, by the end of the placement, for the planning and delivery of 80% of the normal teaching timetable. As my confidence and competence grew, it was immensely satisfying to note that children did not feel the need to refer to the classroom teacher if she were in the room; the children no longer saw me as a teaching assistant, but as a teacher in my own right.
>
> At this point, I continued to receive valuable feedback from my mentor, who observed my teaching and provided support and constructive criticism where necessary. I continued to develop and refine my technique, as I rapidly made the transition from 'back-seat observer' to a fully fledged 'real teacher'.

Every route into teaching will have different expectations for the specific characteristics and build-up of responsibilities in school placements during the course. Training providers will take into account your prior experience of working with children and teaching and your personal subject knowledge in order to individualise the training programme for you.

Task 1.3.5 Reflecting on teaching experiences

Reflect on a particular experience or episode from which you have gained significant insight into an aspect of your learning about teaching while on placement. Write an account that analyses the links between this experience in school and some aspect of your reading of educational research.

SUMMARY

Unless the practicum helps to teach prospective teachers how to take control of their own professional development and to learn how to continue learning, it is miseducative, no matter how successful the teacher might be in the short run.

(Zeichner, 1996)

As a beginning teacher, initially it will be difficult to understand what an experienced teacher does to be effective, but gradually, as you progress through your school placements, you will develop an understanding of the craft, science and art of teaching. Becoming a reflexive practitioner is crucial to this process. As Chris stated right at the beginning, your placements will be some of the most challenging experiences of your training. Being proactive is vital, and having an aspirational disposition for both you and the children will make the process more positive, increasing the likelihood that you become successful and gain QTS. Progressing through school placements may sometimes feel like a roller coaster, as you will undoubtedly experience highs and lows; it is hard to accept that your trajectory is less likely to be like a straight line graph heading upwards, and more like a scattergram with a general upward trajectory. During these often intensive, stressful periods, it is important that you take care of yourself and, as far as possible, retain a work–life balance. Make time for *all* the SPICES of life – the Spiritual, Physical, Intellectual, Creative, Emotional and Social aspects, some of which are easy to forget during school placements. First-hand experiences in schools are obviously vital in your preparation to become a teacher, and in this unit we have attempted to articulate considerations that will help you to become a successful, 'fully developed professional' who has control of their own professional development and continues learning.

ANNOTATED FURTHER READING

McGregor, D. and Cartwright, L. (2011) *Developing Reflective Practice: A Handbook for Beginning Teachers*, Maidenhead: Open University Press.

This trainee-friendly, practical guide will help you understand reflective practice in teaching. The book clearly explains some of the best-known theories on reflective practice and then shows how reflection on and in practice can have a positive impact on classroom performance. The very real problems faced by beginning teachers are brought to life through the use of rich case studies, as well as extracts drawn from the reflective journals of those starting their teaching career.

Hattie, J. (2012) *Visible Learning for Teachers: Maximizing Impact on Learning*, London: Routledge.

This book is written with trainee teachers in mind and champions student teacher perspectives. It links the biggest ever research project on teaching strategies to practical classroom implementation and includes step-by-step guidance on topics such as lesson preparation, interpreting learning and feedback during the lesson and post-lesson discussions. It also contains a useful checklist that enables you to plot your own progress towards 'visible learning inside'.

FURTHER READING TO SUPPORT M-LEVEL STUDY

Hagger, H., Burn, K., Mutton, T. and Brindley, S. (2008) 'Practice makes perfect? Learning to learn as a teacher', *Oxford Review of Education*, 34(1): 159–78.

> This journal article presents research conducted with twenty-five student teachers, following a 1-year postgraduate course within two well-established, school-based partnerships. The authors' findings show that, although the student teachers all learned from experience in school, the nature and extent of that learning varied considerably. The success the trainees had in making the most of their placements was determined by their attitudes and dispositions. Awareness of these dimensions could be helpful as a diagnostic tool when exploring your own attitude towards learning to learn as a teacher.

Hayes, D. (1998) 'Walking on eggshells: the significance of socio-cultural factors in the mentoring of primary school student teachers', *Mentoring and Tutoring: Partnership in Learning*, 6(1/2): 67–76.

> This journal article is helpful in understanding the complex social settings and cultures in which student teachers find themselves. It shows how important it is to realise that school placements are not just about developing teaching skills, but also about learning to recognise, interpret and respond appropriately to a variety of contextual, personal and social factors.

RELEVANT WEBSITES

Reflective Teaching: http://reflectiveteaching.co.uk

> The resources on this website are designed to support the development of high-quality professional judgement and evidence-informed practice. It has further links to the Teaching and Learning Research Programme (TLRP).

REFERENCES

Alexander, R. (2009) *Introducing the Cambridge Primary Review*, October. www.primaryreview.org.uk/publications/introductory_booklet.php

Askew, S. and Lodge, C. (2000) 'Gifts, ping-pong and loops – linking feedback and learning' in S. Askew (ed.), *Feedback for Learning*, London: RoutledgeFalmer.

Burn, K., Hagger, H., Mutton, T. and Everton, T. (2000) 'Beyond concerns with self: the sophisticated thinking of beginning student teachers', *Journal of Education for Teaching*, (26)3.

Calderhead, J. and Shorrock, S. (1997) *Understanding Teacher Education*, London: Falmer Press.

Cartwright, L. (2011) 'How consciously reflective are you?' in D. McGregor and L. Cartwright, *Developing Reflective Practice: A Handbook for Beginning Teachers*, Maidenhead: Open University Press.

Cohen, L. Manion, L. Morrison, K. and Wyse, D. (2010) *A Guide to Teaching Practice*, 5th edn, London: Routledge.

Department for Education (2012) *Teachers' Standards*, London: Department for Education, www.education.gov.uk/publications/eOrderingDownload/teachers%20standards.pdf (accessed 7 January 2013).

Department of Education and Skills (2005) 'National Framework for Mentoring and Coaching', London: Department of Education and Skills, www.curee-paccts.com/files/publication/1219925968/National-framework-for-mentoring-and-coaching.pdf (accessed 22 December 2012).

Dweck, C. (1986) 'Motivational processes affecting learning', *American Psychologist*, 41: 1040–8.

Fletcher, S. (2000) *Mentoring in Schools*, London: Kogan Page.

Furlong, J. and Maynard, T. (1995) *Mentoring Student Teachers: The Growth of Professional Knowledge*, London: Routledge.

Hagger, H., Burn, K., Mutton, T. and Brindley, S. (2008) 'Practice makes perfect? Learning to learn as a teacher', *Oxford Review of Education*, 34(1): 159-78.

Hattie, J. (2012) *Visible Learning for Teachers: Maximizing Impact on Learning*, London: Routledge.

Hayes, D. (1998) 'Walking on eggshells: the significance of socio-cultural factors in the mentoring of primary school student teachers', *Mentoring and Tutoring: Partnership in Learning*, 6(1/2): 67-76.

Hayes, D. (2001) 'The impact of mentoring and tutoring on student primary teachers' achievements: a case study', *Mentoring and Tutoring: Partnership in Learning*, 9(1): 5-21.

Laker, A., Laker, J.C. and Lea, S.J. (2008) 'Sources of support for pre-service teachers during school experience', *Mentoring and Tutoring*, 16(2): 125-40.

Lave, J. and Wenger, E. (1991) *Situated Learning: Legitimate Peripheral Participation*, Cambridge: Cambridge University Press.

McGregor, D. and Cartwright, L. (2011) *Developing Reflective Practice: A Handbook for Beginning Teachers*, Maidenhead: Open University Press.

Moore, A. (2004) *The Good Teacher: Dominant Discourses in Teaching and Teacher Education*, London: Routledge.

Nias, D.J. (1989) *Primary Teachers Talking*, London: Routledge.

Pollard, A. (ed.) (2010) *Professionalism and Pedagogy: A Contemporary Opportunity. A Commentary by TLRP and GTCE*. London: TLRP.

Pollard, A., Anderson, J., Maddock, M., Swaffield, S., Warin, J. and Warwick, P. (2008) *Reflective Teaching: Evidence-Informed Professional Practice*, 3rd edn, London: Continuum.

Rawling, E. (2003) *Connecting Policy and Practice: Research in Geography Education*, Nottingham: BERA.

Sewell, K. (2008) *Doing Your PGCE at M-level: A Guide for Students*, 2nd edn, London: Sage.

Sfard, A. and Prusak, A. (2005) 'Telling identities: In search of an analytical tool for investigating learning as a culturally shaped activity', *Educational Researcher*, 34(4): 14-22.

Zeichner, K. (1996) 'Designing educative practicum experiences', in K. Zeichner, S. Melnick and M.L. Gomez (eds), *Currents of Reform in Preservice Teacher Education*, Columbia University, NY: Teachers College Press.

EXPLORING THE NATURE OF LEARNING AND TEACHING

LOOKING AT CHILDREN

Sandra Smidt

INTRODUCTION

This is a unit about child development. It is designed to help you understand and evaluate some theories about how children develop and learn, why they develop in different ways, and what this will mean for you as a teacher.

As a teacher you will need to know as much as possible about each child you teach. Your knowledge will come through finding out as much as you can about each child's life history, observing children at work and play and talking to them and the significant people in their lives. Knowing something about what theorists have said about how children, in general, develop and about why there are some patterns of development across culture and time will enhance your understanding.

Note: Throughout this unit I will use the convention of referring to 'she' rather than 'he'.

OBJECTIVES

By the end of this unit you should be able to:

- explain why educators need to be both knowledgeable about and critical of some theories of child development;
- critique the work of theorists, practitioners, planners and others in terms of respect for culture and context;
- understand the concept of patterns of development and how and why these vary;
- describe how context, in the sense of family, language, neighbourhood, culture, customs, rituals and other factors, enables children to make sense of the world and of their place in it;
- recognise each child as a competent and unique person, actively involved in making sense of all aspects of the physical, emotional and social worlds she inhabits;
- evaluate current and relevant legislation affecting children, their learning and their rights, and assess the relevance of this to schools and teachers.

Task 2.1.1 What is child development?

Write down anything you know about child development, including the names of any theorists or writers you have heard of. Then read it through and check how many of these words you included:

physical	social	emotional
cognitive or intellectual	context	culture
interaction	identity	communication
language	active learner	make sense of
stages of development	independence	shared focus of attention
play		

Keep this list because you may want to amend it later.

CHILD DEVELOPMENT: WHAT IT IS AND WHY IT MATTERS

All of you reading this unit will have a common-sense definition of child development in your heads. It is clearly a discipline (or an area of study) examining how the human infant develops from dependence to independence. This is in terms of physical, social, emotional and cognitive growth and changes. It is a very wide discipline, encompassing a range of views, and one of the most important things you need to know is that most of what you will encounter in textbooks and in your training will focus on the development of children in the developed world, rather than those in the developing world. This is not a minor issue but carries serious implications in terms of what is *not* addressed. So, in your reading, you are asked to become critical and look out for which child's development is being reflected.

Common-sense knowledge tells us that children throughout the world learn to do complex things. Babies learn to smile at familiar faces, look intently at something they desire, move to the rhythms of music, grasp and hold and then manipulate objects, sit and creep or crawl and then walk and hop and run and jump. They learn to communicate through pointing and gazing, intonation, gesture and spoken language. They become able to express their thoughts and feelings in many ways. And all of this without a single formal lesson.

Books have been written on the subject, and it is only possible in this introductory unit to talk of some key theorists and then point you in the direction of others.

We will start by looking briefly at the work of Piaget, because he has been, and continues to be, so influential. We will then move on to the work of Lev Vygotsky and Jerome Bruner, two great theorists taking a sociohistorical or sociocultural view of development. This means that they always consider the context and culture within which any child is developing. That leads us on to looking at the work of Loris Malaguzzi, who brings much of this together in the preschool provision in Reggio Emilia.

In each case, we will be raising issues that may be contentious. We invite you to make judgements. Later in the unit, we examine the work of some other theorists and writers to give a broader perspective.

FOUR THEORISTS

Jean Piaget was a Swiss biologist who studied his own children as well as groups of children in order to document his thoughts on cognitive development.

- He said that children were actively constructing meaning through their senses and movement. This was highly original and important, because it had been thought that the infant was a blank slate waiting to be written on. This is the introduction of *the child as active learner.*
- He developed a stage model of development with *children moving through age-related stages*, only able to progress when they were cognitively ready to do so. This structure is reflected in our education system. This model focuses largely on the concept of 'readiness' for learning and on what children cannot yet do. Many of those who followed had a focus on what children can do.
- He believed that *young children were egocentric* and could not see things from the perspective of others. Later critics felt that this was incorrect, as even very young children demonstrate that they can put themselves in other people's shoes. Piaget's is a model that does not place emphasis on the social, on interaction with others, on emotion or on context.
- He was *interested in both play and language* and believed that the role of the educator was to set up a learning environment in which there were challenging activities for the learners. So, for him, children learn from the activities and objects they encounter, rather than through their interactions.
- It follows that, for him, the primary role of the educator was to *set out an interesting and challenging learning environment*.

To learn more about his very significant ideas and contribution, read *Introducing Piaget* (2014) by Ann Marie Halpenny and Jan Petterson.

Lev Vygotsky was a Russian psychologist, who died young and whose work was not published in the UK until the 1960s, so that people in the UK only gained access to it at roughly the same time as they encountered the work of Piaget.

- Piaget was interested in how knowledge was acquired; Vygotsky was interested in how knowledge is passed on from generation to generation, which meant he *was deeply concerned with culture*.
- Vygotsky said that children came to understand their world through their interactions with more experienced others, children and adults, and through the use of cultural tools – by which he meant language, art, music, symbols and signs, all of which are developed by groups in society.
- He *shared with Piaget a belief in children as active learners*, but, in believing that learning took place through the interactions learners had with more experienced others, his view is much more social.
- He also *shared with Piaget an interest in play as a mode of learning* and famously said that observing a child at play allows us to see the child 'standing a head taller than himself'. What he meant was that, when a child is playing she is, by definition, interested in what she is doing. The implications are that she will be more involved and more prepared to take chances when solving a problem she has set herself.
- He placed tremendous *emphasis on language*.
- For him, the *role of the educator was to know when and how to intervene* in order to move the child on from what the child could do with help to what she could do alone. To explain this, he developed what was called the '*zone of proximal development*', which is the notional 'gap' between performance and potential.

To learn more about his very significant ideas and contribution, read *Introducing Vygotsky* by Sandra Smidt (2008).

Jerome Bruner was born in the United States and born blind. He has worked in the UK and the USA and written many wonderful books. He is still alive today.

- He was initially concerned with two issues: why so many young children fail in formal education in the UK, and the interactions infants have with their primary caregivers (usually mothers) in the *rituals of early childhood*. He saw this as being the start of intersubjectivity where the child becomes aware of the thoughts and feelings of others.
- He believed it was *essential to take note of culture and context*, which he saw as being critical to learning and development.
- For him the role of the educator was to establish what it was the learner was paying attention to and then intervene, focusing on this, to take learning forward. This sharing of attention is crucial and leads the learner to be able to get deeply involved in whatever it is he or she is doing. In current parlance, it is referred to as '*sustained shared thinking*'. Bruner developed the concept of '*scaffolding learning*', in which the educator supports the child in taking small, measured steps to achieve a higher level of performance or learning.
- He was *very interested in play*, including the playing of games. Related to this was his interest in the role *rules* play in children's development. You have only to observe children engaged in role-playing to see them devising, implementing and changing rules.
- He wrote a great deal about language, focusing on many aspects, but latterly and most importantly on the significance of *narrative*. He believed that possibly the earliest, but also the most powerful, way in which we make sense of who we are, what we are interested in, what has happened to us and what entrances or scares us is through making up stories.
- He was and still is an ardent supporter of the educational provision for young children in Reggio Emilia.

To learn more about his very significant ideas and contribution, read *Introducing Bruner* by Sandra Smidt (2011).

Loris Malaguzzi was born and educated in the wealthy region of Emilia Romagna. Based at Bologna University after the war, he became committed to the idea of providing early childhood education for children that was not run by the church. He was instrumental in helping peasant women in the Reggio Emilia region of Italy to set up a series of nursery schools to provide educational opportunities for very young children. It was the start of a unique and continuing educational experiment.

- Underpinning his work was an ideology based on the notion of *each child being both unique and competent and of every child having access to what he called 'a hundred languages'* – by which he meant the resources (or cultural tools) to allow them to express their thoughts and feelings and theories in as many different ways as possible.
- For him, the role of the educator was *to listen to children* rather than to question or test them; *to take their efforts seriously*; and *to give them access to as many of these languages* as possible – namely music, drawing, painting, dance, language and so on.
- For him, all learning was social.
- He believed that *any educational establishment should belong to those who use it*, and this includes the teachers and children, but also their parents and carers, the cleaners, the cooks and everyone else. This requires respectful sharing, respectful listening and careful documentation.
- He believed that an essential role of schools is to document in detail what the children do and use this as the basis for planning and for sharing with parents/carers.
- He noticed that *children's questions showed what they were thinking* – what he called their theories – and that these could be used to take learning to very complex levels.

• His attitude to education was deeply political and involved him working closely with successive local governments to ensure that all the provision continued to be financed.

To learn more about his very significant ideas and contribution, read *Introducing Malaguzzi* by Sandra Smidt (2013) or the books by Carlina Rinaldi or Via Vecchi, which you will find in the References.

Task 2.1.2 What would they say?

You can now read three small observation notes. The first is my account of something overheard on a London bus. The second was given to me by a student, and the third comes from the work of Charmian Kenner. In each case, analyse what you think Piaget, Vygotsky, Bruner or Malaguzzi would say about the child's development. You are thinking about what the child knows and can do, what she is interested in or paying attention to, and why this matters.

Case study 1

I overheard this on the bus. A man got on with a little girl, no more than 3 years old. They sat beside me, and the little girl said, 'I've got four childs. Have you got four childs, grandpa?' He replied, 'Well, I could say I have got four children. There's your mum and your uncle Sam and you are my grandchild but I could call you my child. And there's Ringo.' There was a brief pause, and then the little girl said, 'But I am my mum's child and Ringo's a dog, so you haven't got four childs'.

Case study 2

We had a group of musicians come and perform to the children, and one of the children in the nursery, who speaks no English yet, got up and came right up to the front and stood watching the girl who was singing, entranced. First she just stood still, and then she started to move, and then dance, and then twirl round, and then clap her hands. At the end, she came up to me and spoke to me, for the first time. Sadly, she was speaking in Yoruba, and I could neither understand nor respond other than with a big smile.

Case study 3

Charmian Kenner worked with young children in inner London and involved them in teaching one another about their first or home languages. Here is an extract from her wonderful book:

> One of the most obvious differences between Arabic and English is directionality: Arabic goes from right to left and English from left to right. Yazan . . . showing his Arabic school textbook in a peer teaching session, pointed to the front cover and stated 'Not the end'. Turning to the back cover, he emphasised 'This is the end'. And to make sure his audience was completely clear about the matter he pointed to the front cover again and said 'This is the first'.
>
> (Kenner, 2004: 41)

KEY IDEAS AND ISSUES

In this section, we are going to look at some important issues relating to child development and not yet addressed, and, as we do this, we will mention the names of additional writers, thinkers, educationalist and theorists.

Placing an emphasis on cultural development

Many people are critical of the fact that the most famous and influential theorists adopt a monocultural view of child development. Some talk of *everybaby* – the notion that every baby is like every other baby – when, in reality, you must know that the world is made up of babies of different genders, from different backgrounds, learning different languages, but all learning and developing.

- *Barbara Rogoff* is an American researcher, deeply interested in the importance of groups and of culture, who looks at children in the developing world and sees how they learn through being active participants in the real-life events of their communities. By this she means shopping, cooking, cleaning, eating meals and so on. She talks of these learners as 'apprentices' and of the learning happening through what she calls '*guided participation*'. Where this is implemented within a classroom setting, it can lead to building a class culture of shared values, cultural tools and expectations.
- *Urie Bronfennbrenner* was an ecologist, concerned with describing the network of contexts available to all children. In his model, which is usually depicted as a series of concentric circles, the child is at the centre, surrounded by the *microsystem*, made up of the home in which are the child, parents and siblings with their own beliefs, customs and culture; the next layer is the *mesosystem*, which defines the interactions between home, school, neighbourhood and religious settings. Then there is the *exosystem*, describing the impact (real or potential) of local industry, parents' workplaces, local government, mass media and school or setting management committee. Finally, and most remote from the child, are the *macrosystems*, which define the dominant beliefs and ideologies operating for that child and his or her family. Into this come things such as laws. This model firmly situates each child in the social and cultural layers, close and remote, that will impact on her development.
- Throughout the world, there are millions of children who grow up knowing more than one language. There are many cognitive advantages to being bilingual, and these include a greater awareness of how language itself operates, which can help with the development of literacy, enhance problem-solving skills and build recognition of the importance of both context and audience. There are many people who have worked in this field, including *Jim Cummins*, *Colin Baker*, *Eve Gregory* and *Charmian Kenner*.
- All of this reminds us that context and culture must always inform our thinking about development.

Placing an emphasis on social development

- *Judy Dunn*'s research focused on very young children and how they came to make sense of the rituals, rules and conventions relating to social interaction. Her study involved her examining interactions in families and, although it was situated within one smallish community or context, it has relevance more widely. Most interestingly, she showed how, early in life, children develop an understanding that others have feelings and needs. It laid the foundation for later work on intersubjectivity.
- *Colwyn Trevarthen*'s seminal work on infants has shed light on this. He found that infants as young as 2 months of age show a different response to someone who speaks to them than to

someone else in the room who remains silent. In his studies of babies together with their primary caregivers, he was able to document the ongoing interchange between the two. Through this, the infant begins to understand the feelings and intentions of the adult. The body of knowledge about intersubjectivity contradicts Piaget's thinking about young children's inability to decentre or see the world from another's perspective.

Placing an emphasis on emotional development

- *Sigmund Freud* is possibly the best-known name here. He spent his life trying to understand and describe emotional development. Through his work with adults, he came to a stage model of emotional development that was (and still is) contentious and not universally accepted. Nonetheless, he was a key figure and exerted an enormous influence over those who followed.
- *Carlina Rinaldi*, who worked very closely with Malaguzzi, tells us that, from birth, the infant is engaged in building a relationship with the world and intent on experiencing it, so that she develops a complex system of abilities, strategies for learning and ways of organising relationships. So she is able to make her own personal maps for her own development and orientation – social, cognitive, emotional and symbolic. She and her co-workers have developed what they call a pedagogy of relationships.
- *Alison Gopnik*, *Andrew Meltzoff* and *Betty Repacholi* propose that development proceeds by a constant process of revision as the child makes sense of her interactions with others. So the child starts out with some assumptions and then tries out her theories, evaluates these and tries again. The child cobbles together her understanding as she interacts with others.

Placing an emphasis on self-esteem and identity

As with many other aspects of child development, thinking about how children develop a sense of themselves – an identity – is changing. Traditionally, it was thought that young children were born unformed and dependent; acquiring an identity was then seen as being about how adults, particularly parents, induct children into the norms and values, beliefs and practices of their community. Another strand of thinking said that children build a sense of themselves as individuals through play and exploration. Both these views depend on the notion of the child being acted on, rather than being the agent of her own identity creation. Most theorists today accept that *the competent child with a unique identity from birth constructs and reconstructs her identity within cultural contexts*. It is thought that both adults and children negotiate multiple and changing, and even competing, identities with the complex multicultural and multiethnic contexts that shape their lives. The United Nations Convention on the Rights of the Child (1989) affirms that every child has the right to a legal identity. This right is activated and safeguarded by the child's birth being registered. From birth, every child begins the journey of constructing a unique personal and social identity that is characterised by a growing awareness of the importance of gender, ethnicity, age and status within the child's immediate community. Before starting school, many children demonstrate a clear understanding of their role and status at home and with their families and community. They begin to understand the impact of how they are treated on their sense of who they are.

Early identities are themselves complex, and they continue to change and grow as children experience new settings, activities, relationships and responsibilities. This might remind you of the work of Bronfenbrenner (1979). In the process, children may form positive, negative and ambivalent feelings about aspects of their changing identity. *Artin Göncü* (1999) tells us that developing personal identity is a dynamic process that is embedded in the child's multiple activities and relationships in the everyday settings of home, community and nursery. Identity is best described as constructed, co-constructed and reconstructed by the child through his or her interactions with parents, teachers, peers and others. These dynamic processes include imitation and identification in shared activities, including imaginative role-play.

Constructing cultural identity, which is the feeling of belonging to a cultural group, is what happens to all children as they make sense of all that they experience within their families. *Nsamenang* believes that family processes are the foundation of identity formation, because it is within the family that the child gets a sense of who she is, which allows her then to refashion this in her encounters with others. Many African cultures emphasise the shared and the social. There is a Zulu saying that, translated, means 'a person is only a person with other people'. Would you say the same is true of Western cultures? Peer cultures enable the child to add to and extend the influence of the family on children's developing identities. Holding fast to your culture is important, and this is not always recognised in schools, where the dominant or host culture is often perceived as the model. This is perfectly summed up in the Swahili saying *Nwacha asili ni mtumwa* – which means he who loses his traditions and culture is a slave.

Task 2.1.3 How has your thinking changed?

Having read the brief notes on a range of thinkers, revise what you wrote about child development in Task 2.1.1. Add to this a short piece on how you think what you have learned will enhance your understanding of children and how they learn and develop. Be sure to focus on how your thinking has changed.

SOME CURRENT AND RECENT RESEARCH

What we learn from neuroscience

As sophisticated imaging devices become more and more refined, we are learning much about what happens within the human brain. Some of it may be familiar to you. You might have been seduced by hearing that playing a CD of Mozart's music would make your baby cleverer, or you might have a child who has to press her 'brain bumps' at school in order to make her succeed. In the early years of analysing brain images, manufacturers of toys and educational equipment jumped on the bandwagon, and some people made a lot of money out of what can only be called dubious myths and claims. I offer these here for you to consider.

- The first myth was that *the first 3 years (or 5, depending on who you read) are the most crucial*, where most learning takes place. It is true that a considerable amount of learning takes place then, but there is no one critical period for all learning. Learning can happen throughout a human lifetime.
- The second myth is that, as one experiment showed that rats, put in what was called an *enriched environment*, showed changes in brain activity, the same should apply to human infants. In reality, it is dangerous to extrapolate from rats to humans, and it has been shown that the original findings could not be replicated. What is more, the myth lead to people making dangerous judgements about what constitutes a 'good' learning environment. You are reminded that we learn wherever we are, through all our activities and interactions. Where poverty impacts on children's lives, there are, of course, serious implications for their physical, social, emotional

and cognitive health, but children do not need fancy equipment and toys in order to learn and develop and thrive.

- Twardosz (2012) talks of what she calls *experience-dependent plasticity*, which involves the modification of existing synapses or connections or the generation of new ones on the basis of individually specific experience. This is what enables individuals to become members of their own culture. So a child in Hanoi might eat using chopsticks, whereas a child in a village in the Sudan might eat with her fingers; Spanish children learn to read text from left to right, whereas children learning Arabic learn to read from right to left. You can see from these examples how learning and memory work. Any child is born into a context of a community, a society, a set of values and customs and beliefs and traditions. The child experiences what exists within her culture. The connections in her brain are affected by what she sees and does. This experience-dependent plasticity occurs throughout life, and there are no sensitive or critical periods. In summary, this says that we *learn through all our experiences, wherever and whenever they take place*.

- Another recent finding is that the brains of children who *make music*, alone or with others, show significant changes. They perform better on a range of measures affecting different areas of learning. Hyde *et al.* (2009) measured behavioural responses and structural changes in the brain after children had had 15 months of weekly half-hour keyboard lessons. The children were aged 6 when they started learning to play, and there was both an experimental group and a control group that participated solely in school music activities. The researchers used a specialised imaging technique to look at the size of the brain and the changes within it. This technique is known as deformation-based morphometry. What they found was that the children having regular weekly keyboard lessons had a greater relative size both in the corpus callosum (which controls motor development) and in the region of the brain controlling hearing. They performed better than the control group on melody and rhythm tests and on a four-finger sequencing task. There seemed to be no differences in visual–spatial or verbal measures between the two groups.

What we learn from non-Western theorists

As you will almost certainly know, the world is shrinking in the sense that poverty, global warming, food crises, absence of jobs and other factors are causing people to migrate, sometimes from the countryside to urban areas, sometimes from one country to another. In your teaching, you are bound to encounter children whose experience will be as different from yours as can be imagined. It is essential that we all start to be aware of this in how we approach children and their families and conceive of their experiences with respect and understanding.

Bame Nsamenang, associate professor of psychology and learning science at the University of Bamenda, Cameroon, and founding director of the Human Development Resource Centre, a research and service facility for young generations, is a respected researcher and writer on African children and their learning and development. His *Handbook of African Educational Theories and Practices* (Nsamenang and Tchombe, 2011) is a collection of chapters written by him and colleagues about what happens within African homes, groups, schools and society and how any or all of that impacts on children. Remember that Africa is a vast and varied continent in which one can find hundreds of languages, styles of learning, attitudes, beliefs, values, customs and cultures. Remember too that the whole continent has suffered, in some way, from colonialism. Nsamenang says that much of current thinking about child development in Africa focuses on the child as being very much the *agent of her own learning and development*. In many African cultures, parents do not consciously raise their children in the sense of getting them ready for each successive stage of a formal education process (as so many do in the West), but create participative spaces where the children emerge and mature by themselves out of one set of developmental tasks into another. This is very similar to some of the examples from South America given by Rogoff, such as the small child who sits and watches older children involved in making tortillas. At first she just watches. Then, perhaps, she is given a lump of dough to play with. Later still she is given one or two necessary tools. Eventually, she is a full participant in the tortilla-making process. It is a process from being co-participants in real-life activities, first as novices within peer groups, and later as recognised, respected and full participants in the life of the family and community. Erny (1981) talks of children 'becoming', and others speak of the driving force being emergence.

Other features of many African childhoods are the role of the oral tradition, community involvement in the life of the child, and a much earlier introduction to becoming independent. Young children are often given real jobs that might be regarded as adult jobs in the West, such as fetching water or chopping yams. Children are also seen as rights-bearers who can contribute to their own development and society. It is worth considering also that the colonial history of Africa means that children today are raised with the coexisting strands of Islamic–Arabic and Western–Christian ideas.

You will find some things that are similar and others not. Many young children are reared by mothers, but, if that is not possible, the child may be cared for by the grandmother or siblings. In parts of Africa, the impact of HIV/AIDS has been to leave some young children as the head of the family. In both the rural and urban areas, formal childcare outside of the home is rare. Young infants learn valuable skills while taking part in domestic activities. This gives young children a sense of their own worth within the family and community. Issues relating to health, safety and nutrition, often caused or exacerbated by poverty, play an enormous role in their lives. However, children develop not only physical and interpersonal skills, but numeracy, motor skills, ideas about work and money, about justice and equity, about what matters and about how to survive. Young children there, as here, learn the expected ways of behaving in relation to parents, grandparents, friends, teachers, strangers and others. Language development there, as here, is strongly dependent on the opportunities provided, and many children grow up knowing more than one language.

That brings us to the *value of bilingualism in learning and development*. We seem still to regard this as a monolingual country, although the evidence is that it is a richly diverse linguistic place. Sadly, research into the positive effects of bilingualism is no longer being funded, and so we are still dependent on the findings of people such as Baker and Cummins. In his *Foundations of Bilingual Education and Bilingualism*, Baker said that bilingual individuals, by knowing two or more words for one object or idea, may have cognitive flexibility giving them the ability to more effectively use devices such as comparison, simile and metaphor. There is a body of evidence that shows just how knowing two or more languages gives children more awareness of language itself. They have enhanced metalinguistic awareness. Metalinguistic awareness is considered 'a key factor in the

Task 2.1.4 The child as an active learner

Most models of child development see the child as an active learner, making meaning through everything she encounters. Most agree that learning is very social in that children learn, not only from things, but from other people, children and adults. How do you think the Foundation Stage Curriculum or the National Curriculum reflects such a view? You are not only allowed, but invited to be critical. And what do you think the implications for pedagogy – your teaching – might be.

development of reading in young children' (Donaldson, 1978) and 'a crucial component of cognitive development because of its documented relation to language ability, symbolic development, and literacy skills' (Bialystok, 1991).

Do refer to the work of *Helen Penn*, *Peter Moss*, *Gunilla Dahlberg* and others. You will find some of their books in the References.

THE IMPLICATIONS OF ALL THIS

By now, you should have started to be able to think about what you can learn about how to teach children from knowing something about child development. What follows should help you consolidate this. We can say the following:

All learning is social: the roles of others in learning cannot be ignored. What this will mean for you as a teacher is that you will need to know as much as possible about the prior experience of your children, and you will need to think very carefully how you can promote learning with others in the classroom. The 'others' who play a role in learning may be teachers, other adults and/or more experienced children. For you, the educator, the importance of this is to ensure that opportunities for interaction between children, and between children and adults, are planned for and exploited. You will need think about where you and the other adults in your room will be and about how you will encourage learners to share, talk, negotiate and collaborate.

Knowledge of and respect for cultural values and cultural tools are vital to successful learning. This implies that all involved in learning/teaching enterprises have to take time and effort to know what experiences and cultural tools their learners have had and ensure that, wherever possible, they have access to using these. You will need to know what languages the children in your class recognise, speak, read and/or write. You need to make as many cultural tools as possible available to the learners.

Building a participative culture within the class or setting is important in developing the principles you bring to your teaching. This will allow you, with your learners, to develop an ethos of sustained shared attention, respect for one another, the use of shared cultural tools, and an environment where questioning, seeking for answers, making things and having a go are embedded. You are trying to create a culture of learners and learning.

Language is the supreme, but not the only, cultural tool essential in planning and organising learning environments. Educators must plan for the use of spoken and written language and other symbolic systems or languages. These must include music and drawing/painting, making and dancing. You should seek to ensure that children can use their first language, where this is the language in which they hold some concepts (both everyday and, in some cases, scientific or abstract) and to offer opportunities for all children to explore and represent things in ways other than in words.

Learning takes place through experience. You must plan and resource activities that are accessible and meaningful to the children. Question the value of asking children to do something meaningless such as colour the big balls blue and the little balls yellow, for example. For younger children, activities should offer first-hand and direct experience to allow for the development of everyday concepts, and for all children they should offer opportunities to create and use symbols, which should enable or enhance the ability to think abstractly.

There are many ways or modes of learning, and all need to be considered. Play is defined as what children do when they are able to follow their own interests and create their own rules. It may well be a dominant mode of learning for younger children, but not, sadly, for those in primary school.

This is despite much work illustrating how much children learn through being in charge of following up their own interests. Your task is to be alert to what children are interested in, so that they will be motivated to raise and answer questions, thus meeting a cognitive challenge and often getting deeply involved in what they are doing so that they can build on what they already know. Listening to stories, making music or expressing ideas through art or drama are all powerful ways of learning, as are climbing, sharing, negotiating and, vitally, questioning. Do read the books by Rinaldi and Vecchi, where you will find some wonderful examples.

Task 2.1.5 Theory in practice

Organise to spend time in one class in a school in which you are doing a placement or practice. Take a notebook with you and see if you can find examples of any of the important issues we have been able to highlight, after our whistle-stop tour of some of the ideas of significant researchers and theorists.

Look for examples of any or all of the following:

- a child or children actively making meaning;
- a child or children raising questions or offering a theory;
- a child or children learning through interaction;
- a child or children showing evidence of understanding the position or feelings of anyone else;
- a child or children having direct or hands-on experience;
- a child or children using signs or symbols in any way;
- a child or children expressing feelings or emotions;
- a young child or children using one thing to stand for or represent another;
- a young child or children communicating effectively with one another;
- children playing different roles;
- the languages of the children being evident in the room;
- the adults listening attentively to the children;
- adults scaffolding children's learning;
- adults giving helpful feedback to a child;
- an adult and a child sharing attention.

I hope this unit will help you decide to be a teacher who adopts a sociocultural view of development and learning, which will help you develop a style of teaching that is interactive, uses cultural tools, focuses on the learner as a competent and curious individual, listens to the learner and thinks carefully about how to take learning forward through scaffolding, where there is sustained shared thinking. There are many modes of teaching, which include listening, making and sharing meaning, observing, giving feedback, modelling, answering, offering resources, and so on.

SUMMARY

In this very brief introduction to an extremely complex and fascinating area, we have only looked at the views of some people who have had an enormous influence on thinking about children, learning, development and childhood. Running through this outline has been the concern to answer the question, 'Why do we, as educators, need to know anything at all about child development?'. After an outline of the most important aspects of the work of writers and theorists, we have looked at some recent and relevant research and the implications of this for teachers. The unit ends with a summary of the contribution this all makes to educators. There are many books you can read on child development. Three are described briefly below.

ANNOTATED FURTHER READING

Donaldson, M. (1978) *Children's Minds*, London: Fontana.

    This is an accessible and important book that has not dated, despite being written 30 years ago. It offers a useful critique of the work of Piaget and reminds us always to think of the competent child who is able to see things from the perspective of others, who insistently makes and shares meaning out of all situations and learns through relationships, questioning, listening, making and communicating.

Gravelle, M. (ed.) (2000) *Planning for Bilingual Learners*, Stoke on Trent: Trentham Books.

    This is a book made up of many voices and offers a framework for those working with children who come with languages other than English. It is relevant because it refers back to recent research, including research into child development.

Smidt, S. (2008) *Introducing Vygotsky: A Guide for Practitioners and Students*, London and New York: Routledge.

    This book aims to discuss the work of Vygotsky in the sort of language that is accessible to everyone. It uses lots of case studies and examples to illustrate some difficult ideas, such as the zone of proximal development. In the same *Introducing . . .* series you will find books on Piaget, Bruner and Malaguzzi.

(M) FURTHER READING TO SUPPORT M-LEVEL STUDY

Kenner, C. and Kress, G. (2003) 'The multisemiotic resources of biliterate children', *Journal of Early Childhood Literacy* 3(2): 179–202.

    This paper argues that children gain access to an enhanced range of communicative resources through familiarity with more than one writing system. Different scripts can be seen as different modes, giving rise to a variety of potentials for meaning-making. In case studies of children's responses to learning Chinese, Arabic or Spanish, as well as English, at the age of 6, they were found to be exploring these potentials in terms of symbol design, spatial framing and directionality. A multimodal analysis shows how children can build up 'embodied knowledges' as they construct different visual and actional dispositions through the bilingual script-learning experience. Such flexibility is likely to be an asset in a world that makes increasing use of multilingual and multimodal communication.

Twardosz, S. (2012) 'Effects of experience on the brain: the role of neuroscience in early development and education', *Early Education and Development* 23(1): 96–119.

    Twardosz writes widely on neuroscience, its implications and dangers. In this paper, she discusses two main themes: first, the findings of research where she reviews (a) the role of experience in shaping the developing brain, (b) individual adaptation to the environment through learning and memory, and (c) the effects of stress on the developing and adult brain. The second is where she addresses controversies about applications of this knowledge to recommendations for parents and teachers regarding the care and education of young children. These include examining some questionable programmes such as BrainGym and addressing the widely held beliefs in the importance of critical periods and enhanced environments. One of her messages is that all infants learn in all environments.

RELEVANT WEBSITES

www.foundationyears.org.uk/early-years-foundation-stage-2012/

www.education.gov.uk/schools/teachingandlearning/curriculum/primary

www.thehdrc.org

The child-driven education: www.ted.com/talks/sugata_mitra_the_child_driven_education.html

www.unicef.org/media/media_62521.html

www.scotland.gov.uk/Resource/Doc/136953/0034036.pdf

REFERENCES

Baker, C. (2000) *Foundations of Bilingual Education and Bilingualism*, 2nd edn, Clevedon: Multilingual Matters.

Bronfenbrenner, U. (1979) *The Ecology of Human Development*, Cambridge, MA: Harvard University Press.

Bialystok, E. (1991) 'Letters, sounds, and symbols: Changes in children's understanding of written language', *Applied Psycholinguistics* 12: 75–89.

Dahlberg, G., Moss, P. and Pence, A. (1999) *Beyond Quality in Early Childhood Education and Care: Postmodern Perspectives*, London: Falmer Press.

Donaldson, M. (1978) *Children's Minds*, London: Fontana.

Erny, P (1981) *The Child and His Environment in Black Africa: An Essay on Traditional Education*, London: Open University Press.

Göncü, A. (ed.) (1999) *Children's Engagement in the World: Sociocultural Perspectives*, Cambridge: Cambridge University Press.

Halpenny, A. and Petterson, J. (2014) *Introducing Piaget: A Guide for Practitioners and Students*, London and New York: Routledge.

Hyde, K., Lerch, J., Norton, A., Forgeard, M., Winner, E., Evans, A.C. and Schlaug, G. (2009) 'The effects of musical training on structural brain development: a longitudinal study', in *The Neurosciences and Music 111: Disorders and Plasticity*, Beth Israel Deaconess Medical Center and Harvard Medical School, Boston: MA.

Kenner, C. (2004) *Becoming Biliterate: Young Children Learning Different Writing Systems*, Stoke on Trent: Trentham Books.

Nsamenang, A.B. and Tchombe, T. (eds) (2011) *Handbook of African Educational Theories and Practices: A Generative Teacher Education Curriculum*, Bamenda, Cameroon: Human Development Resource Centre.

Penn, H. (2005) U*nderstanding Early Childhood: Issues and Controversies*, Maidenhead: Open University Press.

Rinaldi C. (2006) *Dialogue with Reggio Emilia: Listening, Researching and Learning* (Contesting Early Childhood Series), London: Routledge.

Smidt, S. (2008) *Introducing Vygotsky: A Guide for Practitioners and Students*, London and New York: Routledge.

Smidt, S. (2011) *Introducing Bruner: A Guide for Practitioners and Students*, London and New York: Routledge.

Smidt, S. (2013) *Introducing Malaguzzi*, London and New York: Routledge.

Twardosz, S. (2012) 'Effects of experience on the brain: the role of neuroscience in early development and education', *Early Education and Development* 23(1): 96–119.

Vecchi, V. (2010) *Art and Creativity in Reggio Emilia: Exploring the Role and Potential of Ateliers in Early Childhood Education (Contesting Early Childhood Series)*, London: Routledge.

LOOKING AT LEARNING

David Wray

INTRODUCTION

Learning is paradoxical in nature. It can sometimes appear to be a very simple thing. All of us are learning all the time, after all, from the myriad experiences we encounter in our daily lives. I go to a new restaurant and I learn that even smoked salmon can be spoilt if you serve it with too much dill sauce; I read the newspaper and learn a little more about how Bayern Munich are threatening to replace Barcelona as the best football team in the world; I play on my son's Xbox and finally learn how to outwit that alien that's been shooting me in every one of my previous tries. Learning is so simple that we do not question its presence in how we go about our daily activities, for it is as natural to our existence as eating and drinking. Yet, when we encounter difficulties in learning something, we no longer take the learning process for granted. It is only then that our awareness of how we learn is heightened. Learning can suddenly seem very difficult indeed. I remember trying numerous ways of learning Latin declensions at school, until it suddenly struck me I could make a nursery rhyme of them: *lupus, lupe, lupum, lupi, lupi, lupo.* This revelation worked so well, I still have this (useless) knowledge down pat, even now.

Learning is taken for granted as a natural process. Yet, as simple a process as it seems, understanding how we learn is not as straightforward. The existence of numerous definitions and theories of learning, and the significant and, at times, vitriolic debates between adherents of particular theories vouch for the complexity of the process. A look, more or less random, at educational psychology textbooks will illustrate the differences between the views of the 'experts' about what exactly learning is and how we learn. In David Fontana's *Psychology for Teachers* (1985), for example, the author writes, 'Most psychologists would agree that learning is a relatively persistent change in an individual's possible behaviour due to experience' (p. 211). This definition reflects a behaviourist view of learning, for it equates learning with an outcome defined as behaviour. Contrast it with the remarks of Norah Morgan and Juliana Saxton in their *Teaching, Questioning and Learning* (1991), as they argue that:

> effective teaching depends upon recognizing that effective learning takes place when the students are active participants in 'what's going on'. And for effective teaching and learning to occur, teachers must structure their teaching to invite and sustain that active participation by providing experiences which 'get them thinking and feeling', 'get the adrenalin flowing' and which generate in students a need for expression.
>
> (p. 7)

And later: 'Learning springs from curiosity - the *need* to know' (p. 18). Here, learning appears to be defined more by learner engagement with experiences, leading to thought, expression and knowledge - a much broader definition.

So, what is this simple, yet complex, thing called 'learning'? And does it matter how we define it? Will that actually make a difference to how we attempt to go about enabling it to happen in classrooms?

OBJECTIVES

After reading this unit, you should be able to:

1 recognise and describe the main elements of the major theoretical approaches to learning;
2 understand the implications of each of these approaches for classroom teaching.

APPROACHES TO LEARNING

Although there are many different approaches to learning, there are three basic schools of thought about learning theory: behaviourist, constructivist (often referred to as 'cognitivist') and social constructivist. In this unit, I will provide a brief introduction to each theory. For each, I will give a short historical introduction, followed by a discussion of the view of knowledge presupposed by the theory. Next, I will give an account of how learning and learner motivation are treated, before concluding with some discussion of some of the implications for teaching embedded in each theory. A brief overview of the main points of the unit is given in Table 2.2.1.

TABLE 2.2.1 An overview of the main features of learning theories

| | Learning theory | | |
	Behaviourism	Constructivism	Social constructivism
Knowledge	Repertoire of behavioural responses to environmental stimuli	Knowledge systems are actively constructed by learners based on existing structures	Knowledge is socially constructed
Learning	Passive absorption of predefined body of knowledge by learner; promoted by repetition and positive reinforcement	Active assimilation and accommodation of new information to existing cognitive structures; discovery by learners	Integration of pupils into knowledge community; collaborative assimilation and accommodation of new information
Motivation	Extrinsic, reward and punishment (positive and negative reinforcers)	Intrinsic: learners set their own goals and motivate themselves to learn	Intrinsic and extrinsic: learning goals and motives are determined both by learners and extrinsic rewards provided by the knowledge community
Teaching	Correct behavioural responses are transmitted by the teacher and repeated by the pupils; the teacher reinforces these	The teacher facilitates learning by providing an environment that promotes discovery and assimilation/accommodation	Collaborative learning is facilitated and guided by the teacher; group work

BEHAVIOURISM

Brief history

Behaviourism began as a reaction against the introspective psychology that dominated the late nineteenth and early twentieth centuries. Introspective psychologists such as Freud and Jung maintained that the study of consciousness was the primary object of psychology. Their methods relied on introspection, that is, first-person reports of feelings and experiences, both conscious and subconscious. Behaviourists such as B.F. Skinner rejected introspective methods as being subjective and unquantifiable. Instead, they focused on objectively observable, quantifiable events and behaviour. They argued that, as it is not possible to observe objectively or to quantify what occurs in the mind, scientific theories should take into account only observable indicators such as stimulus–response sequences. According to Skinner (1976):

> The mentalistic problem can be avoided by going directly to the prior physical causes while bypassing intermediate feelings or states of mind. The quickest way to do this is to . . . consider only those facts which can be objectively observed in the behaviour of one person in its relation to his prior environmental history.
>
> (p. 23)

For behaviourists such as Skinner, what happens in the mind during processes such as learning would forever be inside 'the black box', and thus not knowable. All that psychologists could do was to observe the behaviours resulting from such internal states.

What is knowledge?

Behaviourists such as Watson and Skinner viewed knowledge as a repertoire of behaviours. Skinner argued that it is not the case that we use knowledge to guide our action, rather 'knowledge is action, or at least rules for action' (1976: 152). It is a set of passive, largely mechanical responses to environmental stimuli. So, for instance, the behaviourist would argue that to say that someone knows Shakespeare is to say that this person has a certain repertoire of behaviour with respect to Shakespeare.

Knowledge that is not actively expressed in behaviour can be explained as behavioural capacities. For example, 'I know a Siamese cat when I see one' can be seen as effectively equivalent to 'I have the capacity to identify a Siamese cat although I am not now doing so' (Skinner, 1976: 154). If knowledge is seen as a repertoire of behaviours, someone can be said to understand something if they possess the appropriate repertoire of behaviour. No reference to unobservable cognitive processes is necessary (pp. 156-7).

What is learning?

From a behaviourist perspective, the transmission of information from teacher to learner is essentially the transmission of the response appropriate to a certain stimulus. Thus, the point of education is to present the learner with the appropriate repertoire of behavioural responses to specific stimuli and to reinforce those responses through an effective reinforcement schedule (Skinner, 1976: 161). An effective reinforcement schedule requires consistent repetition of the material. The material to be learned should be broken down into small, progressive sequences of tasks, and continuous positive reinforcement should be given. Without positive reinforcement, learned responses will quickly become extinct. This is because learners will continue to modify their behaviour until they do receive some positive reinforcement.

What does motivation involve?

Behaviourists explain motivation in terms of schedules of positive and negative reinforcement. Just as receiving food pellets each time it pecks at a button teaches a pigeon to peck the button, pleasant experiences cause human learners to make the desired connections between specific stimuli and the appropriate responses. For example, a learner who receives verbal praise and good marks for correct answers is more likely to learn those answers effectively than one who receives little or no positive feedback for the same answers. Likewise, human learners tend to avoid responses that are associated with negative reinforcements, such as poor marks or negative feedback.

How should you teach?

Behaviourist teaching methods tend to rely on so-called 'skill and drill' exercises to provide the consistent repetition necessary for the effective reinforcement of response patterns. Other methods include question (stimulus) and answer (response) sequences, in which questions are of gradually increasing difficulty, guided practice and regular reviews of material. Behaviourist methods also typically rely heavily on the use of positive reinforcements, such as verbal praise, good marks and prizes. Behaviourists test the degree of learning using methods that measure observable behaviour, such as tests and examinations.

Behaviourist teaching methods have proved most successful in areas where there is a 'correct' response or easily memorised material. For example, although behaviourist methods have proved to be successful in teaching structured material, such as facts and formulae, scientific concepts and foreign-language vocabulary, their usefulness in teaching comprehension and composition is questionable.

As an example of this kind of teaching, some of you will have experienced the use of 'language laboratories' when you were learning a foreign language. In the language lab, you were often presented with stretches of discourse in the target language, which you were required to repeat, and then you were given feedback on the accuracy of this repetition. This experience has been demonstrated to improve learners' knowledge of the particular discourse form, but not of how this should be adapted to other, real-life situations. While I was in the sixth form at school, for instance, I worked with an enthusiastic language teacher who decided we should be introduced to Russian. Through extensive experience of language lab drills, I learned (by rote) how to greet someone in Russian (*Zdrastvwe Olga, kak tee posavaesh?*), how to acknowledge such a greeting (*Spasiba, kharasho, a ti?*) and how to respond (*Spasiba, kharasho*) – these were spoken drills, and so I never did know how this was written down! Unfortunately, the first and only time I tried this out on a Russian speaker, he was not called Olga, and he did not acknowledge my greeting in the 'right' way, and thus left me floundering! My language behaviour was not sufficiently adaptable to cope with the real-life situation.

Behaviourist theories of learning have had a recent renaissance in the field of behaviour management, rather than in content and concept learning. Positive behaviour management is usually taken to involve rewarding acceptable behaviour in pupils (CBG – catch them being good) and ignoring unacceptable. Thus, so the theory goes, pupils will be encouraged to repeat the acceptable behaviour, and the unacceptable will gradually die away. Note that it has usually been argued that, theoretically, unacceptable behaviour, if met with a negative response by the teacher, may in fact be perceived by the pupil as having been rewarded (any attention being better than none for some pupils) and thus will not fade away but be continued. Ignoring it is better. This argument makes good sense theoretically, but you might find it difficult to implement practically!

It is also true, of course, that the reward (positive feedback) that a pupil gains following unacceptable behaviour may come, not from the teacher, but from others in the class. The class clown tends to get his or her rewards from peers rather than from teachers.

Task 2.2.1 A behaviourist approach to teaching

Behaviourist approaches to teaching tend to rely on three basic principles:

1 Break down the desirable end behaviour into small steps.
2 Teach – that is, stimulate and reinforce – each of these steps in the learner.
3 Reinforce increasingly long chains of behaviour until the full end behaviour is finally achieved.

- Think of a teaching event in which you might employ such a set of principles for your teaching. Share your suggestions with colleagues and discuss how applicable this approach might be to teaching.
- Before reading the following section of this unit, discuss with your colleagues what you consider to be the main limitations of behaviourism as a theory of learning.

Task 2.2.2 Skinner vs Chomsky

One of the most significant challenges to behaviourist views of learning came in the field of language acquisition. Skinner's attempt to explain this from a behaviourist perspective came in 1957, in his book *Verbal Behavior*. This produced a devastating review from the noted linguist Noam Chomsky. This review can be read at www.chomsky.info/articles/1967 ----.htm, and a wider attack on behaviourism can be found at www.chomsky.info/articles/ 19711230.htm

When you have read either, or both, of these articles, try to produce a bullet-point summary of the differences between Skinner and Chomsky in terms of their views about learning.

CONSTRUCTIVISM

Brief history

A dissatisfaction with behaviourism's strict focus on observable behaviour led educational psychologists such as Jean Piaget to demand an approach to learning theory that paid more attention to what went on 'inside the learner's head'. An approach developed that focused on mental processes rather than observable behaviour – cognition rather than action. Common to most constructivist approaches is the idea that knowledge comprises symbolic mental representations, such as propositions and images, together with a mechanism that operates on those representations. Knowledge is seen as something that is actively constructed by learners, based on their existing cognitive structures.

Therefore, it relates strongly to their stage of cognitive development. Understanding the learner's existing intellectual framework is central to understanding the learning process.

The most influential exponent of constructivism was the Swiss child psychologist, Jean Piaget. Piaget rejected the idea that learning was the passive assimilation of given knowledge. Instead, he proposed that learning is a dynamic process comprising successive stages of adaptation to reality, during which learners actively construct knowledge by creating and testing their own theories of the world. Piaget's theory has two main strands: first, an account of the mechanisms by which cognitive development takes place; and, second, an account of the four main stages of cognitive development through which, he claimed, all children pass (Piaget, 1962).

The basic principle underlying Piaget's theory is the principle of equilibration (balancing): all cognitive development progresses towards increasingly complex, but *stable*, mental representations of the world. Such stability is threatened by the input of new ideas, and so equilibration takes place through a process of adaptation. One of the reasons why humans have often been quite resistant to new ideas is this inbuilt need for stability in their concepts of the world. Think about the centuries during which people were convinced that the sun orbited the earth, rather than vice versa. It was not until evidence of the falsity of such a belief was overwhelming that most people made the destabilising mental shift to a new set of ideas about the world.

Such adaptation might involve the assimilation of new information into existing cognitive structures, or the accommodation of that information through the formation of new cognitive structures. As an example of this, consider what happens when you enter a novel situation – say, going into a new restaurant. Normally, although you have never been in this particular restaurant before, you will have experience of many similar environments, and thus know what to expect. You know the sequence of events (waiter brings menu, leaves you for a while, returns to ask for your order; if it's a posh restaurant, a different waiter asks you what wine you would like to drink with the meal; etc., etc.) – you know what is expected of you. The 'new' aspects of this restaurant (location, orientation of the room, design of the menus, particular specialist dishes, where the loos are, etc.) are simply new elements of information that you need to assimilate into your mental maps of the world (Piaget used the term 'schema' to refer to one of these mental maps – the plural is variously written as 'schemata' or 'schemas', depending on how classical your education was). If, less usually, this restaurant is way outside your previous experience (suppose it's your first visit to a Japanese restaurant), the process of learning might be more radical. There may be details about the cutlery, plates, order of the courses, appropriate drinks, etc., to come to terms with, and these new features need to be accommodated into an expanded schema of 'restaurant'. Thus, learners adapt and develop by assimilating and accommodating new information into existing cognitive structures.

Piaget also suggested that there are four main stages in the cognitive development of children. In their first 2 years, children pass through a sensori-motor stage, during which they progress from cognitive structures dominated by instinctive drives and undifferentiated emotions (they do not care who picks them up, as long as they satisfy the basic physical drives of hunger, comfort, etc.) to more organised systems of concrete concepts and differentiated emotions (not anyone will do as a food provider – it has to be Mum or Dad). At this stage, children's outlook is essentially egocentric, in the sense that they are unable to take into account others' points of view.

The second stage of development lasts until around 7 years of age. Children begin to use language to make sense of reality. They learn to classify objects using different criteria and to manipulate numbers. Children's increasing linguistic skills open the way for greater levels of social action and communication with others.

From the ages of 7 to 12 years, children begin to develop logic, although they can only perform logical operations on concrete objects and events.

In adolescence, children enter the formal operational stage, which continues throughout the rest of their lives. Children develop the ability to perform abstract intellectual operations and reach emotional and intellectual maturity. They learn how to formulate and test abstract hypotheses without referring to concrete objects. Most importantly, children develop the capacity to appreciate others' points of view, as well as their own.

Piaget's theory was widely accepted from the 1950s until the 1970s. Then, researchers such as Margaret Donaldson began to find evidence that young children were not as limited in their thinking as Piaget had suggested. Researchers found that, when situations made 'human sense' (Donaldson's term) to children, they could engage in mental operations at a much higher level than Piaget had predicted. His theory, particularly that aspect related to the above stages of development, is not now as widely accepted, although it has had a significant influence on later theories of cognitive development. For instance, the idea of adaptation through assimilation and accommodation is still widely accepted, and is incorporated into what is now known as 'schema theory', which we will revisit in the next unit of this book.

What is knowledge?

Behaviourists maintain that knowledge is a passively absorbed repertoire of behaviours. Constructivists reject that claim, arguing instead that knowledge is actively constructed by learners, and that any account of knowledge makes essential references to the cognitive structures within the learner's mind. Knowledge comprises a complex set of mental representations derived from past learning experiences. Each learner interprets experiences and information in the light of their existing knowledge, their stage of cognitive development, their cultural background, their personal history and so on. Learners use these factors to organise their experience and to select and transform new information. Knowledge is, therefore, actively constructed by the learner, rather than passively absorbed; it is essentially dependent on the standpoint from which the learner approaches it.

What is learning?

Because knowledge is actively constructed, learning is defined as a process of active discovery. The role of the instructor is not to drill knowledge into learners through consistent repetition, nor to goad them into learning through carefully employed rewards and punishments. Rather, the role of the teacher is to facilitate discovery by providing the necessary resources and by guiding learners as they attempt to assimilate new knowledge to old and to modify the old to accommodate the new. Teachers must thus take into account the knowledge that the learner currently possesses when deciding how to construct the curriculum and how to present, sequence and structure new material.

What does motivation involve?

Unlike behaviourist learning theory, where learners are thought to be motivated by extrinsic factors such as rewards and punishment, constructivist learning theory sees motivation as largely intrinsic. Because it involves significant restructuring of existing cognitive structures, successful learning requires a major personal investment on the part of the learner. Learners must face up to the limitations of their existing knowledge and accept the need to modify or abandon existing beliefs. Without some kind of internal drive on the part of the learner to make these modifications, external rewards and punishments such as marks are unlikely to be sufficient.

How should you teach?

Constructivist teaching methods aim to assist learners in assimilating new information into existing knowledge, and to enable them to make the appropriate modifications to their existing intellectual frameworks to accommodate that information. Thus, although constructivists accept some use of 'skill and drill' exercises in the memorisation of facts, formulae and lists, etc., they place much greater importance on strategies that help learners to actively assimilate and accommodate new material. For instance, asking learners to explain new material in their own words can help them to assimilate this material, by forcing them to re-express the new ideas in their existing vocabulary. Similarly, providing pupils with sets of questions to structure their reading can make it easier for them to relate the ideas in the reading to previous material by highlighting certain aspects of the text. These questions can also help pupils to accommodate the new material by giving them a clear organisational structure of ideas. Pre-reading questions such as these are referred to by researchers into reading as 'advance organisers'. An extreme example of their usefulness can be seen in the following task.

Because learning is largely self-motivated in constructivist theory, a number of methods have also been suggested that require pupils to monitor their own learning. For instance, the regular use of check-up tests and study questions can enable pupils to monitor their own understanding of material. Other methods that have been suggested include the use of learning journals by pupils to monitor

---

Task 2.2.3 Using schemas to construct meaning

1   Read the following passage, then close this book and try to tell someone else what the passage was about:

> The procedure is actually quite simple. First you arrange things into different groups. Of course one pile may be sufficient depending on how much there is to do. If you have to go somewhere else due to lack of facilities, that is the next step; otherwise you are pretty well set. It is important not to overdo things. That is, it is better to do too few things at once than too many. In the short run this may not seem important, but complications can easily arise. A mistake can be expensive as well. At first, the whole procedure will seem complicated. Soon, however, it will become just another facet of life. It is difficult to foresee any end to the necessity for this task in the immediate future, but then one can never tell. After the procedure is completed one arranges the materials into different groups again. Then they can be put into their appropriate places. Eventually, they will be used once more and the whole cycle will then have to be repeated. However, that is a part of life.

2   Now read the passage again in order to answer the following questions:

- Outline the steps in the process of washing clothes as they are listed in the passage.
- Can you see any end to the necessity for this task in the immediate future?

You should have found that having the questions there to guide your reading made it possible for you to understand a passage that, previously, was incomprehensible. What has happened here is that the questions have 'switched on' the appropriate schema in your mind, allowing details to be assimilated.

their progress and highlight any recurring difficulties. (Modern web logs, or 'blogs', are an electronic version of such journals that are just beginning to be used in classroom learning.)

Constructivists also tend to place a great deal of emphasis upon practical activity, involving the physical manipulation of objects, in teaching such subjects as mathematics and science.

Challenging and pushing forward pupils' ideas are much more likely to happen with this kind of hands-on experience and are well expressed in the proverb much beloved of constructivist learning theorists: 'I hear, I forget; I see, I remember; I do, I understand'.

SOCIAL CONSTRUCTIVISM

Brief history

Social constructivism is a variety of constructivism that emphasises the collaborative nature of much learning. Social constructivism was developed by the Soviet psychologist, Lev Vygotsky. Vygotsky rejected the assumption made by constructivists such as Piaget that it was possible to separate learning from its social context. He argued that all cognitive functions originate in, and must, therefore, be explained as products of, social interactions, and that learning was not simply the assimilation and accommodation of new knowledge by learners: it was the process by which learners were integrated into a knowledge community. According to Vygotsky (1978; this date refers to the translation into English of Vygotsky's work, which was in fact published in the original Russian in the 1930s):

> Every function in the child's cultural development appears twice: first, on the social level and, later on, on the individual level; first, between people (interpsychological) and then inside the child (intrapsychological). This applies equally to voluntary attention, to logical memory, and to the formation of concepts. All the higher functions originate as actual relationships between individuals.

(p. 57)

What is knowledge?

Constructivists such as Piaget saw knowledge as actively constructed by learners in response to interactions with environmental stimuli. Vygotsky emphasised the role of language and culture in cognitive development. According to Vygotsky, language and culture play essential roles both in human intellectual development and in how humans perceive the world. Humans' linguistic abilities enable them to overcome the natural limitations of their perceptions by imposing culturally defined meaning on the world. Language and culture are the frameworks through which humans experience, communicate and understand reality. Vygotsky uses an example to illustrate this. When we look at the symbol on the right we see a clock.

Imagine, though, how a person would perceive this object who has never seen a clock before. He or she would be reduced to describing it, in Vygotsky's words, as 'something round and black with two hands' (1978: 39). (Notice that, here, Vygotsky actually understates his own case, as, in order to describe the two lines in the object as 'hands', you have to have a concept of clock in the first place!)

The essential element that transforms this object into 'clock' is its cultural usage. Vygotsky's point is that language and the conceptual schemes that are transmitted by means of language are essentially social phenomena. As a result, human cognitive structures are essentially socially constructed. Knowledge is not simply constructed: it is co-constructed.

What is learning?

Vygotsky accepted Piaget's claim that learners respond, not to external stimuli, but to their interpretation of those stimuli. However, he argued that constructivists such as Piaget had overlooked the essentially social nature of language. As a result, he claimed, they had failed to understand that learning is a collaborative process. Vygotsky distinguished between two developmental levels: the level of *actual development* is the level of development that the learner has already reached, and is the level at which the learner is capable of solving problems independently. The level of *potential development* (the 'zone of proximal development') is the level of development that the learner is capable of reaching under the guidance of teachers or in collaboration with peers. Learners are capable of solving problems and understanding material at this level that they are not capable of solving or understanding at their level of actual development. The level of potential development is the level in which learning takes place. It comprises cognitive structures that are still in the process of developing, but that can only develop under the guidance of, or in collaboration with, others.

What does motivation involve?

For behaviourists, motivation is essentially *extrinsic* – it depends on positive or negative reinforcement from outside. Constructivist motivation is essentially *intrinsic* – it derives from the learner's internal drive. Social constructivists see motivation as both extrinsic and intrinsic. Because learning is essentially a social phenomenon, learners are partially motivated by rewards provided by the knowledge community. However, because knowledge is actively constructed by the learner, learning also depends to a significant extent on the learner's internal drive to understand.

How should you teach?

If learning is social, then it follows that teaching should ideally use collaborative learning methods. These require learners to develop teamwork skills and to see individual learning as essentially related to the success of group learning. This should be seen as a process of peer interaction that is mediated and structured by the teacher. Discussion can be promoted by the presentation of specific concepts or problems and guided by directed questions, the introduction and clarification of concepts and information, and references to previously learned material. More specific discussion of collaborative teaching and the linked strategies of modelling and scaffolding will be found in the following unit.

NEUROSCIENCE – A NEW INFLUENCE UPON LEARNING THEORY?

A fairly recent development in terms of our attempts to understand processes of learning concerns the insights coming from neuroscience, that is, detailed study at a physical, biological level of the workings of the brain. Such study has begun to suggest some profitable areas to explore, and this is the most that the majority of researchers in the area would claim. However, there have also been a number of other purported outcomes from this research, which have not been well founded.

These claims have been labelled as 'neuro-myths' (OECD, 2002), in the sense that their popularity has spread, not through close scrutiny of research evidence, but through their adoption by commercial teaching programmes. Some of the most widespread of these neuro-myths (or misguided beliefs about neuroscience) include the following claims:

- The brain is static, unchanging, and its parameters and nature are fully set before children begin school. Therefore, teachers need to find ways of understanding and characterising learners according to the perceived natures of their brains (see, for example, the left-brain/right-brain and learning styles neuro-myths below). In fact, one of the most widely accepted conclusions from research in neuroscience is that of neuroplasticity (Hendel-Giller, 2011). Our brains grow, change and adapt all the way through our lives. Thus, all learners are capable of adaptation.
- Some people are left-brained and some are right-brained. This purported division has become a powerful metaphor for different ways of thinking – logical, focused and analytic versus broad-minded and creative, and it probably originated in the split-brain work of Nobel Prize winner Roger Sperry, who noticed differences in the brain when he studied people whose left and right brains had been surgically disconnected. However, in healthy, normal brains, the two sides are very well connected, all parts working together very well.
- We use only 10 per cent of our brains. This is also untrue, according to most neuroscientists. In fact, brain-imaging research has not yet found any evidence of inactive areas in healthy brains. We use all our brains – which does not mean we could not individually use them better!
- Male and female brains are very different. There seems to be absolutely no significant evidence to suggest that the genders learn or should be taught differently. Male and female students may have different *preferences* for what they study, but these are more likely to be culturally determined rather than brain-based.
- The ages 0–3 are more important than any other age for learning. Even though the connections between neurons, called synapses, are greatest in number during this period, there is no evidence (Goswami, 2006) that more will be learned if teaching is timed to coincide with periods of *synaptogenesis*. The evidence suggests that learners can learn anything at any time, and what might prevent them is not the state of their brains but their existing knowledge (and their motivation).
- Children's learning styles can be identified as visual, auditory or kinaesthetic (which, in some schools, means that children wear a badge labelled either V, A or K, showing their learning style, so all their teachers can teach them accordingly). The paper by Sharp, Bowker and Byrne (2008) gives a comprehensive rejection to the learning styles myth.
- Commercial packages that focus upon teaching children a series of simple body movements will have the added advantage of improving the ways the brains of these children work. 'Brain Gym' is the best known of these packages and claims to 'integrate all areas of the brain to enhance learning'. Unfortunately, there is no evidence whatsoever that such activities have any discernible impact upon children's learning.

Although many people in education accept claims such as these as established fact, they are, in fact, very dubiously rooted in research evidence.

Task 2.2.4 Looking at neuro-myths

Here are twenty statements related to the brain and the ways it might be linked to learning. Some of these are correct and some are incorrect – neuro-myths. Can you tell which is which? The answers are given at the end of the unit.

✓ if you think a statement is correct, and ✗ if you think it is wrong

1	Children must acquire their native language before a second language is learned. If they do not do so, neither language will be fully acquired	
2	Boys have bigger brains than girls	
3	If pupils do not drink sufficient amounts of water (= 6–8 glasses a day), their brains shrink	
4	It has been scientifically proven that fatty acid supplements (omega-3 and omega-6) have a positive effect on academic achievement	
5	When a brain region is damaged, other parts of the brain can take up its function	
6	We only use 10 per cent of our brain	
7	The left and right hemispheres of the brain always work together	
8	Differences in hemispheric dominance (left brain, right brain) can help explain individual differences among learners	
9	Brain development has finished by the time children reach secondary school	
10	There are critical periods in childhood after which certain things can no longer be learned	
11	Individuals learn better when they receive information in their preferred learning style (e.g., auditory, visual, kinaesthetic)	
12	Learning occurs through modification of the brain's neural connections	
13	Academic achievement can be affected by skipping breakfast	
14	Normal development of the human brain involves the birth and death of brain cells	
15	Mental capacity is hereditary and cannot be changed by the environment or experience	
16	Environments that are rich in stimulus improve the brains of pre-school children	
17	Children are less attentive after consuming sugary drinks and/or snacks	
18	Circadian rhythms ('body clock') shift during adolescence, causing pupils to be tired during the first lessons of the school day	
19	Regular drinking of caffeinated drinks reduces alertness	
20	Exercises that rehearse co-ordination of motor-perception skills can improve literacy skills	

SUMMARY

The point made at the beginning of this unit was that learning is such a familiar and everyday thing that it is somewhat surprising that defining it has caused such huge debate. However, understanding the main principles of these debates is absolutely crucial if you are successfully to plan for and implement effective learning in your classroom. Learning is what you are mainly there to bring about, so clearly what you think learning is makes a difference to the way you teach. It is, unfortunately, the case, however, that some teachers never really give this issue much thought. Learning is so obviously important that it becomes unproblematic. However, teachers such as yourself, sufficiently interested to read books and units such as this, will know that our intentions as teachers, our *theories* about teaching and learning, do make a difference to how we act in classrooms.

In this unit, I have reviewed the main theoretical approaches to learning and tried to pull out their practical implications. In many ways, you can be an effective teacher if you view learning mainly from a behaviourist, constructivist or social constructivist viewpoint: it is not your choice of theory that makes the difference. What matters is that your strategies for teaching and your teaching actions match the theory you hold about learning. Coherence between your theories and your practices will be much more successful in enabling learning than thinking one thing but doing another.

 ## ANNOTATED FURTHER READING

Donaldson, M. (1978) *Children's Minds*, London: Fontana.
> This was an immensely significant book when it was first published. It brought together recent research into children's learning that fundamentally challenged Piagetian views that learners were limited by the current conceptual development stage they were operating in. It was also noteworthy for being one of the most readable accounts of learning and development ever written.

Joyce, B., Calhoun, E. and Hopkins, D. (1997) *Models of Learning: Tools for Teaching*, Buckingham: Open University Press.
> This is a very useful outline of different models of learning. The writers isolate four 'families' of teaching based on the types of learning they promote: information processing, social/building a learning community, personal and behavioural.

Pritchard, A. (2008) *Ways of Learning*, London: David Fulton.
> This book contains a detailed introduction to the major theories that lie behind children's learning styles. The book explores how to develop learning situations and how to plan and create the best opportunities for effective and lasting learning. It includes coverage of areas such as behaviourism, multiple intelligence, constructivism and metacognition and gives advice on how the theoretical ideas of Piaget, Vygotsky and Bruner can be placed into a classroom context.

Wood, D. (1988) *How Children Think and Learn*, Oxford: Blackwell.
> This is one of the most comprehensive and readable introductions to the study of learning. Wood is very good at relating the theoretical notions he describes so well to their practical implications for teaching. He concludes by arguing that, 'for some time to come, I suspect that the most valuable resources within the classroom will be found in human form', by which he means you – the teacher.

FURTHER READING TO SUPPORT M-LEVEL STUDY

Bransford, J., Brown, A. and Cocking, R. (2000) *How People Learn: Brain, Mind, Experience, and School*, Washington, DC: National Academies Press.

> This is a very comprehensive and well-written account of the major research into the learning process. The section on 'How children learn' is particularly useful as a review of the major learning theories. It is freely available as a PDF download from www.nap.edu/openbook.php?isbn= 0309070368

Siemens, G. (2005) 'Connectivism: a learning theory for the digital age', *International Journal of Instructional Technology and Distance Learning*, 2(1), www.itdl.org/Journal/Jan_05/article01.htm.

> Connectivism is not the same as constructivism. Siemens, in this seminal article, puts forward a theory of learning that he claims better fits with the online, network-based learning that characterises the twenty-first-century digital world. This new theory takes into account the importance of informal as well as formal learning, and the ways we typically use modern technology to support our memories and interactions with others.

 ## RELEVANT WEBSITES

www.chomsky.info/articles/1967----.htm
www.chomsky.info/articles/19711230.htm

> These contain Noam Chomsky's review of Skinner and his attack on behaviourism.

www.emtech.net/learning_theories.htm

> The emTech Learning Theories website contains probably the most comprehensive collection of links on the Internet on the topic of learning theories (and other aspects of education – www.emtech.net). Most of the links are to downloadable articles/papers on topics ranging from operant conditioning to cognitive dissonance.

www.learning-theories.com

> The Learning Theories website provides a useful outline of the principal theories of learning. It also gives access to numerous links to academic and practical material, which will expand your understanding of theories of learning.

 ## REFERENCES

Donaldson, M. (1978) *Children's Minds*, London: Fontana.

Fontana, D. (1985) *Psychology for Teachers*, London: Macmillan.

Goswami, U. (2006) 'Neuroscience and education: from research to practice?', *Nature Reviews Neuroscience* 7: 406-13, www.nature.com/nrn/journal/v7/n5/full/nrn1907.html.

Hendel-Giller, R. (2011) *The Neuroscience of Learning: A New Paradigm for Corporate Education*, Fenton, MO: The Maritz Institute, www.themaritzinstitute.com/Perspectives/~/media/Files/MaritzInstitute/White-Papers/The-Neuroscience-of-Learning-The-Maritz-Institute.pdf.

Joyce, B., Calhoun, E. and Hopkins, D. (1997) *Models of Learning: Tools for Teaching*, Buckingham: Open University Press.

Morgan, N. and Saxton, J. (1991) *Teaching Questioning and Learning*, London: Routledge.

OECD (2002) *Understanding the Brain: Towards a New Learning Science*, Paris: Organisation for Economic Co-operation and Development.

Piaget, J. (1962) *The Language and Thought of the Child*, London: Routledge & Kegal Paul.

Pritchard, A. (2008) *Ways of Learning*, London: David Fulton.

Sharp, J.G., Bowker, R. and Byrne, J. (2008) 'VAK or VAK-uous? Towards the trivialisation of learning and the death of scholarship', *Research Papers in Education*, 23(3): 293-314.

Skinner, B.F. (1976) *About Behaviourism*, New York: Vintage Books.

Vygotsky, L. (1978) *Mind in Society*, Cambridge, MA: Harvard University Press.

Wood, D. (1988) *How Children Think and Learn*, Oxford: Blackwell.

ANSWERS

Task 2.2.4 Looking at neuro-myths

Statement	✓ = correct, ✗ = wrong	
1	Children must acquire their native language before a second language is learned. If they do not do so neither language will be fully acquired	✗
2	Boys have bigger brains than girls	✓
3	If pupils do not drink sufficient amounts of water (= 6–8 glasses a day) their brains shrink	✗
4	It has been scientifically proven that fatty acid supplements (omega-3 and omega-6) have a positive effect on academic achievement	✗
5	When a brain region is damaged other parts of the brain can take up its function	✓
6	We only use 10 per cent of our brain	✗
7	The left and right hemisphere of the brain always work together	✓
8	Differences in hemispheric dominance (left brain, right brain) can help explain individual differences among learners	✗
9	Brain development has finished by the time children reach secondary school	✗
10	There are critical periods in childhood after which certain things can no longer be learned	✗
11	Individuals learn better when they receive information in their preferred learning style (e.g., auditory, visual, kinaesthetic)	✗
12	Learning occurs through modification of the brains' neural connections	✓
13	Academic achievement can be affected by skipping breakfast	✓
14	Normal development of the human brain involves the birth and death of brain cells	✓
15	Mental capacity is hereditary and cannot be changed by the environment or experience	✗
16	Environments that are rich in stimulus improve the brains of pre-school children	✗
17	Children are less attentive after consuming sugary drinks and/or snacks	✗
18	Circadian rhythms ('body clock') shift during adolescence, causing pupils to be tired during the first lessons of the school day	✓
19	Regular drinking of caffeinated drinks reduces alertness	✓
20	Exercises that rehearse co-ordination of motor-perception skills can improve literacy skills	✗

FROM LEARNING TO TEACHING

David Wray

INTRODUCTION

In the previous unit, we examined several important theories of learning, from behaviourism to social constructivism. It will probably have occurred to you that, in planning for the learning you hope and intend will take place in your classroom, you are guided, not by a single theory of learning, but in fact by elements of all these theories. There are useful elements within each of the theories reviewed in the previous unit, and indeed in other theoretical explorations of learning. Planning for teaching is not as simple as just deciding on the particular learning theory you wish to subscribe to. There are, however, a number of important insights into learning that can be used to underpin approaches to teaching, and it is the purpose of this unit to outline these insights and then to develop some principles for teaching that can be derived from them.

OBJECTIVES

After reading this unit, you should be able to:

- discuss some important insights into the nature of learning and recognise the implications of these for teaching;
- describe the basic elements of an apprenticeship approach to teaching, justify such an approach in terms of its foundation in research and theory, and suggest practical examples of the implementation of such an approach.

INSIGHTS INTO LEARNING

Four basic insights into the nature of the learning process have come from research over the past 20 years or so. Each of these has important implications for approaches to teaching.

Learning is a process of interaction between what is known and what is to be learned

It has become quite clear that, in order to do any real learning, we have to draw upon knowledge we already have about a subject. The more we know about the subject, the more likely it is that we shall learn any given piece of knowledge. Learning that does not make connections with our prior knowledge is learning at the level of rote only, and is soon forgotten once deliberate attempts to remember it have stopped.

Learning has been defined as 'the expansion and modification of existing ways of conceiving the world in the light of alternative ways' (Wray and Medwell, 1991: 9). Such a constructivist approach to learning places great emphasis upon the ways in which prior knowledge is structured in the learner's mind and in which it is activated during learning. Theories about this, generally known as schema theories, as they hypothesise that knowledge is stored in our minds in patterned ways (schemas), suggest that learning depends, first, upon the requisite prior knowledge being in the mind of the learner, and, second, upon it being brought to the forefront of the learner's mind.

As an example of this, in the field of learning through reading, try the following task.

Task 2.3.1 Schemas and reading

Look at the following story beginning:

- The man was brought into the large white room. His eyes blinked in the bright light.

Try to picture in your mind the scene so far. Is the man sitting, lying or standing? Is he alone in the room? What sort of room is it? What might this story be going to be about? Now read the next extract:

- 'Now, sit there', said the nurse. 'And try to relax.'

Has this altered your picture of the man or of the room? What is this story going to be about?

After the first extract, you may have thought the story would be set in a hospital, or perhaps concern an interrogation. There are key words in the brief beginning that trigger off these expectations. After the second extract, the possibility of a dentist's surgery may enter your mind, and the interrogation scenario fades.

Each item you read sparks off an idea in your mind, each one of which has its own associated schema, or structure of underlying ideas. It is unlikely, for example, that your picture of the room after the first extract had a plush white carpet on the floor. You construct a great deal from very little information.

Learning from the material you read is exactly like this. It is not simply a question of getting a meaning from what is on the page. When you read, you supply a good deal of the meaning to the page. The process is an interactive one, with the resultant learning being a combination of your previous ideas with new ones encountered in this text.

As another example of this, consider the following sentence:

- Mary remembered her birthday money when she heard the ice-cream van coming.

Without trying too hard, you can supply a great deal of information to the meaning of this, chiefly to do with Mary's intentions and feelings, but also to do with the appearance of the van and its driver's intentions. You probably do not immediately suspect him as a potential child molester! Notice that most of this seems so obvious that we barely give it much conscious thought. Our schemas for everyday events are so familiar that we do not notice when they are activated.

Now compare the picture you get from the following sentence:

- Mary remembered her birthday money when she heard the bus coming.

What difference does this make to your picture of Mary, beyond the difference in her probable intentions? Most people say that she now seems rather older. Notice that this difference in understanding comes, not so much from the words on the page, as from the complex network of ideas that these words make reference to. These networks have been referred to as schemas, and developments in our understanding of how they operate have had a great impact upon our ideas about the nature and teaching of reading comprehension.

Task 2.3.2 The impact of varying the schema

Try out the 'Mary' sentences above on some pupils you have access to (say between the ages of 6 and 11). Do they have the same responses to the sentences as you do? If not, this probably suggests that they have not yet developed the background schemas that you use in reading the sentences.

If they do make similar responses to you, you can extend the activity by using further variations on the original sentence. What schemas does the following activate, for example?

- Mary remembered her gun when she heard the ice-cream van coming.

Or the following?

- Mary remembered her stomach when she heard the ice-cream van coming.

Ask the pupils to think of their own variations and to explain the different impressions each leaves on the reader.

We have explored this issue through the example of reading, but the same interaction between the known and the new happens in any kind of learning. Many teachers have had the experience of asking a young child the apparently simple, mathematical question:

- What is the difference between 6 and 9?

The answer they receive might be 3, or 'one number is upside down', or 'my brother is 9 and he's older than me 'cos I'm 6', depending upon the schema that is activated by the word 'difference'.

You may also have heard the story of the newly qualified teacher who began work with a class of 5-6-year-olds in a rural school. She decided to begin her work with the class by using a topic she was reasonably confident they would be familiar with, so she showed them a picture of a cow. She asked the class, 'Now, who can tell me what this is?', but, to her consternation, not one of them could give her an answer, all of them looking faintly puzzled by the picture. After several equally fruitless attempts to get an answer to this simple question, she eventually became somewhat exasperated. 'Surely *somebody* can tell me what this is? You see them every day.' Eventually, one little boy raised his hand, not to give her an answer but to ask if he could look more closely at the picture. Baffled by now, she allowed him to come closer. He studied the picture for several moments before announcing in a tentative voice, 'I *think* it's a Hereford Jersey cross heifer'.

In this case, the children actually possessed much more background knowledge – a richer schema – than the teacher. Their subsequent learning around this topic would be considerably different from that the teacher had planned.

Task 2.3.3 Conflicting schemas

It would be very useful to work with your colleagues to collect some more examples like this, where the schema being used by the teacher did not coincide with that being employed by the learners. Here are some examples from my own experience:

- One 7-year-old boy once asked me 'How do you spell "friper"?' After some thought, I had to admit this defeated me and I didn't know how to spell it. I asked him if he could tell me the sentence in which he wished to use this word. 'I like friper taters', came the reply!

- One of my students was teaching in a south Wales school and had in his class a boy who was absent from school for a day. On his return, the student asked the boy what had been the problem. He replied, 'Badgers'. The student thought for a while and then took the boy to the class library and began to look for books about badgers, with the idea that they might possibly do a useful piece of project work on the subject. The boy looked increasingly puzzled and eventually stepped back and pointed to his ears, saying, 'Bad yers, sir.'

These are small examples, but, if you can pool your experiences with other colleagues, you might collect a much wider range of activities. The challenge is to think of ways in which these misunderstandings (or 'misaligned schemas') might have been avoided by the teachers.

Learning is a social process

Ideas about learning have progressed significantly away from Piaget's purely 'lone scientist' view of learners as acting upon their environments, observing the results and then, through reflection, modifying or fine-tuning their schemas concerning these environments. Modern learning theory gives much greater recognition to the importance of social interaction and support and has a view of the learner as a social constructor of knowledge. In collaboration with others, learners establish:

- Shared consciousness: a group working together can construct knowledge to a higher level than can the individuals in that group each working separately. The knowledge rests upon the group interaction.
- Borrowed consciousness: individuals working alongside more knowledgeable others can 'borrow' their understanding of tasks and ideas to enable them to work successfully.

From a social constructivist perspective, the most important tool for learning is discussion, or discourse. A lot of research has been carried out to try to understand the qualities of discourse that enhance its effectiveness. Raphael and her colleagues, for example (Raphael *et al.*, 1992), have studied the discourse used by primary-aged pupils as they engaged in discussions about the books they had read. The question leading this research was: How do discussions about books influence 10–11-year-old pupils' ability to talk about literature? A great deal was revealed in the research about the role played by the constitution of the groups, the books they discussed and the writing activities they were asked to complete as a follow-up. For example, it was found that the books chosen needed to have the potential for controversy and the power to elicit emotional responses. Furthermore, writing activities that allowed pupils more flexibility in their responses were more beneficial and led to more interesting discussions than those that demanded more structured responses. Finally, Raphael's research identified some of the more useful roles the teacher could play in such book discussions, such as modelling ways in which they could articulate their personal responses to literature.

The crucial role that the teacher plays in promoting the co-construction of knowledge in classrooms was also shown in the research of Forman *et al.* (1995), who studied the discourse of 11–12-year-old pupils and their teacher as they discussed mathematical problems. The classic pattern of classroom discussion has been found to consist largely of teachers initiating an exchange (usually by asking a question), a pupil responding (answering the question) and a teacher giving feedback on that response. This pattern is known as the Initiation – Response – Feedback (IRF) exchange and has been shown to account for up to 75 per cent of normal classroom discussion. In the Forman study, however, it was found that the pupils, rather than the teacher, were often engaged in evaluating each other's contributions, and the contributions of the teacher were often for the purpose of expanding upon pupils' contributions to the discussion. Similar patterns of discourse have been found in the sequence of research projects reported in Kumpulainen and Wray (2002) and suggest that group discussion, in changing the traditional patterns of classroom discourse, allows and encourages much greater involvement of pupils in learning.

Learning is a situated process

We learn everything in a context. That is not controversial. However, modern learning theorists also suggest that what we learn is the context, as much as any skills and processes that we use within that context (Lave and Wenger, 1991). Psychologists have sought in vain for 'generalisable skills', and all teachers are familiar with the problem of the transfer of learning. Why is it that a child who spells ten words correctly in a spelling test is likely to spell several of these wrongly when writing a story a short while afterwards? And why, to give an example from my own teaching experience, can a 10-year-old boy, who in class is absolutely hopeless with number work, maintain an extended, sensible discussion about horse-racing odds with peers in the playground. 'It's 9 to 4 on but it's going to soften.' Do *you* understand that statement? What will the odds move to if they 'soften'? To 9 to 5 on, or 10 to 4 on? This mathematically challenged pupil had no problem with numbers of this kind. The answer to these conundrums is simply that the learning of skills such as spelling and number knowledge is so inextricably bound up with the context of learning that it cannot easily be applied outside this context.

Traditionally, education has often assumed a separation between learning and the use of learning, treating knowledge as a self-sufficient substance, theoretically independent of the situations in which it is learned and used. The primary concern of schools has often seemed to be the teaching of this substance, which comprised abstract, decontextualised, formal concepts. The activity and context in which learning took place were thus regarded as ancillary to learning – they were useful in terms of motivating the learners, but not fundamental to the nature of the learning.

Recent investigations of learning, however, challenge this separation of what is learned from how it is learned and used. The activity in which knowledge is developed and deployed is now seen as an integral part of what is learned. Learning and cognition, it is now possible to argue, are fundamentally situated.

As an example of this, consider the work of Miller and Gildea (1987) on vocabulary teaching, in which they describe how children are taught words from dictionary definitions and a few exemplary sentences, and compare this method with the way vocabulary is normally learned outside school.

People generally learn words in the context of ordinary communication. This process is startlingly fast and successful. Miller and Gildea note that, by listening, talking and reading, the average 18-year-old has learned vocabulary at a rate of about 5,000 words per year (13 per day) for over 16 years. By contrast, learning words from abstract definitions and sentences taken out of the context of normal use, the way vocabulary has often been taught, is slow and generally unsuccessful. There is barely enough classroom time to teach more than 100–200 words per year. Moreover, much of what is taught turns out to be almost useless in practice. Miller and Gildea give the following examples of pupils' uses of vocabulary acquired in this way:

- Me and my parents correlate, because without them I wouldn't be here.
- I was meticulous about falling off the cliff.
- Mrs Morrow stimulated the soup.

Given the method, such mistakes seem unavoidable. Teaching from dictionaries assumes that definitions and example sentences are self-contained 'pieces' of knowledge, but words and sentences are not self-contained in this way. Using language would be almost impossible without the extra help that the context of an utterance provides. Take all the words in English that directly refer to other words or elements of context – termed by linguists 'indexical' words. Words such as here, now, next, tomorrow, afterwards and all pronouns are not just context-sensitive, they are completely context-dependent. Even words that seem to carry content rather than point to other words – words such as 'word' – are situated. 'I give you my word that a word, unless it is the Word of God, means what I choose it to mean' – is, in a word, context-dependent, each of these 'words' meaning something quite different.

Experienced readers implicitly understand that words are situated. They, therefore, ask for the rest of the sentence or the context before committing themselves to an interpretation of a word. Then, they go to dictionaries with situated examples of the usage in mind. The situation, as well as the dictionary, supports their interpretation. However, the pupils who produced the sentences listed had no support from a normal communicative situation. In tasks such as theirs, dictionary definitions were assumed to be self-sufficient. The extra linguistic props that would structure, constrain and ultimately allow interpretation in normal communication were ignored.

All knowledge is like language. Its constituent parts refer to parts of the world and so are inextricably a product of the activity and situations in which they are produced. A concept, for example, will continually evolve every time it is used, because new situations, negotiations and activities inevitably recast it in a slightly different form. So a concept, like the meaning of a word, is always under construction. All learning is temporary and contextually situated. I remember being very puzzled in one of my early secondary-school science lessons to be informed we were going to make a 'solution'. This sounded interesting: I had envisaged science as being exactly that – finding solutions to the problems of the natural world. When making the solution turned out to be simply a matter of mixing some blue crystals with water and watching them disappear, I could not help asking the teacher what that was the solution to!

Task 2.3.4 Using words with various meanings

Think of some further examples of words and/or concepts that have a multiplicity of meanings depending on the contexts in which they occur. How might you go about teaching some of this diversity of meaning to your pupils?

Learning is a metacognitive process

While reading some particularly densely written background material before writing this unit, I noticed that it was becoming increasingly difficult for me to concentrate on what I was reading. My mind kept drifting to other, lighter, topics, and several times I came to with a jerk to realise that I had understood nothing of the several paragraphs I thought I had 'read'. This was a metacognitive experience, and my comprehension monitoring had alternately lapsed and kicked into action. These terms are probably unfamiliar to many people, yet the processes to which they refer have been increasingly demonstrated to be of special importance in learning and in the operation of many intellectual activities. What do these terms mean?

There are two stages in the development of knowledge: first, its automatic unconscious acquisition (we learn things or how to do things, but do not know that we know these things), and, second, a gradual increase in active conscious control over that knowledge (we begin to know what we know and that there is more that we do not know). This distinction is essentially the difference between the cognitive and metacognitive aspects of knowledge and thought. The term *metacognition* is used to refer to cognition about cognition: thinking about your own thinking.

Metacognition can be differentiated into *metacognitive knowledge* and *metacognitive experience*. Metacognitive knowledge is the relatively stable information that we have about our own thinking processes. This knowledge may be about ourselves, about the tasks we are faced with and about possible strategies for tackling them. I may know, for example, that I have to read things at least twice before I will understand them, that it is much easier to understand texts if they are about a topic about which I already know something, or that it will help me remember information if I jot down key points as I read it.

Metacognitive experience refers to the mechanisms used by active learners as they regulate their own attempts to solve problems. These might include:

- checking the outcome of what has already been attempted;
- planning the next moves in response to a problem;
- monitoring the effectiveness of these attempted actions;
- testing, revising and evaluating strategies for learning.

Although it has been demonstrated that even quite young children can monitor their own activities when working on a simple problem, learners of any age are more likely to take active control of their own cognitive activities when they are faced with tasks of medium difficulty. This is not surprising, as it seems logical that with an easy task there is no need to devote too much attention to it, and with a task that is too hard there is a tendency to give up.

As an example of metacognition in action, we can consider the activity of reading. Good reading has been described as follows:

A good reader proceeds smoothly and quickly as long as his understanding of the material is complete. But as soon as he senses that he has missed an idea, that the track has been lost, he brings smooth progress to a blinding halt. Advancing more slowly, he seeks clarification in the subsequent material, examining it for the light it can throw on the earlier trouble spot. If still dissatisfied with his grasp, he returns to the point where the difficulty began and rereads the section more carefully. He probes and analyses phrases and sentences for their exact meaning; he tries to visualise abstruse descriptions; and through a series of approximations, deductions, and corrections he translates scientific and technical terms into concrete examples.

(Whimbey, 1975: 91)

Although it is, of course, true that all readers do not follow precisely this sequence of actions, recent theories of reading have suggested similarly strategic models for the process. Most characterisations of the reading process include skills and activities that involve what is now termed metacognition. Some of the metacognitive activities involved in reading are:

- clarifying your purposes for reading, that is, understanding the aim of a particular reading task;
- identifying the important aspects of a text;
- focusing attention on these aspects rather than on relatively trivial aspects;
- monitoring ongoing activities to determine whether comprehension is taking place;
- engaging in self-questioning to check whether your aims are being achieved;
- taking corrective action if and when failures in comprehension are detected.

Reading for meaning, therefore, inevitably involves the metacognitive activity of comprehension monitoring, which entails keeping track of the success with which your comprehension is proceeding, ensuring that the process continues smoothly and taking remedial action if necessary.

Although mature readers typically engage in these processes as they read for meaning, it is usually not a conscious experience. Skilled readers tend to proceed on automatic pilot until a triggering event alerts them to a failure or problem in their comprehension. When alerted in this way, they must slow down and devote extra effort in mental processing to the area that is causing the problem. The events that trigger such action may vary widely. One common triggering event is the realisation that an expectation held about a text has not been confirmed by actual experience of the text. For example, in reading a sentence such as 'The old man the boats', the fourth and fifth words will probably cause a revision of your sense of understanding and, therefore, take longer to process.

Realising that you have failed to understand is only part of comprehension monitoring; you also have to know what to do when such failures occur. This involves making a number of strategic decisions, such as:

- reading on: reading more of the text to see if more information can be gained;
- sounding out: examining letters and sounds carefully (this strategy is used most often by younger readers);
- making an inference: guessing a meaning on the basis of textual clues and previous knowledge;
- re-reading: reading the difficult section again;
- suspending judgement: waiting to see if the text provides more clues.

Numerous research studies have examined the operation of metacognition in children's reading, that is, their monitoring of their own comprehension. Overall, there has been a remarkable consistency in the findings of these studies, and it seems that:

- Young children and poor readers are not nearly as adept as older children/adults and good readers, respectively, in engaging in planful activities either to make cognitive progress or to monitor it.

- Younger, less proficient learners are not nearly as 'resourceful' in completing a variety of reading and studying tasks important in academic settings.

The above description has focused on reading, but this only parallels what we know about the importance of metacognition in all areas of learning. Self-awareness appears to be an essential ingredient in success in school. As John Holt put it:

> Part of being a good student is learning to be aware of the state of one's mind and the degree of one's understanding. The good student may be one who often says that he does not understand, simply because he keeps a constant check on his understanding. The poor student, who does not, so to speak, watch himself trying to understand, does not know most of the time whether he understands or not.

(1969: 23)

This is a fundamental problem for young children: being much less aware of the operations of their own minds, and much less able to introspect to find out how their minds are working, they are thus less able to exert any conscious control over their own cognition. There is a strong implication that learning can be improved by increasing learners' awareness of their own mental processes.

PRINCIPLES FOR TEACHING

Arising from these insights, we can derive some clear principles for teaching:

- We need to ensure that learners have sufficient previous knowledge/understanding to enable them to learn new things, and to help them make explicit these links between what they already know and what they are learning.
- We need to make provision for group interaction and discussion as teaching strategies, both in small, teacherless groups and in groups working alongside experts.
- We need to ensure meaningful contexts for learning, particularly in what are often called basic skills. This implies some kind of negotiation of the curriculum for learning. What is a meaningful context for teachers cannot be assumed automatically to be a meaningful context for learners.
- We need to promote learners' knowledge and awareness of their own thinking and learning. This might be done by, for example, encouraging them to think aloud as they perform particular cognitive tasks.

One of the most significant research-based books ever was published in 2012. John Hattie's *Visible Learning for Teachers* (2012) is a thorough account of his meta-analysis of the effects on student achievement of a host of teaching interventions. Hattie distils the results of evaluations of these interventions into what he refers to as 'effect sizes', that is, the size of the effect that the intervention has had on learner achievement. An effect size that is bigger than zero means that achievement has been raised by the intervention. However, in many cases, achievement would have gone up anyway, just through things such as learners growing older and more mature, and so Hattie sets the bar for an effect size to be significant rather higher than zero. He uses the figure of 0.4 as an effect size to take notice of. If an intervention has an effect of 0.4 or higher, then it might be worth other teachers adopting it.

In the appendix to his book, Hattie lists, in order of effect size, those interventions whose effects on achievement have been researched. The highest effect size (and thus, according to Hattie's argument, the most effective teaching intervention) is *Self-reported grades/Student expectations*, with an effect size of 1.44, which we might take to mean getting learners to grade their own achievements in particular tasks and set themselves high targets for future tasks.

Interventions that relate to the insights discussed earlier in this unit are found to have the effect sizes shown in Table 2.3.1.

TABLE 2.3.1 Some effect sizes

Intervention	Effect size
Classroom discussion	0.82
Reciprocal teaching	0.74
Metacognitive strategies	0.69
Prior achievement and knowledge	0.65
Self-verbalisation and self-questioning	0.64
Comprehension programmes	0.60
Peer tutoring	0.55
Cooperative vs competitive learning	0.54
Student-centred teaching	0.54

Source: Hattie (2012)

TOWARDS A MODEL FOR TEACHING

Palincsar and Brown (1984) described a teaching procedure (reciprocal teaching – effect size 0.74, according to Hattie) that began from the principles just outlined and was based upon the twin ideas of 'expert scaffolding' and what they referred to as 'proleptic teaching': that is, teaching in anticipation of competence. This model arose from the Vygotskyan idea that children first experience a particular cognitive activity in collaboration with expert practitioners. The child is first a spectator, as the majority of the cognitive work is done by the expert (parent or teacher), then a novice, as he or she starts to take over some of the work under the close supervision of the expert. As the child grows in experience and capability of performing the task, the expert passes over greater and greater responsibility, but still acts as a guide, assisting the child at problematic points. Eventually, the child assumes full responsibility for the task, with the expert still present in the role of a supportive audience. Using this approach to teaching, children learn about the task at their own pace, joining in only at a level at which they are capable – or perhaps a little beyond this level, so that the task continually provides sufficient challenge to be interesting. The approach is often referred to as an 'apprenticeship approach'. In the apprenticeship approach to reading, for example, the teacher and child begin by sharing a book together, with, at first, most of the actual reading being done by the teacher. As the child develops confidence through repeated sharing of the book, he or she gradually takes over the reading, until the teacher can withdraw entirely.

In mathematics learning, Taylor and Cox (1997) have researched the effects of such apprenticeship approaches. They developed what they termed a 'socially assisted learning approach', which involved teachers modelling the ways they solved mathematical word problems, then encouraging learners to engage in such problem solving using several devices, such as the use of a reflection board in which teachers and pupils could share publicly their representation of a problem, peer collaboration, reflective questioning, scaffolding and quizzes. The pupils experiencing this approach did significantly better on word-problem tests than a control group who just received their normal mathematics teaching. When they analysed in a more detailed way the interactions of the teachers and the pupils, the researchers found that the support offered by the teacher was not a function of the number of questions or statements the teacher made, but rather that these questions/statements came at the right time, when they served to scaffold understanding.

In explaining their results, Taylor and Cox (1997) speculated that success with this type of learning was a result of shared ownership of the learning, in which there were expectations that:

- all members of the group worked on the same aspect of the problem at the same time;
- members externalised their thoughts, including possible wrong approaches and answers;
- members came to agreement among themselves before proceeding;
- as the teaching proceeded, more of the control of the activity was transferred from the adult to the children.

This approach to teaching has been term a 'cognitive apprenticeship' (Collins, 2006), and there appear to be four stages to the teaching process implied by the model.

Demonstration

During this stage, the expert models the skilful behaviour being taught. There is some evidence that learning can be assisted if this modelling is accompanied by a commentary by the expert, thinking aloud about the activities being undertaken. One relatively simple procedure is that of the teacher modelling how he or she tackles the skills being taught, for example, reading or writing, in such a way that the learners have access to the thought processes that accompany these activities.

Joint activity

The expert and the learner share the activity. This may begin by the expert retaining responsibility for the difficult parts, while the learner takes on the easy parts, although, in some teaching strategies, prior agreement is reached that participants will take turns at carrying out sections of the activity. The expert is always on hand to take full control if necessary. One of the best examples of this joint activity is that known as 'paired reading' (Morgan, 1986), in which the teacher (or parent) and the learner read aloud in unison, until the learner signals that he or she is ready to go it alone. The teacher withdraws from the reading but is ready to rejoin if the learner shows signs of difficulty, such as prolonged pausing or reading errors.

Supported activity

The learner undertakes the activity alone, but under the watchful eye of the expert, who is always ready to step in if necessary. In my own work on the reading and writing of non-fiction (Wray, 2013), we found that this was the stage in the process that was most often neglected, and teachers tended to move too rapidly from heavily supporting the children's work to asking them to work without support. Consequently, this is the stage at which most of the practical teaching strategies arising from our work, such as writing frames, were aimed. Such scaffolding strategies play a key role in teaching approaches such as shared and guided reading.

Individual activity

The learner assumes sole responsibility for the activity. Some learners will, of course, move much more rapidly to this stage than others, and the teacher needs to be sensitive to this. It is, arguably, equally as damaging to hold back learners by insisting they go through the same programme of support and practice as everyone else, as it is to rush learners through such a programme when they need a more extensive programme of support.

Task 2.3.5 Using staged interactive teaching

Think of a skill you have taught in a primary school (or are planning to teach). Can you focus your teaching of this skill around the four steps of demonstration, joint activity, supported activity and individual activity? Jot down some notes on how you might use each of these stages in your teaching of this skill.

When you have done this activity, compare your approach with some of the examples given in Wray and Lewis (1997).

SUMMARY

In this unit, I have outlined four major insights that can be derived from a study of learning:

1 Learning is a process of interaction between what is known and what is to be learned.
2 Learning is a social process.
3 Learning is a situated process.
4 Learning is a metacognitive process.

Using these insights I have suggested four key principles for teaching:

1 We need to ensure that learners have sufficient previous knowledge/understanding to enable them to learn new things, and to help them make explicit these links between what they already know and what they are learning.
2 We need to make provision for group interaction and discussion as teaching strategies, both in small, teacherless groups and in groups working alongside experts.
3 We need to ensure meaningful contexts for learning, particularly in what are often called basic skills.
4 We need to promote learners' knowledge and awareness of their own thinking and learning.

These principles are, I have argued, best exemplified by what can be termed an 'apprenticeship approach' to teaching. I hope you will be able to see applications for these principles in all your teaching. The apprenticeship approach has, after all, been used for years to teach all sorts of material to all sorts of people in the world outside school – 'just plain folks', in the terms used by some researchers. Its rediscovery by school teachers was long overdue.

ANNOTATED FURTHER READING

Hattie, J. (2012) *Visible Learning for Teachers*, London: Routledge.

> This is the key text right now for research-led information about teaching. It is hugely influential worldwide, and every teacher should be familiar with the Hattie argument, even if they might disagree about some of the details. One critique that has been made about the approach is that the effect sizes quoted for individual interventions take no account of what happens if interventions are used in tandem with other approaches. Teaching is rarely a case of purely doing one thing, and so, arguably, Hattie misses the point a little here.

Lave, J. and Wenger, E. (1991) *Situated Learning: Legitimate Peripheral Participation*, Cambridge: Cambridge University Press.

> This book contains an exploration of learning as participation in communities of practice. According to the authors, participation moves from the periphery to the 'centre'. Learning is, thus, not seen as the acquisition of knowledge by individuals, so much as a process of *social* participation. This is a seminal text and opened up the concept of situated learning.

Mercer, N. and Hodgkinson, S. (eds) (2008) *Exploring Talk in School*, London: Sage.

> This book consists of a number of papers by leading international researchers who, drawing on the pioneering work of Douglas Barnes, consider ways of improving classroom talk. Chapters cover issues such as classroom communication and managing social relations; talk in science classrooms; using critical conversations in studying literature; exploratory talk and thinking skills; talking to learn and learning to talk in the mathematics classroom; and the 'emerging pedagogy' of the spoken word.

Mercer, N. and Littleton, K. (2007) *Dialogue and the Development of Children's Thinking*, London: Routledge.

> This book draws on extensive research to provide a fascinating account of the relationship between dialogue and children's learning development. It closely relates research findings to real-life classrooms, so that it is of practical value to teachers concerned that their children are offered the best possible learning opportunities. It provides a clear, accessible and well-illustrated case for the importance of dialogue in children's intellectual development.

Wray, D. (1994) *Literacy and Awareness*, Sevenoaks: Hodder & Stoughton.

> If you would like to know more about the concept of metacognition and, in particular, its relation to the teaching of literacy, this book represents a very good start. It includes chapters on metacognition and understanding in reading, awareness and writing, and language awareness.

FURTHER READING TO SUPPORT M-LEVEL STUDY

Kovalainen, M. and Kumpulainen, K. (2005) 'The discursive practice of participation in an elementary classroom community', *Instructional Science*, 33: 213-50.

> This paper outlines and discusses the findings of a fine-grained study of the interactions between children during learning tasks in a primary classroom. It features such aspects as participation rights and their relations to knowledge construction, and the challenges for the teacher in maximising the learning potential of this classroom organisation pattern.

Thomson, P. and Hall, C. (2008) 'Opportunities missed and/or thwarted? 'Funds of knowledge' meet the English national curriculum', *The Curriculum Journal*, 19(2): 87-103.

> 'Funds of knowledge' is a concept developed by the American researchers Gonzales and Moll and relates to the community and cultural knowledge brought to school by children from a range of backgrounds but rarely drawn upon by schools and teachers. The article shows how UK schools, driven by the demands of a national curriculum, actually work against these funds of knowledge in ways that limit the potential achievement of the children they deal with.

RELEVANT WEBSITES

Education Endowment Foundation: http://educationendowmentfoundation.org.uk/toolkit/
> The Education Endowment Foundation has produced this toolkit, which gives research-based information about the effectiveness of particular teaching initiatives, alongside the cost of implementing them. Click on an initiative to find further information about it and the research base that underpins it.

www.infed.org/
> The encyclopaedia of informal education contains a veritable cornucopia of material related to teaching and learning. As well as article-length pieces on a variety of topics, it also has a comprehensive collection of links to take you further into the subject. If you consult no other information from the web about teaching and learning, do look at this site.

REFERENCES

Collins, A. (2006) 'Cognitive apprenticeship', in Sawyer, R. (ed.) *Cambridge Handbook of the Learning Sciences*, Cambridge: Cambridge University Press, pp. 47–60.

Forman, E.A., Stein, M.K., Brown, C. and Larreamendy-Joerns, J. (1995) 'The socialization of mathematical thinking: the role of institutional, interpersonal, and discursive contexts', Paper presented at the 77th annual conference of the *American Educational Research Association*, San Francisco.

Hattie, J. (2012) *Visible Learning for Teachers*, London: Routledge.

Holt, J. (1969) *How Children Fail*, Harmondsworth: Penguin.

Kumpulainen, K. and Wray, D. (2002) *Classroom Interaction and Social Learning*, London: RoutledgeFalmer.

Lave, J. and Wenger, E. (1991) *Situated Learning*, Cambridge: Cambridge University Press.

Miller, G.A. and Gildea, P.M. (1987) 'How children learn words', *Scientific American*, 257(3): 94–9.

Morgan, R. (1986) *Helping Children Read*, London: Methuen.

Palincsar, A. and Brown, A. (1984) 'Reciprocal teaching of comprehension-fostering and comprehension-monitoring activities', *Cognition and Instruction*, 1(2): 117–75.

Raphael, T., McMahon, S.I., Goatley, V.J., Bentley, J.L. and Boyd, F.B. (1992) 'Research directions: literature and discussion in the reading program', *Language Arts*, 69: 55–61.

Taylor, J. and Cox, B.D. (1997) 'Microgenetic analysis of group-based solution of complex two-step mathematical word problems by fourth graders', *Journal of Learning Science*, 6: 183–226.

Whimbey, A. (1975) *Intelligence Can Be Taught*, New York: Dutton.

Wray, D. (2013) 'Principles and practice in teaching extending literacy skills', *The Clearing House: A Journal of Educational Strategies, Issues and Ideas*, 86(1): 11–16.

Wray, D. and Lewis, M. (1997) *Extending Literacy*, London: Routledge.

Wray, D. and Medwell, J. (1991) *Literacy and Language in the Primary Years*, London: Routledge.

DEVELOPING YOUR TEACHING

Samantha Twiselton and Sally Elton-Chalcraft

INTRODUCTION

> Good teaching makes a difference. Excellent teaching can transform lives.
>
> (Alexander, 2010: 279)

Such a responsibility can be quite daunting to anyone contemplating the skills that might be needed for effective primary teaching. This unit will look at the skills and knowledge required for you to be able to create and support successful learning experiences that, ultimately, could transform lives. What you decide to do in the classroom can have a profound influence on the children you work with. In this unit, we unpack factors you need to consider when you plan for the children's learning.

OBJECTIVES

By the end of this unit, you should be beginning to:

- understand that excellent teaching involves being aware of the underlying factors that underpin learning objectives (e.g. organisation of the curriculum; concepts of knowledge; a child's background, prior learning, aptitude etc.);
- understand how knowledge is organised;
- develop strategies to help your own decision-making in the classroom (creativity and knowledge).

KNOWLEDGE AND LEARNING – FOR THE PUPIL AND THE TEACHER

According to Bruner (1996) and many others, learning involves the search for pattern, regularity and predictability. We can only make sense out of the confusion of information continuously bombarding our senses if we can *relate* the pieces of information to each other in some way. If a young child is presented with some bricks and the task of building a tower, this is only likely to be possible if he or she has had some other similar experiences to draw on (e.g. experimenting with bricks and learning something about how they balance, building other simple structures, knowledge of what towers look like, etc.).

Input from a teacher should help children in the formation and discovery of the patterns and rules that are most likely to help them (1) make sense of the experience and (2) generalise it to other experiences. Complex tasks can be broken down into manageable smaller problems, so that the learner can detect patterns and regularities that could not be discovered alone. So a task such as building a tower with bricks can be made possible by the presence of a teacher who helps the pupil through decisions and actions in small steps, while still holding 'the bigger picture' of the ultimate goal of the tower in mind.

The opening quotation is from the final report and recommendations of *Children, Their World, Their Education: Recommendations and Findings of the Cambridge Primary Review*, undertaken by a range of scholars and educationalists (Alexander, 2010). We would argue that, if you encompass the review's suggested principles and aims when designing your lessons, you will thus be engaging in excellent teaching. Alexander's aims (2010: 197) of primary teaching provide a framework that is consistent with (but goes beyond) the 2012 QTS standards. The first few aims call on you to nurture the qualities and capacities of the child, namely, well-being, engagement, empowerment and autonomy; the second group of aims relate to self, others and the world, namely encouraging respect and reciprocity, promoting independence and sustainability, empowering local, national and global citizenship, and celebrating culture and community (Alexander, 2010: 197-9). The third group of aims focus on what should be going on in the classroom, namely, exploring, knowing, understanding and making sense, fostering skill, exciting the imagination and enacting dialogue (Alexander, 2010: 197-9). Other units in Section 2 of this present volume discuss the philosophies and values underpinning the curriculum; here, we restrict our discussion to developing your teaching skills and the learning opportunities you provide. We would argue that teaching ought to be a research-based profession (Elton-Chalcraft *et al.*, 2008), and, in this unit, we show how increasing your own pedagogical knowledge (reading research about teaching and learning), coupled with increasing your own subject knowledge of curriculum areas, can provide an effective learning environment.

Task 2.4.1 An evidence-based profession?

Access the Cambridge Primary Review website (www.primaryreview.org.uk) and read the booklet *Introducing the Cambridge Primary Review* (www.primaryreview.org.uk/downloads/ CPR_revised_booklet.pdf). Consider the extent to which the thinking reflected in this introductory booklet is supported by your experience of what constitutes effective teaching and learning in school. It is also useful to reflect on the notion of teaching as an 'evidence-based profession'. To what extent has this been your experience to date? Does M-level study as part of your ITE course have a role to play in this?

An effective teacher will have an excellent grasp of these fundamental concepts and will be able to break down tasks in ways that will make them achievable, while still remaining consistent with the core ideas that underpin them. This means that core ideas are developed in nucleus as early as possible and are returned to with ever-increasing complexity and sophistication in a 'spiral curriculum', as children's experience and understanding makes them ready for it.

The importance of underlying structures and the role of teachers in helping pupils to make connections is supported by the work of Medwell *et al.* (1998), in which they examined the work of teachers whose pupils made effective learning gains in literacy. In this, they claim that effective teachers are much more likely to embed their teaching in a wider context and to show how specific aspects of literacy relate to each other. They assert that such teachers tend to make connections, both explicitly and implicitly, and to put features of language use into the broader context of texts. Medwell *et al.* found that the effective teachers tended to have more coherent belief systems that led them to pursue an embedded approach, where the more technical aspects of literacy were taught within a broader framework of meaningful contexts. This theme is echoed by the parallel study into effective teachers of numeracy, undertaken by Askew *et al.* (1997), who characterise effective numeracy teachers as being 'connectionist-oriented', which involves a conscious awareness of connections and relationships.

So what does this mean in terms of the knowledge base required by you as a teacher, and how this should be applied in the classroom? This can be a very alarming question for someone learning to be a primary school teacher, as there are so many different subjects in the primary curriculum, each having its own detailed requirements.

QUALITY VERSUS QUANTITY: ORGANISATION OF KNOWLEDGE

The answer to this problem may be helped by Sternberg and Horvath's (1995) attempt to define what is involved in teacher expertise. They comment that there are a number of studies (e.g. Larkin *et al.*, 1980; Chi *et al.*, 1981) that show that it is not so much the *amount* of knowledge that the expert possesses, but *how it is organised* in the memory. In general, experts are sensitive to the deep structures of the problems they solve – they are able to group problems together according to underlying principles. This supports Bruner's model (1996). It seems that the key to being able to teach, for example, history or mathematics is not so much your knowing endless information about the subject, as your understanding some of the key underlying principles and concepts that underpin it.

This is very much supported by one of the author's own study (Twiselton, 2000, 2003, 2004, 2006, 2007; Twiselton and Webb, 1998) of the types of knowledge and understanding that primary student teachers develop as they go through their initial teacher education (ITE) programme. Twiselton found that (partly dependent on how far through the programme they were) these students could be placed into one of three main categories (or points on a continuum) – task manager, curriculum deliverer or concept/skill builder. The task managers (who were likely to be near the beginning of ITE) viewed their role in the classroom in terms of task completion, order and business – without any explicit reference to children's learning. The curriculum deliverers did see themselves as there to support learning, but only as dictated by an external source – a scheme, curriculum or lesson plan – and they struggled to give a rationale for *why what was being taught mattered* in any other terms. In contrast, the concept/skill builders (likely to be at or near the end of ITE) were aware of the wider and deeper areas of understanding and skill needed by pupils that underpinned their learning objectives. Of the three types, the concept/skill builders were much more likely to be able effectively, consistently and responsively to support learning at every stage of the learning experience. The most outstanding quality that separated the concept/skill builders from the other two categories was their ability to see the 'bigger picture' and give a rationale for what they were attempting to do in terms of key principles and concepts. This would appear to be particularly important at a time when policymakers in England swing from one end of the pendulum, a child-centred curriculum, to the other, a subject-focused one. Over the last few years, there has been a somewhat erratic, but nevertheless consistent, desire to make teaching an M-level profession, thus encouraging intending teachers to think beyond the current governmental directives – at time of writing, the Curriculum 2014.

Task 2.4.2 Lesson plans 1

- Choose the subject you feel most confident in – e.g. (1) English; (2) science; (3) religious education.

- Choose a key area within it – e.g. (1) poetry reading and writing; (2) solids, liquids and gases; (3) belief.

- Write the key area in the middle of a piece of paper and write words and phrases you associate with it around the edge – e.g. (1) rhyme, rhythm, verses, language play, imagery; (2) evaporation and condensation, state, materials, properties; (3) beliefs, religious and secular food laws.

- In a different colour, write key words and phrases for all the ways in which this area is important – e.g. (1) it gives a pattern and meaning to chaotic experiences, it expresses emotion, it entertains, it conveys images, it communicates powerful ideas; (2) the changing properties of materials allow us to manipulate our environment; we can manufacture things using these changes; life on land requires the fresh water produced by evaporation and condensation; (3) beliefs and values can often affect action.

- Look at the words and phrases in the two different colours you have used. Is it possible to connect them? For example, (1) rhyme and rhythm help to entertain and impose pattern and meaning, imagery is an effective way of communicating powerful ideas; (2) evaporation and condensation are important examples of key processes we use to manipulate the environment; (3) the way we behave is often influenced by our beliefs and values – so many Muslims fast during Ramadan, and vegetarians do not eat meat. If so, you are connecting the 'what' with the 'why' in the way the concept/skill builders were doing.

- Consider the implications for how these aspects of the subject should be taught to pupils. How can you ensure that they are presented with the 'why' sufficiently?

The next stage is to identify what other factors will be involved, and how this translates into classroom practice. Tables 2.4.1 and 2.4.2 provide some examples of how a similar approach can be taken through planning in Key Stage 1 and Key Stage 2. The commentary shows how the teaching can be directed by the underpinning rationale for the learning objectives.

The lesson plan in Table 2.4.1 shows how a Key Stage 1 lesson can be explicitly and systematically underpinned by key concepts relating to meaning making, purpose and audience.

The lesson plan in Table 2.4.2 shows a very similar approach planned with Year 5.

TABLE 2.4.1 Lesson plan – Year 1/2 – Monday

LESSON PLAN – YEAR 1/2 – MONDAY		
	DESIRED LEARNING OUTCOMES	
T5/6	Recite stories with predictable and repeating patterns and describe story settings and incidents.	
S2	Use awareness of grammar to decipher new words.	
W3	Hear initial and final phonemes.	
KEY LANGUAGE	USE OF ICT	
Setting, character, phoneme, alliteration.	**Clicker**	
ASSESSMENT [make reference to each section of the lesson]		
Shared – yellow group – word choices. **Guided – red group – ability to make sentence orally and in writing.** **Plenary – green group – explanation of choices.**		
USE OF OTHER ADULTS: **Mrs X to support green group in use of clicker.**		
ANTICIPATED MISCONCEPTIONS/DIFFICULTIES: **Support with spelling strategies – reluctance to attempt unknown words – encourage to 'have a go' – use 'magic line'.**		
	ACTIVITIES	COMMENTARY
Introduction Approx. timing – 10 minutes	**Introduce text.** **Look at cover – predict what the characters are thinking (whiteboards).** **Discuss title – explain that we are going to be spending the week thinking about stories with a repeating pattern. Discuss why people like repeating patterns and why such stories are enjoyable. Explain that we are going to be looking at repeating texts so that we can have a go at writing our own later in the week.**	*It is important that pupils are helped to understand the purposes of the texts they look at.* *It is also helpful if there is a concrete goal (e.g. writing their own story based on this one) that is introduced at the beginning and can give meaning and purpose to the week's activities.*

Whole-class work Use of additional support Approx. timing – 20 minutes	Read 'Bear Hunt' – encourage joining in. Cover up words with post-its – time out for words it could be. Show me – ideas. Look at sound effects – time out more words beginning with 'sw' etc. *Additional support – Mrs X focused observation of yellow group word choices on feedback sheet.*	*It is important to emphasise those aspects of the text that define it and make it enjoyable – joining in with repetition is a good way to do this.* *Explain that sound effects might be used in the story the children write – it will be useful to have a bank of words and ideas they can use later.*
Guided group Red group Approx. timing – 20 minutes	1 Introduce 'Rosie's Walk' – explain similar to 'Bear Hunt' in some ways. 2 Strategy check – matching phonemes. 3 Look through text – tell a partner how is same? 4 Review/discuss. 5 Look at text – compare with 'Bear Hunt' – how different? What do we like about each one? 6 Review.	*Frame the whole discussion within the idea of eventually being able to take the best ideas from each book and use them in their own story.* *Remember to keep emphasising the features that make the text enjoyable.*
Independent work Approx timing – 20 minutes	Introduce independent work with whole class. Draw pictures for each stage of story. In pairs: blue group, green group – add simple captions underneath. Yellow group – clicker – put pictures in right order – find captions and paste.	*Explain that the independent work will help with planning their own stories later in the week.*
Plenary	Focus – green group. Blutack sentences on black board — green group read aloud.	*Explain that the captions will help when thinking of sentences for own stories later in the week.*

TABLE 2.4.2 Lesson plan – Year 1/2 – Tuesday

LESSON PLAN – YEAR 1/2 – TUESDAY		
	DESIRED LEARNING OUTCOMES	
T3	Investigate how characters are presented through dialogue, action and description and through examining their relationship with other characters.	
S4	Adapt writing for different audiences.	
KEY LANGUAGE	USE OF ICT	
Characterisation, empathy, perspective, imagery		
ASSESSMENT [make reference to each section of the lesson]		
Shared – yellow group – word choices. Guided – red group – ability to make sentence orally and in writing. Plenary – green group – explanation of choices.		
USE OF OTHER ADULTS: Mrs X to support green group.		
ANTICIPATED MISCONCEPTIONS/DIFFICULTIES: Support with spelling strategies – reluctance to attempt unknown words.		
	ACTIVITIES	COMMENTARY
Introduction Approx. timing – 15 minutes	Look at cover – predict what the characters are thinking (whiteboards). Use freeze frame and thought tracking to follow this up. Could include a hot seat activity. Map out 'Bear Hunt' – focus on one character – list words for each section to show how he is feeling.	*In introducing the text yesterday it will have been important to explain it is going to be used to help consider how characters' perspectives change through the story so that they can write own story showing this.*

Section	Activities	Notes
Whole-class work Approx. timing – 20 minutes	**Read opening passages from 'The Shrieking Face' – look at how author builds up images of how Angus is feeling – time out – show me – write up key words, phrases, sentences.** **Ask for ideas for similar language for 'Bear Hunt' character.** **Teacher demo – 'He was feeling brave and adventurous – like a warrior going into battle.' Time out – paired ideas – supported composition.** *Use of additional support –Mrs X focused observation of yellow group word choices on feedback sheet.*	*It is important that the discussion focuses on the effective use of language for conveying characters' perspectives. Pupils need to keep alive that the purpose is to help them use language effectively in their own stories.*
Guided group Approx. timing – 15 minutes	**Red group – write opening sequence to new version – emphasise figurative language – use examples from shared work as starting point.**	*Keep the reader's needs in mind at all times – read aloud and check for effectiveness.*
Independent work Approx timing – 15 minutes	**Write key words on a story plan for each stage of the story. Write opening sequence.**	*It is important that the pupils understand that this is going to be continued later in the week.*
Plenary – 10 minutes	**Focus – green group.** **Blutack sentences on black board – green group read aloud – consider effectiveness.**	*The focus should be on effectiveness and audience.*

The need for teachers to develop a broad, rich curriculum is strongly promoted. This is set alongside a notion of a very individualised, highly child-centred approach to supporting learning and a strong emphasis on multi-agency working and the sharing of expertise and information. All of this implies a notion of the teacher that goes well beyond the technician who delivers a prescribed curriculum.

This broad, more flexible and child-centred view of the teacher is welcome, but is not without its challenges, particularly for those who are learning to teach. As a student teacher, it is very easy to become so enmeshed in the practicalities of simply 'surviving' in the classroom that it is difficult to focus on underpinning concepts or how to connect these meaningfully to the needs of individual learners. The task below is designed to lead you through a process that will help you to begin to do this in stages, away from the hurly burly of the classroom, and the lesson plans (Tables 2.4.1 and 2.4.2) with commentary should help you to make the link back to the classroom and your planning.

Task 2.4.3 Lesson plans 2

Take a recent lesson plan – ideally one that is your own and that you have already taught. Focus on the learning outcomes that you planned for this lesson. Attempt to answer the following questions:

- Why were these learning outcomes important for these children?
- What importance/usefulness would this learning have beyond this lesson?
- How was the above communicated to the children? Were they aware of why what they were learning mattered?

If you feel able to answer these questions with some confidence, the next step is to analyse the lesson chronologically to work out how well this was communicated at each stage. If possible, identify places where this could have been improved, and how.

If you don't feel able to answer the above questions with confidence, the next step is to replan the lesson, starting with the learning outcomes and rewriting them in a way that you feel can be justified in terms of their importance. You then need to go through the rest of the plan to amend it, to ensure this is clearly and meaningfully communicated to the children throughout the lesson.

KNOWLEDGE AND CREATIVITY

Other sections later in this volume (Section 4, 'Approaches to the curriculum', and Section 7, 'Recent developments' – in particular Unit 7.3 'Creativity and creative taching and learning' (Cremin and Barnes)) discuss the 'what' and 'how' of teaching and learning in more detail; here, we are showing the link between the structural underpinning of lesson planning (why) with the ways in which you can achieve this (what and how) (Elton-Chalcraft and Mills, 2013), together with the where and when (Claxton, 2007).

Boden argues that knowledge and creativity are not opposing forces (2001: 95). For example, children need to know the rules of rhyme, or the tenets of belief, before they can playfully create new poems, or work out their own responses. It is important for teachers to support children's understanding of a curriculum area, but, as we have argued earlier, the organisation of this learning (how we teach) can lead either to mundane completion of tasks (task managers) or effective learning (concept/skills builders). Research in neuroscience tells us that knowledge is contextualised, and teachers need to support the child to make connections in the brain (Claxton, 1997; Heilman, 2005). If the curriculum is seen as a blueprint for learning, Copping (2011) argues, then tasks will not be meaningful. For example, task managers would happily ask children to complete a worksheet about Muslims fasting during Ramadan, perhaps filling in missing words. Concept builders, on the other hand, would have used the Internet/books/Muslim visitors to inform their own subject knowledge, thus enabling the children to explore reasons why many Muslims fast, yet other Muslims choose not to for particular reasons, why the children themselves eat or do not eat certain foods at particular times, etc. Concept builders would make the links between the religious education lesson and the PSHE topic on healthy lifestyle, to discuss what foods the children eat and why, and how this relates to religious food laws. Thus, task managers merely present knowledge – a blueprint – that the children learn, and the children have no interaction with that knowledge. Knowledge is a requisite, as Boden (2001) says, to creating new ideas and concepts and embedding learning in the child's own, personalised web of belief. Kuiper *et al.* (2009) show how children can be encouraged to use resources appropriately to ensure deep learning, using a 'healthy eating' topic. An effective teacher designs creative learning activities and provides creative learning environments that are both fun but also challenge the children (Elton-Chalcraft and Mills, 2013). Claxton (2007) urges the teacher to engage in split-screen thinking – with a dual focus, on both the content of the lesson, and also the learning disposition of the child. In his compelling article, Claxton (2007) suggests teachers build children's 'learning capacity' and encourage children to strengthen their 'learning muscles'. All this requires pedagogical knowledge and understanding, which we outline below.

Task 2.4.4 Creativity and knowledge

Access Denis Hayes's (2011) *Guided Reader to Teaching and Learning*, extract 7, pp. 29–31, TASC (thinking actively in a social context), from Wallace *et al.* (2009). Hayes (2011: 31) asks in what ways are pupils seen as equal partners in learning? How is such a state of working attainable?

Also look at Cedric Cullingford's (2007) passionate article, 'Creativity and pupil's experience of school'. Is Cullingford convincing in his argument about 'children's preferred modes of thinking' (2007: 137)? How does this relate to our discussion of knowledge and concept/skills builders?

Read Claxton (2007) 'Expanding Young People's capacity to learn'. What is your response to Claxton's argument that teachers should be concentrating on children's 'learning muscles', as well as teaching the topic? Do you think this approach is appropriate?

OTHER TYPES OF TEACHER KNOWLEDGE

Any attempt to define all the different kinds of teacher knowledge required in effective practice is bound to hit the problem that the list can be infinitely extended. However, it is worth noting that most people agree that, however you describe it, the knowledge base is wide-ranging and varied, and that different kinds of knowledge are required at different times. Tochon and Munby (1993) studied expert and novice teachers and found that a key characteristic that distinguished the experts was their ability to draw on a wide range of different kinds of knowledge (e.g. the subject, the plan, the individual pupil, the context, etc.) in making one teaching decision. The novices tended to think about one thing at a time and to stick quite rigidly to their plan, regardless of whether the pupil responses, the context, etc., supported this.

Lee Shulman (1987) has classified the knowledge base of teaching in seven categories: content knowledge (better known to us as subject knowledge), general pedagogical knowledge, curriculum knowledge, pedagogical content knowledge, knowledge of learners and their characteristics, knowledge of educational contexts and knowledge of educational ends. Others (e.g. Turner-Bisset, 1999) have expanded this list. The important thing for student teachers to note is not so much the items on the list (though these are useful), but the fact that they are so varied. It is the *drawing together and combining* of these varied factors that are important. For example Devine *et al.* (2013: 83) investigate teacher effectiveness in terms of 'passion, reflection, planning, love for children' and the 'social and moral dimension' of what constitutes good teaching. They argue that, when discussing quality teaching, it is vital to consider sociocultural contexts such as gender, social class and ethnicity (Devine *et al.*, 2013).

The Medwell *et al.* (1998) study found that the subject knowledge of the effective literacy teachers was only fully identifiable when it was embedded within a teaching context:

> Our interpretation of what we have observed is that the effective teachers only knew their material by how they represented it to children . . . through experience of teaching it, their knowledge seemed to have been totally embedded in pedagogic practices.
>
> (p. 24)

They also found that the effective teachers tended to have more coherent belief systems linked to the importance of communication, composition and understanding. This links with Bruner's views about the key components that are the fundamentals of the subject.

In the parallel study of effective numeracy teachers, Askew *et al.* (1997) characterised effective numeracy teachers as being 'connectionist-oriented'. They claimed that the highly effective teachers believed that being numerate required having a rich network of connections between different mathematical ideas.

COMBINING KNOWLEDGE

In Sternberg and Horvath's (1995) study of teaching expertise, three key features are identified. The first is *knowledge*, and we have already considered their claim that the organisation of the knowledge around principles is the central factor. The second and third features are *efficiency* and *insight*. Efficiency is closely linked to experience, in that the claim is that experts are much faster at processing information and making well-informed decisions, partly because what is initially effortful and time consuming becomes effortless and automatic with practice. This is obvious, and one of the most comforting pieces of advice that can be given to student teachers is that, as time goes on, many things that are difficult now become much easier. However, it is worth noting that Sternberg and Horvath (1995) also claim that experts typically spend a greater proportion of time trying to understand the problem, whereas novices spend more in actually trying out different solutions. Sometimes, deciding the best response through more detailed analysis is a much more efficient way of dealing with problems than rushing in without clear judgement.

It can be argued that *insight*, Sternberg and Horvath's third feature of teacher expertise, involves a combination of the first two (knowledge and efficiency). Insight involves distinguishing information that is relevant to the problem solution from that which is irrelevant. This obviously provides the expert teacher with an insight into the situation, which will enable him or her to (1) make the most efficient use of the time available and (2) draw on the most useful areas of knowledge.

Twiselton's study of student teachers (mentioned above; Twiselton, 2000, 2003, 2004, 2006, 2007; Twiselton and Webb, 1998) also involved examining how expert teachers operate. She did this through watching them teach, making detailed notes of their actions and words and interviewing them closely afterwards about how they decided what to do. The extract on page 110 is an example of the notes taken, and Task 2.4.5 helps with understanding how this can be analysed to show how effective teachers constantly assess the situation in order to make the most effective response.

Task 2.4.5 Observing other teachers

- Read through the observation notes 1 overleaf and use the 'Assessment/response' column to make a note of any points at which the teacher (X) appears to be making an assessment or acting on the basis of an assessment made.
- Repeat this with the observation notes 2 on page 111 (from a different teacher).
- What are the differences you notice between the two teachers?

The second set of observation notes were taken from a student teacher (TT) during her first placement. The differences are notable. The student teacher assesses in a limited way and only uses a narrow range of strategies. The expert teacher is constantly assessing and responding, and she uses a range of strategies in doing this. This supports Sternberg and Horvath's (1995) claims that effective teachers demonstrate knowledge, efficiency and insight through their ability to quickly process and analyse a learning experience and draw on a range of conceptual principles to make the best decisions for action.

SUMMARY

It does not require a unit in a book to tell you that teaching is a very complicated business, and that effective teaching requires a wide range of types of knowledge and a large number of skills. In this unit, we have tried to elaborate on some of the more important components of teaching skills and to explore the implications of these for your teaching. It is important to close this unit with a reminder of the importance of quality over quantity. It is not the amount you know, or the number of teaching skills in which you have some competence, that is crucial. Your depth of knowledge and level of confidence in your skills are of much more importance. As you experience teaching, keep asking yourself the 'why' question and keep your eyes and ears open to children's responses. Deeper knowledge and surer confidence in your actions will follow, if this becomes your natural mindset.

Observation notes 1 for Task 2.4.5

Observation notes 1	Assessment/response
9.23 X is talking to child (C1) about her picture of a ladybird: 'Do you want to do some writing to tell everyone about this?' (C1 nods) 'What shall we write?' C1: The ladybird is sitting on a leaf. X: Excellent. Which side shall we start? C1: Over here. **9.25** X: You go ahead and write it and show me in a minute. X is explaining the spider's web pattern to a child (C2). **9.27** X: Can you make the lines go all along the web? It's very important you start at the left and finish on the right because we are practising for writing. Where's the left? Where will you start? (C2 shows her; she observes closely as C2 starts the web) X: Lovely, don't forget to keep your pencil on the line. Nice and slow. **9.30** X: What a lot of lovely writing. I can see some of the letters of your name. Where's the 'm'? C1: Here and here. X: You've done those beautifully. Can you read me your writing now? C1: The ladybird is sitting on the leaf. She has lots of children and they like flying. **9.32** X: Wow! You've added more to it! You told me earlier on that there was a 'l' at the beginning of ladybird. Where might the 'l' have gone here? (C1 points randomly and vaguely) X: Can you read it again and point to the words at the same time? (C1 moves her finger along the line from left to right, but there is no attempt to match up the writing with what she is saying) **9.34** X: Now I'll write my writing. Where shall I start? (C1 shows her; X writes the words and reads them as she does so) X: Let's read it again together. (They read it, X gently holds C1's finger and helps her to point to the words as they read)	

Observation notes 2 for Task 2.4.5

Observation notes 2	Assessment/response
10.10 TT to C1: What does that say? (Points from left to right over the label) (No answer from C1) TT: What does it start with? C1: It's a drink. TT: Yes, but what does it start with? C1: Don't know. TT: It's milk! **10.12** TT to the whole group: Take it in turns to choose a card – see if you can match it. (C2 takes a card) TT: What does that say? (C2 is looking at the picture) C2: Chocolate. TT: Good girl! Put it in the right place. **10.14** (C3 takes a card with a sandwich label) TT: What does that say? Have you got that? C3: It says pizza. TT: It's not pizza. What does it say? It says sandwich! **10.17** (C1 takes a card) TT: What does that card say? (No answer) TT: W . . . C1: Watermelon. TT: Brilliant! **10.19** (C2 takes a card) TT: What does it say? C2: Ice-cream. TT: Have you got ice-cream? (TT points to game card) C2: No. **10.20** TT: Well done!	

ANNOTATED FURTHER READING

Alexander, R. (2010) *Children, Their World, Their Education: Final Report and Recommendations of the Cambridge Primary Review*, London: Routledge.

> An impressive body of research underpins this volume, which covers most aspects of teaching and learning, philosophy and practice. Chapter 7, 'Children's development and learning', Chapter 14, 'Towards a new curriculum', and Chapter 15, 'Re-thinking pedagogy', all contribute to a comprehensive understanding of the complex issues surrounding effective teaching and learning.

Elton-Chalcraft, S., Hansen, A. and Twiselton, S. (2008) *Doing Classroom Research*, Milton Keynes: Open University Press.

> This book has been designed to support those studying at Masters level as part of their initial teacher education programme. However, it has relevance for all who are undertaking school-based research and are interested in the development of teaching as an evidence-based profession.

(M) FURTHER READING TO SUPPORT M-LEVEL STUDY

Claxton, G. (2007) 'Expanding young people's capacity to learn', *British Journal of Educational Studies*, 55(2): 115-34.

> In this article, particularly useful for Masters-level students, Claxton expands his view that hesitancy and unclear knowing are vital aspects of intelligence, and that the teacher's role is to help children to become better learners – increase their 'learning capacity' – as opposed to supporting them to become conformist pupils, which, Claxton argues, can result in learned helplessness.

Cullingford, C. (2007) 'Creativity and pupil's experience of school', *Education 3-13*, 35(2): 133-42.

> Cullingford discusses children's preferred modes of thinking and how teachers can appropriately support children to learn more effectively. This journal article is ideal for Masters-level study concerning relevant curriculum design and appropriate teaching skills. Also useful is Cullingford (2009) *The Art of Teaching: Experiences of Schools*, London: Routledge, where Cullingford discusses the individual nature of the art of teaching.

Devine, D., Fahie, D. and McGillicuddy, D. (2013) 'What is "good" teaching? Teacher beliefs and practices about their teaching', *Irish Educational Studies*, 32(1), Special Issue Research in Education Related to Teacher Accountability.

> This journal article discusses the need for teachers to take into account the broader sociocultural context of the school and the needs of their learners, which will have an influence on the way they construct learning. Masters-level students will find this an engaging read to inform effective classroom practice.

RELEVANT WEBSITES

www.primaryreview.org.uk
> The Cambridge Primary Review website.

REFERENCES

Alexander, R. (2010) *Children, Their World, Their Education: Final Report and Recommendations of the Cambridge Primary Review*, London: Routledge.

Askew, M., Brown, M., Rhodes, V., William, D. and Johnson, D. (1997) *Effective Teachers of Numeracy*, London: Teacher Training Agency.

Boden (2001) 'Creativity and knowledge', in A. Craft, B. Jeffrey and M. Leibling (eds) *Creativity in Education*, London: Continuum, chap. 6.

Bruner, J.S. (1996) *The Culture of Education*, Cambridge, MA: Harvard University Press.

Chi, M.T.H., Feltovich, J.P. and Glaser, R. (1981) 'Categorization and representation of physics problems by experts and novices', *Cognitive Science*, 5(2): 121-52.

Claxton, G. (1997) *Hare Brain Tortoise Mind: Why Intelligence Increases When You Think Less*, London: Fourth Estate Ltd.

Claxton, G. (2007) 'Expanding young people's capacity to learn', *British Journal of Educational studies*, 55(2): 115-34.

Copping (2011) 'Curriculum approaches', in A. Hansen, *Primary Professional Studies*, Exeter: Learning Matters, pp. 23-43.

Cullingford, C. (2007) 'Creativity and pupil's experience of school', *Education 3-13*, 35(2): 133-42.

Devine, D., Fahie, D. and McGillicuddy, D. (2013) 'What is "good" teaching? Teacher beliefs and practices about their teaching', *Irish Educational Studies*, 32(1), Special Issue Research in Education Related to Teacher Accountability.

Elton-Chalcraft, S. and Mills, K. (2013) '"It was the funnest week in the whole history of funnest weeks." Measuring challenge, fun and sterility on a 'Phunometre' scale: A case study evaluating creative teaching and learning with PGCE student teachers and children in a sample of primary schools', *Education 3-13: International Journal of Primary, Elementary and Early Years Education*, DOI: 10.1080/03004279.2013.822904, http://dx.doi.org/10.1080/03004279.2013.822904.

Elton-Chalcraft, S., Hansen, A. and Twiselton, S. (eds) (2008) *Doing Classroom Research: A Step-By Step Guide for Student Teachers*, Maidenhead: Open University Press.

Hayes, D. (2011) *Guided Reader to Teaching and Learning*, London: David Fulton.

Heilman, K. (2005) *Creativity and the Brain*, Hove: Psychology Press.

Kuiper, E., Volman, M. and Terwel, J. (2009) 'Developing Web literacy in collaborative inquiry activities', *Computers & Education*, 52(3): 668-80, www.researchgate.net/publication/220139937_Developing_Web_literacy_in_collaborative_inquiry_activities/file/79e41500812bba381a.pdf&sa=X&scisig=AAGBfm3uf2kxKW2SUmRiOmzQB7r8z2OlrQ&oi=scholarr&ei=uCvbUPfXEYmVOQXc8oCACw&ved=0CDsQgAMoADAA (accessed 24 April 2013).

Larkin, J., McDermott, J., Simon, D. and Simon, A. (1980) 'Expert and novice performance in solving physics problems', *Science*, 208: 1335-42.

Medwell, J., Wray, D., Poulson, L. and Fox, R. (1998) *Effective Teachers of Literacy*, London: Teacher Training Agency.

Shulman, L.S. (1987) 'Knowledge and teaching: foundations of the new reform', *Harvard Educational Review*, 57(1): 1-22.

Sternberg, R. and Horvath, J. (1995) 'A prototype view of expert learning', *Education Research*, 24(6): 9-17.

Tochon, F. and Munby, H. (1993) 'Novice and expert teachers' time epistemology: a wave function from didactics to pedagogy', *Teaching and Teacher Education*, 2: 205-18.

Turner-Bisset, R. (1999) 'Knowledge bases for teaching', *British Educational Research Journal*, 25(1): 39-55.

Twiselton, S. (2000) 'Seeing the wood for the trees: the National Literacy Strategy and initial teacher education; pedagogical content knowledge and the structure of subjects', *Cambridge Journal of Education*, 30(3): 391-403.

Twiselton, S. (2003) 'Beyond the curriculum: learning to teach primary literacy', in E. Bearne, H. Dombey and T. Grainger (eds) *Interactions in Language and Literacy in the Classroom*, Milton Keynes: Open University Press.

Twiselton, S. (2004) 'The role of teacher identities in learning to teach primary literacy', *Education Review: Special Edition: Activity Theory*, 56(2): 88-96.

Twiselton, S. (2006) 'The problem with English: the exploration and development of student teachers' English subject knowledge in primary classrooms', *Literacy*, 40(2): 88-96.

Twiselton, S. (2007) 'Seeing the wood for the trees: learning to teach beyond the curriculum. How can student teachers be helped to see beyond the National Literacy Strategy?', *Cambridge Journal of Education*, 37(4): 489-502.

Twiselton, S. and Webb. D (1998) 'The trouble with English: the challenge of developing subject knowledge in school', in C. Richards, N. Simco and S. Twiselton (eds) *Primary Teacher Education: High Standards? High Status?* London: Falmer.

BUILDING ON FIRM FOUNDATIONS

Early years practice

Sue Rogers and Janet Rose

INTRODUCTION

We have often heard student teachers say that, 'all children do in the early years is play', and that 'early years teachers are just childminders'. Until relatively recently, early years education has suffered from low status, dogged by a wide range of misconceptions about how young children learn and the nature of work in early years settings.

However, the early years sector in the UK has seen an unprecedented period of development and change since the election of the last government in 1997. The sociopolitical agenda to ameliorate the divisive and fragmented nature of early years provision in the UK was (and, arguably, still is) closely bound up with the desire to reduce child poverty and disadvantage and to encourage more lone parents (and in particular mothers) back to work. These aspirations have required a major 'root and branch' approach to services for young children and their families (Anning, 2006), and central to this has been the dual aim to both increase the quantity, and improve the quality, of early education and childcare provision.

Within this context, our task in this unit is to challenge the popular conception that working with young children is easy and of less significance than formal schooling, and to convince you that, as primary school teachers, you need to understand how and in what ways children learn in the early years, and the range of diverse experiences they are likely to have had on arrival in the primary school. We offer also a cautionary note: we acknowledge that a key aim of early years education is to build firm foundations for future learning in the primary school and beyond. However, the purpose of early years education is not simply a preparation for future life or for later schooling, but something that is important in its own right. Understanding this will enable you to build on the firm foundations established in the first 5 years and value the specific characteristics of young children as learners.

OBJECTIVES

This unit will help you to:

- highlight key issues you ought to know about in relation to the early years;
- eliminate any myths that may exist in your perspective of the early years;
- emphasise the importance of the early years and outline key policy initiatives;
- clarify the nature of early years practice.

EARLY YEARS POLICY

> Pre-school children have brains which are more active, more connected and more flexible than an adult's brain.
>
> (Riley, 2003: 3)

It is widely agreed that, from birth, children are powerful, creative and competent learners, and that early years provision should capitalise on this at a time when they are particularly receptive, developmentally, to exploratory, imaginative and social activity. Key questions about what an appropriate curriculum and pedagogy for young children might look like, and how, and in what ways, adults can support the learning and development of children in the early years, have been the major preoccupations of policymakers and early years educators alike in recent years.

The considerable recognition now afforded to the early years of education by policymakers is indicative also of a wider appreciation of the fundamental significance of this phase of childhood in lifelong learning, a view underpinned by a large and robust research literature. For example, there is compelling recent evidence from the neurosciences that testifies to the profound way in which children's earliest experiences affect their developing potential, with long-lasting implications (see, for example, Blakemore and Frith, 2005; Gopnik *et al.*, 1999).

The increasing complexity and demands of contemporary life mean that many children under the age of 5 will have had experiences in one or more different early years contexts, whether they have been cared for by a nanny or childminder, or have experienced group settings such as day nurseries and/or pre-school nurseries or playgroups. Each of these settings will have provided a range of diverse experiences, and, in turn, these will have affected the knowledge, skills and understanding that children bring with them to school. Early education provision has been extended to disadvantaged 2-year-olds via the Early Intervention Grant. Coupled with the current economic climate and sociopolitical trends, the likelihood of children spending time in settings other than the home is set to increase. It is, therefore, imperative that teachers, particularly those working in Key Stage 1, are fully cognisant of the potential range of provision and that they understand the types of experience these children will have had, in order to ease the transition process and be sensitive to the potential impact of these in helping young children to adapt and settle into the school environment. Indeed, the new *Teachers' Standards* refer to the need for teachers to build on pupils' prior experiences (DfE, 2012a).

THE EARLY YEARS FOUNDATION STAGE

Educational provision for children under 5 in the UK is offered within a wide range of diverse settings, in both the maintained and private sectors. These settings include nursery classes, playgroups, childminders, children's centres and reception classes of primary schools. All of these settings now fall within the Foundation Stage, a distinctive phase for children from birth to statutory school age, currently described as 'the term after a child's fifth birthday'. Historically, the fragmented and patchy nature of educational provision has created difficulties and divisions for children, their families and practitioners alike.

In 2006, the Childcare Act provided the legal framework for the creation of the Early Years Foundation Stage (EYFS), implemented in 2008. The EYFS combined and replaced three earlier initiatives (the *Birth to Three* framework of 2002, the *Curriculum Guidance for the Foundation Stage* of 2003 and the *National Standards for Under Eights Day Care and Childminding* of 2003). The EYFS was developed in consultation with key stakeholders in the early years field, including practitioners, and is founded on evidence-based research on early years pedagogy, including international approaches. Under the Coalition government, a revised EYFS has been developed that became statutory from September 2012 (DfE, 2012b). Two main factors need to be taken into consideration in relation to the EYFS:

- The EYFS is intended to create a holistic and coherent approach to the care and education (sometimes referred to as 'educare') of young children – this represents a considerable and welcome development within the early years sector in recognition that the care and education of young children are inseparable and inextricably linked.
- The EYFS is a statutory framework, but it is not intended as a curriculum to be followed, as with the National Curriculum – rather, it is viewed as principles for practice across the early years sector.

The revised EYFS is based on the following principles:

- every child is a *unique child*, who is constantly learning and can be resilient, capable, confident and self-assured;
- children learn to be strong and independent through *positive relationships;*
- children learn and develop well in *enabling environments*, in which their experiences respond to their individual needs and there is a strong partnership between practitioners and parents and/or carers; and
- *children develop and learn in different ways and at different rates*. The framework covers the education and care of all children in early years provision, including children with special educational needs and disabilities.

Building on these principles, the revised EYFS places great emphasis on three key characteristics of effective learning:

- Playing and exploring are the ways in which children engage with their learning – through finding out and exploring, playing with what they know and being willing to have a go.
- Active learning is what motivates children – being involved and concentrating, keeping trying and enjoying achieving what they set out to do.
- Creating and thinking critically – children need lots of opportunities to think, have their own ideas, make links and choose ways of doing things.

It is important to note that these characteristics are concerned with the process of how children learn and the context in which the early years curriculum should be offered. These apply equally to the indoor and outdoor environments.

Much of the old and new EYFS is based on a commitment to 'developmentally appropriate practice', promoting activities that are in tune with the child's individual level of understanding and skills development. Though children are assessed individually, the sociocultural context of children's lives is also recognised, promoting contextually appropriate practice.

What is developmentally appropriate practice?

> Developmentally appropriate practice requires both meeting children where they are – which means that teachers must get to know them well – and enabling them to reach goals that are both challenging and achievable. All teaching practices should be appropriate to children's age and developmental status, attuned to them as unique individuals, and responsive to the social and cultural contexts in which they live.
>
> (National Association for the Education of Young Children, 2009)

Early years practice is commonly associated with the term 'developmentally appropriate practice' (DAP), a term that has particular currency in the USA, but has had a significant influence on early years education in the UK. Blenkin and Kelly (1988) articulated a developmental approach to the early years back in the 1980s, suggesting that education should primarily be concerned with 'human development' rather than knowledge acquisition. Elsewhere in this book, Earl refers to the developmental tradition that 'emphasises the ways in which children develop physically, socially, emotionally and intellectually as a basis for planning and organising learning' (Unit 4.1). The Cambridge Primary Review in the UK has recently confirmed the importance of a developmentally appropriate curriculum for young learners, such as the need for active experience, multisensory approaches and pretend play to promote cognitive development (Goswami and Bryant, 2007). A longitudinal, cross-cultural study on pre-school experiences in ten different countries also shows that developmentally appropriate practice works best for younger children (Montie *et al.*, 2006). Clear links can also be found within the principles of EYFS and the principles behind DAP.

What is contextually appropriate practice?

Practice grows out of political and economic conditions and traditions, rather than scientific research into child development (Penn, 2008). Although DAP endorses a developmental perspective on children's education, we must be careful not to overemphasise the evidence from neuroscience and developmental psychology. Penn calls attention to the many assumptions there are in following a developmental approach, including the capacity to measure 'normality' and the 'compartmentalisation' of development into stages (2008: 14). Similarly, David has highlighted some of the 'pitfalls' of applying developmental theory 'too rigidly' (see Unit 2.1). Moreover, we need to consider, not only developmental aspects, but also the wider context and all the factors that may shape a child's learning and development. No framework or curriculum is 'value-free' or 'context-free' (Penn, 2008: 188). We therefore need to be conscious of the wide range of factors that may influence a child's experiences before entry into Key Stage 1, not just their apparent developmental levels, thereby implementing contextually appropriate practice.

RHETORIC AND REALITY IN THE RECEPTION CLASS

The 'reception class' is the first class of primary school. It receives the new intake of children at age 4 or 5. In England, Scotland and Wales, the statutory school starting age is the term after a child's fifth birthday. However, in practice, most children in England and Wales start school before the statutory age of 5. Changes to the School Admissions Code in 2011 mean that, in practice, most children enter school when they are just four. The stated rationale for this change to one intake per year is its perceived benefits for summer-born children. However, the increase in the number of young 4-year-olds entering school can also be attributed to a range of factors, including falling rolls creating pressure for schools to fill places; pressure from parents for their children to start school earlier, because of a lack of sufficient free, pre-school provision, but also for its perceived educational benefits; and the demands of the National Curriculum to ensure that children have sufficient time in school in order to be 'ready' for Key Stage 1. The impact of this change is felt in reception classes, where provision needs to be made for children who are likely to have different developmental demands owing to their immaturity, but also in pre-school settings across the early years sector, which have been affected educationally and economically by the loss of 4-year-olds to schools.

Studies have highlighted the division between nursery and reception class practice, in spite of the fact that the Foundation Stage was designed precisely to overcome such divisions. A number of specific concerns have been identified and include admission policies that may contribute to the uneven quality of provision for 4-year-olds in reception classes; lower adult-to-child ratios in reception classes, which may reduce effective adult–child interaction; a lack of appropriately trained staff in reception classes, which may lead to over-formal activities; and a reduction in the availability of choice of activity, outdoor access and time and space for active play (David, 1990; Adams *et al.*, 2004; Rogers and Evans, 2008). Others argue that the location of the reception class in school, unlike other separately managed pre-school settings, may result in features of a formal school curriculum percolating down to the teachers and children in the reception class. In turn, this can result in competing discourses of school improvement and school readiness versus a distinctive pedagogy for early childhood (Aubrey, 2004).

Studies of reception class pedagogy explicitly endorse a nursery-style provision for 4-year-olds and argue that there is no compelling evidence that starting school early has lasting educational benefits (Sharp, 2002; Adams *et al.*, 2004). Indeed, opponents of an early school starting age warn that over-formal education, introduced too soon, may be detrimental to children's social well-being and long-term attitude to learning. For example, recent research has highlighted the pressures that are put on early years practitioners to create a more formalised learning environment in reception classes (Rose and Rogers, 2012a). This correlates with other literature that documents how reception class children often experience a watered-down version of Key Stage 1 (Adams *et al.*, 2004; Whitebread and Coltman, 2008; Brooker *et al.*, 2010) and suggests that the situation has not improved. Indeed, it is possible that the pressure to provide more formal activities in reception classes will increase further, as the new EYFS states that one of its aims is to 'ensure children's school readiness' (DfE, 2012b: 2).

The emphasis on skill acquisition in reception classes can be to the detriment of children's motivation to learn, overemphasis on formal reading skills being a classic example of this trend. The Cambridge Primary Review, for example, has noted that any gains have been 'at the expense of [pupils'] enjoyment of reading' (Whetton *et al.*, 2007: 19). Young children's disposition to learning has been a critical factor identified in the literature for educational success (Katz, 1992), suggesting that the 'school-readiness' culture that permeates reception classes may be counter-effective (Rogers, 2010). These issues are compounded by the increasing trend of 4-year-old children entering reception classes who are encountering the effects of 'top-down pressures', as noted earlier. Such trends seem unnecessary, given the well-known evidence that children who start formal school at a later age eventually outstrip English children in academic achievement (Whetton *et al.*, 2007; Alexander, 2009).

As the Cambridge Primary Review has noted:

> the assumption that an early starting age is beneficial for children's later attainment is not well supported in the research and therefore remains open to question, whilst there are particular concerns about the appropriateness of provision for four year olds in school reception classes.
>
> (Riggall and Sharp, 2008)

Task 2.5.1 Principles into practice

- Read the article, Rose, J. and Rogers, S. (2012b) 'Principles under pressure: student teachers' perspectives on final teaching practice in early childhood classrooms', *International Journal of Early Years Education*, 20(1): 43–58.

- Discuss whether the findings in the article echo your own experiences in placement.

- Outline your own principles of early years practice and consider possible challenges you might encounter when applying these principles in the classroom.

THE LEARNING ENVIRONMENT

> A rich and varied environment supports children's learning and development. It gives them the confidence to explore and learn in secure and safe, yet challenging, indoor and outdoor spaces.
>
> (DCFS, 2008, Commitment 3.3)

The above is taken from the old EYFS but offers a useful starting point to consider what an appropriate learning environment for children in the early years should comprise. The debate about what constitutes an appropriate learning environment inevitably draws into its sphere the role of play.

In Northern Ireland . . .

> Learning environments should be secure, interesting and challenging. By adding to and changing these environments, children may be stimulated to pursue new interests, solve problems and generate ideas.
>
> (Council for Curriculum, Examinations and Assessment, 2006: 10)

Source: Council for Curriculum, Examinations and Assessment (CCEA) (2006) *Understanding the Foundation Stage.* Belfast, CCEA Publications.

In Wales . . .

In the Foundation Phase learning environment

> there must be a balance between structured learning through child-initiated activities and those directed by practitioners. A well-planned curriculum gives children opportunities to be creatively involved in their own learning which must build on what they already know and can do, their interests and what they understand. Active learning enhances and extends children's development.
>
> (DCELLS, 2008: 6)

Source: Department for Children, Education, Lifelong Learning and Skills (DCELLS) (2008) *Framework for Children's Learning for 3- to 7-year-olds in Wales.* Cardiff: Welsh Assembly Government (WAG).http://wales.gov.uk/dcells/publications/policy_strategy_and_planning/early-wales/whatisfoundation/foundationphase/2274085/frameworkforchildrene.pdf;jsessionid=A063B61CDC675238A7D3FA3AE765C458?lang=en

The old and revised EYFS both strongly endorse a play-based approach to learning in the early years. In practice, however, implementing a play-based approach can be problematic. First, teachers often feel under pressure to prepare children for formal learning and prioritise literacy and numeracy activities, as noted earlier, which may not be appropriate to developmentally appropriate practice. Second, it is not always clear how much structure to provide. Do children need manufactured and elaborate resources to play? Should play be tied to curriculum objectives, or are the outcomes of play determined by the children? Third, what is the adult role in play? To what extent should adults intervene, and when does intervention become interference?

Few would dispute the fact that one of the key ways in which children up to the age of 5 make human sense (Donaldson, 1978) of the world around them is through their play. We can see this in the earliest sensori-motor play observed in babies and toddlers, involving mainly exploratory activity through the senses and through action on objects. You might be familiar with the tendency of babies to put things in their mouths and throw things. At this stage, children are interested in the properties of things. Take, for example, Sam, who is 10 months old. He is preoccupied with dropping objects from the top of the stairs, repeatedly. Though this behaviour may be difficult for adults to tolerate, it is a vital part of Sam's development in his efforts to make sense of the world around him. He is learning about his impact on the world and early scientific and mathematical concepts, such as gravity, cause and effect and trajectories. This exploratory play gradually changes as children approach their second birthdays, when a profound and uniquely human capacity comes to the fore of children's activity. This is the ability to pretend, seen first in the simple imitations of toddlers and later in the highly sophisticated social pretend play or role-play of 4- and 5-year-olds. It is this social pretence that lays the foundations of many important life skills, such as problem-solving, creative activity and interpersonal relations, as well as being enjoyable and life-enhancing to children as they play.

Of particular interest to those of you working in Key Stage 1 classes is research that demonstrates that children aged 3–5 engage in more pretend play than any other kind of play (see, for example, Corsaro, 2005). Not only is it more prevalent than other kinds of play, but it also becomes highly complex, involving detailed planning and negotiation, and innovation. Developmentally speaking, there are good reasons for this. At around the age of 4, we see children's imaginative play become more complex, as they become more linguistically and socially expert. They have also discovered that other people have minds, and that what they think is not always what others think. This is the emergence of empathy, growing out of a theory of mind acquired at around the age of three. All this is essential to successful pretend play and is also developed within it.

The prevalence of this kind of play occurs precisely at the point at which children enter reception class settings in primary schools, and it continues to develop through to the role-play and other creative activities seen in primary school classrooms. In order to help children develop vivid imaginations, understand social relations and innovate (all transferable skills), it is essential that children are given ample opportunities to engage in social pretence with their peers at this age, and, furthermore, that these experiences are built upon in Key Stage 1 and beyond.

In recognition of the importance of all types of play across the early years phase, early years settings are developed around the concept of 'free flow', continuous play provision, both indoors and outdoors. Classrooms are organised into resource areas to which children have access throughout the day. This approach presupposes choice and autonomy on the part of children, who will have regular and sustained opportunities to access resources independently. Remember that Einstein believed that 'play is research'.

Task 2.5.2 Child-initiated play

Read the following example of real-life practice and consider whether the teacher's aims fulfil her intention:

> A teacher of six year olds is planning an art activity to develop their creative skills. She decides the children will make pine-cone turkeys and collects the range of materials they will use. She sits with a group and demonstrates how they will make them and explains exactly how the materials fit together in particular places to create the turkey. She then supports them in making them, allowing each child to choose five coloured feathers, which she encourages them to count. The children then make the turkeys, but need help with the glueing, sticking and making the pipe-cleaner feet. The children mostly watch the teacher during the whole activity.
>
> (Woyke, 2001)

How you could turn this adult-led activity into one that is child-initiated and allows the child to be more active, creative and independent in the process?

The outdoor environment

Of particular importance since the introduction of the EYFS is the recognition that young children need regular access to outdoor play to enhance their well-being and development in all areas: physical, emotional, social, cognitive and creative. Outdoor spaces offer a range of different learning opportunities to children, not least the freedom to be more active, noisy and exploratory than is possible in indoor spaces. In addition to the obvious physical benefits of being in the outdoors, such activity offers young children a range of multisensory, first-hand experiences, such as feeling the effects of the weather and related temperatures, and experiencing direct contact with the textures, smells and sounds of natural materials, such as wood, grass, ice, earth and water. Research has shown that, not only do young children prefer to play outside, but they play in quite different ways in outdoor spaces. Rogers and Evans (2008) noted that 4- and 5-year-olds engaged in far more complex, sustained and socially developed role-play in outdoor spaces. Children displayed a wider range of social skills to establish and maintain social groups, stayed in character for longer periods, and used open-ended props more creatively, and there were fewer conflicts between children and with adults. The incidence of mixed-gender play was also more frequently observed in the outdoor area. Outdoor play, by its very nature, involves children taking risks that push them beyond their current capabilities and challenge them physically, socially and cognitively. For adults, managing risk is challenging too and may lead to anxieties about how far they can allow children to explore and push boundaries. Certain types of play can also pose a risk to adults' own boundaries about what is acceptable behaviour, particularly within the heavily regulated classroom (Rogers, 2014). As children develop, they move from a situation of dependence and adult-managed experiences to independence and self-management. Gill (2007) argues that there is growing evidence to suggest that, in the developed Western world, an increasingly regulated, risk-averse approach is severely limiting children's opportunities to practise some of the vital skills that would enable them to make this move and to exercise good judgment about what constitutes risk and danger. However, adults may hold an exaggerated view of what constitutes a risk to young children, stemming from their own personal anxiety about potentially threatening situations, about the potential for disorder within the group and a genuine anxiety about litigation while *in loco parentis* (Waite *et al.*, 2011).

THE ROLE OF THE ADULT IN PLAY

It is not simply the material resources that make for a stimulating and effective learning environment for young children. Knowledgeable, skilled and caring adults will create an environment that creates, nurtures and sustains a positive learning ethos that matches the dispositions and characteristics of young children and acknowledges and values cultural diversity and equity. Earlier, we raised some of the dilemmas facing early years practitioners in relation to young children's play and some of the tensions that exist within different pedagogical approaches, both from theorists such as Piaget and Bruner and practitioners themselves, in terms of the amount or level of adult interaction or involvement in children's play activities – in other words, whether practitioners ought to 'develop a child or watch a child develop' (Alexander, 2010: 95). The EYFS compounds this debate by stipulating that 'each area of learning and development must be implemented through planned, purposeful play and through a mix of adult-led and child-initiated activity' (DfE, 2012b: 1.9).

One possible way forward is to reconsider the terms 'adult-led', 'adult-directed', 'child-initiated' and 'child-led' and replace these terms with just two: adult-initiated and child-initiated. Thus,

> by viewing all activities and exchanges as a process of initiation that immediately becomes an interconnected negotiation, rather than as an act of being led or directed by either the child or the adult, we can envisage the adult–child relationship as one that involves interchangeable processes of 'give-and-take' and mutual co-construction.
>
> (Rose and Rogers, 2012b: 9)

We have suggested that this might help early years teachers to 'understand the reciprocal nature of adult–child interactions and might help to diminish uncertainties regarding adult intervention' (Rose and Rogers, 2012b).

A recent research study by Rogers and Evans (2008) studied the role-play activity of 4- and 5-year-olds in reception and Year 1 classes. They found that there was a mismatch between how children viewed their play and the way play was organised in the classroom. Typically, classrooms were set up with structured role-play areas around a particular theme or topic. For example, one classroom developed a shop, and another offered a café. Although these areas were resourced in elaborate and inviting ways, the children paid little attention to the theme, preferring instead to play games of their own choosing. In many instances, the play was difficult to contain and manage within the confines of the classroom. An alternative approach to role-play, well suited to children over the age of 4 and throughout the primary years, is open-ended play, with suggestive rather than pre-specified props.

For example, Kelvin and his friends built a 'ship' from large bricks. They 'sailed' to a 'cave' made from a sheet draped over some chairs. In the 'cave', there were some keys, which they used to lock up the baddies. This example of sustained role-play involving five children lasted for at least 20 minutes. Kelvin, a child with identified special needs, emerged as a 'master player', leading the group and utilising language rarely heard in formal teaching activities. Social relationships were explored, formed and reformed in the course of the play, as children negotiated roles and planned the course of the play.

In this simple example of role-play, we see a wide range of important learning and potential assessment opportunities for the observant adult. However, in order for this type of play to occur, the adult needs to take the following into consideration:

For young children, play is about:

* exercising choice and control over what they do;
* making and developing friendships;
* pretending in a secure context;
* experimenting with materials, ideas, time and place (here and now/fantasy and reality).

For adults, play may be a highly valued activity, but in practice it may be:

* a holding task;
* a reward for good work;
* noisy and disruptive;
* difficult to manage and irrational;
* a low-status activity.

Research shows that adults need to:

* give children real choice about where, with whom, what and how they play;
* give children space (indoors and outdoors) and uninterrupted time to play, revisit, rebuild and recreate ideas with adults and children;
* show children we are interested in their play through co-construction, consultation and negotiation, observation and feedback;
* be knowledgeable others and advocates for play;
* develop outdoor spaces for playful learning where children can exercise greater choice over materials, location and play mates;
* develop open-ended resources and spaces, enabling children to create play contexts and content;
* provide time to play without unnecessary interruptions;
* develop a learner-inclusive environment that encourages children's participation and decision-making;
* encourage sustained shared thinking between adults and children and between children.

(Adapted from Rogers and Evans, 2008)

Sustained shared thinking

Sustained shared thinking involves the adult being aware of the children's interests and understandings and the adult and children working together to develop an idea or skill. The adult shows genuine interest, offers encouragement, clarifies ideas and asks open questions. This supports and extends the children's thinking and helps children to make connections in learning (Sylva *et al.*, 2004).

The Effective Provision of Pre-school Education (EPPE) project findings (Siraj-Blatchford, 2004; Sylva *et al.*, 2004) suggested that the potential for learning through play can be extended by what the researchers have termed 'sustained shared thinking'. This process has officially been incorporated into the EYFS, as noted in the quotation above. This essentially involves adults 'getting involved' in children's thinking, interacting in a shared (verbal or non-verbal) dialogue. In this way, as Siraj-Blatchford explains, adults can act as co-constructors to 'solve a problem, clarify a concept, evaluate activities or extend narratives' (2004: 147). Sustained shared thinking builds on other research that

Task 2.5.3 Sustained shared thinking

Read the following example of a real-life exchange between children and their teacher in a nursery. Evaluate the way in which the practitioner supported the children's thinking.

While playing outside, the children discovered a kitten (toy) stuck in the guttering of the barn area. The group was allowed time to discover the kitten and talk about how they thought it got there and how it could be rescued. (*P* = practitioner)

Child B: Oh, poor kitty, I think she's stuck up there.

Child C: How did it get all the way up there?

P: Oh dear. How do you think the kitten got stuck up there in the first place?

Child A: He climbed up this pipe (pointing to the drainpipe), then went along here and got stuck in here.

Child C: He can't climb up there 'cos he's not real! I think he must have been 'throwded' up there.

P: Who do you think might have done that?

Child C: I don't know but it's not very kind is it? They might have done it on accident.

Child A: Yeah, like this (he mimics throwing an imaginary object accidentally!).

Child E: My daddy 'throwed' the ball through the window by accident. Mummy was cross. He 'breaked' the window!

P: Yes, they might have done it by accident, I can't think that anyone would throw it up there on purpose. Well, I suppose we need to do some good thinking about what to do to help the kitten. How shall we do that do you think?

Child D: I know, I know! We can, we can ask Charlotte to climb up all the way.

Child A: Yeah, I seen Charlotte climb ladders to get that stuff off them tall shelves in the other room.

Child C: Or we can get Jill to do the ladder.

Child B: No, she 'don't' really like 'um' (meaning ladders).

Child C: I know, we can find Graham, he's good with ladders and he fixes stuff.

Child E: Yeah, ask Graham to do it.

P: What do we need to ask Graham?

Child E: Ask him to get the ladders and climb up there.

P: Oh, I see.

Child D: He can climb all the way up to that pipe thing and put it (the kitten) in his pocket.

Child B: He 'don't' want to squash it though. That would hurt it, wouldn't it?

Child A: Poor kitty. I think he's very sad. I don't want him to be sad no more.

Child E: No.

P: Shall we decide what we think we should do then?

Group: Yeah!

P:	Well, you had lots of thoughts and ideas; let's see if we can choose one idea to sort the problem out. You said we need to get a ladder, but who shall we ask to climb up it; you thought it could be Jill, Graham or Charlotte. Who do you think would be best to ask?
Child C:	Graham.
Children A and E:	Yeah, we can ask Graham.
P:	What makes you think Graham will be best for the job of getting the kitten down?
Child E:	He can climb ladders up really high.
Child D:	Yeah, I 'seen' him before on ladders. He can put it (kitten) in his pocket gently, can't he?
Child B:	He mustn't drop her or she'll have a headache and she might die!
P:	I hope she doesn't do that! Okay, so you think Graham can climb the ladder and put the kitten in his pocket gently and bring it back down again?
Child A:	Yeah, really gentle!
Child B:	And then the kitten will live happily ever after!

Source: Bowery (2008)

demonstrates the importance of meaningful, child-initiated and supportive interactions, such as Bruner's (1986) work on scaffolding and learning as a communal activity, inspired by Vygotsky, by Lave and Wenger's (1991) work on situated learning, and by Schaffer's (1996) work on 'joint involvement episodes'.

Apart from helping to develop children's learning, the adult needs to ensure that he or she is sensitive to the children's cues and levels of understanding, supporting them to make connections and transform their learning in a pleasurable and embedded way.

THE FOUNDATION STAGE PROFILE

The Foundation Stage Profile (FSP) is the precursor for the standard assessment tests (SATs) and is intended to provide a 'baseline assessment' of children starting school. Every government-funded setting, including schools, must complete an FSP for every child in the final term of the reception year, or equivalent. In essence, it requires reception class teachers to assess each child in relation to the seventeen Early Learning Goals, along with a brief commentary on the child's skills and abilities in relation to the three key characteristics of effective learning, and to share these assessments with parents and Year 1 teachers. The assessments need to indicate 'whether children are meeting *expected* levels of development, or if they are *exceeding* expected levels, or not yet reaching expected levels (*'emerging'*)' (DfE, 2013; own emphasis) and should consider children's self-assessments. It is intended that Year 1 teachers use the summary profiles to help inform them of individual children's learning and development. The results from these profiles are moderated and collected by local authorities and published nationally. The Standards and Testing Agency has stipulated that these summative assessments should be derived from the ongoing observations of consistent and independent behaviour, undertaken largely in the context of spontaneous (self-initiated) activities and events.

It should be noted that many have criticised these summative profiles and have questioned, among other things, their suitability, their effectiveness in feeding into teaching in Year 1, their over-

In Wales . . .

Educational provision for young children should be holistic with the child at the heart of any planned curriculum. It is about practitioners understanding, inspiring and challenging children's potential for learning. Practitioner involvement in children's play is of vital importance particularly when interactions involve open questioning, shared and sustained thinking.

(DCELLS, 2008: 6)

Source: Department for Children, Education, Lifelong Learning and Skills (DCELLS) (2008) *Framework for Children's Learning for 3- to 7-year-olds in Wales*. Cardiff: Welsh Assembly Government (WAG). http://wales.gov.uk/dcells/publications/policy_strategy_and_planning/early-wales/whatisfoundation/foundationphase/2274085/frameworkforchildrene.pdf;jsessionid=A063B61CDC675238A7D3FA3AE765C458?lang=en

simplification and the way in which they compartmentalise children's learning (British Educational Research Association, 2003). The Assessment Reform Group (1999) has claimed that 'assessment which is specifically designed to promote learning is the single most powerful tool we have for both raising standards and empowering lifelong learners'. There is an increasing call for more formative styles of assessment to take priority. The Researching Effective Pedagogy in the Early Years project has also shown that effective formative assessment directly impacts upon the quality of learning (Siraj-Blatchford *et al.*, 2002).

An alternative form of assessment, namely 'Learning Journeys', is becoming increasingly common practice in early years settings. Indeed, the revised FSP uses Learning Journeys as exemplifications of the way in which practitioners might record children's achievements and use these as evidence for making summative assessments. Such Learning Journeys are largely derived from 'learning stories', developed in New Zealand, whereby early years practitioners carry out regular assessment of children's natural activities, incorporating the observation, assessment and planning cycle within a framework of celebrating children's achievements. These are shared with both the children and parents, alongside discussion and decision-making among the children and staff to plan, enrich and progress children's learning. This style of assessment follows a sociocultural model. It is collaboratively and community based and reflects the learner's personal development rather than performance indicators. It is undoubtedly assessment *for* learning rather than assessment of learning.

TRANSITION FROM THE FOUNDATION STAGE TO KEY STAGE 1

Transition from one key stage to another inevitably presents children and practitioners with both challenges and opportunities. It involves unlearning and relearning, and the teacher's transition practice needs to take this into account. In conversation with reception class children, Rogers and Evans (2008) found that, for some, moving from the Foundation Stage to Key Stage 1 was an exciting prospect, signifying progress and achievement. For others, it was a source of anxiety, perceived as 'hard work', with fewer opportunities to play with friends. It is also a time when competing emotions can result in challenging behaviours:

Transition can be emotionally traumatising as strong internal feelings compete: excitement and fear, anticipation and anxiety, enthusiasm and apathy. Conflicting emotions can quickly and easily result in 'fight or flight' behaviours, and some children either retreat into themselves, become withdrawn or sullen, or begin challenging authority figures such as parents and teachers or get into fights with siblings or peers.

(Smith, 2011: 20)

Task 2.5.4 Supporting transition

Undertake an audit of reception and Year 1 in a school from a child's perspective:

- What do the children see in the Year 1 classroom that is the same as the reception classroom?
- What is different?
- What do the reception children experience that is the same as the Year 1 children?
- What is different?

Now undertake an audit of transition procedures in the school:

- What does the school do to reinforce the similarities?
- What does the school do to accommodate the differences?

Evaluate your findings in terms of the suggestions made in this section about how teachers can support the transition process.

At any stage of education, transition is complex. It is not a straightforward linear process, nor, for that matter, a single event – it involves a complex web of shifting and diverse aspects that need to be taken into account by adults in the school. For example, a series of interactions takes place, invariably involving a change in status and culture and 'continued social activity in which the individual lives, and learns to cope, by adapting to the given social conditions' (Fabian, 2006: 13). Research shows that educational transitions are highly significant to pupils and can be a 'critical factor in determining children's future progress and development' (Fabian, 2006: 4). Smith (2011: 15) also notes that the emotional impact of transition in the early years can have long-term consequences on children's well-being and resilience, as it provides 'an emotional benchmark' for future experiences of change.

With this in mind, it will be helpful to consider the following factors in order to ensure effective transition programmes:

- Children need ample opportunity to become familiar with the new situation through visits to the setting or class and contact with the teacher.
- 'Bridging' activities can form an important part of the process and 'create links between and actively involve children, parents, families, teachers, early childhood services, schools and the local community' (Fabian, 2006: 10).
- Parents need to be properly informed and involved in the transition process.
- Teachers must have appropriate information about the children's prior development and experience (Margetts, 2002), as children may have experienced multiple transitions, e.g. childminder, day nursery, pre-school, home before starting school.

- Rules and rituals are significant issues in the transition process, and assumptions are often made by adults that children will automatically understand these and their complexities.
- The way in which individual children may change from 'comfort zone' to new environment needs to be considered carefully by adults.
- Once the move has taken place, continuity of practice, where possible, is beneficial, with a gradual introduction to new and more formal activities (Smith, 2011).

SUMMARY

This unit has looked at, and should have helped you formulate a view on, a number of issues. First, on the controversial topic of when children should start school. Second, on the most effective ways for young children to learn, and why play is important in early learning. Finally, on the nature of the adult role in early learning and the important part you can play in this.

 ANNOTATED FURTHER READING

Moyles, J. Payler, J. and Georgeson, J. (2012) *Early Years Foundations: An Invitation to Critical Reflection*, Maidenhead: Open University Press.
> This book provides numerous useful chapters offering critical discussion of a range of contemporary issues in early years education.

Rogers, S. and Evans, J. (2008) *Inside Role-play in Early Childhood Education: Researching Children's Perspectives*, London: Routledge.
> An example of classroom research, this book investigates children's perspectives on play in reception classes. It includes introductory chapters on play theories and the nature of the reception class, methodology relating to researching with young children and many examples of children's perspectives of classroom experience.

Rose, J. and Rogers, S. (2012) 'Principles under pressure: Student teachers' perspectives on final teaching practice in early childhood classrooms', *International Journal of Early Years Education*, 20(1): 43-58.
> This article considers the impact of government policy in England and the resultant 'academic shovedown' and 'high stakes' performativity culture in schools. It provides some important evidence of student teachers' experiences on their final teaching practice and identifies various sociopolitical and sociocultural sources of pressures to deliver a more formalised curriculum in reception.

Rose, J. and Rogers, S. (2012) *The Role of the Adult in Early Years Settings*, Maidenhead: Open University Press.
> This book provides a helpful insight into the many different dimensions of the adult role in working with young children. It draws on a range of recent and classic theoretical perspectives and research that will help you to become an effective early years professional.

Siraj-Blatchford, I. and Manni, L. (2008) '"Would you like to tidy up now?" An analysis of adult questioning in the English Foundation Stage', *Early Years*, 28(1): 5-22.
> This article draws on research from the EPPE project. The study focuses attention on effective forms of questioning applied by early years practitioners and makes some significant points about the value of open-ended questions and the links to sustained shared thinking.

Wood, E. (ed.) (2008) *Routledge Reader of Early Childhood Education*, London: Routledge.
> For those who would like more challenging reading, this book brings together a range of chapters and published articles on key issues and perspectives in early childhood education.

FURTHER READING TO SUPPORT M-LEVEL STUDY

Rogers, S. (2011) *Rethinking Play and Pedagogy: Concepts, Contexts and Cultures*, London: Routledge.

Siraj-Blatchford, I. and Mayo, A. (2012) *Major Work International Reader, Early Childhood Education*. London: Sage.

 RELEVANT WEBSITES

www.education.gov.uk/schools/teachingandlearning/curriculum/a0068102/early-years-foundation-stage-eyfs
This is the government site for the new Early Years Foundation Stage.

eyfs.info/
This is a very useful support network and online community website for early years professionals.

 REFERENCES

Adams, S., Alexander, E., Drummond, M.J. and Moyles, J. (2004) *Inside the Foundation Stage: Recreating the Reception Year*, London: ATL.

Alexander, R.J. (2009) *Towards a New Primary Curriculum: A Report from the Cambridge Primary Review. Part 2: The Future*, Cambridge: University of Cambridge.

Alexander, R.J. (2010) *Children, Their World, Their Education*, London: Routledge.

Anning, A. (2006) 'Early years education: mixed messages and conflicts', in D. Kassem, E. Mufti and J. Robinson (eds) *Education Studies: Issues and Critical Perspectives*, Maidenhead: Open University Press/McGraw-Hill, pp. 5–11.

Assessment Reform Group (1999) *Assessment for Learning: Beyond the Black Box*, Cambridge: Cambridge University Press.

Aubrey, C. (2004) 'Implementing the foundation stage in reception classes', *British Educational Research Journal*, 30(5): 633–56.

Blakemore, S. and Frith, U. (2005) *The Learning Brain: Lessons for Education*, Oxford: Blackwell.

Blenkin, G. and Kelly, A.V. (eds) (1988) *Early Childhood Education: A Developmental Curriculum*, London: Paul Chapman.

Bowery, E. (2008) 'Is there a place for the discrete teaching of thinking skills and dispositions in a pre-school curriculum?' Unpublished dissertation, University of Gloucestershire.

British Educational Research Association (BERA) (2003) *Early Years Research: Pedagogy, Curriculum and Adult Roles, Training and Professionalism*, Macclesfield: BERA.

Brooker, E., Rogers, S., Robert-Holmes, G. and Hallett, E. (2010) *Practitioners Experiences of the Early Years Foundation Stage: A Research Report*, London: DCSF.

Bruner, J. (1986) *Actual Minds, Possible Worlds*, Cambridge, MA: Harvard University Press.

Corsaro, W.A. (2005) *The Sociology of Childhood*, 2nd edn, London: Pine Forge Press.

Council for Curriculum, Examinations and Assessment (CCEA) (2006) *Understanding the Foundation Stage*, Belfast: CCEA Publications.

David, T. (1990) *Under Five – Under-educated?* Milton Keynes: Open University Press.

Department for Children Schools and Families (2008) *Statutory Guidance for the Early Years Foundation Stage*, Nottingham: DCSF publications.

DfE (2012a) *Teachers' Standards*, London: DfE.

DfE (2012b) *Statutory Framework for the Early Years Foundation Stage: Setting the Standards for Learning, Development and Care for Children From Birth to Five*, London: DfE.

DfE (2013) *Early Years Foundation Stage Profile Handbook*, London: DfE.

Donaldson, M. (1978) *Children's Minds*, Glasgow: Fontana.

Fabian, H. (2006) 'Informing transitions', in A.-W. Dunlop and H. Fabian, *Informing Transitions in the Early Years*, Milton Keynes: Open University Press.

Gill, T. (2007) *No Fear: Growing Up in a Risk-Averse Society*, London: Calouste Gulbenkian Foundation.

Gopnik, A., Meltzoff, A. and Kuhl, P. (1999) *How Babies Think: The Science of Childhood*, London: Weidenfeld & Nicolson.

Goswami, U. and Bryant, P. (2007) *Children's Cognitive Development and Learning (Cambridge Primary Review: Research Survey 2/1(a))*, Cambridge: Cambridge University Press.

Katz, L.G. (1992) 'What should young children be learning?', in *ERIC Digest*, Urbana, IL: ERIC Clearinghouse on Elementary and Early Childhood Education, ED 290 554.

Lave, J. and Wenger, J. (1991) *Situated Learning: Legitimate Peripheral Participation*, Cambridge: Cambridge University Press.

Margetts, K. (2002) 'Planning transition programmes', in H. Fabian and A.W. Dunlop (eds) *Transition in the Early Years*, London: Routledge, pp. 111-22.

Montie, J.E., Ziang, S. and Schqeinhart, L.J. (2006) 'Preschool experience in 10 countries: cognitive and language performance at age 7', *Early Childhood Research Quarterly*, 21: 313-31.

National Association for the Education of Young Children (NAEYC) (2009) *Developmentally Appropriate Practice in Early Childhood Programs Serving Children from Birth through Age 8*, Position Statement, Washington, DC: NAEYC.

Penn, H. (2008) *Understanding Early Childhood*, Maidenhead: Open University Press.

Riggall, A. and Sharp, C. (2008) *The Structure of Primary Education: England and Other Countries (Cambridge Primary Review: Research Survey 9/1)*, Cambridge: Cambridge University Press.

Riley, J.L. (ed.) (2003) *Learning in the Early Years: 3-7*, London: Paul Chapman/Sage.

Rogers, S. (2010) 'Play and pedagogy: a conflict of interests?', in S. Rogers (ed.) *Rethinking Play and Pedagogy: Contexts, Concepts and Cultures*, London: Routledge.

Rogers, S. (2013) 'Playing and exploring in the early years', in H. Moylett (ed) *Characteristics of Effective Learning*, Maidenhead: Open University.

Rogers, S. and Evans, J. (2008) *Inside Role-play in Early Education: Researching Children's Perspectives*, London: Routledge.

Rose, J. and Rogers S. (2012a) *The Role of the Adult in Early Years Settings*, Maidenhead: Open University Press.

Rose, J. and Rogers, S. (2012b) 'Principles under pressure: student teachers' perspectives on final teaching practice in early childhood classroooms', *International Journal of Early Years Education*, 20 (1): 43-58.

Schaffer, H.R. (1996) 'Joint involvement episodes as context for development', in H. Daniels (ed.) *An Introduction to Vygotsky*, London: Routledge.

Sharp, C. (2002) *School Starting Age: European Policy and Recent Research*, Conference paper, Slough: NFER.

Siraj-Blatchford, I. (2004) 'Educational disadvantage in the early years: how do we overcome it? Some lessons from research', *European Early Childhood Education Research Journal*, 12(2): 5-20.

Siraj-Blatchford, I., Sylva, K., Muttock, S., Gilden, R. and Bell, D. (2002) *Researching Effective Pedagogy in the Early Years (REPEY)*, DfES Research Brief 356, London: DfES.

Smith, H. (2011) 'The emotional impact of transfer: what can be learned from early years practice', in A. Howe, and V. Richards (eds) *Bridging the Transition from Primary to Secondary School*, London: Routledge.

Sylva, K., Melhuish, E.C., Sammons, P., Siraj-Blatchford, I. and Taggart, B. (2004) *The Effective Provision of Pre-school Education (EPPE) Project: Technical Paper 12 - The Final Report: Effective Pre-school Education*, London: DfES/Institute of Education, University of London.

Waite, S., Evans, J. and Rogers, S. (2011) 'A time of change: outdoor learning and pedagogies of transition between Foundation Stage and Year 1', in S. Waite (ed.), *Children Learning Outside the Classroom: From Birth to Eleven*. London: Sage Publications.

Welsh Assembly Governmnt (WAG) (2008) *Framework for Children's Learning for 3- to 7-Year-Olds in Wales*, Cardiff: WAG.

Whetton, C., Ruddock, G. and Twist, L. (2007) *Standards in English Primary Education: The International Evidence (Cambridge Primary Review: Research Survey 4/2)*, Cambridge: Cambridge University Press.

Whitebread, D. and Coltman, P. (eds) (2008) *Teaching and Learning in the Early Years*, 3rd edn, London: Routledge.

Woyke, P.P. (2001) 'What does creativity look like in a developmentally appropriate preschool classroom?' *Earthworm*, 2(3): 15.

PLAY AND EXPLORATION IN LEARNING

Bernadette Duffy and Jo Trowsdale

INTRODUCTION

In this unit, we are looking at the role of explorative learning and play. Although these are stressed in the curriculum documentation for the early years, the Early Years Foundation Stage (EYFS) framework (Department for Education 2012), as children get older and move through their primary education, these key elements for successful learning often receive far less attention then they deserve. This unit argues that it is vital to continue to promote a playful, explorative attitude to learning that promotes the essential learning capacities, such as independence, creative thinking, problem-solving and resilience, that children need for well-being now and success in the future. The best teachers use the ways of thinking encouraged by play and explorative learning to ensure that children are engaged and motivated to learn throughout the primary years and beyond.

This unit covers:

- what we mean by play and explorative learning;
- the importance of play and exploration in children's learning;
- play and exploration in the EYFS and National Curriculum;
- the role of the teacher in promoting children's play and exploration;
- using playfulness to enhance your teaching.

OBJECTIVES

By the end of this unit, you will be confident about:

- the importance and value of play and exploration in promoting learning;
- how to promote play and exploration throughout the primary years;
- how to use playfulness in your own teaching.

WHAT DO WE MEAN BY PLAY AND EXPLORATIVE LEARNING?

In Unit 7.3, Teresa Cremin and Jonathan Barnes make the case for creativity in primary education. Cecil *et al.* (1985) describe exploration and play as part of the creative process, and it is vital that teachers understand these elements, if they are to promote effective learning and well-being.

Explorative learning is about children learning through investigation, speculation, experiment and discovery, stimulated by their curiosity and wondering. It involves children exploring objects, events and ideas, often using all their senses to gather information, and sometimes observing others as part of the investigation. Through such explorations, children construct their own knowledge, find out about what an idea or object is and what it can do, and, because they have been in control of the process, their learning is deeper than if they have simply been presented with the knowledge as a passive recipient (Bruner 1986).

The phrase *'children learn through play'* is much repeated in early years circles, and, as it is used to cover a wide range of experiences, we need to be clear about what we mean by *play*. Although there are a number of theories of play relating to different views about degrees of structure (Bennett *et al.* 1997: 2), most agree that play is freely chosen by the child, controlled by them (Isaacs 1971) and characterised by spontaneity, often without clear final objectives. As there is little or no focus on a predetermined product, children are free to examine all kinds of detail during this period, which they might have missed if they had been concentrating on the end product (Cecil *et al.* 1985). It is also an opportunity to engage the imagination and for ideas from the unconscious to bubble up. As they play, children become aware of patterns and start to see possible connections (Duffy 2006). Playfulness describes an attitude and readiness to explore and discover: to be open to the opportunities of an experience. It is a natural agency for learning that develops from young children's experience of play and can be utilised in a variety of learning contexts.

As children get older, play is often contrasted with work – we divide lesson time from playtime, seeing play as something that happens after serious activity has ceased. Carefully planned, adult-led experiences that enable children to learn specific skills and knowledge are important, but it is often through their play that children test, practise and consolidate the skills, knowledge and understandings they have acquired. Indeed, many would argue that, as knowledge is increasingly easy to access, our society increasingly values conceptual, original and creative thinking and behaviours more and so we must resist over-direction and instead craft our abilities as teachers to facilitate and harness play-based learning (Singer *et al.* 2006: 6).

These notions of play are not confined to children. Cultural anthropologists and theorists argue that the very same characteristics of play are significant to adults, in free and structured forms. Huizinga, for example, suggests that, 'civilization is, in its earliest phases, played. It does not come *from* play like a baby detaching itself from the womb: it arises *in* and *as* play, and never leaves it' (Huizinga 1971: 171). In recent years, the study of neuroscience has enabled us to understand how culture influences affect brain development. Research suggests that, if taught early enough, children can develop unexpected abilities, such being able to see and breathe underwater (Music 2011: 81), or speak another language, for example, if spoken at home. Likewise, the culture of the classroom and the messages about the role of play will affect the brain development of children and their capacities to imagine, empathise, collaborate and problem solve for example.

Task 2.6.1 Play in the learning process

- Through reflecting upon this unit and following through with reading, how would you define the role of play in the learning process?
- What are the key characteristics that make an activity play?
- What are the misconceptions and anxieties that teachers may have about using a playful approach?

As part of the creative process, exploration and play are about an attitude to life. They involve the ability to cope with uncertainty, explore new ideas, look at problems in a variety of ways, the lack of constraint, the existence of choice, creating and recreating. Many creative processes in the arts and business are founded upon the view that exploratory, playful behaviour is key to learning, discovering and making, so that, although an end product is always the goal, its nature is not nor cannot be predetermined, but is in fact defined and refined iteratively and in response to source materials, ideas and context, through explorative and experimental activity.

THE IMPORTANCE OF PLAY AND EXPLORATION IN CHILDREN'S LEARNING

Since Plowden (1967), the role of play in learning has been an influence in curriculum reform. In recent years, perhaps especially since international testing has developed (Mourshed et al. 2010), comparative studies seek to identify the factors and dynamic between factors that best affect learning. Setting curriculum aims, content and standards expected can affect the quality of pedagogy and learning. Yet equally research points towards the importance of a curriculum linking across domains and local, individualised processes being essential to ensuring the progress of individual learners (Department for Education 2011b). Play can be a strong integrator here.

We are born curious: play and exploration are the way in which we express this and are vital to children's learning and development. Babies' brains are designed to enable them to make sense of the world around them. They think, draw conclusions, make predictions, experiment and look for explanations (Gopnik et al. 2001). The skills developed through explorative learning provide the foundations for a playful approach to learning that promotes curiosity, initiative and resilience across the curriculum, throughout the primary years and beyond. Indeed, neuroscientists (Davidson 2000) and evolutionary psychologists increasingly note the value of play in developing cognition and higher human intelligence.

Often, as children get older, play and exploration are sidelined in favour of highly structured activities, with clear goals, inside and outside school. Curriculum demands can make it appear that the best solution is to try to pre-package children's learning to ensure that the whole curriculum is covered. However, exploration at the outset can open up a learning area, so that children can articulate, share and test their current ideas and, by playing with possibilities for next steps, suggest the most relevant and fertile way forward. Such approaches can feed the appetite to engage with more structured learning, enabling a teacher to recognise children's current knowledge and interests, and thus can teach a teacher how to progress and adapt the planning for maximum learning (Dewey 1916; Dale 1954).

Task 2.6.2 Playing and exploring

- What are your memories of playing and exploring at 4 years old, 7 years old, 10 years old, and how do you play as an adult? How and what did /do you do?
- When did you change your play behaviours? What prompted such changes?
- Do colleagues/friends of different ages have similar recollections? Do these reflect changes in society and our attitudes to play inside and outside school?

Promoting imagination and thought

Vygotsky (1978) identified the crucial role of imaginative play in the development of the human mind. He saw the emergence of the imagination in the second year of life as connected with the frustrations children experienced when their desires were not immediately gratified. Whereas babies needs are straightforward and either quickly gratified or forgotten, as children grow, their wishes and aspirations become more complex, less realisable and less capable of instant fulfilment. For example, they want to pour the tea out as adults do and become frustrated when, for safety reasons, they are not allowed to. Imaginative play develops when children experience this frustrating gap between their needs and the gratification of these needs. Such needs cannot be met in the real world, but can be satisfied in the imaginative world: they can pretend to pour the tea. Through imaginative play, children resolve the tensions of everyday life.

Objects may support the imaginative process as 'transitional objects'; these no longer have the meaning they have in the real world, but are used to represent a missing object. For example, children may use stones to represent money while playing shops. The stones act as a prop or pivot to help them engage in the imaginative process (Vygotsky 1978). Initially, transitional objects need to share many characteristics with the object being imagined, but, with practice, the need for physical similarity decreases. Eventually, children no longer require an actual object to support their imaginative play, but can pretend the object is there. As adults, we likewise suspend disbelief and enter the rules of imaginative play when watching theatre, accepting whatever mimed or symbolic use of a prop is suggested by the actors. When older children lose instinctive acceptance of imagined objects in play, the teacher can reaffirm the symbolic and representative role of objects through the practice of imaginative exploration in drama: a cardboard circle, presented convincingly, can symbolise a precious crown. Once children can separate objects and actions from their meaning in the real world, and give them new meanings, they are no longer tied to the concrete world and start to think in an abstract way: beyond the moment and into possibilities.

Promoting well-being and relationships with others

Isaacs (1971) saw play as being essential for development and promoting mental well-being. Through playing and exploring with others, children develop the ability to see things from different perspectives. It is the ability to imagine that enables the child to empathise: to put themselves into the position of another person and understand that other people may have different perspectives, beliefs, intents, desire and knowledge from their own, often referred to as theory of mind (Goswami and Bryant 2007). Through this ability, children develop their understanding of social and cultural expectation and important skills such as self-regulation, negotiation and persuasion (Evangelou et al. 2009). Many schools, explicitly and/or in an embedded way, train children to develop skills for learning such as resourcefulness, self-management, collaboration and resilience (Claxton 2005; Goodbourn et al. 2005, 2007) and celebrate the mix of structure and play-like exploration required to hone such skills.

Promoting physical development

Movement is natural to children, and the importance of physical play should not be underestimated. Babies' first focus for exploration is their own bodies: how arms and legs move, and how to control that movement to achieve their own goals. For the youngest children, physical play will often be spontaneous, *rough-and-tumble* activity, but, as they develop, physical play becomes more complex, involving rules and strategies. Through their physical play, children develop fine and gross motor skills and body confidence.

Recent research argues that, 'we think not just with our minds but with our brains and the rest of our bodies', and that opportunities to develop manual dexterity feed mental agility (Claxton *et al.* 2010: 13). Indeed, limiting movement has been shown to limit thinking, even when movement is routine, abstract or apparently unconnected to the task in hand (Goldin-Meadow and Wagner 2005; Clark 2008). In fact, taking a physical or imaginative excursion from a task can feed thinking (Claxton 2007), suggesting that the discipline of table-bound learning may be counter-productive to thinking and learning.

Promoting language and literacy

Play and exploration with others offer meaningful contexts for children to develop their language and literacy. Negotiating roles, play scenarios and strategies for exploration, explaining ideas and listening to those of others all require good communication skills, and wanting to engage others is an excellent motivation to acquire and develop them.

Children develop their ability to create stories through their imaginative play. Although they start by imitating people around them, as they grow, their ability to imagine influences the scenarios they create, and children do not simply copy what they have seen, but add their own ideas. As children become more skilled, the role of fantasy increases, and they develop scenarios that are no longer restricted to their first-hand experience of the world, but include characters and events from stories and television. Sometimes, children's fantasy play is discouraged and seen as an avoidance of the real world or as reinforcing stereotypical images. However, Paley (1988) presents a persuasive argument for supporting this type of play and using it to stimulate children's storytelling and interest in literacy. Holland (2003) explores this further and documents the work of practitioners who are actively addressing children's interests and finding ways to support them appropriately. Play also provides an important environment for experiential thinking and learning, for testing how effective (or ineffective) language might be for communicating, for recognising the significance of non-verbal communication in knowing and thus understanding the complexity of experience (Damasio 2000; Music 2011: 100).

Through their imaginative play, children develop and extend stories to create their own narratives, using ideas as well as props, as stimulation or provocation. Being able to imagine also initiates the ability to empathise, and thus play feeds, not just creative writing, but also thinking, feeling and interpreting others' behaviour in their daily life and other literary and historical contexts. Through drama-based play at all ages, children can imaginatively engage in role in a range of areas of human experience and also practice adapting language to role and thus extending their language repertoire. Teachers can use drama strategies within any curriculum area, so that subject-specific language and understanding are demanded of children through role. Hot seating, for example, enables children to imagine, rehearse and understand another character, how they might think, speak and feel. With teacher and peer preparation and support, children can recognise and practise new registers, expanding their understanding of language through imagined experience. Children talk themselves into believing in the imagined context, deepening engagement and hearing their own voice reflected back to themselves. A wealth of other possible structures, such as forum theatre or voices in the head, can be used by teachers of children across all key stages to support semi-structured play/play-based learning, where children step, in a structured and protected way, into the shoes of another and try out thinking, feeling and speaking like them (Winston and Tandy 2001; Baldwin 2008; Woolland 2009).

Promoting cross-curricular investigation skills

Through their explorations, children find out about the world around them and, as their skills and understanding develop during the primary years, they are able to deepen their knowledge and find out more. A playful approach motivates this exploration and ensures children are actively engaged. Play provides the opportunity to take risks and find out through trial and error (Isaacs 1971).

As they explore, we can help children to:

* become aware of a problem, new idea or piece of information;
* start to tackle the problem by brainstorming ideas using their existing knowledge to identify connections, similarities and differences;
* ponder and allow ideas to incubate; this may take place over a number of days or minutes;
* have an insight into the problem, a moment of illumination that helps them to understand the problem or the new piece of information;

Example 2.6.1

Key Stage 2 children at a Warwickshire primary school were invited to take on the roles of curators and curate their learning for each other and their community. They were offered, but not limited to using, the display spaces around the school's quad. Children wanted to understand what a curator does and how they could develop such skills and so worked with a professional artist and curator. The challenge initiated a practice of having learning assemblies and wonder walls, where children could pose questions and share the kinds of learning skill they were learning. The very idea of learning rising up from children's interest encouraged curiosity and pondering.

One class was interested in a topical news issue about the Elgin marbles. Pupils explored and presented what knowledge they had already to instigate early research, and through, careful questioning and facilitation by the teacher identified lines of enquiry that children were interested to pursue. Children agreed the storyline, situations, characters and issues they wished to explore through dramatic role-play, working with the teacher in role. They played out several alternatives before becoming clear about the complex issues that informed the question of ownership. They used a mix of scientific and creative process models. Their research informed their in-role imagined exploration and enabled them to explore alterative scenarios. In role, especially, they imagined, 'lived' and reflected in action on the key issues and, out of role, they used such thinking to reflect and decide how to continue their study. Playful exploration enabled them to test ideas presented in the news and in historical texts to inform the interpretation they arrived at. It also enabled them to develop an experience-based understanding of how easily different ideas can be represented and thus how easily we can be influenced.

Their roles reflect those more typical in older play-based learning (Briggs and Hansen 2012). Drawing upon a combination of these motivating, cognitive, embodied and social ways of learning, they practised the skills to develop an experiential understanding of the issues and thus were learning the importance of researching, collaborating and drawing upon a combination of ways of knowing, before establishing their position. They were able to develop an informed opinion that they could justify through the use of playful exploration.

- identify a new understanding or meaningful connection and become aware of a possible solution;
- test the solution or understanding of the idea for themselves or with others, which may lead them to modify their solution or understanding.

PLAY AND EXPLORATION IN THE EYFS AND NATIONAL CURRICULUM

In the EYFS, play is seen as 'essential for children's development, building their confidence as they learn to explore, to think about problems, and relate to others' (Department for Education 2012: 6). The importance of exploration is stressed in the characteristics of effective teaching and learning. Playing and exploring form the first characteristic (Department for Education 2012: 7), and opportunities to play and explore are seen as key to children's engagement. Children need to:

- **find out and explore**: show curiosity about objects, events, people, use senses to explore, engage in open-ended activity, show particular interests;
- **play with what they know**: pretend objects are things, represent experiences in play, take on a role in play, act out experiences with others;
- **be willing to 'have a go'**: initiate activities, seek challenges, show a 'can do' attitude, take a risk, engage in new experiences, learn by trial and error.

These characteristics are important throughout the primary years and should be as evident in Year 6 as they are in reception. The Cambridge Primary Review recommended that the foundation years should be extended into primary schools until at least age 6 (Alexander 2010: 172). The revised National Curriculum does not reflect this view (Department for Education 2011a). It does seek to give schools more freedom over the curriculum, by only specifying the essential knowledge that all children should acquire, freeing schools to design a wider school curriculum that best meets the needs of their pupils and decide how to teach this most effectively. However, there is still a requirement to teach all the foundation subjects alongside the core subjects. The draft documents for English, mathematics and science do include opportunities for play and exploration. For example, mathematics is described as a creative and highly interconnected discipline, and, in science, the importance of developing a sense of excitement and curiosity about natural phenomena is stressed.

It is hoped that schools will be creative in using the revised National Curriculum to design a curriculum that includes play and exploration in each area of the curriculum and uses imaginative and authentic approaches to make connections between areas of the curriculum. A number of schools operate an 'enhanced' or 'creative' curriculum, where children's fortes and interests inform choices within the curriculum. Indeed, many such designed and locally developed curriculum models adopt the play-based roles of older learners proposed by Briggs and Hansen (2012), namely of autonomous and creative learners, investigators, problem-solvers and reflective and social learners. Such models also consider how to plan for and assess play-based learning across both key stages, using structures and examples (Briggs and Hansen 2012: 77-104). A curriculum that maximises the potential of play-based learning thus organises play through 'scaffolding' (Bruner 2006), where tasks are not totally structured, nor is play totally free, but is rather organised in a way that allows a flexible facilitation of play to be directed to intended learning areas. One example of this, which has grown quite a following in the UK, is the 'mantle of the expert' – an approach developed by Dorothy Heathcote (Heathcote and Bolton 1995; Heathcote 2002) in which children are positioned within imagined, authentic contexts 'as if' they are the experts. The focus of the needs presented by a (planned) problem, in addition to the structure's expectation of expertise, can generate collaborative, motivating and purposeful contexts for learning. Any and multiple subject disciplines may come under scrutiny through such an approach. Complex learning happens as children engage in an imagined world and demonstrate an 'ability to plan, concentrate and self regulate as well as engage in complex interpersonal interaction' (Music 2011: 128). The use of drama as a strategy and medium for learning across the curriculum, and how to plan for and assess it, is documented in a number of teaching primary drama sources (Winston and Tandy 2001; Baldwin 2008; Woolland 2009).

THE ROLE OF THE TEACHER IN PROMOTING CHILDREN'S PLAY AND EXPLORATION

Teachers must 'promote a love of learning and children's intellectual curiosity and contribute to the design and provision of an engaging curriculum' (Teaching Agency 2012). Successfully fulfilling this standard requires teachers to draw on approaches that recognise, feed and celebrate children's instinctive playfulness. To be engaged and motivated, children need to be curious and want to learn. Our role is to ensure that there are plenty of opportunities to actively explore, in contexts that are meaningful to the children and that stimulate intrinsic motivation. The teacher needs to be ready to set provocations and resist intervention, to absorb a child's fascination, to witness and watch their focus and challenge so that exploration is genuine. Their interest can thus signal real value for the child's work, and their questioning can enable the child to work to communicate their ideas for themselves and thus deepen their own commitment to learning.

Dweck (2012) emphasises the importance of children developing a mastery orientation, whereby they see their intelligence as growable, rather than a learnt helplessness, and teachers have a key role in this. To explore freely, children need to feel able to take risks, to try things out and experiment, but to do this they need to feel secure and trusted by their teacher. This is especially important when an idea or new connection doesn't work as predicted. It is at the point when children discover that something they thought would work does not, or that a guess was not correct, that they find out something they had not realised before, and learning deepens.

As teachers, we need to see the world through the children's eyes, offer secure relationships that allow curiosity to flourish, and:

- enable children to find their own voice and style, not simply imitate others;
- provide experiences that emphasise exploration and active participation;
- set provocations to feed exploratory learning;
- value children's self-initiated activity by being available and interested;
- help children acquire new skills and identify possibilities;
- recognise that the process may sometimes be more important than the end result;
- resist intervention as a reflex and watch more, know when to be silent, when to encourage, when to inspire and when to help;
- work alongside children as a more experienced learner, modelling learning together;
- establish with the children clear guiding principles, such as rules for use of materials and behaviour;
- extend learning by encouraging critical reflection;
- pause before speaking, giving children the opportunity to communicate their views first;
- offer constructive feedback and encouragement during an activity;
- craft appropriate questions to encourage the child to work to communicate their ideas for themselves and thus deepen their own commitment to learning;
- give children time to respond to our questions and comments.

The traditional classroom power balance between adult and child is disrupted in play-based learning, and this is at the root of many of the features identified above. Frameworks and guidance for teachers wishing to move from structured to more child-led learning suggest ways to situate a planned learning topic within a simulated/imagined real-world setting, to enable playful yet thoughtful experiential learning – for example, learning French in a French café, estimating and measuring dinosaur prints/outlines positioned in the school grounds, designing toys to sell in a toyshop. Such changes may require some support and encouragement, but provide rewarding and more skilful teaching (Briggs and Hansen 2012: 63–90; see 72–4 for a case study example).

Task 2.6.3 Environments for exploration

Think about learning environments and contexts you have experienced as a child and student – how have these promoted or discouraged play and exploration?

Reflecting on these experiences, this unit and your further reading, how would you create an environment that encourages exploration and play for 4-year-olds, 7-year-olds and 10-year-olds. Think about the physical environment, routines that give time to play, and your interactions with the children.

USING PLAYFULNESS TO ENHANCE YOUR TEACHING

Artists often talk about playing with materials to discover new, creative combinations, and scientists emphasise the importance of open-ended exploration, without a focus on a predetermined final outcome. Playfulness remains part of the creative process throughout life. Following Picasso's famous quote, 'Every child is an artist. The problem is how to remain an artist once we grow up', the challenge to the teacher is to retain the imaginative ways of seeing that will enable children to consider different and individual ways of approaching problems and find different solutions.

As teachers, we must be confident about drawing on our own playfulness in our work with children. A playful approach involves flexibility, spontaneity, problem-solving skills, creativity and a readiness to try out and risk 'failure'. An attitude of playfulness enables imaginative possibilities to remain and imaginative leaps to take place (Prentice 1994) and ensures that we are not limited to second-hand information or pre-prepared solutions.

Example 2.6.2

Staff arrived at the entrance to the hall at the beginning of an INSET day, were given a piece of paper cut out like a suitcase and were asked to list on it all the things that got in the way of them being the best creative teacher they could be. They left their baggage outside the hall and then entered to seats laid out as if on a plane. As 'in-flight entertainment', the creative leads offered inspiration about the elements of creative learning staff might focus on. Staff were then invited to take their own 'flights', searching the locality for immediate resources or for ideas about possible partnerships they might pursue to develop learning opportunities. They were encouraged to make new and unexpected connections and to consider how children might be enabled to access these directly. The units of work that were developed from this approach created some of the most engaging learning and engaging teaching the teachers had done to date. Teachers were enabled to imagine, connect and find their own playful impulses, which articulated and modeled playful exploration to children.

Task 2.6.4 Contexts and curiosity

- What contexts (possibly real-world simulations) might inspire your learners to be curious about and persist in learning about a topic you are currently planning?
- What learning opportunities might the context offer? Map as many as you can to the primary curriculum requirements).

SUMMARY

In this unit we have looked at the importance of play and exploration in children's learning. We have identified the key role of the teacher in providing an emotional and physical environment that promotes these key characteristics of effective learning.

The world is changing rapidly, and we do not know the challenges the children we are teaching now will face in their adult lives, but we do know that if they have adopted a playful approach and are confident explorers, open to possibilities, they are more likely to be able to meet them.

ANNOTATED FURTHER READING

Briggs, M. and Hansen, A. (2012) *Play-Based Learning in the Primary School*, London: Sage.
    A theoretically argued, practice-based account of why play-based learning matters, illustrated by examples and ideas for direct use by teachers. The book proposes types of play for older children and offers frameworks for planning and assessing.

Fisher, K., Hirsh-Pasek, K., Golinkoff, R., Singer, D. and Berk, L. (2011) 'Playing around in school: implications for learning and educational policy', in A.D. Pellegrini (ed.) *The Oxford Handbook of the Development of Play*, New York: Oxford University Press.
    These authors argue that playful-learning pedagogies not only promote important academic learning but also build the skills required for success in the twenty-first century. They review current educational trends, playful learning, free play and guided play and how they promote learning and development.

FURTHER READING TO SUPPORT M-LEVEL STUDY

Kuschner, D. (2012) 'Play is natural to childhood but school is not: The problem of integrating play into the curriculum', *International Journal of Play*, 1(3): 242–9.
    An article that explores the innate tensions involved when integrating play into the school curriculum. It proposes that the term play should not be used when developing a play-based curriculum, but that self-directed, play-based pedagogies should indeed be planned for.

RELEVANT WEBSITES

Creative Little Scientist project: www.creative-little-scientists.eu

> Creative Little Scientists aims to bring together creativity and science and mathematics in pre-school and the first years of primary education. The project will propose guidelines, curricula and exemplary materials for teacher training.

Whole Education: www.wholeeducation.org

> Whole Education is a partnership of schools, organisations and individuals that believe that all young people should have a fully rounded education. The partner projects within the site offer a range of models.

The Walker Learning approach: walkerlearning.com.au/info/

> This is an Australian teaching and learning site promoting play for all years of primary education. It is based on research and offers an approach that 'personalises and engages students in active learning alongside explicit and formalised instruction'. Cultural dimensions are designed for the Australian context, but principles can be reapplied.

Mantle of the Expert: www.mantleoftehexpert.com/

> The home of the UK-based, but international, site for schools and teachers developing Mantle of the Expert. It offers training courses, planning models, examples, guidance and video/downloadable resources.

REFERENCES

Alexander, R. (ed.) (2010) *Children, Their World, Their Education. Final Report and Recommendations of the Cambridge Primary Review*, London: Routledge.

Baldwin, P. (2008) *The Primary Drama Handbook: An Introduction*, London: Sage.

Bennett, N., Woods, L. and Rogers, S. (1997) *Teaching through Play: Teacher's Thinking and Classroom Practice*, Buckingham: Open University Press.

Briggs, M. and Hansen, A. (2012) *Play-Based Learning in the Primary School*, London: Sage.

Bruner, J. (1986) *Actual Minds, Possible Worlds*, Cambridge, MA: Harvard University Press.

Bruner, J. (2006) 'Play as a mode of construing the real', in *In Search of Pedagogy: The Selected Works of Jerome S. Bruner*, London: Routledge.

Cecil, L.M., Gray, M.M., Thornburg, K.R. and Ispa, J. (1985) 'Curiosity-exploration-play: The early childhood mosaic', *Early Child Development and Care*, 19: 199–217.

Clark, A. (2008) *Supersizing the Mind*, Oxford: Oxford University Press.

Claxton, G. (2005) *Building Learning Power in Action BLP*, Bristol: TLO.

Claxton, G. (2007) *Hare Brain; Tortoise Mind: Why Intelligence Increases When You Think Less*, London: Fourth Estate.

Claxton, G., Lucas, B. and Webster, R. (2010) *Bodies of Knowledge: How the Learning Sciences Could Transform Practical and Vocational Education*, Seattle, WA: Edge Foundation.

Dale, E. (1954) *Audio-Visual Methods in Teaching* (revised edn), New York: The Dryden Press.

Damasio, A. (2000) *The Feeling of What Happens*, London: Vintage.

Davidson, R.J. (2000) 'Cognitive neuroscience needs affective neuroscience (and vice versa)', *Brain & Cognition*, 42: 89–92.

Department for Education (DfE) (2011a) *Review of the National Curriculum in England: What Can We Learn From the English, Mathematics and Science Curricula of High-Performing Jurisdictions?* London: DfE.

Department for Education (DfE) (2011b) *The Framework for the National Curriculum – A Report by the Expert Panel for the National Curriculum Review*, London: DfE.

Department for Education (DfE) (2012) *Statutory Framework for the Early Years Foundation Stage*, London: DfE.

Dewey, J. (1916) *Democracy and Education: An Introduction to the Philosophy of Education* (1966 edn), New York: Free Press.

Duffy, B. (2006) *Supporting Creativity and Imagination in the Early Years*, Maidenhead: Open University Press.

Dweck, C. (2012) *Mindset: How You Can Fulfil Your Potential*, London: Robinson.

Evangelou, M., Sylva, K., Kyriacou, M., Wild, M. and Glenny, G. (2009) *Early Years Learning and Development Literature Review*, London: DCSF.

Goldin-Meadow, S. and Wagner, S. (2005) 'How our hands help us learn', *Trends in Cognitive Science*, 9(5): 234–41.

Goodbourn, R., Higgins, S., Parsons, S., Wall, K. and Wright, J. (2005) *Learning to Learn for Life: Research and Practical Resources for Foundation and Key Stage 1*, Crediton: Southgate.

Goodbourn, R., Higgins, S., Parsons, S., Wall, K. and Wright, J. (2007) *Learning to Learn for Life 2: Research and Practical Resources for Foundation and Key Stage 2*, Crediton: Southgate.

Gopnik, A., Metfzoff, A. and Kuhl, P. (2001) *How Babies Think*, London: Phoenix.

Goswami, U. and Bryant, P. (2007) *Children's Cognitive Development and Learning (Cambridge Primary Review: Research Survey 2/1(a))*, Cambridge: Cambridge University Press.

Heathcote, D. (2002) 'Contexts for active learning – Four models to forge links between schooling and society', *Journal for Drama and Education*, 19(1) (also presented at the NATD conference).

Heathcote, D. and Bolton, G. (1995) *Drama for Learning: Dorothy Heathcote's Mantle of the Expert Approach to Education*, Oxford: Heinemann.

Holland, P. (2003) *We Don't Play With Guns Here: War, Weapons and Superhero Play in the Early Years*, Milton Keynes: Open University Press.

Huizinga, J. (1971) *Homo Ludens*, Boston, MA: Beacon Press.

Isaacs, S. (1971) *The Nursery Years: The Mind of the Child From Birth to Sixth Years*, London: Routledge.

Mourshed, M., Chijioke, C. and Barber, M. (2010) *How the World's Most Improved School Systems Keep Getting Better*, New York: McKinsey & Company.

Music, G. (2011) *Nurturing Natures: Attachment and Children's Emotional, Sociocultural and Brain Development*, Hove: Psychology Press.

Paley, V.G. (1988) *Bad Guys Don't Have Birthdays*, Chicago, IL: University of Chicago Press.

Plowden (1967) *Children and Their Primary Schools – A Report of the Central Advisory Council for Education (England)*, London: Her Majesty's Stationery Office.

Prentice, R. (1994) 'Experiential learning in play and art', in J. Moyles *The Excellence of Play*, Buckingham: Open University Press.

Singer, D., Michnick Golinkoff, R. and Hirsh-Pasek, K. (eds) (2006) *Play = Learning: How Play Motivates and Enhances Children's Cognitive, Social and Emotional Growth*, Oxford, NewYork: Oxford University Press.

Teaching Agency (2012) *The Education (School Teachers' Appraisal) (England) Regulations 2012*, London: DfE.

Vygotsky, L. (1978) *Mind in Society*, Cambridge, MA: Harvard University Press.

Winston, J. and Tandy, M. (2001) *Beginning Drama 4–11* (2nd edn), London: David Fulton.

Woolland, B. (2009) *Teaching Primary Drama*, Harlow: Longman.

PLANNING AND MANAGING LEARNING

APPROACHING LONG- AND MEDIUM-TERM PLANNING

Jane Medwell

INTRODUCTION

The focus of this unit is longer-term planning: the termly and yearly plans you will use to prepare your teaching across the curriculum. This sort of planning includes long-term planning expressed as school policies and medium-term planning expressed as termly or half-termly planning sheets. Planning at this level is the basis of all your teaching, but it is not something you will easily encounter during your initial training. You should take every opportunity to look at, discuss and question the medium- and long-term plans you encounter.

OBJECTIVES

By the end of this chapter, you should:

- understand the difference between long- and medium-term planning;
- understand the purposes of long- and medium-term planning;
- know the key features of long- and medium-term plans;
- understand the range of issues considered when making long- and medium-term plans;
- be confident in interpreting medium-term plans.

THE IMPORTANCE OF LONG-TERM PLANNING

Long-term planning can often seem like a 'given' in school. When you begin your school-led training or go to a school placement, the planning is already there in the form of National Curriculum documents and school policies. These may even already have been translated into medium-term plans. However, it is important that you understand how long- and medium-term plans are developed, and it is important that you can question the assumptions upon which such plans are based.

Long-term plans for a key stage are usually determined through whole-staff discussion, a process in which you may not be able to be involved. If you do not contribute to long-term planning, then you will always teach what, and how, someone else has chosen, instead of participating in those decisions yourself. One of the most important parts of your initial teacher training or NQT year will be the opportunity to participate in policy reviews.

WHAT ARE YOU PLANNING?

Long-term planning is the process whereby the school team decides how the curriculum is taught across the whole school or key stage. It shows:

*   exactly what the school curriculum is;
*   how the curriculum is covered in terms of breadth and depth;
*   how the curriculum is structured within year groups and across key stages;
*   how much time is allocated to each area of the curriculum in each year group.

Every state-funded school, including academies and free schools, must provide a curriculum that:

*   promotes the spiritual, moral, cultural, mental and physical development of pupils at the school and of society;
*   prepares pupils at the school for the opportunities, responsibilities and experiences of later life.

The curriculum in state-maintained schools in England in the EYFS, Key Stage (KS) 1 or KS2 (and most others) includes the statutory content of the National Curriculum for the relevant key stages. However, schools are not limited by the requirements of the National Curriculum and will want to ensure that the curriculum of the school reflects the mission, purpose and ethos of that school. For academy and free schools, the National Curriculum is not statutory, but many of them have agreed contracts that ensure they cover the National Curriculum, and many independent schools also choose to incorporate the demands of the National Curriculum in their planning. By doing this, schools ensure that children who change schools experience continuity and progression in their learning. The National Curriculum includes the programmes of study for all subjects: English, maths and science, art and design, citizenship, computing, design technology, geography, history, music, PE and, at KS2, foreign languages. In addition, they are required to do personal, social and heath education (PSHE).

The statutory curriculum in the EYFS includes three prime areas and four specific areas of learning and development, which are assessed against the seventeen Early Learning Goals at the end of the reception year, leading to the National Curriculum for schools. Planning for these is still a long-term business, as early years professionals aim to balance the areas of learning and offer both teacher-directed and child-initiated activity.

The documents of the National Curriculum and EYFS are available on the Department of Education and Science (DES) website and give a broad outline of the core content of the curriculum, but not how schools might want to add to this core or how it is to be taught. This is the role of long-term planning in school. Whether or not they are required to follow the National Curriculum, from September 2012, all schools are required to publish information setting out, for each year group, the content of the school's curriculum for each subject. This will usually be on the school website and is a good starting point for you.

Within the subjects of the National Curriculum, the programmes of study set out what children should be taught to know and do. English, maths and science also have notes and guidance, which are not statutory but offer advice to schools and teachers. In the National Curriculum for 2014, the programmes of study for English, maths and science are set out, year by year, for KS1 and two-yearly for KS2. The programmes of study for foundation subjects are set out by key stage. However, this is just a guide, and schools are only required to teach the relevant programme of study by the end of the key stage. So, within each key stage, schools have the flexibility to introduce content earlier or later than set out in the programme of study, or to introduce it in an earlier key stage. This is where the planning decisions made by each school are important.

In the National Curriculum, the attainment targets set out the expected standards of pupils' performance, and, in the most recent curriculum, these specify that at the end of each key stage, pupils are expected to know, apply and understand the matters, skills and processes specified in the relevant programme of study. In practice, as the new curriculum is integrated into schools, the attainment targets will become the statement of what pupils must know and be able to do by the end of each year (or 2-year, for KS2) block of the National Curriculum.

Some key issues taken into consideration when planning for the long term are:

- **breadth** – so that pupils experience the full range of curriculum areas and the key skills discussed above, as well as any additional skills and learning identified as important in the school curriculum;
- **depth** – so there are opportunities for in-depth learning and the chance for children to really develop their own understandings;
- **coherence** – so that natural and meaningful links within and between some subjects are recognised and developed, to help children learn as purposefully as possible;

Task 3.1.1 Beginning to plan a topic

This task aims to get you to consider a popular topic, such as healthy living, where it appears in the National Curriculum, and how this might be taught to children at KS1 and KS2.

Go to the National Curriculum online at www.gov.uk/government/uploads/system/uploads/attachment_data/file/210969/NC_framework_document_-_FINAL.pdf, and look at the science programmes of study.

Science Y2 programme of study (animals, including humans)

Pupils should be taught to:

- describe the importance for humans of exercise, eating the right amounts of different types of food, and hygiene.

This is only a small part of the science curriculum, but it is a huge part of a child's education and will play a very important part in their development, well-being and future self-regulation.

1   Divide up this area of the curriculum into areas for study.
2   Look at other areas of the curriculum. Where might you make natural links with subjects such as PE, maths, English and geography?
3   For each of these areas, think about the spoken language you might develop through study of healthy living.
4   What skills of reasoning, data handling, argument, writing, reading and evaluation might children use when studying this topic?

These links are not evident in the National Curriculum, but it might be that these are the issues you want to plan your curriculum around, rather than just the knowledge.

- **relevance** – so that pupils' activities relate to previous learning, and so that they can understand how the learning is relevant to them;
- **differentiation** – so the needs and progress of pupils are catered for;
- **progression** – so learning develops through sequenced activities, as children go through each term and school year, without undue repetition.

HOW WILL YOU PLAN TO TEACH THE CONTENT?

The content of the statutory curriculum and the needs of the children are two defining factors in what you teach. In long-term planning, you also have to consider:

- how much time is allocated to each area of the curriculum in each year group;
- how the curriculum is structured within year groups and across key stages.

How much time to allocate to learning in each subject, theme or key skill is an important area for negotiation. The working week in school includes activities such as collective worship and assemblies, as well as lessons. It will not be possible to include every learning experience that teachers would like. For instance, a KS2 English co-ordinator might suggest the following allocation of time for English for all KS2 children:

- 1 hour for literacy study every day (5 hours);
- 10 minutes for daily handwriting practice (50 minutes);
- 20 minutes for reading a story or poem to children (1 hour 40 minutes);
- 20 minutes per week for spoken language, planned into other curriculum areas;
- time for setting and doing spelling tests (30 minutes);
- a weekly drama session in the hall (40 minutes);
- a daily 15-minute guided reading/reading activity rota time for all pupils (1 hour 15 minutes).

All these are worthy activities, but, if all were to be timetabled, the English part of the curriculum could consume more than 10 hours of a week in which there are only around 25 teaching hours! Each subject can always justify more time, and school targets, such as a commitment to 2 hours physical education a week, must be taken into account. This is why long-term planning requires decisions about school priorities and about use of time for cross-curricular work.

Although the time available for teaching and learning is finite, there are a number of ways to plan this time so that it is used effectively and helps children to make links between their different areas of learning. Dividing school time rigidly into 'subjects', so that each subject has a weekly allocation, may not be the most effective way to use the time. For instance, rather than having a timed 'lesson' for developing the spiritual, moral, social and cultural lives of children, most schools plan to address this through a range of provision: school assemblies, collective worship, RE, citizenship and whole-school activities, as well as the rules and ethos of the school. This does not mean that spiritual, moral, social and cultural education 'just happens', or that it is a less important aspect of school life than other subjects. The school has a clear policy, and a detailed medium-term plan is derived from it, but it has decided that the best way to address spiritual, moral, social and cultural education is not through a weekly 'lesson'. Similarly, some aspects of English, such as sustained writing or reading comprehension, might focus on the content of other areas of the curriculum, such as science, history or geography topics.

Some schools decide to 'block' subjects, so that children will have a meaningful block of time for a subject, but may not have this subject every week of the year. Children may, for example, do art for one half-term and DT the next, or history one term and a geography topic the next. In this way, the material can be studied, explored and learnt in depth, with an integrity and relevance that would not be possible in 15 minutes per week.

The findings of the Subject to Change report (McCulloch 2011) indicate that many of the most successful schools use carefully constructed themes to deliver learning in a 'rigorous and engaging' way and drive up standards in numeracy and literacy. Some schools plan the whole curriculum in a cross-curricular way, so that the content of the National Curriculum is addressed, but it is done through learning themes or areas that are not designated subjects. Such schemes may be commercial programmes, such as the International Primary Curriculum, a skills-based curriculum or Mantle of the Expert Curriculum (all referenced at the end of this unit), where planning and support can bought in by the school and adapted. Other schools do their cross-curricular planning in house, planning content to make sure the coverage is complete, but arranging teaching for maximum creative opportunity. Two recent curriculum reviews have offered different suggestions for review of the curriculum, but both have identified the need to look across and beyond traditional subject boundaries. An independent review was conducted at the University of Cambridge, and details can be found at www.primaryreview.org.uk/. This review proposed a total replanning of the primary curriculum in schools, but gave very clear purposes for the curriculum, and many schools use this review as the basis for their planning.

In Foundation Stage and KS1, it is very common to find that time is planned around the topic that is the focus of children's learning, with sessions not clearly 'labelled' as particular subjects. The curriculum planning is used to ensure a balanced curriculum, but the need for activities to make sense to the children is more important than the need for labels.

Another example of planning across the curriculum might be the introduction of the teaching of a primary language (teaching a foreign language) at KS1 or KS2. The curriculum includes study of a foreign language for all children at KS2, with an emphasis on communication and study of one language for all modern languages. Schools address the allocation of time for foreign languages (FL) by scheduling a regular FL slot for each class. Other schools will 'block' FL teaching, so that children do it more intensively in a particular term of the school year. In some schools, the Year 6 children have a very intense FL programme in the last term of school, after SATs and at the same time as transition to secondary school is considered, and this gives them a real boost and shot of enthusiasm in preparation for their secondary transition. Other schools will look for opportunities for cross-curricular advantages in teaching FL. They might have a regular FL lesson for all children, but also integrate FL into the school curriculum through assemblies about other cultures, writing to twin schools in English, answering the register in other languages and learning about the target country in geography. This does not actually eat up more curriculum time than the timetabled lesson but, through careful planning, gives the children a much broader experience. Decisions about how to allocate time to FL will depend, not only on the learning goals and time available, but also on who will teach this aspect of the curriculum, what professional development is available to support teachers and what resources are needed. This is true across the curriculum.

In considering how to structure the curriculum within year groups and across key stages, you will have to consider the possibilities and resources available to you and fit into the school approach. The use of expensive resources that must be shared, such as IT suites and halls, is an important consideration. Teacher time and expertise are also valuable resources that need to be planned effectively. A teacher who is particularly qualified or expert in a subject such as music, a foreign language or sport might well spend a good part of their time teaching a whole range of classes. This does not apply only to individual teachers who already have a particular skill or knowledge. Many schools ask teachers to develop particular specialisms, so that their teaching energy can be used effectively. It may also be useful for teachers to concentrate on a smaller range of subjects, so that they can consolidate expertise and make planning and assessment manageable. Some schools will plan to make the teaching (including planning and assessment) manageable by using sets across classes or key stages, or by having teachers teach different parts of the curriculum to a range of classes. These sorts of decision can help to make good use of expertise and to make the learning meaningful and relevant to children. When considering such arrangements, a school staff will weigh them against the lack of continuity caused by a change of teacher and the demands of moving children around between lessons.

The long-term planning undertaken by a school will be expressed through its policies, prospectus and development plan, as well as the school's outline of what will be taught each year. You need to read these documents carefully. You will notice these documents will have review dates and will be regularly considered by staff, so that changes to long-term planning can be made. There are some decisions that will be very clear to you as you work in school but may not be written down – this can include the organisation of sets and groupings and the timing of the school day. If you choose your moment well, mentors and teachers will be happy to discuss these important, but often unwritten, parts of school policy.

ASSESSMENT AND MONITORING PROGRESS IN LONG-TERM PLANNING

One aspect of school planning that is relatively difficult to observe, but has a real influence on long-term planning, is school target setting and monitoring of pupil progress. This happens at a number of levels. Schools, some with the help of their local authority, set targets for the proportions of their pupils' targets, expressed in National Curriculum levels and sub-levels, and aim for children to make a planned rate of progress through the levels and sub-levels of the National Curriculum. Within school, further targets are set for particular key stages and year groups. Each teacher is involved in the tracking of pupil progress, using national iTrack software, against expectations and will have a very clear understanding of the levels of progress made by their children. This tracking allows schools to plan support for groups of children.

School senior managers currently use the Years 2 and 6 SAT results, Year 1 phonics test results, Year 6 spelling, punctuation and grammar (SPAG) test outcomes, optional tests in English and mathematics and a system of ongoing levelling such as Assessment of Pupil Progress (APP) to monitor pupils' progress towards these targets. SAT results are available to schools as summaries of data that can be used to monitor expectations and set targets for schools, key stages and individual year groups. Progress measured in sub-levels and points is monitored through iTrack data. Targets are negotiated with the head, subject co-ordinator and teachers, so that everyone is clear, not only what is to be achieved, but also what action can be taken to help children reach their targets. Such actions might include changes to staffing, such as changing the proportion of teaching assistance or special needs support, the provision of resources or timing of booster classes, one-to-one tuition and other interventions. These decisions exemplify how national targets become school targets and influence long-term and medium-term planning. When you are in school, ask your mentor about the school's targets and your class teacher about pupil tracking.

How the school assesses is also a matter for long-term planning. All schools required to follow the National Curriculum are also required to undertake statutory assessment and report to parents annually (although the arrangements are different in England, Wales and Scotland). However, in addition to the statutory tests such as the phonics test and SPAG test, schools also have to decide how they will conduct their assessment for learning so that it is most useful and underpins teaching, without generating unnecessary work or disrupting teaching. The school will have an assessment policy that is certainly worthy of your attention.

MEDIUM-TERM PLANNING

Medium-term plans will address the National Curriculum and the policies of the school, but will be much more specific than long-term planning. Medium-term planning might be half-termly or termly planning. Plans will be subject or theme specific, but also demonstrate links to other subjects. They will give you much more detail about:

- the organisation and timetable of the particular class, and of any sets or other teaching arrangements;
- learning objectives for the class and sets;
- learning experiences and activities that will take place in the term or half-term;
- continuity and progression in learning – the way the learning is paced and broken up into manageable units.

The medium-term plan in your school will be written well before the start of the term or half-term it applies to. In most cases, it will be written by a group of teachers – either a key stage or year group team. The plan may well be based upon, or use elements from, a previous year's plan, but will never be simply copied. The meetings where plans are written, or those where plans are reviewed, are some of the most useful meetings you can attend.

The role of the medium-term plan is to:

- to provide the detailed framework for classroom practice in a way that can be understood by everyone involved and can be scrutinised by co-ordinators, heads and inspectors (or taken up by a supply teacher, if necessary);
- to identify the nature of work to be covered during the term or half-term and ensure that it covers the requirements set out in the long-term plan and, usually, to identify where pupils need additional provision to ensure the whole class can achieve the objectives for the half-term;
- to reflect the broad principles laid down in the school's policy for the subject and curriculum and ensure that agreed routines and teaching take place;
- to detail the knowledge, skills and processes to be taught during the half-term or term;
- to involve all staff concerned with its teaching in both its writing and subsequent review;
- to give clear guidance about the range of teaching styles, assessment techniques and tracking data needed for the period of the plan.

For you, as a beginning teacher, the medium-term plan has an additional role. It is there for you to discuss with your mentor, teacher, curriculum co-ordinators and teaching assistants. A detailed discussion of the medium-term plan is a very focused way of learning about how the class operates and is the first step in moving towards your responsibilities as a teacher. If you are able to discuss the medium-term plan for one subject with the teacher, you can then identify how you might be involved. Is there an activity you can plan, for instance?

The most important elements of a medium-term plan are:

- the title of the unit of work and identified curriculum areas;
- objectives or learning outcomes: concepts, knowledge, skills and attitudes (related to the National Curriculum programme of study or EYFS curriculum);
- key learning questions derived from objectives for pupils (these are not as simple as you might imagine – you must be well informed in the subject area and anticipate areas of uncertainty or confusion);
- relevant attainment targets, level descriptions and a clear note of what you expect the majority of the class to achieve:

- broad aspects of differentiation, such as how you differentiate for different sets or groups, what additional provision may be planned for some groups, and who will be doing it;
- key vocabulary for pupils;
- broad comments about activities (showing progression and organisation);
- identified assessment tasks, both summative and formative (these might include 'formal assessment tasks' such as a particular piece of writing, a quiz or a mind map at the end of a unit of work, but will also include the lesson outcomes as you go through the unit – these are important formative assessment opportunities).

In addition to these content-specific, medium-term plans, most teachers have very carefully elaborated, but often unwritten, plans for the non-subject-based parts of the curriculum. You need to learn routines, resources, the rules of behaviour, standards and processes of marking and tokens of reward. You should know how your teacher works with the teaching assistants and how plans and assessments are shared among the teaching team. These aspects of class work may be enshrined in policies, but you may need to learn them through observation and discussion. These aspects of the curriculum, the unwritten curriculum, facilitate children's learning, and knowing them marks you out as a teacher.

Task 3.1.2 Influences on planning

Think back to the last piece of medium-term planning in which you were involved. Try to isolate any aspects of the unwritten curriculum applying in your class that influenced your medium-term plans in any way. Examples of features you might suggest include:

- availability of teaching assistants/other adults in the classroom;
- physical aspects of the classroom, e.g. ready availability of a sink;
- rewards systems operating in the class/school.

For each feature, describe how it influenced your planning, and what you might have done (or did do) to moderate the effects of this influence.

SUMMARY

Planning, teaching and assessment are often described as a cycle, because each process is dependent on the others. Teachers devote a considerable amount of their time and energy to planning effectively, something that has now been recognised in teachers' working conditions. There is no perfect teaching plan, because there is no ideal class. Long-term plans are based around a core agreed school curriculum that has had widespread national discussion. However, this is not intended to be the whole school curriculum. The full curriculum a school chooses to do needs to be made relevant and workable in the context of each school, through planning the curriculum, resources and teaching. Even when long-term plans are established, the medium-term plan has to take account of the particular class and situation. Having clear medium-term plans is a very good basis for writing the short-term plans you will be teaching from, but it does not mean those medium-term plans are set in stone. You will find that sometimes teaching does not follow the expected plans, or some outcomes are not what you expect. All teachers make changes to their medium-term plans. They may change the rate at which they address issues, omit or add items or alter the manner or order in which topics are addressed. These changes do not indicate poor medium-term planning – they show that the teacher is making clear assessments of children's performance and evaluating the teaching techniques, pace and strategies necessary for the children to make progress.

ANNOTATED FURTHER READING

'Cambridge Primary Review briefing paper.'
> The aims of a primary curriculum are far from uncontentious. The Cambridge Primary Review Briefing Paper summarises four important views of the aims and values of the primary curriculum; it is available at: www.primaryreview.org.uk/Downloads/Int_Reps/5.Aims-values/RS_1-1_1-2_1-3_1-4_overview_briefing_080118_PU.pdf. The four sets of aims are elaborated in briefings, available at: www.primaryreview.org.uk/themes/aims_and_values_in_primary_education.php

'Framework for the National Curriculum – a report by the Expert Panel.'
> In December 2011, the DFE published the framework for the National Curriculum, which advised the National Curriculum review. Note that the distinction between the National Curriculum and school curriculum and the organisation of the phases of the curriculum originate here. However, recommendations about content, breadth and the layout of the curriculum were not adopted.

Medwell, J. (2007) *Successful Teaching Placement*, Exeter: Learning Matters.
> This book covers, in much greater detail, issues of planning for work with pupils at various stages. It also discusses the implementation of these plans and strategies for successful teaching.

National Curriculum programmes of study.
> The National Curriculum programmes of study for primary schools are available at: www.gov.uk/government/uploads/system/uploads/attachment_data/file/244223/PRIMARY_national_curriculum3.pdf. These seek to raise the level of what pupils and teachers aim to achieve, particularly in the core subjects of English, mathematics and science at primary level. This curriculum aims to ensure all pupils leave primary school able to progress to more challenging study at secondary school. For subjects other than English, mathematics and science, the shorter programmes of study are focused on the essential knowledge and skills to be taught in each subject, giving schools more freedom to develop their own curricula in a way that best meets the needs of their pupils.

'Towards a new primary curriculum.'
> 'An independent review was conducted at the University of Cambridge (2009), and it can be found at www.primaryreview.org.uk/Downloads/Curriculum_report/CPR_Curric_rep_Pt1_Past_Present.pdf. This review is important and invites the reader to ask fundamental questions about the nature of curriculum.

FURTHER READING TO SUPPORT M-LEVEL STUDY

Bell, M., Cordingley, P. and Goodchild, L. (2011) 'QDCA building the Evidence Base Project', Coventry: CUREE.
> Research by CUREE, commissioned by the Qualifications and Curriculum Development Agency (QCDA), examined international evidence around curriculum development and pedagogy. The six

main findings of this report show consistent and clear evidence with regard to the effectiveness and impact of the approach in highly successful schools (p. 3):

1. context-based learning;
2. connecting school-based learning with that in the home;
3. pupil motivation, dialogue and collaborative learning;
4. teaching to existing knowledge and conceptual understanding;
5. increased flexibility in deploying a cross-curricular approach;
6. to teach effectively with sound subject knowledge.

McCulloch, J. (2011) 'Subject to change: Should primary schools structure learning around subjects or themes?' Pearson Centre for Policy and Learning IPN; 9780997854022.

The findings of this report indicate that many of the most successful schools use carefully constructed themes to deliver learning in a 'rigorous and engaging' way. It describes how high-performing schools use creative approaches to enhance subject expertise and drive up standards in numeracy and literacy. Research by Hattie (cited in the report), based on over 6,000 studies into curriculum design, describes the importance of the strategies used by the teacher rather than the content being an indicator of effectiveness.

This report is a thought-provoking, international approach to some of the issues also addressed in the Cambridge Primary Review.

RELEVANT WEBSITES

Draft National Curriculum: www.gov.uk/government/uploads/system/uploads/attachment_data/file/210969/NC_framework_document_-_FINAL.pdf

International Primary Curriculum: www.internationalprimarycurriculum.com/
Curriculum materials for commercial curricula.

Mantle of the Expert: www.mantleoftheexpert.com/about-moe/faqs/what-about-the-international-primary-curriculum-and-mantle-of-the-expert/
Curriculum materials for commercial curricula.

The Foundation Years website: www.foundationyears.org.uk/
This contains a range of non-statutory guidance and other materials produced by the sector to support the framework.

REFERENCES

Department for Education (DfE) (2012) *Statutory Framework for the Early Years Foundation Stage*, London: DfE. Available at: www.education.gov.uk/publications/standard/AllPublications/Page1/DFE-00023-2012

Department for Education (DfE) (2013) *The National Curriculum in England: Key Stages 1 and 2 Framework Document*, London: Department for Education. Available at: www.gov.uk/dfe/nationalcurriculum

McCulloch, J. (2011) 'Subject to change: Should primary schools structure learning around subjects or themes?' London: Pearson Centre for Policy and Learning. Available at: http://thepearsonthinktank.com/wp-content/uploads/2011/04/Subject-to-change-should-primary-schools-structure-learning-around-subjects-or-themes.pdf

APPROACHING SHORT-TERM PLANNING

Jane Medwell

INTRODUCTION

The focus of this unit is short-term planning: the weekly and daily planning you will do to prepare your teaching across the curriculum. Planning at this level is one of your most onerous tasks during training, but it is one of your greatest learning experiences. As you build up your responsibility for planning, you will develop a real understanding of its central importance in teaching. This unit also refers to your use of ICT in teaching and underlines the importance of planning the use of ICT for both you and for the pupils.

OBJECTIVES

By the end of this unit, you should:

- understand the difference between medium-term and short-term planning;
- understand the purposes of short-term planning;
- know the key features of short-term plans;
- be able to critically evaluate examples of short-term planning;
- feel more confident to write some of your plans during school experience.

THE IMPORTANCE OF SHORT-TERM PLANNING

All teachers undertake short-term planning for their teaching. They will do weekly and, sometimes, daily plans. As a trainee, you will do both weekly and daily plans. You will base these on the medium- or long-term plans available to you in schools during your placement or, later in your training, on medium-term plans you may have made yourself. A short-term plan is your tool for adapting the broad objectives of the medium-term planning for the learning needs of your class. This means you may have to add or omit parts of the medium-term plan, rearrange the order in which work is done and plan the way you teach, in detail, so that all the children can learn.

The most obvious reason for planning your lessons carefully is to ensure that you offer children engaging and appropriate lessons. You have to ensure that your lessons address the teaching you have foreseen in medium-term plans in such a way that all the children in the class can understand and explore the issues. As each child is different, you have to plan lessons that present information in ways suitable for all. This is the role of differentiation.

The creation of short-term plans also has a formative role for you as a trainee and is a key training experience in itself. By writing a short-term plan, you are 'rehearsing' your lessons, anticipating challenges and working out exactly what you will do. By evaluating each short-term plan as the basis for the next, you are learning lessons from what you and the children have done. A cycle of planning, assessment, modification and more planning is the basis for children's learning. It is also the basis of yours!

Finally, short-term plans are also a way for you to be accountable, as a teacher and a trainee. Teachers write weekly plans so that they, or other teachers, can work from them and adapt them, but also so that head teachers, colleagues, inspectors and outside agencies can scrutinise and work with the plans. You will write plans so that your teacher and teaching assistants can understand the plans and their roles in them. Teachers and mentors will be able to examine and advise you about these plans, and those assessing your performance can gain insights into your professional thinking. In inspections of initial teacher training (ITT), Ofsted expects outstanding trainees to 'demonstrate through their planning and teaching that their pupils, including those who are disabled and those who have special educational needs, make good progress' (Ofsted, 2012), and so, by doing this, you not only demonstrate your outstanding performance as a trainee, but also prepare for your future as a teacher.

PLANNING FORMATS

The format of your plans will depend on a number of factors, including the age group you are teaching, your course requirements and school practices where you are teaching. You will probably find that completing some sort of grid on the word processor is easiest but it is not essential – clarity is the main issue. There is no single, perfect planning format, and you may find that you want to adapt your format to meet your training needs.

Teachers will usually have a weekly plan, at least for English and maths, but also for each subject, domain or area of learning at Key Stages (KSs) 1 and 2. Where there are strong links across the curriculum or an integrated topic approach, teachers may use a topic or integrated plan. Some of these may be based on commercial schemes such as the International Primary Curriculum, but these will rarely be used unadapted to meet the needs of the children. In Early KS1 and the Foundation Key Stage, the weekly plan will usually be written by at least the teacher and teaching assistant. It may involve a larger team. It will address all the areas of development and will usually be planned around a theme. A good weekly planning format will include most, or all, of the following:

- weekly objectives related to daily tasks;
- references to the relevant curriculum documents;
- task objectives;
- texts, ICT and other resources to be used;
- a summary of each activity for each group, identifying differentiation;
- specific roles for teaching assistants;
- key points for plenary sessions;
- assessment points, often linked to National Curriculum levels or sub-levels, assessment focuses or APP statements.

Weekly plans will break down learning and teaching in such a way that the children can achieve the learning objectives. This is a difficult skill because, as well as knowing everything necessary for medium-term planning, to do weekly plans you need to know what the children have already done, know and can do; the pace the children work at; their individual needs; and the likely response of the children to what you are planning. You will 'predict' these elements of the teaching for the week, but will find that you have to change or amend these weekly plans in response to the children's learning. This is good practice and shows you are using assessments to inform your plans. It is a good idea to amend weekly plans by hand, so that observers can *see* that you are doing this.

Table 3.2.1 shows an example of a format suitable for planning a sequence of lessons. Annotations under the figure give further details about the kinds of material you might include in each section of the plan. It is a good idea to amend weekly plans by hand, so that observers can *see* that you are doing this.

Experienced teachers may teach from their weekly plans, and, as you gain experience, you may too. When you start teaching, you will plan your early lessons and parts of lessons on the basis of the teacher's weekly plans. As your placement progresses, you will be required to write weekly plans (or sequences of lesson plans) for core subjects. You may do this as part of a teaching team, but you will be expected to make a significant contribution and to lead the planning at this level before you can achieve the standards for the award of QTS.

One very important aspect of planning that is best addressed through weekly plans is the issue of routine activities, such as guided group or individual reading and writing, story telling, registration, distribution of maths games or books, story reading, book browsing, spelling tests, handwriting practice, tables practice, mark making, weather recording, show and tell and action rhyme times. These routines are easy to overlook, but they are very important. Patterns of activity that are known to both child and adult are soothing, familiar and powerful learning activities. Your weekly plan needs to be checked to ensure these activities represent the balance you want and that they are planned.

LESSON PLANNING

On the basis of weekly plans, you can construct detailed daily plans. The format depends on the age of the children and what you are planning for. The key elements that you should include are:

- class/group taught;
- time and duration of lesson;
- objectives for the session or lesson;
- reference to the relevant curriculum documents;
- texts, ICT and other resources to be used;
- structure and timings of the lesson;
- summary of each activity for each group, identifying differentiation and what you expect teacher and children to do;
- specific roles for teaching assistants and, usually, a plan for the teaching assistant;
- details of teacher and child activity;
- key vocabulary to be used;
- key questions to be asked;
- key teaching points;
- identified outcomes (how will you assess whether the children have achieved their learning objective?);
- note of pupils' previous experience;
- cross-curricular links;
- identified health and safety issues (such as glue guns, the need to wear coats etc.);
- an evaluation section;
- key points for plenary sessions;
- assessment points (who are you assessing and what do you want to know?); and
- timings.

TABLE 3.2.1 An example format for planning a sequence of lessons

Term/Year:			Teaching group:		
Curriculum subject/Theme/Area(s) of learning:					
Broad learning objectives	Learning objectives	Key Activities	Resources	Cross-curricular opportunities	Planned method of assessment

Broad learning objectives:
Specific references to Early Learning Goals, National Curriculum, Primary National Strategies (PNS) (literacy or maths), Agreed Syllabus for Religious Education

Learning objectives: stating anticipated achievement in one or more of the following:
■ attitudes (show . . .);
■ skills (be able to . . .);
■ knowledge (know that . . .);
■ understanding (develop concept of . . .).
These form the basis of assessment and are judged through planned outcomes

Key activities should:
■ enable learning objectives to be met;
■ include a variety of experiences that progressively develop children's learning;
■ recognise pupils' diverse needs (including pupils with special educational needs (SEN), more able and gifted pupils, and pupils with English as an additional language (EAL);
■ take account of pupils' gender and ethnicity.

Resources should be:
■ influenced by learning objectives;
■ listed in detail;
■ considered with health and safety in mind;
■ related to displays where relevant.

Cross-curricular opportunities should develop significant and planned attitudes, skills, knowledge and understanding *across* the curriculum in, e.g.:
■ English;
■ ICT;
■ PSHE/citizenship;
■ other National Curriculum subjects/areas of learning where significant.

Planned method of assessment should include anticipated evidence:
■ to demonstrate achievement of learning objectives, and to inform assessment and record keeping (may be observational, verbal, written or graphic evidence, depending on activity);
■ to reflect a *range* of assessment methods.

Task 3.2.1 Scrutinising weekly planning

To do this task, you will need a weekly plan and medium-term plan from your placement.

Ensure you know:

- Which parts of the medium-term plan does the weekly plan address?
- Which parts of the relevant curriculum documents does this refer to?
- How long will each lesson or session in the weekly plan be?

Focus on one part of the weekly plan, perhaps English, maths or science.

- What resources are needed for the lessons in the weekly plan?
- What is the balance of whole-class, group and individual work for this week?
- What are the class management challenges for this week?

Discuss your chosen element of weekly planning with your teacher. Possible topics for discussion include:

- How do you ensure that the learning is accessible to all the children in the class?
- How do you differentiate for children who have SEN or are in the gifted and talented register?
- What arrangements are made to include children with SEN?
- What role will a teaching assistant or other adult play in these lessons, and how will they know what to do?
- What do you do if the children do not make the predicted learning gains in one week?
- Will any of these sessions present particular management challenges?

What are the 'routine' activities in this week? Fill in the table and add other activities.

Activity	When	How long/ often	Resources	Content	Teacher action	Pupil response
Welcome/weather, etc.						
Show and tell						
Action rhymes/poems						
Story time						
Spelling test						
Tables practice						
Register						
Handwriting						

You may begin your training by doing lesson plans for every session you teach and, later, when you have more experience, move to teach from your weekly plans. However, always do individual lesson plans when your lesson is being observed, because it helps the observer to see your thinking (and you to do it!). You should also do lesson plans when you are teaching new ideas, are unsure of yourself or the children, or have a specific training target in mind. For instance, if you find it hard to manage time in your lessons with KS2, you will find that planning your lessons in detail, writing predicted times on the plans and reviewing them afterwards really help you to manage time.

PLANNING AN EFFECTIVE LESSON

The research about planning is varied. Brophy and Good (1986) stressed that effective teachers demanded productive engagement with the task, prepared well and matched the tasks to the abilities of the children. Effective lessons tend to be those with a clear structure and shared understandings about what is to be learnt and why, where all children can do the activities and use the learning time effectively, and the teacher assesses progress and evaluates the lessons. All these elements of a successful lesson can be addressed through your planning by focusing on your: lesson structure, management, lesson objectives, differentiation for learning and use of evaluation of lesson plans. All these features will help you to make a lesson engaging and interesting.

Successful lessons have clear beginnings and strong conclusions, with a certain amount of 'academic press' – that is, impetus to complete tasks within the given time. Learning time can be divided up so that it is used productively for learning, and so that the parts of a lesson help children to progress through their tasks. However you structure your lesson, you should always make sure you have a strong, clear structure to a lesson, and that the children know what this is. In this way, the children can learn to use time effectively and experience 'academic press'.

Time spent learning, itself, is a significant factor in the effectiveness of lessons, with research suggesting that the most effective teachers are those who maximise learning time by reducing off-task chatter and managing the class effectively (Silcock, 1993). Transitions from whole-class to group work, effective distribution of resources, and strategies for behaviour management are all parts of lessons where time can be saved through effective planning, thereby maximising learning time for pupils.

Learning to manage the pace of your lessons, so that the teaching and learning are lively and challenging but not rushed, takes time. It is fairly well established that the efficiency of experienced teachers allows them to perform complex procedures in a fraction of the time taken by novices – this is why you need to plan things experienced teachers do not even think about! If you find it difficult to maintain the pace of a lesson, you may want to plan in 5-minute intervals and note down the times on your lesson plans.

Learning objectives are probably the most important points on a lesson plan. You should be absolutely clear about what you want the children to learn, understand or do as a result of your lesson. These lesson objectives must be reasonable and achievable. You may want to reference a National Planning Strategy unit of work on your lesson plan, but phrase your lesson objective accurately, so that the children can achieve it. A single lesson may address or contribute to a unit of work or to the achievement of an Early Learning Goal, but no lesson will completely cover one of these big objectives.

Most importantly, you must make sure your lesson objectives are meaningful. This means they must make sense in terms of the curriculum, so that children are not simply learning a set of assorted skills and knowledge that may (or may not) make sense later. It also means that objectives must be clear to, and understood by, the children. A study of teachers of literacy (Wray *et al.*, 2001) found that effective teachers made sure that even young children understood the wider role of tasks in their learning. You will undoubtedly write up lesson objectives somewhere in the class, such as on the interactive whiteboard (IWB), a sheet of paper or a chart, but, unless you discuss these objectives with children and ensure the children know what they are learning and why, written objectives are just additional wallpaper.

Task 3.2.2 Sharing lesson objectives?

Sharing lesson objectives with the children has become one of the accepted markers of good teaching and is certainly used by inspectors as a means of judging the effectiveness of a lesson. Yet its benefits are not universally accepted. Read the newspaper article on this topic by Philip Beadle (www.guardian.co.uk/education/2007/jan/16/schools.uk1). Beadle concludes his piece with the following:

> But why must children know what the objectives are at the beginning of the lesson? Why can't we ask them to guess what they are going to learn, or tell us what they learned at the end of the lesson? Why can't it be a surprise?

Try to compose *either* a reasoned rebuttal of Beadle's position, *or* a justification for his scepticism about the use of lesson objectives.

Your questioning is an important part of your teaching. The need to ask a range of open and closed questions has been well documented. Brophy and Good (1986) make recommendations from their review of research, which include the need to ensure that questions are clear, that all children are asked questions, that the pace of questioning is adjusted to the task, and that children are given sufficient wait time to answer. They also stress that it is important for questions to elicit correct answers, although, as new material is learnt, the error rate will inevitably rise as a result of children being stretched. More recent characterisations of teaching have stressed the importance of teachers demonstrating, or modelling, the learner behaviour they wish to teach. This includes reading aloud to students, modelling comprehension strategies, modelling writing processes and thinking aloud as you solve mathematical problems. Plan the key points you want to make to the class, the key questions and main skills you want to model. In this way, you can make sure you teach what you intend to teach.

Questioning is only one approach to talk in class and one that may place too much focus on the child. Alexander (2008) emphasises the importance of talk as a tool for learning. This involves the teacher having detailed knowledge of the lesson content and possibilities, but guiding discussion in ways that challenge and develop children's learning. However, there is no magic formula, and different areas of learning may require different approaches to talk (Fisher, 2007).

Differentiation is the way you plan to meet the diverse learning needs of pupils. You will teach the knowledge, skills and understanding in ways that suit the pupils' abilities and previous experience. Differentiation is represented in different forms in your planning:

*   **Presentation** – plan to use a variety of media to present ideas or offer vocabulary or extra diagrams to those who need more support. You will find ICT particularly helpful in preparing different types of presentation on paper, audiotape, screens or IWBs.

- **Content** – select appropriately so that there is content that suits most children, with additional content available to some. For instance: some children may do six calculations where others complete ten. ICT, using the Internet, can offer you a range of content.
- **Resource** – use resources that support pupils' needs such as writing frames, language master word banks or Spellmaster machines for poor spellers. For children with English as an additional language (EAL), you might need to ensure that target vocabulary is available in a written form.
- **Grouping** – group pupils of similar ability for targeted support, or pair children with a more able pupil, teaching assistant or language support teacher.
- **Task** – match tasks to pupils' abilities. This can mean different tasks for different pupils. It is sometimes a good idea to offer different tasks that address the same objectives to different pupils, so that they can achieve success.
- **Support** – offer additional adult or peer assistance, from a TA, language support teacher or more experienced child.
- **Time** – giving more or less time to complete a given task can make the task more suitable to the particular pupils.

Differentiation sounds simple, but it demands really good knowledge of the content, the children, resources and a range of teaching strategies. You will achieve appropriate differentiation by working closely with the teacher, so that you find out what strategies are available and work for these children. Key resources to plan into your lessons will be TAs, language support staff and the individual education plans written for children with special needs.

EVALUATION

Evaluation is a part of planning and also allows you to show you are able to improve your performance through self-evaluation. Evaluation means considering:

- how well the children achieved the learning objectives (assessment);
- how well you planned, taught and managed teaching in relation to your training targets.

Evaluations will usually be brief and will usually focus on two aspects: what you did and what the children learnt. The most useful evaluations focus on particular aspects of your teaching and are the basis of your own training targets. You may be keen to record positive evaluations, but less keen to focus on improvement. However, you should develop your ability to analyse your teaching, especially when you can see an area for improvement. When your evaluation comment identifies work to be done, always say what you propose to do in response. The very best planning is that which clearly uses evidence from children's previous attainment and leads on to influence the planning and teaching of the next session or lesson. This sort of evidence may be the annotations to a lesson plan you make in response to previous evaluations.

BUILDING PLANNING EXPERIENCE

Your early plans on a teaching experience may not be for whole lessons but for short parts of lessons or sessions, such as a whole-class phonics game, a guided reading session for a small group of children or a mental/oral starter in a maths lesson. Planning these parts of lessons gives you the chance to pay attention to detail and really concentrate on some important aspects of using plans, such as:

- ensuring you make your key points clearly;
- maintaining a pace that is brisk and engaging, but not so fast that the children are lost;
- effective questioning and interactive teaching;
- using resources such as the IWB or phonics objects.

Task 3.2.3 Planning a mental/oral starter

Use the planner below to observe a mental/oral starter taught by your teacher. Then plan and evaluate a mental/oral starter or shared literacy session. This may be more detailed than you are used to, but using such detail will help you to construct the mental 'scripts' you need to manage this complex task.

Planner for a mental/oral starter, shared reading or shared writing session

Date		Group/class	
Duration		NC/PNS reference	
Resources		Key vocabulary	
Activity			
Questions			
Less confident	Confident		More confident
Assessment			
Less confident	Confident		More confident
Evaluation			

Planning parts of lessons and teaching them is a good start to building up responsibility for whole lessons.

PLANNING FOR OTHER ADULTS IN THE CLASS OR SETTING

The Class Size and Pupil–Adult Ratios (CSPAR) Project investigated the role of teaching assistants (Rubie-Davies, 2010). This project established that, for TAs to make a real difference to pupil learning, teachers must ensure they are included in planning and assessment. TAs need to understand and support children to engage with the learning processes in the activities, and not just focus on pupils achieving the task. Moreover, it is important that the teacher gets feedback from TAs and uses that information in planning.

To ensure you work effectively with teaching assistants or other adults in class, you may use a set format to present clear expectations of what you would like the TA to do. This will usually include space for the TA to write assessment notes about how well the children achieved the objective. These notes may well affect your future planning.

TABLE 3.2.2 An example of a planning format for a teaching assistant (TA)

Date .... Lesson focus ....
Activity (a brief account of the activity and the TA's role in any whole-class introduction, shared reading, mental/oral, etc.)
Resources needed

Key vocabulary to use	**Key questions to use**
•	•
•	•
•	•

Objectives
1
2
3

For completion by the TA after group work:

Name		Can do	Needs help
	1		
	2		
	3		
	1		
	2		
	3		
	1		
	2		
	3		
	1		
	2		
	3		
	1		
	2		
	3		

Task 3.2.4 Involving a teaching assistant

Arrange a specific time to talk to the TA in your placement class about a lesson in which he/she has assisted. Find out the following:

- What does the TA think the objective of the session was?
- What did the TA understand his/her role to be?
- What key vocabulary did he/she use?
- What resources did he/she prepare?
- How did the TA know what to say and do?
- What additional information would he/she like about class tasks?

When you have this information, you will be able to use it to direct your communication with the TA in your lessons.

PLANNING AND ICT

ICT can assist you in your planning in two main ways. First, the computer is an invaluable tool for planning itself, because it can help with the process and content of planning. Word processing allows you to produce and amend your plans swiftly and effectively. (Alternatively, you can easily spend every evening colour-coding, cross-referencing and wasting time.) The Internet also offers you thousands of ready-made plans for almost any topic, especially on the *Times Educational Supplement* website. These will not be instant solutions to the problems posed by your next lesson, because they do not meet the needs of your particular class. However, they do present you with a spectacular range of ideas and formats. You need to use them, but not rely on them.

The second way that ICT can be useful is in planning for pupil activity. If you are planning to use an IWB or visualiser for your mental/oral starter in a maths lesson, you can make the lesson visually attractive (so that all eyes are attracted to it and are not distracted elsewhere). The content can be tailored to meet the whole range of abilities, and the children can come out and be fully involved in the learning. You might use your computer to produce worksheets for some groups of children, while others use calculators or tablets. To conclude the lesson, your plenary might include the IWB or a demonstration using a projected calculator. The ICT can make the lesson more effective, but only if you plan it carefully.

When you think of using ICT, do not concentrate only on the computer. Children can use audio or video recording to do speaking and listening, reading and writing activities. If children are presenting findings from group work, the visualiser might be the most accessible technology. Do not overlook the use of TV and radio materials. Like computer programmes, they are produced specifically for schools, have helpful teaching guidance and can be very useful if planned carefully.

SUMMARY

An outstanding teacher, in Ofsted's terms, is one who has planning that is thorough and detailed, with clear subject and cross-curricular links. In the plan's assessment, opportunities are identified and annotated accordingly, to show you are using your assessments for planning subsequent teaching. An outstanding teacher's plans show links to speaking and listening, ICT and homework. These plans are what make sure every child learns successfully.

Planning is one of the most time-consuming processes you will engage in, but planning well will help you to become a successful teacher. All successful teaching relies on teachers producing lessons that engage and motivate the children. This is partly down to selecting the right content and partly down to the way the content is dealt with. These issues are planning issues. Use your plans to rehearse and evaluate your lessons and you can be confident, happy and interesting to your class of children.

ANNOTATED FURTHER READING

Bearne, E. (2002) *Differentiation and diversity*, Routledge: London.
> This looks at a set of case studies in a variety of areas of the curriculum, to meet a range of pupil needs.

Gipps, C., Hargreaves, E. and McCallum, B. (2000) *What makes a good primary school teacher?* London: RoutledgeFalmer.
> This accessible book offers an account of the range of teaching, assessing and feedback strategies used by individual 'expert' primary teachers, and how they know or decide which strategy to bring into play, and when.

(M) FURTHER READING TO SUPPORT M-LEVEL STUDY

Wray, D., Medwell, J., Poulson, L. and Fox, R. (2001) *Teaching Literacy Effectively*, London: RoutledgeFalmer.
> This books reports the findings of the Effective Teachers of Literacy project and includes several findings relating to the importance of good planning.

RELEVANT WEBSITES

The *Times Educational Supplement* site: www.tes.co.uk/article.aspx?storycode=6081306&s_cid=Landing_Lesson Plans12
> This site offers access to thousands of lesson plans and has invaluable advice from other teachers about many aspects of planning.

REFERENCES

Alexander, R.J. (2008) *Towards Dialogic Teaching. Rethinking Classroom Talk* (4th edn), York: Dialogos.

Brophy, J. and Good, T. (1986) 'Teacher behaviour and student achievement', in M.C. Wittrock (ed.) *Handbook of Research In Teaching*, London: Collier Macmillan.

Fisher, R. (2007) 'Dialogic teaching: developing thinking and metacognition through philosophical discussion', *Early Child Development and Care*, 177(6–7): 615-31.

Ofsted (2012) *Initial Teacher Education Inspection Handbook*, www.ofsted.gov.uk/resources/initial-teacher-education-inspection-handbook (downloaded July 2013).

Rubie-Davies , C.M. (2010) 'Teacher expectations and perceptions of student attributes: is there a relationship?', *The British Psychological Society British Journal of Educational Psychology*, 80(1): 121-35.

Silcock, P. (1993) 'Can we teach effective teaching?' *Educational Review*, 45(1): 13-19.

Wray, D., Medwell, J., Poulson, L. and Fox, R. (2001) *Teaching Literacy Effectively*, London: RoutledgeFalmer.

ORGANISING YOUR CLASSROOM FOR LEARNING

Peter Kelly

INTRODUCTION

In this unit, I link approaches to organising learning environments to views about how learning takes place, many of which have been discussed in earlier units. Learning is complex, and no one view can fully capture this complexity. However, each view of learning is helpful in understanding and planning for particular aspects of learning. I argue that a balanced approach to classroom organisation draws on each view of learning. Thus, we should use different approaches to promote different types of learning.

OBJECTIVES

Having read this unit, you will be able to:

- recognise the link between views about how learning takes place and approaches to organising your classroom;
- know the key approaches to organising your classroom;
- recognise the scope and limitation of each of these approaches;
- be able to identify appropriate approaches for a particular learning objectives.

ORGANISING LEARNING

How you organise your classroom says a great deal about how you view your children's learning. Colleagues, parents and, perhaps most importantly, children will read much about what you value from those features of classroom life for which you are responsible: the areas of the curriculum you choose to link and focus on; the lessons and activities you plan; the roles you ascribe to other adults in your classroom; how you group and seat the children; the decisions you allow children to take; the resources you provide and the ways in which you make them available; your use of display and of opportunities to learn outside the classroom and school; and so on.

Consider the range of options available to you in relation to just one of these: groupings. Children can be taught as a whole class, in groups or individually. In groups, they might work collaboratively or be provided with differentiated individual tasks. Such tasks might be differentiated in terms of the level of challenge of the task or the level of support the group receives, and so on. Such features are not simple alternatives; those you choose to use and the circumstances in which you choose to use them will say something about your beliefs as a teacher, even if these are largely tacit and the decisions you make are intuitive.

There is a lot of advice available on classroom organisation. This has not always been the case. It was not until the 1960s that the traditional model of teaching – that is, a teacher standing at the front of the classroom, with the children sat facing, working on the same task at the same time – was challenged. Progressive approaches, developed largely from the ideas of Jean Piaget, suggested children should be free to work at different speeds and in different ways, learning from first-hand experiences through active exploration and personal discovery. However, traditionalists argued that such approaches were largely ineffective: there were things that children needed to be taught, such as spelling and grammar, which could not be discovered or left to chance. Thus began an enduring and polarised educational debate.

More recently, a loose consensus has prevailed that recognises that certain approaches favour certain kinds of learning, rather than one approach being best. Nevertheless, the range of approaches suggested can appear daunting. In fact, it is relatively straightforward, if you remain mindful of one thing: how you organise your classroom depends on how you believe children will learn in your classroom.

This unit considers classroom organisation in relation to four views of learning: basic skills acquisition, constructing understanding, learning together, and apprenticeship approaches.

Basic skills acquisition

Once a favourite of traditionalist knowledge-transmission approaches, direct teaching dominates approaches to basic skills teaching in schools as a result of a variety of government frameworks and strategies in the 1990s and 2000s. Originally conceived somewhat behaviouristically as teacher demonstration and student imitation, leading to a period of consolidation and practice, in these strategies direct teaching received a Vygotskian make-over, becoming an interactive approach where the importance of high-quality dialogue and discussion between teachers and pupils is emphasised. However, this was an issue with many teachers, who were less ready to move away from a teacher demonstration and student imitation model towards a more interactive one.

Learning as constructing understanding

Originating in the ideas of Jean Piaget, constructivists see learners as theory builders, developing understandings to make sense of their observations and experiences and modifying these understandings in the light of subsequent observations and experiences, so that they become more generally useful and closer to accepted viewpoints. This perspective has had a huge impact on some curriculum areas, particularly science, where a cottage industry grew in the 1980s researching the alternative understandings and misunderstandings, termed 'alternative frameworks', that children have of the phenomena they encounter. Phil Adey and Michael Shayer's Cognitive Acceleration through Science Education (CASE) has adapted and extended the constructivist approach (Adey *et al.*, 1995). By challenging children's misunderstandings of phenomena, the CASE approach aims to develop the structure of their thinking.

Social learning

Social constructivists, such as Jerome Bruner, cite the ideas of the Russian theorist Lev Vygotsky in positing a central role for talking and listening in learning. Making sense and developing understanding, they assert, are essentially social processes that take place through talk. In the early 1990s, the National Oracy Project, which was unfortunately overshadowed by developments in literacy and numeracy, identified a whole range of ways in which participation with others in activities involving discussion can improve learning: it supports learners in constructing new meanings and understandings as they explore them in words; it allows learners to test out and criticise claims and different points of view as they speak and listen to others; and, importantly, talk provides raw material for learners' own thinking, because, for Vygotsky, thought is an internal, personal dialogue.

Learning as an apprenticeship

The work of social anthropologists such as Jean Lave and Etienne Wenger has illuminated how people learn in everyday contexts. This has led them to reconsider school learning in sociocultural terms. Thus, there are many metaphors that we can adopt for our classrooms: the writer's workshop, the artist's studio, the scientist's laboratory, and so on. In each case, this view suggests, the children act as craft apprentices, engaging in the authentic activities of the community to which the metaphor pertains. So, for children to think as, for example, historians, they have to be helped to act like historians by doing what historians do. The same is, of course, true for scientists or practitioners in any other area of enquiry.

I will now turn to consider approaches relating to each of these views of learning.

Task 3.3.1 Looking for learning

Think back to one particular day during a previous school placement. Write down briefly each of the learning activities that the children engaged in during the day. Consider:

- which areas of the curriculum were addressed and linked;
- the planned lessons and activities;
- the role adopted by the teacher and other adults in the classroom;
- how the children were grouped and seated;
- the decisions that the children took;
- the resources provided;
- use of display;
- opportunities for learning outside the classroom.

Now consider what these features suggest to you about the way in which the teacher (whether it was you or the class teacher) views learning.

Task 3.3.2 Classroom culture

Culture can be described most simply as 'the way we do things round here'. Critically reflect on your answers from Task 3.3.1. How does each of these things contribute to the classroom culture? To help, consider the following questions:

- Is there a learning-centred culture or a working-centred one?
- Is there a teacher-led culture that emphasises pupils acquiring new knowledge and skills, or a student-led culture that emphasises pupils participating in developing new knowledge and skills?
- What metaphor best describes the classroom culture – a factory production line or perhaps a writer's study, an artist's studio or a scientist's laboratory?

You can explore these ideas further by reading Kelly (2005).

CLASSROOM APPROACHES

Basic skills and direct interactive teaching

As a whole-class approach, direct interactive teaching allows children to benefit from involvement with their teacher for sustained periods. However, direct teaching and interaction are also important during individual, paired and group work.

The role of dialogue is emphasised: children are expected to play an active part in discussion by asking questions, contributing ideas and explaining and demonstrating their thinking to the class. However, many studies have found that teachers spend the

majority of their time either explaining or using tightly structured questions. Such questions are mainly factual or closed in nature, and so fail to encourage and extend child contributions or to promote interaction and thinking.

In recent years, new technologies have had a significant impact on direct interactive and whole-class teaching. These include interactive whiteboards, data projectors, and remote devices such as infrared keyboards and graphics tablets.

Good direct interactive teaching is achieved by balancing different approaches:

- **Directing and telling**: sharing teaching objectives with the class, ensuring that children know what to do, and drawing attention to points over which they should take particular care.
- **Explaining and illustrating**: giving accurate, well-paced explanations and referring to previous work or methods.
- **Demonstrating**: giving clear, well-structured demonstrations using appropriate resources and visual displays.
- **Questioning and discussing**: ensuring all children take part; using open and closed questions; asking for explanations; giving time for children to think before answering; allowing children to talk about their answers in pairs before contributing them to the whole class; listening carefully to children's responses and responding constructively; and challenging children's assumptions to encourage thinking.
- **Exploring and investigating**: asking children to pose problems or suggest a line of enquiry.

- **Consolidating and embedding**: through a variety of activities in class and well-focused homework, opportunities are provided to practise and develop new learning; making use of this learning to tackle related problems and tasks.
- **Reflecting and evaluating**: identifying children's errors and using them as positive teaching points by exploring them together; discussing children's reasons for choosing particular methods or resources; giving oral feedback on written work.
- **Summarising and reminding**: reviewing, during and towards the end of a lesson, what has been taught and what children have learned; identifying and correcting misunderstandings; making links to other work; and giving children an insight into the next stage of their learning.

Direct interactive teaching approaches focus on knowledge and skills transmission and acquisition through active learning and interaction. In this, they leave little room for learners to construct their own understandings of phenomena. This is where the following approach is useful.

Constructing understanding

Constructivists believe learners build their understandings of the world from their experiences and observations. They suggest that children bring many misconceptions and misunderstandings to the classroom from their experiences of the world, and assert that the best way to change such misunderstandings is to challenge children to change them themselves through hands-on exploration. For example, in science, children may, from their experiences at home, have formed the misconception that clothes make you warmer. An investigation where chocolate is wrapped in fabric could be used to see if this causes the chocolate to melt. Such information might challenge the children's misconception, and the children would need to restructure their thinking to accommodate the new information that the chocolate is not warmed up; rather it is prevented from cooling or warming as the outside temperature changes.

However, one of the problems here is that it is assumed children will recognise the need to change their thinking or even that they will want to do it. An approach that takes the constructivist approach further is CASE. This can be used to formalise the thinking and restructuring process, as it contains certain key elements that many teachers have adopted or adapted in their own classrooms:

- **Concrete preparation**: the problem is stated in terms that are understandable to the children; that is, so that they see it as a problem. For example, you might ask the children to talk to the person next to them and think about clothes they might choose to take with them on holiday to a very cold country, and why.
- **Cognitive conflict**: children are encouraged to consider a range of possible explanations for causes and effects that may interact in complex ways with each other; for example, children investigating the effects of clothing (identifying features such as fabric type, thickness and shape) on its suitability for a cold location could consider which feature or combination of features is central.
- **Social construction**: now the children work together on the challenging activity to construct new joint understandings. In this, although the teacher asks probing questions to focus debate, the children do most of the thinking. So the children might share each others' discussions and try to come to a consensus.
- **Metacognition**: in this process, the children are helped to become conscious of their own reasoning in order to understand it. In putting pupils in charge of their own learning, it is important to enable them to articulate their own thinking and learning processes.
- **Bridging**: this is the conscious transfer of new ideas and understandings from the context in which they were generated to new, but related, contexts. So the children could apply their new, shared understanding of clothing in cold countries to hot countries.

This approach focuses largely on the learning of the individual. Social learning approaches which follow focus more on what can be achieved by a group working together, with the view that what is done together the individual will eventually become able to do alone.

Social learning

Establishing ground rules

Before engaging in social learning approaches, a number of ground rules need to be established with children. Rules to stop interruptions of all those involved in group work, adults or children, should be negotiated first. Thus, children needing help might be encouraged to take greater responsibility for their learning by seeking support elsewhere, or by doing alternative work until support is available.

Such independent and self-directed learners can be referred to as *autonomous*. The American educationalist Susan Bobbit-Nolan (1995) considers three levels of autonomy. The first is when learners have autonomy or control over the strategies that they use to carry out a task without the guidance of their teacher. Thus, in mathematics, a teacher might teach a variety of strategies for children to undertake three-digit multiplication. The children can then choose which one to use in tackling a problem. Similarly, children might choose the form of recording to use for a science exploration, and so on. At the second level, learners have control over the content of the curriculum, the things to be studied and learned, the objectives of learning. Thus, children might decide to explore something in its own right, or set their own goals for their learning. They might choose an area or theme in history to research, an assignment to write, an experiment to do or a book to read. This is learning for pleasure, following tangents and satisfying curiosities. At the third level, learners are able to judge things for themselves, after taking evidence and various views into account. Thus, the children might make informed decisions about changes to school routines such as playtimes, spending money on new items for class or elections to the school council. They might tackle controversial issues in school and debate these, looking at the perspectives of different parties. This third level of autonomy goes beyond simple independence in accessing resources or completing the teachers' work, and has been called 'intellectual autonomy'. Learners who have intellectual autonomy think for themselves, link their thinking to their experiences and open their minds to new ideas.

Discussions during group work should be democratic: everyone has the right to a say, and for their contribution to be valued. This means that participants should:

- listen attentively to the contributions of others without interrupting;
- speak to each other, looking at the person to whom they are responding;
- take turns and allow everyone an equal opportunity to speak;
- be sensitive to each other's needs;
- try to see things from other people's points of view, even if they disagree with their position;
- give reasons for their views; and
- be prepared to change their viewpoint in the light of new information, and accept others doing the same.

Further, children should understand that it is disrespectful to others if they monopolise the talk or if they ridicule or are unkind about others or their views. Of course, it is often most effective when the children are allowed to come up with rules such as these themselves: with prompting, they can be encouraged to address the key areas. A good place to develop these, together with a regard for these democratic ways of working, is the school council.

Collaborative group work

Group tasks are most effective when children need to share their knowledge, skills and understandings to a common end through some form of problem-solving or open-ended task with one correct solution and many alternatives. In their activity, children's talk will centre initially on their actions, but should be moved towards their understandings.

Research (summarised by Bennett, 1995) suggests the ideal size for groups engaging in collaborative work is four – pairs are too small to generate lots of ideas, threes tend to form a pair and exclude the third member, and groups bigger than four become harder for the children to manage, and so it is less likely that everyone will be fully included. Similarly, mixed-gender and mixed-ability groups tend to be more inclusive and focused and generate the widest range of viewpoints and ideas.

There are two basic forms of task organisation for collaborative work: 'jigsaw' and 'group investigation'. The former requires each group member to complete a sub-task, which contributes to the whole group completing the assigned task. This might be the production of a picture, diagram or piece of writing about, say, Roman villas, for a group display on that topic. In the second, all of the group work together on the same task, with each member of the group being assigned a different role. So the children might create a small, dramatic episode portraying life in a Roman villa. Each child would play a different character, and, in addition, one child might take on the role of director.

So, for example, a group might work together on a 'jigsaw task' to produce a leaflet welcoming newcomers and informing them about the school. Each child might survey a different group of children from across the school to find out what information newcomers would need and benefit from. Particular attention would be paid to the experiences of any newcomers to the school. Then, the group would make decisions together about which areas to address, in what format, etc. Each child could then be allocated the task of developing an aspect of the leaflet, with these being finally brought together for the finished document.

Dialogical enquiry

Dialogical enquiries are discussions in which learners, through language and sometimes supported by written notes and prompts, jointly engage in:

*   working towards a common understanding for all;
*   asking questions and suggesting ideas relating to the evidence on which proposals are based;
*   looking at issues and problems from as many different perspectives as possible;
*   challenging ideas and perspectives in the light of contradictions and evidence, so as to move the discussion forwards.

Examples include book clubs or reading circles, where children discuss their reading and produce new books together. Similarly, writing conferences are extremely valuable, in which writers discuss their writing with their peers. Of course, having such shared dialogues about texts will improve participants' ability to engage in such dialogues alone.

Other opportunities exist in developing home–school learning partnerships in children's work. Thus, in one example, parents of a particular group of young children read the same book with their children at home one evening. During the shared reading, parents wrote down the children's responses to the stories on post-it notes and fixed them to the relevant pages. Next day, these notes became the starting points for discussion between the teacher and the group.

With older children, each child in a group reading the same book together might individually write, predicting the next stage of the story. This writing might provide the starting point for a group discussion about the evidence for each prediction, the likelihood and plausibility of each prediction and the group's preferred outcome. Such a discussion could equally be based on individual group members writing initially from the perspective of one of the characters of the story and providing that character's point of view. The discussion could then consider the story from this variety of perspectives.

In terms of interpretation of data, such discursive enquiries are important, because they can link the process of enquiry to the big ideas of the subject. So, for example, in science, following an investigation of the conditions in which plants grow best, rather than children simply describing the conditions that are most favourable to healthy plant growth, the discussion can focus on ideas about why this might be the case. Perhaps the children's text of the data collected can be compared in their discussion with other writing they have done, which has attempted to explain findings.

Learning through apprenticeship

Apprenticeship models of learning require groups of children to engage in the actual or authentic activities of particular groups. So, for science, children work as scientists, engaging in an enquiry to which the answer is not already known, using the key ideas and tools of science and sometimes working in partnership with others from the local community. For example, Years 5 and 6 children might set up a weather station, or get involved in monitoring environmental changes in an environmental awareness campaign. In doing this, they might involve members of the wider community, contact experts at the Met Office for advice, and so on.

There are many other possibilities for authentic activities in schools. So, in mathematics, Years 1 and 2 children might conduct a traffic survey in order to provide evidence for a letter to the council for some form of traffic control outside school, and Years 5 and 6 children might be helped to cost and plan a residential visit, while children in Years 3 and 4 could run a school stationery shop - ordering, pricing and selling goods in order to make a small profit. Similarly, in geography, children in Key Stage 2 might survey and research the school population growth, using various indicators

Task 3.3.3 Planning for learning 1

Consider how you might plan a series of lessons in one subject area, so that a variety of the above approaches is used. For example, in science, looking at life processes in Years 1 and 2:

- Constructing understanding: growing sunflowers from seed in class, exploring the conditions in which these grow best.
- Group work, discussion: separate groups investigate the effects of one factor on plant growth, making hypotheses beforehand and discussing findings after.
- Authentic activity: set up a garden centre in school, so that the children can grow a variety of plants to sell in time for the summer fair.
- Interactive direct teaching: the children are taught how to write clear instructions so that they can provide buyers at the summer fair with instructions for caring for their plants

Try doing this for another area of learning, for example data handling in mathematics in Year 4.

such as local birth rates, and could be encouraged to identify the implications of their findings. Finally, children from across the school could be involved in making a CD for sale, following their composition of various items for a particular event, such as a school anniversary.

Sometimes, it is important to look at particular areas of study in many different ways. For example, in an essentially historical study of the Battle of the Somme in 1916, older children could engage, not only in a historical enquiry-based approach, be it text or computer based or involving the examination of original artefacts, but also by looking at events through the eyes of poets and novelists, or through the eyes of geographers or scientists. As such, the work of others might be explored, and the children might engage in original work themselves, not only in writing and poetry, but also through the media of music, dance, drama and painting. This would provide the children with a very full and rich learning experience.

Task 3.3.4 Planning for learning 2

Try out some of the activities you have planned for Task 3.3.3 with a group of children. Closely observe the children taking part in two different activities that you have planned and try to answer the following:

- How does their participation differ across the two activities?
- Does one of the activities appear to engage them more than the other?

After the activities, talk to the children involved and try to answer the following:

- What did they think they had to do?
- Why did they think they were doing these activities?
- What did they think they learnt?
- How much did they enjoy them?
- What did they remember most from the activity?

Now look at the work done by the children and critically reflect on this and the answers to the questions above. What does all this tell you about these children's learning?

SUMMARY

The approaches described in this unit are summarised in Table 3.3.1.

Learning is complex, so much so that no one view of learning can fully express this complexity. It is only by considering learning in a variety of ways that we can begin to gain a fuller understanding of its nature, and it is only by planning for such a variety of approaches to address learning as have been described in this unit that we can provide rich and inclusive classroom experiences for our children.

TABLE 3.3.1 Organising your classroom for learning

Approaches to organising your classroom	Learning focus	Broad learning objectives	Strengths	Challenges
Whole class, small group and individual teaching of literacy and numeracy	Basic skills acquisition	To teach fluency and confidence with reading and writing in literacy and with number and calculation in mathematics	An interactive approach where the importance of teacher modelling and high-quality dialogue between teachers and pupils is emphasised	Many teachers have had difficulty adopting fully interactive direct teaching; tendency to be used at whole class levels rather than with individuals or groups; little emphasis on learners own starting points
Constructive science investigations and explorations	Constructing understanding	To develop enquiry and investigative process skills; To develop children's own understandings of phenomena; To apply understandings to new contexts	Starts from children's ideas and perspectives, building on these using direct hands-on experience	Assumes children will notice experiences which don't fit their understandings, challenge their understandings and be able to restructure these to accommodate the new experiences
Group work; discussion; dialogical enquiry	Social learning	To develop collaborative and speaking and listening skills; To see things from different points of view; To develop critical and creative thinking; To develop children's own understandings of phenomena	Supports learners in constructing new meanings and understandings as they explore them together in words; allows learners to test out and criticise claims and different points of view as they speak and listen to others; and provides raw material for learners own thinking	Requires children to have certain basic skills and obey certain ground rules; sometimes difficult to organise; works best when children show areas of autonomous learning
Authentic activity and enquiry	Apprenticeship	To encourage children to act and see the world as scientists, historians, archaeologists, poets, and so on	Outward looking, considering learning as something which takes you outside the classroom; inspiring and motivating	Requires significant time to allow it to happen; often needs access to good quality resources; teachers need to feel confident and have some expertise in the area of activity or enquiry or be able to get in someone who has

ANNOTATED FURTHER READING

Hayes, D. (ed.) (2007) *Joyful Teaching and Learning in the Primary School*, Exeter: Learning Matters.
>This is an interesting take on teaching creatively that looks at a range of approaches to teaching, learning and organisation in different subject areas of the primary curriculum. Chapters that focus particularly on literacy and mathematics teaching in this book include Arthur Shenton's 'The joyful teaching of reading'and Nick Pratt's 'The joy of mathematics'.

Kelly, P. (2005) *Using Thinking Skills in the Primary Classroom*, London: Sage.
>This gives a more detailed consideration of social learning and apprenticeship approaches, together with a wide range of examples and many suggestions for enhancing practice.

Osborn, M., Broadfoot, P., McNess, E., Planel, C., Ravn, B. and Triggs, P. (2003) *A World of Difference? Comparing Learners Across Europe*, Maidenhead: Open University Press.
>Finally, international comparisons are always interesting in relation to classroom organisation. The ENCOMPASS project looked at primary teaching in Denmark, England and France, and this book describes the project and has a chapter on classroom contexts as a reflection of national values.

Pratt, N. (2006) *Interactive Maths Teaching in the Primary School*, London: Paul Chapman.
>This is a look at interactive mathematics teaching in detail.

M FURTHER READING TO SUPPORT M-LEVEL STUDY

Baines, E., Rubie-Davies, C. and Blatchford, P. (2009) 'Improving pupil group work interaction and dialogue in primary classrooms: results from a year-long intervention study', *Cambridge Journal of Education*, 39(1): 95-117.
>This is an interesting article that reports the findings of a study into the potential of group interaction to promote learning. The authors describe how they worked with teachers to develop strategies for enhancing pupil group work and dialogue, and to implement a pupil relational and group skills training programme. They argue that group work can be successfully implemented into everyday school classrooms and improve pupil interactions and high-level discussion, provided teachers take time to train pupils in relational and group working skills.

Webb, N.M., Franke, M.L., De, T., Chan, A.G., Freund, D., Shein, P. and Melkonian, D.K. (2009) '"Explain to your partner": teachers' instructional practices and students' dialogue in small groups', *Cambridge Journal of Education*, 39(1): 49-70.
>These researchers argue that collaborative group work has great potential to promote student learning, but that the role of the teacher in promoting effective group collaboration is often neglected. In their research, they examined the extent to which teachers pressed students to explain their thinking during their interventions with small groups and during whole-class discussions. They argue for teachers to focus on asking probing questions to uncover details of student thinking and problem-solving strategies, as this is of most benefit to student learning.

RELEVANT WEBSITES

Kings College, London: www.kcl.ac.uk/sspp/departments/education/research/crestem/Research/Current-Projects/CogAcc/Cognaccel.aspx
>Research into cognitive acceleration approaches such as CASE has been carried out at Kings College, London, and this site describes some of the work done.

Unicef Child Friendly Schools: www.unicef.org/cfs

> From a more global perspective, Unicef has developed an approach to education development that it calls 'Child Friendly Schools' and that highlights issues of quality in classroom provision and organisation.

International Democratic Education Network: www.idenetwork.org/index.htm

> As an alternative to mainstream educational approaches, Democratic Schools use organisational approaches that seek to give children a say in their own learning, and this site gives an overview. Summerhill School is perhaps the most famous such school; see: www.summerhillschool. co.uk/pages/

REFERENCES

Adey, P., Shayer, M. and Yates, C. (1995) *Thinking Science*, London: Nelson.

Bennett, N. (1995) Managing learning through group work, in C. Desforges (ed.) *An Introduction to Teaching: Psychological Perspectives*, Oxford: Blackwell.

Bobbit-Nolan, S. (1995) Teaching for autonomous learning, in C. Desforges (ed.) *An Introduction to Teaching: Psychological Perspectives*, Oxford, Blackwell.

Kelly, P. (2005) *Using Thinking Skills in the Primary Classroom*, London: Sage.

Mercer, N. (2000) *Words and Minds: How We Use Language to Think Together*, London: Routledge.

Wenger, E. (1998) *Communities of Practice: Learning, Meaning and Identity*, Cambridge: Cambridge University Press.

MANAGING CLASSROOM BEHAVIOUR

Roland Chaplain

INTRODUCTION

Effective classroom management is concerned with maximising pupil engagement with learning – hence, behaviour management, teaching and learning should be viewed as interdependent. The present unit focuses on how to produce a personalised classroom management plan (CMP), taking account of the multilevel nature of behaviour management (see Figure 3.4.1) and emphasising *preventative* rather than *reactive* strategies. Although the target of behavour management is to develop pupils' self-control, this will take more time with some classes and/or individual pupils than others. To address this, the focus shifts from initially establishing authority through teacher control to pupils taking greater responsibility for regulating their own behaviour. As with academic development, pupils of the same age differ in their social development – whereas some will arrive highly motivated to engage with learning, others will need more encouragement.

The Department for Education (2012a) sets out what newly qualified teachers are required to understand and practise in respect of behaviour management. The present author was a member of the DfE consultative group that produced these guidelines, and this unit will reflect key elements – namely, whole-school issues, self-management, teacher–pupil relationships, classroom structures and theoretical knowledge.

OBJECTIVES

By the end of this unit you should understand:

- the multilevel nature of behaviour management in school;
- how to develop your personal classroom management skills;
- how to develop a CMP;
- how to cope with more challenging behaviour;
- how theoretical and research-based evidence informs practice.

FROM WHOLE-SCHOOL ISSUES TO MANAGING CHALLENGING PUPILS

'The most effective schools seem to be those that have created a positive atmosphere based on a sense of community and shared values' (Elton Report, 1989). Achieving this requires attention to different levels of behaviour management, including whole-school issues, classroom management and managing challenging individuals (see Figure 3.4.1). Inconsistency between different levels offers pupils the opportunity to manipulate the system and generates ambiguity and stress for teachers and pupils.

By law, schools 'must ensure they have a strong behaviour policy to support staff in managing behaviour' (Department for Education, 2012b). Behaviour policies should reflect the views and aspirations of *all* stakeholders in a school, including pupils, parents, staff and managers (Chaplain, 1995).

Working with a group in a classroom can create the impression that you are operating in isolation, but *your* classroom is a component of the whole school system, which, through its policies and procedures, can facilitate or undermine your attempts to develop a positive classroom climate (Chaplain, 2003). Schools differ in their aims, expectations and principles and the procedures adopted to care for, control and educate pupils. Similarly structured schools, a few hundred yards apart, can differ substantially in these respects. Those with the right organisational climate can make a difference to pupils' success, despite negative environmental pressures (see Macbeath and Mortimore, 2001). However, the extent of school effects is questioned (Goldstein and Woodhouse, 2000).

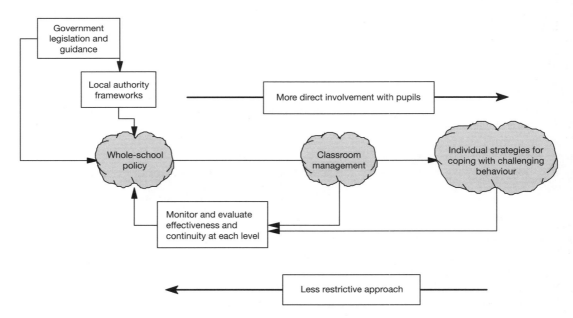

FIGURE 3.4.1 The multilevel model of behaviour management

Note: The whole-school policy is the standard with which both classroom management and individual strategies are compared. As the management function moves from left to right, so does the level of intrusiveness or direct control over pupil behaviour.

Task 3.4.1 Whole-school approaches to behaviour management

Obtain a copy of the behaviour policy from your school and consider the following questions:

* Are the core school rules explicit?
* Does it encourage pupils to make a positive contribution to the school?
* Did pupils participate in developing the school's expectations?
* Are the expectations realistic and teachable?
* Are they in keeping with your own beliefs and theories about managing behaviour?
* What rewards exist for those pupils who behave as expected?
* What sanctions (punishments) exist for those who do not?
* Is there a clear hierarchy of rewards and sanctions?

Compare your school's policy with that of a peer and consider the following:

* In what ways are they similar?
* In what ways are they different?
* How are the school values promoted in school (e.g. through assemblies)?

Task 3.4.2 Understanding disruptive behaviour

Make a list of the disruptive behaviours that cause you most concern. Put them in order of priority, with the most concerning first, and estimate how regularly you think they occur.

Now observe and record how often each actually occurs in your classroom. You can do this using a simple observation pro forma – a number of these can be found in *Pupil Behaviour* (Chaplain, 1995a).

Did your initial perception of their frequency or duration match your observations?

Now list the strategies you plan to use in order to cope with low-level disruptive behaviours.

TEACHER STRESS, PUPIL BEHAVIOUR AND CLASSROOM CONTROL

Teaching is considered to be one of the top three most stressful professions (Health and Safety Executive, 2000). Among the potential stressors in teaching, managing pupil behaviour has been consistently rated as the most stressful element for both trainee and experienced teachers (Chaplain, 1995b, 2008; Mastrilli and Sardo-Brown, 2002). Despite disruptive pupil behaviour being the most common stressor for teachers, many still report being very satisfied with their work (Goldstein, 1995). The main sources of satisfaction for teachers come from features inherent to the job, such as pupils' achievements and positive relationships with pupils (Chaplain, 1995b; Lam and Yan, 2011). Hence, although pupil 'behaviour' is a primary source of stress, it is also the principal source of satisfaction.

Although teachers usually rate extreme behaviour (physical and verbal assault) as their biggest concern, it is relatively rare in the regular classroom. In contrast, low-level disruptive behaviours (e.g. talking out of turn, pupils getting out of their seats, not having equipment, fiddling with equipment) are regularly experienced by many teachers (Elton Report, 1989; Office for Standards in Education, 2006). The cumulative effect can be very stressful. These 'daily hassles' (Kanner *et al.*, 1981) are usually offset by 'daily uplifts', most notably in the form of positive feedback from pupils.

Task 3.4.3 Analysing your strengths and weaknesses

Audit and list your resources (personal strengths) and concerns (potential stressors). Now identify which factors you believe you *can* change, and those outside your control. Consider what changes to make and identify what support you need to cope with the unchangeable.

Task 3.4.4 Causal explanations of misbehaviour

What do you consider to be the main causes of disruptive behaviour?

- **Within pupil** – personality/temperament, part of growing up, children are intrinsically naughty, lack of self-control?
- **Within school** – irrelevant curriculum, teachers' incompetence, poorly managed schools, teachers' attitudes?
- **Within the community** – poor parenting, poverty, lack of discipline in the home/community/society?
- Other reasons.

List your explanations in order of priority. Consider the implications of your explanation. 'Within pupil' and 'within the community' factors are least under your control and hardest to change. In contrast, 'within school' factors are controllable by teachers and, therefore, easier to change. If you found yourself blaming factors outside your control, you are not alone – Lawrence and Steed (1986) found that 78 per cent of teachers blamed misbehaviour on issues outside their control (see also Miller *et al.*, 2000, for pupils' perspectives on the causes of misbehaviour).

MANAGING YOURSELF

Effective classroom management requires attention to what you say and how you say it; checking you are being understood; looking and feeling confident; self-belief in your abilities; and communicating your authority and status as a teacher through verbal and non-verbal behaviour (Chaplain, 2003). Although verbal and, particularly, non-verbal behaviours are central to managing behaviour, they are not always under conscious control. You may plan to communicate something to someone, but, when under pressure, fail, because of emotional interference or lack of confidence (Chaplain, 2003). You will have observed people's habits when feeling under pressure – looking 'nervous', coughing, fidgeting or playing with their hair.

I have observed several teachers saying 'shush' or 'erm' when trying to gain the attention of the class – to no avail. They are busily 'shushing', but the pupils carry on talking – something teachers often do not realise until I show them the video evidence, which surprises them as they were not *aware* of their behaviour. They can remember pupils misbehaving, but nothing about their ineffective *habit*. We are all aware of being told to 'shush' as a young child, and it may indeed work effectively for some teachers – the problem arises when over-learned, 'automatic' responses are ineffective, and we are unaware of using them. Other ineffective strategies retained from childhood that may emerge when we feel under pressure include shouting, screaming and losing our temper. Overcoming such behaviours requires first becoming aware of them (e.g. by videoing yourself), then identifying and over-learning alternative behaviours when not under pressure – taking an active, objective role in self-regulation to improve your skills (see Chaplain, 2003: chapter 3).

Task 3.4.5 Monitoring professional social skills

Video yourself (not your pupils) teaching one or more of your lessons. This can be done subtly using a laptop with an integral camera.

- Was your verbal and non-verbal behaviour as you believed it to be?
- Did you convey all the material that you planned?
- Were your instructions clear?
- Did you check for understanding?

Now plan what changes to make and practise them away from the classroom, and then video yourself again, to monitor change.

There are a number of psychological characteristics that distinguish teachers who cope effectively from those who are regularly distressed attempting to manage pupil behaviour. These characteristics include personality, emotional regulation and self-presentation. Here, I will focus on two specific qualities – locus of control and self-efficacy.

Believing you are able to influence important events in your life ('locus of control'; Rotter, 1966) is central to effective coping. People who believe they can influence important events (internal locus) tend to cope far better than those who believe other people control important decisions for them (external locus). When making your CMP, you should differentiate between factors over which you have control and those over which you have no control. However, sometimes we can overestimate perceived lack of control over situations. Trainee teachers are often reluctant to modify the classroom environment – for example, changing the seating layout – despite being aware that existing arrangements are creating management difficulties for them. Their reason for not making changes is usually because it is 'someone else's' classroom. However, I have yet to meet a mentor who, when asked, said they would not permit a trainee to change the room settings. Hence, this could be brought under the trainee's control simply by the trainee asking if it's OK to move things around to help them teach more effectively.

Teacher self-efficacy is 'a teacher's belief in his or her skills and abilities to be an effective teacher' (Swars, 2005: 139). It is concerned with the question, can I do this? High teacher efficacy is linked to teachers who persist when under pressure (Tschannen-Moran and Woolfolk Hoy, 2001), especially when dealing with challenging behaviour (Cudré-Mauroux, 2011), and who generate more positive and orderly classroom climates (Moore and Esselman, 1992). These differences are consistent among both experienced and trainee teachers with positive correlations between high efficacy and the use of positive classroom management strategies (Gibbs and Powell, 2011) and engagement with learning. In contrast, low self-efficacy is related to lower tolerance of disruptive behaviour and a greater willingness to seek removal of problem children from the classroom (Stanovich and Jordan, 2004). Teachers with positive self-beliefs have a positive effect on pupil engagement – even with regularly disruptive pupils (Chaplain, 2003).

Trainee teachers, unsure of their untested capabilities in managing behaviour, can experience self-doubt and anxiety (Ng *et al.*, 2010), and 'it is difficult to achieve much while fighting self-doubt' (Bandura, 1993: 118).

I observed a trainee teaching a lesson on the four rules of number. She admitted to being anxious (after the lesson) about teaching maths and had decided to write down all her workings on a card, which she held in her hand, checking everything before responding to children's answers or writing examples on the board. However, this behaviour prevented her from maximising interaction with the class (limited eye contact, staying near the whiteboard, talking with her back to the class), because she kept looking at the card. As the lesson progressed, she began confirming pupils' answers to the most elementary calculations from her card (for fear of getting them wrong). Her anxiety arose from her (false) beliefs in her capability in maths (given the examples were all within her ability), undermining her ability to cope. To overcome this problem, she was advised to write worked examples on a flipchart before the lesson (covering the answers with post-it shapes). With the answers available but covered, she could scan the room, move to different areas – by getting pupils to remove the post-it notes – and so maintain the flow of the lesson and project more confidence. A positive teacher efficacy means we think, feel and behave in a more confident manner (Woolfolk Hoy *et al.*, 2009), making pupils feel secure and more likely to respond positively.

Anxiety can make us feel physically tense, removing a valuable non-verbal behaviour – smiling. So make an effort to smile, write a prompt on your plan to remind you of a joke or something that makes you feel good. With classes who are difficult, it can be easy to slip into a negative mindset. It is best to meet such groups at the door. Smile and compliment them. Keep it light hearted. *Do not* linger on the previous unpleasant lesson with a 'I do not want a repeat of the last lesson . . .'. Start each day with a blank slate.

However being overly confident can lead to complacency. Weinstein (1988) found that trainee teachers had unrealistic optimism in thinking that the problems others experienced managing pupil behaviour would not happen to them. Furthermore, Emmer and Aussiker (1990) found that trainee teachers who had difficulty managing classes still had unrealistic beliefs about their ability to control behaviour, which McLaughlin (1991) attributed to the conflict between wanting to care for pupils and the need to control the class. Weinstein (1988) concluded that trainee teachers needed to recognise that care and control can be brought about through teaching well and creating safe, orderly classrooms and should not be viewed as oppositional.

Being self- and context-aware, having realistic and achievable expectations of yourself and your pupils, being prepared to learn through accumulating knowledge from research, and developing your interpersonal skills lead to improved self-efficacy. This will be further enhanced should you find yourself placed with a knowledgeable mentor who is sufficiently experienced in training new teachers (Chaplain, 2008).

Self-monitoring is useful for determining how *all* your behaviours contribute to how you manage your class. Changing how you think, feel and behave is not easy and may feel uncomfortable; the benefits make it worthwhile, but it requires practice to overcome established ineffective habits.

Task 3.4.6 Assess your self-efficacy

Complete Table 3.4.1 by indicating your level of confidence for each area. You should score yourself on a scale of 1–7, with 7 being very confident in your capability, and 1 being not at all confident in your capability.

TABLE 3.4.1 Teaching efficacy rating scale

	Not at all confident ◄——————► Very confident						
	1	2	3	4	5	6	7
Managing whole-class teaching	1	2	3	4	5	6	7
Managing group work	1	2	3	4	5	6	7
Managing pupils with behaviour problems	1	2	3	4	5	6	7
Managing PE lessons	1	2	3	4	5	6	7
Managing aggressive pupils	1	2	3	4	5	6	7
Managing distressed pupils	1	2	3	4	5	6	7
Motivating apathetic pupils	1	2	3	4	5	6	7
Managing low-level disruptive behaviour (e.g. talking out of turn)	1	2	3	4	5	6	7
Teaching your subject(s)*	1	2	3	4	5	6	7

*If you teach more than one subject, indicate your confidence level with each.

- What evidence do you have to support your perceptions?
- Reflect on those areas in which you feel least confident (where you scored 1 or 2) – what resources and/or support do you need in order to raise your self-efficacy in those areas?
- What might prevent you from actively raising your efficacy levels?
- Retest yourself at the end of a term – have your ratings changed, and, if so, why?
- How will you determine improvement – by intuition or by measuring changes in pupil behaviour?
- Do you need to reset your priorities?

DEVELOPING A CLASSROOM MANAGEMENT PLAN

A CMP is not dissimilar to your lesson plan, and specifies:

- how you will organise your classroom for different lessons, including seating arrangements to minimise off-task behaviour;
- your planned classroom behaviour strategies – tactics to deter disruptive (proactive); responses to pupils who occasionally slip off task (reorientation); and responses to more persistent off-task behaviour (reactive) (See Table 3.4.2);
- rewards and sanctions you will use (check they are compatible with your school systems);
- your verbal and non-verbal behaviour;
- contextual priorities (e.g. challenging behaviour).

Your CMP should be informed by, and *reflect*, the expectations of your school's behaviour policy.

TABLE 3.4.2 Classroom behaviour strategies

Preventative tactics	Reorientation tactics	Reactive tactics
Make sure your lessons are interesting	Gaze – sustained eye contact to inform pupils you are aware of what they are doing	Caution – inform what will happen should the unwanted behaviour persist
Teach and reinforce rules and routines	Posture and gesture – use to complement gaze, e.g. raised eyebrow, raised first finger, hands on hips	Remove privileges, e.g. ban from use of the computer or miss a trip
Be clear about what behaviour you expect from your pupils – reinforce and check for understanding	Space invasion – the closer you are to pupils the more control you will have – do not hide behind your desk or 'glue' yourself to the whiteboard – the classroom is your domain to move around as you wish	Require pupil to complete extra work during break times
Be alert to changes based on perceptions of pupils' non-verbal and verbal behaviours (e.g. too quiet/too loud, eye movements, looking out of window)	Restate rules – remind pupils about what is expected	Time out as arranged with colleague or manager in advance – avoid having disruptive pupils wandering around the school – it is of no help to anybody
Scanning – think about positioning in respect of being able to see the whole class at all times to quickly respond to potential disruption	Use individual encouragement to get pupils back on task – 'You have been doing really well so far . . .'	Contract – agree with pupil specific expectations and record successes – review and adjust as necessary
Going up a gear in anticipation of a disruptive event, e.g. new pupils, time of year	Name-dropping – we are all sensitive to hearing our name even when there are several conversations going on – mentioning a non-attentive pupil's name while you are talking will usually get their attention – supplement this, if necessary, with gestures	Removal from class temporarily – working elsewhere in school or with another class
Being enthusiastic even when you're not!	Praising peers in the vicinity of someone off task can be effective, provided the pupil values being praised by you – usually most effective with younger pupils	Suspension from school
Manipulating classroom layout, e.g. planned seating arrangements	Humour – pupils like teachers with a sense of humour, so make use of yours – but not by ridiculing pupils – and ensure it is appropriate to pupils' levels of development	
Using appropriate reward systems for on-task behaviour	Maintain the flow of the lesson by carrying on teaching while moving round the room, using non-verbal gestures and removing anything being played with (e.g. pens) avoid being distracted from what you have to say	
Awareness of pupils' goals		
Getting lesson timings right		

Note: These are some examples of effective tactics, but you should modify to suit your teaching styles and the expectations of your school's behaviour policy.

How you structure your CMP is a matter of personal choice – you may have a separate plan or, alternatively, integrate with your general lesson plan. Do remember to keep a separate, detailed record of different strategies you have tried and their success rate, for future planning.

MAKING AN EARLY IMPACT ON YOUR CLASS

We form impressions of other people in a few seconds (Ambady and Rosenthal, 1993), and these impressions often remain unchanged for long periods of time. Hence, the first part of your CMP should consider the type of impression you wish to make. In your early visits to the classroom, you will be observing, which can feel uncomfortable, as pupils are inquisitive and will want to know all about you, weighing you up. You will want to settle in and learn the ropes, but do not be too friendly with the pupils, as you will eventually have to establish your authority with the whole class. This is not to suggest you should be standoffish or hostile – just remember to convey your status and authority as a teacher. Your first lesson may be relaxed, with pupils being quite passive (Ball, 1980), but, at some point, they will test your ability to establish and maintain behavioural limits, so make sure you are clear about your expectations and convey them to your pupils.

It is essential to pay attention to detail, especially in your early lessons. Your CMP should detail how you will:

- teach and reinforce your behavioural expectations;
- teach and reinforce classroom routines;
- use verbal and non-verbal behaviours to control the class – especially at critical points in the lesson (see Table 3.4.2);
- reward required behaviour (see Table 3.4.3);
- respond to disruptive behaviour (see Table 3.4.3);
- organise the physical layout of the classroom.

These procedures are not exclusive to early lessons, as they represent good, professional practice. Adjust your learning plans and CMP over time, as your relationship with classes changes and you become more practised – experiment and rise to new challenges.

CONVEYING YOUR EXPECTATIONS: RULES AND ROUTINES

All lessons have similar patterns; for example, getting the attention of the class, conveying information, managing feedback, managing transitions, monitoring and responding to unwanted behaviour, and so on. Whether your teaching is enhanced or undermined by any or all of the above depends on devising and applying appropriate, enforceable and effective rules and routines. Rules set the limits to pupils' behaviour (Charles, 1999). Whereas whole-school (core) rules are designed primarily to produce harmonious relationships among pupils, the main purpose of classroom rules is to maximise pupil engagement with learning. Effective rules provide pupils with a physically and psychologically safe, predictable environment (Chaplain, 2003) and work in a preventative way to establish and keep order and maintain momentum through the lesson. To gain maximum effect, rules should be:

- **positively worded** – tell pupils what they *can do* rather than what they *cannot do*, e.g. 'be polite', as opposed to 'don't be rude'; negatively framed rules are not effective long term (Becker *et al.*, 1975);
- **few in number** – long lists of rules will not be remembered – focus on key concerns, e.g. follow directions; keep hands, feet and objects to yourself; I would recommend having no more than five;

- **realistic** – have rules that are age-appropriate, enforceable and achievable by your pupils;
- **focused on key issues** – personal safety, safety of others, cooperation and facilitating learning;
- **applied consistently** – intermittent or selective reinforcement of rules will render them ineffective; for instance, if putting hands up to answer questions is a rule, and you respond positively to those pupils who shout out a *very* competent answer, then reprimand someone else for shouting out an unsophisticated answer, you are sending out mixed and unhelpful messages to pupils.

TABLE 3.4.3 Examples of hierarchical rewards and sanctions

Rewards	Example	Sanctions	Example
Verbal praise private	Quiet word, 'John that's excellent work'	Gesture	Raised first finger, thumbs down
Verbal praise public	Teacher and class applaud individual	Prolonged gaze	Hold eye contact (with frown)
Public display of positive behaviours	Star/points chart – cumulative points; gets postcard to parents	Rule reminder	'What do we do when we want to ask a question?'
Classroom awards	Certificates, badges or superstar of the day/week award	Physical proximity	Move closer to pupil – perhaps stand behind him/her – say nothing
Contact home (either for accumulated star/points or exceptional good behaviour)	Notes/cards/phone calls	Verbal reprimand	'I am very unhappy with your behaviour'
		Public display	Remove points from star chart
Special privileges	Helping around school, attending an event	Separate from group in class or keep back at playtime	Adjust length of time to suit needs/age of pupil
Tangible rewards	Book token, sweets, pens	Record name	Write name on board
School award	Certificates, tokens	Removal from classroom	Teach outside normal teaching area
		Refer to SMT	Send to deputy (as per school policy)
		Contact parents	Letter/phone home
		Invite parents to school	For informal/formal discussion
		Behavioural contract	Short, focused on specific expectations
		Separation from group	Individual teaching or special class
		Suspension	For an agreed period
		Review contract	As a basis for return
		Exclusion	

When taking over a class from another teacher, it is important to consider his or her expectations in relation to your own, and whether this will affect the way in which you establish your rules. If you adopt the rules of the existing teacher, do not assume the pupils will necessarily respond in the same way to you – they will not inevitably associate you with a particular rule – so teach the behaviour you require explicitly, even if it means repeating what they may already know.

Display your rules prominently and keep reminding pupils about them subtly until they are established. Be creative, perhaps using cartoons or pictures to liven up your display.

Task 3.4.7 Rules and expectations

- Think of four or five essential rules that embody your behavioural expectations.
- Look again at the school behaviour policy – are your expectations similar?
- Discuss with your classroom teacher/mentor how he/she originally established rules with the class.
- Do you feel confident applying them?
- What, if any, changes would you make?
- Justify your changes.

USING ROUTINES TO MAXIMISE ON-TASK ACTIVITY

Schools, like most organisations, operate through a series of established routines. Although rules provide the framework for the conduct of lessons, they are few in number, and so teachers rely on many routines to provide the link between expectations and action. Routines are usually organised around times, places and contexts. Effective teachers spend considerable time in their early encounters with their classes teaching them routines (Emmer and Worsham, 2005), which, when practised, become automatic, leaving more time for teaching. Jones and Jones (1990) found that up to 50 per cent of some lessons was lost to non-teaching routines, such as getting out equipment and marking work, and so efficient routines provide a real learning bonus. The following paragraphs consider pivotal routines in more detail.

Entering the classroom

How pupils enter your classroom sets the scene for the lesson – charging noisily into a room is not the best way to start a lesson, so consider how you might control this initial movement. One way is to greet your pupils at the door, look pleased to see them and remind them what they are expected to do when they go into class. Have an engaging activity waiting for them that has a time limit and is, preferably, linked to a reward. Physically standing by the door reduces the likelihood of pupils charging in, but, if they do, call them back and make them repeat the procedure correctly.

Getting the attention of the class

This can be done by using verbal or other noises, silence or puppets.

- **Using noise** – such as ringing bells, tapping the desk, clapping, asking pupils to show their hands or sit up straight. Which method you choose depends on your personal style and school policy.

However, make sure that you explain beforehand what the signal is and what you want pupils to do when they hear it. I witnessed one teacher, working with a 'lively' class, use a tambourine to gain attention part way through the lesson, but the teacher had omitted to let pupils know beforehand. Although it made everyone jump (including me!), it was not associated with any required behaviour. A more effective method would have been to tell the class in advance, 'Whenever I bang the tambourine I want you all to stop what you are doing and look at me'.

- **Using silence** – some teachers find they can gain attention using non-verbal signals, such as folding their arms, putting hands on hips, raising eyebrows or frowning. Using non-verbal gestures can be very powerful – indeed, the more you use body language to manage behaviour the better, as it minimises disruption to the flow of your lesson. However, to be effective, it requires you to feel confident about your presence and to *teach* the pupils to associate a particular behaviour with a particular expectation.
- **Using puppets** – a large, figurative hand puppet can be very effective in behaviour management (see puppetsbypost.com). Introduce the puppet and say that it will only come out if everyone is quiet – because it is nervous. If the noise level gets too high, put the puppet away. Snail puppets that only emerge if pupils are behaving as required are also excellent. They can also be used as a reward; for example, the best-behaved group is allowed to have the puppet sitting at its table. Pupils are usually very attentive and empathetic towards puppets, so they can be used to aid the pupils' socio-emotional development. We have had excellent results when using them with pupils from Foundation Stage to Year 6.

Briefing

Take time to ensure that pupils understand exactly what is required from them at each stage of the lesson – unless you want those pupils who find it hard to pay attention wasting time asking other pupils what they should be doing. Taking time in your first lessons may be difficult if you are anxious about being in the spotlight – if this is so, use prompts to remind yourself to speak slowly and carefully (writing 'SLOW' on your lesson notes). Write instructions, key words and questions on the board to support your verbal inputs – *do so before the lesson*, so that you can maintain eye contact and scan the whole class while briefing them. You might also consider using consistent, colour-coded writing to differentiate instructions, key words, questions, etc., so that pupils recognise more easily what is expected of them.

Distributing equipment

Issuing equipment in advance can create a distraction, with pupils fiddling with it while you are talking – whereas issuing it after you have finished talking can disrupt a settled group. Choosing which one to use depends on how the class responds to you and each other. If you issue equipment in advance, make sure you tell pupils beforehand not to touch the equipment, rather than having to correct afterwards. Always check all your equipment before the lesson – do not assume that people will have returned the electrical experiment kit complete with wires untangled, otherwise you may find yourself spending 20 minutes sorting it out, giving pupils the opportunity to misbehave.

Moving bodies

Often overlooked when planning lessons, keeping control of pupils on the move, both in and out of the classroom, requires careful planning if it is to be efficient and safe. Always specify in advance exactly what you require people to do (including supporting adults). If moving a class to a different location, think before the lesson about the group dynamics in the same way you would plan a learning activity. Plan where to position yourself in relation to the group to maintain your view of everyone you are responsible for. Reinforce those individuals who are behaving correctly to encourage the other pupils to copy them.

Checking for understanding

Throughout your lesson, check that pupils are clear about your expectations. Where appropriate, support your verbal instructions with written ones – especially when working with pupils who have attention difficulties. Avoid repeatedly asking the same child or group and encourage all pupils to ask relevant questions if in doubt.

Task 3.4.8 Classroom routines

- List the routines you consider important in your classroom. How do you plan to teach them to your pupils?
- Make a list of your key routines and rate them in terms of efficiency.
- Do they work?
- Could they be made more efficient?

REWARDS AND SANCTIONS

The existence of rules and routines does not guarantee they will be followed. For them to be established and maintained, they need to be reinforced. From a psychological perspective, a reinforcer is any consequence that strengthens the behaviour it follows (see Figure 3.4.2). In contrast, a sanction (punishment) is any consequence that reduces or stops undesirable behaviour. Behaviour may be reinforced by a reward (e.g., praise or food), but may also be reinforced by what a *teacher* thinks is punishment. For example, telling a pupil off for persistent calling out in class provides the pupil with individual attention. Hence, it can be reinforcing and result in repetition of the behaviour to gain more attention. The Teaching Agency now requires trainee teachers to 'know how to apply rewards and sanctions to improve behaviour' (Department for Education, 2012a). To be effective requires attention to detail that is following the principles of the behavioural approach (see Porter, 2006, for a comprehensive review of behavioural and cognitive behavioural approaches).

Rewards and sanctions need to be fit for purpose – the reward must be something the pupils like, and the sanction(s) something they do not like. It is unwise to assume that *you* know what pupils like or do not like. One way of discovering what pupils' value is to ask them to complete a simple 'All about me' questionnaire, in which they indicate their favourite subjects, lessons, hobbies, music, sports and learning styles.

Reinforcing acceptable behaviour does not mean issuing rewards haphazardly; rather, they should be managed through a reinforcement schedule. See Table 3.4.3 for examples of reinforcers and sanctions. Initially, an abstract reinforcer, such as praise, could be given for every occurrence of the desired behaviour, but then, over time, given intermittently to maintain effectiveness (see Figure 3.4.3 for an outline of the process). Praise should be warm and natural, appropriate to the pupil's level of development, varied and creative. However, until you have established a working relationship with the class, it is useful to use tangible rewards alongside praising the required behaviour – the

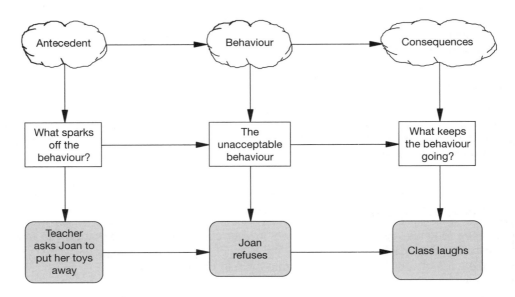

FIGURE 3.4.2 An A–B–C model of behaviour

reward being accessed by acquiring points, stars or raffle tickets. The raffle tickets are particularly effective, as any pupil who earns at least one ticket has a chance of winning, unlike points systems, where some individuals will conclude that they can never win a prize. Whenever you issue a point, star or ticket, praise the pupil's *specific* behaviour simultaneously. In that way, they will learn to associate praise from you with a rewarding experience, a process known as contiguity.

Always make reference to the specific behaviour and not the pupil when issuing rewards or sanctions, e.g., 'I am pleased to see everyone on this table has put all their equipment back in the correct place'. Share the rewards for positive behaviour with the whole class; with difficult pupils, focus on catching them behaving as required, however rare that might be in the early days. When punishing unacceptable behaviour, do so in a way that suggests disappointment in having to do so, rather than anger or contempt. Encourage more withdrawn pupils to contribute by building waiting time into your questions: 'I am going to be asking about X in five minutes, so start thinking about it now'. Teach more enthusiastic pupils to wait their turn, without disengaging them from learning: 'Thanks for putting your hand up all the time, Kylie, but I am going to ask someone else to answer this one'.

Make a list of your planned sanctions and familiarise yourself with them; keep them to hand as reference to avoid using higher-order sanctions prematurely, especially when you feel under pressure. Furthermore, when threatening sanctions, always offer the opportunity to respond positively. For example, 'Jack, you have left your seat again, despite being reminded of the rule. Now you can either sit down and stay there or stay in at break for five minutes.' Should Jack continue to ignore the rule say, 'Jack, you are already staying in for five minutes, now either sit down or you will be staying a further five minutes.' Whatever sanction you threaten, be sure to carry it through, otherwise a future repetition of the unwanted behaviour is more likely.

Plan to start each new day on a positive note, whatever happened the day before – feeling negative in advance will focus your attention on negative behaviour, which will produce a cyclical event, reflecting negativity in your behaviour, generating further negative pupil behaviour, and so on.

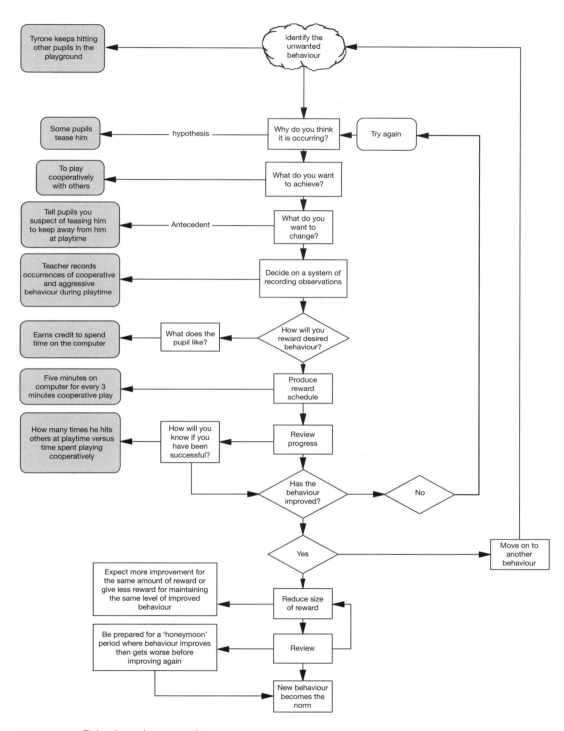

FIGURE 3.4.3 Behaviour change cycle

CLASSROOM LAYOUT

There is evidence to demonstrate a correlation between seating arrangements and pupil behaviour (Steer, 2005). For example, sitting boys with girls tends to reduce disruption (Merrett, 1993), and children organised in rows tend to be less disruptive than when organised in groups (Wheldall and Lam, 1987). However, these findings need to be considered in relation to the nature of the learning task and the level of academic and social functioning of the children (see, for example, Finn and Pannozzo, 2004).

Movement around the classroom should be free-flowing. Where this is not the case, there is potential for disruption – some individuals will use every opportunity to push past, nudge or dislodge the chair or whiteboard of other pupils (Chaplain, 2003).

Task 3.4.9 Classroom layout

Consider the layout of your classroom. Is there sufficient room to move easily between the furniture?

Make a drawing of the classroom and cut out the various pieces of furniture. Try moving them around to see which arrangement gives the least disruptive flow around the room. Try this online classroom layout design tool: http://classroom.4teachers.org/

Where is the best place to stand to address the whole group? (Do not assume it is by the whiteboard.) Can you scan the whole room easily from where you stand when teaching?

Monitor your movement during a lesson (video record or ask someone to record your movements) – do you spend equal amounts of time with each group?

How might you organise your tables so as to make the transition from group work to pairs most efficient?

COPING WITH CHALLENGING BEHAVIOUR

Some pupils will persistently challenge your authority, with behaviour ranging from defiance and refusal to work to physical and verbal aggression. Members of such groups are heterogeneous and include pupils with temporary difficulties as well as persistent difficulties, e.g., ADHD or other behavioural emotional or social difficulty, who may require specialist interventions.

When dealing with challenging behaviour, do not interpret such behaviour as a personal 'assault' – pupils seldom behave this way because they hate you, and you will gain nothing if you get angry. Instead, reprimand pupils in an assertive way. Do not become preoccupied with descriptive categories (e.g. ADHD) - focus on the behaviour itself and record carefully what they do, when and where they do it - making sure you *include positive behaviour*, however infrequent. Keeping a record of positive behaviours not only provides an uplift when times are tense, but also gives useful insight into the pupil's currency - i.e. what motivates them to behave appropriately. A useful tool for observing challenging behaviour is the strengths and difficulties questionnaire available free from www.sdqinfo.com.

Keep things in perspective and do not lose your sense of humour. Managing challenging pupils can require considerable effort and can be frustrating, which inhibits problem-solving and creativity.

It is not uncommon for teachers to question their own ability and lower self-efficacy, which reflects in their behaviour – a change that pupils recognise and respond to negatively – making the situation worse. Finding humour in the situation can be sufficient to influence events positively (Molnar and Lindquist, 1989). Focus on controlling your emotions and on believing that the situation can be coped with, if not completely controlled. Even situations that are so awful that you have to grin and bear it won't last forever. Do not be afraid to ask for help with extreme pupils, especially where physical aggression is involved. If you anticipate an aversive reaction (e.g. aggressive outburst) to a particular event, arrange for a supportive adult to be around in advance of that time.

The DfE recently issued guidelines on restraining aggressive pupils, and details can be found on www.education.gov.uk/publications/standard/publicationDetail/Page1/DFE-00028-2012. Fortunately, such occurrences are rare, and most common behaviours can be dealt with through developing your knowledge of established interventions (see Chaplain and Smith, 2006).

Dealing with challenging behaviour requires attention to several issues, including the following:

*   **Be consistent** with whatever approach you adopt. Challenging pupils are looking for structure and security and will repeatedly challenge you until they realise you mean business. They act like people playing slot machines and will keep pressing your buttons until they hit the jackpot (make you angry). Do not let them – keep calm and focused. Remember, there are no quick fixes, so prepare for the long haul!
*   **Classroom organisation** – seating arrangements. Position challenging pupils near the front, so that there are no pupils between them and you to distract or provide an audience. This places you in close proximity while addressing the class, making monitoring and controlling their behaviour easier, for example through direct eye contact and using hand gestures. Putting aggressive pupils with groups for *all* activities is likely to create disruption, as they may cause arguments and fights, or make bullets for others to fire. This is not to suggest that they should live in isolation, but think about the nature of the learning task and (classroom permitting) try having them work on separate tables for individual tasks.
*   **Learning** – carefully organise their time and the sequencing/size of their learning tasks. If concentration is an issue, break down their learning into smaller, achievable, progressive units, vary the tasks, emphasise visual learning, use colours and shapes to help them organise their work and change their tasks frequently. It is also helpful to have a clock visible and indicate how long they are required to stay on task; the clock provides a visual reference point and helps maintain focus. Specify exactly what you want them to do and provide visual reminders of important instructions.
*   **Support** – where you have a teaching assistant, plan in advance who will deal with a disruptive pupil and who will take responsibility for the rest of the class – this eliminates ambiguity and inconsistency.
*   **Changing behaviour** – focus on observable behaviour and avoid describing a pupil as 'always badly behaved'. List the behaviours causing concern, then gather detailed observations of what occurs before the unwanted behaviour (antecedent), the behaviour itself and what happens afterwards (consequence), along with how frequently it occurs (see Figure 3.4.2).

Use your observations to hypothesise why the pupil is behaving in this way – in Figure 3.4.2, it could be the antecedent (asking Joan to put her toys away) or the consequences (other pupils laughing when she defies you). Next, decide what you want Joan to do instead of being defiant and what to reward her with for behaving appropriately. The process requires attention to detail and is outlined in Figure 3.4.3. (For detailed practical methods to help pupils' develop self-control, see Chaplain and Freeman, 1998; Chaplain, 2003; Chaplain and Smith, 2006.)

SUMMARY

This unit has outlined some key factors to consider when developing your CMP. It is essential to keep in mind that effective classroom behaviour management is strongly influenced by whole-school attitudes and practices, as well as your interpersonal skills and classroom organisation. Additional reading has been provided to assist you in extending your knowledge of the relevant areas, which you are strongly recommended to do in order to advance your behaviour management skills.

ANNOTATED FURTHER READING

Canter, L. and Canter, M. (2001) *Assertive Discipline: Positive Behavior Management for Today's Classroom)*, Los Angeles, CA: Canter & Associates.
> Although aimed at the US market, this text offers helpful guidance on developing a discipline plan and managing difficult behaviour.

Chaplain, R. (2003) *Teaching Without Disruption in the Primary School: A Model for Managing Behaviour*, London: RoutledgeFalmer.
> A comprehensive account of the theory and practice of behaviour management, including whole-school issues, classroom management and how to cope with challenging pupils.

Porter, L. (2006) *Behaviour in Schools: Theory and Practice for Teachers*, Buckingham: Open University Press.
> A useful sourcebook reviewing some key theories on behaviour management, their underlying philosophy and practical application.

Robertson, J. (1996) *Effective Classroom Control: Understanding Teacher–Student Relationships*, London: Hodder and Stoughton.
> Advice on establishing and maintaining authority in the classroom, with an emphasis on non-verbal communication.

FURTHER READING TO SUPPORT M-LEVEL STUDY

Guo, Y., Justice, L.M., Sawyer, B. and Tompkins, V. (2011) 'Exploring factors related to preschool teachers' self-efficacy', *Teaching and Teacher Education*, 27: 961–8.
> This study examined the relationship between preschool teachers' efficacy and pupil's engagement with learning using a quantitative methodology. The findings highlight the relationship between teacher collaboration with colleagues, pupil engagement and teacher efficacy. Social support from colleagues has also been identified as an important buffer to stress. The authors also question whether increased teaching experience necessarily results in improved teaching skills or increased sense of efficacy.

Sanson, A., Hemphill, S. and Smart, D. (2004) 'Connections between temperament and social development: A review', *Social Development*, 13: 142–70.
> Although sociocultural experiences affect social development, this paper reviews research into the role of temperament in childrens' social development. Temperament is an important stable behavioural style, observed in children from an early age, and is concerned with a child's ability to pay attention, impulsiveness, anger and emotional control, and it has implications for the development of behaviour problems in school. The review considers a wide range of methodological issues, including operational definitions and cross-discipline findings.

RELEVANT WEBSITES

Department for Education – Behaviour and Discipline in Schools (2012): www.education.gov.uk/aboutdfe/advice/f0076803/behaviour-and-discipline-in-schools-a-guide-for-headteachers-and-school-staff]
> This site contains advice and information for teachers (and heads and governors) on behaviour and discipline in schools, including an overview of staff powers and duties.

Department for Education – Ensuring Good Behaviour in Schools (2012): www.education.gov.uk/aboutdfe/advice/f0076882/ensuring-good-behaviour-in-schools
> Outlines the government's plans to support teachers in providing a safe and structured environment for effective teaching and learning.

REFERENCES

Ambady, N. and Rosenthal, R. (1993) 'Half a minute: predicting teacher evaluations from thin slices of behaviour and physical attractiveness', *Journal of Personality and Social Psychology*, 64: 431–41.

Ball, S.J. (1980) 'Initial encounters in the classroom and the process of establishment', in P. Woods (ed.) *Pupil Strategies*, London: Croom Helm.

Bandura, A. (1993) 'Perceived self-efficacy in cognitive development and functioning', *Educational Psychologist*, 28: 117–48.

Becker, W.C., Englemann, S. and Thomas, D.R. (1975) *Classroom Management*, Henley-on-Thames: Science Research Associates.

Chaplain, R. (1995a) *Pupil Behaviour*, Cambridge: Pearson.

Chaplain, R. (1995b) 'Stress and job satisfaction: a study of English primary school teachers', *Educational Psychology: An International Journal of Experimental Educational Psychology*, 15(4): 473–91.

Chaplain, R. (2003) *Teaching Without Disruption in the Primary School: A Model for Managing Behaviour*, London: RoutledgeFalmer.

Chaplain, R. (2008) 'Stress and psychological distress among secondary trainee teachers', *Educational Psychology: An International Journal of Experimental Educational Psychology*, 28(2): 195–209.

Chaplain, R. and Freeman, A. (1998) *Coping with Difficult Children*, Cambridge: Pearson.

Chaplain, R. and Smith, S. (2006) *Challenging Behaviour*, Cambridge: Pearson.

Charles, C.M. (1999) *Building Classroom Discipline from Models to Practice*, 6th edn, New York: Longman.

Cudré-Mauroux, A. (2011) 'Self-efficacy and stress of staff managing challenging behaviours of people with learning disabilities', *British Journal of Learning Disabilities*, 39(3): 181–9.

Department for Education (2012a) *Improving Teacher Training for Behaviour*, London: The Stationery Office.

Department for Education (2012b) *Guide for heads and school staff on behaviour and discipline*, London: The Stationery Office.

Elton Report (1989) *Discipline in Schools: Report of the Committee Chaired by Lord Elton*, London: HMSO.

Emmer, E. and Aussiker, A. (1990) 'School and discipline problems: How well do they work?' in O. Moles (ed.) *Student Discipline Strategies: Research and Practice*, Albany, NY: SUNY Press.

Emmer, E.T. and Worsham, M.E. (2005) *Classroom Management for Middle and High School Teachers*, 7th edn, Boston, MA: Allyn & Bacon, Prentice Hall.

Finn, J. and Pannozzo, G. (2004) 'Classroom organization and student behavior in kindergarten', *Journal of Educational Research*, 98(2): 79–92.

Gibbs, S. and Powell, B. (2011) 'Teacher efficacy and pupil behaviour: the structure of teachers' individual and collective efficacy beliefs and their relationship with numbers of children excluded from school', *British Journal of Educational Psychology*, 82(4): 564–84.

Goldstein, S. (1995) *Understanding and Managing Children's Classroom Behaviour*, New York: Wiley.

Goldstein, H. and Woodhouse, G. (2000) 'School effectiveness research and educational policy', *Oxford Review of Education*, 26(3/4): 353-63.

Health and Safety Executive (HSE) (2000) *The Scale of Occupational Stress: A Further Analysis of the Impact of Demographic Factors and Type of Job*, Contract Research Report 311/2000, London: HSE.

Jones, V.F. and Jones, L.S. (1990) *Comprehensive Classroom Management*, 3rd edn, Needham: Allyn & Bacon.

Kanner, A.D., Coyne, J.C., Schaever, C. and Lazarus, R.S. (1981) 'Comparison of two modes of stress measurement: daily hassles and uplifts versus major life events', *Journal of Behavioural Medicine*, 4: 1-39.

Lam, B. and Yan, H. (2011) 'Beginning teachers' job satisfaction: the impact of school-based factors', *Teacher Development: An International Journal of Teachers' Professional Development*, 15(3): 333-48.

Lawrence, J. and Steed, D. (1986) 'Primary school perceptions of disruptive behaviour', *Educational Studies*, 12(2): 147-57.

MacBeath, J. and Mortimore, P. (eds) (2001) *Improving School Effectiveness*, Buckingham: Open University Press.

McLaughlin, H.J. (1991) 'The reflection on the blackboard: student teacher self-evaluation', *Alberta Journal of Educational Research*, 37: 141-59.

Mastrilli, T. and Sardo-Brown, D. (2002) 'Novice teachers' cases: a vehicle for reflective practice education', *Chula Vista*, 123: 56-62.

Merrett, F. (1993) *Encouragement Works Best*, London: David Fulton.

Miller, A., Ferguson, E. and Byrne, I. (2000) 'Pupils' causal attributions for difficult classroom behaviour', *British Journal of Educational Psychology*, 70: 85-96.

Molnar, A. and Lindquist, B. (1989) *Changing Problem Behaviour*, San Francisco, CA: Jossey-Bass.

Moore, W. and Esselman, M. (1992) 'Teacher efficacy, power, school climate and achievement: A desegregating district's experience'. Paper presented at the annual meeting of the American Educational Research Association, San Francisco, April.

Ng, W., Nicholas, H. and Alan, W. (2010) 'School experience influences on pre-service teachers evolving beliefs about effective teaching', *Teaching and Teacher Education*, 26: 278-89.

Office for Standards in Education (Ofsted) (2006) *Improving Behaviour*, London: Ofsted.

Rotter, J.B. (1966) 'Generalised expectancies for internal versus external control of reinforcement', *Psychological Monographs*, 91: 482-97.

Stanovich, P.J. and Jordan, A. (2004) 'Inclusion as professional development', *Exceptionality Education Canada*, 14(2/3): 169-88.

Steer, A. (2005) *Learning Behaviour: Lessons Learned* (Steer Report), London: DCSF/Institute of Education, University of London.

Swars, S.L. (2005) 'Examining perceptions of mathematics teaching effectiveness among elementary preservice teachers with differing levels of mathematics teacher efficacy', *Journal of Instructional Psychology*, 32(2): 139-47.

Tschannen-Moran, M. and Woolfolk Hoy, A. (2001) 'Teacher efficacy: capturing an elusive construct', *Teaching and Teacher Education*, 17: 783-805.

Weinstein, C. (1988) 'Preservice teachers' expectations about the first year of teaching', *Teaching and Teacher Education*, 4: 31-41.

Wheldall, K. and Lam, Y.Y. (1987) 'Rows versus tables II: the effects of classroom seating arrangements on classroom disruption rate', *Educational Psychology*, 7(4): 303-12.

Woolfolk Hoy, A., Hoy, W.K. and Davis, H. (2009) 'Teachers' self-efficacy beliefs', in K. Wentzel and A. Wigfield (eds) *Handbook of Motivation in School*, Mahwah, NJ: Lawrence Erlbaum.

HANDLING DIFFICULTIES IN SOCIAL, EMOTIONAL AND BEHAVIOURAL DEVELOPMENT

Janice Wearmouth

INTRODUCTION

This unit focuses on difficulties experienced by children who demonstrate features of social, emotional and behavioural problems. Research tells us that schools play a critical part in shaping a young child's identity as a learner (Bruner, 1996). Use of the terms 'emotional and behavioural difficulties' (Warnock Report, 1978) or 'social, emotional and behavioural difficulties' as a label for some students who behave inappropriately is not always helpful to teachers. Poulou and Norwich (2002: 112) conclude, from a review of international studies, that the more teachers think student behaviour stems from problems within students themselves, such as the 'child's innate personality', 'the more they experience feelings of "stress" and even "helplessness"', and the less they feel able to cope with difficult behaviour.

The new *Teachers' Standards for Qualified Teacher Status*, introduced from September 2012 (Department for Education, 2012a) require teachers to take responsibility for promoting good behaviour in classrooms and elsewhere, have high expectations and maintain good relationships with pupils. As a teacher, you can minimise the possibility of poor behaviour in your classroom and put yourself in a much stronger position if you recognise that appropriate behaviour can be taught

OBJECTIVES

By the end of this unit, you should:

- be familiar with frames of reference that are commonly used in educational institutions to research and understand challenging behaviour and social and emotional difficulties and to form the basis for conceptualising effective responses;
- be aware of ways that difficult behaviour can be addressed in schools in relation to these frames of reference;
- understand that learning environments that are designed to support children to engage with their learning will reduce the possibility of undesirable behaviour in the first place;
- be familiar with a range of effective responses when children's behaviour is extremely challenging.

(Rogers, 2013). Children can learn to make conscious choices about behaviour, even where it is associated with a genetic or neurological condition (Wearmouth *et al.*, 2005).

FRAMEWORKS FOR UNDERSTANDING DIFFICULT BEHAVIOUR

The frameworks for understanding problematic behaviour in schools really matter. Antisocial or challenging behaviour in classrooms and around the school is sometimes explained as a problem that stems from the student him/herself and his/her family. This may be the case with some students. However, student behaviour in schools does not occur in a vacuum (Watkins and Wagner, 2000). All students' behaviours are situated in a social context and can be interpreted as resulting from interactions between people and their environments or social events. We begin the discussion here with an outline of the principles of behavioural psychology, which is probably the most common theoretical framework underpinning behaviour management in schools. We continue by looking at biological and neurological explanations for difficult behaviour and exemplify these with attention deficit/hyperactivity disorder (ADHD) and difficulties associated with autism and Tourette syndrome. We then discuss issues of withdrawn behaviour associated with emotional deprivation and conclude by examining bullying behaviour.

Behavioural methodologies

Commonly, research into difficult behaviour is based on principles from behavioural psychology (Skinner, 1938; Baer *et al.*, 1968). Behavioural methodologies hold that all (mis)behaviour is learned. There are two different ways of looking at this. First, research over a long period of time (Glynn, 2004) suggests that elements of a setting may exert powerful control over behaviour. It may be that something about a particular learning environment, for example the physical properties or the presence or behaviour of an adult, has provoked good, or alternatively poor, behaviour, and that the young people have come to associate good, or poor, behaviour with that setting. In behaviourist terms, we would consider that the setting has created 'antecedent conditions' for that good, or poor, behaviour to occur. As a teacher, therefore, if you can work out what these antecedent conditions are, you can modify (mis)behaviour through intervening in that environment and altering the setting in which the behaviour occurs. Second, particular behaviour can be learned if it is rewarded and, thus, reinforced, especially if this is done in a consistent, predictable way. Many behaviourist principles were derived from work with laboratory animals. In a famous sequence of trial-and-error learning tasks related to the effective use of rewards, rats learned to press levers in order to find food (Skinner, 1938). Learning involved the formation of an action–response association in the rats' memory: pressing the lever resulted in a reward – finding food. If the reward of food was removed, the rats' behaviour would gradually cease through 'extinction'. Translating this interpretation into human terms, pupils can learn how to behave appropriately in response to positive reinforcement (rewards). Where young people behave badly, you might work out whatever it is that seems to be reinforcing (rewarding) this behaviour and remove the reward(s). Whenever individuals behave more appropriately, you might reward them in a way that recognises the greater acceptability of the new behaviour.

The opposite of positive reinforcement is negative reinforcement. From this view, you can discourage undesirable behaviour and reinforce compliance in classrooms by making classroom or school rules and the consequences for unacceptable behaviour very clear. Pupils may learn acceptable or appropriate behaviour through avoidance of punishment.

Practical applications of behaviourist principles for teaching appropriate behaviour and controlling what is unacceptable are discussed later in this unit.

Neurological and biological explanations of behaviour

Sometimes, behaviour that you may experience as challenging to yourself as the teacher or to the welfare and academic progress of the other young people may relate to an underlying condition or dysfunction.

Attention deficit/hyperactivity disorder

One such condition is ADHD, 'characterised by chronic and pervasive (at home and school) problems of inattention, impulsiveness, and/or excessive motor activity which have seriously debilitating effects on individuals' social, emotional and educational development, and are sometimes disruptive to the home and/or school environment' (Norwich *et al.*, 2002: 182) .

A diagnosis of ADHD may result in a prescription for psychostimulants.

> The medication stimulates areas of the brain regulating arousal and alertness and can result in immediate short-term improvements in concentration and impulse control. The precise mechanism is poorly understood and the specific locus of action within the central nervous system remains speculative.

> (British Psychological Society, 1996: 50-1)

Some researchers suspect that stimulants work through the release of neurotransmitters, powerful chemical messengers. Many researchers suspecte that ADHD may result from problems related to communication between neurons in the brain that communicate through neurotransmitters passed between them. Methylphenidate (Ritalin) is the most widely used stimulant, prescribed in the form of tablets to be taken regularly.

There are particular concerns about the use of such psychostimulants, including the effects and side effects of these drugs and ethical considerations about the lack of adequate monitoring of the day-to-day classroom learning and behavioural outcomes of medication (British Psychological Society, 1996: 51-2). Prescribing a drug may provide an insufficient response to supporting pupils in how to behave more appropriately. 'We have evidence that children given the diagnosis ADHD don't attend, don't wait and don't sit still. But just because they don't do all these things does not mean that they cannot do them' (British Psychological Society, 1996: 23). The use of psychostimulants is not the only response to ADHD, as we discuss later in this unit.

Autism

It is highly likely these days that you will meet young people in schools who have been diagnosed as having an autistic spectrum disorder (ASD). Autism is a condition that is generally thought to affect communication, cognition and learning. In 1943, Leo Kanner identified a small group of young children who faced a difficulty that seemed to centre around excessive focus on the self. He called it 'early infantile autism' from the Greek αυτος (*autos*) meaning 'self' (Kanner, 1943). These children appeared unable to relate to people and social situations from early life and experienced profound 'aloneness', failure to use language fluently to communicate and an anxious and obsessive desire to maintain sameness. Some seemed to have a fascination for objects that are handled with skill in fine motor movements, a good rote memory, oversensitivity to stimuli, and apparently good cognitive potential.

Around the same time as Kanner, Hans Asperger, in 1944, used the term 'autistic' to denote a range of attributes bearing a similarity to that commented on by Kanner. This range included extreme egocentricity and an inability to relate to others, speech and language peculiarities, repetitive routines, motor clumsiness, narrow interests, and non-verbal communication problems (Wing, 1996).

Additional features to those already seen by Kanner included sensory sensitivities and unusual responses to some sensory experiences: auditory, visual, olfactory (smell), taste and touch. Asperger also noticed an uneven developmental profile, a good rote memory, very narrow special interests and motor coordination difficulties. Asperger syndrome now commonly refers to a form of autism used to describe people at the higher end of the autistic spectrum (National Autistic Society, 2013). Delay in language development is not likely. One in ten people with ASD have what appear to be extremely well-developed skills in one specific area. These skills are often found in mathematical and calendrical calculations, and areas such as music and art. In autism, however, three-quarters of the population have difficulties in learning, some at a severe level.

Wing and Gould (1979) identified a 'triad of impairments' in a broader group of 'autistic' children: difficulty in social interaction, for example appearing aloof and indifferent to other people, social communication, both verbal and non-verbal, and imagination. Each area within the triad implies particular behaviours. A child who lacks social understanding is unlikely to understand unwritten social rules, recognise others' feelings or seek comfort from others. Children often find it hard to understand and interpret other people's thoughts, feelings and actions. Autistic children may appear to behave 'strangely' or inappropriately, and may often prefer to be alone. Difficulties in social communication mean that people on the autistic spectrum often find it hard to understand the meaning of gestures, facial expressions or tone of voice. Difficulties with social imagination mean people with ASDs are unable to think and behave flexibly, predict what will or could happen next and understand the concept of danger. They may also find it hard to engage in imaginative play, prepare for change and plan for the future, and cope in new or unfamiliar situations. This may result in restricted, obsessional or repetitive activities, and difficulties in developing the skills of playing with others.

You will find discussion of ways to support children with ASD in classrooms later in this unit.

Tourette syndrome

Tourette syndrome is an example of a neurological disorder characterised by motor and vocal tics: repetitive, stereotyped, involuntary movements and vocalisations. Motor tics are, commonly, sudden, brief, repetitive movements that may include eye blinking and other vision irregularities, facial grimacing, shoulder shrugging and head or shoulder jerking, or, more dramatically, touching objects, hopping, jumping, bending, twisting or motor movements that result in self-harm, such as punching oneself in the face (National Institute of Neorological Disorders and Stroke, 2005). Vocalisations often include repetitive throat-clearing, sniffing or grunting sounds – or, at the extreme, 'coprolalia' (uttering swear words) or 'echolalia' (repeating the words of others). People with Tourette syndrome often report that tics are preceded by a sensation in the affected muscles, a 'premonitory urge' that builds up to the point where it is expressed. Excitement, anxiety or particular physical experiences can trigger tics.

Across the world, the prevalence among schoolchildren 'ranges from 1 to 10 per 1000' (Piacenti *et al.*, 2010: 1929). Evidence from family studies suggests that Tourette syndrome may be genetic (National Institute of Neorological Disorders and Stroke, 2005). Tics tend to start in early childhood, peak before mid-teens and improve subsequently. Approximately 10 per cent of children have symptoms lasting into adulthood.

Medication can be prescribed for severe tics. The most effective appears to be antipsychotics. However, these 'rarely eliminate tics and are often associated with unacceptable sedation, weight gain, cognitive dulling, and motor adverse effects', such as tremors (Piacenti *et al.* 2010: 1930). Other ways to address these problems are suggested below.

Emotional problems in childhood

One theory of human development that has influenced educational provision for young children whose behaviour is antisocial is attachment theory (Bowlby, 1952). Babies quickly attach themselves emotionally to their adult carers and progress through well-recognised stages towards maturity. Successful development depends on needs being adequately met at an earlier stage. Where this is not so, then children will persist in inappropriate attachment behaviour, being over-anxious, avoidant, aggressive or incapable of warm attachment and positive human relationships (Harris-Hendriks and Figueroa, 1995; Bennathan, 2000). Learning, personality and behaviour difficulties can result from inadequate early care and support from parents who struggle with poverty, damaged relationships and harsh and stressful living conditions (Boxall, 2002).

Approaches in schools to address problems of insecure attachment in early childhood are outlined later in the unit.

Bullying behaviour

You may well find that bullying behaviour is a concern in the schools in which you teach.

Task 3.5.1 Personal reflection of the experience of 'bullying'

Take a few minutes to reflect on your own school experiences:

- Do you have experience of being bullied, or even of being a bully yourself? Or perhaps you saw someone being bullied? How did this make you feel?
- How would you define what constitutes 'bullying' behaviour? How far do you think this behaviour was related to the characteristics of you as the victim or bully, and/or to the other person/people involved? How far was it related to the context in which the behaviour occurred?
- How did it all start?
- Is it possible to identify the cycle of its development?
- Did you (or the victim) try to resist the bullying in any way?
- What might have been done to stop the bullying behaviour that you experienced or perpetrated?
- How did it all end?

Comment

How did you feel when you were carrying out this activity? Did you feel any of the same emotions that you did in your experience of bullying?

Bullying means behaviour, repeated over time, that intentionally hurts others, physically or emotionally (Department for Education, 2012b). It includes:

- bullying related to race, religion and culture;
- bullying pupils with disabilities or special educational needs;
- sexist bullying and harassment;

- bullying pupils because of their sexuality or perceived sexuality;
- cyberbullying, using mobile phones and the Internet.

Bullying is often associated with an imbalance of power between victim and perpetrator. Once the victim reacts to the bullying by showing signs of stress, bullies may experience pleasure from feelings of dominance. The cycle of bullying may continue over a long time and intensify. The victim may fight back or find ways to avoid the bullying by hovering around teachers or staying at home. If the bullying is extremely serious, and the bully is over the age of 10, the bully could be prosecuted for a criminal offence, for example, assault or harassment. If the bully is under 10, it may be possible to take legal action for negligence against the school and the local authority for failure in their duty of care to the pupil.

Under the Children Act 1989, bullying is a child protection concern when there is 'reasonable cause to suspect that a child is suffering, or is likely to suffer, significant harm'. If so, staff should report concerns to their local authority children's social care. Schools may need to consult a range of external services to support pupils who are bullied, or address underlying issues contributing to children's bullying behaviour (Department for Education, 2012b).

Rigby (2002) warns against assuming that the descriptors 'bully' and 'victim' suggest a stable personality trait. Many who bully in younger years do not repeat this behaviour later. Some who bully in one situation would never do so in another. Thinking of bullies as socially inadequate (Field, 1999) may be an oversimplification. On measures of self-esteem, school bullies are average, but tend to be less able to imagine another's viewpoint (Rigby, 2002) and to be more likely to experience feelings of depression (Slee, 1995). Despite the risk of stereotyping, there is some consensus about the correlates of victimisation. For example, victims of bullying may have low self-worth and self-esteem, be non-assertive and have poor social skills, be introverted, relatively uncooperative and physically less strong than others, be physically shorter, lonely and isolated, and prone to anxiety, depression and suicide (Rigby, 2002: 139–40).

A crucial factor that explains the severity of bullying in schools is the behaviour of bystanders. Research in this area began in 1964, after a New Yorker, Kitty Genovese, was murdered. Neighbours heard her screams but failed to assist her (Atkinson *et al.*, 1993). Social psychologists researching 'bystander apathy' found that the presence of others often deters individuals from intervening in difficult situations where they could assist the person in trouble. However, a training programme focusing on raising awareness of bystander apathy can be shown to make a difference to the preparedness of bystanders to help peers in schools.

Further approaches to dealing with bullying behaviour in schools are outlined later.

APPLYING BEHAVIOURIST PRINCIPLES TO MANAGE BEHAVIOUR IN SCHOOLS

There is a lot of evidence to demonstrate that approaches derived from behavioural methodologies are effective in establishing positive behaviour in schools and reducing incidents of disruption or challenging behaviour. Antecedent conditions, in other words the physical properties – for example space, arrangement of desks – objects – for example easy availability of well-organised resources – and adults in classrooms, playgrounds and other areas in the school, may exert a very powerful control over pupil behaviour. It is very important that you think about this, because, as a teacher, you are in a very good position to make changes in the learning environment that can affect young people's behaviour and bring about improvement where required. There is also a lot of evidence to show that the way in which teachers reward behaviour, sometimes inadvertently, by their own actions can be a very strong reinforcer of good, or poor, behaviour. As a teacher, you are also in a good position to reflect on what reinforces the behaviour you wish to see in your pupils, and what you would like to see improve. Whatever you do, you need to know that changing pupil behaviour using behaviourist approaches depends on consistency. It is essential, therefore, that you are very consistent in your own behaviour.

Establishing conditions that support appropriate behaviour in classrooms

The classroom is the most important place in the education system and the place where you can establish your own norms and expectations of positive pupil behaviour. 'Classroom climate', that is 'the collective perception of pupils of what it feels like, in intellectual, motivational and emotional terms, to be a pupil in any particular teacher's classroom', influences 'every pupil's motivation to learn and perform to the best of his or her ability' (Hobby and Smith, 2002: 9). A research report on what works in schools in terms of promoting positive behaviour and learning (Department for Education and Skills, 2006) notes that pupils will look towards you as the teacher for a sense of security and order, an opportunity to participate actively in the class and for it to be an interesting and exciting place. Discussing and establishing the right to feel safe, learn without disruption and be respected and treated fairly are essential as the basis for instituting clear rules and routines (Rogers, 2013).

Classroom management and the effective teacher

One of the very well-known approaches to managing behaviour across the whole school is Canter and Canter's (1992) *Assertive Discipline*. These authors assert (p. 12) that students need to know 'without doubt' what teachers expect, what will happen if they choose not to comply, and that appropriate behaviour will be recognised. To be what they call an 'assertive' teacher, you would communicate your expectations confidently and reinforce your words with actions. Teachers who are able to control classes most effectively are those who can command respect and, often but not always, those whom pupils like (Elton, 1989; Department for Education and Skills, 2006). These teachers know how to get the best out of children.

The reverse of the effective teacher is, of course, the teacher who is ineffective in managing pupil behaviour. Examples of teachers whose behaviour establishes antecedent conditions that predispose to poor pupil behaviour include:

> teachers who lack confidence in their own ability to deal with disruption and who see their classes as potentially hostile. They create a negative classroom atmosphere by frequent criticism and rare praise. They make use of loud public reprimands and threats. They are sometimes sarcastic. They tend to react aggressively to minor incidents. Their methods increase the danger of a major confrontation not only with individual pupils but with the whole class.
>
> (Elton, 1989: chapter 3, paragraph 8)

Social and Emotional Aspects of Learning

The link between the quality of teaching and pupil behaviour, the importance of consistently applied policy and practice, and an understanding that good behaviour will not necessarily just happen have been accepted by central government (Department for Education and Skills, 2006). In the mid-1990s, the Department for Children, Schools and Families in England commissioned curriculum materials to be used as part of schools' personal, social and health education programmes. This material is known as *Social and Emotional Aspects of Learning (SEAL): Improving behaviour, improving learning*. Primary SEAL has been available since 2005, and secondary since 2007. The programme is based on a number of social and emotional aspects of learning: self-awareness, managing feelings,

Task 3.5.2 Reflecting on the qualities of effective classroom teachers

Note down what, in your experience, are the most important qualities of the classroom teachers who experience the least disruptive behaviour by pupils? How do these teachers behave in the classroom?

How far do you measure up to your list of qualities?

How far do you agree with Elton (1989), who concluded that, to be effective, teachers should:

- have good subject knowledge;
- be able to plan and deliver lessons that are coherent and engage pupils' attention;
- be able to relate to young people and encourage good behaviour and learning;
- deal calmly and firmly with inappropriate behaviour;
- establish positive relationships with their classes, based on mutual respect;
- be able to create a classroom ethos in which pupils lose popularity and credibility with classmates by causing trouble;
- recognise potential disruptive incidents, choose an appropriate means to deal with them early on and prevent escalation;
- know what is going on around them;
- know how pupils react to each other and to teachers;
- be in full control of their own behaviour and model the good behaviour they expect of pupils.

motivation, empathy and social skills. The underpinning assumption is that all children benefit from support to understand and manage their feelings, work cooperatively in groups, motivate themselves and develop resilience in the face of setbacks.

> Evidence shows that well-designed SEAL programmes contribute to school improvement through better academic results, more effective learning, better behaviour and higher school attendance. SEAL supports inclusion and contributes to reducing the need for exclusions providing staff and pupils with ways of managing and resolving conflict. [. . .] A whole school approach and continued professional development (CPD) are essential to the success of SEAL in schools.
>
> (www.pshe-association.org.uk/uploads/media/27/7415.pdf,
> accessed 24 June 2013)

'Circle time'

Particularly in primary schools, but in some secondary schools also, you may well come across the initiative 'Circle time' (Mosley, 1996), which was designed to resolve disputes between pupils. If you wish to set up this approach, it is very important first to establish the clear expectation that the views of others will be listened to with respect in your classroom. This approach has a long history. In many traditional communities, the circle is a symbol of 'unity, healing and power' and can be found in the traditions of groups as diverse 'as the North American Indians and Anglo Saxon monks' (Tew, 1998: 20). In schools, 'Circle time' is a meeting following strict protocols of involving all participants in discussion. Both teachers and students are bound by rules that stipulate no one may put anyone down, no one may use any name negatively, and, when individuals speak, everyone must listen. Everyone has a turn and a chance to speak. Members of the class team suggest ways of solving problems, and individuals can accept or politely refuse help (Wearmouth *et al.*, 2005: 184). If a student breaks the protocol, a visual warning is given. If this persists, time away from the circle follows.

Ways to reinforce positive behaviour and reduce incidence of disruption

In Rogers's (2013) view, a child's background is no excuse for poor behaviour. Key to motivating pupils to choose appropriate behaviour are 'positive reinforcers': teacher praise, rewards of various sorts and positive communications with parents. As Berryman and Glynn (2001) comment, behaviour learnt most readily has consistent positive consequences: social attention, praise, recognition, access to favourite activities, and so on. It is really important that you inform parents about the good things their children are doing and their positive achievements, as well as your concerns.

Canter and Canter advocate that, as a teacher, you should aim to be assertive in your approach to pupils and should establish a classroom discipline plan with three parts: rules, positive recognition and consequences. You should provide positive, predictable consequences, with a limited number of rules. If children disrupt the lesson, they should take ownership of this, and you should remind them what the rules are: 'Jayson . . . you're calling out . . . Remember our class rules for asking questions, thanks' (Rogers, 2013: 238). You can give younger children a non-verbal cue to appropriate behaviour and show them clearly what is expected.

Your own behaviour as a teacher is very important in modelling and reinforcing specific ways of behaving in particular situations. In doing so, it is really important for you not to allow yourself to be drawn into a power struggle that some pupils find rewarding and that is likely to reinforce the way they are behaving. Students may imitate negative as well as positive behaviour, however, so, for example, the use of abusive or sarcastic language should be avoided at all costs. You should:

model ways of resolving conflict which respect the rights of students to learn and feel safe, and

- meet the needs of both parties, that is, provide win-win outcomes wherever possible
- bring an end to the conflict, or at least reduce it
- do not leave either party 'wounded'.

(Sproson, 2004: 319)

There are a number of techniques that can enable you to avoid power struggles with pupils:

- Some young people may take pleasure in not doing what they are asked immediately, especially if there is an audience of peers. In this situation, Rogers (2013: 240), among others, advocates that you build in a brief 'take-up' period for pupils to respond: 'Craig . . . Deon . . . you're chatting – it's whole-class teaching time'. Make the request, walk away so as to imply compliance, and acknowledge compliance when it happens.
- The 'broken record' approach (Rogers, 2013: 240) also allows you, as the teacher, to repeat a request calmly without being drawn into the kind of argument. For example, as Sproson (2004: 320) exemplifies:

Teacher: John, start your work, thanks.
John: It's boring.
Teacher: John, start your work, thanks.
John: Didn't you hear what I said?
Teacher: Start your work, thanks.
John: This lesson's just so boring . . . (picking pen up – if you're lucky!)
Teacher: Pleased to see you getting down to work – well done.

- Pupils bringing inappropriate objects into the classroom, or engaging in inappropriate activities, might be given what Rogers (2013: 242) calls 'directed choices'. My own sister, as a newly appointed member of staff in a school where the whole class had been suspended the previous term, was once in a situation where teenage girls brought long sticks into her mathematics lesson – to test her out, as they later admitted. She simply responded by directing their choices: 'Shall I put them in this cupboard or that one? I'll keep them safe for you till the end of the day.' They never asked for them back.
- It is important for you to distinguish between the primary (target) behaviour that is of concern and secondary behaviours that are just intended to annoy. Secondary behaviours (sighs, looks, and so on) can be ignored, and take-up time can be allowed to comply with the original request.
- Finally, you may be able to address inappropriate and/or disruptive or even aggressive behaviour by defining another behaviour that is incompatible with the undesirable behaviour, modelling this and reinforcing it with positive consequences. For example, some schools that have experienced problems of aggressive bullying or even violent behaviour at break times organise group games to avoid antisocial behaviour.

RESPONDING TO ADHD

We have already seen that the use of drugs is not a complete answer to controlling the behaviour of children identified as having ADHD. Children whose behaviour is seen as extremely challenging can also sometimes be taught alternative behaviours that offer a sense of belonging and increase self-control (Rogers, 2013), using approaches based on behaviourist principles. The British Psychological Society (1996: 47–8) identified seven approaches that focus on the effects of consequences through positive reinforcement, training in the reduction of behaviour viewed as problematic, and response cost, that is mild punishment designed to make the undesirable behaviour more difficult and more of an effort to perform. 'Several studies showed that behaviour management and medication were most effective when combined' (British Psychological Society, 1996: 47–8).

Rogers advocates the use of individualised behaviour management programmes where behaviour is very challenging. Behavioural methodology is a scientifically based technology, and so the first requirement is a clear definition of the target behaviour. For instance, if a child is thought to be 'hyperactive', an operational definition of behaviours such as 'out of seat' will be required. Once the behaviour has been operationally defined, there should be systematic observational sampling across times of day, situations, nature of activity, person in charge and so on. Such observations need to be taken over a period of several days to establish the baseline level of responding. Once the baseline can be clearly seen, an analysis detailing the following three stages should be carried out: (1) the antecedent event(s), that is, whatever starts off or prompts the undesirable behaviour; (2) the observable behaviour; (3) the consequence(s). When a consequence seems to be reinforcing a behaviour, then that consequence should be removed. It may be that, by telling the child off, you are maintaining and reinforcing a child's 'attention-seeking', for example. If the positive reinforcement is removed, the occurrences of that behaviour should reduce. This is not always easy to achieve, of course, and it may be that you will need to work out alternative, incompatible behaviour, as outlined above.

At the same time as making clear to pupils what behaviours are unacceptable, individualised behaviour management strategies should also provide opportunities for modelling, rehearsing and reinforcing behaviours that are acceptable (Rogers, 2013: 167–9). For example, a teacher might explain to the child what his/her current behaviour looks and sounds like, and how it affects the other students in the classroom: 'Do you mind if I show you what you do when . . .?' It is also important to model the desired behaviour to the student: 'Let me show you how I want you to . . .' The student might then be encouraged to copy this behaviour. In the classroom, the teacher should acknowledge any positive changes in the student's behaviour with positive verbal encouragement. It is important to recognise that this type of intervention involves the skilful manipulation of both antecedents and consequences, and that training takes place in the context where problem behaviour occurs.

Potentially unsafe or abusive behaviour should be addressed very assertively: '[That language] is not a joke to me – it stops now'. 'Kyle . . . put the scissors down, on the table – now' (Rogers, 2013: 243–4). If it is necessary to remove a student from a group of peers, this can be achieved 'by asking the other students to leave. It may be more appropriate, and safer, to bring other staff to the place where the student is, rather than the other way around' (Dunckley, 1999: 10).

Physical restraint is a last resort that should only be used to manage a dangerous situation. There is a difference between physical restraint, to hold a student still until aggression (hitting, kicking, punching others) subsides, and punitive incarcerations, such as locking the student away for extended periods of time, as can occur when the principles of 'time out' are misunderstood, or misapplied, often in the heat of the moment (Cornwall, 2004). Writing from a New Zealand perspective, Dunckley (1999) comments that students, 'in an agitated state require guidance and direction to increase their sense of security . . . where possible and appropriate give a choice, time for the student to respond, then, after an appropriate time, follow through with consequences' (Dunckley, 1999: 16)

It is very important to minimise the risk of physical confrontation in the first instance, rather than having to take action after the event. However, many of us have experienced situations when confrontations cannot be avoided. In such cases, Smith notes:

> [If] the student continues to be defiant or provocative, and, if the worst comes to the worst, you have to be sure that you can manage the situation should the student attempt a physical challenge. Once started, confrontations sometimes develop very quickly and unpredictably, so that it is foolish to initiate one and then find that it has gone out of control and escalated into a situation which cannot be managed successfully, becoming demeaning and undignified.
>
> (Smith, 2004: 261–2)

Whatever you do, you should familiarise yourself with school policies, which should indicate when restraint can be used.

Responding to autistic spectrum disorders

Commonly, approaches to addressing difficulties associated with autism and/or Aspergers syndrome are based on behavioural principles. In a classroom, you might address the learning and behavioural needs of children on the autistic spectrum in a number of ways. For example, you can pay close attention to clarity and order, reduce extraneous and unnecessary material in order that children know where their attention needs to be directed, and maintain a predictable physical environment, with very predictable and regular routines, ensuring that everything is kept in the same place. You might teach children agreed signals to be quiet or to call for attention. You might provide specific low-arousal work areas free from visual distractions and find out how you can make headphones available to reduce sound. You might also provide a visual timetable, with clear symbols to represent the various activities for the day, and a simple visual timer with, for example, an arrow that is moved across a simple timeline to show how much time has passed and how much is left.

In order to develop greater understanding of personal emotions, you might teach children in a very deliberate, overt and structured way to name their feelings and relate these to their own experiences, predict how they are likely to feel at particular times and in particular circumstances, and recognise the signs of extreme emotions such as anger. A visual gauge showing graduated degrees of anger in different shades of colour might be helpful to you here.

You might also teach pupils, again very deliberately and in small steps, to identify and name others' feelings, link these to possible causes and identify appropriate responses to others' emotions. They might, for example, keep a feelings diary in which they record times when they feel happy, sad or frightened, and what they can do about this. You might use art, drama and social stories to identify the different kinds of emotion and/or explore their physical aspects and/or talk through situations that need to be resolved. Above all, it is important for you to get to know the pupil really well and to understand his/her individuality, strengths, weakness, likes and dislikes, and so on.

Responding to Tourette syndrome

Children with Tourette syndrome often cope well in mainstream classrooms. However, frequent tics can interfere with academic performance or disrupt social relationships. Children with Tourette syndrome benefit from a learning environment flexible enough to accommodate their learning needs. This may imply special arrangements if the tics disrupt the pupil's ability to write, or problem-solving with the pupil to reduce stress in classrooms or during examinations.

In recent years, particular interventions, based on behaviourist approaches, have been developed that seem to be effective in reducing tic severity (National Institute of Neorological Disorders and Stroke, 2005). For example, Piacenti *et al.* (2010: 1930) describe the main components of 'habit reversal training' as tic-awareness and 'competing-response' training. Awareness training comprises self-monitoring of tics and signs that a tic is about to occur. Competing-response training involves deliberately engaging in an alternative, socially acceptable behaviour that is not physically compatible with the tic, as soon as the premonitory urge is felt. For vocal tics, the most common competing response that is taught is slow, rhythmic breathing from the diaphragm.

ESTABLISHING ATTACHMENT TO ADDRESS ANTISOCIAL BEHAVIOUR IN EARLY CHILDHOOD

Attachment theory has influenced the development of 'nurture groups' in some infant schools, originally in the Inner London Education Authority in 1970-1 and, more recently, in other local authorities. The nurture group attempts to create the features of adequate parenting with opportunities to develop trust, security and positive identity through attachment to an attentive, caring adult. Features include: easy physical contact between adult and child; warmth, intimacy and a family atmosphere; good-humoured acceptance of children and their behaviour; familiar, regular routines; a focus on tidying up; provision of food in structured contexts; opportunities to play and appropriate adult participation; adults encouraging children's reflection on troublesome situations and their own feelings; and opportunities for children to develop increasing autonomy (Wearmouth, 2009).

If you teach in early years settings, you may well come across the *Boxall Profile* (Bennathan and Boxall, 2000). This is an observational tool, based on attachment theory and developed to identify children's developmental needs and the levels of skills they possess to access learning. It was originally standardised for children aged 3-8 years to support work in nurture groups, but has recently been developed for use in secondary schools.

INTERVENTIONS TO ADDRESS BULLYING BEHAVIOUR IN SCHOOLS

Responses to bullying behaviour in schools often fall into one of two categories. There are those that assume bullying is an antisocial act, to be reduced by applying various types of punishment. Typically, any violation of rules is addressed through 'rules, sanctions and zero tolerance for rule infractions' (Rigby, 2002: 238). Other responses focus on establishing respectful behaviour between people to minimise bullying. From this view, 'positive improvement in behaviour between people can be brought about through instruction, persuasion and modelling of respectful behaviour' (Rigby, 2002: 238). In England, government guidance advises that schools should discipline pupils who bully, inside or outside the school. State schools should have an anti-bullying policy (Department for Education, 2012b) setting out how bullying should be dealt with in the school. At the same time, the school should investigate reasons for the bullying and whether bullies also need help.

Bullies trade in secrecy, not from their peers but from adults. Breaking through this secrecy is crucial in addressing bullying of any kind. There need to be clear, school-wide consequences for bullying, otherwise the bully will continue in the belief that s/he can continuity with impunity (Olweus, 1978). Such consequences need to be set out in a formal process for dealing with bullying behaviour in an educational context that emphasises rights-respecting behaviour. These consequences will be:

- known in advance and published in a school-wide policy document
- explained to all students in relation to what the school means by bullying
- discussed within classroom meeting time, during the establishment phase of the year, and at times when the school experiences any spate of bullying behaviour.

(Rogers, 2003: 129)

SUMMARY

'Difficult' neighbourhoods tend to produce more 'difficult' children than neighbourhoods in more affluent circumstances (Watkins and Wagner, 2000), but economic impoverishment in the neighbourhood does not necessarily lead to disruptive behaviour in schools (Rutter *et al.*, 1979; Office for Standards in Education, 2001). Even in areas of disadvantage, good classroom management, as well as interventions with individual students, can make a difference to student behaviour, learning and future life chances. It is crucial for teachers to understand that belonging is a fundamental human need (Maslow, 1943). As Rogers (2003) notes, young people spends a third of their day at school. During that time, teachers are in a position to provide structured frameworks within which these young people can be taught alternatives to unacceptable behaviour that offer a sense of belonging and increase self-control.

 ## ANNOTATED FURTHER READING

Applying behaviourist principles to teach and manage behaviour

Bill Rogers, an Australian educator, has written a number of books and articles on addressing challenging behaviour in schools that may be interpreted as using the principles of behavioural psychology. His work tends to be very practical, and you may find some of the following material very useful in devising ways to manage behaviour in schools.

Rogers, B. (1994) 'Teaching positive behaviour to behaviourally disordered students in primary schools', *Support for Learning*, 9(4): 166-70.

> Although this article appears dated, it very usefully outlines a systematic and principled way to address behavioural issues at primary level.

Rogers, B. (2004) *Behaviour Recovery*, London: Paul Chapman.

> This book is focused on teaching positive behaviour, in particular where things have gone wrong.

Rogers, B. (ed.) (2009) *How to Manage Children's Challenging Behaviour*, London: Sage.

> This book brings together contributions from practising teachers that suggest ways to tackle disruptive and challenging behaviour, with a commentary by Bill Rogers.

Rogers, B. (2012) *You Know the Fair Rule: Strategies for Positive and Effective Behaviour Management and Discipline in Schools*, London: Pearson.

> This book is concerned with establishing good, effective classroom management strategies to prevent disruptive and difficult behaviour developing in the first place, planning behavioural interventions and resolving conflict in schools.

 # FURTHER READING TO SUPPORT M-LEVEL STUDY

Evaluating nurture groups

Cooper, P. and Whitehead, D. (2007) 'The effectiveness of nurture groups on student progress', *Emotional and Behavioural Difficulties*, 12: 171-90.

> This is a national evaluation of the effectiveness of nurture groups (NGs), which you might choose to read. This study attempts to assess the effectiveness of NGs in promoting positive social, emotional and educational development. The study set out to measure: the effects of NGs in promoting pupil improvement; the extent to which these improvements generalised to mainstream settings; and the impact of NGs on whole schools. Statistically significant improvements were found for pupils who had attended NGs in terms of social, emotional and behavioural functioning.

Reflecting on restorative justice

Wearmouth, J., McKinney, R. and Glynn, T. (2007) 'Restorative justice: two examples from New Zealand schools', *British Journal of Special Education*, 34(4): 196-203.

> You might like to read this if you are interested in reading about an approach to bullying, and disruptive behaviour generally, that in some ways is similar to circle time, that of restoration rather than punishment.
>
> Both examples come from a New Zealand Maori context and interventions undertaken with young men whose behaviour was of concern in school and in the local neighbourhood. The interventions operated through traditional Maori protocols to shift the focus away from individuals on to the whole community, in order to focus on putting things right between all those involved in the wrong-doing. These examples show how the use of traditional community conflict resolution processes was able to resolve tensions, make justice visible and re-establish harmonious relations between the individuals, the school and members of the community.

 # RELEVANT WEBSITES

The Department for Education website contains advice and guidance for schools about their legal powers and duties in relation to behaviour and attendance. You might find this useful:

> www.education.gov.uk/schools/pupilsupport/behaviour

A number of charities that focus on particular kinds of behaviour also offer help and guidance to teachers. For example Tourettes Action is to be found at:

    www.tourettes-action.org.uk/62-advice-for-teachers.html

The National Autistic Society provides support for those dealing with children on the autistic spectrum:

    www.autism.org.uk

The National Health Service has a website that gives an overview of AD/HD from a medical perspective at:

    www.nhs.uk/Conditions/Attention-deficit-hyperactivity-disorder/Pages/Treatment.aspx

 # REFERENCES

Atkinson, R.L., Atkinson, R.C., Smith, E.E. and Bem, D.J. (1993) *Introduction to Psychology*, 11th edn, Fort Worth, TX: Harcourt Brace College Publishers.

Baer, D.M., Wolf, M.M. and Risley, T.R. (1968) 'Some current dimensions of applied behavior analysis', *Journal of Applied Behavior Analysis*, 1: 91–7.

Bennathan, M. (2000) 'Children at risk of failure in primary schools', in M. Bennathan and M. Boxall *Effective Intervention in Primary Schools: Nurture Groups* (2nd edn), London: David Fulton, pp. 1–18.

Bennathan, M. and Boxall, M. (eds) (2000) *Effective Intervention in Primary Schools: Nurture Groups*, London: David Fulton.

Berryman, M. and Glynn, T. (2001) *Hei Awhina Matua: Strategies for Bicultural Partnership in Overcoming Behavioural and Learning Difficulties*, Wellington: Specialist Education Service.

Bowlby, J. (1952) 'A two-year-old goes to hospital', *Proceedings of the Royal Society of Medicine*, 46: 425–7.

Boxall, M. (2002) *Nurture Groups in School: Principles and Practice*, London: Paul Chapman.

British Psychological Society (BPS) (1996) *Attention Deficit Hyperactivity Disorder (ADHD): A Psychological Response to an Evolving Concept*, Leicester: BPS.

Bruner, J. (1996) *The Culture of Education*, Cambridge, MA: Harvard University Press.

Canter, L. and Canter, M. (1992) *Assertive Discipline: Positive Behaviour Management for Today's Classroom*, Santa Monica, CA: Lee Canter and Associates.

Cornwall, J. (2004) 'Pressure, stress and children's behaviour at school', in J. Wearmouth, R.C. Richmond, T. Glynn and M. Berryman (eds) *Understanding Pupil Behaviour in Schools: A Diversity of Approaches*, London: Fulton, ch. 20, pp. 307–21.

Department for Education (DfE) (2012a) *Teachers' Standards for Qualified Teacher Status*, London: DfE.

Department for Education (DfE) (2012b) *Preventing and Tackling Bullying: Advice for Head Teachers, Staff and Governing Bodies*, London: DfE.

Department for Education and Skills (DfES) (2006) *Learning Behaviour: Principles and Practice – What Works in Schools* (Steer Report), London: DfES.

Dunckley, I. (1999) *Managing Extreme Behaviour in Schools*, Wellington, New Zealand: Specialist Education Services.

Elton, Lord (1989) *Enquiry into Discipline in Schools*, London: DES.

Field, E.M. (1999) *Bully Busting*, Lane Cove, New South Wales: Finch Publishing Pty.

Glynn, T. (2004) 'Antecedent control of behaviour in educational contexts', in J. Wearmouth, R.C. Richmond and T. Glynn (eds) *Understanding Pupil Behaviour in Schools: A Diversity of Approaches*, London: Fulton.

Harris-Hendriks, J. and Figueroa, J. (1995) *Black in White: The Caribbean Child in the UK Home*, London: Pitman.

Hobby, R. and Smith, F. (2002) *A National Development Agenda: What Does it Feel Like to Learn in Our Schools?* London: The Hay Group.

Kanner, L. (1943) 'Autistic disturbances of affective contact', *Nervous Child*, 2: 217–50.

Maslow, A. (1943) 'A theory of human motivation', *Psychological Review*, 50(4): 370–96.

Mosley, J. (1996) *Quality Circle Time in the Primary Classroom: Your Essential Guide to Enhancing Self-Esteem, Self-discipline and Positive Relationships*, Cambridge: LDA.

National Autistic Society (2013) 'The genetics of autism spectrum disorders', www.autism.org.uk/working-with/health/screening-and-diagnosis/the-genetics-of-autism-spectrum-disorders.aspx (accessed 24 June 2013).

National Institute of Neorological Disorders and Stroke (NINDS) (2005) *Tourette Syndrome Fact Sheet*, Bethesda, MD: NINDS.

Norwich, B., Cooper, P. and Maras, P. (2002) 'Attentional and activity difficulties: Findings from a national study', *Support for Learning*, 17(4): 182–6.

Office for Standards in Education (Ofsted) (2001) *Improving Attendance and Behaviour in Secondary Schools*, London: Ofsted.

Olweus, D. (1978) *Aggression in the Schools: Bullies and Whipping Boys*, New York: Wiley.

Piacentini, J., Woods, D.W., Scahill, L., Wilhelm, S., Peterson, A.L., Chang, S., Ginsburg, G.S., Deckersbach, T., Dziura, J., Levi-Pearl, S. and Walkup, J. (2010) 'Behavior therapy for childrenwith Tourette Disorder', *Journal of the American Medical Association*, 303(19): 1929–37.

Poulou, M. and Norwich, B. (2002) 'Cognitive, emotional and behavioural responses to students with emotional and behavioural difficulties: a model of decision-making', *British Educational Research Journal*, 28(1): 111–38.

Rigby, K. (2002) *New Perspectives on Bullying*, London: Jessica Kingsley.

Rogers, B. (2003) *Behaviour Recovery*, Melbourne, Victoria: ACER Press.

Rogers, B. (2013) 'Communicating with children in the classroom', in T. Cole, H. Daniels and J. Visser *The Routledge International Companion to Emotional and Behavioural Difficulties*, London: Routledge, ch. 26, pp. 237–45.

Rutter, M., Maughan, B., Mortimore, P. and Ouston, J. (1979) *Fifteen Thousand Hours: Secondary Schools and their Effects on Children*, London: Open Books.

Skinner, B.F. (1938) *The Behaviour of Organisms*, New York: Appleton Century Crofts.

Slee, P.T. (1995) 'Peer victimization and its relationship to depression among Australian primary school students', *Personality and Individual Differences*, 18(1): 57–62.

Smith, C. (2004) 'Confrontation in the classroom', in J. Wearmouth, R.C. Richmond and T. Glynn (eds) *Addressing Pupils' Behaviour: Responses at District, School and Individual Levels*, London: Fulton, ch. 16, pp. 248–66.

Sproson, B. (2004) 'Some do and some don't: teacher effectiveness in managing behaviour', in J. Wearmouth, T. Glynn, R.C. Richmond and M. Berryman (eds) *Inclusion and Behaviour Management in Schools*, London: Fulton, ch. 18, pp. 311–21.

Tew, M. (1998) 'Circle time: a much neglected resource in secondary schools', *Pastoral Care*, September: 18–27.

Warnock Report (1978) *Special Educational Needs, Report of the Committee of Enquiry into the Education of Handicapped Children and Young People, Cmnd. 7212 Department of Education and Science*, London: HMSO.

Watkins, C. and Wagner, P. (2000) *Improving School Behaviour*, London, Paul Chapman.

Wearmouth, J. (2009) *A Beginning Teacher's Guide to Special Educational Needs*, Buckingham: Open University Press.

Wearmouth, J., Glynn, T. and Berryman, M. (2005) *Perspectives on Student Behaviour in Schools: Exploring Theory and Developing Practice*, London: Routledge.

Wing, L. (1996) *The Autistic Spectrum: A Guide for Parent and Professionals*, London: Constable.

Wing, L. and Gould, J. (1979) 'Severe impairments of social interaction and associated abnormalities in children: epidemiology and classification', *Journal of Autism and Developmental Disorders*, 9, pp. 11–29.

ORGANISING EFFECTIVE CLASSROOM TALK

Lyn Dawes

Teachers must value the relationship between the talk they use for teaching, and the talk they hope to inspire their pupils to use for learning.

(Smith and Higgins, 2006: 500)

INTRODUCTION

Most children arrive at school able to talk. Children are rarely taught how to use spoken language in the same way that they are taught literacy and numeracy. Because of this, they may never learn how to share and negotiate a range of points of view, how to listen attentively to others, how to evaluate what they hear and provide a considered response. Children who are not helped to understand these important skills get by in various ways. Some express themselves by shouting, sulking, asserting themselves or ignoring others. Some say very little when faced with alternatives, choices or problems. However, children need to know how to talk to one another, in order to learn effectively. An inability to communicate with others through talk is a true deprivation, and it is unnecessary, because, in classrooms, we can teach children how to engage one another in discussion. This is not just a social skill, but a crucial capacity, enabling access to educational opportunities. Effective talk – talk for learning – does not just happen, but is a product of planning, teaching and organisation. We need to make sure that every child learns ways to share their ideas through talk. A focus on talk for learning is essential if all are to benefit from classroom activities.

OBJECTIVES

This unit will help you to:

- consider the crucial importance of classroom talk for learning;
- identify ways that teachers use talk for learning;
- understand when and how to move between different sorts of talk;
- raise children's awareness of their classroom talk and its impact on others.

THE CRUCIAL IMPORTANCE OF CLASSROOM TALK FOR LEARNING

Children learn, not just through experience, but by talking about what they are doing. Talk precipitates thought, as children share ideas and comment on what they observe. In this way, children help one another to generate new understanding and stimulate curiosity, imagination and interest. Children talking may articulate tentative or more firmly entrenched ideas, make suggestions or offer information. The chance to listen to children's talk allows us some useful insight into their thinking. In whole-class settings, talk with a teacher can provide children with new information. Even more importantly, children can hear and consider a range of alternative points of view, and classroom talk has the social function of helping the child to learn how effective communication goes on as ideas are raised and negotiated. The 2014 Primary National Curriculum emphasises both the importance of children's talk, and the importance of direct teaching of the relevant skills:

> The National Curriculum for English reflects the importance of spoken language in pupils' development across the whole curriculum – cognitively, socially and linguistically [. . .] Pupils should develop a capacity to explain their understanding of books and other reading, and to prepare their ideas before they write. They must be assisted in making their thinking clear to themselves as well as to others and teachers should ensure that pupils build secure foundations by using discussion to probe and remedy their misconceptions. Pupils should also be taught to understand and use the conventions for discussion and debate.
>
> (Department for Education, 2013)

We can usefully teach children how to explain their understanding generally. In primary classrooms, even the most literate children are only just beginning to learn through reading and writing. Talk is the medium through which much learning goes on, as children become involved in a range of activities. Teachers have the responsibility to make sure that every child has the opportunity to speak out in class as an everyday occurrence. This requires some organisation, because, as educationalists, we cannot be satisfied with casual conversation; we need to organise the sort of educationally effective talk that we know will help everyone to develop, think and learn. So it is that we need to organise talk for learning. To do so, we need to be able to say what *talk for learning* is, and to be able to describe what it sounds like and achieves.

WHAT IS TALK FOR LEARNING?

We can start by saying what it is not. Every teacher is aware that children's talk is not so easily focused on learning. Children are marvellous beings: imaginative, funny, charming and inconsequential, but also anarchic and self-centred. Classrooms put children in a social setting in which much is expected of them in terms of behaviour and concentration. They can, and do, use language in ways we find difficult. They contradict one another, are unkind, insensitive or rude; they come up with irrelevant or oblique comments; they shout, laugh or don't speak at all; they make jokes and distract others; they talk but do not listen; their concentration wavers, and their thoughts drift off to their homes, games or friends. This is all fine – we want our children to be natural, chatty and confident. But we also want them to focus their minds on the educational task in hand. So we comment on talk in terms of behaviour: 'Everyone's being lovely and quiet'; 'Stop talking now please'; 'You need to listen, and you can't listen if you're talking'.

Classes do need to learn how to be quiet and attentive. They also need to learn how and why to talk to one another in ways that support everyone's learning.

Whole-class talk

Children's everyday experiences and their willingness to offer ideas for joint consideration by the class are invaluable resources. Children may rely on the teacher to tap into the minds of others on their behalf. Ensuring access to this rich seam of imagination and information requires teachers to establish a positive relationship with children, based on an understanding that everyone's ideas will be valued. Developing an environment in which children feel that they can be open can be a slow process, but can be helped by direct teaching of the knowledge, skills and understanding needed to contribute to whole-class talk.

Group talk

Children's expectations of their contribution to group talk differ enormously from what we optimistically imagine. The moment adult attention is withdrawn, a group left to work alone may find it very hard to focus on the artificial, complex and sometimes less than fascinating learning intentions that the curriculum demands. Again, direct tuition of talk skills and an understanding of why talk is so important for learning can help children to take part in effective discussions with one another in a small-group setting. The chance to hear a range of ideas or points of view can be truly motivating; there is a positive feedback loop in operation, which means that children taught how to discuss things enjoy the experience and are better able to stay on task.

So what is talk for learning? Talk for learning is educationally effective talk; it is talk that is focused on the task in hand, is inclusive and equitable, and helps everyone to gain new understanding, or to articulate their inability to understand. Like everything else good that goes on in classrooms, it is unlikely to happen unless we organise it; we cannot leave this to chance. We can consider ways of organising talk for learning in two common classroom contexts:

- whole-class talk between teacher and class: *dialogic teaching*;
- children working in groups with their classmates: *exploratory talk*.

Much (though by no means all) talk for learning falls into these two contexts. A brief description of each follows, with references to further information and a summary of key points in Tables 3.6.1 and 3.6.2.

DIALOGIC TEACHING

Using dialogue as a way of thinking and learning has a long history in education (Alexander, 2006; Scott and Asoko, 2006). Dialogic teaching can be described as teaching in which the teacher is aware of the power of dialogue and creates opportunities to engage every child in dialogue. For example, during whole-class work, children are expected to contribute, not just brief answers, but more lengthy explanations in which they go into detail about what they do, or do not, know or understand. Others listen attentively and are prepared to contribute themselves. In this way, children work together to discuss, reflect on and modify their ideas. The teacher orchestrates the discussion to lead children through a line of thinking. Crucially, there is time to deliberate and listen to tentative ideas. An effective lesson may contain dialogic episodes in addition to more authoritative episodes, in which the teacher sums up or clarifies the discussion and offers clear explanations.

What does dialogic teaching look and sound like?

During dialogic teaching, the class and teacher have the same aims for their learning and are engaged in pursuit of knowledge and understanding through talk. Dialogic teaching is characterised

TABLE 3.6.1 Dialogic teaching: talk between a teacher and a class of children

Purpose	Children summarise and share their thinking; express hypothetical ideas; admit to lack of understanding; listen to and reflect on other points of view; follow a line of reasoning. Exploring children's thoughts.
Organisation	Everyone can see and hear one another.
During dialogic teaching . . .	Children pay attention to each other's words; take extended turns; ask one another questions or challenge ideas; follow up on what they hear. The teacher chains responses into a coherent whole; orchestrates the talk; may speak very little themselves.
Talk tools	What is your opinion/idea . . .? Could you say more? Have you considered . . .? Choose someone who might contribute next . . . What if . . .? Remember what * said . . .? Who would like to challenge that . . .? What is your question/idea . . .? That's helpful because . . .
Ground rules	Children are prepared to explain their thinking; ask questions; admit lack of understanding; reason; listen attentively and follow the discussion. Teacher elicits contributions and maintains a focus on a line of thinking or reasoning.
Outcomes	Shared understanding and developing knowledge. Respect for ideas. Awareness of the limits of understanding, leading to productive questioning and learning.
Notes	Children may need input in active listening. Some may have an unwillingness to contribute or take an extended turn, and need positive support. There may be problems with admitting to lack of understanding. Children need to know that their contributions are of value to others.

by purposeful listening, a willingness to offer ideas or make problems with learning explicit, and teacher contributions that keep the children talking. This might mean that one child is encouraged to hold the floor, or another to talk about problems with their work in a way that helps their classmates to identify solutions or strategies. Contributions are linked to generate an overall 'bigger picture', through which children can make connections with previous learning. A feature of dialogue is that questions are raised, which, instead of leading to immediate and brief answers, lead to further questions, a discussion of detail or an admittance that more information is required. Such talk fosters children's natural curiosity.

EXPLORATORY TALK

Exploratory talk is talk in which children engage one another in a good discussion. Children can learn to take part in exploratory discussions that continue when the group has no adult present. Members of such groups draw on what they have been taught about talk for learning. They are aware of the importance of their talk and take responsibility for their own learning and that of the others in their group. Each child is invited or encouraged to contribute. All information is shared. Opinions are backed up with reasons and discussed with respect. In addition, the talk may be hesitant, as half-

TABLE 3.6.2 Exploratory talk: talk between groups of children with no adult support

Purpose	Inclusive talk to enable joint problem solving; sharing of ideas, opinions and reasons; negotiation.
Organisation	Three children seated near one another, around a table.
During exploratory talk . . .	All are invited to contribute; ideas and opinions are offered with reasons; information is shared; the group seeks to reach agreement; everyone listens; the group is on task.
Talk tools	What do you think? Why do you think that? I agree because . . . I disagree because . . . What do we know about . . .? I think . . . Shall we decide that . . . Wait a minute . . . But . . .
Ground rules	Everyone is invited to speak by others; contributions are treated with respect; reasons are asked for, and given; ideas are considered fully before agreement is reached.
Outcomes	Group agreement on a joint solution, idea or course of action. Group responsibility for decisions. Children support one another's thinking.
Notes	The task must necessitate discussion. Children need preparation; they must have an awareness of talk for learning, and have thought about and created a set of their own shared class ground rules for exploratory talk.

formed ideas are tentatively suggested, or particular points may be taken up and elaborated in some detail. Children may not be aware that this is what we require when we ask them to work in a group; direct teaching of the essential skills and understanding is necessary (Mercer and Littleton, 2007).

Exploratory talk requires shared motivation and purpose, which can be generated by direct teaching of the 'ground rules' that support discussion (Dawes, 2008). By creating and using their own class ground rules for talk, children are freed from having to negotiate social barriers and can really concentrate on engaging with the task in hand. Exploratory talk enables children in a group to achieve more than each child would alone, whatever their ability. Crucially, they simultaneously internalise the structures of reasoned, equitable discussion. By doing so, they learn a powerful and transferable way of thinking, which they can put to use when faced, alone, with a range of classroom and out-of-school problems.

What does exploratory talk look and sound like?

Children work closely in groups, using exploratory talk. That is, they are able to use questions as talk tools: 'What do you think?', 'Why do you think that?'; and as prompts: 'Can you say what you know about . . .', 'Tell us what happened . . .'. They can be heard to offer hypothetical ideas: 'What if . . .', 'But . . .'; and to elaborate on ideas: 'Yes, but remember when we did this before, we . . .'. They listen attentively to one another, and their talk is courteous and purposeful, characterised by a degree of challenge and explicit reasoning. The group of children is aware of the underlying rules that govern effective discussion and aims to adhere to them, in order to negotiate an agreement.

WHEN AND HOW TO MOVE BETWEEN TYPES OF TALK

We can plan talk for learning without being able to say precisely how the talk will proceed in all classroom situations. We have to rely on our professional expertise to decide when and how to switch between types of talk. But we can generalise a little to say that:

• **Whole-class introductory dialogue** requires authoritative input, such as clear instructions and information. Also, we might use the sorts of question that simply check for items of knowledge: 'What did we do last week?', 'Remind us of the difference between an isosceles and equilateral triangle?', 'Where do herons lay their eggs?'. Some of these questions might be targeted at individuals and often have a behavioural function; the question 'Jason, what is your answer to this?' is a way of ensuring Jason's involvement without actually saying, 'Are you listening, Jason?'. After more than 5 minutes of such questions, children are not usually learning much. Some children always involve themselves with this particular sort of closed questioning; some do just the opposite. It is not motivating to think of answers to questions when you know that the questioner already knows the answer they want.

   Introductions benefit from more complex dialogue, in which we ask genuine questions: 'What do you already know about . . .', 'Has anyone heard of anything about this that might help us . . .?', 'What is your experience of this . . .?'.

• **Group work** requires children to engage one another in exploratory talk. The teacher's role is, first, to ensure that the children have been taught the structures of exploratory talk and, second, to listen in, support the children's work and move on. We can model exploratory talk as we move around the groups: 'Could you give a reason please?', 'Does anyone have any more information we can think about?', 'Has everyone been asked for their ideas?'.

   A problem with exploratory talk is that a persuasive argument can sway a whole group into believing things that are not necessarily true. However, as the talk is part of an ongoing classroom dialogue, the group is subsequently able to hear other ideas from their classmates and can reconsider. Ideas established during discussion may not be firmly held until the child has had a chance to check them against practical experience and the ideas of others. Thinking about new ideas – 'weighing things up' and reflecting on how new ideas fit with one's own current thinking – is a learning process and an invaluable experience for a child. The chance to reject or accept an idea enables children to understand that they are responsible for their own learning and to create their own ideas as they speak, listen and think with others.

Task 3.6.1 Children's classroom talk

Listen carefully to children's classroom talk in two contexts – a whole class in discussion with a teacher, and a small-group discussion with no adult support. Ask yourself questions about the purpose, organisation and outcomes of the talk.

• **Purpose**: What is the purpose of the talk? Is everyone aware of this purpose? Is the talk fulfilling its purpose?
• **Organisation**: Who is organising the talk? How do people bid for turns? Who gets a turn and why? What happens to people who do not get a turn? Is any of the talk to do with behaviour management? Does the talk always stay on task?
• **Outcomes**: What are the outcomes of the talk? What have different individuals learned about (1) the topic under discussion, (2) their position in the classroom, (3) how to communicate effectively with others?

- **Whole-class closing plenary sessions** require dialogue that brings together the children's ideas from their group work, linked into a coherent line of thinking. The teacher's role is to ensure that there is plenty of time for talk, and to orchestrate the dialogue. In addition, there is often the necessity for some authoritative summary information. Dialogic teaching can be thought of as including episodes of talk and episodes of authoritative teacher input, which will later contribute to further dialogue. Plenary discussion should bring out children's thinking about new concepts, and also about the quality of the talk that took place in their group work. They can suggest who offered ideas, listened, asked an important question, and so on.

RAISING CHILDREN'S AWARENESS OF TALK FOR LEARNING

Organising effective talk involves raising children's awareness of the power of spoken language. We must clarify the expectation that every child will contribute to the learning of others through sharing their thoughts. Some children may never have imagined that this is the case. Others may have a very good idea of why we ask them to contribute, but may find themselves unable to do so in an unsupportive context.

For children in class, their teachers act as models for the sorts of structure that make talk educationally effective. The phrases we use in whole-class talk, such as 'What do you think?' or 'Can you say a bit more about . . .?', are what we want children to say to each other. Encouraging someone to keep talking, making links between contributions, rephrasing and summing up are all skills children learn from experience, especially if they happen often and are explicitly discussed as talk strategies.

If we are honest, we know that group work can go wrong. The classroom becomes too noisy, or little learning seems to be happening. When children are in discussion in small groups, the teacher cannot know what every child is saying. Children in a group may bicker or simply ignore one another; they may feel that helping others is not helping their own learning, or that others are 'cheating' if they want to talk about their answers. It is instructive to ask children what they think of group work.

However, we know that talk is essential for learning. This is a real paradox and a problem for every teacher. We want to ensure effective group talk, because what is the alternative? We must insist on quiet. The command 'Please be quiet!' immediately confines each child to their own thoughts . . . sometimes, an uneasy silence reigns. Silence is a behaviour management strategy and not always conducive to developing minds. No doubt quiet has some value, but not if it is overused, and not when a child is trying to puzzle something out, explain something, use a recently heard word, ask a question or find out a missing piece of information. And silence cannot guarantee that children are thinking and learning about the topic in hand.

So, 'talk lessons' are necessary – that is, before you expect them to conduct a good discussion, children need direct teaching about exploratory talk. We need to make explicit the usually hidden 'ground rules' that keep a discussion on track (Dawes, 2008, 2011).

What talk skills are needed? Simply put, children need to:

- listen;
- stay on task;
- include everyone;
- know how to challenge one another;
- always respect contributions;
- ask questions;
- elaborate and explain;
- offer their ideas with reasons.

This list can be used to devise learning intentions for lessons that focus on each skill in turn. There are plenty of contexts for talk in curriculum areas. Plenary discussions about the effectiveness of talk can help children to build up an awareness of their ability to contribute to one another's learning, and can help groups to establish an ethos of exploratory talk. Importantly, the child's own 'voice' (their accent, bilingualism, vocabulary and dialect) is valued, not diminished, by learning this extension to their talk repertoire.

So, we can discuss and model relevant talk skills during introductory sessions, identify them as learning intentions, and review them during plenary sessions, so that children can evaluate the difference good talk makes. Children need constant chances to reflect on what they have said and heard, in order to examine what they have learned, and how, and who from. They need opportunities to identify particular talk episodes that helped them to understand, or caught their imagination, or made them feel puzzled. They need to acknowledge who it is that has contributed orally. It has to be made clear to children that knowledge and understanding are not simply contained in the teacher, computers or books, but in the class as a whole, and that, by talking and thinking together, such understandings can be profitably shared. They can usefully learn the term 'interthinking' – thinking aloud together – as a description of the spoken mechanism for creating joint understanding (Littleton and Mercer, 2013). Children given a direct insight into the idea of interthinking, and taught the skills to take part in interthinking, can see how and why to find out what others think. They can articulate their own ideas. They can include themselves in the everyday educational conversations of their classroom. For some children, this makes a huge difference to their engagement. For others, it overcomes barriers caused by wider social issues, or their personal inhibitions. For all children, interthinking is a life skill.

Task 3.6.2 Understanding interthinking

Read 'Learning to think together and alone', in Mercer and Littleton (2007), *Dialogue and the Development of Children's Thinking*, pp. 55–82. Discuss with colleagues the value and purpose of interthinking and strategies for enabling children to talk about talk and their own thinking in school. How might you, as the teacher, model this?

Without shared ground rules, children in an unsupervised group will generally talk as they would in the playground or at home. Children unused to thinking that what they say is important are almost bound to misunderstand what we mean when we ask them to 'Talk about this with your group . . .' Indeed, they may believe that, if they talk about their work, they are somehow cheating, or, worse, they will be teased or even ridiculed by classmates. For the child who is interested in talking about the task, the barriers may be insurmountable, as more and more lures to join in with off-task conversation are thrown out. A group of children arguing about what happened at break time or discussing last night's television programmes, instead of talking about the activity they are engaged in, might not seem very unusual. After all, some social talk can help children cohere. But it is actually very worrying. If every chance to talk is a chance to forget about school work, children are unknowingly rejecting a major part of their learning throughout their primary years. This is unfair to them, especially as those most vulnerable to failure in the education system may well be those frittering away their time in class in superficial chatter.

Task 3.6.3 Children's rules for classroom talk

Work with a group of three or four children. Ask them to discuss their ideas with you.

- When they are working in a group with classmates, who do they like to work with and why? Who helps them to learn? Who stops them learning? What do they like or dislike about working in a group with other children? Why do they think that teachers ask them to work in groups?
- Ask the children to suggest a list of five or six 'rules', which, if applied, would help a group to work well together. (Try to persuade them not to start these with the word 'Don't!') Compare their suggestions with the ground rules for exploratory talk in Table 3.6.2.
- Have the same discussion with other groups, or with the whole class. Collate ideas to establish a class set of ground rules for exploratory talk. Check that everyone agrees with the rules and will try to follow them. Devise an activity that requires group discussion and ask the children to try to apply their rules. Evaluate the talk: did the rules help everyone to join in and share ideas? If not, can the class alter them?

PLANNING FOR EXPLORATORY TALK

Organising effective classroom talk requires planning: planning for the teaching of exploratory talk; planning for the creation of time to develop and consider ideas through dialogue; and planning for group talk, in which children can make the most of the opportunity to interthink. Of course, children do need to work individually sometimes, but, sometimes, the chance to discuss resources, ideas and problems can promote the sort of collaborative learning that is the advantage of being part of a class.

We can foreground talk for learning by having paired learning objectives. That is, we can pair up a learning objective for talk with the curriculum learning objective. In this way, we can teach skills that are tailored to class or individual needs, practise their use, and reflect on their effectiveness in closing plenary discussions, within highly relevant contexts. In addition, the other key feature of a talk-focused lesson plan is that it includes some time set aside for discussion. Talk invariably takes longer than you would imagine, and an effective discussion can last and last; there is a limit to time in any classroom situation. However, unless you plan for discussion time, none will happen, and children will lose the chance to articulate, develop and reflect on their ideas, to use new vocabulary and to generally think things through properly.

Example 3.6.1 is a brief example of a lesson outline, with science as a context for the talk.

Suggestions for further work using talk for learning objectives

- Identify and use objectives for specific talk skills in curriculum lessons.
- Choose one particular objective, teach the skills directly and integrate throughout a week.
- Ask children to identify their particular problems with speaking and listening in class.
- Make the link between speaking, listening, thinking and learning explicit at all times.
- Encourage children to see that learning cannot happen unless certain sorts of talk go on – and unless voices are modulated, contributions are thoughtful and everyone in the class is included in effective discussions.
- Create a 'speaking and listening for thinking and learning' display.

Example 3.6.1 Science (friction) and talk lesson

Learning objectives

To be able to:

- offer reasons and evidence for views, considering alternative opinions;
- listen to a speaker, making (mental) notes on the talk;
- identify some starting ideas about the topic of friction.

Introduction

Share learning objectives, asking children to recall their ideas about the importance of talk for learning and how it might best proceed. Ask children to explain to one another what the words *reasons*, *evidence* and *alternative opinions* mean; then share with the class.

Ask the children to think about friction (give a brief example by rubbing hands); explain that we need to find out what everyone already knows, so that it can be shared.

Group work

Ask groups to discuss the following *Talking Points* (Dawes, 2012) to decide whether their group thinks that each statement is true or false, or if their group is unsure. Stress that uncertainty is valuable: it leads to questioning and learning. Remind the groups of the importance of asking everyone for ideas, opinions and reasons. No writing is needed.

Talking Points: friction

Are these statements true or false, or is your group unsure? Make sure you give reasons for what you say.

1 Grip is another word for friction.
2 Friction always happens when surfaces are moving against each other.
3 Friction is usually a nuisance.
4 Trainers have friction built into the soles.
5 You can't stop friction happening.
6 Bikes work because of friction.
7 Friction is a force.
8 Air resistance, which makes parachutes work, is a sort of friction.
9 There is no friction on the moon.
10 You can't slide on a carpet because of friction.

Mini-plenary

During discussions, focus the children on active listening and ask them to try to remember something that they think particularly interesting from their group talk.

Plenary

1 **Science**: Choose a Talking Point to discuss. Ask groups to contribute ideas about friction, especially if their group was unsure. Remind them that *uncertainty* is helpful, because it is a way for everyone to learn. What were contradictory opinions? Ask groups to explain their ideas and reasons.

Once all opinions have been heard, ask children to comment on one another's ideas, using positive language and challenging others using the talk tool, 'I disagree because . . .'. Chain the discussion into coherent lines of thinking. Encourage children to nominate who they want to hear from next, and encourage children to take extended turns when talking. Sum up, or ask a child to sum up, the outcome of the discussion.

2 **Talk for learning**: Ask the class to suggest classmates who offered ideas, listened well, gave good reasons, summed up discussions and helped negotiation. Help the children to understand that you have, as yet, done no teaching about friction, but that they have learned by sharing their understanding through speaking and listening.

Ask children to reflect, recall and share examples of productive talk; who gave an *opinion* and what was their *reason*? How did your group *negotiate* ideas with another group? What were *key points* of the discussion? Can anyone offer to *compare* the ideas they heard? Who would you describe as *articulate*? Do you consider the class to have had a *productive discussion*? How do you know? What have we learned about *talk for learning*? What is important about talk for learning? How does it help us to *think*? In what ways is it difficult? How can we get round the problems to make sure that classroom talk helps us all to think and learn?

This session would be followed by practical activity in which children have a chance to learn about friction through experience.

Task 3.6.4 Talk for learning

- Decide on a year group that interests you.
- Decide on a specific discussion skill relevant to your class (e.g. asking for and giving reasons, asking a question, active listening and responding, elaborating, explaining, summing up). You will need to think of a relevant context for talk, but keep the lesson focused on the talk, not the context!
- Now choose a curriculum area and devise a lesson that incorporates talk skills and understanding. In particular, carefully plan your plenary questions, which will enable children to reflect on talk for learning and to value one another's contribution to their learning.
- Teach the lesson and evaluate what happened. Ask the children for their comments.

LISTENING AND RESPONDING

It's easy to forget about listening as a skill. As teachers, we learn how to help children listen – or appear to listen – and schoolchildren learn how to seem to be listening. However, active listening is extremely important. A child who is genuinely listening has access to new thinking. Listening improves motivation. We often talk to whole classes of children; it's worth evaluating such talk to check on its effectiveness. The 'traditional' interaction between teacher and children in a classroom has been called IRF; that is, initiation, response and feedback. Here are two examples, in which the teacher both initiates an exchange with a child, and provides feedback:

I: What is the gas we need to breathe in from the air?
R: Nitrogen.
F: Hmm, no –
I: What is the gas we need to breathe in from the air?
R: Oxygen.
F: Yes, right.

In both cases, a brief answer is required, and the teacher knows that answer. The class of children knows that the teacher has a 'right' answer in mind and will guess until they discover it. It is a common classroom game. Some children always take part in it; some, never. It does not help children to develop their thinking or their discussion skills, and it is unrelated to active listening. A study undertaken by the Institute of Education (Kyriacou and Issit, 2008) looked at children learning mathematics and found that the IRF structure persists as very prevalent. They point out that teachers need to think about how to approach their classroom conversations, in order to avoid the IRF trap (which we have all fallen into sometimes!). Characteristics of more effective talk are identified; space precludes discussion of all of them, but two already mentioned throughout this unit are:

- enhancing pupils' self-knowledge of how to make use of teacher–pupil dialogue as a learning experience;
- encouraging high-quality pupil dialogue.

A third characteristic is 'transformative listening'. The report suggests some talk for learning teaching strategies that involve transformative listening. The teacher:

(a) asks a question to which *they do not know* the answer;
(b) responds to pupils' suggestions;
(c) asks for feedback from the whole class;
(d) asks a pupil to explain their ideas to the class.

(Adapted from Kyraicou and Issit, 2008)

Such strategies can all have the effect of broadening the scope of the discussion, involving children, and thus supporting thinking and learning. The key thing is to help children to listen by showing them that, in return, you will listen to them; and to ask stimulating and creative questions that you do not already know the answer to. We want children to explain, comment, hypothesise and elaborate. So, it is not only the initiation questions that we ask, but also the feedback we give learners, that merit some reflection and attention – can we keep them talking, encourage them to talk to one another, and help them to build understanding based on this scaffold of talk?

Listening is key to learning, and yet we teachers often think that children just *do not listen*. Why don't they? Do we become part of the background noise to be blanked out, are our questions inauthentic, and would they listen better to us if we listened better to them? We can teach listening in parallel with teaching talk skills. Such tuition is time well spent.

SUMMARY

We cannot just leave classroom talk to chance. Children arrive in our classrooms knowing how to talk, but may not have particularly considered the specialised sort of talk, so important for classroom learning, that is exploratory talk. Talk is such an everyday medium that children may take it for granted, not knowing that they can learn as much about talk as they do about reading and writing in classrooms. Talk can be so bound up with classroom behaviour that its crucial function of stimulating and developing thinking may be unclear to children.

Dialogic teaching is a means to move whole classes through steps of reasoning, hypothesis and deduction, by valuing contributions and encouraging reflection. By employing a dialogic approach and simultaneously teaching children how to engage one another in exploratory talk, we offer them a powerful means to work on their own thinking and that of others. Exploratory talk is educationally effective talk – talk for learning – and children need an awareness of what it is and why it's important. The everyday occurrence of talk for learning can only happen if we organise classrooms by planning: there needs to be time for talk; resources and activities must merit discussion; and the teaching of children how to talk to one another must go on constantly. Effective teachers move between different types of talk as a lesson proceeds. Every child needs to know how and why to listen actively, if they are to develop their thinking and make the most of learning opportunities.

Engaging children in talk for learning helps teachers to develop effective classroom relationships. Talking about what they are doing with their group helps to motivate children and focus their interest. The busy hum of a classroom in which children are discussing their work – a sure sign of a well-organised teacher – is a happy feature of effective primary schools. Teachers want to hear children talking: it is an indication of learning and a sign that children are practising the talk skills that will help develop their minds throughout their education.

ANNOTATED FURTHER READING

Mercer, N. and Littleton, K. (2007) *Dialogue and the Development of Children's Thinking: A Sociocultural Approach*, London: Routledge.
> An accessible and richly documented text that argues for the importance of spoken dialogue in children's intellectual development.

FURTHER READING TO SUPPORT M-LEVEL STUDY

Mercer, N. (2008) 'The seeds of time: why classroom dialogue needs a temporal analysis', *Journal of the Learning Sciences*, 17(1): 33-59.
> 'The relationship between time, talk, and learning is intrinsically important to classroom education [. . .] The coherence of educational experience is dependent on talk' (p. 55).

Smith, H. and Higgins, S. (2006) 'Opening classroom interaction: the importance of feedback', *Cambridge Journal of Education*, 36(4): 485-502.
> 'Hence it is arguable that it is neither the act of asking questions itself, nor, as we have argued, the types of questions teachers ask, which limits pupil response. Rather, it is the feedback given in reaction to pupil responses and the historical precedence of the perception of teacher intent this engenders, which either opens or restricts classroom interaction. Using such conversational tactics as regular alternatives to evaluative feedback means that pupils will come to expect the purpose of questions as a tool to focus their minds on a problem to be jointly solved, in order to arrive at a shared and possibly new understanding' (p. 500).

RELEVANT WEBSITES

www.learningandteaching.info

thinkingtogether.educ.cam.ac.uk

www.education.gov.uk/schools/teachingandlearning/curriculum/nationalcurriculum2014

http://eppi.ioe.ac.uk

REFERENCES

Alexander, R. (2006) *Towards Dialogic Teaching*, York: Dialogos.

Daniels, H. (2001) *Vygotsky and Pedagogy*, London: RoutledgeFalmer.

Dawes, L. (2008) *The Essential Speaking and Listening: Talk for Learning at Key Stage 2*, London: Routledge.

Dawes, L. (2011) *Creating a Speaking and Listening Classroom: Integrating Talk for Learning at Key Stage 2*, London: Routledge.

Dawes, L. (2012) *Talking Points: Discussion Activities in the Primary Classroom*, London: Routledge.

Department for Education (2013) The National Curriculum, www.gov.uk/government/collections/national-curriculum.

Kyriacou, C. and Issit, J. (2008) *What Characterises Teacher–Pupil Dialogue to Promote Conceptual Understanding in Mathematics Lessons in England in Key Stages 2 and 3?* Evidence for Policy and Practice Information and Co-ordinating Centre (EPPI-Centre) Social Science Research Unit: Report 1604R.

Littleton, K. and Mercer, N. (2013) *Interthinking: Putting Talk to Work*, London: Routledge.

Mercer, N. and Littleton, K. (2007) *Dialogue and the Development of Children's Thinking: A Sociocultural Approach*, London: Routledge.

Scott, P.H. and Asoko, H. (2006) 'Talk in science classrooms', in V. Wood-Robinson (ed.) *Association of Science Education Guide to Secondary Science Education*, Hatfield: Association for Science Education (ASE).

Smith, H. and Higgins, S. (2006) 'Opening classroom interaction: the importance of feedback', *Cambridge Journal of Education*, 36(4): 485–502.

VALUING, ORGANISING AND MANAGING LEARNING OUTSIDE THE CLASSROOM

Simon Catling

INTRODUCTION

Opportunities for learning outside the classroom are highly valued. Almost every primary schoolchild studies and learns in their school grounds through various cross-curricular subjects and activities during the year. Annually, several million off-site primary pupil visits take place. Providing experience for young children to learn through activities in the real world is important to primary teachers. The government's *Learning Outside the Classroom Manifesto* (DfES, 2006) endorsed, emphasised and encouraged the value, importance and role of extending children's learning into the school's grounds, the local environment and further afield. Learning outside the classroom builds on the vital and engaging experiences initiated through work in outdoor learning environments in the Foundation Stage, where it is a matter of routine for young children to learn in their outdoor area and through visits to such sites as a forest school, a shop and the park. Outdoor learning is not a new approach for schools, although it is not as widespread as usually assumed and may even be declining. You will consider why it is valued, constraints on learning out of the classroom and how such work can be undertaken effectively.

OBJECTIVES

By the end of this unit you should be able to:

- appreciate the value and benefits of out-of-classroom learning;
- identify opportunities in your own planning and teaching where you can use out-of-classroom learning;
- plan effectively for out-of-classroom learning.

These objectives reflect the requirements in the *Teachers' Standards* for trainee teachers. Planning for out-of-classroom work involves meeting the standards for teaching, including 'setting high expectations which inspire, motivate and challenge pupils' (Standard 1), planning and teaching 'well structured lessons' (Standard 4), and 'managing behaviour effectively to ensure a good and safe learning environment' (Standard 7) (DfE, 2012).

Across the unit, you will read case studies that used out-of-classroom learning opportunities in the school grounds and beyond. They illustrate a range of intentions, foci and organisational matters. Reflect on what they illuminate and relate them to the discussions about the value of such work and the range of activities, organisation and management that are outlined.

Task 3.7.1 Reflecting on your own out-of-classroom learning experience

Consider your own experience studying outside, whether in primary or secondary school, accompanying or organising taking children out of their classroom.

(a) Describe an activity you did, where you did it, for how long.
(b) List what you think you were intended to learn.
(c) Identify the most encouraging and least engaging aspects of your experience.
(d) Reflect on what you feel you really learned from this out-of-class activity.
(e) Explain what you most value about out-of-classroom learning, and why.

OUT-OF-CLASSROOM LEARNING IN THE NATIONAL CURRICULUM

The National Curriculum requirements for Key Stages 1 and 2 make negligible direct reference to out-of-classroom learning (DfE, 2013a). It is referred to directly in reference to *fieldwork* in the geography programmes of study, where it is essential in making observations and gathering information in studies of local neighbourhoods and urban centres, of physical and human geographical features, processes, variations and patterns, and in developing children's mapping skills. It is inferred in developing children's understanding of science processes, methods and content, particularly where children need to observe, measure and record data when investigating the natural and human-constructed world in both key stages. It is evidently implicit in physical education when working outside with children in individual and team activities. In history, local study across the key stages will involve investigating the local area, and there will be visits to such places as museums and heritage sites – just as these will be vital in religious education. For art and design, English and language studies, and design and technology, the outdoor environment in and beyond school can be an inspiration, as can visits to concert halls, art galleries and other venues. There will be opportunities to use and develop mathematical and computing skills and understandings in outdoor enquiries.

Waite (2011b) and colleagues have demonstrated the range of learning and teaching opportunities that are available and can be employed to foster primary children's learning in and of the range of curriculum subjects through out-of-classroom experiences, tasks and investigations. Whichever subject or area, there is a real need to make use of outdoor learning opportunities as an integral aspect of the normal planning, teaching and learning that children experience, not as an 'add-on' (e.g. see Davis, 2010; Pound and Lee, 2011; Cooper, 2012; Scoffham, 2013). This implies that out-of-classroom learning should be a regular context and source for children's learning through working on and off the school's site, not used infrequently.

Case study 1 The Coombes School: a whole school philosophy and approach

The Coombes School is a nursery and primary school renowned for its use of and commitment to its outdoor environment. Its philosophy is founded on 'education offering children and ourselves as the adult group, authentic experiences through which we can start to understand ourselves and our relationship with the world around us' (Rowe and Humphries, 2012: 7). A key aspect in the school's approach is to make consistent and effective use, across the curriculum, of its rich and evolving school grounds, founded on the beliefs that: the outdoors is important to and valuable for children's learning, in and beyond school; any playground can be enhanced through stimulating and 'memorable learning adventures' (p. 10); children's values about the environment can be engaged through experiences in it; and learning outdoors means taking risks in learning, with encounters and activities that engage understanding and foster confidence. The outdoors is also an arena for personal, social, physical and emotional learning. Outdoor activities are planned, timed and purposeful, but are such a normal part of the children's schooling that, while different groups work outside at the same time, the children maintain focus and respect each other and their planned activities. Such activities are subject-based and/or cross-curricular studies, involving environmental, musical, dramatic enactment and historical learning, or are language, mathematics, science, spiritually or art based. Since the start of the 1970s, the school grounds have been developed and enhanced to provide a myriad of opportunities for teaching and learning. The school makes off-site visits and invites in visiting specialists for workshops, bringing the outside world into the school. The outdoors and outside world are both special and everyday. The Coombes School integrates these as core to school life and at the heart of children's learning (Rowe and Humphries, 2012).

VALUING OUT-OF-CLASSROOM LEARNING

The essence of learning outside the classroom is the opportunity for 'first-hand experiences . . . to make subjects more vivid and interesting for pupils and enhance their understanding' (Ofsted, 2008: 7). Learning beyond the classroom is a dynamic aspect of children's experience. This view argues strongly that it is vital for all children, providing learning in its own right and initiating and extending value to their classroom experiences. Well planned and taught, such learning enhances children's knowledge, understanding and skills across the curriculum, providing opportunities and foci that are not available in the classroom. It fosters children's motivation, self-confidence and interpersonal learning (House of Commons Education and Skills Committee, 2005; Stagg *et al.*, 2009; Waite, 2011a, 2011b; Beames *et al.*, 2012). The case for children's learning out of the classroom is well supported by research.

Learning outside the classroom provides a variety of opportunities and benefits for children's learning (Rickinson *et al.*, 2004; Ofsted, 2008; Nundy *et al.*, 2009; Vascellaro, 2011; Sedgwick, 2012; Council for Learning Outside the Classroom, 2013), many of which are outlined in Figure 3.7.1. These *foci* and *benefits* refer to cognitive outcomes, values and attitudes, *and* to personal and interpersonal learning. These opportunities can be pursued and developed in a variety of settings, within and beyond the school's grounds, which may involve being in the outdoors, but can equally be undertaken indoors beyond the child's own school. Figure 3.7.2 identifies a variety of *sites* that might be used in out-of-classroom learning.

There are challenges in undertaking out-of-classroom activities (House of Commons Children, Schools and Families Committee, 2010). Table 3.7.1 identifies several of these. Such challenges need to be resolved when organising working outside the classroom. You need to remember that risk assessments and health and safety regulations are for your security as a teacher, as well as for the children's

Examples of *foci* for out-of-classroom learning for developing knowledge, understanding and skills:

- the natural environment, e.g. the school 'wild area';
- human settlements, e.g. a local village or urban area study;
- community activities, e.g. bulb planting in green spaces, drama or music group;
- nature-society interactions, e.g. visits to nature reserves;
- environmental issues, e.g. contentious planning proposals and developments;
- investigative skills, e.g. using quadrants learnt through science investigations led by field centre staff;
- culture and the arts, e.g. visit to a religious centre or to a concert;
- changes in society over time, e.g. a visit to a historical site.

Examples of *foci* for out-of-classroom learning about oneself and relationships:

- self-awareness, e.g. reflecting on personal outdoor learning experiences;
- building confidence, e.g. through tree climbing in a forest school site;
- personal experiences, e.g. in making a residential visit for the first time and interrelating with peers, teachers and other adults in a different, perhaps novel situation;
- engaging and enhancing curiosity, e.g. through a nature reserve or museum visit;
- working with and relating to others, e.g. through working together on small-group fieldwork tasks;
- a spiritual sense, e.g. senses of wonder and awe through close observations in an art gallery;
- emotional engagement, e.g. through drama enactments in a heritage or wild environment;
- developing interests, e.g. being captivated by objects in a museum;
- personal capabilities, e.g. self-management and communication.

Examples of *benefits* resulting from out-of-classroom learning:

- greater understanding of enquiry-based research, e.g. from investigating stream flow, erosion, transportation and deposition;
- greater information about the local environment, e.g. through recognising historical features;
- increased knowledge and understanding of scientific, geographical and social processes, e.g. about mini-beasts and people's uses of shops and cafes;
- recognition of personal values and feelings, e.g. in relation to heritage conservation;
- fostering attitudes to the future of an environment, e.g. a relic woodland, or to ones' personal treatment of the environment;
- developing new or improved skills, e.g. in orienteering and communication;
- developing or reinforcing positive behaviours, e.g. in taking care not to leave litter or in working with others in community activities;
- personal development, e.g. in building self-confidence through completing new challenges;
- developing inter-personal skills and relationships, e.g. through team working on an outdoor project;
- improved understanding of other people's values, e.g. religious values.

FIGURE 3.7.1 Examples of opportunities provided by learning outside the classroom

safety. Planning out-of-classroom learning requires understanding the benefits such opportunities provide and finding ways to overcome the potential difficulties considerately and safely. Appreciating the value of out-of-classroom learning sets a positive basis for achieving this (Ofsted, 2008).

The range of possible out-of-classroom *sites* that can be used to support, develop and motivate learning include:

- the school grounds, play areas, habitats, equipment, gardens;

- the built environment: urban/suburban areas around school, local streets, park, local shops, new developments;

- the built environment: suburban/urban areas in similar and contrasting localities;

- the rural environment: landscapes, farmland, villages/hamlets;

- wilderness areas;

- rivers, streams, ponds, lakes, canals, waterfalls;

- rural or city farms, botanic gardens;

- parks, allotments, gardens;

- industrial sites, waste disposal sites, reservoirs;

- other school sites;

- tourist information centres;

- heritage sites, castles, historic houses and gardens;

- museums, science centres, National Park centres, zoos;

- field study centres, nature study centres, urban studies centres, science centres;

- theatres, drama and dance workshops, art galleries, concert halls;

- planning offices, old people's homes, community centres;

- shopping centres/malls, supermarkets;

- library, local history and archive centre;

- town hall, civic centre;

- sacred sites, places of worship.

FIGURE 3.7.2 A variety of possible sites for out-of-classroom activities

TABLE 3.7.1 Possible challenges to out-of-classroom learning opportunities

Challenges	Possible concerns
1 **Planning ahead**	Organising out-of-classroom activities requires forethought and careful planning, whether going into the school grounds, the neighbourhood or a site some way away. It may require rearranging the class timetable.
2 **Resources and organisation: from funds to time to staffing**	Visits to museums and similar venues involve costs that may need to be contributed to by parents, who are not always in a position to do so. Taking children outside involves organising other adult support, and informing the adults about the activities they will supervise. Time is needed to walk to nearby sites, and public or private transport bookings must be made in advance, and time must be factored in for travel. There is the need to oversee the children on the bus/coach, have sick bags, etc.
3 **Health and safety concerns**	You must be fully acquainted with the school's and local authority's guidance on health and safety and school visits and follow procedures. Teachers and parents have heightened concerns about how safe children will be, whether from traffic, walking, farm visits, etc. However, perceived risk of accidents far exceeds the reality of very few accidents during out-of-classroom activities and visits.
4 **Personal confidence in taking children out**	Taking children out requires confidence. Going into the school grounds, locally or further afield, means knowing what these places are like, what can be studied and how safely, and setting suitable challenges in the children's tasks. Often, a lack of training or opportunities to accompany experienced colleagues taking children out lies at the root of such concerns. Feeling that personal subject knowledge and information about features, such as plants or birds, is inadequate for making best use of the school's grounds or the local area can inhibit some teachers in taking children outside.
5 **Managing the children**	A frequent concern is managing children's behaviour outside the classroom. It is vital that you are well prepared and that the children understand what is required of them. They need to understand the tasks they will do, perhaps because they have been involved in creating them. You need to be consistent with your classroom expectations, and the adults with you must know these and be consistent too. Ensure the children know how they must respond when you or their group adult wants their attention while out of the classroom.
6 **Risk assessment**	You must undertake or have seen a completed a risk assessment of a potential, even familiar, site. Making judgements about risks involves taking responsibility for decisions about the possible hazards and ways to overcome them.
7 **Regulations and requirements**	The number of forms to complete and the regulations to check can be numerous when you take children off the school site, though it is decreasing. Visits off site involve obtaining permission from the head teacher. Be organised well in advance.
8 **Curriculum demands**	There is a perception that the demands, in particular in teaching and learning in the core subjects, constrain opportunities to take children out of the classroom. There are issues of justification in terms of the time involved and 'lessons missed'. Although teachers may feel that learning outdoors has value, they have concerns that it may take too much time and not provide the outcomes that classroom-based activities will.

Task 3.7.2 Taking children out of the classroom

Use the Ofsted (2008) evaluation, *Learning Outside the Classroom*, to review the benefits and challenges of taking children to work outside the classroom. Go to the Ofsted website and examine recent subject reports for a variety of subjects to see what positive and critical points are made about learning outside the classroom. Use the references for this unit, and others you find in journals, to read more widely. What further opportunities and barriers for schools and classes are noted? How is it suggested these can be overcome?

ORGANISING FOR LEARNING OUTSIDE THE CLASSROOM

This section discusses matters you need to consider, organise for and manage when working with children outside the classroom (DfES, 1998; Salaman and Tutchell, 2005; Hoodless *et al.*, 2009; Waite, 2011b).

Deciding why to go out of the classroom

First, you must consider *why* you might take the children out of the classroom for teaching and learning activities. As with all activities, this is about what you want the children to learn and why using the school grounds or going off site will enhance and extend the children's learning. Such learning might be well planned and ordered, or it might be open-ended. You need to consider how working outside/off site meets your *learning intentions* and/or your *intended objectives/outcomes*. Think where it fits into the *sequence* of activities planned for the topic and how it contributes to the focus of study *at that time*. Identify the *relevant children's experience* it draws on or develops, and whether it provides new experiences and why.

Case study 2 In the school garden: transforming a space

Alicia enjoyed gardening and felt that her Year 3 children would benefit from taking responsibility for such an activity in the school's grounds. She discussed her proposal with her head teacher and agreed a site in the grounds that was in a relatively unused area and that contained good soil. She introduced the idea to her class as part of an environmental project linked with health and developing botanical knowledge. The children inspected the site and considered what they might grow there, how they needed to organise and manage their cultivation and what it might help them learn. They were fully involved in initiating the project, in its development, including linking it with meals they might eat seasonally, tending the plot during school days and holidays, and recording and communicating what they were doing for themselves and others in the school to promote a caring attitude to the garden (see Gaylie, 2011; Passy and Waite, 2011; Williams and Brown, 2012).

Deciding where to take the children

Having decided to provide learning activities and opportunities outside the classroom, you must consider *where* you will take the children. You may look at a particular area or features in the school grounds for a science investigation; you might take the children into the local area as part of a geographical enquiry they have planned; you could involve the children in a historical re-enactment at a country house, working with its education staff. You might visit a concert hall to hear a recital.

In each case, you need to have decided where the most appropriate *location/site/centre* is to take the children for the learning you are planning, whether it is possible to take the children there *when* you want to (visits to centres, zoos, museums, theatres, etc., need booking *well* in advance), and what *alternative sites* there are if you cannot book your first choice.

Meeting the schools' policies for taking children outside

Primary schools have policies for off-site visits and health and safety matters. Before undertaking work outside, you must check with the person responsible for granting permission (either the head or a designated teacher) and find out what the school's visits policy states and how it complies with government and local authority regulations (Council for Learning Outside the Classroom, 2013; DfE, 2013b). It presents the specific requirements the school has relevant to its particular circumstances, for instance concerning children whose English is limited or who have particular learning and/or behavioural needs, and what happens for a child unable to accompany a visit off site. It will cover health and safety matters, if these are not cross-referenced to a separate policy. Working in the school grounds and off the school site means complying with good-practice and common-sense approaches to planning and organising your classroom teaching and in managing behaviour. The school will have a view on the support of other adults working with you, but you will need to check this if there is no such statement in the school's visits policy.

When taking the children off site, for however long, there are organisational matters you need to check (Stagg *et al.*, 2009). Use the *checklist* in Table 3.7.2, particularly for when you are planning a visit to a site some distance away and need to travel by public transport or coach. Many of these points apply when you take the children out of school to sites locally.

Checking the site

When you take children into the school's grounds, you must check that the sites you plan to use are appropriate and accessible and that any potential hazards have been muted (Bianchi and Feasey, 2011). It is an opportunity to foster the children's understanding of hazards and risk in a safe environment, perhaps allaying misperceptions and increasing rational awareness. Children might check the grounds and make their own risk assessment. You should check if other staff plan to take children outside when you intend to. Do this properly, in advance, not just in the playtime before you go out.

If you plan to undertake fieldwork or study off site, you must make a *reconnaissance* visit to the location first, whether it is a local site, a museum, a religious building, a field centre or anywhere else. There are two prime reasons for doing this. One is to check for any risk factors associated with the site. The other is to identify and review the potential for, and opportunities available at, the site. A site *opportunities assessment* allows you to examine and consider the site, whether the local park or a museum, for what it offers related to the topic you are planning and what other possibilities there might be for visits with other foci during different topics. For instance, a museum may well have a variety of sections of value in other history topics, or it may contain a picture gallery that might be a stimulus for an approach in the context of 'Take One Picture' (www.takeonepicture.org). A field studies centre may offer opportunities to take young children away for an overnight stay as part of their social learning and for exploratory activities, while your initial intent might be to investigate it for a comparative locality and river and landscape studies. Table 3.7.3 offers a way to record the affordances that places and sites offer. A good opportunity to explore the potential of a site is for you to use this format to examine the school's grounds.

TABLE 3.7.2 A checklist for planning and reviewing off-site work

	Checklist items	Date started	Date completed
1	Check school policies for off-site visits, including health and safety		
2	Identify reasons and objectives for working off-site		
3	Obtain permission from head or designated teacher		
4	Select location(s) for visit		
5	Check date(s)		
6	Undertake site visit and complete school risk assessment forms or obtain and review the site's own risk assessment for visiting parties		
7	Book visit with those who run the site/centre		
8	Book transport and check timings (as required)		
9	Collect contributions (if required) and keep accounts		
10	Write to parents about visit and request signed permission slips (unless already covered by school's approach)		
11	Introduce visit, purpose and activities to children; involve children in planning aspects of their work		
12	Ensure site staff know about any particular needs for your party, such as access for wheelchair users and children with particular educational needs		
13	Brief teachers, teaching assistants and other adults; allocate responsibilities for children and roles in case of emergency		
14	Know emergency procedures; access mobile phone; leave lists of participants, route and contact points in school		
15	Have plans in place for contingencies, such as where to eat lunch if it is wet, or what to do with the children if the coach breaks down		
16	Ensure awareness of key locations at the visit site, such as where the toilets, meeting places and kiosk or shop are, and which places are to be 'out-of-bounds' or time limited		
17	Organise resources/equipment and responsibility for return		
18	Make payments (as needed)		
19	Write letters of thanks (from children/yourself)		
20	Evaluate visit; note modifications for future site use; with the children review what has been learnt and gather their views about the site		

TABLE 3.7.3 A site opportunities assessment form

Visit site:		Date visited:
The variety of and particular features/areas of the site with potential		
Aspects of the site to consider for other visits and foci	Potential areas of learning (subjects, topics, personal, social, etc.) that may be initiated and/or enhanced	Possible foci and activities, noting additional resources
Aspects of the site you should check for safety, using your school's or the site's risk assessment form		

You need to have completed or checked a *risk assessment form*, certainly if you are going off site. If you are visiting a managed site, such as a country house or nature reserve, it is likely that the education staff will have undertaken their own risk assessment for school parties; it is vital that you review this to ensure that all the matters you have noted on your visit and that you are aware of concerning your children are accounted for properly and safely.

Your off-site visit will involve travel, whether a walk locally or the use of public transport, a school minibus, a coach or parents' vehicles. You should check or gather information about the route. When you walk to a local site, you must have walked the route you will use beforehand.

You should ensure that you have planned for emergencies. A contingency plan might cover such possible events as rain at an outdoor site (are you aware of, and/or have you arranged to use, a nearby shelter?) or not having been informed of a change of plan at the site, and unforeseen occurrences such as when the minibus or coach breaks down on the journey or a child becomes ill (who takes responsibility for the child and what do they do?). Although you cannot be expected to plan for every eventuality, those that might occur (such as rain: check the 5-day weather forecast) ought to be planned for. You should always have one or more alternative activities for use at the site if the tasks planned prove to be inappropriate or are completed more speedily than anticipated. You should know who to contact if you need to leave the site earlier than expected, or if you are delayed.

Case study 3 *Exploring environmental print: taking the curriculum off site*

Peter planned to give his multilingual Year 4 class opportunities to widen their vocabulary using the local streets (Cotton, 2011). On his reconnaissance, he identified the high street as a rich source of road and building print signs, shop names, and bus, van and lorry vocabulary. He visited the local supermarket to view print on aisle signs and goods, from food to magazines. He checked these sites for suitable locations for groups of children to work, and discussed matters with the supermarket manager to enable the children to work in the store, arranging a day and time that suited both the school and the supermarket. He planned his activities as an element in his literacy teaching, but was conscious that this would help the children to develop their environmental awareness and knowledge to support future local studies and their lives outside school.

MANAGING LEARNING OUT OF THE CLASSROOM

Planning teaching and learning outside the classroom

Planning a teaching session out of the classroom requires the same level and quality of planning as for any lesson. It is important to consider your teaching approach and the types of activity that the children will do. Figure 3.7.3 outlines a range of teaching approaches used to engage children in out-of-classroom learning in a variety of ways, from the more traditional to the more adventurous (Kimber and Smith, 1999; Knight, 2011; Waite, 2011b; Sedgwick, 2012). When deciding your approach, be clear about your purpose and the level of children's active learning involvement that you want. An aspect of working outside the classroom should involve the children considering how doing so has supported and challenged their thinking about their learning, from their views on the sites of learning to their engagement with learning and what they have learnt.

It is important to lead into fieldwork or a visit lesson/day, not least to ensure children come appropriately dressed for the activities they will do. In an *enquiry-based research* approach, for instance, the children will have been involved in planning some or all of their tasks. For their study of a wasteland site, they might have identified, with their teacher, the specific questions and topics they will pursue at the site, have agreed the teams to undertake the tasks, and have organised the way they will measure, record, evaluate the quality and describe the potential of the site, so that they can bring back useful information for analysis and future planning. Beforehand, they may, using photographs and video, have undertaken a classroom-based risk assessment and identified precautionary approaches. Their preparation may have taken two or more lessons before the fieldwork.

The fieldwork or visit itself needs to be carefully planned, whether for half an hour or much of the day. Table 3.7.4 provides an example of a lesson plan. There may be more detail in this plan than you usually provide, but it is important to be thorough, as planning for work outside the classroom and off site is done less frequently. This example includes some key points that need to be planned into the lesson. Look particularly at the lesson sequence.

Vital for an effective lesson will be your use of resources for activities and recording information, perceptions and what is seen. You may well have developed a survey sheet or questionnaire with the children, who will need clipboards and spare pens or to have taken art materials. However, technologies offers a number of possibilities here. For instance, the use of digital still and video cameras enables records of views, activities (from pond dipping to interviews) and items of particular interest to be brought back to the classroom for further analysis and evaluation. Tape recorders provide another alternative to writing answers. Tablets and laptop computers can be used by children and adults to make notes or link to portable sampling technologies, such as stream flow meters. Simpler equipment, such as compasses, magnifying glasses, collecting containers and quadrants, should be to hand as relevant. Locating where features and items are can be undertaken using global positioning system technologies, and some digital data recorders will give locations, for instance, of photographs. Such technological records enable evidence to be revisited in a variety of ways in the classroom following a visit. Their use needs to be planned for in advance.

Reading the environment:
Children observe signage in the outdoors, e.g. the variety of symbols, colours and logos to be seen on buildings, signs and vehicles and who they are for; understanding the range of environmental print encountered daily, from food labels to street names and direction information; identifying the variety of visible tessellations and other patterns from building shapes to pavement to car park layouts; and being aware of the range of sounds and smells and their sources.

Site investigation:
Children undertake observations, measurements and recording to find out information, e.g. about particular artefacts in a museum, the uses of shops in a local street, or river flow. This might involve using digital recording devices, whether cameras, gauges or timers with computers.

Enquiry-based research:
Children engage in planning the studies they undertake, the focus of and approaches to investigations, and the recording and follow up, e.g. researching how a particular site is managed, or using interview questions they devise to investigate the roles of people in a religious centre.

Problem solving:
Children tackle a particular problem identified at a site, e.g. what specific objects are or evidence in relation to a particular event in the past, mapping an area, or identifying ways to improve or change a site.

Creating outdoors:
Children become involved in such activities as a garden and growing project within their school grounds or in helping to enhance a site in the neighbourhood; designing and helping to build features and dens for their school grounds; and using immediate and other sites as sources for inspiration for drawing and painting, photography and dramatic improvisation.

Re-enactment:
Children use role play or dramatic recreations of people's lives and events, possible in costume, from times in the past or at another place elsewhere in the world. This requires orientation to the context at the start and debriefing at the end about what as been learned.

Guided walk:
Children are guided around a site, e.g. a museum or historic building or on an urban or rural trail, where particular features, etc are pointed out or which they observe and record using a variety of methods, from photographs to drawings, using descriptive vocabulary, and identification cards, discussing and making notes on what they see.

'Free' exploration:
Children, for instance at a forest school site or in a demarcated safe urban park area, explore the area and respond to how it makes them feel and what they can do alone or with others; or are encouraged to undertake a range of activities such as an earth walk sensing the place through touch by tree-hugging and climbing, smelling scents and listening for and to natural sounds.

Adventurous activities:
Children visit sites and centres with qualified staff who provide them with challenges and elements of risk in safe environments to extend or develop their range of experiences outdoors, encouraging children to become increasingly risk aware in ordinary places, such as their streets, and less visited places such as industrial sites, managed landscapes and wild areas. This can involve children exploring the boundaries of their comfort zone and their personal responses to challenge and risk.

'Being' outside:
Children undertake activities in an outside setting which they might ordinarily undertake in a classroom or hall, such as physical education activities, drama, listening to, creating and playing music, hearing and telling stories and writing.

FIGURE 3.7.3 Teaching approaches used in out-of-classroom studies

Subject: Geography – Local Area Study	**Children**: 26 – Year 5
Context and focus: What does street furniture tell us about the place it is in?	**Time/Duration**: 2 hours 15 minutes

Learning Outcomes – Children will be able to:

• identify different categories of street furniture;

• record the location of the street furniture accurately on a large scale map;

• give reasons for their judgements about the purpose and usefulness of street furniture.

Background to the current lesson:

• 5th lesson in local study unit, first off-site;

• Children have fieldwork experience in school grounds and off-site;

• Have recorded on maps but not used quality ratings;

• Children have devised street furniture key and quality rating scale for use;

• Children have discussed what they recall to be in the streets to investigate.

Risk assessment outcome: Overall accident risk low

• All involved will walk to the sites from school along familiar roads;

• Wide pavements to sites and along streets selected;

• Traffic at time of day less heavy;

• Large open space to meet at the centre of area, toilets nearby.

Lesson Sequence [Introduction, Main Activity, Conclusion]:

Introduction (20 minutes)

1. Check children understand purpose of fieldwork: to annotate a local map for types of street furniture, rating for usefulness, using agreed key and rating scale.

2. Review, through discussion, variety of street furniture they expect to see: signs (directions, information), posts (traffic lights, lighting), advertising notices (hoardings, A-stands), furniture (seats, benches), and safety fixtures (bollards, railings).

3. Check children have maps, keys, rating scales, clipboards. Ensure partners paired up, children know adult overseen by (5 groups), understand how to undertake tasks. Check they know their survey area. Toilet check.

Main activity (1 hour 30 minutes)

4. Go out as a class, each group with adult, walk to open space by bank (15 mins). Check all present. Groups/adults move to areas.

5. On each street group identifies street furniture, maps, rates these. Pairs state rating judgements; group agrees fair quality rating, record. In turn, pairs take photographs of selected street furniture. Repeats for 2 streets (45 mins)

6. At set time, regroup at open space. Count children. Children list 3 points on back of map about: helpfulness or not of street furniture observed. (15 mins)

7. Return. (15 minutes)

Conclusion (25 minutes)

8. Pairs check maps/notes, ensure legible, symbols and rating judgements clear.

9. Plenary, pairs comment on variety/usefulness of street furniture. Discuss purpose, value, environmental impact of street furniture.

Subsequent lesson(s): Same groups share information, prepare maps, ratings, comments on judgements about usefulness of street furniture in area surveyed; prepare report on role, quality, effectiveness of street furniture surveyed; make proposals for changes (if needed).

Support/differentiation:

2 TAs, 2 parent helpers responsible for groups of 4 children. Children in mixed pairs. 2 children (slow at recording) with same TA. 2 children (concentration and behaviour support) with me. 2 children (ESL) with TA.

Assessment opportunities [observed by adults]

• Do children identify a variety of street furniture types (use categories)?

• Do children mark locations accurately on map (recording)?

• Can children give reasons for some ratings (making judgements)?

Resources:	**Cross-Curricular Links**:
• A4 enlarged, modified street map: survey streets	• Literacy – speaking and listening
• Street furniture key, rating key	• Thinking skills – making judgements
• Clipboards, digital cameras	

FIGURE 3.7.4 An example of a fieldwork lesson plan

Managing the children

Among the challenges to making the most of out-of-classroom learning is managing the children in what is usually a less familiar situation, unless this becomes your regular practice. You should take account of the points made elsewhere in this section and Section 6 about managing children's classroom behaviour, planning and organising for learning, and diversity and inclusion. Essential to managing children in out-of-classroom learning are the following five elements:

- Ensure that you are well informed about the site and its opportunities and constraints and have planned well for the work the children will undertake.
- Use the expectations, standards and routines you have established with the class, so that the children know that there is consistency expected in the ways they work and behave with those in their class in every learning and teaching environment. If teaching staff and other adults at a centre will be working with the children, know about their ways of working and tell them about your expectations of, and routines with, the children.
- Ensure that the children have been involved in the preparation for the work outside the classroom, whether it is only for a short while in the school's grounds or the local area or for a full day's visit to another location. This gives the children much greater 'ownership' of the tasks and increases the likelihood that they will be focused and engaged.
- Ensure that the other adults working with the children know and maintain the expectations and standards and are properly briefed on, and understand, the tasks and what is required of the children. If you have children with particular needs who may find working outside the classroom rather unfamiliar, challenging or even threatening, and whom you wish to monitor and support to keep on task, or whose confidence you wish to build, plan for the adults they will work with and vary the tasks to meet their needs.
- Be clear to the children about the organisation of the work out of the classroom, so that they know the cues to listen for and follow what they are asked to do, who to go to and what to do in an emergency (such as an urgent toilet need), and the timings of their activities, such as when they will have lunch (if part of the visit), when they will change activities, and when and where they gather to return to class or school.

You may wish to organise the groups children are in, and the group work they will undertake with them, so that they work as effectively as they do in the classroom setting, or you might take the opportunity to provide fresh challenges when you are confident that the children will respond positively to these. For such group work, you will need to have briefed the adults working with them, to ensure that they foster the interactive and dialogic nature of good group work, to ensure mutually collaborative outcomes.

Case study 4 A local geography study: investigating off site

Phil's class is undertaking fieldwork in the high street for its local geography study. Involving teaching assistants and parents, the Year 5 children examine how well the local council, shops and other businesses have provided access for people with disabilities and infirmities. The children map the accessibility of doorways, the benefits and hindrances of street furniture, pavement access and road crossing points, using a rating scale to judge the quality of access. They work in groups, with a designated area to map and take digital photographs of good and poor examples they identify, which are to be used later in a display showing their findings and outlining their proposals for action. The children were involved in planning their fieldwork, which included developing awareness of the risks of undertaking studies along a street that many of them knew well. During his risk assessment, Phil took photographs to show the children, so they could discuss potential hazards and how they would safely undertake their tasks. Phil uses sites outside school because he feels that, for geography, science and history, it is vital to go into the real world that these subjects are about. He argues that children can 'see further' by going outside, because such fieldwork extends their observations in a disciplined and 'disciplinary' way.

Following up work undertaken outside the classroom

The lesson plan in Table 3.7.4 includes follow-up activities. These help to settle the children when they return to class and encourage them to think about key points from their research. You should do this, if only for a few minutes, when you arrive back before lunch or the end of the day, before the children disperse. It is not helpful to them simply to complete activities outside and leave, without time to 'gather themselves together', to receive some brief feedback from you about how the session has gone, and to know there will be a follow-up soon. As one in a series of lessons in their topic, you should plan to follow up out-of-classroom work over one or more lessons. Consider how you will use the enthusiasm generated by the work outside the classroom, how the children can work on the information they have gathered, what types of outcome you want to see, and what resources and support are needed to complete the work.

Evaluating the experience

You should always evaluate out-of-classroom studies. You may have collected new information from a museum, a field centre or a mosque to add to topic resources. The children may have engaged in unfamiliar approaches to learning that might be applied in other outdoor contexts and in class. You need to know what the children feel they gained from their experience. Such matters are important, because you need to appreciate how out-of-classroom learning has been beneficial for the children, how effectively it fitted into your planned learning sequence, whether the site and activities are worth using again, and in what ways you might improve future out-of-classroom activities. You can evaluate the experience immediately, to record key points straight away, and at the end of the topic, when you judge how well such activities contributed overall to the children's learning. You may wish to involve the children, hearing their views about their experiences. In this context, you might look at your own and the children's responses to the out-of-classroom experience, what had the most or least impact, the appropriateness of the site to the topic, the limitations of what you did, what you might change, whether you would use the site again, and if you can apply what you learn to other teaching and learning, in class and out of doors.

Task 3.7.3 Planning for out-of-classroom learning

Either for a unit you have taught *or* for one you might teach, *evaluate* or *plan* a sequence of three lessons:

- the lead-in lesson to the out-of-classroom studies;
- the lesson in the school grounds or off site;
- a follow-up lesson after the out-of-classroom work.

Use the advice in each sub-section above to help you in your planning and/or evaluation. Use Figure 3.7.3 as a guide to selecting your approach(es) to teaching and learning.

Task 3.7.4 The value of learning outside

Taking children out of the classroom to enhance their learning makes considerable demands on teachers. This unit has presented the benefits and value of such learning contexts. It has outlined the organisational and planning demands involved and noted some of the constraints on these. Ofsted (2008) and others (House of Commons Children, Schools and Families Committee, 2010; Waite, 2010) have noted that the use of the out-of-classroom environment, whether on or off the school site, outside or indoors, is less well used than it needs to be. What are the pragmatic and philosophical arguments that teachers and others might use to challenge the value of learning outside? How would you critique and debate such arguments? In which literature do you find, and what are, the strongest arguments made for the value and benefits for children and teachers in teaching and learning outside the classroom?

SUMMARY

Learning outside the classroom is essential for every child (DfES, 2006). Although it is not as widespread as desired, this view seems to be beyond dispute (Waite, 2010, 2011b; Beames *et al.*, 2012). Using the school grounds and off-school sites, nearby and distant, enhances each primary curriculum subject. Some subjects, such as geography, require children to work outside to gather data for their studies at various times. In PE, the outdoor environment, for sport and more adventurous activities, is an essential teaching and learning site. Not only does work in English, mathematics, science, art and design, history, RE, design and technology, and computing benefit from children using real-world experiences in their studies, but such opportunities are essential for improved learning and achievement. For primary languages, there are real opportunities too. Waite and Pratt (2011) argue that the sites of learning, as places for and about learning, have evident impacts. Learning outside the classroom is embodied learning, in the sense of being in a place, of children engaging practically, cognitively and affectively, and in its experiential nature, personally and socially. It is about direct and primary involvement, as well as about reflection. Much more often than not, it is memorable, and its impact goes beyond the nature of the planned activities.

ANNOTATED FURTHER READING

Beames, S., Higgins, P. and Nicol, R. (2012) *Learning Outside the Classroom: Theories and Guidelines for Practice*, London: Routledge.

> The authors explore the contexts for using out-of-classroom learning across the curriculum, with an emphasis on meaningful practice for children. Using a variety of examples of outdoor teaching and learning, they identify principles for practice in local environments. They provide advice on approaches to, and organising, learning outside the classroom. They explain how learning outside can promote children's curiosity, engagement and responsibility, while considering the links with

environmental concerns, sustainability and community connections, and extol the value of outdoor learning across the curriculum. It is well grounded, practical and provides a variety of case studies of practice.

Waite, S. (ed.) (2011) *Children Learning Outside the Classroom*, London: Sage.

> This edited book covers early years and primary school practices in fostering and engaging in learning out of the classroom. The variety of chapters consider aspects of Foundation Stage practices, learning outside in the context of a range of subjects, core and foundation, and in off-school-site contexts, such as forest school, residential centres and national parks. It is theoretically and practically grounded, based on the authors' experience and analysis. Recognising constraints, it nonetheless advocates out-of-classroom learning unequivocally.

 ## FURTHER READING TO SUPPORT M-LEVEL STUDY

Bentsen, P. and Søndergaard Jensen, F. (2012) 'The nature of *udeskole*: outdoor learning theory and practice in Danish schools', *Journal of Adventure Education & Outdoor Learning*, 12(3): 199–219.

> Outdoor learning has been advocated as a vital approach for learning well beyond the UK, but there is limited access to literature on how it is received and used elsewhere. This article examines relevant background literature and provides a survey of practice in 'outdoor school' to outline teachers' approaches. It raises concerns and possibilities about 'outdoor school', noting that Danish schooling is subject to increasing accountability. The article raises a number of questions, issues and possibilities that are pertinent to British primary out-of-classroom learning. You should explore the comparison with developing outdoor learning practices in the UK.

Humberstone, B. and Stan, I. (2011) 'Outdoor learning: primary pupils' experiences and teachers' interaction in outdoor learning', *Education 3-13*, 39(5): 529–40.

> This study is based on research in a residential setting in the Well-Being and Outdoor Pedagogies project. Very many primary children go on school journeys, particularly during their final primary year. This paper focuses on aspects of learning and teaching with Year 4 children in a particular context, using ethnographic research. What is important to consider is its focus on children's perspectives and on teacher–pupil interactions and relationships, which are essentially positive, though it raises a number of vital points about power and control when examining a 'critical incident' during the observed study. You might reflect on how the matters discussed are relevant to school grounds and local-area out-of-school organisation, management and learning.

 ## RELEVANT WEBSITES

Association for Science Education: www.ase.org.uk

Council for Learning Outside the Classroom: www.lotc.org.uk

Forest School Association: www.forestschoolassociation.org

Geographical Association: www.geography.org.uk

Historical Association: www.history.org.uk

Learning Through Landscapes: www.ltl.org.uk

Outdoor Learning, Scotland: www.educationscotland.gov.uk/learningteachingandassessment/approaches/outdoorlearning/index.asp

School Journeys Association: www.sjatours.org

The Institute of Outdoor Education: www.outdoor-learning.org

UNESCO: Teaching and Learning for Sustainable Development: www.unesco.org/education/tlsf/mods/theme_d/mod26.html

Wales GEM: Out-of-Classroom-Learning: www.gem.org.uk/res/advice/ball/res_out.php

REFERENCES

Beames, S., Higgins, P. and Nicol, R. (2012) *Learning Outside the Classroom: Theories and Guidelines for Practice*, London: Routledge.

Bianchi, L. and Feasey, R. (2011) *Science beyond the Classroom Boundaries for 7–11 Year Olds*, Maidenhead: McGraw Hill/Open University Press.

Cooper, H. (ed.) (2012) *Teaching History Creatively*, London: Routledge.

Cotton, H. (2011) 'English and language outside the classroom', in S. Waite (ed.) *Children Learning Outside the Classroom*, London: Sage, 66–79.

Council for Learning Outside the Classroom (2013) *Policy and Curriculum Planning*, www.lotc.org.uk/plan-deliver-lotc/policy-and-curriculum-planning/ (accessed 12 August 2013).

Davis, J. (2010) *Young Children and the Environment*, Cambridge: Cambridge University Press.

DfE (2012) *Teachers' Standards*, www.gov.uk/government/publications/teachers-standards (accessed 12 August 2013).

DfE (2013a) *The National Curriculum in England: Framework Document*, www.gov.uk/dfe/nationalcurriculum (accessed 12 September 2013).

DfE (2013b) *Health and Safety: Advice on Legal Duties and Powers*, http://media.education.gov.uk/assets/files/pdf/h/dfe%20health%20and%20safety%20advice%2003%2006%2013.pdf (Accessed 12 August 2013).

DfES (1998) *Health and Safety of Pupils on Educational Visits*, London: DfES, static.zsl.org/files/haspev-1179.pdf (accessed 10 August 2013).

DfES (2006) *Learning Outside the Classroom Manifesto*, Nottingham: DfES Publications, www.lotc.org.uk/about/manifesto (accessed 10 August 2013).

Gaylie, V. (2011) *Roots and Research in Urban School Gardens*, New York: Peter Lang.

Hoodless, P., Bermingham, S., McCreery, E. and Bowen, P. (2009) *Teaching Humanities in Primary Schools*, Exeter: Learning Matters.

House of Commons Children, Schools and Families Committee (2010) *Transforming Education Outside the Classroom*, London: The Stationery Office.

House of Commons Education and Skills Committee (2005) *Education Outside the Classroom*, London: The Stationery Office.

Kimber, D. and Smith, M. (1999) 'Field work, visits and work outside the classroom', in M. Ashley (ed.) *Improving Teaching and Learning in the Humanities*, Lewes: Falmer, pp. 101–18.

Knight, S. (2011) *Risk and Adventure in Early Outdoor Play: Learning from Forest Schools*, London: Sage.

Nundy, S., Dillon, J. and Dowd, P. (2009) 'Improving and encouraging teacher confidence in out-of-classroom learning: the impact of the Hampshire Trailblazer project on 3–13 curriculum practitioners', *Education 3–13*, 37(1): 61–73.

Ofsted (2008) *Learning Outside the Classroom: How Far Should You Go?* www.ofsted.gov.uk/resources/learning-outside-classroom (accessed 12 August 2013).

Passy, R. and Waite, S. (2011) 'School gardens and Forest Schools', in S. Waite (ed.) *Children Learning Outside the Classroom*, London: Sage, 162–75.

Pound, L. and Lee, T. (2011) *Teaching Mathematics Creatively*, London: Routledge.

Rickinson, M., Dillon, J., Teamey, K., Morris, M., Young Choi, M., Sanders, D. and Benefield, P. (2004) *A Review of Research on Outdoor Learning*, Preston Montford: Field Studies Council.

Rowe, S. and Humphries, S. (2012) *The Coombes Approach: Learning Through an Experiential and Outdoor Curriculum*, London: Continuum.

Salaman, A. and Tutchell, S. (2005) *Planning Educational Visits for the Early Years*, London: Paul Chapman Publishing.

Scoffham, S. (ed.) (2013) *Teaching Geography Creatively*, London: Routledge.

Sedgwick, F. (2012) *Learning Outside the Primary Classroom*, London: Routledge.

Stagg, C., Smith, P., Thomas, A. and Warn, C. (2009) *Off the Premises Handbook*, London: Optimus Education.

Vascellaro, S. (2011) *Out of the Classroom and Into the World*, New York: New York Press.

Waite, S. (2010) 'Losing our way? The downward path for outdoor learning for children aged 2-11 years', *Journal of Adventure Education and Outdoor Learning*, 10(2): 111-26.

Waite, S. (2011a) 'Teaching and learning outside the classroom: personal values, alternative pedagogies and standards', *Education 3-13*, 39(1): 65-82.

Waite, S. (ed.) (2011b) *Children Learning Outside the Classroom*, London: Sage.

Waite, S. and Pratt, N. (2011) 'Theoretical perspectives on learning outside the classroom: relationships between learning and place', in S. Waite (ed.) *Children Learning Outside the Classroom*, London: Sage, 1-18.

Williams, D. and Brown, J. (2012) *Learning Gardens and Sustainability Education*, London: Routledge.

APPROACHES TO THE CURRICULUM

THE AIMS OF
PRIMARY EDUCATION

Justine Earl

INTRODUCTION

This unit focuses on the aims of primary education. It encourages readers to reflect upon aims that are inherent within different philosophies of education, as well as to consider their own views of the aims of primary education. It takes readers from the conception of the English National Curriculum towards the proposals for the near future, examining the aims stated in each policy document.

By considering the importance of educational aims, it is hoped that readers can revisit and evaluate their own sense of purpose in their role, and reflect on the important connections between their values, beliefs and practice.

OBJECTIVES

By the end of this unit, you will:

- have a greater understanding of the aims of education;
- have reflected upon the relationship between educational aims and educational practice, and be familiar with some well-known historical examples;
- have considered the specific aims of primary education, as well as the values that underpin them;
- have thought about your own philosophy of primary education, and be aware of the practical implications of philosophical thinking in education.

WHAT ARE AIMS, AND WHY DO WE NEED THEM?

You might think that discussions of educational aims are not very practical or useful. You might think that they are overly theoretical and will not help you to survive in the classroom. We hope that it will become clear by the end of this unit that this is a mistaken view, as any sensible discussion about educational practice is always built on top of a foundation of aims. A teacher who is skilled in a technical sense, but who lacks a clear sense of their subject or lesson, will almost certainly offer the pupils an unsatisfactory experience. The same can be said for education as a whole.

Aims define the point of an activity: what it seeks to achieve; where it should go.

The difficulty is that there is no simple, overriding aim of education with which all of us – teachers, parents, academics, policymakers – can agree and to which we all aspire. There are numerous possible aims. Taken individually, these aims often seem legitimate and reasonable. Placed together, however, it often becomes apparent that some aims are incompatible with others. For example, in introducing its educational reforms in England and Wales in the 1980s, the government identified a number of principles, such as educational standards and excellence, parental choice and participation, professional accountability, market forces and consumer satisfaction, economy, efficiency and effectiveness (Le Métais, 1995). Some have suggested that there are real tensions between pairs of these principles. For example, the call for parental choice and the promotion of market forces may be incompatible with the demand for equality.

Skills and competencies are important if one wishes to become a good teacher, but they are really very little more than tools used to help realise some goal. Without this goal – this *aim* – the tools become rather pointless.

The solution to this apparent problem is not like the solution to a crossword puzzle, in which you simply need to find the correct answer. This is because educational aims are inseparable from educational *values* and *principles*. Values are concerns about what ought to be. A value can be understood as a belief that need not rely on facts or evidence. Values go beyond mere statements of fact towards more ambitious, yet more ill-defined aspirations.

To make this point more clearly, turn to Task 4.1.1.

Ultimately, you, as a professional, will have to come to some judgement for yourself. At some stage, every teacher needs to ask him or herself, 'What am I trying to achieve?', 'What are my goals as a teacher?' and 'What are my aims of education?'.

Task 4.1.1 Which aims?

An international review of the stated aims of educational systems from around the world came up with the following composite list (Tabberer, 1997):

- excellence
- individual development
- social development
- personal qualities
- equal opportunity
- national economy
- preparation for work
- basic skills
- foundation for further education
- knowledge/skills/understanding
- citizenship/community/democracy
- cultural heritage/literacy
- creativity
- environment
- health/physical/leisure
- lifelong education
- parental participation

1 Give this list to friends and family and ask them to select what, for them, reflects most closely the main aims of education. Which aims are most frequently selected? Which are not selected at all?
2 If you are working in a school, ask to see a policy document that contains that school's aims. How do these aims reflect the list?
3 What is your view? Which aims do you think capture your personal philosophy?

Values influence our aims, which, in turn, influence every aspect of the education we offer our pupils. Figure 4.1.1 illustrates one way about thinking about the relationship between values, aims and practice.

Values and aims direct decisions about school and class organisation (are pupils grouped according to age, ability or interest? How much say do parents and outside groups have? What is the nature of the authority of the teacher?). Decisions of this sort will influence the type of curriculum offered (subject-based or theme-based? Broad and balanced or narrow and specialist? Which subjects receive most time, which receive least?), and these questions influence the selection of appropriate teaching styles and materials (teacher-centred or learner-centred? Memorising facts or problem-solving? Teacher as authority, as friend, as resource?). Finally, the types of assessment strategy employed, if they are to have any purpose at all, need to reflect the aims of the education process.

There are good reasons to suppose that talk of aims will be relevant to you throughout your training. As a citizen, you have the same right as everyone else to hold and express your view on what education is for, and to contribute to the communal discussion about the aims and character of education. As a teacher, you have an even greater responsibility to be clear to yourself and others what your aims are, and be prepared to argue and defend them (Haydon, 1995). It is very difficult to identify universally shared values and aims. Committed professionals need to make decisions at each stage of the teaching process about how to interpret their values and aims in terms of practice. For this reason, we do not have one type of school, with one type of curriculum, teaching approach and assessment.

In Wales . . .

The Welsh Assembly Government (WAG) states that the purpose of schools is to 'enable all children and young people to develop their full potential by acquiring skills, knowledge, understanding and attitudes, including personal, social and emotional skills, to enable them to become economically, socially and personally active citizens and lifelong learners' (DCELLS, 2008: 10).

In addition to this, WAG also states that, in Wales, 'The ethos needs to reflect the values inherent in Wales, including the importance of the Welsh language within the context of a bilingual country with its unique culture and traditions' (DCELLS, 2008).

Source: Department for Children, Education, Lifelong Learning and Skills (DCELLS) (2008) *School Effectiveness Framework: Building Effective Communities Together*. Cardiff: Welsh Assembly Government (WAG). http://dera.ioe.ac.uk/7732/1/1331.pdf

---

AIMS AND PRACTICE: SOME HISTORICAL EXAMPLES

The point has already been made that educational practice cannot be separated from notions of aims. In order to exemplify this, we will consider the educational theories of three influential thinkers: Plato, Jean-Jacques Rousseau and John Dewey. These thinkers have been selected because each has had a significant influence on the way people think about the ways education should be conceived and carried out. Also, they have the virtue of coming from different places and times from our own. This distance should make it easier for us to talk about aims and practice, without being constrained by our assumptions of the way education *ought to be*.

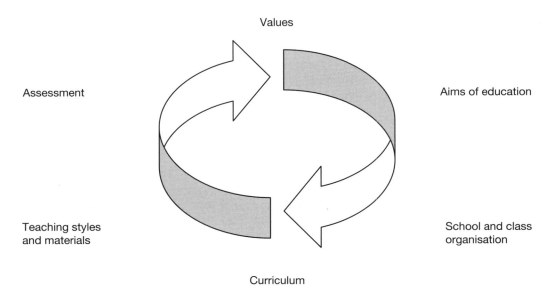

Values

Assessment

Aims of education

Teaching styles
and materials

School and class
organisation

Curriculum

FIGURE 4.1.1 Values, aims and practice
Source: adapted from Le Métais (2004)

Plato

The ancient Greek philosopher Plato (428–348 BCE) wrote about education in a number of his works, but his best known treatment is in the book that has come to be known as *The Republic* (Bloom, 1991). Plato, a student of Socrates and the teacher of Aristotle, is said to have founded the first university – his Academy, near Athens.

Much of Plato's work is presented in the form of dialogues, or question-and-answer discussions in which a student, or 'seeker', is led to uncover gaps in his/her reasoning by a teacher, or 'expert'. This method of teaching has come to be known as the 'Socratic Method' (after Plato's teacher) and characterises the presentation of educational ideas in *The Republic*, as well as Plato's view that such dialogues are a powerful method for developing a student's understanding, as their subject knowledge comes through questioning, not teaching. Although this might at first appear a somewhat progressive teaching style, Plato makes it clear that the teacher–student relationship is not one of equals – the teacher is in control.

To understand Plato's educational theory, it is necessary to understand his views of politics. For him, the central issue is that of justice or right-living – the just person lives a life of harmony. This harmonious life expresses itself in two ways. First, as a member of a community, the just person lives a life that is appropriate to his/her social group. Soldiers, farmers, leaders and manufacturers all contribute to the just state, but each needs to stay in their place in the order: they need to know their place.

Second, just as the state needs order and harmony, so does the individual. We all have appetites and passions, as well as a capacity for reason and reflection. The different elements within us relate directly to the different roles within the state: our appetites (which equate to the producers) and our passions (the soldiers) must remain under the control of the higher, rational part (the leaders).

When our appetites and passions overtake our reason, we become disturbed and disordered, just as a state becomes unstable if the lower orders take control from their leaders.

For Plato, then, the aim of education is to produce certain types of people, the just, and a certain type of state, the just society, in which each of the different elements keeps its proper place in the order. How can we recognise where different people fit in this order? Plato's view is that humans are made up of a body that is perishable and a soul, which is immortal. Some souls are better than others. In Plato's terms, some of us have gold in our souls, whereas other, progressively less worthy people have iron and bronze. The highest function of education, therefore, is to develop those with souls of gold (Moore, 1974) and to lead them to see beyond superficial appearances towards an understanding of another level, the world of eternal, changeless reality.

So, how does this view of education translate into practice? First, if there really are different qualities of people, it follows that they will require different forms of schooling. Second, young children of quality who are not yet ready for the strains of philosophical training need to develop their senses, their love of beauty, order and harmony. Third, as children get older, they need to be inspired by tales of heroes and great leaders. Fourth, they need to ensure that their bodies are strong enough to house their souls, and so the young need a period of rigorous physical training. Finally, only once the few have shown themselves to be fit will they be taught the secrets necessary for leadership. Only if these steps are followed will the state be kept safe, harmonious and just.

Rousseau

Jean-Jacques Rousseau (1712–78) was born in Switzerland and grew up in France. His book *Emile* (Bloom, 1979) is generally regarded as the most significant text on education since Plato's *Republic*. Rousseau lived shortly before the French Revolution, and his writing is often credited as being influential in setting the intellectual scene for that great political change.

Rousseau's 'other' great book is *The Social Contract*, which begins with the famous and chilling lines: 'Man was born free, and he is everywhere in chains' (Cranston, 2004). This quotation captures his view that we are born good, but are corrupted by the evils of society. Rousseau called for an abandonment of the French society of his day, which he thought corrupt and unjust, and the emergence of a new kind of society, based on the real interests and engagement of its members (as opposed to just the aristocrats). The government, in this new system, would be based on what he called the 'General Will', the rational, informed will of all members of society, guided by principles of 'liberty, equality and fraternity'. There is always a danger in such democratic structures that individuals and minority groups are exploited. So, Rousseau was forceful in advocating freedom of thought, independence and individualism of members and, of course, education.

Rousseau's *Emile* is a call for 'a return to nature', and his goal of education is the 'natural man' and an educational system 'according to nature'. Quite what he means by 'nature' is a matter of some interpretation. Certainly, there is a strong 'green' element in Rousseau's writing. However, he means much more than modern environmentalism. In some parts of *Emile*, it seems that nature equates to the way things are in the natural world, within which children live as human animals. So, Rousseau stresses the importance of treating a child as a child, and not as a mini-adult (as was the fashion of his day). Ultimately, childhood should be characterised by a life of experience, rather than knowledge, of sensation rather than reason. In another part of *Emile*, it seems that Rousseau has a somewhat different understanding of the term 'nature'. Here, he places much greater emphasis on the natural person as one who has yet to be corrupted by society. A third view, offered by Rousseau's critics, is that his natural man is really the middle-class citizen of his new society, who is independent of thought, yet able to play a constructive part in society, without being overtaken by it (Moore, 1974).

The relationship between Rousseau's views of childhood and education and modern, so-called 'child-centred' or progressive education is clear. It is not surprising, then, that he has been blamed by some traditionalists for the anti-intellectual, antisocial forms of schooling that they claim have become endemic in recent decades. This is, perhaps, a little harsh, as Rousseau clearly recognised the need for both intellectual and social engagement. He stressed, however, that studying from books, initiation into academic disciplines and learning about the social world should occur when the individual is mature enough to benefit from them and not be corrupted by them. Before that time, during childhood, s/he should be educated using personal experience.

Dewey

John Dewey (1859-1952) was born in an America evolving into a major industrial nation, yet was still influenced by the ethos of the frontier, with its emphasis on enterprise, independence and merit. He is acknowledged as one of the most influential educational philosophers of modern times, and, although he is sometimes portrayed as Rousseau's intellectual heir, and the father of modern, child-centred education, he really marks a different tradition altogether.

Like both Plato and Rousseau before him, Dewey's views on education were greatly influenced by his views on children's nature. Born in the year that Charles Darwin published *The Origin of Species*, Dewey saw humans as active, problem-solving creatures, who are continually seeking to overcome challenges from their environment. By the time they enter school, they have already experienced a great deal and bring with them innate instincts to communicate, construct, inquire and express themselves. Children also bring their interests, and it is a basic task of the teacher to make use of these interests and instincts by guiding the child's activities at school. Dewey divides childhood into three developmental stages: the period of 'play', which is characterised by spontaneous, child-led activity; the 'techniques' period, during which the child learns to follow simple procedures; and the period of 'reflective attention', when an overtly critical problem-solving is developed. At each stage, the emphasis is on the child's activity, which gradually becomes more specific and outcome-orientated as the child grows older.

Underlying Dewey's philosophy is the aim of educating a certain type of person: an individual fit for a democracy. However, unlike the writers we met earlier, he is very suspicious of any theory of

Task 4.1.2 Educational aims and philosophies

Reflect upon the different visions of education offered by Plato, Rousseau and Dewey. Each has a distinctive view of education, and of its aims, as well as of childhood and children. Also, each, whether implicitly or explicitly, has a view of the role of *primary education* within their vision.

Outline the aims of primary education within each of these approaches. Can you recognise aspects of these aims in modern education and schooling? Consider, in particular, these contexts:

- the Foundation stage;
- independent 'preparatory' schools;
- self-proclaimed 'child-centred' schools;
- the school with which you are most familiar.

education that has an 'end' in mind, whether it be Plato's 'leader' or Rousseau's 'natural man'. For Dewey, education cannot really have an aim beyond itself: the end point of education is more education. This does not mean that Dewey thought of education as distinct from society; on the contrary, he was keen for schools to prepare for life in the 'real world'. Therefore, schools should present their students with real problems, which stem from their own interests. Many of these problems may originate in the social settings in which children work co-operatively and collaboratively. Education, according to Dewey, therefore, is fundamentally concerned with developing children's innate interests and abilities by leading them to operate in the world of practical problems.

WHAT ARE THE AIMS OF PRIMARY EDUCATION?

Is there a quintessential character of 'primary' education? Are there aims that are special to the primary phase and that set it apart from other aspects of pupils' learning and experience? One important writer, reflecting on changing practices and on different approaches around the world, has been led to ponder: 'We encounter so little uniformity of practice that we might feel inclined to ask whether the word "primary" is anything more than a label denoting a stage of compulsory schooling' (Alexander, 1984: 11). Can that be all that is special about primary education: the age of the pupils? Or is there something else; is there something special and distinctive about the primary phase?

Historically, there have been some discrete traditions associated with primary education (see Alexander, 1984; Pollard and Tann, 1997):

*   **The elementary tradition**: This is a form of educational practice and provision associated with a concentration on the so-called '3R's' (reading, 'riting and 'rithmetic), and with a strict approach to discipline.
*   **The developmental tradition**: This approach emphasises the ways in which children develop physically, socially, emotionally and intellectually, as a basis for planning and organising learning.
*   **The preparatory tradition**: This tradition sees primary education as a 'preparation' for later schooling, during which children learn the more traditional, subject-based knowledge.

To some extent, these traditions need not be mutually exclusive. It is quite possible to envisage a school claiming to support all three approaches. For example, it might claim to be respectful of children's developmental needs, while still recognising their need to learn the basics of literacy and numeracy, as well as the foundations of good behaviour, so that they are prepared for the more traditional business of secondary schooling. However, this would miss the purpose of the classification, which is to reflect upon the dominating aim – the driving purpose that defines and, to some extent, restricts what is offered in the name of primary education. Our imagined school might very well claim to represent all three traditions, but the true test comes when time and resources are limited, or when external inspectors demand evidence of its achievement. Does the school push forward its exemplary record in reading, writing and arithmetic, and flawless disciplinary record, or does it claim that it has devised a curriculum that is responsive and respectful of each child's developmental needs, which means that not all children can read or add up, because they are not all ready for these skills? Or does it boast of its outstanding SATs results or high success rate in winning places in selective secondary schools?

THE CURRENT NATIONAL CURRICULUM FOR ENGLAND

So far, in this unit, it has been asserted that aims for education are inseparable from values and moral purposes. You have been asked to consider this and to begin to reflect on your own view of education and your beliefs about its purpose. These beliefs will help to shape all the decisions you make and all the actions you take in your professional career.

Reviews into international educational aims have found that they are broadly influenced by two main ideas: child-centred education and socio-economic concerns (Shuayb and O'Donnell, 2008). Child-centered philosophies lead to educational aims that, unsurprisingly, focus on the whole child, encompassing the social and emotional development of pupils, as well as their cognitive and creative needs. This means that a curriculum emerging from this ideology champions the value of play in the early years and focuses on the individual pupil's competencies and requirements as they develop through the primary phase.

Socio-economic educational aims focus on the need to prepare pupils for their place in the world of work, in a constantly changing economy. Attainment in subject areas such as mathematics and English is seen as important as is the acquisition of key skills.

Shuayb and O'Donnell (2008) found that, from the start of the twenty-first century, in countries such as England, Sweden and the Netherlands, socio-economic principles merged, to a certain extent, with those of personalised learning. This created a 'hybrid' of purposes that could be seen as contradictory. Can preparing an individual for his or her place in the economic world be served by an individualised approach to education?

The previous National Curriculum for schools in England (slimmed down, but otherwise essentially unchanged since 1999) sets out a strong statement that mixes together values, aims and purposes in its handbook:

> A belief in education, at home and at school, as a route to the spiritual, moral, social, cultural, physical and mental development, and thus the well-being, of the individual. Education is also a route to equality of opportunity for all, a healthy and just democracy, a productive economy, and sustainable development. Education should reflect the enduring values that contribute to these ends. These include valuing ourselves, our families and other relationships, the wider groups to which we belong, the diversity in our society and the environment in which we live. Education should also reaffirm our commitment to the virtues of truth, justice, honesty, trust and a sense of duty.
>
> At the same time, education must enable us to respond positively to the opportunities and challenges of the rapidly changing world in which we live and work. In particular, we need to be prepared to engage as individuals, parents, workers and citizens with economic, social and cultural change, including the continued globalisation of the economy and society, with new work and leisure patterns and with the rapid expansion of communication technologies.
>
> (Department for Education and Employment/Qualifications and Curriculum Authority, 1999)

In Northern Ireland . . .

The aim of the Northern Ireland Curriculum (NIC) is 'to empower young people to develop their potential and to make informed and responsible choices and decisions throughout their lives' (CCEA, 2007: 4). This includes developing the young person as an individual, as a contributor to society and as a contributor to the economy and the environment. Underpinning this is the aim to build desirable attitudes and dispositions, such as moral character, community spirit, tolerance, flexibility, self-belief, pragmatism, concern for others, personal responsibility and curiosity.

Source: Council for Curriculum, Examinations and Assessment (CCEA) (2007) *The Northern Ireland Curriculum: Primary.* Belfast, CCEA Publications.

Task 4.1.3 Key aspects of the curriculum

Revisit the statement from the current English National Curriculum handbook above. The following is a list of some of the key words and phrases from the statement:

- spiritual, moral, social, cultural;
- physical and mental development, well-being;
- equality of opportunity for all;
- healthy and just democracy;
- productive economy and sustainable development;
- enduring values;
- relationships;
- diversity;
- our environment;
- truth, justice, honesty, trust and a sense of duty;
- preparation for place in the economic world;
- the changing world;
- citizenship;
- globalisation;
- communication technologies.

1 Which of these do *you* believe to be key, in order of importance?
2 Apply your list to a subject: choose a subject taught in the primary curriculum with which you feel familiar. Consider to what extent the key aspects you listed translate into the content of that subject and that subject's pedagogy.

For example, you might choose to think about English/literacy. If you have selected *the environment* as a key phrase from the National Curriculum statement, consider how the subject of English can contribute to the notion of valuing the environment: what in its content and what in your pedagogical approach? What have you observed in the teaching of English that does this?

Of course, a national curriculum delivers its aims and purpose through all the subjects, and not one in isolation. The ethos of the school and the manner of teaching are part of this delivery too. However, by considering just one subject, you may be able to develop your thoughts about to what extent specific content and subject-relevant approaches relate to the aims of the curriculum.

THE FUTURE OF THE CURRICULUM IN ENGLAND

The Cambridge Primary Review (CPR) was a rigorous and wide-ranging, research-based inquiry into the primary curriculum, undertaken from 2006 to 2009. The final report drew on surveys of published research; extensive consultation through written submissions from individuals and organisations; focus-group meetings; and use of official statistical, test and inspection data from a range of government and official agencies. The CPR promotes a primary curriculum driven by, and built on, carefully considered aims.

An important chapter of the CPR final report (Chapter 12: 'What is primary education for?') acknowledges the challenges involved in defining educational aims. It sets out key questions asked of respondents during the process of the review:

- What is primary education for?
- To what needs and purposes should it be chiefly directed over the coming decades?

- What core values and principles should it uphold and advance?
- Taking account of the country and the world in which our children are growing up, to what individual, social, cultural, economic and other circumstances and needs should it principally attend? (p. 174).

Questions such as these are not simple or straightforward. Defining educational aims is not possible without asking challenging questions.

The report goes on to point out four key things to remember when attempting to answer such questions:

1 educational aims must look to the future, as well as present, needs of children;
2 previous attempts at defining aims for education have not been very successful – statements have often been brief and almost meaningless;
3 grand, overarching statements of aims have rarely been translated into the details of policies or into practices;
4 aims must be relevant to all in the community to which they relate, and they must shape what pupils actually do and experience in schools.

Because the CPR is informed by a large amount of research evidence and wide consultation, it is perhaps inevitable that the recommended aims are not neat and tidy. The twelve aims of the CPR come from reflecting on all manner of educational aspects, for example: balancing individual and societal needs; community and citizenship; addressing disadvantage; material desires and global needs; the 3Rs and beyond; the whole child and faith and spirituality (Alexander, 2010: 184).

The CPR's twelve aims for primary education are grouped as follows:

- The individual:
  - well-being;
  - engagement in learning;
  - empowerment of pupils;
  - autonomy and sense of self.
- Self, others and the wider world:
  - encouraging respect and reciprocity;
  - promoting interdependence and sustainability;
  - empowering local, national and global citizenship;
  - celebrating culture and community.
- Learning, knowing and doing:
  - exploring, knowing, understanding and making sense;
  - fostering skill;
  - exciting the imagination;
  - enacting dialogue.

(Alexander, 2010: 197-9)

It would take careful consideration, time and hard work to apply such aims effectively to the whole school curriculum, the organisation of subjects, the creation of coherent plans and the activities that the children experience. Hard work such as this is vital, and, by reading this unit, you are beginning to undertake it. You are beginning the important journey of reflection by considering what you believe education is for. As we have seen, attempts to simplify educational aims can result in broad, vacuous statements that rarely result in related actions. The aims of the CPR 'unashamedly reflect values and moral purposes, for that is what education is about, and they are designed to empower children to manage life and find new meaning in the 21st century' (Alexander, 2010: 200). It is hard to argue with this statement.

THE PROPOSED CURRICULUM FOR ENGLAND: AIMS FOR PRIMARY EDUCATION IN THE DRAFT NATIONAL CURRICULUM PROPOSALS

The first draft proposals for the English National Curriculum primary subjects of English, mathematics and science were published by the Department of Education on 11 June (Department for Education, 2012a, 2012b, 2012c, 2013).

These proposals emerged from the National Curriculum Review, launched on 20 January 2011. From January to December 2011, the review was advised by an expert panel, consisting of Professor Mary James, Associate Director of Research for the University of Cambridge, Professor Dylan Wiliam from the Institute of Education, Professor Andrew Pollard of the University of Bristol and the University of London, and chaired by Tim Oates of Cambridge Assessment. Members of this panel have since distanced themselves from the proposed curriculum (Pollard and James, 2011).

Following publication, there commenced a period of public consultation.

AIMS IN THE DRAFT NATIONAL CURRICULUM DOCUMENTS FOR ENGLISH, MATHEMATICS AND SCIENCE

The original draft documents contained very little in terms of aims, despite the work of the expert panel. The panel wrote at length about aims in Chapter 2 of its report, *The Framework for the National Curriculum: A Report by the Expert Panel for the National Curriculum Review* (Department for Education, 2011). This chapter referred to extensive international research and the education frameworks of 'high-performing jurisdictions' (p. 13), thus reflecting the government's desire to emulate these successful international contexts. The expert panel recommended aims at a number of levels, as advocated by the Cambridge Primary Review (Alexander, 2010).

These levels were described as being:

- Level 1: affirming system-wide educational aspirations for school curricular;
- Level 2: specifying more particular purposes for schools and for their curricula;
- Level 3: introducing the goals for the programmes of study for particular subjects.

(Department for Education, 2011: 14)

The 2012 draft proposals only offered aims at Level 3. This would suggest that the content of each subject is more important than the overarching values, principles and purposes of education. Contrast this approach with the description of the aims of the CPR earlier in the unit.

However, on 11 June 2012, Michael Gove, Secretary of State for Education, wrote to Tim Oates as chair of the expert panel. In this letter, Gove wrote:

> I agree with your clear recommendation that we should define the aims of the curriculum. We need to set ambitious goals for our progress as a nation. And we need clear expectations for each subject. I expect those aims to embody our sense of ambition, a love of education for its own sake, respect for the best that has been thought and written, appreciation of human creativity and a determination to democratise knowledge by ensuring that as many children as possible can lay claim to a rich intellectual inheritance.

> We will consult on how those aims should be defined, with a deliberate emphasis on representing the views, and evidence, produced by those currently teaching who have achieved the highest standards and stretched all their students most effectively. And we will continue to ensure that any change takes into account the experience of other nations with successful school systems.

Task 4.1.4 Aims of the curriculum

Reflect on the first paragraph from Michael Gove's letter, above. What key words do you notice? How do these demonstrate the Secretary of State's underlying values? With which do you agree?

Now re-read the second paragraph from his letter. Who does he want to consult on the aims of the curriculum? Why are these people particularly important? What key words represent the values and purposes here?

How would you contribute to a consultation about the definition of aims?

In February 2013, the renewed drafts for English, mathematics and science were published, as were the first offerings for the other National Curriculum subjects. The subjects were, as promised, prefaced by a statement of aims for the curriculum as a whole:

- The National Curriculum provides pupils with an introduction to the core knowledge that they need to be educated citizens. It introduces pupils to the best that has been thought and said; and helps engender an appreciation of human creativity and achievement.
- The National Curriculum is just one element in the education of every child. There is time and space in the school day and in each week, term and year to range beyond the National Curriculum specifications. The National Curriculum provides an outline of core knowledge around which teachers can develop exciting and stimulating lessons.

(Department for Education, 2013: 6)

It could be argued that only the first point is an aim. The second simply sets out how to use the National Curriculum to plan the work of a school. The first aim is, yet again, broad, general and not primary specific. You may now want to review what you have understood so far in this unit and reflect on whether this aim offers you anything as a student teacher.

THE 2013 NATIONAL CURRICULUM PROPOSALS AT SUBJECT LEVEL

Whatever the stated overarching aims of a curriculum are, it seems sensible that the content of subjects meets them. It is questionable whether this is the case in the 2013 drafts.

It is also possible to argue that the content of individual subjects does not always relate to the stated subject-level aims. For example, in the draft proposals for English, the stated overarching aim is: 'to promote high standards of literacy by equipping pupils with a strong command of the written and spoken word, and develop a love of literature through widespread reading for enjoyment'.

It is questionable whether this aim is reflected in the content of the subject. For example, the use of the phrases 'love of literature' and 'reading for enjoyment' in the introductory aims cannot be tracked satisfactorily through the content requirements for the subject (Wyse, 2012).

Another example of this is the treatment of spoken language. The introductory section of the subject states: 'the National Curriculum for English reflects the importance of spoken language in pupils' development – linguistic, cognitive and social – across the whole curriculum'.

Teachers are told to ensure that pupils' confidence and competence develop in spoken language. However, the programmes of study for each year group *only* include detail for reading and writing. This is an example of aims not being translated into the content of a subject; content that will ultimately guide the experiences of pupils in many classrooms.

THINKING AGAIN ABOUT YOUR OWN PHILOSOPHY OF PRIMARY EDUCATION

> Education as such has no aims. Only persons, parents and teachers, etc. have aims, not an abstract idea like education.

(Dewey, 1916: 107)

Studies suggest that most teachers enter the profession with a strong sense of values and aims (Thomas, 1995). You are probably the same. I hope that you have had the opportunity to reflect upon these, and perhaps you have reconsidered them or modified them, in some way. In reflecting on your own conceptions of the aims of primary education, two points need to be stressed. First, your aims come from somewhere. Just as Plato, Rousseau and Dewey all reflect aspects of their culture and time in their philosophies of education, we cannot separate ourselves from our upbringing, schooling and cultural values. Although we might like to think that we generate our views through raw intelligence and reason alone, the reality is that our individual beliefs often reflect our upbringing, previous experiences and social background. This is why we can find it difficult to change our aims, as their source can date back many years and be closely associated with our conception of ourselves as people. Second, we need to remember that our aims will influence what we do, both inside and outside the classroom. Our aims are revealed in our behaviour and, thus, in our teaching (Pollard, 2002).

SUMMARY

To some extent, all teachers have to work within a framework of aims, prescribed by a national curriculum, but there is room for the development and articulation of your personal views and philosophy. Aims help give teachers a sense of direction and purpose in their professional work; different aims are associated with different teaching practices, curriculum organisation and assessment procedures. As such, they are serious matters and deserve careful consideration and critical examination.

 ## ANNOTATED FURTHER READING

Pollard, A. and Tann, S. (1997) *Reflective Teaching in the Primary School: A Handbook for the Classroom*. London: Continuum.
> This practical textbook has become something of a classic. Although it covers a great amount of material of relevance to primary practitioners, its implicit demand that we reflect upon our actions and the thinking behind them makes this a valuable resource for those wishing to consider aims in real-life contexts.

Pring, R. (2004) *Philosophy of Education: Aims, Theory, Common Sense and Research*. London: Continuum.
> A challenging, thought-provoking series of chapters, examining different aspects of educational theory, and introducing the reader to a range of relevant authors and texts.

Walker, D.F. and Soltis, J.F. (2004) *Curriculum and its Aims*. New York: Teachers College Press.
> This book from the US offers an accessible introduction to the issue of educational aims. It uses case studies to exemplify the practical implications of different theoretical positions and offers a useful further reading section.

 # FURTHER READING TO SUPPORT M-LEVEL STUDY

Alexander, R. (2012) Neither national nor a curriculum *Forum*, 54:3, 369–84.
> This article brings us up to date with Robin Alexander's view on the proposed new curriculum. Here can be found a range of research-supported objections to the draft proposals, including the lack of clearly defined aims. Unsurprisingly, Alexander takes us back to the CPR. The article can be found at: www.robinalexander.org.uk/wp-content/uploads/2012/04/Forum-Neither-national-nor-a-curriculum-2012.pdf

Cunningham, P. (2002) Primary aims and educational change: the aims of primary education project in historical perspective *Education 3-13: International Journal of Primary, Elementary and Early Years Education*, 30:1, 12–16.
> This article provides a useful, detailed, historical perspective on the aims of primary education and the constantly changing educational landscape. It revisits a research project undertaken in the 1970s that examined the views of 300 primary teachers on what they believed the aims of primary education to be. Over a decade since this article was written, it is possible to ask: what now: what has changed and what is still the same?

 # RELEVANT WEBSITES

The Cambridge Primary Review Trust www.primaryreview.org.uk/

Canterbury Christ Church University Faculty of Education Blog www.consider-ed.org.uk/

The Institute of Education Blog http://ioelondonblog.wordpress.com/

The Philosophy of Education Society of Great Britain www.philosophy-of-education.org/

 # REFERENCES

Alexander, R. (1984) *Primary Teaching*. Eastbourne: Holt, Rinehart and Winston.

Alexander, R. (ed.) (2010) *Children, Their World, Their Education. Final Report and Recommendations of the Cambridge Primary Review*. London: Routledge.

Bloom, A. (tr.) (1979) *Emile: or, On Education*. New York: Basic Books.

Bloom, A. (tr.) (1991) *The Republic of Plato*. New York: Basic Books.

Cranston, M. (tr.) (2004) *Jean-Jacques Rousseau: The Social Contract*. London: Penguin.

Department for Education (DfE) (2011) *The Framework for the National Curriculum: A Report by the Expert Panel for the National Curriculum Review*. London: DfE.

Department for Education (DfE) (2012a) *The National Curriculum for English Key Stages 1 and 2* (Draft). London: DfE.

Department for Education (DfE) (2012b) *The National Curriculum for Mathematics Key Stages 1 and 2* (Draft). London: DfE.

Department for Education (DfE) (2012c) *The National Curriculum for Science Key Stages 1 and 2* (Draft). London: DfE.

Department for Education (DfE) (2013) *The National Curriculum in England Framework Document for Consultation*. London: DfE.

Department for Education and Employment/Qualifications and Curriculum Authority (1999) *English National Curriculum Handbook*. London: HMSO.

Dewey, J. (1916) *Democracy and Education*. New York: Free Press.

Gove, M. (2012) Secretary of State letter to Tim Oates regarding the National Curriculum Review, 11 June 2012, available online at www.education.gov.uk/schools/teachingandlearning/curriculum/nationalcurriculum/b0075667/national-curriculum-review-update (accessed November 2012).

Haydon, G. (1995) Aims of Education. In S. Capel, M. Leask and T. Turner (eds), *Learning to Teach in the Secondary School*. London: Routledge.

Le Métais, J. (1995) *Legislating for Change: School Reforms in England and Wales, 1979–1994*. Slough: NFER.

Le Métais, J. (2004) Values and Aims in Curriculum and Assessment Frameworks. In S. O'Donnell, C. Sargent, R. Brown, C. Andrews and J. Le Métais (eds) *INCA: The International Review of Curriculum and Assessment Frameworks Archive*. London: QCA.

Moore, T.W. (1974) *Educational Theory: An Introduction*. London: Routledge and Kegan Paul.

Pollard, A. (2002) *Reflective Teaching*. London: Continuum.

Pollard, A. and James, M. (2011) Letter from Andrew Pollard and Mary James to Michael Gove, 10 October 2011, available online at www.bera.ac.uk/system/files/AP%20%2526%20MJ%20Letter%20to%20MG%20101011%20%28redacted%29.pdf (accessed 18 May 2013).

Pollard, A. and Tann, S. (1997) *Reflective Teaching in the Primary School: A Handbook for the Classroom*. London: Continuum.

Shuayb, M. and O'Donnell, S. (2008) *Aims and Values in Primary Education: England and Other Countries (Primary Review Research Survey 1/2)*. Cambridge: University of Cambridge Faculty of Education.

Tabberer, R. (1997) Primary Education: Expectations and Provision. In S. O'Donnell, C. Sargent, R. Brown, C. Andrews and J. Le Métais (eds) *INCA: The International Review of Curriculum and Assessment Frameworks Archive*. London: QCA.

Thomas, D. (1995) *Teachers' Stories*. Buckingham: Open University Press.

Wyse, D. (2012) *The Primary English Curriculum: Command of Language or Language Of Command?* Institute of Education blog, available online at http://ioelondonblog.wordpress.com/2012/07/25/the-primary-english-curriculum-command-of-language-or-language-of-command/ (accessed November 2012).

THE CURRICULUM

Dominic Wyse

INTRODUCTION

The primary curriculum in the different countries of the UK has been subject to increasing attention from politicians over the last 25 years. Since political devolution, the curricula of the different countries in the UK has diversified from England's. In spite of all the controversy and change since 1988, you will see that the curriculum model in England remains very similar to the first statutory curriculum from 1862. Although there were signs that an emphasis on creativity might lead to a new progressivism, things are once again much more uncertain. The unit concludes with a vision for the future primary curriculum.

OBJECTIVES

By the end of this unit you should:

- understand about the aims of the curricula at Foundation Stage and Key Stages 1 and 2;
- appreciate that the history of the curriculum is an important aspect of continuing debates;
- be starting to think about how teachers make professional decisions about the curriculum in the best interests of the children that they teach;
- have some ideas about how a future curriculum might look.

As part of your preparation for school experience, you will have become more familiar with national curricula. The Early Years Foundation Stage (EYFS) requirements (from birth to age 5) are shown at the Department for Education website (www.education.gov.uk/aboutdfe/statutory/g00213120/eyfs-statutory-framework). For the later years, the requirements of the National Curriculum for England are shown at www.gov.uk/government/collections/national-curriculum. In spite of the importance of the National Curriculum, in relation to what all primary teachers must teach, you may find that, once you start your school experience, the statutory requirements are rarely referred to. This is because schools' long-term and medium-term planning has often been discussed, agreed and written down over a considerable period of time. Once this thinking has been translated from the National Curriculum into teaching plans, the official documents are not really needed so much. This can make it difficult for student teachers to appreciate the links between the National Curriculum and school planning. Another area in which it is sometimes difficult to see the links with the statutory documents is the extent to which some of the important opening statements of national curricula are genuinely reflected in classroom practice. These opening statements, such as aims, principles and values, should be very important, because, in theory, it is these that guide everything else in the documents, and in practice.

The introduction of the EYFS and the associated assessment through the EYFS Profile by the New Labour government in 2008 marked a new inroad by government into the compulsory education curriculum. Subsequently, in common with other curriculum developments carried out by the Conservative–Liberal Democrat government, a government-commissioned review (Tickell, 2011) resulted in a streamlined EYFS curriculum and its assessment. The aims for the 2012 EYFS are expressed as overarching principles:

Overarching principles

VI. Four guiding principles should shape practice in early years settings. These are:

- every child is a **unique child**, who is constantly learning and can be resilient, capable, confident and self-assured;
- children learn to be strong and independent through **positive relationships**;
- children learn and develop well in **enabling environments**, in which their experiences respond to their individual needs and there is a strong partnership between practitioners and parents and/or carers; and
- **children develop and learn in different ways and at different rates**. The framework covers the education and care of all children in early years provision, including children with special educational needs and disabilities.

(Department for Education, 2012: 2)

Another significant feature of the EYFS is the Early Learning Goals, which are assessed by the Early Years Foundation Stage Profile, which is part of the extensive statutory assessments in England at age 6 (the phonics screening check), 7, 11 and 16 (at the end of 2013 the government proposed new national assessment arrangements which were subject to a public consultation). Many people remain unhappy about the amount and nature of testing of children in England and the way such testing is used to hold schools and teachers accountable.

The curriculum for children in the early years is organised around the areas of learning and development:

The areas of learning and development

1.4 There are seven areas of learning and development that must shape educational programmes in early years settings. All areas of learning and development are important and inter-connected. Three areas are particularly crucial for igniting children's curiosity and enthusiasm for learning, and for building their capacity to learn, form relationships and thrive. These three areas, the *prime* areas, are:

- communication and language;
- physical development; and
- personal, social and emotional development.

1.5 Providers must also support children in four *specific* areas, through which the three prime areas are strengthened and applied. The specific areas are:

- literacy;
- mathematics;
- understanding the world; and
- expressive arts and design.

(Department for Education, 2012: 4)

The EYFS curriculum emphasises physical, personal, social and emotional development, but the primacy of core curriculum areas, such as language and literacy, and mathematics, is clear in the location and emphasis of subjects in the 'prime areas' and 'specific areas' of the new curriculum, with a corresponding weaker emphasis (particularly compared with the previous version of the EYFS) on the arts and creativity.

As far as the primary curriculum is concerned, the two aims and the subjects of the National Curriculum for primary schools are stated in the Education Act 2002 (see Figures 4.2.1 and 4.2.2). You can see from section 80(1)(a) that religious education and religious worship are singled out in the legal requirements for schools in England and Wales. An important question is whether the wording of the two aims is appropriate for the twenty-first-century world that children are living in. For example, is pupils' 'spiritual' development correctly positioned as the first priority of the first of the two aims? And, to what extent does the education system prepare children for adult life? Finally, if the state is going to establish aims for the National Curriculum (which is a moot point itself), to what extent does the curriculum as a whole genuinely reflect the aims? White's (2004) analyses have found a disjuncture between National Curriculum aims in England and the programmes of study, something that was not the case in Northern Ireland, where White was invited to support the development of the curriculum.

Task 4.2.1 Religious education, religion and the curriculum

The Church of England and the Catholic Church have had a profound influence on the English education system, including involvement in the funding of schools, the legal necessity for a daily act of worship, and the place of religious education (RE) as a subject. Given that, in most other countries, this is not the case, and in some their national curricula are completely secular, to what extent do you think the influence of religion is a positive aspect of the curriculum in England?

When the National Curriculum was first proposed, there was overwhelming resistance to the fact that it should be introduced at all, as Haviland (1988) showed. However, one of the strong arguments mounted in favour of the National Curriculum was that pupils across England and Wales were receiving an uneven education, which could include considerable repetition of subject matter, a situation that could be exacerbated if children moved areas to different schools. There were also well-founded claims that some groups of children, particularly minority ethnic ones, were subject to low expectations, reflected in the curricula that were delivered to them. A national curriculum was seen as a solution to these problems, because it would ensure that all children had an *entitlement* to a continuous and coherent curriculum (one of four *purposes* of the National Curriculum). However, exposing children to the *same* curriculum does not necessarily lead to the fulfilment of their entitlement. I would argue that a curriculum that is informed by pupils' interests, needs and rights is more likely to give them their entitlement than a uniform one that is legally imposed.

Despite the resistance to the National Curriculum, it was introduced in 1988. Following many complaints that it was overburdening schools, it was revised in 1993, but the revisions did little to reduce the load. In spite of three significant reviews of the primary curriculum in 2009, the National Curriculum has remained very similar to the previous versions; to understand the reasons for this, we need to look back in time.

HISTORY OF THE CURRICULUM

The idea of the curriculum being dominated by the 3Rs (Reading, wRiting and aRithmetic) is a very old one. In 1862, Parliament finally agreed a legal document called the Revised Code of 1862. This introduced the idea that children over the age of 7 would be examined in the 3Rs by an inspector. Children were grouped by age into different 'standards' that had certain requirements (see Table 4.2.1)

78 General requirements in relation to curriculum

(1) The curriculum for a maintained school or maintained nursery school satisfies the requirements of this section if it is a balanced and broadly based curriculum which –

    (a) promotes the spiritual, moral, cultural, mental and physical development of pupils at the school and of society, and

    (b) prepares pupils at the school for the opportunities, responsibilities and experiences of later life.

(2) The curriculum for any funded nursery education provided otherwise than at a maintained school or maintained nursery school satisfies the requirements of this section if it is a balanced and broadly based curriculum which –

    (a) promotes the spiritual, moral, cultural, mental and physical development of the pupils for whom the funded nursery education is provided and of society, and

    (b) prepares those pupils for the opportunities, responsibilities and experiences of later life.

80 Basic curriculum for every maintained school in England

(1) The curriculum for every maintained school in England shall comprise a basic curriculum which includes –

    (a) provision for religious education for all registered pupils at the school (in accordance with such of the provisions of Schedule 19 to the School Standards and Framework Act 1998 (c. 31) as apply in relation to the school),

    (b) a curriculum for all registered pupils at the school who have attained the age of three but are not over compulsory school age (known as 'the National Curriculum for England'),

    (c) in the case of a secondary school, provision for sex education for all registered pupils at the school, and

    (d) in the case of a special school, provision for sex education for all registered pupils at the school who are provided with secondary education.

(2) Subsection (1)(a) does not apply –

    (a) in relation to a nursery class in a primary school, or

    (b) in the case of a maintained special school (provision as to religious education in special schools being made by regulations under section 71(7) of the School Standards and Framework Act 1998).

(3) The Secretary of State may by order –

    (a) amend subsection (1) so as to add further requirements (otherwise than in relation to religious education or sex education),

    (b) amend subsection (1)(b) by substituting for the reference to compulsory school age (or to any age specified there by virtue of this paragraph) a reference to such other age as may be specified in the order, and (c) amend any provision included in subsection (1) by virtue of paragraph (a) of this subsection. (Education Act 2002)

FIGURE 4.2.1 The aims of the current National Curriculum

83 Curriculum requirements for foundation stage

(1) For the foundation stage, the National Curriculum for England shall comprise the areas of learning and may specify in relation to them –

  (a) the knowledge, skills and understanding which pupils of different abilities and maturities are expected to have by the end of the foundation stage (referred to in this Part as 'the early learning goals').
  (b) the matters, skills and processes which are required to be taught to pupils of different abilities and maturities during the foundation stage (referred to in this Part as 'educational programmes'), and
  (c) assessment arrangements.

(2) The following are the areas of learning for the foundation stage –
  (a) personal, social and emotional development,
  (b) communication, language and literacy,
  (c) mathematical development,
  (d) knowledge and understanding of the world,
  (e) physical development, and
  (f) creative development.

(3) The Secretary of State may by order amend subsection (2).

84 Curriculum requirements for first, second and third key stages

(1) For the first, second and third key stages, the National Curriculum for England shall comprise the core and other foundation subjects specified in subsections (2) and (3), and shall specify attainment targets, programmes of study and assessment arrangements in relation to each of those subjects for each of those stages.

(2) The following are the core subjects for the first, second and third key stages –

  (a) mathematics,
  (b) English, and
  (c) science.

(3) The following are the other foundation subjects for the first, second and third key stages –

  (a) design and technology,
  (b) information and communication technology,
  (c) physical education,
  (d) history,
  (e) geography,
  (f) art and design,
  (g) music, and
  (h) in relation to the third key stage –
    (i) citizenship, and
    (ii) a modern foreign language.

(4) In this section 'modern foreign language' means a modern foreign language specified in an order made by the Secretary of State or, if the order so provides, any modern foreign language.

(5) An order under subsection (4) may –

  (a) specify circumstances in which a language is not to be treated as a foundation subject, and
  (b) provide for the determination under the order of any question arising as to whether a particular language is a modern foreign language.

(6) The Secretary of State may by order amend subsections (2) to (5). (Education Act 2002)

FIGURE 4.2.2 The subjects of the current National Curriculum

TABLE 4.2.1 The curriculum specified by the Revised Code of 1862

48.	Standard I	Standard II	Standard III	Standard IV	Standard V	Standard VI
Reading	Narrative in monosyllables.	One of the narratives next in order after monosyllables in an elementary reading book used in the school.	A short paragraph from an elementary reading book used in the school.	A short paragraph from a more advanced reading book used in the school.	A few lines of poetry from a reading book used in the first class of the school.	A short ordinary paragraph in a newspaper, or other modern narrative.
Writing	Form on blackboard or slate, from dictation, letters, capital and small, manuscript.	Copy in manuscript character a line of print.	A sentence from the same paragraph, slowly read once, and then dictated in single words.	A sentence slowly dictated once by a few words at a time, from the same book, but not from the paragraph read.	A sentence slowly dictated once, by a few words at a time, from a reading book used in the first class of the school.	Another short ordinary paragraph in a newspaper, or other modern narrative, slowly dictated once by a few words at a time.
Arithmetic	Form on blackboard or slate, from dictation, figures up to 20; name at sight figures up to 20; add and subtract figures up to 10; orally from examples on the blackboard.	A sum in simple addition or subtraction, and the multiplication table.	A sum in any simple rule as far as short division (inclusive).	A sum in compound rules (money).	A sum in compound rules (common weights and measures).	A sum in practice or bills of parcels.

Teachers were paid 8 shillings for each child who passed the examination of the 3Rs in their standard. A failure in any one of the 3Rs would mean that the grant was reduced by 2 shillings and 8 pence. Four shillings were awarded for general merit and attendance. This system, known as 'payment by results', had two main problems: (1) the stress on the children due to the examination system; (2) the focus on the 3Rs, resulting in a very narrow curriculum (Curtis and Boultwood, 1964). Payment by results was suspended from 1895, to be replaced by more freedom for primary teachers represented by the Education Act 1902 and the publication of the significant handbook *Suggestions for the Consideration of Teachers and Others Concerned in the Work of Public Elementary Schools*. Until 1926, the legal powers established in the Elementary Code meant that the Board of Education held the right to approve the school curriculum and timetable through the work of inspectors. In 1926, the regulations were revised, and any reference to the subjects of the curriculum was removed (Cunningham, 2002).

It wasn't until much later, in the 1960s, that government began to take a strong interest in the curriculum once more. The idea of the primary curriculum as a 'secret garden' was coined by David Eccles (Minister of Education from 1954 to 1957 and again from 1959 to 1962) in a debate on the Crowther Report in the House of Commons in March 1960. It became a very powerful slogan, especially in the subsequent attempt by the government to set up a Curriculum Study Group in the Ministry of Education, in the face of opposition from teacher unions. The result was the Schools Council, which had more teacher representation and less dominance by civil servants than the Study Group. Shirley Williams, as Prime Minister James Callaghan's Secretary of State for Education and Science, initiated the Great Debate. She called on local education authorities (LEAs) to account for the curriculum in a way to which her broad powers under the 1944 Act entitled her. These powers had not, hitherto, been exerted conventionally in respect of the curriculum, especially given post-war sensitivities about curriculum control in totalitarian states, and possibly some respect for the professional judgement of teachers (Cunningham, 2009, personal communication). Prime Minister James Callaghan's Ruskin College speech clearly signalled government's intention to take more control of the curriculum. As you saw at the beginning of the unit, this control was maximised in the Child Care Act 2006 and has steadily increased to the present day through the imposition of the national strategies. The 'secret garden' has become a national park.

Cunningham (2002) points out that LEA teachers' centres were an important catalyst for new ideas and practices, and he claims that their influence has been unduly neglected by historians of the teaching profession. The year 1902 marked the beginning of progressivism, which, through the first 70 years of the twentieth century, was increasingly influenced by courses provided by LEAs. From my own point of view, I still remember the excitement of taking part in courses run by the Inner London Education Authority, later involvement in the Language in the National Curriculum project while working in Bradford, and subsequent courses run by Kirklees LEA when I worked in Huddersfield. However, I'm not sure that the progressive ideas emerging from teachers' centres were as universally influential as has been suggested. Let me take an example from the teaching of English. 'The real book approach' is a progressive approach to the teaching of literacy that has frequently been blamed for alleged poor standards in reading, but the number of teachers who use such an approach is frequently exaggerated. Research (Wyse, 1998) has shown that, at various periods in time, a maximum of about 4 per cent of schools appeared to use such progressive approaches to the teaching of literacy. Simpson (1996) confirms this figure in his comment that, in spite of the Plowden Report's claim (Central Advisory Council for Education, 1967; a report that is seen as a classic account of progressive teaching) that many of the old beliefs about primary teaching had been 'blown away', only 4 per cent of schools had rejected streaming (a good indicator of more traditional teaching approaches), which was in contradiction to the report's recommendations. This lack of change in teacher practice continued in spite of the fact that LEA teachers' centres and universities may have promoted progressive educational ideas. Alexander (1995) recognised this when he spoke about the change in the collective culture of schools contrasting with continuity in the privacy of classrooms:

> English primary education in 2000 is nineteenth-century elementary education modified – much modified, admittedly – rather than transformed. Elementary education is its centre of gravity. Elementary education provides its central point of reference. Elementary education is the form to which it most readily tends to regress.
>
> (Alexander, 2000: 147)

One of the most damaging aspects of the lack of change is the separation of core and foundation subjects, which Alexander (2004) has called a crude '"basics" and the rest' curriculum, which you saw was first statutorily implemented in the revised code of 1862.

CREATIVITY AND THE CURRICULUM

The period since the Education Reform Act 1988, which first established the modern National Curriculum, has seen year on year increases in government control of primary and early years education. Heavy prescription through the National Curriculum, national strategies, testing, targets and league tables of test results have resulted in an impoverished curriculum (Wyse and Torrance, 2009), in spite of some schools' ability to resist such control and maintain their philosophies of teaching and learning. Amid this stormy landscape, a lifeline emerged in the unexpected form of another government report. The National Advisory Committee on Creative and Cultural Education (NACCCE) was established in February 1998 to make recommendations on the creative and cultural development of young people through formal and informal education. There were some powerful messages in the report:

> The real effect of the existing distinction between the core and foundation subjects now needs to be carefully assessed in the light of ten years' experience. It appears to have reduced the status of the arts and humanities and their effective impact in the school curriculum.
>
> (NACCCE, 1999: 75)

As a way of reducing curriculum content and addressing the neglect of subjects such as music and art, the report recommended: 'In order to achieve parity, the existing distinction between core and foundation subjects should be removed' (p. 87). Unfortunately, this recommendation was not followed when the National Curriculum 2000 was put into place, nor has it been to date, as, yet again, English, maths and science are to be the core curriculum. The NACCCE report seemed to strike a chord with many people in education who were deeply unhappy about the mechanistic and bloated curriculum that had been followed since 1988.

In spite of overwhelming support for the NACCCE report, politicians were not quick to act. *Excellence and Enjoyment: A Strategy for Primary Schools* (Department for Education and Skills, 2003) subsumed the literacy and numeracy strategies and was the third major national strategy from the period between 1997 and 2003. It came on top of an unprecedented number of government interventions in primary education. In spite of teachers' feelings of 'intervention overload', it was anticipated keenly, because of the growing consensus that educational policy in England was too prescriptive, and that this was impacting negatively on creative teaching and creative learning. It was hoped that fundamental reforms might result in a more appropriate level of professional autonomy for teachers, including the opportunity to teach more creatively, with fewer constraints.

The document did indeed include words such as 'freedom' and 'empowerment', and, on page 18, for the first time after the executive summary, the word 'creativity' appeared:

> 2.11 Some teachers question whether it is possible to exercise their curricular freedom, because of the priority the Government attaches to improving literacy and numeracy. But as Ofsted reports have shown, it is not a question of 'either', 'or'. Raising standards and making learning fun can and do go together. The best primary schools have developed timetables and teaching plans that combine creativity with strong teaching in the basics.
>
> (Department for Education and Skills, 2003: 18)

It is true that it is not impossible to teach creatively and to help children learn creatively in spite of government constraints, but there is a more important consideration: what is the *best* way to achieve creativity, and might part of this mean abolishing national statutory testing of all children?

In 2010, the European Commission published the final report on its study of creativity and innovation (Cachia *et al.*, 2010). The study addressed the role of creativity in primary and secondary education in twenty-seven member states of the European Union. The findings in relation to curricula included the perception that there was, in general, insufficient encouragement for creativity, caused in many cases by a lack of clear definitions and understanding. The findings also showed that excessive curriculum content was regarded as a common barrier to creativity. In spite of commitment to curricula, frequently stated by teachers, conventional teaching methods such as 'chalk and talk' were regarded as an obstacle to creativity, because this kind of formal teaching is less likely to lead to creativity. Primary teachers were considered to be more likely than secondary teachers to promote creative learning and active learner-centred approaches in class. Summative assessment processes were recognised as a barrier, whereas more versatile assessment processes were perceived as an enabler. Revision of curricula to include more creativity therefore requires parallel revisions in assessment systems, if creativity is to flourish. Within the UK, the study by the Institute for Prospective Technological Studies noted that Northern Ireland's and Scotland's curriculum texts had the most prominent use of the term creativity.

In England, creativity featured in the aims for the primary National Curriculum from 1999 onwards. The handbook and accompanying website for the National Curriculum also included creativity in 'Promoting skills across the curriculum' as part of a thinking skills section. At a later date, an extra section called 'Learning across the curriculum' was added to the online version of the National Curriculum. This section contained extensive requirements and guidance about how creativity could be fostered in the curriculum. In 2010, following the Rose review of the primary curriculum commissioned by the New Labour government, a new primary curriculum was published online that required pupils 'to create', 'to develop creativity skills' and 'to develop creativity'. However, in 2011, the new Conservative-Liberal Democrat Coalition government simply removed the new curriculum from the government website and initiated yet another review of the National Curriculum. At the same time, the guidance on promoting skills across the curriculum material (including the creativity guidance) was also removed from the National Curriculum website, because it was deemed non-statutory. From 2012 onwards, it appeared that creativity was no longer going to have a significant profile in the National Curriculum in England, unlike in many other countries.

In Wales, the foundation phase curriculum includes creativity as part of thinking skills in its 'Skills across the curriculum' section. 'Developing thinking' is described as thinking across the curriculum through the processes of planning, developing and reflecting, in order that pupils can make sense of their world. It is argued that these processes enable children to think creatively and critically. Uniquely, Wales includes 'Creative development' as a discrete foundation stage 'area of learning'. This is summarised as follows:

> Children should be continually developing their imagination and creativity across the curriculum. Their natural curiosity and disposition to learn should be stimulated by everyday sensory experiences, both indoors and outdoors. Children should engage in creative, imaginative and expressive activities in art, craft, design, music, dance and movement. Children should explore a wide range of stimuli, develop their ability to communicate and express their creative ideas, and reflect on their work.

> (Department for Children, Education, Lifelong Learning and Skills, 2008: 10)

In addition, Wales's 'Skills framework for 3- to 19-year-olds' includes the claim that the developing-thinking section of the framework is underpinned by creative and critical thinking, although metacognition seems to be the strongest focus.

Northern Ireland also locates creativity within its 'Thinking skills and personal capabilities' framework, which advocates the provision of worthwhile experiences across the curriculum that allow pupils to develop skills, including being creative. Examples include seeking questions and problems to solve, making new connections, valuing the unexpected and taking risks.

Unlike the other nations, Scotland does not have a separate and explicit framework promoting thinking skills and creativity; instead, creativity is built into the experiences and outcomes across the curriculum areas. Scotland also includes a 'Learning across the curriculum' section, but creativity is not identified as a separate strand, as it is in Wales and was in England.

The strongest commitment to creativity, as evident from national curricula in the UK, is seen in Wales's National Curriculum, particularly in its identification of a separate area of learning to complement the inclusion of creativity as part of thinking skills. However, Scotland's inclusion of creativity as a theme that is built into the experiences and outcomes is perhaps the most logical conception, because creativity is a process and disposition, rather than a subject/area of learning. Although the inclusion of creativity as part of thinking skills in three of the nations is welcome, there is a danger that this categorisation of creativity is somewhat limited. Although creativity is characterised by divergent thinking, this is only one important part of what it means to be creative. However, its inclusion in thinking skills sections in national curricula is often characterised by additional descriptions that indicate a much broader understanding of creativity.

It is of great regret that, at the time of writing, England's proposals for programmes of study for the new National Curriculum (2013) have very little attention to creativity, compared with the previous National Curriculum (1999). Quite apart from the lack of opportunity this will entail for the nation's children, the retrogressive proposals will reflect badly on a country with a historical legacy of creative teaching and learning that is highly regarded internationally.

Task 4.2.2 Thinking about national curricula

- What changes would you like to see made to the curriculum?
- What are your views about a subject-led curriculum?
- Has the emphasis on English and maths since 1997 been a reasonable one?
- In what ways are teachers developing a more creative curriculum?
- Which aspects of the curriculum are you excited about teaching? Which ones are you less confident about? What will you do to improve your confidence?

VISIONS FOR THE PRIMARY CURRICULUM

In 2012, Wyse *et al.* published the first book-length analysis to compare the National Curricula in England, Northern Ireland, Scotland and Wales. The book explores the idea of national educational policy being influenced by transnational policy trends, and includes historical perspectives on the development of national curricula, paying particular attention to the National Curriculum texts and research evidence on the implementation of national policies. One of the findings of the work was to identify the increasingly stark differences between national curricula in England and national curricula in the other three nations, as a result of political devolution. The policy in Scotland is particularly noteworthy. In Scotland, the Education (Scotland) Act 1980 very clearly gave power over the curriculum to local authorities: '(2) In any such school the education authority shall have *the sole power* of regulating the curriculum and of appointing teachers' (The Education (Scotland) Act 1980, section 21, p. 13; italics added). This early legislation was an important feature of the greater democratic involvement of educators in its system. A recent study in Scotland indicated very strongly that teachers mediated curriculum direction and guidance in relation to their own existing practice (Hulme *et al.*, 2009). In England, the Education Reform Act 1988 put the power to develop a national curriculum in the hands of the government through the Secretary of State for Education:

> Duty to establish the National Curriculum
>
> 4.–(1) It shall be the duty of the Secretary of State so to exercise the powers conferred by subsection (2) below as–
>
> (a) to establish a complete National Curriculum as soon as is reasonably practicable (taking first the core subjects and then the other foundation subjects); and
> (b) to revise that Curriculum whenever he considers it necessary or expedient to do so.
>
> (Chapter 40, section 4: 3)

Another difference between the curriculum in England and the curriculum in Scotland is that the Curriculum for Excellence is a through curriculum that covers birth to 18, rather than the position in England with different curricula for different phases of the education system.

In order to understand the practical implications of the National Curriculum in Scotland, which is called the Curriculum for Excellence (Scottish Government, 2011), let us take one area, 'languages' (note this more appropriate title, as opposed to the National Curriculum subject title 'English', in England). In the *experiences and outcomes* element of the curriculum, the five major sections in the language requirements are all divided up into the *organisers* of: listening and talking, reading, and writing ('mode' might have been a more appropriate description in relation to language). The requirements are preceded by a list of aspects that pupils are expected to have opportunities to engage with. These include, 'engage with and create a wide range of texts' (p. 24). An interesting feature of the language of these aspects and the requirements more generally is the use of the personal pronoun 'I', implying that the curriculum is pupil-centred. For example, 'I develop and extend my literacy skills when I have opportunities to: communicate, collaborate and build relationships' (p. 24). Another interesting feature is the *Enjoyment and choice* strand, which is the first column in the first section of the tables that are used to organise the requirements for each organiser. For the teaching of writing, the requirements in the primary education stages include, 'I enjoy creating texts of my choice and I regularly select subject, purpose, format and resources to suit the needs of my audience' (p. 33). This is indeed a powerful statement. The opportunity for pupils to choose what to write (in the fullest sense, including topic, form and ways of working) is something that has very rarely been seen in practice since the process writing approach of the 1990s (Wyse, 1998). Like Northern Ireland, Scotland's National Curriculum texts include extensive descriptions of the rationales for the experiences and outcomes material and its organisation.

Primary phase National Curriculum development in England has suffered from a lack of rigour, understanding and coherence as a result of poor government interventions. In the summer of 2012, a number of the mistakes that had dogged National Curriculum development since the 1980s looked likely to be repeated. The most serious of these were the following: (a) the lack of transparency in selection of people to advise on the curriculum; (b) insufficient attention to the range of relevant evidence; (c) an undue emphasis on comparison with other countries in international league tables, as opposed to greater democratic attention to consideration of aims; (d) dubious pubic consultations; (e) weak proposals for programmes of study.

Unlike, for example, Scotland's attempts over many years to fully engage society in developing a shared curriculum, from 2010 onwards, ministers in England opted for an expert group to make recommendations to a dedicated group of civil servants in the Department for Education, and, hence, rejected the opportunity for a longer-term, more considered and democratic process to build a national curriculum fit for the twenty-first century. Even accepting many of the recommendations of the National Curriculum expert group appointed by education Minister Nick Gibb proved impossible, as was clearly documented (see www.bera.ac.uk/content/background-michael-gove's-response-report-expert-panel-national-curriculum-review-england).

I have offered a critical account of National Curriculum developments in England, and so, finally, I want to identify what I think are some of the key considerations for the development of better curricula. One of the most important things about the curriculum in future is that the model needs to be relevant from the early years up to the end of schooling, and should genuinely prepare pupils for higher education and lifelong learning. As we have seen in this unit, the current model for early years differs from the model for primary years. I propose Figure 4.2.3 as a starting point for thinking about the curriculum.

A curriculum model that reflects learning and teaching throughout life needs to put the individual's 'self' at the centre. It is the individual person's motivation to learn and their interests that will sustain learning throughout life. A new curriculum will need to encourage teaching that explicitly encourages pupils to find areas of work that motivate them and to pursue these in depth, even at the very earliest stages of education. Children's rights to participate in all matters that affect them should not be an abstract item in the programmes of study for citizenship, but a daily reality in their lives (Wales's National Curriculum uniquely is built on the UN Convention on the Rights of the Child). Role-play and drama will be a recurrent medium for reflecting on the self and others. Physical development, including health, will be nurtured as part of this focus.

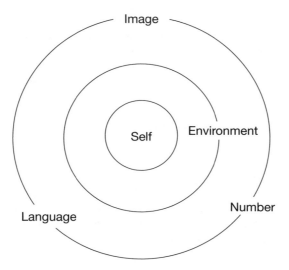

FIGURE 4.2.3 Proposed curriculum model

The environment in which learning takes place is vital to sustain the self. In spite of futuristic claims about learning electronically from home, a place called school will still be the main arena for learning, but it should be one that is not a grimy, damp, cold, boomy building: it should be architecturally inspiring. It should be a place where the crafts of life, such as the preparation and sharing of food and the performing of and listening to music, are centre stage. The social interaction provided by the home and community will form an integrated link with the social interaction provided by the school's curriculum. Sights, sounds and exploration of the world, beginning with the immediate surroundings, will form part of the environmental curriculum. Investigations will take place, problems will be solved, and things will be made. All of this will be set in the context of active participation in working towards a sustainable environmental future for the world.

Learning centred on image – both still and moving, icons, logos, signs, symbols – will no longer be neglected, in view of the dominant role these things have in our daily lives, and have done for many years. The counting and categorisation of entities, ultimately leading to the beautiful abstraction of mathematical symbols, will remain a powerful focus for learning about number. Language in all its linguistic contexts, including text and talk, will also remain a powerful focus and one that unites all other aspects of this curriculum.

Information technology (IT) will not be a subject. Do we have P and P, or paper and pencils, as a subject in the curriculum? No. IT will be central to the work of schools, just as any other basic resource is. It will not be used as the latest solution to all our problems, but it will, whenever appropriate, enrich the possibilities for learning and teaching, and its natural influence will continue to grow.

My key considerations are most likely to be realised by a curriculum organised, not by traditional subjects, but by areas of learning. Is my suggestion that we abandon the current, subject-dominated core/foundation curriculum particularly radical? Not really. As one example of practice, the Royal Society for the encouragement of Arts, Manufactures and Commerce has been working with schools, developing their 'Opening Minds' curriculum for a number of years. Opening Minds is a curriculum that more than 500 schools have trialled. It is not based on subjects but a series of 'competences' that pupils are expected to acquire through curriculum content decided by schools. As another example of alternative curricula, the primary curriculum developed by the International Baccalaureate Organisation organises its curriculum around six themes. Consider, also, higher education, which offers hundreds of subjects, and continues to add new ones, that combine a range of understanding and skills that would benefit from preparation by a different curriculum model in schools. However, the reason that these changes have not been made before, and why the curriculum is still entrenched in the nineteenth century, is that it requires our political leaders to have the knowledge, understanding and courage to change legislation and revolutionise the primary education system in order to bring it into the twenty-first century.

Task 4.2.3 Other national curricula

Examine a national curriculum from another country. Discuss the similarities and differences between England's National Curriculum and that from the other country, then agree two or three changes that you think would be of benefit to the National Curriculum in England.

SUMMARY

In this unit, we have discussed the aims of the curriculum at Foundation and Key Stages 1 and 2, and have explored how teachers make professional decisions about the curriculum for their pupils. It is recommended, therefore, that you build on these discussions by reading the recommendations below, in order to widen your knowledge and understanding of the primary school curriculum.

ANNOTATED FURTHER READING

Department for Education (2011) *The Framework for the National Curriculum: A report by the Expert Panel for the National Curriculum Review*, London: DfE.
> Thorough, research-based review, with recommendations based on a selection of evidence. Interesting to compare this with the government's actions subsequently.

Kelly, A.V. (2009) *The Curriculum: Theory and Practice*, 6th edn, London: Sage.
> An excellent overview of issues that combines comprehensive definitions with necessary political analysis. The comments about the increase in political interference with the curriculum, revealed through the author's reflections about the six editions of this book, are fascinating.

Wyse, D., Baumfield, V., Egan, D., Gallagher, C., Hayward, L., Hulme, M., Leitch, R., Livingston, K., Menter, I. and Lingard, B. (2012) *Creating the Curriculum*, London: Routledge.
> The first book-length analysis of the National Curricula in England, Northern Ireland, Scotland and Wales. The opening chapter contextualises the themes of the book and the UK in a wider international perspective. Chapters include direct comparison of curriculum texts, e.g. language, PSE, creativity, etc.

FURTHER READING TO SUPPORT M-LEVEL STUDY

Boyle, B. and Bragg, J. (2006) 'A curriculum without foundation', *British Educational Research Journal*, 32(4): 569-82.
> Reveals evidence of the narrowing of the curriculum in England.

Wyse, D. and Torrance, H. (2009) 'The development and consequences of national curriculum assessment for primary education in England', *Educational Research*, 51(2), 213-28.
> One of the articles in a special issue of the journal that was focused on National Curriculum and assessment.

RELEVANT WEBSITES

Cambridge Primary Review: www.primaryreview.org.uk/
> This website contains links to the evidence for the large-scale, wide-ranging independent review of primary education headed by Robin Alexander and based at the University of Cambridge's Faculty of Education.

Children, Schools and Families Committee: www.publications.parliament.uk/pa/select.htm
> This House of Commons Select Committee's report on the National Curriculum was one of the most important education reports of the 2000s.

International Review of Curriculum and Assessment Frameworks Internet Archive: www.inca.org.uk/
INCA's archive is a useful resource for comparing different countries.

National Curriculum: www.education.gov.uk/schools/teachingandlearning/curriculum/primary
This is the home of the National Curriculum for England.

www.education.gov.uk/childrenandyoungpeople/earlylearningandchildcare/delivery/education/a0068102/early-years-foundation-stage-eyfs
The Early Years Foundation Stage curriculum requirements are shown here.

REFERENCES

Alexander, R.J. (ed.) (1995) *Versions of Primary Education*, London: Routledge and The Open University.

Alexander, R.J. (2000) *Culture and Pedagogy: International Comparisons in Primary Education*, Oxford: Blackwell.

Alexander, R.J. (2004) 'Still no pedagogy? Principle, pragmatism and compliance in primary education', *Cambridge Journal of Education*, 34(1): 7–33.

Cachia, R., Ferrari, A., Ala-Mutka, K. and Punie, Y. (2010) *Creative Learning and Innovative Teaching. Final Report on the Study on Creativity and Innovation in Education in the EU Member States*, Seville: European Commission. Joint Research Centre. Institute for Prospective Technological Studies.

Central Advisory Council for Education (1967) *Children and Their Primary Schools* (The Plowden Report), London: HMSO.

Cunningham, P. (2002) 'Progressivism, decentralisation and recentralisation: local education authorities and the primary curriculum, 1902–2002', *Oxford Review of Education*, 28(2–3): 217–33.

Curtis, S.J. and Boultwood, M.E.A. (1964) *An Introductory History of English Education Since 1800* (3rd edn), London: University Tutorial Press.

Department for Children Education, Lifelong Learning and Skills (2008) *Framework for Children's Learning for 3 to 7-year-olds in Wales*, Cardiff: Welsh Assembly Government.

Department for Education (2012) *Statutory Framework for the Early Years Foundation Stage*, Runcorn: Department for Education.

Department for Education and Skills (DfES) (2003) *Excellence and Enjoyment: A Strategy for Primary Schools*, London: DfES.

Haviland, J. (1988) *Take Care, Mr Baker!* London: Fourth Estate.

Hulme, M., Baumfield, V. and Payne, F. (2009) 'Building capacity through teacher enquiry: the Scottish Schools of Ambition', *Journal of Education for Teaching*, 35(4): 409–24.

National Advisory Committee on Creative and Cultural Education (1999) *All Our Futures: Creativity, Culture and Education*, Sudbury: DfEE.

Scottish Government (2011) *Curriculum for Excellence*, at www.ltscotland.org.uk/

Simpson, D. (1996) 'Progressivism and the development of primary education: an historical review', *History of Education Society Bulletin*, 58(Autumn): 55–63.

Tickell, C. (2011) *The Early Years: Foundations for Life, Health and Learning. An Independent Report on the Early Years Foundation Stage to Her Majesty's Government*, London: DfE.

White, J. (ed.) (2004) *Rethinking the School Curriculum: Values, Aims and Purposes*, London: RoutledgeFalmer.

Wyse, D. (1998) *Primary Writing*, Buckingham: Open University Press.

Wyse, D. and Torrance, H. (2009) 'The development and consequences of national curriculum assessment for primary education in England', *Educational Research*, 51(2): 213–28.

THE NATIONAL CONTEXT FOR THE CURRICULUM

Carrie Ansell and Deborah Nicholson

INTRODUCTION

Prior to the introduction of the National Curriculum in 1988, the school curriculum was largely determined at local level, but, throughout the 1970s and 1980s, public debate about education, schools and the curriculum grew. This debate culminated in the introduction of a statutory National Curriculum by the Department for Education and Science in 1988, which heralded an era of increasingly centralised control of education. During the last half of the twentieth century, the National Curriculum and other non-statutory guidance (and the support structures and assessment associated with these) have become part of the mechanism by which government education policy becomes enacted within schools.

A school's curriculum involves a complex interplay of beliefs, attitudes, skills, knowledge and understanding. It is no surprise, therefore, that what is taught in our schools, as well as how it is taught, is a matter of debate between those who subscribe to different values, who have different aims for education, who have different views on the kind of knowledge that the curriculum should contain or who question whether a national curriculum is needed at all (see Kelly, 2009, for detailed discussion of such issues). Throughout this unit, we will be discussing the draft 2013 National Curriculum and the *Statutory Framework for the Early Years Foundation Stage* and non-statutory guidance for England. For details of the curriculum in Wales and Northern Ireland, see www.wales.gov.uk/curriculuminwales and www.ccea.org.uk. For details of the curriculum for Scotland see Unit 4.4.

OBJECTIVES

By the end of this unit, you should:

- understand the rationale and context for the emergence of a national curriculum;
- be familiar with the current aims, structures and content of the National Curriculum/Early Years Foundation Stage curriculum;
- have analysed the draft 2013 National Curriculum, with a particular focus on English as a case study of moving from policy into curriculum practice;
- have considered the advantages and disadvantages of a statutory national curriculum;
- have reflected on possible future developments of the National Curriculum and examined alternative curricula that focus on creative and cultural development.

THE EMERGENCE OF A NATIONAL CURRICULUM

The Education Act 1944 did not lay down any requirements for the school curriculum (other than the inclusion of religious education). This gave schools and individual teachers great freedom to determine what was taught. There have been many significant educational and political changes during the last 70 years that have affected this position, and some of the key events relating to the curriculum are outlined below.

The rise of progressive education

In the 1950s and 1960s, the 11+ examination was widely used to assess which type of school children would attend at the end of their primary years. In 1953, the first secondary comprehensive (non-selective) school opened, and local education authorities began to abandon the 11+ examination. Changes aimed at modernising the primary and secondary curricula, such as the introduction of 'modern maths' and 'creative writing', began to be made. In 1967, the Plowden Report (Central Advisory Council for Education, 1967) argued for an active, experiential and child-centred curriculum for primary schools. This report both reflected and gave further impetus to changes that were already happening within some schools. Although the extent of progressive practice with primary schools in the 1960s and 1970s is difficult to quantify, this shift in thinking and practice brought to the fore the tensions between child-centred views of education and more traditional, performance-based views.

In Northern Ireland . . .

In Northern Ireland, the last 11+ exam was held in November 2008. The 11+ was officially discontinued in Northern Ireland, but has re-emerged as a different selective process. For the time being, two consortia of schools have emerged: the Association for Quality Education and another grouping known as the Post Primary Transfer Consortium, which is driven mainly by the Council for Catholic Maintained Schools. Although both tests are based on the Northern Ireland Key Stage 2 Curriculum, the tests for the two consortia differ in structure, style and format.

Source: www.elevenplusexams.co.uk/schools/regions/northern-ireland-11-plus

The 'Great Debate'

The so-called rise of progressive educational ideas and practices led to a public debate via parliamentary questions, newspaper articles and academic publications. New practices, such as the introduction of mixed-ability classes, the use of competency-based assessment and the spread of informal and 'play'-based approaches in primary schools, were attacked as leading to a decline in educational standards. In response, in 1974, the government set up the Assessment Performance Unit to monitor standards in mathematics, English and science and to provide statistical evidence.

In 1976, the then prime minister, James Callaghan, opened what he called the 'Great Debate' on education in a speech, in which he discussed the need for changes in education. The major concerns at the time centred around beliefs that there were too many variations in approaches to the curriculum between schools, and that there was an imbalance in the subjects being taught, with too much emphasis placed on the humanities rather than science and technology. These factors, among others, were said to be the cause of a general decline in standards.

In reality, the two major studies of classroom practice in primary schools – Primary Assessment Curriculum Experience and the Observational and Classroom Learning Evaluation – that took place in the mid-1970s found little evidence of the 'progressive', inquiry-based curriculum said to be prevalent in primary schools at that time.

Task 4.3.1 Concerns about the curriculum

Look at the list of concerns about the curriculum in 1976. Discuss the following questions:

- Which of these concerns are under discussion in relation to today's schools?
- What would you consider to be robust evidence to prove or disprove these concerns?
- Do you consider that any of the concerns listed above have been 'solved' or have become less pressing since 1976?

The introduction of a core curriculum

Following the Great Debate, the government began to exercise some control over the curriculum.

Throughout the 1980s, the idea of a 'core curriculum', which gave greater attention to 'the basics', began to be promoted. Critics saw this as a narrowing of the curriculum, with the potential for a split between 'the basics' and the rest of the curriculum (which could be seen as less important). These decades of intense debate and increasing official control of the curriculum culminated in the Education Reform Act 1988, which introduced the National Curriculum for the first time. The curriculum contained the statutory statements and non-statutory guidance concerning the curriculum every child should study between the ages of 5 and 16. It set out the structural details of how the curriculum would operate:

- core and foundation subjects to be studied by all pupils;
- attainment targets defining progress through knowledge, skills and understanding in every subject;
- programmes of study – the content, skills and processes that must be taught during each key stage;
- assessment arrangements for assessing each pupil at or near the end of key stages.

The National Curriculum Council and the Schools Examination and Curriculum Council were set up to oversee the new curriculum. The titles of subsequent quangos have changed constantly under new government directives, and, on 1 April 2013, the National Council for Teaching and Leadership was formed by the DfE, following the merger of the Teaching Agency and National College for School Leadership.

In 2000, the National Curriculum came into force. The subject content was slimmed down, and citizenship was included for the first time; the aims, purposes and values were stated explicitly, and further non-statutory guidance and learning across the curriculum guidelines were included. This revised document – *The National Curriculum Handbook for Primary Teachers in England* (Department for Education and Employment/Qualifications and Curriculum Authority, 1999), statutory at the time of writing until September 2014 (Table 4.3.1), shows the content and assessment of the current National Curriculum and its division into key stages.

TABLE 4.3.1 Content and assessment of the National Curriculum in England 2013 and the Early Years Foundation Stage 2012

Key Stage	Age	Year	Statutory curriculum 2005	Statutory assessment
Foundation Stage	3–4		**Statutory document** *Statutory Framework for the Early Years Foundation Stage* 7 areas of learning	The EYFS Profile (reception year)
	4–5	R	**3 prime areas:** · Communication and language · Physical Development · Personal, Social and Emotional development **4 specific areas:** · Literacy · Mathematics · Understanding the world · Expressive Arts and Design Each area of learning has a set of related Early Learning Goals	
Key Stage 1	5–7	1–2	**Statutory document** *The National Curriculum in England Framework document July 2013* **Core subjects** English, mathematics, science	Year 1 Phonics Screening Check Teacher assessment and national tests in English and mathematics in Year 2
Key Stage 2	7–11	3–6	**Foundation subjects** Art and Design, Citizenship, Computing, Design and Technology, Languages (introduction of a 'foreign language' at KS2), Geography, History, Music, Physical Education Statutory teaching of Religious Education	National tests in core subjects, with a new test in grammar, punctuation and spelling replacing writing introduced in 2013 (summer term, Year 6)
Lower		3–4		
Upper		5–6		
Key Stage 3	11–14	7–9	As Key Stages 1 and 2 with the addition of MFL, Sex and relationship education	National tests in core subjects (summer term, Year 9)

During the period of 2008–9, there were a total of three curriculum reviews, which resulted in a period of great uncertainty. One of these, the 'official' *Independent Review of the Primary Curriculum*, led by Sir Jim Rose, was set up in response to a request from the Secretary of State as part of the *Children's Plan* (December 2007). One of its main aims was to provide greater scope for flexibility and creativity in the curriculum. Despite this, criticism of the review focused on the narrow brief, lack of any real independence or intention to change the current testing regime inherent in the present curriculum and, in relation to literacy, the fundamental absence of speaking and listening, with the emphasis being on the 'basics' of reading and writing.

An independent review of the primary curriculum was also set up by Robin Alexander, of Cambridge University, in October 2006. The main purpose of the Cambridge Primary Review was:

> to begin to make a real difference to the character and quality of English primary education over the first decades of the 21st century, and to the contribution which that education makes to individual lives and the collective good, at a time of change, uncertainty and growing concern about the future.

The review culminated in numerous research and interim reports and eventually the publication of *Children, Their World, Their Education* (Alexander, 2010). The Rose Report was published shortly before the Cambridge Review final report, which, according to Mick Waters, then head of curriculum at the QCDA, acted as a 'pre-emptive strike' against some inconvenient truths. Nevertheless, both reports at the time seemed to offer educators the hope of greater cross-curricular approaches, which could potentially open up the narrow curriculum and engage children in meaningful learning experiences.

In May 2010, the Conservative–Liberal Democrat Coalition government came into office and decided to ignore all these reviews and set up one of their own. As part of the planning for the review, the government sought information about what other countries did, particularly the highest performing jurisdictions, including Singapore, Finland and Hong Kong. The Education Secretary did take up some of the approaches looked at, in particular the consideration of the setting of high expectations as key to improving England's performance in international terms. He expressed an intention to 'set the same level of high expectations, especially for those subjects which are central to school accountability' (Gove, 2012). These subjects – mathematics, science and English – received the closest focus in the review, which laid out the content that each child was expected to learn in each year. In mathematics, for example, there would be 'additional stretch' and an expectation that children would be more proficient in arithmetic and the use of written methods. Programmes of study in the foundation subjects would be much shorter, to allow for 'maximum innovation' (Gove, 2012).

The latest proposed revision of this National Curriculum, and the revised programmes of study for English, mathematics, science and physical education, due to be implemented in September 2014, had, therefore, greater focus on core subjects and a return to the 'essential building blocks of education'. Luke (cited in Wyse *et al.* 2013) describes this as 'an enacted curriculum of basic skills, rule recognition and compliance'. It could be argued that primary schools would, following this revision, be dominated by the curriculum rather than the child. This was policy development that purported to give teachers greater freedom, and yet was highly prescriptive in nature. As we shall see from the case study of the English curriculum, teachers were told not just *what* to teach, but *how* to teach it.

In Northern Ireland . . .

In 1992 the first Northern Ireland Curriculum was introduced – similar in structure to that in England and Wales but with a few points of distinction in relation to subjects and cross-curricular themes. It was found in practice to be much too overloaded and, in 1996, was revised with a significant amount of content removed but remaining unchanged in structure. In 1999 the then Minister gave permission for the CCEA to undertake a fundamental review of the statutory requirements of the curriculum. Following a 5 year period of research, review and consultation, a new and quite different statutory curriculum was approved in 2004. Legislation has now been passed for the phased introduction of that curriculum beginning in September 2007 over a 3 year period. Among the changes now being introduced is a new Foundation Stage for the first 2 years. The new National Curriculum (2013), in each of its stages, is now almost devoid of statutory requirements relating to subject content. This enables teachers to choose appropriate content for the particular pupils they are teaching. The statutory requirements now mostly concern the skills and competences that children are expected to develop rather than to the content that they must learn. There is emphasis on information management skills and on thinking skills, problem solving and creativity. The result of these changes is that, from 2007, there will be much greater divergence between the statutory curriculum in NI and that in England.

Source: www.bbc.co.uk/northernireland/schools/pdf/NIschools_curriculumOverview.pdf

In Wales . . .

The National Literacy Programme and Numeracy Programme set out the actions the Welsh government intends to implement to improve literacy and numeracy standards in Wales. The Literacy and Numeracy Framework (LNF), which became a statutory part of the curriculum in September 2013, aims to 'help teachers of all subjects to identify and provide opportunities for learners to apply literacy and numeracy across the curriculum' (DfES, 2013: 4).

The LNF's relationship to the whole curriculum is 'to help bring about coherent approaches to developing literacy and numeracy across the curriculum. It also informs teachers of all subjects about how they can provide opportunities for learners to apply literacy and numeracy across the curriculum' (see: http://wales.gov.uk/topics/educationandskills/schools home/literacynumeracy/lnframework/lnfrelationship/?lang=en).

The LNF will replace the number and communications components of the non-statutory skills framework, and the thinking and ICT components remain in place as guidance on these skills, with the view to addressing these separately at a later date. It will also be used for formative assessment by teachers.

Source: Department for Education and Skills (DfES) (2013) *National Literacy and Numeracy Framework (LNF)*. Cardiff: Welsh Assembly Government (WAG). http://learning.wales.gov.uk/docs/learningwales/publications/130415-lnf-guidance-en.pdf

The early years curriculum

In 2000, the 'Foundation Stage' was introduced as a distinct phase for children aged 3–5, and the Education Act 2002 extended the National Curriculum to include the Foundation Stage.

The 2012 *Statutory Framework for the Early Years Foundation Stage* (Department for Education, 2012b) replaced the 2008 statutory framework that aimed to help children achieve the *Every Child Matters* (ECM) five outcomes – be healthy; stay safe; enjoy and achieve; make a positive contribution; and achieve economic well-being. The guiding principles remained the same: that every child is a *unique child*, learns through *positive relationships*, in *enabling environments*, and that *children develop and learn in different ways and at different rates*, but this 2012 framework saw the introduction of seven areas of learning and development. These were divided into three prime areas: communication and language, physical development, and personal, social and emotional development – and four specific areas: literacy, mathematics, understanding the world and expressive arts and design. It stated that all the areas were of importance and interconnected, and that each area should be implemented through purposeful play, with practitioners responding to children's needs and interests. This emphasis on communication as a prime area has been praised by early years educators. Unfortunately, this influence has not spread to the July 2013 National Curriculum Framework document (Department for Education, 2013), as speaking and listening have been reduced to eleven statements that apply to all year groups.

A national assessment system for the Foundation Stage, replacing local baseline assessment schemes, was also introduced. Called the Early Years Foundation Stage Profile, the slimmed down 2012 Profile, with seventeen instead of sixty-nine Early Learning Goals, required all registered early years providers to assess each child in the final term in which he or she reaches the age of 5, and no later than 30 June in that term. The results of the profile should be shared with the parent or carer of the child and the Year 1 teacher. Criticism focused on the Progress Check for 2-year-olds, which is said to contradict the principle of the 'unique child', and others have said that the profile was still too prescriptive, with a continued emphasis on Early Learning Goals overly concerned with phonics as the prime approach for reading and writing. The argument was that these may encourage teachers to resort to using formal teaching methods with children who are far too young, in order to ensure goals are achieved. This, in turn, may cause increased stress, with parents being told that their children are failing at a very young age. Comparisons have been made with alternative curricula in other countries, which wait until children are 6 or 7 before introducing formal elements of reading and writing. There is evidence to show that this has little effect on standards (Clark, 2012; Twist *et al.*, 2012).

THE AIMS AND STRUCTURES OF THE NATIONAL CURRICULUM

Values, aims, purposes and principles

See Task 4.3.2, page 290.

Programmes of study and attainment targets

The *programmes of study* are legally binding statements that set out:

- the knowledge, skills and understanding that must be taught;
- the breadth of study – the contexts, activities, areas of study and range of experiences through which the knowledge, skills and understanding are taught.

Task 4.3.2 Aims and purposes

When asked the purpose of education, young children often reply that its purpose is 'to help you get a job'. Teachers may argue that the purpose has become increasingly to pass tests such as SATs, and that teaching is 'by numbers', with little attention paid to social class and inequality (Taubman, cited in Wyse *et al.*, 2013). Do you think there are other purposes to education?

- Reflect on what you think are the values, aims and purposes of education. Then read the section 'Values and purposes underpinning the school curriculum' in the *National Curriculum Handbook* (Department for Education and Employment/Qualifications and Curriculum Authority, 1999).
- Summarise the two aims and four purposes in the handbook. Compare your ideas with those.
- Now consider what you think are the aims and values underpinning the draft National Curriculum (Department for Education, 2012a).
- Discuss why is it important to be explicit about the values and purposes underpinning any national curriculum.

In the 2013 National Curriculum, attainment was said to be measured through pupils reaching the expected knowledge, skills and understanding of the matters taught in the relevant programme of study, whereas attainment targets in the 1999 National Curriculum clearly set out the criteria for the knowledge, skills and understanding that pupils were expected to have by the end of each key stage. Most attainment targets were divided into eight, progressively more challenging level descriptors. These level descriptors provided the basis for making judgements about pupil performance, and the expected attainment at each key stage is shown in Table 4.3.2. The removal of the level descriptors from the 2013 draft curriculum aimed to help ensure that schools make certain that all pupils reach the required standard. The expectation is that teachers will move on when all children have mastered the content in the programme of study. Teachers will always need to consider that there will be some pupils who may move more slowly or more quickly in their learning, because of their particular abilities and aptitudes.

TABLE 4.3.2 National Curriculum attainment target levels

Range of levels at which the great majority of pupils are expected to work		Expected attainment for the majority of the pupils at the end of the key stage	
Key Stage 1	1–3	At age 7	2
Key Stage 2	2–5	At age 11	4
Key Stage 3	3–7	At age 14	6

National tests (see Section 5) at the end of each key stage (and teacher assessment at Key Stage 1) are still used to grade attainment. These saw an increase under the Conservative-Liberal Democrat Coalition government that introduced the statutory Year 1 phonics 'check' in 2011 and the spelling, grammar and punctuation test at the end of Key Stage 2 in 2013. Schools inform parents of the individual results of these formal tests for their child, and the overall school results are made public. Teachers also assess children's work and moderate standards within the school.

Schemes of work and other National Curriculum support materials

Schools are expected to show how they will cover the National Curriculum through outlining their own school curriculum, which must be published online. There is no statutory way in which a school must set out its curriculum; head teachers and teachers can plan their own schemes to take account of their own context and the choices available to them within the curriculum. Each school can specify in its own way the year-by-year detail of its curriculum in every subject.

To support teachers in understanding how the programmes of study can be translated into practical schemes of work, the QCA provided exemplar schemes of work in all subject areas except for English and mathematics (where support with planning was provided via the Primary National Strategies). The personalisation of centrally provided support materials was officially encouraged. In *Excellence and Enjoyment* (2003) – the Department for Children, Schools and Families statement of its vision for primary education – schools were encouraged to be more innovative and creative and use the freedom they have to plan a more flexible curriculum. Although many teachers found these resources helpful, critics saw them as a way of controlling and strengthening the official approach to the curriculum. Despite the revision of the Primary Frameworks in 2006 that aspired to give greater flexibility, many still regarded the primary national strategies as promoting an essentially objectives-led curriculum that reinforced the 'input–output' model of assessment. However, the encouragement for schools to be more flexible was welcomed by most educationalists as evidence of a changing ethos, after several years of increasingly centralised control. At the time of writing, some schools continue to use these schemes of work and the Primary National Strategy documents to ease the planning burden and to familiarise themselves with the planning process, despite the dismantling of the QCDA and Primary National Strategy in 2012.

A REVIEW OF THE ENGLISH NATIONAL CURRICULUM – A CASE STUDY OF POLICY INTO PRACTICE

The teaching of reading has been an area of debate and controversy for many years in England. The *Independent Review of the Teaching of Early Reading* (Rose, 2006) is a key document that has been instrumental in a shift in the way reading is now taught. It emphasised a conceptual framework for reading known as the 'Simple view of reading', which sees reading as having two sides: word recognition and language comprehension. It suggested that systematic synthetic phonics should be the prime way to teach reading, and this became the requirement, backed up by funding for schools to provide resources and training. Both the Coalition and recent Labour governments have relied heavily on the research of Johnston and Watson (2004) in Clackmannanshire to underpin this requirement, research that has been seriously challenged (Wyse and Styles, 2007). In the Schools White Paper of 2010, the Education Secretary, Michael Gove, stated the intention to ensure all trainee teachers were 'instructed' in how to 'implement' this approach:

> The central priority for the first years of primary schooling must be learning to read. Unless children have learned to read, they can't read to learn. Which is why we will improve teacher training to provide authoritative instruction in the implementation of systematic synthetic phonics.

The use of systematic synthetic phonics is now enshrined in the new *Teachers' Standards*, which came into effect in 2012 (Department for Education, 2012c), requiring all new teachers to: 'if teaching early reading, demonstrate a clear understanding of systematic synthetic phonics'.

Many practitioners in schools, supported by researchers in this particular field of literacy, objected to being directed to teach reading to young children using a synthetic phonics approach and not being able to use other approaches alongside this.

This background of government direction of the way children are taught to read provided part of the context that explains the nature of the review of the primary English National Curriculum. In a letter (2012) to the expert panel that was set up to advise on the development of the new curriculum, the Education Secretary, Michael Gove, made the following comments:

> In English, the new Programme of Study will ensure high standards of literacy. Pupils will be taught to read fluently and develop a strong command of the written and spoken word. We will strengthen the focus on the fundamentals of phonics, grammar and spelling. There will also be a much stronger emphasis on reading widely for pleasure.

The expressed aims for English in the draft 2013 National Curriculum reflect a view of what English is for that moves away from the creativity in language and literacy that many teachers had begun to develop, towards that focus on the 'fundamentals' and also promotion of 'high standards'.

The overarching aim for English in the draft 2013 National Curriculum is to promote high standards of literacy by equipping pupils with a strong command of the written and spoken word, and to develop a love of literature through widespread reading for enjoyment. The National Curriculum for English aims to ensure all pupils:

- read easily, fluently and with good understanding;
- develop the habit of reading widely and often for both pleasure and information;
- acquire a wide vocabulary, an understanding of grammar and knowledge of linguistic conventions for reading, writing and spoken language;
- appreciate our rich and varied literary heritage;
- write clearly, accurately and coherently, adapting their language and style in and for a range of contexts, purposes and audiences;
- use discussion in order to learn; they should be able to elaborate and explain clearly their understanding and ideas;
- are competent in the arts of speaking and listening, making formal presentations, demonstrating to others and participating in debate.

'The National Curriculum should set out only the essential knowledge and understanding that all children should acquire and leave teachers to decide how to teach this most effectively.' Despite these assurances in *The Importance of Teaching* White Paper (Department for Education, 2010) of giving teachers more flexibility in how to teach, the new curriculum for English is more prescriptive than the 1999 document. Each programme of study is set out year by year for Key Stage 1 and two-yearly for Key Stage 2 in English, and there are appendices that specify features of spelling, grammar and punctuation that should be taught within the programmes of study. Combined with the spelling, grammar and punctuation test at the end of Year 6, this could be seen as likely to encourage teachers to work through this list, rather than to consider the needs of each child and try to provide a broad and balanced curriculum. Teachers will need to use all their skill and expertise in building on each child's experience and understanding, and their creativity and imagination to see how this can be done.

Responses to this draft document from national bodies, including the United Kingdom Literacy Association (UKLA) and the National Association for Language Development in the Curriculum (NALDIC), welcomed the emphasis on reading for pleasure and reading aloud. There had been widespread use of extracts in classrooms during the time of the National Literacy Strategy, when teachers found little time for reading whole texts (Frater, 2000), and this was found to fragment and diminish the reading experience and achievement of children, particularly boys. Even when the renewed Primary Framework for Literacy and Mathematics (2006) encouraged more flexibility and creativity, reading aloud to classes was not routine in many schools. It has been recognised as a key practice in effective teaching of reading by many researchers; for example, the Teachers as Readers research project that began in 2006 emphasised the importance of teachers' knowledge of children's literature and frequent reading to and talking about books with children.

Concerns from respondents about the draft document focused on the prescriptive elements and what was perceived as having been lost:

- Speaking and listening are fundamentally lacking as a programme of study.
- Emphasis on reciting and presentation, although to be welcomed, is not enough, and there is little reference to drama, oral storytelling or exploratory talk.
- The range of texts is restricted, with no mention of digital literacy, multimodal texts or multicultural texts.
- EAL learners come to school with a range of language and learning needs. They will learn English in different ways and at different rates of progression. Such diversity in primary classrooms requires a more flexible approach to teaching English language and literacy.
- The idea that no other decoding strategies other than systematic synthetic phonics are mentioned is a narrow view of what readers do.
- Access to texts could be limited for younger children to those that are 'decodable'.
- The emphasis in teaching writing is on transcription before composition, and this may limit what children are enabled to write.
- The large appendices may lead to teachers focusing too heavily on technical aspects of literacy.

Task 4.3.3 Case study: English National Curriculum 1

- Examine the draft 2013 National Curriculum for English Key Stages 1 and 2.
- Look at the programmes of study and compare these to the programmes of study in the 1999 curriculum. What do you notice about the recognition of speaking and listening?
- What do you think the speaking and listening programme of study should look like? Explain your thinking.

Task 4.3.4 Case study: English National Curriculum 2

- Discuss what you think are the advantages and disadvantages of a focus on the 'fundamentals' in the English curriculum, such as phonics, grammar and spelling.

A CURRICULUM FOR THE TWENTY-FIRST CENTURY – THE DEBATE CONTINUES

Curriculum development never remains static for long, and, as society changes, the kind of curriculum it wants and needs in its schools is likely to change also.

In December 2006, the Teaching and Learning in 2020 Review Group published their 2020 Vision report of teaching and learning, with a focus on what personalised learning might look like in schools in 2020. The group described personalised learning as 'a highly structured and responsive approach to each child's and young person's learning, in order that all are able to progress, achieve and participate' (Teaching and Learning in 2020 Review Group, 2006). The recommendations included embedding assessment for learning, with pupils taking ownership of their learning, and engaging parents and carers in children's learning.

Previously, the report, *All Our Futures: Creativity, Culture and Education* (NACCCE, 1999) had also argued for a national strategy for creative and cultural education. Current debate still centres around how schools can create an adaptable and creative curriculum that has personal meaning for the children they teach. A recent report, 'ImagineNation: The Case for Cultural Learning' (Cultural Learning Alliance, 2011), talks of the importance of unlocking individual potential, and pupils exercising decision-making and developing skills such as empathy and communication. This tension between creating a curriculum that excites and interests children, particularly in the face of a narrow curriculum that emphasises standards and the mechanics of learning, is apparent. Jean Anyon's research into social class and the hidden curriculum demonstrated that the kind of pedagogy that emerges from a narrow curriculum can reinforce curriculum inequality (Anyon, 1980). Adopting a critical and questioning perspective will continue to remain crucial for teachers who are passionate about putting children at the centre of their learning (Driscoll *et al.*, 2012).

WHERE NEXT? THE IMPORTANCE OF TEACHING OR LEARNING TO LEARN?

In the paper *The Importance of Teaching* (Department for Education, 2010), there is an obvious dichotomy between government interpretation that there was too much prescription in the 1999 National Curriculum and, on the other hand, the government giving specific instruction as to the best approach to teach early reading and mathematics. In this traditional, subject-based curriculum, with a reductive model speaking and listening as a programme of study, it is hard to see how reciprocal dialogue and children's choices, needs and interests will be promoted.

Prior to this, there had been a growing interest in the aspects of learning that were to be found in the 'Learning across the National Curriculum' section of the 1999 National Curriculum document. These aspects of learning include:

- Key skills – problem-solving, communication, application of number, information technology, working with others, improving own learning and performance.
- Thinking skills – enquiry, information processing, reasoning, creative thinking, evaluation.

Campaigns to promote 'learning to learn' (Claxton, 2002) and research and development into this were under way by the Department for Children, Schools and Families (DCSF) (for example, *Excellence and Enjoyment: Learning and Teaching in the Primary Years*, 2003) and a wide range of organisations and academics (for example, the Campaign for Learning; the Economic and Social Research Council's (ESRC) Learning How to Learn research project; and Claxton, 2002).

The *Primary Curriculum Futures* report from the 2008 Cambridge Primary Review (Conroy *et al.*, 2008) referred to the curriculum of the future having a focus on 'understanding for learning', and a shift away from traditional subjects towards integrated content. It identified alternative curricula, such as the Somerset Critical Skills course, the Reggio Emilia approach and Philosophy for Children (see, for example, Haynes, 2002), which have as their underpinning beliefs creativity and children as self-determining agents of their learning.

A curriculum that encourages teachers to become both learners and researchers of learning with children may appear to be the way forward, as thinking skills, citizenship and 'learning to learn' attributes become increasingly important for employment and participation in society. Projects (for example 5 × 5 × 5 = creativity) that are endeavouring to foster creative enquiry and to empower children have already proved the transformative nature of this kind of curriculum for both children and teachers. Building in time for teachers to reflect and engage in professional dialogue and development seem to be at the heart of creative learning in these contexts (Bancroft *et al.*, 2008).

The International Primary Curriculum (IPC), now adopted by an increasing number of schools, is similarly underpinned by an ethos of creativity, personal learning and an international perspective. Schools that adopt this 3–11 curriculum place value on purposeful learning goals, which include 'subject goals', 'personal goals' and 'international goals'. In addition to developing knowledge and understanding in a range of subjects, children will develop personal goals emphasising qualities and dispositions such as enquiry, resilience, morality, communication, thoughtfulness, cooperation, respect and adaptability. The IPC is said to help children to become aware of global issues and comparisons between people and countries. Units of work are organised thematically around themes such as 'Inventions and machines', with 'entry points' ideas that inspire pupils to learn about forthcoming units.

For further exploration of the IPC, visit www.greatlearning.com/ipc/.

THE ADVANTAGES AND DISADVANTAGES OF A NATIONAL CURRICULUM

Now you have looked at why the National Curriculum was created and how it is structured and assessed, considered a case study of how government curriculum policy becomes practice and looked at how the curriculum continues to change and evolve, you will probably have begun to form your own opinions on whether a national approach to the curriculum is a good idea. Those who support the introduction and continued development of a national curriculum and non-statutory guidance argue that it has a crucial role to play in addressing several educational issues. These include:

- **Providing an entitlement curriculum** for all pupils, regardless of ability. The curriculum applies to all children, and there is guidance on inclusion for children with special education needs, those for whom English is an additional language and pupils with disabilities.
- **Ensuring progress and continuity**, through subjects, between key stages and across schools.
- **Addressing inequality of provision** and educational opportunity between schools, by ensuring schools do not offer widely varying curricula.
- **Raising standards**. The curriculum levels provide a measure against which individual progress and attainment can be judged. They also provide national assessment data against which schools can be judged in comparison with schools with similar intakes.
- **Improving communication, transparency and accountability**. Parents and the wider public know what is taught in schools and the progress that can be expected. Schools must report on the progress of individuals to parents. Governments and local authorities can monitor the results of investments in professional development and curriculum innovations. Education is very costly, and governments and the public have a right to know if their money is being spent effectively.

Those who have concerns about the role of a national curriculum point to:

- **A lack of conceptual clarity** in the aims and purpose of the National Curriculum and a particular view of the nature of knowledge and how it is acquired and measured.
- **The ideological dominance of the official views** and discourse; for example, at subject level, an emphasis on standard English and synthetic phonics, or, at the conceptual level, the implicit message that this is the only correct approach to the curriculum.
- **A diminution in teacher professionalism and autonomy**, with teachers increasingly told what to teach and how to teach it, leaving no space for professional judgement. ·

- **Restrictions on pupil choice and creativity**. The curriculum leaves little space for pupils to pursue areas of particular interest or go outside the proscribed curriculum. Critics argue whether this prepares children for the kind of flexible, self-motivating environments in which many will spend their adult working lives, or whether it allows them to develop as fully rounded individuals.
- **The crowded nature of the curriculum**, which can lead to superficial understanding in order to achieve coverage.
- Concerns regarding **the reliability of national tests** and their impact on what is taught.

Task 4.3.5 Do we need a national curriculum?

- Consider the arguments for and against a national curriculum.
- Which to you seem the most compelling? On balance, do you consider we should retain or abandon or modify our National Curriculum?

Task 4.3.6 Analysing your views on the National Curriculum

Make use of arguments from further reading and theory in order to analyse your views on the National Curriculum.

SUMMARY

This brief overview of the development of the National Curriculum shows the move from teacher and school autonomy to an increasingly centralised control of the curriculum. As society continues to evolve and technology to advance, new demands are made on the curriculum. Debates now focus on what is needed to be an imaginative, articulate and emotionally mature learner who is actively engaged with their culture and community (Cultural Learning Alliance, 2011) and how digital and communication technologies can enable learners to collaborate and participate in this process. Qualities such as developing critical thinking skills, managing information and establishing relationships are being given high status. A curriculum that 'energises everyone' (Hulme and Livingston, 2013) and encourages them to think laterally will be essential in such a fast-moving, global world. It has been noted that it is not basic literacy and numeracy that are needed in a global knowledge economy (Coulby, cited in Ward and Eden, 2009). A recent Ofsted report found that an inappropriate or dull curriculum will not inspire pupils or generate high standards (Ofsted, 2011). After several years of a centrally controlled, content-driven curriculum, some schools are now developing more autonomy within their curriculum. However, this change only remains possible through strong leadership and shared vision. Head teachers who push the boundaries of curriculum development have to continually steer a fine line between being held accountable and striving to develop a flexible and transformative curriculum. Keeping an entitlement curriculum for all that is relevant to young people's lives, with an emphasis on creativity and flexible learning skills, is now the challenge for all those engaged in curriculum development.

ANNOTATED FURTHER READING

Conroy, J., Hulme, M. and Menter, I. (2008) *Primary Curriculum Futures (Primary Review Research Survey 3/3)*, Cambridge: University of Cambridge Faculty of Education.
> This interim report from the Primary Review (now the Cambridge Primary Review) gives an overview of research and a discussion of issues arising from changes in education policy in recent years.

Johnson, M. (2007) *Subject to Change: New Thinking on the Curriculum*, London: ATL.
> The foreword by Mick Waters from the QCA refers to a book that, 'asks searching questions and provides serious argument. It is a positive book, looking for a better future for learning, and in so doing seeks out the treasure of the curriculum'.

Kelly, A.V. (2009) *The Curriculum: Theory and Practice*, 6th edn, London: Sage.
> Kelly summarises the findings of curriculum research, and considers the nature and development of the curriculum and the importance of examining curriculum development. He takes a critical look at recent curriculum development and the introduction of the National Curriculum.

Pollard, A. and Triggs, P. (2000) *What Pupils Say: Changing Policy and Practice in Primary Education*, London: Continuum.
> This gives a view of the curriculum from the pupils' perspective. This book looks at the impact of the introduction of the National Curriculum on pupils and their experiences in the classroom.

Wyse, D., Baumfield, V., Egan, D., Gallagher, C., Hayward, L., Hulme, M., Leitch, R., Livingston, K., Menter, I. and Lingard, B. (2013) *Creating the Curriculum*, London: Routledge.
> This is a highly accessible book that is grounded in research and encourages educators to critically reflect on what an effective and meaningful curriculum looks like in good practice.

Use the following suggested journal articles and reports to support your critical thinking about a curriculum that focuses on the 'fundamentals' of the core subjects.

FURTHER READING TO SUPPORT M-LEVEL STUDY

Campbell, E. (2012) 'Teacher agency in curriculum contexts', *Curriculum Inquiry*, 42(2): 183-90.
> Campbell discusses the role and influence of teachers in creating new interpretations of curriculum expectations and policies, including views of teachers as moral practitioners and the idea of teacher agency.

Cremin, T., Burnard, P. and Craft, A. (2006) 'Pedagogy and possibility thinking in the early years', *International Journal of Thinking Skills and Creativity*, 1(2): 108-19.
> This article reports on a study into what characterises possibility thinking in young children and what teachers can do to support this in terms of pedagogical approaches. It enables the teacher to consider how to organise time and space for creativity.

RELEVANT WEBSITES

www.5x5x5creativity.org.uk/
> Arts-based action research organisation that supports children in their exploration and expression of ideas, helping them develop creative skills for life.

Cambridge Primary Review, Final Report: www.primaryreview.org.uk/

Campaign for Learning: www.campaign-for-learning.org.uk

Cultural Learning Alliance: www.culturallearningalliance.org.uk/userfiles/files/FINAL_ImagineNation_The_Case_for_Cultural_Learning.pdf

Economic and Social Research Council's Learning How to Learn research project: www.campaign-for-learning.org.uk/cfl/learninginschools/projects/learningtolearn/index.asp

IPC Curriculum: www.greatlearning.com/ipc/

NALDIC response to the primary National Curriculum proposals: www.naldic.org.uk/eal-advocacy/eal-news-summary/260812

Review of the draft 2013 National Curriculum documents: www.education.gov.uk/schools/teachingand learning/curriculum/nationalcurriculum

UKLA response to the proposed programme of study for English (2012): www.ukla.org/news/uklas_response_to_the_proposed_programmes_of_study_for_english_2012/

For reports and articles on the draft 2013 National Curriculum for English, including a further summary of policy analysis, see also www.literacytrust.org.uk/policy.

 # REFERENCES

Alexander, R.J. (ed.) (2010) *Children, Their World, Their Education: Final Report of the Cambridge Primary Review*, London: Routledge.

Anyon, J. (1980) 'Social class and the hidden curriculum of work', *Journal of Education*, 162(1, Fall), accessed online at: http://cuip.uchicago.edu/~cac/nlu/fnd504/anyon.htm

Bancroft, S. Fawcett, M. and Hay, P. (2008) *Researching Children Researching the World: 5 × 5 × 5 = Creativity*, Stoke-on-Trent: Trentham Books.

Central Advisory Council for Education (1967) *Children and Their Primary Schools (Plowden Report)*, London: HMSO.

Clark, M. (2012) *Literacies in and for a Changing World: What is the Evidence?* Accessed online at: www.ecswe.org/downloads/publications/QOC-V3/Chapter-5.pdf

Claxton, G. (2002) *Building Learning Power: Helping Young People Become Better Learners*, Bristol: TLO.

Conroy, J., Hulme, M. and Menter, I. (2008) *Primary Curriculum Futures (Cambridge Primary Review Research Survey 3/3)*, Cambridge: University of Cambridge Faculty of Education.

Cultural Learning Alliance (2011) 'ImagineNation: the case for cultural learning', accessed online at: www.culturallearningalliance.org.uk/userfiles/files/FINAL_ImagineNation_The_Case_for_Cultural_Learning.pdf

Department for Children, Schools and Families (DCSF) (2003) *Excellence and Enjoyment: Learning and Teaching in the Primary Years*, London: DCSF.

Department for Education (DfE) (2010) *Schools White Paper: The Importance of Teaching*, London: DfE.

Department for Education (DfE) (2012a) Draft National Curriculum documents for primary English, mathematics and science. London: DfE, accessed online at: www.education.gov.uk/schools/teachingandlearning/curriculum/a00210036/sosletter

Department for Education (DfE) (2012b) *Statutory Framework for the Early Years Foundation Stage*, London: DFE.

Department for Education (DfE) (2012c) *Teachers' Standards*, London: DfE, accessed online at www.education.gov.uk/publications/eOrderingDownload/teachers%20standards.pdf

Department for Education (DfE) (July 2013) *The National Curriculum in England Framework document*. London: DfE.

Department for Education and Employment/Qualifications and Curriculum Authority (DEE/QCA) (1999) *The National Curriculum Handbook for Primary Teachers*, London: HMSO.

Driscoll, P., Lambirth, A. and Roden, J. (2012) *The Primary Curriculum: A Creative Approach*, London: Sage.

Frater, G. (2000) 'Observed in practice, English in the National Literacy Strategy: some reflections', *Reading*, 34(3): 107-12.

Gove, M. (2012) Secretary of State letter to Tim Oates regarding the National Curriculum Review, 11 June 2012, accessed online at: www.education.gov.uk/schools/teachingandlearning/curriculum/nationalcurriculum/b0075667/national-curriculum-review-update

Haynes, J. (2002) *Children as Philosophers: Learning Through Enquiry and Dialogue in the Primary Classroom*, London: RoutledgeFalmer.

Hulme, L. and Livingston, K. (2013) 'Curriculum for the future', in D. Wyse *et al.*, *Creating the Curriculum*, London: Routledge.

Johnston, R. and Watson, J. (2004) 'Accelerating the development of reading, spelling and phonemic awareness skills in initial readers', *Reading and Writing: An Interdisciplinary Journal*, 17: 327-57.

Kelly, A.V. (2009) *The Curriculum: Theory and Practice*, 6th edn, London: Sage.

NACCCE (1999) *All Our Futures: Creativity, Culture and Education*, Sudbury: DfEE.

Ofsted (2011) 'Excellence in English: What we can learn from12 outstanding schools', accessed online at: www.ofsted.gov.uk/resources/excellence-english

Rose, J. (2006) *Independent Review of the Teaching of Early Reading*, London: DfES.

Teaching and Learning in 2020 Review Group (2006) '2020 Vision: Report of the Teaching and Learning in 2020 Review Group', accessed online at: http://dera.ioe.ac.uk/6347/1/6856-DfES-Teaching%20and%20Learning.pdf

Twist, L., Sizmur J., Bartlett, S. and Lynn, L. (2012) 'PIRLS 2011: Reading achievement in England', Research report, NFER.

Ward, S. and Eden, C.E. (2009) *Key Issues in Education Policy*, London: Sage.

Wyse, D. and Styles, M. (2007) 'Synthetic phonics and the teaching of reading: the debate surrounding England's "Rose Report"', *Literacy*, 41(1): 35-42.

Wyse, D., Baumfield, V., Egan, D., Gallagher, C., Hayward, L., Hulme, M., Leitch, R., Livingston, K., Menter, I. and Lingard, B. (2013) *Creating the Curriculum*, London: Routledge.

THE SCOTTISH CONTEXT FOR THE CURRICULUM

Sue Ellis and Jenny Carey

INTRODUCTION

The curriculum in Scotland seeks to define and frame the core ideas and experiences that are most important for learning and teaching. Although it is not easy to design a curriculum framework that provides support and direction while allowing flexibility, this is what Scotland's *Curriculum for Excellence* (CfE) seeks to do. Allowing for flexibility is important, so that each school's curriculum can meet the needs of, and build from the experience of, the local community. Flexibility also allows the curriculum to be responsive to new social contexts and new political priorities for education, as well as to new research understandings of how best to develop learning. The challenge is to create a framework that promotes development, allows educators to be effective and efficient in a variety of contexts and ensures that curriculum intentions are not lost during implementation.

OBJECTIVES

This unit describes how curriculum policy is made in Scotland and outlines how CfE is enacted in schools and local authorities. By the end of this unit, you should be able to:

- explain who shapes curriculum development in Scotland, and some of the key bodies and documents that help them;
- explain some of the advantages and disadvantages that the Scottish Curriculum framework offers;
- describe CfE, how it shapes practice and pedagogy and the demands on, and expectations of, teachers;
- consider how the context of implementation may impede or facilitate change.

CURRICULUM POLICY IN SCOTLAND

Scotland has its own legislative framework for education. There is no legally enforceable 'national curriculum', and all curriculum and assessment guidelines are non-statutory. This means that the curriculum is not a rigid, centrally determined programme of study.

Pupils enter primary school in the year of their fifth birthday. There is one intake per year, in August, and the ages of children at the start of Primary 1 range from 4 years, 6 months to 5 years, 6 months. Children leave primary school when they have completed Primary 7. Children from the age of 3 years are entitled to nursery education, but it is not compulsory.

Education is the responsibility of the Cabinet Secretary for Education and Lifelong Learning, who, with the Education Ministerial Team, and on the advice of Scottish government policy departments, sets overall policy and strategy. The body charged with leading and supporting schools and local authorities to implement these policies, including curriculum policies, is *Education Scotland*. The remit of Education Scotland is wide: it is responsible for providing curriculum and assessment advice, for school and local authority inspections, for monitoring national attainment, curriculum implementation and innovation, and it is also responsible for stimulating creativity and innovation, providing evidence-based advice and for building the capacity of educational providers and practitioners (local authorities, schools, teachers and parents) to improve. Education Scotland produces a range of professional development resources, for example, *Journey to Excellence* (Education Scotland 2012), it runs GLOW, the Scottish schools' digital network, and, with the Scottish Qualifications Authority (SQA), it produces the National Assessment Resource (NAR) to provide assessment advice, support materials and exemplars for assessing CfE (Scottish Qualifications Authority 2012). It also produces Her Majesty's Inspectorate of Education (HMIE) inspection reports, and runs development support networks and advisory committees. It works closely with the *General Teaching Council for Scotland*, which is responsible for professional standards, setting out the expectations for entry into teaching, for leadership and management and for career-long professional learning.

The annual Scottish Survey of Literacy and Numeracy is used to monitor national performance at P4, P7 and S2, alternating between literacy and numeracy (Scottish Government 2011). Scotland also participates in the OECD Program for International Student Assessment, which surveys the attainment of 15-year-olds in maths, literacy and science, but it withdrew from the Progress in International Reading Literacy Study and the Trends in International Mathematics and Science Study. HMIE provides school and local authority inspection reports and, when necessary, summarises these into 'Journey to Excellence' cameo reports, which illustrate the good practice in particular curricular areas.

Task 4.4.1 Education Scotland *Journey to Excellence*

Read some of the Education Scotland *Journey to Excellence* documents on the website: www.journeytoexcellence.org.uk

Think about:

(a) the nature of this process of evaluation and how it could be used to enhance and support your own teaching and learning experiences in school;
(b) how far the process on its own can provide insights into the curriculum and pedagogy and the extent to which it must be supplemented with reading about research and pedagogy in a specific subject area.

Then, list three specific implications for advancing your own teaching.

The management of school education rests with the thirty-two local authorities in Scotland. Most local authorities offer support in the form of local development plans and professional development courses, and organise working parties to create curriculum resources and guidance on planning and assessment. The curriculum in schools is the formal responsibility of the head teacher, who prepares development plans to show how the school is developing its curriculum to meet local and national priorities. The head teacher must ensure that teachers deliver a suitable curriculum, and that appropriate frameworks for teaching, assessment, monitoring and reporting are in place.

POLICY ON TESTING AND ASSESSMENT

Scottish policymakers know that assessment policies can have unintended consequences. The first national assessment policy, introduced in 1991, highlighted the importance of evidence from a range of sources and introduced national literacy and mathematics tests to confirm teacher judgements. Tests were chosen by the teacher from a bank of test items. They were to be sat only when the teacher judged a child to have attained a level, and teachers' professional judgements were to be prioritised over children's test performances (Scottish Exam Board 1993). However, local authorities used test results to set attainment targets for schools, and there were numerous reports of children being rehearsed for tests and retaking them many times. CfE brought in a different kind of testing regime, the NAR, which appears to be designed to prevent such practices by providing highly contextualised assessment tasks. These exemplify CfE assessment within levels, with teachers expected to use evidence from a broad range of contexts to check how a learner is progressing and that learning is secure (Education Scotland 2011; Education Scotland n.d.). However, it is not clear how the unfocused assessments of the NAR provide useful data for teachers, schools or local authorities. Many local authorities have introduced their own baseline assessments for literacy and numeracy and pay commercial companies to track pupil progress using externally devised summative assessments. A previous formative assessment initiative, *Assessment is for Learning* (AifL) (Black et al. 2002; Hutchison and Young 2011), is assumed to underpin teacher understandings of assessment in CfE, but AifL remains unevenly embedded into schools and so continues to be a focus for many school learning communities. The document *Assessment for CfE: Strategic Vision and Key Principles* (Education Scotland, n.d.) sets out the assessment approaches officially in use in Scotland.

Task 4.4.2 Assessment by primary school educators

Read the document *Assessment for CfE: Strategic Vision and Key Principles* (Education Scotland, n.d.).

Summarise the different kinds of *assessment* that primary school educators are expected to use. The document uses the terms 'attainment' and 'achievement'. Achievement is a wide term encompassing social, emotional and physical success, both in and out of school. 'Attainment' has a narrower meaning, used when pupils have met specific cognitive learning outcomes in their school curriculum. The document does not refer to 'ability' at all; the evidence of 'ability' is vulnerable to factors such as experience, opportunities or the openness of the task, and one can be 'able' but not attain, or attain without being able. The sociological term 'Matthew Effects' captures some aspects of this. Now:

1 Read Stanovich (1986) and think about how Matthew Effects may apply in other areas of the curriculum.
2 To what extent to you feel this document is influencing practice in the schools with which you are familiar? Which aspects would benefit teaching and learning in the schools, were they to be given greater focus?
3 Why is it important to have both *summative* and *formative assessment* information? What could happen to teaching and learning if a primary teacher were over-reliant on one or the other?

Website activity

Using all the information given so far, draw a diagram to show how the curriculum is shaped and developed in Scotland.

Compare your diagram with that of a colleague on the course.

THE PRIMARY CURRICULUM: A CURRICULUM FOR EXCELLENCE

CfE was introduced in 2004 to provide 'a curriculum that will fully prepare today's children for adult life in the 21st century, be less crowded and better connected, and offer more choice and enjoyment' (SEED 2004: 3). It represents both a genuine desire to make the education system work for children and a confidence that the Scottish educational community can deliver effective change. It aims to provide a single curriculum for 3-18-year-olds, supported by a simple and effective structure for assessment that frees up more time for young people to achieve and allows teachers the freedom to exercise judgement on appropriate learning.

The starting point is that the curriculum should not focus solely on narrow definitions of attainment and progression, nor on detailing sets of teaching content and tasks. The four capacities that define the purposes of the curriculum (see Figure 4.4.1) focus attention on building social, emotional and intellectual capacity. CfE extends the influence of curriculum policy beyond subject areas, giving explicit recognition to the importance of interdisciplinary links, to the ethos and life of the school as a community within wider society, and to the importance of providing opportunities for wider achievement.

Task 4.4.3 The purposes of the curriculum

Look carefully at Figure 4.4.1: Purposes of the curriculum from 3 to 18.

Think about one curricular area that you have seen taught in schools. To what extent do you think the teaching delivered these purposes? How would you change or adapt the teaching to enable it to better meet the purposes outlined in *A Curriculum for Excellence*.

A Curriculum for Excellence divides the curriculum into eight areas: health and well-being; mathematics and numeracy; languages and literacy; religious and moral education; sciences; social subjects; technologies; and expressive arts. Health and well-being, literacy and numeracy must be developed across learning by every teacher, at every level, regardless of curriculum area or the formal exam focus of secondary school teachers.

In each subject area, *A Curriculum for Excellence* details five levels of experiences and outcomes, covering the age range 3-18: Early (pre-school and P1); First (by the end of P4 or earlier); Second (by the end of P7 or earlier); Third (S1-3) and Fourth (S4-6). By defining the curriculum in terms of experiences as well as outcomes, the design seeks to promote coherent progression in both content *and* the types of learning experience, to smooth the transitions between the nursery, primary and secondary sectors.

Successful learners

With
- enthusiasm and motivation for learning
- determination to reach high standards of achievement
- openness to new thinking and ideas

and able to
- use literacy, communication and numeracy skills
- use technology for learning
- think creatively and independently
- learn independently and as part of a group
- make reasoned evaluations
- link and apply different kinds of learning in new situations

Confident individuals

With
- self respect
- a sense of physical, mental and emotional well-being
- secure values and beliefs
- ambition

and able to
- relate to others and manage themselves
- pursue a healthy and active lifestyle
- be self aware
- develop and communicate their own beliefs and view of the world
- live as independently as they can
- assess risk and take informed decisions
- achieve success in different areas of activity

To enable all young people to become

Responsible citizens

With
- respect for others
- commitment to participate responsibly in political, economic, social and cultural life

and able to
- develop knowledge and understanding of the world and Scotland's place in it
- understand different beliefs and cultures
- make informed choices and decisions
- evaluate environmental, scientific and technological issues
- develop informed, ethical views of complex issues

Effective contributors

With
- an enterprising attitude
- resilience
- self-reliance

and able to
- communicate in different ways and in different settings
- work in partnership and in teams
- take the initiative and lead
- apply critical thinking in new contexts
- create and develop
- solve problems

FIGURE 4.4.1 The purposes of the curriculum from 3 to 18: the four capacities

Source: www.ltscotland.org.uk/curriculumforexcellence/curriculumoverview/aims/fourcapacities.asp

The framework seeks to provide focus, but not to be so content-laden as to leave little space for innovative teaching or spontaneously responding to children's interests and needs. The planning principles emphasise the importance of focusing on what is most appropriate for the pupils and the school context:

- challenge and enjoyment,
- breadth,
- progression,
- depth,
- personalisation and choice,
- coherence,
- relevance.

ACTIVE LEARNING

CfE requires a change of mindset for all sectors. For example, the Early Level promotes continuity and progression and encourages a less 'transmission oriented' approach to teaching young children in schools; instead of requiring pupils to be 'ready for school', schools should become 'ready for children' (Stephen and Cope 2003). CfE requires nurseries and schools, for the first time, to have shared understandings of early years learning and child-centred approaches (Stephen *et al.* 2010; Martlew *et al.* 2011). The result has been the introduction of 'active learning' approaches to early years classes in schools, and an increase in play-based activities, including spontaneous play, sociodramatic play and play as a planned and structured activity (Learning Teaching Scotland 2007). However, schools have implemented this in various ways, with varying degrees of success. Initially, many set up 'active learning' or 'structured play' rooms, and infant classes were timetabled to use these once or twice a week. Now, some schools employ 'soft-start' initiatives, which may serve to 'settle' young children, but may equally get the business of play out of the way in the first half hour of the day before moving to teacher-directed learning. Others have bought a huge number of resources to organise a carousel of activities each day. However, although children are certainly active as they move from desk to desk, it is not clear that these necessarily offer children possibilities to deepen their learning, or investigate and explore their understandings through meaningful contexts (Stephen *et al.* 2009, 2010).

Implementing curriculum change is always problematic. There are many reasons why teachers can be slow to adopt new initiatives. Eisner identifies a passive resistance, in which 'experienced teachers tend to . . . ride out the wave of enthusiasm, and then just float until the next wave comes' (1992: 616). There can also be a tendency for teachers to embrace aspects that concur with current practice, but to overlook or dismiss ideas that require change, and there can be a tendency to focus on activities, materials and classroom organisation, rather than on the deeper pedagogical principles (Spillane 2000). For some early years teachers, 'active learning' has required a large leap. They have been presented with visions of 'good practice' developed in nursery settings, premised on a staffing ratio of one adult to eight children, but must deliver in a school setting with a staffing ratio of one to eighteen at best, and often very much higher. Translating nursery 'good practice' to the school context requires a grounded understanding of early years pedagogy, of what is 'active' about learning and a grounded model of practice that recognises the various ways that children can be dynamic agents in their own development (Wood and Attfield 2005). Active learning is not something that can be copied from one establishment to another, and a clear 'vision' of what active learning looks like in classrooms when it 'engages and challenges children's thinking using real-life and imaginary situations and crosses all curricular areas' (Scottish Government 2007: 5) is still developing. The challenges class teachers face in planning, recognising and guiding intended, potential and spontaneous learning in this model need to be more fully researched and understood. This work has begun in relation to support for language development (Fisher 2008; Martlew *et al.* 2010), the role of the environment as the 'third teacher', and exploration and investigation (Rinaldi 2006).

Active learning for older children requires responsive and contextualised planning to balance direct teaching with demonstrations of what, why and when such learning is useful. However, uncertainties about the role of the teacher, how to foster creativity and engagement, the role of the learning environment, of planning and of self-directed, independent learning remain. For some, this has meant a return to carousel activities, but others have adopted interdisciplinary and collaborative approaches ('rich tasks') exemplified by Scottish Storyline (Bell and Harkness 2006), novel studies or literature circles (Allan *et al.* 2005). These are collaborative and make space for 'personalisation and choice' by allowing pupils to shape the context and focus of their learning. It is an approach that accords with recent policy and research studies highlighting the impact of engagement on learning and attainment (Guthrie and Humenick 2004; OECD 2010; Ellis and Coddington 2013).

Task 4.4.4 Active learning

Most schools have endeavoured to implement changes to their practice to adopt 'active learning', but understandings can vary.

1 How would you characterise the differences between 'active learning' and 'activity based learning'?
2 Work with others to think of examples of highly effective 'active approaches' to learning in the early years, and some less effective examples. What makes the difference? What are the implications for teachers' planning in terms of input, tasks, resources, environment, time, observations, interactions and evaluations? Stephen *et al*. (2010) and Martlew *et al*. (2011) may help you to think about this.
3 Think about the role of the teacher in planning and implementing Scottish Storyline, literature circles or novel studies. What are the mechanisms used in each approach to foster personalisation and choice, challenge, coherence and depth? What other ways have you seen these principles exemplified in schools?

RESEARCH PERSPECTIVES

At its heart, CfE recognises that learning is socially and culturally mediated. It has the potential to power school systems and curricula in ways that draw explicitly on sociocultural, ethnographic and cognitive research to create new dialogues about education. It allows spaces for professional creativity in connecting curriculum design directly to the social and cultural learning experiences in children's home communities. CfE demonstrates educational integrity by focusing on the issues that are central to the quality of children's lives: it is a curriculum that learners can influence and where health and well-being, literacy and numeracy are the responsibility of every teacher, in every sector, at every level.

However, John MacBeath (2008) reminds us that school organisation and curricula have changed little since Victorian times. Attempts to revolutionise schools and schooling have not worked. In MacBeath's words, 'The future never happened' (MacBeath 2008: 940). The design of buildings, school hierarchies, staffing structures, teaching arrangements, pedagogical conventions, planning and monitoring procedures, and tests combine to produce our traditional curricula and learning experiences. Without big changes to these elements, radical, bottom-up curriculum change, in which learner experiences forge new ways of seeing and learning in the curriculum, will not happen.

To be successful, CfE must undoubtedly challenge and change the thinking of players at every level of the system, if it is to be enacted in classrooms in ways that support, rather than destroy, its spirit. School systems tend to favour conformity, but CfE success is likely to produce less uniformity and more diversity. For teachers, making sense of this diversity requires a strong professional knowledge base; simply copying other schools will not do.

The Donaldson Report (Donaldson 2010) recognises the need for strong, research-based knowledge in initial and continuing professional development. However, to deliver the secure professional knowledge and to enact constructivist, evidenced-based approaches to pupil learning, classroom pedagogy and curriculum design, teachers need to be exposed to complex analyses of practice. They need to resist presenting innovations as activities or resorting to abstract rhetoric in place of grounded research. This requires high-quality conversations about the curriculum that can only take place in research-oriented schools, where curriculum innovation and evaluation are significant parts of the job for teachers, head teachers and local authorities. It requires everyone – local authority managers, educators, children, parents, the media, employers and politicians – to see and understand education as a complex process with many outcomes, rather than a one-dimensional commodity. Primary teachers will need a strong, informed and assertive professional voice to steer such conversations, and, to develop this, it will be important to mobilise research knowledge at every level of the system. The role of classroom-focused research that develops curriculum and pedagogical knowledge will be crucial.

Task 4.4.5 Curriculum for Excellence

CfE gives great scope for teachers, schools and local authorities to create a curriculum that works for them. It contrasts with the more centralised, top-down curriculum approaches in England or the USA. Top-down models can be positioned in two ways. They can be seen negatively, as ignoring the teaching capacity that exists in schools, positioning teachers as passive conduits for the curriculum and making curricular decisions highly vulnerable to single-issue pressure groups. They can also be seen positively as building capacity, by compelling teachers to engage with new pedagogies, providing clear frameworks that focus decisions on evidence and mitigating the worst effects of a weak teacher.

Devolved curriculum models, such as CfE, offer more potential to engage teachers and to capitalise on the good practice and emotional investment that already exist in schools. However, they may leave teachers unsupported in making evidence-based decisions or analysing curriculum changes, forcing them to rely on their own, unexplored and possibly limited past experiences. Critics argue that the dream of teachers making clear judgements based on research and robust analyses of evidence is simply a dream. Research studies on rolling out educational reforms, however, show that the contexts in which programmes are implemented are at least as important to their effectiveness as the content or the design features of the programme (Datnow *et al*. 2002); Eisner comments, 'Educators know experientially that context matters most in the "chemistry" that makes for educational effectiveness' (Eisner 2004: 616).

How important do you think teachers' curriculum content knowledge is for successful CfE? What do you think are the important things to bear in mind when considering the pros and cons of CfE in your own experience of schools?

Task 4.4.6 Radical change?

To what extent do you agree with MacBeath's analysis? How far does it concur with what you have read and experienced?

What four things would you change in the structure and organisation of primary schools that would revolutionise teaching and learning and ensure that CfE succeeds? Justify your choices with reference to your own experience, research and theory.

Compare your ideas with those of a colleague.

SUMMARY

The discussion of curriculum guidelines and how they are implemented can seem awfully dry and boring. There is a great temptation for student teachers to focus on the immediate job of teaching the children, without thinking about the big picture. It is part of every teacher's professional responsibility to think about what matters in education, and to ensure that the curriculum works to deliver this. The key points from this unit are that curriculum guidelines are a crucial aspect of a complex, dynamic picture, and that the process of implementation is all-important.

 ## ANNOTATED FURTHER READING

Bryce, T.G.K. and Humes, W.M. (eds) (2013) *Scottish Education*, 4th edn. Edinburgh: Edinburgh University Press.
    This is the most comprehensive text on Scottish education. Each chapter is designed to give an explanatory overview of policy and practice and identify key issues for the future.

Priestley, M. and Minty, S. (2012) *Developing Curriculum for Excellence – Summary of findings from research undertaken in a Scottish local authority.* Stirling: University of Stirling. Available at: http://www.ioe.stir.ac.uk/research/projects/documents/StirlingCfEresearch-report_March2012.pdf (accessed December 2012).
    This is an early report of a small-scale study into how teachers are implementing CfE, the difficulties they encounter, the parts of the policy framework that are producing positive outcomes and those that are not.

SEED (2004) *A Curriculum for Excellence.* Edinburgh: HMSO.
    A highly readable document that sets-out the framework and vision for the new curriculum. It is worth returning to this many times.

 ## FURTHER READING TO SUPPORT M-LEVEL STUDY

Bearne, E. and Marsh, J. (eds) (2007) *Literacy and Social Inclusion: Closing the Gap.* Stoke on Trent: Trentham Books.

Datnow, A., Hubbard, L and Mehan, H. (2002) *Extending Educational Reform: From One School to Many.* New York: RoutledgeFalmer.

 ## REFERENCES

Allan, J., Ellis, S. and Pearson, C. (2005) *Literature Circles, Gender and Reading for Enjoyment: Report to the Scottish Executive Education Department.* SEED website, available at: www.scotland.gov.uk/Publications/2005/11/SRLitCir

Bell, S. and Harkness, S. (2006) *Storyline: Promoting Language Across the Curriculum*, Royston: UKLA.

Black, P., Harrison, C., Lee, G., Marshall, B. and Wiliam, D. (2002) *Working Inside the Black Box*, London: King's College.

Datnow, A., Hubbard, L. and Mehan, H. (2002) *Extending Educational Reform: From One School to Many*, New York: RoutledgeFalmer.

Donaldson, G. (2010) *Teaching Scotland's Future: The Donaldson Review*, Edinburgh: Scottish Government.

Education Scotland (n.d) *Assessment for CfE: Strategic Vision and Key Principles*, Edinburgh: Scottish Government. Available at: www.educationscotland.gov.uk/publications/a/publication_tcm4645133.asp (downloaded December 2012).

Education Scotland (2011) *A Curriculum for Excellence – Building the Curriculum 5: A framework for Assessment*, Edinburgh: Scottish Government. Available at: www.educationscotland.gov.uk/Images/AssessmentforCfE_tcm4-565505.pdf (downloaded December 2012).

Education Scotland (2012) *Journey to Excellence*, Glasgow: Scottish Government. Available at: www.journeyto excellence.org.uk/index.asp (downloaded December 2012).

Eisner, E.W. (1992) Educational Reform and the Ecology of Schooling. *Teachers College Record*, 93(4), 610–27.

Eisner, E.W. (2004) Artistry in teaching, *Cultural Commons*. Available at: http://infed.org/mobi/elliot-w-eisner-connoisseurship-criticism-and-the-art-of-education/ (retrieved 30 April 2009).

Ellis, S. and Coddington, C. (2013) Reading engagement: review of the research. In K. Hall, T. Cremin , B. Comber and L. Moll (eds) *International Handbook of Research on Children's Literacy, Learning, and Culture*, Part 11, Chapter 17. Oxford: Wiley-Blackwell.

Fisher, J. (2008) *Starting from the Child* (3rd edn). Berkshire: Open University Press.

Guthrie, J.T. and Humenick, N.M. (2004) Motivating students to read: evidence for classroom practices that increase reading motivation. In P. McCardle and V. Chhabra (eds) *The Voice of Evidence in Reading Research*, pp. 329–55. New York: Erlbaum.

Hutchinson, C. and Young, M. (2011) Assessment is for learning in the accountability era: empirical evidence from Scotland. *Studies in Educational Evaluation*, 37(1): 62–70.

Learning Teaching Scotland (2007) *Taking Learning Outdoors; Partnerships for Excellence*. Available at: www.educationscotland.gov.uk/resources/t/genericresource_tcm4410524.asp

MacBeath, J. (2008) Do schools have a future? In T.G.K. Bryce and W.M. Humes (eds) *Scottish Education: Third Edition – Beyond Devolution*, Chapter 105, pp. 939–48. Edinburgh: Edinburgh University Press.

Martlew, J., Ellis, S., Stephen, C. and Ellis, J. (2010) Teacher and child talk in active learning and whole-class contexts: some implications for children from economically less advantaged home backgrounds. *Literacy*, 44(1): 12–19. Wiley Blackwell.

Martlew, J., Stephen, C. and Ellis, J. (2011) Play in the primary school classroom? The experience of teachers supporting children's learning through a new pedagogy. *Early Years*, 18(4): 315–29.

OECD (2010) *PISA 2009 Results: Learning to Learn – Student Engagement: Strategies and Practices* (Vol. III), Paris: OECD.

Rinaldi, C. (2006) *In Dialogue With Reggio Emilia: Listening, Researching and Learning*, Routledge: Oxford.

Scottish Exam Board (1993) *The Framework for National Testing*, Edinburgh: SOED.

Scottish Government (2007) *A Curriculum for Excellence Building the Curriculum 2: Active Learning in the Early Years*. Available at: www.educationscotland.gov.uk/images/Building_the_Curriculum_2_tcm4-408069.pdf

Scottish Government (2011) *Scottish Survey of Literacy and Numeracy (SSLN) 2011 – Publication of Numeracy 2011 Results*, Edinburgh: Scottish Government. Available at: www.scotland.gov.uk/Topics/Statistics/Browse/School-Education/SSLN

Scottish Qualifications Authority (2012) *National Assessment Resource (NAR)*, Edinburgh: Scotland. Available at: www.educationscotland.gov.uk/learningteachingandassessment/assessment/supportmaterials/nar/assessmentmaterials/index.asp (downloaded December 2012).

SEED (2004) *A Curriculum for Excellence*, Edinburgh: HMSO.

Spillane, J.P. (2000) Cognition and policy implementation: district policymakers and the reform of mathematics education. *Cognition and Instruction*, 18(2): 141–79.

Stanovich, K.E. (1986) Matthew Effects in reading: some consequences of individual differences in the acquisition of literacy. *Reading Research Quarterly*, 21: 360–407.

Stephen, C. and Cope, P. (2003) An inclusive perspective on transition to primary school. *European Educational Research Journal*, 2(2): 262-76.

Stephen, C., Ellis, J. and Martlew, J. (2009) Turned on to learning 2: Active learning in primary one. *Applied Educational Research Scheme, Research Briefing*, 8. Available at: www.ioe.stir.ac.uk/staff/documents/AERSresearchbrief8_000.pdf (accessed December 2012).

Stephen, C., Ellis, J. and Martlew, J. (2010) Taking active learning into the primary school: a matter of new practices? *International Journal of Early Years Education*, 18(4): 315-29.

Wood, E. and Attfield, J. (2005) *Play, Learning and Early Childhood Curriculum* (2nd edn). London: Paul Chapmen Publishing.

ASSESSMENT

ASSESSMENT FOR LEARNING

Formative approaches

Eleanore Hargreaves, Caroline Gipps and Alison Pickering

INTRODUCTION

Assessment for Learning (AfL) is a particular approach to assessment used by teachers in classrooms. It is not the same as the standardised tests or SATs you may give, but rather is a way of using informal assessment during ordinary classroom activities to improve learning. Here, assessment is seen as an integral part of the learning and teaching process, rather than being 'added on' for summative purposes. This approach brings with it a rather different relationship between teacher and learner than in traditional models of assessment, as the pupil needs to become involved in discussions about learning and assessment tasks, including learning objectives, the assessment criteria (success criteria), their performance and what they need to do to progress: the relationship is more of a partnership, with both pupil and teacher playing a role. We know that, with appropriate guidance, children as young as 6 or 7 can exercise considerable self-direction and benefit from doing so.

Although there are many different interpretations of how AfL would ideally work, early defining sources were those of the Assessment Reform Group (ARG) (1999) and of Black and Wiliam (1998), who showed that improving children's learning through assessment depended on five, deceptively simple, key factors:

- the provision of effective feedback to pupils;
- the active involvement of pupils in their own learning;
- adjusting teaching to take account of the results of assessment;
- a recognition of the profound influence assessment has on the motivation and self-esteem of pupils, both of which are crucial influences on learning;
- the need for pupils to be able to assess themselves and understand how to improve.

This unit will attempt to unpack two key issues: first, the nature of the feedback given to learners to help them understand the quality of their work and inspire them to consider how to progress in their learning; and, second, the active engagement of the learner, which is essential for promoting the learner's self-direction.

Since the publication of the ARG's summary of research-based principles of AfL (Assessment Reform Group, 2002) and the DCSF's policy document of 2008 called *Assessment for Learning* (Department for Children, Schools and Families, 2008), teachers have had clear guidance on introducing AfL strategies. However, how much teachers' approaches to learning have changed to accompany the new strategies is a matter of debate. Some research suggests that AfL strategies are most effective where the 'spirit' as well as the 'letter' of AfL has been embraced (Marshall and Drummond, 2006). The ten principles of effective teaching and learning identified by the ARG (see www.aaia.org.uk) nonetheless form the basis of current strategies of learning and teaching in many classrooms. Some of the ARG's ten principles are addressed in this unit, and suggestions are made for putting them into practice.

OBJECTIVES

By the end of the unit you should be able to:

- understand the key factors associated with AfL;
- develop a range of strategies that will facilitate improved learning/teaching;
- recognise that pupils' self-direction in assessment is a powerful tool in raising achievement in the classroom.

AFL: FROM THEORY TO PRACTICE

The ten principles of AfL

Assessment for Learning should be part of the effective planning of teaching and learning

A teacher's planning should provide opportunities for both learner and teacher to obtain and use information about progress towards learning goals. It also has to be flexible to respond to initial and emerging ideas and skills. Planning should include strategies to ensure that learners understand the goals they are pursuing, why they are pursuing them and the criteria that could be applied in assessing their work against these. How learners will receive feedback, how they will take part in assessing their learning and how they will be helped to make further progress should also be planned, ideally in negotiation with the pupils themselves.

Assessment for Learning should focus on how pupils learn

The process of learning has to be in the minds of both learner and teacher when assessment is planned and when the evidence is interpreted. Learners should become as aware of the 'how' of their learning as they are of the 'what'. Up-to-date research into how the learning process works needs to be recognised (see, for example, Hargreaves, 2012).

Assessment for Learning should be recognised as central to classroom practice

Much of what teachers and learners do in classrooms can be described as assessment. That is, tasks and questions prompt learners to demonstrate their knowledge, understanding and skills; what learners say and do is then observed and interpreted, and judgements are made about how learning can progress. These assessment processes are an essential part of everyday classroom practice and involve both teachers and learners in reflection, dialogue and decision-making. These definitions of assessment expand its meaning beyond tests to include all forms of inquiry into the learner's progress.

Assessment for Learning should be regarded as a key professional skill for teachers

Teachers require the professional knowledge and skills to: plan for assessment; observe learning; analyse and interpret evidence of learning; give feedback to learners; and support learners in self-assessment. Teachers should be supported in developing these skills through initial and continuing professional development. Today, there is research to indicate that continuing professional development can be most effective when it is continuous, integrated into the school's agenda, collaborative and inspired by sources beyond the school too. One effective means of developing the skills of AfL has been the Teacher Learning Community within the individual schools, whereby a group of teachers meet together every 6 weeks and report back on AfL strategies with which they have experimented in the classroom (see Wiliam, 2008).

Assessment for Learning should be sensitive and constructive because any assessment has an emotional impact

Teachers should be aware of the impact that comments, marks and grades can have on learners' confidence and enthusiasm and should be as constructive as possible in the feedback that they give. Comments that focus on the work rather than the person are more constructive for both learning and motivation. A student who is distracted by negative – or even positive – personal comments is less likely to be focusing on learning (see Torrance, 2012).

Assessment for Learning should take account of the importance of learner motivation

Assessment that encourages learning fosters motivation by emphasising progress and achievement rather than failure. Comparison with others who have been more successful is unlikely to motivate learners. It can also lead to their withdrawing from the learning process in areas where they have been made to feel they are 'no good'. Motivation can be preserved and enhanced by assessment methods that protect the learner's autonomy, provide some choice and constructive feedback, and create opportunity for self-direction.

Assessment for Learning should promote commitment to learning goals and a shared understanding of the criteria by which they are assessed

For effective learning to take place, learners need to understand what it is they are trying to achieve and why they are trying to achieve it – and they must also want to achieve it. Understanding and commitment follow when learners have some part in deciding goals and identifying criteria for assessing progress. Communicating assessment criteria involves discussing their importance and meaning with learners, using terms that they can understand, providing examples of how the criteria can be met in practice and engaging learners in peer and self-assessment.

Learners should receive constructive guidance about how to progress

Learners need support in order to plan the next phases of their learning. Teachers should:

- pinpoint the learner's strengths and advise on how to develop them;
- be clear and constructive about any weaknesses and how they might be addressed;
- provide opportunities for learners to improve upon their work.

Assessment for Learning develops learners' capacity for self-assessment so that they can become reflective and self-managing

Reflective and self-managing (or self-directed) learners seek out and cultivate new skills, new knowledge and new understandings. They are able to engage in self-reflection and to identify how to progress in their learning. Teachers should support learners to take charge of their learning through developing the skills of reflection and self-assessment and allow pupils to take their own initiatives for progressing learning at times.

Assessment for Learning should recognise the full range of achievements of all learners

AfL should be used to enhance all learners' opportunities to learn in all areas of educational activity. It should enable all learners to achieve their best and to have their efforts recognised. (Adapted from Assessment Reform Group, 2002.)

PLANNING FOR AFL

The inspection framework in England for 2012 tells us that: 'Inspectors consider the planning and implementation of learning activities across the whole of the school's curriculum, together with teachers' marking, assessment and feedback to pupils' (Ofsted, 2012).

Effective planning enables you to provide learning opportunities that match the needs of all the children. It should include the following:

*   objectives that focus on learning; the task then becomes the vehicle for the learning;
*   strategies for finding out what the children already know, so that you can pitch the learning/teaching at the appropriate level;
*   an element of pupil choice;
*   ways in which you can share the 'bigger picture' with the children, so that they know what they are aiming for;
*   mini-plenaries, so that the children can regularly reflect back on the bigger picture;
*   opportunities for peer and self-assessment, with and without teacher support.

Sharing the bigger picture

From the start, discuss the success criteria with your pupils. Articulate exactly what it is you will be assessing. In writing, for example, a success criterion might be 'a descriptive piece of writing using a range of adjectives'. Teachers and pupils can create the success criteria together. Figure 5.1.1 shows a pupil self-assessment sheet for a history topic. You can display a large version on the wall and have an individual copy for each child. There are three levels of attainment here, which can either be used for pupil self-assessment or peer assessment.

Task 5.1.1 Pupil assessment sheet

Referring to Figure 5.1.1, choose another area of the curriculum and construct a similar sheet.

Discussion during the sessions and mini-plenaries

Discussions take place before, during and after each lesson, as well as outside the classroom, so that the teacher can check the children's understanding and judge their progress. Discussion also provides a vehicle for a continued sharing of the learning objectives. Here are some strategies for doing this:

What was it like to live here in the past?

Must

- understand that St Paul's School was different in the past;
- make comparisons between the school in the past and as it is today.

Should

- recognise features of the school building and know how it has changed over time;
- enquire about some of the people who have worked at the school (both pupils and staff) and understand differences in working conditions at different times;
- be able to use a range of historical sources in a variety of ways.

Could

- describe and compare features of the school and identify changes on a time line;
- select and combine information from different sources.

FIGURE 5.1.1 Pupil self-assessment sheet

- Before the lesson, have discussions with the children to ascertain what they already know about the subject, in order that you can plan the work effectively to include different levels of understanding. Identify in your planning the children you wish to support in that lesson.
- Once you have identified children's misconceptions or unexpected responses, you can follow up your individual discussion during the session to clarify these.
- Monitor the children's progress throughout the lesson by asking them questions about the task and then sharing with them targets for the next steps in their learning.
- At intervals during the session, remind the children of the lesson objectives, then ask children to feed back to the class what they have found out so far, and what they still have to do to complete the task.
- Ask the children to evaluate their own progress against the success criteria given.

QUESTIONING

Effective questioning is the key to good teacher assessment; make sure you know which questions to use and when you will use them. Teachers are always asking questions, but, in order to develop higher-order thinking skills, it is important to ask open-ended, provocative and child-centred questions (see Table 5.1.1). Harris and Williams have suggested that open-ended questions 'provoke speculation and extend the imagination' (2012: 375). The use of open questioning is critical in encouraging children to develop and then offer their own opinions. This occurs when the teacher acknowledges that these opinions are a valid response, rather than assessing whether they are 'right' or 'wrong'. This open-ended approach to questioning is much more productive than a closed questioning technique, where only one response is deemed 'correct' by the teacher, leaving the children guessing what the teacher wants to hear, rather than basing their response on their own ideas. Ask follow-up questions to make the children think more deeply. (For details of 'convergent' or 'divergent' questions, see Pryor and Crossouard, 2008; Harris and Williams, 2012.) Table 5.1.1 illustrates some questions designed to elicit higher-order thinking, which may be posed by either teacher or other pupils (King, 2002: 2).

TABLE 5.1.1 How open-ended questions encourage thinking skills

Type of question	Responses
What do you notice about . . .?	Descriptive observations
What can you tell me about . . .?	Inviting recalled information but content chosen by the children
What does it remind you of?	Seeing patterns/analogies
Which things do you think belong together? Why do you think that?	Seeing patterns/classifying and creative explanations
What do you think will happen next?	Creative predictions
What happened after you did that?	Descriptive reasoning/cause and effect/conclusions
Why do you think that happened? I wonder why it did that?	Creative hypotheses/explanations
Do you think you could do it differently?	Evaluation/reflective analysis
I wonder what made you think that?	Reflective self-awareness/metacognition
Anything else? Or?	Neutral/inviting more of the responses listed above

Thinking time ('wait' time)

To encourage this process of high-level thinking, children must be given time to think more deeply before responding to questions. Once you have asked a question, allow the children 'thinking time' before listening to their responses. This has a twofold effect. First, it encourages pupils to think more deeply and fosters higher-order thinking skills, and, second, it builds the confidence of those pupils who take longer to respond. Teacher expectation is important here, expecting a response from every child. A useful technique for encouraging this is the use of 'discussion' or 'talk partners'. The child first shares their ideas with a partner, before some children are selected to share their response with the teacher and the class. This does require careful planning of partnerships to be effective, and frequent changes of partners can offer children exposure to a wider range of ideas. In this way, the children can test their ideas with their peers and perhaps adjust their thinking before offering a response, which in turn helps them feel more confident about voicing a response. During these peer discussions, the teacher has an opportunity to find out any misconceptions that the children may hold, or indeed areas of the topic that excite them. S/he may use a randomising method to choose who responds in front of the class each time, for example, using raffle tickets or lolly sticks with names on. The information s/he gains from every child can be fed into planning, making it more personalised.

PEER AND SELF-ASSESSMENT

An increased awareness of the role of the learner in the assessment process has led to changes in approaches to teaching involving more dialogue between pupils and teachers in the setting and adaptation of the assessment process. Learners are more aware, not only of what they learn, but how they learn and what helps them learn. Pupils can assess themselves and can learn from their own and others' assessments. This, in turn, leads them to reflect on how they learn. Children should

Task 5.1.2 Questioning to encourage thinking skills 1

- Table 5.1.1 shows a range of questions designed to help children think in sophisticated ways. Apply this technique to a specific curriculum area.
- Ask a colleague to observe your teaching session and comment on your inclusion of the following aspects of questioning. You could reciprocate by observing his or her teaching and then share your findings.
    - asking questions to assess the children's starting points in order to adapt learning and teaching;
    - asking a range of questions to develop understanding;
    - using thinking time and 'talk partners' to ensure all children are engaged in answering questions;
    - giving the children opportunities to ask questions before and after the session;
    - creating a question board related to a particular topic and encouraging children to 'post' on this;
    - having an agreed time to discuss the questions with the children.

Task 5.1.3 Questioning to encourage thinking skills 2

Reflect on how the information you have obtained in Task 5.1.2 then impacted on your planning for this aspect of the curriculum.

be involved, not only in their own, but also in peer assessment. This gives children a central role in learning and is a really important shift from the teacher having all the responsibility for assessment to a position of sharing goals, self-evaluation and setting their own targets (see Read and Hurford, 2010).

This approach can be highly motivating, but must be endorsed by a supportive classroom ethos, which should include clear guidelines for the children in terms of supporting and guiding each other's learning. There must, for example, be a clear focus and structure for the lesson. Children need a set of success and assessment criteria (see 'Planning for AfL', above) by which to judge the success of their learning, and avoiding marks or grades is essential. These can be negotiated with the children. Consider some of the following methods of engaging your children in their own assessment. Notice that the final example is a class's assessment of its own learning strategies, not just focused on a particular curriculum domain.

(a) In Mr Zak's class, before starting any new topic of learning, the pupils describe what they already know about that topic and what they would like to know about that topic. Mr Zak then teaches the topic in accordance with what the pupils have told him. Sometimes he invites pupils to teach some parts, if they have a good knowledge about it.

(b) In Miss Sophie's class, each month pupils are asked to do 'self-assessments'. They look back at the work they have done over the past month, notice progress made since the previous month, and write down in a Learning Log specific tasks they need to do in order to achieve the targets they have been set. Sometimes they work in collaboration with a peer-assessor.

(c) Before the class does any work or project, teacher Mrs Han asks the class to suggest what features a good end product would include. For example, when writing a creative story, the children suggested that the story would be interesting to read. When all the criteria are agreed, they are written for everyone to see. At the end of the work or project, the pupils assess each other against these agreed criteria.

(d) Mr Nat's Year 5 class uses a system of peer assessment. When an assignment is finished, two peers read the assignment. The author of the assignment then assesses it against agreed criteria (making judgements about its value). The two peers then give *provocative* feedback, asking the author questions that will make the author think more deeply about the topic. No judgements are made by the peers, only by the author him/herself. The author may then rework the assignment.

(e) In Mrs Yasmina's class, there are two big noticeboards pinned up at the front of class. One is titled: 'What helps our learning', and the other is titled: 'What hinders our learning'. At the end of each day, the children reflect on their day's learning and contribute factors for each noticeboard. They then discuss how they can decrease the hindrances and increase the helping factors.

Task 5.1.4 Self-assessment

Support your pupils to assess themselves or their peers using one of the methods described above.

FEEDBACK

Effective feedback to children provides information to support self-assessment and suggests steps that will lead to progress. Feedback through written comments should refer back to the learning goals set at the beginning of the session and should be constructive. We know that many teachers focus on spelling, punctuation, grammar or the structure of the piece of work, often omitting to comment on children's learning of the specific lesson objective. It can help to keep the presentational factors as *separate but constantly important* criteria, but on *each individual occasion to emphasise comments that relate directly to the specific learning and assessment objectives* for that lesson.

A useful way of thinking about/describing feedback is whether it is evaluative, descriptive or provocative. All too often, teachers provide evaluative feedback in the form of grades and short (usually non-specific) comments, praise or censure. This kind of feedback tells pupils whether they are doing well or not, but it offers little direction for moving their learning forward. Regular critical, evaluative feedback, without guidance for how to improve, can lower motivation and self-esteem. Descriptive feedback, however, relates to the task at hand, the learner's performance and what they might do to improve in relation to specified learning objectives. Provocative feedback, finally, is less directive and inspires the learner to think more deeply and engage further, or to extend their imagination in relation to learning goals.

The ideal situation is when the teacher can discuss and annotate work with the child present, so that progress can be negotiated together. However, this is not always possible, and so the teacher writes comments for the child to read and then gives them time to consider the comments. Here is a Year 5 pupil, Esther's, description of the teacher's feedback during a lesson on using adjectives. The feedback led Esther to reflect further about adjectives and additionally encouraged her to draw on her own resources for progress:

[The teacher has told Esther not to use 'silly' as her adjective.]

Interviewer: Do you remember why [the teacher] said not to use 'silly'?

Esther: Well, normally she says, because we're not 5, we're Year 5, and we can actually think of much better words than just 'silly' or 'stupid' or something like that. You can think of much better words, because you've got a big thesaurus in your brain.

Interviewer: Indeed . . . All right, then [teacher] gave you some advice, not just about what you were doing today, but always – she said the word 'always'. She said, 'It always helps to read your work out loud.'

RECOGNISING AND CELEBRATING CHILDREN'S WORK

You need to consider how a child's successful learning is recognised. Build in time for reflection at the end of the day or the week. In an early years setting, good learning may be celebrated in a discussion at the end of each session, taking the opportunity to point out what makes it worthy of comment. Another method of highlighting good learning is by taking photographs, which can be displayed as a slide show on a computer screen, providing a permanent reminder for both child and teacher. Some teachers simply display a chosen piece of work on the wall or on a bookstand, so that everyone can share that pupil's success. It is important to involve the class sometimes in pointing out the learning that is particularly appropriate and to focus specifically on learning processes, not only its products. Praise in the form of 'excellent' or a reward/high grade for completed work does little to direct learning processes and can encourage children to avoid risk-taking or asking questions in the future.

Task 5.1.5 Questions to ask yourself in relation to your planning for AfL

- Does the assessment allow children multiple ways to demonstrate their learning across the range of curriculum activities?
- Does it assess the ways in which learning has taken place?
- How do you ensure that feedback from assessments allows the children opportunities to develop and progress in their learning by linking your comments to agreed success criteria and indicating the next phase to encourage further learning?
- How do assessment outcomes influence session planning and modifications to future curriculum planning?
- How will you/should you keep track of this?

Task 5.1.6 Peer reflection

You have had an opportunity to evaluate your practice in relation to pupil self-assessment and questioning. Now ask one of your peers to observe another lesson and comment on another two of the principles of AfL identified by the ARG. You can then observe your peer's class and share your comments to help each other learn. Remember that your comments should focus only on the aspects requested by the colleague you observe: you are not assessing their competence, but rather helping them to learn.

SUMMARY

*Assessment **for** learning* as opposed to *assessment **of** learning* is part of ongoing learning and teaching, and is not a 'bolt-on'. Its aim is to assess all areas of the curriculum, and, in order to achieve this, it uses a wide range of strategies to secure a range of opportunities to find out about each child. It leads to a recognition of what a child can already do and the identification of progress they might now make in their learning, so that they can proceed at a pace appropriate for them. This is done by a mixture of teacher-led assessment and pupils' sharing in the assessment process, so that they can eventually assess their own work and set appropriate targets. Although there is currently a national debate on the extent to which AfL strategies raise attainment, many teachers in England and especially Scotland, as well as in diverse countries across the world, have described AfL as transforming their children's learning and their own experiences of teaching. When this happens, it seems to involve the teacher and pupils in a whole new approach to learning and teaching in which the teacher–learner relationship is freshly negotiated, and pupils take a greater lead over directing their own learning.

 ## ANNOTATED FURTHER READING

Read, A. and Hurford, D. (2010). '"I know how to read longer novels" – developing pupils' success criteria in the classroom'. *Education 3-13*, 38, 1, 87-100.

> In this paper, also suitable to support M-level study, the authors identify issues with the practical application of AfL in the primary classroom. They note a theoretical shift from teacher-generated to pupil-generated success criteria and seek to explore what this might look like in practice in the classroom. They develop a model for generating pupil-based success criteria, based on AfL principles, which they introduce to a Year 5 classroom. They conclude that the innovative teacher may use such an approach in the primary classroom, but they raise some issues that need to be addressed, such as the children's familiarity with the subject matter being assessed.

Stobart, G. (2008) 'Reasons to be cheerful: Assessment for Learning'. In: G. Stobart (2008), *The Uses and Abuses of Assessment*. London: RoutlegeFalmer.

> In this amusingly written chapter on AfL, Gordon Stobart provides a thorough survey of what AfL has been defined as, how this concept has developed in relation to learning theories, and what its implications are for classrooms. It is certainly useful as an M-level reading and provides an insight into the ARG's thinking, as Stobart was a founder member of the ARG. Stobart flags up the issue of teachers implementing the strategies of AfL without engaging with the 'spirit' of the strategies, that is, understanding how they might support learning most effectively. He gives considerable attention to classroom feedback, given its close relationship to enhanced learning.

 ## FURTHER READING TO SUPPORT M-LEVEL STUDY

Hargreaves, E. (2013) 'Inquiring into children's experiences of teacher feedback: reconceptualising Assessment for Learning'. *Oxford Review of Education*, 39, 2, 229-46.

> This article is suitable for M-level reading. This paper reports on the longitudinal study of nine 'profile' children in a UK school (which was described earlier in this unit in relation to Esther's comments on feedback). The children were observed and video-filmed in threes, twos or individually, during literacy and numeracy lessons, across two terms, from January to July 2010. The video-recordings were shown

to the children who had been filmed later the same day, being stopped at frequent intervals to allow the participants to comment on specific feedback incidents. The children claimed that learning was frustrated by overly directive feedback, and that their learning benefited when the teacher's feedback included substantial but not burdensome detail. The children felt their learning was supported by feedback reminder cues, and they noticed that negative and positive feedback provoked emotions that could interfere with or support learning. The article concludes by suggesting that AfL might be conceptualised as a classroom conversation in which children, as well as teachers, assess how teacher feedback relates to children's learning, which would itself constitute a major contribution to their autonomous learning

Torrance, H. (2012) 'Formative assessment at the crossroads: conformative, deformative and transformative assessment'. *Oxford Review of Education*, 38, 3, 323-42.

This article is suitable for M-level reading, although more demanding than the three readings suggested above. In the article, Harry Torrance suggests that the theory and practice of formative assessment (AfL) seems to be at a crossroads, even an impasse. Different theoretical justifications for the development of formative assessment have been apparent for many years. However, practice, although quite widespread, is often limited in terms of its scope and its utilisation of the full range of possible approaches associated with formative assessment. The paper reviews the issue that the aim of AfL is, ostensibly, to develop independent and critical learners, whereas, in practice, highly conformative assessment procedures are being designed and developed. The paper argues that educators need to attend to the divergent possibilities inherent in formative assessment, if the full potential of AfL is to be realised as a transformative practice.

RELEVANT WEBSITES

Ofsted (2012): www.ofsted.gov.uk/publications/

www.aaia.org.uk

REFERENCES

Assessment Reform Group (ARG) (1999) *Assessment for Learning: Beyond the Black Box*. London: ARG/Nuffield Foundation.

Assessment Reform Group (ARG) (2002) Assessment for Learning: 10 Research-based Principles to Guide Classroom Practice. Available online at www.aaia.org.uk

Black, P.J. and Wiliam, D. (1998) 'Assessment and classroom learning'. *Assessment in Education*, 5, 1, 7-74.

Department for Children, Schools and Families (DCSF) (2008) *Assessment for Learning*. London: DCSF.

Hargreaves, E. (2012) 'Teachers' classroom feedback: still trying to get it right'. *Pedagogies*, 7, 1, 1-15.

Harris, D. and Williams, J. (2012) 'The association of classroom interactions, year group and social class'. *British Educational Research Journal*, 38, 3, 373-97.

King, A. (2002) 'Structuring peer interaction to promote high-level cognitive processing'. *Theory into Practice*, 41, 1, 33-9.

Marshall, B. and Drummond, M.J. (2006) 'How teachers engage with AfL: lessons from the classroom'. *Research Papers in Education*, 21, 2, 133-49.

Pryor, J. and Crossouard, B. (2008) 'A socio-cultural theorisation of formative assessment'. *Oxford Review of Education*, 34, 1, 1-20.

Read, A. and Hurford, D. (2010) '"I know how to read longer novels" – developing pupils' success criteria in the classroom'. *Education 3-13*, 38, 1, 87-100.

Torrance, H. (2012) 'Formative assessment at the crossroads: conformative, deformative and transformative assessment'. *Oxford Review of Education*, 38, 3, 323-42.

Wiliam, D. (2008) 'Developing classroom practice: meeting regularly in teacher learning communities is one of the best ways for teachers to develop their skill in using formative assessment'. *Educational Leadership*, 65, 4, 36-42.

ASSESSMENT FOR LEARNING

Summative approaches

Kathy Hall and Kieron Sheehy

INTRODUCTION

In this unit, you will have the chance to reflect on what summative assessment is, its uses and its potential impact on learners. You will also be able to consider some aspects of current policy on assessment. We start by considering some basic questions about summative assessment and by linking it with formative assessment. We will go on to identify purposes of summative assessment, as well as sources of assessment evidence, and we will explain what counts as good evidence of learning. We also consider standard assessment tests (SATs) in the context of summative assessment, and we finish by inviting your views on current assessment policy.

OBJECTIVES

By the end of this unit you should be able to:

- define summative assessment and relate it to formative assessment;
- explain why it is important to assess learners in a variety of contexts and know the kinds of assessment task that are effective in generating good evidence of learning;
- identify ways in which schools might use summative assessment information to feed back into teaching and learning;
- describe some aspects of the national policy on assessment and offer an informed opinion about the current emphasis on different assessment purposes and approaches.

WHAT IS ASSESSMENT AND WHY DO IT?

Assessment means different things in different contexts, and it is carried out for different purposes. There is no simple answer to what it is or why we do it. Indeed, one of the most important messages that we would like you to take away from this unit is that assessment is not a simple or innocent term. Assessing learning is not a neutral or value-free activity – it is always bound up with attitudes, values, beliefs and sometimes prejudices on the part of those carrying out the assessment and on the part of those being assessed. When we make assessments of children's learning, we are always influenced by what we bring with us in terms of our previous experiences, personal views and histories. Children's responses to assessment are influenced by what they bring with them – their previous experiences and their personal views.

Summative assessment sums up learning

Most recent sources on assessment refer to two important types. One is summative assessment, the other is formative assessment. Sometimes, summative assessment is termed 'assessment of learning' (AoL), and, in recent times, formative assessment is associated with 'assessment for learning' (AfL). These newer terms are useful, as they give an insight into the purpose of assessment that is involved in each case. In the previous unit (5.1), the area of formative assessment is addressed in more detail.

As the term implies, summative assessment tries to sum up a child's attainment in a given area of the curriculum. Summative assessment is retrospective: it looks back at what has been achieved, perhaps over a term, year or key stage. Formative assessment, on the other hand, is prospective: it looks forward to the next steps of learning. However, debate continues over whether and how summative and formative assessment should be distinguished (Black and Wiliam, 2007; Torrance, 2012). As we explain in a moment, we consider that the use to which assessment information is put is also helpful in determining whether it is labelled summative or formative.

SOURCES OF ASSESSMENT EVIDENCE

Assessing learning is about collecting information or evidence about learners and making judgements about it. The evidence may be based on one or more of the following:

- what learners say;
- what learners do;
- what learners produce;
- what learners feel or think.

The information or evidence may come from learners' responses to a test, such as a spelling test; a classroom activity, such as a science investigation; a game or a puzzle; or a standard assessment task or test such as the SATs. It may come from a task or activity that is collaborative, that is, one where several pupils work together on the same problem. It may come from a task that pupils do on their own, without interacting with other children.

We suspect that you will have observed children and made judgements about them in many of those settings, and you may have noted down some of your observations and/or shared them with the class teacher or tutor when you were on teaching practice.

PURPOSES OF SUMMATIVE ASSESSMENT

As a new teacher, you will be meeting children whom you have not taught, or may not have even met previously. In these situations, you might wish to gain an overview of each pupil's progress. This is particularly so when children are transferring between different stages of schooling, and the classwork is different. Summative assessment is used frequently in these contexts, because obtaining a summary of what learners know or can do helps the teacher to decide what to teach next.

Summative assessment is carried out for several purposes. First, it provides you with a summary of learners' achievements that will inform your future teaching and, of course, your planning for future learning. (This is close to the notion of formative assessment described in Unit 5.1.) Second, it provides valid and accurate information that can be shared with parents about their children's progress. Third, summatively assessing learning provides a numerical measurement that can be used in league tables – the purpose being to make schools accountable.

Before reading on, try to put these purposes in order of importance for yourself as a classroom teacher.

We suspect this exercise is not that simple to do. Assessing learners for the purpose of helping you to plan your teaching can't easily be accommodated alongside assessing learners for the purpose of rendering the school or class accountable through the publication of league tables. League tables call for assessment methods that are reliable, in that they are comparable across all schools and across the country as a whole, and valid, in that they offer an account of what is considered important to know at various stages of schooling. As Black *et al.* (2003: 2) note, these are 'exacting requirements'. Reliability and comparability are not major issues if, on the other hand, you are seeking evidence to help you decide what to teach next.

For the purpose of generating league tables, as Black *et al.* (2003) note, the main assessment methods are formal tests (not devised by teachers). These are usually isolated from day-to-day teaching and learning, and they are often carried out at special times of the year. In contrast, assessments designed to inform your teaching are usually more informal, they may be integrated into your ongoing teaching, and they are likely to be carried out in different ways by different teachers. In the light of the previous sentence, you may well wonder what the difference is between summative and formative assessment, and indeed some research challenges the distinction in the first place (Threlfall, 2005). However, in line with the work of Black and Wiliam (1998), we are reluctant to label the latter as formative assessment.

As we see it, the salient feature of formative assessment is that learners themselves use the information deriving from the assessment to bridge the gap between what they know and what they need to know (see Hall and Burke, 2003, for a full discussion). Collecting information to inform your teaching is in itself no guarantee that learners will use this information to move forward in their learning.

PRODUCING GOOD EVIDENCE OF ACHIEVEMENT

It is important to appreciate that summative assessment can take a variety of forms – it need not, indeed should not, just be a written test. In addition, it is important for you as a teacher to try to anticipate how pupils might respond to the demands of an assessment task. In 1987, Desmond Nuttall wrote a paper describing the types of task or activity that are good for assessing learning. Such tasks, he says, should be concrete and within the experience of the individual; they should be presented clearly; and they should be perceived by the pupils as relevant to their current concerns.

Being able to respond to a task by using different methods – for example, making, doing, talking and writing – allows learners to demonstrate their learning in a variety of ways. The value of varied approaches to assessing learning is that they help learners really show what they know or can do. For example, a learner who is not a very skilled writer may be better able to demonstrate their historical knowledge through talk or through a combination of written work and oral work. Think about your own history as a pupil – do you feel that a written test enabled you to demonstrate what you really knew? Would other ways have been more appropriate for assessing your competence in different curriculum areas?

The use of a variety of ways of assessing learning (often referred to as 'multiple response modes') allows adults to have evidence of learning from a variety of contexts, and to avoid making judgements about learning based on single sources of evidence, such as, say, a pencil and paper test. This results in information that is more accurate and trustworthy than results deriving from just one assessment in just one situation. You could say that it is more valid and dependable. By looking across several instances in which a child uses, say, reading, the teacher and teaching assistant gain valuable information about that child as a reader.

Judgements based on the use of a variety of sources of assessment information are, of course, more demanding on time and resources. This means teachers and policymakers have to consider the appropriate balance to obtain between the validity and trustworthiness of assessment evidence on the one hand, and manageability and cost on the other. Teachers' summative assessment appears to work well when they make decisions about the programme of work and what needs to be assessed within it when they have helped develop the assessment criteria and can examine a range of pupil work (Harlen, 2005). Reviewing teachers' use of summative assessment, Harlen (2005) also highlighted a need for teachers to be aware of potential bias in their judgements – for example, a 'halo' effect, where one pupil characteristic (such as gender or an identification of special educational needs) may influence the teacher's judgement about their performance on academic tasks or activities.

Tick sheets and portfolios

Some teachers use 'tick sheets' to summarise a child's achievements at a point in schooling. This type of assessment is also summative. What is your view of this approach in the light of the previous section about good assessment evidence?

The tick-sheet, yes/no approach might be manageable for very busy practitioners and could provide a useful overview of a child's learning. However, it is likely to be too crude to offer a really meaningful account of learning and usually it offers no source of evidence or little evidence regarding the context in which the assessment took place. Mary Jane Drummond, an expert on early years education, says that a tick-sheet approach may hinder the production of a 'rich respectful account' (1999: 34) of a child's learning.

Portfolios offer a useful way of keeping evidence of learning. For example, your pupils might have an individual literacy portfolio, into which they put lists of books read, written responses to stories, non-fiction writing, drawings or paintings in response to literature, and so on. They may include drafts of work, as well as finished pieces of writing. You might then use this evidence to write short summary accounts of your pupils, which in turn could be used as a basis of discussion at a parents' evening.

As well as individual portfolios, some schools keep 'class' or 'school' portfolios, where they put samples of pupil work. They may annotate the samples with reference to context and the standards met. So, for example, contextual annotations might include the date, whether the piece of work was the result of pupils collaborating or an individual working alone, whether the teacher helped, or whether it was done independently. Annotations about the standard met might include a grade or a score and a comment indicating how closely the work met a National Curriculum standard or level description (see p. 210). This kind of portfolio sometimes acts as a vehicle for teachers to share their interpretation of the standards, not just among themselves but also with parents and with pupils.

SUMMATIVE ASSESSMENT AND TEACHER ASSESSMENT

As well as the external testing regime of SATs, teachers assess and report on their pupils via teacher assessment – they are required to 'sum up' their pupils' attainments in relation to National Curriculum levels. As we noted earlier, in order to offer defensible and trustworthy accounts of their attainment, you need to assess pupils in a variety of contexts and in a variety of ways, but any assessment is only as good as the use to which it is put. Some writers refer to this concept as 'consequential validity', as what is considered important are the consequences of the assessment – what happens to the assessment information once it is collected. Is it used to inform teaching, to enable the production of league tables or to summarise achievement for parents, or for the next teacher?

Recent changes across the UK have given teachers more responsibility for summative testing (Black *et al.*, 2011). Previous mandatory tests at 7, 11 and 14 have ceased in Northern Ireland. In England, previous 'national' tests for 7-year-olds have been replacement by an approach based on teacher assessment, and, in Scotland, such external tests have not been part of primary school practice (Black *et al.*, 2011).

Assessment information, including that obtained via SATs and, especially, teacher assessment, can be used in a way that supports teaching and learning. We will explain this with reference to the way some teachers use level descriptions.

Level descriptions have been used in all four parts of the UK. They are summary statements that describe the types and range of performance that pupils are expected to demonstrate at various stages in their schooling. Teachers have to judge which level 'best fits' a child's performance for each area of the curriculum. This involves cross-checking against adjacent levels in a scale and considering the balance of strengths and weaknesses for each particular child.

What use is made of level descriptions? Does the process of allocating levels to pupils' achievements inform teaching and learning? A study conducted in six different schools in six different local education authorities (LEAs) in the north of England sought to understand how primary teachers were using level descriptions (Hall and Harding, 2002). On the basis of many interviews, over 2 years, with teachers and LEA assessment advisers, and observations of assessment meetings, two contrasting approaches to the process of interpreting and using level descriptions in schools were identified. The approaches are described as *collaborative* and *individualistic*. To illustrate, we will describe just two of the schools – East Street and West Street (not their real names), which show these contrasting tendencies.

A collaborative approach

East Street School is a large, inner-city primary school of more than 400 pupils, all but 5 per cent of whom are from ethnic minority backgrounds. East Street has an assessment community that is highly collaborative, with teachers, parents and pupils having many opportunities to talk about assessment and how and why it is done. The staff frequently meet to discuss the purposes of assessment in general and of their ongoing teacher assessment in particular. They talk about what constitutes evidence of achievement in various areas of the curriculum and they compare their judgements of samples of pupil work. They use a range of tools, such as school portfolios and sample material from the Qualifications and Curriculum Authority (QCA), to help in their assessment tasks and to ensure that they are applying the level descriptions consistently. They strive to include pupils, parents and other teachers as part of that assessment community.

An individualistic approach

West Street School is a larger-than-average primary school, serving a varied socio-economic area in a northern city. Pupils are drawn from a mixture of privately owned and council-maintained housing, and the school has a sizeable number of pupils from educationally disadvantaged backgrounds. West Street reluctantly complies with the demands of national policy on assessment.

Teachers here work largely in isolation from each other in interpreting and implementing assessment goals and, especially, in interpreting level descriptions and using portfolios and evidence. There is no real attempt to involve interested groups, such as parents and pupils, in assessment discussions. The staff tend to view national testing as an unhelpful, arduous intrusion.

What all of this tells us is that schools vary a great deal in how they implement national assessment policy. Some teachers reluctantly comply with the policy, whereas others make it work for the benefit of all interested parties in the school. To be more precise, some teachers use level descriptions in a way that supports assessment *for* learning and assessment *of* learning.

To become a collaborative assessment community, staff need time to develop their expertise. They need time to talk about and share their practices in a culture that shares the expectation that adults too are valued learners.

Task 5.2.1 Assessment – different approaches

- Study Table 5.2.1, which summarises the assessment approach in East Street and West Street schools.
- Suggest some reasons for the difference in approach in the two schools.
- Practice in most schools is probably somewhere in between these two. Make a note of which practices listed for East Street you are aware of from your experience in school recently.

TABLE 5.2.1 Assessment communities and assessment individuals

Collaborative (East Street School)	Individualistic (West Street School)
Goals	
Compliant and accepting	Reluctant compliance and resistance
Processes	
(1) Level descriptions: interpretation is shared; (2) portfolio: in active use; (3) exemplification materials: owned by teachers; a mixture of school-devised and QCA materials; (4) evidence: planned collection; variety of modes; assessment embedded in teaching and learning; emphasis on the process; (5) common language of assessment; (6) commitment to moderation (cross-checking of interpretations of evidence)	(1) Level descriptions: little or no sharing of interpretations; (2) portfolio: dormant; (3) exemplification materials: QCA not used; commercially produced materials used by some individuals; (4) evidence: not used much; assessment often bolted on to learning and teaching; emphasis on products; (5) uncertainty/confusion about terms; (6) weak or nonexistent moderation
Personnel	
Whole school; aspirations to enlarge the assessment community to include pupils, parents and other teachers	Year 2 teachers as individuals; no real grasp of the potential for enlarging the assessment community
Value system	
Assessment seen as useful, necessary and integral to teaching and learning; made meaningful through collaboration	Assessment seen as 'imposed' and not meaningful at the level of the class teacher

The use of level descriptors within the UK is likely to change. At the time of writing, the minister of education has proposed that 'the current system of levels and level descriptors should be removed and not replaced' (Department for Education, 2012a). The nature of any new assessments is under review, with the steer that the emphasis in the new programmes of study on what pupils should know and be able to do will help to ensure that schools concentrate on making sure that all pupils reach the expected standard, rather than on labelling differential performance (Department for Education, 2012a).

This implies that the new approach will be summative and 'external'. However, the nature of the outcomes that will be examined are not yet known, and so the effect of such changes on collaborative assessment practices within schools remains to be seen.

SUMMATIVE ASSESSMENT AND SATS

Summative assessment does not just refer to the kinds of end-of-key-stage assessment carried out in schools in England and known as SATs (there are no SATs in Wales, Scotland or Northern Ireland). Although these external tasks and tests are indeed summative, they are not the only kind of summative assessment that goes on in schools. However, because of their 'high stakes' – that is, schools' ranking in league tables depends on them – they are accorded very high status in practice in schools, and people sometimes make the mistake of assuming that summative assessments means SATs. In England, children are assessed in this way in Years 2, 6 and 9, when they are approximately 7, 11 and 17 years of age. There is also statutory assessment for children in the final year of the foundation stage (Department for Education, 2012a).

Table 5.2.2 illustrates the range of SATs undertaken by pupils in English primary schools in 2012.

Optional tests also exist for children in Years 3, 4 and 5 in English and mathematics. These tests are published by the government, but they are marked internally, and their results are not published.

A significant issue is not the amount of testing itself, but the impact that such assessments have on pupils or on practice within schools (Whetton, 2004).

TABLE 5.2.2 SATs undertaken by pupils in English primary schools

Early Years Foundation Stage profile	Typically age 5
Phonics screening check at the end of Year 1	Typically age 6
Key Stage 1 (KS1) tasks and tests during Year 2	Typically age 7
Key Stage 2 (KS2) English grammar, punctuation and spelling test (beginning May 2013)	Typically age 11
KS2 National Curriculum tests in English and maths taken at the end of Year 6	Typically age 11

The use of performance scales (P scales) is a requirement when reporting attainment for pupils with special educational needs who are working below level 1 of the National Curriculum. Performance scales are used at the end of Key Stage 1, Key Stage 2 and Key Stage 3 for reporting teacher assessment in English, mathematics and science to the Standards and Testing Agency. P scales are also used for reporting teacher assessment to parents in other National Curriculum subjects

Source: adapted from Department for Education (2012a)

THE IMPACT OF 'HIGH STAKES' ASSESSMENT ON PUPILS

Many researchers on assessment, including ourselves, have written about the impact on pupils of different assessment purposes and practices (Harlen and Deakin Crick, 2002). The research shows that schools feel under pressure to get more of their pupils achieving at higher levels in national tests. This pushes some teachers, especially those who have classes about to take national tests, to spend more time and energy on helping pupils to get good at doing those tests. This is often referred to as 'teaching to the test', and it means there is less time to actually develop pupils' skills and understanding in the various areas of the curriculum.

This is exactly what we found in a study of Year 6 pupils in urban areas of disadvantage (Hall *et al.*, 2004). The external pencil and paper tests, which are designed to offer evidence to the government about how schools are raising standards, received enormous levels of attention in the daily life of pupils in the schools that were part of our study. Such is the perceived pressure in schools to do well in league tables that they sometimes feel unable to place sufficient emphasis on assessment designed to promote learning across the curriculum, or on assessing learning through a variety of modes. Summative assessment can even become seen as the goal of teaching. George W. Bush, a former president of the USA, visited an east London primary school. After listening to a story being read to the children, he commented on the importance of literacy to the teachers: 'You teach a child to read, and he or her [*sic*] will be able to pass a literacy test' (cited in Yandell, 2008).

In situations where passing a test is seen as the purpose of teaching, the children's learning experiences become focused towards this end. Yandell (2008) described how pupils, studying a play, were only given photocopies of the 'SATs' sections of the text and never read the play itself. Reviewing a range of evidence concerning the impact of high-stakes summative testing led Wyse and Torrance (2009: 224) to conclude that it can drive teaching in 'exactly the opposite direction to that which other research indicates will improve teaching, learning and attainment'.

There are many other potential consequences for pupils. High-stakes tests can lead teachers to adopt transmission styles of teaching and thus disadvantage pupils who prefer other, more creative ways of learning. Practice tests, when repeatedly undertaken, can have a negative impact on the self-esteem of lower-achieving pupils. Research from outside the UK suggests that pupils' expectations about the purpose of assessment reflect badly on summative approaches (Black, 2003): for example, pupils believing that summative assessment was entirely for their school's and parents' benefit. Children who did less well in such assessments felt that their purpose was to make them work harder. It was a source of pressure that resulted in pupil anxiety and even fear.

Pupils used to a diet of summative assessments, based on written tests and on only a few curriculum areas (often numeracy and literacy), can take time in adapting to more formative approaches. The same can be true for teachers. For example, in response to calls for formative assessment, many teachers produce formal summative tests that mimic the statutory tests. This again reflects the perceived importance of SATs. Weeden *et al.* (2002: 34) make the point that the more important a quantitative measure becomes, 'the more it is likely to distort the processes it is supposed to monitor'.

High-stakes testing might also influence the way you respond to and feel about the children in your class. 'How many teachers of young children are now able to listen attentively in a non-instrumental way without feeling guilty about the absence of criteria or the insistence of a target tugging at their sleeve' (Fielding, cited in Hill, 2007). There is clearly an emotional/affective factor that is often overlooked in seeking the objective viewpoint that summative assessments are seen as presenting. Robert Reinecke highlights this:

> Assessments, formal or informal, considered or casual, intentional or not, powerfully affect people, particularly students. The assessment climate that students experience is a crucial component of instruction and learning. Students' assessment experiences remain with them for a lifetime and substantially affect their capacity for future learning . . . emotional charge is part of the character of assessment information.
>
> (1998: 7)

For any assessment to have a positive impact on children's learning, the way in which performance results are used and communicated is vitally important.

The phonics screening test is intended to be a 'light-touch assessment to confirm whether individual pupils have learnt phonic decoding to an appropriate standard' (Department for Education, 2012b). Children are examined on their ability to identify a series of isolated non-words and words. However 'light touch' it was intended to be, one can see how such a statutory test, whose results provide information at school, local authority and national level, could have a profound effect on classroom practice and pedagogy. Dombey (2011) argues that the assessment will distort the process of learning to read, and the United Kingdom Literacy Association (2012) questioned its usefulness as a summative assessment for all readers. The statutory assessment of English grammar, punctuation and spelling has yet to happen at the time of writing this unit; however, this will comprise a series of short-answer questions in different formats (Standards and Testing Agency, 2012). The extent to which these become high stakes will be revealed.

DIFFERENCES IN TESTING ACROSS THE UK

Key Stage 2 requirements are that 'Teachers are required to make their statutory teacher assessments, at the end of the key stage, for each eligible learner in the following subjects: English Welsh first language (if the learner has followed the Welsh programme of study) or Welsh second language: Mathematics and Science' (Department for Education and Skills, 2013: 9).

Pupils in England and in Northern Ireland are subjected to more testing than their peers in other parts of the UK. However, after decades of external summative assessment, there now appears to be a shift towards teacher assessment (Leung and Rea-Dickens, 2007). Teachers in Scotland, for instance, decide when their pupils are ready to take the external tests. Teachers at Key Stage 1 in Wales are no longer obliged to assess their pupils for the purpose of compiling league tables, and teacher assessment is used for statutory reporting at ages 11 and 14 (Leung and Rea-Dickens, 2007). This followed a review of assessment practices that questioned whether the hard data extracted by external assessments were worth the negative consequences (Daugherty, 2008, 2009). Teacher assessment is now used in Wales for statutory reporting at 11 and 14 years (Daugherty, 2008, 2009), with teachers working in 'cluster groups to maximise the consistency' of their assessments (Daugherty, 2008: 80). Scotland has developed an overall approach that emphasises formative testing (for details of these approaches, please see the 'Relevant websites' section at the end of this unit).

The following is a short extract from an important policy document in England, *Excellence and Enjoyment: A Strategy for Primary Schools*. It tells you what head teachers think is the best way of summarising a learner's achievements:

> At our head teacher conferences, head teachers argued that a teacher's overall, rounded assessment of a child's progress through the year (taking into account the regular tests and tasks that children do) was a more accurate guide to a child's progress at this age [Key Stage 1] than their performance in one particular set of tasks and tests.
>
> (Department for Education and Skills, 2003: 2.29)

In Wales . . .

All learners in their final year of the Foundation Phase and Key Stages 2 and 3 must be assessed through teacher assessment.

(DfES, 2013b: 7)

Foundation Phase (FP) requirements are that teachers are required to make their statutory teacher assessments at the end of the Foundation Phase against three of the Areas of Learning: Personal and Social Development, Well-being and Cultural Diversity; Language, Literacy and Communication Skills and Mathematical Development.

(DfES, 2013b: 9)

Source: Department for Education and Skills (DfES) (2013) *Statutory assessment arrangements for the end of Foundation Phase and Key Stages 2 and 3.* Cardiff: Welsh Assembly Government (WAG). http://wales.gov.uk/docs/dcells/publications/130219-statutory-assessment-arrangements-2012-13-booklet-en.pdf

Because head teachers in England are so concerned about testing at Key Stage 1, the government decided to commission research to see whether an approach that focuses more on teachers' judgements about pupils' progress throughout the year could result in accurate and rigorous assessments. Currently, teacher assessment of progress across the key stage is the main focus, supported by tests in maths, reading and writing. A sample of schools is externally moderated each year, with the rest carrying out internal moderation exercises. Guidance recommends a standardisation to check consistency of judgements before assessments are made (Department for Children, Schools and Families, 2008). Once the teachers have concluded their assessments, internal moderation is carried out. Typically, this will be a sample of one or two pupils' work per teacher (Department for Children, Schools and Families, 2008). This practice is useful for formative aspects (see Unit 5.1) and also for

In Northern Ireland . . .

In Northern Ireland, statutory assessment of Cross-Curricular Skills (Communication and Using Mathematics) at Key Stages 1 and 2 takes the form of teacher assessment, with moderation. Teacher assessments are carried out using the statutory levels of progression provided for the purpose. The use of assessment tasks within the assessment arrangements for end of key stage pupils (Years 4 and 7) is a key element in the Council for Curriculum, Examinations and Assessment's support of teachers' assessment judgements and in facilitating effective moderation. Teachers are advised not to regard tasks as 'tests'; nor should they be used by teachers to determine their summative judgements. They should be regarded as one element of ongoing teacher assessment, alongside samples of work from across the curriculum, to support the summative judgements made. Teachers are advised to use a variety of sources of assessment information to inform their judgements about the standard attained by their pupils. Once a teacher has considered the range of assessment information available to him/her, a level-based summative judgement is required for Communication and Using Mathematics, for pupils in Years 4 and 7.

Source: www.nicurriculum.org.uk/docs/assessment/assessment_arrangements/keytages_1and2/English/AA_English_1and2_Jan13.pdf

Task 5.2.2 Testing – what do you think?

- Note down some advantages and disadvantages of testing all children at ages 7 and 11.
- Why do you think England, in particular, places such a strong emphasis on external testing for accountability purposes?

teachers' in-school summative assessment (see Department for Children, Schools and Families, 2008, for details of standardisation and moderation processes).

We would suggest that external testing in primary schools is part of a wider social preoccupation with measuring, league tables and auditing. If you consider other social services, for example the health service and the police service, you find a similar push towards accountability in the form of league tables. England has experienced all of this to a greater degree than other parts of the UK. Education in England seems to be more politicised than in other parts of the UK, and politicians in England are less inclined to be influenced by professional groups such as teachers and researchers. This means that, in turn, such groups have less power in educational decision-making in England than their counterparts have in Scotland, Wales and Northern Ireland.

A CRITIQUE OF CURRENT ASSESSMENT APPROACHES

Dylan Wiliam, a researcher on assessment over many years, has expressed concern about the narrowing effect on the curriculum of teachers teaching to the test – a point we noted earlier in this unit. Here are some key questions he poses.

- Why are pupils tested as individuals, when the world of work requires people who can work well in a team?
- Why do we test memory, when in the real world engineers and scientists never rely on memory: if they're stuck, they look things up.
- Why do we use timed tests, when it is usually far more important to get things done right than to get things done quickly?

He favours an approach that would support teachers' own judgements of pupil achievement, and believes that this approach should replace all forms of testing, from the earliest stages through to GCSE and A-levels. He points out that this happens in Sweden. This is how he justifies his argument:

> In place of the current vicious spiral, in which only those aspects of learning that are easily measured are regarded as important, I propose developing a system of summative assessment based on moderated teacher assessment. A separate system, relying on 'light sampling' of the performance of schools, would provide stable and robust information for the purposes of accountability and policy-formation.

(Wiliam, 2002: 61-2)

He goes on to say that his preferred approach 'would also be likely to tackle boys' under-achievement, because the current "all or nothing" test at the end of a key stage encourages boys to believe that they can make up lost ground at the last minute' (pp. 61-2).

He envisages that there would be a large number of assessment tasks, but not all pupils would undertake the same task. These good-quality assessment tasks would cover the entire curriculum, and they would be allocated randomly. This would guard against teaching to the test, or, as he puts it, 'the only way to teach to the test would be to teach the whole curriculum to every student' (p. 62).

He suggests that schools that taught only a limited curriculum, or concentrated on, say, the most able pupils, would be shown up as ineffective.

Task 5.2.3 A different approach – what do you think?

- What do you think of Wiliam's ideas?
- Do you think his suggestions are more in line with what we know about learning and assessment, especially what we know about the impact of testing on pupils?
- Do you think his suggestions are feasible?
- How would these groups view his ideas: parents, pupils, teachers, politicians?

SUMMARY

In this unit, we have sought to define and describe summative assessment and ways of using it. We have also highlighted the (mostly negative) impact on learners of testing, especially 'high stakes' testing. Whatever the national policy on external testing, as a class teacher you will have a powerful influence over how you assess your pupils. In turn, how you assess your pupils will have considerable influence on how they perform, on how motivated they become as learners, and on how they feel about themselves as learners. You are likely to influence the kind of lifelong learners they become.

To recap the major points of the unit, we suggest that you revisit the learning objectives we noted on the first page. As you do this, you might consider the different ways in which you could demonstrate your understanding and knowledge of the topic.

ANNOTATED FURTHER READING

Hall, K., Collins, J., Benjamin, S., Sheehy, K. and Nind, M. (2004) 'SATurated models of pupildom: assessment and inclusion/exclusion', *British Educational Research Journal*, 30(6): 801-17.
Harlen, W. (2005) 'Teachers' summative practices and assessment for learning: tensions and synergies', *The Curriculum Journal*, 16(2): 207-24.
Reay, D. and Wiliam, D. (1999) '"I'll be a nothing": structure, agency and the construction of identity through assessment', *British Educational Research Journal*, 25(3): 343-54.
> These three articles provide evidence about the impact of high-stakes summative assessment on pupils and teachers, and on teaching and learning.

Gipps, C. (1994) 'Developments in educational assessment: what makes a good test?' *Assessment in Education*, 1(3): 283-91.
> Although more than a decade old, this article provides an excellent account of what makes a good test.

FURTHER READING TO SUPPORT M-LEVEL STUDY

Black, P., Harrison, C., Hodgen, J., Marshall, B. and Serret, N. (2011) 'Can teachers' summative assessments produce dependable results and also enhance classroom learning?' *Assessment in Education: Principles, Policy & Practice*, 18(4): 451-69.

> This research is based on a longitudinal study of teachers' opinions and practices and addresses the issue of how summative assessments might be used to positive effect within the classroom. Five key features of summative assessment practice are presented.

Wyse, D. and Torrance, H. (2009) 'The development and consequences of national curriculum assessment for primary education in England', *Educational Research*, 51(2): 213-28.

> This key paper reviews evidence about the development of National Curriculum assessment in England and the impact of national curriculum assessment. The article gives an excellent insight into the impact of high-stakes testing in education on teachers and pupils.

RELEVANT WEBSITES

Assessment is for Learning (AifL): www.scotland.gov.uk/Publications/2005/09/20105413/54156

> Information about National Assessments and examples of tasks, which are open to anyone to browse, can be found at this site.

Department for Education: www.education.gov.uk

> A useful source for details of assessment initiatives mentioned in the chapter and the results of statutory tests.

Northern Ireland Curriculum: www.nicurriculum.org.uk

> This has information on Northern Ireland's curriculum and assessment arrangements.

Primary Assessment - Making Summative Assessment Work for You: www.teachers.tv/video/3360

> Professor Wynne Harlen, whose work is referred to in this unit, takes part in a discussion of teacher's summative assessments.

Primary Assessment - The Welsh Experience: www.teachers.tv/video/3361

> This looks at how teachers in Wales are assessing and moderating their work across phases, following the removal of statutory testing at Key Stages 2 and 3.

Scottish Government site on Curriculum and Assessment: www.scotland.gov.uk/Publications/2005/09/20105413/54156

> This is a useful source of further information regarding AifL.

REFERENCES

Black, P. (2003) *Testing: Friend or Foe? Theory and Practice of Assessment and Testing*, London: Routledge Falmer.

Black, P. and Wiliam, D. (1998) *Inside the Black Box*, London: Kings College.

Black, P. and Wiliam, D. (2007) 'Large-scale assessment systems: design principles drawn from international comparisons', *Measurement: Interdisciplinary Research and Perspectives*, 5(1): 1-53.

Black, P., Harrison, C., Lee, C., Marshall, B. and Wiliam, D. (2003) *Assessment for Learning: Putting it Into Practice*, Buckingham: Open University Press.

Black, P., Harrison, C., Hodgen, J., Marshall, B. and Serret, N. (2011) 'Can teachers' summative assessments produce dependable results and also enhance classroom learning?' *Assessment in Education: Principles, Policy & Practice*, 18(4): 451–69.

Daugherty, R. (2008) 'Reviewing National Curriculum assessment in Wales: how can evidence inform the development of policy?' *Cambridge Journal of Education*, 38(1): 77–91.

Daugherty, R. (2009) 'National Curriculum assessment in Wales: adaptations and divergence', *Educational Research*, 51(2): 247–50.

Department for Children, Schools and Families (2008) Primary Framework for Literacy and Mathematics. Available at: http://webarchive.nationalarchives.gov.uk/20100202100434/nationalstrategies.standards.dcsf.gov.uk/node/84445 (accessed October 2009).

Department for Education (2012a) Testing and Assessment. Available at: www.education.gov.uk/schools/teaching andlearning/assessment (accessed December 2012).

Department for Education (2012b) Phonics Screening Check FAQs. Available at: www.education.gov.uk/schools/teachingandlearning/pedagogy/a00198207/faqs-year-1-phonics-screening-check#faq2 (accessed December 2012).

Department for Education and Skills (DfES) (2003) *Excellence and Enjoyment: A Strategy for Primary Schools*, London: DfES.

Department for Education and Skills (DfES) (2013) *Statutory Assessment Arrangements for the End of Foundation Phase and Key Stages 2 and 3*, Cardiff: Welsh Assembly Government.

Dombey, H. (2011) 'Distorting the process of learning to read: The "light touch" phonics test for six year olds', *Education Review*, 23(2): 23–33.

Drummond, M.J. (1999) 'Baseline assessment: a case for civil disobedience?', in C. Conner (ed.) *Assessment in Action in the Primary School*, London: Falmer, pp. 3–49.

Hall, K. and Burke, W. (2003) *Making Formative Assessment Work: Effective Practice in the Primary Classroom*, Buckingham: Open University Press.

Hall, K. and Harding, A. (2002) 'Level descriptions and teacher assessment: towards a community of assessment practice', *Educational Research*, 40(1): 1–16.

Hall, K., Collins, J., Benjamin, S., Sheehy, K. and Nind, M. (2004) 'SATurated models of pupildom: assessment and inclusion/exclusion', *British Educational Research Journal*, 30(6): 801–17.

Harlen, W. (2005) 'Trusting teachers' judgement: research evidence of the reliability and validity of teachers', *Research Papers in Education*, 20(3): 245–70.

Harlen, W. and Deakin Crick, R. (2002) 'A systematic review of the impact of summative assessment and tests on students' motivation for learning' (EPPI-Centre Review, version 1.1), in Research Evidence in Education Library, London: EPPI-Centre, Social Science Research Unit, Institute of Education.

Hill, D. (2007) 'Critical teacher education, New Labour in Britain, and the global project of neoliberal capital', *Policy Futures in Education*, 5(2): 204–25.

Leung, C. and Rea-Dickins, P. (2007) 'Teacher assessment as policy instrument: contradictions and capacities', *Language Assessment Quarterly*, 4(1): 6–36.

Nuttall, D. (1987) 'The validity of assessments', *European Journal of the Psychology of Education*, 11(2): 109–18.

Reinecke, R.A. (1998) *Challenging the Mind, Touching the Heart: Best Assessment Practice*, Thousand Oaks, CA: Corwin Oaks.

Standards and Testing Agency (2012) *2013-2015 Key Stage 2 English Grammar, Punctuation and Spelling Test Framework: End of Key Stage 2 Framework for Assessment 2013-2015*. STA: Crown Copyright.

Threlfall, J. (2005) 'The formative use of assessment information in planning: the notion of contingent planning', *British Journal of Educational Studies*, 53(1): 54–65.

Torrance, H. (2012) 'Formative assessment at the crossroads: conformative , deformative and transformative assessment', *Oxford Review of Education*, (December), 37–41.

United Kingdom Literacy Association (2012) UKLA Analysis of Schools' response to the Year 1 Phonics Screening Check, July, 1–5.

Weeden, P., Winter, J. and Broadfoot, P. (2002) *Assessment: What's In It For Schools?* London: Routledge Falmer.

Whetton, C. (2004) Reflections on Fifteen Years of National Assessment: Lessons, Successes and Mistakes, Paper presented at the 30th International Association for Educational Assessment Conference, Philadelphia, PA, 13-18 June.

Wiliam, D. (2002) 'What is wrong with our educational assessment and what can be done about it?', *Education Review*, 15(1): 57-62.

Wyse, D. and Torrance, H. (2009) 'The development and consequences of national curriculum assessment for primary education in England', *Educational Research*, 51(2), 213-28.

Yandell, J. (2008) 'Mind the gap: investigating test literacy and classroom literacy', *English in Education*, 42(1): 70-87.

DIVERSITY AND INCLUSION

PROVIDING FOR INCLUSION

Christopher Robertson

INTRODUCTION

This unit explores new developments in policy, provision and practice for children with special educational needs (SENs) in England, and the implications of these for trainee and beginning teachers. It is recommended that the content of the unit is considered together with that in Unit 6.2, 'Providing for differentiation', because effective differentiation, based on the premise that schools and teachers seek to welcome all learners, is at the heart of making good provision for children with SENs.

OBJECTIVES

By the end of the unit, you should have:

- an increased understanding of the rationale for including almost all pupils with SENs in mainstream school settings;
- an awareness of the key SEN policy initiatives that inform the development of provision and practice in schools;
- reflected upon how to develop your own teaching skills with regard to children with SENs;
- an understanding of the importance of collaborative support in meeting the needs of children with SENs and their families.

PRINCIPLES (CONTEXT)

It is estimated that about a fifth of children in schools in England experience a difficulty in learning at some point during their education and are identified as having an SEN. Over the past 30 years, a sophisticated system of identification, assessment and intervention procedures, based on the 1981 Education Act, has provided a statutory framework for meeting the needs of children with SENs and their families. During this period, the vast majority of children with SENs have been taught in mainstream school environments, and a small percentage of children - between 2 and 4 per cent - with more complex needs have been taught in special schools, resource bases and units.

In the latter years of the 1980s, professional and parental concerns began to emerge regarding the quality of SEN provision in mainstream schools. In the name of what was then termed 'integration', it seemed that too many children with SENs were expected to 'sink or swim', without enough professional attention being given to how they could be supported effectively in ways that enabled them to participate fully in school life and to achieve good educational outcomes. This led to the publication of the first *Code of Practice on the Identification and Assessment of Special Educational Needs* in the early 1990s (Department for Education 1994). The code set out comprehensive statutory and non-statutory advice and guidance on many aspects of SENs, and it was aimed at education professionals in the main, including teachers, and, to a lesser extent, parents of children with SENs. However, one of its key purposes was to provide a clear support *framework for mainstream schools* to use, with a view to ensuring that integration for children with SENs would work in the future. Three new ways of making this happen were introduced.

First, a 'staged' approach to assessment and provision was introduced. This recognised that some children required a little additional support in school, and this could be provided through well differentiated teaching (stage 1). Other children required more focused support, with clearly articulated learning goals set out in an individual education plan (IEP) (stage 2), and some children warranted additional advice and support provided by specialist teachers or health or social care professionals, which would be delivered through the vehicle of an IEP (stage 3). A small number of children might require a yet more detailed assessment of their needs, leading in some instances to the drawing up of a Statement of Special Educational Needs by the local authority. Children with statements might attend mainstream or special schools. Their needs would be complex and require significant additional resourcing, for example through the provision of specialist teaching, therapy and access to specialist equipment and facilities.

Second, the introduction of IEPs, referred to above, became a formal requirement for schools. The expectation was that schools would have IEPs in place for children they assessed as needing focused teaching and support at stages 2 and 3 of the Code of Practice. IEPs would be characterised by SMART (specific, measurable, achievable, relevant, timely) target setting.

Third, all mainstream schools were required to appoint a designated teacher as SEN coordinator (SENCO). The SENCO would be responsible for the day-to-day operation of a school's SEN policy, liaising with fellow teachers, and for coordinating provision for children with SEN.

This new approach to meeting the needs of children with SENs, described here, did encourage schools and teachers to take responsibility for pupils who too often were regarded as someone else's problem (Croll and Moses 1985, Moore and Morrison 1988). However, towards the end of the 1990s, it became apparent that the code had also created new problems for mainstream schools. The introduction of a staged approach to assessment and provision led to some children simply being labelled as 'SEN stage 2 or stage 3', with teachers looking to an IEP designed and delivered by a SENCO as a teaching and learning panacea, preferably provided in a withdrawal teaching context rather than the ordinary classroom. IEPs were not having a significant impact on the learning of children either. Too often, children were given far too many imprecise targets that lacked a focus on educational outcomes. SENCOs, instead of supporting class teachers in the writing of IEPs and the monitoring of their impact on learning, often took on sole responsibility for writing all IEPs and the delivery of them. Responsibility for teaching children with SENs did not, it seems, become part of everyday practice in a lot of primary school classrooms. This was recognised by the government in research-based guidance for SENCOs (Department for Education and Employment 1997a). This research-informed advice sought to help schools and teachers take greater ownership of their SEN pupils through the use of more effective IEPs in classroom contexts (Tod, Castle and Blamires 1997). It also clarified the role of the SENCO, linking it to strategic management and collaboration with teachers, and the implementation of SEN policies designed to have a direct impact on classroom practice.

In 2001, a revised *Special Educational Needs Code of Practice* was published (Department for Education and Skills 2001). It took account of some of the difficulties that schools experienced in implementing the first code and clarified advice on the use of IEPs and the role of the SENCO. The revised code also replaced the staged approach to assessment and provision with a more action-focused, 'graduated' response. This approach to meeting the needs of pupils encouraged teachers to use an 'assess-teach-monitor-review' approach, and to use evidence from this process to decide – with a SENCO – whether a child might need either more or less support to make good educational progress. It also emphasised, in practical terms, one of the code's central messages, that *all* teachers are teachers of children with SENs.

The 2001 code is still in force today and will remain so until a new version is implemented. It is anticipated that this will be from September 2014 (subject to approval by Parliament), following the implementation of the Children and Families Act, the legislation that sets out formal SEN policy requirements that schools must adhere to. Indicative comments on new legislation and the accompanying are included in the last section of this unit.

In Northern Ireland . . .

The law dealing with special education needs in Northern Ireland is contained in the Education (Northern Ireland) Order 1996, as amended by the Special Educational Needs and Disability (Northern Ireland) Order 2005 (SENDO). The Department of Education has provided guidance for Education and Library Boards and schools in Northern Ireland in the form of a Code of Practice on the Identification and Assessment of Special Educational Needs and also a Supplement to the Code of Practice, effective from 1 September 2005, which was produced as a result of SENDO.

Source: Department of Education for Northern Ireland (DENI) (2009) *Every School a Good School: The Way Forward for Special Educational Needs and Inclusion*. Bangor, DENI.

Task 6.1.1 Supporting children with special educational needs

- What is your experience of supporting children with SENs in mainstream classes?
- Can you give an example of group or individualised support that you think worked well, or less well, for a child with SENs?

SPECIAL AND INCLUSIVE EDUCATION DEBATES

Both the current and pending versions of the Code of Practice acknowledge that mainstream and special schools have key, complementary roles to play in the education of children with SENs. This represents what might be regarded as a middle-ground policy approach, or one of significant compromise. During the latter years of the 1990s, it appeared that the government of the day was planning to adopt a more radical approach that involved a major move away from the use of special school provision (Department for Education and Employment 1997b).

In retrospect, although the government referred to international developments in inclusive schooling, and most notably the United Nations Educational, Scientific and Cultural Organisation (UNESCO) *Salamanca Statement and Framework for Action on Special Needs Education* (UNESCO 1994), it never seriously considered introducing legislation that would require *all* children with SENs to be placed in mainstream schools. By 2004, this became clear when, in a policy update publication, *Removing Barriers to Achievement: The Government's Strategy for SEN*, the following statements were made:

> Inclusion is about much more than the type of school that children attend: it is about the quality of their experience; how they are helped to learn, achieve and *participate* fully in the life of their school.
>
> (Department for Education and Skills 2004: 25; emphasis added)

In Northern Ireland . . .

Similarly Northern Ireland SEN policy states, 'inclusion is not simply about where a child is taught; it is about the quality of a child's experience of school life, including both the formal and informal curriculum, in and beyond the classroom' (DENI 2009: 8).

Source: Department of Education for Northern Ireland (DENI) (2009) *Every School a Good School: The Way Forward for Special Educational Needs and Inclusion*. Bangor, DENI.

> We want to break down the divide between mainstream and special schools to create a unified system where all schools and their pupils are included within the wider community of schools.
>
> (Department for Education and Skills 2004: 35)

The emphasis here is on participation rather than placement. It is an acknowledgement that 'inclusive' mainstream provision can be ineffective if it is only seen in terms of being the best or only place for children with SENs to be taught. Just a year later, Mary Warnock, author of the influential Warnock Report (Department of Education and Science 1978), which helped create the modern system of special education in England, went further, arguing that:

> the idea of inclusion should be rethought insofar at least as it applies to education at school. If it is too much to hope that it will be demoted from its present position at the top of the list of educational values, then at least let it be redefined so that it allows children to pursue the common goals of education in the environment within which they can best be taught and learn.
>
> (Warnock 2005: 48)

This apparent rejection of a previously held commitment to inclusion was linked to the view that small schools, and special schools in particular, should play a greater role in the education of children with SENs. Policy and provision for children needed to focus on 'a common enterprise of learning, rather than being necessarily under the same roof' (Warnock 2005: 35).

The consequences of Warnock's recantation were significant. Politicians debated the issue, and a Parliamentary inquiry (House of Commons Education and Skills Committee 2006) recommended that the government should define what it meant by inclusive education much more clearly. This debate continues today and is likely to do so for many years to come, despite the publication of the United Nations Convention on the Rights of Persons with Disabilities in 2006, which calls upon countries that have signed and ratified it to make every effort to realise the right to inclusive education (Article 24) (United Nations 2006). For example, the United Kingdom signed and ratified the Convention in 2009, but did so in a qualified way, noting that its interpretation of inclusive education recognised the role of special schools as integral to an inclusive system and the need on occasions for some children with SENs to be taught in schools outside their local communities.

Critical appraisals of the issues involved in this have been written by Cigman (2007), Norwich (2008a, 2008b), Warnock and Norwich (2010) and Slee (2011). It is important for trainee and beginning teachers to be aware of different perspectives on the organisation of education for children with SENs. This involves thinking about the complex arguments involved and recognising the wide range of views held by politicians, policymakers, parents and education professionals. At a more practical level, it is also important to consider how 'I can become an effective teacher of *all* the children I work with, including those with a special educational need'.

Task 6.1.2 'Limits' to inclusion

Drawing on your experience of working in schools, what, if any, are the 'limits' to including children with SENs in mainstream schools and classrooms? In responding to this question, consider:

- your own beliefs and values;
- practical issues.

TEACHING AND LEARNING

The current *Teachers' Standards* (Department for Education 2012) make it clear that teachers must:

- set goals that stretch and challenge pupils of *all* backgrounds, abilities and dispositions;
- be accountable for pupils' attainment, progress and outcomes;
- be aware of pupils' capabilities and their prior knowledge, and plan to build on these.

The Standards also require that teachers demonstrate good subject knowledge and, if they are teaching early reading (specifically the systematic teaching of synthetic phonics) or early mathematics, a secure grasp of appropriate teaching strategies. Put simply, teaching approaches deemed effective for the majority of primary-age children will also be appropriate to use when teaching pupils with SENs. This view has been well supported during the past 30 years, most notably in research-based books that have explored the concept of inclusive pedagogy (e.g. Hart 1996; Loreman *et al.* 2010). Other books have set out similar arguments, but linked effective classroom teaching for *all* to wider aspects of school organisation that challenge influential approaches designed to improve pupil attainment through setting, streaming and high-stakes summative testing (e.g. Corbett 2001; Swann *et al.* 2012). Reviews of SEN teaching approaches (Davis and Florian 2004; Lewis and Norwich 2005) have made it difficult to argue for the use of highly specialised (distinct, different and additional) teaching approaches, with dyslexia being a particular – and politically sensitive – case in point (Elliot 2012). Instead, and in response to the *Teachers' Standards* requirement for teachers to be able to 'respond to the strengths and needs of *all* pupils', what is important is that teachers:

- carefully differentiate, using approaches that are effective in helping pupils to learn;
- have a secure understanding of how a range of factors can inhibit pupils' ability to learn, and how best to overcome these;
- are aware of the physical, social and intellectual development of children and adapt their teaching accordingly;

- make use of and evaluate teaching approaches that engage pupils and support them, including distinctive approaches that have a proven track record in improving outcomes.

(Wording adapted from the *Teachers' Standards*, Teaching Standard 5, Department for Education 2012)

The distinctive approaches referred to here will include those set out in professional development materials linked to the Inclusion Development Programme and Advanced Training materials for Special Educational Needs and Disability, online resources targeted at improving the skills of teachers in relation to children with high-incidence SENs. Currently, some of these materials can be found at: www.idponline.org.uk. In future, they are likely to available via the National Association for Special Educational Needs (nasen) website at: www.nasen.org.uk. These resources can be used by individual teachers or a group of staff, and they focus on supporting children with: autism; dyslexia and specific learning difficulties; social, emotional and behavioural difficulties; moderate learning difficulties; and speech, language and communication needs. They were developed in response to concerns identified by the Department for Education and Skills (2004) and more recently in the Lamb Inquiry report (Lamb 2009). Both highlighted the need for teachers to be better trained to meet the SENs of children attending mainstream schools.

Alongside the development of resources designed to address a long-standing skills gap (Hartley 2010), it has increasingly become apparent that, rather than focusing solely on problems associated with the SEN 'label' or specific 'impairments' (e.g. autism, attention deficit and hyperactivity disorder, dyspraxia, dyslexia . . . the listing could go on and on), what is imperative is that teachers focus on improving educational and related outcomes for children through the use of effective interventions. Helpful guidance on literacy interventions, with both a generic and SEN focus, has recently been published (Brooks 2013). Although there is no equivalent research-informed resource focusing on mathematics, practice-focused books by Bird (2012), Chinn (2011, 2012) and Clausen-May (2005) are directly applicable to meeting the needs of children with and without SENs. Broader aspects of learning – for example, the development of motivation, confidence, memory and metacognitive skills – are also important for pupils with SENs and can be incorporated into a whole-school approach, as Reid (2007) has shown.

In a major review of SEN provision in England, Ofsted (2010) expressed a concern that too many schools used 'low attainment and relatively slow progress as the principal indicators of a special educational need'. The review called for schools and teachers to pay greater attention to supporting children to achieve better learning outcomes, and this involved having higher aspirations and making use of more appropriate interventions. Since then, the government has introduced the Pupil Premium, providing schools with additional funding to be targeted at particularly disadvantaged groups of

In Wales . . .

In Wales, it is set out, when planning for inclusion, that schools should actively seek to remove the barriers to learning and participation that can hinder or exclude pupils with additional learning needs. This includes: having key personnel in a position to drive school improvement; monitoring of learning and teaching, and promotion of effective practice; and making effective use of attainment data to improve teaching and learning.

Source: Welsh Assembly Government (WAG) (2006) *Inclusion and Pupil Support*. Cardiff: WAG. http://wales.gov.uk/dcells/publications/policy_strategy_and_planning/schools/inclusion andpupilsupport/guidance/introduction/introductioninclusionpupil2.pdf?lang=en

children. Most notably, this funding is aimed at improving the attainment of children who are entitled to free school meals, and this includes a high number of children who also have SENs. Again, the focus is on matching interventions to the needs of children. Too often, it seems, interventions have been used without any serious reflection on their impact. To address this concern, the Education Endowment Foundation (2013) has developed a 'toolkit' of interventions with the aim of helping schools and teachers to consider carefully in relation to impact and cost (value for money). Some of these interventions may be used to support children with SENs. Some may be used to support other vulnerable groups of children, and others as school-wide approaches to improving attainment.

It is worth noting that children with SENs can be particularly susceptible to having some particularly odd or ineffective interventions incorporated into their learning experiences. Some of these (for example, teaching approaches based on simplistic, and sometimes downright wacky, interpretations of neuroscience) are discussed in a thought-provoking, edited book by Adey and Dillon (2012).

Task 6.1.3 Interventions

Look at the interventions included in the Teaching and Learning Toolkit. This can be found at: educationendowmentfoundation.org.uk/toolkit

- Consider how these are being used in your school to help children with special educational needs.
- Are they making a positive difference, in your view? If not, what interventions do you think could be more effective?

COLLABORATIVE SUPPORT

Trainee and beginning teachers can sometimes feel isolated and overwhelmed when presented with the familiar mantra 'all teachers are teachers of children with special educational needs'. Although this unit is clear in saying that this is the case, teachers should always have access to the advice and support of a trained SENCO. The SENCO in a primary school takes lead responsibility for SEN provision. An increasing number of SENCOs are members of school leadership teams and many have designated 'non-contact' time to enable them to carry out most or all of the following responsibilities:

- overseeing the day-to-day operation of the school's SEN policy;
- coordinating provision for children with SENs;
- liaising with, advising and contributing to the in-service training of fellow teachers and other staff;
- liaising with the relevant designated teacher where a looked-after pupil has SENs;
- advising on a graduated approach to providing additional SEN support;
- ensuring that records of all children with SENs are kept up to date (to support plans and decisions made in relation to individual children);
- liaising with parents of children with SENs;
- liaising with early years providers and secondary schools, educational psychologists, and health, social care and independent or voluntary bodies who may be providing SEN support and advice to a child and their family;
- being a key point of contact with external agencies, especially the local authority and local authority support services;

- liaising with potential next providers of education to ensure a child and their parents are informed about options and a smooth transition is planned;
- collaborating with curriculum coordinators so that the learning for all children is given equal priority;
- ensuring with the head teacher and school governors that the school meets its responsibilities under the Equality Act 2010 with regard to reasonable adjustments and access arrangements.

(Adapted from Department for Education 2013)

This detailed listing of SENCO responsibilities highlights the importance of the role. It also sets out expectations of the SENCO for trainee and beginning teachers. They can expect, as an entitlement, to access regular advice and support from the SENCO in their school. This also means that teachers should actively seek guidance and help whenever they feel that they need it. The role of the SENCO is likely to become even more important in the future, as mainstream primary schools take on greater responsibility for SEN pupils than ever before (Robertson 2012). It is also worth noting here that a growing number of beginning teachers take on the role of SENCO within the first few years of their careers and complete the mandatory National Award for Special Educational Needs Coordination.

Another challenge that many trainee and beginning teachers encounter is the deployment of teaching assistants to support children's learning and other needs effectively. The role of teaching assistants has come under close scrutiny in recent years, and major substantive research by Blatchford *et al.* (2012) has shown that providing additional support for pupils with SENs can be counter-productive and lead to poorer educational outcomes. In a primary phase-specific study of adult support for children with Statements of SENs (for children with moderate learning difficulties and behavioural, emotional and social difficulties), Webster and Blatchford (2013) found that the role of teaching assistants could actually create a barrier between the child receiving support and the person with lead responsibility for her or his learning, the class teacher. Unfortunately, these significant research findings have been wilfully misinterpreted by some commentators, who argue that they point to the need for schools to stop employing teaching assistants (Robertson 2013). Others, including the Education Endowment Foundation referred to in the previous section, have argued a little too simplistically about the lack of impact that teaching assistants make, without considering more complex commentaries written by the authors of key research studies. In fact, as Russell *et al.* (2012) are careful to note, the real challenge is for school leaders, SENCOs and teachers to examine how best they can optimise the skills of teaching assistants, with a clear focus on teaching. Trainee and beginning teachers have a role to play, bringing new and fresh ideas of their own to discussions. However, they may also seek advice on teaching assistant deployment from SENCOs, other teachers with responsibility for this deployment and, of course, from experienced and effective teaching assistants themselves.

Trainee and beginning teachers can sometimes feel daunted by the prospect of working 'in partnership' with parents of children with SENs. This is not surprising, given that some parents may, for a variety of reasons, have concerns about their child that might be expressed in terms of what can be perceived as blaming the teacher or school. Reading the Lamb Inquiry report on parental experiences of the special educational system in England (Lamb 2009) helps to explain why some parents can feel angry or upset about provision for their child, the lack of it, or bureaucratic assessment procedures. It is also worth noting, however, that relatively straightforward approaches to honest communication can be used by teachers, SENCOs and head teachers to make a positive difference to the education of children with SENs, as Robertson (2010) and Laluvein (2010) make clear. For trainee and beginning teachers, it is important that they are directly supported when liaising with families of children with SENs.

Task 6.1.4 SENCO support

- Can you identify ways in which a SENCO you have worked with has been able to support you in your work with children with SENs?
- If support has not been provided or has been ineffective, can you think about why this has been the case. For example, has the SENCO been fully timetabled with class teaching commitments?
- Consider how a teaching assistant you have worked with has made a positive difference to the education of a child or group of children with SENs.
- Finally, can you give an example of a parent/carer who has helped you to understand the difficulties in learning that their child experiences? How has this informed your teaching?

A NEW SEN LANDSCAPE

Earlier in this unit, it was noted that new SEN legislation is due to be implemented in England from September 2014. The rationale for this legislation, associated regulations and a new Special Educational Needs Code of Practice, was set out in a Government Green Paper, *Support and Aspiration: A New Approach to Special Educational Needs* (Department for Education 2011). It is beyond the scope of this unit to outline forthcoming changes to SEN policy, procedures and provision, because definitive statutory and non-statutory advice and guidance have not yet been published. However, drawing on ideas set out in *Support and Aspiration*, it is clear that the government wants to improve the SEN system and considers that it is necessary to do so, because, under the current system, too many parents of children and young people with SENs, and professionals who support them, experience frustration when it comes to providing services in a timely and effective way. The government is also concerned that too many pupils with SENs achieve poor educational and life outcomes.

With these concerns in mind, we can expect a new SENs system to be introduced in England from September 2014 onwards. Key features of this system are likely to include the following:

- a stronger requirement (with a duty set out in law) for education, health and social care services to work in partnership to support children and their families across the 0–25 age range;
- the introduction of a new approach to identifying SENs in early years and school settings as soon as a child's difficulties become apparent;
- replacement of School Action and School Action Plus 'categories' of SENs with a new, school-based, level of SEN support that emphasises the importance of using delegated special needs funding effectively through the use of targeted intervention programmes;
- outcomes-focused advice that encourages schools to make their own decisions about approaches to support and intervention, without needing to use IEPs;
- a new single assessment process leading to an Education and Health Care Plan (EHCP) to replace current SEN assessment procedures and the provision of statements for children with more complex needs;
- the setting out by all local authorities of a local offer of SEN services available to support children with SENs and disabilities – developed in partnership with parents and children and young people – and made available in easy-to-understand formats;
- a stronger role for schools (including academy and free schools) in determining their local offer to children with SENs and their parents;

- the option of using personal budget for parents of children eligible for EHCPs to enable them to purchase personalised services and resources;
- a greater choice of schools for parents, so that they can decide whether they wish their child to attend a mainstream or special school setting.

Some of new features of the SEN system are already piloted in different areas of England through the work of government-funded Special Educational Needs and Disability Pathfinder projects. Information about these projects can be found at: www.sendpathfinder.co.uk. The progress of the Pathfinders is being carefully evaluated and should inform the final and definitive proposals for a new SEN system.

The possible implications of a new SEN policy framework for mainstream schools and SENCOs have been appraised by Robertson (2012). This appraisal is, of course, tentative, and it is more important for trainee and beginning teachers to be alert to the publication of the definitive version of the new Special Educational Needs Code of Practice. In the past, the code has often been regarded as 'essential reading' for SENCOs, but not for other teachers in primary schools. Given that the code will make it clear that mainstream schools and all teachers working in them will have greater responsibility – within a new legal framework – with regard to meeting the needs of children with SENs, reading it should no longer be optional.

Task 6.1.5 Special Educational Needs Code of Practice

When the final version of the new *Special Educational Needs (SEN) Code of Practice: for 0 to 25 years* (provisional title) is published in Spring 2014 (subject to Parliamentary approval), do make sure that you have access to a copy. The Code, due to be implemented from 1 September 2014, sets out essential statutory guidance and advice for teachers and other stakeholders with an interest in special education. It will be available to read online or download at: www.education.gov.uk.

Make sure that you read the introduction and the summary sections that set out the principles underpinning the Code. Then read the chapters that set out guidance and advice on: a family-centred system, the local offer and the role of schools.

SUMMARY

The vast majority of primary-age pupils who may have an SEN are taught in mainstream schools. During the past 30 years, a systematic approach has been developed to identify and carefully assess this group of children. At the current time, this approach is based on principles, advice and guidance set out in the 2001 *Special Educational Needs Code of Practice* (Department for Education and Skills 2001). The code has been very useful in helping schools and teachers to meet the needs of children with SENs through carefully planned individual teaching arrangements that are provided within the ordinary classroom or on a withdrawal basis. Too often, however, these teaching arrangements have also been shown to be ineffective: for example, when a teacher relies solely on the support of a teaching assistant to work with a child, instead of taking lead responsibility her or himself;

or when a teacher, or school as a whole, identifies significant numbers of children in terms of 'special educational needs', without ensuring first that good classroom teaching is being offered to all children in a setting.

With these concerns in mind, new SEN legislation is due to be introduced in England from September 2014, and primary school teachers can expect to be working with an entirely new Special Educational Needs Code of Practice. This will strengthen requirements for schools and teachers to identify and assess the needs of all their pupils effectively. It will also emphasise the importance of putting the right interventions in place for the right pupils at the right time, and ensuring that the outcomes of these are monitored and evaluated.

The emphasis on outcomes does not mean that trainee or beginning teachers will be left alone to meet the needs of all children with SENs in their classes. Yes, they should expect to teach children with a diverse range of needs, but they should do so with the support of a collaborative, whole-school approach to SENs. This will involve a close working relationship with the school's SENCO and its teaching assistants, and a positive approach to working with parents of children who may be experiencing difficulties in learning. This shared approach to responsibility will be premised on a commitment to meeting the needs of children with SENs in the ordinary classroom wherever this is possible, but variants to this type of provision may make good educational sense, as long as these do not lead to unnecessary or prolonged forms of separation for some pupils.

 # ANNOTATED FURTHER READING

Adey, P. and Dillon, J. (eds) (2012) *Bad Education: Debunking Myths in Education*, Maidenhead: Open University Press.

> This edited book is *not* about SENs. However, its themes of school organisation, teaching methods and learners all have a direct bearing on the education experienced by children with SENs. Chapters on grouping, teaching assistants, social and emotional intervention programmes, learning styles, intelligence and neuroscience all have implications for teachers for the practice of special education. Readers should be prepared to discover that some established 'theories' that inform school organisational and pedagogic practice do not stand up to scrutiny.

Boyle, C. and Topping, K. (eds) (2012) *What Works in Inclusion*, Maidenhead: Open University Press.

> This edited text looks closely at the practice of inclusive education, focusing on the reality of school life and factors that enable teachers have a positive impact on the learning of children and young people with a wide range of special and additional needs.

Elliott, J. and Place, M. (2011) *Children in Difficulty: A Guide to Understanding and Helping*, 3rd edn, London: Routledge.

> This book presents thoughtful and positive insights into the experiences of a range of children and young people who may experience difficulties during their education. These include children with eating disorders, attention difficulties and problems of compliance. The authors draw on extensive research evidence to help teachers understand difficulties experienced by children, and their framework for 'helping' children is well worth using.

Ellis, S., Tod, J. and Graham-Matheson, L. (2012) *Reflection, Renewal and Reality: Teachers' Experience of Special Educational Needs and Inclusion*, Birmingham: NASUWT.

> This highly readable research report is unusual in reporting the experiences and views of over 1,500 teachers on the realities of teaching children with SENs in a wide range of school settings. Key

themes include: working with government policy; training, support and development needs; the deployment of support staff; behaviour and special educational needs; local authority and other external support.

FORUM (2013) 'This way out: teachers and pupils escaping from fixed-ability thinking and practice', *FORUM*, Special Issue, 55(1).

> This special issue of the journal is well worth reading as a whole. It includes fifteen articles that explore and challenge many of the assumptions and practices associated with school improvement and effectiveness. Some of these address issues pertaining to SENs, and others explore broader aspects of schooling. The articles make excellent use of evidence to illustrate how schooling could be both different and better.

Frederickson, N. and Cline, T. (2009) *Special Educational Needs, Inclusion and Diversity: A Textbook*, 2nd edn, Maidenhead: Open University Press.

> This book (the 2nd edition) provides a comprehensive discussion of special education, with particular reference to the UK (England). It looks in detail at the needs of a wide range of pupils with SENs and outlines practical strategies for effective and inclusive classroom practice. It also 'signposts' a wide array of useful further reading and resources.

Runswick-Cole, B. and Hodge, N. (2009) 'Needs or rights? A challenge to the discourse of special education', *British Journal of Special Education*, 36(4), 198–203.

> This article is interesting in the way that it makes use of Reggio Emilia approaches to education in Northern Italy. In doing so, the authors reject the term special education, preferring Reggio Emilia's use of the term rights, and arguing that, by adopting its use, we might develop less exclusionary practices in our schools and related settings.

FURTHER READING TO SUPPORT M-LEVEL STUDY

Armstrong, D. and Squires, G. (eds) (2012) *Contemporary Issues in Special Educational Needs: Considering the Whole Child*, Maidenhead: Open University Press.

> This edited book offers clear and challenging insights into key aspects of special education, in terms of its conceptualisation, provision and practice. Its up-to-date content includes chapters that can be read as stand-alone introductions to 'big issues' that will continue to inform debates about the nature of effective policy and the impact of this on children, young people and their families.

Slee, R. (2013) 'How do we make inclusive education happen when exclusion is a political predisposition', *International Journal of Inclusive Education*, 17(8), 895–907.

> In this article, Roger Slee examines the struggle for inclusive education in international contexts. He discusses past and present challenges to inclusion, its failures and successes. He argues that we can and should continue the struggle for inclusion, but that we need to do so with a clear focus on broader democratic reform of schooling.

RELEVANT WEBSITES

National Association for Special Educational Needs: www.nasen.org.uk

> The National Association for Special Educational Needs (nasen) website includes information for a wide range of education professionals working with children who have special educational needs. It includes a members area, but a lot of the material on the site is available to non-members. During 2014, nasen will be launching, with government support, a new online SEN Gateway, and this will be accessible via its website. The aim of the gateway is to provide a 'one-stop shop' that provides high-quality information, resources and training.

Council for Disabled Children: www.councilfordisabledchildren.org.uk/what-we-do/strategic-reform-partner-work

> The Council for Disabled Children (CDC) is the government's named strategic partner in the planning

and implementation of SEN reforms in England. From September 2014, it is anticipated that new SEN legislation, supported with a new SEN Code of Practice, will be implemented. The CDC website provides regular and accurate updates on changes taking place and how these will impact on education professionals, parents, children and young people.

Optimus Education: www.optimus-education.com/hubs/special-educational-needs-hub

Optimus Education runs a successful online SEN hub. Access is via subscription and provides information about all aspects of SEN policy, practice and provision. The hub also includes case study material and downloadable resources.

 # REFERENCES

Adey, P. and Dillon, J. (eds) (2012) *Bad Education: Debunking Myths in Education*, Maidenhead: Open University Press.

Bird, R. (2012) *The Dyscalculia Toolkit: Supporting Learning Difficulties in Maths*, London: Sage.

Blatchford, P., Russell, A. and Webster, R. (2012) *Reassessing the Impact of Teaching Assistants*, London: Routledge.

Brooks, G. (2013) *What Works for Children and Young People with Literacy Difficulties*, 4th edn, The Dyslexia-SpLD Trust; see: www.interventionsforliteracy.org.uk.

Chinn, S. (2011) *The Trouble with Maths: A Practical Guide to Helping Learners with Numeracy Difficulties*, London: Routledge (David Fulton/nasen).

Chinn, S. (2012) *More Trouble with Maths: A Practical Guide to Helping Learners with Numeracy Difficulties*, London: Routledge (David Fulton/nasen).

Cigman, R. (ed.) (2007) *Included or Excluded: The Challenge of the Mainstream for Some SEN Children*, London: Routledge.

Clausen-May, T. (2005) *Teaching Maths to Pupils with Different Learning Styles*, London: Paul Chapman.

Corbett, J. (2001) *Supporting Inclusive Education: An Inclusive Pedagogy*, London: RoutledgeFalmer.

Croll, P. and Moses, D. (1985) *One in Five: The Assessment and Incidence of Special Educational Needs*, London: Routledge and Kegan Paul.

Davis, P. and Florian, L. (2004) *Teaching Strategies and Approaches for Pupils with SEN: A Scoping Study*, Research Briefing RB516, Nottingham: DfES.

Department for Education (1994) *Code of Practice on the Identification and Assessment of Special Educational Needs*, London: DfE.

Department for Education (2011) *Support and Aspiration: A New Approach to Special Educational Needs and Disability*, London/Norwich: The Stationery Office.

Department for Education (2012) *Teachers' Standards*, London: DfE; available for download at: www.education.gov.uk.

Department for Education (2013) *Indicative Draft: The 0-25 Special Educational Needs Code of Practice*, London: DfE.

Department for Education and Employment (1997a) *The SENCO Guide: Good Practice for SENCOs; Individual Education Plans; Developing Effective SEN Policies in Schools*, London: DfEE.

Department for Education and Employment (1997b) *Excellence for All Children: Meeting Special Educational Needs*, London: The Stationery Office.

Department for Education and Skills (2001) *Special Educational Needs Code of Practice*, Nottingham: DfES Publications.

Department for Education and Skills (2004) *Removing Barriers to Achievement: The Government's Strategy for SEN*, Nottingham: DfES Publications.

Department of Education and Science (1978) *Special Educational Needs: Report of the Committee of Enquiry into the Education of Handicapped Children and Young People* (Warnock Report), London: HMSO.

Education Endowment Foundation (2013) *Teaching and Learning* Toolkit; see: http://educationendowment foundation.org.uk/toolkit.

Elliott, J. (2012) 'The dyslexia debate', in P. Adey and J.Dillon (eds) *Debunking Myths in Education*, Maidenhead: Open University Press.

Hart, S. (1996) *Beyond Special Needs: Enhancing Children's Learning Through Innovative Thinking*, London: Paul Chapman Publishing.

Hartley, R. (2010) *Teacher Expertise for Special Educational Needs: Filling the Gaps*, London: Policy Exchange; see: www.policyexchange.org.uk

House of Commons Education and Skills Committee (2006) *Special Educational Needs: Third Report of Session 2005-06*, Vol. 1 (HC 478-1), London: The Stationery Office.

Laluvein, J. (2010) 'Variations on a theme: parents and teachers talking', *Support for Learning*, 25(4), 194-9.

Lamb, B. (2009) *Lamb Inquiry: Special Educational Needs and Parental Confidence*, Nottingham: DCSF Publications.

Lewis, A. and Norwich, B. (2005) *Special Teaching for Special Children? Pedagogies for Inclusion*, Maidenhead: Open University Press.

Loreman, T., Deppeler, J. and Harvey, D. (2010) *Inclusive Education: Supporting Diversity in the Classroom*, London: Routledge.

Moore, J. and Morrison, N. (1988) *Someone Else's Problem: Teacher Development to Meet Special Educational Needs*, London: Falmer Press.

Norwich, B. (2008a) *Dilemmas of Difference, Inclusion and Disability: International Perspectives and Future Directions*, London: Routledge.

Norwich, B. (2008b) 'What future for special schools and inclusion? Conceptual and professional challenges', *British Journal of Special Education*, 35(3), 136-43.

Ofsted (2010) *The Special Educational Needs and Disability Review: A Statement is Not Enough*, London: Ofsted.

Reid, G. (2007) *Motivating Learners in the Classroom: Ideas and Strategies*, London: Paul Chapman.

Robertson, C. (2010) 'Working in partnership with parents', in F. Hallett and G. Hallett *Transforming the Role of the SENCO: Achieving the National Award for SEN Coordination*, Maidenhead: Open University Press.

Robertson, C. (2012) 'Special educational needs and disability co-ordination in a changing policy landscape: making sense of policy from a SENCO's perspective', *Support for Learning*, 27(2), 77-83.

Robertson, C. (2013) 'Future of teaching assistants: let's wilfully misinterpret the evidence', *SENCO Update*, 147(July), 6.

Russell, A., Webster, R. and Blatchford, P. (2012) *Maximising the Impact of Teaching Assistants: Guidance for School Leaders and Teachers*, London: Routledge.

Slee, R. (2011) *The Irregular School: Exclusion, Schooling and Inclusive Education*, London: Routledge.

Swann, M., Peacock, M., Drummond, M.J. and Hart, S. (2012) *Creating Learning Without Limits*, Maidenhead: Open University Press.

Tod, J., Castle, F. and Blamires, M. (1997) *Individual Education Plans: Implementing Effective Practice*, London: David Fulton.

UNESCO (1994) *The Salamanca Statement and Framework for Action on Special Needs Education*. Adopted by the World Conference on Special Needs Education: Access and Quality. Paris: UNESCO.

United Nations (2006) *Convention on the Rights of Persons with Disabilities*; see: www.un.org/disabilities.

Warnock, M. (2005) *Special Educational Needs: A New Look*, London: Philosophy of Education Society of Great Britain.

Warnock, M. and Norwich, B., with Terzi, L. (ed.) (2010) *Special Educational Needs: A New Look*, 2nd edn, London: Continuum.

Webster, R. and Blatchford, P. (2013) *The Making a Statement Project Final Report: A Study of the Teaching and Support Experienced by Pupils with a Statement of Special Educational Needs in Mainstream Primary Schools*; see: www.schoolsupportstaff.net/mast.html.

PROVIDING FOR DIFFERENTIATION

Eve Bearne and Rebecca Kennedy

INTRODUCTION

Differentiation is one of those 'iceberg' terms in teaching – what you see on the surface covers something much bigger. However, not only does it have underlying complexities, it is also one of those concepts that teachers assume 'everyone knows' the meaning of. The DfE *Teachers' Standards* document states that a teacher must 'adapt teaching to respond to the strengths and needs of all pupils', knowing 'when and how to differentiate appropriately, using approaches which enable pupils to be taught effectively' (Department for Education, 2012: 8). This is all well and good, but there is no clear consensus about what the term means and implies. It is linked in many teachers' minds with 'mixed ability teaching', but there is still considerable debate about what it might look like in the classroom and just what 'ability' is. Some place greater emphasis on curriculum provision, whereas others see differentiation as more linked with individual progress. Most recently, differentiation has been linked with narrowing the gaps between the achievements of different groups of learners. The Ofsted framework for school inspection points out that: 'When evaluating the achievement of pupils, inspectors consider how well . . . gaps are narrowing between the performance of different groups of pupils, both in the school and in comparison to those of all pupils nationally' (Ofsted, 2012b: 18).

However, as well as seeing the progress of specific groups as important, this includes an awareness of individual pupils' needs: 'The most successful schools were those that had identified the particular needs of their pupils and then designed a distinctive curriculum to meet those needs' (Ofsted, 2011: 5).

As with many classroom issues, the answer often lies in the combination of providing a suitable curriculum to ensure progression for all learners, while catering for the needs and experiences of individuals.

OBJECTIVES

By the end of this unit, you should be able to:

- see the links between differentiation, diversity and difference;
- understand the importance of providing a differentiated approach to the curriculum for a diverse range of learners;
- understand the main approaches to differentiation;
- develop some practical strategies to provide differentiated approaches to learning.

So what does differentiation look like? Figures 6.2.1-4 show examples of how some teachers see differentiation.

Figure 6.2.1 shows how learning objectives relate to individuals. The teacher describes this as 'making one thing accessible to all, through an acknowledgement of different learning styles and experiences and a knowledge of individuals' "baseline" knowledge and skills'.

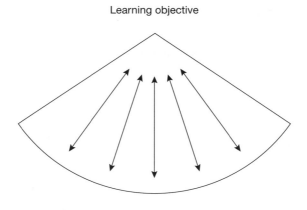

FIGURE 6.2.1 Description of differentiation – teacher 1

Figure 6.2.2 shows three different ways of reaching a learning destination. The teacher came across this in an in-service session and felt it aptly summarised her views. Route A is by bus, where the passenger depends on the driver; Route B shows how a traveller might choose between a range of different vehicles; in Route C, the traveller gets to the destination in her or his own way. The teacher writes: 'The transport enables all students to access the curriculum through means which suit their individual needs.'

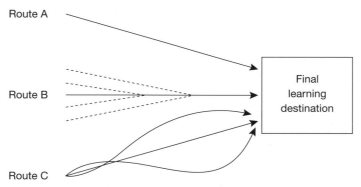

FIGURE 6.2.2 Description of differentiation – teacher 2

Figure 6.2.3 shows a swimming pool. The teacher writes: 'Differentiation is ensuring that every child can find their depth in every lesson but also challenging them to swim. If we don't support/encourage child A to take chances, [he or] she will never leave the shallows.'

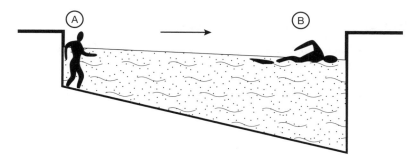

FIGURE 6.2.3 Description of differentiation – teacher 3

Figure 6.2.4 shows something like a fairground carousel, with pupils on the ride. The teacher explains:

> At the top of the central pole are the teacher's expectations for the unit, lesson etc. The teacher controls the ride to ensure the pupils are supported and able to succeed but each child's ride is slightly different and their experiences may be different. There are points around the ride which mark where each learner is but they are all on the continuum/progression to reach the highest central point. The teacher acts to control and bring it all together with the use of differentiation and a common goal.

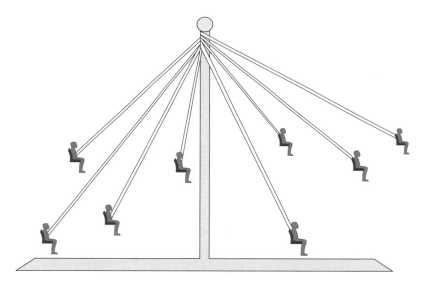

FIGURE 6.2.4 Description of differentiation – teacher 4

The first teacher emphasises providing for the different qualities, knowledge and experiences of every learner, while aiming for common learning objectives for all; the second recognises the importance of developing pupils' independence and creativity; the third sees it as important to create an environment that allows learners to feel secure enough to push themselves further; and the fourth acknowledges the teacher's central role in helping all children achieve. These descriptions indicate the variations that experienced teachers may have in mind as they consider differentiation. They also share a concern to provide for individual differences within a common curriculum.

Task 6.2.1 Describing differentiation

What does differentiation mean to you? How would you depict it? Draw a sketch or diagram and write a few words of explanation to describe differentiation. You might then compare your ideas with others in your group and with the examples in Figures 6.2.1–4 and discuss with your tutor the range of descriptions of differentiation gathered by the group. A group list would be a good starting point for a definition.

DIFFERENTIATION, DIFFERENCE AND DIVERSITY

In general terms, differentiation is about how far the curriculum is appropriate for groups of learners with particular needs. This does not only mean considering special educational needs (SEN), including the group defined as gifted and talented, but takes into account the differences between what a young learner at the Foundation Stage may need, in contrast to an appropriate curriculum for pupils at Key Stage 2. Such a general approach would also consider differences between schools, settings and their communities. For example, a school where there are many multilingual pupils will adjust its curriculum to make the most of its linguistic diversity; or a school where pupils have to travel long distances may adopt specific approaches to home–school liaison. In this general sense, differentiation means providing an appropriate curriculum, within national guidelines, for the particular school. In its more specific usage, differentiation refers to provision of learning opportunities and activities for individuals in particular classrooms. This often includes a concept of 'matching' the task or activity to the child's experience, knowledge and skills.

Ofsted emphasises educational attainment and the need to provide for different groups of pupils to reach national standards, but it is worth being cautious about categorisations of the 'differences' between learners. Ainscow *et al.* (2007: 9) argue that 'differences are never neutral', as descriptions of learners are necessarily constructed according to prevailing educational values. Recently, for example, attention has been given to children in receipt of free school meals (Department for Education, 2011), but these children do not necessarily comprise a 'group' in terms of provision for learning:

> Children entitled to free school meals (FSM) encompass the full spectrum of needs and backgrounds in the school community, including white and minority ethnic pupils, looked after children, gifted and talented (G&T) children and those with special educational needs (SEN).
> (Department for Children, Schools and Families, 2009: 7)

Similarly, attention has been given to boys' 'under-achievement' (see Unit 6.5), but, again, neither 'boys' nor 'girls' comprise undifferentiated groups.

There are, of course, many links between differentiation and inclusion. The Ofsted inspection framework includes a requirement to evaluate: 'the extent to which schools provide an inclusive environment which meets the needs of all pupils, irrespective of age, disability, gender reassignment, race, religion or belief, sex, or sexual orientation' (Ofsted, 2012b: 13), whereas Ainscow and Sandill (2010) argue that inclusive education is: 'increasingly seen more broadly as a reform that supports and welcomes diversity amongst all learners' (Ainscow and Sandill, 2010: 401-2).

However, whereas inclusion is largely concerned with equity in terms of individual rights and curriculum entitlement, differentiation focuses on the management of teaching and learning, including:

- identifying pupils' knowledge, experience, skills and learning preferences;
- planning for a variety of ways in to learning;
- classroom organisation for learning;
- using resources (material and human);
- response to the outcomes of activities or units of work and assessment of achievement in order to plan for future learning.

The Education Reform Act 1988 legislated for every pupil's entitlement to a curriculum that is broad, balanced, relevant and 'subtly' differentiated. In 1992, the National Curriculum Council referred to providing a curriculum suitable for 'differences in the abilities, aptitudes and needs of individual pupils' (National Curriculum Council, 1992: 67). Twenty years later, Ofsted (2012a) noted that the most effective lessons were characterised by, among other qualities, 'differentiation used effectively to ensure that activities and teaching were matched to pupils' specific learning needs' (Ofsted, 2012a: 19). The DfE expects teachers to 'adapt teaching to respond to the strengths and needs of all pupils' and to 'use and evaluate distinctive teaching approaches to engage and support them' (Department for Education, 2012: 8).

In addition, a teacher must 'set goals that stretch and challenge pupils of all backgrounds, abilities and dispositions' (Department for Education, 2012: 8). However, taking account of difference and diversity is complex. In addition to acknowledging that learners may use a range of approaches according to the task/context and/or time of day, differentiation that genuinely allows for diversity needs to consider:

- differences in learning approaches, strategies or preferences;
- the time individuals take to complete tasks;
- particular strengths and difficulties in some areas of the curriculum;
- physical and medical differences;
- variations in fluency of English, which may not be the first or home language;
- the range of previous experiences brought to the classroom.

Providing for the needs of different learners means having some sense of where they are in their learning at any specific time. This, in turn, implies having some sense of where you want them to be, so that, before planning for any unit of work or series of activities, the teacher will need to have a clear idea of learning objectives. This will need to be accompanied by useful pupil records of progress, so that the learning can be matched to individuals or groups. Grouping pupils is common classroom practice, but the reasons for grouping have to be clear. Some activities require grouping pupils according to their common achievements, for example in guided reading, where grouping is determined by a perceived common level of reading competence. At other times, teachers will opt for 'mixed ability' groups.

Grouping pupils can be trickier than it may at first appear, as, even if learners can be grouped according to common qualities, they may not form genuinely homogeneous groups. It is by no means a simple matter to group according to ability, because it begs the question 'ability in what?'. There is a danger in making generalised judgements. It is all too easy to assume that someone who has difficulty with spelling, or reading or mathematics is 'less able'. Such convenient definitions are best avoided; they are inaccurate and misleading and, in the end, give no help to either teacher or pupil. It is better to be precise and to describe the skills rather than the pupil, for example 'less fluent in reading; accurate in mental mathematics'.

Not only does each person's 'ability' vary according to the task or curriculum area, it also varies according to what the teacher makes it possible for the pupil to achieve. Observing pupils at work – in physical education (PE), art, design and technology, or as they work on-screen together – and listening to their talk in science or maths, for example, can reveal a great deal about the learning

Task 6.2.2 Reflecting on your own abilities

Think about your own 'abilities'. Are you good at everything? Some people are very good at spatial awareness in team sports, whereas others read music fluently. Some find mental calculations easy; some are good at constructing 3D objects; some express ideas elegantly through dance; others are successful at solving abstract problems.

- What are your strengths? What areas of your learning need, or have needed, support? Make a few notes, then compare your reflections with others in your group.
- How diverse are you as a group of learners? Discuss with your tutor the implications this diversity has for planning teaching and learning.

strengths and needs of particular pupils. Such observations help to provide descriptions of what learners can do that avoid unhelpful labels and overgeneralisations.

IDENTIFYING THE RANGE OF LEARNERS

Over the last 20 years, perhaps primarily because of the work of Howard Gardner on multiple intelligences (Gardner, 1993, 1999), there has been considerable attention paid to learning styles. This concept is at one and the same time seductive (how neat to be able to categorise the learning styles of our pupils and so teach accordingly) and misleading, as many of the most popular instruments and models vary: in intended application (many were developed for industry); in theoretical underpinning; and in the extent to which they can be considered reliable, as Coffield puts it: 'the research field of learning styles is theoretically incoherent and conceptually confused' (Coffield, 2012: 220). As with any categorisation, there are dangers. Labelling pupils may not be helpful, as this can take attention away from teaching approaches and the importance of learning contexts. Added to that, categorisations can ignore the fact that many learners use a variety of approaches to learning, according to circumstances, prior learning and experience and what is on offer in terms of teaching. Coffield (2012) also quotes John White, Emeritus Professor of Philosophy of Education at the Institute of Education, on the potential dangers of 'a new type of stereotyping' (White, 2005, cited in Coffield, 2012: 222).

Rather than seeing qualities as fixed, like the colour of one's eyes, it is better to take account of diversity in planning for teaching, but also to aim to extend the range of learning approaches through specific teaching and discussing learning with the learners themselves.

Differences in learning approaches, strategies or preferences

From the readings in Task 6.2.3, it is evident that it is important to see learners as individuals, with particular strengths and preferences. Some may approach learning by taking in whole concepts and then attending to detail, whereas others build from detail to broad concepts. The versatile learner is the one who has been able to develop both kinds of learning to fit specific purposes. Some learners show more of a tendency to take intellectual risks in learning, while others are much more cautious, at least at first. Although learners may show a predisposition towards more innovative or more speculative approaches, education should help them to decide when it is better to be adventurous and when it is better to be more carefully decisive. It is important to remember that no approach is necessarily 'better' than another. As Hargreaves points out (2005: 20), a key aim for educators is to help develop independence in learners.

Task 6.2.3 Learning styles

Read the chapter, 'Learning styles: unreliable, invalid and impractical and yet still widely used', by Frank Coffield (2012), or the free download *About Learning* (2005), edited by David Hargreaves, available at: www.demos.co.uk/files/About_learning.pdf?1240939425 (accessed 12 May 2013).

- What are the implications for your own classroom practice?
- How might you cater for children's different approaches to learning without being too narrowly categorical about 'styles'?
- How might you develop a vocabulary to talk about learning with pupils?

Task 6.2.4 Identifying learning preferences

Have a look at these comments on their own learning made by a range of 9- and 10-year-olds. What do they tell you about their learning preferences?

- I worked it out by thinking about what we'd done last time.
- I can't be bothered to work out all those fiddly bits.
- I like to find out all the facts from the Internet.
- Being under pressure helps me to learn.
- It helps me if I know what to do.
- We've been shown how to do different investigations so I use the best way of doing it.
- I like maths when things are hard.
- I have a big board of words in my mind that I know how to spell.
- I like to make models and inventions.
- I like trying things out . . . I don't like being interrupted when I've got a good idea.
- I want to learn how to be a good social person; a good group would be a boff, two friends and me.
- If it's got writing on it, I'll read it.

You may find it tricky to tie some of these down. That is perfectly understandable and simply serves to demonstrate the problems of trying to make hard and fast categorisations of learners. However, they should help you discuss with your tutor the issues about 'learning styles'. It also offers a chance to consider how to move young learners towards independence, taking account of their different strengths and struggles.

Pupils' particular strengths and difficulties

Specific strengths or difficulties with learning can often be associated with pupils who give cause for concern. This can be because the pupil's learning may not be thriving, or because the teacher feels that more could be done to support or extend particular learners. 'Cause for concern' may include pupils with statements of SEN, but it can be wider than that. One teacher describes the range of pupils giving cause for concern:

Alex struggles with writing. He often spends a lot of time thinking about what he has to write and the result is that very little ends up on the paper. Sometimes it can take an hour to get one sentence on the paper. He is a sensitive boy with a vivid imagination and good memory. So the ideas are there, but he seems to stumble with the writing and doesn't see the urgency of writing.

Rehan is very hard working, always completes homework, is reticent in class but written work is of a very high standard. He needs to be extended and challenged intellectually.

Jo is an avid learner of facts – knows all the names, habits and habitats of birds – but does not have any friends in the class and so it's difficult to set up collaborative activities. Also, although reading is fluent, I'm not sure how much reading between the lines goes on.

Kris is bright and attentive and reads a lot but written work is neat and 'safe'.

A 'special educational need' can mean catering for those who enjoy learning and excel, or who might be described as being gifted and talented in some aspects of learning, as well as those who struggle.

Identifying pupils who might be described as gifted and talented is an aspect of diversity that has come to prominence over the last few years. Unit 7.5 provides an overview, but, to ensure these pupils are not forgotten when thinking about differentiation, they are also noted here. Very able children often show outstanding potential or ability in one area or in several or all areas of the curriculum. This might not be in traditional academic learning, but could be in physical, creative, spatial, mechanical or technical learning. Pupils' abilities could be so well developed that they operate significantly in advance of their peers, or a pupil might show outstanding talent in just one area of learning, again outstripping others of their age. Whether their abilities are in a range of areas or just one, such pupils require extra learning experiences in order to support and extend the identified ability.

Generally, however, it is often the 'strugglers' who come to attention first in the classroom. You might have observed pupils who:

- have low self-esteem;
- are capable, but frustrated because they don't have the means, vocabulary, strategies or techniques to write what they want to say;
- do not yet speak English fluently;
- only skate on the surface of text when reading aloud and don't understand what they're reading;
- 'can't think what to write' because they are paralysed by fear of failure;
- have poor techniques;
- do not value their own experience;
- lack motivation;
- are restless – wanderers, diverters;
- can write with technical accuracy but do not seem to have their own voice;
- are naturally slow at working;
- have hearing loss/sight loss/difficulties with manual dexterity;
- are too proud to ask for help;
- have language or neurological disorders;
- have so many ideas they find it hard to follow one through.

Bilingual/multilingual pupils

Again, it is important to avoid generalisations. Bilingualism is perhaps best seen as a continuum of proficiency in speaking (and often writing) more than one language, which varies according to the

Task 6.2.5 How do teachers provide support for different learners?

- Select one or two of the descriptions above and consider how pupils displaying these characteristics might be supported and moved on in their learning. If possible, recall any strategies you have observed teachers using, or that you have used yourself.
- Discuss with your tutor the practical implications of offering support for strugglers.
- Add to this list as you consider bilingual/multilingual learners and gender issues. What strategies have you seen teachers use to cater for language diversity and for gender differences?

social contexts of language use, for example: with peers who speak the same language; with peers who don't; with older people or relatives; or at school, work or worship (see Unit 6.6). Everyone, including apparently monolingual people, uses a set of language variations, and so it is worth trying to find out about:

- the languages/dialects used in school, in lessons, at break time with friends;
- the languages used in the home;
- any language classes attended out of school.

Gender

Issues of gender often focus on boys' under-achievement, although concerns about boys' achievements in learning generally are not new. While any under-achievement is a proper concern for everyone involved in education – parents, teachers and pupils – it is wise not to take on generalised observations about boys, girls and learning, without asking a few questions or gathering first-hand information (Bearne, 2007). Contexts differ, and pupils' attitudes, motivation and achievements will be influenced by a variety of home-, classroom- and school-based factors. Careful observation and monitoring are essential so that teaching approaches can be developed that will support boys' – and girls' – achievements (see Unit 6.5).

Task 6.2.6 Managing classrooms for diversity

The survey by Ainscow *et al.* (2007) (*Cambridge Primary Review: Research Survey 5/1*; www.primaryreview.org.uk) argues that 'currently dominant constructions [of diversity] conceal as much as they reveal, and mislead as much as they guide' (pp. 17–18). After reading the survey, consider the implications for managing classrooms for diversity.

What does the emphasis on the role of practitioners mean in terms of classroom practice aimed at catering for the kinds of diversity that you have observed in the classroom?

You might also like to look at chapter 8, 'Children, diversity and equity', in Alexander (2009).

APPROACHES TO DIFFERENTIATION

Considering diversity involves looking, not only at the qualities and potential of different learners, but also at the provision that is made to support and build on that potential. As you have already considered, some learners find diagrams, maps and webs useful in shaping and representing ideas; some read pictures more accurately than written text; some think best in sequences, using lists to help organise ideas and actions; others have a more random or spontaneous way of dealing with things. For sustained work, some people need background noise, whereas others need absolute silence. The next move, after identifying the range of learners, is to identify the range of contexts and opportunities for learning that are on offer and that seem successful and effective.

Creating a school environment for learning

The aspects of differentiation that balance issues of equity and entitlement with access to the curriculum are most apparent at whole-school level. The environment is critical in allowing or blocking access to learning, and so it is worth considering first of all how hospitable to diversity the physical setting of the school is. Figure 6.2.5 offers a checklist. You might think that these aspects of differential provision seem peripheral, but they are, in fact, a reflection of a general approach to diversity within the school.

- Are the notices accessible to those who read iconic or pictorial texts more readily than print?
- Are the languages of the school community genuinely represented (not just as a poster of 'greetings')?
- Is there easy access for those whose mobility is hampered?
- How is pupils' work displayed and presented? Is it only 'the best' or a wider representation?
- How accessible is the library or resource centre? What provision has been made for diversity here? Does it have books of maps, photographs, technical manuals etc.?
- How does the school reflect an environment that celebrates different areas of the curriculum – for example, are maths work, science, design and technology displayed as much and as frequently as art and writing?

FIGURE 6.2.5 The school as hospitable to diversity – review 1

The classroom environment

What messages does the classroom give about the status or value given to the diversity of the pupils? Figure 6.2.6 provides a checklist of the classroom setting, as the physical environment reflects the thoughts of the teacher about what provision for diversity means.

It is worth remembering, however, that the physical context for learning is only part of the environment. Even more significant in supporting the diverse needs of learners is the environment of opportunity, expectation and challenge offered by the teacher. This might include:

- modelling and demonstrating processes and approaches;
- offering pupils chances to experiment and try things out for themselves;
- creating an environment where failing is seen as part of learning and is a stepping stone to trying again;
- building on successes.

- Are there special areas for activities – technical, practical, role-play, listening, working on-screen, problem-solving?
- What do the displays suggest about accessibility to different approaches to learning? Are there pictures, maps, diagrams, written texts, photographs, three-dimensional objects?
- What about the pupils' input into displays and the visual environment? Is the work or display material all selected and mounted by the adults?
- Is there variety in the curriculum areas on display?
- How does the classroom operate as an environment for inclusion? What about the height of shelves and the use of space?
- What messages about gender and culture are signalled by the materials and books used?

FIGURE 6.2.6 The classroom as hospitable to diversity – review 2

Task 6.2.7 Observing school approaches to differentiation and diversity

This task and the following two ask you to make some observations in a school. If you are not likely to be making a school visit soon, you will need to complete the review by thinking back to a school that you are familiar with.

- When you have completed the review in Figure 6.2.4, discuss your notes with one or two colleagues. What differences did you find between the schools? What similarities? How can you account for these?
- A second means of finding out the school approach to differentiation is to look at school policy documents. Ask the school for a copy of its equal opportunities, special needs and or gifted and talented policies (or look for these online on the school website). Look at the policy for specific subjects. What guidance do these policies give about differentiation?
- You may have found some gaps as well as some useful guidance. With your tutor, outline some guidelines that might be included in a school or particular subject policy to support appropriate differentiation.

It is often assumed that intervention for learning is about teachers 'doing things' in the classroom. In fact, the most effective intervention happens before a teacher ever reaches the classroom – in the process of planning and organising activities and approaches.

Managing groups

Flexible planning for differentiation raises issues about how groups are constituted and how they might be varied. Strategies to organise groups may depend on social factors as well as learning objectives, so that pupils might be grouped according to:

- friendship patterns;
- expertise or aptitude relative to the task or subject;

Task 6.2.8 Reviewing how the classroom environment provides for diversity

- Complete the review of the physical environment of the classroom in Figure 6.2.5 and observe how your teacher creates an environment of opportunity, expectation and challenge.
- Discuss with your tutor the relationship between the tangible environment of the physical setting and the intangible environment of the teacher's attitudes and aspirations for the pupils.

- a mix of abilities relative to the task or subject;
- gender/gendered identity;
- home language;
- pupils' own choices;
- the content of the activity.

Whenever teachers plan for the management of learning, there is an implicit question about classroom control. This is fundamental to successful group work, and so it is important to teach pupils to work productively in groups. This might mean:

- negotiating ground rules for turn-taking and dealing with disagreements;
- giving written prompts to guide discussion;
- developing ways of time-keeping for fair chances to contribute;
- using role-play and simulations;
- reviewing and evaluating with the pupils the ways in which they managed (or did not manage!) to work together. (See Unit 3.5 for further support.)

All the observations you make in school will help you to think about how best to manage group work in your own teaching. (See also Unit 3.5.)

Task 6.2.9 Observing group work

Either by observing during a day in your current school or by remembering a particular classroom, make notes about the ways in which work is organised:

- Is there a balance between whole-class teaching, group work, paired work and individual work?
- Are the pupils working *in* groups or *as* groups?
- Following one pupil, note the variations in groups that that child is involved in during the day.

Compare your observations with those of others in your group. From your discussions, make a list of the criteria used by the teachers to decide on how to group the pupils. Was it always by perceived ability? Discuss with your tutor the advantages and disadvantages of grouping according to any specific criterion.

Provision – planning for input and activities

For certain activities, differentiation is unnecessary, although attention to diversity will be important. In drama work, for example, activities are likely to be 'open access'; in PE, differentiation will be decided by criteria that will be different from those for maths. In long- and medium-term planning for classes and groups, teachers make decisions about learning objectives: the facts, concepts, strategies they want the class to learn in the course of a term or a year, as well as in the extended teaching unit in each subject area; what experiences they want them to have; what attitudes they want them to develop (see Unit 3.1). In terms of input, decisions might be made about factual information, the concepts and the vocabulary that will be used to help learners grasp content and ideas. At this point, it is important to start with what the learners already know, in order to build on existing knowledge. At the same time, planning will identify what new information or concepts individuals and the group as a whole might now be introduced to (see Unit 5.1).

In shorter-term planning for specific learning outcomes (see Unit 3.2), teachers may differentiate by providing different tasks within an activity to cater for different levels of ability. In its worst manifestation, this version of differentiation is represented by three different worksheets – one with mostly pictures and few words; one with more words, more densely packed, and one picture; and a third with lots of words and no pictures. This kind of 'worst-case' practice gives very powerful negative impressions to all the learners in the classroom. It is more like division than differentiation. Although recognising that these things are done with the best of intentions in order to cater for the range of pupils, it is wrong to assume that ability is linked only with reading print text. Also, if differentiated tasks assume that certain individuals or groups will only be able to cope with a limited amount of new information, this can run the risk of excluding pupils who might be able to cope with more ambitious learning objectives. The challenge to the teacher is to find ways of framing tasks that can not only genuinely stretch all the learners, but that might provide for the variety of approaches to learning.

These teachers describe their approaches to differentiated input and tasks:

> When I plan for a unit of work I make sure that I include visual stimuli and ICT, some activity-based and some writing tasks and some group and individual work.

> I try to vary the teaching approaches between and within lessons, scaffolding and extending where appropriate. When the children work in guided writing groups I might ask one child to write a paragraph about the setting, another to re-tell the story we'd read, and another to invent a story. In whole-class teaching I'll use a drama strategy for one activity and scaffold the learning, adjusting as I notice how individuals are doing.

> I use writing frames and word mats which have personal prompts including individual targets and success criteria linked to the learning objectives and perhaps key vocabulary matched to the child's ability. In maths I might give some children number squares if they need them (some might not) or give others particular apparatus.

Resources and support

Although it is important to identify a range of material resources to cater for the preferences of all learners – for example, ICT, digital texts, listening stations, audio equipment, pictures, photographs, maps, diagrams and print – it is also important to acknowledge and use the range of human resources available in the classroom, for example teaching assistants (TAs). In some schools, TAs are given responsibility for planning parts of the teaching, and the best practice is when practitioners and TAs plan jointly, particularly for group work. Although TAs are often used to support children who are experiencing difficulties, it can be just as effective, or even more effective, if the support is given to different groups, including those described as gifted and talented. The key lies in making sure that support time is carefully allocated according to the requirements of the curriculum and the children involved. (See Unit 8.2 for a full discussion of working with other adults in the classroom.) However, support need not only be seen in terms of the adults in the classroom, or peer support; it might also mean use of ICT or other tools for learning, e.g. prompts, scaffolds, texts etc. Perhaps the most critical element in considering this area of provision for diversity is to do with teacher time. There is never enough time to give the individual support that a teacher almost inevitably and continuingly wants to offer. Group and paired work, self- and peer-evaluation, support from adults or other pupils, collaborative revising and proofreading all help in offering differentiated support.

These teachers describe their approaches to differentiating by support:

> I find that I do differentiate by support, although with the older pupils I teach it has to be done subtly to avoid upsetting individuals. I tend to use paired work a lot, basing the pairs on different things – sometimes I suggest the pupils choose their own learning partners; at other times I select a more confident mathematician, for example, to work with someone who finds some of the concepts difficult. But I do think it's important to avoid making social divisions. In group work I'll sometimes select groups according to having someone who is more confident in literacy to take notes working with others who may not be quite so fluent and I also make the criteria for working in groups explicit so that everyone feels valued whatever role they take on.

> Of course, the TA is an important part of differentiated support but I don't really like the usual practice of putting her with the least able group – whatever that means. It's not good for her because it doesn't stretch her professionally and it means that I don't get to work with them and give them some focused support. We discuss things at the beginning of the week and sometimes she'll be working with the more able – she's particularly interested in science so I tend to ask her to work with the able scientists quite often. At other times I'll work with them and she'll work with other groups. She's also very good with ICT so she might work with individuals at certain times either to consolidate skills or to extend the exceptional pupils.

Outcome, response and assessment

Many teachers favour differentiation by outcome, but this can be seen as a less organised way to cater for the range. If differentiation by outcome is to be genuinely effective, it has to be allied with response to help move learners on, and that response has to be based on a clear view of the learning outcomes aimed for in a series of lessons or a unit of work. This teacher explains why she prefers to differentiate at this stage of the teaching process:

> I find individual feedback particularly powerful in moving learning forward. When I'm marking a pupil's work I identify strengths and areas for development. My feedback links to exactly what each pupil needs and what the next steps in learning are. Of course I focus on the learning objective but the development points are personal. I always identify part of the writing that could be improved and discuss or comment on how this might happen. After I've marked work I'll gather together pupils with the same needs and teach a guided session. For example, in guided writing I'd gather together the children who have been over-using adjectives or writing sentences that are too detailed. I also use the plenary to teach children to edit and improve their work. I might ask them to work in different pairs to find the most powerful use of language in their writing. Then I ask them to underline the part that presents the reader with the image, for example. I use oral sentence stems to encourage them to explain their thinking to their partner like: *The most powerful sentence in my writing is . . . because it makes the reader . . .*

This enables me to consolidate the learning, to make judgements on children's understanding and develop their ability to self-evaluate.

Outcomes can be both tangible and intangible. Tangible products (written or diagrammatic work, craft or art work, displays of physical activities or drama activities) provide obvious opportunities for assessment across a range of areas and kinds of ability. However, intangible outcomes are equally open to observation and assessment: increased confidence; the ability to carry out a particular operation or to present ideas orally; new-found enthusiasm or the articulation of concepts that have been understood; or the use of a language to talk about the subject or learning itself (metalanguage). Equally, response need not always be written. The end points of learning are often used to assess how well pupils have achieved, but, if assessment is to inform future teaching and learning, there may be a need for a diversity of kinds of assessment and variation in times when those assessments are carried out. Response to the outcomes of learning, by teachers and pupils, makes the process of learning explicit and acknowledges different abilities.

Teachers are continually making assessments and judgements – minute by minute, hour by hour, day by day – as they work alongside pupils. Those assessments are based on implicit criteria of what counts as success and will necessarily be adjustable to take into account all the learners in the classroom. That is a teacher's professional expertise, but it is important to make criteria explicit. In doing so, a teacher can check that he or she is using a differentiated range of types of assessment that will accurately describe the achievements of a diverse set of learners (see Units 5.1 and 5.2).

SUMMARY

Differentiation involves providing a curriculum that allows for the progress of all learners, but that will specifically cater for the needs of different groups of pupils and the diverse strengths, needs and abilities of individual learners. It involves planning for teaching approaches that will build on the knowledge, concepts, skills and prior experiences of the pupils in the class. It also means balancing knowledge of the range of learners with the content of learning and managing and evaluating teaching and learning to try to move all learners on successfully. Judgements about lesson content, pace of learning, levels of challenge, management of groups in the classroom, use of support and response to individuals and groups for successful differentiation are part of the developed expertise of teachers. You are just starting on that professional journey; thoughtful observation and planning will help you to begin effective, supportive and stimulating differentiation.

 ## ANNOTATED FURTHER READING

Ainscow, M., Booth, T. and Dyson, A. (2003) *Understanding and Developing Inclusive Practices in Schools*, Swindon: ESRC.

> This study, carried out by a research network that was part of the Economic and Social Research Council's Teaching and Learning Research Programme, highlights the relationship between externally imposed requirements to raise standards and a school-based commitment to inclusion and equity.

Bearne, E. (ed.) (1996) *Differentiation and Diversity in the Primary School*, London: Routledge.
> There are few books dealing with differentiation in the primary school. This edited collection has sections on definitions; differentiation and literacy; mixed-ability learners; assessment; and school policies for differentiation. Although written some time ago, the content is still highly relevant, and there are practical suggestions as well as reflective chapters.

Coffield, F. (2012) 'Learning styles: unreliable, invalid and impractical and yet still widely used' in P. Adey and J. Dillon (eds) *Bad Education: Debunking Myths in Education*, pp. 215-30.
> This chapter is based on research carried out by Frank Coffield, David Moseley, Elaine Hall and Kathryn Ecclestone. It provides an overview of a systematic and critical research review of learning styles and their implications for methods of teaching, presenting a clear, coherent and balanced analysis.

Special Children
> This magazine, published monthly by Questions Publishing, is a source of relevant articles; see: http://specialchildren-magazine.com

Support for Learning: British Journal of Learning Support
> This journal, published on behalf of nasen, is also valuable; see: www.nasen.org.uk

FURTHER READING TO SUPPORT M-LEVEL STUDY

Alexander, R. (ed.) (2009) *Children, Their World, Their Education: Final Report and Recommendations of the Cambridge Primary Review*, London: Routledge.
> Chapter 8, 'Children, diversity and equity', argues that all aspects of childhood are shaped by culture, and that, 'England today is a country of exceptional cultural diversity' (p. 110). With regard to the influences of poverty, gender and ethnicity, it notes the views of some witnesses that the education system exacerbates inequalities and offers some suggestions for addressing these problems.

McPhillips, T., Shevlin, M. and Long, L. (2012) A right to be heard: learning from learners with additional needs in literacy, *Literacy* 46 (2) pp 59-65.
> Pupils in Northern Ireland and the Republic of Ireland who have additional needs in literacy were consulted about how their learning experiences could be improved, revealing that they had a keen awareness of how their specific difficulties might be supported.

RELEVANT WEBSITES

Cambridge Primary Review: www.primaryreview.org.uk
> See particularly: Blatchford, P., Hallam, S., Ireson, J., Kutnick, P. with Creech, A. (2008) Classes, groups and transitions: structures for teaching and learning. Institute of Education and Kings College, University of London (http://gtcni.openrepository.com/gtcni/bitstream/2428/26653/1/RS_9-2_report_160508_Structures_for_teaching_learning.pdf; accessed 12 May 2013).

Demos: www.demos.co.uk
> See particularly: Hargreaves, D. (2005) *About Learning*, Demos: London. There are other interesting articles about education available on this site (accessed 12 May 2013).

Differentiation in Action, Teachers TV (2011): www.tes.co.uk/teaching-resource/Differentiation-in-Action-Primary-6084160/
> How one teacher handles primary pupils of varying achievement in a school in Bethnal Green, London (accessed 12 May 2013).

2020 Vision: Report of the Teaching and Learning 2020 Review Group (Department for Education and Skills, 2006): http://dera.ioe.ac.uk/67347/1/6856-DfES-Teaching%20and%20Learning.pdf Accessed 12 May 2013.

REFERENCES

Ainscow, M., Conteh, J., Dyson, A. and Gallanaugh, F. (2007) *Children in Primary Education: Demography, Culture, Diversity and Inclusion (Cambridge Primary Review: Research Survey 5/1)*, Cambridge: University of Cambridge Faculty of Education. Available online at: www.primaryreview.org.uk (accessed 12 May 2013).

Ainscow, M. and Sandill, A. (2010) Developing inclusive education systems: the role of organisational cultures and leadership, *International Journal of Inclusive Education* 14 (4) pp 401-16.

Alexander, R. (ed.) (2009) *Children, Their World, Their Education: Final Report and Recommendations of the Cambridge Primary Review*, London: Routledge.

Bearne, E. (2007) 'Boys (girls) and literacy: towards an inclusive approach to teaching', in E. Bearne and J. Marsh (eds) *Literacy and Social Inclusion: Closing the Gap*, Stoke on Trent: Trentham Books.

Coffield, F. (2012) 'Learning styles: unreliable, invalid and impractical and yet still widely used' in P. Adey and J. Dillon (eds) *Bad Education: Debunking Myths in Education*, pp. 215-30.

Department for Children, Schools and Families (2009) *Narrowing the Gaps: Leadership for Impact*. Available online at: www.essex.gov.uk/Business-Partners/Partners/Schools/One-to-one-tuition/Documents/Narrowing%20the%20gaps%20leadership%20for%20impact.pdf (accessed 12 May 2013).

Department for Education (2011) Disadvantaged pupils - what you need to know. Available at: www.education.gov.uk/schools/pupilsupport/premium/a0076062/disadvantaged-pupils (accessed 12 May 2013).

Department for Education (2012) *Teachers' Standards*, May 2012. Available online at: www.education.gov.uk/publications/eOrderingDownload/teachers%20standards.pdf (accessed 12 May 2013).

Gardner, H. (1993) *Frames of Mind: The Theory of Multiple Intelligences*, 2nd edn, London: Fontana Press.

Gardner, H. (1999) *Intelligence Reframed: Multiple Intelligences for the 21st Century*, New York: Basic Books.

Hargreaves, D. (2005) *About Learning*, Demos: London.

National Curriculum Council (NCC) (1992) *Starting Out With the National Curriculum*, York: NCC.

Ofsted (2011) Excellence in English: what we can learn from 12 outstanding schools, May 2011, No. 100229.

Ofsted (2012a) Moving English forward: action to raise standards in English, March 2012, No. 110118.

Ofsted (2012 b) The framework for school inspection, No. 120100.

PROVIDING FOR SPECIAL EDUCATIONAL NEEDS

Noel Purdy

INTRODUCTION

> Every teacher should expect to teach children with SEN – and we must ensure that they are equipped with the skills to do so effectively.
>
> (Department for Education and Skills, 2004, section 3.9)

It is clear from many influential reports over recent years that much more is now expected of mainstream teachers than in the past in relation to meeting the needs of children and young people with special educational needs (SEN). For instance, the Bercow Report (Department for Children, Schools and Families, 2008) into children with speech, language and communication needs, the Lamb Report into parental confidence and SEN (Department for Children, Schools and Families, 2009) and the Cambridge Primary Review (2010) all made recommendations that teachers should be better equipped to meet the needs of pupils with a wide range of different SEN.

Initial Teacher Education (ITE) has, however, struggled to keep up with these raised expectations. Indeed several reports have been critical of the preparation of student teachers to meet the challenges of teaching children with SEN in mainstream schools. In 2008, an Ofsted report, *How Well New Teachers Are Prepared to Teach Pupils With Learning Difficulties and/or Disabilities* (Ofsted, 2008) identified considerable differences in practice and quality of preparation in ITE in England; limited evaluation of the long-term outcomes by providers; and an over-reliance on schools to provide the bulk of the teaching; this, in turn, meant that new teachers often failed to receive guidance in a wide enough range of learning difficulties. Barton (2003), Winter (2006) and Hodkinson (2009) also found evidence of inadequate preparation of teachers in many cases, especially in shorter PGCE courses. For instance, Winter (2006) found that 89 per cent of the student teachers in her study did not feel that their ITE prepared them for teaching children with SEN in inclusive classrooms, and that there was a very real need and desire for more focused preparation, both as stand-alone courses and also 'permeated' through subject disciplines.

The need for quality preparation for teachers is clear, given that almost a fifth of the school population in England has SEN, and over half of all children with statements of SEN in England are placed in mainstream schools (Department for Education, 2012a).

It is far beyond the scope of this introductory unit to provide detailed practical guidance in relation to meeting the needs of children with specific SEN; however, student teachers are advised to follow the general principles at the end of the unit and to consult the texts suggested in the annotated further reading section on page 382.

OBJECTIVES

By the end of this unit you should have:

- an awareness of the development of the UK policy context of SEN over recent years;
- an understanding of current expectations of mainstream teachers in relation to SEN;
- an appreciation of government plans for the immediate future of SEN provision;
- an understanding of the main principles involved in seeking to meet the needs of children with SEN in primary schools.

THE DEVELOPMENT OF UK POLICY IN RELATION TO SEN

Perhaps the most significant report to date in relation to SEN in the UK was the *Report of the Committee of Enquiry into the Education of Handicapped Children and Young People* (HMSO, 1978), commonly referred to as the Warnock Report after the chair of the committee, Mary Warnock. This influential report led to legislation in the 1981 Education Act and transformed the conceptualisation of special education in the UK by advocating a focus by teachers on children's 'special educational needs' (as a means to giving them access to learning) rather than on their 'handicap' or disability.

Prior to the changes in legislation resulting from the Warnock Report, there existed a rigid system of eleven categories of 'handicap' (blind, partially sighted, deaf, partially deaf, delicate, diabetic, educationally subnormal, epileptic, maladjusted, physically handicapped and those with speech defects), which dated back to the 1944 Education Act. The regulations at that time also prescribed that children who were blind, deaf or epileptic, had physical disabilities or were aphasic were 'seriously disabled' and *had* to be educated in special schools. They also stipulated that children with other disabilities might attend 'ordinary schools', but only if adequate provision for them was available. Before the 1970 Education Act, some children with severe disabilities had even been deemed 'ineducable'. In rejecting the medical model of disability (with its focus on a child's deficit or impairment), the Warnock Report heralded a new approach that aimed to remove the obstacles to progress for children with SEN:

> The purpose of education for all children is the same; the goals are the same. But the help that individual children need in progressing towards them will be different. Whereas for some the road they have to travel towards the goals is smooth and easy, for others it is fraught with obstacles. For some the obstacles are so daunting that, even with the greatest possible help, they will not get very far. Nevertheless, for them too, progress will be possible, and their educational needs will be fulfilled, as they gradually overcome one obstacle after another on the way.
>
> (HMSO, 1978, section 1.4)

The Warnock Report not only coined the term 'special educational needs', but is important for a number of other reasons: it rejected once and for all the notion that some children with the most severe disabilities are 'ineducable' and asserted that 'education, as we conceive it, is a good, and a specifically human good, to which all human beings are entitled' (section 1.7); it suggested that 'up to one in five' (section 3.3) children will require a form of special educational provision at some stage during their school careers, thus broadening the term and removing the notion of a fixed or irreversible label; it endorsed the policy of 'integration' (now more commonly referred to as the 'inclusion') of children with SEN into mainstream schools; it introduced the principle that parents should be engaged in meaningful dialogue as 'equal partners' in the education of their children; and it safeguarded the educational provision for the small minority of children with more severe or complex needs by laying an obligation on local authorities to make special educational provision for any child judged to be in need of such provision based on a multidisciplinary assessment of need (known as the 'statement'). There have been many subsequent policy developments, but perhaps the most significant was the introduction of the National Curriculum (Education Reform Act, 1988), which established the notion that all children were entitled to have access to the same curriculum. However, this also marked the beginning of the standards and performance agendas in schools, which are often perceived to have had a negative impact on the inclusion of children with SEN.

In Wales . . .

The SEN Code of Practice for Wales provides practical advice to Local Education Authorities, maintained schools, early years settings and others on carrying out their statutory duties to identify, assess and make provision for children's special educational needs.

(WAG, 2004: xi)

Source: Welsh Assembly Government (WAG) (2004) *Special Educational Needs Code of Practice for Wales*. Cardiff: Welsh Assembly Government (WAG). http://wales.gov.uk/docs/dcells/publications/120705sen codeofpracticeen.pdf

---

Task 6.3.1 Special educational needs

Warnock (2005) argues that the concept of SEN must be 'broken down', and that we must abandon the common practice of referring to children with SEN (or 'SEN pupils') as one homogenous group. Think of three pupils you have come across who have SEN. To what extent are their barriers to learning the same/different? Why might a single label of SEN be unhelpful in planning to meet the needs of these children?

LEGAL DEFINITION OF SEN

The term 'special educational needs' was first defined in the Education Act 1981 and more recently in the Education Act 1996:

A child has special educational needs . . . if he (or she) has a learning difficulty which calls for special educational provision to be made for him (or her).

A child has a learning difficulty if he (or she):

(a) has significantly greater difficulty in learning than the majority of children of his age;
(b) has a disability which either prevents or hinders him from making use of educational facilities of a kind generally provided for children of his age in schools within the area of the local education authority;
(c) is under compulsory school age and is, or would be, if special educational provision were not made for him, likely to fall within paragraph (a) or (b) when of that age.

Special educational provision means:

(a) in relation to a child who has attained the age of two, educational provision which is additional to, or otherwise different from, the educational provision made generally for children of his age in schools maintained by the local education authority (other than special schools);

(b) in relation to a child under that age, educational provision of any kind.

(Education Act 1996, section 312)

A more inclusive term of 'additional support needs' (ASN) has been introduced in recent years in Scotland (Education Additional Support for Learning Scotland Act, 2004) which refers to any child or young person who, for whatever reason, requires additional support to benefit from their school education. This definition encompasses any factor that might relate to social, emotional, cognitive, linguistic, disability, or family and care circumstances.

SEN AND THE INCLUSION DEBATE

There has been considerable focus in recent years on *where* children with SEN should be taught, whether wholly in mainstream classes or special schools, or in dual placements, where children can be integrated at certain times or for certain subjects, according to their individual needs. The polarity of opinion on this subject is often very evident. Some would argue (for instance, Rustemier, 2002) that, although the UK has signed up to pro-inclusion international agreements, such as the United Nations Convention on the Rights of the Child (United Nations, 1989) and the Salamanca Statement (UNESCO, 1994), financial and legislative support for separate special schooling continues as before. Others, including Mary Warnock herself, would contend that inclusion has not always worked and, indeed, can at times be experienced as a 'painful kind of exclusion' for some children (Warnock, 2005: 39), and that there remains a need for separate schooling for children with the most severe and complex needs.

Another perspective is, however, emerging, and here the focus is not on *where* children with special educational needs are taught, but rather on *how* they are taught. Frederickson and Cline (2009: 8), for instance, argue that the concept of SEN must be seen as 'the outcome of an interaction between the individual characteristics of learners and the educational environments in which they are learning', emphasising the degree to which the child has responded to their current learning environment and suggesting how the environment might be adapted to meet those learning needs more effectively. The degree of school/classroom adaptation is, therefore, vitally important. This is confirmed in Ofsted's report into *Inclusion: Does it Matter Where Pupils Are Taught?* (Ofsted, 2006), which found that the most significant factor in promoting the best outcomes for pupils with learning difficulties and disabilities was not the *type* but the *quality* of provision. The report found, further, that pupil progress depended less on whether the placement was in a mainstream or special school, and more on the availability of high-quality, specialist teachers and a commitment by school leaders to creating opportunities for meaningful inclusion.

THE CODE OF PRACTICE

Needless to say, in working with children with SEN, teachers are often more interested in practical guidance rather than legal definitions. In this regard, students are referred to the most recent Code of Practice (Department for Education and Skills, 2001). The Code of Practice sets out practical advice to local authorities and schools on how best to carry out their statutory duties to 'identify, assess and make provision for children's special educational needs' (Department for Education and Skills, 2001: iii). Although the code itself is not a piece of legislation, local authorities, schools and early education settings 'must have regard to it. They must not ignore it' (p. iii). Nonetheless, the code makes clear that there remains a duty on these bodies to decide, in light of the guidance provided in the Code of Practice, what to do in each individual case. The Code of Practice provides guidance in areas such as the identification of SEN, the role of the SEN co-ordinator (SENCo), pupil participation, individual education plans (IEPs), statements (and their annual review), and working with parents and other agencies. Such detailed guidance is, however, underpinned by the following general principles (Department for Education and Skills, 2001, section 1:5):

- a child with special educational needs should have their needs met;
- the special educational needs of children will normally be met in mainstream schools or settings;
- the views of the child should be sought and taken into account;
- parents have a vital role to play in supporting their child's education;
- children with special educational needs should be offered full access to a broad, balanced and relevant education, including an appropriate curriculum for the foundation stage and the National Curriculum.

In the spirit of the Warnock Report's recommendations, the Code of Practice acknowledges (Department for Education and Skills, 2001, section 7:52) that there are no 'hard and fast categories' of SEN, that each child is unique, and that there is a wide spectrum of needs that are often interrelated. Nonetheless, the Code of Practice does indicate that children will have needs and requirements that may fall into at least one of four areas:

- communication and interaction;
- cognition and learning;
- behaviour, emotional and social development;
- sensory and/or physical.

LEVELS OF PROVISION OF SUPPORT IN MAINSTREAM PRIMARY SCHOOLS

In seeking to meet the needs of children with SEN in mainstream primary schools, the Code of Practice sets out three distinct levels of provision (although there are proposals to revise these to just two – see below). These are School Action, School Action Plus and the Statement of Special Educational Needs. Each of these will be considered briefly in turn.

School Action

This refers to interventions that are 'additional to or different from those provided as part of the school's usual differentiated curriculum offer and strategies' (section 5:43). In such a case, a teacher may notice that a child is making little or no progress, despite expected levels of differentiated teaching and, in the case of sensory or physical difficulties, despite the provision of specialist equipment. The class teacher should, in consultation with the child's parents, seek further support, in the first instance from the SENCo. All available information should be gathered, and there may be occasional liaison with external agencies for advice, but the class teacher remains responsible for working with the child on a daily basis and for planning and delivering an individualised programme. Intervention at this level might include different learning materials, specialist equipment or further staff development. An IEP should be drawn up, in consultation with parents and the pupil (where possible), implemented and reviewed on a regular basis (see section below).

School Action Plus

This level of provision is triggered whenever children, despite focused intervention at the initial School Action stage, continue to make little or no progress over a long period. At this level, schools seek the help of external support services, those provided by either the local authority or outside agencies, who will usually see the child in school (if possible), review current provision and advise on new and appropriate targets and teaching strategies. Further assessment (for instance by an educational psychologist) may also be required. Based on the observations, assessments and discussions, a revised IEP will be written with fresh strategies, which will be implemented, as far as possible, in the normal classroom setting.

Statement of Special Education Needs

Where the planned interventions at School Action and School Action Plus have both failed to meet the learning needs of a child, the school (or parents, or another agency, such as health authorities or social services) may make a request to a local authority that a statutory assessment be carried out. Here, the local authority will need documentary evidence of the child's progress, the child's SEN, the range of strategies and resources that have been put in place to date, the child's IEPs and details of regular reviews, assessment details and the views of the parents, child and other professionals involved. The possible outcomes of the statutory assessment by the local authority (which must include evidence of the views of parents and the ascertainable views of the child, in addition to the progress reports and appropriate educational, medical, psychological and social services advice) are the issuing of a Statement of Special Educational Needs (which places a statutory obligation on the local authority to provide the recommended support) or a decision that a statement is not necessary. Where a statement is issued, a child will still require an IEP, irrespective of whether the recommended placement is in a mainstream or special educational context. The Code of Practice sets out a flowchart of the statutory assessment process that guarantees that the period from the receipt of a request for a statutory assessment or the issue of a notice to parents to the issue of the final copy of the statement should normally be no more than 26 weeks. The Statement of Special Educational Needs must follow a prescribed format, to include details of the child and their parent(s); their SEN; the recommended special education provision; the recommended type and name of school where the child's needs will best be met; and details of a child's non-educational needs and provision. Parents have full access to the reports written as part of the statutory assessment and have the right to be present at any observation or assessment carried out as part of the process.

INDIVIDUAL EDUCATION PLANS

As a primary school teacher, you are currently expected to understand, follow and possibly contribute to an IEP for all children who have SEN. The Code of Practice provides details of the content of IEPs, which must be written for all children with SEN (at School Action, School Action Plus and with Statements) and notes (section 5:50) that the IEP should include information about:

- the short-term targets set for or by the child;
- the teaching strategies to be used;
- the provision to be put in place;
- when the plan is to be reviewed;
- success and/or exit criteria;
- outcomes (to be recorded when IEP is reviewed).

Moreover, the Code of Practice continues that the IEP should be 'crisply written' (section 4:27) and focus on just three or four targets, to be chosen from those relating to the key areas of communication, literacy, mathematics, and behaviour and social skills. The IEP should be discussed with the child and the parents, and should be reviewed ideally termly, but at least twice a year, again in consultation with the parents.

Several recent research studies have, however, cast doubt on the extent to which pupils are truly involved in the process of IEP writing and the extent to which they know and understand the targets that have been set for them. For instance, in a report on the contribution of IEPs to the raising of standards for pupils with SEN, Ofsted (1999) found that many primary schools admitted that the limited involvement of pupils in the formulation of their IEP targets was a weakness. More recently, Goepel (2009), in a small-scale study of pupils, their parents and teachers, found a lack of consistency in terms of the involvement by the child and the parents in the IEP process. When the child's views were not taken into account, the pupil saw the IEP as ineffective and did not give it their allegiance, which in turn led to a lack of engagement by the pupil. Goldthorpe (2001) argues further that a consensus is necessary, not just between teachers, but between teachers, the child and the parents. In all of this, it is important, as Frankl (2005) notes, that the IEP does not become a burdensome, bureaucratic paperwork exercise (especially for the SENCo), and that the focus remains on helping the individual child make progress in their learning.

Task 6.3.2 Constructing the IEP

Read Goepel's 2009 article, 'Constructing the Individual Education Plan: confusion or collaboration?'. Identify the main opportunities and challenges of involving pupils to a greater extent in the construction of IEP targets. How might this be applied to the primary context?

RECENT GOVERNMENT PROPOSALS IN RELATION TO SEN

In Wales . . .

The Welsh Assembly Government is proposing to replace the statutory framework for the assessment and planning of provision for children and young people with SEN with a simpler, more person centred and integrated system for children and young people with additional needs (AN). Their proposed description of AN is 'that a child or young person would be deemed to have an additional need if they have a greater difficulty than the majority of persons of the same age, which can encompass significant problems due to their: physical or sensory needs; communication needs; ability to learn or their social and emotional development' (DfES, 2012: 16).

Source: Department for Education and Skills (DfES) (2012) Consultation Document - Forward in partnership for children and young people with additional needs: Proposals for reform of the legislative framework for special educational needs. Cardiff: Welsh Assembly Government (WAG). http://wales.gov.uk/docs/dcells/consultation/120710senconsultationen.pdf

At the time of writing, the government is embarking on an ambitious overhaul of the SEN system, with the intention of implementing the changes from 2014. The process began with the publication, in March 2011, of the Green Paper entitled *Support and Aspiration: A New Approach to Special Educational Needs and Disability* (Department for Education, 2011). There followed a period of public consultation that attracted 2,378 responses. The government subsequently announced, in September 2011, that twenty 'pathfinders' would test out the proposals contained in the Green Paper, in a pilot scheme covering thirty-one local authorities and their Primary Care Trust partners.

Following the public consultation, the government published *Support and Aspiration: A New Approach to Special Educational Needs and Disability – Progress and Next Steps* (Department for Education, 2012b), in which it responded to the consultation and set out the progress made and the next steps in taking forward its plans. In September 2012, the *Draft Legislation on Reform of Provision for Children and Young People with Special Educational Needs* (The Stationery Office, 2012) was presented to parliament by the Secretary of State for Education. It is hoped that this will form part of the planned Children and Families Bill.

The main proposals are as follows:

- a single assessment process (from birth to age 25) that is more streamlined, involves children, young people and families more effectively, and is completed quickly;
- an Education, Health and Care Plan (EHC Plan) (to replace the current Statement), which aims to bring services together and is focused on improving outcomes. Legal protection, offered through the EHC Plan, will be extended for the first time to young people over 16 in further education;
- an offer of a personal budget for families with an EHC Plan, although such families will not be forced to take up that option;
- a requirement for local authorities and health services to plan and commission services that children, young people and their families need;
- a requirement for local authorities to publish a 'local offer', which would set out the support they could offer to children and young people with SEN, and their families, from 0–25;
- the introduction of mediation opportunities for disputes between parents and local authorities in an attempt to make the process less adversarial; children with SEN (as well as their parents) will have the right to appeal to the tribunal if they are unhappy with their support;
- School Action and School Action Plus will be replaced by a single, school-based SEN category for children whose needs exceed what is normally available in schools (to be known as Additional SEN Support).

Already, initial steps have been taken as part of the government's reforms. These include the launch of a new sponsorship scheme for teachers and support staff, to extend their knowledge and expertise in working with children with SEN and disabilities; the publication of additional training resources by the Teaching Agency; an increase in the number of placement opportunities in special schools for Initial Teacher Training; and the inclusion within the new Standards for Qualified Teacher Status (QTS) of a continued focus on meeting the needs of all children, including those with SEN (Department for Education, 2012c: 8). Importantly, the new Ofsted framework (Ofsted, 2012) highlights that inspectors will consider, not just the extent to which the education provided by the school meets the needs of all the pupils at the school, including those with SEN, but also how well such children have achieved since joining the school.

In March 2013, the government published an 'indicative draft' of its new Code of Practice. Entitled *The (0–25) Special Educational Needs Code of Practice* (Department for Education, 2013), this represented a work in progress and was to be followed later in 2013 by a final draft, before being put before Parliament for approval so that it can come into force with the Children and Families legislation in 2014. Notwithstanding the provisional nature of the new code, it is clear that it aims to extend SEN provision beyond the school years, to ensure that every child is given the best chance to succeed in life:

> Professionals who work with the fifth of children and young people who have a special educational need (SEN) should strive to enable them to achieve at school and college, and make a successful transition to adulthood, including finding paid work, living independently and participating in their community.
>
> (Department for Education, 2013, section 1.1)

The proposed new 0-25 EHC Plan will, for the first time, give children and young people with more complex needs clear rights and protections in further education and training, in the same way as they would have in school. The new 0-25 SEN Code of Practice also redefines SEN to include children or young people with a disability (rather than just a learning difficulty), thus incorporating the Equality Act 2010. As before, bodies will have to fulfil a statutory duty towards children with SEN by following the guidance set out in the new 0-25 SEN Code of Practice.

In place of the current system of School Action and School Action Plus, the revised code proposes one single model of 'Additional SEN Support', through which a child's or young person's needs can be met without an EHC Plan. Additional SEN Support will be provided by the school (with, where necessary, input from external services and providers), following consultation and agreement with the pupil and their parents.

Although the government had originally proposed to 'remove advice on using IEPs' (Department for Education, 2011), following parental feedback during the consultation process, the latest draft of the new Code of Practice reaffirms the value of the (renamed) Additional SEN Support Plan, which 'focuses on what outcomes are expected and the support that the school, college and any relevant agencies will provide' (Department for Education, 2013, section 5.6). Furthermore, a review of the Additional SEN Support plan should be held 'at least once a term' to review progress and outcomes.

Task 6.3.3 Impact of government proposals

In light of your experience to date of teaching children with SEN, which of the government proposals outlined above do you think will have the most significant impact, and why?

MEETING THE NEEDS OF CHILDREN WITH SEN: WHERE DO I BEGIN?

In learning to be a primary school teacher, students are often naturally apprehensive and, indeed, sometimes 'scared' at the prospect of teaching so many children with so many different types of SEN (see Richards, 2010). It would be foolish to make a selection of particular SEN in this unit and to offer 'teaching tips' as quick-fix solutions to complex individual situations. Instead, and in seeking to move from fear to confidence, the following advice is offered:

- Take advantage of the courses available during your ITE on the most common and challenging SEN (e.g. moderate learning difficulties; speech, language and communication difficulties; social, emotional and behavioural difficulties; autism; dyslexia), and thus try to develop your understanding of the particular learning needs of different children with SEN.

- Consider also the need to make adaptations to the learning environment, the task set and your teaching style, rather than focusing solely on the child's learning characteristics (see Department for Education and Skills, 2001, section 5.6). Differentiation is essential.
- Be aware of the particular targets set in a child's IEP (soon to become the Additional SEN Support Plan) and plan your teaching to facilitate the meeting of those targets. This necessitates knowledge and understanding of the particular child, their needs and the barriers to their learning, as well as the particular targets themselves. However, in your planning, you should also remember to take into account the whole-school provision, which might include, for instance, evidence-based group interventions for literacy, numeracy or social skills support.
- Realise that you are not alone: ask for advice and support from more experienced teachers, and especially from the school SENCo.
- Always seek the support of the child's parents/guardians as 'equal partners', as they can offer unrivalled insights into the child's needs and also help to reinforce at home the strategies you are implementing in class.
- Keep abreast of the government's planned changes to SEN provision, which should begin to come into effect in 2013-14. This will have significant impact on the provision of support for children with SEN (see above).
- Take every opportunity to develop your own skills and understanding, through professional development courses and/or membership of professional organisations (e.g. National Association for Special Educational Needs (nasen)).
- Remember that each child with SEN is unique. Although knowledge of key policy and legislation is a requirement, and although an understanding of key aspects of common SEN is very useful, it is crucial that you take time to get to know the individual strengths and needs of each individual child with SEN in your primary classroom, including an understanding of their lives outside school.

Task 6.3.4 Children's context

The Cambridge Primary Review (2010) concludes that expert teachers should possess knowledge of *children*, knowledge of *subject*, but also knowledge of children's *context* (recognising the importance of family and community). Think of two pupils with SEN. Explain the nature of the children's SEN, how the barriers to their learning depend on the curricular area in question (are the barriers different in mathematics, history, art and design?) and the extent of contact you or the school have with the pupils' families.

SUMMARY

In this unit, we have examined the current levels of SEN provision in schools and provided guidance on how planning should be used to support children with SEN in meeting learning targets. The policy context for SEN is changing rapidly, and, in this unit, we have considered the development of the concept of SEN from its origins in the Warnock Report (HMSO, 1978) to the most recent policy proposals of the current Coalition government (Department for Education, 2013). Notwithstanding recent developments in SEN policy, we have concluded that nothing is more important than a teacher's willingness to engage with an individual child and to seek to meet their learning needs, while drawing on the support of parents, teachers and other professionals.

ANNOTATED FURTHER READING

Frederickson, N. and Cline, T. (2009) *Special Educational Needs, Inclusion and Diversity* (2nd edn), Maidenhead: Open University Press.

> This is an authoritative textbook on SEN, which offers a balance between theory, research and practice. The authors are careful to offer practical strategies to promote inclusion, while recognising and supporting diversity. This second edition provides new chapters on inclusion and diversity, assessment for learning, autism and sensory needs, as well as interesting sections on recent legislation and the contribution of neuroscience to our understanding of SEN.

Peer, L. and Reid, G. (eds) (2012) *Special Educational Needs – A Guide for Inclusive Practice*, London: Sage.

> This edited volume contains chapters written by a range of experts on different SEN, and includes many practical suggestions to promote the successful inclusion of children with SEN. Some of the topics covered include dyslexia, ADHD, Asperger Syndrome and ASD and dyspraxia. The book sets out to represent the many different perspectives on SEN – research, policy, practice, parents and the children themselves. Discussion points, case studies and summaries help make this a highly accessible text.

Westwood, P. (2011) *Commonsense Methods for Children with Special Educational Needs* (6th edn), London: Routledge.

> This seminal publication offers sound, practical advice on assessment and intervention, embedded within a clear theoretical context supported by current research and classroom practice. Topics covered include autism, physical disabilities, sensory impairments, managing classroom behaviour, reading difficulties, writing difficulties, difficulties with mathematics and, in this most recent edition, a new chapter on identifying and meeting the needs of gifted and talented pupils.

FURTHER READING TO SUPPORT M-LEVEL STUDY

Calder, I. and Grieve, A. (2004) 'Working with other adults: what teachers need to know', *Educational Studies*, 30 (2): 113–26.

> This research article argues that teachers need to be much better prepared to manage effectively the growing number of other adults in their classrooms, including SEN classroom assistants. The article is based on the Scottish primary context and makes an argument that is transferable to any mainstream setting, stressing the need for teachers to take the lead in managing, training, motivating and supervising assistants and in developing effective collaborative structures.

Richards, G. (2010) '"I was confident about teaching but SEN scared me": preparing new teachers for including pupils with special educational needs', *Support for Learning*, 25 (3): 108–15.

> This article is based on a small-scale research study carried out with a group of student teachers taking part in short, focused SEN placements in schools. The findings are very positive, with the students reporting higher levels of confidence and skills as a result of their experience. Implications are discussed for ITE, particularly in ensuring that the quality of the experience is maintained, even when offered to the entire student population.

RELEVANT WEBSITES

Mencap: www.mencap.org.uk

> Mencap works in partnership with people with a learning disability through over 500 affiliated local groups throughout the UK. This site provides details of Mencap's projects, campaigns and resources.

nasen: www.nasen.org.uk

> nasen aims to promote the education, training, advancement and development of all those with special and additional support needs. This site offers details of professional development opportunities and membership, as well as information about nasen's journals (*British Journal of Special Education*, *Support for Learning*, *Journal of Research in Special Educational Needs*) and the popular magazine *Special*.

TES Special Needs Teaching Resources: www.tes.co.uk/sen-teaching-resources

> This site provides thousands of free resources for SEN teachers, including lesson plans, activities, games, worksheets and classroom resources.

REFERENCES

Barton, L. (2003) *Inclusive Education and Teacher Education: A Basis for Hope or a Discourse of Delusion?* London: Institute of Education.

Cambridge Primary Review (2010) *Children, Their World, Their Education – Final Report and Recommendations of the Cambridge Primary Review* (R. Alexander, ed.), London: Routledge.

Department for Children, Schools and Families (2008) *The Bercow Report: A Review of Services for Children and Young People (0-19) with Speech, Language and Communication Needs*. Available online at: www.education.gov.uk/publications/eOrderingDownload/Bercow-Report.pdf (accessed December 2012).

Department for Children, Schools and Families (2009) *Lamb Inquiry: Special educational needs and parental confidence*. Available online at: http://webarchive.nationalarchives.gov.uk/20130401151715/https://www.education.gov.uk/publications/eOrderingDownload/01143-2009DOM-EN.pdf (accessed December 2012).

Department for Education (2011) *Support and Aspiration: A New Approach to Special Educational Needs and Disability* (Green Paper). Available at: www.education.gov.uk/publications/standard/publicationDetail/Page1/CM%208027 (accessed December 2012).

Department for Education (2012a) *Special Educational Needs In England*. Available online at: www.education.gov.uk/rsgateway/DB/SFR/s001075/sfr14-2012v2.pdf (accessed December 2012).

Department for Education (2012b) *Support and Aspiration: A New Approach to Special Educational Needs and Disability – Progress and Next Steps*. Available online at: www.gov.uk/government/uploads/system/uploads/attachment_data/file/180836/DFE-00046-2012.pdf (accessed December 2012).

Department for Education (2012c) *Teachers' Standards*. Available online at: www.education.gov.uk/publications/eOrderingDownload/teachers%20standards.pdf (accessed December 2012).

Department for Education (2013) *Indicative Draft: The (0-25) Special Educational Needs Code of Practice*. Available online at: http://media.education.gov.uk (accessed May 2013).

Department for Education and Skills (2001) *Code of Practice*. Available online at: https://www.education.gov.uk/publications/eOrderingDownload/0581-2001-SEN-CodeofPractice.pdf (accessed December 2012).

Department for Education and Skills (2004) *Removing Barriers to Achievement: The Government's Strategy for SEN*, Nottingham: Department for Education and Skills.

Education Act (1944) London: HMSO.

Education Act (1970) London: HMSO.

Education Act (1981) London: HMSO.

Education Act (1996) London: HMSO.

Education Additional Support for Learning Scotland Act (2004) Edinburgh: Scottish Government.

Education Reform Act (1988) London: HMSO.

Frankl, C. (2005) 'Managing Individual Education Plans: reducing the load of the special educational needs coordinator', *Support for Learning*, 20 (2): 77-82.

Frederickson, N. and Cline, T. (2009) *Special Educational Needs, Inclusion and Diversity* (2nd edn), Maidenhead: Open University Press.

Goepel, J. (2009) 'Constructing the Individual Education Plan: confusion or collaboration?', *Support for Learning*, 24 (3): 126–32.

Goldthorpe, M. (2001) *Effective IEPs through Circle Time*, Wisbech: Learning Development Aids.

HMSO (1978) *Report of the Committee of Enquiry into the Education of Handicapped Children and Young People (The Warnock Report)*, London: HMSO.

Hodkinson, A. (2009) 'Pre-service teacher training and special educational needs in England 1970–2008: is government learning the lessons of the past or is it experiencing a groundhog day?', *European Journal of Special Needs Education*, 24 (3): 277–89.

Ofsted (1999) *The SEN Code of Practice: Three Years On. The Contribution of Individual Education Plans to the Raising of Standards for Pupils With Special Educational Needs*. Available online at: www.ofsted.gov.uk/resources/sen-code-of-practice-three-years (accessed December 2012).

Ofsted (2006) *Inclusion: Does it Matter Where Pupils Are Taught?* Available online at: www.ofsted.gov.uk/resources/inclusion-does-it-matter-where-pupils-are-taught (accessed December 2012).

Ofsted (2008) *How Well New Teachers Are Prepared to Teach Pupils with Learning Difficulties and/or Disabilities*. Available online at: www.ofsted.gov.uk/resources/how-well-new-teachers-are-prepared-teach-pupils-learning-difficulties-andor-disabilities (accessed December 2012).

Ofsted (2012) *The Framework for School Inspection*. Available online at: www.ofsted.gov.uk/resources/framework-for-school-inspection-january-2012 (accessed December 2012).

Richards, G. (2010) '"I was confident about teaching but SEN scared me": preparing new teachers for including pupils with special educational needs', *Support for Learning*, 25 (3): 108–15.

Rustemier, S. (2002) *Social and Educational Justice: The Human Rights Framework for Inclusion*, Bristol: Centre for Studies in Inclusive Education.

The Stationery Office (2012) *Draft Legislation on Reform of Provision for Children and Young People with Special Educational Needs*. Available online at: www.official-documents.gov.uk/document/cm84/8438/8438.pdf (accessed December 2012).

United Nations (1989) *The United Nations Convention on the Rights of the Child*. Available online at: http://treaties.un.org/pages/viewdetails.aspx?src=treaty&mtdsg_no=iv-11&chapter=4&lang=en (accessed December 2012).

UNESCO (1994) *The Salamanca Statement and Framework for Action*. Available online at: www.unesco.org/education/pdf/SALAMA_E.PDF (accessed December 2012).

Warnock, M. (2005) *Special Educational Needs: A New Look*, Philosophy of Education Society of Great Britain (Impact).

Winter, E. (2006) 'Preparing new teachers for inclusive schools and classrooms', *Support for Learning*, 21 (2): 85–91.

RESPONDING TO CULTURAL DIVERSITY AND CITIZENSHIP

Pam Copeland and Des Bowden

INTRODUCTION

> Education for diversity is fundamental if the United Kingdom is to have a cohesive society in the 21st century.

> (Ajegbo, 2007)

This unit is for teachers who are hoping to develop an understanding of, and who are ready to implement a real commitment to, cultural diversity in their teaching. It explores the issues, challenges and opportunities that face schools, teachers and children in an ever-diverse, multicultural, twenty-first-century classroom.

OBJECTIVES

By the end of this unit you will have understood:

- the issues surrounding diversity;
- entitlements to diversity;
- obstacles to entitlement to diversity;
- the value of diversity awareness;
- challenges in the classroom;
- teacher attitudes to diversity.

The population of the UK continues to be diverse in terms of ethnicity, religion, language and culture, and the Census 2011 data show that England and Wales have become more ethnically diverse, with increasing numbers of people identifying with minority ethnic groups. The white ethnic group has decreased in size; although it is still the majority, the trend is apparent: the white ethnic group accounted for 86.0 per cent of the usual resident population in 2011, a decrease from 91.3 per cent in 2001 and 94.1 per cent in 1991. Indeed, in the 2011 Census, London has become so diverse that the white ethnic group is no longer in the majority: about 55 per cent of London's population is non-white. It is a clear sign of this great diversity that London claims some 300 languages are spoken throughout its streets (Johnson, 2012).

Religious affiliations are also changing. The 2011 Census reports a drop in number of Christians from 71.7 per cent in 2001 to 59.3 per cent in 2011; at the same time, the number of Muslims increased from 3.0 per cent to 4.8 per cent, and those reporting no religion increased from 14.8 per cent to 25.1 per cent. The most common non-UK countries of birth for usual residents of England and Wales in 2011 were India, Poland and Pakistan. Poland showed by far the largest percentage increase in the top ten countries of birth, with a ninefold rise (897 per cent) over the last decade, following its accession to the EU in 2004. Of the total population of some 4 million, from 2001 to 2011, some 2.9 million are foreign born, and these now make up some 13 per cent of the total population. The level of immigration over the last 20 years has been unprecendented. This diversity also has a great spatial and locality variation. For example, 94 per cent of the population in the north east are white, whereas in Newham, 43.5 per cent of its population are Asian/Asian British, compared with 29 per cent white; in Harrow, 42.7 per cent are Asian/Asian British, and 42.3 per cent are white . Altogether, some 1 million (4 per cent) households in England and Wales were recorded has having no English speakers, from a total of 23,366,000 households. Ethnic minorities often tend to be spatially concentrated in terms of where they live. The degree to which the new, diverse peoples should be integrated or separated is often a matter of personal choice, but there are societal drivers that interact to encourage segregation. This is partly a cultural issue, but also controlled by social (e.g. language, housing allocation) and economic (e.g. job market) factors, but, in some areas of some cities, there is more or less a racial/ethnic segregation, such as the Ladypool Road and Sparkbrook areas of Birmingham. Indeed, this is the essence of multiculturism; the opposite and increasingly more politically favoured philosophy is that of integration.

Over time, integration does seem to occur more or less organically; for example, great concentrations of Jewish people in the East End of London and the central area of Birmingham are no longer clearly identifiable. These people have prospered, developed and moved out into wider society. Indeed, Ed Milliband, the leader of the Labour party, who has familial roots traceable back to Jewish immigration into the East End, has recently (December 2012) recognised the failings of past immigration policies and has moved towards integration, not assimilation, as a political goal. He reminded his listeners that, in the Olympics, one-third of Team GB medal winners had parents or grandparents born outside this country. There is great strength in diversity, but not where it leads to isolation and separation. He thought that all people should be able to speak and communicate in English and suggested much of the funds spent on translating official documents might be better spent on teaching people English. Although Conservative thinkers might suggested that it was the poor policies of past Labour governments that failed to deal with immigration, there is broad agreement that integration might be the way forward, to allow people to be proud of their cultural roots but also proud to be British.

> I have no doubt that there are plenty of scroungers and fraudsters out there, but in my experience what immigrants want the most is acceptance and the chance to show their commitment to the society that has given them freedom and hope.
>
> (Johnson, 2012)

This unit investigates this diversity and develops strategies for use in school for identifying, sharing and working with this wealth of difference. It develops an understanding of the issues concerned with identities that children inhabit. It tries to promote an understanding of the different people in the UK today, and how children contribute to this diverse society. Teachers and schools have the difficult task of helping their children challenge and evaluate different standpoints from their own, and educating them to develop an informed view of diversity and, hopefully, become part of a more cohesive society.

Children in the UK can inhabit a range of identities that are as confusing as they are defining, not only for themselves, but also for others. It is for teachers to gain an understanding of these dilemmas and to devise appropriate learning episodes that contribute to a curriculum tailored to the individual needs of the children in their unique setting. This should be their entitlement for education for diversity. Which national cricket team should a Bangladeshi boy living in Birmingham support? Where does his identity rest? What rights does he have to his own cultural mores?

There is much encouragement from government educational policies to work towards the goal of more a cohesive and united society. The Ajegbo (2007) Report, *Effective Leadership in Multi-Ethnic Schools* (National College for School Leadership, 2005) and Ofsted (2013a) are strong in their encouragement of understanding diversity and working towards a cohesive curriculum that reflects, understands and celebrates the values of today's multicultural society, and indeed there is a UNESCO convention on the protection and promotion of the diversity of cultural expressions (2005).

For schools, the current driver for ensuring pupils' spiritual, moral, social and cultural development lies, not so much within the new primary curriculum, but rather from the new Ofsted framework for schools (2013b). This spiritual, moral, social and cultural development will be a significant focus in all lesson observations, as well as overall school effectiveness.

However, there is political debate over the speaking of English. Whereas the use of native languages is a strong cultural cement, the lack of spoken English is a challenge and often prevents access to a range of services offered by the host country. The debate hinges around the controversial issue of whether government and local councils should spend about £7 million per year on translating non-essential documents into a variety of languages, or whether this money might be better spent teaching English to non-speakers. There is a strong feeling that people who have jobs that bring them into direct contact with the public should be able to speak English.

In Wales . . .

In the Foundation Phase, 'The concept of cultural diversity encompasses acceptance and respect. It means understanding that each individual is different and unique. By providing a safe, positive and nurturing environment children will have opportunities to share and explore these differences' (DCELLS, 2008a: 9).

Key Stage 2,

> builds upon the Personal and Social Development, Well-Being and Cultural Diversity Area of Learning in the *Foundation Phase Framework for Children's Learning for 3- to 7-year-olds in Wales* and progresses into the 14–19 Learning Core components that relate to PSE such as Personal, Social, Sustainability and Health Matters, Attitudes and Values, and Community Participation.

(DCELLS, 2008b: 3)

Source: Department for Children, Education, Lifelong Learning and Skills (DCELLS) (2008a) *Personal and Social Development, Well-Being and Cultural Diversity*. Cardiff: Welsh Assembly Government (WAG). http://wales.gov.uk/dcells/publications/policy_strategy_and_planning/early-wales/whatisfoundation/page4/sevenareas/personaldiversity/socialdeve.pdf?lang=en

Source: Department for Children, Education, Lifelong Learning and Skills (DCELLS) (2008b) *Personal and social education framework for 7 to 19-year-olds in Wales*. Cardiff: Welsh Assembly Government (WAG). http://wales.gov.uk/subsites/personalsocialed/publications/pseframework/pseframeworke.pdf?lang=en

In Northern Ireland . . .

Northern Ireland policy for cultural diversity fits firmly within the

> emerging concept of 'additional need', which recognises and encompasses the diversity within the classroom. That wider concept moves away from the in-child deficit model and recognises that many children at some time, and for a number of reasons, experience barriers to learning.
>
> (DENI, 2011: 16)

Source: Department of Education for Northern Ireland (DENI) (2011) *Every School a Good School: Supporting Newcomer Pupils.* Bangor, DENI.

CASE STUDIES IN MODERN DIVERSITY

The following case studies demonstrate the challenges and benefits of living a plural society on a range of scales. The example of Leicester shows the plurality of a modern British city. On a school level, the study of Brook Primary School highlights the benefits and richness that a multicultural school can offer. The individual study of George Alagiah shows how people may have a range of identities, determined by racial, cultural, social and economic circumstances.

Case study 1

Urban diversity – Leicester

Based on the 2001 census data and supplementary evidence, Leicester was likely to become the UK's first plural city. It was likely to become one of the first cities in England to have a majority of people with an ethnic minority background. This was owing to a range of factors, including higher birth rates among ethnic minority groups, increases in existing populations through family consolidations and increases in the numbers of new arrivals. If this trend continued, it was possible that Leicester would reach this milestone some time after 2011. The 2011 Census showed that 50.6 per cent of the population were classified as white, and 37.1 per cent were classed as Asian/Asian British. The Asian population is predominantly Indian, from either East Africa or from Gujarat in India. Other, much smaller Asian populations include Bangladeshis and Pakistanis. The black population in Leicester comprises two groups - those of Caribbean origin and those of African origin. This range of ethnic groups has led to the fact that 45 per cent of the pupils in Leicester schools say that English is not their preferred language (www.oneleicester.com).

Case study 2

School diversity – Brook Primary School

Brook Primary School is a popular, oversubscribed, inner-city school that achieves excellent results, at or above the national average at Key Stage 1 (in 1997, reading: 91 per cent; writing: 85 per cent; mathematics: 91 per cent) and well above the national average at Key Stage 2 (English: 80 per cent; mathematics: 80 per cent; science: 98 per cent).

The number of free school meals taken was higher than the local education authority (LEA) average (41 per cent) at 48 per cent in 1997, according to school data. Attendance was in line with the national average. Brook Primary is clearly a very good school, meeting the needs of its pupil intake.

This is particularly striking in the UK context, given the profile of the school's intake. The children attending the school come from very diverse backgrounds. According to school data collected in 1997, 28 per cent were of black Caribbean origin, 6 per cent were black African, and 12 per cent 'black other', mainly children of dual heritage. Children of South Asian origin make up less than 3 per cent of the intake (Indian: 1 per cent; Pakistani: 1 per cent). Only 37 per cent of children in the school were classified as from a UK white background. The remaining 17 per cent consisted of small numbers of children from a wide variety of other language backgrounds, including children with the following home languages: Arabic, Bengali, Chi, Danish, Dutch, Fante, Farsi, French, French Creole, German, Greek, Gujarati, Hindi, Italian, Luo, Norwegian, Polish, Portuguese (some from Angola), Punjabi, Spanish, Swedish, Tagalog, Urdu, Yoruba and others. One of the biggest groups was Portuguese speakers (nine children, including those of Portuguese, Mozambican and Angolan parentage), followed by Arabic speakers (eight) and Yoruba speakers (seven).

At the time of the last Ofsted visit in 1995, 15 per cent of the children were assessed as needing English language support. By 1997, this had risen to 23 per cent, according to school records, but was still less than the LEA average of 30 per cent learners with English as an additional language (EAL).

However, these language survey data do not illustrate the true complexity of the school's intake. Many of the children were of mixed ethnic group parentage; for example, one child categorised as 'Indian' had a Goan father and lived with a white UK mother. This is not an exceptional case, for this is an inner-city area in which multi-ethnic cultural groupings and diverse new cultural forms are emerging, in which traditional or heritage cultures are only one element among other constructions of identity, signalled in clothing, choice of music, choice of food and other affiliations.

This new urban, changing social background was also seen in the school records on the children's religious affiliations. Although the majority (60 per cent) of parents claimed to be Christian, as many as 31 per cent claimed to have no religious affiliations at all. There were only 4 per cent Muslim, then 2 per cent Hindu, 1 per cent Buddhist and 1 per cent Jewish children (adapted from the Standards Site; see: www.standards.dcsf.gov.uk)

The challenge of diversity facing the teacher today varies across the country. Inner cities have a particular mix of ethnic groups and mixed-heritage children. With the expansion of the European Union (EU) and the right to work in any member state, there has been an increase in in-migration of new member states' workers, and these are not always concentrated in large cities. The eastern European farm workers in East Anglia form significant minority groups amid traditional white British communities; for example, 12.1 per cent of Boston's population hold non-British European passports. Towns such as Slough and Reading have all received large numbers of Polish and other nationals.

Teachers are also faced with serious issues about the education of non-European nationals, both as refugees and as illegal immigrants.

Case study 3

Personal identities – George Alagiah

George Alagiah was born in Colombo, Sri Lanka, on 22 November 1955, to Tamil parents. The Tamils were a minority group in Sri Lanka. His father was an engineer, and they moved to Ghana in 1961, where George completed his primary education. They then moved to the UK and lived in Portsmouth, at a time when there was an unhappy intrusion of race into politics. After reading politics at Durham, he followed a career as a journalist and author, which led to him becoming a prominent BBC presenter. He married Frances Robathan, from a British family, with whom he has had two sons. He writes of the gentle clash of cultures, as his mother wore a red sari, and his mother-in-law a floral patterned suit. He claims not to have found race an impediment: 'If you're hungry enough, you work that much harder'. But he recognises that multiculturism may not be the answer, as it results in almost ghetto-like communities of poor and isolated people (Alagiah, 2011; online). His is the kind of extended rainbow network of relationships, spanning countries and continents, that has become a conventional feature of the migrant experience.

ENTITLEMENT TO DIVERSITY EDUCATION

> Multi-cultural education that celebrates diversity is an important part of responding to the kaleidoscope of cultural attributes in the school and the community. Children will be living in a more globalised world where the old barriers of geography will no longer be relevant. Children in all parts of UK (rural, inner-city, suburban) need to understand and respect a range of different cultural heritages. Minority ethnic children, like all children, are entitled to appropriate diversity education through their experiences in school, both in the overt curriculum and within the ethos of the school.
>
> (Claire, 2006)

Schools are under a legal obligation to promote good race relations and provide full equality of opportunity for all children (Race Relations Amendment Act 2000). However, recent policy statements have improved on these baseline requirements. For example, the National Curriculum (2007) has a specific section on 'Identity and cultural diversity', which considers diversity in the curriculum, planning for identity and cultural diversity learning, and community cohesion. This comes from the cross-curriculum dimensions, which:

> provide important unifying areas of learning that help young people make sense of the world and give education relevance and authenticity. They reflect the major ideas and challenges that face individuals and society . . . Dimensions can add a richness and relevance to the curriculum experience of young people. They can provide a focus for work within and between subjects and as a whole, including routines, events and ethos of the school.
>
> (Qualifications and Curriculum Authority, 2009)

Ajegbo (2007) recommends that schools recognise the 'pupil voice' and have systems in place so these voices can be heard (such as school councils and other mechanisms for discussion). Head teachers and their governors are required to meet statutory requirements for diversity. The National College for School Leadership ensures that training for diversity is an essential component of leadership. All schools are encouraged to audit their curriculum to establish their provision for diversity and multiple identities. There are many audit tools available for this process that help map the school's provision (for example, www.education-support.org.uk/teachers/ids/audit-and-action-plan-primary/). Schools should build active links between and across communities, with diversity understanding as the focus. Ajegbo further recommends the appointment of 'advanced skills teachers' with a responsibility for diversity training, and suggests that points on the pay scale be awarded to teachers taking special responsibility for diversity.

The *Every Child Matters* (ECM) (Department for Education and Skills, 2004) agenda puts the emphasis on the needs and aspirations of each individual pupil, so that they can make the best possible progress in developing as responsible citizens and making a positive contribution to society. Learners are at the heart of the curriculum, but all learners have a set of cultural diversity experiences that need to be understood and appreciated, so that learning can be more effective. Teachers are encouraged to be more flexible and to develop localised curricula relevant to the needs and aspirations of their children, their schools and their communities. Learners are encouraged to be a focal part of their own learning journey.

The former Qualifications and Curriculum Authority's (QCA) *Big Picture of the Curriculum* (2008), which was part of the government's *Children's Plan*, put identity and cultural diversity as one of its overarching themes, and this had a significance for individuals and society and provided relevant learning contexts.

The extensive Cambridge Primary Review (Alexander, 2009) was a major independent survey and analysis of primary school education that had been ongoing since 2004. Of its ten major themes, Theme 5 is diversity and inclusion. It warns that recognising diversity in school may not be a straightforward exercise:

> differences between children are constructed rather than simply described, and . . . the constructs embodied in official statistics and policy texts tend to dominate discourse in primary education currently. These constructions favour simplistic and evaluative categorisations which conceal as much as they reveal about diversity.

This review went on to encourage individual schools to develop approaches to diversity that meet the needs of their children and the local community.

The Ofsted inspectors' handbook (2013b) updated for 2013 states:

> Evidence of pupils' spiritual, moral, social and cultural development can be found, for example, where pupils:
>
> - are reflective about beliefs, values and more profound aspects of human experience, using their imagination and creativity, and developing curiosity in their learning
> - develop and apply an understanding of right and wrong in their school life and life outside school
> - take part in a range of activities requiring social skills
> - develop awareness of and respect for diversity in relation to, for example, gender, race, religion and belief, culture, sexual orientation and disability
> - gain a well-informed understanding of the options and challenges facing them as they move through the school and on to the next stage of their education and training

Task 6.4.1 Provision for diversity

Use these questions to consider the provision for diversity in a school known to you:

- Do our primary schools attend fairly and effectively to the different learning needs and cultural backgrounds of all their pupils?
- Do all children have equal access to high-quality primary education?
- If not, how can this access be improved?
- How can a national system best respond to the wide diversity of cultures, faiths, languages and aspirations that is now a fact of British life?
- Of what is identity constituted in a highly plural culture, and what should be the role of primary education in fostering it?
- How can primary schools best meet the needs of children of widely varying abilities and interests?
- How can schools secure the engagement of those children and families who are hardest to reach?

(www.primaryreview.org.uk)

- develop an appreciation of theatre, music, art and literature
- develop the skills and attitudes to enable them to participate fully and positively in democratic modern Britain
- respond positively to a range of artistic, sporting and other cultural opportunities
- understand and appreciate the range of different cultures within school and further afield as an essential element of their preparation for life.

OBSTACLES TO ENTITLEMENT TO DIVERSITY

Ajegbo (2007) recognises that the quality of education across the nation is uneven and suggests the following issues may prevent a coherent diversity curriculum being implemented:

- insufficient clarity about flexibility and customising the curriculum;
- lack of confidence in schools to engage in diversity issues;
- lack of diversity training opportunities;
- lack of proper consideration for the 'pupil voice';
- tenuous or non-existent links to the community.

Other challenges facing teachers wishing to develop diversity awareness in their school include:

- embedding it in a single subject, such as religious education, and not in others;
- lack of planning for integration of newcomers into the learning environment;
- concentration on famous British people;
- narrow selection of reading materials in the library;
- stereotypes in school displays;
- stereotypes in geography (e.g. all Africans are starving and live in mud huts);
- lack of empathy in questioning children who are different from the teacher;
- not recognising that some children do not have Christian names;
- exoticising minority children;
- tokenism;
- language;
- unwillingness to face controversial issues;
- unacknowledged racism.

VALUE OF DIVERSITY AWARENESS: BEYOND TOKENISM

Ajegbo (2007) believes that 'education for diversity is crucial not just for the future well-being of our children and young people but for the survival of our society'.

If children are to develop as successful learners, confident individuals and responsible citizens, it is essential for them to understand and have respect for cultures, religions and identities.

The most successful teaching and learning for diversity occur when there is a whole-school commitment. This includes governors and staff, children, support staff and the local community, working together on the whole-school ethos, which includes the taught and learned curriculum as well as the hidden curriculum. Too many schools celebrate cultural diversity without really understanding the nature of that diversity.

FLEXIBILITY AND THE CURRICULUM

Ever since 2002, in the QCA's *Designing and Timetabling the Primary Curriculum* (Qualifications and Curriculum Authority, 2002), schools have been encouraged to adopt more flexible approaches to the curriculum by customising the basic entitlement to learning to create their own distinctive and unique curricula. Some schools have shown innovative ways to include this flexibility, by:

1   using appropriate resources, such as artefacts and images, to show diversity within and between cultures and groups:
    *   ensuring choice of examples provide balance;
2   presenting a broad and balanced view of culture, identity and diversity:
    *   giving learners accurate and objective views;
    *   avoiding presenting minority groups as problematic;
    *   looking for commonalities between groups.
3   questioning commonly held opinions and stereotypes (e.g. migration in the UK is a recent occurrence):
    *   challenging media portrayal of different countries and peoples;
4   creating an open climate (using ground rules and distancing techniques when dealing with controversial issues):
    *   encouraging learners to take pride in their identity and culture;
    *   encouraging learners to draw on their own experience.

DIVERSITY AND INCLUSION

TeacherNet produces a Community Cohesion Resource Pack, and Ofsted (2009) produces a booklet for inspecting community cohesion. *Who Do We Think We Are?* (www.wdwtwa.org.uk) is a readily available scheme of work designed to help teachers deliver diversity lessons at Key Stages 1 and 2.

Task 6.4.2 Racism

Consider the influence of racism on people such as Mary Seacole, Nelson Mandela, Anne Frank and Stephen Lawrence and develop a scheme of work to include activities that will enhance the learners' empathy.

SCHOOL CONFIDENCE IN ADDRESSING DIVERSITY ISSUES

Many teachers feel that they do not have the experience or understanding to deal with diversity issues. At one level, it is treating individuals with politeness and respect, but this can be confounded by language difficulties. In some cases, female teachers may not be shown the same sort of respect as male teachers by certain minority groups. Schools need to develop their staff to feel confident in their approach to dealing with controversial issues. This could be through taking a certain viewpoint, or playing devil's advocate, or adopting a neutral stance. At the beginning of any teaching episode, every child needs to gain an understanding of which approach the teacher is adopting.

Lack of diversity training

Increased training opportunities are being made at school, regional and national levels. The Training and Development Agency for Schools (TDA) has spent more than £1.5 million between 2002 and 2006 in respect of diversity training. More opportunities are becoming available, as the government pushes the diversity agenda. It is suggested that diversity training should be part of initial teacher training courses, giving newly qualified teachers the opportunity to spread their understanding to staff as they take up posts in school (Ajegbo, 2007).

The children's voice

This is concerned with giving a real say in what goes on in school. Most schools now have a school council. Some of these are strong and allow children to join in by making decisions on the nature of the school and its curriculum. Ajegbo (2007) reports that, in some schools, children are routinely asked for their feedback on all aspects of school life, being involved in staff selection processes and working with teachers on schemes of work. In these schools, children are seen as part of the solution, not part of the problem.

Tenuous community links

These may be addressed by engaging children, their parents and the wider community in the daily life of the school. The extended school day, with breakfast clubs and after-school activities, offers opportunities for more people to come into school and for the school to play a more important role in the community.

CHALLENGES IN THE CLASSROOM

Teachers frequently encounter difficult classroom situations.

Various languages

Languages may be both barriers and bridges to learning. There are dangers for some to confuse not understanding a language with low ability. The child receiving language help and the other children need to be informed about the nature of the EAL support in the classroom.

Short-term children

Some schools receive more or less transient children, such as those from a travellers' community, army children or the children of short-term migrants. Their inclusion in the classroom needs to be carefully managed, and their learning needs need to be catered for. As they move on, a teacher should supply a report on their progress and achievement.

Task 6.4.3 Watching children

Next time you are in school, take time to watch specific children who might be vulnerable, in the playground and on those occasions where children choose partners or group members. Isolation and marginalisation can be a signpost for more overt bullying away from teachers' eyes. Who is being left out? Who is hanging around on the sidelines?

- Can you find out why some children are popular and others are not?
- Does the school's equal opportunities policy have anything to say about bullying and name calling? How is this monitored and dealt with?

(Adapted from Claire, 2006)

BULLYING AND NAME-CALLING OF MINORITY ETHNIC GROUPS

Name-calling is probably one of the more frequently encountered expressions of racial hostility. Picking on individuals or small groups is also seen as bullying. Children need to be made aware that this type of behaviour is unacceptable – not only that, they need to understand why it is unacceptable. They may need to consider what their feelings might be if the situation were reversed. Moralising tends not to work in the face of opposing attitudes. Just to forbid such behaviour is controlling rather than educating. No Name-calling Week runs annually in January and is a week of educational activities aimed at ending name-calling in school and providing schools with the tools and inspiration to launch a continuing dialogue about ways of eliminating bullying (www.nonamecallingweek.org).

It is hard to counter entrenched attitudes of racism, possibly learned from the family; nevertheless, racism is illegal, and children need to be made aware of their right not to be bullied. Teachers need to be vigilant about bullying in their school, and it may be a suitable topic for the school council to consider.

CONTROVERSIAL ISSUES

Teachers have to deal with controversial issues for many reasons, and sometimes they are unavoidable. They may result in exciting classroom learning and, indeed, reflect partly what it means to be human, and they may help children make connections between areas of learning. They will help children develop value positions.

The former QCA suggested that, 'Education should not attempt to shelter our nation's children from even the harsher controversies of adult life, but should prepare them to deal with such issues knowledgeably, sensibly, tolerantly and morally' (Qualifications and Curriculum Authority, 1998: 56).

A strategy for dealing with controversial issues is for the teacher to take a known stance and argue the issue with the children from there. The teacher may:

* be an impartial chairperson (procedural neutrality);
* speak from his or her viewpoint (stated commitment);
* present a wide variety of views (balanced approach);
* take an opposing position (devil's advocate).

Task 6.4.4 Tokenistic gestures or real understanding?

Consider these issues:

* Is learning a Caribbean song in music really improving diversity awareness?
* Does circle time raise awareness of difference?
* Are travellers' children ethnic minorities?
* Do all children in your school celebrate Christmas?
* Does making a curry make you more culturally aware?
* Does dressing up in native clothes improve understanding of other people?

TEACHER ATTITUDES

Sometimes, it is the teacher's attitude that is the concern in the classroom. Teachers need to acknowledge and decide how to deal with their own prejudices and viewpoints, and to consider how to represent their personal opinions in the classroom. Low expectation of certain children and perceived typical behaviour problems are often associated with teachers' own stereotypical views. Children need children's diversity.

Task 6.4.5 Human rights

Use the European Convention on Human Rights (www.hrcr.org/docs/index.html) and the United Nations' Declaration of the Rights of the Child (www.un.org/cyberschoolbus/humanrights/resources/child.asp) to critically evaluate the level of equality in society.

Task 6.4.6 Teaching diversity

Critically evaluate the following paragraph and consider its implications for teaching diversity in the context of government policy and delivery in a specific primary school:

> Teachers who are required to work within the framework of categorical constructions are nonetheless capable of moving beyond those constructions and of developing new responses in a 'spirit of transformability'. An example may serve to illustrate this point. Dyson and Gallannaugh (2007) report how a primary school participating in the Understanding and Developing Inclusive Practices project faced a situation in which many of its pupils appeared unable to make adequate progress in writing using the strategies that were favoured by the then National Literacy Strategy. Faced with this situation, and with considerable external pressure to raise attainment, the school could have opted simply to intensify its existing approaches. Instead, it sought to understand why its pupils were not responding, and came to the conclusion that they lacked the life and language experience they needed to profit from established approaches. Instead, therefore, of intensifying its teaching of reading, the school opted to embark on an experiential approach in which children participated in activities designed to extend their experience, in which they were then encouraged to talk about those experiences and in which only then, if at all, were they expected to write.
>
> (Ainscow *et al.*, 2007: 16)

Task 6.4.7 Role play and debate

Multiculturalism and integration

Assign roles to learners/groups of learners such as (this is only a suggested list of categories):

1 elderly members of the Sikh community;
2 young, middle-class people of Indian origin;

3 recent arrivals of Polish origin;

4 members of the white community;

5 Pakistani restaurant owners;

6 British communities living in Cyprus/Spain.

The learners can investigate the perceptions of living in Britain from the point of view of the various groups by considering the following.

Ed Miliband, Labour party leader, said Britain needed to fashion a new integration strategy which rejected two opposing views. He rejected the idea that immigrants should assimilate totally by abandoning their culture, and he rejected a traditional view of multiculturalism in which different communities live side by side but separately.

He said:

> Some people say that what we should aim for is assimilation, whereby people who have come here do so only on the condition that they abandon their culture. People can be proudly, patriotically British without abandoning their cultural roots and distinctiveness.

> But there is another idea we should also reject: the belief that people can simply live side by side in their own communities, respecting each other but living separate lives, protected from hatreds but never building a common bond – never learning to appreciate one another. We cannot be comfortable with separation. It blocks opportunities, leaving people at the margins. And it breeds ignorance, suspicion and prejudice.

Debate whether each group would prefer to live in a multicultural or an integrated Britain.

SUMMARY

This unit has started to address the dialogue currently surrounding diversity in the classroom. It has considered the challenges posed and suggests some solutions to help combat what is seen by many teachers, children and schools as one of the major issues in school today.

Encouraging multicultural education to be an integral part of the school ethos and embedding it in the curriculum are the first stages towards real inclusion and equal opportunity for all children. It should be part of the whole-school ethos, embraced by all members of the school community. The unit highlights the need to be able to directly tackle racism and racial and other stereotyping, so that a relevant, meaningful and coherent curriculum can flourish. This curriculum needs to be designed to be appropriate for the whole school, in the local community. It should be challenging, exciting and inclusive, meeting the unique needs of the children and helping all concerned to develop a cohesive society, based on mutual understanding, tolerance and respect.

ANNOTATED FURTHER READING

Alagiah, G. (2006) *A Home from Home: From Immigrant Boy to English Man*, London: Little, Brown.
> This is an account of his journey from Sri Lankan boy to English man. He describes the immigrant's experience and the transition he undergoes, and, in the process, Alagiah considers the debate about multiculturalism and British identity, presenting his experiences as documentary evidence about the problems and advantages of 'multicultural' policies.

Claire, H. and Holden, C. (eds) (2008) *The Challenge of Teaching Controversial Issues*, Stoke-on-Trent: Trentham.
> This is an authoritative book that offers much practical support in teaching controversial issues, including diversity, in the primary school. It helps teachers to understand their own role and be equipped with effective approaches to sensitive and complex issues.

Elton-Chalcraft, S. (2009) *It's Not Just About Black and White, Miss: Children's Awareness of Race*, Stoke-on-Trent: Trentham.
> This book provides research-based evidence on what children themselves think about cultural diversity and about efforts to counter racism in their schools. It is empirical, child-centred research that tells educators what they need to know. It was conducted with a sample of Year 5 pupils in two predominantly white and two diverse schools, all of whom were themselves involved in the research process. The book offers the children's voices and their surprising and challenging ideas.

Huddleston, T. (2007) *Identity, Diversity and Citizenship: A Critical Review of Educational Resources*, London: ACT. Available online at: www.citizenshipfoundation.org.uk/lib_res_pdf/0747.pdf (accessed November 2009).
> This review aims to present a critical overview of what is currently available, with a view to helping teachers select appropriate resources for use with their learners. The usefulness of the resources in supporting teachers concerned with identity and diversity is appraised.

Maylor, U. and Read, B. (2007) *Diversity and Citizenship in the Curriculum*, London: London Metropolitan University/DfES.
> This research report provides an up-to-date analysis of diversity in the curriculum. It includes relevant case studies and provides insight on the nature of Britishness.

FURTHER READING TO SUPPORT M-LEVEL STUDY

Drydakis, N. (2012) The effect of ethnic identity on the employment of immigrants. *Review of Economics of the Household*, Springer.
> This study evaluates the effect of ethnic identity on the employment level of immigrants in Greece. Treating ethnic identity as a composite of key cultural elements, the estimations suggest that employment is positively associated with assimilation and integration and negatively associated with separation and marginalisation. In all cases, assimilation provides the highest employment returns, whereas marginalisation provides the highest employment losses. This study adds to the literature by setting up hypotheses and directly measuring immigrants' ethnic identity commitments. The current results have potentially important implications for post-immigration policies, indicating that assimilation and integration policies may be beneficial in terms of labour market outcomes.

Ford, R., Morrell, G. and Heath, A. (2012) '"Fewer but better"? Public views about immigration', in A. Park, E. Clery, J. Curtice, M. Phillips and D. Utting (eds.), *British Social Attitudes: The 29th Report*, London: National Centre for Social Research, available online at: www.bsa-29.natcen.ac.uk (© NatCen Social Research 2012).
> This is a detailed investigation of the data collected on British attitudes to immigration, and the evidence suggests the British public perhaps takes a more sophisticated and nuanced view of the issues pertaining to immigration, multiculturalism and integration than politicians seem to recognise at present, and, setting aside the current constraint, Britain would benefit from a policy response that reflected this nuance.

RELEVANT WEBSITES

International Convention on the Elimination of All Forms of Racial Discrimination: www.equalityhumanrights.com/human-rights/our-human-rights-work/international-framework/international-convention-on-the-elimination-of-all-forms-of-racial-discrimination/

European Convention on Human Rights: www.hrcr.org/docs/index.html

National Curriculum: www.education.gov.uk/schools/teachingandlearning/curriculum

No Name-calling Week: www.nonamecallingweek.org

Mixed Britannia: Telling the story of mixed race Britain, a BBC 2 documentrary series (three programmes) hosted by George Alagiah (through BBC iPlayer).

United Nations Declaration of the Rights of the Child: www.un.org/cyberschoolbus/humanrights/resources/child.asp

Who Do We Think We Are?: www.wdwtwa.org.uk

REFERENCES

Ainscow, M., Conteh, J., Dyson, A. and Gallanaugh, F. (2007) *Children in Primary Education: Demography, Culture, Diversity and Inclusion (Cambridge Primary Review: Research Survey 5/1)*, Cambridge: University of Cambridge Faculty of Education.

Ajegbo, K. (2007) *Diversity and Citizenship in the Curriculum: Research Review*, London: DfES.

Alagiah, G. (2011) What it's like to be mixed-race in Britain. *BBC News Magazine*, 2 October. Available online at: www.bbc.co.uk/news/magazine-15019672 (accessed 2 January 2014).

Alexander, R. (2009) PISA 2012: Time to grow up? Available online at: www.primaryreview.org.uk (accessed 2 January 2014).

Claire, H. (2006) 'Education for cultural diversity and social justice', in J. Arthur and T. Cremin (eds) *Learning to Teach in the Primary School*, London: Routledge, pp. 307–17.

Department for Education and Skills (DfES) (2004) *Every Child Matters: Change for Children*, Nottingham: DfES.

Dyson, A. and Gallannaugh, F. (2007) National policy and the development of inclusive school practices: a case study, *Cambridge Journal of Education*, 37(4): 473–88.

Johnson, B. (2012) Let's not dwell on immigration but sow the seeds of integration. *Daily Telegraph*, 15 December.

National College for School Leadership (2005) *Effective Leadership in Multi-ethnic Schools*. Available online at: http://dera.ioe.ac.uk/5312/ or www.nationalcollege.org.uk/download (accessed November 2009).

Ofsted (2009) *Inspecting Maintained Schools' Duty to Promote Community Cohesion: Guidance for Inspectors*, London: Ofsted.

Ofsted (2013a) Evaluating pupils' spiritual, moral, social and cultural development. Subsidiary Guidance No. 110166, April.

Ofsted (2013b): Supporting the inspection of maintained schools and academies. Subsidiary Guidance No. 110166, January, p. 30, paragraph 126 and pp. 37–38, paragraphs 37–8. Available online at: www.ofsted.gov.uk/resources/subsidiary-guidance-supporting-inspection-of-maintained-schools-and-academies.

Qualifications and Curriculum Authority (QCA) (1998) *Education for Citizenship and the Teaching of Democracy in Schools*, London: QCA.

Qualifications and Curriculum Authority (QCA) (2002) *Designing and Timetabling the Primary Curriculum*, London: QCA.

Qualifications and Curriculum Authority (QCA) (2008) *A Big Picture of the Curriculum*, London: QCA.

Qualifications and Curriculum Authority (QCA) (2009) *National Curriculum: Cross-curriculum Dimensions*, London: QCA.

UNESCO (2005) Convention on the Protection and Promotion of the Diversity of Cultural Expressions, Paris, 20 October.

RESPONDING TO GENDER DIFFERENCES

Elaine Millard and Louise Wheatcroft

INTRODUCTION

This unit discusses the influence of gender on attitudes to schooling in general and the development of literacy in particular. While working through it, you will be asked to think carefully about the way in which society conveys its messages about what it means to be a boy or a girl and some strategies that you might adopt for ensuring that all pupils are encouraged to develop effective learning skills, irrespective of their gender.

OBJECTIVES

By the end of this unit, you should:

- be clear about what is meant by gender, differentiating its role from that of sex and considering its interaction with race and class;
- have an informed opinion of the role played by gendered cultural capital in determining school success and under-achievement;
- be able to identify some common patterns of behaviour that militate against individual performance and know how to combat them;
- begin to connect children's experiences of home with their school learning;
- gain more insight into the part children's own (gendered) interests can play in motivating learning.

BACKGROUND TO THE ISSUE

In education in the 1970s and 1980s, it was girls' under-achievement in maths and science that was a major concern. This was successfully addressed by a range of initiatives targeted particularly at increasing girls' access to these subjects, and girls began to match and, in some cases, outperform boys in all subjects. At the beginning of the twenty-first century, the concern for girls' education was replaced, in most anglophone nations (Australia, Canada, New Zealand, USA, UK), with more strident debates about a perceived 'underperformance' by boys. Boys' under-achievement in education in schools in general, and in literacy in particular, has become a global concern, evoking an anxious response from governments across the Western world. In England, primary girls' literacy levels have remained stubbornly better than those of boys since statistics obtained from the regime of national testing through standard assessment tests (SATs) were made public. Moreover, although this led to a whole raft of strategies being introduced and followed for over a decade to support boys' schooling, boys have not yet 'caught up'.

In the UK, girls continue to outperform boys across a variety of subjects at every age, most markedly in literacy and in reading tests. In 2012, in the Key Stage 2 reading tests, 90 per cent of girls and 84 per cent of boys achieved level 4 or above in reading (DfE, 2012). In fact, girls outperformed boys in English, reading and writing, with significant differences in attainment, whereas in maths and science there continued to be little difference between them. In 2012, the GCSE results showed a similar trend, with girls significantly outperforming boys at A* grade and at A*–C, this time in all subjects,

In 2012, the National Literacy Trust published a report by the Boys' Reading Commission, which examined the gender gap in reading. The results confirmed that there had been little national improvement in decreasing the gap in boys' and girls' reading attainment throughout the previous decade. Moreover, the issue was not just a concern for schools in England: the most recent Progress in International Results in Literacy Study (PIRLS) study (2011), an international study comparing the reading attainment and attitudes of 10-year-olds, reported that, in nearly all of the countries surveyed, girls outperformed boys, with little reduction in the reading achievement gap (Mullis *et al.*, 2012).

From the way that the media reports gender differences in examination results each summer, you might be forgiven for thinking that not a single boy in the classes you meet will willingly sit down to read or write, nor will any boy be able to achieve his best. The anxiety over boys' achievements has been further fuelled by those, often male, commentators who, speaking up for the importance of reforming boys' education, have suggested that schooling has become overly feminised through the predominance of female teachers, particularly in the primary stages of schooling (Bleach, 1998), and therefore does not cater effectively for the particular needs of boys (Biddulph, 1997; Hannan, 1999). Their recommendations have included the abandonment of coursework (unfair, because girls do it better!); boys-only classes; boys seated next to girls to discipline their learning; the recruitment of greater numbers of male primary teachers to create 'role models'; and a more 'boy-friendly' reading curriculum. The general burden of these accounts has been that boys are held back by the system, and so it is the system that requires modification. This was most vividly portrayed at the time by the late Ted Wragg's views on the subject, reported in the *Times Educational Supplement* (TES) in 1997 (Wragg, 1997) and accompanied by an image entitled 'Chained males – How boys are held back'. It showed boys in short-trousered school uniforms, dragging a ball and chain behind them. Wragg's views can be taken either as providing a practical summary of issues raised earlier by research, or contributing to one of the periodic national moral panics about literacy-related issues (or basic skills). Interestingly, more than 10 years later, an American, Michael Gurian, who describes himself as an author, business consultant and social philosopher, promoted a similar message in *The Purpose of Boys* (Gurian, 2009). It is a concern that has not gone away.

Education policymakers in the UK have supported a number of research programmes, including The Raising Boys' Achievement project 2000–4 (DfES, 2005), to examine the differences in attainment revealed by the current system of assessment and, from them, have produced a series of publications that address key aspects of boys' motivation and performance in relation to the literacy curriculum. Research recommendations included suggestions about 'boy-friendly reading' and more appropriate writing genres and subject matter, such as using an interest in sports to motivate learning, greater use of new technologies and better male role models both in schools and in society in general. In 2010, such was the media attention on the gender gap and boys' under-achievement in literacy that the BBC, as part of a collection of programmes on educational issues, produced a television series called *Gareth Malone's Extraordinary School for Boys*, featuring Gareth Malone, choirmaster and television presenter, in which a range of 'boy-friendly' approaches for motivating boys to read and write was explored as part of an experiment.

However, it is also argued that a preoccupation with the needs of boys can be divisive and cause schools to neglect the specific needs of girls, while ignoring their real gains in achievement. Skelton and Francis (2003) suggest that girls' needs have, in fact, been sidelined by government policy and media attention on the issue of boys' under-achievement. The taking of a competing-victims stance means that a better understanding of the issue is prevented from being fully explored, and critics of government policy insist that it is important to be clear about which boys and which girls are being discussed, and that cultural and class differences need also to be considered (Skelton and Francis, 2003; Watson *et al.*, 2010). In 2008, still concerned about the gender gap in attainment, the government launched 'The Gender Agenda', resulting in two publications; *Gender Issues in schools: What Works to Improve Achievement for Boys and Girls* and *Gender and Education Mythbusters: Addressing Gender and Achievement: Myths and Realities* (DCSF, 2009a, 2009b). Interestingly, one of the key messages from the documents is that any interventions that are implemented to address boys' under-achievement in literacy should not detrimentally affect girls, and that any initiative should also consider how gender, social class and ethnicity interact in their particular setting (Gillborn and Mirza, 2000). In the Boys' Reading Commission (National Literacy Trust, 2012), it was recommended that approaches that effectively support boys should be equally girl-friendly. 'They are perhaps better thought of as quality teaching' (National Literacy Trust 2012: 6).

Nevertheless, despite these reservations, most commentators suggest that more boys would perform better if they were provided with different teaching and learning approaches from those currently dominating teachers' planning. The key to understanding the 'boys' issue' is rooted firmly in the cultural differences inscribed in femininities and masculinities in society. Without this understanding, teachers may become trapped in responding to a competing-victims scenario, where either boys' or girls' needs are afforded primacy at any given time, and so one group is always regarded as underprivileged, and the curriculum is merely tweaked to remedy the perceived problem, without real thought being given to the underlying issues. An example of this is demonstrated in the work of Steve Biddulph, who began by focusing his writing for parents on the disadvantages experienced by boys (Biddulph, 1997), but who has recently published a book outlining the problems identified with being a girl, particularly focusing on body image (Biddulph, 2013).

The irony of a 'moral panic' (Cohen, 1973) about boys' performance in school is that current debate draws its arguments from a theoretical basis for understanding differences in educational aspirations and achievements that is firmly grounded in the feminist perspective and a pro-woman lobby, which some of the commentators seek to challenge. As noted above, the 1970s' and 1980s' educational focus was on girls' under-achievement, rather than any perceived problems experienced by boys, although, looking back at examination results with hindsight, boys' weaker achievement in English literature and their poorer uptake of modern foreign languages were then already marked.

As Carrie Paechter has suggested, in this period, girls were regarded in many quarters as 'the other sex' (a process described as 'othering') or as 'boy(s) gone wonky' (1998: 7), and their achievements were often compared unfavourably with those of boys of the same age or simply left unacknowledged, for example in relation to their preferred sports, or their chosen areas of study. The emphasis was getting girls into science and technology, and not boys into English literature or art history. Hilary Wilce, writing for the TES in 1995, summed up the conditions that prevailed for girls in school at that time:

> Boys dominated the playgrounds, the computers, the Bunsen burners, and teachers' time and attention; men dominated the headships and pay scales. A majority of all teachers, men and

women, said science classes mattered less for girls than boys, while girls were less likely than boys to get the remedial help they needed.

(Wilce, 1995)

Mercifully, most of these conditions have changed, particularly in relation to girls' achievements in maths and science and women teachers' achievement of higher status and managerial roles. However, it is still very important to think about issues such as the distribution of teacher attention in the classroom, or the biasing of curriculum choices when planning a scheme of work or selecting a focus for learning.

As someone preparing to teach, you will need to be both well informed in your judgements and have a well-thought-out strategy for supporting all pupils' learning, rather than a dependence on the gender stereotypes that predominate in the popular press and in some current advice on managing boys' schooling. Therefore, before you consider what key researchers and curriculum advisers have had to say on the topic, it is important for you to take time to think through the influence of gender on education from your own standpoint.

Task 6.5.1 Thinking about the influence of gender on people's experience

Your schooling

- How far do you think boys and girls of your own generation were given equal opportunities to succeed in school?
- Were there any times at school and in your later experiences of education that you thought you were treated differently from members of the opposite sex?
- Did boys and girls of your generation share similar career aspirations?
- Did boys and girls of your generation behave as well as each other, or as badly as each other in school?
- Do male and female members of your family share the same interests, particularly in reading tastes?
- Which family members were most proactive in helping you learn to read?
- Have you observed any differences in the treatment of boys' and girls' achievements and behaviours in school today?

About teaching

- Did equal numbers of men and women of your acquaintance 'always want to be a teacher'?
- Now you have chosen to teach, what do your friends make of your choice? Do you think they would respond differently if you were of the opposite sex?
- Do men and women choose similar subjects as their specialism in school – who, for example, is in charge of literacy, or in charge of ICT?

Comment

It is hoped that all of you found fewer differences in the access to education for all than were reported in earlier research studies and can report a sensitivity in schools to the individual learning needs of boys and girls of whatever race, class or gender. You may, however, have noted that there are still differences in how boys and girls, men and women position themselves in relation to education, and may have views on how this influences both their achievement in school and their future employment. This unit will now consider the issues that lie behind these influences and offer ways of understanding the role that gender plays in shaping an individual's experience of school and engagement with her or his own education.

DEFINITIONS

The first point to clarify is the definition of gender as it is employed in the debate, distinguishing it from sex. Whereas the term 'sex' is used to signify the biological differences between male and female, 'gender' designates the patterns of behaviour and attitude attributed to members of each sex that are an effect of experiences of education, culture and socialisation. Whereas sex is conventionally categorised by binary oppositions of male and female, gender has a less determined division, embracing a spectrum of experiences and ways of self-presentation and identity markers, so that an individual may adopt a feminine gender without being biologically female, and vice versa. This means that both sexes respond either in accordance with, or in opposition to, what they take to be the gender role ascribed to their biological sex. These roles tend to emphasise differences between the sexes, rather than common patterns of similarity and correspondence. Glance at any children's television programme, toy catalogue or favoured Internet website to see how aspects of masculine identity and femininity are clearly signalled to the participating reader/viewer.

Put simply, sex is a biological given, but gender is socially and culturally constructed. All current evidence supports the idea that boys and men are more concerned to establish themselves as not female than vice versa, and that 'masculine' roles are therefore under greater scrutiny and more vulnerable to peer pressure. There have been several different explanations of how gender understanding influences choice and interest.

Gender regime

Gender regime refers to the accepted version(s) of masculinity or femininity as practised in a particular community or institution, such as the family, peer group, school or place of employment. It encompasses differences in patterns of behaviour, interests and relationships expected of boys and girls, men and women. In relation to schooling, Kessler *et al.* (1985) argued that young people were caught up in overlapping gender regimes, the most powerful influence of all being the peer group, which defines what is 'cool' for each sex, both in and out of a school context.

Habitus

Related to this concept of a 'regime' is Pierre Bourdieu's theory of the habitus (Bourdieu, 1990). Bourdieu's term denotes taken-for-granted ways of thinking, which, although socially constructed, are so ingrained in an individual as a result of embodied action that they appear natural and 'durably incorporated in the body'. What this implies is that human behaviour is often heavily influenced by dispositions of action, thought and attitude, created from previous experiences of both success and failure in contexts influenced by class, family, education and social groupings. Such behaviours are, therefore, neither entirely voluntary nor completely determined.

Another way of thinking about the influence of habitus on gender-inflected behaviour is by using the concept of 'doing gender'. The following examples are given by Hilary Claire in her introduction to the Association of Teachers and Lecturers' 2004 publication, *Gender in Education 3-19: A Fresh Approach*:

When a woman sits with her knees together and a man sprawls; when a woman stops talking because someone else has butted in, or jumps up to clear the table; when a man becomes the spokesperson for a mixed group, or takes over in managing a joint project – they are 'doing gender'. Girls and boys learn to do gender from the earliest age with positive and negative reinforcements at every turn, which, for most of us, are extremely difficult to ignore or unlearn.

(Claire, 2004a: 13)

Cultural capital

This is another concept taken from the work of Bourdieu and his colleague Jean Passeron (1977 [1970]), which accounts for the cultural advantages bestowed on individuals from their own family and its position in society, rather than from mere economic power. It is used to understand and explain distinctions in cultural knowledge, taste and preference, which place individuals in positions of either social advantage or disadvantage in relation to dominant forms of education and experience. Cultural capital strongly influences educational opportunity and confers power and status on those whose capital is deemed to demonstrate their superiority. Further, Bourdieu argues that the value ascribed to specific aspects of cultural knowledge is dependent on the predilections, education and practices of the dominant elite already educated into particular tastes, as, for example, books rather than websites, classical rather than rock or pop music, theatre rather than television, world cinema rather than American movies. In terms of culture, men's activities often attract higher status than those practised by women. It has often been observed, for example, that primary teachers' lower status than that of other professionals is a result of the preponderance of women teachers in our first schools.

You will find a fuller discussion of both habitus and cultural capital in relation to literacy in *Differently Literate* (Millard, 1997: 20–3).

Task 6.5.2 Cultural capital and the curriculum

- How does the current National Curriculum (DfE, 2013a, 2013b) reinforce particular notions of national cultural capital?
- Are there any aspects of the curriculum that appear to be given a higher status?
- Why do you think this is?

Identity work

Sex and gender are key components of personal identity and, arguably, the first attributes that we register about someone we encounter, whether casually in the street or, more permanently, in relation to friends, colleagues and partners. Our upbringing and social interactions all provide us with strong messages about what it is to be a man or a woman and how we should present ourselves and interact socially. Carrie Paechter (1998) gives a very full account of the interrelationship of these two categories. Her chapter on 'Gender as a social construct' in *Educating the Other* will help you to understand these distinctions more fully. She argues that much of what is taken for granted as 'natural' in Western society, as regards sex and gender, is not only socially constructed but also male-centred. Biological explanations have been used to support prevailing social inequalities by making gender roles seem to be a natural state (as in 'boys will be boys'). Further, she reminds us that, although in the majority of cases gender identity is related to biological sex, this is not a necessary relation, and in some cases the two are unrelated.

Gender is, therefore, relational, and, most importantly, the differences expressed in gender roles involve power relations in which, as argued above, 'masculine' activities are usually perceived to have higher status than feminine ones; for example, basketball is considered a more interesting sport than netball, carpentry more skilful than needlecraft or cookery. Because of the power relation inherent in constructed gender differences, boys are under greater pressure from their peer group to conform to what is acceptably 'male' (Martino, 2007). Masculine identity, therefore, is more precarious and, therefore, more constrained and defended than femininity; this leads to there being more restricted behavioural possibilities for males than for females, with boys showing a tendency to be homophobic and misogynistic in classroom interactions and punitive of those who step 'out of line'. Becky Francis, who has shown how gender policing impacts on gendered power relations in both primary and secondary classrooms, reports:

> So, from pre-school ages onwards children engage in what Davies calls 'gender category maintenance work'. This involves behaving in stereotypical ways to demonstrate their gender allegiance, but also in policing other children to ensure that they do the same. It is this kind of behaviour that results in gendered trends in classroom behaviour and interaction.
>
> (Francis, 2005: 42)

It is clear that school plays a significant role in shaping children's sense of self, and it is, therefore, important to take account of the role category maintenance may play in reinforcing, or maintaining, gender stereotypes in classroom interactions.

GENDER AND SCHOOL DISCIPLINE

In broad generalities, it has been found that many boys find accommodating themselves to school expectations a far more difficult task than most girls do. In particular, working-class boys and black boys are reported as finding school regimes oppressive and often seek to subvert the power of their teachers and other authorities (Phoenix, 2004). The issues created for boys by schooling has also been described by a number of sociologists, who identified key groups of boys who create their identities in opposition to schooling (Willis, 1977; Mac an Ghaill, 1994; Connell, 1995; Martino, 2007).

The findings of a wide range of studies related to behaviour are summed up below. Teachers find boys more disruptive in school, and the attention they demand holds back girls.

Task 6.5.3 Adult–child interactions

Take time to consider some of the ways shown in Table 6.5.1 in which adults have been shown to interact with children and think about their consequences for learning, filling in the right-hand column with your views. Two have already been completed to provide examples; however, please think of your own examples and explanations for these items.

- Boys use diversionary tactics to disrupt classroom management.
- Boys' peer culture endorses 'messing about' in class – it is 'uncool' for them to be seen to work, and the dominant groups mock boys who wish to study.
- Boys are less diligent about completing homework (particularly 'learning' or 'reading' work).

- Boys seek to occupy the 'action zone' in the lessons they enjoy, gaining more opportunities for interaction with teachers (Randall, 1987; Shilling, 1991).
- Boys are reprimanded more often than girls – it is estimated that the ratio of praise to blame is as low as 1:3 for boys.
- Boys' disruptive behaviour annoys girls and prevents them from working as well as they intend.
- Boys' name-calling can deter less dominant boys and many girls from feeling confident in proffering ideas and comments in class.
- Girls are more quietly inattentive and so may slip out of a teacher's sight.

TABLE 6.5.1 Adult–child interactions and the consequences for learning

Interaction	Consequences
Adults, through their earliest interactions, treat boys and girls very differently	This reinforces gender roles, and, from an early age, boys and girls begin to emphasise their differences from each other
Boys are encouraged to be more active than girls and participate more frequently in boisterous play	Boys find sitting down for an extended length of time tedious
Boys and girls are provided with different kinds of toys	
Girls are provided with a wider range of writing and drawing materials	
Girls often spend more time working with, and talking to, adults	
The early reading of boys and girls, particularly in relation to popular culture, conveys different messages about what it is to succeed	

Think about which of these findings match your own experience and decide what implications they may have for your practice. Discuss your ideas with your tutor and other teachers in training. Identify areas you might concentrate on addressing in specific lessons. Think about how these relate to the teachers' standards. Which standards are linked to adult–child interactions?

Comment

One of the most common issues raised by boys consulted by researchers is that they are 'picked on more than girls', and it is clear from classroom observational research that the teacher's gaze is frequently directed at the boys, focusing on their behaviour and using closed questioning as a disciplinary tactic (have you been listening?), rather than adopting a strategy that avoids confrontation (can you find your own solution to this problem?).

In managing classroom behaviour, you need to show fairness by dealing with both boys and girls in similar ways. Your 'ground rules' for the behaviour you expect should be applicable to all, and, when you deviate from them, you need to be able to give a clear expectation of what has made you change your rules.

GENDER AND READING

It is in matters of literacy that most concern has been expressed about gender differences. Earliest attention to this difference focused on achievements in reading, and every survey of children's reading interests conducted since the seminal work of Whitehead *et al.* (1977) has shown that boys and girls have quite different reading tastes (Hall and Coles, 1999; Maynard *et al.*, 2008). In general, girls are also far more committed readers (Sainsbury and Schagen, 2004; Clark, 2012a,). Research shows that children's enjoyment of reading is strongly linked to attainment. The more children read, the more successful readers they become, and the more they wish to read. The National Literacy Trust's annual literacy survey in 2011 (in Clark 2012a) shows that boys still report that they do not enjoy reading as much as girls do; they are less likely to read outside school than girls; they are less likely to perceive themselves as readers than girls; they have different reading preferences to girls; and more boys than girls struggle with reading. Further, it has been shown that girls' predominant tastes in reading choices, which favour narratives and life-like experiences, more closely match the demands of the current English curriculum (DfEE, 1999), giving them a better start in school tasks (Millard, 1997; Barrs and Pidgeon, 1998). Twist and Sainsbury (2009) also argue that, not only are there differences in boys' and girls' reading preferences, which can have an impact on their responses to texts in reading tests, but that there are differences in their test-taking strategies, suggesting that the reading tests used to indicate reading attainment are, therefore, gender biased. Michael Rosen, writer and former Children's Laureate, when consulted for the Boys' Reading Commission Report (National Literacy Trust, 2012) argued that curriculum and assessment strategies encourage closed questioning about texts, which leads to boys having negative attitudes towards reading tests. He suggests that teachers need to provide more opportunities for talk around texts, rather than asking pupils only to respond to set questions. Moss (2011) also warns that, as long as performance indicators drive policy, the development of a quality literacy curriculum will be hard to achieve.

Both boys' and girls' interests need to be taken into account when selecting resources for both independent and whole-class reading, and these need to include a wide and varied range of texts, including non-fiction, magazines and screen-based texts. Further, it is important to ensure that all pupils are able to experience a rich diet of well-crafted narratives and hear them read well. The experience of reading aloud and 'performing' powerful texts embeds an understanding of the rhythms as well as the language of both poetry and prose, and it is essential to create time for some texts to be read and reread. Given an appropriate opportunity, the least able and the unwilling readers can enjoy reading to younger pupils, if enabled to prepare properly. Parents and carers are usually very pleased to help with practice for performance.

When discussing issues related to reading and responding in writing, boys may be embarrassed by requests to reveal aspects of their personal lives and generally have less experience of sharing feelings with their peers than girls. Given appropriate contexts, however, boys can be interested in exploring their own concerns, but the choice of context for this needs handling sensitively. Drama, poetry and fiction allow many opportunities for discussing important personal issues through considering the interrelationship of characters, experiences and events. The importance of developing empathy, a cornerstone of social and emotional aspects of learning (SEAL), makes it important to share texts, with both boys and girls, that focus on character development and emotions, rather than always selecting for adventure, plot and action. It is also equally important to think about different cultures' responses to narrative and storytelling and weave other ethnic interests into your choices too.

A particularly useful way of categorising children's reading is provided by data from a sustained research project conducted by Moss and Attar (1999), in which the reading events in particular schools were analysed and related to children's understanding of what messages their attainment carries. They identified three distinct kinds of event, which they designated as: reading for proficiency; reading for choice; and procedural reading. Drawing out gender differences in the experiences they recorded, they suggested it is the proficiency frame for reading that creates most gender differentiation, with the less proficient boy readers masking their lack of competence by selecting non-fiction texts as their main reading choices. Moss (2008) later warns against a popular assumption that many weaker boys' interest in non-fiction, such as the very popular Usborne information texts, will support the development of their reading proficiency. She argues that their choice of text is picture-led and involves little more than scanning for impressive images to talk about with friends. To encourage a more thoughtful, analytical response to non-fiction, more appropriate to enquiry, you will need to set the reading of non-fiction within an appropriate context.

When catering for different reading tastes in individual reading, it is also important that a focus on gender does not simply reinforce the differences in range and breadth of the texts that all pupils encounter, and girls' preferences are not ignored when providing for boys' perceived interests. At the time of writing, the revised National Curriculum for English is still in draft form; however, it appears that it will include a greater emphasis on established works of English literature. One of the aims stated in the curriculum is 'to develop a love of literature through widespread reading for enjoyment' (DfE, 2013b). This has always been part of the National Curriculum, and many strategies have been tried to create more enthusiastic boy readers. Despite this, girls continue to report enjoying reading more than boys do. Not only this, but research by Twist and Sainsbury (2009) on the 2008 SATs reading test has shown that girls performed better than boys when responding to the literary questions. It will, therefore, be interesting to see what provision the new curriculum will advise to promote more equal access and participation.

Task 6.5.4 Book audit

Examine the books on just one shelf in your classroom that you are currently making available for sustained reading in your class.

- Ask yourself if you are providing your class with texts and their related activities that reflect a wide range of children's current interests.
- Take time to discuss the roles ascribed to men and women, boys and girls in these texts, and help your children to think more critically about representation and stereotyping.
- Are there significant differences of representation from that in the books you read as a pupil in school?
- Are there particular issues related to access to learning that you need to address, such as access to computers, preparedness for writing and time to share ideas with others?

GENDER AND WRITING

Differences in reading choices have been shown to have consequences, not only for children's reading in school, but also for developing their confidence as writers (Millard, 1997; Barrs and Cork, 2001). More of girls' writing shows evidence of traditional narrative influences and structures, whereas boys frequently draw on film or oral narrative structures, producing action-packed stories (Marsh, 2003; Millard, 2005; Willett, 2005). This may make boys appear less competent writers in relation to narratives produced in response to school criteria. Boys are often made aware of teachers' disapproval of their preferred content in story writing, which makes them less confident or motivated to write.

Again, it is important to ensure literacy activities from a wealth of different narratives, short stories, tales and children's novels are shared – not just a selection of excerpts to demonstrate specific language points. Digital and other multimodal texts, including the structure of computer games, can also afford interesting stimuli for writing (Millard, 2000). A report on *Young People's Writing in 2011* for the NLT by Clark (2012b) showed that girls enjoy writing more than boys, and, although both boys and girls engage in reading and creating digital texts in their home literacy practices, girls also tend to write more in technology-based formats such as emails, text messages and messages on social networking sites.

When discussing writing in literacy work, draw attention to successful uses of language in both boys' and girls' written work. For example, Millard's research (2005) found that boys often employed a wider range of vocabulary and used action verbs more effectively, whereas girls spent more time developing the setting of a story or creating character. Help classes to analyse and comment on each other's work by sharing their most interesting pieces and highlighting achievements. Here are some comments made by Year 5 girls on stories that had been written by boys:

> My favourite part is where you find arrows firing across the room. I also liked the flame-pit room with a flaming fire. I think 'find a rope and swing for your life' is an original idea. I like the spiders and their sharp fangs. In fact I like everything.

> I think your title is brilliant and so is your blurb. I like 'the mummy with gleaming eyes' and 'bubbly paper wrapped round it'. I like your pictures of the mummies. My favourite room is the dark chamber.

And a boy's comments on a girl's story:

> I liked page two best. It has a brilliant description of the witch. I would have liked a picture of her though. The most interesting bit was where you discover the treasure. It was good how you could click your fingers to escape the magic.

Interestingly, only one boy in this particular group chose a girl's story to report on, whereas girls were equally interested in the stories written by both boys and girls (Castle of Fear Project; see Millard, 2005). It is important to get boys and girls sharing their work and understanding differences of language use in order to expand both groups' repertoires of image and vocabulary.

It is also frequently noted that most girls have greater concern for presentation in all forms of language work, and often do more than is required of them, whereas many boys are happy with the bare minimum. To counter this, you need to place greater emphasis on fewer finished pieces of work, rather than completing numerous notes and exercises. Setting fewer writing tasks will encourage both genders to see both the composition and presentation phases as more important. Encourage the use of word-processing as well as handwriting to achieve well-set-out work and use the concept of design (Kress and Van Leeuwen, 2006) rather than handwriting alone as a way of judging good presentation. A range of media for creating meaning, such as PowerPoints, weblogs and simple poster designs, will help the overall development of both boys' and girls' use of appropriate language, design and presentation skills.

Make a class collection of stories and poems to promote both better presentation skills and an opportunity to learn from each other's work. This could be stored online, and children could be encouraged to read work from the collection to children in other classes or share with parents and school visitors, as well as each other. Let the children make the selection themselves, giving specific reasons for the choices they make, based on the language used. From the selection, identify each pupil's writing strengths, so that these can be drawn on for discussion in later writing sessions.

Comment

There is insufficient space here to consider in detail the particulars of differences in the affordances created by writing in a variety of modes, some of them electronic. However, these are important in understanding differences in pupils' responses to the written texts required in school. In research studies (Millard, 1997, 2000, 2003), the focus has been on the differences in boys' and girls' approaches to writing, demonstrating that more boys than girls make use of visual forms to create meaning. It is important to understand each individual's writing preferences as thoughtfully as you do for their reading and encourage them in trying out varied ways of both planning and presenting texts. All pupils need to experience a wide range of ways of making meanings and to not be limited to what they already do, as when, for example, boys are allowed to use graphics and girls to write reams. A focus on text types and ways of framing writing that informed much of the National Literacy Strategy, if not limited to a mechanical reproduction of form for practice, has proved very effective in supporting all children's written work, particularly that of boys. The challenge is to match the genre you are teaching to your pupils' interests and preferences, in a process termed 'fusion' (Millard, 2000).

GENDER AND ORAL WORK

In oral work, it is girls who are more often placed at a disadvantage in both whole-class and mixed groupings. In whole-class settings, teachers have been found to direct more of their questions at boys, often for management of their behaviour, and, in all kinds of group work, boys manage to dominate talk, even in small mixed groups, so that both girls and quiet boys may have problems in making themselves or their views heard. However, the same boys often leave the written recording of discussions to girls, while taking charge of representations (Davies, 1998).

The first thing to do is to look closely at your own habits of questioning to promote more thoughtful responses from all pupils. In group work, it is important not only to select members to work together and ensure that all your pupils have experience of working in both mixed and single-sex groups, but also to define their roles carefully. Homophobic attitudes have been found to limit who speaks and what can be said in group work (Guasp, 2009). The ridiculing of alternative viewpoints should always be challenged, and very clear strategies for cooperative work should be set out. It is more productive if you encourage your classes to draw up guidelines for good habits of working together for themselves.

Talk is gaining increasing importance as an essential part of pupils' school experience, its value being emphasised by Sir Jim Rose in the final report of his *Independent Review of the Curriculum* (2009) and in the Cambridge Primary Review (Alexander, 2010). Boys have been characterised as particularly enjoying argument, competition and disputation (Davies, 1998). These aspects of language can be built into many classroom activities, particularly through the use of role-play and simulations. Girls will also benefit from safe challenges provided by working in role. You should be careful to 'protect' all children in role, especially the least confident ones; see Heathcote (2002) for an account of this approach. Despite the importance educators place on oracy, it is disconcerting to note that, in the aims of the current draft of the proposed English curriculum (DfE, 2013b), speaking and listening appear at the bottom of the list, despite being the key to all aspects of literacy and one aspect of learning in which many boys feel most confident.

A ROLE FOR POPULAR CULTURE

Although English and language work in school concerns itself largely with what is judged by adults to be appropriate literature, out-of-school, pleasurable narratives are available in a much wider range of forms, including comics, magazines, television, film, videos, computer games and so on. Many of these texts are interconnected, so that a film, a comic, a computer game and a popular book may share a common narrative source and main characters. These narratives have wide currency with all groups of children and are important in the development of friendships and peer groups (Dyson, 1997; Marsh, 2003; Marsh and Millard, 2003; Willett, 2005). As Marsh argues:

> Popular culture, media and new technologies offer a myriad of opportunities for deconstructing these representations of gender and developing critical literacy skills, skills which are essential in order to challenge the stereotypes which perpetuate literacy myths, including those relating to underachievement.

(Marsh, 2003: 73)

Marsh and Millard (2003) have examined the role that popular media can play in creating motivation, particularly among pupils who find conventional school work unappealing (more frequently boys). You need to be aware of your own classes' popular interests and use them for these aspects of language work (see Dyson, 1997; Marsh, 2003; Millard, 2003; Willett, 2005). There are, however, disadvantages to popular texts, as they are often more marked by gendered interests than resources more commonly made available in school. Commercial interests deliberately frame them to appeal specifically either to boys or girls by reinforcing ideas of typical interests; for example, football and Star Wars for boys, home-making and Barbie dolls for girls. However, because of their wide circulation and the personal interest invested in them, they provide a very rich source of ideas for writing and discussion and can provide good opportunities for challenging stereotypes that limit expectations.

Task 6.5.5 Examining popular texts

Examine a range of popular texts for children that include paper-based and digital texts, such as comics, magazines and websites for children.

- How are gender stereotypes reinforced?
- How might you use popular texts in the classroom to challenge gender stereotypes?
- How might you use popular texts to engage and motivate pupils?

GENDER AND CHOICE

As was discussed in the earlier section on identity, in Western cultures, girls are often freer to participate in activities that are seen as having a masculine bias, for example football or computing, than boys, who often feel unable to take up interests that are perceived by their peers as feminine, for example French or dance. Tomboys have more credibility than cissies! One example of such limitations occurs if reading in school appears to many boys to be associated with women and girls. This is because it is mothers and other female members of their families who, for the most part, help with early reading, and book choice in school sometimes seems skewed to the kind of psychological story in which nothing very exciting happens (Millard, 1997). If things are to change, such gender limitations need to be addressed in the same way in which earlier gender research addressed girls' disenchantment with science. The first step towards this is to consider how concepts of masculinity work to limit expectations in literacy.

Hegemonic masculinity

Hegemony is a term introduced by Antonio Gramsci to refer to prevalent ideas that have become naturalised, accepted without question and used to justify the status quo of an institution or cultural practice within a particular society. In the Western world, there is a prevailing view that accepts gender as a binary division, biologically fixed, with masculinity occupying a dominant, assertive role. Hegemonic masculinity is present in the narratives of popular novels and films, in characters such as James Bond or Batman.

Hegemonic masculinity in schools works similarly to validate a male peer-group culture based on music, technology and sport, which expects challenges to authority; it often rejects schooling as uncool and endorses messing about in class, expecting achievement through effortless ability (Mac an Ghaill, 1994; Connell, 1995; Martino and Meyenne, 2001; Phoenix, 2004). Mac an Ghaill caricatured this version of masculinity in older students as being dominated by the three 'f's (fighting, fucking and football; 1994: 58, 108–9). Its binary opposite has been labelled 'emphasised femininity' (Connell, 1995). Connell suggests that the cultural ideal that is celebrated for women is about sociability, fragility, passivity and, above all, compliance with male desire. Emphasised femininity is constructed in a subordinated relationship to hegemonic masculinity in ways that reinforce masculine power.

It can be argued that one of the main reasons for girls' greater achievement in education and the workplace has been the result of changing conceptions of femininity in society as a whole, brought about by the educational work of the second wave of feminists, who focused on questioning women's role in society. In schools in the 1980s, the changing role of women and the possibilities opening up for girls in the professions were very much on the agenda. By contrast, there have been relatively few attempts in this or any other anglophone country to challenge the traditional place of men in society or to understand the role that hegemonic (dominant) masculinity plays in determining and limiting boys' educational opportunities. This is an issue you may wish to begin to debate with your colleagues.

Warning: Because of the negative influence of peer-group pressure, which 'polices' the maintenance of this view of masculinity, attempts to address boys' relatively poorer performance, particularly in literacy activities, using teaching strategies that focus on the interests associated with hegemonic masculinity, will not change deep-seated attitudes and learning behaviour. It is important that, as a teacher, you make time to discuss with the boys how the world works for them and the difficulties they might encounter without greater flexibility in role and expectations.

This discussion of gender difference has asked you to think carefully again about the current emphasis on boys' educational needs, while stressing that it is of equal importance to keep in mind the preferred interests of the girls in your classes. Most of the points that have been raised about gender are as relevant to the sound development of girls' education as they are to that of boys'. Both boys' and girls' interests should be taken into account when selecting resources and activities associated with literacy. It is important that both boys and girls are helped to make choices and judgements about their own work, preferred learning styles and competencies. Avoid the easy adoption of supposedly 'boy-friendly' resources that address a very limited set of expectations. Not all boys dislike reading or are interested in sport and conflict, for example. Boys' behaviour in general may present many teachers with greater difficulty, but that is not always the case, and so the rules made for a good classroom ethos should treat both girls and boys fairly and equally.

GENDER, ETHNICITY AND CLASS

Gender identity and its relationship to boys' schooling and achievement have now been on the agenda for more than 10 years of the new century, and many individual strategies adopted have proved effective in particular contexts. However, the focus on boys' needs has taken place at the expense of a more thoughtful consideration of educational disadvantage and an understanding of the intercalation of other markers of identity, such as ethnicity and gender. As Gillborn and Mirza stated in their 2000 report for Ofsted, *Educational Inequality*: 'social class and gender differences are . . . associated with differences in attainment, but neither can account for persistent underlying ethnic inequalities' (cited in Claire, 2004b: 23). The statistical evidence on which Gillborn and Mirza's judgements rest can be found in Hilary Claire's summary of the report (Claire, 2004b). Nevertheless, Claire herself emphasises a point they make that, 'in all the data, gender is a factor in unequal attainment and that their recommended strategies to reduce inequalities of "race"/ethnicity are equally applicable to class and gender' (Claire, 2004b).

The principles recommended in this unit emphasise the importance of understanding the cultural experience of each individual pupil in each class set, and, therefore, questions of class and ethnicity that influence both interest in and orientation to learning should always inform both your understanding and planning.

Task 6.5.6 Gender, ethnicity and class

In the new *Teachers' Standards* implemented in 2012, a number of standards relate to a teacher's ability to consider gender, ethnicity and class when planning children's learning experiences:

1 Set high expectations that inspire, motivate and challenge pupils: set goals that stretch and challenge pupils of all backgrounds, abilities and dispositions.
2 Promote good progress and outcomes by pupils: demonstrate knowledge and understanding of how pupils learn and how this impacts on teaching
3 Demonstrate good subject and curriculum knowledge: have a secure knowledge of the relevant subject and curriculum areas, foster and maintain pupils' interest in the subject, and address misunderstandings.
4 Plan and teach well-structured lessons: promote a love of learning and children's intellectual curiosity; contribute to the design and provision of an engaging curriculum within the relevant subject area.

- Reflect on your own teaching and performance against the standards and consider how you have considered the cultural experience of the pupils that you have taught.
- How have you achieved this through your planning?
- How have you used resources to motivate learners/boys/girls/under-achievers?
- How have you motivated learners through your choice of activities and learning experiences?
- How have your assessment strategies enabled all learners to demonstrate what they have learned?
- How have you engaged boys and girls in reading and writing?
- How have you provided for the different interests and passions of your pupils?

Task 6.5.7 Taking it further through research work

Those of you who are interested in conducting your own research in this area, whether as part of work towards an M-level qualification, or in order to address a specific need of your current context, may wish to consider working on a small project in your place of work. Here are some ideas you might choose to follow up:

- As recommended by Watson *et al.* (2010), widen the range of literacy materials that you use to engage pupils by investigating the current reading interests of the boys and girls in your class. Find out what types of text they are enjoying and explore ways to incorporate literacy materials from children's out-of-school experiences in your literacy lessons.
- Conduct a piece of action research. Identify a small group of children or individuals who are under-achieving and identify some approaches that would benefit both boys and girls in your class. Implement an approach and evaluate the effectiveness of the intervention.
- Observe boys and/or girls in the role-play area or in the writing area. What can you find out about how they enact and develop stories/narratives or about when and why they choose to write? How can this learning be used to inform your practice?
- Devise a questionnaire to survey the literacy experiences and interests of your colleagues or fellow students. Analyse the responses in relation to teaching experience, age and gender. Do your findings hold any implications for planning the school's continuing professional development requirements?

SUMMARY

Despite the many changes that have improved the position of both girls and women in society, Western culture is still saturated with notions of gender difference, often with an accompanying assumption that there are 'natural' attributes of the sexes that are best acknowledged as fixed. Questions of masculine identity have not been analysed with the same amount of scrutiny, even when stereotypical masculine responses result in poorer orientation to both schools and schooling. This unit, in helping you to think otherwise about the role of gender in schooling, has stressed the importance of developing a pedagogy rooted firmly in the sociocultural lives of children, which is sensitive to their ethnicity, class, previous experiences and preferred ways of learning, as well as their gendered identity.

ANNOTATED FURTHER READING

Millard, E. (1997) *Differently Literate: Boys, Girls and the Schooling of Literacy*, London: Falmer.
> Many of the main concepts on which this unit are based are found in this book. It also contains the research methodology useful in guiding you in how to find out about your classes' interests in reading and writing. In particular, it recommends collecting 'stories of reading' from all the children you teach, by asking them to write about their own journey into reading.

Moss, G. (2008) *Literacy and Gender: Researching Texts, Contexts and Readers*, London: Routledge.

> Here, you will find an excellent analysis of further research methodologies, including accounts of important findings from Moss's own research. Her focus is on the structures of schooling and, in particular, the 'literacy events' that shape children's perceptions of what is expected of them in the literacy curriculum. Her analysis of types of reader and their response to classroom tasks is particularly useful in helping you understand how your organisation in the classroom contributes to the construction of readers and their self-identity.

Skelton, C. and Francis, B. (eds) (2003) *Boys and Girls in the Primary Classroom*, Maidenhead: Open University Press.

> In this book, you will find ways of developing your classroom practice in many of the areas discussed in this unit. It includes chapters on the following issues: working with children to deconstruct gender; the role of gender in the playground; aspects of transfer; issues of identity, status and gender; gender and special educational needs; and literacy, gender and popular culture.

Watson, A. Kehler, M. and Martino, W. (2010) 'The problem of boys' literacy underachievement: raising some questions', *Journal of Adolescent and Adult Literacy*, 53(5): 356-61.

> In this article, Watson *et al.* express concerns about the way in which boys and girls are often presented as competing victims. They suggest that the issue is oversimplified and it should include consideration of a number of other factors, such as social class, race, ethnicity and sexuality, as well as gender. They argue that it would be more productive to challenge culturally and socially constructed understandings of masculinity.

 FURTHER READING TO SUPPORT M-LEVEL STUDY

Moss, G. (2011) 'Policy and the search for explanation for the gender gap in literacy attainment', *Literacy*, 45(3): 111-18.

> Moss considers how a heavy focus on performance data has impacted upon issues relating to gender, literacy and attainment. Moss suggests that policymakers, in wanting quick-fix solutions, have exacerbated the issue and reinforced stereotypes. Moss recommends that what is needed is time for teachers and researchers to reflect on the issue, focusing on the quality of the curriculum, through creating an extended and inclusive curriculum that engages pupils and allows them to step beyond narrowly defined gendered interests.

Twist, L. and Sainsbury, M. (2009) 'Girl friendly? Investigating the gender gap in national reading tests at age 11', *Educational Research*, 51(2): 283-97.

> In this research, Twist and Sainsbury examine the performance of boys and girls in the 2008 reading test and explore the differences in their responses to questions on different types of text and to different types of question. This research suggests that, although children's affective responses to the subject matter of the tests affect attainment, it is a much more complex issue. Questions arise over the effectiveness of reading tests in assessing attainment. This article relates to the article by Moss above on the effectiveness of using performance data to drive practice

 RELEVANT WEBSITES

The BBC School Season of television programmes: www.bbc.co.uk/tv/seasons/schoolseason

The DfE website holds a number of reports and articles on gender: www.education.gov.uk/search/results ?q=gender

DfE *Teachers' Standards* 2012: http://webarchive.nationalarchives.gov.uk/20130401151715/https://www.education. gov.uk/publications/eOrderingDownload/teachers%20standards.pdf

Examination results: www.jcq.org.uk/examination-results/gcses/gcse

National Literacy Trust gender and literacy research pages: www.literacytrust.org.uk/search?q=gender
> A very comprehensive research index that you can use to follow up specific issues in relation to literacy and gender.

The National Literacy Trust also hosts all the policy documents related to government research and initiatives to raise boys' achievements on:

www.literacytrust.org.uk/sitemap_overview#initiatives

Times Educational Supplement (TES): www.tes.co.uk

REFERENCES

Alexander, R. (2010) *Children, Their World, Their Education: Final Report and Recommendations of the Cambridge Primary Review*, London: Routledge.

Barrs, M. and Cork, V. (2001) *The Reader in the Writer*, London: CLPE.

Barrs, M. and Pidgeon, S. (1998) *Boys and Reading*, London: CLPE.

Biddulph, S. (1997) *Raising Boys*, London: Thames.

Biddulph, S. (2013) *Raising Girls*, New York: HarperCollins.

Bleach, K. (1998) *Raising Boys' Achievement in Schools*, Stoke-on-Trent: Trentham Books.

Bourdieu, P. (1990) *The Logic of Practice*, Cambridge, Polity Press.

Bourdieu, P. and Passeron, J. (1977 [1970]) *Reproduction in Education, Society and Culture* (trans. Richard Nice), London: Sage.

Claire, H. (ed.) (2004a) *Gender in Education 3-19: A Fresh Approach*, London: Association of Teachers and Lecturers. Available at: www.atl.org.uk/Images/Gender%20in%20education%203-19.pdf

Claire, H. (2004b) 'Mapping "race", class and gender: a summary of the report by David Gillborn and Heidi Mirza', in H. Claire (ed.) *Gender in Education 3-19: A Fresh Approach*, London: Association of Teachers and Lecturers.

Clark, C. (2012a) *Children's and Young People's Reading Today. Findings From the 2011 National Literacy Trust's Annual Survey*, London: National Literacy Trust.

Clark, C. (2012b) *Young People's Writing in 2011. Findings From the National Literacy Trust's Annual Literacy Survey*, London: National Literacy Trust.

Cohen, S. (1973) *Folk Devils and Moral Panics*, St Albans: Paladin.

Connell, R.W. (1995) *Masculinities*, St Leonards, NSW: Allen and Unwin.

Davies, J. (1998) 'Taking risks or playing safe: boys' and girls' talk', in E. Millard and A. Clark (eds) *Gender in the Secondary School Curriculum*, London: Routledge.

DCSF (2009a) *Gender and Education Mythbusters: Addressing Gender and Achievement: Myths and Realities*, Nottingham: DCSF.

DCSF (2009b) *Gender Issues in School – What Works to Improve Achievement for Boys and Girls*, Nottingham: DCSF.

DfE (2012) *National Curriculum Assessments at Key Stage 2 in England 2012*. Available at: www.gov.uk/government/uploads/system/uploads/attachment_data/file/219204/sfr19-2012.pdf

DfE (2013a) *National Curriculum in England: Primary Curriculum*. London: DfE. Available at: www.gov.uk/government/collections/national-curriculum

DfE (2013b) *English Programmes of Study for Key Stages 1-2*. Available at: http://media.education.gov.uk/assets/files/pdf/e/english%20-%20key%20stages%201%20and%202.pdf

DfEE (1999) *The National Curriculum: Handbook for Primary Teachers in England*, London: QCA.

DfES (2005) *Raising Boys' Achievement*, London: HMSO.

Dyson, A.H. (1997) *Writing Superheroes: Contemporary Childhood, Popular Culture, and Classroom Literacy*, New York: Teachers College Press.

Francis, B. (2005) 'Classroom interaction and access: whose space is it?', in H. Claire (ed.) *Gender in Education 3-19: A Fresh Approach*, London: Association of Teachers ad Lecturers. www.atl.org.uk/Images/Gender%20in%20education%203-19.pdf

Gillborn, D. and Mirza, H. (2000) *Educational Inequality: Mapping Race, Class and Gender* (HMI 232), London: Ofsted.

Guasp, A. (2009) *Homophobic Bullying in Britain's Schools: The Teachers' Report*. Available at: www.stonewall.org.uk/teachersreport (accessed November 2009).

Gurian, M. (2009) *The Purpose of Boys: Helping Our Sons Find Meaning*, San Francisco, CA: Jossey-Bass.

Hall, C. and Coles, M. (1999) *Children's Reading Choices*, London: Routledge.

Hannan, G. (1999) *Improving Boys' Performance*, Oxford: Heinemann Educational Publishing.

Heathcote, D. (2002) 'Contexts for active learning: four models to forge links between schooling and society', Paper presented at the NATD conference, February.

Kessler, S., Ashden, D., Connell, R. and Dowsett, G. (1985) 'Gender relations in secondary schooling', *Sociology of Education*, 58(1): 34-48.

Kress, G. and Van Leeuwen, T. (2006) *Reading Images. The Grammar of Visual Design*, London: Routledge.

Mac an Ghaill, M. (1994) *The Making of Men*, Buckingham: Open University Press.

Marsh, J. (2003) 'Super hero stories: literacy, gender and popular culture', in C. Skelton and B. Francis (eds) *Boys and Girls in the Primary School*, Buckingham: Open University Press.

Marsh, J. and Millard, E. (2003) *Literacy and Popular Culture in the Classroom*, Reading: Reading and Language Centre Publications.

Martino, W. (2007) 'Policing masculinities: investigating the role of homophobia and heteronormativity in the lives of adolescent school boys', *Journal of Men's Studies*, 8(2): 213-16.

Martino, W. and Meyenne, B. (eds) (2001) *What About the Boys? Issues of Masculinity in Schools*, Buckingham: Open University Press.

Maynard, S., Mackay, S. and Smyth, F. (2008) 'A survey of young people's reading in England: borrowing and choosing books', *Journal of Librarianship and Information Science*, 40: 239-53.

Millard, E. (1997) *Differently Literate: Boys, Girls and the Schooling of Literacy*, London: Falmer.

Millard, E. (2000) 'Aspects of gender: how boys' and girls' experiences of reading help to shape their writing', in J.Evans (ed.) *The Writing Classroom: Aspects of Writing and the Primary Child*, London: David Fulton.

Millard, E. (2003) 'Transformative pedagogy: towards a literacy of fusion', *Reading, Literacy and Language*, 37(1): 3-9.

Millard, E. (2005) 'Writing of heroes and villains: fusing children's knowledge about popular fantasy texts with school-based literacy requirements', in J. Evans (ed.) *Literacy Moves On*, Portsmouth, NH: Heinemann.

Moss, G. (2008) *Literacy and Gender: Researching Texts, Contexts and Readers*, London: Routledge.

Moss, G. (2011) 'Policy and the search for explanation for the gender gap in literacy attainment', *Literacy*, 45(3): 111-18.

Moss, G. and Attar, D. (1999) 'Boys and literacy: gendering the reading curriculum', in J. Prosser (ed.) *School Cultures*, London: Chapman.

Mullis, I.V.S., Martin, M.O., Foy, P. and Drucker, K.T. (2012) *PIRLS 2011 International Results in Reading*, Boston, MA: TIMSS & PIRLS International Study Center.

National Literacy Trust (2012) *Boys' Reading Commission*, NLT: London.

Paechter, C. (1998) *Educating the Other: Gender Power and Schooling*, London: Falmer.

Phoenix, A. (2004) 'Learning styles and gender', in H. Claire (ed.) *Gender in Education 3-19: A Fresh Approach*, London: Association of Teachers and Lecturers.

Randall, G. (1987) 'Gender differences in pupil-teacher interactions in workshops and laboratories', in M. Arnot and G. Weiner (eds) *Gender Under Scrutiny*, London: Hutchinson in association with The Open University.

Rose, J. (2009) *Independent Review of the Primary Curriculum: Final Report*, London: DCSF.

Sainsbury, M. and Schagen, I. (2004) 'Attitudes to reading at ages nine and eleven', *Journal of Research in Reading*, 27(4): 373-86.

Shilling, C. (1991) 'Social space, gender inequalities and educational differentiation', *British Journal of Sociology of Education*, 12(1): 23-44.

Skelton, C. and Francis, B. (eds) (2003) *Boys and Girls in the Primary Classroom*, Maidenhead: Open University Press.

Twist, L. and Sainsbury, M. (2009) 'Girl friendly? Investigating the gender gap in national reading tests at age 11', *Educational Research*, 51(2): 283-97.

Watson, A. Kehler, M. and Martino, W. (2010) 'The problem of boys' literacy underachievement: raising some questions', *Journal of Adolescent and Adult Literacy*, 53(5): 356-61.

Whitehead, F., Capey, A.C., Maddren, W. and Wellings, A. (1977) *Children and Their Books*, School's Council Research Studies, London: Macmillan.

Wilce, H. (1995) 'Different drums for gender beat', *Times Educational Supplement*, 15 September.

Willett, R. (2005) 'Baddies in the classroom: media education and narrative writing', *Literacy*, 39(3): 142-8.

Willis, P. (1977) *Learning to Labour: How Working Class Kids Get Working Class Jobs*, London: Saxon House.

Wragg, T. (1997) 'Oh boy', editorial, *Times Educational Supplement*, 16 May. Available at: www.tes.co.uk/search (accessed February 2013).

RESPONDING TO LINGUISTIC DIVERSITY

Anny Northcote

INTRODUCTION

> Language is not only a tool for communication and knowledge but also a fundamental attribute of cultural identity and empowerment, both for the individual and the group. Respect for the languages of persons belonging to different linguistic communities therefore is essential to peaceful cohabitation.
>
> (UNESCO, 2003)

The languages that we hear and see around us in our communities and classrooms in Britain enrich society and contribute to developing all children's understanding of the wider world. Statistics show that 16.8 per cent of primary-age children speak languages other than English (DfE, 2012b); also, the number of languages spoken as a first language is this country is over 300. This multilingual society we live in should be as much recognised and supported within the education system as in all areas of government and society.

OBJECTIVES

By the end of this unit you should have:

- an understanding of the meaning of linguistic diversity;
- an understanding of bilingual children's range of linguistic skills;
- knowledge of key responses to linguistic diversity in education;
- an awareness and understanding of practical strategies to support bilingual learners in the classroom.

HISTORICAL RESPONSES TO LINGUISTIC DIVERSITY

In the UK, children and their families speaking languages other than English has been predominantly regarded as a problem by successive governments. Even today, with advances made in our understanding of how children best acquire an additional language, there is still the demand that English should become the first language of families with other mother tongues.

The idea that bilingual families should speak in English at home stems from a notion, prevalent in the 1960s, that children and their families needed to be assimilated into the wider society through conforming to the language and culture of that society. To achieve this, bilingual learners new to English were withdrawn from the 'normal' classroom context and put into 'special' English classes (Levine, 1990) or 'language centres'. This took them away from their peers and a natural environment in which they could hear and engage in the new language. The focus was solely on learning new language skills, which ignored the actual linguistic competence of the learner (Levine, 1990). Children new to English were marginalised and without full access to the curriculum. There was, at this time, the danger of perceiving 'immigrant' children as deprived, disadvantaged and handicapped owing to their own background and the unfamiliarity of the wider society's language and culture (Gregory, 1996).

There was a shift in the 1970s that acknowledged a linguistic and cultural pluralism within the expanding move to comprehensive education. In 1975, *A Language for Life* (Bullock Report) (Department of Education and Science, 1975) presented a comprehensive study of language and English learning and teaching. This included a very powerful chapter on the importance of a child's home language, which stated that:

> no child should be expected to cast off the language and culture of the home as he crosses the school threshold, nor to live and act as though school and home represent two separate and different cultures which have to be kept firmly apart.
>
> (Department of Education and Science, 1975: 286, 20.5)

The next decade saw some advances in recognising bilingual learners in their acquisition of a new language within a more positive understanding of a multicultural society: one that recognised cultural and linguistic diversity. The support for bilingual learners became more sustained and specialist, although all teachers were considered to be responsible for the learning and language needs of the bilingual pupils. Mother-tongue teaching was introduced in some areas, particularly in the early years, but this was limited and seen predominantly as part of a transition from the home language to English. The Swann Report, *Education for All* (Department of Education and Science, 1985), reported that there were still major concerns around the lack of progress in the advance of a pluralist society that recognised diversity, achievement and minority ethnic communities in a positive way.

The last 20 years have seen a change in the understanding of the needs of bilingual children, as Ofsted reports and subsequent research have highlighted aspects of under-achievement, which has led to some redress through the revision of the National Curriculum and the National Strategies, paying greater attention to inclusion, and some additional funding for local authorities and schools. However, the Ethnic Minority Achievement Grant (Department for Education and Skills, 1999) was cut in 2011, and, although some funding has been devolved to local authorities or schools (DfE 2012a), it is no longer a ring-fenced grant.

As we enter another period of change, with a new curriculum due to start in September 2014, there is little development in government thinking on the learning of bilingual children. The emphasis has shifted back to a more assimilationist rather than pluralistic model, and children with English as an additional language (EAL) are given scant recognition other than within the *Equalities Impact Assessment*, in which,

> the national curriculum inclusion statement makes it clear that teachers should set high expectations for all pupils, including . . . pupils with EAL, and reaffirms the need for schools to take account of their duties under equal opportunities legislation that covers disability, sex, sexual orientation, gender identity, and religion or belief. We understand that some pupils will access the national curriculum in ways that are different to others, and will progress at different

rates. This, however, is a matter of pedagogy and good teachers will always adapt their teaching approach to meet the needs of their pupils. In practice this means ensuring that the national curriculum is taught in ways that enable all pupils to have an equal opportunity to succeed.

(Department for Education, 2013)

LANGUAGE, IDENTITY AND LINGUISTIC DIVERSITY

Language is a key aspect of our identity. It is the main form of communication, and all children use a range of language(s) when they are with family members, friends and teachers, whatever the first language. The standard English taught in school is one of these. When we talk about identity, on the surface this can mean our gender, nationality, religion and even what we look like and the clothes we choose to wear. However, not everything is static. It could be argued that identity is dynamic and changes to suit the needs of the occasion or situation we find ourselves in. It can be negotiated and socially constructed through interactions, relational practices and events. Language plays a key role here, as the prime tool for such interactions. Bilingual children often find themselves in different situations that require different cultural and linguistic responses. In this sense, the diversity is within them and their lives – they are linguistically diverse. However, when we consider the phrase 'linguistic diversity' in our schools, we are mainly talking about the different languages spoken in a particular context, whether it is national, regional or specific to a certain school.

In Wales . . .

Wales' vision is,

> to have an education and training system that responds in a planned way to the growing demand for Welsh-medium education, reaches out to and reflects our diverse communities and enables an increase in the number of people of all ages and backgrounds who are fluent in Welsh and able to use the language with their families, in their communities and in the workplace.

(WAG, 2010: 4)

Source: Welsh Assembly Government (WAG) (2010) *Welsh-medium Education Strategy*. Cardiff: Welsh Assembly Government (WAG). http://wales.gov.uk/docs/dcells/publications/100420welshmediumstrategy en.pdf

Of course, linguistic diversity is diverse in itself and varies from school to school. In some areas, there will be schools with a wide range of languages spoken by a large number of children. There will be schools where there is one main language other than English that is spoken by the majority, and schools where there may only be a few speakers of a minority language other than English. The combinations are varied, but the key is that we live in a culturally and linguistically diverse country, and, if you can acknowledge that your language is central to your identity, so is everybody else's.

It is a challenge for policymakers, concerned with ensuring that children are educated to meet the demands of society, while at the same time protecting the right to be different in relation to the varied ethnic and linguistic population (UNESCO, 2003).

In Northern Ireland . . .

Northern Ireland policy states, 'The whole island of Ireland faces the challenge of creating an inclusive primary school culture, which not only welcomes newcomer pupils but turns the linguistic, cultural and ethnic diversity to the educational advantage of all' (DENI, 2011: 21).

Source: Department of Education for Northern Ireland (DENI) (2011) *Every School a Good School: Supporting Newcomer Pupils.* Bangor, DENI.

Task 6.6.1 Language survey

Find out about languages spoken by children in a school you know. What do you know about the languages? Where are they spoken in the world? Choose one of them and explore the story of migration behind the speakers of the language now settled in your area.

- Are there spoken dialects that differ from the written standard?
- How and where do children study their home language?
- How are children categorised in terms of their language?
- Does the language relate to their religion, and is this always the case?

Be careful not to make assumptions or apply the same conclusion to all speakers of a certain language.

BILINGUALISM AND BILINGUAL LEARNERS

This is an area within which definition and distinction are complex (see Baker, 2011). The focus for the purpose of this unit is to consider the individual bilingualism of a learner within the educational context. When we talk about a child being bilingual, this does not necessarily mean that the speaker is fully competent and fluent in at least two languages. Although this 'balanced bilingualism' may be one end of the continuum, it is more likely that children in school may have varying levels of operating in two or more language domains. Children new to English do not have 'no language', but are likely to be highly proficient users of at least one language, which is referred to as the first or home language in this unit. The term bilingual is intended to focus you on the potential of the learner and to avoid negative labels such as 'non-English speakers'. This more positive approach can also be seen in the shift from the term English as a second language (ESL) to English as an additional language (EAL), in which English is seen in addition to an already well-established knowledge and understanding of at least one other language. As bilingual learners become more proficient in an additional language, they are frequently able to switch between the languages as movement between linguistic communities demands. Also, you need to remember that bilingual learners are not a homogeneous group, either as learners or in their proficiency in English. Their first language may not be viewed in the same way by the majority in society. Those languages more familiar to UK society, such as French, German, Spanish and other western European languages with a Roman alphabet, may appear more acceptable than South Asian and African languages. Discrimination is evident, particularly against groups seen to be religiously or culturally 'different', which can affect the learning and achievement of some children. It is, therefore, important to maintain positive images of all children, even when their background is not that familiar.

The rest of this unit explores the issue of linguistic diversity in our schools and classrooms and considers your knowledge and understanding of such diversity and, in particular, how to support bilingual learners, both in their acquisition of English and in ensuring that they have meaningful access to learning and the curriculum. The approach is one that starts from what bilingual children already know about language and the actual language that they bring to the classroom. Not only does this establish the foundation for the learner acquiring the new language, but also adds to the knowledge and understanding of language for all children. Questions frequently asked by student teachers are explored through what research tells us and what this might mean in action. There are ideas for the classroom as well as tasks for you to enhance your own research into the issues that affect and interest you in particular.

ACKNOWLEDGING CHILDREN'S FIRST LANGUAGE IN THE CLASSROOM

There is a considerable body of research that explores the relationship between acquisition of the first language and that of an additional language, particularly when that language is acquired subsequently rather than simultaneously. Cummins and Swain (1986) explore this relationship through a theory of interdependence, which suggests that second language acquisition is influenced by the extent to which the first language has developed. If the first language is strong, acquisition of the second may be relatively easily acquired.

Lambert (1974) considers that learning an additional language, within the same set of cognitive and social factors as those of acquiring the first language, leads to 'additive bilingualism'. Positive values and high status given to the first language provide an enriched context in which the second language is an additional tool for thought and communication. The learner is able to build on what they implicitly know about language and how to use it and adapt or adopt this to the new language.

Opposite to this is 'subtractive bilingualism', in which skills in the first language are not deemed to be a basis for acquiring the second language, and a new set of linguistic skills have to be learned. In this instance, the value placed on the first language is low. Subtractive bilingualism can lead to a diminishing of the first language, while at the same time not allowing the additional language to be fully developed. This may result in difficulties in acquiring the additional language and prevent children being able to show their true cognitive level. Their capacity and potential for learning may be wrongly viewed in a negative light. Therefore, the concepts of additive and subtractive bilingualism are important when discussing the relationship between first and subsequent language acquisition. This also opens the debate on the positive cognitive aspects of being bilingual. The ability to speak two or more languages has been shown to contribute to cognitive understanding and to thinking, reasoning and problem-solving skills, as well as to being more confident in social intercultural contexts (Baker, 2011).

In fact, there is evidence that support for the first language of bilingual learners at academic levels is key to academic success in the additional language. Cummins (2000) shows how children's cognitive and academic language proficiency (CALP) in their first language can be transferred to an additional language, owing to the underlying linguistic proficiency being a key factor in learning.

Therefore, it is possible that older children who arrive in the classroom at the early stages of acquiring English, but with a strong command of their first language, are generally found to acquire an additional language more rapidly than those who are not as skilled. Once concepts are developed, making connections becomes easier – the new language gives new labels to the well-established concepts.

In reality, it can be hard to engage children in the classroom in their first language, particularly where there are small numbers of bilingual learners, or a range of languages spoken by individual children rather than groups. However, if you understand the role first language plays in the acquisition of an additional language, and the language skills are valued and recognised as key to learning, you need to make the experience of learning a positive one, building on the bilingual learners' linguistic backgrounds in their learning of English. The ethos of the classroom plays an important role here, and recognising a child's bilingualism and, therefore, enhancing self-esteem can go some way to ensuring that the child's identity is seen as important, and that diversity is beneficial for all children. As a teacher who encourages diversity and open discussion between adults and children and among peers, you will see that, when children use their first language with each other in the classroom, there is a positive effect on their learning. A school that values the languages and cultures of the community will find that the bilingual children are more likely to be successful in their acquisition of English and in their learning (Department for Education and Skills, 2003). All this is not just for the benefit of the bilingual learners, but for all children and adults. It increases language and cultural awareness, supporting communication between groups and encouraging a positive response to a multicultural society. Where there are few bilingual learners in a school, it may seem daunting to consider their needs, but the same principles can apply. An example of integrating a new bilingual child into the classroom where there are no other bilingual learners can be seen in the following case study.

Case study

Year 1 and 2 class (Spring Term)

Marco is a five year old Italian boy who started school in the UK in the previous autumn term. He was new to English when he arrived. At that time his mother spoke a little English and gave him good support, which has continued.

Marco settled well socially in class and soon began visiting friends out of school time. The classroom context provided lots of opportunities for play and modelling of spoken English by peers and adults. Marco really enjoyed himself in this context and particularly enjoyed retelling stories, which he soon began to do in English.

The teacher included lots of resources in Italian in displays and other materials. The whole class became interested in Marco's language and supported Marco well, even trying out some Italian words.

In recent years, there has been an opportunity for languages to become part of the curriculum, particularly in Key Stage 2, with the introduction of primary languages, often referred to as modern foreign languages. *Languages for All: Languages for Life* (Department for Education and Skills, 2002) established a commitment to language learning for every pupil throughout Key Stage 2. Not only does this strategy recognise that children starting to learn other languages early are more receptive to the new languages, but it also gives us the opportunity to promote the languages already spoken by numbers of children in school. The document states that, 'learning another language opens up access to other value systems and ways of interpreting the world, encouraging intercultural understanding and helping reduce xenophobia' (Department for Education and Skills, 2002). The opportunity to introduce such languages as Urdu, Polish and even Mandarin, alongside the more commonly accepted European languages, is available, although the reality is that the languages taught tend to be French, followed by Spanish and German, rather than languages spoken in the local community. Although learning a language is a central aspect, it also includes a strong commitment to knowledge about language (KAL) and intercultural understanding. This provides a good platform for extending our awareness and understanding of the world and the people we share it with. The teaching of foreign languages in Key Stage 2 is to continued in the 2014 curriculum, with primary schools able to decide which language(s) to teach. In the *Equalities Impact Assessment*, it is recognised that:

> a significant proportion of respondents expressed the view that pupils with English as an additional language – many of whom are from minority ethnic backgrounds – would benefit in particular from this development as they are experienced language learners and therefore in a position to build on concepts of language learning they have already acquired.
>
> (Department for Education, 2013)

SUPPORTING HOME LANGUAGES IN THE CLASSROOM

To help develop a positive ethos, consider the following:

- Allow and encourage children to speak and work in their own language, recognising that the first language is valued.
- Learn some key vocabulary and phrases, such as numbers, days of the week, hello/goodbye, and encourage children to do this too.
- Explore stories, books and poetry through the first language, maybe with the help of a teaching assistant, and introduce the English version with props, puppets or through drama.
- Encourage talk partners to use home languages in whole-class and group work.
- Create a graphics/writing area with different scripts, giving all children opportunities to practise the range of symbols using different materials.

For more fluent bilingual learners, encourage them to continue to explore texts using the home language with peers or adults. Similarly, encourage pupils to use the first language as well as English when engaged with investigative and problem-solving tasks.

Task 6.6.2 Observing spoken language

Observe the use of language(s) of a bilingual learner in the classroom and playground. Record the different ways the child uses language to communicate with peers and adults.

- Does the context influence the child's confidence when speaking?
- What do your observations tell you about the child's understanding and use of home language and English? Similarly, encourage pupils to use the first language as well as English when engaged with investigative and problem-solving tasks.

TEACHING ENGLISH EFFECTIVELY IN A LINGUISTICALLY DIVERSE CLASSROOM

Acquiring an additional language has similarities to acquiring the first language. Learners of school age start by picking up words, before putting them together in two- or three-word phrases, as they tackle the syntactic structure of the new language. The similarities are important, but it is also important to recognise the differences. The most important of these is that bilingual learners already know implicitly how a language works and are generally proficient users. They will also have conceptual understanding similar to that of their peers, and will relate the language to the context. Bilingual learners are not less intelligent, nor linguistically disadvantaged (Baker, 2011). On the contrary – they have a skill in being able to speak and possibly read and write in more than one language, as their understanding of English progresses. Not speaking English must not be viewed as a disability and should not be equated with special educational needs (SEN).

However, it is important to recognise that some bilingual learners may have SEN, not linked to their additional language acquisition. Children giving cause for concern need to be assessed carefully, preferably by involving professionals who know and understand the language and culture of the pupil (Hall, 2001).

Another issue is that there is often a mismatch between home and school. Children coming from a different country may have experienced a different form of education, such as a transmissive model, and need time to adjust.

Learning through play and experimentation is a successful approach for all young children and gives a strong context in which opportunities for the new language can be used for social and intellectual engagement. In the Foundation Stage, this should be common practice, which can be enhanced through a range of resources that reflect the linguistic and cultural diversity of the community. The Statutory Framework for Early Years Foundation Stage endorses good practice by stating that: 'For children whose home language is not English, providers must take reasonable steps to provide opportunities for children to develop and use their home language in play and learning, supporting their language development at home' (Department for Education, 2012a).

Stories are also central to the primary curriculum and an excellent resource for supporting bilingual learners, particularly when supported by visuals, available on film, DVD or audio cassette, preferably in the home language as well as English.

Don't be surprised if some bilingual learners choose not to speak at these early stages. A silent period is quite common, and, of course, during this time the child is engaging and, most importantly, listening. Bilingual learners acquire a new language most successfully if there is a meaningful context for learning to take place within which they can listen, experiment, hypothesise, adapt or adopt the language. In some cases, in Key Stage 1, and particularly in Key Stage 2, you may need to reassess your planning and teaching approaches, providing more opportunities for investigative and problem-solving tasks, using visual and physical resources.

SUPPORTING BILINGUAL LEARNERS

Learners at different stages of learning English

This is a very common and likely scenario. As for all children, learning contexts should be carefully planned, with the intention to build on the strengths of the learner and address their specific needs, which will vary from one bilingual primary to another.

One aspect to consider is how to group children, and frequently teachers may place the new pupil with speakers of the same language. Although it may be appropriate to have a pupil new to English working alongside one with the same home language, but more proficient in English, other factors need to be taken into consideration, such as experience, friendship, gender and interest. It is also important to consider the 'new' child's approach to learning. Research by Chen and Gregory (2004) shows how two Chinese girls, one aged 9 and new to Britain, the other born here and now 8, work together. It sheds light on how children may perceive learning a new language and, when given the chance, control their learning. The newly arrived older girl's insistence on what she wants to know and how she wants to learn may come from her previous experience of schooling, as well as her wish and determination to take on a new language. The younger girl's need to act as translator and teacher stretches her language abilities, allowing her to become more aware of her own bilinguality. Chen and Gregory argue that the interaction can only be successful if there is an element of trust, respect and reciprocity between the two girls, which has to be in a setting that facilitates such interaction. They see the learning context, not as one in which the 'able' English speaker scaffolds the other, but as one in which a synergy is created, in which the roles of the more experienced and the novice are more complex.

Placing bilingual children together in one group is rarely appropriate and is, in fact, a form of withdrawal in the classroom rather than inclusion. Labelling them as 'the EAL group', which may be common practice, is demeaning and misguided.

To understand this, you need to consider further what has been stated previously – that children learn best when engaged in activities with speakers of English who can model the language appropriate to the task and to the cognitive level of the child. A collaborative approach to learning is one that is recognised as good practice for all children, and a stimulating learning environment that allows for children to take risks can give positive support for the bilingual learner. However, although some of their learning needs may be similar to those of pupils whose first language is English, they also have different linguistic needs, particularly at the early stages, by the fact that they are learning through another language and come from cultural backgrounds and communities where there may be differing expectations of education. This means that, even if you only have one or two bilingual learners in your class, it is still important to find out about them and consider their needs.

Another important factor is how you assess children's development of English. The first thing to note is that no formal assessment should be done too early, and, even then, any assessment of language has to start from the understanding of the child acquiring EAL. All local authorities and schools should have descriptors that show the developmental steps against which to build a picture of each bilingual learner's achievements in the new language. However, at the heart of this must be an understanding that proficiency in understanding written texts takes longer than the spoken language, and this will vary depending on each child's age, educational background and other factors.

Cummins (1984a, 1984b) distinguishes between 'basic interpersonal communicative skills' (BICS) and the aforementioned CALP. BICS refers to the oral fluency of the bilingual learner, which may take up to 2 years to achieve. CALP is more concerned with the demands of the curriculum, particularly in terms of literacy skills, which take longer – between 5 and 7 years. This is somewhat dependent on when a bilingual learner begins to acquire a new language, and whether or not he or she is already literate in the first. The main point is that you will often hear teachers say that a bilingual pupil is good at speaking and listening, but, in spite of this fluency, finds writing and reading tasks harder than monolingual peers.

In summary, you need to consider several areas when planning for bilingual learners (Gravelle, 2000). The social, cultural, linguistic and cognitive aspects need to be teased out, alongside the learner's previous experience. The demands of the task need to then be considered for you to decide what support is needed.

Types of support

For children new to English:

- give them time to adjust to the new situation and to tune into the new language – don't pressurise them to speak, but include them in the established routines and activities of the class, making them feel welcome;
- allow them to be silent if they choose to and know that this is fine;
- ensure activities are considered for their linguistic content – but keep the conceptual element at an appropriate challenging level for their age; ensure that activities are considered in terms of their cultural content and relate to previous learning and social experiences;
- centre activities around spoken English until confident that the child is able to engage with written texts through their own reading and writing; this may be quite soon with children in Key Stage 2 who are already literate;
- ensure that activities include active participation of the learners – stories, songs, rhymes, turn-taking games, investigative and problem-solving tasks with good-quality support materials provide opportunities to engage the child and give a scaffold for the linguistic component;
- consider supportive grouping with children who will provide a language model and be encouraging in a collaborative learning context;
- always have high expectations – look at what children can do, are interested in and enjoy.

For children more advanced in spoken English, but who need further support with accessing written texts, particularly in Key Stage 2:

- give plenty of opportunities to discuss language and linguistic devices in a way that builds on the children's own interest of a range of fiction and non-fiction texts, and their own reading and writing;
- engage in language play, such as jokes, riddles, jingles and tongue-twisters, which give an understanding of the subtleties and nuances of language and develop a colloquial fluency;
- set up discussion groups around literature that encourage children to focus on the text to support their comments and questions;
- consider close work with subject-related texts.

Task 6.6.3 Planning and teaching to support bilingual learners in English

Plan a sequence of activities (Foundation Stage) or a unit of work (Key Stages 1 and 2). Consider the points above that are relevant to your context and plan two or three tasks to support the different bilingual learners in your class. Also consider the learning culture of the classroom, as well as specific activities.

PARENTS AND THEIR EXPECTATIONS

Partnership between home and school is crucial to ensure bilingual learners and their families get the best help they can for academic success. All parents want their children to do well in school, and, for families settling in a new country, where the majority language is not their home language, there is an added dimension to achieving that success. All schools will have an admissions policy, which should include gathering information about the child's linguistic and educational background and which should be available to you.

Learning to speak, read and write English is high on the list of priorities for bilingual families, and one role of the school is to discuss with parents how that is done and the support they can give. Being aware of the issues around how their children acquire English and the value of being bilingual is often a relief to parents, who think maintaining their home language may be disadvantageous to learning English. We need to show it is not, emphasising that communication in the child's first language is the best way to support children's learning in school.

However, some parents of bilingual learners may not feel comfortable coming into school, and there needs to be some positive engagement to change such a situation. A tried and tested approach is one of sharing stories, culture and customs at book-making workshops, involving children and their parents writing stories in different languages. Projects that involve the community groups that bring together parents, siblings and teachers to discuss issues, as well as research into the children's range of literacy practices, have revealed a great deal about children's language and literacy experiences outside school, which are rich and varied (Gregory, 1996; Sneddon, 2003). Mismatch between home and school can be one of the most detrimental factors affecting a child's progress, with no exception when it comes to bilingual children, and needs careful consideration.

Gonzalez *et al.* (2005) provide some excellent insight into how the relationship between teachers and parents can be supportive, if schools really come to understand the cultural practices and resulting knowledge of children in their classes. The recognition of children's social experiences concurs with Vygotsky's thinking that intellectual development cannot be explained separately from experience, which is located in social, cultural and historical contexts. Such contexts for learning are successful when the child is comfortable, yet challenged, and, through guided participation and co-construction of meaning, the learning is supported.

The relationship between siblings is another aspect to be considered when making links between home and school. It may often be the older sibling who, once settled in school, is able to support the parents and the younger children in making sense of educational practices. For example, understanding the literacy practices of the home has frequently been recognised as a way of mediating the familiarity of home with the new world of the school. Once again, the sociocultural aspects of learning a new language and recognition of different cultural norms are crucial in our understanding of diversity.

Task 6.6.4 Communication and language

Read the paragraph on page 428 concerning Cummins's (1984a, 1984b) distinction between BICS and CALP.

- What do you consider to be the key points of Cummins's research?
- How do other models of bilingualism referred to in this unit relate to this?
- How do these ideas relate to other theories of learning that you know?
- From this reflection and analysis, consider in your planning and through assessment how you can scaffold the learning for those pupils who may be causing some concern in their progress in reading and, in particular, writing in English.

SUMMARY

In this unit, you have been introduced to what it means to be bilingual, including some theoretical perspectives and ways to support children in the classroom, recognising home language as a positive force, not one that hinders their learning of English. Research into the learning and achievement of bilingual children is increasing, although the future of addressing their needs is still a politically charged arena. Under-achievement of certain minority ethnic groups continues to be an issue, and, in spite of all the research into heightening our understanding of how pupils acquire an additional language, there have been no major structural changes to support this. We do not live in a culturally neutral society, nor in one that is free from prejudice and racism. Socio-economic status is also a strong determiner of success, and this range of causal factors cannot be tackled solely within education.

This picture makes it more important that the curriculum and the types of interaction we can establish in schools and classrooms should be there to promote academic success for all children. An integration into the mainstream, while clearly positive, must be done systematically and with appropriate resources, including bilingual teachers and assistants, if we are serious about supporting bilingual learners to achieve their potential. Therefore, a greater understanding among all teachers of bilingual children, their linguistic and cultural backgrounds, their families and communities is essential, if any sense of social equity can be turned into positive achievement.

Therefore, as new teachers soon to enter the profession, it is crucial that you are aware of the issues in order to support your own planning for bilingual learners. It is not as daunting a task as is sometimes perceived. As discussed in this unit, it is not about a separate curriculum for children with a learning disability, but about an enhanced curriculum for all children within which there are varied opportunities for children to extend their linguistic repertoires.

A greater understanding about how bilingual learners acquire an additional language and develop literacy skills gives insight into how all children learn to read and write, and how talk in educational contexts is part of an extended literacy curriculum. As was stated at the beginning of this unit, the range of languages spoken in this society and the cultures and communities in which they thrive can only enrich our schools and the lives of all children to become more tolerant and understanding of the backgrounds, linguistic and cultural, that present us with such diversity.

ANNOTATED FURTHER READING

Baker, C. (2011) *Foundations of Bilingual Education and Bilingualism*, 5th edn, Clevedon: Multilingual Matters.
A very readable and engaging text that discusses comprehensively issues of bilingualism, learning and diversity, as well as educational policies. The author draws on a range of established research into what it means to be bilingual and how to address this in schools and classrooms. He also discusses such issues as language minorities and whether we should consider linguistic assimilation or diversity. There are also study and practical activities suitable for student teachers.

Drury, R. (2007) *Young Bilingual Learners at Home and School: Researching Multilingual Voices*, Stoke-on-Trent: Trentham Books.

> An ethnographic study of three young bilingual learners, at home and in nursery, that explores issues around learning, language, culture and how their engagement and progress are observed, or not, by professionals and practiners. The children's stories will open your eyes on bilingual children and their learning within a sociocultural analysis.

Edwards, V. (2009) *Learning to be Literate: Multilingual Perspectives*, Clevedon: Multilingual Matters.

> This books considers bilingualism and literacy and how different countries tackle the issues of multilingualism at an individual and societal level. It is a practical as well as theoretical book, with useful case studies and activities to explore how language in education is considered in policy, with particular reference to bilingual education and the power of literacy.

 # FURTHER READING TO SUPPORT M-LEVEL STUDY

Gonzalez, N., Moll Luis, C. and Amanti, C. (eds) (2005) *Funds of Knowledge: Theorizing Practices in Households, Communities and Classrooms*, New York and London: Routledge.

> This research study reveals so much that is relevant to working with children whose cultural and linguistic background may not be that of the majority community. The understanding of children's lives is opened to the teachers involved, from which a reconsideration of curriculum context and pedagogy shows a changing level of achievement when participants are actively engaged in learning in a world they recognise. A seminal work, which is relevant to how sociocultural contexts are varied yet accessible.

Safford, K. and Drury, R. (2013) The 'problem' of bilingual children in educational settings: policy and research in England, *Language and Education*, 27, 1, pp 70–81.

> A review of policy and research on language diversity and how different contexts support bilingual children. This is well embedded in understanding of second language learning and pedagogical approaches and consideration of how a monolingual national curriculum and assessment procedures may disadvantage the young child learning English as an additional language.

 # RELEVANT WEBSITES

NALDIC, The National Association for Language Development in the Curriculum: www.naldic.org.uk

> This website covers a wealth of resource materials to enhance the educational achievement of pupils from diverse backgrounds. It includes research articles, debates and ideas for the classroom, including for teaching EAL. It is the national subject association for teaching EAL.

ROTA, Race on the Agenda: www.rota.org.uk

> Although not specifically dedicated to education, this keeps a clear watching brief on education policy in relation to black and minority ethnic pupils.

 # REFERENCES

Baker, C. (2011) *Foundations of Bilingual Education and Bilingualism*, 5th edn, Clevedon: Multilingual Matters.

Chen, Y. and Gregory, E. (2004) '"How do I read these words": bilingual exchange teaching between Cantonese-speaking peers', in E. Gregory, S. Long and D. Volk (eds) *Many Pathways to Literacy*, London: RoutledgeFalmer.

Cummins, J. (1984a) *Bilingualism and Special Education: Issues in Assessment and Pedagogy*, Clevedon: Multilingual Matters.

Cummins, J. (1984b) 'Wanted: a theoretical framework for relating language proficiency to academic achievement among bilingual pupils', in C. Rivera (ed.) *Language Proficiency and Academic Achievement*, Clevedon: Multilingual Matters.

Cummins, J. (2000) *Language. Power and Pedagogy: Bilingual Children in the Crossfire, Bilingual Education and Bilingualism* series, Clevedon: Multilingual Matters.

Cummins, J. and Swain, M. (1986) *Bilingualism in Education*, London: Longman.

Department for Education (2013) *Reform of the National Curriculum in England: Equalities Impact Assessment*. DFE-00106-2013.

Department for Education (DfE) (2012a) *School Funding Reform: Next Steps towards a Fairer System*. DFE-00029-2012.

Department for Education (DfE) (2012b) *Statistical First Release, Schools, Pupils and their Characteristics*: January.

Department for Education and Skills (1999) *Raising the Attainment of Minority Ethnic Pupils*, London: Ofsted.

Department for Education and Skills (2002) *Languages for All: Languages for Life: A Strategy for England*, London: DfES.

Department for Education and Skills (2003) *Aiming High: Raising the Achievement of Minority Ethnic Pupils*, London: Ofsted.

Department of Education and Science (DES) (1975) *A Language for Life* (The Bullock Report), London: HMSO.

Department of Education and Science (DES) (1985) *Education for All* (The Swann Report), London: HMSO.

Gonzalez, N., Moll Luis, C. and Amanti, C. (eds) (2005) *Funds of Knowledge: Theorizing Practices in Households, Communities and Classrooms*, New York and London: Routledge.

Gravelle, M. (ed.) (2000) *Planning for Bilingual Learners*, Stoke-on-Trent: Trentham Books.

Gregory, E. (1996) *Making Sense of a New World*, London: Paul Chapman Publishing.

Hall, D. (2001) *Assessing the Needs of Bilingual Learners Living in Two Languages*, 2nd edn, London: David Fulton.

Lambert, W.E. (1974) 'Culture and language as factors in learning and education', in F.E. Aboud and R.D. Meade *Cultural Factors in Learning and Education*, Bellingham, WA: Fifth Western Washington Symposium on Learning.

Levine, J. (ed) (1990) *Bilingual Learners and the Mainstream Curriculum*, London: Falmer.

Sneddon, R. (2003) 'What language do you speak at home?', in *The Best of Language Matters*, London: CLPE.

UNESCO (2003) *Education in a Multilingual World*, Education Position Paper, Paris: UNESCO.

RECENT DEVELOPMENTS

LISTENING TO THE VOICES OF YOUNG PEOPLE IN SCHOOL

Carol Robinson

INTRODUCTION

In recent years there has been a growing move within the UK, as well as in other countries, to consider pupils' perspectives and 'voices' on aspects of school-related issues, including learning and teaching. Pupil voice work involves engaging with pupils about issues that matter to them and that affect their experiences in school. This unit focuses on pupil voice work, what it 'looks like' in the school context and the significance of it for both teachers and pupils. Within this unit, we start by considering the terms used when referring to pupil voice work, and we then outline factors that have led to an increased importance now being placed on pupils' voices. We go on to identify ways in which teachers can listen to the voices of those they teach and consider how implementing such practices can make learning more meaningful for pupils and, as a result, improve the learning and experiences of young people in schools. We also consider the benefits of pupil voice work from teachers' perspectives and give ideas on how teachers can work towards developing and implementing strategies focused on listening to, and making learning meaningful for, the pupils with whom they work.

OBJECTIVES

By the end of this unit you should:

- understand the term 'pupil voice' and have an insight into the origins of this work;
- be familiar with school practices that promote listening to pupils' voices and be aware of the barriers around such practices;
- be aware of the benefits, for both teachers and learners, of incorporating pupil voice work into school practices;
- have developed ideas about how you can listen to pupils within your school, with a view to making lessons more meaningful and enhancing pupils' enjoyment of lessons.

'PUPIL VOICE', 'PUPIL ENGAGEMENT' AND 'PUPIL PARTICIPATION': WHAT DO THESE TERMS MEAN?

There are various terms used to relate to the concept of listening to pupils to elicit their perspectives about aspects of their school experiences. For example, you are likely to come across the terms 'pupil voice', 'student voice' and 'learner voice', as well as the terms pupil, student and learner 'engagement' and 'participation'. Each of these terms broadly relates to the move to consult pupils and provide opportunities for pupils to voice their opinions about matters that concern them and that affect their learning and other school experiences.

The term 'pupil voice', often used synonomously with the terms 'student voice' and 'learner voice' (Robinson and Taylor 2007), tends to be used as an all-encompassing term referring to working with students to elicit their perspectives on matters relating to any aspect of school life. It is about teachers and other adults in schools wanting to know and learn from pupils about their experiences, and it is concerned with encouraging pupils to participate in, and voice their opinions on, any issues that impact on their life in school, either directly or indirectly. In extreme cases, if schools were to fully embrace pupil voice work, this would result in schools being run in a democratic way, with pupils' voices being equal to those of the adults in the school. In such cases, pupils would have the opportunity to be involved in decision-making processes in every aspect of schooling, including, for example, policy, financial- and environmental-related decisions, as well as decisions about teaching and learning. Thus, staff and students would have a shared responsibility for the development of all practices and policies within their school.

According to Flutter and Rudduck (2004: 5), 'pupil participation' implies inclusion or membership of a community in which pupils are respected contributors. It relates to pupils being given an active and direct involvement in school matters at some level. The notion of participation suggests that pupils are invited to respond and contribute to some decision-making, usually with an institution-driven agenda, but they are not active participants in all school decision-making arenas. Often, the arenas in which pupils are invited to participate and offer their opinions are those areas that are considered to be non-threatening to the adults in the school, for example, decisions relating to the decor of the school toilets or the choice of charity to which money from a school fund-raising event should be donated.

The term 'pupil engagement' commonly has two different meanings attributed to it. It can refer to the excitement and investment a pupil feels towards an aspect or issue that is of interest to them (Cheminais, 2008). However, it can also relate to pupils being active partners and shaping their experiences of school. Similar to the notion of pupil voice work, pupil engagement in this latter sense is concerned with listening to individual and collective perspectives about matters that relate to their experiences of school, including issues of teaching and learning; this work may have institution-driven or pupil-driven agendas (Robinson, 2012).

For the purpose of our work in this unit, the term 'pupil voice' will be used to relate to measures taken to encourage pupils to voice their opinions, and to become involved in decision-making processes, relating to any school-related issues, whether these be pupil- or institution-driven. We will focus in particular on pupil voice work in relation to pupils' experiences of learning and teaching in school, and acknowledge that, in schools where pupil voice work is taken seriously, such work has the potential to influence teachers' pedagogies and practices.

LEGISLATION PROMPTING THE MOVE TOWARDS LISTENING TO THE VOICES OF YOUNG PEOPLE IN SCHOOLS

Agencies working with young people and government departments in a number of countries, including Australia, Canada, New Zealand, the UK and the USA, have placed an increasing importance on pupils' voices in recent years. Much of this work has stemmed from the United Nations Convention on the Rights of the Child (UNCRC) (United Nations, 1989). In particular, Article 12 of the UNCRC states:

> State parties shall assure to the child who is capable of forming his or her own views the right to express those views freely on all matters affecting the child, the views of the child being given due weight in accordance with the age and maturity of the child.

Lundy (2007: 927) explored the interpretation of Article 12 in detail and acknowledged that the Article comprises two key elements: the right for children and young people to (a) express a view and (b) have their view be given due weight. Thus, the UNCRC gives children the right to freedom of opinion and the right to be heard and take part in decisions that affect them; this was a major factor that contributed to the positive recognition of student voice work in schools.

Following the UNCRC, in 1991 Fullan posed the question, 'What would happen if we treated the student as someone whose opinion mattered?' (Fullan, 1991: 170). At this time, the notion of taking pupils' opinions into account was relatively new for most schools; however, this idea, coupled with the implications of the UNCRC, served to open up spaces for consideration to be given to how schools might be improved, for the benefit of the whole school community, through listening to the voices of the pupils within them.

In recent years, although educational reforms within England have focused largely on raising students' and schools' achievements based on performance, there have been a number of Acts and reforms within England that have recognised and promoted the importance of listening to the voices of young people in schools. These include, for example, the Education Act 2002 (Department for Education and Skills, 2002), which requires that schools consult with pupils. In 2003, the Department for Education and Skills (DfES) prepared a document entitled *Working Together: Giving Children and Young People a Say*; within this, it drew up draft guidance notes on pupil participation. This guidance was designed to help schools and local authorities organise opportunities for pupils to develop their 'skills as active citizens' and to prepare them for involvement in decision-making processes (Rudduck and McIntyre, 2007, 8). Following this, in 2004 the government published *Every Child Matters: Change for Children* (Department for Education and Skills, 2004), which brings together ways in which public services are working towards improved outcomes for children, young people and families into a national framework. Central to the *Every Child Matters* legislation is that all children should have a say in decisions affecting their lives.

The voices and views of children and young people were taken into consideration and informed the government's *Children's Plan* (Department for Children, Schools and Families, 2007); and, in 2008, the document, *Working Together: Listening to the Voices of Children and Young People* (Department for Children, Schools and Families, 2008) outlined the importance, and significant benefits, of taking account of children's and young peoples' views when working with them. Together, these documents reflect the general principles of the UNCRC and, collectively, they have contributed significantly to making pupil voice work a recognised part of working with young people in England.

Although more recent legislation within England has not specifically promoted listening to the voices of pupils in schools, the recent regulations relating to the appraisal of teachers' standards has implications for the extent to which teachers are expected to consider the needs of the pupils with whom they work. In September 2012, new *Teachers' Standards* (Department for Education, 2012) were introduced to replace both the previous standards for Qualified Teacher Status (QTS) and the core professional standards published by the Training and Development Agency for Schools. The new standards set a clear baseline of expectations for the professional practice and conduct of teachers from the point of qualification, and will apply to the vast majority of teachers, regardless of their career stage. They will be used to assess all trainees working towards QTS and those completing their statutory induction period; they will also be used to assess the performance of all teachers subject to the Education (School Teachers' Appraisal) (England) Regulations 2012.

Within the new *Teachers' Standards*, it is stated that a teacher must 'set high expectations which inspire, motivate and challenge pupils' (Department for Education, 2012: 7), and must 'manage behaviour effectively to ensure a good and safe learning environment' (Department for Education, 2012: 8). Within this latter standard, there is also an expectation that teachers 'manage classes effectively, using approaches which are appropriate to pupils' needs in order to involve and motivate them' (Department for Education, 2012: 9). Implicit within these two standards is the expectation that teachers have built relationships with pupils which have enabled them to gain insights into individual pupils' interests, capabilities and preferred ways of learning, and are aware of and understand the sort of work and activities that are most likely to inspire, motivate and challenge them.

Within the Ofsted Framework for School Inspection (Ofsted, 2012), it is stated that one of the areas on which school inspections will focus when evaluating the quality of teaching in the school is 'the extent to which teachers enthuse, engage and motivate pupils to learn and foster their curiosity and enthusiasm for learning' (Ofsted, 2012: 15). Similar to the points made above in relation to the new *Teachers' Standards*, implicit within this expectation is the implication that, in order to enthuse, engage and motivate pupils, teachers first need to have knowledge of individual pupils in terms of their interests, capabilities and preferred ways of learning. Within the Ofsted Framework for School Inspection, it also states that, 'School inspection will: focus on pupils' and parents' and carers' needs by taking account of pupils' and parents' and carers' views when Ofsted plans and carries out inspections' (Ofsted, 2012: 11); thus pupils' voices will continue to be listened to as part of the school inspection process.

WHY IS IT SO IMPORTANT TO LISTEN TO PUPILS?

Imagine a classroom in which teachers teach only what they think learners ought to know, where there is no space for pupils to ask questions or voice opinions on areas of interest to them, where pupils are not encouraged to learn through discovery, and where learners are simply passive recipients within a process. Alternatively, imagine a school in which pupils feel listened to, respected and valued as individuals, where their views are important to the teachers they work with, where teachers want to know what interests and motivates the pupils, and where pupils feel confident about taking responsibility for aspects of their learning – a school in which pupils are encouraged to participate in assessing their work and setting future goals, and where learners feel a sense of belonging to the classroom and the wider school.

Task 7.1.1 Listening environments

Of the two situations described above, in which of these would you expect pupils to thrive? Why?

Task 7.1.2 Taking pupil voice work forward in your classroom

- Define what you understand by the term 'pupil voice work'. Reflect on your experiences of pupil voice work in your classroom to date. Which pupils participate? In what ways do they participate?
- Identify one area of your work in the classroom in which you would like to move pupil voice work forward (this could relate to either a curriculum area or an aspect of your practice, such as assessment). What do you hope to achieve by involving pupils? What steps will you take to ensure the voices of all pupils are heard?

HOW CAN LISTENING TO PUPILS BE OF BENEFIT TO THEM?

Children and young people tend to enjoy school more when they are listened to and their views are taken seriously, when they are treated with respect and when they feel valued and included. Where schools enable pupils to become active participants in the school and in their learning, and where pupils are provided with opportunities to have a say in their learning, this is more likely to result in them developing a sense of belonging to the school.

Flutter and Rudduck (2004: 7-8) report on findings from Jelly *et al.* (2000), who consulted pupils in a special needs school. They found clear evidence that consulting pupils about their learning enhanced self-esteem and confidence, promoted stronger engagement and motivation to learn and encouraged pupils to become more active members of the school community. Similarly, Rudduck and McIntyre (2007: 152) found that pupil consultation tends to enhance pupils' commitment to, and capacity for, learning, through strengthening self-esteem, enhancing attitudes to school and learning, developing a strong sense of membership and developing new skills for learning. Furthermore, where students are actively involved in contributing to discussions and decisions about teaching and learning, Flutter and Rudduck (2004) found that this led to them developing a deeper understanding of the learning processes and promoted their development in higher-order thinking skills.

HOW CAN LISTENING TO PUPILS BENEFIT TEACHERS?

Listening to the voices of pupils is a key component in constructing a discourse of respect, empowerment and citizenship in schools; it can help schools to become learning communities, rather than knowledge factories, that serve the needs of the majority of the pupils within them (Busher, 2012).

Bragg and Fielding (2005) found that pupils are able to give valuable feedback to teachers in relation to their learning, and this in turn can inform their future practice. Where pupils' views are heard on teaching and learning issues, you and other supportive adults in school can gain an insight into pupils' perspectives on what helps and what hinders their learning. Finding out about pupils' perspectives on aspects of their school experiences, including learning, may take you outside of your comfort zone in terms of the sort of dialogue in which you want to engage with pupils. The outcome of listening to pupils, however, can be hugely beneficial, as you are able to receive helpful feedback that can increase your awareness of the learning needs of those you teach. An increased understanding and awareness of how pupils learn can be of great help when analysing and reflecting on your own performance and can serve to help inform and improve your own practice. Research has found that, where teachers listen to pupils' opinions, this results in them being able to understand more easily how pupils learn most effectively and, as a result, leads teachers to reconsider and make changes to aspects of their own teaching practice (Flutter and Rudduck, 2004). Rudduck and McIntyre (2007) found that consultations with pupils can lead to improved teacher awareness of pupils' capacities for learning, and it can help teachers gain new perspectives and a renewed excitement about their teaching.

A further benefit of consulting with pupils is that a more collaborative relationship between the teacher and the pupils tends to develop, the outcome of which is likely to lead to improvements in the quality of pupil learning. Thus, the better you understand pupils and their learning, the more effective your teaching and their learning will be.

Creating listening classrooms can create a positive culture within the school and help teachers to identify factors that contribute towards helping pupils' learning and their enjoyment of learning, as well as identifying factors that create barriers to learning. Thus, listening to the voices and opinions of pupils has the potential to transform teacher-pupil relationships, improve the conditions of learning and lead to improvements in teachers' practices, through teachers learning from pupils about ways in which their teaching can become more effective and more meaningful to those within their class.

WHAT DOES PUPIL VOICE WORK LOOK LIKE IN SCHOOLS?

The processes involved in listening to pupils within school should be more than features on inspection frameworks about pupils' involvement and participation in school. Genuine pupil voice work involves listening to pupils about matters that are important to them, rather than merely listening to pupils about issues that you and other adults in the school want to know.

When thinking about pupil voice work, it is important to remember that there is more than one voice; there are as many voices as there are pupils, and care must be taken to listen to the voices of all pupils, not just the articulate, able, elite minority and those familiar with the language used by teachers. The views of all pupils, including minority groups and less positive learners, are important. We also need to consider that work relating to pupils' voices can refer to more than the spoken word, that is, it also refers to the actions, behaviours and attitudes of pupils, as well as a pupil's choice to remain silent, as each of these are ways in which pupils can chose to display their opinions. For pupil voice work to be authentic, those with authority within schools must be open to genuinely listening to pupils' perspectives on any issue that is important to the pupils themselves, and to the possibility of making changes to school policy and practices as a result of this.

Fielding (2008) suggests some questions for teachers to consider when embarking on pupil voice work; for example: Who is allowed to speak? To whom? What are they allowed to speak about? What language is encouraged or allowed? Who decides the answers to these questions? How are those decisions made? How, when, where, to whom and how often are these decisions communicated? In relation to listening, he suggests we ask: Who is listening? How and why? When planning consultations with pupils, in order to help think of ways to make pupil consultations inclusive for all learners, it would be beneficial to ask yourself the above questions.

In order to build 'listening schools', the development of positive working relationships between teachers and pupils is crucial; however, it takes time and perseverance by the whole school community to build such relationships. Constructing respectful cultures within schools is one of the key features of the UNICEF UK's Rights Respecting Schools Award (RRSA); taking on board the ideas of the RRSA may help schools in their endeavour to work towards building an ethos of respectful cultures. The RRSA, which was developed in 2004, helps schools use the UNCRC as their values framework. Over 2,000 primary, secondary and special schools in England, Wales, Scotland and Northern Ireland are now registered for the award. A study involving schools registered on the RRSA found that, where schools adopted the principles of the RRSA, both adults and young people reported positive relationships between teachers and pupils, based on mutual respect and collaboration (Sebba and Robinson, 2010).

GUIDING PRINCIPLES WHEN LISTENING TO PUPILS' VOICES

Thomson points out (2011: 25) that student representation is often tokenistic and seems more about students being *seen* to be involved in schools' processes, rather than being active partners of change. In order to avoid such tokenistic involvement of pupils, the following principle should be considered:

- There should be a genuine desire to hear what pupils have to say.
- It should be acknowledged that there are many voices, not just one unified voice.
- Teacher-pupil relationships should be based on mutual respect, and adults in the school should acknowledge that pupils have the right to express their views on matters affecting them.
- *All* pupils should be encouraged to have an active, rather than passive, involvement in discussions.
- Situations should be created where pupils feel confident that they can speak freely about what is on their mind, rather than feeling they ought to say what they think you or other adults want to hear.
- Pupils need to know that, if they express their views, they will be taken seriously, and this won't be held against them, no matter how controversial their views are.
- The topics about which pupils are asked to offer their opinion should not be trivial.
- It should be acknowledged that pupils may express their views through more than the spoken word.
- When pupils express their views, adults in school should demonstrate, through their responses, that pupils' opinions are valued.
- Voices that offer an alternative view and do not align with the generally accepted school ethos should be listened to.
- Where pupils suggest a change in policy or practice and this cannot be done for whatever reason, these reasons should be explained to pupils, rather than their opinions being simply dismissed.

Thus, for pupil voice work to be authentic, those with authority within schools must be open to genuinely listening to pupils' perspectives on any issue of importance to the pupils themselves, and to the possibility of making changes to school policies and practices as a result of this. You may, however, also need to consider how you would react to antisocial voices in school. These voices should not be dismissed, it may be that some pupils are frustrated by particular situations, and their voices appear antisocial; however, their opinions need to be considered with equal weight to those opinions that are offered in, what teachers consider to be, more acceptable ways.

WAYS IN WHICH YOU CAN ENGAGE WITH PUPILS

Schools need to develop practices to encourage pupils to voice opinions and to encourage the adults who work with them to listen to pupils as part of their everyday practice. Some schools have a school council, and many run circle times during which teachers listen to pupils' perspectives on particular issues. In addition, some schools encourage 'pupils as researchers' projects, which involve pupils conducting their own research within schools. The aim of these projects is to determine pupils' opinions, with a view to making changes in school as a result of the research findings. For pupil voice work to be embraced in schools, opportunities should be created for all pupils to voice their opinions on all school issues of importance to them. There should be a real desire for teachers to hear pupils' perceptions on any aspect of their school experience, and to listen to the ideas they have on how to enhance these experiences. Pupils can be involved in making decisions about the running of the school by, for example, taking on pupil governors' roles and by participating in management committees.

Teachers can also encourage a culture of pupil participation in the classroom by engaging with pupils about pedagogy and practice in a way that empowers pupils. For example, pupils can be invited to comment on their learning, as well as on the teaching strategies and conditions for learning (Rudduck and McIntyre, 2007). You, as the teacher, can pose simple questions to pupils during your day-to-day working with them, in order to determine their perceptions of what motivates/demotivates them, what enhances/diminishes their enjoyment of lessons and what increases/reduces barriers to learners engaging in learning.

Task 7.1.3 Motivating pupils

Think about what interests you and motivates you to learn. Do you know what interests and motivates pupils in your class? If not, spend some time finding out. You might ask pupils, either individually, in small groups or as a class group:

- What activities help you to learn best? Why?
- Which activities do you enjoy the most? Why?
- What stops you from learning? Why?
- What would your ideal lesson be like? Why?

NON-VERBAL WAYS OF 'LISTENING' TO PUPILS

As well as listening to pupils verbally, pupils can also 'voice' their opinions through non-verbal means. Several literature sources provide details of the processes implemented by schools to enhance their efforts to listen to the voices of their pupils (Rudduck et al., 1996; Fielding, 2001; MacBeath et al., 2003; Rudduck and Flutter, 2004).The box below includes some suggestions of ways in which pupils can express their views in non-verbal ways.

- Drawing, painting, taking photos of, or role-playing, different situations; for example, situations that they either like or dislike in school.
- Posting their opinions in a posting box – this way pupils can remain anonymous if they wish.
- Writing a log about, for example, what aspects of lessons they enjoy and why.
- Completing questionnaires, sentence-completing exercises or surveys on an aspect of their school experience. Pupils could be involved in the writing and administering of these.
- Engaging pupils in ballots and elections.

Pupils could also be given more choice and freedom in lessons and tasks, for example, choosing for themselves which level of work to complete when there is work prepared for varying ability ranges within the class.

Task 7.1.4 Who gets listened to? About what?

Consider the processes currently in place to listen to pupils in your classroom about:

- environmental issues, such as the school toilets or the playground;
- learning and teaching issues;
- policy/organisational issues.

Whose voice gets listened to? How often? How can less assertive and less confident pupils be encouraged to participate and have more of a say in each of the above?

PUPIL PARTICIPATION

For pupil voice work to be effective, there needs to be a degree of pupil participation; that is, adults and pupils need to work together to ensure the voices and views of pupils are heard and valued in relation to decisions that affect them. In 2008, the Department for Children, Schools and Families produced a booklet entitled *Working Together: Listening to the Voices of Children and Young People* (Department for Children, Schools and Families, 2008). Within this, it suggested that different levels of learner participation take place in schools. Drawing on work by Shier (2001), it advocated that levels of learner participation could be viewed as shown in Figure 7.1.1.

Children share power and responsibility for decision-making

Children are involved in the decision-making process

Increasing empowerment and responsibility

Children's views are taken into account

Children are supported in expressing their views

Children are listened to

FIGURE 7.1.1 Levels of participation

Task 7.1.5 Levels of pupil participation

- At which level would you position the pupils you teach?
- Does this position vary in different circumstances? If so, why?
- Think about the way you engage with pupils on one specific aspect of work, e.g. the teaching of numeracy. At what level would you currently position the pupils? Where would you like to position them in six months' time? What steps can you take to achieve this?

Task 7.1.6 Developing pupil participation in the wider school context

- In an 'ideal' world, in which aspects of schooling do you consider pupils should have a say? Consider, for example, whether, and, if so, to what extent, you consider pupils should be involved in discussions and decisions relating to school policies, teaching and learning issues, financial and environmental issues. In what ways does your thinking correspond and/or conflict with your school's values and aims?
- How could you determine pupils' views on which aspects of the wider school context (outside the classroom) they would like to be involved in? Once you have ascertained this, what steps could you take to involve pupils as active partners in one aspect of the wider school context?
- How will you ensure opportunities are available for all pupils to voice their opinions?

MAKING LEARNING MEANINGFUL

Pupils are more likely to be fully engaged in lessons where teaching is 'based on a sound knowledge and understanding of each child's needs' (Miliband, 2004: 8). The move to consider the needs of individual pupils stems from the national policy on personalised learning in England, which was launched in 2004. Within this policy, David Miliband advocated that, in order to make learning personalised to each individual pupil, teaching needs to be shaped around the ways different youngsters learn, and the unique talents of every pupil need to be developed and nurtured (Miliband, 2004). Although the term 'personalisation of learning' is not commonly used now, the ideas behind Miliband's speech remain and are part of the move to listen to the voices of, and engage with, young people in schools, with a view to making learning meaningful for all pupils. Pupils are more likely to be engaged with learning if they are involved in having a say in the ways in which they learn, by being given the opportunity to, for example, decide what they would like to learn and choose how to present their work. The key challenge for the teacher with regard to considering the needs of individuals is how to cater simultaneously for all the different needs of learners in one class.

For teachers to make learning meaningful for all pupils, they need information about the attainment and past progress of each of the pupils with whom they work. Pupils can be encouraged to take some responsibility for making their learning meaningful and relevant, with the help of teachers if need be, by identifying specific targets for them to work towards and deciding upon the best pedagogic approach to meet these targets. In classrooms where pupils are encouraged to take some responsibility for their learning, there are regular opportunities for pupils to discuss their progress with teachers, and for teachers to actively involve learners in the setting and reviewing of their progress towards these targets.

If teachers are serious about pupils taking responsibility for learning, pupils need to be involved in the assessment of their work; that is, pupils need to be equipped with the necessary skills to help them judge the quality of their work, and they need to be aware of what they are doing well and what they need to do in order to improve their work. Research by Black *et al.* (2002) demonstrated that learning is dramatically enhanced when pupils know what it is they are aiming for, and they do even better when they play some part in deciding how to set about achieving their aims.

Learning is made more meaningful for learners when their prior learning is taken into account, where learners have some say in what, when and how they learn, and where pupils' interests and aspirations are taken into account.

Task 7.1.7 Making learning meaningful for all pupils

Think about a lesson you have recently conducted. Did the lesson give pupils the opportunity:

(a)   to have responsibility for deciding at what level to learn?
(b)   to assess what they had learned?

If yes, what key factors needed to be in place for both (a) and (b) to happen? If no, how could you have planned the lesson differently to allow both (a) and (b) to happen?

Task 7.1.8 Enhancing the relevance of pupils' learning

Identify ways in which you could use your knowledge of pupils in your class to support and challenge them within one curriculum area throughout (a) next term and (b) next year.

* Which pupils or groups of pupils do you think will be the most difficult to reach? What can you do to help reach these groups?
* What resources/training would be of help to you in order to facilitate taking the needs of individual pupils into account?
* Identify ways in which you could make your teaching more relevant to the needs of individual pupils in your class within one curriculum area, throughout (a) next term and (b) next year.

BARRIERS TO PUPIL VOICE WORK

For teachers, listening to the voices of pupils means facing up to being open to criticism, which can generate personal and interpersonal insecurities. Teachers may be anxious about pupils' criticism of aspects of their work and may be wary of the unpredictability of learners' comments and views.

The fear by some senior staff of 'losing control' (Busher and Cremin, 2012) and an unwillingness of teachers to recognise the legitimacy of different perspectives on schooling, including students' perspectives, can create barriers to pupil voice work (Robinson and Taylor, 2007).

As teachers, you may lack support from others in your school to work towards encouraging pupil voice work, and you may feel constrained owing to the pressure of the curriculum you are expected to get through and feel you lack time to listen to pupils as well. Some teachers may not agree with pupils being given opportunities to express their opinions in relation to teaching and learning issues. They may believe that pupils are not capable or sufficiently mature to be consulted about teaching, and may want full control of this aspect of their work. Some teachers may resent pupils' voices being listened to, if they feel they are listened to more than theirs. A further barrier to pupil voice work is the existence of power relations between staff and pupils in schools. The greater the existence of the power relations, the less likely it is that pupils will feel at ease to voice their opinions, especially in areas such as learning and teaching, which have traditionally been seen as a domain fully controlled by teachers.

Task 7.1.9 Enhancing the degree of pupil voice work in schools

- Consider how you might gain pupils' perceptions about the degree to which their voices are heard (a) within your classroom and (b) in the wider school context.
- How do school practices affect the degree to which different groups of pupils are listened to?

Choose one way, which you have not tried previously, in which you could listen to pupils about an aspect of their school experiences (for ideas on this, see the box at the bottom of page 444).

- Would you foresee any barriers to taking this work forward? If so, how might these be overcome?

SUMMARY

This unit has given you an introduction to how work around pupil voice can be incorporated into everyday classroom practices. If pupil voice work is to be taken seriously and become embedded within your school, opportunities need to be provided for pupils to be given a voice on all aspects of their school life. If schools are to listen to the whole body of pupils, they need to acknowledge that there are multiple voices, and that these voices are constantly changing. There should not be situations where schools favour only those with a language and culture similar to that of the school, or favour those whose voices fit neatly with the existing school ethos.

Making learning meaningful for pupils and encouraging pupils to take some responsibility for their learning promotes confidence and capacity building in individual pupils. It gives pupils some power over what and how they learn, and encourages pupils to take more responsibility for their learning, from setting targets to assessing their work. It is the normative goal of pupil voice work to challenge the structures and processes of power that create barriers to the voices of pupils being heard and curtail the opportunity to embed equality of voice for all in the life of the school (Robinson and Taylor, 2007). It may be that, in some schools, teachers and pupils will need to change their understanding of what it is to be a teacher and what it is to be a pupil, in order to allow pupils' voices to play a more significant role in their schools.

ANNOTATED FURTHER READING

Cheminais, R. (2008) *Engaging Pupil Voice to Ensure that Every Child Matters: A Practical Guide*, London: Routledge.

> This publication provides a practical guide to support teachers who wish to strengthen the engagement of pupils' voices in their everyday practices in schools. It includes models of good practice and resources that can be used in pupil voice development work.

Department for Children, Schools and Families (DCSF) (2008) *Personalised Learning: A Practical Guide*, DCFS-00844-2008, London: DCFS.

> This publication discusses the key features of personalised learning and how these can be promoted in schools. It covers, among other areas, target setting and tracking, assessment, pupil grouping, curriculum organisation and the extended curriculum. The publication was developed to support schools in implementing personalised learning and to help them move to a system based on progression, underpinned by assessment for learning, with relevant interventions such as one-to-one support.

Department for Children, Schools and Families (DCSF) (2008) *Working Together: Listening to the Voices of Children and Young People*, DCFS-00410-2008, London: DCFS.

> This guidance discusses the principles and benefits of pupil participation and outlines a range of opportunities that can be provided by schools to increase levels of pupil participation.

Robinson, C. and Fielding, M. (2010) 'Children and their primary schools: Pupils' voices', in R. Alexander (ed.) *The Cambridge Primary Review Research Surveys*, pp. 16–48, London: Routledge.

> This chapter forms part of an edited book comprising the twenty-eight research surveys that together formed the Cambridge Primary Review, England's biggest review of primary education in over 40 years. The chapter focuses on the views of primary school pupils in relation to various aspects of their primary schooling, including the purposes of primary schooling; learning and teaching within primary schools; the primary curriculum; and assessment within primary schools.

Sebba, J. and Robinson, C. (2010) *Evaluation of UNICEF UK's Rights Respecting Schools Award*, London: UNICEF UK.

> UNICEF UK's Rights Respecting Schools Award (RRSA) started in 2004, and more than 2,000 primary, secondary and special schools are now registered for the award in England, Wales, Scotland and Northern Ireland. It helps schools use the United Nations Convention on the Rights of the Child (UNCRC) as their values framework. A major part of working towards the award involves schools listening to the voices of pupils and developing a culture of respect in all aspects of school life, as well as developing a culture of respect in pupils as they move outside school. The evaluation assessed the impact of the RRSA on the well-being and achievement of children and young people in the participating schools.

FURTHER READING TO SUPPORT M-LEVEL STUDY

Busher, H. (2012) 'Students as expert witnesses of teaching and learning', *Management in Education*, 26(3): 113–19.

> Within this article, the author advocates that student voice is a key component in constructing discourse, empowerment and citizenship in schools, and that listening to and acting upon the views of students can lead to improvements in pedagogical and organisational practices. The article takes

the position that students are expert observers of school life and teachers' practices, and draws on research with students in primary and secondary schools to explore students' perspectives in relation to such practices.

Robinson, C. and Taylor, C. (2007) 'Theorising student voice: values and perspectives', *Improving Schools*, 10(1): 5-17.
This article explores the core values that underpin and inform student voice work. The authors argue that student voice work is an inherently ethical and moral practice, and that at the heart of student voice work are four core values: a conception of communication as dialogue; the requirement for participation and democratic inclusivity; the recognition that power relations are unequal and problematic; and the possibility for change and transformation. Throughout the article, complexities that arise in theorising student voice work are highlighted.

RELEVANT WEBSITES

Economic and Social Research Council (ESRC), *Consulting Pupils about Teaching and Learning* project: www.consultingpupils.co.uk
This site provides details of a major ESRC-funded project conducted in 2000-3. One of the aims of the project was to support teachers who wanted to develop ways of enhancing pupil engagement and achievement through consulting pupils and increasing opportunities for participation (accessed January 2013).

Pupil voice teaching resources: www.tes.co.uk/pupil-voice-whole-school-teaching-resources/
This site includes links to free teaching resources relevant for pupil voice work, including lesson plans, worksheets and teaching ideas. It is free to join this site (accessed January 2013).

Pupil Voice Wales: www.pupilvoicewales.org.uk
This site provides practical advice on how to involve children and young people within school activities and decision-making processes. The advice given is based on the premise that professionals working with young children must realise that every child has a right to be involved, and that children and young people of all ages and backgrounds have a valuable contribution to make, and suitable platforms should be provided to enable all children to contribute. The site gives separate advice for each of nursery, primary and secondary settings (accessed January 2013).

Department for Education (May 2012) *Teachers' Standards*: www.education.gov.uk/publications/eOrdering Download/teachers%20standards.pdf
These new *Teachers' Standards* set a clear baseline of expectations for the professional practice and conduct of teachers, from the point of qualification, and will apply to the vast majority of teachers, regardless of their career stage (accessed January 2013).

REFERENCES

Black, P., Harrison, C., Lee, C., Marshall, B. and Wiliam, D. (2002) *Working Inside the Black Box: Assessment for Learning in the Classroom*, London: Department of Education and Professional Studies, King's College, University of London.

Bragg, S. and Fielding, M. (2005) '"It's an equal thing . . . it's about achieving together": student voice and the possibility of radical collegiality', in H. Street and J. Temperley (eds) *Improving Schools Through Collaborative Enquiry*, pp. 105-34, London: Continuum.

Busher, H. (2012) 'Students as expert witnesses of teaching and learning', *Management in Education*, 29(3): 113-19.

Busher, H. and Cremin, H. (2012) 'Constructing ethnographies in schools in performative times. Perspectives of students, teachers and researchers on educational research processes', in D. Beach, B. Jeffrey, G. Troman and G. Walford (eds) *Performativity and Ethnography in Education in the UK: Effects, Consequences and Agency*, Milton Keynes: Open University Press.

Cheminais, R. (2008) *Engaging Pupil Voice to Ensure That Every Child Matters: A Practical Guide*, London and New York: Routledge.

Department for Children, Schools and Families (DCSF) (2007) *The Children's Plan: Building Brighter Futures: Summary*, Norwich: The Stationery Office.

Department for Children, Schools and Families (DCSF) (2008) *Working Together: Listening to the Voices of Children and Young People*, DCSF-00410-2008, London: DCSF.

Department for Education (DfE) (2012) *Teachers' Standards*, May. Available at www.education.gov.uk/publications/eOrderingDownload/teachers%20standards.pdf (accessed January 2013).

Department for Education and Skills (DfES) (2002) *The Education Act Statutory Instrument 2002*, London: DfES.

Department for Education and Skills (DfES) (2003) *Working Together: Giving Children and Young People a Say*, DfES/0492/2003, Nottingham: DfES.

Department for Education and Skills (DfES) (2004) *Every Child Matters: Change for Children*, DfES/1081/2004, Nottingham: DfES.

Fielding, M. (2001) 'Students as radical agents of change', *Journal of Educational Change*, 2: 123–41.

Fielding, M. (2008) 'Interrogating student voice: pre-occupations, purposes and possibilities', in H. Daniels, H. Lauder and J. Porter (eds) *The Routledge Companion to Education*, London: Routledge.

Flutter, J. and Rudduck, J. (2004) *Consulting Pupils: What's In It for Schools?* London: RoutledgeFalmer.

Fullan, M. (1991) *The New Meaning of Educational Change*, New York: Teachers College Press.

Jelly, M., Fuller, A. and Byers, R. (2000) *Involving Pupils in Practice: Promoting Partnerships with Pupils with Special Educational Needs*, London: David Fulton.

Lundy, L. (2007) '"Voice" is not enough: conceptualizing Article 12 of the United Nations Convention of the Rights of the Child', *British Educational Research Journal*, 33(6): 927–42.

MacBeath, J., Demetriou, H., Rudduck, J. and Myres, K. (2003) *Consulting Pupils: A Toolkit for Teachers*, Cambridge: Pearson.

Miliband, D. (2004) *Personalised Learning: Building a New Relationship with Schools*, Speech at the North of England Education Conference, Belfast, 8 January, London: DfES. Available at www.education.gov.uk/publications/eOrderingDownload/personalised-learning.pdf (accessed January 2013).

Ofsted (April 2012) *The Framework for School Inspection: Guidance and Grade Descriptors for Inspecting Schools in England under Section 5 of the Education Act 2005, from January 2012*, Manchester: Ofsted. Available at: www.ofsted.gov.uk/resources/090019 (accessed January 2013).

Robinson, C. (2012) 'Student engagement: What does this mean in practice in the context of higher education institutions?', *Journal of Applied Research in Higher Education*, 4(2): 94–108.

Robinson, C. and Taylor, C. (2007) 'Theorising student voice: values and perspectives', *Improving Schools*, 10(1): 5–17.

Rudduck, J. and Flutter, J. (2004) *How to Improve your School: Giving Pupils a Voice*, London: Continuum.

Rudduck, J. and McIntyre, D. (2007) *Improving Learning Through Consulting Pupils*, London: Routledge.

Rudduck, J., Chaplain, R. and Wallace, G. (1996) *School Improvement: What Can Pupils Tell Us?* London: David Fulton.

Sebba, J. and Robinson, C. (2010) *Evaluation of UNICEF UK's Rights Respecting Schools' Award*, Final report, London: UNICEF UK.

Shier, H. (2001) 'Pathways to participation: Openings, opportunities and obligations', *Children and Society*, 15: 107–17.

Thomson, P. (2011) 'Coming to terms with "voice"', in G. Czerniawski and W. Kidd (eds) *The Student Voice Handbook: Bridging the Academic/Practitioner Divide*, Bingley: Emerald Group Publishing Ltd.

United Nations (1989) *UN Convention on the Rights of the Child: General Assembly Resolution 44/25*, New York: United Nations.

LEARNING AND TEACHING LANGUAGES

Carrie Cable and Cynthia Martin

INTRODUCTION

Many primary schools are now teaching languages, and some have been doing so for many years. Language is closely linked to identity: developing children's knowledge about language (KAL) and their language skills will help learning across the curriculum. Languages are often seen as a means of enriching the curriculum and as a way of responding to diversity within our society and preparing children for participation in an increasingly globalised world.

Teachers are often enthusiastic about languages teaching, either because they are linguists or have some facility in languages, or, alternatively, because they feel they missed out on languages learning during their school days. Learning languages in primary schools is not simply a preparation for more intensive study at secondary school, but an opportunity to develop children's interest in, and enthusiasm for, languages and language learning in a context where there are opportunities for more holistic and cross-curricular learning. Although each school currently has the freedom to organise the teaching of languages in a way that best suits its situation, all primary teachers need to be able to teach languages to their classes, either as discrete lessons or by reinforcing the teaching of specialist teachers and through developing language awareness and intercultural understanding.

OBJECTIVES

By the end of this unit, you should have:

- reflected on your own knowledge of languages and how you developed this;
- developed your understanding of the value of languages in society;
- increased your understanding of the place and importance of languages in the primary curriculum;
- increased your awareness of a range of approaches to teaching languages.

HISTORY AND CONTEXT

Languages teaching in primary schools is not new, and some readers may remember learning languages themselves at primary school. However, the publication of the Burstall report (Burstall *et al.* 1974), a longitudinal study of children's attitudes and performance that suggested children gained little from starting their study of languages prior to secondary school, had a major impact on primary provision across the country in the latter part of the last century. It was not until the introduction of a National Curriculum at the turn of the century that guidelines and schemes of work for the teaching of languages in the primary phase were produced (Department for Education and Employment 1999; Qualifications and Curriculum Authority 2000), although these were non-statutory. The publication of *Languages for All: Languages for Life A Strategy for England* (Department for Education and Skills 2002) marked a significant turning point, as the then government accepted that there were strong social, economic and political arguments for languages learning.

> In the knowledge society of the 21st Century, language competence and intercultural understanding are not optional extras; they are an essential part of being a citizen. Language skills are also vital in improving understanding between people here and in the wider world, and in supporting global citizenship by breaking down barriers of ignorance, and suspicion between nations.
>
> (Department for Education and Skills 2002: 12)

As a result, the English Labour government decided to introduce languages teaching *within curriculum time* as an entitlement in Key Stage 2, for Years 3-6, (ages 7-11), although many schools have decided to also teach languages to children in Reception and Key Stage 1 (ages 5-7) (Department for Education and Skills 2002: 15).

There has long been a debate about the optimum age at which to start learning another language in a school setting. Some argue for an early start, because young children are more open to new experiences, and others argue that older learners learn more quickly, owing to more finely developed language learning strategies. Edelenbos and colleagues (Edelenbos *et al.* 2006: 26), in a report for the European Commission, conclude that an early start offers a longer overall period for learning, but that continuity from year to year and high-quality teaching are vital.

Ironically, at the same time as language learning was being introduced into primary school, proposals to reduce the mandatory curriculum in secondary schools were being considered. In 2004, learning a language at Key Stage 4 (ages 14-16) ceased to be a compulsory part of the curriculum. Partly as a consequence of this decision, the numbers of pupils sitting a modern foreign language exam at GCSE level (age 16) fell by more than 200,000 between 2002 and 2010. In order to arrest this decline, in January 2011, the Department for Education introduced an English Baccalaureate at age 16, an award for pupils who achieve high GCSE grades (A*-C) in a combination of five core academic subjects, including a modern language. Consequently, numbers taking GCSEs in a language have begun to rise again.

The previous Labour government invested heavily in training and support, with a view to languages becoming statutory in a revised primary curriculum to be introduced in 2010 (Department for Children, Schools and Families 2009). However, the Coalition government embarked on a fresh review of the curriculum in 2011. In 2012, the Department for Education announced that languages would become mandatory for 7-year-olds in the new revised draft primary curriculum, to be introduced from 2014 (Department for Education 2013). Whereas, previously, schools were free to choose the language(s) they taught, the government intends to restrict choice to French, German, Italian, Mandarin, Spanish and Latin or Ancient Greek, although schools will be free to teach another language in addition to these.

Scotland, Wales and Northern Ireland have their own provision for (foreign) languages teaching. In Scotland, a long standing Modern Languages in the Primary School initiative, which began with a pilot in 1989 (Low *et al.* 1995), resulted in 1998 in a recommendation by Her Majesty's Inspectorate of Education that all children in the upper primary years, P6 (age 9-10) and P7 (age 10-11), should have the opportunity to learn another language in curriculum time. In 2004, Scotland introduced a new 3-18 Curriculum for Excellence, which requires a wider cross-curricular approach and an emphasis on structures and building confidence to speak in a sustained manner.

In Wales, languages are included as a non-statutory element in the guidance for the Key Stage 2 curriculum (Welsh Assembly Government 2008). In Northern Ireland, primary schools are encouraged to teach other languages as part of the languages and literacy area of learning, although no specific guidance is provided (Council for the Curriculum, Examinations and Assessment (Northern Ireland) 2007).

In Northern Ireland . . .

The Department of Education for Northern Ireland states:

> Any education system that is responsive to the future wellbeing of the society that it serves must be able and willing to put forward a vision that supports the development of the language skills that will allow us to take our place in a future increasingly characterised by multilingual exchange and international cooperation.
>
> (DENI 2011: 6)

Source: Department of Education for Northern Ireland (DENI) (2011) *Languages for the Future: Northern Ireland Languages Strategy*. Bangor, DENI.

In Wales . . .

In Wales, at Key Stage 2, there is a non-statutory framework for modern foreign languages with the rationale that,

> The learning of a foreign language supports pupils' literacy and oracy, building on and complementing the skills acquired in English and Welsh. Modern foreign languages enrich the primary curriculum, providing a valuable educational and enjoyable cultural experience for all pupils. Learning a foreign language brings pupils into contact with aspects of the culture of other countries and they develop a greater understanding of their own lives and communitiesthrough exploring those of others.
>
> (DCELLS 2008: 26)

Source: Department for Children, Education, Lifelong Learning and Skills (DCELLS) (2008) *Modern Foreign Languages in the National Curriculum for Wales*. Cardiff: Welsh Assembly Government (WAG). http://wales.gov.uk/dcells/publications/curriculum_and_assessment/arevisedcurriculumforwales/national curriculum/modernforeirnlanguagesnc/mfleng.pdf?lang=en

There are also policies or provision for Welsh-medium teaching in Wales, Gaelic-medium teaching in Scotland and Irish-medium teaching in Northern Ireland that aim to support the development of bilingual education and bilingualism in the respective countries/languages. The Republic of Ireland has a separate Irish curriculum for schools, where teaching is through the medium of Irish. The *Gaeilge* curriculum is presented in two separate sections: the first for English-medium schools, and the second for Gaeltacht and all-Irish schools. For more information, see the websites at the end of this unit.

Community languages

However, in contrast to the provision for the study of Gaelic, Irish and Welsh, community languages teaching across the UK rarely takes place in mainstream schools, even though, in 2012, it was estimated that over a million primary and secondary school pupils in England have a first language known to or believed to be a language other than English (Department for Education 2012). Teaching and learning of community or heritage languages tend to take place in classes provided and organised by communities, sometimes supported by the governments of other countries. These classes take place after school or at weekends. It is only at secondary level that some schools make provision for the teaching of community languages within the upper secondary school curriculum (ages 14–16) or submit students for GCSE examinations in their community languages. CILT, the former National Centre for Languages, published a booklet, 'Positively plurilingual', which summarises findings from its 2005 UK survey of community languages and aims to support the development of plurilingualism within our society.

Mainland Europe

In contrast, in mainland Europe, English is the main language taught in the majority of primary schools, largely owing to the position of English as a global language. Furthermore, children start learning English earlier and study it for longer and for more hours in total than children in the UK and other English-speaking jurisdictions. (Edelenbos *et al.* 2006; DfES 2006; Tinsley and Comfort 2012).

Task 7.2.1 Reflection on learning languages

- Reflect on your own experience of learning another language at home or in school. What made this a successful experience for you?
- Think about your competence in another language. How does this make you feel?
- Jot down your ideas and share them with colleagues.

LEARNING AND TEACHING LANGUAGES – METHODS AND APPROACHES

Approaches to learning and teaching languages have changed over time and been influenced by different theories of learning and of learning language. Previous methodologies have included grammar-translation, in which modern languages were taught in a similar way to the Classics; the direct method, which attempted to mimic the way in which learners learned their mother tongue; and the audio-lingual approach, which used language laboratories and tape recorders as a stimulus to drill new language habits. Since the late 1970s, variations on communicative language teaching (CLT) have been developed internationally. This approach emphasises the genuine communication of meaningful messages. Learners practise in pairs by means of information gap tasks, in which one has information that their partner does not and that they must seek to discover. CLT is more pupil-centred than previous methods and is an eclectic mix of problem-solving, dealing with the unpredictable and the use of authentic materials, alongside new language presented, practised and produced in a particular sequence.

A more intensive form of CLT is content and language integrated learning, derived from immersion teaching in parts of Canada, where part of or the whole curriculum may be taught through the medium of French. In England, initiatives have generally sought to teach an aspect of the curriculum through the medium of another language. *Children must be learning new content* and not just rehearsing already learned knowledge, as it is this new learning that they find intrinsically motivating. In London, an ambitious example is Wix Primary School, where children are able to learn for half the week in English and half in French, and follow both the English and French primary curricula.

However, some primary schools have sought to make their languages teaching more task-based, becoming adept at linking languages extensively to other aspects of the curriculum. Here, one teacher explains what they do:

> I know Year 5 best . . . after Christmas we do 'keeping healthy' as our Science unit, so that is why we are doing the 'healthy eating' unit then, because it is an obvious link. In the summer term we do 'Earth, sun and moon' as the Science unit, so we do a lot of work on the planets and the order from the sun and things like that. In Year 6 because they are getting ready to leave school the last one we did was 'nôtre école'.

(Cable *et al.* 2010: 139)

Task 7.2.2 Comparing teaching and learning in languages and English

Think about these approaches to teaching languages/what you have observed in schools. Then consider what you have learnt/observed about teaching English.

- What are the similarities and differences between the two approaches?

Individually, or as a group, you might wish to make a list under headings such as: role of teacher, role of learners, listening, speaking, reading, writing, whole-class activities, pair/group work tasks, interactions between teacher and pupils, use of ICT, resources.

TEACHING LANGUAGES IN PRIMARY SCHOOLS

In England, three models predominated in the primary schools studied by Driscoll *et al.* (2004) and Muijs *et al.* (2005): language sensitisation, language awareness and language competence.

The different approaches can be placed along a spectrum ranging from language competence, where the intention is that children should develop real competence, usually in a single language, through sensitisation, in which the emphasis is more on fun, developing positive attitudes and basic conversational skills, and language awareness, where the intention is to explore features of a number of languages, and compare and contrast them to English. Of these, the one likely to be adopted by the current government is language competence, although there are still proponents of an approach combining sensitisation and language awareness. We discuss these options briefly below.

Language competence

This model aims to develop the four language skills: listening, speaking, reading and writing. There are often staged objectives in terms of learning and usually some form of formative and summative assessment.

Language sensitisation

In this approach, a different language may be taught each term or year, and children are not expected to become competent in the language being taught but to develop elementary conversational skills and some KAL (e.g. comparing and contrasting similarities and differences in languages and cultures, which they will then be able to apply to other language learning). Other, bilingual adults can become involved, and the languages chosen for study may reflect the languages spoken in the local community. Cultural awareness is an important element and includes developing knowledge and understanding of our own and other multilingual, multicultural societies and developing children's ability to reflect on their own assumptions, values and beliefs. Teaching typically takes place in short sessions and through incidental opportunities for learning linked to routines or projects.

Language awareness

This model owes much to the work of the late Eric Hawkins, who believed that children need to develop sound foundations for learning languages before they focus on learning one specific language (Hawkins 2005), and that this is best achieved in primary schools through a focus on exploring a variety of languages and making comparisons with English. Children are encouraged to examine the sounds, ways of expressing meaning, the scripts and writing systems, the roots of languages and how languages are used in different contexts and for different purposes in different societies and situations. Because discussion of language characteristics takes place in English, the demands on a teacher's foreign language competence are minimal. Some schools have adopted this kind of language awareness approach for younger children. Coventry Local Authority created the 'Language Investigator' scheme, devised as part of the Language Learning Pathfinders between 2003 and 2005 (Muijs *et al.* 2005). These resources enable children to compare features of a number of languages, including some in their own locality. According to Ofsted (2005: 8), this innovative multilingual programme 'provided a strong foundation for later, or simultaneous learning of one or two specific languages' through investigative activities that built on children's work in literacy, as well as developing their early understanding of how languages work.

A second project, which is a flexible mix of sensitisation and language awareness, is the multilingual *Discovering Language* programme, based on learning the basics of up to six languages over Key Stage 2, each of which is drawn from different language families and may include Latin. Which combination of languages and how the programme is structured are determined by the school. Resources for non-specialist teachers are available in French, German, Spanish, Japanese, Punjabi, Latin and Esperanto. This programme has been evaluated by a team at the University of Manchester (Barton *et al.* 2009).

Such programmes help meet the objectives of community cohesion and appreciation of linguistic diversity, providing an inclusive, non-hierarchical view of language and culture.

> ### Task 7.2.3 My language knowledge and awareness
>
> How much do you know about other languages spoken in the UK?
>
> - Ask someone to tell you about a language you don't speak, including a few common words or greetings.
> - Try to identify some similarities and differences (between English and the new language you have been exposed to).
> - Prepare a 2-minute presentation and share your new knowledge with others.

THE KEY STAGE 2 FRAMEWORK FOR LANGUAGES

This non-statutory Framework (Department for Education and Skills 2005) lays out learning objectives, suggested learning opportunities and outcomes relating to three core strands: oracy, literacy and intercultural understanding, and two cross-cutting strands: KAL and language learning strategies. The inclusion of 'objectives and outcomes' reflects an expectation that children will progress in their learning and achieve a certain standard in oracy and literacy in at least one language by the time they leave primary school. Achievement of the objectives relies on children receiving sustained teaching (the intention is for 1 hour a week). A degree of teacher language knowledge and confidence in teaching languages is important and becomes increasingly so as children move through to the upper stages of Key Stage 2.

Oracy

Oracy is defined as' listening, speaking and spoken interaction' (Department for Education and Skills 2005: 7) and is the focus in the initial stages, with an emphasis on exposure to the sound patterns of the new language. Initially, children are expected to listen, recognise, respond to and perform simple words and phrases, but, by Year 6, to understand spoken texts, read aloud or recite texts, initiate and sustain conversations and tell stories.

Literacy

Children are expected to progressively apply their developing knowledge of sounds to the letters (or characters) of the new language and gradually build up their reading and writing skills, so that, by Year 6, they can read a range of short, authentic texts and write sentences from a model and independently. They are expected to apply their developing knowledge to a range of text types, including: 'simple stories, poems, information texts, advertisements, letters, messages – in paper and electronic form' (Department for Education and Skills 2005: 8).

Intercultural understanding

Intercultural understanding is viewed as an essential part of being a citizen, and language competence is viewed as contributing to this understanding. The aims are to enable children to develop a better understanding of other people, their lives, traditions and cultures, and in so doing to identify similarities and differences and reflect on their own lives. Teaching can take place both within language lessons and more broadly as part of cross-curricular learning. One Year 6 teacher explained:

For intercultural understanding for Year 6, one our units is called Passport to the World, so the children have to do work on that . . . so they would each take a country, which they would research, and then we have presentations . . . it's absolutely fantastic, you learn a huge amount.

(Cable *et al.* 2010: 59)

Knowledge about language

Children develop their KAL through making comparisons between languages and reflecting on similarities and differences. This helps them to see patterns, rules and conventions in languages and can encourage reflection, questioning and experimentation. It can contribute to children's understanding of how both the new language, English and other languages they speak work. Cable *et al.* (2010: 93) noted the following example of a short KAL moment within a longer Year 3 lesson:

The teacher asked pupils in English what differences they noticed between the spellings of months in English and French. Pupils commented that they all started with the same letter, that months from September onwards 'all started the same', that if you 'turned the ending round' they would be spelled the same as in English. The teacher asked whether they had the same number of syllables.

Language learning strategies

These are a range of teaching and learning strategies to support memorisation and recall: using rhythm (chanting, clapping and beating out), rhymes and songs, mime, physical response and mouthing words silently are some examples. Others include making comparisons between languages, guessing based on context or prior knowledge and applying knowledge learned in one context to a new situation.

OTHER ESSENTIAL FEATURES OF THE KEY STAGE 2 FRAMEWORK FOR LANGUAGES

It is important to see the strands summarised above as linked and complementing each other. Although the framework contains examples of the learning opportunities children should be provided with each year and suggestions for teaching activities with progression built in, it *does not* prescribe which languages should be taught, by whom they should be taught or how. Although the National Languages Strategy (Department for Education and Skills 2002: 15) initially recommended that children should learn at least one language of European origin, other languages, including community languages, were not excluded. Furthermore, because the learning objectives are skills-based, they can be applied to any language. Consequently, in addition to the more common languages of European origin, in a small number of schools children are learning Turkish, Greek or Somali, for example. Not surprisingly, however, the majority of schools teach French.

STAFFING

The dominance of French has come about because the choice of language is often determined by the skills, knowledge and confidence of staff and the languages that children will be able to study at secondary school. Some primary schools employ secondary specialists to teach languages, especially where they have established good working relationships with secondary schools, many of which are specialist language colleges. The majority of schools prefer to employ teachers who are primary language specialists and familiar with primary pedagogy (Wade and Marshal 2009). Some are employed specifically to teach languages, others are full-time members of staff who teach languages for part of their working week and their own class for the rest. Elsewhere, class teachers teach their own classes, usually with the support of a subject leader who provides training, advice and suggestions for lessons to those who may initially lack confidence. Sometimes, teachers are supported by foreign language assistants or bilingual parents. Different approaches suit different schools, and a number of schools combine several staffing models.

The pedagogic approach varies according to the teacher's training and qualifications, both in terms of teaching generally and specifically in teaching languages in the primary school. However, it can broadly be described as communicative, with an initial emphasis on speaking and listening. Key aims are to make language learning enjoyable and motivate learners to develop language skills and understanding of other cultures. Teachers model language, provide lots of opportunities for repetition and revisiting vocabulary and phrases, using rhyme, chants, songs, games and role-play to enable children to practise language in whole-class situations and in pairs. The interactive whiteboard is a key resource, but teachers also use authentic artefacts, puppets, stories, flash cards, labels, dual-language books, poems, play scripts, matching and sequencing activities and individual computers to support literacy development and the growth of intercultural understanding. The example below provides a flavour of what is possible.

> All the children in Key Stage 2 worked on the story of *Les Trois Petits Cochons* with varying degrees of complexity and engagement. Years 3 and 4 learnt through songs and games, they developed an awareness of the vocabulary by listening to the story and repeating individual phrases so that they could join in with the Year 6 production e.g. '*Non, non, non, crient les petits cochons*', '*Attention au grand loup méchant*'. Year 6 worked on their characters in class. They wrote what each character might say with support from the model provided using drawing and speech bubbles. To help with comprehension and memorisation they translated some phrases into English. To help with their pronunciation, they crossed out letters that were not pronounced e.g. 's' of '*trois*'. Older children discussed ways to adapt the script e.g. one Year 5 child suggested a story about 'the three wolves and the big black pig'.
>
> (Cable *et al.* 2010: 87)

PROGRESSION, ASSESSMENT AND ACCREDITATION

As children's study of languages continues throughout Key Stage 2, teachers become more aware of the need to ensure their teaching provides progression. Many teachers assess children's achievements and progress informally, but more and more are seeking ways to keep a more formal record. With the increasing importance given to personalisation, self-assessment and assessment for learning, some schools have found that 'My Languages Portfolio' provides one way of doing this.

> They [the teachers] can use that [Language Portfolio] then to inform planning, so you can differentiate any work that they do and the kind of resources in front of them. Some children will have pictures without words, some children will have pictures of the Spanish words and some will have pictures in English and the Spanish word, depending on what their need is, and that's something (we) try to do a lot more.
>
> (Cable *et al.* 2012: 373)

The 'My Languages Portfolio' is a junior version of the European Language Portfolio developed by the Council of Europe and comprises:

- **My Language Biography** – a personalised learning diary making children aware of their achievements as they learn.

- **My Dossier** – where learners can file work and materials to illustrate the achievements recorded in the *Language Biography* or *Language Passport*.
- **My Language Passport** – an overview of the learner's knowledge and experiences of different languages based on a series of 'can do' statements, and of their cultural experiences.

The Council of Europe has been at the forefront of language developments over many years. In 1996, the Council published the Common European Framework of Reference (CEFR) for languages, with six reference levels from A1 (beginner) to C2 (mastery) as a means of grading an individual's language proficiency (Council for Europe, 2001). Indeed, the European Language Portfolio uses simplified CEFR level descriptors to assess children's development in each of the four skills. Hasselgreen *et al.* (2011) have published a handbook to support the assessment of children's reading and writing from age 9, which is similarly linked to the CEFR. However, it should be noted that the Early Language Learning in Europe project found that these CEFR level descriptors were not entirely suited to primary children, having been originally designed for older learners. It is important that, whatever method is adopted, assessment is based on good primary practice and the way younger children learn in primary school.

Task 7.2.4 Exploring research

For a *national* picture, look at the *Languages Learning at Key Stage 2: A Longitudinal Study* (Cable *et al.* 2010) and, to place their findings in an international context, consider Tinsley and Comfort (2012).

Make a note of the key findings from these two reports and be prepared to discuss these with your colleagues. Is there any aspect that surprised you?

Use the following website to explore further research reports: www.primarylanguages.org.uk

SUPPORT FOR TEACHING AND LEARNING

Resources

The resources teachers use depend on their role in teaching languages and the approach the school adopts. Many teachers directly involved in teaching languages as a discrete subject make their own materials.

The former Qualifications and Curriculum Development Authority developed a non-statutory scheme of work to sit alongside the Key Stage 2 Framework. Many local authorities have also produced their own schemes of work, and several commercial publishers have developed resources for teaching French and, to a growing extent, Spanish and German, which similarly draw on Framework objectives, providing 'ready made' schemes of work.

You will find many web-based resources for teachers to download and use, the most important of which are listed at the end of this unit.

Languages in the community

Finding out about the languages children already speak is a vital part of any teacher's role. It is important to ascertain whether they are continuing to learn to read and write these languages at home or in community or supplementary schools. In a world where we are trying to encourage children to learn new languages, we must not overlook the ones they already know and those in which they may be developing literacy (or able to do so with appropriate support inside school as well as outside). Respect for children's languages and cultures is a major part of every teacher's role. Over 17 per cent of children in primary schools (National Association for Language Development in the Curriculum 2012) already speak a language other than English. Many have considerable knowledge about language and language learning strategies – their knowledge and skills are a resource to be valued and drawn on. Consulting and involving parents, making contact with teachers in community and supplementary schools to share ideas and investigating the languages spoken by all members of staff are crucial means of developing your own language and cultural awareness.

> Learning other languages gives us insight into the people, culture and traditions of other countries, and helps us to understand our own language and culture. Drawing on the skills and expertise of those who speak community languages will promote citizenship and complement . . . the promotion of social cohesion.
>
> (Department for Education and Skills 2002: 12)

Task 7.2.5 Exploring resources to support my teaching

Access one of the websites listed at the end of this unit (if you are working in a group, you might like to choose different sites or work in pairs).

Start to build up a list of websites that will be useful in the future and keep a summary of how they may be able to support your teaching. Share your findings with others in your group.

ENTHUSIASM FOR LANGUAGES

Children in primary schools are overwhelmingly enthusiastic about learning languages. They are motivated by the range of engaging activities their teachers offer, including story telling and imaginative use of the interactive whiteboard. Children learning English as an additional language and those with learning difficulties often excel, because most children are starting learning from the beginning together. Affective factors such as developing a positive attitude to languages and cultures and to learning in general are identified by teachers as key drivers for primary language learning.

SUMMARY

All teachers will be involved in teaching languages in the future and need to prepare by developing their own knowledge and skills. You may already be able to speak, read and write other languages, or you may need initially to learn alongside children and seek the advice of more knowledgeable others, who may be advisers, other teachers, children or parents. This unit has set out the background to the growth of primary languages, introduced some approaches to teaching languages in primary schools and provided suggestions for you to explore to develop your own teaching.

ANNOTATED FURTHER READING

Kirsch, C. (2008) *Teaching Foreign Languages in the Primary School,* London: Continuum.
>   This book combines coverage of theories of language learning and approaches to pedagogy with practical suggestions for teaching and case studies.

Martin, C. (2008) *Primary Languages: Effective Learning and Teaching,* Exeter: Learning Matters.
>   This book expands the discussion of the optimum age to begin learning languages and supports teachers in exploring the requirements of the Key Stage 2 Framework for Languages.

FURTHER READING TO SUPPORT M-LEVEL STUDY

Barton, A., Bragg, J. and Serratrice, L. (2009) 'Discovering Language' in primary school: An evaluation of a language awareness programme, *Language Learning Journal,* 37(2): 145-64.
>   In this paper, the authors evaluate a language awareness programme introduced into seven primary schools. They consider the responses of children, parents, teachers and head teachers to the initiative and possible implications for primary languages teaching and learning.

Cable, C., Driscoll, P., Mitchell, R., Sing, S., Cremin, T., Earl, J., Eyres, I., Holmes, B, Martin, C. and Heins, B. (2012) Language learning at Key Stage 2: findings from a longitudinal study, *Education 3-13: International Journal of Primary, Elementary and Early Years Education,* 40(4): 363-78.
>   This paper provides an overview of a longitudinal research project examining the teaching and learning of languages in forty primary schools. Key issues for future provision are discussed.

RELEVANT WEBSITES

Support for teaching and learning

Primary Languages: www.primarylanguages.org.uk
>   An excellent website providing information on policy and research, training and continuing professional development and ideas for best practice, supported by video sequences related to the Key Stage 2 Framework for Languages (accessed 17 May 2013).

Association for Language Learning: www.all-languages.org.uk
>   This website by the National Association for Language Teachers provides information about developments in the world of languages for all languages and sectors. Membership of ALL ensures that you receive weekly ALL-net updates about local and national language events, including the annual conference, at which there is a primary strand (accessed 17 May 2013).

Speak to the Future: www.speaktothefuture.org
>   Discover all about the campaign for languages and its ambitious objectives setting out the value of learning and using languages in all sectors of education and at all stages of life (accessed 17 May 2013).

Scotland's National Centre for Languages SCILTL: www.scilt.org.uk
>   Information about languages developments and resources in Scotland and links to the revised Scottish curriculum - A Curriculum for Excellence (accessed 17 May 2013).

Language Learning in Scotland: A 1 + 2 approach: www.scilt.org.uk/A12ApproachtoLanguageLearning/tabid/1715/Default.aspx
>   The Scottish Government published a final report in May 2012, with the aim of establishing a new model for learning and teaching languages in schools in Scotland.

The National Centre for Languages in Wales: www.ciltcymru.org.uk/primary/
> Your gateway to advice and support for language teaching and learning in the primary school, with resources, practical teaching ideas, and the latest news and research about primary languages in Wales, in particular guidance drawn from the outcomes of the Key Stage 2 MFL Pilot Project (2003–9) (accessed 17 May 2013).

Northern Ireland Centre for Information on Language Teaching and Research (NICILT): www.qub.ac.uk/schools/SchoolofEducation/nicilt
> Based at Queen's University Belfast, NICILT aims to serve all sectors and stages of education in Northern Ireland and support the implementation of national objectives in language learning and teaching, including early language learning (accessed 17 May 2013).

Department for Education for Northern Ireland: www.deni.gov.uk
> The Department for Education commissioned a study to develop a languages strategy for Northern Ireland. A revised curriculum was introduced in 2007–8, including a primary languages initiative. You can also find out more about Irish Gaelic medium teaching in Northern Ireland on this site (accessed 17 May 2013).

Department for Education and Skills Republic of Ireland: www.education.ie/en/The-Education-System/Primary
> This website gives information on Irish Gaelic medium teaching at primary school in the Republic of Ireland, as well as languages within the whole primary curriculum (accessed 17 May 2013).

Our Languages Project: www.ourlanguages.org.uk
> The 'Our Languages Project' was a DCSF-funded initiative to promote community languages and develop greater synergy between languages teaching in mainstream and complementary schools, involving ninety schools across England between 2007 and 2009 (accessed 17 May 2013).

Language awareness through language investigation: www.language-investigator.co.uk/index.htm
> An alternative approach to language teaching developed in 2003–5 in Coventry Local Authority as part of the DfES-funded KS2 Pathfinder project, which takes account of the needs of non-specialist teachers (accessed 17 May 2013).

Discovering Languages: http://sha.org.uk/Home/About_us/Projects/Discovering_language/Discovering_language
> Here you will find details of the materials for teaching a carousel of several languages, either prior to a course in a typical language such as French, or alongside another main European language (accessed 17 May 2013).

Language of the month website: www.newburypark.redbridge.sch.uk/langofmonth/
> This website offers free resources for promoting language awareness, including videos of children teaching their home languages, resources for putting up language displays and a booklet with more than 100 ideas for celebrating community languages (accessed 17 May 2013).

Schemes of work: http://webarchive.nationalarchives.gov.uk/20100612050234/; www.standards.dfes.gov.uk/schemes3/subjects/primary_mff/?view=get (accessed 17th May 2013); www.primarylanguages.org.uk/resources/schemes_of_work/qcda_schemes_of_work.aspx (accessed 17th May 2013)
> The former QCDA Schemes of Work for French, Spanish and German at Key Stage 2 have been archived, but at time of writing were available at the above addresses.

Assessment and recording

General information: www.primarylanguages.org.uk/teaching_and_learning/assessment_and_recording.aspx (accessed 17 May 2013)

My Languages Portfolio, Junior European Language Portfolio: www.primarylanguages.org.uk/resources/assessment_and_recording/european_languages_portfolio.aspx (accessed 17th May 2013)

Languages ladder currently archived at: www.education.gov.uk/publications/standard/publicationDetail/Page1/DCSF-00811-2007

Asset Languages: www.assetlanguages.org.uk/teachers/primary.asp (accessed 17th May 2013)
> Information about a scheme to measure children's progress in small steps in each of the four language skills. Options are available for teacher assessment and for external assessment.

REFERENCES

Barton, A., Bragg, J., and Serratrice, L. (2009) 'Discovering Language' in primary school: an evaluation of a language awareness programme, *Language Learning Journal*, 37(2): 145-64.

Burstall, C., Jamieson, M., Cohen S. and Hargreaves, M. (1974) *Primary French in the Balance*, Windsor: NFER Publications.

Cable, C., Driscoll, P., Mitchell, R., Sing, S., Cremin, T., Earl, J., Eyres, I., Holmes, B., Martin, C., with Heins, B. (2010) *Languages Learning at Key Stage 2: A Longitudinal Study Final Report*. DCSF Research Report RR 198. London: DCSF. Available at: www.education.gov.uk/publications/standard/publicationDetail/Page1/DCSF-RB198 (accessed 17 May 2013).

Cable, C., Driscoll, P., Mitchell, R., Sing, S., Cremin, T., Earl, J., Eyres, I., Holmes, B., Martin, C. and Heins, B. (2012) Language learning at Key Stage 2: findings from a longitudinal study, *Education 3-13: International Journal of Primary, Elementary and Early Years Education*, 40(4): 363-78.

Council for the Curriculum, Examinations and Assessment (Northern Ireland) (2007) *The Northern Ireland Primary Curriculum*. Available at: www.nicurriculum.org.uk/docs/key_stages_1_and_2/northern_ireland_curriculum_primary.pdf (accessed 17 May 2013).

Council for Europe (2001) *Common European Framework of Reference for the Learning and Teaching of Languages*, Cambridge: Cambridge University Press.

Department for Children, Schools and Families (2009) *Independent Review of the Primary Curriculum: Final Report*. Available at: http://publications.teachernet.gov.uk (accessed 5 May 2009),

Department for Education (2013) The National Curriculum in England Framework document for consultation. Available at: www.education.gov.uk/schools/teachingandlearning/curriculum/nationalcurriculum2014/b00220600/draft-national-curriculum-programmes-of-study (accessed 17 May 2013).

Department for Education and Employment (DfEE) (1999) *Handbook for Primary Teachers in England Key Stages 1 and 2 Guidelines for MFL at Key Stage 2*, London: DfEE/QCA.

Department for Education and Skills (DfES) (2002) *Languages for Life: Languages for All: A Strategy for England*, Nottingham: DfES Publications.

Department for Education and Skills (DfES) (2005) *The Key Stage 2 Framework for Languages*, Nottingham: DfES Publications.

Department for Education and Skills (DfES) (2006) *The Language Review*, Nottingham: DfES Publications.

Driscoll, P., Jones, J. and Macrory, G. (2004) *The Provision of Foreign Language Learning for Pupils at Key Stage 2*, DfES Research Report RR572, Nottingham: DfES Publications.

Edelenbos, P., Johnstone, R. and Kubanek, A. (2006) *The Main Pedagogical Principles Underlying the Teaching of Languages to Very Young Learners*, Final Report of the EAC 89/04, Lot 1 study. Brussels: European Commission. Available from: http://ec.europa.eu/languages/documents/doc427_en.pdf (accessed 17 May 2013).

Hasselgreen, A. Valedaité, K., Maldonado-Martin, N. and Pizorn, K. (2011) *Assessment of Young Learner Literacy Linked to the Common European Framework for Languages*. Graz: ECML.

Hawkins, E. (2005) Out of this nettle, drop out, we pluck this flower, opportunity: rethinking the school foreign language apprenticeship, *Language Learning Journal*, 32: 4-17.

Low, L., Brown, S., Johnstone, R. and Pirrie, A. (1995) *Foreign Languages in Primary Schools: Evaluation of the Scottish Pilot Projects. Final Report to Scottish Office*, Stirling: Scottish CILT.

Muijs, D., Barnes, A., Hunt, M., Powell, B., Arweck, E., Lindsay, G. and Martin, C. (2005) *Evaluation of the Key Stage 2 Language Learning Pathfinders*, London: DfES.

National Association for Language Development in the Curriculum (2012) EAL statistics. Available at: www.naldic.org.uk/research-and-information/eal-statistics (accessed 17 May 2013).

Ofsted (2005) *Implementing Languages Entitlement in Primary Schools: An Evaluation of Progress in Ten Pathfinder Schools*. Available at: www.ofsted.gov.uk/resources/implementing-languages-entitlement-primary-schools (accessed 17 May 2013).

Qualifications and Curriculum Authority (QCA) (2000) *Modern Foreign Languages a scheme of work for Key Stage 2*, London: QCA.

Tinsley, T. and Comfort, T. (2012) *Lessons From Abroad. International Review of Primary Languages. Research Report*. CfBT Education Trust.

Wade, P. and Marshall, H. (2009) *Primary Modern Foreign Languages, Longitudinal Survey of Implementation of National Entitlement to Language Learning at Key Stage 2. Final Report*. DCSF Research Report RR127. Available at: www.education.gov.uk/publications/standard/publicationDetail/Page1/DCSF-RR127 (accessed 10 January 2013).

Welsh Assembly Government, Department for Children, Education, Lifelong Learning and Skills/Llywodraeth Cynulliad Cymru, Yr Adran Plant, Addysg, Dysgu Gydol Oes a Sgiliau (2008) *Modern Foreign Languages Guidance for Key Stages 2 and 3*. Available at: http://wales.gov.uk/docs/dcells/publications/090109 modernen.pdf (accessed 17 May 2013).

CREATIVITY AND CREATIVE TEACHING AND LEARNING

Teresa Cremin and Jonathan Barnes

INTRODUCTION

Nurturing learner creativity is a key aim for many schools. Teachers and school leaders continue to see the development of creativity as an essential part of their job. They recognise that an appropriate climate for creative thought and activity has to be established (Ofsted, 2006, 2009), and know that pressures to improve standards in 'the basics' can crowd creativity out of the curriculum.

In a world dominated by technological innovations and rapid change, creativity is a critical component; human skills and people's imaginative and innovative powers are key resources in a knowledge-driven economy (Robinson, 2001, 2009). As social structures and ideologies continue to change, the ability to live sustainably with uncertainty and deal with complexity is essential. So organisations and governments all over the world are now more concerned than ever to promote creativity (Craft, 2011).

As primary professionals, it is our responsibility to steer the creative development of young people in our care. In the first decade of the twenty-first century, creativity was given a high profile in education policy and the media; 'creative development' was named as an Early Learning Goal in the Early Years Foundation Stage (EYFS) (Department for Children, Schools and Families, 2008) and highlighted in aspects of the primary curriculum. Children were expected to think creatively, make connections and generate ideas, as well as problem solve. More recently, with a change of government, the revised EYFS (Department for Education, 2012) acknowledges that, alongside 'playing and exploring' and 'active learning', the third characteristic of effective learning is 'creating and thinking critically'. In relation to the forthcoming primary curriculum however, indications suggest that explicit references to creativity may be few. Nonetheless, there is professional recognition that developing the creativity of the young cannot be left to chance (e.g. Cooper, 2013; Scoffham, 2013).

Academic explorations of creative teaching and teaching for creativity continue to expand (e.g. Jeffrey and Woods, 2009; Dismore *et al.*, 2008; Cremin *et al.*, 2009, 2012; Sawyer, 2011; Craft *et al.*, 2013), and teachers still seek innovative ways to shape the curriculum in response to children's needs. Creative teaching should not be placed in opposition to the teaching of essential knowledge, skills and understandings in the subject disciplines; neither does it imply lowered expectations of challenge or behaviour. Rather, creative teaching involves teaching the subjects in creative contexts that explicitly invite learners to engage imaginatively and that stretch their generative, evaluative and collaborative capacities.

However, many teachers still feel constrained by perceptions of a culture of accountability. You too may already be aware of the classroom impact of an assessment-led system. Such pressure can limit opportunities for creative endeavour and may tempt you to stay within the safe boundaries of the known. Recognising that tensions exist between the incessant drive to raise measurable standards and the impulse to teach more creatively is a good starting point, but finding the energy and enterprise to respond flexibly is a real challenge. In order to do so, you need to be convinced that creativity has an important role to play in education, and believe that you can contribute, both personally and professionally. You may also need to widen your understanding of creativity and creative practice in order to teach creatively and teach for creativity.

OBJECTIVES

By the end of this unit you should have:

- an increased understanding about the nature of creativity;
- an awareness of some of the features of creative primary teachers;
- a wider understanding of creative pedagogical practice;
- some understanding of how to plan for creative learning.

CREATIVE PRACTICE

A class of learners express interest as they collaborate to create three-dimensional representations of Egyptian gods to add to the classroom museum. Earlier that morning, at this Northamptonshire primary school, the 6–7-year-olds had discussed their options, generated ideas and listened to others. Then, in groups, they sought to turn their ideas into action. Operating independently of their teacher, they found resources in their classroom and others, monitored their activities and discussed their work. A wide variety of representations were created, and new ideas were celebrated and appraised. Later, the children wrote instructions for making their images and added them to their huge class book, which contained DVDs of other cross-curricular activities. However, their ability to recall, explain and discuss the finer points of this carefully planned and executed project two terms later was an even richer testimony to the enjoyment and depth of creative learning involved.

In this school, as in many others, the staff had adopted a more creative approach to the curriculum, influenced in part by the significant achievements of what were then called 'creative schools' (Ofsted, 2003, 2006; Eames *et al.*, 2006). This trend was encouraged by many initiatives, including the report *Nurturing Creativity in Young People* (Roberts, 2006), and Creative Partnerships (2002–11), a government-funded initiative that encouraged schools to develop more innovative ways of teaching. It showed that creative and collaborative projects inspired and fostered creative skills and raised children's and young people's confidence and aspiration (Eames *et al.*, 2006).

The focus on creative learning has since shifted. Creativity in schools was overshadowed by what became known as the 'cultural offer' in 2008 (McMaster, 2008), and the Creative Partnerships programme ended in 2011. A 'cultural education' agenda took the former position of creative education, and creativity is currently barely mentioned in education policy documents; for example, in music education guidance, creativity only appears in the context of the 'creative industries' (Henley, 2012). Nonetheless, it plays a key role economically, and, with increasing evidence of a close relationship between creativity and social and psychological well-being (Barnes, 2013), teachers continue to seek innovative ways of teaching to increase motivation and develop creative learning.

In Wales . . .

This document for Foundation Phase pupils, age 3–7 years, sets out in its introduction that:

Children should be continually developing their imagination and creativity across the curriculum. Their curiosity and disposition to learn should be stimulated by everyday sensory experiences, both indoors and outdoors. Children should engage in creative, imaginative and expressive activities in art, craft, design, music, dance and movement.

(DCELLS, 2008: 4)

Source: Department for Children, Education, Lifelong Learning and Skills (DCELLS) (2008) *Creative Development*. Cardiff: Welsh Assembly Government (WAG). http://wales.gov.uk/dcells/publications/policy_strategy_and_planning/early-wales/whatisfoundation/page4/sevenareas/creativedevelopment/creativedeve.pdf?lang=en

SO WHAT IS CREATIVITY?

Creativity is not confined to special people or to particular arts-based activities, nor is it undisciplined play. It is, however, notoriously difficult to define. It has been described as 'a state of mind in which all our intelligences are working together', involving 'seeing, thinking and innovating' (Craft, 2000: 38) and as 'imaginative activity fashioned so as to produce outcomes that are both original and of value' (National Advisory Committee on Creative and Cultural Education, 1999: 29). Creativity is possible wherever human intelligence is actively engaged and is an essential part of an effective education: it includes all areas of understanding and all children, teachers and others working in primary education. Indeed, it can be demonstrated by anyone in any aspect of life, throughout life.

It is useful to distinguish between high creativity and ordinary creativity, between 'big C creativity' (exemplified in some of Gardner's (1993) studies of highly creative individuals, such as Picasso, Einstein and Freud) and 'little c creativity', which Craft (2001) highlights. This latter form focuses on the individual agency and resourcefulness of ordinary people to innovate and take action. Csikszentmihalyi suggests that each of us is born with two contradictory sets of instructions – a conservative tendency and an expansive tendency, but warns us that, 'If too few opportunities for curiosity are available, if too many obstacles are put in the way of risk and exploration, the motivation to engage in creative behaviour is easily extinguished' (1996: 11).

In the classroom, developing opportunities for children to 'possibility think' their way forwards is, therefore, critical (Craft, 2001; Burnard *et al.*, 2006; Cremin *et al.*, 2006a). This will involve you in immersing the class in an issue or subject and helping them ask questions, be imaginative and playfully explore options, as well as innovate. At the core of such creative endeavour is the child's identity. Their sense of self-determination and agency and their understanding of themselves as unique thinkers able to solve life's problems are essential ingredients of their success, resilience and general health (Marmot, 2010). From this perspective, creativity is not seen as an event or a product (although it may involve either or both), but a process or a state of mind involving the serious play of ideas and possibilities. This generative, problem-finding/problem-solving process may involve rational and non-rational thought and may be fed by the intuitive, by daydreaming and pondering, as well as by the application of knowledge and skills. In order to be creative, children may need considerable knowledge in a domain, but 'creativity and knowledge are two sides of the same psychological coin, not opposing forces' (Boden, 2001: 102) and enrich each other.

Imaginative activity can take many forms; it draws on a more varied range of human functioning than linear, logical and rational patterns of behaviour (Claxton, 2006). It is essentially generative and may include physical, social, reflective, musical, aural or visual thinking, involving children in activities that produce new and unusual connections between ideas, domains, processes and materials. When children and their teachers step outside the boundaries of predictability and are physically engaged, this provides a balance to the sedentary and too often abstract nature of school education. Creative learning is often collaborative and uses mind and body, emotions, eyes, ears and all the senses, in an effort to face a challenge or solve a problem. In less conventional contexts, new insights and connections may be made through analogy and metaphor, and teachers become the 'meddlers in the middle' (McWilliam, 2008), not the 'sage on the stage' of more transmissive modes of education. Modes of creative thinking, such as the 'imaginative-generative' mode, which produces outcomes, and the 'critical-evaluative' mode, which involves consideration of originality and value (National Advisory Committee on Creative and Cultural Education, 1999: 30), operate in close interrelationship and need to be consciously developed in the classroom.

The process of creativity, Claxton and Lucas (2010) suggest, involves the ability to move freely between the different layers of our memories to find solutions to problems. They propose a metaphor of the mind based on the concept of three layers of memory that impact upon our thinking: an upper layer or *habit map*, which is a map of repeated patterns of behaviour; an *inner layer*, comprised of individual conscious and unconscious memories; and an *archetypal layer*, laid down by our genes. Others see the creative mind as one that looks for unexpected likenesses and connections between disparate domains (Bronowski, 1978). Csikszentmihalyi (1996) wisely suggests, however, that

Task 7.3.1 Creativity

Read a chosen chapter of either Vera John-Steiner's fascinating book, *Creative Collaboration* (2000), or Chappell *et al.*'s more recent *Close Encounters* (2011), which expands upon Steiner's argument with reference to 'dance partners for creativity'. Consider the degree to which you see creativity as individualised or collective, subject-specific or generalised. Discuss the consequences of your views for classroom practice.

Task 7.3.2 Ownership of learning

Relevance, ownership and control of learning, as well as innovation, have all been identified as key issues in creative learning in children (Jeffrey and Woods, 2009). Imaginative approaches involve individuals and groups in initiating questions and lines of enquiry, so that they are more in charge of their work, and such collaboration and interaction help to develop a greater sense of autonomy in the events that unfold.

- To what extent have you observed children taking control of their learning, making choices and demonstrating ownership of their own learning? Think of some examples and share these in small groups.
- To what extent was the work also relevant to the children? Were they emotionally or imaginatively engaged, building on areas of interest, maintaining their individuality and sharing ideas with one another?
- If you have seen little evidence of these issues, consider how you could offer more opportunity for relevance, ownership and control of learning in the classroom.

creativity does not happen inside people's heads, but in the interaction between an individual's thoughts and the sociocultural context. When one considers examples of both big C and little c creativity, this explanation seems to make the most sense, as the social and cultural context of learning is highly influential.

It is clear, too, that creativity is not bound to particular subjects. At the cutting edge of every domain of learning, creativity is essential. It depends in part on interactions between feeling and thinking across boundaries and ideas. It also depends upon a climate of trust, respect and support, an environment in which individual agency and self-determination are fostered, and ideas and interests are valued, discussed and celebrated. Yet we have all experienced schools that fail to teach the pleasure and excitement to be found in science or mathematics for example, or that let routines and timetables, subject boundaries and decontextualised knowledge dominate the daily diet of the young. In such sterile environments, when formulae for learning are relied upon, and curriculum packages are delivered, children's ability to make connections and to imagine alternatives is markedly reduced. So, too, is their capacity for curiosity, for enquiry and for creativity itself.

CREATIVE TEACHING AND TEACHING FOR CREATIVITY

The distinction between creative teaching and teaching for creativity is helpful in that it is possible to imagine a creative teacher who engages personally and creatively in the classroom, yet fails to provide for children's creative learning. Responsible creative professionals are not necessarily flamboyant performers, but teachers who use a range of approaches to create the conditions in which the creativity of others can flourish. Creative teachers also recognise and make use of their own creativity, not just to interest and engage the learners, but also to promote new thinking and learning. Their confidence in their own creativity will enable them to offer the children stronger scaffolds and spaces for emotional and intellectual growth.

In Northern Ireland . . .

The importance of creativity, both in pedagogy and also as a theme that underpins the learning experiences of pupils, is regarded by educationalists as fundamental to the teaching and learning process. With this in mind, the competences have been designed to enhance professional autonomy, both at an individual and collective level, in a way that encourages creative and innovative approaches to teaching and which, in turn, develops in pupils the ability to think creatively. Indeed, the ability to think creatively, and the innovation it encourages, is central to any modern education system that strives to enhance the life chances of children and young people.

(GTCNI, 2009: 8)

Source: GTCNI (2009) *Teaching: the Reflective Profession.* Belfast, GTCNI.

Research undertaken in higher education, with tutors teaching music, geography and English, suggests that creative teaching is a complex art form – a veritable 'cocktail party' (Grainger *et al.*, 2004). The host gathers the ingredients (the session content) and mixes them playfully and skilfully (the teaching style), in order to facilitate a creative, enjoyable and worthwhile party (the learning experience). Although no formula was, or could be, established for creative teaching, some of the ingredients for mixing a creative cocktail were identified, albeit tentatively, from this work. However, the elements are not in themselves necessarily creative, but the action of shaking and stirring the ingredients and the individual experience of those attending are critical, if the 'cocktail party' is to be successful. The intention to promote creative learning appeared to be an important element in this work.

The session content included: placing current trends in a wider context and extensive use of metaphor, analogy and personal anecdotes to make connections. The teaching style included: multimodal pedagogic practices, pace, humour, the confidence of the tutors and their ability to inspire and value the pupils. In relation to the learning experience, the themes included involving the pupils affectively and physically and challenging them to engage and reflect. Together, these represent some of the critical features of creative teachers and creative teaching that combine to support new thinking.

Task 7.3.3 Teaching as cocktail party

- Consider the metaphor of teaching as cocktail party for a moment. In what ways do you think it captures the vitality of teaching – the dynamic interplay between teachers, children and the resources available? Select one or two of the features, such as humour or personal anecdotes. Do you make extensive use of either? Remember, the research indicates that such features are employed with others at the 'cocktail party'.
- Consider your previous teachers. Which were the most creative? Did they create successful cocktail parties in which you felt valued and engaged, took risks, made connections and developed deep learning? How did they achieve this?

PERSONAL CHARACTERISTICS OF CREATIVE TEACHERS

It is difficult to identify with any certainty the personal characteristics of creative teachers. Research tends to offer lists of propensities that such teachers possess (e.g. Fryer, 1996; Beetlestone, 1998). Common elements noted in these various studies include:

- enthusiasm, passion and commitment;
- risk-taking;
- a deep curiosity or questioning stance;
- willingness to be intuitive and/or introspective;
- gregariousness and introspectiveness;
- a clear set of personal values;
- awareness of self as a creative being.

This list encompasses many of the personal qualities you might expect in any good teacher, except perhaps the last. Sternberg (1999) suggests that creative teachers are creative role models themselves - professionals who continue to be self-motivated learners, who value the creative dimensions of their own lives and who make connections between their personal responses to experience and their teaching. In addition, a clear set of values, reflecting fair-mindedness, openness to evidence, a desire for clarity and respect for others, are important and among the attitudinal qualities embedded in creative teaching. So, too, is a commitment to inclusion and a belief in human rights and equality. Such attitudes and values have a critical role in creative teaching and are, perhaps, best taught by example.

FEATURES OF A CREATIVE PEDAGOGICAL STANCE

The intention to promote creativity is fundamental. There are a number of features of a creative pedagogical stance that you may want to consider in relation to your teaching and observation of other creative professionals.

A learner-centred, agency-oriented ethos

Creative teachers tend to place the learners above the curriculum and combine a positive disposition towards creativity and person-centred teaching that actively promotes pupils who learn and think for themselves (Sawyer, 2011). Relaxed, trusting educator–learner relationships exist in creative classrooms, and the role of the affect and children's feelings play a central role in learning in such contexts. Such relationships foster children's agency and autonomy as learners (Cremin et al., 2006a). A learner-oriented ethos will also involve you showing patience and openness, reinforcing children's creative behaviour, celebrating difference, diversity and innovation, as well as learning to tolerate mild or polite rebellion (Gardner, 1999). If you adopt such a person-centred orientation, you will be shaping the children's self-esteem and enhancing their intrinsic motivation and agency. You might, for example, explicitly plan for small groups to shape and plan for themselves how they might investigate melting, by giving them enormous 'ice eggs' (made from balloons filled with water and frozen) and telling an imaginary tale of how these came to be in your possession (see Craft et al., 2012).

A questioning stance

Creativity involves asking and attempting to answer real questions; the creative teacher is seen by many as one who uses open questions and who promotes speculation in the classroom, encouraging deeper understanding and lateral thinking (Cremin et al., 2006a; Cremin, 2009b). In the context of creative teaching, both teachers and children need to be involved in this process of imaginative thinking, encompassing the generation of challenging and unusual questions and the creation of possible responses. The questioning stance of the teacher has been noted as central to children's possibility thinking, and the importance of question-posing and question-responding has been documented (Chappell et al., 2008). You could, for example, play with the idea of 'book zips', new books that have invisible zips which prevent children opening them! (Zipped plastic bags or magical tales often help to extend the patience necessary!). Groups can generate questions about characters, plot, setting et al. and respond to other group's questions (see Cremin, 2009a).

Creating space, time and freedom to make connections

Creativity requires space, time and a degree of freedom. Deep immersion in an area or activity allows options to remain open, and persistence and follow-through to develop. Conceptual space allows children to converse, challenge and negotiate meanings and possibilities together. For example, through employing both film and drama in extended units of work, teachers raised boys' standards and creativity in writing (Bearne et al., 2004). Through adopting the role of 'Davis Jones', an archaeologist and the brother of Indiana Jones, you could, for example, trigger historical enquiry and exploration (see Cooper, 2013).

Employing multimodal, intuitive teaching approaches

A variety of multimodal teaching approaches and frequent switching between modes in a playlike and spontaneous manner appear to support creative learning (Cremin et al., 2009). The diversity of pattern, rhythm and pace used by creative teachers is particularly marked (Woods, 1995), as is their use of informed intuition (Claxton and Lucas, 2004). As you teach, opportunities will arise for you to use your intuition and move from the security of the known. Give yourself permission to go beyond the 'script' you have planned and allow the children to take the initiative and lead you, for such spontaneity will encourage you to seize the moment and foster deeper learning (Cremin *et al.*, 2006b). In geography, for example, you might nurture creative play through opportunities for transforming and adapting places, making dens, yurts, shelters or tree houses perhaps (see Scoffham, 2013).

Prompting full engagement, ownership and ongoing reflection

In studying an area in depth, children should experience both explicit instruction and space for exploration and discovery. Try to provide opportunities for choice and be prepared to spend time developing their self-management skills so that they are able to operate independently. Their engagement can be prompted by appealing to their interests and passions, by involving them in imaginative experiences and by connecting learning to their lives (Cremin *et al.*, 2009). A semi-constant oscillation between engagement and reflection will become noticeable in the classroom as you work to refine, reshape and improve learning. The ability to give and receive criticism is also an essential part of creativity, and you will need to encourage evaluation through supportive and honest feedback (Jeffrey, 2006). For example, using drama to teach mathematical concepts prompts engagement and deep learning (see Pound and Lee, 2011).

Modelling risk-taking and enabling the children to take risks too

The ability to tolerate ambiguity is an example of the 'confident uncertainty' to which Claxton (1997) refers when discussing creative teachers – those who combine subject and pedagogical knowledge, but also leave space for uncertainty and the unknown. You will gain in confidence through increased subject knowledge, experience and reflection, but your assurance will also grow through taking risks and having a go at expressing yourself. Risk-taking is an integral element of creativity, and one that you will want to model and foster. The children, too, will need to feel supported as they take risks in safe, non-judgemental contexts.

To be a creative practitioner, you will need more than a working knowledge of creativity and the prescribed curriculum. You will need a clear idea of your values, a secure pedagogical understanding and a secure knowledge base, supported by a passionate belief in the potential of creative teaching to engage, inspire and educate. Such teaching depends, in the end, upon the human interaction between teachers and pupils and is also influenced by the teacher's state of mind. The creative teacher, it is proposed, is one who is aware of, and values, the human attribute of creativity in

Task 7.3.4 Creative engagement

Read the first chapter of Ken Robinson's *The Element* (2009).

- Consider with others when you feel in your 'element' and try to identify what the features of your engagement are in such contexts?
- How do these relate to the aspects of creative practice described above – are there parallels, and, if not, what might this reveal about the degree to which creative engagement can be prescribed or fostered?

themselves and actively seeks to promote this in others. The creative teacher has a creative state of mind that is both exercised and developed through their creative practice and personal/ professional curiosity, connection-making, originality and autonomy (Cremin *et al.*, 2009). Such practice is, of course, influenced by the physical, social, emotional and spiritual environments in which teachers and children work.

CREATING ENVIRONMENTS OF POSSIBILITY

You may have been to a school where creativity is planned for and fostered, and where there is a clear sense of shared values and often a real buzz of purposeful and exciting activity. Such schools have a distinctive character that impacts upon behaviour, relationships, the physical and ethical environment and the curriculum. An ethos that values creativity will, according to most definitions, promote originality and the use of the imagination, as well as encourage an adventurous attitude to life and learning. In such environments of possibility, packed with ideas and experiences, resources and choices, as well as time for relaxation and rumination, physical, conceptual and emotional space is offered.

The social and emotional environment

Taking creative risks and moving forward in learning are heavily dependent upon an atmosphere of acceptance and security. Children's well-being is widely recognised as important, in its own right and to support their creativity, but can only be fostered by a secure ethos. However, creative schools may display apparently contradictory characteristics. The ethos may be simultaneously:

*   highly active and relaxed;
*   supportive and challenging;
*   confident and speculative;
*   playful and serious;
*   focused and fuzzy;
*   individualistic and communal;
*   understood personally and owned by all;
*   non-competitive and ambitious.

Since Plato, many have argued that there are links between involvement in creative acts and a general sense of well-being. More recent research in cognitive neuroscience (Damasio, 2003) and positive psychology (Seligman, 2004; Huppert *et al.*, 2005) has suggested that the state of well-being promotes optimum conditions in mind and body, and ensures constructive and secure relationships. A perceived link between discovering one's own creativity and feeling a sense of well-being (Barnes *et al.*, 2008) has led some to make arguments for a revaluation of curricula, in favour of educational programmes that offer frequent, planned and progressive creative opportunities across every discipline (Barnes, 2005).

The physical environment

The physical environment in a school that promotes creativity is likely to celebrate achievement and individuality and can be a valuable teaching resource. Children's views on this are important and deserve to be taken into account (Burke and Grosvenor, 2003). Projects have shown how creative thinking in the context of focused work on improving the school building, grounds or local areas can achieve major citizenship objectives and high-level arts and literacy targets in an atmosphere of genuine support and community concern (Barnes, 2007, 2009).

Active modes of learning and problem-solving approaches that include independent investigation require accessible resources of various kinds, so that the richer and more multifaceted a range you can offer the better. This supports genuine choice, speculation and experimentation, happy accidents and flexibility. An environment of possibility in which individual agency and self-determination are fostered and children's ideas and interests are valued, shared and celebrated depends upon the presence of a climate of trust, respect and support in your classroom/school. Creativity can be developed when you are confident and secure in both your subject knowledge and your knowledge of creative pedagogical practice; then you will seek to model the features of creativity *and* develop a culture of creative opportunities in school.

PLANNING FOR CREATIVITY

Open-ended learning opportunities that offer space for autonomy and collaboration and have real-world relevance can be created through extended and creative units of work, encompassing multiple subjects. These can be enriched by regularly involving the expertise of partners from the creative and cultural sector; Ofsted (2006) suggests such partnerships can enrich learning and raise children's expectations and achievements. Seek to plan coherent learning experiences in which 'school subjects [are seen as] resources in the construction of the curriculum, rather than determinants of its overall structure and emphasis' (Halpin, 2003: 114). In planning such creative units of work, you will want to build on insights from research. The following ten research-informed suggestions are worth considering:

- Create a **positive, secure atmosphere** in which risks can be taken (Seltzer and Bentley, 1999; Grainger *et al.*, 2005).
- Profile a **questioning stance** and frame the work around children's interests and questions (Cremin *et al.*, 2006a; Craft *et al.*, 2007b).
- Ensure a range of **practical and analytical, open-ended** activities (Cremin *et al.*, 2006a).
- Emphasise **learner agency** and individual and cooperative thinking and learning (Cremin *et al.*, 2006a; Craft *et al.*, 2007a).
- Agree **clear goals**, some of which are set and owned by the learners (Csikszentmihalyi, 2002; Jeffrey and Woods, 2009).
- Build **emotionally relevant links** to the children's lives, offering opportunities for **engagement and enjoyment** (Fredrickson, 2003; Barnes, 2007).
- Integrate a manageable number of **relevant subjects/areas of learning** (Gardner, 1999; Barnes, 2007).
- Involve developmentally appropriate **progression** in skills, knowledge and understanding .
- Set the work in a wider framework that includes **concepts, content and attitudes** (Grainger *et al.*, 2004; Cremin, 2009b).
- Provide supportive **assessment** procedures that build security and include time and tools for reflection (Adey and Shayer, 2002).

CREATIVE CURRICULA IN ACTION

Two examples bring such a curriculum, centred upon creative learning, to life. A whole-school community from Tower Hamlets made a winter visit to Canary Wharf, less than 500 metres from the school gates. Many pupils had never been there. The event was grasped as an opportunity to collect as much information as possible. None of the collected impressions could have been gathered from websites or written sources, and so the visit was a genuine investigation, involving every age group – traffic surveys, rubbings, observations of people walking, collections of geometric shapes, still images framed by 'key' describing words, moving images, sensory descriptions of sights, sounds and smells, intricate 360º drawings, mosaics or trees imprisoned in stainless steel, stone and scaffolded containers. Every moment, morning or afternoon, was fully used in information gathering. Children and adult supporters collected digital, drawn, listed, tallied, acted and heard data from a variety of contrasting sites around the wharf.

The library of collected and remembered objects, images and sensations was brought back to school and formed the basis of the curriculum for the next few weeks. Creating responses from these disparate sources involved very different paths in each class, from Nursery to Year 6. One Year 2 class made a 'sound journey' using mapping and musical skills and knowledge. Groups of five or six composed music to capture different places on their journey and linked them with other compositions of 'walking music'. Separate teams then mapped their journeys using techniques learned in the previous term, and the resultant maps were used as graphic musical scores. A mixed group created large and imaginative abstract constructions from bamboo and tissue and applied decoration from rubbings and drawings, expressing their experience of the towering buildings at the wharf.

Children, along with their co-learning teachers, presented their compositions, artworks, mathematical investigations, stories and dramas to the rest of the school in a series of assemblies. These were especially appreciated across the school, because everyone had shared in the same initial experience. The whole project was evaluated through a continuous blog kept by children, teachers, artists and teaching assistants. Their challenge, like yours, is to take account of individual differences in learning, help each child become a self-regulated learner, and ensure appropriate coverage of the areas of learning and their attendant knowledge bases.

In another context, a class from a rural school decided, through discussion, to concentrate on the value of community in a 2-day project for the website Engaging Places (www.engagingplaces. org.uk/home). They divided into teams of five and went on walks up and down the street in which the school stood. Each group decided upon a sub-theme: improving the community, describing the community now and the community in the future, problems in the community, or litter and the community. After this first decision, the children used the walk as a data-gathering opportunity. The description group used cameras and viewfinders to record the different ages and materials of houses in the street, but also used sound recorders to collect the vastly different sounds at either end of the street. In class on their return, they combined the sound-based and visually based impressions on a street map, which they constructed with great enthusiasm. Bursts of creativity occurred as pairs decided how to represent the street and the sounds and images they had collected. Eventually, the group decided on a 3D street map, with press-button recordings of different sounds in four different parts of the street. The litter group arrived at a double focus. They decided to design and make attractive dustbins and an anti-littering video. This involved storyboarding, rehearsals, acting, filming and editing. The wild and wacky litter bins were planned in detail and made in model form for a presentation in the school and at a national launch of Engaging Places. Evaluation was crucial at every stage of these activities.

Careful planning for such creative learning experiences is important and perhaps best done in collaboration with others. Some will last a term, others just a few days, but all will seek to involve the children in real, purposeful and imaginatively engaging experiences.

SUMMARY

Creative teaching is a collaborative enterprise that capitalises on the unexpected and variously involves engagement, reflection and transformation, patterned at such a rate as to invite and encourage a questioning stance and motivate self-directed learning. Creative learning involves asking questions, exploring options and generating and appraising ideas, as the learner take risks and imaginatively thinks their way forwards, making new or innovative connections in the process. New thinking happens at the meeting places of different ideas and approaches, and it also takes place when new links occur between people. Many of the examples in this unit show both adults and children involved in thinking and learning together, which can be a key generator of creativity. We hope you will choose to teach creatively and promote creativity through your planning, and will build in choice and autonomy, relevance and purpose in engaging environments of possibility – environments both inside and outside the classroom.

For more ideas on teaching creatively across the curriculum, see the series that accompanies this handbook. Edited by Cremin, it includes books on *Teaching English* (Cremin, 2009a), *Mathematics* (Pound and Lee, 2011), *Science* (Davies, 2010), *History* (Cooper, 2013), *Geography* (Scoffham, 2013) and *Music* (Burnard and Murphy, 2013) – *Creatively*. New books in the series being developed included *Teaching PE, Art, RE* and *Languages – Creatively*.

ANNOTATED FURTHER READING

Craft, A. (2005) *Creativity in Schools: Tensions and Dilemmas*, London: RoutledgeFalmer.
> This is an informative and engaging read that raises more questions than answers as Craft explores principles and practice, policy and research and identifies an agenda for development, both at the level of the classroom and on a wider scale.

Jeffrey, B. and Woods, P. (2009) *Creative Learning in the Primary School*, London: Routledge.
> This book explores features of creative teaching and learning in the context of contemporary policy reforms in England. It is accessibly written and well informed, highlighting the inventiveness of teachers and the role of pupils as a powerful resource for creative learning.

Sawyer, R. (ed.) (2011) *Structure and Improvisation in Creative Teaching*, New York: Cambridge.
> This edited collection from the US provides practical advice for teachers wishing to become more creative professionals. It highlights the need for teachers to respond artfully to curricula and the unexpected demands of classroom interactions.

FURTHER READING TO SUPPORT M-LEVEL STUDY

Craft, A., Cremin, T., Burnard, P., Dragovic, T. and Chappell, K. (2012) 'Possibility thinking: an evidence-based concept driving creativity?', *Education*, 3(13): 1-19.
> This paper examines empirical evidence about possibility thinking with 8-11-year-olds. It highlights the core features as question-posing, question-responding, self-determination, intentional action, development, being imaginative, play/playfulness, immersion and innovation.

McWilliam, E. (2008) 'Unlearning how to teach', *Innovations in Education and Teaching International*, 45(3): 263-9. This paper argues that good teachers are creative 'meddlers in the middle', who spend less time instructing and more time participating, often as a co-workers, designers and experimenters alongside children.

 ## RELEVANT WEBSITES

NACCCE report, *All Our Futures: Creativity, Culture and Education*: www.cypni.org.uk/downloads/ alloutfutures.pdf

Ofsted's Expecting the Unexpected: www.ofsted.gov.uk/publications/

Creative Little Scientists: www.creative-little-scientists.eu/

 ## REFERENCES

Adey, P. and Shayer, M. (2002) *Learning Intelligence: Cognitive Acceleration from 5 to 15 Years*, London: Open University Press.

Barnes, J. (2005) '"You could see it on their faces . . ..": the importance of provoking smiles in schools', *Health Education*, 105(5): 392-400.

Barnes, J. (2007) *Cross-Curricular Learning 3-14*, London: Sage.

Barnes, J. (2009) 'The integration of music with other subjects, particularly in art forms', in J. Evans and C. Philpott (eds) *A Practical Guide to Teaching Music in the Secondary School*, London: Routledge.

Barnes, J. (2013) 'Drama to promote social and personal well-being in six-and seven-year-olds with communication difficulties: the Speech Bubbles project', in *Perspectives in Public Health,* Royal Society for Public Health, London: Sage.

Barnes, J., Hope, G. and Scoffham, S. (2008) 'A conversation about creative teaching and learning', in A. Craft, T. Cremin and P. Burnard (eds) *Creative Learning 3-11 and How We Document It*, London: Trentham, pp. 125-34.

Bearne, E., Grainger, T. and Wolstencroft, H. (2004) *Raising Boys' Achievements in Writing*, Leicester: UKLS and PNS.

Beetlestone, F. (1998) *Creative Children, Imaginative Teaching*, Buckingham: Open University Press.

Boden, M. (2001) 'Creativity and knowledge', in A. Craft, B. Jeffrey and M. Liebling (eds) *Creativity in Education*, London, Continuum, pp. 95-102.

Bronowski, J. (1978) *The Origins of Knowledge and Imagination*, New Haven, CT: Yale University Press.

Burke, C. and Grosvenor, I. (2003) *The School I'd Like: Children and Young People's Reflections on an Education for the 21st Century*, London: Routledge.

Burnard, P., Craft, A. and Cremin, T. (2006) 'Documenting "possibility thinking": a journey of collaborative inquiry', *International Journal of Early Years Education*, 14(3): 243-62.

Burnard, P. and Murphy, R. (2013, forthcoming) *Teaching Music Creatively*, London: Routledge.

Chappell, K., Craft, A., Burnard, P. and Cremin, T. (2008) 'Question-posing and question-responding: at the heart of possibility thinking in the early years', *Early Years: An International Journal of Research and Development*, 28(3): 267-86.

Chappell, K., Rolfe, L., Craft, A. and Jobbins, V. (2011) *Close Encounters: Dance Partners for Creativity*, London: Trentham.

Claxton, G. (1997) *Hare Brain, Tortoise Mind: Why Intelligence Increases When You Think Less*, London: Fourth Estate.

Claxton, G. (2006) 'Mindfulness, learning and the brain', *Journal of Rational Emotive and Cognitive Behaviour Therapy*, 23: 301-14.

Claxton, G. and Lucas, B. (2004) *Be Creative: Essential Steps to Revitalize your Work and Life*, London: BBC.

Claxton, G. and Lucas, B. (2010) *New Kinds of Smart*, Milton Keynes: Open University Press.

Cooper, H. (2013) *Teaching History Creatively*, London: Routledge.

Craft, A. (2000) *Creativity across the Primary Curriculum: Framing and Developing Practice*, London: RoutledgeFalmer.

Craft, A. (2001) 'Little c: creativity in craft', in A. Craft, B. Jeffrey and M. Liebling (eds) *Creativity in Education*, London: Continuum.

Craft, A. (2011) *Creativity and Education Futures: Learning in a Digital Age*, London: Trentham.

Craft, A., Cremin, T. and Burnard, P. (eds) (2007a) *Creative Learning 3-11 and How To Document It*, London: Trentham.

Craft, A., Cremin, T., Burnard, P. and Chappell, K. (2007b) 'Teacher stance in creative learning: a study of progression', *Journal of Thinking Skills and Creativity*, 2(2): 136-47.

Craft, A., Cremin, T., Hay, P. and Clack, J. (2013) 'Creative primary schools: developing and maintaining pedagogy for creativity', *Ethnography and Education*, 9.1.

Craft, A., Cremin, T., Burnard, P., Dragovic, T. and Chappell, K. (2012) 'Possibility thinking: an evidence-based concept driving creativity?' Education 3-13, 1-19.

Cremin, T. (2009a) *Teaching English Creatively*, London: Routledge.

Cremin, T. (2009b) 'Creative teaching and creative teachers', in A. Wilson (ed.) *Creativity in Primary Practice*, Exeter: Learning Matters.

Cremin, T., Barnes, J. and Scoffham, S. (2009) *Creative Teaching for Tomorrow*, Margate: Future Creative.

Cremin, T., Craft, A. and Burnard, P. (2006a) 'Pedagogy and possibility thinking in the early years', *Journal of Thinking Skills and Creativity*, 1(2): 108-19.

Cremin, T., Chappell, K. and Craft, A. (2012) 'Reciprocity between narrative, questioning and imagination in the early and primary years: examining the role of narrative in possibility thinking', *Thinking Skills and Creativity*, 9: 135-51. Available at: http://dx.doi.org/10.1016/j.tsc.2012.11.003

Cremin, T., Goouch, K., Blakemore, L., Goff, E. and Macdonald, R. (2006b) 'Connecting drama and writing: seizing the moment to write', *Research in Drama in Education*, 11(3): 273-91.

Csikszentmihalyi, M. (1996) *Creativity: Flow and the Psychology of Discovery and Invention*, New York: Harper.

Csikszentmihalyi, M. (2002) *Flow: The Classic Work on How to Achieve Happiness*, London: Rider.

Damasio, A. (2003) *Looking for Spinoza: Joy, Sorrow and the Feeling Brain*, Orlando, FL: Harcourt.

Davies, D. (2010) *Teaching Science Creatively*, London: Routledge.

Department for Children, Schools and Families (DCSF) (2008) *Statutory Framework for the Early Years Foundation Stage*, London: DCSF.

Department for Education (DfE) (2012) *Statutory Framework for the Early Years Foundation Stage*, London: DfE.

Dismore, H., Barnes, J. and Scoffham, S. (2008) *A Space to Reflect: Creative Leadership and the Science of Learning*, London: Creative Partnerships London North.

Eames, A., Benton, T., Sharp, C. and Kendall, L. (2006) *The Impact of Creative Partnerships on the Attainment of Young People*, Slough: NFER.

Frederickson, B. (2003) 'The value of positive emotions', *American Scientist*, 91: 300-5.

Fryer, M. (1996) *Creative Teaching and Learning*, London: Paul Chapman.

Gardner, H. (1993) *Frames of Mind: The Theory of Multiple Intelligences*, London: Fontana Press.

Gardner, H. (1999) *The Disciplined Mind*, New York: Simon and Schuster.

Grainger, T., Barnes, J. and Scoffman, S. (2004) 'Creative teaching: a creative cocktail', *Journal of Education and Teaching*, 38(3): 243-53.

Grainger, T., Goouch, K. and Lambirth, A. (2005) *Creativity and Writing: Developing Voice and Verve in the Classroom*, London: Routledge.

Halpin, D. (2003) *Hope and Education*, London: Routledge.

Henley, D. (2012) *Cultural Education in England*, London: Department for Culture, Media and Sport/DfE.

Huppert, F., Baylis, N. and Keverne, B. (2005) *The Science of Well-being*, Oxford: Oxford University Press.

Jeffrey, B. (ed.) (2006) *Creative Learning Practices: European Experiences*, London: Tufnell Press.

Jeffrey, B. and Woods, P. (2009) *Creative Learning in the Primary School*, London: Routledge.

John-Steiner, V. (2000) *Creative Collaboration*, New York: Oxford University Press.

McMaster, M. (2008) *Supporting Excellence in the Arts: From Measurement to Judgement*, London: DCSF.

McWilliam, E. (2008) 'Unlearning how to teach', *Innovations in Education and Teaching International*, 45(3): 263–69.

Marmot, Sir M. (2010) *The Marmot Review: Fair Society Healthy Lives*, London: Marmot Review. Available at: www.ucl.ac.uk/marmotreview

National Advisory Committee on Creative and Cultural Education (1999) *All Our Futures: The Report of the National Advisory Committee on Creative and Cultural Education*, London: DfEE/DCMS.

Ofsted (2003) *Expecting the Unexpected: Developing Creativity in Primary and Secondary Schools*, HMI 1612, E-publication. Available at: www.ofsted.gov.uk

Ofsted (2006) *Creative Partnerships: Initiative and Impact*, London: Ofsted. Available at: www.creative-partnerships.com (accessed November 2009).

Ofsted (2009) *Twenty Outstanding Primary Schools: Excelling against the Odds*, Manchester: Ofsted.

Pound, L. and Lee, T. (2011) *Teaching Mathematics Creatively*, London: Routledge.

Roberts, P. (2006) *Nurturing Creativity in Young People: A Report to Government to Inform Future Policy*, London: DCMS.

Robinson, K. (2001) *Out of Our Minds*, London: Capstone.

Robinson, K. (2009) *The Element: How Finding Your Passion Changes Everything*, London: Allen Lane.

Sawyer, R. (ed.) (2011) *Structure and Improvisation in Creative Teaching*, New York: Cambridge.

Scoffham, S. (ed.) (2013) *Teaching Geography Creatively*, London: Routledge.

Seligman, M. (2004) *Authentic Happiness*, New York: Free Press.

Seltzer, K. and Bentley, T. (1999) *The Creative Age: Knowledge and Skills for the New Economy*, London: Demos.

Sternberg, R. (ed.) (1999) *The Handbook of Creativity*, Cambridge: Cambridge University Press.

Woods, P. (1995) *Creative Teachers in Primary Schools*, Buckingham: Open University Press.

THINKING SKILLS

Robert Fisher

INTRODUCTION

> We need to think better if we are to become better people.
>
> (Paul, aged 10)

In recent years, there has been growing interest across the world in ways of developing children's thinking and learning skills (Fisher, 2005). This interest has been fed by new knowledge about how the brain works and how people learn, and evidence that specific interventions can improve children's thinking and intelligence. The particular ways in which people apply their minds to solving problems are called *thinking skills*. Many researchers suggest that thinking skills are essential to effective learning, although not all agree on the definition of this term (Moseley *et al.*, 2005). If thinking is how children make sense of learning, developing their thinking skills will help them get more out of learning and life. This unit looks at the implications of research into ways to develop thinking children, thinking classrooms and thinking schools.

OBJECTIVES

By the end of this unit, you should be able to:

* inform your understanding of 'thinking skills' and their role in learning;
* understand some key principles that emerge from research into teaching thinking;
* identify the main approaches to developing children's thinking;
* see how you might integrate a 'thinking skills' approach into classroom teaching and research.

WHAT ARE THINKING SKILLS?

Thinking skills are not mysterious entities existing somewhere in the mind. Nor are they like mental muscles that have a physical presence in the brain. What the term refers to is the human capacity to think in conscious ways to achieve certain purposes. Such processes include remembering, questioning, forming concepts, planning, reasoning, imagining, solving problems, making decisions and judgements, translating thoughts into words, and so on. Thinking skills are ways in which humans exercise the *sapiens* part of being *Homo sapiens*.

Some critics claim that there are no general thinking skills, and that all thinking must be about specific aspects of knowledge or linked to a particular subject in the school curriculum. However, different fields of learning can have shared aspects, and, although a subject such as history may have a particular content, this does not mean it has no links to thinking in other subjects, for example in the need to give reasons and analyse evidence.

Nor does a focus on thinking mean ignoring the role of knowledge. Knowledge is necessary, but simply knowing a lot of things is not sufficient, if children are to be taught to think for themselves. Children need knowledge, but they also need to know how to acquire it and use it. 'Knowledge comes from other people', said Leo, aged 11, 'but thinking comes from yourself . . . or should do.'

It is true that thinking must be about something, but people can do it more or less effectively. The capacity, for example, to assess reasons, formulate hypotheses, make conceptual links or ask critical questions is relevant to many areas of learning. As Gemma, age 10, put it: 'To be a good learner you need to practice training your mind.'

We usually refer to skills in particular contexts, such as being 'good at cooking', but 'skills' can also refer to general capacities in cognitive performance, such as having a logical mind, a good memory, being creative or analytical, and so on. A thinking skill is a practical ability to think in ways that are judged to be more or less effective or skilled. However, learning a skill is not enough, for we want children to use their skills on a regular basis and get into the habit of thinking critically, creatively and with care. Good thinking requires that cognitive skills become habits of intelligent behaviour learned through practice, and children tend to become better at, for example, giving reasons or asking questions, the more they practise doing so.

Psychologists and philosophers have helped to extend our understanding of the term 'thinking', by emphasising the importance of *dispositions*, such as attention and motivation, commonly associated with thinking. This has prompted a move away from a simple model of 'thinking skills' as isolated cognitive capacities, to a view of thinking as inextricably connected to emotions and dispositions, including 'emotional intelligence', which is our ability to understand our own emotions and the emotions of others (Goleman, 2006), or what Lipman, founder of Philosophy for Children, describes as 'caring thinking'.

In England, as elsewhere, the curriculum is no longer seen simply as subject knowledge, but as being underpinned by the skills of lifelong learning. Good teaching is not only about the achieving curriculum objectives, but is also about developing general capacities to think, remember and learn. The last 50 years have seen a burgeoning of research across the world into the teaching of thinking, developing 'teaching for thinking' approaches in new directions, integrating them into everyday teaching to create 'thinking classrooms', and developing whole-school policies to create 'thinking schools'.

If thinking skills are the mental capacities we use to investigate the world, to solve problems and make judgements, to identify every such skill would be to enumerate all the capacities of the human mind, and the list would be endless. Many researchers have attempted to identify the key skills in human thinking, and the most famous of these is Bloom's taxonomy (Bloom and Krathwohl, 1956). Bloom's taxonomy of thinking skills (what he called 'the cognitive goals of education') has been widely used by teachers in planning their teaching. He identifies a number of basic, or 'lower-order', cognitive skills – knowledge, comprehension and application – and a number of 'higher-order' skills – analysis, synthesis and evaluation. Table 7.4.1 shows the various categories identified by Bloom and the processes involved in the various thinking levels.

You could plan or analyse many learning activities in terms of the above categories. For example, when telling a story, a teacher might ask the following kinds of question:

1   **Knowledge**: What happened in the story?
2   **Comprehension**: Why did it happen that way?

3 **Application**: What would you have done?
4 **Analysis**: Which part did you like best?
5 **Synthesis**: Can you think of a different ending?
6 **Evaluation**: What did you think of the story? Why?

Bloom's taxonomy built on earlier research by Piaget and Vygotsky that suggested that thinking skills and capacities are developed by *cognitive challenge*. Teachers need to challenge children to think more deeply and more widely and in more systematic and sustained ways. Or, as Tom, aged 10, put it: 'A good teacher makes you think . . . even when you don't want to.' One way in which you, as a good teacher, can do this is by asking questions that challenge children's thinking.

TABLE 7.4.1 Bloom's taxonomy

Cognitive goal	Thinking cues
1 Knowledge (knowing and remembering)	Say what you know, or remember, describe, repeat, define, identify, tell who, when, which, where, what
2 Comprehension (interpreting and understanding)	Describe in your own words, tell how you feel about it, what it means, explain, compare, relate
3 Application (applying, making use of)	How can you use it, where does it lead, apply what you know, use it to solve problems, demonstrate
4 Analysis (taking apart, being critical)	What are the parts, the order, the reasons why, the causes/problems/solutions/consequences
5 Synthesis (connecting, being creative)	How might it be different, how else, what if, suppose, putting together, develop, improve, create in your own way
6 Evaluation (judging and assessing)	How would you judge it, does it succeed, will it work, what would you prefer, why you think so

Task 7.4.1 Questions for thinking

Choose a story, poem, text or topic that you would like to use with children as a stimulus for their thinking. Using Bloom's taxonomy, create a series of questions to think about and discuss after you have shared the stimulus with them. List your questions under Bloom's six categories: knowledge, comprehension and application, analysis, synthesis and evaluation.

WHY ARE THINKING SKILLS IMPORTANT?

Thinking skills are important because mastery of the 'basics' in education (literacy, maths, science, etc.), however well taught, is not sufficient to fulfil human potential, nor to meet the demands of the labour market or of active citizenship. Countries across the world are recognising that a broad range of competencies is needed to prepare children for an unpredictable future. These higher-order thinking skills are required, in addition to basic skills, because individuals cannot 'store' sufficient knowledge in their memories for future use. Information is expanding at such a rate that individuals require transferable skills to enable them to address different problems, in different contexts, at different times, throughout their lives. The complexity of modern jobs requires people who can comprehend, judge and participate in generating new knowledge and processes. Modern, democratic societies require citizens to assimilate information from multiple sources, determine its truth and use it to make sound judgements.

The challenge is to develop educational programmes that enable all individuals, not just an elite, to become effective thinkers, because these competencies are now required of everyone. A 'thinking skills' approach suggests that learners must develop awareness of themselves as thinkers and learners, practise strategies for effective thinking and develop the habits of intelligent behaviour that are needed for lifelong learning. As Paul, aged 10, said: 'We need to think better if we are to become better people.'

WHAT DOES RESEARCH TELL US ABOUT THINKING?

Research in cognitive science and psychology is providing a clearer picture of the brain and the processes associated with thinking (Smith, 2004). This brain research has some important implications for teachers. For example, we now know that most of the growth in the human brain occurs in early childhood: by the age of 6, the brain in most children is approximately 90 per cent of its adult size. This implies that intervention, while the brain is still growing, may be more effective than waiting until the brain is fully developed. Cognitive challenge is important at all stages, but especially in the early years of education.

Dialogue is the primary means for developing intelligence in the human species. The large human brain evolved to enable individuals to negotiate, through dialogue, the complexities of social living. The capacity for dialogue is central to human thinking. Human consciousness originates in a motivation to share emotions, experience and activities with others. This 'dialogic' capacity is more fundamental than writing or tool use. It is through dialogue that children develop consciousness, learn control over their internal mental processes and develop the conceptual tools for thinking (Fisher, 2009). No wonder recent research emphasises that teacher–pupil interaction is the key to improving standards of teaching and learning (Alexander, 2006; Hattie, 2008; Higgins *et al.*, 2011).

Psychologists and philosophers have helped to extend our understanding of the term 'thinking' by emphasising the importance of *dispositions*, such as attention and motivation, commonly associated with thinking (Claxton, 2002). This has prompted a move away from a simple model of 'thinking skills' as isolated cognitive capacities to a view of thinking as inextricably connected to emotions and dispositions, including 'emotional intelligence', which is our ability to understand our own emotions and the emotions of others (Goleman, 2006).

THE IMPORTANCE OF METACOGNITION

There is also a growing realisation that we need not only to teach cognitive skills and strategies, but also to develop the higher 'metacognitive' functions involved in metacognition. This involves making learners aware of themselves as thinkers and how they process/create knowledge by 'learning how to learn'.

Metacognition involves thinking about one's own thinking. It includes knowledge of oneself: for example, what one knows, what one has learned, what one can and cannot do, and ways to improve one's learning or achievement.

Metacognition involves two levels of reflection:

*   knowledge of thinking: includes awareness of self, task and strategy;
*   self-regulated thinking: includes ability to self-evaluate, and self-manage learning.

Metacognition also involves skills of recognising problems, representing features of problems, planning what to do in trying to solve problems, monitoring progress and evaluating the outcomes of one's own thinking or problem-solving activity.

Metacognition is promoted by helping pupils to reflect on their thinking and decision-making processes. It is developed when pupils are helped to be strategic in organising their activities and are encouraged to reflect before, during and after problem-solving processes. The implication is that you need to plan time for debriefing and review in lessons, to encourage children to think about their learning and how to improve it. This can be done through discussion in a plenary session, or by finding time for reflective writing in their own thinking or learning logs.

In practice, we prompt metacognitive discussion by asking metacognitive questions at different levels of cognitive challenge. First is the level of *cognitive description*, when we ask children to describe what they have been thinking and learning, as when we ask: 'What have you read/learnt?'. We then seek *cognitive extension*, by probing their thinking more deeply, as when we ask: 'What does . . . mean?'. We should also encourage their *cognitive regulation* by asking them, for example: 'What does a good learner/reader/writer do?'. Other metacognitive questions to ask children include:

*   **Before a task**: How will you do this? What might help? What strategy could you use?
*   **During a task**: Is it working? What is difficult? Is there another way, what could you try?
*   **After a task**: What went well? What have you learned? What do you need to remember for next time?

The human mind is made up of many faculties or capacities that enable learning to take place. Our general capacity for understanding or *intelligence* was once thought to be innate and unmodifiable. As a child once put it: 'Either you've got it or you haven't'. The notion of inborn intelligence that dominated educational practice until the mid-twentieth century was challenged by Vygotsky, Piaget and others, who developed a constructivist psychology based on a view of learners as active creators of their own knowledge. Some researchers argue that intelligence is not one generic capacity, but is made up of multiple intelligences (Gardner, 1999). Howard Gardner's multiple-intelligence theory has had a growing influence in recent years on educational theory and practice, although not all are convinced of its claims. Whether intelligence is viewed as one general capacity or many, what researchers are agreed upon is that it is modifiable and can be developed.

In teaching for metacognition, we want to strengthen children's belief that their intelligence and ability to learn can improve, and teach them to set goals, plan, monitor and evaluate their own learning and, as far as possible, to be self-directed in their thinking and learning.

KEY PRINCIPLES IN TEACHING FOR THINKING

Key principles that emerge from this research include the need for teachers and carers to provide:

- **cognitive challenge**, challenging children's thinking from the earliest years;
- **collaborative learning**, extending thinking through working with others;
- **metacognitive discussion**, reviewing what children think and how they learn.

This research and the pioneering work of Reuven Feuerstein, who created a programme called Instrumental Enrichment, Matthew Lipman, who founded Philosophy for Children, and other leading figures, such as Edward de Bono, creator of 'lateral thinking', have inspired a wide range of curriculum and programme developments (Fisher, 2005). These include a range of teaching approaches that you could use, including 'cognitive acceleration', 'brain-based' approaches (such as 'accelerated learning') and 'philosophical' approaches that aim at developing the moral and emotional, as well as intellectual, aspects of thinking – caring and collaborative, as well as critical and creative thinking. These are discussed on pages 490–6.

By the end of the twentieth century, there was a widespread realisation that 'key' or 'core' skills of thinking, creativity and problem-solving lay at the heart of successful learning and should be embedded in primary and secondary school curricula. When the Department for Education and Employment (DfEE) in England commissioned Carol McGuinness (1999) to review and evaluate research into thinking skills and related areas, key points that emerged from her study were that:

- pupils benefitted from being coached in thinking;
- not one model but many approaches proved effective;
- success was due to pedagogy (teaching strategies), not specific materials;
- strategies were needed to enable pupils to transfer thinking to other contexts;
- teachers needed professional support and coaching to sustain success.

SHOULD THINKING BE TAUGHT IN SEPARATE LESSONS OR ACROSS THE CURRICULUM?

Research suggests that one-off 'thinking' lessons are less effective than teaching thinking and learning strategies that can be applied in subjects (such as CASE; see page 490) or as dialogic strategies across the curriculum. McGuinness (1999) points out that the most successful interventions are associated with a 'strong theoretical underpinning, well-designed and contextualised materials, explicit pedagogy and teacher support'.

In England, the revised National Curriculum (Department for Education and Employment, 1999) included thinking skills in its rationale, stating that thinking skills are essential in 'learning how to learn'. The list of thinking skills identified in the English National Curriculum is similar to many such lists: information processing, reasoning, enquiry, creative thinking and evaluation. Any good lesson or learning conversation will show evidence of some or all of these elements. They focus on 'knowing how', as well as 'knowing what', not only on curriculum content, but on learning how to learn. See Table 7.4.2 for ways in which they can be related to Bloom's taxonomy.

In recent curriculum developments, such as the Personal Learning and Thinking Skills framework (Qualifications and Curriculum Authority, 2009), in England, as elsewhere, the curriculum is no longer seen simply as subject knowledge, but as being underpinned by the skills of lifelong learning. Good teaching is not just about achieving particular curriculum objectives, but also about developing general thinking skills and learning behaviours. Since the McGuiness review (1999) and reference to developing thinking skills in the National Curriculum, interest in the teaching of thinking has

TABLE 7.4.2 Thinking skills linked to Bloom's taxonomy

Thinking skills	Bloom's taxonomy
Information processing	Knowledge, comprehension
Enquiry	Application
Reasoning	Analysis
Creative thinking	Synthesis
Evaluation	Evaluation

In Wales . . .

From September 2013, while the Communication and Number components in the non-statutory document have been replaced by the statutory Literacy and Numeracy Framework, in Wales the Thinking and ICT components in this skills framework remain in place to guide schools on these important skills.

> Developing thinking can be defined as developing patterns of ideas that help learners acquire deeper understanding and enable them to explore and make sense of their world. It refers to processes of thinking that we have defined as plan, develop and reflect. These processes enable learners to think creatively and critically to plan their work, carry out tasks, analyse and evaluate their findings, and to reflect on their learning, making links within and outside their formal learning environment. Although we are born with a capability to think, there is ample evidence that we can learn to think more effectively.
>
> (DCELLS, 2008: 10)

Source: Department for Children, Education, Lifelong Learning and Skills (DCELLS) (2008). *Skills Framework for 3 to 19-year-olds in Wales*. Cardiff: Welsh Assembly Government. http://wales.gov.uk/dcells/publications/curriculum_and_assessment/arevisedcurriculumforwales/skillsdevelopment/SKILLS_FRAMEWORK_2007_Engli1.pdf?lang=en

In Northern Ireland . . .

At the heart of the Northern Ireland Curriculum lies an explicit emphasis on the development of skills and capabilities for life-long learning and for operating effectively in society. The five broad strands that are identified in the Northern Ireland Framework for thinking skills include, managing information, thinking, problem-solving and decision-making, being creative, working with others, and self-management. The framework does not stand-alone nor is it isolated from the traditional areas of the curriculum. Rather, it is intended that the skills and capabilities highlighted in the framework are developed and assessed *in and through* the Areas of Learning at each Key Stage. This will give opportunities for their development to be reinforced and make it easier for teachers and pupils to make connections and see relationships.

Task 7.4.2 Identifying thinking skills

Identify, in a lesson plan or observation of a classroom lesson, the thinking skills that are being developed as general learning objectives. Look for evidence that the children are engaged in information processing, reasoning, enquiry, creative thinking and evaluation.

The following proforma could be used for recording the evidence.

Identifying thinking skills

What thinking skills are pupils developing and using in this lesson?
Identify examples of:

Information processing
Finding relevant information
Organising information
Representing or communicating information

Reasoning
Giving reasons
Making inferences or deductions
Arguing or explaining a point of view

Enquiry
Asking questions
Planning research or study
Engaging in enquiry or process of finding out

Creative thinking
Generating ideas
Imagining or hypothesising
Designing innovative solutions

Evaluation
Developing evaluation criteria
Applying evaluation criteria
Judging the value of information and ideas

burgeoned in the UK. Research has shown that interventions work, if they have a strong theoretical base, and if teachers are enthusiastic and well trained in the use of a programme or strategy. Teachers are developing 'teaching for thinking' approaches in new directions, integrating them into everyday teaching to create 'thinking classrooms', and developing whole-school policies to create 'thinking schools'.

HOW DO WE TEACH THINKING IN THE CLASSROOM?

Researchers have identified a number of teaching strategies you can use to help stimulate children's thinking in the classroom. These approaches to teaching thinking can be summarised as:

- cognitive acceleration;
- brain-based techniques;
- philosophy for children;
- teaching strategies across the curriculum.

Cognitive acceleration

CASE

Philip Adey and Michael Shayer developed the original Cognitive Acceleration through Science Education (CASE) project in the 1980s and early 1990s, applying the theories of Piaget on 'cognitive conflict' to Key Stage 3 science. Their work now extends into other subjects and age groups and has, perhaps, the best research and most robust evidence of the impact of thinking skills in the UK (Shayer and Adey, 2002).

The following is a typical format of a CASE lesson for thinking that builds in time for cognitive and metacognitive discussion:

1 **Concrete preparation**: stimulus to thinking, introducing the terms of the problem.
2 **Cognitive conflict**: creates a challenge for the mind.
3 **Social construction**: dialogue with others, discussion that extends thinking.
4 **Metacognition**: reflection on how we tackled the problem.
5 **Bridging**: reviewing where else we can use this thinking and learning.

CASE lessons have also been developed for young children under the title 'Let's Think!' and aim to raise achievement by developing Year 1 pupils' general thinking patterns and teachers' understanding of children's thinking.

During Let's Think! lessons, young children work with a teacher in groups of six, and each activity takes about 30 minutes. The session is completely oral, with discussion based on a range of objects. At the beginning of the session, the teacher helps agree a common language to describe the objects being used. Having established the vocabulary and the concepts involved, the teacher sets the challenge of the activity. One popular activity in this schema is called the 'hoop game', in which children are required to put orange toy dinosaurs in one hoop and T-Rex dinosaurs in another hoop. The challenge is that one of the dinosaurs is an orange T-Rex. This is very perplexing for pre-operational children, because they have to utilise two pieces of information about the dinosaur and find a solution to the problem. The children work together as a group to come to a solution or a number of possible solutions to solve the task. They discuss their ideas and make suggestions. The teacher guides them, without being obvious, towards the idea of overlapping the hoops and putting the wayward dinosaur in the intersection.

As in other discussion-based approaches, children are encouraged to state whether they agree or disagree with each other by giving a reason. For example, they are taught to say, 'I think . . . because' or 'I disagree with you because . . .'. The activities are designed as problems to be solved, thus creating a context for developing thinking. Children are given a challenge and are required to work collaboratively, in order to plan and evaluate their own and others' thinking strategies.

The teacher then gets the children to think about their thinking (metacognition) through asking such questions as, 'What do you think we are going to have to think about?' and 'How did you get your answer?', rather than, 'Is your answer correct?'. Of course, you do not need the Let's Think! materials to apply this teaching strategy to any area of the curriculum.

What the Let's Think! approach aims to do is to accelerate cognitive development between two types of thinking. The first type of thought is what Piaget called 'pre-operational', when children still find it difficult to engage in what adults perceive as rational thought. The next stage, which Piaget described as 'concrete operational', involves manipulating at least two ideas in order to produce a third, new idea, which is what the sessions encourage the children to do. 'Let's Think!' aims to accelerate the transition between the two types of thought in order to help pupils make better sense of their learning and improve general achievement. It does this by ensuring that teaching includes cognitive challenge, collaborative activity and children thinking about how they think and learn.

'Thinking maths' lessons for primary children are part of a related project called Cognitive Acceleration in Mathematics Education (CAME). These lessons involve discussion-based tasks in maths that aim to develop children's conceptual thinking rather than the mechanics of doing the maths. They differ from open-ended investigations in that each lesson has a specific concept to develop. The activities are planned to generate group and whole-class discussion, rather than written work, with an emphasis on 'how did you get your answer?' rather than 'what is the answer?'. As the CAME approach suggests, if your emphasis in teaching is, 'How did you get your answer?' rather than 'Is your answer correct?', it is a far more productive way of generating children's thinking and learning.

Brain-based techniques

Accelerated learning

Many educationalists are influenced by recent research into how the human brain works and draw on some of the implications of this research for teachers and schools. Accelerated learning and multiple-intelligence approaches all draw on these broad ideas, together with research into learning styles. The common feature is the reliance on brain research to inspire teaching techniques in the classroom.

There are many theories of learning styles. They are rooted in a classification of psychological types and the fact that individuals tend to process information differently. Different researchers propose different sets of learning style characteristics, but many remain unconvinced by their claims that children learn best through using one preferred style (Coffield *et al.*, 2004).

Accelerated learning approaches include applying VAK learning styles to teaching. VAK stands for:

- **visual** – learning best through pictures, charts, diagrams, video, ICT, etc.;
- **auditory** – learning best through listening;
- **kinaesthetic** – learning best through being physically engaged in a task.

For example, in teaching a class to spell a word, a teacher might show them how to chunk the word into three pieces and emphasise this by using different colours for each section of the word and asking them to visualise it in their heads. The teacher might also ask them to write the word in the air with their fingers. Accelerated learning emphasises the importance of including a range of learning experiences – visual, verbal and physical – in your teaching, so that children are challenged to think in different ways. (For more on Alistair Smith's approach to accelerated learning, see: www.alite.co.uk)

These and other 'brain-based' teaching strategies, such as 'Brain Gym' (which uses simple but challenging aerobic exercises to focus the mind and stimulate the brain), offer much scope for research in the classroom (see www.braingym.org.uk).

De Bono

According to Edward de Bono, we tend to think in restricted and predictable ways. To become better thinkers, we need to learn new habits. His teaching strategy, known as 'thinking hats', helps learners try different approaches to thinking. Each 'thinking hat' represents a different way to think about a problem or issue. Children are encouraged to try on the different 'hats' or approaches to a problem to go beyond their usual thinking habits (de Bono, 2000). The 'hats', together with questions you might ask, are as follows:

- White hat = information: **What do we know?**
- Red hat = feelings: **What do we feel?**
- Purple hat = problems: **What are the drawbacks?**
- Yellow hat = positives: **What are the benefits?**
- Green hat = creativity: **What ideas have we got?**
- Blue hat = control: **What are our aims?**

De Bono claims that the technique is widely used in management, but little research has been published on its use in education. Some teachers have found it a useful technique for encouraging children to look at a problem or topic from a variety of perspectives. It encourages us, and our children, to think creatively about any topic and to ask: 'Is there another way of thinking about this?'.

Philosophy for children

A pioneer of the 'critical thinking' movement in America is the philosopher Matthew Lipman. Originally a university philosophy professor, Lipman was unhappy at what he saw as poor thinking in his students. They seemed to have been encouraged to learn facts and to accept authoritative opinions, but not to think for themselves. He became convinced that something was wrong with the way they had been taught in school when they were younger. He, therefore, founded the Institute for the Advancement of Philosophy for Children and developed, with colleagues, a programme called Philosophy for Children, used in more than forty countries around the world (see http://cehs. montclair.edu/academic/iapc/). Lipman believes that children are natural philosophers, because they view the world with curiosity and wonder (Lipman, 2003). It is children's own questions, stimulated by specially written philosophical stories, that form the starting point for enquiry or discussion.

Stories for Thinking

Many resources have been developed that adapt Matthew Lipman's approach to Philosophy for Children to the needs of children and teachers in the UK. 'Stories for Thinking' is one such approach (Fisher, 1996). The aim, through using stories and other kinds of stimulus for philosophical discussion, is to create a *community of enquiry* in the classroom (see: www.sapere.org.uk). Encouraging children to question and discuss what they do not understand is fundamental to this teaching method. Researchers have reported striking cognitive gains through this approach in the classroom, including enhancing verbal reasoning, self-esteem and dialogic skills (Topping and Trickey, 2007).

In a typical Stories for Thinking lesson, the teacher shares a 'thinking story' with the class. They have 'thinking time', when they are asked to think about anything in the story that they thought was strange, interesting or puzzling. After some quiet thinking time, the teacher asks for their comments or questions and writes each child's questions on the board, adding their name after their question. The children then choose from the list of questions which one they would like to discuss. The teacher invites the children to comment and asks who agrees or disagrees with particular comments made. If children do not give reasons or evidence from the story for their opinions, the teacher asks 'Why do you think that?' or 'Have you got a reason for that?'.

When asked the value of a Stories for Thinking lesson, one child said: 'You have to ask questions and think hard about the answers'. Another said: 'Sometimes you change your mind and sometimes you don't.' A third reply was: 'It is better than just doing reading or writing because you have to say what you really think.'

Teachers note that, in Stories for Thinking lessons, in which they may also uses poems, pictures, objects or other texts for thinking, the children have become more thoughtful, better at speaking and listening to each other, better at questioning and using the language of reasoning, more confident in posing creative ideas and in judging what they and others think and do, and more confident about applying their thinking to fresh challenges in learning and in life (Fisher, 2013).

What stories or other forms of stimulus could you use to really engage your children in thinking? How could you create an enquiring classroom?

Task 7.4.3 Creating a thinking classroom

What would a thinking classroom look like?

- Collect words to describe what a thinking classroom might look like. These might include some reference to the teacher's behaviour, children's behaviour, classroom environment or kinds of activity that help children to think and learn well.
- Sort your ideas into small groups and give each group a heading that you think appropriate.
- Choose one idea from each group and consider how you could develop this in your classroom.

Teaching strategies across the curriculum

A growing number of programmes and strategies aim to help teachers develop children's thinking and learning across the curriculum, such as Thinking Actively in a Social Context (TASC) and Activating Children's Thinking Skills (ACTS). It is difficult to evaluate the success of these and other interventions because of the many variables involved in the teaching situation. There is much scope here for your own research into teaching strategies in the classroom and for developing new strategies.

A number of specific teaching strategies have been identified to help stimulate children's thinking in different subject areas. For example, 'Odd One Out' is a teaching technique to identify pupils' understanding of key concepts in different subjects. A teacher might, in a numeracy lesson, put three numbers on the board, such as 9, 5 and 10; or, in science, three materials; or, in English, three

Task 7.4.4 Evaluating concepts

Choose a concept related to thinking or learning skills, such as creative thinking (or creativity), critical thinking (or reasoning), information processing, enquiry (or questioning) or evaluating (or assessment) as a focus for a small-scale investigation.

Try collecting data in the following ways:

- **Find out from others:** Find out what others think of this concept through reading or Internet research, and by interviewing children and/or colleagues, asking what this concept means to them.
- **Investigate for yourself**: Observe a lesson to collect evidence about what happens in the classroom in relation to teaching and learning related to the concept you have chosen.

After collecting some data, evaluate what you find. Review, critically analyse and evaluate your data and draw conclusions about what you have learned from this investigation. Think in what ways teaching policy or practice might be modified in light of your research.

characters to compare and contrast – then ask the children to choose the 'odd one out' and to give a reason. Teachers who use this strategy claim it can reveal gaps in the knowledge taught and the knowledge and vocabulary that the children are then able to use. The children think of it as a game and are used to thinking up examples and ideas that show their thinking in different curriculum subjects. This approach encourages creative thinking and reasoning (Higgins *et al.*, 2001). Can you think of three things and give reasons why one, two or each of them might be the odd one out?

Mind mapping

Many approaches include the use of thinking diagrams – 'mind maps' or 'concept maps' – as aids to making thinking visual and explicit.

Concept mapping is an information-processing technique with a long history. Tony Buzan developed this technique into a version he calls 'mind mapping' (Buzan, 2006). Concept maps are tools that help make thinking visible and involve writing down, or more commonly drawing, a central idea and thinking up new and related ideas that radiate out from the centre. Children, by focusing on key ideas written down in their own words and then looking for branches out and connections between the ideas, are mapping knowledge in a manner that can help them understand and remember new information. A simple concept map might be used to map out the connections between characters in a story. Children might also draw maps from memory, to test what they remember or know. Teachers have found concept maps helpful in finding out or revising what children know, and the technique is especially popular when used in pairs or groups. Children can learn the technique from an early age, and many find it motivating. As one young child put it: 'Concept mapping gets you to think and try more.' Concept mapping is a useful teaching and revision technique for extending thinking and making it visually memorable.

When you are planning your next topic or activity with children, think of ways of making your own or your children's thinking visible, for example by creating a 'mind map' of a story, a process or collection of ideas.

Computers and thinking

Research shows that there are several ways in which ICT could particularly enhance information-processing skills. ICT enables multiple and complex representations of information, for example allowing learners to think with a richer knowledge base. As James, aged 8, said: 'I didn't know there was so much to know!'

Educational software can act like a teacher to prompt and direct enquiry through asking questions, giving clues and suggesting avenues of investigation. It can also act as a resource while learners discuss and explore ideas, for example prompting reflection around a simulation. Networks via the Internet, including video conferencing, can allow children to engage directly in collaborative learning and knowledge-sharing with others who are not physically present.

The main criticism of the computer as a tutor model is that directed computer teaching does not allow children to be creative learners, able to think and make connections for themselves, and so is unlikely to support the development of higher-order thinking. This can be transformed, however, by collaboration around ICT activities, which has been shown to have the potential to enhance the learning of transferable thinking skills.

Effective collaborative learning still needs to be structured. Learners should be taught how to reason and learn together, before they are asked to work collaboratively with ICT, because having to articulate and explain strategies to others is more likely to lead to transfer than just doing things without thinking or talking them through. In the lesson plenary, by reflecting on this process of collaborative problem-solving, the teacher can help children to 'bridge' their thinking, from their experience with, for example, Logo or another computer program to different areas of the curriculum.

Computers can help develop children's thinking skills when used as part of a larger dialogue about thinking and learning (Wegerif, 2002). The challenge for you as a teacher is to find ways to use the computer to encourage thinking with, and discussion between, children.

Task 7.4.5 Planning for teaching thinking

- Choose a teaching strategy or approach from published materials that aims to develop children's thinking skills.
- Think how you might use this strategy or approach in a chosen area of the curriculum.
- Plan a lesson that incorporates this strategy, identifying a specific thinking or learning skill in your lesson objectives.
- Share your plan or teaching ideas with others.
- Teach and evaluate your lesson for thinking!

Recent test results show that standards in schools are rising – but slowly. Could the teaching of thinking provide a key to raising achievement? The experience of many teachers suggests that, when pupils are taught the habits of effective thinking, they grow in confidence, their learning is enriched, and they are better prepared to face the challenges of the future. Children think so too – as Arran, aged 9, put it: 'When you get out in the real world you have to think for yourself; that's why we need to practise it in school.' Research suggests that the most successful approaches to teaching thinking are dialogic teaching methods (such as Philosophy for Children), Piagetian approaches (such as CASE) and assessment for learning (AfL) (Hattie, 2008; see also Unit 5.1 of this volume). *Toolkit of Strategies to Improve Learning*, published by the Sutton Trust (Higgins *et al.*, 2011), a research summary into cost-effective teaching strategies, identified 'effective feedback' and teaching for 'metacognition and self-regulation' as having the greatest impact on improving learning and attainment (see website below). However, other approaches, not so well supported by research, may be found useful by teachers and provide a good focus for their own research. Good teaching is about helping children to think for themselves, which is why it is both a challenge and an adventure.

SUMMARY

In recent years, there has been much research into ways of developing children's thinking and learning skills. This has been informed by growing knowledge about how the brain works, how people learn, and how teaching approaches can help improve children's ability to think and learn. The phrase 'thinking skills' refers to many of the capacities involved in thinking and learning, skills fundamental to lifelong learning, active citizenship and emotional intelligence. Research shows that the key to raising standards in education is through teaching that promotes cognitive challenge, interactive dialogue with and between children and metacognitive review. These and other teaching strategies can help raise standards of achievement and create thinking children, thinking classrooms and thinking schools.

 ## ANNOTATED FURTHER READING

Fisher, R. (2005) *Teaching Children to Think*, 2nd edn, Cheltenham: Stanley Thornes.
> This book discusses the nature of thinking and thinking skills and explores the development of thinking skills programmes and how they can be implemented in the classroom.

Fisher, R. (2009) *Creative Dialogue: Talk for Thinking*, London: Routledge.
> This is a guide to dialogic learning, presenting practical research-based ways of teaching children to be more thoughtful and creative, and to learn more effectively through talk for thinking in the classroom. It includes advice on using dialogue to support AfL and ideas for developing listening skills and concentration.

Fisher R. (2013) *Teaching Thinking: Philosophical Enquiry in the Classroom*, 4th edn, London: Continuum.
> A guide to using philosophical discussion in the classroom to develop children's thinking, learning and literacy skills.

Hattie, J. (2008) *Visible Learning: A Synthesis of Over 800 Meta-analyses Relating to Achievement*, London: Routledge.
> This, the largest ever overview of education research, suggests that raising the quality of teacher-pupil interaction is the key to improving education. Encouraging pupils to question their teachers on what they do and do not understand is identified as the single most effective teaching method. Other effective approaches identified include Piagetian programmes (such as CASE) and AfL.

FURTHER READING TO SUPPORT M-LEVEL STUDY

Burke, L.A. and Williams, J.M. (2009) 'Developmental changes in children's understandings of intelligence and thinking skills', *Early Child Development & Care*, 179(7): 949–68.
> This study extends previous research on the development of children's concepts of intelligence and produces new data on children's understandings of effective thinking and thinking skills. During semi-structured individual interviews, children aged 5 , 7 and 11 years old were asked questions regarding their understanding of intelligence and thinking, the relation between effort and ability, the stability of intelligence and their knowledge of specific thinking skills. Results showed developmental trends in children's understandings of intelligence and specific thinking skills.

Jones, H. (2010) 'National Curriculum tests and the teaching of thinking skills at primary schools – parallel or paradox?' *Education 3-13*, 38(1): 69–86.
> This article is based on findings from a questionnaire-based research project that investigated the relationship between National Curriculum tests and the teaching of thinking skills in primary schools. Analysis of the data indicated a negative impact of these tests on the teaching of thinking skills. In examining the results, the principles underlying both the National Curriculum tests and the teaching of thinking skills are discussed and found to be in conflict.

RELEVANT WEBSITES

Department of Education: Articles on improving pupils thinking and reasoning skills: www.education.gov.uk/schools/toolsandinitiatives/tripsresearchdigests/a0013261/themes-thinking-skills

Sapere: www.sapere.org.uk/
> This site promotes philosophy for children throughout the UK.

The Sutton Trust Toolkit: www.cem.org/attachments/1toolkit-summary-final-r-2-.pdf
> The *Toolkit of Strategies to Improve Learning* (2011) evaluates teaching strategies, including teaching for metacognition.

Times Educational Supplement (TES): www.tes.co.uk/thinking-skills-whole-school-teaching-resources/
> Provides a range of resources for teaching thinking skills.

Thinking Skills and Creativity: www.journals.elsevier.com/thinking-skills-and-creativity/
> *Thinking Skills and Creativity* is a journal of peer-reviewed articles on teaching for thinking and creativity.

Society for Advancing Philosophical Enquiry and Reflection in Education (SAPERE): www.sapere.org.uk/
> Visit this site for more on philosophy for children.

REFERENCES

Alexander, R. (2006) *Towards Dialogic Teaching: Rethinking Classroom Talk*, 3rd edn, Cambridge: Dialogos.

Bloom, B. and Krathwohl, D.R. (1956) *Taxonomy of Educational Objectives, Handbook 1: Cognitive Domain*, New York: David McKay.

Buzan, T. (2006) *The Mind Map Book*, London: BBC Active Publications. See also: www.mind-map.com (accessed November 2009).

Claxton, G. (2002) *Building Learning Power: Helping Young People Become Better Learners*, Bristol: TLO.

Coffield, F., Moseley, D., Hall, E. and Ecclestone, K. (2004) *Should We Be Using Learning Styles: What Research Has to Say to Practice*, London: Learning Skills and Development Agency.

de Bono, E. (2000) *Six Thinking Hats*, 2nd edn, London: Penguin.

Department for Education and Employment (DfEE) (1999) *The National Curriculum: Handbook for Primary Teachers in England*, London: DfEE.

Fisher, R. (1996) *Stories for Thinking*, Oxford: Nash Pollock.

Fisher, R. (2005) *Teaching Children to Think*, 2nd edn, Cheltenham: Stanley Thornes.

Fisher, R. (2009) *Creative Dialogue: Talk for Thinking*, London: Routledge.

Fisher, R. (2013) *Teaching Thinking: Philosophical Enquiry in the Classroom*, 4th edn, London: Continuum.

Gardner, H. (1999) *Intelligence Reframed: Multiple Intelligences for the 21st Century*, New York: Basic Books.

Goleman, D. (2006) *Social Intelligence*, New York: Bantam.

Hattie, J. (2008) *Visible Learning: A Synthesis of Over 800 Meta-analyses Relating to Achievement*, London: Routledge.

Higgins, S., Baumfield, V. and Leat, D. (2001) *Thinking Through Primary Teaching*, Cambridge: Chris Kington.

Higgins, S., Kokotsaki, D. and Coe, R.J. (2011) *Toolkit of Strategies to Improve Learning: Summary for Schools Spending the Pupil Premium*, Sutton Trust.

Lipman, M. (2003) *Thinking in Education*, 2nd edn, Cambridge: Cambridge University Press.

McGuinness, C. (1999) *From Thinking Skills to Thinking Classrooms: A Review and Evaluation of Approaches for Developing Pupils' Thinking*, Research Report RR115, London: DfEE.

Moseley, D., Baumfield, V., Elliott, J., Higgins, S., Miller, J. and Newton, D.P. (2005) *Frameworks for Thinking: A Handbook for Teaching and Learning*, Cambridge: Cambridge University Press.

Qualifications and Curriculum Authority (QCA) (2009) *Personal Learning and Thinking Skills*, London: QCA.

Shayer, M. and Adey, P. (2002) *Learning Intelligence*, Buckingham: Open University Press.

Smith, A. (2004) *The Brain's Behind it: New Knowledge About the Brain and Learning*, London: Continuum.

Topping, K.J. and Trickey, S. (2007) 'Impact of philosophical enquiry on school students' interactive behaviour', *International Journal of Thinking Skills and Creativity*, 2(2): 73–84.

Wegerif, R. (2002) *Literature Review in Thinking Skills, Technology and Learning*. Available online at: www.futurelab.org.uk (accessed November 2009).

GIFTED AND TALENTED

Deborah Eyre and Marcelo Staricoff

INTRODUCTION

> We need to take particular steps to serve the needs of gifted and talented children.
> (Department for Education and Skills, 2003: 41)

The idea that gifted and talented children need particular consideration during their primary schooling is one that has now been recognised for many years. Indeed, managing the learning needs of all the children in a primary classroom, regardless of their abilities, remains one of the greatest challenges for teachers.

Gifted and talented children is the term applied to those children who are achieving, or have the potential to achieve, at a level substantially beyond the rest of their peer group. It does not mean just the infant Mozart or the child Einstein, but rather refers to the upper end of the ability range in any cohort. Every primary teacher, therefore, needs to know how to teach the children working within this top end of the spectrum in any of the subject areas, and to be familiar with the techniques for creating high levels of intellectual challenge in the classroom. On the whole, these children can be some of the most rewarding to teach, and, provided that you create a classroom in which they can thrive, they will generally repay you handsomely. Conversely, if they are under-challenged, they can become disruptive and difficult.

This unit is designed to help you to create a classroom that meets the needs of your gifted and talented children by creating an intellectually lively and challenging learning environment. By creating this kind of environment to meet the needs of your gifted children, you will also provide benefits for the whole class and raise overall expectations (Staricoff, 2005). In this unit, we will consider how to identify the gifted or talented children in your class, ways to create an overall learning environment that encourages high levels of achievement and techniques for planning challenging tasks.

OBJECTIVES

By the end of the unit, you should be beginning to:

- understand how to recognise gifted and talented children;
- know how to create a suitable classroom learning environment;
- develop techniques for planning challenging tasks.

WHO ARE THE GIFTED AND TALENTED?

Identifying who is gifted or talented is not as important in the primary school as making provision for them. You need to concentrate on making the right provision, and then it is easy to spot who is gifted. The reason for this is that giftedness is not something that we are born with and will always be evident, whatever the circumstances; it is rather more complicated than that. Current thinking suggests that we are born with certain predispositions, and that they give us the capacity to excel in particular areas. However, this does not mean we will automatically excel, only if we develop those predispositions. For predisposition, we might substitute the more commonly used educational term, potential.

An easy way to think about giftedness is as an equation:

potential + opportunities/support + personal drive = high achievement (giftedness)

Therefore, for giftedness to emerge, children must meet the right opportunities and be given appropriate support throughout their entire childhood. It is not a question of 'pushing' or 'hot-housing', but instead of inspiring, engaging, coaching and supporting; not holding children back by having preconceived ideas about what a 6-year-old or a 10-year-old can/should do, but equally not pushing them forward at a rate that makes them uncomfortable.

Therefore, the main focus in primary education should be on creating the right opportunities, offering appropriate support and helping the child to develop a desire to learn and to achieve. Also to act as a 'talent spotter', recognising indicators of outstanding ability as and when they begin to emerge. As you will already know, most researchers think that ability is multidimensional, so you don't have to be good at everything, just outstanding at something, to be considered gifted.

It is important to keep in mind that children defined as gifted or talented are simply normal children, with all the usual personality characteristics of their age group. They are diverse in their personalities and interests, and it is no more possible to attribute an extensive range of personality characteristics to gifted children than it would be to children with, say, dyslexia. Don't be surprised if you find you have a gifted child in your class who is naughty or immature; giftedness is simply about intellectual ability, and that is only one aspect of any child. As far as intellectual characteristics are concerned, most gifted and talented children are of above-average ability generally, but have specific areas of outstanding strength.

IDENTIFYING THE GIFTED AND TALENTED

Outstanding ability in some areas, or in some children, can be detected very early. If, in the Early Years Foundation Stage, you have a child who uses an extensive vocabulary and exhibits an easy facility with language, then they will stand out from others in the class. Equally, a child who, when introduced to simple number patterns, then makes up much more complex ones of his or her own (e.g. using large or negative numbers) is obviously mathematically able. These types of children who stand out from their peers are known in the literature as 'precociously gifted' and are usually identified early.

> A child in Reception surprised us all with his explanation of how the simple number sequence we were looking at in fact carries on to infinity! He then proceeded to demonstrate a very advanced conceptual knowledge of numbers going on for ever!
>
> (Teacher, Hertford Infant and Nursery School)

In Wales . . .

Wales has devised a set of standards to enable schools to provide a clear framework to support more able and talented pupils:

> The Standards will help schools to develop an action plan for their provision, and will ensure that their approach is inclusive. The Standards will cover all aspects and will support a whole school approach to raising standards. Inspection has shown that schools that provide well for able pupils, generally provide well for all pupils because individual needs are focussed upon across the curriculum.
>
> (DCELLS, 2008: 12)

Source: Department for Children, Education, Lifelong Learning and Skills (DCELLS) (2008) *Meeting the Challenge: Quality Standards in Education for More Able and Talented Pupils*. Cardiff: Welsh Assembly Government (WAG). http://wales.gov.uk/pubs/circulars/2008/meetingthechallenge/meetingthechallenge.pdf?lang=en

A second group of children start to emerge as they progress through school. In primary school, some children with the potential to perform highly will start to forge ahead of others as soon as school introduces them to high-quality learning opportunities in the formal curriculum. They will readily acquire the knowledge, skills and concepts associated with their domains of strength. For these individuals, identification becomes a relatively straightforward process, because the gap between their performance and that of their peers grows rapidly. They will be the 'star performers' in your class. They may well be recognisable in Foundation Stage or Key Stage 1, but will almost certainly be on the gifted and talented register by Key Stage 2.

The 'precociously gifted' and 'star performers' usually identify themselves, but there are other indicators that can help you, as a teacher, to spot who else might be gifted. One of the best early indicators is not so much about outstanding performance relative to others, but rather about substantial interest. The child who is fascinated by music, or number or language and seeks to play games with it. (Linguistically able children often, for example, make up terrible jokes using word puns.) As formal school progresses, each stage brings a chance for children to collide with new opportunities and to discover their areas of particular strength.

If children are exposed to initiatives such as the image of the week or the poem of the week, where they are encouraged to critique a work of art or a poem and encouraged to express how these stimuli makes them feel, one can very easily spot the gifted child whose insight, originality of thought and depth of explanation are consistently and significantly more developed than those of their peers.

Playfulness should not be restricted to the Early Years Foundation Stage; you may be playful at any stage, and, in fact, the more skilled you become in an area, the more scope there is to play. Once you know that a story has to have a beginning, a middle and an end, you can start to create ones that don't! A key technique for teaching gifted and talented children is to encourage them to be intellectually playful. Teach them the rules and then help them to move beyond them. The techniques and ideas included within this unit are designed to equip you with the practical ideas that will enable you to deliver the whole curriculum through an 'intellectually playful' approach, regardless of the age group or subject that you are teaching (Westbury Park Primary School, 2003).

Task 7.5.1 Talent spotting

Spend a few minutes thinking about the children in your class. Can you identify any who fit the categories we have looked at? Do you have any 'precociously gifted'? Who are your 'star performers'?

- Over a day or two, observe your class and see if you can spot any intellectually 'playful' children.
- Use the Classroom Quality Standards for Gifted and Talented Education (National Strategies, 2009) in order to identify your strengths and to identify any areas that could improve your provision for gifted and talented children within your classroom.

Families play a large part in the intellectual development of young children. Any signs of ability or 'playfulness' will be nurtured in most families, especially if the area of interest coincides with the interests of other members of the family. If a pair of professional musicians find their child shows an interest in music, they will encourage and support its development in quite a structured way. Equally, a family of academics might encourage questioning or investigation. An entrepreneurial family will encourage entrepreneurship, etc. This means that it is hard for you, as a teacher, to distinguish between raw potential and nurtured achievement. Howe (1995) suggests that, in the right circumstances, anyone can be coached to become gifted. This may be an extreme view, but, nevertheless, help from home can assist those with potential to appear 'precocious' and, perhaps more worryingly, can lead to some children being seen as gifted in their early years of schooling, when in fact they are really just well coached. These children will inevitably begin to find schooling more difficult as they move through school, when the conceptual demands increase, and their performance will become less remarkable.

The reverse of parent support is, of course, the results of lack of parental support. Gifted children from homes where intellectual support and opportunity are lacking are more reliant on the school making those opportunities and support available. These children will not show up in the 'precociously gifted' category and will never be your 'star performers', unless you, as a teacher, take action. You need to spot their 'playfulness' or insightful comments and structure their learning to help them make rapid progress in the formal curriculum. It is your job to look below the surface, especially with children from disadvantaged backgrounds.

Whether children come from a supportive or non-supportive family background, it is essential that the school works very hard to develop a close triangular relationship between the child, the school and the family. Effective triangulation benefits all parties and helps the child perceive that learning is not just a process that is restricted to when they are at school, but something that they should be encouraged to engage in throughout their day and throughout their lives. Engaging the families with their child's learning can transform the way that the child and the family interact with the process of learning, and may help to cancel out any negative feelings that families may have been harbouring from their own schooling and unconsciously transmitting to their child. This partnership can also be very beneficial when a child comes home excited about having being stimulated intellectually by something they have encountered at school. Home learning tasks are often accompanied by instructions for parents, so that the child can act as the teacher at home and feel that they are adding something special to their parents' understanding and knowledge base.

Five ways to spot gifted children

- Assessment of achievement through a variety of assessment measures (precocious).
- Particularly at Foundation Stage and Key Stage 1, children who are interested in an area and actively seek to pursue it, enjoying it for its own sake (playful).
- Pupils who appear to master the rules of a domain easily and can transfer their insights to new problems (precision).
- Pupils who observe their own behaviour and, hence, utilise a greater variety of learning strategies than others (self-regulation).
- Pupils who exhibit any of the characteristics above, plus a tendency towards non-conformity in the given domain (originality).

A very real problem in identifying gifted and talented children in primary school is confusion between the acquisition of skills and real intellectual ability. Giftedness is about cognitive ability, the ability to think. Skills are important, but not all gifted children acquire basic skills quickly, and this can hold back intellectual development.

In thinking about this, you may find it helpful to think of a particular skill, such as learning to read, as being like learning to drive. The length of time it takes you to pass your driving test is not an indicator of how good a driver you will eventually be. You can't be an expert driver without acquiring the basic skills (passing the test), but it is how you apply those skills later that makes the difference. So too in school. Acquiring the skills is important, but it is how you use and apply them that differentiates between acceptable and outstanding performance. It is important for a teacher to create a classroom environment in which children are encouraged to develop a high level of self-esteem and in which they feel motivated to want to use and apply these skills, as they recognise that this approach will lead to them achieving their very best.

Case study

Jack, aged 7, is a linguistically gifted child with an exceptional vocabulary. He learned to talk at 12 months and never makes grammatical errors. He never needs to redraft his ideas because he has immense fluency with language. However, he finds some of the skills associated with learning to read (decoding text) or to write (forming letters) difficult, even though he is expert at plot and character. This discrepancy is because the aspects he finds difficult require visual or physical coordination, which is not an area of strength for him. He needs support in these. This mismatch between ability and skill can lead to a very frustrating period for some gifted children, as they are accustomed to learning easily. If they are not helped to master basic skills, then under-achievement is inevitable. However, once these 'tools' are acquired, then progress is very rapid. This inability to master some of the basic skills quickly is one of the reasons that some gifted children are not recognised at primary school. Jack may well have been overlooked if his teacher had not been 'talent spotting'.

We have talked very little about the role of SATs or other tests in the identification process. They are, of course, crucial and an integral part of the school's methodology for identifying gifted children. If a child performs well on the test, then that should be seen as a key indicator. However, it is also important to look beyond test data, especially in Foundation Stage and Key Stage 1. Tests should be seen as one indicator, rather than the sole indicator. Evidence-based teacher assessment is crucial in this process, so use the tests, but also keep your antenna alert for undiscovered talent. One way of making sure that you are maximising your chances of spotting undiscovered talent is to adapt, for your own circumstances, the excellent practice that occurs in the EYFS, that is to be always alert to catch 'children at learning' and recording these significant achievements on a daily basis. If you are lucky enough to have a teaching assistant or other adults in the classroom, a great deal can be achieved by providing them with post-it notes or sticky labels to record these moments as they happen. It is a fantastic way of building up a true picture of a child over time.

Often now, when you are observed by senior management or by inspectors, you will notice that they also look for the immediacy in a child's learning and the progress they make in the short space of time they are with you. Observations have moved away from the judgement of how good a teacher you are towards placing the emphasis on how well all groups of children are learning. Gifted and talented children will definitely be one of the groups that they will focus on, and so it is very important to be able to discuss with the observers or inspectors the range of formative assessment tools that you deploy in order to inform yourself of the progress that the gifted and talented children are making, on a daily basis, in your classroom.

It is very important to realise that each teacher is responsible for ensuring that the gifted and talented children within their class are making good progress, and not to think that this is just the job of the gifted and talented coordinator.

CREATING THE LEARNING ENVIRONMENT

Gifted and talented children are first and foremost children, and much of what they need is exactly the same as for other children. They need to be treated like other children and expected to behave accordingly. If the following is the basis by which you set your classroom climate for all children, then gifted children will also thrive.

Gifted and talented children need to:

- have a secure environment in which they feel happy to display ability;
- experience intellectual challenge, sometimes having to struggle to achieve;
- take risks and not be worried about sometimes making mistakes;
- relax and have fun;
- comply with the class rules and code of conduct;
- know that they can ask searching questions and get a considered response;

In Northern Ireland . . .

There is no formula that any school should adopt to develop provision for Gifted and Talented students. Any strategies which are developed will emanate from the strengths of the staff, the needs of the pupils and the opportunities that arise from the community activities and the personnel involved. A system of education which caters for the diversity of pupils' needs is founded on the belief that students first need enriching opportunities to discover their strengths and interests. Once identified, these strengths and interests can be nurtured and supported and potential developed into performance.

(CCEA, 2007: 97)

Source: Council for Curriculum, Examinations and Assessment (CCEA) (2007) *Gifted and Talented Pupils: Guidelines for Teachers*. Belfast, CCEA.

- receive praise when they do well or put a lot of effort into doing things well;
- be recognised as an individual, with strengths and weaknesses;
- be able to discuss meaningfully with the teacher (current research suggests that effective feedback is one of the most effective way of raising standards and of closing the gap of achievement).

Creating a secure environment

Each of the items in the above list is particularly important for gifted and talented children. The secure environment is perhaps the most important of all. Gifted children who are achieving highly do stand out, and this can cause difficulties. Sensitive children will notice that they stand out and may not find it easy. It is not 'cool to be bright'. In some schools, and in some classrooms, gifted children will learn that drawing attention to what you know leads to being called 'clever clogs', or earns you the reputation as the class 'boffin'. If you are a sensitive child, this can be very damaging, and such children soon learn to hide their ability and, in some cases, deliberately under-achieve in order to remain unnoticed. Less sensitive children may continue to draw attention to themselves and become socially ostracised. Gifted children do need to learn how to manage their ability, so that they do not continually show off and try to outperform everyone else, but equally they should not have to be ashamed of their ability. It is something to celebrate. If you are really committed to celebrating diversity in your classroom, then it should be easy to accommodate the gifted and talented children. Circle time is, for example, a good way of addressing the needs of gifted individuals and also can be used to help them to recognise the different strengths other children have.

If you are trying to 'talent spot', then it is essential that you create a classroom climate where children are happy to reveal their ability. The best way to do this is to focus all your children on learning and deliberately draw attention to the different strengths individuals in the class bring to the class's learning. More generally, make it clear that everyone is expected to do their best, and it is evidence of achievement through hard work that is rewarded, not just achievement. A piece of research (Eyre *et al.*, 2002: 10), looking at primary school teachers who were very good at teaching gifted and talented children, found that all the successful classrooms were positive, pacey and purposeful, with a focus on hard work, fun and recognition of individual effort and achievement. They were not classrooms characterised by serious and earnest endeavour, but rather a context where children and teachers enjoyed the challenge of learning and the satisfaction of progress and success, these being the attributes that contribute towards creating an intellectually playful classroom environment.

The intellectually playful classroom

The intellectually playful classroom can be created by the following:

(a) Establish high expectations

Of course, in order for gifted children to both emerge and to excel, you have to have high expectations regarding what you think can be achieved. The learning objectives must be ambitious and clear, and you need to ensure that the children are aware of them. Gifted children make intellectual connections between what they are learning now, what they learnt before and the long-term learning objective. They like you to take them into your confidence and for you to tell them not only what is going to happen, but also why you are doing it, and where it is leading. By Years 5 and 6, many gifted children will want an overview of the term, or at least the half-term, because this information helps them to gain control of their learning and become more independent. If they know you are going to do the

Greeks, then they may begin to read about them. They may line up their relatives to make sure they give them relevant presents for Christmas, and they are likely to help you make the lessons more engaging. Of course, you do not need to have a special conversation with your gifted and talented about the overall scheme of work; just tell the whole class.

A key element in creating a good learning environment is learning to value each child as an individual and knowing their strengths and weaknesses. Even the most gifted children are better at some things than others, and they often suffer from people expecting them to be able to do everything equally well. They may find it hard to ask for help, and some will be real perfectionists, who find even minor failures hard to take. You can help here by creating an approach where 'having a go' is highly valued, even more than 'getting it right'. Make comments, such as 'That's a really good suggestion, I can see why you thought that, but . . .' or 'I used to think . . . but then I found out' etc. Encourage children to take intellectual risks and not worry if they are wrong. Einstein said that clever people are those who make their mistakes fastest. Help your class to see that making mistakes is good, if we examine them carefully and learn from them. It helps us move forward. Try using some examples of famous people who made big mistakes on the way to discovering great things. (Science can provide particularly good examples, as science is about refuting or confirming existing theories.)

(b) Develop purposeful teacher–pupil interactions

Gifted and talented pupils like to work with people who have greater levels of expertise than themselves. In school, this is usually the adults, and especially the teacher. It can also, in many schools, be other children of similar ability. Gifted children value teachers who habitually discuss with their class and who are willing, on occasion, to discuss in depth with the individual. To make this happen, it is important to focus on four areas:

- teacher questions
- pupil questions
- teacher explanation
- pupil explanation.

Task 7.5.2 Asking good questions

Teacher questions can stimulate thinking and are a very useful way to differentiate for the most able. Try directing a series of particularly searching questions towards a confident child who you know to be gifted and let everyone listen as the argument is developed.

Discuss with your tutor your questioning technique. How frequently do you ask open questions that require children to think or offer an opinion? Most teachers ask too many closed questions, which are designed merely to confirm whether the child understands, rather than open up new thinking.

Look at how to improve your questioning skills. (Wragg and Brown, 1993, is a good starting point, as is the guidance from the literacy and numeracy strategies.)

Asking the right questions is a two-way process, and, as children move through primary school, you need to help them to become questioners. They need to pose questions and query findings, not take information at face value. This can begin very early, and 'book talk' is a good way to engage with this agenda. If you begin by asking, 'what questions could we ask about this book?', and do this quite regularly, then your gifted children will start to pose similar questions when they read. Aidan Chambers' book, entitled *Tell Me* (1993), has a great set of ideas for this. This technique works equally well with a historical picture or a map. Any stimulus can be used in this way to get children thinking. In GCSE history, original sources are used, and students judge the reliability of the source. This kind of technique can easily be used in Key Stage 2 and even younger. All children can take part when this is a general classroom activity, but, with your gifted children, you should encourage, and later expect, them to take this analytical approach to all their work, not just when you have set up a particular task. For gifted pupils, it should become a way of thinking, not just an activity.

In a similar way, you can use your teacher explanations to create thinking. Don't just describe and convey information. Try to set it as a query, or use it to make connections with previous learning. Encourage your gifted children to describe what they have learnt/found out in such a way as to make it appealing to others – perhaps for a specific audience, e.g. a younger class or the school governors. Explanations that have a real purpose are much more engaging than feedback sessions.

(c) Develop excellent classroom management

The key to meeting the needs of all the children in your class, including the gifted, is time management. Well-established classroom routines create the space for one-to-one work with individuals. Make sure the classroom is laid out in such a way as to enable children to collect materials independently. Ensure that you prevent disruptive behaviour by having a clear code of behaviour and a consistent approach to dealing with misbehaviour. Make sure your instructions are clear and unambiguous. Create ways of working in the classroom that everyone adheres to, e.g. where to put books for marking. Most of all, always make sure you have planned carefully and have everything you need for the lesson.

(d) Introduce a number of initiatives that are designed to challenge gifted children in the primary classroom

Much of what constitutes good classroom provision generally is also good provision for the gifted. You need to ensure that these elements are in place generally in your classroom, before looking at specific challenges for the gifted.

* careful planning
* clear learning objectives
* target-setting
* high expectations
* variety of approach
* assessment for learning
* good evaluation.

One way to ensure that your classroom is set up with all of these characteristics is to devote the first week with your new class to a 'learning to learn' week. The aim of this week is to introduce all the children to a number of initiatives that will equip them with the tools, values and aptitudes that will ensure that all children are able to view themselves as successful learners and perceive learning as something that they will enjoy, secure in the knowledge that they now have the tools and strategies that will enable them to keep getting better and better at learning and at fulfilling their potential.

The 'learning to learn' week enables you to develop:

* a set of shared values for the class that will allow all children to thrive as individuals;
* a classroom that promotes a thought-provoking, challenge-rich and enquiry-based learning environment, where the children feel able to take risks with their learning, learn at their own

pace, pursues individual interests and develop a high level of self-esteem and a lifelong love of learning;

- a 'thinking skills' toolbox for every child, with the ideas, language and resources that they will need to be able to thrive throughout the year.

Typically, a 'learning to learn' week would include:

- Whole-class agreements on what values go to make a learning environment where all children can thrive.
  - Try setting up with your class a set of values, rather than a set of rules: values are more powerful than rules, as they enable you to develop desired characteristics in the way the children 'are', rather than in how you may want them to 'behave'. For example, through being 'respectful', the children are encouraged to respect each other and school property, but also, very importantly, each other's views. Similarly, if one of your class values is being 'ambitious', then all children will be encouraged to try tasks to their best of their ability and to challenge themselves, as this is an accepted culture in your class (Hertford Infant and Nursery School Ofsted Report, 2012).

- Models of learning and how these can help with removing the fear of 'not knowing' or 'getting things wrong'.
  - Try asking the children to describe to you how they view themselves as learners – for example, they may say that, for them, it's like driving on a motorway, sometimes they are in the slow lane, sometimes in the middle lane and sometimes they are cruising in the fast lane. Each child's model of learning can then be displayed in your classroom and referred to throughout the year – a great way to make children realise that learning can be difficult at times, but it is only when it is difficult that they are actually learning, i.e. if they already know it, they are not learning. This can be referred to as the 'joy of not knowing' (Staricoff, 2012).

- The attributes and behaviours that contribute to becoming a successful lifelong learner.
  - Try researching the attributes that contribute to successful lifelong learners and adapting these to your age group – linking each of the attributes to an animal enables the children to empathise with a certain characteristic that they associate with the animal, and they are thus motivated to develop this characteristic themselves – for example, a snail perseveres, and thus children learn to be like a snail and not give up (Staricoff, 2006, Chapter 7).

- The initiatives that enable children to structure their thinking and develop their curiosity for learning and their higher-order thinking skills.
  - Try starting each day with an open-ended challenge; this is a fabulous way to enthuse all children with a love of learning, as they can all access each challenge, and the children don't perceive it as formal learning. As these are all open-ended, they are fantastic vehicles for gifted and talented children to engage in and keep pursuing in their own time, for example, 'the answer is 5; what is the question?' can lead to what is 1 + 4, how many days in a week not counting the weekend, what is the square root of 25 – these starters have enormous scope for open-ended thinking and enabling the gifted and talented children to thrive as individual and creative thinkers (Staricoff and Rees, 2005).

- The initiatives that enable practitioners to deliver the curriculum in an open-ended way, so that all children can contribute to the learning, while, at the same time, giving the gifted and talented children opportunities to take the concepts being discussed into a 'deeper' or 'broader' context.

- Try turning your learning objective from a statement of what you intend to teach to a question of what you intend the class to learn – this is very powerful, as it immediately encourages discussion in the classroom (community of enquiry) and allows you, very naturally, to derive the success criteria for the task, alongside the children, as the class begins to try to answer the question; for example, if you change the learning objective from 'To learn the properties of 2D shapes' to 'Can we investigate the properties of 2D shapes?' or even 'Do 2D shapes exist?', you will reinforce the community of enquiry and the philosophical approach to the curriculum that can have such an impact on the way the children perceive and enjoy their learning (Staricoff, 2007).

Once the 'learning to learn' week has been established, gifted children will be challenged, both by the way in which they are required to operate in class, and by the tasks they are given to do. These two elements support each other. In designing tasks for gifted and talented children, it is useful to consider what we know about their learning (Shore, 2000: 173).

- Gifted pupils do not seem to use strategies that others never use.
- Gifted pupils differ from others in the creativity and extent to which they draw upon a repertoire of intellectual skills that are, nonetheless, available to others.
- They demonstrate expert performance by using metacognition, strategy flexibility, strategy planning, hypothesis, preference for complexity and extensive webbing of knowledge about both facts and processes.
- They think like experts, even though they may lack some of the skills of experts.

So there is nothing that is unique to the gifted children in your class. The above do, however, give some good clues on designing tasks to challenge the gifted. If gifted children think like experts, then consider what experts in the subject consider to be important and try to include it. If gifted children are original and creative in their solutions to problems, give them tasks that encourage this, and don't be surprised if they fail to give you the text-book answer. If they see learning as a complex, interwoven web, then help them to make those connections and allow them to complexify the original task, to make it more interesting and demanding. Try differentiation by self, i.e. they suggest ways in which the core task set for the whole class could be made more demanding. Don't forget they are the ones with the brains; don't do everything for them.

TASKS TO HELP CHILDREN ENGAGE IN ADVANCED THINKING

It is helpful to consider what, in addition to the acquisition of the knowledge, skills and concepts that we hope all children will achieve, we should expect of gifted children. The following are behaviours you should seek to engender:

- greater reflection;
- exploration of a variety of viewpoints;
- consideration of difficult questions;
- formulation of individual opinions;
- problem-solving and enquiry;
- connections between past and present learning;
- regular use of higher-order thinking (analysis, synthesis and evaluation);
- independent thinking and learning.

How might you do this? A good way is by designing enquiry-based tasks:

- Think independently – what do you think was the reason?
- Reflect – why do you think that happened?

- Recognise connections in learning – can you think of another time when that happened? Or – compare these two accounts.
- Explore ideas and choose a 'best' solution – which of these would be the most appropriate for . . .?
- Justify ideas – which of the following would be best? Give reasons for your choice.
- Explain ideas using appropriate technical language – yes that's right, that is called a . . .
- Solve problems and recognise the strategy used – what made that successful?
- Think about real problems – how could we stop mud getting on the classroom carpet?
- Encourage to use a wide vocabulary – can you find a better word for . . .?
- Order and marshall ideas – tell me/draw/write the different steps you took to do that experiment.
- Explore conflicting ideas – was Robin Hood a good man?

This enquiry-based approach helps gifted children to develop the higher-level thinking skills that will enable them to perform at an advanced level. There are a variety of hierarchies of thinking skills in the education literature, but all share a view that the higher-order thinking involves concepts such as comparison, analysis, reworking of ideas (synthesis), invention and evaluation of worth/value. Unit 7.4 in this book, by Robert Fisher, looks in more detail at general use of thinking skills. When creating challenge for the gifted, simply focus on the top-level skills.

These kinds of enquiry-based task are a good way to create challenge for the gifted, but they do not always have to be given to a specific group of children. Sometimes, the task may require advanced reading or mathematical skills and, therefore, can only be offered to a specific group, but often enquiry tasks can be designed with challenge for the gifted in mind, but then made available to all. The gifted will simply offer better, more sophisticated and more original solutions. This brings us back to identification. If you offer these types of task to all children, then the outcomes may surprise you. You may 'talent spot' potentially gifted children you had not recognised before.

BREADTH, DEPTH AND PACE

There are three ways in which you plan for gifted children to experience learning outside that made available to all. You can add breadth, depth or pace to the normal curriculum offer.

Breadth (sometimes called enrichment) can be defined as adding additional material at broadly the same cognitive level; for example, studying more about a particular period of history, or reading more widely around the core subject. It does not require the acquisition of new skills, but may emphasise the opportunity to use and apply existing ones. Breadth can also include learning a completely new subject, in addition to those studied by others. An example here might be a Key Stage 2 after-school Latin club. Breadth is useful, because using and applying learned skills are good ways to consolidate them and also create a context for devising original ideas. Introducing children to new areas can also help children discover their abilities by widening their horizons, and, as this is a key role for primary schools, adding breadth to the curriculum for all children (as well as those identified as gifted) should be seen as a key strategy in challenging the gifted and talented.

In adding breadth to the curriculum, the greatest risk is inevitably overload. If you want your gifted children to experience additional learning, then also consider what you could excuse them from. Gifted children are no more industrious than others and don't like having extra work.

Depth (sometimes called extension) refers to an increase in cognitive level achieved by taking the existing focus of work and going into greater depth. It usually involves learning new material, including new skills and concepts. Good classroom provision should include a mix of breadth, depth and pace, but perhaps depth is the most important. It is about learning how to think intellectually. There are many ways to achieve depth, but here is an example you might like to try. Take a solvable puzzle, e.g. a crossword or a word search, and first ask all the class to solve it and then ask the gifted children to create one of their own. In order to create a puzzle, you need to consider how the puzzle works, and this requires you to deconstruct it. Talk about how it functions and why it works. Can they make one? Can they make one that is even better than the one they solved? Why is it better? This takes you into much deeper territory. Equally, you might add depth by selecting an area that experts value but that does not appear in the primary curriculum. Historiography is a good example here. If you have very able children in Key Stage 2 looking at the Victorians, then you might take a Victorian (maybe from your local area) who was considered a hero in his or her time and is now less valued (or vice versa), and consider how the society in which we live shapes our view of history. Use some first-hand resources such as newspaper articles. These are very easy to access on the Internet.

A practical way to increase depth is by bringing experts into the classroom, using people from the wider community, from museums or science centres, using authors or academics, using parents or local experts. These events are great for all children, but think carefully about whether a proportion of the time could be spent with a smaller group, developing high-level skills or exploring more advanced concepts.

Pace is about moving through the existing curriculum faster than other children and is sometimes called acceleration. (Acceleration should not be confused with accelerated learning, which is something quite different.) In practice, whatever strategies you adopt will involve the gifted children moving ahead of their peers in the formal curriculum, and this is entirely appropriate. In general planning, you should always look at the more advanced levels in the National Curriculum as a key way of creating challenge for the gifted and talented. The National Curriculum is a spiral curriculum, and so concepts recur, and skills are revisited. When planning a lesson, you should consider what the next learning objective in this area would be, and if it would be suitable to include it in this lesson for some children.

The best provision for gifted children is through a mix of depth, breadth and pace. When planning the scheme of work, it is usually easy to see which might work best, but ensure that you do not rely too heavily on any single one.

Task 7.5.3 Breadth, depth and pace (B-D-P)

Create three tasks for use in your classroom. Task 1 must add breadth, task 2 depth, and task 3 pace.

Implement them and then reflect on the following with your tutor:

- why you chose them;
- how you created them;
- who in your class experienced them and why;
- how they worked in practice;
- what you have learned from the process.

There is no single way to create challenge for your gifted and talented children, but make sure you aim high and use resources that will help you help to create well-informed, thinking children. The following ideas may get you started.

1   Investigate or problem-solve using a 'plan/do/review' approach.
2   Work from difficult texts or intensively on one text.
3   Use a variety of texts/pictures/artefacts, to compare and contrast.
4   Record in an unusual way. Use fewer words rather than more.
5   Role-play. Think from someone else's point of view.
6   Provide choice in how children handle the content.
8   Create tasks that require decision-making.
9   Create tasks with no single correct answer.
10 Provide the answer; they set the questions.
11 Create an element of speed; set journalistic deadlines.
12 Introduce technical language. Speak and think like an expert.

SUMMARY

Meeting the needs of gifted and talented children is part of meeting the needs of all. By focusing on high expectations and talent spotting, you may well find more gifted children than you expect and, at the same time, create a learning environment that is challenging and fun for all. The aim for a primary school is to ensure that its gifted and talented children reach secondary school with a desire to learn and the skills to do so, so that they can go on to achieve highly.

 # ANNOTATED FURTHER READING

Eyre, D. (1997) *Able Children in Ordinary Schools*, London: David Fulton.
> This book provides practical strategies for both senior managers and classroom teachers to meet the needs of gifted and talented children. It explores the issues and problems surrounding good provision and suggests why schools have found this area so difficult.

Rockett, M. and Percival, S. (2002) *Thinking for Learning*, London: Continuum.
> This book is very useful in that it amalgamates the worlds of thinking skills and accelerated learning and provides practitioners with practical ideas for the classroom.

Staricoff, M. and Rees, A. (2005) *Start Thinking*, Birmingham: Imaginative Minds Publishers.
> This book provides practitioners with easy-to-implement resources that will stimulate and inspire all children through challenge in the classroom. The open-ended nature of these challenges means that gifted and talented children are able to derive great satisfaction from tackling each one.

 # FURTHER READING TO SUPPORT M-LEVEL STUDY

Coates, D. (2009) Developing challenging science activities for gifted pupils through action research. *Education 3–13*, 37, 3, 259–68.
> This article focuses on a methodology by which teachers can change/develop their ability to create classroom challenge.

Dimitriadis, C. (2012) Provision for mathematically gifted children in primary schools: an investigation of four different methods of provision. *Educational Review*, 64, 2, 241-60.
    This article takes a practical look at ideas for primary provision.

 ## RELEVANT WEBSITES

London Gifted & Talented: www.londongt.org
    This is an excellent website, specialising in classroom challenge, critical thinking, personalisation, quality-first teaching, independent learning, assessment for learning, urban education, disadvantaged learners and collaborative e-learning.

 ## REFERENCES

Department for Education and Skills (DfES) (2003) *Excellence and Enjoyment*, London: DfES.

Chambers, A. (1993) *Tell Me*, Stroud: Thimble Press.

Eyre, D., Coates, D., Fitzpatrick, M., Higgins, C., McClure, L., Wilson, H. and Chamberlin, R. (2002) *Effective Teaching of Able Pupils in the Primary Classroom*, Birmingham: National Primary Trust.

Hertford Infant and Nursery School Ofsted Report (2012) Available at: www.ofsted.gov.uk/inspection-reports/find-inspection-report/provider/ELS/114368 (accessed 14 January 2014).

Howe, M. (1995) What can we learn from the lives of geniuses? In J. Freeman (ed.) *Actualizing Talent*, London: Cassell.

National Strategies (2009) The Classroom Quality Standards for Gifted and Talented Education: a subject focus, Ref: 00256-2009LEF-EN.

Shore, B.M. (2000) Metacognition and flexibility: qualitative differences in how gifted children think. In R.C. Friedman and B.M. Shore (eds) *Talents Unfolding: Cognition and Development*, Washington, DC: American Psychological Association.

Staricoff, M. (2005) G&T Provision through a Thinking Skills Approach, *NACE Newsletter*, 66, 13-16.

Staricoff, M. (2006) Learning power in practice. In *Powerful Learning in the Primary Classroom*, Chapter 7, London: Sage.

Staricoff, M. (2007) Here comes philosophy man; philosophising the primary school curriculum, *Gifted Education International*, 22, 2/3, 182-91.

Staricoff, M. (2012) *Hertford Infant and Nursery School Prospectus 2010-2011*. Available at: www.thelifecloud.net/schools/HertfordInfant (accessed 14 January 2014).

Staricoff, M. and Rees, A. (2005) *Start Thinking*, Birmingham: Imaginative Minds Publishers.

Westbury Park Primary School (2003) Case Study One, Primary Leadership Paper, 10, 18-20.

Wragg, E.C. and Brown, G. (1993) *Questioning*, London: Routledge.

UNPACKING ICT

Peter Twining

INTRODUCTION

Digital technology has changed many aspects of our lives, and there has been considerable talk about the potential of ICT to transform education. This has been accompanied by substantial financial investment in hardware and software in schools. For example, a survey of 1,317 primary and secondary schools estimated that maintained schools in the UK had ICT budgets totalling approximately £547.4 million in 2013-14 (BESA 2012). Although funding for professional development has been low compared with the overall ICT spend, there has been dedicated government funding for ICT CPD. For example, between 2000 and 2003, every teacher in the UK was provided with ICT training funded by the New Opportunities Fund, at a total cost of £230 million, and, between 2009 and 2013, successive English governments devoted £9.4 million to funding Vital (www.vital.ac.uk) to support teachers in making even better use of digital technology.

Despite the claimed potential of, and massive investment in, ICT in education, it seems to have made little impact in schools. Trend *et al.* (1999) referred to this as a 'reality rhetoric gap'. In 2012, a study commissioned by Nesta 'to analyse the use of technologies for learning around the world and draw out lessons for innovation in the UK education systems' (Luckin *et al.* 2012: 6) found that 'evidence of digital technologies producing real transformation in learning and teaching remains elusive' (Luckin *et al.* 2012: 8). Indeed, in January 2012, the English Minister of Education declared that 'ICT in schools is a mess' (Gove 2012).

In this unit, we will unpack what we mean by ICT before going on to explore three different facets of its use in schools: digital technology and its organisation in schools; the subject that used to be

OBJECTIVES

By the end of this unit, you should have begun to:

- clarify your use of terminology related to digital technologies in education;
- understand some ways in which learning to program can support the development of children's problem-solving skills;
- recognise ways in which digital technology changes subject knowledge, and thus the curriculum;
- be aware of ways in which digital technology provides additional approaches to teaching, and thus changes pedagogy;
- think about the potential impacts of digital technology on your practice.

called ICT but has been renamed Computing; and the cross-curricula use of digital technology. By providing you with some questions to focus your own thinking about digital technologies in education, and practical examples to exemplify the potential and develop your expertise, we hope to take a small step to enhancing the impact of digital technology on your teaching and your pupils' learning.

DEFINING ICT

One of the reasons that ICT has not had the scale of impact that people have claimed it will have is confusion about why we are using ICT in education, and what impacts we want it to have.

Task 7.6.1 Why should we use ICT in education?

A project called Discussing ICT, Targets and Aspirations for Education, or dICTatEd for short, identified nineteen different rationales for using ICT in education (dICTatEd 2002).

- Read the list of rationales in Figure 7.6.1.
- Rank the rationales and list the three rationales that you think are first, second, and third most important.
- Write brief notes explaining and justifying your choice.

---

1. In order to learn IT skills
2. As a tool to achieve traditional teaching and learning goals across the curriculum
3. In order to extend and enrich learning across the curriculum
4. In order to motivate learners
5. As a catalyst for educational change
6. Because of the impact of ICT on the nature of knowledge
7. In order to fundamentally change teaching and learning
8. As a tool to support learners in thinking about their own learning
9. In order to provide access to the curriculum for those who might otherwise be excluded from it
10. In order to increase productivity in education
11. In order to reduce the cost of education
12. In order to make education more efficient
13. As a substitute for teachers
14. In order to reward learners
15. As preparation for living in a society that is permeated with technology
16. As preparation for work (employment)
17. In order to support and stimulate the country's economic development
18. In order to impress stakeholders (e.g. inspectors, funders, prospective parents/students)
19. In order to reduce inequalities between students/pupils with differential access to ICT outside formal education

---

FIGURE 7.6.1 Rationales for using ICT in education
Source: dICTatEd (2002)

Your response to Task 7.6.1 will reflect your vision of education and, hence, the sorts of impact that you believe that ICT should have. The Educational Innovation Framework (EdIF) (Twining 2012a, 2012b) identifies that an innovation, such as the use of ICT, can impact on practice in qualitatively different ways, by:

- **supporting** existing practice, leaving both the curriculum and pedagogy fundamentally unchanged, but increasing efficiency or effectiveness;
- **extending** practice, by changing curriculum and/or pedagogy, but in ways that could have been achieved without using the innovation (in our case, without using digital technology);
- **transforming** practice, by changing curriculum and/or pedagogy, but in ways that could only realistically have been achieved with the innovation (in our case, digital technology).

Figure 7.6.2 provides a diagrammatic representation of the impact dimension of the EdIF, where the innovation is the use of digital technology.

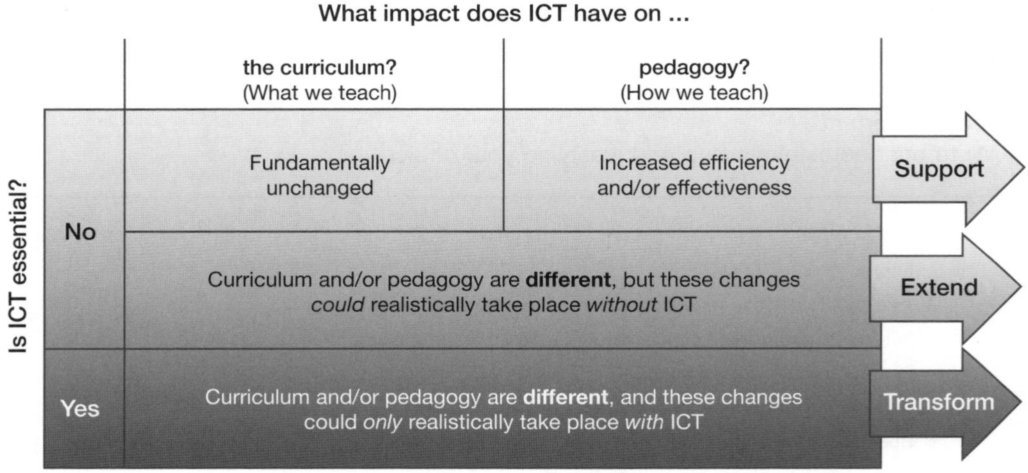

FIGURE 7.6.2 Summary of the categories of impact that use of ICT might have

Source: adapted from Twining (2012a)

As Figure 7.6.2 illustrates, the Impact dimension of the EdIF is based on three questions that it is useful to consider when thinking about the use of digital technology in your teaching:

- What impact does digital technology have on the curriculum (what we teach)?
- What impact does digital technology have on pedagogy (how we teach)?
- Is digital technology essential in order to achieve these impacts, or could they have been achieved in some other way?

The last question is particularly important, as it gets you to think about the extent to which the use of digital technology is more appropriate than some other approach.

The confusion about why we want to use ICT in education is compounded by confusion about what people mean when they use the term ICT. It is commonly used to mean:

- the equipment itself, including hardware, software, networks etc., which I will refer to as digital technology;

Task 7.6.2 Support, Extend or Transform?

Think of one or two examples of ICT being used that supports, extends or transforms practice in schools. Note your examples in the table below.

	Example 1	Example 2
Support		
Extend		
Transform		

If you had to choose 'the best' two ways of using ICT from your examples, which two would you choose, and why? Note down your answers.

- the subject traditionally called ICT, which was renamed Computing in the English National Curriculum, where the focus is on learning about the technology and its underpinnings;
- the use of digital technology across the curriculum (in subjects other than Computing), which I will refer to as ICT from now on.

In the remainder of this unit, we explore each of these three areas in a little more detail.

THINKING ABOUT THE EQUIPMENT (DIGITAL TECHNOLOGY)

One of the major challenges for schools is ensuring that all their pupils have appropriate and equitable access to digital technology in school. Traditionally, schools have provided all of the technology that pupils use in their lessons. This might be organised in computer labs, as a single machine or clusters of machines in classrooms or shared areas, or sets of laptops that could be borrowed for use by groups of children (from individuals to whole classes). A small percentage of schools have moved towards ensuring that every pupil in a class, year group or across the school has their own mobile device. More recently, two developments have driven schools to consider a range of alternative models of provision. First, funding all of the technology that pupils need to have access to in the twenty-first century has become increasingly difficult for schools. Second, it seems clear that many pupils have ever-greater access to increasingly powerful mobile technology at home, and often in their pockets. This is leading many schools to consider hybrid models of provision of digital technology, with the pupils being allowed to bring in their own mobile devices, and the school providing both the technical infrastructure to allow those devices to connect to the Internet and provision for those pupils who are unable to supply their own equipment. Table 7.6.1 summarises the main models of provision of digital technology in schools. In practice most schools use a mix of two or more of these main models.

In Wales . . .

Hwb (http://hwb.wales.gov.uk), Wales' bilingual virtual learning environment is a space for teachers and educators to share and access a range of digital tools and resources that will support the learning of all 3–19-year-olds in Wales, with the opportunity to create and share their own resources and work collaboratively.

Source: Hwb – Towards a Digital Future, http://wales.gov.uk/topics/educationandskills/schoolshome/raisingstandards/hwb/?lang=en (December 2012)

TABLE 7.6.1 The main models of digital technology provision in schools

Model	Description	Who pays
Desktop	Computer lab, individual or clusters of machines in classrooms or shared areas	The school
Mobile loan	Sets of mobiles (e.g. laptops, tablets, iPods) lent out for short periods of time	The school
1:1 computing	Every pupil has a mobile device; all devices are the same	May be funded by the school, a parental lease scheme or bought outright by parents
Bring your own device (BYOD)	Pupils can bring in their own mobile devices and can connect to the school WiFi to access the Internet and/or school network; the school controls which devices can be connected and what they can access – usually by requiring the MAC address for the device to be pre-registered and then using some management software to restrict and monitor access	The home provides mobile devices for (most) pupils; the school provides the network infrastructure and provides mobile devices for pupils who do not have home provision
Bring your own technology (BYOT)	Pupils can bring in their own mobile devices and connect to the school WiFi to access the Internet; devices do *not* have to be pre-registered – any Internet-enabled device will be able to connect	The home provides mobile devices for (most) pupils; the school provides the WiFi and provides mobile devices for pupils who do not have home provision

There is growing evidence that mobile devices have many advantages over computer labs or even classroom-based desktop machines. For example, an early study of the use of tablet PCs in UK schools concluded that, 'Tablet PCs have the potential to enhance learning and this goes beyond what is possible with other technologies', so long as there is 'a robust ICT infrastructure, including wireless networking' (Twining *et al.* 2005: 22). Technology, of course, has moved on since then. A more recent study of tablets in Scotland (not to be confused with tablet PCs) found that the use of tablets, such as the iPad, had many positive impacts on teachers, pupils, parental engagement and the achievement of curriculum goals (Burden *et al.* 2012). This study also concluded that the single most important factor determining the success of the use of tablets was personal 'ownership', in the sense of each member of staff and pupil having a dedicated device, which they could use at home as well as in school. For further information on the use of mobile devices in school, including practical advice on digital technology strategies, see http://edfutures.net.

Task 7.6.3 Home provision of Internet-enabled technology

Create a survey that you can use to find out about your pupils' home access to the Internet and Internet-enabled mobile devices. For the mobile devices, include questions about whether they have sole or shared use of the device, and whether or not they would be allowed, able and willing to bring the device(s) into school. Once you have designed your survey, get the head teacher's permission to use it, before sending it home with your pupils, and ask their parents to help them fill it in. Then collect in all the responses and analyse the data.

To simplify this whole process, you could use the Your Own Technology Survey (YOTS). Schools can register with YOTS (free of charge) and are then provided with a dedicated web link to a questionnaire that they can get their pupils (with their parents/guardians) to complete. The school can then download reports on their pupils' (anonymous) data. See www.yots.org.uk for more details.

Once you have collected your data, answer the following questions:

1 What proportion of my pupils has access to the Internet at home?
2 What proportion of my pupils has sole use of an Internet-enabled mobile device at home?
3 What proportion of my pupils would be allowed, able and willing to bring an Internet-enabled mobile device in to school?

Then think about the implications of your answers to questions such as:

4 Will I be disadvantaging some of my pupils if I set homework that requires Internet access? If so, what can I do to overcome that problem?
5 Could I supplement the digital technology that is available to my class in school by allowing pupils to bring in their own mobile devices? If I were going to do that, what are the other issues that I would need to consider?

Many schools are currently exploring one-to-one computing models and, increasingly, BYOD and BYOT. Underpinning bring-your-own models of provision is an assumption that sufficient numbers of pupils will have access to a suitable mobile device and will be allowed, able and willing to bring that device into school on a regular basis. The next activity gives you a chance to explore your pupils' access to Internet-enabled mobile devices and the extent to which they could, in reality, use those in school, if the school permitted them to.

TEACHING COMPUTING

Digital technology has permeated all of our lives. If our role as educators is to prepare pupils to become happy and effective members of society, then we need to educate them about digital technology. This has three elements:

* **Computer science** – which at its core is about being able to design, create and control computerised systems.
* **Information technology** – which is about being able to decide what digital technologies to deploy in different contexts to achieve specific goals.

- **Digital literacy** – which encompasses being well-informed and competent users of digital technologies to: find, evaluate and manipulate information; represent ideas in creative and multimodal ways; and interact and communicate safely. This includes understanding how digital technologies impact on you as an individual and on societies and cultures.

In August 2011, Eric Schmidt, chairman of Google, condemned the British education system and said Britain was, 'throwing away your great computer heritage . . . I was flabbergasted to learn that today computer science isn't even taught as standard in UK schools' (Robinson 2011). This fed into a heated debate that was taking place at the time about the state of computing in schools and the need to reintroduce 'rigorous computer science' into school curricula, with an emphasis on computer programming.

Computer programming has a long tradition in schools, going back to the early 1980s and the work of Seymour Papert, the father of Logo. Central to Papert's argument about the importance of Logo was its power to enable pupils to make their thinking visible and thus support them in reflecting upon that thinking, identifying errors and finding ways to correct them (Papert 1980, 1993, 1994). Programming in Logo also encapsulated key elements of what might rather grandiosely be called 'computational thinking'. These include:

- identifying a problem you are trying to solve (e.g. I am at A and want to get to B);
- being clear about your starting position (Where is A in relation to B?);
- being clear how you will know if you have solved your problem (How will I know when I have got to B?);
- if you cannot solve your problem in one step, then breaking it down into a series of sub-problems, each of which you can solve (I can't go directly from A to B because that obstacle is in the way, so I will go from A to C and then from C to B).

You will immediately have recognised these as basic problem-solving strategies, of the sort that we regularly try to help our pupils develop. Programming is particularly good at supporting people in learning to problem-solve, because of the way in which it:

- forces you to be explicit and precise;
- encourages you to break down problems into sub-problems;
- gives you very clear feedback on whether or not your proposed solution (the program) works;
- allows you to correct your mistakes and try again.

In the next activity, you are going to try out a programming activity without a computer!

Task 7.6.4 attempts to mimic programming a computer. If you were programming a real computer using a language such as Logo or Scratch, then it would be easier to record the program and correct (or debug) it.

Scratch is a visual programming language that is free to download and supported by a large community of educators. Follow these links to find out more:

- http://scratch.mit.edu/ – the home of Scratch, where you can download the software, explore other people's programs (Projects) and find lots of support materials;
- www.vital.ac.uk/content/programming-scratch-0 – a set of nine video tutorials for teachers in KS2 and early KS3 on starting to use Scratch.

For further information about computing, join Computing at School (www.computingatschool.org.uk) or Naace (www.naace.co.uk).

Task 7.6.4 Programming without a computer

For this activity, you should work in groups of either two or four. Each group should have two teams, let's call them A and B, with one or two people in each team.

You need the following resources:

- four identical sets of Lego bricks (two sets for each team);
- a small screen (e.g. a folder or large book) set up between the two teams;
- paper and writing implements for each team.

The teams then follow these instructions:

- Each team builds 'a model' out of their first set of bricks (Set 1), making sure that the other team cannot see what they have built.
- Once your team has built its model, write down instructions explaining *exactly* what you did to create it (no pictures are allowed).
- When both teams have finished, they each give the other team their instructions and the other set of bricks (Set 2) – being careful *not* to let them see the original model they have made.
- Each team then tries to follow the other team's instructions.
- When both teams have finished following the other team's instructions, they take turns to compare their models. For example, Team A compares its original model with Team B's copy of the model – if they are not identical, then they try to work out where the instructions went wrong, and correct them. They then swap and compare Team B's original model with Team A's copy.

Think of ways in which you could adapt (differentiate) this activity to use with children who have different levels of competence.

Although learning about Computing is important, it is only a small fraction of the challenge for you as a teacher. You will spend a relatively short amount of time teaching Computing compared with all the other subjects.

USING DIGITAL TECHNOLOGY ACROSS THE CURRICULUM (ICT)

In the world outside school, digital technology has impacted on almost every discipline. Whether you are a sports person, a historian, geographer, journalist, engineer or chemist, the nature of what you do and how you do it has been changed by digital technology. For example, the sorts of question that historians can ask and the ways in which they can attempt to answer them are different because of the power of digital technology to organise and interrogate large data sets (such as census data).

It seems reasonable to assume that the subjects we teach in school should bear some relationship to their corresponding disciplines outside school, and, thus, if digital technology has changed the discipline, then it should also *change the curriculum* for that subject. This might be referred to as 'embedded technology'.

In Northern Ireland . . .

The Northern Ireland Curriculum states,

> ICT across the curriculum has the potential to transform and enrich pupils' learning experiences and environments. It can empower pupils, develop self-esteem and promote positive attitudes to learning. The creative use of ICT also has the potential to improve pupils' thinking skills, providing them with opportunities to become independent, self-motivated and flexible learners.

Source: www.nicurriculum.org.uk/key_stages_1_and_2/skills_and_capabilities/uict/what_is_UICT/using_ict.asp#top, accessed 23 September 2013

Task 7.6.5 Thinking about embedded technology

Developing children's literacy is one of the most important aspects of your role as a primary school teacher.

- Write down what you think it means to be literate today.
- If you had been answering that question 100 years ago, how would your response have been different?
- Do you think that digital technologies change the relative importance of traditional literacy skills, such as reading and writing (including handwriting), and, hence, change what you should teach your pupils? Write notes to explain and justify your answers.

Digital technology also provides us with additional strategies for teaching: it *extends pedagogy*. This might be referred to as Technology Enhanced Learning (TEL). For example, an interactive whiteboard *can* enable us to move from a teacher-dominated form of whole-class teaching to one that is much more interactive and dynamic (though, in practice, this is often not the way in which interactive whiteboards have been used by teachers). Perhaps a better example is the way in which digital technology provides opportunities for pupils to:

- take greater control of, and responsibility for, finding information (via the Internet);
- present information in new ways, including through multi- and hyper-media;
- share their work with real audiences, beyond the classroom.

Task 7.6.6 Thinking about TEL

On the facing page is a schematic diagram showing the layout of 'furniture' in four classrooms. Below are descriptions of the digital technology provision in each of those classrooms.

A The 'board' is an interactive whiteboard connected to a laptop by a cable. There are no other computer devices.

B   The 'board' is a whiteboard (not interactive), with a data projector that is connected wirelessly to a tablet. There are no other computer devices.

C   The 'board' is a large monitor/TV that can connect wirelessly to any mobile device. The teacher and every pupil have their own mobile device.

D   The 'board' is a large monitor/TV. The table surfaces are large touchscreen computer displays (in effect, each table is one shared computer). The teacher can replicate what is displayed on any of the tables on the 'board'. She can also transfer whatever is on one table/computer to any or all of the other ones.

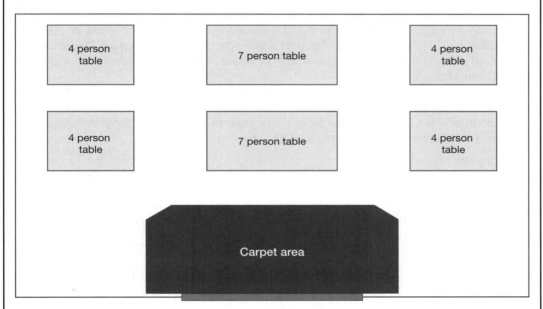

The 'board'

For each class configuration, jot down some ideas about what you think the most effective ways would be to teach in that classroom.

Which of these classrooms would you feel most comfortable teaching in? Why?

There are lots of possible ways in which you might teach effectively in each of the configurations described in the last task. What works will depend upon a range of factors, including the curriculum objectives, other educational goals, your expertise and the pupils who are being taught. Technology should never determine your pedagogy, and you should always think about whether there might be other, better ways of achieving your goals - taking us back to the third question that the EdIF Impact dimension asks you to consider.

You may have decided that all three activities were effective, or that, for your particular children, some of them would not be appropriate. This reflects the complexity of supporting learning and is why teaching requires you to make professional judgements based on your understandings of what education is for, how children learn and the pedagogical strategies that are available to you.

Task 7.6.7 Is there a better way?

Think about each of the following activities or scenarios. For each, note down whether you think its impact falls into the Support, Extend or Transform category, and the extent to which you think it might be an effective pedagogical approach for the age group that you are hoping to teach. Explain and justify your answers.

- **Sugar-coated learning** – Go to BBC Bitesize (www.bbc.co.uk/bitesize/) and try out one or two activities that are targeted at the pupils that you will be teaching.
- **Explaining my work** – Pupils use a tool such as ScreenChomp to record a mini lesson on how to solve a maths problem and then share that with their friends or pupils in another class. (If you are unfamiliar with ScreenChomp, then search for ScreenChomp in YouTube and watch one of the explanatory videos, e.g. www.youtube.com/watch?v=5__7UMtHyS8).
- **Blogging** – Pupils share their work with each other and with their parents by posting to their class blog. (If you are unfamiliar with blogging in primary schools, then watch a video in which a Year 1 teacher talks about how he uses a class blog with his pupils: www.youtube.com/watch?v=6tm_1UoQGvE.)

	Sugar-coated learning	Explaining my work	Blogging
Impact (Support, Extend, Transform)			
Effective? (yes/no)			
Explanation			

SUMMARY

This unit has just touched the surface of some of the issues you need to think about in relation to digital technology, Computing and ICT in education.

Your pupils will inevitably be immersed in a world in which digital technology impacts on many aspects of their lives. You will need to be able to help them become effective users of technology who understand the ways in which it impacts on them and the wider society in which they live. As a competent teacher, you also need to understand how digital technology changes the curriculum and should be aware of the full range of teaching strategies that are available to you. Most importantly, you need to be able to make professional judgements about which pedagogical strategies are the most appropriate in different contexts. Thinking about the three questions that the EdIF highlights, and in particular the extent to which using digital technology is the optimal way to achieve your educational goals, will help you to do this. Remember to stay focused on your educational goals and the needs of your particular pupils, and avoid being drawn into using technology for its own sake.

ANNOTATED FURTHER READING

Shaffer, D.W. (2006) *How Computer Games Help Children Learn*. New York: Palgrave Macmillan.
> A thought-provoking book that not only identifies how computer games can enhance learning, but, in so doing, fundamentally challenges how we think about education.

Voogt, J. and Knezek, G. (2008) *International Handbook of Information Technology in Primary and Secondary Education*. London: Springer.
> This two-volume heavyweight contains a huge wealth of information about educational technology, from a wide range of international perspectives.

Walsh, M. (2010) Multimodal literacy: What does it mean for classroom practice? *Australian Journal of Language and Literacy*, Vol. 33, No. 3, pp.211-39.
> This article explores the impact of digital technology on language and literacy practices in primary classrooms. The context for the discussion is the Australian education system, which is moving towards having a national curriculum.

FURTHER READING TO SUPPORT M-LEVEL STUDY

Livingstone, S. (2012) Critical reflections on the benefits of ICT in education. *Oxford Review of Education*, Vol. 38, No.1, pp.9-24.
> This article explores two possible explanations for why schools have been slow to embed digital technology into teaching: the lack of convincing evidence that it improves learning, and the tension about whether digital technology should be supporting or transforming traditional pedagogy.

McDougall, A., with Murnane, J., Jones, A. and Reynolds, N. (eds) (2010) *Researching IT in Education: Theory, Practice and Future Directions*. New York: Routledge.
> Although this book is aimed at those who want to conduct research on ICT in education, it also provides valuable insights for those who want to be able to make sense of the published research literature in the field.

RELEVANT WEBSITES

EdFutures.net: http://edfutures.net
> This wiki provides a wealth of information about the use of digital technologies in education, including information about 1:1 computing, BYOD, BYOT and other issues related to the provision of digital technology in schools.

Computing At School (CAS): www.computingatschool.org.uk
> This is an invaluable source of information and support for teachers interested in teaching computer science.

The ICT Association (Naace): www.naace.co.uk
> Naace is a membership organisation for all those with an interested in the use of digital technology in schools – spanning ICT, embedded technology and TEL.

 # REFERENCES

BESA (2012) *Information and Communication Technology in UK State Schools: Full Report – Volume II Provision and Spending*. London: BESA.

Burden, K., Hopkins, P., Male, T., Martin, S. and Trala, C. (2012) iPad Scotland Evaluation. Hull: University of Hull. Available at: http://is.gd/6BwPPv (accessed 23 November 2012; registration required).

dICTatEd (2002) Discussing ICT, aspirations & targets for education. Available at: http://med8.open.ac.uk/dictated/rationales.php (accessed 4 December 2012).

Gove, M. (2012) Speech at BETT Show 2012. London: DfE. Available at: http://is.gd/fX4EIN (accessed 23 November 2012).

Luckin, R., Bligh, B., Manches, A., Ainsworth, S., Crook, C. and Noss, R. (2012) Decoding learning: the proof, promise and potential of digital education. London: Nesta. Available at: www.nesta.org.uk/library/documents/DecodingLearningReport_v12.pdf (accessed 23 November 2012).

Papert, S. (1980) *Mindstorms: Children, Computers and Powerful Ideas*. Brighton: The Harvester Press.

Papert, S. (1993) *Mindstorms: Children, Computers and Powerful Ideas*, 2nd edn. London: Harvester Wheatsheaf.

Papert, S. (1994) *The Children's Machine: Rethinking Schools in the Age of the Computer*. London: Harvester Wheatsheaf.

Robinson, J. (2011) Eric Schmidt, chairman of Google, condemns British education system. *The Guardian*, 26 August. Available at: http://is.gd/OQMXV0 (accessed 21 November 2012).

Trend, R., Davis, N. and Loveless, A. (1999) *Information and Communications Technology*. London: Letts Educational.

Twining, P. (2012a) What role should ICT play in compulsory education in the 21st Century? *BETT*, 11 January, London.

Twining, P. (2012b) The Education Innovation Framework. EdFutures.net. Available at: http://edfutures.net/index.php?title=EdIF (accessed 11 December 2012).

Twining, P., Evans, D., Ralston, J., Selwood, I., Jones, A., Underwood, J., Dillon, G. and Scanlon, E. (2005) Tablet PCs in schools: Case study report. Coventry: Becta. Available at: http://is.gd/ayI4gN (accessed 23 November 2012).

EARLY READING

*Julie Bowtell and Suzy Holding
with Eve Bearne*

It is possible that children may develop the skills of reading but lack the disposition to use them unless their reading experiences encourage autonomy, enthusiasm, achievement and a sense of enjoyment.

(UKLA, 2008)

INTRODUCTION

Over many years, much debate has been generated about how best to develop the skills of reading, especially in the early years. Despite state interventions such as the Primary National Strategy in England, constant monitoring by Ofsted and much hard work by teachers, international rankings indicate that children in England read independently less, and that their disposition to enjoy reading is lower than for many children in other countries. Further, the Progress in International Reading Literacy Study (PIRLS) of 2006 indicated that reading attainment in England had fallen significantly (Twist *et al.*, 2003, 2007). In the 2011 PIRLS (Twist *et al.*, 2012), although enjoyment in, and motivation for, reading had improved, nonetheless a fifth of those surveyed responded that they did not like reading, and 53 per cent responded that they liked it 'somewhat'; hardly a glowing endorsement. This is a matter of concern, as reading achievement affects potential development both academically and socio-economically (OECD, 2002: 3). So there is an imperative to find ways of promoting both achievement and enjoyment in reading.

Debates about how best to raise standards of reading have often focused on methods and materials, rather than dealing with the essential business of what children, parents and teachers understand reading to mean. Unfortunately, much public comment about reading tends to be, not only alarmist, but also uninformed. Positions are often polarised, with, on the one hand, a commonplace view that learning to read is pre-eminently a matter of matching sounds to letters or combinations of letters, and, on the other hand, a view that reading is a complex matter of, not only drawing meaning from print, but also appreciating the cultural influences on texts and the ways they are read. In addition, reading instruction is now a political matter, with governments legislating about the correct method for teaching reading.[1] In England, systematic synthetic phonics has been espoused as the favoured means of initial teaching, and phonics is spoken of as 'a fundamental body of knowledge' in the English national curriculum. Further, it is a statutory requirement that only phonically decodable texts should be read independently by beginning readers (Department for Education, 2013).

However, although teaching phonics systematically has always been an essential part of teaching reading, it is evident that becoming a reader is much more complex than mastering phonic correspondence. Committed and accomplished readers expect the words they decode to make sense, which means that are able to self-regulate their reading from an early stage, correcting themselves as they makes miscues (Campbell, 2011). Reading as an act requires a range of cueing systems to make sense of print, but, in addition, becoming a reader involves behaviours about reading: learning to discriminate and choose, developing reading stamina, finding one's way around texts of all kinds – in print and on screen. Home and community experience will also contribute to a child's growing sense of what reading means and can do, so that, in considering early reading, it is important to take a broader view (González *et al.*, 2005; Gregory and Williams, 2000).

OBJECTIVES

By the end of this unit, you should be able to:

- explain some of the background to current approaches to teaching early reading, with particular reference to phonics teaching;
- debate the strengths of different views;
- recognise the difference between 'learning to read' and 'becoming a reader';
- understand the importance of providing a rich reading diet;
- consider the responsibilities of a teacher of reading.

HISTORY: WHY WE ARE WHERE WE ARE

In the last 50 years (and more!), there have been shifts in preferred methods of teaching reading in the early years: for example, the introduction of the Initial Teaching Alphabet in the 1960s, critiques of reading schemes in the 1970s and 1980s and the advocacy of a 'real books' approach (Waterland, 1988). Despite these changing fashions, teaching reading was seen as a multilayered and complex matter (UKLA, 2006). From the inception of the National Literacy Strategy (Department for Education and Employment, 1998), there has been heightened emphasis by government on a preferred approach to teaching reading, formalised in the *Independent Review of the Teaching of Early Reading* (known as the Rose Review; Rose, 2006) as the Simple View of Reading. This history shows that the teaching of reading is ever-evolving and never static. So teachers of reading cannot be complacent; they need to understand the body of knowledge already existing and be comfortable with future developments in reading and alert for opportunities to expand their own knowledge, skills and expertise.

THE SIMPLE VIEW OF READING

This is the prevailing view of the relationship between decoding and comprehension. Gough and Tunmer (1986) presented the Simple View of Reading as a formula:

decoding (D) × language comprehension (LC) = reading comprehension (RC)

stressing that both sides of the equation must be present for reading for meaning to occur. Rose (2006) developed this equation into a diagram format, presenting the equation as a model with two axes (see Figure 7.7.1) (see also: www.teachingtimes.com/news/the-simple.htm for a very clear explanation of the history and development of this view).

Word recognition encompasses the use of phonic cues and information to decode, plus knowledge of tricky words and high-frequency words to enable efficiency and speed in reading words. It is expected that these aspects will be learned quickly. Although all readers will use word recognition and phonic knowledge to decode unfamiliar words and phrases, this is a finite body of knowledge and should be time limited in terms of teaching. In contrast, language comprehension continues

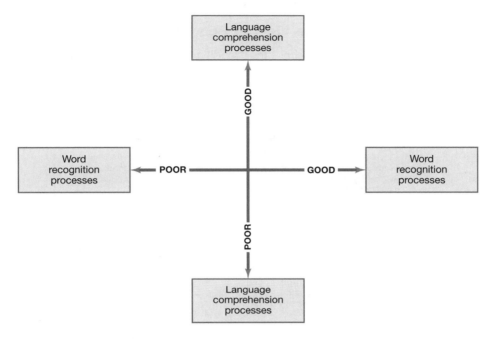

FIGURE 7.7.1 The simple view of reading
Source: Rose (2006: 40)

throughout life – we are regularly challenged by new ideas when we read. Language comprehension varies from person to person and is probably 'infinite in range' (Lewis and Ellis, 2006: 16).

Consider this very simple text in terms of comprehension:

> Alex was going to the fair. She wondered if there would be a roundabout. She didn't want to be late so she turned the radio on.

To understand this text, children must use a range of reading strategies, including:

- understanding letter sounds, words, concepts and ideas to determine the meaning of sentences and to build mental representations of situations described;
- applying background knowledge about fairs that is essential to make the inferences necessary to link the first two sentences and create a coherent mental representation: if you do not know that there are different rides at a fair, then why should Alex wonder if there would be a roundabout? In addition, you need to know that roundabouts are a kind of fairground ride, so as not to confuse them with traffic islands;
- having background knowledge about radio stations giving time checks, for the third sentence to make sense; otherwise, wanting to know the time and turning the radio on makes no sense;
- bringing to bear cultural influences, which are inevitably used in understanding written texts, and they are implicit in the Simple View of Reading (Stuart *et al.*, 2008).

The four quadrants of the Simple View of Reading enable children's progress to be measured and monitored along the two dimensions of the model. However, the Simple View of Reading should not be seen as implying that there is a ceiling on children's reading development, as readers in the top right quadrant still have more to learn about the reading process.

Task 7.7.1 The Simple View of Reading

Match these children's comments about their reading to the Simple View of Reading (see Figure 7.7.1).

JULIA

My teacher says I read slowly and don't always get it right.

But my teacher also says that I enjoy discussing stories and that I'm really good at remembering all the details of what has been read to me, and what I've seen on TV and of everything that happens in school.

FATIMA

My teacher says that I can read accurately and quite fluently – and I have a really good knowledge of high frequency words.

But my teacher also says that I often appear to be unable to remember what I've read or what has been read to me – or to have understood a lot of the detail of the stories she reads.

LEE

My teacher says that I struggle to read even simple texts and I don't know many phonemes yet.

And my teacher says that I don't seem able to discuss the books I've read – or answer questions about stories I've heard – or talk much about things which have happened to me.

My teacher says I read a lot from the reading scheme and from my favourite Mr Gum books.

My teacher also says that I can talk in an informed way about what I've read and that I play a full part in class discussions about books and literature, and I can build on what other children say.

ALISTAIR

What does this tell you about the model?[2]

STAGES IN EARLY READING DEVELOPMENT

In order to play to the strengths of the child's current reading abilities and interests, it is helpful to recognise the stages that children progress through in getting to grips with print. The first stage is logographic reading (Frith, 1980), where very young children are able to recognise print and logos in the environment by the distinctive features of font, shapes and colour. They see the golden arches of McDonalds and suddenly want a Happy Meal! In the same way, they recognise the logos on supermarket plastic bags, traffic signs and car badges. This is not letter-by-letter reading, but, significantly, at this stage children understand that a message has been encoded, and that the symbol has meaning, denoting a message of interest. Shop and packaging logos give opportunities to teach about phonemes. Similarly, web providers employ the universality of symbols in order to provide ease of reading access for all. Young children are adept at navigating through this medium. Notice how they use a mouse, can swipe a screen, use a cursor and other computer conventions and show an awareness of the symbols on a remote control.

In the logographic stage of reading development (Frith, 1980), a child's own name is very often the first word recognised. Many young children will initially see their own name as a logo, using the significant features of the distinctive shape of the first letter, any ascenders and descenders and possibly the length of the word as familiarly recognisable. Learning to write their name enables children to begin to understand the principles of the alphabetic code and appreciate that letters are used to represent and encode words, ideas and messages, moving them towards the alphabetic stage of reading development (Frith, 1980). When children begin to point at print and ask adults to read it to them, they have made a cognitive breakthrough, actively recognising the concept of representing and encoding. Their growing interest in print in the environment and in books provides an appropriate starting point for systematic phonics teaching.

THE PHONICS DEBATE

Teaching reading has always included phonics. What is different is the current emphasis on synthetic, rather than analytic, phonics. The National Curriculum for English (2013) favours the synthetic phonics approach:

> Teachers should also ensure that pupils continue to learn new grapheme–phoneme corres-pondences (GPCs) and revise and consolidate those learnt earlier. The understanding that the letter(s) on the page represent the sounds in spoken words should underpin pupils' reading and spelling of all words.

> (Department for Education, 2013: 16)

But what are the differences? In 2003, in a report for the Department for Education and Skills, Greg Brooks defined the two phonics approaches as follows:

> Synthetic phonics refers to an approach to the teaching of reading in which the phonemes associated with particular graphemes are pronounced in isolation and blended together (synthesised). For example, children are taught to take a single-syllable word such as cat apart into its three letters, pronounce a phoneme for each letter in turn /k, æ, t/, and blend the phonemes together to form a word.

> Analytic phonics refers to an approach to the teaching of reading in which the phonemes associated with particular graphemes are not pronounced in isolation. Children identify (analyse) the common phoneme in a set of words in which each word contains the phoneme under study. For example, teacher and pupils discuss how the following words are alike: *pat*, *park*, *push* and *pen*.

> (Brooks, 2003: 11-12)

There is no established body of evidence that synthetic phonics is a better method of early reading instruction than analytic phonics. Indeed, in terms of teaching letter–sound relationships, a systematic research review by the National Reading Panel (NRP) (2000) in the US concluded that there is no evidence that working with phonemes (as in the synthetic phonics approach) is more effective than working with slightly larger analytic units (onset-rime):

> Explicit, systematic phonics instruction is a valuable and essential part of a successful classroom reading program. However, there is a need to be cautious in giving a blanket endorsement of all kinds of phonics instruction . . .

> . . . phonics teaching is a means to an end. To be able to make use of letter–sound information, children need phonemic awareness. That is, they need to be able to blend sounds together to decode words, and they need to break spoken words into their constituent sounds to write words.

Programs that focus too much on the teaching of letter–sound relations and not enough on putting them to use are unlikely to be very effective.

(National Reading Panel, 2000)

The differences between a synthetic phonics approach and an analytic phonics approach is sometimes characterised as 'part-to-whole' (synthetic) and 'whole-to-part' (analytic). Part-to-whole depends on letter–sound relationships; whole-to-part emphasises onset and rime, where the initial part of the syllable is the onset, and the unit below the level of the syllable is the rime, for example: *s/in*; *th/ink*; *str/ong*.

However, as the NRP emphasises, whatever the approach, phonemic awareness is the goal.

TEACHING PHONICS

The teaching and learning of phonics are underpinned by phonemic awareness, which involves the processes of blending and segmenting plus applying the alphabetic principle through knowledge of the alphabetic code. Blending is when the constituent phonemes in a word are run together, smoothed, merged and synthesised, in order to decode that word. Segmenting is when the word is pulled apart, or broken down into its constituent phonemes. The skills of blending and segmenting are mutually beneficial and supportive (Ofsted, 2011a). Blending and segmenting are, in the words of the Rose Review (2006), 'reversible processes': that is, if you can blend the sounds together to read a word, you should also be able to identify and break down (segment) the individual sounds in a word you hear to spell it.

The alphabetic code

Hepplewhite (2011) defines the alphabetic code as 'the reversible relationship between the discrete sounds we can identify in speech and the letters or letter groups which are code for the sounds' (p. 1). For educational purposes, it is generally accepted that there are forty-four phonemes in spoken English (see the companion website). As English contains only twenty-six letters, it is immediately clear that there is not a direct relationship between spoken and written language, and sounds and letters. English does not have a transparent correspondence in the way that some languages do, for example, Gujarati and Italian. This makes English such an interesting and fascinating language to learn to read and spell.

Letter names and letter sounds

There can be concerns about whether or not to teach letter names as well as phonemes, in case this could be confusing. However, as many children start school already knowing the alphabet, it is important to acknowledge this prior knowledge as a strength. These children have a means of talking about print, as the letters of the alphabet are the metalanguage we all use to discuss letters and words. Knowing that each symbol has a name as well as a sound (phoneme) can help children to be flexible in their approach and move them away from a possible one-letter-one-sound mentality.

PHONIC PHASES

Children's phonic knowledge develops along a continuum. It is helpful to separate this into distinct phases, so that it is easier to plan systematically from EYFS to KS2. Phonic understanding starts with young children's ability to discriminate sounds in the environment. This phonological awareness is a fundamental precursor to listening for discrete letter sounds and is a necessary foundation for all future phonic learning. Children must be able to hear and say sounds in words (phonemes) before they are expected to read and write them. In addition, they need to be able to pick out individual sounds from the barrage of background noise in a classroom or a busy playground. Making a distinction between listening and hearing enables children to develop the skills of phonemic awareness: the ability to discriminate the smallest of sounds in speech (Medwell *et al.*, 2011).

Application of phonics

However, planning opportunities for children to apply their phonic knowledge after a discrete phonics session is crucial. Application of phonics is best developed through daily games and activities highlighting phonic examples in real-life contexts and the children using their phonic knowledge in reading and writing meaningful texts. Motivating contexts such as this enable children to apply new knowledge at least six times, so that it moves from working memory to long-term memory and becomes effortless and automatic (Apthorp, 2006).

Task 7.7.2 Application of phonic knowledge

Applying phonic knowledge in the early stages is often dependent on high-quality play that uses themes, characters and activities relevant to the children and affords them opportunities to find enjoyment in using the new elements of their phonic programme.

Read the account, *'Was that brilliant or what?' Engaging reception children in phonics: Lambton Primary School*, on www.ofsted.gov.uk/resources/good-practice-resource-engaging-reception-children-phonics-lambton-primary-school (Ofsted, 2012a).

Discuss the ways in which the staff were supporting and developing the children's phonic knowledge.

THE YEAR 1 PHONICS SCREENING CHECK

In an educational arena that demands accountability, it is inevitable that aspects of children's reading will be measured. At the end of Year 1, all children's use of phonics and their ability to blend phonemes to decode unfamiliar words are assessed. This screening check demands that the children read twenty 'real' words and twenty 'pseudo' words.

Recent research (UKLA, 2012; NFER, 2013) has revealed that teachers and head teachers overwhelmingly felt that the check did not give any information that they did not already know, and it took valuable teaching time. Many stated that the outcome of the phonics check, which is being used as an indicator of reading skills, did not reflect children's reading abilities, as children who were already achieving level 2 comprehension did not pass the screening check. It was evident from the survey data that all schools already teach phonics on a regular basis and use assessment data to monitor children's progress in decoding skills. All were firm supporters of phonics as one aspect of learning to read. However, there was criticism of both the Year 1 check and an over-emphasis on phonics teaching. Comments included:

> I appreciate this was a phonics test not reading test, but it is very difficult to understand why it would be done in isolation as a readiness to read measure. Reading is a much more complex

issue and although we value the introduction of phonics very highly this appears a crude measure which I hope will be reviewed.

We were in the pilot last year and only 22% met the expected level, yet 47% achieved level 3 in the teacher assessment and reading SAT test this year! It just proves that phonics is only a very small part of learning to read and has no bearing on being an able reader.

A further concern was that the check misidentified pupils who are beyond the stage of phonetic decoding as readers; in several cases, successful, fluent readers did less well in the check than emergent readers, and, in some cases, reading confidence was affected:

Children scored 40 who cannot read fluently with expression.

All children in the cohort assessed on an NfER reading progress test have a reading age above their chronological age. About half have a reading age more than 12 months above their chronological age. A child of 6y 5m with an assessed reading age of 8 years failed the test.

The failures in the test were entirely due to the nonsense words. Most children could read all the real words using both phonics and other strategies. The children had had practice in nonsense words but most tried to turn the nonsense words into sense ('storm' for 'strom' etc.) . . . The most able children who did manage the nonsense words slowed right down from being fluent expressive readers to sounding out every word phoneme by phoneme, even words they knew.

This phonics check has in no way supported them to learn to read and has in some cases affected their confidence in themselves as readers.

(UKLA, 2012)

Task 7.7.3 The phonics screening check

- Read: www.education.gov.uk/schools/teachingandlearning/pedagogy/a00198207/faqs-year-1-phonics-screening-check
- Consider the arguments put forward in this DfE article and the comments by the teachers who completed the UKLA survey.
- What are the implications for assessing children's reading in the early years?

See also the NFER interim evaluation report for the phonics screening check; this supports the UKLA survey results (www.gov.uk/government/uploads/system/uploads/attachment_data/file/198994/DFE-RR286A.pdf).

BARRIERS TO LEARNING TO READ – WHAT PREVENTS SUCCESS?

Adults forget how they learned to read; only unsuccessful readers remember the details of their struggles . . .

(Meek, 1982: 9)

It is best, of course, to try to ensure that barriers do not occur in the first place. There is no cure-all for children who have 'atypical' needs, knowledge or prior experience (Brien, 2012). Poverty can be a barrier to achievement in general, but this is not inevitable. In fact, the best teachers enable children to learn to read regardless of socio-economic circumstances, ethnic background or special educational needs (Taylor *et al.*, 2000; Allington, 2001; Taylor and Pearson, 2002, cited in Dombey *et al.*, 2010).

Barriers include:

- **Insufficient phonological awareness**: The ability to hear sounds in general (gross listening) and individual sounds in words (fine listening) underpins children's future success for decoding. Teachers need to give credence to the important foundation skills of discriminating between gross and fine listening in the development of phonemic awareness.
- **Ineffective word level reading skills**: Children need the skills to decode and recognise unfamiliar and tricky words in a print-rich environment (Rose, 2006). Through careful observation of children's decoding abilities, and an understanding of the beginner reader, the teacher will be able to plan steps to enable children to progress through the phonic phases.
- **Poor oral language skills**: Communication is the engine of a young child's learning. Children need to be talking and actively listening in order to drive their understanding of their world. An abundance of first-hand experiences with the opportunities for meaningful discussion are key.
- **Lack of print experience**: Teachers who flood their classrooms with a broad and varied diet of fiction, non-fiction and poetry are most successful in promoting successful reading development. Teachers and children need to seek out, show and interact with print in the environment, in books and on the Internet.
- **Negative attitudes to reading**: Reading is the key to lifelong learning and requires a positive attitude. It is a teacher's job to hand over the key to the children by enthusiastically promoting the written word, maintaining resilience and the EYFS (Department for Education, 2012) 'have a go' disposition.
- **Low self-esteem**: Young readers must be encouraged and praised for their beginning efforts at reading. Every detail of the reading process must be noticed by the teacher and celebrated.

SELECTING TEXTS FOR LEARNING TO READ

The new National Curriculum for English (2013) requires that, for Year 1 children:

> Alongside this knowledge of GPCs [grapheme–phoneme correspondences], pupils need to develop the skill of blending the sounds into words for reading and establish the habit of applying this skill whenever they encounter new words. This will be supported by practising their reading with books consistent with their developing phonic knowledge and skill. At the same time they will need to hear, share and discuss a wide range of high-quality books to develop a love of reading and broaden their vocabulary.
>
> (Department for Education, 2013: 16)

Alongside this is the statutory requirement that, for independent reading, Year 1 children should:

- read aloud accurately books that are consistent with their developing phonic knowledge and that do not require them to use other strategies to work out words;
- re-read these books to build up their fluency and confidence in word reading.

Restricting independent reading to such phonically decodable books seems not only nonsensical but very difficult indeed on a practical level. A rich diet of literature must also include books that promote reading for pleasure from texts that interest, excite and motivate young children in the early stages of learning to read.

On the website you will find advice for selecting books for developing readers.

READING FOR PLEASURE

Knowledge of the children's reading experience and preferences is vital in promoting reading for pleasure, because it is intrinsically linked to reading behaviour, attitude and attainment (Clark and De Zoysa, 2011). Moreover, reading for pleasure is not predicated on where you live, where you come from, what languages you speak, what you have and what you do not have. Reading for pleasure depends on a reader's positive self-concept, a tendency to read and a reported enjoyment of, or interest in, reading. It is this necessary foundation that enables lifelong reading to flourish. The National Curriculum, the EYFS and Ofsted recognise the importance of reading for pleasure and the value of encouraging a reader's response to a broad range of texts (Ofsted, 2011b, 2012b, 2013; Department for Education, 2013). In the words of the DfE (2013: 14), teachers should 'establish an appreciation and love of reading' because reading 'opens up a treasure-house of wonder and joy for curious young minds'.

Alongside reading instruction, children will be enjoying shared reading experiences of quality picture books, poetry, songs and rhymes. It is through these experiences that children come to relish what books (and other texts) can offer and begin to see how reading can be both a reflection of personal experience and a window to look out on other people's experiences. Reading enables us to imagine, enact, relive and understand our lived experience.

A key to providing children with creative and enlivening experiences linked with reading is the reading teacher (Commeyras *et al.*, 2003). Reading teachers – teachers who read and readers who teach and who are knowledgeable and socially interactive about what they read about children's texts – are best placed to foster engagement in, and commitment to, reading in their classes. Such teachers model their own love of reading in various ways, but all spend time talking about their reading practices and providing space for children to talk about theirs (Cremin, 2013).

See website for examples of how talk feeds into early reading development.

SKILL AND WILL

Although reading instruction is critically important in developing successful readers, a study into schools as reading communities (Cremin *et al.*, 2009) argues that it is crucial to consider both 'the skill and the will' to read. Currently, the research suggests, teachers tend to focus on skill rather than developing the will – or commitment to reading. Figure 7.7.2 represents the distinctions between reading instruction and reading for pleasure.

Task 7.7.4 Are you a reading teacher?

A survey by Cremin *et al*. (2008) asked, among other things, for teachers to list six children's picturebook makers and six poets for young children.

- Without talking to anyone else or looking things up, try this yourself.
- Share your list with others – this will begin to build a useful repertoire of books that you might use to promote children's reading for pleasure.

Reading Instruction is oriented towards:	Reading for Pleasure is oriented towards:
Learning to read	Choosing to read
The skill	The will
Decoding and comprehension	Engagement and response
System readers	Lifelong readers
Teacher direction	Child direction
Teacher ownership	Child ownership
Attainment	Achievement
The minimum entitlement (A Level 4)	The maximum entitlement: (A reader for life)
The Standards Agenda	The Wider Reading Agenda

FIGURE 7.7.2 Distinctions between reading instruction and reading for pleasure
Source: Cremin *et al.* (2009)

Working with families and homes

While developing a reading community within the school, it is important to establish genuine partnerships with homes over reading. Very often, home–school 'partnerships' are governed by the school telling parents/carers how they intend to teach their children to read and how homes can co-operate. Although such information is important to share, there is rarely traffic the other way, with schools inviting families to let them know about the children's home reading and viewing experience. A more fruitful way of developing partnerships is for the school to assume that children have 'funds of knowledge' (González *et al.*, 2005) that include literacy-related experiences and to seek to discover what these are, so that they can be built on to promote successful and satisfying reading for children (Cremin *et al.*, 2012).

SUMMARY

Research has shown that teachers can ensure success by providing young children with a rich environment that offers challenging and inspiring opportunities for experiential learning (Medwell *et al.*, 1998). The development and use of communication in all its forms are at the heart of young children's learning. Ultimately, it is not phonics programmes or reading schemes that teach children to read: it is the teacher. Published commercial schemes cannot anticipate what children will need at each stage in their learning. All the significant adults in a young child's life – their family and teachers – can provide the appropriate models for how written language is used. Even the best materials in the world do not teach themselves, as all resources need to be mediated. It is the 'human connection between reader and text and teacher that consistently provides the reading lesson' (Goouch and Lambirth, 2011: 8). Teachers who are readers and readers who teach are most likely to inspire and support committed, discriminating and successful early readers.

ANNOTATED FURTHER READING

Jolliffe, W., Waugh, D. and Carss, A. (2012) *Teaching Systematic Synthetic Phonics in Primary Schools*, London: Sage.

> This book gives a comprehensive overview of the place of systematic synthetic phonics in teaching reading, with a useful two-part division into 'Subject knowledge for teachers' and 'Effective pedagogy'. Here is a good starting point for further in-depth study, with information needed for analysis of some of the factors contributing to successful teaching of reading. Sections of research focus give the reader access to expert opinion, background theory and supporting ideas.

Lockwood, M. (2008) *Promoting Reading for Pleasure in the Primary School*, London: Sage.

> This book includes strategies for promoting reading for pleasure both at a whole-school level and individual classroom level, focusing separately on early years and later primary years. There is a topical and relevant chapter devoted to getting boys reading for pleasure and enjoyment. The salient topics of pupil choice, resources, role models, different reading media and cross-curricular reading are addressed. Lockwood helpfully considers reading inside and outside the classroom, and there are several useful sections on involving parents and the wider community.

Ofsted (2010) Reading by six: how the best schools do it. Available at: www.ofsted.gov.uk/resources/reading-six-how-best-schools-do-it

> This document outlines excellent practice in the teaching of reading in twelve primary schools. Ofsted maintains that these schools enable children to read through a rigorous and sequential approach to developing speaking and listening and teaching reading, writing and spelling through systematic phonics. It concludes that success is based on a determination that every child will read, regardless of socio-economic factors, ethnicity, home language and most special educational needs or disabilities.

 FURTHER READING TO SUPPORT M-LEVEL STUDY

Lewis, M. and Ellis, S. (2006) *Phonics: Practice, Research and Policy*, London: Sage in association with UKLA.

> The range of chapters in this collection gives readers the opportunity to consider all aspects of the phonic debate. This book covers the place of phonics in the teaching of early reading, analyses classroom approaches to phonics teaching and also outlines the important links between phonics and spelling.

Wyse, D. and Goswami, U. (2008) 'Synthetic phonics and the teaching of reading', *British Educational Research Journal*, 34 (6): 691–710.

> In this paper, Wyse and Goswami critically analyse the research evidence presented to support the change to synthetic phonics in the teaching of reading. It also includes useful insights into the distinctions between 'synthetic', 'systematic', 'contextualised' and 'discrete' phonics learning and teaching.

 RELEVANT WEBSITES

The following websites are useful for finding reviews of children's books:

Books for Keeps http://booksforkeeps.co.uk/

The English Association: www2.le.ac.uk/offices/english-association/primary/ea-plus

REFERENCES

Allington, R. (2001) *What Really Matters for Struggling Readers: Designing Research-Based Programs*, New York: Longman.

Apthorp, H. (2006) 'Effects of a supplemental vocabulary program in third grade reading/language arts', *Journal of Educational Research*, 100 (2): 67–79.

Brien, J. (2012) *Teaching Primary English*, London: Sage.

Brooks, G. (2003) *Sound sense: the phonics element of the National Literacy Strategy. A report to the Department for Education and Skills*. London: DfES.

Campbell, R. (2011) *Miscue Analysis in the Classroom*, Leicester: United Kingdom Literacy Association.

Clark, S. and De Zoysa, S. (2011) *Mapping the Interrelationships Between Reading Enjoyment, Attitudes, Behaviour and Attainment*, London: National Literacy Trust.

Commeyras, M., Bisplinghoff, B.S. and Olson, J. (2003) *Teachers as Readers: Perspectives on the Importance of Reading in Teachers' Classrooms and Lives*, Newark, NJ: International Reading Association.

Cremin, T. (2013) Exploring teachers' positions and practices: a case study of one poetry teacher. In S. Dymoke., A. Lambirth and A. Wilson (eds) *Making Poetry Matter: International Research Perspectives on Poetry Pedagogy*, London: Bloomsbury.

Cremin, T., Mottram, M., Bearne, E. and Goodwin, P. (2008) 'Exploring teachers' knowledge of children's literature', *Cambridge Journal of Education*, 38 (4): 449–64.

Cremin, T., Mottram, M., Collins, F., Powell, S. and Safford, K. (2009) 'Teachers as readers: building communities of readers', *Literacy*, 43 (1): 11–19.

Cremin, T., Mottram, M., Collins, F., Powell, S. and Drury, R. (2012) 'Building communities: teachers researching literacy lives', *Improving Schools*, 15 (2): 101–15.

Department for Education (DfE) (2012) *Statutory Framework for the Early Years Foundation Stage*. Available at: www.education.gov.uk/publications/standard/AllPublicationsNoRsg/Page1/DFE-00023-2012 (accessed 8 March 2013).

Department for Education (DfE) (2013) *The National Curriculum in England: Framework Document for Consultation*. London: DfE.

Department for Education and Employment (DfEE) (1998) *The National Literacy Strategy: Framework for Teaching*, London: Crown Copyright.

Dombey, H. with Bearne, E., Cremin, T., Ellis, S., Mottram, M., O'Sullivan, O., Öztürk, A., Reedy, D., Raphael, T. and Allington, R. (2010) *Teaching Reading: What the Evidence Says*, Leicester: United Kingdom Literacy Association.

Frith, U. (ed.) (1980) *Cognitive Processes in Spelling*, London: Academic Press.

Gamse, B.C., Bloom, H.S., Kemple, J.J. and Jacob, R.T. (2008) *Reading First Impact Study: Interim Report* (NCEE 2008-4016), Washington DC: National Center for Education Evaluation and Regional Assistance, Institute of Education Sciences, US Department of Education.

González, N., Moll, L. and Amanti, C. (2005) *Funds of Knowledge: Theorizing Practices in Households, Communities, and Classrooms*, New Jersey: Lawrence Erlbaum.

Goouch, K. and Lambirth, A. (2011) *Teaching Early Reading and Phonics*, London: Sage.

Gough, P.B. and Tunmer, W.E. (1986) 'Decoding, reading and reading disability', *Remedial and Special Education*, 7: 6–10.

Gregory, E. and Williams, A. (2000) *City Literacies: Learning to Read Across Generations and Cultures*, London: Routledge.

Hepplewhite, D. (2011) *The Two-Pronged Approach to Synthetic Phonics Teaching: Systematic and Incidental*. Available at: www.phonicsinternational.com/Debbie_RRF_Two_pronged_handout.pdf (accessed 8 March 2013).

Lewis, M. and Ellis, S. (2006) *Phonics: Practice, Research and Policy*, London: Sage in association with UKLA.

Medwell, J., Fox, R., Poulson, L. and Wray, D. (1998) *Effective Teachers of Literacy*, Exeter: Exeter University.

Medwell, J., Moore, G., Wray, D. and Griffiths, V. (2011) *Primary English Knowledge and Understanding*, London: Sage.

Meek, M. (1982) *Learning to Read*, London: Bodley Head.

National Foundation for Educational Research (2013) *Evaluation of the Phonics Screening Check: First Interim Report*. Available at: www.gov.uk/government/uploads/system/uploads/attachment_data/file/198994/DFE-RR286A.pdf (accessed 19 December 2013).

National Reading Panel (2000) *Teaching children to read: an evidence-based assessment of the scientific research literature on reading and its implications for reading instruction*. Washington DC: NICHD. Available at: www.nichd.nih.gov/publications/pubs/nrp/Pages/findings.aspx (accessed 23 March 2013).

OECD (2002) *Reading for change: Performance and engagement across countries: Results from PISA 2000. Executive summary*. OECD.

Ofsted (2011a) *Getting them reading early*. Available at: www.ofsted.gov.uk/resources/getting-them-reading-early (accessed 8 March 2013).

Ofsted (2011b) *Excellence in English*. Available at: www.ofsted.gov.uk/resources/excellence-english (accessed 8 March 2013).

Ofsted (2012a) *'Was that brilliant or what?' Engaging reception children in phonics: Lambton Primary School, Manchester*. Available at: www.ofsted.gov.uk/resources/good-practice-resource-engaging-reception-children-phonics-lambton-primary-school (accessed 8 March 2013).

Ofsted (2012b) *Moving English forward*. Available at: www.ofsted.gov.uk/resources/moving-english-forward (accessed 8 March 2013).

Ofsted (2013) Subject professional development materials: English. Available at: www.ofsted.gov.uk/resources/subject-professional-development-materials-english (accessed 8 March 2013).

Rose, J. (2006) *Independent Review of the Teaching of Early Reading*. Available at: http://webarchive.nationalarchives.gov.uk/20130401151715/https://www.education.gov.uk/publications/standard/publicationdetail/page1/DFES-0201-2006 (accessed 23 March 2013).

Stuart, M., Stainthorp, R. and Snowling, M. (2008) 'Literacy as a complex activity: deconstructing the simple view of reading', *Literacy*, 42(2): 59–66.

Taylor, B.M. and Pearson, P.D. (eds) (2002) *Teaching Reading: Effective schools, Accomplished Teachers*, Mahwah, NJ: Lawrence Erlbaum.

Taylor, B.M, Pearson, P.D., Clark, K. and Walpole, S. (2000) 'Effective schools and accomplished teachers: lessons about primary grade reading instruction in low income schools', *Elementary School Journal*, 101: 121–65.

Twist, L., Sainsbury, M., Woodthorpe, A. and Whetton, C. (2003) *PIRLS Progress in International Literacy Study, National Report for England: Reading all over the world*. Slough: NFER.

Twist, L., Schagen, I. and Hodgson, C. (2007) *Readers and Reading: National Report for England PIRLS 2006*. Slough: NFER.

Twist, L., Sizmur, J., Bartlett, S. and Lynn, L. (2012) *PIRLS 2011: Reading achievement in England*. Research Brief DFE-RB262. Available at: www.education.gov.uk/publications/standard/publicationDetail/Page1/DFE-RB262 (accessed 23 March 2013).

UKLA (2006) *Submission to the Review of Best Practice in the Teaching of Early Reading*, Leicester: UKLA.

UKLA (2008) *Evidence contribution to the Primary Review: Independent Review of the Primary Curriculum*. Leicester: UKLA.

UKLA (2012) 'Phonics Screening Check fails a generation of able readers', UKLA, University of Leicester. Available at: www.ukla.org/news/phonics_screening_check_fails_a_generation_of_able_readers (accessed 9 March 2013).

Waterland, L. (1988) *Read with Me: An Apprenticeship Approach to Reading*, Stroud: Thimble Press.

NOTES

1   In 2001, the US Senate passed the No Child Left Behind Act, including the mandation of Reading First, a programme to remedy reading failure in low-achieving schools. This consisted of direct instruction in the 'essential components' of reading (phonemic awareness, phonics, vocabulary, fluency and comprehension), taught as separate skills, to children in Grades 1–3. Billions of dollars were spent on the programme, which involved nearly 6,000 schools. However, the official evaluation, which involved 128 schools, on eighteen sites in twelve states, found that its adoption brought no significant improvements to children's comprehension (Gamse *et al.*, 2008). Congress has since eliminated further funding for the Reading First programme.

2   Task 7.7.1 The Simple View of Reading answers: Julia: Poor word recognition, good language comprehension. Fatima: Good word recognition, poor language comprehension. Lee: Poor word recognition, poor language comprehension. Alistair: Good word recognition, good language comprehension.

PARTNERSHIP IN PRACTICE

THE CHANGING ROLE OF THE TEACHER

Tony Eaude

INTRODUCTION

This unit considers the primary teacher's role and how this has been affected by recent changes to legislation and policy. It should be read in the light of Hayes's earlier unit, Unit 1.2, 'Professionalism and trainee teachers', as such changes are based on, and create, new views of what professionalism involves. The first half of this unit considers how the primary school teacher's role has evolved and different views of professionalism, including those in the *Teachers' Standards*, to highlight both continuities and changes. The second half discusses how three aspects of government policy – on the curriculum, inspection and school structures – affect, or might affect, teachers in primary schools; and then the wider role of the class teacher, including working with other professionals and with parents/carers. The tasks are designed to encourage you to relate general principles to your own experience, given the importance of reflection, professional judgement and continuing professional development.

OBJECTIVES

This unit should help you:

- be aware of how the primary class teacher's role and views of teacher professionalism have evolved and how the *Teachers' Standards* reflect this;
- recognise the need to relate your professional attributes, knowledge and understanding and skills to your own role and context;
- understand more of how changes to the curriculum, inspection and school structures affect how primary school teachers work;
- reflect further on the challenges and opportunities of teaching in a primary school.

THE HISTORICAL AND CULTURAL BACKGROUND

When revising this unit for a new edition, I was surprised at how out of date the policies and changes highlighted in 2009-10 seem in 2013. A new government has introduced changes to the requirements to gain qualified teacher status (QTS) and to the curriculum, inspection and school structures. Yet, in many ways, the primary class teacher's role remains remarkably similar to that of elementary school teachers in the late nineteenth century. For example, in the elementary schools, one (usually female and unqualified) teacher covered a fairly narrow curriculum, for a whole class, aided, if at all, only by one or more older children. The current emphasis on literacy and numeracy has a long history, despite the importance of breadth and balance, especially for young children (see Alexander, 2010: 242–3). Traditionally, teachers in British primary schools have been seen as generalists, working with one class most of the time, undertaking a wide range of tasks, both academic and pastoral, and able to teach all, or most, subjects. Although the introduction of more specialist teaching, technological changes and the involvement of other adults in the classroom, either as support staff or replacing the class teacher, has altered this to some extent, the model has remained remarkably durable.

In other countries, the role has been seen differently. For instance, in Scandinavia, most teachers are educated to Masters level, with an emphasis on pedagogy – an understanding of teaching based on the wider context of how children learn, and, especially in France and central Europe, the focus of the teacher's work is largely academic, with pastoral work delegated to others. Alexander (2000) provides fascinating insights into how teaching approaches – and the training expected – are shaped by, and shape, different beliefs about education in five countries. Therefore, the cultural assumptions behind any curriculum and the structures to select, support and oversee teachers – as well as the teachers' own beliefs – affect both the role and status of teachers and how any teacher actually works with children.

THE TEACHER AS A PROFESSIONAL

In England, the twentieth century saw long struggles to ensure that primary school teachers had to be qualified, and then to make teaching a graduate profession. However, although teaching has for many years been called a profession, teachers have never been seen as professionals like doctors, lawyers or architects. One reason is the widespread belief that teaching is really just applied common sense, a view that no one would ever take of dentistry! Yet, as Eaude (2012) argues, young children's learning is very complicated, and how best to enable this is far from obvious. So, primary teachers need to be, and act as, professionals.

Among the typical characteristics of a profession are:

- mastery of a knowledge base requiring a long period of training;
- tasks that are inherently valuable to society;
- a desire to prioritise the client's welfare;
- a high level of autonomy;
- a code of ethics to guide practice.

(Adapted from John, 2008: 12)

Most teachers would agree on the importance of all of these, though many complain about the extent of interference in what and how to teach. Autonomy has reduced with the growing expectation that teachers will be accountable, especially in terms of results. Despite being true of all professions, it has affected teachers strongly, although they retain considerable autonomy in *how* to teach. Although many teachers, especially when new to the profession, may expect to be told what to do, exercising judgement remains an integral part of being a professional, because school and government priorities change, and even more because how young children respond is never entirely predictable, one reason why teaching them is so challenging and rewarding.

Professionalism is closely linked to being thoughtful and reflective about teaching. Schon's (1987) distinction between reflection-on-action (on what has happened) and reflection-in-action (about what is happening to inform immediate decisions) is useful. The former involves thinking about, and planning, how to teach in the light of school policies, schemes of work and experience; reflection-in-action involves taking decisions on the spur of the moment, in response to particular situations. This is something good teachers are constantly doing, based on their own skills and experience and knowledge and understanding, especially of how children learn.

Pollard and Tann (1994: 9–10) identify six main features of reflective teaching:

*   an active concern with aims and consequences;
*   a process in which teachers monitor, evaluate and revise their own practice continuously;
*   competence in methods of classroom enquiry;
*   attitudes of open-mindedness, responsibility and whole-heartedness;
*   teacher judgement, informed both by self-reflection and insights from educational disciplines; and
*   collaboration and dialogue with colleagues.

These may look difficult, especially the third, but being a class teacher with young children is not easy. As Eaude (2012) indicates, this does not just require subject knowledge, but a high level of craft and personal/interpersonal knowledge. In other words, primary class teachers need practical as well as theoretical knowledge and a good ability to relate to young children, as well as an understanding of how children learn in a wide range of subject areas. The previous set of professional standards broke these into professional *attributes*, *knowledge and understanding* and *skills*. Many of these are tacit, or hard to identify, and even harder to learn, with their successful application depending on practice and experience and the specific context in which they are used. However, these are areas to develop over your career, if you are going to act as a professional, rather than just a technician.

Task 8.1.1　What are the key features of a successful teacher?

Think about the features of one teacher you have worked with, or observed working with young children. Consider the ones suggested below and add your own.

*   Which particular attributes did s/he demonstrate – enthusiasm, strictness, empathy . . .?
*   What professional knowledge did s/he use – subject knowledge, behaviour management, knowledge of individual children . . .?
*   Which professional skills did you see – in terms of planning, giving feedback, asking questions . . .?

Be specific. For example, how did s/he use subject knowledge? Or what was good about his/her feedback?

Now, preferably with another person, do the same for yourself, but make sure you focus mainly on the positives – you will find there are plenty, even when a lesson has not gone well. From this, decide on your strengths and what you need to work at developing, but remember, we are all different, and so it is not just a case of trying to copy one teacher you admire.

M-LEVEL CHALLENGE

Sometimes, people talk about 'a born teacher'. Does this idea make any sense? To what extent do you believe that becoming an outstanding or expert teacher comes naturally or can be learned?

Decide five aspects that distinguish an outstanding primary class teacher from a good one. Discuss this with another student or teacher. To what extent do your ideas and priorities coincide?

THE *TEACHERS' STANDARDS*

The new *Teachers' Standards* (DfE, 2012) are intended to show clearly what is expected for a teacher to gain QTS. Although it is likely that other standards for more experienced teachers will be replaced by a new 'Master Teacher Standard', setting out the characteristics of excellent teachers, this has not yet been finalised.

The *Teachers' Standards* are in two parts, one related to teaching, the other to personal and professional conduct. The first part states that a teacher must:

1   set high expectations that inspire, motivate and challenge pupils;
2   promote good progress and outcomes by pupils;
3   demonstrate good subject and curriculum knowledge;
4   plan and teach well-structured lessons;
5   adapt teaching to respond to the strengths and needs of all pupils;
6   make accurate and productive use of assessment;
7   manage behaviour effectively to ensure a good and safe learning environment;
8   fulfil wider professional responsibilities.

Each of these items is broken down into between three and five subheadings (see Department for Education, 2012, for the detail of these).

The second part is shorter, defining the behaviour and attitudes required throughout a teacher's career, emphasising the need to uphold public trust in the profession, having regard to the school's ethos, policies and practices and setting an example, and understanding and always acting within statutory frameworks. As a professional, you are expected to conduct yourself appropriately both in and out of school. Remember that acting professionally extends beyond the school gate, so that, for instance, putting pictures of yourself 'having a good time' on to social media may be inappropriate and very unwise.

Although the *Teachers' Standards* provide a useful starting point, they do not, in my view, capture the complexity of teaching a class of young children, with their different interests, abilities and needs, over a whole year, across the whole curriculum (see Eaude, 2012: 56, for my list of twelve propositions on this). As a primary school teacher, you may find yourself taking on many roles in any one day: a story-teller, a subject specialist, a shoulder for a parent or a colleague to cry on, a manager of a team of other adults, a wiper-up, a guide . . . It is very hard to capture exactly what makes a good teacher, because the necessary knowledge and skills vary according to the context and who the teacher is working with at any one time. So teaching a class of 10-year-olds in a large urban school will require a different balance of attributes, knowledge of policies and ability to liaise with other professionals from that involved in working in a nursery unit in a small town, and meeting

In Northern Ireland . . .

The GTCNI has published twenty-seven professional competences for teachers in Northern Ireland, which have been organised within three broad areas: professional values and practice, professional knowledge, and understanding professional skills and application. The document states:

> Teachers, in discharging their responsibilities engage first and foremost as individuals with a sense of moral purpose and responsibility and it is the interaction between mission, ethical understanding, and professional knowledge that the mystery that is never far from the heart of good teaching is to be found.
>
> (GTCNI, 2009: 5)

Source: GTCNI (2009) *Teaching: the Reflective Profession.* Belfast, GTCNI.

In Wales . . .

The *Revised Professional Standards for Education Practitioners in Wales* has fifty-five standards that teachers must meet at the end of their induction period and throughout their teaching career. Each standard covers three main aspects: professional values and attributes, professional knowledge and understanding, and professional skills.

> The overall purpose of the professional standards is to raise standards of teaching and to improve learner outcomes throughout Wales. The professional standards articulate the understandings, knowledge and values that our teachers, leaders and Higher Level Teaching Assistants must demonstrate. They provide a framework to enable practitioners to identify their performance management objectives and to choose the most appropriate professional development activities.
>
> (DfES, 2011: 1)

Source: Department for Education and Skills (DfES) (2011) *Revised professional standards for education practitioners in Wales*. Cardiff: Welsh Assembly Government (WAG). http://wales.gov.uk/docs/dcells/publications/110830profstandardsen.pdf

Task 8.1.2 What factors affect the teacher's role in a context that you know?

Think about factors that affect your job or the one you hope to have: you may not know the answers, but these are all things to consider, or find out, in applying for jobs and when you start. How will the following affect you as a teacher?

- which class or group and the age of the children you teach;
- the area that the school serves, its size, whether it is a faith school;
- the level of responsibility you are expected to take on;
- school policies on planning, schemes of work and timetable;
- the relationships among staff and more subtle expectations, such as how you might relate to the community, or how you are expected to dress.

M-LEVEL CHALLENGE

In your second year of teaching, you have been asked to co-ordinate a subject area that you have not studied since school, as well as being a class teacher.

What might be the main challenges and tasks initially? Some areas to think about are resources, professional development (for yourself or others) and schemes of work, but add your own. Where, and from whom, would you look for advice and support?

the needs of a child with a physical disability will need a different balance from that involved in teaching a class of high-attaining Year 6 mathematicians.

No list can cater, entirely, for three key elements:

- the specific role and context in which teachers operate;
- the external expectations placed on them; and
- individual teachers' beliefs and understanding about teaching and learning.

This emphasises the importance of teachers being adaptable and thinking how best to use, and develop, their knowledge, understanding and skills, depending on the specific context.

THE CURRICULUM AND THE TEACHER'S ROLE

The curriculum is an important, but not the only, influence on how teachers teach. Elementary school teaching involved *delivering* a fairly narrow curriculum. In the 1960s and 1970s, there was more emphasis on *facilitating* the child's learning and on the humanities and the arts, with considerable autonomy for teacher (and often the child). However, recent trends have emphasised literacy and numeracy and the class teacher *managing* a team of adults to ensure that all children can access a range of curricular opportunities, adapted to the children's own needs.

The introduction of the National Curriculum, after 1989, based on 'core' and 'foundation' subjects, led to a greater emphasis on curriculum content and measurable outcomes, especially in the core subjects, English, maths and science. This was designed to ensure a consistent entitlement for all children, with inspection making the results publicly available. The National Literacy and Numeracy Strategies, in the late 1990s, were explicit about how primary teachers should teach in these subject areas. *Excellence and Enjoyment* (Department for Education and Skills, 2003) emphasised that children should enjoy learning and use their creativity, as well as attaining high standards. Subsequent reviews have tried to strike a balance between prescription and teacher autonomy and between maintaining high standards in the core subjects and leaving space for innovation and breadth and balance. Although the Cambridge Primary Review (Alexander, 2010: 241-3) discusses a series of reports arguing for a broad and balanced curriculum as a route into high standards, the pressure for results often means that schools focus heavily on literacy and numeracy, especially in Year 6.

A new National Curriculum will be introduced in England from September 2014. The Government promised to reduce the amount of prescription, focusing mainly on the core subjects, leaving space for schools to develop their own school curriculum, of which the National Curriculum is only part. However, the level of detail in the Programmes of Study for primary schools - and the emphasis on systematic, synthetic phonics - has led many teachers to worry about how much space there will be for the humanities (history and geography) and the expressive arts (art, music and drama). It is uncertain to what extent these changes will change what, and how, primary teachers are expected to teach, but inspection and testing seem likely to continue to exert a strong influence on this.

There will always be a tension between how much content should be prescribed and how much left to individual schools' and teachers' discretion, and to what extent, and when, children should be taught to be subject specialists or generalists. However, any curriculum needs to be adapted and differentiated according to children's needs – for those with English as an additional language, those who are gifted and talented, those with special educational needs. This is essential if the National Curriculum being an entitlement for all children is to be a reality. Twiselton's (2006) research characterises some student primary teachers as 'task managers', with little emphasis on children's learning, some as 'curriculum deliverers', where the focus is more on learning, but largely based on external demands, and some as 'concept/skill builders', where teachers encourage children's broader learning and application of concepts and skills, rather than just completion of tasks.

Although the curriculum highlights what governments deem most important at any one time, head teachers often have their own priorities. For example, some may put pressure on teachers to ensure that the children perform well in SATs, even if other opportunities are restricted, and some will encourage artistic and cultural experiences more than others. However, enabling all children to learn successfully depends crucially on the skill and judgement of teachers in deciding how to take children's different abilities, backgrounds and cultures into account and build on their prior learning, and so seeing themselves as creating, not just delivering, the curriculum.

Task 8.1.3 How does the current curriculum reflect your own beliefs about what, and how, children should learn?

What are the advantages and disadvantages of having a national curriculum? What are the assumptions behind the current National Curriculum (2013) about:

- how young children learn?
- the teacher's role?
- the aims of education for primary age children?

In which respects do you share these assumptions? And in which respects do you differ?

M-LEVEL CHALLENGE

Bruner (2006: 141) wrote,

> we have learned that there is no such thing as *the* curriculum, there is only *a* curriculum; it is very specific to a particular situation and a particular student, and it will vary. For, in effect, it's an animated three-way conversation between a learner, someone who is somewhat more expert in an area of study and a body of knowledge that is difficult to define but that exists in the culture.

- What are the implications for how primary school teachers should teach?
- What are the challenges and opportunities in creating a broad and balanced curriculum, in a school you know well?

HOW INSPECTION AND SCHOOL STRUCTURES AFFECT THE TEACHER'S ROLE

Ofsted (the Office for Standards in Education) was established in 1993 to make schools, and teachers, more publicly accountable, and to enable parents and others to know about the quality of individual schools. SATs (tests) in English and maths were used to inform the inspection reports and to create league tables, with schools that did not achieve what was deemed an acceptable level expected to improve rapidly. Where this is the case, teachers are usually expected to focus even more on improving results in literacy and numeracy. Inspection has become a key influence on how schools, and teachers, allocate their time, so that most primary teachers – and children – spend a majority of the week on literacy and numeracy.

The Ofsted Inspection Framework (Ofsted, 2013, paragraphs 103–5) emphasises that inspectors must make an overarching judgement on the quality of education provided in the school. To do this, they must first make four key judgements on:

- the achievement of pupils;
- the quality of teaching;
- the behaviour and safety of pupils;
- the quality of leadership in, and management of, the school.

In addition, they must also consider:

- pupils' spiritual, moral, social and cultural development (SMSC); and
- the extent to which the education provided meets the needs of the range of pupils, and in particular those who have a disability and those with special educational needs.

This may seem unremarkable, but the 'high-stakes' aspect of inspection has tended to make heads – and teachers – very conscious of ensuring that they do what they think Ofsted will approve of. This leads to an emphasis on data, target-setting and monitoring, which can be very time consuming and often leads to teachers feeling pressured. However, the importance ascribed to SMSC highlights the need to balance a focus on literacy and numeracy with other areas of the curriculum and the pastoral and wider aspects of the teacher's role.

The present government has encouraged, or in some cases forced, schools to become academies, and so responsible to the Secretary of State rather than to local authorities and free to set many of their own policies. For instance, they do not need to follow the National Curriculum, can vary the length of the school day and may have a sponsor influencing how the school is run. As more primary

Task 8.1.4 Inspection and the class teacher's role

A major focus of inspection is on results in literacy and numeracy. To what extent does this mean that children should spend most of their time on these subjects? What advantages and disadvantages might there be for children:

- with English as an additional language;
- who are talented at music or art;
- who have behavioural and emotional difficulties?

(Remember the list of areas above that the Ofsted framework highlights in how inspectors will make their judgement.)

schools become academies, they are likely to introduce changes, some of which you may welcome, others less so. The reduced role of local authorities may make it less likely that you will have access to good continuing professional development and support, although good schools will make provision for this.

THE TEACHER'S WIDER ROLE

The primary teacher's role has always extended beyond what happens with children in the classroom. For example, this has involved reporting to, and working with, parents/carers, liaising with other teachers and visiting artists and poets, and contributing to whole-school events, such as Christmas productions, and, usually, to extracurricular activities. Aspects of this are discussed in other units, but this section considers the implications for the teacher's role.

We saw that teacher professionalism increasingly involves *managing* a range of learning opportunities for children, rather than just direct teaching. Planning will often entail working with other teachers in the same year group or key stage, but there are many other adults to plan with, or for, and to liaise with. Some will be highly qualified, others less so. Some may only visit the school occasionally. Some will work in the class, others with small groups or individuals, while others, such as learning mentors or specialist teachers, may offer individual support. For instance, for 10 per cent of your timetable, someone else will replace you for planning, preparation and assessment (PPA) time, and for another 10 per cent in your first year of teaching. Where those covering PPA time are less skilled, teachers may find that they are asked to provide lesson plans, although this is not a requirement. You are likely to have at least one teaching assistant (and possibly more), whether working alongside you or with a separate group, whom you will need to consider in your planning.

Although you will probably welcome such support, and this has the potential to improve children's learning opportunities, these all make demands in planning, liaising and ensuring that the class teacher keeps track of what is happening in all subject areas, as well as knowing about individuals' progress, making links across the whole curriculum and supporting those children who find working with a range of adults difficult. This may also give the teacher limited opportunities to work with the whole class for a sustained period.

Schools, and teachers, are expected to liaise closely with other professionals. Among these are:

*   health professionals such as school nurses and doctors;
*   teachers with specific expertise in a particular disability, such as sensory impairment or autism;
*   educational psychologists, who offer assessment and advice to schools and parents/carers, usually for children at the higher stages of the SEN code of practice;
*   educational social workers, who provide support, especially on attendance; and
*   social workers, especially with looked-after children (those vulnerable children whom a court (usually) has determined that the local authority has a particular duty to 'look after').

Many of these have specific expertise, to support individual children directly and/or help teachers meet their needs. Some have designated responsibilities in supporting parents/carers or monitoring children's welfare, and, often, professionals from other agencies have different procedures and ways of working, for instance in relation to confidentiality. Although much of the liaison is likely to be undertaken by senior colleagues, especially the head teacher or the SENCO, class teachers have an important role, for instance reporting concerns or being part of reviews. The class teacher, as the professional who sees children and parents/carers most frequently, is vital in noticing possible indicators of concern. For example, irregular attendance may indicate problems at home, or a child who becomes withdrawn or aggressive may need psychological support. Most serious is teachers' responsibility in relation to recognising the need for child protection, signs of which may be immediate, such as a bruise or a burn, or more long term and harder to identify, such as emotional abuse. All schools must have a child protection policy, with which all teachers should be familiar. This must be followed – with the first action usually being to share concerns with a senior colleague. As a rule of thumb, if in doubt, discuss your concerns with a more experienced teacher.

Working with parents/carers, and the benefits of doing so, are dealt with in more detail in other units. Liaising with them is a normal part of what teachers do. In the early years, especially, contact may be frequent and often informal. Class teachers have to report to, and discuss children's progress with, parents/carers more formally. Usually, this is constructive and helpful for parents/carers and teachers, although time constraints mean that these discussions are often rushed. Therefore, you must prepare well and ensure that parents/carers have time to raise key points and ask questions, as this is a two-way process. Sometimes, it is necessary to arrange separate meetings, and the need to inform, or involve, other professionals because of concerns about children's safety can, sometimes, strain relationships with parents/carers. However, remember that senior and more experienced colleagues are usually willing to help, with advice or by taking the lead.

Task 8.1.5 Planning support for a child with special educational needs

(This task is best done with someone else or in a small group.)

Imagine that you are the teacher of a class of whichever age you know best. In the class, a little girl, Paula, has a hearing impairment and speech and language difficulties.

- What information would you hope to have before you start teaching Paula?

List the other adults within and outside the school whom you would expect to be involved, including the professionals listed above and other adults, including support staff and midday supervisors and parent/carer(s).

- What would you hope to gain from each?
- What do you think you can offer to each of them? And to the process of assessment?
- Which aspects of your classroom environment or your teaching may need to be considered to ensure that Paula is fully integrated into the class and her additional needs can be met? Think, for example, of induction, equipment, grouping, use of support staff, timetable, activities outside the classroom etc.

M-LEVEL CHALLENGE

What are the challenges that teachers encounter when liaising, or working with, other professionals, especially those who are not teachers, in terms of:

(a) understanding each other's roles;
(b) time and responsibilities; and
(c) different belief systems and ways of working, such as confidentiality?

(See Atkinson *et al.*'s 2005 article for a brief review of some of the complexities of working with other professionals and the key factors involved in doing so successfully.)

SUMMARY

This unit has emphasised how complex the primary teacher's role is and the extent to which it requires professional judgement, drawing on a range of professional attributes, knowledge and understanding and skills, to make policies and initiatives work in the classroom.

Learning to be a teacher may mean that you will, initially, concentrate on the mechanics of teaching. However, changes in expectations of teachers and the knowledge and skills they require emphasise the importance of continuing professional development. This does not just involve courses, but reflection, reading, planning, evaluation of one's own teaching, moderation, coaching/mentoring, discussion (sometimes on one's own; where possible with others) – in many subject areas and classroom management. As a teacher can often feel isolated, remember to work with, and seek advice from, other colleagues and take whatever opportunities you can to see other, experienced teachers at work. They are usually happy to offer guidance, and schools benefit from the up-to-date knowledge and energy that new teachers bring. The variety of the primary school teacher's role is one reason why it is so rewarding, offering the chance to enrich many children's lives – and your own – but you need to ensure that you keep a good work–life balance by not taking on too much.

ANNOTATED FURTHER READING

Alexander, R. (ed.) (2010) *Children, Their World, Their Education - Final Report and Recommendations of the Cambridge Primary Review*. London: Routledge.
> The report of a major independent review of primary education, which is fairly daunting, but summarises a wealth of research.

Eaude, T. (2011) *Thinking Through Pedagogy for Primary and Early Years*. Exeter: Learning Matters.
> A book designed to help students explore the complexities of teaching in the primary and early years.

Pollard, A. (2002) *Reflective Teaching*. London: Continuum.

Pollard, A. (2002) *Readings for Reflective Teaching*. London: Continuum.
> Two linked books that, though large, are well worth dipping into, especially for short extracts, to set you thinking about different aspects of teaching. New editions of both were due to be published in 2014.

(M) FURTHER READING TO SUPPORT M-LEVEL STUDY

Atkinson, M., Doherty, P. and Kinder, K. (2005) Multi-agency working: models, challenges and key factors for success. *Journal of Early Childhood Research*, 3(1), 7-17.
> A short but thoughtful and practical article about the complexities of 'joined-up' working involving different agencies such as education, health and social services. It highlights areas that can be problematic when one is working with other professionals and key factors in doing so successfully.

Twiselton, S. (2006) The problem with English: the exploration and development of student teachers' English subject knowledge in primary classrooms. *Literacy*, 40(2), 88-96.

An article that uses English as an example to explore why, and in what ways, subject knowledge is important, arguing that what matters is how this is applied to enhance children's learning, and that teachers must see themselves not just as curriculum-deliverers, but as concept/skills builders.

RELEVANT WEBSITES

Reflective teaching: www.reflectiveteaching.co.uk
    A website that is constantly updated with articles to encourage reflective practice.

REFERENCES

Alexander, R. (2000) *Culture and Pedagogy – International Comparisons in Primary Education*. Oxford: Blackwell.

Alexander, R. (ed.) (2010) *Children, Their World, their Education – Final Report and Recommendations of the Cambridge Primary Review*. London: Routledge

Atkinson, M., Doherty, P. and Kinder, K. (2005) Multi-agency working: models, challenges and key factors for success. *Journal of Early Childhood Research*, 3(1): 7–17.

Bruner, J. (2006) *In Search of Pedagogy, Volume 11 – The Selected Works of Jerome S. Bruner*. London: Routledge.

Department for Education (2012) *Teachers' Standards*, www.education.gov.uk/schools/leadership/deployingstaff/a00205581/teachers-standards1-sep-2012

Department for Education and Skills (2003) *Excellence and Enjoyment: A Strategy for Primary Schools*: http://web archive.nationalarchives.gov.uk/20081230134948/nationalstrategies.standards.dcsf.gov.uk/primary/publications/literacy/63553/

Eaude, T. (2012) *How Do Expert Primary Classteachers Really Work? A Critical Guide for Teachers, Headteachers and Teacher Educators*. Northwich: Critical Publishing (www.criticalpublishing.com).

John, P. (2008) The predicament of the teaching profession and the revival of professional authority: a Parsonian perspective. In D. Johnson and R. Maclean (eds) *Teaching: Professionalization, Development and Leadership*. Berlin: Springer (springer.com).

Ofsted (2003) *School Inspection Handbook*, www.ofsted.gov.uk/resources/school-inspection-handbook.

Pollard, A. and Tann, S. (1994) *Reflective Teaching in the Primary School*. London: Cassell.

Schon, D. (1987) *Educating the Reflective Practitioner: Toward a New Design for Teaching and Learning the Professions*. San Francisco, CA: Jossey Bass.

Twiselton, S. (2006) The problem with English: the exploration and development of student teachers' English subject knowledge in primary classrooms. *Literacy*, 40(2): 88–96.

WORKING TOGETHER

Other adults in the classroom

Jenny Houssart and Andreas O. Kyriakides

INTRODUCTION

A common feature of contemporary primary classrooms is the presence of other adults employed to work alongside the teacher. Such adults are known by different names; we will generally use the phrase teaching assistant (TA) here. They present a considerable opportunity for both teachers and pupils, but making the most of them is not straightforward. Current and recent guidance for initial teacher education stresses that teachers need to communicate and work effectively with others, recognising their contributions and showing a commitment to collaborative working. These themes also occur throughout the literature and in our research data, which we draw on here.

We start by considering the growth in TA numbers and the debate about their effectiveness. Next, we discuss TAs with a general role, followed by those assigned to individuals. Finally, we consider issues related to TA training and development. We draw on our own interviews with TAs, first, in sections called 'TAs talking', where we give a range of views, and, second, in 'sharing strategies' sections, where we offer practical examples of strategies that our interviewees and the teachers they work with have found effective.

OBJECTIVES

By the end of this unit, you should have started to:

- be aware of factors that have led to the increase in TA numbers;
- be aware of some key research findings related to TAs' roles;
- consider the opportunities and potential challenges arising from the presence of other adults in primary classrooms;
- develop strategies for working collaboratively with TAs.

THE WHY AND WHO OF SUPPORT STAFF

The majority of primary teachers no longer work alone in classrooms. The large increase in the number of adults other than teachers working in schools is due to three main factors:

- increased opportunities for children considered to have special educational needs to attend mainstream schools;
- the advent of the National Literacy and Numeracy Strategies, later the Primary National Strategy;
- changes in workload management, brought about by the 'National agreement'.

These factors apply to different degrees across the United Kingdom; the first has had impact worldwide. A range of research examines the changing role and impact of support staff.

Research round-up (part 1): the evolving role of support staff

Butt and Lance (2009) consider how workforce reforms in the UK have impacted the role of TAs and conclude that TAs are now more closely involved with children's learning. Issues raised include ambiguity with job descriptions and line management. The changing roles of support staff are also a key theme of research by Barkham (2008), who identifies the introduction of the Literacy and Numeracy Strategies as a factor in increasing the involvement of TAs with learning. Concerns raised include lack of time for teachers and TAs to plan together and TAs' poor pay and conditions. Hancock and Eyres (2004) consider TAs' role in implementing the Literacy and Numeracy Strategies and argue that their role is undervalued in official reports.

A large-scale study, with an emphasis on quantitative data, was the Deployment and Impact of Support Staff (DISS) project, carried out in England and Wales. One article reporting on this project (Blatchford *et al.* 2011) explores the 'Positive approaches to learning' (PAL) and academic progress of pupils who work with support staff. Results on PAL are often positive. Results on academic progress suggest that pupils working with support staff make less progress than others; the authors claim this is not explained by the characteristics of these pupils. One suggestion in the paper is that this is because pupils who receive such support have less contact with the teacher and the curriculum as a result.

There is general agreement in the research that TAs have increasing involvement in teaching and learning. However, the research is inconclusive about their impact, particularly if seen in terms of pupil progress. Research has also considered the profile of support staff and exactly how they are deployed. We now consider these issues.

Who are support staff, and how can their backgrounds be used?

TAs in UK schools were once seen as mainly white and female, with modest qualifications and often with their own primary aged children. This led in the past to TAs being known by some as 'Mums' army' (Ainscow 2000, cited in Kerry 2005) and to be associated in school folklore with parent helpers, working on a voluntary basis to perform tasks such as washing paint pots. Kerry outlines the change in attitudes and practices from the time when TAs were often seen in this way and goes on to offer a typology for conceptualising the roles of TAs, which includes the categories carer/mentor, behaviour manager, curriculum supporter and mobile paraprofessional (p377).

Changes in the role of TAs are confirmed by a study from an industrial-relations perspective (Bach *et al.* 2006), which comments on the growing diversity of the TA workforce, as well as changes in TA roles. They note the ethnic diversity of the TA workforce in some areas, as well as TAs with differing career aspirations. A large study by Russell *et al.* (2005, p180) also notes the range of TA qualifications, with those in their study ranging from having no qualifications to degrees or higher degrees, with the majority having their highest qualification at either GCSE or A level. There is agreement in the literature that TAs are now a more diverse group, engaged in a wider range of tasks. They possess a range of skills and qualities, as the following examples illustrate.

TAs talking (part 1): background and experience

> Yes. I was an interior designer for about twenty years and I have my own business and things ... And I'd started going into my son's primary school to read ... and that's what got me started ... And it sounds a bit clichéd, but it's a bit more meaningful than worrying about people's curtains and cushions and things, so that's really what got me started. So I went along for the interview with various odd dressing-up pictures, really, that I made with my son ... I thought, 'Well, I've got to show I know *something* about kids'.
>
> (Audrey)

> I did a training ... years ago. Mediation for youth offenders ... I was trained to be ... a mediator that goes to young offender's homes ... But I think that's been useful. Elements of that have stayed with me. And I know that when I'm speaking to children ... I do use the skills that I know. I have worked voluntarily in settings with young children ... Just helping to run playgroups and things like that. Or maybe just being a big kid yourself helps, you know [*Laughter*].
>
> (Charlene)

> I know how to teach these things because I have a child of my own in primary school ... I know what to ask, what to expect from the child ... If you can't teach it, if you can't explain it yourself to the child he will not be able to understand it. I'm seeing this from my own perspective as a mother ... I believe that the way you explain something to a child is very important.
>
> (Diana)

Task 8.2.1 TA experience

- How would you make the most of the skills and experience of each of the assistants considered above?
- Have a conversation with a TA in the school you work in to find out their experience and consider how this might be used.

Sharing strategies: drawing on individual strengths

The examples below, drawn from our research, show how some schools try to make the most of the expertise that individual TAs bring.

- Several of the TAs we interviewed reported that schools make use of the experience they gained from their *previous employment*, or voluntary work. For example, Tony, who had worked as a chef, started a cookery club and worked with the teacher to develop activities related to taste tests as part of a topic on chocolate.
- Some TAs had experience of children and adults with *particular needs* that schools could draw on, sometimes by assigning the TA to work with an individual child, sometimes by involving the TA in discussions about meeting the needs of various children. For example, Kate, who supported a child in a wheelchair, came from a family where children had particular physical needs.

- For some, living in the *local community* was important in helping them to understand the children. For Obi, her voluntary work teaching Swahili at a Saturday school contributed to her informal role in supporting children from East African communities, both in praising their progress in Swahili and in discussing with them the differing expectations in different school systems.

TEACHING ASSISTANTS AS PART OF A CLASSROOM TEAM

TAs work in a range of ways, and schools will often take the strengths and experiences of individual assistants into account when making decisions about this. However, the two basic alternatives are for them to be assigned to one or more learners with special educational needs, or to be assigned to a class or classes, with their particular role within the class decided in conjunction with the class teacher. We consider this sort of general TA next.

Research round-up (part 2): general classroom support

Several research projects have focused on TAs assigned to work with a particular class. An example is a project in Scotland reported by Woolfson and Truswell (2005), in which additional assistants were placed in primary schools in disadvantaged areas. Each assistant was placed in a class to work under the direction of, and in partnership with, the class teacher. The aims of the project were to improve the quality of learning, impact positively on pupils' personal and social development and encourage parental involvement. Evaluation of the project suggests that these aims were met, with particular success in the first two. The authors also suggest that assistants are more likely to be effective when they work closely with the class teacher, and their effectiveness can be enhanced by the provision of more opportunities for liaison between class teachers and assistants. This call for teamwork is echoed elsewhere: a report by Ofsted (2002) on the quality and impact of the work of TAs in primary schools sees close partnership between TAs and teachers as key.

A detailed consideration of ways in which teachers and TAs might work together is presented by Cremin *et al.* (2005). They used an intervention strategy to develop three classroom models: *room management*, involving assigning specific roles to each adult; *zoning*, where responsibilities are divided according to classroom geography; and *reflective teamwork*, where adults develop integrated ways of working together, based on thorough discussion. Each model was introduced to two schools for use in literacy lessons. They reported increased pupil engagement in all cases. All three models stressed enhanced teamwork and role clarity, and the findings suggest that these are the key features, rather than the details of the models, which can all be seen as having advantages and disadvantages.

Task 8.2.2 TA and teacher role agreement

- Consider the three models presented by Cremin *et al.* (2005). What do you consider the advantages and disadvantages of each model? Can you suggest other ways of agreeing roles?
- Think about the class you work in, or one you are familiar with. How does the agreement of roles between the TA and teacher in this class match those suggested by Cremin *et al.*?

Varying levels of clarity about roles was a common theme in our interviews with TAs. The extracts below show the range of experiences, from having virtually no direct instructions about what to do, to feeling totally involved as part of a team. The middle example, suggesting the TA would like to know more about the thinking behind planning, was echoed by many other interviewees.

TAs talking (part 2): general classroom support

It's funny, actually, because I thought I would get a lot more direction when I started this job. I thought I would be asked to do things: 'Could you do this? Could you do that?' . . . I do use my initiative and the teacher I've been working with for the last two years didn't really ask me to do anything.

(Charlene)

I have a great deal of respect for the teacher I'm with now . . . even though we work on a very equal platform, the planning is planned really . . . One thing I find frustrating is that, alright, we've seen the weekly plans . . . Just sort of knowing the understanding and the reasoning behind it, really, I think. So yes, in an ideal world, it would be nice to be a part of the planning.

(Margaret)

She's really made me enthusiastic as well, because she's enthusiastic. And she's confident, and she makes me confident. She includes me in the planning and the team teaching. She takes my advice on things . . . She kind of values my ideas, which is a great boost of confidence, and makes you believe a little bit more in yourself. And the kids really pick up on it as well.

(Sheena)

Sharing strategies: agreeing roles and responsibilities

The quotations above suggest that TAs feel that both they and the children benefit if they are involved by the teacher. This still leaves questions about the nature of the involvement and how teachers and TAs find time to communicate. Here are some practical suggestions that have worked for the TAs named and their teachers:

- Some TAs have a role in *assessing children's learning*. For Marion, this happens at the start of a lesson, when the teacher introduces a topic to the whole class. The teacher indicates particular learners he would like Marion to observe in the introduction, making judgements about their understanding and providing support if necessary. When Margaret works with groups of learners, her support includes marking their work during the lesson and explaining what she is writing to the children, a process agreed with the class teacher. Pria also has a role in marking work and received specific training from the deputy head about the school's marking policy before she was asked to do this.
- When TAs are assigned to a group of children for the middle part of the lesson, they may have a role in *adapting work*, sometimes to assist children with difficulties. Jan listens to the teacher's introduction to work, so that, if she has to repeat the instructions later, she uses the same words and ideas, possibly in simplified form. Margaret has developed strategies for breaking down and going over ideas, using whiteboards and practical equipment. Crucially, Jan and Margaret see their role as supporting children to enable them to do the work, not as doing the work for them. Rita works in a classroom where extension activities are planned by the teacher, and Rita can decide when children would benefit from these.
- Finding time to *liaise with teachers* can be challenging. Sheena is allowed some planning time with the teacher out of the classroom. Others use short periods of time inventively. Tony works

with older primary children who do some work in sets. The children organise themselves to return from sets to classes, and Tony uses this short time every day to feed back information to the teacher about children he has supported during sets. Pauline writes brief information about children's responses to tasks and how much help they needed on post-its, which she gives to the teacher. Lola has a short pro forma that she completes at the end of sessions supporting groups, to give the teacher an outline of how the session progressed and how the children responded.

SUPPORTING INDIVIDUALS

In many countries, TAs have been used increasingly to support individual children with special needs and to enable them to attend mainstream school. In the research round-up below, we draw on literature discussing this practice in England, Cyprus and the USA. Other countries using this system include Scotland (Woolfson and Truswell 2005) Northern Ireland (Abbott *et al.* 2011), Finland (Takala 2007) and New Zealand (Rutherford 2012). A strength of this system is that the TA may work alongside one child for several years, getting to know them well. Such TAs are sometimes linked to a unit within the school for children with a particular need, or have attended specialist training or liaised with external experts who visit the school. They sometimes form a relationship with the child's parents.

Despite the advantages, potential drawbacks exist. A key issue can be misunderstanding about who is responsible for the child's education. Role clarity is important here, and teachers should also understand the contribution TAs responsible for individuals can make.

Research round-up (part 3): TAs' support for individuals

Considerable international research and debate exist concerning the use of TAs assigned to support individual children. A study carried out in two schools in Cyprus (Angelides *et al.* 2009) identified a range of practices across the schools leading the authors to conclude that the role of 'companions' (a direct translation of their Greek title) in relation to inclusion was contradictory. They found instances where the presence of the 'companion' increased the child's participation in the learning process and encouraged relations with other children. However, they also give examples where the companions hindered inclusion, by reducing interaction between the pupil and the teacher or by completing work for the pupil. Sometimes, dependence on the companion appeared to be encouraged, and time spent with the companion was at the expense of time spent with other students. Teachers interviewed as part of this study had different expectations of companions. Some expected them to take much responsibility for teaching the child, whereas others felt they, as teachers, should retain that responsibility. Similar findings have arisen in studies in other countries.

Giangreco (2003), writing from a USA perspective, makes a strong case for teachers engaging with pupils with disabilities, even though they are assigned individual assistants. He maintains that teachers should not expect the assistant to take responsibility for educating the child, but should work with the assistant in a supportive way.

Although a TA may be assigned to a named child, they may be deployed in a more integrated way to meet the child's needs. Such practices were found by Rose (2000) in a case study of a school in England with a high proportion of pupils with special educational needs. The assistants had a wider role than working with the individuals they were assigned to; the implication is that this is the school's policy. Points are made about the importance of teamwork and effective communication.

TAs talking (part 3): supporting individuals

> Sometimes yes I spoke with the teacher . . . but mostly I would say I did what I did by my own.
>
> (Kate)

> When they have a test I'm saying to him to try his best. Okay, I help him but I am not going to tell lies to the teachers, right? They got to know him, they know how much he understands.
>
> (Dorothy)

> Each person has to do his job. Teachers have to teach and TAs have to do their job as TAs. Teachers take three times our salary and even more.
>
> (Eva)

Task 8.2.3 TA support interviews

Having made your own daily observations of the way a TA supports a child, conduct individual interviews with the classroom teacher, the TA, the parents of the child and with some of the child's peers. Ask them what impact they think TA support has on the child's progress (both in terms of cognition and socialisation). Compare the views of the five resources (yourself included) and draw conclusions about TAs' contribution to the inclusion of children with special needs in mainstream schools. Specify three ways in which you can use your conclusions to maximise children's progress.

Sharing strategies: supporting individuals

- Diana draws upon three resources to assist children with special needs in lessons: (a) the learning objectives set by the special education teacher for each child; (b) her own experience as a parent; (c) relatives' advice.
- Lynn relies on the ways the teacher shows in the classroom to teach. She also thinks that her communication with the child's parents has a positive impact on the child's long-term achievement.
- Susan supports a 10-year-old boy who sometimes becomes upset or aggressive during mental mathematics sessions, which he finds difficult. Susan works alongside the boy for these sessions, using tasks adapted by the teacher to suit his needs. If necessary, Susan will accompany him out of the room and use strategies to help him calm down and relax.
- Pauline is assigned to work with a boy diagnosed as on the autistic spectrum. In mathematics lessons, she usually starts a lesson alongside him, using strategies to help him focus. When these strategies prove successful, she works alongside others in the group, a strategy agreed with the teacher, partly to encourage his independence.

TEACHING ASSISTANTS' TRAINING AND DEVELOPMENT

We have hinted above at the variation in training and development available to TAs and how that is likely to affect the support they can offer. We now turn explicitly to this issue.

Research round-up (part 4): TAs' training and development

In the UK and many other countries, no formal training or qualifications are required to be a TA. Lack of training is raised as an issue by many studies (e.g. Butt and Lance 2009). However,

TAs increasingly have qualifications and specific training for the job, although many – including some TAs – see this as inadequate or patchy. Abbott *et al.* (2011), in Northern Ireland, focused on the training needs of support staff who worked with pupils with different special needs. The assistants consulted overwhelmingly said they would like more training, including training aimed at giving them a deeper understanding of the various syndromes and conditions they dealt with. Given the increasing role of TAs in numeracy and literacy, they are increasingly likely to receive training in these areas. An example is the Specialist Teacher Assistant programme, an Open University programme for TAs, with a focus on English and mathematics. An evaluation of TAs completing the course, by Swann and Loxley (1998), reports that almost all felt they had increased knowledge and confidence, but this was not necessarily reflected in wider roles in their schools. The authors conclude that increasing TAs' competence does not necessarily lead to changes in their role; this is in the hands of schools and teachers. This underlines the importance of teachers who work alongside TAs being aware of the training they have received.

Mistry *et al.* (2004) report on a case study from a school for 4–9-year-olds in England that examines the role of support staff . Recommendations include a need for training for support staff, to support their work, and for teachers, in order to enable them to manage adults more effectively. This reflects the fact that, traditionally, teachers received no such training, and many started their careers expecting that they would work alone in the classroom. Current and recent requirements, however, are that teachers will begin their careers aware of ways of working alongside support staff.

TAs talking (part 4): training and development

We have training . . . it's in my contract. Not all of us are contracted into joining INSET, . . . But it's cool. I want to. It's important, I think. I find them really useful, actually . . . those TAs who perhaps don't really feel that they want to move on don't have to attend.

(Dorian)

I actually found out about it (Aspergers) in my foundation degree . . . because I was actually doing a few modules where they spoke about autism, and I thought, 'Okay, I work with a boy, that rings a few bells'.

(Salma)

Certainly, it would have been useful if I attended some seminars with regard to subject matter. Because you will offer much more to the children.

(Hara)

It depends on the level of the child. With this child I am working with, I don't need anything because he doesn't understand anything. But if I worked with a different child who understood and I was always next to him I would want to help him.

(Dorothy)

There's no need to attend any seminars about how to help children understand mathematics because then you get into the teacher's job.

(Mary)

Sharing strategies: training and development

•   For many TAs, part of their role involves working with individuals or groups considered to need additional support on intervention programmes in English and mathematics. These normally consist of pre-prepared materials and instructions and are ideally accompanied by appropriate training. For example, Tony attended training for catch-up literacy, and, in line with the

Task 8.2.4 Views of the TAs

- What do you think about the differing views of the TAs quoted in 'TAs talking (part 4)' about the need for training or development related to subject matter? Do you agree with Dorothy's assertion that this is not required if the children supported are working on simple (to adults) tasks?
- How do the views and experiences of the TAs in your school compare with those expressed in 'TAs talking (part 4)'?
- Discuss the implications of the aforementioned views.

programme's expectations, the deputy head with responsibility for literacy also attended, so that there was a member of staff with overall responsibility with whom the TA could discuss issues. In Jodie's school, training for TAs working on intervention programmes was led by the deputy head, who carried out some activities with a group of children, observed by TAs.

- Several TAs received training and guidance relevant to the specific needs of individuals they support. Pauline had attended several courses outside the school on supporting children on the autistic spectrum. Sometimes, outside agencies visit the schools and share expertise with TAs and teachers. For example, a speech and language specialist visited Jan's school to deliver sessions to a small group of children while Jan watched. After 6 weeks, Jan took over the sessions, while the specialist watched and supported. After that, the specialist made occasional visits. Sometimes, a special unit or department exists inside the school, and the department staff share their expertise with TAs; Jodie received support on working with hearing impaired children from specialists within her school.
- Some TAs are involved in training in their schools alongside the teachers. Dorian's contract states that attending INSET within the schools is part of her job, and she is positive about sessions she has attended, for example about boys and writing. In Barbara's school, TAs attend staff meetings concerned with materials used for teaching mathematics, such as number lines, and literacy training. Thus, teachers are aware of the training the TAs have had and can make the most of it. This is only usually possible when training is provided during the working day, or when TAs work and are paid for sufficient hours to attend meetings after school.

SUMMARY

This unit offers strong examples of positive practice in primary classrooms where teachers work alongside other adults. When TAs have a general supporting role in the classroom, there is a range of models for agreeing the respective roles of the teacher and TA. Whichever model is used, it is clarity of roles that enhances the experience of both adults and children. When TAs work mainly or entirely with individual learners with particular needs, the teacher still has overall responsibility for learning, but should recognise, value and utilise the knowledge and expertise brought by the TA. The TA workforce varies from those with no qualifications to graduates, and some may have studied on work-based foundation degrees or attained higher-level teaching assistant (HLTA) status. All will bring with them tacit knowledge acquired in a range of contexts, and many will have expertise related to the particular needs of learners they support. If TAs and teacher work as a team to develop effective practice, they are better placed to meet the needs of all learners.

ANNOTATED FURTHER READING

Angelides, P., Constantinou, C. and Leigh, J. (2009) The role of paraprofessionals in developing inclusive education in Cyprus, *European Journal of Special Needs Education*, 24(1), 75-89.

> A study of the role of 'companions' in Cyprus indicates the internationally acknowledged confused status of their contribution towards provision of effective inclusive education.

 FURTHER READING TO SUPPORT M-LEVEL STUDY

Blatchford, P., Bassett, P., Brown, P., Martin, C., Russell, A. and Webster, R. (2011) The impact of support staff on pupils' 'positive approaches to learning' and their academic progress, *British Educational Research Journal*, 37(3), 443-64.

> A report of findings from the DISS project, including discussion of whether pupils supported by TAs make more progress.

Cremin, H., Thomas, G. and Vincett, K. (2005) Working with teaching assistants: three models evaluated, *Research Papers in Education*, 20(4), 413-32.

> Three classroom models (room management, zoning, reflecting teamwork) are suggested as methods of teacher-TA collaboration.

 RELEVANT WEBSITES

Teachfind: http://archive.teachfind.com/ttv/www.teachers.tv/ta.html

> Under the Teaching assistants' link, there are videos, features and quick tips helpful for the enhancement of TAs' role.

Institute of Education: www.ioe.ac.uk/research/departments/phd/5619.html

> Provides a range of articles and reports arising from the DISS study.

 REFERENCES

Abbott, L. McConkey, R. and Dobbins, M. (2011) Key players in inclusion: Are we meeting the professional needs of learning support assistants for pupils with complex needs? *European Journal of Special Needs Education*, 26(2), 215-31.

Angelides, P., Constantinou, C. and Leigh, J. (2009) The role of paraprofessionals in developing inclusive education in Cyprus, *European Journal of Special Needs Education*, 24(1), 75-89.

Bach, S., Kessler, I. and Heron, P. (2006) Changing job boundaries and workforce reform: the case of teaching assistants, *Industrial Relations Journal*, 37(1), 2-21.

Barkham, J. (2008) Suitable work for women? Roles, relationships and changing identities of 'other adults' in the early years classroom, *British Educational Research Journal*, 34(6), 839-53.

Blatchford, P., Bassett, P., Brown, P., Martin, C., Russell, A. and Webster, R. (2011) The impact of support staff on pupils' 'positive approaches to learning' and their academic progress, *British Educational Research Journal*, 37(3), 443-64.

Butt, G. and Lance, A. (2009) 'I am *not* the teacher!': some effects of remodelling the roles of teaching assistants in English primary schools, *Education 3-13*, 37(3), 219-31.

Cremin, H., Thomas, G. and Vincett, K. (2005) Working with teaching assistants: three models evaluated, *Research Papers in Education*, 20(4), 413-32.

Giangreco, M. (2003) Working with paraprofessionals, *Educational Leadership*, 61(2), 50-3.

Hancock, R. and Eyres, I. (2004) Implementing a required curriculum reform: teachers at the core, teaching assistants on the periphery? *Westminster Studies in Education*, 27, 223-35.

Kerry, T. (2005)Towards a typology for conceptualizing the roles of teaching assistants, *Educational Review*, 57(3), 373-84.

Mistry, M., Burton, N. and Brundrett, M. (2004) Managing LSAs: an evaluation of the use of learning support assistants in an urban primary school, *School Leadership and Management*, 24(2), 125-37.

Ofsted (2002) *Teaching Assistants in Primary Schools: An evaluation of the quality and impact of their work*. HMI 434 (London, OFSTED).

Rose, R. (2000) Using classroom support in a primary school, a single school case study, *British Journal of Special Education*, 27(4), 191-6.

Russell, A., Blatchford, P., Bassett, P., Brown, P. and Martin, C. (2005) The views of teaching assistants in English key stage 2 classes on their role, training and job satisfaction, *Educational Research*, 47(2), 175-89.

Rutherford, G. (2012) In, out or somewhere in between? Disabled students' and teacher aides' experiences of school, *International Journal of Inclusive Education*, 16(8), 757-74.

Swann, W. and Loxley, A. (1998) The impact of school-based training on classroom assistants in primary schools, *Research Papers in Education*, 13, 141-60.

Takala, M. (2007) The work of classroom assistants in special and mainstream education in Finland, *British Journal of Special Education*, 34(1), 50-7.

Woolfson, R. and Truswell, E. (2005) Do classroom assistants work? *Educational Research*, 47(1), 63-75.

PARTNERSHIPS WITH PARENTS

John Ryan and Stephen Griffin

INTRODUCTION

This unit focuses on building effective, purposeful and long-lasting relationships with parents/carers. For the purposes of this unit, the term 'parents' should be taken to include carers also – single parents, grandparents, foster carers or older siblings, acting *in loco parentis*. After the Education Acts 1988 and 1992, parents have been increasingly described as 'partners' in their children's education. Coupled with the move towards greater parental choice in terms of the schools parents can send their children to, such as academy primary schools, there has also been an increased transparency of school performance data, via Ofsted reports, league tables and the publication of exam results; parents are viewed as key stakeholders in the educational process and, more recently, the choice of schools. The Coalition government has encouraged parents and independent groups in England to set up their own schools under the academy scheme – called free schools. The first 24 opened in September 2012, and yet the current government's prediction of 55 opening in the

OBJECTIVES

By the end of this unit you should:

- have an understanding of the need to ensure that you develop secure relationships with the parents of pupils in your class, during school placement, the first year of teaching and subsequent years of teaching;
- recognise and understand the importance of purposeful and structured working relationships with parents;
- know of effective ways of liaising and communicating with parents;
- have an appreciation of the need for trust and understanding as the foundation for successful relationships between parents and school;
- know the range of partners and external agencies with which a primary school has to work in order to support children and parents;
- begin to have some strategies as a trainee teacher or newly qualified teacher (NQT) and begin to establish sound home–school links;
- understand the impact of recent Coalition government educational policy upon schools and the implications of these changes for parents.

autumn 2012, with a further 114 opening in 2013, has yet to be achieved. *Excellence and Enjoyment* (Department for Education and Skills, 2003), introduced under the previous Labour government and still used currently in primary schools, directly stresses 'partnership beyond the classroom', where primary schools 'review their strategies for involving parents in their children's education'. The power of parental involvement should not be underestimated – the Organisation for Economic Co-operation and Development (OECD) has suggested that family social background and involvement accounts for 29 per cent of variation in pupil educational outcomes (2001 Program for International Student Assessment (PISA) study, in Goldstein, 2004). In an attempt to support children from disadvantaged backgrounds, the Coalition government has extended provision available for the organisation known as CANparent – an organisation established to give parents of children under 5 years old £100 vouchers to purchase parenting lessons from independent organisations, e.g. the national Childcare trust; however, this is currently still a trial and only available to parents in England in certain areas. Therefore, it is evident that greater collaboration with parents needs to be a key aim in improving educational outcomes for children.

PROFESSIONAL REQUIREMENTS

It is important to recognise that, not only is parental involvement desirable in achieving positive educational outcomes, but it is also a professional requirement of all teachers, as detailed in the new *Professional Standards* published in 2012.

The qualified teacher status (QTS) standards (Training and Development Agency for Schools, 2007) are divided into three sections:

- professional attributes;
- professional knowledge and understanding;
- professional skills.

The implementation of a concise set of standards, which apply to teachers at the point of entry to the profession, as well as to experienced practitioners, will, according to the government, enable the following: 'an overarching set of standards establishes a platform for the coherent approach to Initial Teacher Education (ITE), induction and continuing professional development (CPD) that the profession aspires to' (Training and Development Agency for Schools, 2007). Running through all these standards is a theme of being respectful towards all learners and considerate and committed to raising their achievement. The new standards are organised as separate headings, numbered 1–8. Under each section, there are bullets and subheadings. These subheadings should not be referenced as separate standards and should be used advisedly. For example, under section 8, we see the introduction of the role of parents for the first time. Despite the government's acknowledgement of the importance of schools working effectively with parents, the new standards now have only one reference to parental engagement. However, included in standard Q8 is an emphasis on the need for trainee (and indeed all) teachers to ensure the importance of working alongside parents:

- Communicate effectively with parents with regard to pupils' achievements and well-being, young people, colleagues, parents and carers.

(Training and Development Agency for Schools, 2012: Q8)

Under the current Coalition government, there has been increasing concern regarding the teaching of reading and basic mathematic strategies. These now form an integral part of Ofsted inspections and ITE provision. As such, parents' understanding of pedagogical approaches in primary school, such as the teaching of synthetic phonics as the preferred method for teaching reading and a move towards an instrumental approach for the teaching of mathematics, has now increased.

HISTORICAL OVERVIEW

Historically, in England, the home and the school have been two distinct and separate realms of a child's life. The role that parents have as educators has, therefore, been underdeveloped in the past. The Hadow Report (1931) highlighted the importance of a child-centred curriculum, but it was not until the Plowden Report (Department of Education and Science, 1967) that recognition was attributed to the vital role that parents can play in their child's education: 'One of the essentials for educational advance is a closer partnership between the two parties (i.e. schools and parents) to every child's education' (Department of Education and Science, 1967: 102).

As well as highlighting parental involvement, it also suggested strategies as to how this could be implemented, the most significant being Parent Teacher Associations (PTAs) – a common feature of our schools today. More recently, Desforges and Abouchaar discussed the obvious link between input from home and attainment in school: 'Parental involvement has a significant effect on children's achievement and adjustment even after all other factors (such as social class, maternal education and poverty) have been taken out of the equation' (2003: 9.2.2).

As teachers, you need to ensure that this is constructively built on and you have a secure understanding of pupils' cultural capital (Bourdieu, 1986). This can be understood as the set of dispositions that enable certain groups of pupils to succeed more readily at school than others; that is, they receive linguistic ability from their parents and have access to certain forms of culture, such as the theatre and the 'arts', which are reflected heavily in the school curriculum. It is these predisposed skills that give them the advantage, whereas pupils from less privileged backgrounds may struggle to access the curriculum for this very reason.

Under the last Labour government, strong links between parents and schools were encouraged. In particular, strategies such as Early Intervention and Sure Start were seen as integral to supporting child development and fostering links with parents. More recently, the Coalition government, although acknowledging the importance of its Early Intervention Grant as a means of supporting successful practice, has reduced overall funding. Inevitably then, schools remain at the forefront of 'early intervention', and all teachers, including NQTs, need to be mindful of promoting positive relationships with parents and outside agencies who support children and their families.

The government's *Excellence and Enjoyment* (Department for Education and Skills, 2003) outlines three proposals to ensure that parental involvement is maximised. These are:

* providing parents with information;
* giving parents a voice;
* encouraging parental partnerships with schools.

A wide range of strategies have been adapted in primary schools to ensure that the above have been implemented and followed. These will be discussed throughout this unit.

As recently as 30 years ago, children who did not achieve the national expectation were labelled as 'educationally subnormal' or even 'unteachable'. It was not until 1978 that the concept of 'inclusion' and 'inclusive education' was introduced into primary pedagogy by the publication of the Warnock Report, thus giving all children with special educational need (SEN) the entitlement to attend mainstream education. Dearing (1993) noted that one in five children will have some form of SEN at various stages throughout their school life. As an NQT, you need to become familiar with the SEN Code of Practice (Department for Education and Skills, 2001), currently being utilised in schools, and the philosophy behind the policy for inclusion and removal of barriers to learning; however, at the time of writing this unit, current government policy is being changed relating to SEN and the SEN Code of Practice. You need to be familiar with the current Coalition's stance and the proposed changes to the current SEN Code of Practice. At the time of writing this unit, the current government is in the process of making wide-ranging proposals to support children and young people with SEN and their families. This is the biggest reform in provision for some 30 years. As NQTs and student teachers, you need to be aware that these proposals will affect mainstream provision significantly. The major changes, according to the government's Green Paper, 'Support and aspiration: a new approach to SEN and disability' (DfE, 2011), that will affect you as a mainstream teacher, include the following:

* The old system of statementing is set to be reformed, with the disappearance of the categories of School Action and School Action Plus. In its place will be a new kind of statement that brings together the medical and educational needs of the child.
* There will be a lot more focus on the attainment and progress of lower-attaining pupils in published school performance data.
* The 'bias towards inclusion' is to end, and the Green Paper suggests that parent power may prevent the closure of special schools, which could be saved with free school status.
* Parents will also be able to express a preference for their child to attend a particular school, and this should be met, unless this would not provide the best education for the child, disrupt the education of other children or be an inefficient use of resources.

With the introduction of the Children Act 2004, it could be argued that most primary schools are more proactive than ever at investigating strategies to ensure parents are actively involved in their child's education. In January 2003, a national Workforce Remodelling Agreement was signed by school workforce unions, local government employers and the government. The purpose was to support schools in raising standards and tackling workload issues for staff. It also enabled many schools to have more autonomy as to how to organise the structure of their staff. One of the results was that many schools now employ a principal parent officer (PPO) or parent support adviser (PSA). Often, these roles are carried out by class teachers or TAs and complement the common core of skills and knowledge for children's workforce staff of the *Every Child Matters* (ECM; see below) agenda and are aligned to the Children's Workforce Development Council induction standards. The current Coalition government is currently looking at changing outcomes and processes relating to ECM, but it is still referred to in current practice in educational settings.

The recent Green Paper relating to changes in the SEN Code of Practice states:

> Our proposal for a single category of SEN would make it easier for schools to plan and deliver the right support and provide clarity for families on the help their child can expect to receive, whether it is a normally available tailored approach (such as support delivered through one of the Every Child programmes) or something specific to SEN.

Roles concerned with initial training, as well as staff working with children, young people and their families, are receiving increased attention in relation to ensuring children receive the best possible start in education. Under the previous government, the Department for Children, Schools and Families (DCSF) funding was expanded to ensure the utilisation of school-based PSAs, as outlined in the Children Act 2004 (Department for Education and Skills, 2004). The roles of teachers and parents may be different, but the ambitions that they have for children are very similar, if not identical. Teachers are contributing and adding to the learning process that has already, hopefully, been begun by the parents.

A brief history of the ECM agenda would be useful, as these major reforms, although soon to be replaced, are common practice in schools and are starting points for proposed changes by the Coalition government. In 2003, the previous government published the ECM Green Paper (see Department for Education and Skills, 2004). This coincided with the public inquiry into the death of

Victoria Climbié, known as the Laming Report (Health Committee, 2003), which outlined huge failings in systems in place to protect children. According to Reid, the ECM agenda, 'proposes the most radical changes in services for children and their families since the Children Act 1989' (Reid, 2005: 12). This agenda and its philosophy constitute a radical change, which incorporates protection yet places more emphasis on prevention.

One of the previous government's visions was, by implementing ECM, to support the principle of personalisation, as well as supporting the work schools were already doing in order to raise educational standards. Five outcomes were identified that were significant to the well-being of all children. As NQTs, and indeed as any grade of teacher, it is useful to still refer to the following five outcomes as a way to ensure that all children meet ways to:

- be healthy;
- stay safe;
- enjoy and achieve;
- make a positive contribution;
- achieve economic well-being.

At the heart of the ECM agenda was the recognition that parents play a significant role in supporting their child's education and are key educators themselves. The publication *Every Parent Matters* (Department for Education and Skills, 2007) goes so far as to suggest that, 'Parents and the home environment they create are the single most important factor in shaping their children's well-being, achievements and prospects'. The Coalition government has made clear its continued commitment to ensuring relevant data and information relating to schools' overall performances are shared in a more transparent way with parents.

Common Assessment Framework

Under the Coalition government, the Common Assessment Framework (CAF) is still a key part of delivering frontline services in an attempt to integrate and focus on the needs of children and young people. It should be a standardised approach used by practitioners, such as teachers, in order to assess children's additional needs and decide how these should be met.

These procedures are again utilised in schools and, in many cases, have taken over more significance than ECM outcomes. If, for any reason, a child in your class is not progressing towards the five ECM outcomes, you need to discuss your concerns with the designated teacher, and CAF procedures will have to be employed for the child. The process that this may take will vary in each local authority and may include:

- pre-assessment checklist;
- discussion with designated teacher;
- consent from parents;
- checking with other professionals/CAF;
- undertaking CAF;
- allocating lead professional;
- coordinating services.

As an NQT, it is very unlikely that you will lead the CAF and be known as the 'lead professional', but, as a class teacher, your evidence and contributions will be very significant, which is why it is essential to keep rigorous and up-to-date records of pupils' progress in relation to all areas of the curriculum and the five outcomes of ECM. Parent permission must be sought before a CAF is carried out on their child, and only CAF-trained professionals may undertake one.

The purpose of carrying out a CAF is to stimulate early intervention in cooperation with families and encourage multi-agency working. It is anticipated by the government that such an approach will prevent overlap or repeating information gathering and thus provide better and more appropriate services for families. For example, after completing a CAF for a child in your class, all practitioners may well help the parents access other services, such as health, social care or housing.

There are instances when a CAF may not be deemed appropriate. The most important one could be, for example, that you, as a class teacher, are worried about significant harm being done to the child. In such cases, you need to raise your concerns with the designated teacher in school and adhere to confidentiality. Another reason may be that you are aware of the needs of the child or family, but your service, that is school, can meet these needs. In such a case, you would need to involve outside agencies and be guided by senior members of staff or the designated teacher.

ADVANTAGES OF SECURE RELATIONSHIPS WITH PARENTS

Research (Bastiani, 2003; Desforges and Abouchaar, 2003) has shown that involving parents in their children's education can help remove barriers to learning, raise attainment and improve attitudes and behaviour. It is widely believed that primary schools, working in partnership with parents to support their children's learning and development, can expect significant and lasting benefits. Among these are improved, as well as consistent, levels of attainment, coupled with a more positive attitude towards behaviour and attendance.

O'Hara (2008: 14) highlights the importance of communicating with parents and suggests six practical ways to ensure that teachers and parents have effective dialogue:

- regular parent–teacher contact;
- joint teaching/work in the classroom;
- home visits;
- whole-school events;
- school handbooks/prospectuses;
- letters, notices and circulars.

In a recent survey by Lewis *et al.* (2007: 2), primary head teachers were asked what were the most effective ways of involving parents in their child's education. The findings indicated that over 90 per cent of primary schools used the following:

- school newsletters;
- special events for parents (e.g. information/discussion evenings);
- gathering parents' views as part of school self-evaluation;
- encouraging parents to contact/or visit the school.

When considering behaviour of pupils in the classroom, Rogers (2000) contends that there are some behavioural issues outside the school or classroom environment that teachers or the school cannot influence. Similarly, Charlton and David (1993: 207) state that, 'much behaviour at school seems to be independent of home influences'. It could, therefore, be argued that some childrens' lives are split into two distinct parts: home and school. Thus, it is vital that, in order to provide a consistent and effective approach to the education of children in primary-phase education, both academically and socially, parents and teachers cooperate and form what Cooper and Olson (1996) term a healthy 'alliance'. The Steer Report (2005) placed similar emphasis on this crucial relationship, asserting that good, as well as effective, communication between the school and home is essential for appropriate behaviour.

Research by Miller and Rollnick (2002) outlined that many teachers have rather a negative view of parents of children in their class. This chimes with findings from the Elton Report (1989: 133), which concluded, 'our evidence suggests that teachers' picture of parents is generally very negative. Many teachers feel that parents are to blame for much misbehaviour in schools'. Yet the value of healthy parent-teacher relations has been strongly emphasised within the behavioural discourse (Barnard, 2004; Cooper and Olson, 1996; Addi-Raccah and Ainhoren, 2009), as well as Selwyn (2011a, b) who observe that, 'the notion of the "engaged parent" has become a key element of governmental policy

Task 8.3.1 An intervention case study

Read the following and consider the questions afterwards.

Case study

Before early intervention

Jamie had been receiving help at school in Year 2 from the Behaviour Support Service owing to his aggressive behaviour. However, over the summer, his behaviour worsened, and his mother was concerned that the transition to Key Stage 2 in a Year 3 class may mean that he would not get the same level of support. She contacted the PPO, who agreed to liaise with other agencies. A check on the data held for Jamie revealed incomplete records, and Jamie's health visitor confirmed concerns about his sleep routines and an outstanding referral for speech therapy, while the school revealed concerns about Jamie's and his mother's difficulties.

After early intervention

The school undertook a CAF process with Jamie's mother and, from that, planned how services could come together to form a 'team around the child', including an education welfare assistant, a health visitor and a teacher. As a result, the education welfare assistant worked with Jamie at home and at school; a re-referral for speech therapy was made; and the health visitor continued to offer support to his mother, suggesting strategies for dealing with his behaviour. You, as class teacher, acted as the first point of contact for the family, and information was shared on request with the other specialists about Jamie's behavioural difficulties. Owing to this integrated approach to identifying and addressing the causes of Jamie's behaviour, Jamie's family now feels they are receiving coordinated support that meets his needs. His re-referral for speech therapy was prioritised, owing to his needs being set within a broader context of his educational and social development, and the team continues to work with Jamie and his family to achieve more improvement.

- How do you think Jamie's school might have been more proactive in easing transition to Key Stage 2 for him and his family?
- As Jamie's class teacher, you are acting as the first point of contact. This means that you would have to make time to talk his parents. How do you enable face-to-face communication with parents?
- You would also have to liaise with other professionals, in order to deliver accurate information and to share it appropriately. What skills might you need to develop in order to do this effectively?

efforts to improve educational standards and reduce inequalities' (2011: 314). Despite this, these potential relationships are not always fully utilised and realised, and, as a teacher new to the profession, it could be advantageous for you to be proactive in forming appropriate and effective relationships with parents.

The survey also described that the majority of primary schools actively sought strategies to involve their PTAs. However, the survey highlighted that socio-economic factors influenced the amount of involvement from the PTA or even if the school had a PTA. Whether on placement or when you qualify as an NQT, you need to ensure that you know the strategies employed by the school to ensure that parents are involved in their child's education. Recently, online communication and virtual learning environments (VLEs) have been identified as strategies to involve parents in school life. This is going to have an impact on your daily routine, and you may be requested to contribute to such forums, so you need a confident and capable approach to ICT. Lewis *et al.*'s (2007: 3) survey also outlines other strategies that head teachers feel they use to actively involve parents in primary education:

- parents' forums/focus groups;
- online communication/VLEs;
- family learning/parent-child workshops;
- as parent governors.

FIRST IMPRESSIONS

Recent initiatives at both a national and local level have encouraged greater collaboration between the two (schools and parents). For example, many schools now offer parents the opportunity to observe lessons and to discuss the new teaching methods employed.

To this end, it is essential that you seek out opportunities to forge meaningful and appropriate links with parents of the children in your class. Outside formal meetings such as parents' evenings, this can be done effectively by taking the opportunity to be 'seen' at key times. It is often the case that many home-school partnerships never reach their potential because the school is seen as being remote and distant from the home. When you also consider that there may be significant numbers of parents whose own experience of schooling was negative, it is not surprising that they are reticent to 'cross the threshold' and approach teachers comfortably. For these parents, school may still represent an unhappy and less than productive period of their lives. Also, the demands on parents who may work full time or look after younger children may mean that they are less active than they would like to be regarding the teaching and learning of their children. Therefore, it is your duty as teachers to reach out and open up the possibilities of home-school partnerships.

A key time to achieve this aim is at the beginning and end of the school day. Although you need to be mindful of ensuring a prompt start to lessons, if you are visible and welcoming in the morning,

Task 8.3.2 Relationships with parents

- **Action point**: Introduce yourself to parents at either the beginning or end of the school day – make a point of remarking positively on an achievement each child has made.
- **Task**: During your non-contact time (or NQT time), visit other schools (or compare approaches while on school placements) to research how they ensure that parents are involved with their children's education. Report your findings to your mentor, line manager or tutor.

it sends a clear message to parents and children alike. This is especially important at the beginning of a new school year. Both the parents and the children will be keen to meet the new teacher, and your presence will ensure that you have a positive influence throughout the year. As formal parents' meetings may not take place until later in the school year, a quick personal introduction is an effective means of establishing a relationship sooner.

HOME READING

A considerable amount has been written about how to involve parents in school-based reading programmes. Halsall and Green (1995), Leseman and De Jong (1998), Hammett *et al*. (2003) and Dombey *et al*. (2006) have all sought, through their interventions, to increase children's academic performance by manipulating and maximising the home literacy environment (HLE).

The HLE is one of the child's first influences in learning basic literacy skills. The importance of this environment has been long recognised. Educators are stating that children must be read to and must have opportunities to improve their own reading (Badian, 1988; Burgess *et al*., 2002; Dombey *et al*., 2006). It is important that parents should feel confident in supporting their children's learning on an everyday basis, as children learn from those closest to them and care about the reactions that they receive from those adults. It is even more important that parents who do not feel confident in their role of supporting their child in reading or learning receive support from the child's class teacher and the school. There should be clear methods employed by the school to support parents in helping their children:

> This recognition of the importance of understanding the process of learning to read is both hopeful and liberating; it shows how important is the role of the parent as well as the teacher, and accepts that there are many things that can be done to help, most of which are not very technical or complicated.

(Cullingford, 2001: 15)

While in school, whether on placement or in your first year of teaching, you need to become familiar with the school's policy on home reading and how this is encouraged. It must be acknowledged that the parents' role in all learning is crucial. The environment that they provide at home can help to cultivate their children's vital literacy skills. Many parents are willing to continue to help their children in many ways, and it is your role as class teacher to promote these and to ensure that children benefit from them: 'Parental involvement in children's academic development is of vital importance, partly because it contributes to a sense of purpose and achievement' (Aunola *et al*., 2002: 313).

DEALING WITH DIFFICULT SITUATIONS

As discussed previously, as teachers we are aware of the benefits that supportive parents have for the achievement of their children. Research (Edwards and Warin, 1999; Aunola *et al*., 2002; Desforges and Abouchaar, 2003; Hammett *et al*., 2003) also highlights the enormous benefits that parents can bring to school when the values and ethos are shared between home and school. However, we need to be aware of the problematic nature of school when this is not the case. The work of Edwards and Warin (1999) raises many issues concerning the assumptions that schools make considering adequate and appropriate support from parents. They reached the conclusion that many schools were keen to utilise parents as 'long arms' for the schools' own purposes, and not as equal partners. They concluded that the ways in which schools enhance parental involvement is rather one-sided. This can be problematic if parents and the school have opposing views and values. As an NQT, you may find that not all parents are as supportive as you would hope.

A shared language concerning the nature of school is vital, and staff in primary schools have to be aware that this may not be the case for the majority of parents, so that schools have to take steps to ameliorate the feeling of failure, the feeling that education is of little or no value, and that school represents a legitimate target for verbal and physical abuse. It is vital that, if you are abused physically or verbally, your line manager or a senior teacher is informed immediately. It is against this background that your role as an NQT or trainee teacher may sit. When you are appointed, you will need local knowledge of the school and an understanding of the issues that families may bring: domestic violence, child protection, alcohol and substance abuse, teenage pregnancies, joblessness and so on. Despite this, it is important to state that, as an NQT (or indeed any teacher), you should not make assumptions about parents and families that are unfounded.

You will also need a working knowledge of agencies and training opportunities for parents. The role of any NQT in a whole-school context is that of supporting families and children, as well as staff. This is crucial in building and developing a shared vision, where the outcomes ensure that every day matters for every child, and where parents and staff are given the tools, knowledge and understanding to enable this.

Task 8.3.3 Managing parent helpers

How would you respond to the following?

- A parent helper begins to discuss their child with you during a science lesson.
- A parent helper has led a design technology task (e.g. making puppets) with a group of children, but it has come to your attention that the children merely observed the process, rather than becoming actively involved in the activity.
- At the end of the school day, an agitated parent approaches you stating that their child is being bullied and that you have failed to deal with it.

Discuss these with a fellow NQT or your school mentor and decide upon a clear, structured course of action.

One of the most challenging, yet rewarding, aspects of your NQT year, after teaching and learning, is the relationship between yourself and parents. Research (Bastiani, 2003; Desforges and Abouchaar, 2003) shows that, where the partnership between home and school is supportive, with shared values and expectations, this contributes greatly to the outcomes for the child. In order for this to happen, there needs to be a good relationship between home and school that facilitates open and honest communication. This does not just mean 'talking' to parents when there are concerns about the pupil, but taking the time to celebrate the child's achievements on a day-to-day basis, so that, when the difficult conversations have to take place, they do so against a background of 'perceived fairness'. It is imperative, therefore, that all school policies are consistently adhered to by all staff. Such policies may include the following, which you should find and read:

- behaviour policy;
- SEN policy;
- teaching and learning policy;
- whole-school policy;
- assessment policy;
- emotional literacy policy;
- homework policy.

All policies should be followed with transparency, so that parents are kept informed about their children's behaviour and attainment at every stage.

All primary schools need to work hard to develop positive relationships with parents. This can be a challenge. It is, therefore, important that, as part of the induction process or while on placement, you as an NQT or trainee teacher have the opportunity to sit in at both formal and informal parent discussions. This will provide you with an opportunity to observe how such a meeting is structured, to observe the body language and the language used by the teacher, and to see how any issues are resolved. It is suggested that, should an NQT need to have a 'difficult conversation' with a parent, they discuss it with their mentor or line manager first, in order to 'rehearse' the points, and that the mentor or line manager should also be at the meeting with the NQT, whether this is formal or informal. There should be some reflection following the meeting, to critically analyse your responses and set common agreements after such meetings.

If appropriate, it would be extremely useful for NQTs to attend any parents' coffee mornings (or similar activities) from time to time. This allows parents to get to know the NQT in a different setting and also provides NQTs with the opportunity to observe the other staff's relationships with parents. If the school has PPOs or PSAs, such professionals will be able to provide NQTs with a different kind of support. They will know the parents very well and may well have information about the whole family that the NQT needs to be aware of, on a need-to-know basis, before seeing the parents. You should be careful of making generalisations or labelling parents unduly.

PARENTS' EVENINGS

Parents' evenings form part of a teacher's statutory duties (Department for Education and Skills, 2009) and are an important fixture of the school year. Many schools will operate a termly parents' evening, where parents are invited in to discuss their child's progress. It is also worth mentioning that parents' evenings may vary in their nature. Pastoral parents' evenings are often held at the start of the academic year to allow discussion around specific issues of transition and settling into a new class. These meetings may well be held with the acknowledgement that it is too early to discuss academic progress, and, as such, the discussion will centre on the happiness and disposition of the child and friendship groupings. It may also be an opportunity for the teacher to share information regarding the curriculum. As was mentioned previously, these early meetings are particularly useful as a means of building purposeful relationships.

As with other aspects of school life, parents' evenings require careful planning to ensure success. It goes without saying that parents will expect to see their children's work marked effectively, with purposeful, formative comments. Also, it will help to make a few notes about each child prior to the meeting and be prepared to make notes during the meeting, should the need arise. Often, parents may use the meeting to air particular concerns about their child that you may not be able to respond to immediately without some investigation (e.g. a bullying issue). In this case, it is important that you offer the parents a particular time to meet at a later stage, when you have more information at hand.

It is always worth opening the meeting by asking the parents whether they have any particular concerns that they wish to discuss. This will allow for an open and frank dialogue. You must be also mindful that parents themselves are useful sources of information, as the Cambridge Primary Review (Alexander *et al.*, 2009) suggests: 'Teachers need to establish more fruitful links between home and school which build on the support for children's learning that already exists in the home and community'. This highlights the need for the partnership between teachers and parents to be a two-way process.

Task 8.3.4 Audit of parental involvement

- While on placement, or during your first year of teaching, you may want to research the school's overall success at encouraging effective parental involvement. For example, an audit could be carried out by you and a working party on strategies currently being utilised by your school.
- Alternatively, you may want to carry out action research on a group of parents relating to current government thinking. The results and findings of the research could be shared with the school's senior management team and governors.

Any results of your research could form the basis of revisiting existing school policies on parental involvement.

Remember that the purpose of the meeting with parents is to report on the child's progress, but it is also an opportunity to enhance pupil learning by empowering the parents with knowledge that will help them support their child. Therefore, you will need to communicate pupil targets clearly and make suggestions as to how these can be supported at home. As these meetings operate (for the most part) on scheduled appointments, it is necessary to keep an eye on the time. It is inevitable that you will, on occasion, run over time, but, in the interests of all parents, it is important to keep an eye on the clock. If you find that a particular issue requires more time, you may have to arrange to meet at a later date.

Task 8.3.5 Parents' evenings

- Consider what types of note might be useful when preparing for a meeting with parents.
- How would you explain to parents how best to support their child at home in the following areas:
    - literacy
    - numeracy?
- Consider what course of action you would take in the following scenarios:
    - A parent complains that their child is being bullied by an older child from the local secondary school on the way home.
    - A parent wishes to withdraw their child from the sex education lessons that are due to take place the following week.
    - A parent is concerned that their child is not being challenged enough at school.
    - A parent asks your advice about getting a home tutor to support their child with numeracy.

Discuss these with your mentor or tutor.

PARENT GOVERNORS

All primary schools are run by a governing body, which works alongside the head teacher and senior management team to ensure that pupils receive a high standard of education. The governing body in primary schools is made up of:

- parent governors (elected by parents);
- staff representatives (elected by school staff);
- local authority governors (appointed by the local authority);
- community governors (members of the local community appointed by the governing body);
- for some schools, people appointed by the relevant religious body or foundation;
- up to two sponsor governors (appointed by the governing body).

As an NQT, it is very unlikely that you will be a school governor; nevertheless, this is entirely possible. As with all teachers, when you become an NQT you do need to become familiar with the role of the governing body. Governors probably form the largest volunteer group in major cities in the country, with around 350,000 governor places in England, and so they perform an important job on behalf of the community.

The main role of any governing body is to ensure the smooth running of the school and to promote pupil achievement. Parent governors need to ensure that the views of the parents are reported to their local authority. Alongside other governors, they should also be involved in the following duties: setting the strategic direction of the school; approving the school budget; reviewing progress against the school development plan; and appointing as well as supporting the head teacher. As with all governors, a parent governor may be viewed as a critical friend. It would be beneficial, as a new member of staff, to be proactive and informally introduce yourself to any parent governors at your school.

Schools have always actively sought the opinions of parents and, from May 2007, have had a duty to take account of the views of parents. All schools are encouraged to review their current practice in relation to this and consider enhancing such arrangements by setting up a parent council. Ultimately, the governing body will decide whether to set up a parent council and may appoint a working group to take responsibility for its establishment and management. The purpose of such councils needs to be clear and shared with all the school. One of the advantages of such an approach is that it opens up the school and allows parents who are less involved in the school, owing to full-time work commitments, to become more active in their children's education. This allows the school to present ample evidence of engaging all parents, and to provide positive responses to the section of the self-evaluation form relating to parental involvement.

Task 8.3.6 Home–school agreements

With permission from the head teacher, obtain examples of home–school agreements from your school, consider the provisions in them and then explore any issues raised. For example:

- Are all parents able to support their children?
- Are there any cultural differences between the curriculum and values at home?
- What are the significant issues that parents have concerns about?

Use these as a basis for a discussion with your school parent governor, with a view to proposing an action plan for dissemination at a staff meeting.

PARENTAL EXPERTISE

Another strategy to encourage closer relationships between parents and schools is to maximise on the expertise of parents and other members of the community. Contributions to the development of the curriculum by support from outside agencies and parents has become increasingly common over recent years. The willingness of parents to share their experiences with a group of children can provide a renewed vigour and inspiration to an existing unit or scheme of work. Parents who are, for example, nurses, postal workers, police officers, community artists, technicians or workers for the fire service could be utilised effectively by schools to enhance learning. Parents with particular interests or hobbies, or who have visited places of interest, or who have lived in different countries, could also be involved by being invited to the class (or a small group of children, if the whole class is too daunting) as visiting speakers.

It is vital that, if you are going to use the suggestions above, you arrange a meeting before any planned activities, in order to ensure that the work or talk that any visitor is going to lead is appropriate for the children in your class. You will also need to refer to the school's policy on Criminal Record Bureau checks, to ensure that the correct protocols for adult visitors in class are followed. It is also important that follow-up work is planned for, and shared with, such parents, in order to celebrate the impact that their expertise may have had on a group of children. This work does not necessarily have to be in written form, thus encouraging all children to express their engagement with the visiting speakers.

Such an approach could ensure that you value as well as respect parents' contributions, and the children in your class will notice that you have a two-way relationship with parents.

Task 8.3.7 Using parents' expertise

Read the case study and discuss the questions with a peer or mentor.

Case study

Yasmin's father is a staff nurse at the local hospital, and the newly appointed class teacher, working in Year 5, is keen to use his expertise. Yasmin's father is invited to come and speak to the Year 5 class, and the class teacher tells him to prepare 'something about healthy eating'. On arriving in school, Yasmin's father shares with the class a PowerPoint presentation of thirty-three slides (with mostly words) that he has used on a recent INSET day. He also talks to the children for 30 minutes on nutrition and dietetics. Throughout the talk, advanced scientific vocabulary and terminology are used. At the end of the talk, the children and class teacher cannot think of any questions to ask, and there is a long, rather embarrassing pause until the teacher asks the class to thank Yasmin's father by giving him a round of applause.

- How could the class teacher have avoided this situation?
- What should the class teacher have done prior to Yasmin's father visiting the class or school?
- How could the class teacher have maximised on the parent's expertise?
- What follow-up activities could have been planned, if the presentation had been pitched at the appropriate level?
- Why is it important to liaise clearly and in advance with any visitors?

SUMMARY

In this unit, we have endeavoured to highlight the importance of purposeful, open and structured relationships with parents as a means of ensuring the best possible education for the children in school. At the heart of this is the acknowledgement that parents are partners in their children's education and, as such, are key educators themselves. We have suggested that there are many ways in which these partnerships can be developed and supported in school, and the tasks are a good starting point for this. It is our view that establishing strong home–school links is essential when it comes to ensuring that the individual potential of pupils is realised.

 ## ANNOTATED FURTHER READING

Department for Education and Skills (DfES) (2007) *Every Parent Matters: Creating Opportunity, Releasing Potential, Achieving Excellence*, London: DfES.

> If you wish to understand better the key role that parents can play in education and the emphasis that government is placing on partnership, this publication is a useful starting point. The report offers a literature review of the research in this area and highlights the various initiatives that are taking place at present. In particular, the bibliography is a good source of references that provide further evidence of the efficacy of teacher–parent partnerships in improving educational outcomes.

Lewis, K., Chamberlain, T., Riggall, A., Gagg, K. and Rudd, P. (2007) *How Are Schools Involving Parents in School Life? Annual Survey of Trends in Education: Schools' Concerns and their Implications for Local Authorities* (LGA Research Report 4/07), Slough: NFER.

> This gives a clear overview as to how secondary and primary schools try to engage parents. It is a relevant, up-to-date publication that highlights some of the contentious issues around this topic.

 ## FURTHER READING TO SUPPORT M-LEVEL STUDY

Abdullah, A.G.K, Seedee, R., Alzaidiyeen, N.J., Al-Shabatat, A., Alzeydeen, H.K. and Al-Awabdeh, A.H. (2011) 'An investigation of teachers' attitudes towards parental involvement', *Educational Research*, 2(8): 1402-8. Available at: www.interesjournals.org/ER

> This journal article discusses teachers' attitudes towards parents and their involvement in their children's education in Jordan, and whether individual teacher characteristics (such as age, qualifications and experience) have an impact upon these relationships. It will be useful for you to analyse the findings of the research and consider whether we might find parallels in England. What cultural differences might impact upon the teacher–parent relationship?

Selwyn, N., Banaji, S., Hadjithoma-Garstka, C. and Clark, W. (2011) 'Providing a platform for parents? Exploring the nature of parental engagement with school learning platforms', *Journal of Computer Assisted Learning*, 27(4): 314-23.

> This journal article considers how the utilisation of technologies can further support parental involvement in children's education. It will be useful for you to consider carefully just how such technologies might provide a support for parents. The report suggests that most learning technologies used for this purpose provide mostly 'one way traffic' from the school to the home. What might the barriers to engagement be? How might these be overcome?

RELEVANT WEBSITES

Department for Education: www.education.gov.uk
> Type 'parent support advisers' into the search box and follow the links.

Department For Education Teaching Agency: www.education.gov.uk/get-into-teaching
> Merging with National College for School Leadership from 1 April 2013.

REFERENCES

Addi-Raccah, A and Ainhoren, R. (2009) 'School governance and teachers' attitudes to parents' involvement in schools', *Teaching and Teacher Education*, 25(6): 805–13

Alexander, R. (ed.) (2009) *Children, Their World, Their Education: Final Report and Recommendations of the Cambridge Primary Review*, London: Routledge.

Aunola, K., Nurmi, J.-E., Niemi, P., Lerkkanen, M.-K. and Rasku-Puttonen, H. (2002) 'Developing dynamics of achievement strategies, reading performance and parental beliefs', *Reading Research Quarterly*, 37(3): 310–27.

Badian, N. (1988) 'The prediction of good and poor reading before kindergarten entry: a nine-year follow-up', *Journal of Learning Disabilities*, 21: 98–103.

Barnard, W. (2004) 'Parent involvement in elementary school and educational attainment', *Children and Youth Service Review*, 26(1): 39–62.

Bastiani, J. (2003) *Materials for Schools: Involving Parents, Raising Achievement*, London: DfES.

Bourdieu, P. (1986) 'The forms of capital', in J.G. Richardson (ed.) *Handbook of Theory and Research for the Sociology of Education*, Santa Barbara, CA: Greenwood Press.

Burgess, S.R., Hecht, S.A. and Lonigan, C.J. (2002) 'Relations of the home literacy environment (HLE) to the development of reading abilities: a one year longitudinal study', *Reading Research Quarterly*, 37(4): 408–26.

Charlton, T. and David, K. (1993) *Managing Misbehaviour in Schools*, New York: Routledge.

Cooper, K. and Olson, M. (1996) 'The multiple 'I's of teacher identity'. In M. Kompf, T. Boak, W. R. Bond and D. Dworet (eds), *Changing Research and Practice: Teachers' Professionalism, Identities and Knowledge*, London, Falmer Press.

Cullingford, C. (2001) *How Children Learn to Read and How to Help Them*, London: Kogan Page.

Dearing, R. (1993) *The National Curriculum and its Assessment: Final Report*, London: SCAA.

Department for Education (2011) *Support and Aspiration: A New Approach to Special Educational Needs and Disability – A Consultation*, London: Stationery Office Limited.

Department for Education and Skills (DfES) (2001) *Special Educational Needs Code of Practice*, DfES/581/2001, London: DfES.

Department for Education and Skills (DfES) (2003) *Excellence and Enjoyment: A Strategy for Primary Schools*, London: DfES.

Department for Education and Skills (DfES) (2004) *Every Child Matters: Change for Children in Schools*, DfES/1110/2004, London: DfES.

Department for Education and Skills (DfES) (2007) *Every Parent Matters: Creating Opportunity, Releasing Potential, Achieving Excellence*, London: DfES.

Department for Education and Skills (DfES) (2009) *School Teachers' Pay and Conditions Document 2009*, London: DfES.

Department of Education and Science (DES) (1967) *Children and Their Primary Schools* (Plowden Report), London: HMSO.

Desforges, C. and Abouchaar, A. (2003) *The Impact of Parental Involvement, Parental Support and Family Education on Pupil Achievement and Adjustment: A Literature Review* (Research Report RR433), London: DfES.

Dombey, H., Ellis, S., Pahl, K. and Sainsbury, M. (2006) 'Handbook of Early Childhood Literacy', *Literacy*, 40(1): 29-35.

Edwards, A. and Warin, J. (1999) 'Parental involvement in raising the achievement of primary school pupils: why bother?', *Oxford Review of Education*, 25(3): 325-41.

Elton, R. (1989) *Discipline in Schools*, London: HM Stationery Office.

Goldstein, H. (2004) 'International comparisons of student attainment', *Assessment in Education: Principles, Policy and Practice*, 11(3): 319-30.

Hadow, W.H. (1931) *Report of the Consultative Committee on The Primary School*, London: HM Stationery Office.

Halsall, S. and Green, C. (1995) 'Reading aloud: a way to support their children's growth in literacy', *Early Childhood Educational Journal*, 23: 27-31.

Hammett, L., van Kleeck, A. and Huberty, C. (2003) 'Patterns of parents' extratextual interactions during book sharing with preschool children: a cluster analysis study', *Reading Research Quarterly*, 38(4): 442-68.

Health Committee (2003) *The Victoria Climbié Inquiry: Report of an Inquiry by Lord Laming*, London: The Stationery Office.

Leseman, P.P.M and De Jong, P.F. (1998) 'Home literacy: opportunity, instruction and social-emotional quality predicting early reading achievement', *Reading Research Quarterly*, 33: 294-391.

Lewis, K., Chamberlain, T., Riggall, A., Gagg, K. and Rudd, P. (2007) *How Are Schools Involving Parents in School Life? Annual Survey of Trends in Education 2007: Schools' Concerns and their Implications for Local Authorities* (LGA Research Report 4/07), Slough: NFER.

Miller, W.R. and Rollnick, S. (2002) *Motivational Interviewing: Preparing People for Change*, 2nd edition, New York: Guilford Press.

O'Hara, M. (2008) *Teaching 3-8 (Reaching the Standard)* (3rd edn), London: Continuum.

Reid, K. (2005) 'The implications of Every Child Matters and the Children Act for schools', *Pastoral Care in Education*, 23: 12-18.

Rogers, B. (2000) *Behaviour Management: A Whole-School Approach*, Thousand Oaks, CA: Sage.

Selwyn, N. (2011a) *Education and Technology: Key Issues and Debates*, London: Continuum.

Selwyn, N. (2011b) *Schools and Schooling in the Digital Age: A Critical Perspective*, London: Routledge.

Steer, A. (2005) *Learning Behaviour: The Report of the Practitioners' Group on School Behaviour and Discipline*, Nottingham: DfES Publications.

Training and Development Agency for Schools (TDA) (2007) *Professional Standards for Teachers: Qualified Teacher Status*, London: TDA.

UNDERSTANDING THE TEACHER'S PASTORAL ROLE

Ben Whitney

INTRODUCTION

One of the key characteristics of the British system of education is that it is based on a holistic understanding of children. Despite increasing use of continuous testing and examination outcomes as the preferred ways of monitoring schools' effectiveness, there are clearly many factors that will influence a child's ability to learn at school, not only their intellectual capacity or the quality of their teaching. 'Welfare' factors may not be as evident in the Ofsted Framework as they used to be under the 'Five Outcomes', but they are still there, and the link between under-attainment and personal or social deprivation has to be specifically addressed, or pressures from the rest of a child's life will inevitably impact on their learning. The best hope of reducing the impact of these wider issues is to try to address them while children are still young, if at all possible.

Despite the emphasis on greater school autonomy, government thinking over the last decade has moved education professionals to the centre of arrangements for meeting children's overall needs. Local authority services that used to be delivered by education and social care in isolation are now far more integrated, and schools are expected to take increasing responsibility for co-ordinating the multi-agency support that some children need. (This unit uses local authority (LA) throughout, as it is no longer appropriate to talk about a distinct 'local education authority' (LEA), in isolation from other children's services.) Together with the development of extended schools, and a greater emphasis on early years provision, this has led to a radical repositioning of schools, and those who work in them, to the heart of family support, alongside their strictly educational functions.

Key responsibilities are:

- promoting and monitoring pupils' school attendance and the reasons given for their absence;
- determining whether absences are authorised or unauthorised, according to school policy, and ensuring appropriate and timely responses;
- sharing concerns about children at risk of 'significant harm';
- helping parents to access services and support for 'children in need';
- understanding the role of key professionals both inside and outside the school, under agreed inter-agency child welfare procedures.

Although many of these responsibilities will also be addressed by non-teaching colleagues, you cannot teach a child you never see, or if they are constantly preoccupied with the effects of their negative experiences at home. Making sure that children actually attend school as the law requires, and that all education staff play an appropriate part in carrying out the duty to keep them safe are both crucial. This unit explores the relevant legal frameworks involved in these tasks and gives practical guidance about both managing attendance and dealing with concerns related to child protection and safeguarding.

OBJECTIVES

By the end of this unit, you should:

- be familiar with the legal framework within which the wider pastoral responsibilities of schools are carried out;
- appreciate the appropriate duties of a teacher for monitoring attendance and working with both parents and non-teaching colleagues to ensure that absences are followed up and school or individual targets are met;
- become more aware of the in-school procedures that should be in place to safeguard children and protect them from the risk of 'significant harm';
- understand the role of the teacher when working with colleagues from outside the school, such as education welfare officers and social workers.

SCHOOL ATTENDANCE

Legal framework

Since at least the Education Act 1870, there has been a sense that education is compulsory between certain ages. In the early days, this was a gradual process of prising children away from the other activities that might occupy them as an alternative and holding parents in some way legally accountable for ensuring they received at least an elementary level of instruction. It is an open question whether there has ever been a total acceptance that education should come first in the lives of all children. (The rules were, for example, set aside during both world wars, when many older children returned to the workplace, and some children and young people still end up out of school for a variety of reasons.)

Provision is certainly more universal with younger children, but the ever-greater numbers of children in pre-school education may give a misleading impression. It is only a generation or two since large numbers went through the system and into unskilled, if generally available, work, with little or no formal qualifications to show for the previous 10 years. Judging by the extent of poor literacy and numeracy in the current adult population, many must have been simply going through the motions. The importance to every child's future prospects of what you do at school, from age 3 or 4, is a relatively recent idea.

Despite all the current concerns about 'truancy', unauthorised absence (the correct term) has risen only very slightly since the current recording system was introduced in the early 1990s. Attendance has certainly risen more. But, somehow, the absences seem to matter more now. Even if a commitment to regular attendance cannot be assumed, it has certainly become the majority view, with an ever-increasing period of time over which the child is required to participate, and with a growing expectation that either training or further education should be the norm even beyond that.

Critics might suggest that, if our education system was good enough, everyone would want their children to go anyway! However, some element of legal encouragement has always been retained and, along with it, the existence of the 'School Board Man' (*sic*) and the contemporary equivalent in the LA's Education Welfare Service/Attendance Service, in order to encourage the reluctant. Parents and children have a daily choice. Even the most stimulating and well-organised school needs to be aware of what may have to be done to ensure its pupils attend as they should. Early intervention at Key Stages 1 and 2 may reduce the risk of greater problems later. The signals you send then can make a real difference.

Absence is not necessarily an indicator of major family problems or an antisocial attitude in either child or parent. Some children just skip school occasionally, perhaps showing an entirely natural avoidance of something difficult or less than exciting, without necessarily repeating the behaviour. Parents sometimes have other, more urgent priorities to deal with, and school just has to wait till tomorrow. Much use of attendance and absence procedures is just a routine response to everyday problems, and many situations are capable of relatively easy resolution through prompt action by school staff.

All schools should have practical procedures in place for promoting attendance and following up absences. These may include class competitions, individual targets, text-messaging, meetings with parents, focused action plans with at-risk individuals and efficient pastoral care. However, some cases of non-attendance are but the tip of an iceberg, where not being at school is only the presenting problem betraying something much greater underneath. There are many vulnerable groups of children who cannot be expected to attend school while all else crumbles in chaos around them. These include those whose families are in crisis; those experimenting with gangs, drugs, alcohol or other substances; those with major mental health needs; many children in the public care system; the victims of exploitation, abuse and discrimination; child carers; and those grappling with the implications of homelessness, acute poverty and domestic violence. These children, in particular, will need 'joined-up' solutions to their problems.

The law seeks to be realistic in recognising that 100 per cent attendance is not necessarily required, allowing for 'sickness and other unavoidable cause' (Education Act 1996, s 444). There is considerable discretion given to head teachers that enables situations that are less than perfect to be regarded as nonetheless satisfactory. It is often more appropriate to adopt a 'welfare' approach where children have complex needs or there is major disruption to their family life.

However, there is also an expectation that schools and local authorities will use their statutory enforcement powers against parents more extensively. There are particular issues in relation to 'persistent absentees', that is, those with attendance under 85 per cent or at risk of it. These statutory tasks cannot be done without teachers, so it is important that you get to know what these responsibilities are and the context in which they operate. If there is to be a legal response, it will be your class register that provides the evidence. (See Department for Education, 2013a, for detailed guidance.)

Registration regulations

Twice-daily registration should be a significant part of the school day. Try to make it feel like something important has been missed if the child isn't there. Attendance registers must be kept strictly in accordance with the regulations (Education Act 1996, s 434(6)). Should a parent be prosecuted for failing to ensure their child attends, head teachers will be required to account to the court for any discrepancies or mistakes in the register. Any dispute between the parent and the LA about whether, for example, a given absence should have been authorised will require the personal evidence of the head teacher in explaining the criteria used.

As almost every classroom teacher at Key Stages 1 and 2 will be involved in actually marking the register, whether manually or by computer, schools *must* have written and consistently applied attendance policies that enable parents to know what the rules are and that ensure good practice by all staff. The decision about whether or not to authorise an absence determines whether or not the parent is committing an offence. Many schools authorise too generously or may never have established clear policies and procedures that are consistently applied. It should be clear to you whose responsibility it is to make a decision and what procedures are in place for clarifying any uncertainties or challenging parents' explanations for absence.

Registers have always had to be marked at the beginning of each half-day session. This is still the requirement for the morning, but there can be some discretion about when to mark afternoon registers. This was intended to catch those who go missing during the afternoon, but also raises a number of problems, and few schools have seen the need for change, although many schools have systems for lesson-by-lesson monitoring in addition to the official sessional mark.

There are five registration categories, one of which must be used for every half-day session for every child of compulsory school age:

- present on site;
- authorised absent;
- unauthorised absent;
- approved educational activity off site (counts as present);
- school 'closed' for that session for that pupil (not counted).

The category of 'approved educational activity' enables schools to count those who are receiving their education away from the premises for a legitimate reason, such as an educational visit or attending an alternative provision, as 'present' for statistical purposes (provided they actually turned up!). The previous regulations classed all those not on the premises as 'authorised absent', even if the child was where they were supposed to be. This was plainly unreasonable, and this change has given schools a welcome flexibility.

Education Act 1996

This outlines the basic legal obligations on parents and replaced the relevant sections of the Education Act 1944 and the Education Act 1993, from 1 November 1996.

Duty of parents

Section 7 of the Education Act 1996 says,

> The parent of every child of compulsory school age shall cause him to receive efficient full-time education suitable:
>
> (a) to his age, ability and aptitude, and
> (b) to any special educational needs he may have, either by regular attendance at school or otherwise.

Prosecution of parents

Parents (not children) commit an offence if a registered pupil does not attend 'regularly' (s 444(1) and 444(1A)). This duty includes any adult looking after the child, even if they are not actually related (although not staff from public agencies). Technically, any absence is an offence, unless authorised by the school. Enforcement is the responsibility of the LA where the school is (not the LA in which the child lives, if this is different). These proceedings, which can be based only on unauthorised absences, are carried out by LA officers, who may be known by a variety of titles: education welfare officer, education social worker or attendance enforcement officer. Referral thresholds and criteria should be widely known throughout the school.

Anti-social Behaviour Act 2003 and Education (Penalty Notices) (England) Regulations 2004

New powers came into force from 2004 (in England only) that have given LAs the option of formalising their responses to non-attendance, but without the need for a court appearance. A penalty notice, along similar lines to a speeding fine, enables a parent to discharge their liability for unauthorised absences by paying a penalty. From September 2013, penalties are £60 if paid within 21 days, or £120 if paid within 28 days (per parent and per child). Payment must be made in full, not by instalments. A written warning must be issued first, and so most LAs are not using them 'on the spot', but as part of a formal procedure where the parent is deemed primarily responsible for the absence. Some schools expect them to be used for all unauthorised holidays in term time, although this can only be with the agreement of the LA.

There is also the capacity for parents to be summonsed for the enhanced offence under s 444(1A) of 'parentally condoned unauthorised absence'. Some LAs may now use these more serious proceedings rather than s 444(1), where an actual court appearance is considered appropriate. Convictions at this level carry a maximum fine of £2,500 and up to 3 months in prison, although this is very rare. The effectiveness of prosecution has always been a matter of some debate. Research suggests that it is effective in about two-fifths of cases, in that the children concerned subsequently improved their attendance (National Foundation for Educational Research, 2003). However, many LA officers also report that the proceedings often make little difference, that fines may be unpaid or that the threat of court action is often more effective than actually going ahead with it. Timely action by the school in the early stages almost certainly stands the best chance of success. It is essential for everyone to maintain a focus on raising attendance and challenging absence as part of the everyday life of the school. Attendance should never be assumed; it always has to be promoted, encouraged and rewarded, just like any other achievement.

Task 8.4.1 Attendance 1

Devise an incentive scheme to raise attendance in a class or year group.

- What kinds of prize might be appropriate, and how would they be awarded?
- Will they go to the children with the best attendance or those who show most improvement? How will it work?
- Is it the children, or the parents, who need the encouragement? What difference might this make to the kinds of reward available?
- How might peer pressure best be used to encourage those who find regular attendance difficult?

If your scheme is used, make sure it is included in the school's attendance policy and all parents are made aware of it.

Task 8.4.2 Attendance 2

Analyse attendance and absence figures in your school, perhaps for the current and previous year. There should be plenty of data available from computerised records and census returns.

- Do the data identify any patterns or trends?
- Is attendance rising or falling?
- Are some groups of pupils more likely to be absent? What might be the reasons for this?
- How many children are present less than 85 per cent of the time, and what is being done about them?
- How much of the absence is authorised by the school, and for what reasons, e.g. family holidays?
- What is the balance between authorised and unauthorised absences?

What does your analysis suggest about which children should be the focus for the school's attendance-raising strategy?

CHILD PROTECTION AND SAFEGUARDING

Inter-agency procedures

Teachers are not required to be experts at recognising child abuse, especially when new to the profession. That is not your responsibility, any more than a doctor can assess a child's special educational needs or reading performance. Child protection is an inter-agency process from start to finish, but all those working with children must be clear about their own role, not act some other person's role. Despite a sometimes negative public perception, considerable progress has been made in recent years, but services are subject to almost continuous change.

A very large percentage of child protection concerns arise at school. This is not surprising. Children spend more time there than almost anywhere else; relationships with the adults there are important, especially to younger children. Safeguarding continues to be an important element of the revised Ofsted Framework, even though there is no longer a specific separate rating. Section 157/175 of the Education Act 2002, in force from 1 June 2004, requires staff in every school, whatever its status (including the independent sector, academies, free schools etc.), to cooperate with the Local Safeguarding Children Board's procedures. In ensuring that this legal duty is carried out, the governors or proprietors must 'have regard' to the current DfE guidance (Department for Education, 2013b). LA officers may also be involved, but all school staff should expect to take individual responsibility for child protection in their own right.

The task of teaching (and non-teaching) staff is:

- to be sufficiently confident to recognise those situations that give most cause for concern;
- to refer them appropriately within the school's own and inter-agency procedures and support the child's need for longer-term protection if required.

Categories of abuse

Concerns about possible child abuse must be identified under four standard categories, as outlined in government guidance *Working Together to Safeguard Children* (HM Government, 2013):

- **physical abuse** – non-accidental cuts, bruises, fractures, wounds, burns, bites, poisoning, etc.;
- **emotional abuse** – extreme or persistent denial of love, care, attention and security;
- **sexual abuse** – not only sexual activity, but may also involve video, photography or 'grooming' (preparation for abuse) and the Internet;
- **neglect** – persistent failure to meet a child's basic need for food, warmth, protection, safety, etc.

If your concern suggests the child may be at risk of 'significant harm' under s 47 of the Children Act 1989, as outlined in the categories above, parental consent is not required to make a referral in the child's best interests. The school's child protection policy should make this clear. Parents can often be informed of the referral, unless this would put the child at increased risk of harm, but never make this decision alone. Always seek advice from your senior designated member of staff (DMS) who is responsible for managing the process, based on the information you have received or seen.

Prevention of abuse is always preferable to waiting for a more serious incident. Other welfare concerns are more appropriately seen as 'children in need', under s 17 of the Children Act 1989. With parental agreement, referral may be made to other agencies for support, on a voluntary basis. This process may involve use of the Common Assessment Framework (CAF), or local equivalent, which enables a variety of professionals to work together more effectively in meeting the child's needs, according to a plan agreed with the parents. Schools will be central to this process.

The curriculum

A child protection concern may arise indirectly, rather than by direct disclosure or because a member of staff sees an injury, and often when you least expect it! Almost any subject area contains the potential for the child to choose that moment to share what is on their mind. Children generally trust their teachers and do not always see the significance of what they are saying. They may write about their experiences at home in a poem, or give an indication in a practical lesson that the nutrition standards are unacceptable. They may talk about how their parents punish them, or use language that is attempting to describe sexual activity, when faced with a entirely conventional topic. Children choose to disclose, when they are ready, and to whom; and so the teacher must always be ready too, even if 'child abuse' was nowhere near their expectations for that particular lesson. The curriculum is also an essential element in teaching children about e-safety, where they may be putting themselves at considerable risk of exploitation.

Making referrals

Referrals to a social worker or (in an emergency) to the police would normally be made by the school's DMS, on receipt of information from the child, a parent, a colleague or other source, although action may still be required, even if they are not available. If you have concerns about a child, you should always discuss them with the designated person or other senior member of staff, to clarify whether referral under child protection procedures is appropriate. Always pass on disclosures of abuse under the four categories above, and any related allegations, together with children with significant or suspicious injuries.

You do not have to establish first whether or not it is abuse; that is the job of the investigating agencies, not the school. Evidence of possible physical abuse makes a referral particularly urgent, partly as the child may need medical attention, but also because any injury needs to be seen and assessed by a qualified medical practitioner as quickly as possible. These cases should be raised as early as possible in the school day, to give maximum time for a response while the child is safe at school.

Children should not be promised confidentiality, or, if you do promise it, be prepared to break it, if the child then makes a disclosure of alleged abuse or you have other information that requires you to use the school's child protection procedures. You cannot protect such a child by yourself. Written records should be kept carefully within the school. When the child changes school, records should be passed or copied to the new designated person as far as is possible. The ideal place for the child's whole protection history is in their current school.

Investigation and assessment

Following referral from any source, the social worker (jointly with the police, if potential criminal charges are involved) will carry out an assessment of risk to the child. This will usually involve them contacting other relevant agencies that know the family, including other schools, and may include a strategy discussion/meeting with key professionals. The social worker will advise on when to contact the family and who will do it. (It is always helpful if the referrer receives a notification of the outcome of this initial assessment, even if no further action is being taken.) If necessary, they will make home visits, involve the child's parent, arrange to have the child medically examined, and so on. Where the child is old enough, they may be interviewed on DVD about what has happened. This can then be used as evidence in any subsequent court proceedings.

Many cases are resolved quickly, with practical advice and support to the parents, or programmes to deal, for example, with basic care, alcohol abuse or domestic violence. Other cases, where sex offences and assaults or severe family breakdown and neglect are involved, will require much longer involvement. Court proceedings may be taken, or arrangements may be made for the child to be cared for by other members of the family or foster carers. Where children continue to live in situations of risk, a child protection conference may be called.

Initial child protection conferences and child protection plans

Conferences are often required at short notice. It is essential that a representative of the school attends the conference for any school-aged child, even if other education officers have also been invited. A written report may be required. The conference is an opportunity for all professionals involved with the family to consult about how they may best be protected and, in particular, to decide whether the child needs an ongoing child protection plan. If so, a keyworker (social worker) and a Core Group will be appointed – someone from the child's school should always be a member of the Core Group. An outline plan will be drawn up immediately, and the Core Group will all be responsible for meeting regularly and for undertaking a more extensive assessment.

When a child has a child protection plan, the DMS must decide who needs to be told. This should be on a need-to-know basis and should certainly include the person with day-to-day responsibility for marking their attendance record. Procedures should be agreed about what to do if the child is absent or if further concerns are identified at school. The child's status must be reviewed every 6 months (after the first 3 months).

Policy issues

There must be a written policy for child protection within the school, which should be made known to all staff and parents (see Ofsted, 2011, for examples of best practice). This will set out general principles, the duty to make referrals, and so on, including wider issues such as staff and volunteer appointments, arrangements for criminal record bureau (CRB)/disclosure and barring service (DBS) checks, the prohibition of corporal punishment, the use of restraint, curriculum issues and complaints procedures. Staff, especially those newly appointed, should have access to clear procedures within the school covering required documentation and defined responsibilities.

Ensuring such policy and procedures are in place is the responsibility of the senior management team, the governing body and the DMS, who must all work together to ensure a coordinated approach. Training must be available to both teaching and non-teaching staff. This will normally be part of the role of the DMS, but additional training from LA and other specialists may also be available.

Allegations against teachers or other staff

Some child abuse cases raise additional issues, because the abuse is complex, involves a number of adults or children or because the person who is the subject of the allegation is a professional or volunteer rather than a parent. This is the context in which any concern about an adult within a school will be investigated. There is always the possibility that someone may seek to exploit their position as a consequence of relationships established at a school. (The CRB/DBS process continues to identify a significant number of people who seek to be teachers but are clearly not suitable.) Especially since the Soham case and other high-profile cases involving teachers, nursery workers and others in a 'position of trust', it is essential that a school's child protection policy and procedures include an awareness of such a risk.

There is understandable concern among many teachers that careers may be irreparably damaged on the basis of flimsy or malicious allegations by children. It may reassure you to know that this is actually extremely rare. Most allegations have their roots in an incident of some kind, although some do end up only as 'unproven' one way or the other, which is generally unsatisfactory. It is always better for a school to anticipate possible risks and to seek to prevent all reasonable risk of misunderstandings and false allegations. Proper policy and procedures are also likely to deter any individual seeking to use the school as a basis for inappropriate relationships with pupils. Agreed procedures should be applied both to teaching staff and to any volunteers and non-teaching staff who have direct contact with children, especially if they will be unsupervised or involved in high-risk activities, such as supervising children dressing and undressing or being alone with children in cars, and so on.

It is important to draw a distinction between complaints and allegations that involve misconduct or unprofessionalism, and those that specifically raise child protection concerns. Any concern that involves the possibility of harm to a child or a criminal offence involving a child should always be discussed by the head teacher with senior LA officers (usually known as local authority designated officers (LADOs)), and advice should be taken from outside the school. If child protection procedures are needed, investigations are carried out by social workers and the police, as with any other referral, co-ordinated by the LADO. Head teachers, governors and LA officers must not carry out investigations themselves in these circumstances. If inter-agency action is required, there will be a strategy meeting at an early stage to agree a corporate approach. The views of the head teacher on any incident will be listened to carefully at this stage.

Corporal punishment, restraint and staff conduct

Teachers may occasionally need reminding that they are prohibited by law from using any form of punishment intended to inflict pain, including 'hitting, slapping or shaking' a child. Neither may they 'intimidate or humiliate' a child or make them carry out any kind of 'degrading punishment' (Education Act 1996, ss 548-50). This is a higher standard than that applied to parents. Teachers are permitted to use 'reasonable restraint' to protect a child or other children, but this must be in ways that are defined by clear, written procedures within the school.

Parents should be informed of the legitimate use of restraint or physical searches, where the head teacher is satisfied that the member of staff has acted appropriately. If parents are not satisfied, they may still choose to go the police or social care themselves. It will usually help to agree a staff code of conduct to avoid the risk of any misunderstanding about, for example, sharing private mobile phone numbers, contacting pupils by email or meeting up with pupils outside school. This is in everyone's interests.

Task 8.4.3 Child protection 1

You have been asked to assist in providing a report on a child for a child protection conference. Ask to see a report that has been produced by another member of the school staff and consider what it includes. What do you see as the most important information for a school report to contain? Talk to the teacher or other representative who submitted the report and attended the conference and ask them what it felt like. If possible, attend a conference yourself, if only as an observer. Remember the need for careful confidentiality in all these discussions.

Task 8.4.4 Child protection 2

Carry out an evaluation of child protection procedures in a school where you are working, in the light of the guidance, *Keeping Children Safe in Education* (Department for Education, 2013b).

- What information is made available as part of induction?
- Is there a written policy, and who knows about it?
- Are there children with a child protection plan, and, if so, what does this mean for their class teacher?
- Does the school, in your judgement, meet all the requirements of the guidance?
- What strengths and weaknesses have you identified? Discuss your findings with the school's senior leadership team and recommend any necessary changes in policy or procedures.

SUMMARY

These may not be the issues that initially attracted you to the idea of being a teacher. Perhaps you thought that other people would be responsible for these sensitive areas. It is true that teachers are primarily employed to teach, and that schools may now contain a variety of other professionals in a supportive role, but the wider pastoral care of pupils still cannot happen without you. It will only enhance your effectiveness in the classroom if you can show the child that you understand them as a person. It may just have to be you who is needed to respond to a serious concern for their welfare. That is an immense privilege, but one for which it pays to be well prepared.

ANNOTATED FURTHER READING

Department for Education (DfE) (2013) Keeping children safe in education. London: DfE.
> First produced in conjunction with s 175 of the Education Act 2002 and now revised, this statutory circular provides comprehensive guidance to schools on safeguarding children and safe recruitment and should be the basis of all local policy and procedures. Available at: www.education.gov.uk/publications

Department for Education (2013) Advice on school attendance. London: DfE.
> A summary of the duties placed on all schools and local authorities, including detailed guidance on the management of registration. Available at: www.education.gov.uk

HM Government (2013) Working together to safeguard children. London: DfE.
> The inter-agency statutory guidance and framework for the work of Local Safeguarding Children Boards. Available at: www.education.gov.uk

Whitney, B. (2007) *Social Inclusion in Schools*, London: David Fulton/Routledge.
> This is an overview of a range of social and pastoral issues that may prevent children from accessing education, and what can be done about them.

Whitney B (2014) 'Just Ticking the Box?: Refocusing School Attendance'. Available from www.ypd-books.com
> An overview of law and practice in relation to school attendance which keeps the needs of the child at the centre. More details are available on the author's website: www.ben-whitney.org.uk

FURTHER READING TO SUPPORT M-LEVEL STUDY

Davies, C. and Ward, H. (2012) Safeguarding children across services: messages from research, DfE/Jessica Kingsley.
> A comprehensive review of inter-agency practice in keeping children safe from harm, which contains numerous examples of best practice.

Ofsted (September 2011) *Safeguarding in Schools: best practice*, Ref. 100240.
> An extremely useful overview of the most effective work in a sample of schools.

RELEVANT WEBSITES

Department for Education: www.education.gov.uk

This website contains examples of good practice, latest guidance, etc. For 'school attendance', go to www.education.gov.uk/schoolattendance, and for useful advice on national and local safeguarding arrangements, type 'safeguarding children' into the home page search box.

Your LSCB will have an extremely useful website containing local procedures, etc. This is indispensible for best practice. Details can be obtained from your DMS.

REFERENCES

Department for Education (2013a) Advice on school attendance. Available at: www.education.gov.uk

Department for Education (2013b) Keeping children safe in education. Available at: www.education.gov.uk

HM Government (2013) Working together to safeguard children. Available at: www.education.gov.uk

National Foundation for Educational Research (NFER) (2003) *School Attendance and the Prosecution of Parents: Effects and Effectiveness*, London: NFER.

Ofsted (2011) *Safeguarding in Schools: Best Practice*, Ref. 100240.

YOUR PROFESSIONAL DEVELOPMENT

APPLYING FOR JOBS AND PREPARING FOR YOUR INDUCTION YEAR

Jane Medwell

INTRODUCTION

Your ITT confers the award of QTS, which is the first step in your career. Gaining QTS is rather like passing your driving test – you will be safe to teach a class, but will still have plenty to learn about teaching and very limited experience to draw upon. The next step in your training comes during your year as an NQT. After passing your induction period, you can be employed as a teacher in a maintained school. You only get one chance to pass induction, and so it is important you find the right job to do it in. Towards the end of your training, you will devote considerable energy to finding the right job for you. This is a job that you feel happy in and one that offers you the professional development you need to become a better teacher. By preparing your goals for the induction year thoughtfully, you can ensure you get the support you need in your NQT year. This unit should help you.

OBJECTIVES

By the end of this unit, you should:

- understand the role of the NQT year;
- know how to look for a teaching post;
- be able to begin to write job applications;
- be able to start work on objectives for your NQT year;
- have considered the priorities for your NQT year.

APPLYING FOR A TEACHING JOB

During your training, you may start to apply for jobs. This will necessitate some personal decisions about what area you aim to work in, in what sort of school you would like to work, how far your domestic commitments allow you to commute each day and whether you want a full-time post. This is the time to be realistic, because your first teaching post is so important. It is no use finding the perfect post if you have to leave for work at 6 a.m. every day to get there, or doing your NQT year in a school that does not suit you and your educational beliefs. Deciding where to apply and what sorts of school to apply to is the first step.

Jobs suited to NQTs (starting in September) are advertised at any time from the previous October to the June or July before you start. If you have a target area, you must not miss the job advertisement for that area or job. Teaching posts are usually advertised by individual schools or by NQT 'pools', whereby a group of schools recruit together. You must make sure you check the systems in place in your target areas – it is not uncommon for schools to advertise individually *and* be part of a local authority (LA) cluster or teaching school pool that recruits for a group of schools. Look first at the websites for the borough, LA or Teaching School Alliance (TSA) you are interested in. This will tell you where they advertise teaching posts. Perhaps surprisingly, jobs are still usually advertised in the *Times Educational Supplement* (TES) (Friday) and/or local newspapers, as well as on Internet sites such as e-teach and the electronic TES. You may be able to arrange to have regular bulletins sent to you directly from the LA or TSA in which you are interested.

When you respond to an advertisement, the school or education authority will send you an information pack and details of how to apply for a job. Your ITT provider will give you further information about how to apply for a job, and you should also look at all the information offered by your union.

Applying for jobs will take time and raises a number of issues for you. You will:

- want to use your training experience positively in writing your application;
- need time out from your course for preparation, visits and interviews;
- want to ask for references and ensure your referees are clear about what is required.

In Wales . . .

All providers must ensure that all those who are assessed as meeting the QTS Standards receive and are supported in completing a Career Entry and Development Profile, are informed about the statutory arrangements for the induction of newly qualified teachers and have been helped to prepare for these.

(DCELLS, 2009: 157)

Source: Department for Children, Education, Lifelong Learning and Skills (DCELLS) (2009) *Becoming a Qualified Teacher: Handbook of Guidance (2009)*. Cardiff: Welsh Assembly Government (WAG). http://wales.gov.uk/docs/dcells/publications/090915becomingateacheren.pdf

In Northern Ireland . . .

In Northern Ireland, teachers in the controlled sector are employed by one or other of the five Education and Library Boards. Application forms are obtained from and returned to the individual boards. Teachers in the maintained sector are employed by the Council for Catholic Maintained Schools (CCMS), which was brought into existence by the Education Reform (Northern Ireland) Order 1989. Application forms are obtained from and returned to CCMS.

Source: www.education-support.org.uk/teachers/induction-epd/early-professional-development/

USING YOUR EXPERIENCE POSITIVELY IN YOUR APPLICATION FOR A TEACHING POST

You will be given support in applying for a teaching post in your ITT programme, but it is important that your application includes insights from your ITT course and placements and shows that you can learn from your experiences. When you write in response to an advertisement for a teaching post or for details of an NQT pool, you will receive a person specification for the job. This may be general, simply listing a number of attributes sought in a successful applicant, such as appropriate teaching placement experience, ability to plan deliver, monitor and evaluate children's learning, and so on. Alternatively, there may be very specific requirements associated with a school. As an NQT, you will not be expected to co-ordinate a curriculum area in your induction year, but the school may well be seeking staff with particular areas of expertise.

There are two main types of written application for primary and early years teaching posts: the LA or school application form, which usually includes a personal statement or letter of application, or your own curriculum vitae (CV) and letter of application. The information pack you receive from the school or LA will tell you what is required.

Complete application forms neatly and accurately and in a way that demonstrates enthusiasm. The usual rules for form filling apply: read the instructions carefully and follow them; write a draft first (and keep it for future reference); do not leave gaps but write N/A (not applicable); check all your dates and have all your information to hand; make sure your writing is neat, spell correctly and make sure your personal statement (or letter) is effective. Plan plenty of time to fill in your application and make sure you have done a thorough review of your record of professional development or training plan.

Task 9.1.1 Reviewing your progress towards the *Teachers' Standards*

You review your progress throughout your training, but when you apply for jobs is a key review point, and so we suggest you conduct a thorough review just before you complete an application. Doing this helps you to:

- remember and revisit all the training tasks you have done – assignments, school tasks and even visits, some of which may have taken place a while ago;
- bring to mind all the training opportunities you took up on placement;
- identify progress you have made towards demonstrating the *Teachers' Standards*;
- decide what constitutes evidence of your progress towards the *Teachers' Standards* and to store this appropriately;
- prepare a portfolio of work in preparation for a job interview (see below);
- begin to formulate your areas of interest, strength and weakness for your NQT year (see below).

Go through your record of professional development (or training plan), reviewing your placement reports and academic work against the *Teachers' Standards*. Identify four areas where you have made progress and four areas in which you would like to improve.

You will be required to write either a supporting statement or a letter of application as part of an application form. The first thing you should do to prepare this is to examine thoroughly the person specification and/or job description, to work out what the school or LA is looking for. Then read the instructions for completing the form or letter very carefully. Filling out this form is a chore, but it is your chance to market your skills. Do not be too modest or make impossible, exaggerated claims. The completed form will be slightly embarrassing, because it spells out your achievements and qualities, but it should not be untruthful. Mentors, personal tutors and teachers will help you to prepare your application, and you should discuss a draft of your letter of application, supporting statement or CV (whichever is requested) with your tutor or mentor. Arrange a time in advance, as you cannot expect staff necessarily to be available at short notice.

There are many ways of writing your letter of application or supporting statement, and there is no perfect template, but there are some key points you should bear in mind. Give a brief overview of your training (but do not repeat everything you have put in the application form) and mention your degree and any relevant projects, experiences or previous work. It is important to identify why *you* are the candidate who would suit this post, so say why you are applying for this job, in particular. Include any local links, faith issues or visits to the school.

Your teaching placements during training are very important, and so reference to your formal school placements should include when you did the placement, what year groups you have taught and the level of responsibility you took, but do not use up all your letter space by repeating what you have put on the form. Refer to special features of the placement, such as open-plan schools or team teaching. You could also refer to your placements to illustrate an aspect of your learning or an enthusiasm you have developed during your training. Such references could be to examples of how you plan, teach, monitor and evaluate learning outcomes, behaviour management strategies, work with parents and so on.

Write a little about your vision or beliefs for early years or primary education and the principles that underpin your practice. This might include beliefs about how children learn, classroom management, teaching styles, for instance. If you can illustrate with an example of how you have learned this on your course or school placement, this can be very effective. This sort of information gives the school a flavour of you as a teacher.

Another part of your letter will include details of your personal experiences: leisure activities, interests or involvement with children. Make these relevant to your work as a teacher and be explicit about what skills you have.

One of the easier ways to organise this information is to identify a number of subheadings taken from the person specification or job description, such as:

- teaching experiences (placements);
- commitment to teaching;
- knowledge, skills and aptitudes;
- planning and organisation;
- strengths and interests;
- personal qualities.

Organise your information under these headings. You can then remove your subheadings and have a well-organised letter to discuss with your mentor, tutor or careers adviser. Write in the first person, check your grammar and use interesting adverbs and adjectives to lift the text. If in doubt, ask a friend to proof-read your letter before you talk to your mentor or tutor.

Task 9.1.2 Using a person specification

Using the suggested bullet points for a person specification (see above), review your experience, qualifications and knowledge skills and aptitudes. Go through each point asking yourself:

- What evidence do I have that I meet this criterion?
- What have I learnt about this on my placements and in my course of study?
- What else do I need to be able to do to achieve this?
- What do I want to focus on in my continuing professional development (CPD) during the induction year.

Use the headings below to organise your information:

- Teaching experiences (placements)
- Commitment to teaching
- Knowledge, skills and aptitudes
- Planning and organisation
- Strengths and interests
- Personal qualities.

Write a letter of application, of not more than two sides of A4, setting out your experience, knowledge, skills and aptitudes and views about education. Discuss this general draft with your mentor, tutor or teacher and ask them to tell you about the impact and impression it makes. This letter can then form the basis of other letters that are tailored to suit a particular post.

THE CURRICULUM VITAE

In applying for your first teaching post, you may find yourself writing a CV for the first time. Your CV sets out the important information about you on two sides of A4. Preparing for this is similar to preparing to fill in a form, but you will need to print it out on good-quality white paper. As with the letter, prepare a general CV well in advance, but adapt it for each application, so that it matches the person specification.

There are some things you should omit from a CV, such as your date of birth, age, marital status or ethnic origin. Photographs of yourself are not necessary for CVs for teaching posts and can trigger subconscious prejudice. Do not include failures on your CV – aim to keep it focused on what you have achieved and why you match the school's needs. You should also leave out previous salary information or reasons for changing jobs, which are irrelevant.

The following should be included on your CV:

- Contact details: Make sure that these are guaranteed routes to reach you. Ideally, include your postal address and any telephone numbers you have (landline and mobile). Schools will not expect to contact you through social networking sites, and you should not include these – it creates the impression that you do not know where to draw professional boundaries.
- Your gender, if it is not obvious from your name.
- A short skills summary or supporting statement (see below).

- Your work experience and placement experiences – most recent first (any positions you held more than about 10 years ago can be left out).
- Your education: This is best organised as follows: primary, secondary, further, higher.
- Your qualifications, listed with the most recent first, including results.
- Interests: only real and genuine ones, e.g. any sports in which you actively participate. If these hobbies and interests can convey a sense of your personality, all the better. Include any non-teaching qualifications that may have arisen from your hobbies or interests here too.
- Membership of professional associations (not including unions).
- Nationality, National Insurance number and referee details can be included at the end of your CV.

A skills summary need only be around 200 words, but you can still cover a lot of ground. It should be written in the first person. Every word must have a use, and grammar should be immaculate. Do not just repeat what experience you have had – your achievements, accountability and competence are more important, and this is where you can really bring these out. Aim to give a sense of your creativity, personal management and integrity – the reader will want to see that you have strong communication skills and, perhaps, even leadership potential. When writing a skills summary, some people prefer to include a short bulleted list of around six key skills.

With only two sides of A4, the layout of a CV is important, and you need to be economical with space. Although the page should not look cluttered, excess space will look messy and ill thought through.

- Present your contact details across the top of the first page (like a letterhead) to preserve space.
- Use a clear, standard font such as Times New Roman or Arial.
- Avoid abbreviations unless they are universally understood.

If you really cannot fit everything on to two sides of A4, try reducing the font size slightly. This will mean the print is still large enough to read, but will give you a little more room to play with. There really is not too much difference between 12 and 11 point in terms of readability.

When you have designed your CV on screen, print off a draft version and try to view it through fresh eyes. Is it likely to grab the attention of a reader within a few seconds? Is it visually pleasing? Are there any errors? It is a good idea to ask someone else to cast an eye over it, as it is easy to miss typos on documents you have been working on yourself.

Writing a CV is not a one-off task. Once you have completed your CV (see the example in Figure 9.1.1), you will need to keep it up to date and make sure it is tailored to each application you use it for. It is not enough to send out a standard CV.

REFEREES

You will usually be asked to supply the names, positions and contact details of two referees. The first should be a senior member of staff in your ITT provider. Check carefully who this should be. It is common for universities to use the name of the head of department, even though your tutor will probably actually write the reference. It is essential to get this name right for two reasons. If you do not get a first reference from your ITT provider, the job advertiser will usually assume you have something to hide. Second, the reference system in a large ITT provider will be geared up for a swift response, but it will only work if you get the right name. The wrong name will slow down your reference and may put you at a disadvantage.

Your second referee should usually be from your placement school – your mentor, class teacher or head teacher. Ask whether the mentor or head teacher is prepared to offer you a reference. In most

Paula Grey
Eastleigh Cottage, 35 Thornton Hill, Cardiff CF21 9DE
Telephone: 0128 213 3567, mobile: 07337 632077, email: Paulie@yahoo.com

I am a newly qualified teacher trained to teach across the curriculum with the 5–11 age group. My previous work experience as an accountant has enabled me to develop an understanding of management in a large multinational corporation as well as demonstrable communication skills. Part of my role was the delivery of internal training for new staff. During my initial teacher training I taught in an inner-city Key Stage 1 class and in two Key Stage 2 classes in a school with a large multiracial population. In addition to my teaching, I ran a successful 'Get Into Reading' after-school workshop for parents, which crossed age and cultural boundaries and was recognised by the head and governors as a constructive addition to the wider school culture.

Education

Primary:	1984–1990 Abbey Primary School, Cardiff
Secondary:	1990–1995 Newport High School for Girls, Newport
Further:	1995–1997 Newport Sixth Form College, Newport
Higher:	1997–1999 University of Reading BA
	1999–2007 Membership of the Society of Chartered Accountants
	2008–2009 Institute of Education, University of London PGCE

Qualifications

PGCE:	Primary
Degree:	Archaeology and Statistics 2.1
A levels:	Mathematics A, Statistics A, Physics B, General studies B
GCSEs:	Mathematics A, English literature A, English language B, Physics B, History A, ICT A, Art B, Geography B, French A, Biology B

Professional development

During my initial teacher training I completed an LA-run 'Levelling Mathematics' course and attended a 'Developing Storysacks' training day.

Work experience

2004–2005:	ITT placements: High Five School, Camden and Nelson Mandela Primary School, Westminster
1999–2004:	British International Bank, London, Accountant
1997–1999:	Vacation positions with Marks and Spencer and Dillons, Cwmbran

Interests

I have run a local Brownies group for some years. I also run to keep fit and have completed the London marathon.

Additional qualifications

Full, clean driving licence
South Glamorgan County Junior Football Coaching

Nationality

British

National Insurance number

TY123456B

References

Referees available on request

FIGURE 9.1.1 A sample CV

cases, a reference is offered gladly. Professionals will not write a bad reference for anyone, but would decline to offer a reference if they could not truthfully recommend you. Mentors and head teachers will never decline to offer a reference simply because they do not want the effort.

Be quite clear who you intend to name as a referee. You might want to discuss this with your mentor or head, so that you get the best reference. Will you name the mentor him or herself, or the headteacher? Check that you know the full name, title and professional position of your referee and make sure that the mentor or head has your contact details and that you have theirs. You should contact them to let them know when you use their name as a referee in any application. Be clear about anything you would like your referee to mention (such as participation in out-of-school events) or avoid mentioning, such as a disability or illness. Say when you expect to be applying for jobs and whether these will be exclusively teaching jobs or will include things such as vacation jobs or voluntary work. Give your referee a copy of your CV and a summary of your strengths as part of the process of asking for a reference. Schools that you have applied to may ring your second referee for an informal reference, particularly if you are applying for a job locally. You want your referee to be prepared for this and to speak warmly about you, rather than be surprised and feel caught out.

VISITS AND INTERVIEWS DURING YOUR TRAINING

When you are considering applying for a job, you may be invited to look around the school, or you may ask to look around a school. Some schools schedule specific times and take a large number of applicants around the school together. This sort of tour is a very good way to find out about a school and whether it will suit you. However, it can present problems because of the time it takes out of your training programme, especially if you are applying for posts at some distance. You must consider the impact of absence from school or university on your training and the cumulative impact of multiple visits, particularly as this is often a time when you are on school placement. You have to complete a certain amount of placement time in school and take sustained responsibility for the class on final placement, and a large number of visits could affect the outcome of your placement, as well as the way your commitment to your placement school is seen. It may be better to try to visit schools after the end of the school day, or to explain to schools that your placement commitments prevent you from visiting informally.

On interview day, you will be given a tour of the school prior to interview, and you would have the opportunity to withdraw from the interview after this if you did not think the school would suit you. If you apply for a job through a teaching pool, you will usually go for an interview for the pool first and may then be invited to look around schools that have jobs available. This is a different sort of school visit from the informal, pre-interview visit mentioned above, because you will be looking at a school to see whether you would take a job there. You should go on these visits, but be aware of the time consideration mentioned above.

When you have applied for a post and are invited to interview during training time, you should ask your tutor or mentor for permission to attend, thus missing the taught sessions or school placement that day. In practice, this is a courtesy, and you will always be given permission to attend interviews. It is a good idea to ask your mentor, tutor or class teacher to help you to prepare for interview, and such preparation might take a number of forms:

- Discuss 'hot' topics in the educational press or recent initiatives in school. Identify and discuss issues in the TES or another publication with a colleague, tutor or teacher. This will help you to explore the issues from another perspective. Consider what the effects of new ideas are for teachers, schools and children.

- Role play a 'mock' interview with your tutor, mentor, teacher or another trainee. This can help you to conquer nerves and prepare your interview manner. Practise framing your replies at interview – a pause to think, for example, rather than rushing in and babbling. What sort of body language do you want to exhibit – or avoid? Consider how you will conclude the interview and what your final impression is to be.

Your interview may include a task such as teaching a class or group, planning a lesson or making a presentation to the interview panel. If a letter of invitation states (or hints at) this, do not be afraid to telephone the school to ask for details of the year group, subject required, technology available and time parameters of the task. Many schools leave the details vague and expect you to enquire.

Ask a tutor or teacher to help you to plan any teaching you are asked to do as part of your interview, but make sure you go to them with plenty of ideas and suggestions. It is not uncommon to be asked to teach something to a class. You will not be able to prepare a perfect lesson, because you do not know the children, but you can still use a lesson plan to show that you know the relevant curricula, have good ideas, know a range of teaching strategies, are aware of a range of resources and have a good manner with children. Your tutor or mentor may be able to spot obvious faux pas or overambitious plans if you ask to discuss them.

Always re-read a copy of your application before you go to interview and prepare some questions to ask the panel at the end of the interview. It is perfectly acceptable to find that all your questions have been answered in the recruitment process (say so), but not to seem clueless.

INTERVIEW PORTFOLIOS AND INTERVIEWS

As a trainee, you will be maintaining a training plan or record of professional development that contains evidence to demonstrate your achievement of the *Teachers' Standards*. This will contain examples of your assessment and planning, placement assessment reports, observation notes, written assignments, mentor meeting notes and other evidence.

You may be asked to take this training plan or record with you to interview or to bring a portfolio. Even if you are not asked to bring a portfolio, you may want to do so. You can offer this to your interviewers – they do not have to spend much time looking at it, but it does indicate you are well prepared and professional.

Consider how you can create the best impression to someone who does just looks through your portfolio (the flick factor). For example, anything on the back of facing pages is unlikely to be seen, so either put less important pages here, or have a single-sided portfolio with all pages facing the reader. Make sure your photos are well displayed, as they have a disproportionate impact. Although your portfolio may not command much time or attention, by preparing it, you are not only demonstrating professionalism, but also getting the chance to present a tailored image of your achievements to the panel, in addition to your written application.

When you are interviewed for a teaching post, the panel will usually include the head teacher and governors, as well as LA representatives or staff from other areas of the school organisation. They will have agreed the questions to be asked of all candidates before the interview. When you answer questions, it is perfectly appropriate to pause and think before replying, and you should not feel under pressure to rush in and say the first thing you think of. Schools are concerned with 'safe recruitment' and may ask questions about your relationships with pupils or that deal with issues of e-safety, such as, 'A pupil contacts you on Facebook. How do you respond?'. These are important questions, so consider responses carefully. (A pupil should not be able to contact you on Facebook, nor should a primary child be using it.)

Interview portfolio

An interview portfolio can be a substantial document, but, more usually, is a slim document containing some of the following:

- Title and content page, preferably with a photo of you in a teaching situation.
- Concise CV.
- Placement assessment reports (one or more).
- A really good lesson plan or two, some examples of the work associated with the lesson and the lesson evaluation.
- An example of your assessment.
- A mentor, tutor or class teacher observation of a lesson that picks out a strength.
- A sample mentor meeting summary (to show you are focused and organised).
- An example of a piece of your written work (and the marking sheet) if relevant.
- A few photos of you teaching. Choose these carefully, as you really want to present a particular image. Generally, you might choose one photo of you 'at the front' teaching a large group or class, one of you looking sensitive with a group and, ideally, one of you teaching elsewhere – perhaps on a school visit or outside. Remember, choose photos to suit that job. If the school is very ICT conscious, make sure there is a picture of you using ICT. If the school is keen to improve its physical education, a photo of your gym session would not go amiss! Make sure you follow your placement school policy on photo use and that the school, teachers and children are not identifiable.
- One or two photos of displays, school visits you have been on, after-school clubs or assemblies you have led.
- Any evidence of your special interests – coaching certificates, first aid, cookery, etc.

In addition to your interview with the panel, you will often be interviewed by pupils who are representatives of the school council, who will be the voice of the pupils in the appointment process. They, too, will have agreed on the areas they want to ask candidates about. Think about what the pupils are looking for – usually consistency, fun and warmth. It is a good idea to ensure you have an appropriate joke ready, in case you are asked!

INDUCTION FOR NEWLY QUALIFIED TEACHERS

Induction for NQTs is compulsory, follows ITT and is the foundation for CPD throughout your career. The induction period must be undertaken by NQTs who wish to work in maintained schools and non-maintained special schools, but is not necessary for academies, independent schools or free schools. The induction period may also be done while working in independent schools, academies and free schools, but not all of them offer this. You can usually complete induction part time, but it will take longer than the usual year. Check when you apply for a job, as failure to do a recognised induction period will mean you cannot be employed as a qualified teacher in maintained schools. You do not have to complete your induction period immediately after your ITT, and there is currently no time limit, but this changes, and so you should check this on the Department for Education website (www.education.gov.uk/schools/leadership/deployingstaff/newstaff/b0066959/nqt-induction). In the same way, supply work of less than a term does count towards the induction period, but check this, as it may change.

Task 9.1.3 Using CARE to give a reflective answer to interview questions

The mnemonic CARE (context, action, result, evaluation) can help you give positive answers to interview questions. For instance, a common question might be, 'Describe a time when you have dealt with a disruptive pupil?'. You might answer:

> I had a lesson during my second placement when one pupil in my class became very agitated and would not let me carry on my lesson [context]. I had discussed this possibility with my class teacher when we looked at the school policy so, after I have given the pupil an amber warning, I sent two children to contact the TA in my companion class, as we had agreed [action]. The TA worked with my disruptive pupil until she could take part in the lesson, so that the other children could work and she didn't feel excluded [result]. That experience really brought home the importance of school policy and preparing for every situation [evaluation] so that the class can make progress.

Try to apply the CARE framework to these questions and think about how you would answer them:

- How would you teach phonics to Year 1 children?
- A parent comes into school and accuses another pupil of breaking their son's glasses. How would you handle it?
- Tell us about an exciting activity you have planned.

In Wales . . .

'All NQTs must successfully complete Induction to continue teaching in a maintained school or non-maintained special school. As with ITT, NQTs should play an active role in their Induction' (DCELLS, 2009: 158).

Source: Department for Children, Education, Lifelong Learning and Skills (DCELLS) (2009) *Becoming a Qualified Teacher: Handbook of Guidance (2009)*. Cardiff: Welsh Assembly Government (WAG). http://wales.gov.uk/docs/dcells/publications/090915becomingateacheren.pdf

---

During the induction period, you have to demonstrate you can meet the *Teachers' Standards*, over a sustained period. You will have an individualised programme of support during the induction year, from a designated induction tutor in your school. This includes observations of your teaching by school staff and induction tutors, you observing more experienced teachers in different settings, and a formal review of progress three times during the induction year. You will also have the opportunity to attend school-centred, in-service provision and, often, external courses. During your induction year, you will not teach more than 90 per cent of a normal timetable (not including the 10 per cent PPA time), to allow your induction to take place.

The head is responsible for registering you with an appropriate body for induction (which can be the LA, the Independent Schools Teacher Induction Panel or a teaching school induction provider) and will make a final recommendation as to whether you have passed or failed your induction period.

The appropriate body makes the final decision, and there is a right of appeal to the National College for Teaching and Leadership in England or the General Teaching Council for Wales, in Wales. The DfE guidance on induction (Department for Education, 2013) is available on the DfE website. You should ensure you check it.

PLANNING AND MONITORING YOUR INDUCTION YEAR

At the end of your ITT, you should prepare for your induction year and see it as CPD. You should evaluate, monitor and seek the appropriate experiences to ensure you can meet the *Teachers' Standards* consistently. During your induction year, there are clear induction responsibilities for the head teacher, the induction tutor and you, the NQT.

Your head teacher will register you with an appropriate induction body, the National College for Teaching and Leadership and the governors and will ensure you have an appropriate timetable and induction tutor. It will be your head who eventually reports your assessments to the appropriate body, and the head will monitor your induction. However, the day-to-day support will come from your induction tutor, who will offer you the guidance, coaching and mentoring you need and arrange for you to observe good practice. The induction tutor will observe your teaching and discuss the observations with you. During the induction year, the induction tutor will make and report three formal assessments of your ability to meet the *Teachers' Standards*. This will be based on observations of your teaching and discussions with you. You will have copies of all the assessment forms, and it is your duty to keep those forms, seek the help you need and raise any concerns about your induction support.

NQT induction is all about you, and your role in your induction is central. You should see it as an opportunity to demonstrate your strengths and seek the training you need to develop as a teacher. You will discuss how to use your reduced timetable to meet your own professional targets with your induction tutor, and it will be up to you to demonstrate and provide evidence against the relevant standards at each assessment meeting. This should sound familiar – it is very similar to the process of continuous reflection, evaluation and action you took during your ITT.

The starting point of your induction year is the targets for yourself you set as you complete your ITT. These will give you a basis for discussion at your first meeting with your induction tutor and help you to appear professional and focused on your professional development in a new setting. The same *Teachers' Standards* apply, not only to your ITT, but also to your induction year, and the difference in assessment of ITT and induction is that your induction year gives you the chance to demonstrate an ability to address the *Teachers' Standards* consistently.

As you come to the end of your ITT programme, you will want to think about how far you have come in your professional development. This process is likely to be a natural part of your ITT programme. Your ITT provider will also help you to understand your own role in your induction, and this meeting will help you to think about your experience from before, during and outside your formal training programme, including your placements, and to identify your key achievements and aspirations in relation to teaching.

You should aim to set targets that:

- reflect and build on the strengths in your practice;
- develop aspects of the teacher's role in which you are particularly interested;
- provide more experience, or build up your expertise, in areas where you have developed to a more limited extent so far.

Task 9.1.4 Preparing your targets for induction

- At this stage, which aspect(s) of teaching do you find most interesting and rewarding? What has led to your interest in these areas? How would you like to develop these interests?
- As you approach the award of QTS, what do you consider to be your main strengths and achievements as a teacher? Why do you think this? What examples do you have of your achievements in these areas?
- In which aspects of teaching would you value further experience in the future?

  For example:

  – aspects of teaching about which you feel less confident, or where you have had limited opportunities to gain experience;
  – areas of particular strength or interest on which you want to build further.

- At the moment, which of these areas do you particularly hope to develop during your induction period?
- As you look ahead to your career in teaching, you may be thinking about your longer-term professional aspirations and goals. Do you have any thoughts at this stage about how you would like to see your career develop?

Record your responses to these questions for discussion with your induction tutor at the start of the induction year. Because it is the document you will be taking to show your induction tutor, you may want to word-process your answers and include evidence. This shows your induction tutor not only your IT skills, but also your professional approach.

Task 9.1.5 Using your record of professional development to prepare your induction targets

Note down your response to the questions above, where you might find evidence to support your thinking, and/or the reasoning that led you to this response. You will want to draw on evidence that is already available in your record of professional development or training plan, for example:

- reports on your teaching during your placements;
- observation reports written by your mentor, class teacher or course tutor;
- examples of your planning for placement;
- records of targets and objectives set during your ITT programme;
- your own audits of your progress towards the QTS Standards;
- course assignments or subject audits.

Task 9.1.6 Framing your targets professionally

Consider an excerpt from the answers to some of these questions noted by Sophie and Alex, below.

- As you approach the award of QTS, what do you consider to be your main strengths and achievements as a teacher?

    Sophie: I think I am a caring person and relate well to the children. I have really got on well with teachers but I have not had a chance to work with a TA. I want to work with a TA.

    Alex: My placement reports identify my relationships with the children and teachers as one of my strengths. My final report suggested that good relationships with the children was part of my success at managing the class and my second placement report noted that I had worked particularly closely with other teachers in planning and assessment. I now want to develop my experience of planning for a TA in the classroom, as I have not experienced this.

- In which aspects of teaching would you value further experience in the future?

    Sophie: I have not really had the chance to teach children with EAL during my placement and I would like to do much more of this and really cater for the EAL children in my class.

    Alex: Although I have had training sessions and done an assignment about teaching children with EAL, my practical experience has been limited. In my induction year I would like to develop my experience of planning for and teaching children with EAL with the support of a more experienced teacher. I want to develop a reasonable repertoire of practical strategies.

Which answers:

- use evidence well?
- emphasise experience?
- balance strengths and weaknesses?
- offer the best indication of what action might be required?

The targets and evaluation you make at the end of you ITT will enable the school that employs you to:

- understand your strengths and experiences by the end of ITT;
- support your professional development through your NQT year;
- support constructive dialogue between NQTs and induction tutors;
- make links between induction, CPD and performance management.

At your meeting with your induction tutor, you will identify your targets and actions for the beginning of your induction, based on this evaluation. If you have maintained a record of professional development or a training plan as part of your ITT training, keeping a record of your induction will not be totally unfamiliar. It simply continues the target-setting-action–review cycle that you will be used to, will help you to make the most of your first job and your induction year and will carry you through your career. The guide issued by the National Union of Teachers on Induction (NUT, 2013) spells out the process of the induction year in some detail.

SUMMARY

This chapter gives you a broad overview of the whole topic of moving on in your professional development and training. You will need to allocate a substantial amount of time and attention to securing the right first teaching post, but when you have, you have real opportunities to develop as a professional. To do this, you must carry out a clear-eyed, realistic review of your achievements and further professional development needs and put these into your targets for induction.

- When applying for jobs, enlist the support of your mentor or tutor. They can look at applications and offer you mock interviews.
- Start considering applications early and allow plenty of time.
- Prepare each job application carefully, making sure you use the application format they want and that you set out your abilities and skills appropriately.
- Ensure you name the appropriate referees and that you have asked them if you may use them as referees.
- Use evidence from your training plan (or record of professional development) to prepare an interview portfolio. Make sure it presents the image you want for each job.
- The induction year has its own standards for induction, and setting targets for these is a final task of ITT.
- Ensure you know about your strengths and targets as an NQT before you meet your course tutor or mentor. You are responsible for negotiating these targets with your induction tutor when you get your induction post. Use your records and your final meeting with your ITT tutor to prepare.

 ## ANNOTATED FURTHER READING

Association of Graduate Careers Advisory Services (AGCAS) (2012-13) Getting a Teaching Job in Schools: A Guide to Finding Your First Appointment. AGCAS.
  Detailed information about applying for a teaching post is available in this publication.

Department for Education (December 2013) Induction for Newly Qualified Teachers (England).
  DfE guidance on induction, Induction for Newly Qualified teachers (England) is available on the DfE website at: www.education.gov.uk/aboutdfe/statutory/g00212895/induction-nqts-england. This site also provides detailed guidance about induction and links to the Teachers' Standards.

FURTHER READING TO SUPPORT M-LEVEL STUDY

Cordingley, P. and Bell, M. (2012) Understanding What Enables High Quality Professional Learning – A Report on the Research Evidence. Coventry: CUREE; London: Pearson. Available at: www.curee.co.uk/files/ publication/%5Bsite-timestamp%5D/CUREE-Report.pdf

> This report reviews a range of research to try to answer the question: 'What are the characteristics of high-quality professional learning for teachers?'. The report suggests that teachers' professional development is more likely to benefit students if it is:
>
> * collaborative, involving teachers working together to share their practice and try out new approaches;
> * supported by specialist expertise;
> * focused on improving outcomes for learners;
> * sustained over time;
> * aimed at connecting practice to theory, and theory to practice.
>
> It will repay study as you plan for your own professional development beyond your NQT induction year.

Totterdell, M., Woodroffe, L., Bubb, S. and Hanrahan, K. (2004) The impact of NQT induction programmes on the enhancement of teacher expertise, professional development, job satisfaction or retention rates: a systematic review of research on induction. In: Research Evidence in Education Library. London: EPPI-Centre, Social Science Research Unit, Institute of Education. Available at: http://eppi.ioe.ac.uk/cms/ Default.aspx?tabid=307

> The main aim of this report was to identify and map studies that could shed light on the impact of induction programmes for NQTs on teacher performance, career development and retention rates. Findings suggest that:
>
> * The goals of an induction programme must be clear.
> * New teachers need to be given reduced teaching loads and opportunities for collaborative planning, target-setting and reviews with their mentors.
>
> Effective training and development need to be available to support new teachers, their mentors and their head teachers.

 RELEVANT WEBSITES

Times Educational Supplement: www.tesjobs.co.uk

The Guardian (Tuesdays): www.jobsunlimited.co.uk

The Daily Telegraph (independent schools): www.telegraph.co.uk

The Independent (Thursdays): www.independent.co.uk

> Most school vacancies are advertised in the above publications. Some of these operate an electronic job alert system.

Independent Schools Council Information Service (ISCIS): www.iscis.uk.net

Incorporated Association of Preparatory Schools (IAPS): www.iaps.co.uk

> The above two websites offer general information about teaching in the private sector.

NASUWT: www.teachersunion.org.uk

NUT: www.teachers.org.uk

ATL: www.atl.org.uk

> Your union is an excellent source of help, advice and support in applying for a teaching post.

Eteach: www.eteach.com

Prospects: www.prospects.ac.uk
>Other useful online resources for finding a teaching post are available at the above websites.

Teachers' Standards (May 2012): www.education.gov.uk/publications/eOrderingDownload/teachers%20standards.pdf

Department for Education (May 2012) Induction for Newly Qualified Teachers (England): www.education.gov.uk/schools/leadership/deployingstaff/newstaff/b0066959/nqt-induction/useful-resources-for-nqt-induction
>The statutory provisions that underpin this guidance are ss 135A, 135B and 141C(1)(b) of the Education Act 2002, and the Education (Induction Arrangements for School Teachers) (England) Regulations 2012.

 ## REFERENCES

Department for Education (2013) Statutory Guidance on Induction for Newly Qualified Teachers (England). London: DfE. Available at: http://media.education.gov.uk/assets/files/pdf/s/statutory%20guidance%20revised%20june%202013.pdf

National Union of Teachers (NUT) (2013) Induction. London: NUT. Available at: www.teachers.org.uk/files/NUT_Induction_Guide-13-14.pdf

UNDERSTANDING AND PLANNING YOUR CONTINUING PROFESSIONAL DEVELOPMENT

Kit Field and Chris Randall

INTRODUCTION

The world of continuing professional development (CPD) is fast changing. The emphasis on CPD within *The Children's Plan* (Department for Children, Schools and Families, 2007), subsequent documentation and literature has changed since 2010 and the election of the Coalition government. Curriculum changes and the proposed introduction of the English Baccalaureate have signalled a return to a more traditional, subject knowledge-based curriculum. The introduction of Teaching Schools at the heart of alliances of schools and the continued commercialisation of CPD have led to a form of deregulation of CPD, and the belief that teaching is a craft (Gove, 2010) has enabled schools to pay a bigger role in supporting a form of CPD that promotes teachers supporting teachers, and accountability for it resting with schools, their results and Ofsted ratings. Reports from many sources, including the remit for teaching schools (National College of School Leadership, 2012), stress the need for CPD focused on core skills and modern foreign languages.

The disbanding of the General Teaching Council (England) (GTC(E)) has removed a collective view of a code of conduct/practice for CPD, and the removal of Training and Development Agency (TDA) funding to support Masters-level study, including the ending of the much trumpeted Masters in Teaching and Learning, places a greater emphasis on apparently less expensive forms of CPD.

New national professional standards for all teachers, coupled with stringent performance management procedures, tie CPD in with a sense of professional entitlement and obligation. For new teachers, engaging with CPD represents an essential component of being a professional. CPD is multi-dimensional and is a means of (re-)professionalising the teaching workforce, providing a degree of self- and professional esteem, as well as the means of improving school performance and implementing a wide range of national strategies. Research has shown (Gray, 2005, for example) that CPD has not been a major success in more recent years, with teachers expressing little respect for what has been on offer, and head teachers being prepared to divert funding towards more pressing priorities. With such an emphasis in recent legislative documentation, it comes as no surprise that built into the processes of CPD is a need to demonstrate a link between engagement by teachers and a positive and visible impact.

OBJECTIVES

By the end of this unit, you should:

- understand the complexity of, and the need to redefine, CPD;
- recognise the roles of the many professional agencies associated with CPD;
- acknowledge the need to be proactive in organising your own CPD, from planning stages to identifying the impact;
- recognise the links between CPD and performance management;
- appreciate the need for ongoing professional learning and development;
- appreciate what constitutes effective CPD from the perspectives of the 'system', the 'individual', the 'school' and the 'profession'.

POLICY SHIFT

The continued piecemeal approach to CPD that has led to a 'cluttered playing field' has provoked policy changes. The (then) TDA wrote to local authorities (LAs) in 2008 to launch a 'Leading CPD in Schools Project', identifying barriers and challenges to effective CPD. These included:

- **cultural**: changing staff perceptions of the value and nature of CPD;
- **capacity**: using resources such as time and money effectively;
- **operational**: identifying the needs of the staff, developing CPD opportunities and evaluating impact;
- **specific**: addressing current initiatives such as performance management, new professional standards and extending CPD to the wider workforce.

The argument was that understanding these challenges is essential to shaping the range and nature of support to develop effective CPD leadership.

The Coalition government has striven to build upon the apparent successes of City Challenges in London, Manchester and the Black Country. The notion of school-to-school support, coupled with an enthusiasm to accelerate the academies programme, has resulted in many deep-seated implications for CPD.

The Schools White Paper, *The Importance of Teaching* (Department for Education, 2010), set out the Coalition government's intention to develop a national network of teaching schools, based on the model of teaching hospitals, to lead the training and professional development of teachers and head teachers and increase the number of national and local leaders of education. This is underpinned by a commitment to head teachers of excellent schools working to support other schools. The White Paper also stated that this will involve 'giving outstanding schools the role of leading the training and professional development of teachers and headteachers'.

The establishment of teaching schools led to new forms of CPD driven by schools that have proven track records. Andy Buck, of the National College for School Leadership (NCSL), presented the concept around the country throughout 2011. Among the functions of the new teaching schools are CPD, support for weaker schools, the development of regional talent pools and leadership development. By creating an elite of high-performing schools and of local and national leaders of education, the aim is to identify sources of excellence and to facilitate inter-school support and co-operation.

In addition, it is highly recommended that teaching schools work with a strategic partner from the higher-education sector, i.e. a university provider of teacher education.

It is not clear whether universities will be a strategic partner or whether they might only be involved as a provider whose services can be purchased. However, in many cases, teaching schools are seeking support for Masters-level accreditation of CPD undertaken, linked to school improvement intervention, plans and priorities. In addition, teaching school partners can include commercial companies. This includes companies that develop and sell educational resources, as well as those that design and deliver training and CPD. Academy sponsors could also be partners.

The National Association of School Teachers/Union of Women Teachers (n.d.) argues that the programme is built on the principle of competition and the idea that the market should determine what training and CPD are provided.

The fear is that increased marketisation will reduce schools' willingness to collaborate and co-operate, that multiple 'suppliers of CPD' will emerge, without any form of quality control, and that the policy will benefit the vast range of private providers looking to expand their training packages to schools, often at high cost and in the absence of any national benchmarking of quality assurance.

The justification for this argument is that, by giving individual teaching school alliances responsibility for the design and delivery of training and CPD locally, it will lead to wide variation in the quality of what is provided. Several reports have indicated that certain groups of professionals have found it more difficult to access CPD and, therefore, to be identified as having potential for promotion and career development (e.g. McNamara *et al.*, 2008, 2009).

The implication is that individual teachers must be more proactive in seeking their own CPD, but drawing on the opportunities available. Masters-level qualifications remain a respected currency, and the abolition of the GTC(E) and its Teaching and Learning Academy has removed another form of professional recognition. Higher-level qualifications remain the only form of recognition beyond local reputation.

In Northern Ireland . . .

The Department of Education for Northern Ireland states, 'The quality of an education system cannot exceed the quality of its teachers . . . Teachers must therefore be properly supported in their work' (DENI, 2011: 12)

Source: Department of Education for Northern Ireland (DENI) (2011) *Count, Read: Succeed: A strategy to improve outcomes in literacy and numeracy.* Bangor, DENI.

WHY CPD?

Experienced teachers only have to reflect on their careers over the years to acknowledge the changes in educational expectations. Changes in curriculum, new understandings and learning theories, new technologies, the establishment of independent , state-funded schools and new forms of governance, all demand new ways of working. The adage that teachers are born and not made can easily be challenged. No teacher can rely on skills and competences from the past. What a teacher may be good at may not be relevant for the future.

Periodically, the Department for Education (DfE) issues priorities for attention – often emerging from reports emanating from Ofsted. Current priorities include the development of a phonics approach to learning to read, behaviour management and provision and support for children with special educational needs and disabilities (SEND).

WHAT IS CPD?

CPD is the term used to ensure teachers continuously improve and adapt to current and future circumstances. There are, self-evidently, three aspects to CPD: *continuing*, *professional* and *development*.

Continuing

Society is ever changing. If one goal of education is to prepare young people today for the world of tomorrow, no teacher can rely on lessons learned yesterday. Teachers must engage in learning for practical reasons. A former government CPD strategy (Department for Education and Employment, 2001) mentions the need for pupils to develop an enthusiasm for lifelong learning, as it is seen to be key to success in adult life. Such an enthusiasm is more likely to develop if young people see their teachers modelling such practices.

In addition, O'Brien and MacBeath (1999) note that lifelong learning in the form of CPD is increasingly regarded as an important means of contributing to the creation of more effective schools, and as integral to learning organisations.

The starting point for this argument is initial teacher education (ITE). The years 2007-8 saw the introduction of two forms of university-led teacher training. A *Professional* Graduate Certificate of Education provides training at degree level, whereas a *Postgraduate* Certificate in Education provides the opportunity to accrue a number of M-level credits during the training process. Most institutions enable participants to gain 40-60 M-level credits, whereas some offer 90 or even 120 credits. This enables participants to pick up further credits once in post as a newly qualified teacher (NQT) or even later in the teaching career. This provides a basis for *continued* studies from the outset. The logical justication for this is that lifelong learning leads to the development of a learning organisation, which continuously and collectively re-evaluates its purposes and seeks ways to develop the most effective and efficient ways of reaching its goals. Improvement is continuous if learning is ongoing.

Continuous and continuing learning is not problematic. It involves individual learning and developing along with colleagues, but also individually. The core 'business' of a school is teaching and learning. All teachers, therefore, have access to teaching and learning situations all day, prompting one Secretary of State for Education to assert that teachers learn best from and with other teachers (Morris, 2001), a statement that rings ever more true today. This does suggest the need for contact, communication and regular access to other teachers. New national professional standards for teachers emanating from the Teaching Agency (TA) are no longer tiered to represent career development, but form the basis of the appraisal of all teachers, whatever the stage of their career. Success is not measured by demonstrating higher-level standards, but by demonstrating an improvement in all standards. With proposals that teachers' pay should be linked to levels of performance, this belief in continuous improvement against a standard set of measures is being strengthened. It is becoming more difficult to build a career development plan from addressing a higher-level set of standards, but more through demonstration of competence through performance management procedures and linked CPD. Putnam and Borko (2000) condemn the traditional view that teachers should 'find their own style' (p. 19), in that it encourages a paradigm of privacy. For them, the development of a community of practice (Wenger, 1999) leads to the establishment of a common theory and language and opportunities to challenge assumptions. 'Continuing' professional development relies on regular interaction with colleagues.

Professional

The word 'professional' is problematic. Certainly, Morris (2001) uses the term to draw approval for the strategy from teachers: '[CPD] . . . is part of the re-professionalisation of what teachers should do, shout as loudly as we possibly can that, yes, we demand a lot of teachers.'

Rose (2009) similarly commends existing practices and the attempts of teachers to develop as professionals, notably in processes associated with assessing pupil progress (APP).

Professionalising teachers, for others (for example, Whitty, 2000), means providing independence and self-governance. Within the current government's approach, teachers are encouraged to take responsibility for their own professional development, but more in line with school performance levels and development priorities. The model of linking union learning representatives to school-based CPD leaders in Scotland (Alexandrou, 2006) is now not on the agenda. Success as a teacher is demonstrated through the acknowledgement of Ofsted grades (Outstanding), and it is these teachers who are able to support colleagues to attain the same standard of performance.

Evidently, characteristics of the 'restricted professional' (Hoyle, 1975) are applicable. Action is intuitive, and learning is derived from the work base. Experience rather than theory is used to justify action. Teachers are not encouraged to become 'extended professionals', that is, to locate practice in a broader political and social context. The extent to which teaching is 'value-led' is also questionable. The 'values' are imposed, present in standards for all qualified teachers. The values have not emerged from the profession itself.

Performance management procedures are very much tied in with school performance priorities, and the role of a mentor/coach serves the function of supporting individuals within the context of the need to link to school development plans, which themselves are engaged in implementing government-led policies and curriculum plans. The recommendation that phonics should be the 'prime approach' to teaching reading, in the report *Phonics and Early Reading* (Rose, 2006), serves as an example.

Academies and free schools, however, are free from such pressure and are able to recruit teachers without qualified teacher status and are not obliged to follow a national curriculum.

Development

Development can mean several things in the context of CPD. First, it can relate to personal growth and understanding within a community of practice and, therefore, relate to the unique contribution an individual makes (Tsui *et al.*, 2008). Second, it can relate to career development, and, third, it can relate to school development and the extent to which the school achieves its own priorities through improved, or more focused, teacher practice. From a government perspective, development can mean the extent to which schools and, therefore, teachers have successfully implemented national strategies, or attained required standards of performance. Last, and perhaps the least well covered in the literature, is the development of the profession, in terms of its prestige and the esteem in which it is held.

A TYPOLOGY OF CPD

As the above intimates, CPD can be used for different purposes. These purposes overlap – one form of CPD can serve more than one purpose. Field (2011) presents a taxonomy of CPD, consisting of four forms. Indeed, Field argues that these are dimensions of CPD.

To categorise these into four extreme types, and to recognise intermediate forms, involves a collection of views on what constitutes CPD and a consideration of to what extent each relates to others.

Individual-led

Individual-led CPD involves a focus on intra-personal learning through high-level, cognition-based courses. This reveals a focus on 'thinking skills', which need to be converted into action and professional learning. A recognition of multiple applications, across curriculum disciplines, but with an accent on the creative and artistic, appeals to individual-led learning. The individual teacher has to master learning and then apply and evaluate to ascertain the impact and success of that learning.

Individual-led CPD often consists of self-study, the observation of fellow practitioners and the extension of existing experience and expertise. New knowledge emanating from the teacher's working context is representative of this form of CPD.

Other key features relate to the belief that teachers develop as professionals in stages. Huberman (1993, 1995) identifies five stages and recommends the deployment of particular activities appropriate to the individual teacher's stage of development (launching one's career, stabilising, facing new challenges, 'plateauing', final phase). Indeed, the stages can be seen to be characterised by attitudes displayed at the different career stages. These include 'coping', 'consolidation', 'experimentation', 'evaluation', 'self doubt' and 'disenchantment'. Taking these into account, individuals will learn from different activity types (role-plays, problem-solving, debates and discussions, micro-teaching, observing others, being observed, buzz sessions and action learning, for example). An individual-led approach to CPD involves an acceptance of, and an active provision of, choices and options designed to address individual needs.

Individual-led CPD has to be negotiated. It is demanding of high levels of self-awareness and of resources available, and an ability to recognise and articulate personal needs and wants. It, therefore, demands a system that is flexible and responsive to individual teachers' needs, which can change at different points in time.

Case study 1

After being appointed as assistant head teacher at a very large, inner-city primary school, I was negotiating performance management targets with my head teacher for the coming academic year. We decided together that it would be an excellent idea to complete the 'Leadership Pathways' year-long course with the National College of School Leadership (NCSL). This decision was taken after we discussed my individual needs, as a previous middle leader at the school, and we agreed that, although I had a lot of very good leadership and management skills, we also identified that there were many attributes and skills involved in leadership that I certainly needed to develop. Strategic awareness was going to be vitally important, and dealing with challenging people and difficult situations would also be beneficial to consider.

The performance management process in itself was a very good professional development activity: having the opportunity to discuss your strengths and areas to develop is hugely valuable. This then enabled me to feel confident that my head teacher had a shared understanding of my thoughts and feelings in relation to my role within the school. I was also able to gain a strong insight into her views and opinions. As a result of this meeting, I felt extremely confident that I was not expected to be an outstanding assistant head teacher immediately. I felt very comfortable that I had a lot to learn, and the expectations were that I would undertake training, engage in everyday experiences and grow into the role.

The Leadership Pathways training was incredibly valuable. It involved attending core day sessions, led by the NCSL, with other colleagues in leadership and management positions. We developed our knowledge of skills and attributes related to leadership and engaged in role-play activities to enhance and support us in coping with difficult experiences; we also completed a number of tasks and activities related to real problems back at school. This enhanced my understanding of how to deal with a variety of school-based situations, giving me reasoning and rationale. I was able to put a lot of this into practice and immediately see the impact of what I had learned.

The NCSL also ensured that, through this training, we had a 'coach' who was based in our school. I was coached by my deputy head teacher. I also had to 'lead' a project based in school, relating to my roles and responsibilities. Over the course of the academic year, we had to engage in ten coaching sessions.

The power of coaching is incredible: having a colleague who can question what you are doing, enabling you to clarify and justify the way in which you are doing things, really supports you to think things through. I really enjoyed the coaching sessions and felt quite empowered; the deputy head teacher was able to offer huge advice and support, as well as challenging me. As a result of this, I really grew as a leader. I became a very confident and articulate member of the Leadership Team. I was able to actively listen, not only to advise.

System-led

System-led CPD is usually centrally organised. It may be, but is not necessarily, the case that the CPD offer marries well with individuals' ambition and aspiration. What actually 'individualises' system-led CPD is the reflection process, which follows input, that is, digesting, absorbing, and experimenting with what is learnt at the input sessions. A positive impact resulting from training is facilitated by coaching and mentoring and task-based approaches. Reflection is clearly a major feature of individual-led CPD, yet an extension of system-led CPD. System-led CPD is usually designed and promoted from the centre as a means of assuring quality and effectiveness, in line with externally imposed performance indicators for the school as a whole.

System-led CPD is attractive to policymakers. The political force of government agencies, supported by an army of LA officers to encourage compliance to ideas and the embedding of new practices, is measurable in terms of classroom impact. It is, therefore, also deployed in order to introduce new, authority-led innovations. System-led CPD is characterised by a predominance of training methods and little time to share and discuss.

Case study 2

We heard from the head teacher that my school was unlikely to score well in Ofsted, and was in danger of slipping below floor targets. The message was clear: we needed to improve, or nobody knew what the consequences would be. Not far away there is a very high-performing school, and staff were recruited in to help us – a school improvement intervention. So-called expert teachers were contracted to our school for the equivalent of a day a week. I was attached to an expert maths teacher. Initially, I talked her through our plans – what we taught when and what we expected in terms of pupil progress. The expert teacher questioned why we set such low objectives, and I explained that it was related to our expectations, given the difficult intake we had.

Second, the expert teacher arranged to attend some lessons and give feedback on my teaching, but also, more importantly, on the learning of the pupils. The feedback showed that I was not ambitious enough for my pupils, and the expert teacher provided me with the opportunity to observe her in action. I was very impressed with the levels of engagement.

We also organised some after-school sessions for targeted pupils, those who we felt could improve, as a result of scrutinising the data. Parents were informed, and we promised to feed back to parents on their child's progress on a regular basis, and to suggest activities with which they could help.

Although I initially felt demoralised, the outcome was great. My 'expert' quickly became a critical friend, a coach and a mentor for me. The levels of attainment of pupils shot up, and I luckily realised that I had spent too much time focusing on my teaching and not enough on the pupils' learning. What was interesting, as I reflect, is that my own and my school's development was driven by an inspection and league-table system. We all learnt how to play that system in a way that was not at the expense of professional integrity.

Profession-led

Profession-led CPD is concerned with individuals using their learning in order to improve collective performance. Professional development is not perceived as a series of events a teacher might be urged to attend, but an integral part of being a teacher. Development is both an entitlement and an obligation. The stance is that teachers are concerned primarily with learning, and, therefore, to neglect their own learning would be inconsistent and unprofessional. For some, CPD is a natural experience, whether planned or incidental, which is intended to lead to an improved quality of education. Profession-led CPD is a necessary part of being a teacher that serves to characterise teaching as a profession.

The profession does extend beyond teachers themselves and involves a range of agencies, including LAs, private providers, higher-education institutions, the National College for Leadership and, increasingly, inter-school activity . Profession-led CPD can bond and bind any competing interest of such bodies. A dogged persistence to improve learning for pupils is at the heart of all CPD offered by such groups. The essential component is the commonality of goals, rather than the differences between the forms of provision.

Case study 3

My own CPD experience was driven by my own desire to be recognised by my profession as an expert. Masters-level credits, and ultimately a qualification, meant that what I was doing was recognised by an internationally valid award. In addition, I took part in a programme known as the 'Teaching and Learning Academy'. This enabled the GTC, as well as an academic institution, to show respect for my own development. It is important to be recognised, but also to know that the continuous improvement in pupils' learning, for which I strive, shows how the teaching profession values success.

My awards were related to an improvement project I undertook. I wanted to improve boys' literacy. I observed teachers in another school, I deconstructed my own practice by relating my teaching to literature, and to my observations. I then introduced some new ideas, and evaluated the impact of these. I then wrote this up in the form of a portfolio, with a connecting narrative. Suddenly my work took shape, and the recognition gave it a significance beyond my own classroom. I became a representative of good professional practice.

Institution-led

Institution-led CPD is essentially one concerned with localised school improvement. Contemporary models of evaluation contain an emphasis on the impact of development in the classroom, and its relationship with pupil learning outcomes. More and more CPD takes place in and between schools and is linked to school improvement plans.

It is the consideration of effective CPD and models of evaluation and impact that bring attention back to the school. The connections to the outside world are important and valued, and yet, without a close relationship with the school, CPD is not valued by those who lead and who are accountable. In this way, institution-led CPD is closely related to organisational culture. Not only does CPD reflect the culture of a school, it shapes the ethos and attitudes. Institution-led CPD relies on collaboration, teamwork and sharing. It mitigates cultures of individualism and balkanisation. On the negative side, such a focus can lead to an inward approach, mitigating against a culture of critical enquiry and reflection.

Case study 4

When I first started teaching there was one thing that every teacher enjoyed going on – a course. Some of them lasted for more than one day . . . and always included a lunch. Looking back, I didn't learn a lot. It wasn't that my self or my colleagues didn't have anything to say about our 'course' when we got back to school – we did – in fact we could all talk at length about the quality of the refreshments and the all important lunch.

I missed the point!

Sometimes it wasn't all my own fault, it is hard to learn, after all, if someone talks *at* you for 5 hours and you only look interested because when they started discussions at 9 a.m., they made the promise of letting you go early if we could get 'through the slides' as quickly as possible.

Things did change for me – thank God!

After 4 years of teaching, I moved into a new role as an Advanced Skills Teacher to coach other people on how to use Interactive Whiteboards, and it changed me forever. First, and most importantly, it was a unique and brave opportunity by a forward thinking Local Authority to take 'the course' to the classroom i.e. instead of sitting in a hotel for 5 hours being told how to do something, you actually did it at base, having a go and learning by your mistakes. It dramatically changed my philosophy on Professional Development. In one school term of coaching alongside teachers who were hungry to make use of something new in their classrooms, I understood the statistics at last: 'you remember 10% of what you hear, 20% of what you see and 90% of what you participate in'.

My belief in coaching has stayed with me ever since. Now, as a Head teacher, our school votes on the next effective teaching strategy they want to really hone, someone brave lets everyone watch them have a go at it, then we all talk about how it went – simple but effective. Our Staff Meetings are strictly Professional Development Meetings too – no business – just Teaching and Learning. Sometimes it still bites me on the bum, I'll be talking to someone about their CPD in Performance Management and we'll audit the 'courses attended' in the last 12 months. It shocks me sometimes to think about the money that can be wasted. The average course can cost up to £300 and supply an extra £200 . . . £500 'going on a course'. Some courses are brilliant, of course, but nothing can match evaluating where you really are as a teacher, thinking about what you need to do next, seeing it in action with your own children and then having a go.

In a nutshell, you don't have to go on a course – most of the time you just need to sit in the classroom next door or let someone sit in yours!

Task 9.2.1 Dimensions of CPD

Read the examples of CPD above, which can be seen to be related to the four dimensions of CPD. Do you think they exemplify the dimension described? What do you see to be the advantages and disadvantages of focusing CPD on a particular dimension?

FORMS OF CPD

Professional development activities can take may forms. Each can be shaped to contribute to all the dimensions above, and some activities lend themselves to more than others. Councils did provide a list of activity types, engagement with which does constitute forms of CPD:

- attendance at a course or conference;
- in-school training using the expertise available within the school, e.g. team teaching, coaching/ mentoring, skills in classroom observation, sharing existing expertise;
- school-based work through accessing an external consultant/adviser or relevant expert, such as an advanced skills or lead teacher;
- school visit to observe or participate in good and successful practice, e.g. visit to a school or subject area with similar circumstances, a training school;
- secondments, e.g. with a regional or national organisation, an exchange or placement, e.g. with another teacher, school, higher education, industry, international exchange, involvement with governing body;
- shadowing opportunities to observe experienced colleagues in another setting;
- opportunities to participate in award-bearing work from higher education or other providers such as the National College for the Leadership of Schools and Children's Centre;
- research opportunities;
- distance learning, e.g. relevant resources, training videos, reflection, simulation;
- practical experience, e.g. national test or exam marking experience, opportunities to present a paper, contribute to a training programme, co-ordinate or support a learning forum or network, become involved in local and national networks;
- job enrichment/enlargement, e.g. a higher level of responsibility; front lining working in someone else's job, job sharing, acting roles, job rotation, shadowing;
- producing documentation or resources such as a personal development plan, teaching materials, assessment package, ICT or video programme;

- coaching and mentoring – receiving or acting in these roles, acting as or receiving the support of a critical friend, team-building activity;
- partnerships, e.g. with a colleague, group; subject-, phase-, activity- or school-based; team meetings and activities such as joint planning, observation or standardisation, special project working group, involvement in School Improvement Partnership Network, Network Learning Community;
- creating an improved learning environment within the school.

Task 9.2.2 Forms of CPD

What combination of the CPD activities above do you think constitutes:

- profession-led CPD?
- system-led CPD?
- individual-led CPD?
- institution-led CPD?

None of these should exist in isolation from each other. The extent to which they benefit the individual, the institution or the profession as a whole depends upon structure and planning. An outcome of appraisal/performance management should be an agreed CPD plan for each individual teacher. It is the responsibility of the CPD leader in each school to co-ordinate and organise in such a way that all stakeholders benefit.

PLANNING YOUR CPD

In Wales . . .

The Welsh government has developed the practice, review and development process, which is an integrated system of professional standards, CPD and performance management.

> Practice, review and development (PRD) describes what all effective practitioners do: practice – they teach, lead and support learning; review – they reflect critically on a range of data and evidence about their practice to ensure it has improved learner outcomes and to identify priorities for further professional development; and development – they seek opportunities to increase and deepen their knowledge, understanding and skills in order to address development priorities and to continually improve their practice.

> (WG, 2013)

Source: Welsh Government (WG) (2013) *Your Career*. Available at: http://learning.wales.gov.uk/your career/?lang=en (accessed 31 May 2013).

A ten-stage process is recommended (see Figure 9.2.1). The 'critical path' explained below serves to analyse the process, and to enable the identification of training and development needs in relation to the agenda. It also offers a synthesis of the separate procedures and overall process.

The 'reviewee' refers to the teacher. A reviewer is what is traditionally referred to as an appraiser, but clearly incorporates the role of a coach and mentor. The 'school' is represented by the CPD leader. Each of the ten stages (reviewee) is explained below.

Stage 1 – self-audit against standards

In order to support future career development, the teacher should rate his or her performance against the professional standards to the level of performance to which he or she aspires. One approach is to annotate each standard using an 'MIC' approach. 'M' means that a level of performance against a standard should be maintained. 'I' means that the teacher should strive to improve. 'C' means 'change', in that the school should attempt to provide opportunities for such a standard to be met.

Stage 2 – express aspirations

Self-audits (see above) do lend themselves well to deficit approaches, through the identification of weaknesses. By stating aspirations, teachers may look to the future and build on existing strengths with defined purposes in mind.

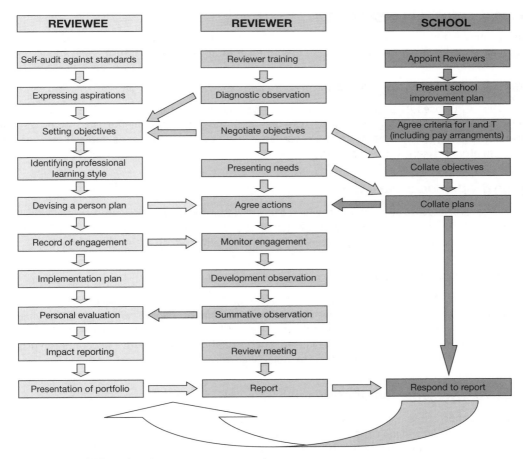

FIGURE 9.2.1 The CPD and performance management process

Stage 3 – set objectives

The negotiation of targets/objectives with a reviewer/coach/mentor is essential. With the need to demonstrate development, it is necessary to agree the criteria against which judgements relating to success are made.

Stage 4 – identify professional learning style

Different people, in different circumstances, learn in different ways. It is important for professionals to have a role in determining how they will be supported in achieving the agreed targets. This means drawing from a wide range of CPD types.

Stage 5 – devise a personal plan

A personal plan will consist of the identification of learning activities, as well as the means and evidence by which the learning can be demonstrated. Timelines and feedback mechanisms should be agreed. This plan can be the basis of a personal log for future use.

Stage 6 – record of engagement

It is recommended that a log of activity should be accompanied by reflective commentaries or a personal narrative, to embed the learning and to foresee advantageous future applications.

Stage 7 – implementation plan

Too often, CPD loses its potential effectiveness once teachers return to their day-to-day activity. Reflection and implementation of new strategies and understandings in the classroom, through careful planning, should be formally recorded. This stage recommends judicial use of the coach/mentor to support development.

Stage 8 – personal evaluation

This stage is related to the extent to which the individual has been stimulated through the CPD process, and the extent to which he or she has improved practice. This involves consideration of statistical and qualitative evidence. Often, individuals benefit from an external viewpoint.

Stage 9 – impact reporting

Impact reporting demands a consideration of how the CPD process has impacted upon others. These will include pupils, colleagues and other stakeholders. A claim of 'impact' will need to be evidence-based and evaluative. It is recognised that direct causal links between CPD engagement and pupil learning outcomes cannot be firmly established, but correlations and narrative accounts can provide clear indicators of success in relation to the objectives agreed under stage 3.

Stage 10 – presentation of portfolio

The presentation stage covers several factors. It enables acknowledgement and recognition – key factors in motivation and job satisfaction (Herzberg, 1987). It may be used for accreditation purposes, provides evidence for accountability purposes and should inform the next CPD/performance management cycle.

The pivotal point of the ten-stage process is the review/appraisal stages (3–5). Working with a reviewer serves as a bridge between the individual and the organisation. The following reflection activity illustrates how a teacher who meets induction standards and who is working towards threshold might interact with his reviewer.

Task 9.2.3 Planning your CPD

From the information you have to hand, prepare stages 1,2 and 3 of the above, i.e.:

- What do you need to achieve?
- What are you good at and what do you want to build on?
- What do you want to achieve?
- What types of CPD do you think would help you to achieve these?

KEY STAKEHOLDERS

Many organisations are involved in CPD, not least the individual teacher who has a moral obligation to learn and develop for the benefit of those s/he teaches. Schools themselves must be proactive in identifying needs and providing opportunities for teachers to learn how to address those needs. Increasingly, schools are part of alliances and partnerships that themselves are obliged to draw on internal resources to support others.

For maintained schools and teachers working in them, LAs remain key stakeholders. LAs remain the employer of teachers in such schools and, therefore, have statutory and moral obligations. For example, it is the LA that signs off teachers' induction year, and, therefore, there remains a responsibility for brokering suitable CPD when needed and/or desired. Links with other 'educare' organisations, such as social services, Children's and Community Centres, hard-to-reach families and parents, all rely on LA engagement. The wider agenda associated with integrated services is, therefore, reliant upon LA engagement. Lastly, local accountability for pupil results, attendance and behaviour fall under the auspices of the LA.

Teaching schools are key proponents of school-to-school support. Teaching schools must be outstanding in all Ofsted categories, and, therefore, equal coverage across the country is not guaranteed. As a consequence, not all schools form part of a Teaching School Alliance, and they may seek to link with other organisations for school improvement and CPD purposes.

Academy Trusts can and do provide support and guidance for the academies that they sponsor. Several trusts (e.g. ARK, Ormiston) now support twenty or more academies and, through their sponsors (often industry representatives), offer professional development opportunities for teachers. In a similar way to Teaching School Alliances, Academy Trusts recognise the efficiency and cost-effectiveness of drawing on internal staff and resources for CPD purposes. Links to universities for accreditation purposes give their own forms of provision a wider acknowledgement and recognition.

The NCSL has provided the infrastructure for teaching schools, examining suitability and providing guidance on how to operate. The NCSL is clearly a major player in the CPD field. In addition, it assesses applications from organisations to become licensed providers of national leadership programmes at five levels. By supporting and providing professional recognition for middle leaders, assistant and deputy heads, aspiring head teachers, 'beyond headship' and system leadership, it is the NCSL that provides career pathways for those seeking a leadership and management route.

This has prompted a culture of entrepreneurialism. For example, an organisation, OLEVI, franchises CPD courses across the country, in particular to support teachers moving from 'good' to 'outstanding' teacher. OLEVI is the trading arm of a successful school in Kent and provides services across the whole country. OLEVI's link with a school enables it to offer credible courses, which (according to its own website publicity):

- are designed and facilitated by experienced school leaders and teachers, the Outstanding Teacher Programme gives good (and outstanding) teachers a set of high level skills and strategies that enable them to become consistently and sustainably outstanding. It helps them to:
- demonstrate higher level understanding of teaching and improve learning for their pupils
- coach colleagues in their own school and in other schools to raise performance levels
- create a proactive school culture where the quality of teaching and learning is observed, discussed, challenged and enhanced
- increase the job satisfaction and create opportunities for further leadership and career progression.

Universities remain key stakeholders. By offering accreditation opportunities for those involved in school improvement, school-based and school-led Masters courses, which can build upon credit accrued during a teacher's training period, it is universities that service the 'individual-led' dimension of CPD. Action research and impact evaluation studies also link universities to the institution-led dimensions of CPD.

There are many 'for profit' and 'not for profit' private providers in the CPD marketplace. These include large, multinational companies (e.g. SERCO, Pearson) and education-specific providers (e.g. CfBT, Best Practice).

SUMMARY

The very title of this unit emphasises the need for teachers to organise, plan and manage their own CPD. Much needs to go into the plans – account must be taken of purposes, approaches, requirements and the relationship with performance management and, therefore, agreed performance standards.

CPD is more than 'keeping up to date' – it contributes to job satisfaction, professional morale and status and school improvement. Being a professional is, in part, concerned with professional autonomy matched by responsibility and accountability. Evaluating the impact of CPD undertaken can be seen to reinforce learning and development, and provide the opportunity to share and disseminate good practice. Impact studies do contribute towards a view of an evidence-based profession.

 ANNOTATED FURTHER READING

The proliferation of new approaches to, and indeed of providers of, CPD for teachers means there are few recent academic evaluative texts. Literature related to the concept of CPD and the impact of CPD is a little dated but does exist. Academic journals, such as *Professional Development in Education*, offer an insight into international trends and relevant book reviews. Reports and texts worthy of reading are as follows:

Gordon, S.P. (2004) *Professional Development for School Improvement: Empowering Learning Communities*, Boston, MA: Pearson.

> Gordon provides an American perspective. He cleverly builds a view of CPD based upon an 'onion metaphor'. By unpeeling each layer, Gordon is able to examine the interrelationships between school leadership and CPD provision. The view that values and principles are at the core of CPD is reassuring and does help readers to build their own understanding, based on their own stance as teachers. Strategies and approaches to suit the individual can be traced to the teacher's values, enabling a real tailoring from the practitioner perspective.

Guskey, T.R. (2002) 'Does it make a difference? Evaluating professional development', *Educational Leadership*, 59: 45–51.

> For many, Guskey is *the* CPD guru. His views on evaluation have informed the debates concerning impact across the world. Guskey identifies five layers of evaluation: participants' reaction; participants' learning; institutional support and change; participants' use of new knowledge and skills; and student learning outcomes.
>
> He explains the need for depth of evaluation studies and explains that to not address the five layers is to provide a superficial and insufficient evaluation report. For him, evaluation is too often a brief, one-off event. CPD must focus on the classroom, but the whole school culture, climate and structures need to be supportive. Consequently, Guskey explains that CPD can contribute in small steps towards a big change. When collective effort and collegiality are essential, CPD can bring teams together, and affective factors (such as attitudes, enjoyment and motivation) usually follow recognition of success. In these ways, Guskey coincidentally provides the means to inform CPD planning.

The professional publication *CPD Update* (Optimus Publishing) provides up-to-date professional articles and guidance on CPD.

 ## FURTHER READING TO SUPPORT M-LEVEL STUDY

Bolam, R. and Weindling, D. (2006) *Synthesis of Research and Evaluation Projects Concerned With Capacity-Building Through Teachers' Professional Development*, London: GTCE.

> This synthesis of CPD research and policy provides an excellent overview of what is seen to be successful in the field. It provides hard evidence to support successful approaches to CPD, enabling the identification of principles of best practice.

Bubb, S. and Earley, P. (2004) *Leading and Managing Continuing Professional Development: Developing People, Developing Schools*, London: Paul Chapman.

> As the title suggests, Bubb and Earley provide an explanation of how effective, well-planned CPD can work hand in glove with school improvement. The book explains well how CPD can be informed by key players, including the TDA and GTC(E). It offers very up-to-date guidance and advice, ensuring that any approach designed does meet statutory requirements. Bubb and Earley base their studies on the premise that CPD empowers teachers, thereby placing the emphasis on the 'professional' at the heart of CPD.

 ## RELEVANT WEBSITES

International Professional Development Association: www.ipda.org.uk

> This site contains updates on the world of CPD, an opportunity to join blogs related to CPD, and access to the association's refereed journal, *Professional Development in Education*. The site also provides information on the association's annual conference and events in England and other countries.

National College for Leadership of Schools and Children's Services: www.nationalcollege.org.uk
Look here for descriptors and programmes for development routes for leadership and management.

Continuing Professional Development Research: http://webarchive.nationalarchives.gov.uk/20130401151715/
https://www.education.gov.uk/publications/standard/publicationDetail/Page1/RB659
This research brief summarises an evaluation of the impact of Continuing Professional Development
(CPD). The evaluation was carried out on behalf of the Department for Education and Skills (DfES)
by a research team from the University of Warwick and the University of Nottingham.

Teacher Research: www.teacherresearch.net
This website shows how teachers in schools can initiate and sustain educational research within
their everyday work in their classroom. Teachers as researchers are often supported by a process
of 'research mentoring', integrating mentoring into action enquiry. Teachers and research mentors
are 'experts' whose skills, values and understandings complement and enrich one another's practice.

National Foundation for Educational Research: www.nfer.ac.uk
The NFER provides independent evidence to support and promote improvement in learning and
teaching. You will find examples of research projects that can be used to inform your own
understanding of best practice.

REFERENCES

Alexandrou, A. (2006) *EIS Learning Representatives: An Evaluation of the Educational Institute of Scotland's
First Cohort of Learning Representatives*, Edinburgh: Educational Institute of Scotland.

Department for Children, Schools and Families (2007) *The Children's Plan: Building Brighter Futures*, London:
The Stationery Office.

Department for Education (2010) *The Importance of Teaching: The Schools White Paper 2010*, London: HMSO

Department for Education and Employment (DfEE) (2001) *Learning and Teaching: A Strategy for Professional
Development*, London: DfEE. Available at: http://webarchive.nationalarchives.gov.uk/20130401151715/
https://www.education.gov.uk/publications/standard/publicationDetail/Page1/RB659 (accessed November
2009).

Field, K. (2011) 'An audit tool for identifying the most appropriate forms of CPD for staff', *CPD Update*: 6-8.

Gove, M. (2010) 'Seizing Success', ministerial address to the National College of Leadership Conference,
Nottingham, 17 June.

Gray, L.S. (2005) *An Enquiry into Continuing Professional Development for Teachers*, Cambridge: University of
Cambridge Centre for Applied Research in Educational Technologies (CARET).

Herzberg, F.I. (1987) 'One more time: how do you motivate employees?', *Harvard Business Review*, 65(5): 109-20.

Hoyle, E. (1975) 'Professionality, professionalism and control in teaching', in V. Houghton, R. McHugh and
C. Morgan (eds) *Management in Education: The Management of Organisations and Individuals*, London:
Ward Lock Educational/Open University Press.

Huberman, M. (1993) *The Lives of Teachers*, London: Cassell.

Huberman, M. (1995) 'Professional careers and professional development: some intersections', in T.R. Guskey
and M. Huberman (eds) *Professional Development in Education: New Paradigms and Practices*, New York:
Teachers' College Press.

McNamara, O., Howson, J., Gunter, H., Sprigade, A. and Onat-Stelma, Z. (2008) *Women Teachers' Careers*,
Birmingham: NAS/UWT.

McNamara, O., Howson, J., Gunter, H. and Fryers, A. (2009), *The Leadership Aspirations and Careers of Black
and Minority Ethnic Teachers*, Birmingham: NASUWT, and Nottingham: National College.

Morris, E. (2001) Keynote speech at the DfEE launch of The National Strategy for CPD, 1 March.

National Association of School Teachers and Union of Women Teachers (NAS/UWT) (n.d.) *Teaching Schools*,
Birmingham: NAS/UWT.

National College of School Leadership (NCSL) (2012) System Leadership Prospectus. Nottingham: NCSL.

O'Brien, J. and MacBeath, J. (1999) 'Co-ordinating staff development: the training and development of staff development co-ordinators', *Journal of In-Service Education*, 25(1): 69–84.

Putnam, R.T. and Borko, H. (2000) 'What do new views of knowledge and thinking have to say about research on teacher learning', in B. Moon, J. Butcher and E. Bird (eds) *Leading Professional Development in Education*, London: RoutledgeFalmer/Open University, pp. 11–29.

Rose, J. (2006) *Phonics and Early Reading: An Overview for Head Teachers, Literacy Leaders and Teachers in Schools, and Managers and Practitioners in Early Years Settings*, London: DCSF.

Rose, J. (2009) *Independent Review of the Primary Curriculum*. Available at: www.educationengland.org.uk/documents/pdfs/2009-IRPC-final-report.pdf

Tsui, A., Edwards, G., Lopez-Real, F., Kwan, T., Law, D., Stimpson, P., Tang, R. and Wong, A. (2008) *Learning in School-University Partnership: Sociocultural Perspectives*, New York: Routledge.

Wenger, E. (1999) *Communities of Practice: Learning, Meaning and Identity*, Cambridge: Cambridge University Press.

Whitty, G. (2000) 'Teacher professionalism', *New Times Journal of In-Service Education*, 26(2): 281–96.

TEACHING, RESEARCH AND FURTHER QUALIFICATIONS

Cathy Burnett

INTRODUCTION

> One of the fascinating aspects of the last year has been how my attempts to get closer to the children's learning have given me a greater understanding of myself, not just as a teacher but as a learner . . . The children and I have, in a sense, been travelling along the same road. They and I have both been engaged in the same process of taking time to stop . . . to stop and talk about, to stop and look at, to stop and reflect on the work we are involved in. That taking time to stop and look has, I think, given me insights into the children's learning; given the children insights into and consciousness of their own learning, and given me insights into my own practice as a teacher.
>
> (Strauss, 2002: 227)

The previous units in this book have given rich, wide-ranging support for learning to teach in the primary school, and together they provide a firm basis for embarking on a career in teaching. One of the most exciting – and perhaps troubling – dimensions of learning to teach, however, is that the learning never stops. We cannot underestimate the complexity of teaching, of developing inclusive approaches to facilitate all our pupils' learning, while responding to their emotional and social needs and organising classes of children given limited space and resources. Moreover, we find that approaches that work well for one child or in one context do not work for others, that policy changes place new demands on us as professionals, or that there are broader societal shifts – such as developments in new technologies – which have implications for education. We never 'master' teaching, but rather engage in ongoing reappraisal as we review, interrogate and re-evaluate how we are supporting children's learning, and the values and beliefs that underpin what we do.

This unit explores how engaging with research, possibly through further qualification, can help you reflect on your practice more deeply and make informed decisions about your work. It is likely that you will have already engaged in research-based work during initial teacher education, for example conducting small-scale investigations or child studies. This unit describes how research can support you throughout your career. Research will help you gain new insights, build your confidence to refine or innovate, and sometimes generate the evidence to justify why you should continue to do what you are already doing. After discussing different perspectives on teacher research, the unit explores how you can challenge your own assumptions about practice, with a particular focus on approaches to gaining children's perspectives on their learning. It also provides guidance on critical engagement with existing research. Finally, it explores how you can become involved in research and considers the benefits of collaboration.

OBJECTIVES

By the end of this unit, you will be able to:

- identify how engagement with research will support ongoing critical reflection on your practice;
- engage critically with the work of other researchers;
- consider how your practice is underpinned by certain ways of thinking, values and beliefs;
- identify how you can use research to explore children's perspectives;
- recognise the value of engaging in collaborative, research-focused activities.

WHAT IS RESEARCH AND WHY IS IT IMPORTANT TO PROFESSIONAL DEVELOPMENT?

Teachers constantly make choices and decisions. In doing so, they gather evidence through talking to children, observing what they do and analysing what they produce. As they make sense of all this, they draw conclusions about how children are learning and respond in the light of these. Teachers work in busy, complex environments, and consequently much of this sense-making is tacit, and decisions to act are often rapid. However, these processes of gathering evidence and drawing conclusions are very similar to those we associate with research. Engaging in research is essentially about engaging in these processes more systematically. It means slowing down – as the teacher quoted at the beginning of this unit suggests – to look more deeply and perhaps differently at what is happening. This involves being explicit about the questions you want to investigate and deciding which research approaches will generate the kinds of understanding you need to answer these questions. It means collecting and analysing data in an organised manner and considering different ways that these might be interpreted. Ultimately, it means communicating the results to others, so that they can learn from what you have found out. Here, Chris Bailey, assistant head teacher, reflects on his Masters research project:

> I decided to look closely at an area of my practice in which I felt I was already successful in certain aspects but wanted to improve in others. I had recent experience of using animation in the classroom, with children creating short films using stop-frame techniques. I believed that there were clear benefits to using this approach, but also felt that children working in groups on this kind of activity were not being as productive as they could be. I audio-recorded the children working in small groups, produced transcripts and analysed their conversations, to gain an insight into the nature of their discussions while they were working. I also involved the children, seeking their opinions on three different pedagogical approaches to organising group-work. Using enquiry gave me a deeper insight into the children's perspectives on their learning. This led me to re-think the kinds of tasks I set and the way I supported children to work collaboratively.

Much teacher research involves *action research*, through which teachers research and develop their own practice, collecting evidence and using what they learn from this to inform what they do.

Over the years, there have been a series of government-funded initiatives designed to engage teachers in action-research projects focused on raising attainment. However, action research is about more than enhancing provision for particular groups of children. It is also about generating theory. Importantly, when we refer to theory, we do not mean something that is divorced from practice. We are talking about an ongoing, two-way, or reflexive, relationship between how we understand practice and our actions. As McNiff and Whitehead (2005: 4) argue, 'Practice (what you do) informs theory (what you think about what you do), and theory (what you think) informs practice (what you are doing). Theory and practice transform continuously into each other in a seamless flow.'

A focus on using teachers' research to generate understandings has led some to see practitioner research as a 'path to empowerment' (Kincheloe, 2003); engaging in research can enable teachers to take charge of what they do, going beyond implementing local or national policy or responding to research generated in other contexts. From this perspective, teacher research should be driven by teachers' questions, rather than those imposed by their head teachers or the government. Central to this is a critical stance. Teacher research is not just about finding 'what works' to raise attainment, but interrogating the assumptions, values and beliefs that underpin policy and practice (Carr and Kemmis, 1986). This emphasises the relationship between the specific contexts in which teachers work and broader social, cultural and political contexts. As Hardy and Ronnerman argue (2011: 462),

> Changed practice can only come about as a result of sustained and concerted inquiry on the part of teachers into the nature of their work, in specific locations, and in the knowledge that this work is being undertaken under broader, influential social conditions.

Task 9.3.1 Considering relationships between research and teaching

Knobel and Lankshear suggest that a teacher who is involved in research is also a 'thinker, troubleshooter, creator, designer and practitioner' (Lankshear and Knobel, 2004: 11).

Discuss what you feel is meant by each of these terms in relation to your teaching role, using examples from your own experience or of practice you have observed or read about.

Next, order the terms from 'most' to 'least' to represent the extent to which you feel you have had opportunities to fulfil each of these roles in your teaching experience to date. Consider what has enabled you to do so, and any barriers you have faced.

Discuss how you think research might support you in carrying out these different roles as you embark on your career.

HOW CAN RESEARCH HELP YOU THINK DIFFERENTLY ABOUT PRACTICE?

Importantly, when individual teachers and researchers look at evidence, they often notice very different things and have different ways of interpreting what they do notice. In her book, *Listening to Stephen Read*, Kathy Hall (2003) illustrates this powerfully by presenting interviews with four experts on the teaching of reading, all of whom have different beliefs about what reading involves and, consequently, how children can best be supported to become readers. The interviews focus on

In Northern Ireland . . .

The GTCNI states that, so as to be creators of knowledge and theory builders, teachers should act as:

> researchers and change agents; in seeking a deeper understanding of their practice or in seeking to plan for change, teachers use a variety of evaluation and action research techniques to collect and interpret findings, to inform their thinking and decision making.

(GTCNI, 2007: 9)

Source: GTCNI (2007) *Teaching: the Reflective Profession.* Belfast, GTCNI.

their analysis of evidence of 8-year-old Stephen's reading. They each draw different conclusions about him as a reader and the kinds of experience that might be appropriate for him. The book not only helps us understand different perspectives on reading, but also illustrates how different theoretical understandings mean that we arrive at different conclusions when we analyse evidence.

Task 9.3.2 Reflecting on own assumptions when analysing practice

With a group of colleagues, watch a video of children interacting around a shared task. This could be a video of children you have taught or one of the many videos of classroom practice found on websites such as the Teachers TV video archive, available via the TES website (www.tes.co.uk). Individually, jot down what you notice about how the children interact and how this is supporting their learning.

Afterwards, draw two conclusions about these children's interactions based on what you have noted. Take turns with your colleagues to share and justify your observations.

Discuss reasons for any differences – both in what you noticed and in your explanations. Which theories – implicit or explicit – did you draw on as you made sense of what you observed? For example, did these relate to assumptions about each individual child, or to features such as the task or the setting?

As discussed above, all teachers draw on theories, as they interpret what learners are doing and what they need. These may be explicit (based on values and beliefs that they clearly express) or implicit (evident in what they do and the assumptions they make as they do so).

Research can help us re-examine some of the implicit theories that underpin everyday practice. In their book, *Turnaround Pedagogies*, Barbara Comber and Barbara Kamler (2005) describe how they worked with a group of teachers to develop a series of research projects through which newly qualified teachers collaborated with more experienced colleagues. The projects aimed to achieve a 'turnaround' in how teachers saw what was going on in classrooms and the resources children brought with them to school. Following work by Moll *et al.* (1992) and Thompson (2002), Comber and Kamler supported teachers to recognise and investigate what children *could* do and *did* know, rather than what they could not do. They then used their collective experience to decide how to respond to what they found.

Another way of gaining a different perspective – or perhaps a turnaround – is to research children's experiences of school. Children will learn what counts in classrooms from what happens when they enter them, the resources they can access, the way their spaces are bounded and regulated, and the kinds of response given to what they do and say. In developing practice, Bath argues that teachers therefore, 'need to constantly reflect upon and question what they do and the messages that practice transmits to the children in their care' (Bath, 2009: 3). Alison Clark and Peter Moss (2011) recommend using participatory methods to enable parents, children and practitioners to build a 'mosaic' of a child's experiences. This involves supplementing traditional research methods such as observation with participatory methods, such as inviting children to take photographs, give tours, create maps or role-play. The range of evidence is then used to stimulate reflection and dialogue about children's experiences and feelings and how to respond to these.

The following studies all used participatory methods to investigate children's perspectives:

- Caroline Bath (2009) asked children to share their experience of transition to school. Methods included voting slips, discussions about dilemmas presented in stories and an activity called 'Who chooses', through which children identified who made particular choices about what they did as they started school.
- Rachel Levy (2011) investigated young children's views of themselves as readers, for example through their responses to puppets and small world figures. Her work highlighted that some children made easy transitions between reading at home and at school, whereas others found this process difficult and lost confidence.
- Anne Kellock (2011) invited her pupils to take photographs and devise captions to present views on their school environment. As well as learning a great deal herself, she felt that her pupils gained from the opportunity to explore their experiences and gain insights into each other's perspectives.

Task 9.3.3 Thinking differently about a focus area

Identify an aspect of your teaching experience to date that has caused you concern or raised questions for you. This could, for example, be linked to an area of the curriculum, the experiences of a particular group of children, or the broader school environment. Summarise the evidence you currently have that has led you to identify this issue. Identify what you think you already know about this and your possible explanations for how things are. Note these on a network diagram. Now consider what you could investigate to help you gain a deeper understanding of this area. What kind of evidence might you collect to gain a different perspective? Whose perspectives might you investigate? How might you involve children or parents and carers in this process? How might the wider context – such as school, local or national policy – be relevant here? Annotate your initial diagram with these areas for further investigation. It will help to talk through your ideas with a friend – can they provide other possible explanations? Or suggest other areas for enquiry?

USING EXISTING RESEARCH

The previous sections have suggested that carrying out your own research is important for your professional development. You also need to continue to be aware of educational research done by others, for example academics based in universities, and/or commissioned by organisations. This is important because such research may provide new insights or introduce new approaches. It is also important when research is being used to justify local or national policy developments; looking at the original research can help you adopt an informed position about what is being recommended. Masters programmes will, of course, introduce you to research relevant to your particular interests. You can also find various digests written for teachers that provide summaries of research linked to particular topics. Such digests can be very useful in finding out about a range of recent research. It is important to be aware, however, that they are inevitably selective, and you may find other useful sources. Moreover, just as you need to think about how your own ways of thinking influence your practice, you also need to consider how others' ways of thinking – informed by their assumptions, values and beliefs – have helped shape their research. Many would argue that research can never simply provide us with evidence of 'what works' (Biesta, 2007). Learning is always highly contextualised, and what 'works' in one context may not in others. If we are going to evaluate a piece of research, we need to identify how values, beliefs and assumptions have influenced: what researchers tried to find out, how they went about this, and what they concluded. This means approaching research reports or summaries critically.

One aspect of being critical involves evaluating how the study was conducted and judging whether or not the ideas presented seem justified. This involves considering whether methods used were well chosen to generate the kinds of insight the researchers claim to have made. You might consider, for example, the research tools used, the range of participants or the scale of the study. It is important, though, not to dismiss a study simply because it is small scale or because it used qualitative approaches. Qualitative approaches can generate valuable data that allow you to better understand complex issues and the experiences of learners. Critical evaluation of qualitative studies involves deciding whether the researchers' approach to the study enabled them to gain rich and detailed insights into the experiences or practices of the individuals, groups, classes or schools studied.

Another aspect of being critical involves considering how useful a study is in terms of thinking about or developing practice, and how it adds to what is already known about an area. There are various ways in which a study may be valuable. It may provide evidence that suggests that a particular approach is worth trialling. Alternatively, it may generate a new way of looking at what you do, or lead to further questions relevant to your situation. In any case, as explored above, you need to try and identify the values, beliefs and assumptions (implicit and explicit) that informed the study and decide whether you feel these are appropriate.

Some questions to support critical reading of research articles and reports

- Which research questions did the researchers want to answer? How far did their research approaches and methods enable them to answer these questions?
- Which claims do they make, based on their findings? How far are these justified by the evidence presented?
- How do the findings connect to your current understanding and beliefs relating to this area, or to existing research?
- What implications do any recommendations have for your and others' practice?
- Do any issues or questions remain unresolved?
- Which values, beliefs and assumptions have informed the choice of research question, research approaches, methods, data analysis and conclusions?

Task 9.3.4 Critical review of research

Identify a report or journal article based on a recent piece of research that has been linked to a policy development at local, regional or national level. These can be difficult to locate, but policy documents will usually reference the research that has informed them. Alternatively, if you can identify the name of the lead researcher, an Internet search for their name should generate their university website, which will include references to her/his work.

Use the questions above to support your critical reading of the report or article.

Next, search for media reports that refer to the policy developments based on this research. How far do the media reports reflect the conclusions you have drawn through your own critical reading?

GETTING INVOLVED IN RESEARCH

In Wales . . .

The MEP is a practice-based Masters programme that started in September 2012 and is designed to enhance and support the teaching practice and professional development of Newly Qualified Teachers (NQTs). It also offers professional development for experienced teachers, as they can apply to become an external mentor on the MEP programme, providing support for both NQTs in their induction year and guidance while they are undertaking their MEP. This guidance will be: identifying professional needs and learning outcomes to be achieved for each taught module; providing support to enable teachers to carry out classroom-based research; and providing feedback on the progress made.

Source: Welsh Government (WG) (2013) *Masters in Educational Practice (MEP)*. Available at: http:// learning.wales.gov.uk/yourcareer/mastersineducationalpractice/?lang=en (accessed 31 May 2013).

In practical terms, teachers often become involved in research through a postgraduate programme of professional development, such as a Masters in Education. Indeed, you may gather credits towards a Masters degree during initial teacher education and have opportunities to gain further credits through modules aimed at those in their first year of teaching. Universities run a variety of Masters courses, including generic programmes with a broad range of options and those with a specific focus such as literacy, inclusion or leadership. During a Masters programme, you are likely to engage in a series of practitioner-led enquiries designed to research aspects of your work. Programmes will support you in reflecting critically on your practice, exploring it from different perspectives and developing your skills as a teacher-researcher. As well as directly contributing to the development of your practice and thinking, Masters work can have many other benefits. Below, Sally Roberts describes her experience of a Masters in Education:

> I enrolled on a Masters in Education for Primary Mathematics specialists after my head teacher suggested that it could support me in my role as maths coordinator. I was initially concerned that it would be time consuming, and might not help me in the areas that I wanted to develop as a teacher and subject leader.

The course has had a huge impact on my practice. It has made me more methodical in how I plan my lessons, particularly in maths, but increasingly in other subjects too. Not only have I read in depth about each of the main areas of mathematics, and across the primary age range, I've learned how to research effective teaching strategies in other areas of the curriculum too. This has developed my confidence hugely and given me a greater enthusiasm for teaching maths in fun and engaging ways. Furthermore, as the course progressed, I made a number of good friends who I was able to pinch ideas from and share practice with. I hadn't realised how useful being part of a learning community could be, for both my professional development and for allowing my pupils to develop links with pupils from other schools. I am still in touch with some of these teachers and find it interesting to learn about what other schools are doing and what's working well.

As a result of completing my course, I have led training meetings with staff and parents and introduced whole school initiatives in the subject of mathematics. Importantly, I feel like I am somebody who is more equipped to support other teachers and certainly feel more valued and more employable. Although the course was at points quite demanding in terms of time, it was incredibly worthwhile.

As Sally describes, working with colleagues to investigate and develop practice can be very rewarding. There are many opportunities for collaboration, in addition to those provided by Masters programmes. For many years, local education authorities have facilitated professional networks. Recent changes in the funding, organisation and administration of schools, however, have meant that groups of teachers may be more likely to meet together in other contexts, for example as part of collaborative research projects conducted within Teaching School Alliances or special interest groups. Teachers increasingly exchange ideas and engage in professional discussion through online communities, for example participating in the forums managed by the *Times Educational Supplement* (www.tes.co.uk), or through following teachers' blogs. Opportunities may also arise to engage in collaborative research projects with university-based researchers.

You may choose to join one of the many associations that promote the development of a particular subject. Joining a subject association or attending a subject association conference can provide you with rich opportunities to: learn about recent research and/or present your own research, meet colleagues from elsewhere and even work with others to play an active part in influencing policy. Subject associations also sometimes offer small grants for research projects. Julie Rayner, deputy head teacher, reflects on her involvement with the United Kingdom Literacy Association (UKLA):

As a teacher of 12 years, developing pedagogical subject knowledge and keeping up to date with theoretical viewpoints can be difficult. School-based professional development is usually directed by school development issues, linked to patterns of pupil attainment across the school. Working with those outside my school has given me an opportunity to reflect more broadly on how children learn and meant that I am more up-to-date with new developments. I have attended two UKLA conferences and this has allowed me to access innovative and thought provoking practice from across the world. This in turn has helped me to question my own practice and curriculum. Recently I have been working with the editorial board for The English Association/ UKLA magazine, *English 4-11*. Being able to edit articles has been an interesting process. I think I play an important role as I can read from a 'layperson's' point of view and am able to suggest points that might make articles more teacher friendly.

Task 9.3.5 Investigating subject associations

In a group, each select a subject association from the list below. Visit its website and investigate the support and opportunities the association provides. Report back to the rest of the group.

- Association for Physical Education: www.afpe.org.uk
- Geographical Association: www.geography.org.uk
- NAACE – the IT association: www.naace.co.uk
- National Association for Language Development in the Curriculum: www.naldic.org.uk
- National Association for Primary Education: www.nape.org.uk
- National Association for Special Educational Needs: www.nasen.org.uk
- National Association for the Teaching of English: www.nate.org.uk
- National Association of Music Educators: www.name.org.uk
- National Drama: www.nationaldrama.org.uk/nd/
- The Association for Science Education: www.ase.org.uk/home/
- The Association of Teachers of Mathematics: www.atm.org.uk
- The Design and Technology Association: www.data.org.uk
- The Historical Association: www.history.org.uk
- The National Society for Education in Art and Design: www.nsead.org/home/index.aspx
- United Kingdom Literacy Association: www.ukla.org

You can also identify subject associations through the Council of Subject Associations website: www.subjectassociation.org.uk

SUMMARY

This unit has explored the role of research in supporting ongoing critical reflection on practice. It has emphasised that this involves not only a process of asking questions and collecting and analysing evidence, but also being prepared to examine the values and beliefs that underpin what you do and how you think about your work. It has suggested that collaborating with others is an important part of this process and also highlighted the need to keep up to date with research conducted by others and review this critically. Research has an important role in professional development, and it is hoped that the examples provided here will inspire you to keep investigating and interrogating practice throughout your career.

ANNOTATED FURTHER READING

Cohen, L., Manion, L. and Morrison, K. (2011) *Research Methods in Education*, 7th edn, London: Routledge.
   This gives practical guidance on designing and conducting research, including a very useful overview of research methods.

Gonzalez, N., Moll, L. and Amanti, C. (2005) *Funds of Knowledge: Theorizing Practices in Households, Communities and Classrooms*, London: Routledge.

> A compelling account of a study from the USA, through which teachers investigated the life experiences – and 'funds of knowledge' – children brought with them to school. The book explores how such learning can be used to transform children's school experiences.

McNiff, J. and Whitehead, J. (2005) *Action Research for Teachers: A practical guide*, London: David Fulton.

> A very practical and accessible book, providing advice for each stage of designing, conducting and reporting action research.

 ## FURTHER READING TO SUPPORT M-LEVEL STUDY

Biesta, G. (2007) 'Why what works won't work: evidence-based practice and the democratic deficit in educational research', *Educational Theory*, 57 (1): 1–22.

> This article raises questions about the kind of research that is most appropriate in informing the development of classroom practice.

Clark, A. (2005) 'Listening to and involving young children: a review of research and practice', *Early Child Development and Care*, 175 (6): 489–505.

> This article reviews a range of approaches to researching with young children. Although focused specifically on the early years, methods described and issues raised are relevant to those working with primary children.

 ## RELEVANT WEBSITES

Research-informed practice digests produced by the Department for Education: www.education.gov.uk/schools/toolsandinitiatives/tripsresearchdigests

Collaborative Action Research Network: www.esri.mmu.ac.uk/carnnew

> CARN is an international network that aims to raise the profile of action research and support its development.

 ## REFERENCES

Bath, C. (2009) *Learning to Belong: Young Children's Participation at School*, London: Routledge.

Biesta, G. (2007) 'Why what works won't work: evidence-based practice and the democratic deficit in educational research', *Educational Theory*, 57 (1): 1–22.

Carr, W. and Kemmis, S. (1986) *Becoming Critical: Education, Knowledge and Action Research*, Lewes: Falmer.

Clark, A. and Moss, P. (2011) *The Mosaic Approach*, 2nd edn, London: National Children's Bureau.

Comber, B. and Kamler, B. (2005) *Turnaround Pedagogies: Literacy Interventions for At-Risk Students*, Newtown, Australia: Primary English Teaching Association.

Hall, K. (2003) *Listening to Stephen Read: Multiple Perspectives on Literacy*, Buckingham: Open University Press.

Hardy, I. and Ronnerman, K. (2011) 'The value and valuing of continuing professional development: current dilemmas, future directions and the case for action research', *Cambridge Journal of Education*, 41 (4): 461–72.

Kellock, A. (2011) 'Through the lens: accessing children's voices in New Zealand on well-being', *International Journal of Inclusive Education*, 15 (1): 41–55.

Kincheloe, J. (2003) *Teachers as Researchers: Qualitative Inquiry as a Path to Empowerment*, 2nd edn, London: RoutledgeFalmer.

Lankshear, C. and Knobel, M. (2004) *A Handbook for Teacher Research: From Design to Implementation*, Maidenhead: Open University Press.

Levy, R. (2011) *Young Children Reading at Home and at School*, London: Sage.

McNiff, J. and Whitehead, J. (2005) *Action Research for Teachers: A Practical Guide*, London: David Fulton.

Moll, L., Amanti, C., Neff, D. and Gonzalez, N. (1992) 'Funds of knowledge for teaching: using a qualitative approach to connect homes and classroom', *Theory into Practice*, 31 (2): 132-41.

Strauss, P. (2002) 'No easy answers: the dilemmas and challenges of teacher research', in C. Day, J. Elliot, B. Somekh and R. Winter, *Theory and Practice in Action Research*, Oxford: Symposium Books, 221-32.

Thomson, P. (2002) *Schooling the Rustbelt Kids: Making the Difference in Changing Times*, Stoke on Trent: Trentham Books.

INDEX